International Directory of

COMPANY HISTORIES

International Directory of
COMPANY
HISTORIES

VOLUME 56

Editor

Tina Grant

St J

ST. JAMES
PRESS®

THOMSON
✦ ™
GALE

Detroit • New York • San Diego • San Francisco • Cleveland • New Haven, Conn. • Waterville, Maine • London • Munich

THOMSON
™
GALE

International Directory of Company Histories, Volume 56
Tina Grant, Editor

Project Editor
Miranda H. Ferrara

Editorial
Erin Bealmear, Joann Cerrito, Jim Craddock,
Stephen Cusack, Peter M. Gareffa,
Kristin Hart, Melissa Hill, Margaret
Mazurkiewicz, Carol A. Schwartz, Christine
Tomassini, Michael J. Tyrkus

Imaging and Multimedia
Randy Bassett, Lezlie Light

Manufacturing
Rhonda Williams

LIBRARY OF CONGRESS CATALOG NUMBER 89-190943

ISBN: 1-55862-486-4

BRITISH LIBRARY CATALOGUING IN PUBLICATION DATA

International directory of company histories. Vol. 56
I. Tina Grant
33.87409

Printed in the United States of America
10 9 8 7 6 5 4 3 2 1

CONTENTS

Company Histories

PREFACE

The St. James Press series *The International Directory of Company Histories (IDCH)* is intended for reference use by students, business people, librarians, historians, economists, investors, job candidates, and others who seek to learn more about the historical development of the world's most important companies. To date, *IDCH* has covered over 6,100 companies in 56 volumes.

Inclusion Criteria

Most companies chosen for inclusion in *IDCH* have achieved a minimum of US$25 million in annual sales and are leading influences in their industries or geographical locations. Companies may be publicly held, private, or nonprofit. State-owned companies that are important in their industries and that may operate much like public or private companies also are included. Wholly owned subsidiaries and divisions are profiled if they meet the requirements for inclusion. Entries on companies that have had major changes since they were last profiled may be selected for updating.

The *IDCH* series highlights 10% private and nonprofit companies, and features updated entries on approximately 45 companies per volume.

Entry Format

Each entry begins with the company's legal name, the address of its headquarters, its telephone, toll-free, and fax numbers, and its web site. A statement of public, private, state, or parent ownership follows. A company with a legal name in both English and the language of its headquarters country is listed by the English name, with the native-language name in parentheses.

The company's founding or earliest incorporation date, the number of employees, and the most recent available sales figures follow. Sales figures are given in local currencies with equivalents in U.S. dollars. For some private companies, sales figures are estimates and indicated by the abbreviation *est.* The entry lists the exchanges on which a company's stock is traded and its ticker symbol, as well as the company's NAIC codes.

Entries generally contain a *Company Perspectives* box which provides a short summary of the company's mission, goals, and ideals, a *Key Dates* box highlighting milestones in the company's history, lists of *Principal Subsidiaries, Principal Divisions, Principal Operating Units, Principal Competitors,* and articles for *Further Reading.*

American spelling is used throughout *IDCH*, and the word "billion" is used in its U.S. sense of one thousand million.

Sources

Entries have been compiled from publicly accessible sources both in print and on the Internet such as general and academic periodicals, books, annual reports, and material supplied by the companies themselves.

Cumulative Indexes

IDCH contains three indexes: the **Index to Companies**, which provides an alphabetical index to companies discussed in the text as well as to companies profiled, the **Index to Industries**, which allows researchers to locate companies by their principal industry, and the **Geographic Index**, which lists companies alphabetically by the country of their headquarters. The indexes are cumulative and specific instructions for using them are found immediately preceding each index.

Suggestions Welcome

Comments and suggestions from users of *IDCH* on any aspect of the product as well as suggestions for companies to be included or updated are cordially invited. Please write:

The Editor
International Directory of Company Histories
St. James Press
27500 Drake Rd.
Farmington Hills, Michigan 48331-3535

AB	Aktiebolag (Finland, Sweden)
AB Oy	Aktiebolag Osakeyhtiot (Finland)
A.E.	Anonimos Eteria (Greece)
AG	Aktiengesellschaft (Austria, Germany, Switzerland, Liechtenstein)
A.O.	Anonim Ortaklari/Ortakligi (Turkey)
ApS	Amparteselskab (Denmark)
A.Š.	Anonim Širketi (Turkey)
A/S	Aksjeselskap (Norway); Aktieselskab (Denmark, Sweden)
Ay	Avoinyhtio (Finland)
B.A.	Buttengewone Aansprakeiijkheid (The Netherlands)
Bhd.	Berhad (Malaysia, Brunei)
B.V.	Besloten Vennootschap (Belgium, The Netherlands)
C.A.	Compania Anonima (Ecuador, Venezuela)
C. de R.L.	Compania de Responsabilidad Limitada (Spain)
Co.	Company
Corp.	Corporation
CRL	Companhia a Responsabilidao Limitida (Portugal, Spain)
C.V.	Commanditaire Vennootschap (The Netherlands, Belgium)
G.I.E.	Groupement d'Interet Economique (France)
GmbH	Gesellschaft mit beschraenkter Haftung (Austria, Germany, Switzerland)
Inc.	Incorporated (United States, Canada)
I/S	Interessentselskab (Denmark); Interesentselskap (Norway)
KG/KGaA	Kommanditgesellschaft/Kommanditgesellschaft auf Aktien (Austria, Germany, Switzerland)
KK	Kabushiki Kaisha (Japan)
K/S	Kommanditselskab (Denmark); Kommandittselskap (Norway)
Lda.	Limitada (Spain)
L.L.C.	Limited Liability Company (United States)
Ltd.	Limited (Various)
Ltda.	Limitada (Brazil, Portugal)
Ltee.	Limitee (Canada, France)
mbH	mit beschraenkter Haftung (Austria, Germany)
N.V.	Naamloze Vennootschap (Belgium, The Netherlands)
OAO	Otkrytoe Aktsionernoe Obshchestve (Russia)
OOO	Obschestvo s Ogranichennoi Otvetstvennostiu (Russia)
Oy	Osakeyhtiö (Finland)
PLC	Public Limited Co. (United Kingdom, Ireland)
Pty.	Proprietary (Australia, South Africa, United Kingdom)
S.A.	Société Anonyme (Belgium, France, Greece, Luxembourg, Switzerland, Arab speaking countries); Sociedad Anónima (Latin America [except Brazil], Spain, Mexico); Sociedades Anônimas (Brazil, Portugal)
SAA	Societe Anonyme Arabienne
S.A.R.L.	Sociedade Anonima de Responsabilidade Limitada (Brazil, Portugal); Société à Responsabilité Limitée (France, Belgium, Luxembourg)
S.A.S.	Societá in Accomandita Semplice (Italy); Societe Anonyme Syrienne (Arab speaking countries)
Sdn. Bhd.	Sendirian Berhad (Malaysia)
S.p.A.	Società per Azioni (Italy)
Sp. z.o.o.	Spólka z ograniczona odpowiedzialnoscia (Poland)
S.R.L.	Società a Responsabilità Limitata (Italy); Sociedad de Responsabilidad Limitada (Spain, Mexico, Latin America [except Brazil])
S.R.O.	Spolecnost s Rucenim Omezenym (Czechoslovakia
Ste.	Societe (France, Belgium, Luxembourg, Switzerland)
VAG	Verein der Arbeitgeber (Austria, Germany)
YK	Yugen Kaisha (Japan)
ZAO	Zakrytoe Aktsionernoe Obshchestve (Russia)

$	United States dollar	K	Zambian kwacha
£	United Kingdom pound	KD	Kuwaiti dinar
¥	Japanese yen	L	Italian lira
A$	Australian dollar	LuxFr	Luxembourgian franc
AED	United Arab Emirates dirham	M$	Malaysian ringgit
B	Thai baht	N	Nigerian naira
B	Venezuelan bolivar	Nfl	Netherlands florin
BD	Bahraini dinar	NIS	Israeli new shekel
BFr	Belgian franc	NKr	Norwegian krone
C$	Canadian dollar	NT$	Taiwanese dollar
CHF	Switzerland franc	NZ$	New Zealand dollar
COL	Colombian peso	P	Philippine peso
Cr	Brazilian cruzado	PLN	Polish zloty
CZK	Czech Republic koruny	PkR	Pakistan Rupee
DA	Algerian dinar	Pta	Spanish peseta
Dfl	Netherlands florin	R	Brazilian real
DKr	Danish krone	R	South African rand
DM	German mark	RMB	Chinese renminbi
E£	Egyptian pound	RO	Omani rial
Esc	Portuguese escudo	Rp	Indonesian rupiah
EUR	Euro dollars	Rs	Indian rupee
FFr	French franc	Ru	Russian ruble
Fmk	Finnish markka	S$	Singapore dollar
GRD	Greek drachma	Sch	Austrian schilling
HK$	Hong Kong dollar	SFr	Swiss franc
HUF	Hungarian forint	SKr	Swedish krona
IR£	Irish pound	SRls	Saudi Arabian riyal
ISK	Icelandic króna	TD	Tunisian dinar
J$	Jamaican dollar	W	Korean won

International Directory of

COMPANY HISTORIES

Affinity Group Holding Inc.

2575 Vista Del Mar
Ventura, California 93001
U.S.A.
Telephone: (805) 667-4100
Fax: (805) 667-4454
Web sites: http://www.rv.net; http://www.trailerlife.com

Private Company
Incorporated: 1992 as Affinity Group Inc.
Employees: 1,627
Sales: $431.1 million (2002)
NAIC: 511120 Periodical Publishers; 511130 Book
    Publishers; 721211 RV (Recreational Vehicle) Parks
    and Campgrounds; 813410 Civic and Social
    Organizations

Affinity Group Holding Company is the parent company of several businesses, including Affinity Group, Inc. (AGI), that provide goods and services to the outdoor recreation market, primarily recreational vehicle (RV) enthusiasts. Through its subsidiaries, the company owns and operates the Camping World chain of retail stores for RV parts and camping equipment and oversees several clubs for RV owners, including the Good Sam Club, Coast to Coast, Camping World's President's Club, Motorhome America Club, as well as Golf Card International. AGI publishes books, such as campground directories and buyer's guides, and consumer magazines, including *Trailer Life, Highways, MotorHome,* and several regional publications. Another publication, *RV Business,* serves the recreational vehicle industry. Through several Internet sites and a cable television show, AGI provides technical and non-technical information to RV enthusiasts and act as forums for RV-related businesses. The company publishes several magazines for other outdoor recreational activities, including *ATV Sport, American Rider, Woman Rider,* and *Thunder Press.*

Early Organization

Stephen Adams, a private investor and entrepreneur, formed AGI in 1992 to oversee three companies—TL Enterprises, Coast to Coast, and Golf Card International—serving the outdoor recreation market.

The roots of AGI go back to 1941, however, with the publication of *Trailer Life* magazine, established by an association of trailer manufacturers. At ten cents a copy, the publication provided practical information on trailer repair and maintenance and featured articles on travel destinations.

In 1958, Art Rouse, an advertising executive, purchased *Trailer Life.* Ten years later, Rouse formed Trailer Life Publishing Company to oversee operations of that magazine as well as other publications he had initiated. Among the Trailer Life repertoire was an annual directory, *RV Campground and Services,* which proved seminal to RV enthusiasts and sold more than 300,000 copies each year. Also during this time, the company introduced *Motorhome Life,* later renamed *MotorHome,* a consumer magazine providing useful information appropriate to the RV lifestyle, including product tests and reviews, travel destinations and outdoor recreational activities, as well as humor and general interest material.

Rouse also purchased *Trail-R-News,* best known perhaps as the initiator of the Good Sam Club, founded in 1966 to provide a system of volunteer assistance to RV owners in trouble while on the road. The name Good Sam referred to the biblical principle of the Good Samaritan, and club members identified themselves by placing on their RVs a sticker depicting the cartoon character Good Sam. The club established *Hi-Way Herald* magazine, which later became known as *Highways* magazine, as its official publication. It also provided a variety of RV-related services, such as insurance programs, begun in 1978, and emergency road service, started in 1985, as well as discounts off the nightly rate at more than 2,000 private campgrounds nationwide. Another holding, *RV Business,* established as *RV Retailer* in 1972, covered issues of concern to recreational vehicle manufacturers, dealers, and insurers.

The company soon began diversifying beyond the RV world, offering publications of interest to those who enjoyed other modes of transportation. *Rider* magazine and *Bicycle Rider* for motorcycle and bicycle enthusiasts, respectively, were introduced.

Key Dates:

1941: *Trailer Life* magazine is started by a trailer manufacturer association.
1958: Art Rouse purchases *Trailer Life* and develops other publications for RV enthusiasts under the company name Trailer Life Publishing Co.
1966: The Good Sam Club is established as a volunteer protection organization for RV owners.
1988: Stephen Adams purchases Trailer Life Publishing, now known as TL Enterprises.
1992: Affinity Group Inc. (AGI) is formed to oversee three companies: TL Enterprises, Coast to Coast, and Golf Card International.
1994: The acquisition of Woodall Publications adds seven regional publications to AGI.
1997: AGI acquires Camping World chain of retail stores.
2000: RVtoday begins to air on cable television; the first Great North American RV Rally is a big success.
2003: The company begins development of retail destinations for RV travelers.

Trailer Life Publishing, renamed TL Enterprises (TLE), also broadened its reach in the late 1970s by purchasing Benbow Valley RV Resort, a campground in northern California with deluxe facilities and a golf course.

In 1986, as part of a diversification and acquisition plan, American Bakeries purchased TLE. At that time the company was recording approximately $37 million in annual revenues, primarily from subscriptions to *Trailer Life*, with a circulation of over 300,000 subscribers, and *MotorHome*, with more than 120,000 subscribers. With over 480,000 members paying annual dues of $15, the Good Sam Club accounted for about one-third of revenues.

American Bakeries had also acquired Camp Coast to Coast Resorts, a national, membership-based network of RV campgrounds. Formed in 1972, Coast to Coast served membership resorts comprised of nearly 200,000 members; members could use any of more than 400 resorts in the network on a reciprocal use basis. Combining Coast to Coast with TLE allowed for an expansion of services from the Good Sam Club to Coast to Coast members. Members of each of these clubs had similar interests and backgrounds, largely retirees or pre-retirees who had raised their children and paid their mortgages, giving them the leisure time and financial foundation to enjoy long-term travel and recreation.

Consolidation Moves in the 1990s

Colorado entrepreneur Steve Adams acquired TLE and its sister company, Coast to Coast, in 1988. Adams was a veteran of the advertising, publishing, and communications industries, having established Adams Outdoor Advertising and having controlling ownership interests in several other related companies. TLE and Coast to Coast provided the basis for expanding products and services available to club members and customers in the outdoor recreation market. In 1990 TLE purchased The

Golf Club, formed in 1973 to provide special rates and golfing opportunities for its members. Membership included discounted rates at over 360 country club resorts and two rounds of golf at more than 1,660 18-hole golf courses in the United States and overseas. The acquisition included the club's official publication, *Golf Traveler*.

The formation of Affinity Group Inc. in 1992 provided an umbrella company for Adams' existing companies and new acquisitions. With the May 1994 acquisition of the Woodall Publications Corporation, AGI obtained several regional magazines designed for RV enthusiasts, including *Carolina RV, Florida RV Traveler, Northeast Outdoors,* and *Texas RV*. The acquisition also included Woodall's Campground Directory, the company's flagship publication established in the late 1930s.

AGI acquired the San Francisco Thrift and Loan in 1996, renaming it Affinity Bank, for the purpose of providing financial services to its customers and club members. While continuing to provide full banking services to its existing base of four million customers, Affinity Bank developed services that catered to the on-the-road lifestyle of RV owners. Banking transactions took place over the telephone, with each customer assigned to a regular representative, if preferred. In 1997 the bank opened a second branch at AGI's headquarters in Ventura, California. Banking operations were then reorganized as Affinity Bank Holdings Inc., an entity independent of AGI.

AGI augmented the goods and services it provided to the RV niche market when, in April 1997, the company acquired Camping World, a chain of retail stores supplying RV aftermarket parts and camping equipment. Based in Bowling Green, Kentucky, the first Camping World store opened in 1966. The company added a mail-order catalog and opened 29 additional stores as RV travel became more popular, particularly in the 1980s and 1990s. Camping World formed the President's Club to extend special discounts and benefits to regular customers. As separate companies, Camping World and AGI had cooperated successfully on marketing programs with RV manufacturers, dealers, and consumers. The acquisition broadened the customer base for both companies, while saving costs by integrating redundant operations.

Also in 1997, AGI purchased Ehlert Publishing and successfully integrated that unit into the AGI publications division. The acquisition included several magazines catering to specific outdoor recreational activities, such as *Snowmobile Magazine, SnowGoer, WaterCraft World WaterCraft Business*. Ehlert acquired or started other publications, including the trade publications *Ehlert Powersports Business* and *Boating Industry*.

Late 1990s and Beyond

AGI found a new outlet for providing goods and services to its customers through the Internet, developing a variety of web sites, including individual sites to promote each club and its services. Some sites provided a limited extension of specific publications, such as *Trailer Life* and *MotorHome* magazines, while others provided specific services, such as RVSearch.com, where interested parties could buy or sell new and used RVs. The concept had originated in 1995 as a phone-and-mail operation, but the electronic version simplified the service. Sellers provided basic information and photos, and the site matched a vehicle to a potential buyer from a database of interested individuals.

In 2000 the company launched RV.NET which provided information and links of value to RV owners. The site contained a catalog of RV-related products and services, including financing, insurance, emergency road service, and extended warranties. Information included an RV repair manual and a campground directory. Members could make a change of address, order or extend magazine subscriptions, or order books from Trailer Life Books, such as the *RV Buyers Guide*. The site provided links to AGI clubs and magazines, to Camping World, and other RV-related web sites.

AGI's broad reach to RV enthusiasts through clubs, publications, and the Internet culminated in a new annual event, the Great North American RV Rally. First held in Gillette, Wyoming, in July 2000, the rally differed from similar events in that it was designed to attract a broad base of RV enthusiasts. Members of the Good Sam Club, Coast to Coast, and the President's Club, as well as readers of the company's RV publications, attended the event. The rally featured entertainment, educational seminars, and an exhibition by more than 250 suppliers and manufacturers of RV-related goods and services. Camping World held a sweepstakes, giving away a recreational vehicle, while the Good Sam Club celebrated its millionth member. The Great North American RV Rally attracted 11,000 people in over 5,000 RVs and was considered a great success.

AGI also expanded its national presence by launching a cable television show called ''RVtoday.'' The 30-minute show brought information found in AGI publications to a video format. ''RVtoday'' contained segments about new products, road tests on vehicles, technical advice, and features on RV campgrounds and travel destinations. After a pilot show in June 2000, regular broadcast began on the Nashville Network in April 2001. The following September the show moved to the Outdoor Life Network, airing three times a week.

The Internet continued to be an important avenue of promoting AGI's services. In June 2001 the company launched adventuremall.com. Operated by a new subsidiary, Adventure Mall, Inc., the site provided space for professional dealers and private individuals to advertise their sport vehicles for sale. These included recreational vehicles, motorcycles, all-terrain vehicles, personal watercraft, and sport utility vehicles. Related information included pricing guides, financial and insurance services, and rental referrals.

In October 2002 AGI introduced the RV Finance Program through the Good Sam Club. RV loan services included funding for private party and dealer/broker purchases, loan prequalification and refinancing, as well as equity cash-outs. Club members complete an application online at NADAguides.com, the website of NADA Appraisal Guides, publisher of recreational vehicle and other vehicle valuations.

In January 2003 RVtoday began its third season on cable television and its first season as an in-house production. In response to viewer input, the new season shows featured cooking and ''how-to'' segments. The 26 episodes ran five days per week, but expanded to seven days in March, continuing to air on Outdoor Life Network.

In March 2003 AGI launched rvSearch.com to make RV dealer advertising easier. The site allowed dealers to upload photos and information about an RV on three of nine available web sites. AGI also combined the advertising potential of its magazines and the Internet through a promotion on rvSearch. The program allowed customers to place a classified advertisement on the website and in *Trailer Life*, *Motorhome*, or *Highways* magazine for a special low rate.

During the early 2000s AGI also developed the idea of creating RV retail destinations. Specifically, the company initiated partnerships with independent RV dealers to locate Camping World stores next to the dealerships. Camping World preferred situations which allowed the company to share space under one roof with an RV dealer. Ideally, a common lobby area would house a customer lounge and offices, but each retailer's sales area would be separate. Also, Camping World wanted to establish comprehensive RV retail developments that provided for all of the needs of the RV lifestyle. Each destination could provide a gasoline station, a convenience store, a restaurant, a waste dump, access to the Internet, and limited banking.

Camping World established five dealer partnerships, with the largest retail destinations in Palm Springs, California, and in Stuart, Florida, both near interstate highways. The Palm Springs site, called Indio RV Mall, involved a 25,000 square foot Camping World Supercenter on a 60-acre site with eight RV dealerships. In Stuart the company planned an 18,000 square foot store on a site to be shared with Florida Outdoors, a dealer of RVs, all terrain vehicles, and personal watercraft. Another partnership, with the Hart City RV Supercenter in Elkhart, Indiana, involved a sharing a 60,000 square foot indoor showroom. Camping World expected all the sites to be completed by the end of 2003.

In conjunction with the new program, Camping World upgraded business and operating systems and updated the store design. Stores took on a contemporary feel with a rustic, outdoor style. Camping World expanded its merchandise mix, adding snacks and traditional camping equipment, such as tents and sleeping bags. The company adapted the product mix to local geographic and seasonal requirements. The changes succeeded in increasing the average check amount. Camping World reported same store sales growth of 9.8 percent in 2002, contributing to companywide average sales growth of 6.4 percent; Affinity Group revenues of $431.1 million net $12 million in profit in 2002.

Principal Subsidiaries

Affinity Group, Inc.; TL Enterprises, Inc.; Golf Card International; Adventure Mall, Inc.; Camping World, Inc.; Ehlert Publishing Group.

Principal Competitors

Cendant Corporation; Kampgrounds of American, Inc.; Outdoor Resorts of America, Inc.; REI Equipment, Inc.; Thousand Trails, Inc.

Further Reading

''Affinity Group Inc. (AGI) Pursues 'Strategic Alliances' with Retail Dealers,'' *RV Business,* March 2002, p. 7.

"Affinity Launches New Site January 1, 2000," *Trailer Life*, January 2000, p. 28.

"American Bakeries Co. Will Pay $40 Million for TL Enterprises," *Wall Street Journal*, June 24, 1986, p. 1.

Crider, Jeff, "Coast to Coast's Miller Eyes Growth of Membership Firm," *RV Business,* April 2003, p. 20.

Epstein, Jonathan D., "Publisher of Affinity Group Magazines Opens No-Branch Bank for RV Crowd," *American Banker*, May 5, 1997, p. 9.

Goldenberg, Sherman, "Affinity, Camping World Meld Operations," *RV Business*, January 1998, p. 14.

——, "AGI Becomes the News," *RV Business*, September 2000, p. 4.

——, "The New Age of Camping World," *RV Business,* November 2002, p. 81.

"Good Sam Celebrates Hitting Million-Member Mark," *RV Business*, October 2000, p. 24.

Lee, W.A., "Chasing a Moving Target," *American Banker,* October 13, 2000, p. 1.

Leonard, Barbara, "What a Web We Weave," *Trailer Life*, February 2000, p. 6.

Manly, Lorne, "Affinity Group Scoops up Ehlert," *Folio: the Magazine for Magazine Management*, October 1, 1996, p. 16.

"New Club for Upscale Motorhome Owners," *Motorhome*, October 2001, p. 28.

Pattison, Kermit, "RV News Firm Rides to Success; Affinity Group Moves Operations to Ventura," *Daily News of Los Angeles*, January 15, 1996, p. T1.

Peterson, Brent, "Coast to Coast Hires Miller as President, Celebrates 30 Years," *RV Business,* September 2002, p. 8.

Reed, Dixie, and John Sullaway, "AGI Draws Throngs of RV Enthusiasts to Second Great North American Rally," *RV Business*, May 2001, p. 13.

Sullaway, John, "AGI's Camping World Unit Announces Three New U.S. Retail Developments," *RV Business,* March 2003, p. 8.

Sullaway, John, and Bev Edwards, "AGI North American Rally Draws 11,000 RVers to Wyoming," *RV Business*, September 2000, p. 7.

—Mary Tradii

Alcoa Inc.

Alcoa Corporate Center
201 Isabella Street
Pittsburgh, Pennsylvania 15212-5858
U.S.A.
Telephone: (412) 553-4545
Fax: (412) 553-4498
Web site: http://www.alcoa.com

Public Company
Incorporated: 1888 as The Pittsburgh Reduction
     Company
Employees: 127,000
Sales: $20.2 billion (2002)
Stock Exchanges: New York American Swiss Australia
     Brussels Frankfurt London
Ticker Symbol: AA
NAIC: 331312 Primary Aluminum Production; 331314
     Secondary Smelting, Refining, and Alloying of
     Aluminum

The largest aluminum manufacturer in the world, Alcoa Inc. produces aluminum and alumina for automotive, aerospace, commercial transportation, construction, packaging, and other markets. Active worldwide in all major elements of the industry, Alcoa's operations include mining, refining, smelting, fabricating, recycling, and developing technology. In addition to its numerous industrial applications, Alcoa aluminum is used in beverage cans and such consumer products as Reynolds Wrap aluminum foil and Alcoa Wheels. In 2003 the company employed 127,000 people in 39 countries.

Company Origins: 1888

Alcoa was founded in 1888 in Pittsburgh, Pennsylvania, under the name The Pittsburgh Reduction Company. Its founders were a coalition of entrepreneurs headed by Alfred Hunt, a metallurgist who had been working in the steel industry, and a young chemist named Charles Martin Hall. Pittsburgh Reduction's sole property was a patented process for extracting aluminum from bauxite ore

by electrolysis, which Hall had invented in the woodshed of his family house in 1886, just one year after his graduation from Oberlin College. Hall's discovery had promised to make aluminum production economical for the first time in history. Later in 1886, Hall had taken his process to a smelting company in Cleveland, Ohio, but left in 1888 after it showed little interest. One of his associates there, who had also worked with Hunt at another company, introduced the two men, and Pittsburgh Reduction was started as a result of their meeting.

Despite its relative abundance, few practical uses existed for aluminum because it was so expensive to extract. By 1893, however, Hall's process allowed Pittsburgh Reduction to undercut its competitors with aluminum that had been produced at a lower price. The company then faced two challenges: to generate a larger market for aluminum by promoting new uses for the metal and to increase production so that it could cut costs even further through economies of scale. Efforts in the former area proved most successful in the manufacturing of cooking utensils, so much so that the company formed its own cookware subsidiary, Aluminum Cooking Utensil Company, in 1901. Aluminum Cooking Utensil adopted the Wear-Ever brand name.

Pittsburgh Reduction also began the process of vertical integration, insuring itself against the day when Hall's patent would expire and it would no longer have a monopoly on his process. In the mid-1890s, it began acquiring its own bauxite mines and power-generating facilities. This process continued after the death of Alfred Hunt, who had served as president since founding the company. In 1899 Hunt, an artillery captain in the Pennsylvania militia was sent to Puerto Rico with his battery during the Spanish-American War and succumbed to malaria there. He was succeeded by R.B. Mellon of the Mellon banking family, which had loaned the company much of its startup capital and controlled a substantial minority stake. The Mellons, however, had been content to let the engineers run the company. Arthur Vining Davis, a partner who had joined Pittsburgh Reduction only months after its founding, acted as president during this time, and the Mellons formally ceded power to him in 1910. In 1907 The Pittsburgh Reduction Company changed its name to Aluminum Company of America, but eventually went by the shortened form of Alcoa. In 1914 Davis became the

Company Perspectives:

At Alcoa, our vision is to be the best company in the world in the eyes of our customers, shareholders, communities and people. We expect and demand the best we have to offer by always keeping Alcoa's values top of mind.

Integrity: Alcoa's foundation is our integrity. We are open, honest and trustworthy in dealing with customers, suppliers, coworkers, shareholders and the communities where we have an impact. Environment, Health and Safety: We work safely in a manner that protects and promotes the health and well being of the individual and the environment. Customer: We support our customers' success by creating exceptional value through innovative product and service solutions. Excellence: We relentlessly pursue excellence in everything we do, every day. People: We work in an inclusive environment that embraces change, new ideas, respect for the individual and equal opportunity to succeed. Profitability: We earn sustainable financial results that enable profitable growth and superior shareholder value. Accountability: We are accountable individually and in teams for our behaviors, actions and results. We live our Values and measure our success by the success of our customers, shareholders, communities and people.

company's last surviving link to its early days when Charles Martin Hall died, leaving an estate worth some $45 million.

Post-World War I Expansion

Alcoa had virtually created the market for aluminum, and its only competition came from foreign producers, who were hindered by high tariffs. Alcoa also benefited from rising demand from the automobile industry; by 1915, 65 percent of all new aluminum went into automotive parts. The outbreak of World War I ended the threat from foreign producers, and Alcoa even became an exporter. Annual production rose from 109 million pounds to 152 million pounds between 1915 and 1918, with much of it going to Great Britain, France, and Italy. At home, the vast majority of Alcoa's output was used for military applications.

The export boom that the war had fostered made it seem natural that Alcoa should expand its overseas operations once hostilities ended. Throughout the 1920s, the company acquired factories, mines, and power-generating facilities in Western Europe, Scandinavia, and, most prominently, in Canada. Late in the decade, however, the difficulty of managing far-flung operations, combined with a rising tide of economic nationalism abroad, made Alcoa's position overseas increasingly untenable. In 1928 it divested all of its foreign operations except its Dutch Guyana bauxite mines, spinning them off as Aluminum Limited, based in Montreal and headed by Edward Davis, A.V. Davis's brother. Aluminum Limited was renamed Alcan Aluminum Limited in 1966. In 1929 Arthur Vining Davis retired as president and became chairman. He was succeeded by Roy Hunt, the son of Alfred Hunt.

At home, the general economic boom carried Alcoa with it, but between 1929 and 1932, during the early years of the Great

Depression, sales fell from $34.4 million to $11.1 million. Alcoa laid off half of its workforce in this time, slashed wages for those who remained, and cut back its research-and-development budget. Demand for aluminum did not recover until 1936. Even so, Alcoa's market share remained unchallenged, as it was still the only aluminum smelter in the United States thanks to its technological lead and economies of scale—a position that had not gone unnoticed.

Alcoa had been having antitrust run-ins with the Justice Department since 1911, but all of the blows had glanced off of it until U.S. Attorney General Homer Cummings filed suit in 1937, charging monopolization and restraint of trade on Alcoa's part. The trial lasted from 1938 to 1940 and was the largest proceeding in the history of U.S. law to that time. A district court ruling in 1942 found in favor of Alcoa, but the government appealed. In 1945 an appeals court sustained that appeal. In his decision, Judge Learned Hand ruled that although Alcoa had not intended to create its monopoly, the fact remained that it had a monopoly on the domestic aluminum market in violation of antitrust law and it would be in the nation's best interest to break it up. Hand's decision became a landmark in the history of judicial activism, although it did leave open the question of how Alcoa's grip on aluminum was to be broken.

Meanwhile, of course, the United States had entered World War II. Demand for aluminum skyrocketed. Alcoa, however, proved to be unable to keep up with the increases in demand, disappointing the War Department. During the war the government financed new plants that were built and run by Alcoa, but also encouraged the development of other aluminum producers. As the tide of the war shifted in favor of the Allies in 1944, the U.S. government began deliberations on how to dispose of these plants, which would soon become surplus capacity. As a result, a solution to the problem of how to carry out Hand's ruling became apparent. The Alcoa plants that the government had financed would be sold off to two new rivals: Reynolds Metals Company and Permanente Metals Corporation, owned by industrialist Henry Kaiser. Reynolds and Permanente were to buy the plants at cut-rate prices. In effect, this divestiture created an oligarchy where there had formerly been a monopoly. In 1950 a district court decree carved up the U.S. aluminum market between the three: Alcoa would get 50.9 percent of production capacity, Reynolds 30.9 percent, and Kaiser Aluminum & Chemical Corporation, as Permanente Metals was renamed, 18.2 percent.

Roy Hunt retired in 1951 and was succeeded by Irving Wilson. During the 1950s, Alcoa's share of U.S. production capacity declined as it expanded more slowly than Reynolds and Kaiser. Faced with increased competition, Alcoa also found itself without any brand-name recognition on which to capitalize in the consumer products arena; Reynolds, by comparison, had established a name for itself quickly with its Reynolds Wrap aluminum foil. Nevertheless, booming demand for aluminum, the result of successful wartime experiments in using the metal to build military aircraft, helped compensate for decreased market share. Despite increased competition, Alcoa remained the industry's largest member and its acknowledged price leader.

Davis retired in 1957, ending his 69 years of service with Alcoa. He was succeeded by Wilson, and Frank Magee became

Key Dates:

1888: Alcoa is founded in Pittsburgh, Pennsylvania, under the name The Pittsburgh Reduction Company.
1901: The company forms its own cookware subsidiary, Aluminum Cooking Utensil Company.
1907: The Pittsburgh Reduction Company changes its name to Aluminum Company of America (Alcoa).
1928: Alcoa divests all of its foreign operations except its Dutch Guyana bauxite mines, spinning them off as Aluminum Limited, based in Montreal and headed by Edward Davis.
1945: An appeals court ruling finds Alcoa guilty of antitrust violations, calling for a breakup of the company's monopolistic hold on the aluminum market.
1958: Alcoa joins with Lockheed and Japanese manufacturer Furukawa Electric Company, forming Furalco to produce aluminum aircraft parts for Lockheed.
1972: Alcoa decides to sell its technology to other manufacturers on a large scale, a significant departure from previous policies.
1987: Paul O'Neill becomes chairman and CEO of Alcoa and begins to institute a major revitalization program for the business.
1998: Alcoa moves to new headquarters as part of a major restructuring.
1999: Alain J.P. Belda succeeds O'Neill as CEO; company officially adopts the name Alcoa Inc.
2000: Alcoa acquires Reynolds Metals Company for $5.8 billion.

president and CEO. Alcoa came out of the brief recession of 1957–58 by realizing that it would have to internationalize and diversify in order to ensure its future. In 1958 Alcoa joined with Lockheed and Japanese manufacturer Furukawa Electric Company to form Furalco, which would produce aluminum aircraft parts for Lockheed. Also that year, Alcoa became a player in what was then the largest takeover battle in British corporate history when it negotiated a friendly acquisition of a stake in struggling British Aluminum, Ltd. The acquisition was aborted, however. Alcoa had been approached by British Aluminum Chairman Lord Portal, Viscount of Hungerford, who had neglected to consult his major stockholders before closing the deal. Thus, when Reynolds and British manufacturer Tube Investments made a substantially sweeter bid, a bitter struggle ensued. Institutional investors sold their shares to the Reynolds and Tube venture and Alcoa lost out. The fight over British Aluminum became a sensation in Britain not only because of the sheer spectacle of foreign interests vying for control of a major domestic corporation, but also because hostile takeovers were considered a breach of etiquette in British finance. What came to be known as The Great Aluminum War split British investment banks between the old-line, established houses that backed Alcoa and Portal, and the upstart firms that supported Reynolds and Tube.

Undeterred by this setback, Alcoa went on to spread its mining operations into other parts of the world, reestablishing an international presence it had not had since it spun off Alcan. Back home, the company moved aggressively into producing finished aluminum products. In 1959 it acquired Rome Cable and Wire Company. The next year, it purchased Rea Magnet Wire Company and Cupples Products Company, a manufacturer of aluminum curtain walls and doors. Both Rome and Cupples eventually had to be divested, however, because of antitrust objections.

When John Harper became president and CEO in 1963, Alcoa found its profit margins squeezed by increased competition, high overhead, and a generally low market price for aluminum. One of Harper's solutions was to move more aggressively into manufacturing finished products, which provided higher returns than smelting. On his initiative, Alcoa began producing sheet metal for aluminum cans, which became more popular among beverage consumers in the 1960s after the invention of the pop-top, and aerospace parts. In 1966 the company posted a record profit, finally exceeding a mark it had set ten years before.

1970s: Recycling and Diversification

High labor costs, dramatically high-energy prices, unpredictable bauxite prices, a slower national economy, and new competitors trying to break up the aluminum oligarchy all conspired against Alcoa in the 1970s. Sales and other operating revenues grew from $1.8 billion to $4.6 billion between 1972 and 1982, but profits as a percentage of gross income remained below historical levels. High interest rates forced Alcoa to slow its expansion and concentrate on paying down existing debt. In 1972 the company also decided to sell its technology to other manufacturers on a large scale, something it had been loath to do in the past.

W.H. Krome George succeeded John Harper as chairman and CEO in 1975, and Alcoa began to show new signs of life. In the late 1970s it seized upon recycling as an alternative to the high cost of smelting, although somewhat later than rival Reynolds. By 1979 Alcoa was reprocessing 110 million pounds of scrap aluminum. By 1985 that figure would rise to over 500 million pounds and recycling would account for 19 percent of the company's aluminum ingot capacity. George, who was more scientifically oriented than his predecessors, also led Alcoa into expansive research into high-tech applications of aluminum. By the time George retired in 1983, he had started the company on the path once again to developing new high-strength alloys for use in the aerospace business. Other areas of research and development, often pursued as joint ventures with other companies, included alumina chemicals, satellite antennae, and computer memory discs.

George's successor, Charles Parry, took over in 1983, and was even more committed to diversifying Alcoa. His goal, he said, was that half of the company's revenue should come from non-aluminum sources by 1995. Immediately, Alcoa began scouting around for companies to acquire, particularly in high-tech fields. At the same time, however, Parry's vigor in attempting to reshape the company was not well received in all quarters. He was attempting to radically change corporate thinking in a short period of time even as he continued the layoffs and plant closures that George had begun in an effort to cut costs, and employee morale suffered. Many did not see how he could create new business worth between $7 billion and $9 billion from scratch in less than ten years. Although Alcoa made only minor acquisitions during Parry's tenure, which ended in 1987, the directors became concerned that the deals that Parry proposed to make would not fit in well. Some worried that the risks involved were more appropriate to a young company just starting up, not a major corporation nearing its centennial.

Even George became uncomfortable with his successor, and in 1986 he led the search for Parry's replacement. Aware of his board's discontent, Parry took an early retirement in 1987. He was replaced by Paul O'Neill, former president of International Paper Company and deputy director of the Office of Management and Budget during the administration of President Gerald R. Ford. O'Neill's appointment was largely George's doing; the two had met because of the latter's directorship at International Paper.

Cost-Cutting and Strategic Acquisitions in the 1990s

Under O'Neill, the first outsider ever to run Alcoa, the company slowed its diversification and refocused on its core aluminum business. In 1990 it formed a joint venture with Japanese manufacturer Kobe Steel, Ltd. to make sheet metal for aluminum cans and parts for automakers for the Asian market. O'Neill had also sought to revitalize employee morale and ensure product quality by emphasizing safety as a primary concern, and by instituting a profit sharing plan.

Combined profits for 1988 and 1989 more than doubled Alcoa's total for the first eight years of the decade, providing an early sign that the changes instituted by O'Neill were working. By 1991, the revitalization of the aluminum business under O'Neill's watch had achieved great strides. A billion-dollar program to modernize its plants was finished that year, long-term debt had been whittled down, and the company's research and development budget had been increased significantly. Important changes in the structure of Alcoa also were underway during the early 1990s, as O'Neill pursued his agenda of "reinventing" the venerable aluminum giant. Two layers of corporate management were stripped away, including the company's presidential post, exposing 24 business units that were ceded autonomous control over their respective operations. Each of these business units reported directly to O'Neill, who exerted considerable sway over the company's operations despite his desire to give the business units an unprecedented amount of power.

However, two developments outside Alcoa's control affected the early years of the 1990s, hampering the company's progress under O'Neill's decisive rule. The collapse of the Soviet Union had a disastrous effect on the world aluminum market, causing prices to fall to the lowest in history. The Soviets exported an average of 250,000 metric tons of aluminum a year before the Berlin Wall came down, but when revolution swept communism aside and left Russia in a precarious financial position, aluminum shipments exported from the former Soviet Union increased exponentially. In dire need of cash, Russia was shipping an average of 1.2 million metric tons of aluminum per year during the early 1990s, flooding the market and drastically reducing the price of aluminum. Aluminum, which sold for $1.65 a pound in 1988, was priced at $.53 a pound by 1993, the lowest price ever recorded.

To make matters worse, a worldwide recession settled in during the early 1990s as aluminum prices plummeted. The effects of the recession had a more lasting hold on Alcoa's fortunes than the fall of the Soviet empire. The company trimmed its payroll by 2,000 in 1992, the first major layoff since 1986, as depressing financial totals were tallied at the company's headquarters. Alcoa lost $1.1 billion in 1992 and recorded a paltry $4.8 million gain in 1993. Despite the bad news, O'Neill remained steadfast to his revitalization plan and focused his attention on reducing the company's healthcare costs, which were rising by 11 percent a year and costing the company nearly $200 million annually. "Our productivity improvements," he declared, "are effectively being eaten up by health care costs."

By the mid-1990s, O'Neill's reputation for running a tight and efficient enterprise had helped Alcoa realize a marked recovery from the ills of the early 1990s. Alcoa's net income rose from $4.8 million in 1993 to $375.2 million in 1994 and up to $790.5 million in 1995, while annual sales increased from $9 billion to $12.5 billion. As the company charted its course for the late 1990s and the new century ahead, O'Neill continued to hold a tight rein on spending, vowing to cut $300 million from Alcoa's annual sales and administrative costs by the end of 1997, which would produce a savings of 25 percent.

Toward this end, O'Neill spent $150 million in 1995 to upgrade Alcoa's computer technology system to a customized, state-of-the-art network. By linking Alcoa's businesses across the globe and facilitating the fluid transfer of information and ideas between operations, the system promised to increase the efficiency of bookkeeping, production and delivery cycles, and other corporate functions. Another key initiative of O'Neill's restructuring vision was to move the company from its 1952 headquarters to a new, $40 million facility on the Allegheny riverfront. Vital to the new corporate headquarters was the emphasis on open space and the leveling of hierarchy as a way of fostering employee interaction and productivity. As Martin Powell, one of the principal architects on the project told the *New York Times,* "It is a design driven by function, not status. People will be more visible and more accessible." O'Neill himself even went so far as to give up his own executive office in favor of a common cubicle. The move was complete by 1998.

Ultimately, O'Neill aimed to increase Alcoa's revenues from $13 billion to $20 billion by the new millennium. But in 1997 the price of aluminum remained depressed, and demand, particularly in the United States, continued to falter. As beverage companies sought to increase their profit margins by packaging drinks in eye-catching and unconventional plastic bottles, the long-held primacy of aluminum can packaging, which had accounted for 20 percent of all aluminum sales in North America and whose efficiencies were unrivaled, began to erode. To reach his ambitious revenue target by the year 2000, O'Neill would have to pursue aggressive strategies to continue cutting costs and increasing market share.

One such strategy was to drive up demand for aluminum in the auto industry. This was a challenging objective, as steel was generally a much less expensive material for manufacturing cars, and as auto manufacturers had already invested heavily in equipment designed to handle steel. Still, with fuel efficiency standards on the rise, there was reason to believe that lighter weight aluminum would gain appeal. Alcoa had begun in the early 1990s to court car companies including Audi and Chrysler to cooperate in aluminum car projects. While all-aluminum cars remained a thing of the future, Alcoa nonetheless made incremental strides to penetrate the industry. In 1995, for example, anticipating increased foreign demand for its lightweight, forged aluminum bus and truck wheels, the company announced plans to invest $30 million to begin manufacturing the wheels in Europe. In addition to wheels automakers were amenable to the use of aluminum in transmissions, doors, and roof racks.

To better position itself to take advantage of these areas of demand, in 1998 Alcoa spent $2.8 billion to purchase Atlanta-based Alumax, then a leader in the business of aluminum extrusion for the automobile and construction industries. The acquisition put Alcoa first in the extrusion business, expanding its overseas exposure, especially in emerging markets in China and India. This was seen as an important step toward insulating Alcoa from the cyclical nature of the raw aluminum market.

Indeed, an aggressive course of international acquisitions—including significant deals in Australia, Italy, and Spain—became increasingly important to Alcoa's growth strategy for the 1990s. The biggest move, however, came in 1999, when Alcoa secured a $4.8 billion deal to take over the Reynolds Metals Company, shortly after the consolidation of three of its biggest rivals, Alcan Aluminum of Canada, Pechiney of France, and Alusuisse Lonza Group of Switzerland. While companies were powerless to control the price of aluminum, they could maximize their profit-per-pound of metal sold by merging various operations and excising overlapping expenses. Although Alcoa's 1997 bid to buy certain assets from Reynolds was terminated after the Justice Department cited antitrust concerns, the 1999 deal won regulatory approval because of the complementary nature of the two businesses. Fulfilling O'Neill's lofty goal, the merger brought Alcoa's projected earnings for 2000 to $24 billion and enabled the company to retain its position as the world's number one aluminum producer. The merger was completed in 2000.

New Leadership for a New Century

In 1999, O'Neill's protégé, Alain J.P. Belda, succeeded him as CEO. Announcing his own, even loftier goal of growing the company—now officially renamed Alcoa Inc.—to a $40 billion concern by 2004, Belda continued to pursue a bold course of strategic acquisitions and cost-cutting. In 2000, Belda angled to secure Alcoa's stake in the aerospace industry with the $2.9 billion purchase of Cordant Technologies, a leading supplier of aluminum airplane parts and solid-fuel rockets. The following year, the company reached a further agreement to complete the purchase of Howmet International, Cordant's biggest business and the number one manufacturer of jet engine castings. Belda projected a combined cost savings of $425 million from the Reynolds and Cordant deals.

Still, in spite of Alcoa's shrewd strategic gains, the company remained vulnerable to the metals market, which continued to founder, and in January 2002, Alcoa posted its first quarterly loss since 1994. Later that year Alcoa announced plans to realign its businesses to better focus on the aerospace, automotive, and commercial transportation markets. By early in 2003, with sales still flat, the scope of the restructuring initiatives included the dismissal of 8,000 employees worldwide and the divestiture of the company's underperforming assets, especially in Europe and South America. Belda remained steadfast in his belief that these initiatives would afford the company increased flexibility to focus on and profit from its core businesses.

Principal Subsidiaries

Alcoa Brazil Holdings Co.; Alcoa Building Products, Inc.; Alcoa Closure Systems International, Inc.; Alcoa International Holdings Company; Alcoa Latin American Holdings Corporation; Alcoa Laudel, Inc. Alcoa Power Generating Inc.; Alcoa Securities Corporation; Alcoa (Shanghai) Aluminum Products Company Limited (China); Alcoa World Alumina LLC; Alumax Inc.; Howmet International Inc.; Cordant Technologies Holding Company; Gulf Closures W.L.L.; Reynolds Metals Company; Shibazaki Seisakusho Limited (Japan).

Principal Competitors

Alcan Inc.; Nippon Light Metal Company, Ltd.; Norsk Hydro ASA.

Further Reading

"Alcoa, the Microcosm," *Financial World*, June 25, 1991, p. 76.

Arndt, Michael, "Alcoa Wants One of These, and One of Those . . . ," *Business Week*, September 11, 2000, p. 63.

Arndt, Michael, "How O'Neill Got Alcoa Shining," *Business Week*, February 5, 2001, p. 39.

Baker, Stephen, and David Woodruff, "Alcoa Wants to Take Its Show on the Road," *Business Week*, August 1, 1994, p. 58.

Baker, Stephen, and Nicole Harris, "What's Foiling the Aluminum Can," *Business Week*, October 6, 1997, p. 106.

Carlisle, Anthony Todd, "Alcoa's Steely Course Prevails," *Pittsburgh Business Times*, December 30, 1996, p. 1.

Deutsch, Claudia H., "Alcoa Seeks to Acquire a Competitor," *New York Times*, August 12, 1999, p. C1.

Klebnikov, Paul, " 'Absolutely Trashed,' " *Forbes*, April 12, 1993, p. 86.

McGough, Robert, "The Spoiler," *Financial World*, February 18, 1992, p. 22.

Regan, Bob, "On Road Dead Ahead O'Neill Sees 'Black' As Others See 'Red,' " *American Metal Market*, October 13, 1993, p. 1.

Schroeder, Michael, "The Quiet Coup at Alcoa," *Business Week*, June 27, 1988.

Smith, George David, *From Monopoly to Competition: The Transformation of Alcoa, 1888–1986*, Cambridge: Cambridge University Press, 1988.

Stewart, Thomas A., "A New Way to Wake Up a Giant," *Fortune*, October 22, 1990.

Swaney, Chriss, "About Real Estate; Alcoa Vacating Its Downtown Pittsburgh Landmark," *New York Times*, July 24, 1996, p. A22.

—Douglas Sun
—updates: Jeffrey L. Covell and Erin Brown

amazon.com.

Amazon.com, Inc.

1200 12th Avenue, Suite 1200
Seattle, Washington 98114
U.S.A.
Telephone: (206) 266-1000
Fax: (206) 266-1821
Web site: http://www.amazon.com

Public Company
Incorporated: 1997
Employees: 7,800
Sales: $3.9 billion (2002)
Stock Exchanges: NASDAQ
Ticker Symbol: AMZN
NAIC: 45411 Electronic Shopping and Mail-Order
　　Houses

Considered a pioneer in online retailing, Amazon.com, Inc. expanded during the late 1990s to offer the "Earth's Biggest Selection" of books, CDs, videos, DVDs, electronics, toys, tools, home furnishings and housewares, apparel, and kitchen gadgets. Through third-party agreements, Amazon.com also sells products from well-known retailers including Toysrus.com Inc., Target Corporation, Circuit City Stores Inc., the Borders Group, Waterstones, Expedia Inc., Hotwire, National Leisure Group Inc., and Virgin Wines. Sometimes criticized for its focus on market share over profits, Amazon.com put investor fears to rest when it secured its first net profit during the fourth quarter of 2001.

The Early 1990s: Beginnings

Throughout the 1990s, the popularity of the Internet and World Wide Web swept across the world, and personal computers in most businesses and households got hooked up in some form or another to Internet providers and Web browser software. As use of the Internet became more prevalent in society, companies began looking to the Web as a new avenue for commerce. Selling products over the Internet offered a variety of choices and opportunities. One of the pioneers of e-commerce was Jeff Bezos, founder of Amazon.com.

In 1994, Bezos left his job as vice-president of the Wall Street firm D.E. Shaw, moved to Seattle, and began to work out a business plan for what would become Amazon.com. After reading a report that projected annual Web growth at 2,300 percent, Bezos drew up a list of 20 products that could be sold on the Internet. He narrowed the list to what he felt were the five most promising: compact discs, computer hardware, computer software, videos, and books. Bezos eventually decided that his venture would sell books over the Web, due to the large worldwide market for literature, the low price that could be offered for books, and the tremendous selection of titles that were available in print. He chose Seattle as the company headquarters due to its large high-tech work force and its proximity to a large book distribution center in Oregon. Bezos then worked to raise funds for the company while also working with software developers to build the company's web site. The web site debuted in July 1995 and quickly became the number one book-related site on the Web.

In just four months of operation, Amazon.com became a very popular site on the Web, making high marks on several Internet rankings. It generated recognition as the sixth best site on Point Communications' "top ten" list, and was almost immediately placed on Yahoo's "what's cool list" and Netscape's "what's new list." The site opened with a searchable database of over one million titles. Customers could enter search information, prompting the system to sift through the company database and find the desired titles. The program then displayed information about the selection on a customer's computer screen, and gave the customer the option to order the books with a credit card and have the books shipped in a just a few days.

Unlike its large competitors, such as Barnes & Noble and Borders, Amazon.com carried only about 2,000 titles in stock in its Seattle warehouse. Most orders through Amazon.com were placed directly through wholesalers and publishers, so no warehouse was needed. Amazon.com would simply receive the books from the other sources, then ship them to the customer. At first, the company operated out of Bezos' garage, until it was clear that it was going to be a success, necessitating a move to a Seattle office, which served as the customer support, shipping, and receiving area. It was interesting that, because of the Internet, such a small venture could realize such a broad scope so quickly; within a month of launching the web site, Bezos and Amazon.com had filled orders from all 50 states and 45 other countries.

As a pioneer in the world of Internet commerce, Amazon.com strived to set the standard for web businesses. With that goal in mind, Bezos went to work on making the web site as customer friendly as possible and relating the site to all types of customers. For those people who knew what book they were looking for and just wanted quick performance and low cost, Amazon.com offered powerful search capabilities of its expanded 1.5 million-title database. The company also began offering 10 to 30 percent discounts on most titles, making the prices extremely affordable. For other customers who were just looking for something to read in a general area of interest, Amazon.com offered topic areas to browse, as well as lists of bestsellers, award winners, and titles that were recently featured in the media. Finally, for people who could not decide, Amazon.com offered a recommendation center. There a customer could find books based on his or her mood, reading habits, or preferences. The recommendation center also offered titles based on records of books the customer had purchased in the past, if they were return customers to the site.

Other hits with customers were the little touches, such as optional gift wrapping of packages, and the "eye" notification service, which sent customers e-mails alerting them when a new book in their favorite subject or by their favorite author came into stock. The site also offered the ability for customers not only to write their comments about different books and have them published on the site, but to read other customers' comments about books they were interested in buying.

Going Public in 1997

After less than two years of operation, Amazon.com became a public company in May 1997 with an initial public offering (IPO) of three million shares of common stock. With the proceeds from the IPO, Bezos went to work on improving the already productive web site and on bettering the company's distribution capabilities.

To help broaden the company's distribution capabilities, and to ease the strain on the existing distribution center that came from such a high volume of orders, in September 1997 Bezos announced that Amazon.com would be opening an East Coast distribution center in New Castle, Delaware. There was also a 70 percent expansion of the company's Seattle center. The improvements increased the company's stocking and shipping capabilities and reduced the time it took to fill customers' orders. The Delaware site not only got Amazon.com closer to East Coast customers, but also to East Coast publishers, which decreased Amazon.com's receiving time. With the new centers in place, Bezos set a goal for the company of 95 percent same-day shipping of in-stock orders, getting orders to the customers much faster than before.

Another growth area for Amazon.com was the success of its "Associate" program. Established in July 1996, the program allowed individuals with their own web sites to choose books of interest and place ads for them on their own sites, allowing visitors to purchase those books. The customer was linked to Amazon.com, which took care of all the orders. Associates were sent reports on their sales and made a 3 to 8 percent commission from books sold on their sites. The Associates program really began to take off in mid-1997, when Amazon.com formed partnerships with Yahoo, Inc. and America Online, Inc. Both companies agreed to give Amazon.com broad promotional capabilities on their sites, two of the most visited sites on the Web. As the success continued, Amazon also struck deals with many other popular sites, including Netscape, GeoCities, Excite, and AltaVista.

As the company continued to grow in 1997, Bezos announced in October that Amazon.com would be the first Internet retailer to reach the milestone of one million customers. With customers in all 50 states and now 160 countries worldwide, what had started in a Seattle garage was now a company with $147.8 million in yearly sales.

Further Expansion in 1998

As Amazon.com ventured into 1998, the company continued to grow. By February, the Associates program had reached 30,000 members, who now earned up to 15 percent for recommending and selling books from their web sites. Four months later, the number of Associates had doubled to 60,000.

The company's customer database continued to grow as well, with cumulative customer accounts reaching 2.26 million in March, an increase of 50 percent in just three months, and of 564 percent over the previous year. In other words, it took Amazon.com 27 months to serve its first million customers and only six months to serve the second million. This feat made Amazon.com the third largest bookseller in the United States.

Financed by a $75 million credit facility secured in late 1997, Amazon.com continued to reshape its services in 1998. To its catalog of over 2.5 million titles, the company added Amazon.com Advantage, a program to help the sales of independent authors and publishers, and Amazon.com Kids, a service providing over 100,000 titles for younger children and teenagers.

Amazon.com also expanded its business through a trio of acquisitions in early 1998. Two of the companies were acquired to further expand Amazon.com's business into Europe. Bookpages, one of the largest online booksellers in the United Kingdom, gave Amazon.com access to the U.K. market. Telebook, the largest online bookseller in Germany, added its German titles to the mix. Both companies not only gave Amazon.com access to new customers in Europe, but it also gave existing Amazon.com customers access to more books from around the world. The Internet Movie Database (IMD), the third acquisition, was used to support plans for its move into online video sales. The tremendous resources and information of the IMD served as a valuable asset in the construction of a customer-friendly and informative web site for video sales.

Key Dates:

1995: Amazon.com debuts on the Web.
1997: The company goes public; Amazon.com becomes the first Internet retailer to secure one million customers.
1998: Amazon.com enters the online music and video business; companies are acquired in the United Kingdom and Germany.
1999: The firm expands into selling toys, electronics, tools, and hardware; Bezos is named Time Magazine's ''Person of the Year.''
2001: Amazon.com reports its first net profit during the fourth quarter.

Another big change in 1998 was the announcement of the company's decision to enter into the online music business. Bezos again wanted to make the site as useful as possible for his customers, so he appealed to them for help. Several months before officially opening its music site, Amazon.com asked its bookstore customers and members of the music profession to help design the new web site.

The music store opened in June 1998, with over 125,000 music titles available. The new site, which began operations at the same time that Amazon.com debuted a redesigned book site, offered many of the same helpful services available at the company's book site. The database was searchable by artist, song title, or label, and customers were able to listen to more than 225,000 sound clips before making their selection.

Amazon.com ended the second quarter of 1998 as strong as ever. Cumulative customer accounts broke the three million mark, and as sales figures for Amazon.com continued to rise, and more products and titles were added, the future looked bright for this pioneer in the Internet commerce marketplace. With music as a part of the company mix, and video sales on the horizon, Bezos seemed to have accomplished his goal of gathering a strong market share in the online sales arena. As Bezos told *Fortune* magazine in December 1996: ''By the year 2000, there could be two or three big online bookstores. We need to be one of them.''

Growth Continues: 1999 and Beyond

As such, the company's focus on growth continued. In 1999, it launched an online auction service entitled Amazon Auctions. It also began offering toys and electronics and then divided its product offerings into individual stores on its site to make it easier for customers to shop for certain items. During the holiday season that year, the firm ordered 181 acres of holiday wrapping paper and 2,494 miles of red ribbon, a sign that Bezos expected holiday shoppers to flock to his site as they had in the two past years. Sure enough, sales climbed to $1.6 billion proving that the founder's efforts to create an online powerhouse had indeed paid off. In 1999, Bezos reached the upper echelon of the corporate world when *Time* magazine honored him with its prestigious ''Person of the Year'' award.

While Amazon.com's growth story was remarkable, Bezos' focus on market share over profits had made Wall Street uneasy and left analysts speculating whether the company would ever be able to turn a profit. Sales continued to grow as the company added new products to its site—including lawn and patio furniture and kitchen wares. The company however, continued to post net losses. To top it off, the ''dot-com boom'' of the late 1990s came to a crashing halt in the early years of the new millenium as many startups declared bankruptcy amid intense competition and weakening economies.

Bezos remained optimistic, even as Amazon.com's share price faltered. During 2001, the company focused on cutting costs. It laid off 1,300 employees and closed a distribution facility. The company also added price reduction to its business strategy, which had traditionally been centered on vast selection and convenience. Amazon.com inked lucrative third-party deals with such well-known retailers as Target Corporation and America Online, Inc. By now, products from Toysrus.com Inc., Circuit City Stores Inc., the Borders Group, and a host of other retailers were available on the Amazon.com site.

Amazon.com's strategy worked. In 2001, sales grew to $3.12 billion, an increase of 13 percent over the previous year. During the fourth quarter, Amazon.com reached a milestone that many had regarded as unlikely; it secured a net profit of $5 million. In 2002, the company launched its apparel store, which included clothing from retailers The Gap and Lands' End. Overall, the company reported a net loss of $149 million for the year, an improvement from the $567 million loss reported in 2001. In the fourth quarter of 2002 however, the firm secured a quarterly net profit of $3 million—the second net profit in its history.

While securing quarterly net profits was a major turning point for the young company, a July 2002 *Business Week* article warned, ''after seven years and more than $1 billion in losses, Amazon is still a work in process.'' Indeed, the company's foray into providing the ''Earth's Biggest Selection'' had yet to prove it could provide profits on a long-term basis. Nevertheless, Bezos and his Amazon team remained confident that the firm was on the right track. With $3.9 billion in annual sales, Amazon.com had without a doubt come a long way from its start as an online book seller.

Principal Subsidiaries

Amazon Global Resources, Inc.; Amazon.com.dedc, LLC; Fulfillco.ksdc, Inc.; Amazon.com.kydc, Inc.; Amazon.com Commerce Services, Inc.; Amazon.com Holdings, Inc.; Amazon.com International Sales, Inc.; Amazon.com LLC; Amazon.com Payments, Inc.; NV Services, Inc.; Amazon Fulfillment Services, Inc.; Amazon.com@Target.com, Inc.

Principal Competitors

Barnes & Noble Inc.; CDNow Inc.; eBay Inc.

Further Reading

''Chewing the Sashimi with Jeff Bezos,'' *Business Week*, July 15, 2002.
Colker, David, ''Amazon Delivers Profit for the Second Time,'' *Los Angeles Times*, January 24, 2003.

Green, Lee, "Net Profits," *Spirit Magazine*, March 1998, pp. 52–54, 126–28.

Haines, Thomas, "Amazon.com Sales Grow While Loss Widens," *Seattle Times*, January 23, 1998, p. C1.

Hansell, Saul, "Amazon's Risky Christmas," *New York Times*, November 28, 1999.

Hazleton, Lesley, "Jeff Bezos: How He Built a Billion Dollar Net Worth Before His Company Even Turned A Profit," *Success*, July 1998, pp. 58–60.

"How Amazon Cleared the Profitability Hurdle," *Business Week*, February 4, 2002.

"Jeffrey Bezos," *Chain Store Age Executive*, December 1997, p. 124.

Jeffrey, Don, "Amazon.com Eyes Retailing Music Online," *Billboard*, January 31, 1998, pp. 8–9.

Martin, Michael, "The Next Big Thing: A Bookstore," *Fortune*, December 9, 1996, pp. 168–70.

Perez, Elizabeth, "Store On Internet Is Open Book: Amazon.com Boasts More Than 1 Million Titles On The Web," *Seattle Times*, September 19, 1995, p. E1.

Rose, Cynthia, "Site-Seeing," *Seattle Times*, March 10, 1996.

Soto, Monica, "Amazon Layoffs: What's It All Mean?," *Seattle Times*, February 5, 2001.

Zito, Kelly, "Amazon CEO Tells of Life at the Top," *San Francisco Chronicle*, December 23, 1999, p. B1.

—Robert Alan Passage
—update: Christina M. Stansell

It's Where America Swims™

Anthony & Sylvan Pools Corporation

6690 Beta Drive, Suite 300
Mayfield Village, Ohio 44143
U.S.A.
Telephone: (440) 720-3301
Toll Free: (877) 307-7946
Fax: (440) 720-3303
Web site: http://www.anthonysylvan.com

Public Company
Incorporated: 1996
Employees: 460
Sales: $158.4 million (2002)
Stock Exchanges: NASDAQ
Ticker Symbol: SWIM
NAIC: 235710 Concrete Contractors

Anthony & Sylvan Pools Corporation is America's largest, and only, publicly traded installer of in-ground residential concrete swimming pools and spas. The company, based in Mayfield Village, Ohio, serves 22 metropolitan markets in 16 states and operates 40 sales and design centers. In 2002 Anthony & Sylvan installed some 6,000 pools, which come in more than 40 shapes and may be as large as 1,200 square feet. A basic in-ground spa costs around $12,000, while on the upper end a pool with spa, stone deck, and appropriate landscape work can cost in excess of $100,000. In addition to building new pools, the company offers pool maintenance services, refurbishes existing pools, and sells pool-related items such as chemicals, filters, pumps, and heaters, as well as flotation devices and poolside accessories.

Postwar Origins

The two companies that make up the legacy of Anthony & Sylvan, Anthony Pools and Sylvan Pools, were both formed in the years just after the end of World War II and took advantage of the major postwar building boom. Sylvan Pools was launched in 1946 in the Philadelphia, Pennsylvania, area by Herman Silverman, who borrowed $500 to start the business.

Not only was he able to successfully grow his pool business, he became wealthy from real estate ventures. (Silverman was also one of novelist James Michener's closest friends, and he published a book about their relationship following Michener's death in 1997.) Sylvan Pool became the leading pool installer in the Northeast and branched out to the Southeast as well as Texas and Nevada. In 1969 the Cincinnati-based conglomerate KDI Corporation acquired an 80 percent interest in Sylvan Pools and took over the management of the business.

KDI was an amalgamation of unlikely assets. In addition to swimming pools it was involved in defense-related electronics, plastics technology, and film distribution. Although conglomerates with diverse interests may have been in vogue in the 1950s and 1960s, they were clearly out of style by the 1980s, when they became the object of corporate raiders who recognized the breakup value of such enterprises. During the first half of the 1980s KDI fended off a number of hostile takeovers. Finally in 1986 Ariadne Australia Ltd. succeeded in acquiring a controlling interest and installed former auto executive Eugene A. Cafiero as its chairman, chief executive officer, and president. Two years later, when the Australian parent company began to reconsider its investment, Cafiero led an investor group in a $275 million leveraged buyout. As a result the company, comprised of 18 subsidiaries, was saddled with excessive debt and in 1989 was forced to begin shedding assets. Five electronics companies were sold by the end of the year and the selloff continued in 1990. With a poor economy causing many people to cut back on luxury items, the business of the Sylvan Pools subsidiary was adversely impacted. KDI was forced to restructure, and Cifiero was essentially forced out in the fall of 1993. As part of the divestiture of assets Sylvan Pools was sold to California-based General Aquatics Inc., maker of swimming pool equipment. In 1996 General Aquatics acquired Anthony Pools and merged its operations with Sylvan.

The history of Anthony Pools followed a path similar to Sylvan, becoming part of a conglomerate. Phil Anthony founded the company in southern California in 1947 and, like Silverman on the East Coast, he took advantage of the postwar building boom to establish a thriving enterprise. Bernard Forester took over the company in 1973 and began to diversify

Company Perspectives:

"Where America Swims" is more than a slogan. It represents our base of more than 350,000 pools installed over the past 50 years and a reputation synonymous with quality and integrity.

beyond the seasonal swimming pool business, acquiring a wide range of businesses that he placed under the corporate shell of Anthony Industries, which he operated out of the Los Angeles, California, suburb City of Commerce. Forester's approach was to target recreational and sporting goods companies that had some brand-name recognition and were leaders in small niche markets. In 1974 Anthony acquired Hilton Active Wear, a Chicago company that produced bowling shirts, athletic jackets, and other imprintable items. Anthony also bought a mobile home manufacturer, which it later sold. In the 1980s Anthony became heavily involved in skiing, buying the Seattle-based K2 brand of skis and later adding the Olin brand. Further acquisitions included Shakespeare Fishing Tackle and Shakespeare Electronics & Fiberglass. The monofilament produced for fishing lines also found a market outside of sporting goods, used in weed cutters and such industrial applications as laminated paperboard and packaging. In addition to using fiberglass to make fishing poles the subsidiary began to produce fiberglass poles for street lights. It also produced insulating wall sheathing under the Thermo-Ply brand, which became America's leading brand. Anthony augmented Shakespeare's offerings by buying Stearns Water Safety Products, makers of life vests. It also moved into another sporting goods niche by acquiring Pro-Flex full suspension bikes. Moreover, Anthony added to its pool business by acquiring Automatic Solar Covers, a San Dimas, California, company that specialized in motorized pool covers. To build on strong pool sales on the West Coast and in the Sunbelt, Anthony Pools opened a Chicago office to serve the Midwest. While conglomerates like KDI Corporation were struggling, Anthony Industries posted a string of strong results in the late 1980s. Sales improved from $231.8 million in 1986 to $382 million in 1989. Net profits during this period grew from $1.9 million in 1986 to $13.4 million in 1989. Anthony's traditional pool business remained strong, contributing 25 percent of sales.

As the economy sputtered in the early 1990s, however, Anthony began to feel the effects of the slowdown. Revenues fell to $376 million in 1990 and net income to $1.7 million. The company instituted some cost-cutting measures, trimming staff and eliminating underperforming products. It also began to take on the business of rehabilitating older pools, an area that it had previously referred to independent contractors. K2 began to produce snowboards, after years of ignoring the product line, and found ways to distribute outside of its normal sales channels. As a result of such changes, Anthony improved its net earnings to $6.6 million in 1991 despite a further drop in revenues to $370 million. The company returned to its previous growth mode in 1992 when revenues topped $400 million and net profits reached $8.5 million.

In the early 1990s Anthony Industries began to pursue an aggressive strategy that would make it one of the top multi-line

sporting goods companies. Again it looked to make niche acquisitions as well as to use current subsidiaries to branch into new product lines. The company established a presence in the camping and outdoor market with the 1995 purchase of Wilderness Experience, makers of backpacks and outdoor apparel. Anthony added to its outdoor brands later in the year when it acquired innovative backpack manufacturer Dana Design. K2, during the mid-1990s, relied on product extension for growth, creating an entire line of snowboards and bindings and also eight models of upscale in-line skates. Anthony Industries' most recognizable brand was no longer Anthony Pools but K2, and the pool business was becoming less connected to the conglomerate's future plans in the sporting goods and recreation equipment area. In 1995 the subsidiary contributed just 12 percent of the parent's total revenues of $544 million. Early in 1996 Anthony Pools was sold to General Aquatics, and Anthony Industries subsequently changed its name to K2.

1990s Merger

General Aquatics combined its swimming pools assets to create Anthony & Sylvan Pools Corporation, which instantly became America's largest installer, with annual sales in the range of $150 million. The company, which established its headquarters in Doylestown, Pennsylvania, changed corporate parents a year later when in May 1997 Ohio-based Essef Corporation acquired General Aquatics and in the process inherited Anthony & Sylvan. Essef was formed in 1954 and produced plastics, fiberglass, and other materials used to make swimming pool filters as well as pressurized containers at water treatment plants. It was the swimming pool industry that contributed most of the company's sales, although in the 1980s it appeared that the computer industry's demand for plastic housings for personal computers would overshadow Essef's traditional source of sales. Optimism over the company's move into computers, however, was short-lived as its heavy reliance on a single customer, IBM, proved to be an ill-considered strategy.

When Essef acquired General Aquatics, experts believed that Essef was primarily interested in the swimming pool accessories and equipment operations. A manufacturing company, Essef appeared poorly suited to operate a swimming pool business, which was more of a sales and marketing operation.

Essef's management indicated from the outset that it planned to spin off Anthony & Sylvan but it soon opted to bide its time instead as it realized that the subsidiary, the only swimming pool installer with any kind of national presence, was in an excellent position to roll up smaller companies and gain an even greater market share and wider reach. Essef hired an investment banking firm to study the market and suggest a strategy on how to proceed with the swimming pool business, ultimately deciding to spin off the subsidiary and hold an initial public offering (IPO). Not only was this plan expected to help Anthony & Sylvan in its consolidation efforts, it eliminated business conflicts for Essef, which sold swimming pool products such as heaters, pumps, and filters to local swimming pool construction companies that were in competition with Anthony & Sylvan.

In the meantime, Anthony & Sylvan already began to bring smaller pool installers into the fold. Early in 1998 it acquired Tango Pools, a major Las Vegas pool maker. In September

Key Dates:

1946: Herman Silverman starts Sylvan Pools in Pennsylvania.
1947: Phil Anthony starts Anthony Pools in California.
1969: KDI Corporation acquires Sylvan.
1996: Anthony & Sylvan is formed as a subsidiary of General Aquatics.
1999: Anthony & Sylvan is spun off as an independent company.

1998 it acquired Pools by Andrew, a well-established Florida company that gave Anthony & Sylvan a foothold in the Florida market. In that same month, the company filed for a public sale of $22.5 million of common shares with the Securities and Exchange Commission, but with a cold market for IPOs the offering was postponed until August 1999, when it was finally completed in conjunction with the sale of Essef to Minnesota-based Pentair, Inc., manufacturer of pumps and electrical equipment. As part of the deal, Anthony & Sylvan assumed $17 million of Essef's debt.

Now an independent company, which began trading on the NASDAQ SmallCap Market, Anthony & Sylvan moved its corporate headquarters to Mayfield Village, Ohio and subsequently opened a sales, design, and installation office there to serve the northeast Ohio region. The company's chairman and chief executive officer, Stuart Neidus, announced a strategy of gaining greater market share by opening even more sales offices and to leverage their size and reach to establish relationships with national home builders, to become the pool developer for their projects. In 2000 the company opened new sales offices in the existing markets of Ft. Myers and Naples, Florida; Houston; and Las Vegas, and also looked to such new markets as Pittsburgh, Reno, Nevada, Phoenix, and Tucson. Because the company relied on local subcontractors to do construction, opening these offices was relatively inexpensive. Anthony & Sylvan achieved some external growth in 2000 by acquiring Cardinal Pools of Austin, Inc., a move that strengthened the company's presence in Texas (it already had operations in Dallas and Houston). In 2001 the company added to its Florida market share by opening a retail outlet in the Tampa area.

Despite a softening economy in 2001 that threatened to result in a slowdown in the pool industry, Anthony & Sylvan was able to continue its expansion efforts, due in large measure to its geographic diversification, which provided some shelter from underperforming markets. Net sales in 2000 totaled $175.7 million but fell to $167.7 million in 2001. As the economy worsened in 2002 Anthony & Sylvan was forced to take some steps to adjust to difficult conditions. It closed underperforming divisions in Orlando and southeastern Florida. Nevertheless, net sales in 2002 dropped to $158.4 million, the result of a 10.8 percent decrease in new pool construction, and the company posted a net loss of $2.2 million. The situation was mitigated somewhat by a 2.5 percent increase in the average selling price for new pools. In spite of these disappointing results and the continuation of poor economic conditions, Anthony & Sylvan still retained high hopes for the future, as it continued to pursue plans to expand within existing markets and enter new ones, achieved either through start-ups or by acquisition.

Principal Competitors

Shasta Inc.

Further Reading

Fickes, Michael, "Anthony & Sylvan: Where East Meets West," *Swimming Pool/Spa Age,* November 30, 1998.

Hardin, Angela Y., "Pool Maker Set To Test Waters in More Markets," *Crain's Cleveland Business,* January 17, 2000, p. 5.

Kowalczyk, Nick, "Pool Installer Makes Waves," *Plain Dealer,* August 1, 2001, p. C1.

Paris, Ellen, "A Conglomerate That Works," *Forbes,* November 28, 1988, p. 52.

Prizinsky, David, "Essef Eyes Big Splash in the Pool Business," *Crain's Cleveland Business,* April 13, 1998, p. 3.

——, "Essef's Swimming Pool Unit Plans Dive into IPO Market," *Crain's Cleveland Business,* September 28, 1998, p. 3.

—Ed Dinger

attachmate™

Attachmate Corporation

3617 131st Avenue Southeast
Bellevue, Washington 98006
U.S.A.
Telephone: (425) 644-4010
Toll Free: (800) 426-6283
Fax: (425) 747-9924
Web site: http://www.attachmate.com

Private Company
Incorporated: 1984
Employees: 1,275
Sales: $319 million (2001 est.)
NAIC: 511210 Software Publishers; 334119 Other
    Computer Peripheral Equipment Manufacturing

Attachmate Corporation is one of the largest privately held software companies in the world, operating as a developer of software for e-business and Web services technology. The company's strengths are in allowing personal computers to communicate with and to emulate mainframe computers, historically the primary repositories of corporate data. Attachmate's customers are Fortune 500 corporations and federal and state governments. The company operates on a global scale, serving customers in Europe, the Middle East, Africa, Latin America, Asia, and Australia. Domestically, the company maintains offices in nearly 50 cities. Attachmate is managed and owned by its founder, Frank Pitt.

Origins

In the January 27, 1997 issue of *Forbes,* Ann Marsh wrote: "A great barrier to new technologies is the investment people have in the old ones. That's why the United States hasn't embraced the metric system. It's why the un-ergonomic Qwerty keyboard survives. And it's how Frank Pritt made a small fortune." Pritt, Attachmate's founder, could not have known he would make a fortune with his start-up venture. Indeed, his first experience associated with Attachmate's founding was anxiety-ridden shock. All signs pointed to a quick failure. Pritt was retired when he launched his start-up company. In December

1982, with the idea of starting Attachmate, Pritt composed his resignation letter from Harris Corp., mailed the letter to his boss in California, and left his sales and marketing position behind him. He then went home to have lunch.

Pritt's intention was to create a company that made software capable of connecting mainframe computers to a fledgling but fast-growing breed of computers: the desktop. Corporations were keen on incorporating desktop, or personal computers, within their operations, but they also were reluctant to give up their trusted mainframes. Pritt sought to bridge the gap separating the old technology with the new technology by developing a product that enabled desktops to emulate the monitor of a mainframe. Known as connectivity, or terminal emulation, the process of allowing mainframe computers to "talk" to personal computers and networks promised to be a big business as the computing revolution leaped forward. By using a program that turned a personal computer's screen into a facsimile of a mainframe's old terminal, corporations could use both their existing equipment and invest in the future. Further, the program would allow employees to access information on the mainframe without memorizing a long string of commands and performing as many as 15 different steps. Pritt foresaw great demand for this backward-looking technology, but his heart dropped while eating lunch at home.

As he sat at his kitchen table, Pritt flipped through an issue of *Computer World* and saw an advertisement for IRMA. Pritt was looking at a product made by a company—Alpharetta, Georgia-based Data Communications Associates (DCA)—that was offering a product identical to the one he intended to make. IRMA was available for immediate shipment. Pritt's product existed only in his mind.

Nevertheless, Pritt pressed ahead with his career as an entrepreneur, resolving to forget that DCA existed and that IRMA was already to market—a difficult feat of denial given that DCA's Bothell, Washington, headquarters stood only several miles north of his base in Bellevue, Washington. Pritt used his retirement money to start Attachmate and immediately faltered. In a June 18, 1993 interview with the *Puget Sound Business Journal,* Pritt explained what happened next. "I had lots of technical problems getting started," he said. By the time I got on the market every competitor I had was already there [and] the product wasn't quite as ready as the customers were. We had a lot of customer problems and I wasn't very successful in raising outside money. I was about to run out of money by mid-1984 and the product wasn't working the way we thought.''

Having eschewed the voices of reason by going to market belatedly, Pritt again flew in the face of conventional wisdom. He laid off some of his workforce, fixed the product's flaws, and did something rarely witnessed in the software industry at the time. Pritt got rid of Attachmate's distributor and dealer marketing methods and assembled a direct sales force. Although his tactic was unconventional, Pritt was convinced that the reasoning behind this move was sound. In his June 18, 1993 interview with the *Puget Sound Business Journal,* he remarked: ''Our product was going into a sophisticated environment that required a lot of expertise and knowledge to sell. What we found out was that distributors and dealers didn't have good product knowledge. So we did something that was considered a no-no and set up our own direct sales force.'' Pritt also made two other important moves, each designed to beat back his competitors and give Attachmate a toehold in a burgeoning market. The company focused on designing extra features only a small portion of the market needed, theorizing that eventually the rest of the market would demand the added features. The design strategy gave Pritt's product its name, a terminal emulation package marketed under the name Extra. Pritt also turned his attention directly to DCA, offering customers the opportunity to trade in IRMA for Extra, a marketing ploy that later became commonplace in the computer industry.

Growth in the 1980s

After Pritt revamped his product and implemented his new marketing strategy, Attachmate began to record robust growth. As Pritt had hoped, mass demand for the added features included in Extra occurred, giving Attachmate a secure and sizeable position in the market it belatedly entered. Annual sales reached $5.3 million in 1986, rose to $13.6 million in 1987, and jumped to $31 million in 1987. Vigorous financial growth ensued, giving the company a $90 million sales volume by 1991, when Pritt, then in his early 60s, decided to step back from his responsibilities at the Bellevue-based company. He no longer enjoyed his work as much as he once had, and he needed someone to shepherd Attachmate's evolution from a start-up venture into a full-fledged corporation. Pritt turned to a friend for help, hiring G. Wayne Smith as Attachmate's president and chief executive officer. Pritt cut back his duties to those assigned to a chairman, taking responsibility for strategic planning and monthly reviews of Attachmate's performance.

In the wake of the transition in leadership, Attachmate's sales continued their energetic rise. In 1992, the company generated $123 million in sales, representing nearly a ten-fold increase during a five-year period. Not along afterwards, speculation abounded regarding Attachmate's conversion to public ownership. During the period of speculation about the company's initial public offering (IPO) of stock, Smith left and Pritt returned as Attachmate's president and chief executive officer. The IPO rumors swirling around the industry ended in May 1994, when speculation turned to anticipation. Pritt filed a preliminary prospectus with the Securities and Exchange Commission (SEC), confirming the company's intention to complete an IPO. The proposed IPO was expected to raise between $87 million and $101 million, but in July 1994 the IPO was scuttled, with poor market conditions given as the reason for the withdrawal. Not long afterwards, Attachmate filed an amended IPO document with the SEC, but backed out again. Following these two aborted attempts at an IPO, Pritt stunned the connectivity software community with an announcement.

1994 Merger Creates Industry Leader

In November 1994, Pritt announced he was embracing his old nemesis. The following month, Attachmate merged with $241 million-in-sales DCA, creating the largest company devoted to connectivity software in the world. The union of the two companies created an enterprise with nearly $400 million in annual revenues, 2,200 employees, and control of 35 percent of the worldwide market for terminal emulation, a greater market share than its closest rival, IBM, which controlled 23 percent of the global market. The merged company retained the Attachmate name and used Bellevue as its headquarters. Leadership of the company was drawn from both sides of the merger. Pritt served as chairman and chief executive officer, while DCA's chairman, chief executive officer, and president, James Lindner, took on the responsibilities of Attachmate's president and chief operating officer. As the two senior executives worked on amalgamating the two companies, plans were announced for another attempt at completing an IPO, perhaps as early as nine months after the merger was completed.

Problems surfaced within months of Attachmate's merger with DCA. Pritt handed the chief executive officer title to Lindner and began spending much of his time at his second home in Newport Beach, California, performing his duties as Attachmate's chairman while living in what was essentially semi-retirement. Left largely in control of Attachmate's entire operations, Lindner attempted to answer a question posited in the January 27, 1997 issue of *Forbes:* ''What would Attachmate do for a living when the last mainframe died?''

Lindner began searching for a new identity for Attachmate, attempting to redefine the company in anticipation of a time when the old mainframe technology at last became moribund. He recast Attachmate as ''the intranet company,'' releasing a Web browser whose existence was lost in one of the most contentious product wars of the 1990s. In the ferocious fight between Microsoft and Netscape, Attachmate's software floundered. By 1997, the company's browser failed to attract even 500 new customers a month. Another attempt by Lindner to redefine Attachmate met with equal disaster. In 1996, the company released server software for personal computer networks, but the introduction angered the last company any software developer wanted to anger. Microsoft, which had been promot-

---

Key Dates:

1982: Frank Pritt founds Attachmate.
1994: Attachmate merges with DCA.
1996: A failed diversification brings Pritt back to Attachmate's headquarters.

---

ing Extra to customers of its own server software, lashed out. The software giant severed all joint marketing agreements with Attachmate and began giving preferential treatment to the Bellevue company's competitors. In June 1996, Attachmate dropped its server software product line. One month later, Pritt moved back to Bellevue and fired Lindner, taking back the titles of chief executive officer and president. "I'm going to keep my finger in the pie," he vowed in a November 1, 1996 interview with the *Puget Sound Business Journal*.

Pritt Returns to Attachmate

In the post-Lindner period, Pritt grappled with getting his company back into shape. He reduced the company's workforce by at least 400 employees and restructured internal operations. However, the company remained plagued for years by the mistakes made during the mid-1990s. Attachmate was unprepared for the explosive rise in the use of the Internet in corporate settings and found itself trailing competitors for the remainder of the 1990s. Although corporations continued to rely on mainframes to store a majority of their information by the end of the 1990s, the core of Attachmate's business was ensconced in a dying sector, as companies increasingly turned to the Internet and server-base networks to store data. Against the backdrop of this ominous news, Attachmate became a dramatically smaller company. By the beginning of 2001, after three substantial lay-offs in little more than a year, the company employed 1,200

workers, nearly half the size of the company's workforce six years earlier.

For the 21st century, Attachmate was attempting to orient itself toward a market capable of sustaining long-term growth. Pritt broadened the company's reach, extending its involvement into developing software used to manage access to enterprise applications and databases. The company also developed desktop management software, development tools, and connectivity hardware. For a company that had once registered great success in assisting the evolution from old technology to new technology, its future depended on its own ability to evolve.

Principal Subsidiaries

Attachmate Unisys Group.

Principal Competitors

Computer Associates International, Inc.; International Business Machines Corporation; WRQ, Inc.

Further Reading

Baker, Sharon, "Attachmate's Fearless Founder Ignored Rival's Big Head Start," *Puget Sound Business Journal*, June 18, 1993, p. 51.
——, "Pritt: Everyone Keeps Guessing as Attachmate Keeps Growing," *Puget Sound Business Journal*, December 23, 1994, p. 13.
——, "Pritt Steps in at Attachmate," *Puget Sound Business Journal*, November 1, 1996, p. 1.
Berst, Jesse, "Attachmate: Look for It on the IPO Slate," *PC Week*, September 18, 1995, p. 79.
Marsh, Ann, "Why Frank Pitt Docked His Yacht," *Forbes*, January 27, 1997, p. 104.
Meisner, Jeff, "Attachmate Struggling to Shift Gears," *Puget Sound Business Journal*, February 2, 2001, p. 3.

—Jeffrey L. Covell

Aurora Casket Company, Inc.

10944 Marsh Road
Aurora, Indiana 47001
U.S.A.
Telephone: (812) 926-1111
Toll Free: (800) 457-1111
Fax: (812) 926-0208
Web site: http://www.auroracasket.com

Private Company
Incorporated: 1890 as Aurora Coffin Company
Employees: 900
Sales: $118 million (2001)
NAIC: 339995 Burial Casket Manufacturing

Aurora Casket Company, Inc. is the largest privately owned casket company in the United States. It produces more than 150,000 caskets a year, which are priced from $400 to $5,000. Aurora also makes urns and other cremation-related products. The business has been in the family since it was founded by John Backman in 1890. It has embraced e-commerce as a means of connecting with both consumers and funeral directors; about a third of the company's orders come through the Internet.

Many of the workers at Aurora are descendants of those who worked there in previous generations. It is "a family company serving a family profession." Aurora acquired Clarksburg Casket Co. of West Virginia, another family-run firm, in 2000. Clarksburg's hardwood caskets complemented those offered by Aurora's sales partner in Quebec, Victoriaville Casket Ltd. Aurora markets its products to funeral directors through 60 service centers across the United States.

Origins

Colonel John J. Backman formed the Aurora Coffin Co. in 1890. Southern Indiana was a good source of pine, and the company's caskets were sold in-state, as well as in Kentucky and Ohio. In the beginning, 30 workers made the caskets by hand.

Backman's son, Bill Backman, and son-in-law Bill Barrott entered the business in the 1920s. The two families would form the company's stable ownership for decades. They also took distinctive roles in management, with the Backmans concentrating on business and finance, and the Barrotts focusing on production and marketing.

Aurora began making mostly metal caskets in the 1940s. Presses and dies were acquired by 1947, enabling mass production of what had previously been tooled mostly by hand. The area in which the company was located was a great source for skilled metal workers from the automotive industry of Indiana and the tool-making tradition of Cincinnati, just a few miles to the west.

Wooden casket production was phased out in 1954. Aurora rolled out stainless steel caskets in 1966. This quickly became the fastest growing segment of the metal casket market. Aurora also made caskets from carbon steel and copper. Several processes would continue to be done by hand, such as sanding and buffing the exterior finishes and sewing fabric in the casket interiors.

A Canadian Partner in 1988

Aurora stopped selling coffins in Canada in 1973 due to a rise in the U.S. dollar and Canadian tariffs. A 15 percent tariff kept Aurora from returning to the Canadian market until a U.S.-Canada free trade agreement in the late 1980s. In December 1988, Aurora announced an agreement to sell its up to 2,000 steel coffins a year through Quebec's Victoriaville Casket Ltd., Canada's largest maker of wooden coffins. At the same time, Aurora would be selling up to twice as many of Victoriaville's wooden coffins in the United States. The U.S. duty on wooden coffins from Canada was 5.1 percent; both it and the Canadian tariff were being phased out over a ten-year period.

Surveys ranked Aurora either the second or third-largest producer of caskets in the business in the early 1990s. (In-state rival Batesville Casket Co., a subsidiary of Hillenbrand Industries Inc., was the largest.) Aurora had 600 employees, up from 400 a decade earlier. It had sales of about $50 million a year and was growing between 7 and 10 percent a year, according to *Indiana Business*. The plant was producing about 500 units a day. Trends affecting the industry, such as increased lifespan

Company Perspectives:

Colonel Backman established his company on three basic principles that he believed crucial to success. First, he insisted that the quality of his caskets set the standard for the industry. Second, he established a process to provide his customers with the products that best met their needs, as well as a superior level of service. Finally, he ensured his customers that they would be treated fairly and honestly within the bounds of a family business.

Key Dates:

1890: Colonel John J. Backman forms Aurora Casket.
1947: The company's acquisition of presses speeds metal casket manufacture.
1966: Aurora's stainless steel caskets are introduced.
1992: Aurora acquires the largest mechanical press in the casket industry.
1997: Urn manufacturer Meierjohan-Wengler Inc. is acquired.
1998: Mountain States Casket Co. and J&B Casket Co. are acquired.
2000: Clarksburg Casket Co. is acquired.
2003: Cotrim Hardwood Parts Co. and Hastings Casket Co. are acquired.

and the growing popularity of cremation, have been factors in Aurora's fortunes in recent decades.

In late 1992, Aurora acquired a 2,500-ton mechanical press from a Canadian automotive metal products company. Buying the press, relocating it, and rebuilding a 5,000-square-foot addition to house it cost Aurora $1.2 million. The press was the largest in the casket industry and increased both Aurora's capacity and range of products. It also served as a backup for the company's 500 ton and 1,000 ton presses.

Longtime employee William E. Barrott III became company president in September 1993. He succeeded William D. Backman, Jr., who became chairman and CEO. The company had sales of $80 million a year and 600 employees.

In 1994, the company got a moment on the silver screen during Tim Burton's film *Ed Wood,* which featured a recreation of Bela Lugosi as Count Dracula in a funeral parlor.

Aurora's headquarters underwent a $2.5 million expansion in 1995. The washer system was moved from the paint facility to a 15,000-square-foot addition to accommodate increasingly stringent environmental regulations. A 9,500 square foot sales and marketing building, with showroom, was also added to host a variety of customer service activities for funeral directors. The total size of Aurora's plant was 400,000 square feet. The company had 50 service centers around the country.

Acquisitions in the Late 1990s and Early 2000s

Aurora made a number of acquisitions in the late 1990s. Meierjohan-Wengler Inc., bought in 1997, was a maker of cremation urns, bronze plaques, and other funeral supplies. It had been founded in 1992. Mountain States Casket Co. of Salt Lake City was acquired from owner John Platt in 1998. Mountain States served funeral homes in Utah, Idaho, Colorado, Nevada, and Wyoming. In the same year, Aurora picked up the J&B Casket Co., based in Fargo, which served markets in Montana and the Dakotas. Aurora bought Clarksburg Casket Co. of Clarksburg, West Virginia in 2000. Clarksburg made hardwood caskets and had about 140 employees. Aurora president William Barrott said the Clarksburg line complemented that of its Canadian partner, Victoriaville.

Clarksburg was another venerable casket manufacturer, founded in 1906 by Frank Wilson. It also remained family managed; control of the company passed to Mark Garrett, grandson-in-law of the founder, in 1981.

These acquisitions helped push Aurora to $110 million in sales in 1999, when the company had 800 employees. Aurora had also launched an online technology initiative in 1998 and would soon be considered a pioneer in e-commerce.

Online in the 21st Century

A content-rich educational web site, funeralplan.com, was launched by Aurora in December 2000. It featured informative articles, interactive funeral planners, and allowed users to post online obituaries free. The ''Ask the Experts'' section provided advice from 15 experts in areas such as grief counseling and pre-need insurance. Funeralplan.com had three million visitors in 2001. Executive vice-president of operations told *Indiana Business Magazine* that the Internet was a good way to deliver information. ''You've got a family that needs information, needs it quickly and efficiently, and they probably know very little going in,'' he said. In addition, having casket selection information online spared families from visiting a room full of empty coffins.

Aurora had also developed Family Advisor software to help bereaved families cope with burial planning. About 150 funeral homes across the United States had it installed. When installed on a laptop, the software allowed funeral directors to visit bereaved families in their homes, saving them a visit to the funeral home.

Another online site, Memorial-markers.com, allowed funeral directors to design memorials online. By the end of 2002, more than 30 percent of Aurora's sales to funeral homes came online, reported *Indiana Business.*

Growth by acquisition continued in 2003. In March, Aurora acquired Cotrim Hardwood Parts Co. of Tennessee, which made hardwood caskets and cremation products and supplied hardwood parts to the furniture industry. The next month, Aurora bought Hastings Casket Co. of Nebraska. Hastings Casket's distribution center in Nebraska supplied funeral homes in Nebraska, Colorado, Kansas, South Dakota, and Wyoming; the acquisition enhanced Aurora's national distribution.

Principal Subsidiaries

Clarksburg Casket Co.; Meierjohan-Wengler Inc.

Principal Competitors

Hillenbrand Industries Inc. (Batesville Casket Co.); Matthews International; Service Corporation International; York Group Inc.

Further Reading

"Barrott to Head Aurora Casket," *Cincinnati Post*, September 25, 1993, p. 7C.

Beck, Bill, "Indiana Manufacturing Firsts," *Indiana Business Magazine*, January 1995, pp. 16ff.

Boyer, Kerry, "New Press Giving Aurora Casket More Capacity," *Greater Cincinatti Business Record*, March 15, 1993, p. 1.

Boyer, Mike, "Aurora Buys Another Casket Firm," *Cincinnati Enquirer*, April 24, 2003, p. D3.

Brothers, Perry, "Job Outlook Is Good for Grads Who Worked," *Cincinnati Enquirer*, May 15, 1997.

"Dot-Com Funeral?," *Indiana Business Magazine*, December 1, 2002, p. 6.

Gherson, Giles, "U.S. Business Plots Its Free Trade Push: Continental Market Seen as Barriers Fall," *Financial Post* (Toronto), Sec. 1, September 5, 1988, p. 1.

Hannagan, Charley, "Timing Was Bad for Potential Marsellus Suitor," *The Post Standard/Herald Journal*, April 18, 2003, p. C6.

Kerfoot, Kevin, "Aurora Casket Co. Begins $2.5 Million Expansion," *Indiana Manufacturer*, May 1, 1995, p. 12.

Mei Fong, "The Web@Work: Casket Royale," *Wall Street Journal*, August 27, 2001, p. B4.

Melcher, Rachel, "Aurora Casket Launches Computer-Based Showroom," *Business Courier Serving Cincinnati-Northern Kentucky*, June 23, 2000, p. 8.

Myers, George, Jr., "Software Helps Bereaved Cope," *Columbus Dispatch* (Ohio), August 6, 2001, p. 7E.

Nyden, Paul J., "Indiana-Based Funeral Supplies Giant Buys Clarksburg, W.Va. Casket Company," *Charleston Gazette*, October 12, 2000.

"Portable CMM Cuts Time to Program Five-Axis, Hole-Drilling Machine Tool from Eight Hours to 15," *Modern Machine Shop*, July 1995, pp. 124ff.

"Road Kill; Bits and Bytes from the New-Media Front," *Advertising Age*, June 26, 1995.

"Salt Lake Casket Maker Sold to Indiana-Based Industry Leader," *The Enterprise* (Salt Lake City), October 19, 1998, p. 3.

Shen, Fern, "Gold King Tut Casket Is the Chic Way to Go; 3,000 Funeral Directors Meet in Md., Study Trends," *Washington Post*, October 22, 1989, p. B3.

Spaid, Ora, "Aurora Casket Company," *Indiana Business*, February 1, 1991, p. 36.

"State Helping in Purchase of Harrison Casket Maker," *Charleston Daily Mail* (West Virginia), November 18, 2000, p. 11A.

Tallmer, Jerry, "When Horror Was at Its Most Horrible; Dark Days of Ed Wood," *The Record*, September 28, 1994, p. C8.

"U.S. Firm Renews Canadian Sales with a Coffin-Swap Arrangement," *Tornoto Star*, December 30, 1988, p. C3.

Whitford, Marty, "Casket Manufacturers Test Watertight Seals," *Rubber & Plastics*, October 10, 1994, p. 19.

—Frederick C. Ingram

AWB Ltd.

528 Lonsdale Street
Melbourne 3000 VIC
Australia
Telephone: (+61) 3-9209-2000
Fax: (+61) 3-9209-2350
Web site: http://www.awb.com.au

Public Company
Incorporated: 1939 as the Australian Wheat Board
Employees: 485
Operating Revenues: A$2.33 billion ($1.31 billion)
  (2002)
Stock Exchanges: Australian
Ticker Symbol: AWB.AX
NAIC: 424510 Grain and Field Bean Merchant
  Wholesalers

AWB Ltd. is redefining itself for the new century. Formerly government-regulated Australian Wheat Board, AWB Ltd. is transforming itself into a publicly listed, vertically integrated agribusiness. Nonetheless, AWB retains its monopoly position as the country's sole wheat and grains exporter through its unique single-desk system that not only maximizes prices for its farmer-shareholders but also contributes to ensuring Australian wheat exports' high-quality reputation. Australian grain production, which averages 35 million tons per year, accounts for less than 5 percent of the total world wheat market. However, because the country exports as much as 80 percent of its wheat production, the country ranks among the world's top five wheat exporters. Although wheat accounts for 90 percent of AWB's export business, the company also markets barley, sorghum, oilseeds, and pulses. AWB is especially active in the Asian markets, where wheat is slowly replacing more traditional rice and other grains as a staple food. The company's main markets include Iran, Indonesia, Japan, Egypt, and South Korea; AWB has also been a strong supplier of wheat to Iraq. In addition to its core export business, AWB has been investing in grain storage facilities in Australia and in feed and flour milling operations elsewhere. The company's attempt to acquire the milling assets of Australia's Goodman Fielder—worth

some 40 percent of the total Australian market—were thwarted because of competition concerns. Instead, the company has taken a major shareholding stake in Futuris, which controls Australian agricultural services group Elders, and has expressed an interest in acquiring Grainco, which provides agricultural logistics services. AWB's freely tradable Class B shares are listed on the Australian Stock Exchange. The company's Class A shares are restricted to a pool of 38,000 grain farmers, each of whom must grow a minimum of 100 tons of wheat per year. This class of shareholders elect the majority of AWB's board of directors.

Origins

Wheat farming began in the Australian colonies in the early part of the 19th century but remained limited until the development of the country's railway system. By the middle of the century, however, the accessibility of increasing portions of the country spurred farming development. Grains, and especially wheat, became an important crop, and by the beginning of the 20th century had become largely centered on the states of New South Wales, Victoria, and South Australia. Western Australian became another important grains-growing region at the end of the first decade of the century. In the 1930s, Queensland developed into another major Australian grain-grower.

Australia emerged as a prominent wheat exporter at the end of the 19th century when the colony's limited population led it to seek markets for its expanding wheat production. The United Kingdom became the most significant market for the country's grain exports and remained so until the 1960s. In the early years of the 20th century, Australian farming was dominated by independent and typically family-owned farmers, a situation that left the country's wheat production financially vulnerable. At the same time, farmers were unable to invest in updated farming technologies.

The outbreak of World War I led to significant changes in the country's grain export system as a large number of the country's farmers joined the war effort, causing wheat production to drop sharply. The Australian government responded by setting up the first Australian Wheat Board, which took over marketing of the country's wheat exports. By the end of the war, the Wheat Board had succeeded not only in granting farmers a strong measure of financial security but had also established the highest wheat prices in decades. The first Australian Wheat Board was disbanded after the war, however.

During the 1920s, a number of Australian states set up temporary agricultural cooperatives to fill in the gap left by the shutdown of the Wheat Board. In the meantime, wheat production expanded strongly throughout the decade, in part because of the Australian government's policy of setting aside land for returning soldiers after the war. By the end of the decade, wheat production in some parts of the country had risen some 400 percent. At the time, Australia, with its apparently limitless natural resources, remained heavily reliant on its agricultural sector.

Grain Farmer Protection in the 1930s

The collapse of the worldwide economy during the 1930s, and the Australian government's response to it, set in motion the emergence of a new and more lasting Australian Wheat Board. With the nation's economy floundering, the government, believing it could grow its way back to economic prosperity, launched a program in 1930 based on the slogan: "Grow More Wheat." The collapse of many small farms over the next decade led to the emergence of a growing number of large-scale producers.

The increases in Australia's wheat production in the meantime had placed the country's smaller, independent farmers more or less at the mercy of "parasitical" wheat buyers both at home and on the export market. Indeed, throughout the 1930s, the worldwide international grain trade was dominated by just five companies: Cargill, Continental Grain, Andre, Louis Dreyfus, and Bunge and Born.

The emergence of large-scale grain producers led to an increasing number of complaints from smaller farmers as the larger farms were better equipped financially to negotiate with the grain traders, thereby forcing down wheat prices. In 1938, the Australian government enacted legislation under the Wheat Industry Assistance Act in order to create new taxes that would standardize prices on domestic flour prices and wheat exports.

Australian Wheat Board Created

With the outbreak of World War II, national security imperatives brought about the creation of a new Australian Wheat Board (AWB) by the Commonwealth Government in 1939. The AWB was given the authority to oversee the marketing, storage, shipping, pooling, and payment, including advance payments, of the country's wheat output.

The AWB implemented its first wheat pricing stabilization measures in 1940, which took effect after the 1941–42 growing season. The policy provided for guaranteed prices, created a stabilization fund, and put in place new growing licenses. The AWB continued to adjusting its stabilization policies throughout the war. By the end of the war, the necessity and desirability of maintaining a postwar stabilization policy found general acceptance. Nonetheless, an initial attempt to legislate a peacetime stabilization failed in 1946. It was only in 1948, when production controls were dropped from the legislation package, that the Australian government finally passed the Wheat Industry Stabilization Act.

Postwar Growth

Under the AWB, which initially controlled both the domestic wheat and wheat export sectors, Australia's wheat exports grew strongly. By the 1950s, the country exported some 60 percent of total wheat production, and the wheat industry accounted for some 15 percent of the country's total export sales. By the 1980s, exports had risen to account for 80 percent of total production. In the meantime, however, Australia's the expansion of the country's industrial sector had reduced the wheat export market to just 5 percent of total exports.

Nonetheless, Australian wheat gained a reputation as a quality leader on the international grains market. The AWB had been instrumental in leading genetic research to improve both the variety and quality of the country's grains crops. The AWB's efforts resulted in the introduction of a number of grains brands, including the well known Australian White Wheat. This development led the board to institute a classification system that divided the country's grains brands into some fifty or more grades targeted for specific foods and feed markets. At the same time, AWB's "single-desk" system allowed it to control the quality and purity of its exports, thus winning it steady customers against a number of international competitors.

The AWB began to shift its export focus from the United Kingdom and other western markets—where grain production remained heavily subsidized—to more promising markets in the Middle East as well as in rapidly developing Asian countries. As Western influences took hold in these markets, consumer preferences slowly began to shift away from a reliance rice consumption to adopt wheat-based foods. In 1960, the board began marketing wheat to China; by the end of the 1960s, the company's Chinese exports had grown to a significant share of its total.

Privatization and Deregulation

In the 1980s, the Australian government, then led by Prime Minister Robert Hawke, began an attempt at deregulating much of the country's state-dominated industries, including the wheat industry. In 1989, the Hawke government passed the Wheat Marketing Act, which stripped the domestic grains market from AWB's control. The same legislation also created a separate Wheat Industry Fund, which was administered by the Australian Wheat Board. The deregulation of the domestic market led to the creation of a number of new businesses, including Grainco and GrainCorp.

AWB remained the state-controlled wheat export monopoly into the late 1990s. By then, however, deregulation caught up to

Key Dates:

1939: Australian Wheat Board is created to oversee war-time domestic and export wheat markets.
1948: The Wheat Industry Stabilization Act is passed.
1989: Australia's domestic wheat market is deregulated and the Wheat Industry Fund is created under AWB management.
1998: The Wheat Export Authority, which effectively guarantees AWB's monopoly on wheat exports, is created.
1999: AWB takes over Wheat Industry Fund and issues Class A and Class B shares.
2001: AWB goes public, changing its name to AWB Ltd.
2003: AWB begins acquiring shares in Futuris and enters merger talks with Grainco.

the grains export market as well. In 1998, the government, now under John Howard, passed the Wheat Marketing Amendment Act, which created a new Wheat Export Authority (WEA) to take over the AWB's regulatory powers. Yet the legislation that created WEA also in effect affirmed the AWB's monopoly over wheat exports by granting it a veto over third-party requests for bulk exports. (Third parties were, however, allowed to export smaller quantities of grains.)

The Australian government remained under heavy pressure, both from the major international grains trading groups such as Cargill, as well as other governments, including the United States, which, under the Bush administration, lobbied the Australians to abandon the single-desk system. In the meantime, the Australian government continued the process of privatizing the AWB. In 1999, the government placed the Wheat Industry Fund under the AWB's direct control. The government then issued shares in the AWB, granting Class A shares, which were non-tradable and non-transferable, to grains growers that averaged at least 100 tons over a three-year period and Class B shares to shareholders in the Wheat Industry Fund. Under the terms of the Fund transfer, however, AWB was required to maintain at least 75 percent of the Fund, which by then totaled A$600 million.

A Public Company in the 21st Century

The Australian Wheat Board reached the end of the privatization process in 2001, when it changed its name to AWB Ltd. and listed its Class B shares on the Australian stock exchange. The newly public company announced its intention to develop into a full-scale, vertically integrated agribusiness. AWB began a series of investments, including adding grain storage operations as well as taking shares in milling and feed businesses in a number of chiefly Asian markets.

Yet AWB was thwarted in its first attempt at large-scale vertical expansion in Australian. The company had made a bid to purchase the milling operations of Goodman Fielder, which would have given it control of some 40 percent of the Australian and New Zealand milling markets. However, the government body regulating monopolies and mergers struck down the deal due to competition concerns in 2002.

Instead, AWB looked elsewhere for expansion. At the beginning of 2003 the company began buying shares in Futuris, a diversified business which controlled, among other companies, the Elders agricultural services group. By May 2003, AWB, amid a new drought that threatened grain production and exports, began merger talks to acquire grain-growing group Grainco. A month later, the Australian High Court upheld AWB's monopoly on grain exports, defeating a suit brought against the company by would-be rival NEAT Domestic Trading. At the same time, a four-month investigation by the Australian Senate concluded that AWB's monopoly should be placed under an independent review board in order to guard against potential conflicts of interest between the company's obligations to its grower-owners and to shareholders of its publicly listed stock. Despite the uncertainty over its status, AWB Ltd. remained committed to developing itself as a major international agribusiness in the new century.

Principal Subsidiaries

AWB International (AWBI) Limited; AWB Finance Limited; AWB Seeds Ltd.

Principal Competitors

Cargill International S.A.; Cenex Harvest States Cooperatives; Royal Cebeco Group Cooperative UA; Ets Jean Soufflet; Canadian Wheat Board.

Further Reading

"AWB Head Sees More Growth," *Business Asia*, April 2002, p. 19.
"Grainco Australia Remains in Merger Talks with GrainCorp and AWB," *Asia Pulse News*, May 13, 2003.
Easdown, Geoff, "Monopoly Secure," *Herald Sun*, June 20, 2003, p. 85.
Frith, Bryan, "AWB Harvest Futuris," *Australian*, February 14, 2003, p. 20.
Whitwell, Greg, and Diane Sydenham, *A Shared Harvest: The Australian Wheat Industry 1939–1989*, Macmillan: South Melbourne, 1991.
Wyatt, Stephen, "Australian Wheat Monopoly May Soon Be Overturned," *Financial Times*, January 12, 2001, p. 38.

—M.L. Cohen

Awrey Bakeries, Inc.

12301 Farmington Road
Livonia, Michigan 48150-1747
U.S.A.
Telephone: (734) 522-1100
Toll Free: (800) 950-2253
Fax: (734) 522-1585
Web site: http://www.awrey.com

Private Company
Incorporated: 1910 as Awrey & Sons
Employees: 420
Sales: $80 million (2003 est.)
NAIC: 311812 Commercial Bakeries; 311813 Frozen
   Cakes, Pies, and Other Pastries Manufacturing;
   311821 Cookie and Cracker Manufacturing

Awrey Bakeries, Inc. is one of the leading producers of frozen baked goods for the U.S. food service trade. The company makes a number of different items including cakes, cookies, Danish pastries, doughnuts, and croissants, which are used by restaurants, hotels, schools, hospitals, and other institutional customers. About one-tenth of the firm's business comes from retail sales of its own branded goods, which are available only in the state of Michigan. Awrey Bakeries is owned by members of the Awrey family and executives of the firm.

Early 1900s Beginnings

Awrey Bakeries got its start in 1910 in the home of Fletcher and Elizabeth Awrey, who were living in Detroit, Michigan, after moving there from Canada. To help make ends meet, Elizabeth Awrey began to bake breads and pastries in her wood-fired oven and selling the goods to their neighbors. When sons Wilbur, Elton, and Thomas began to help sell the baked goods door-to-door, the business started to grow. In 1914 the Awreys opened a retail outlet on Tireman Avenue in Detroit, where the firm's first "volume baking" was begun. Two bakers were hired along with three women who finished cakes, assembled products, and minded the store.

Over the next four years two more storefronts were added, and the Awreys purchased a Model T Ford truck to make deliveries from the Tireman bakery to the stores. The three Awrey sons were now involved in every aspect of the business and excelled at finding new markets, such as high school cafeterias and lunching workers at Detroit auto plants.

As sales increased the Awreys began to expand their baking plant and staff. By 1923 there were 25 employees working in production, and in 1929 the company began installing mechanized baking equipment. Awrey & Sons, as the firm was now known, was operating 32 stores by the end of the decade. The firm was also again selling baked goods door-to-door, which it had returned to in 1923 with a group of independent salesmen who owned their own trucks.

The Great Depression did not slow the company's expansion, and it had 55 units in operation by 1933. By 1940 this number had increased to 91. During World War II growth was put on hold in part because of a shortage of sugar due to rationing.

Supermarket "Service Counters" Fuel Postwar Expansion

After the war Awrey's growth resumed, aided by the increasing popularity of supermarkets. The large grocery stores of this era typically contained several departments operated by outside concessionaires, and Awrey "service counters" were set up in many such stores around the Detroit area. By 1950 the company had 120 locations, including both individual stores and supermarket concessions, and was also operating a home delivery service. This period saw the introduction of the "Kissing Kids" line of products. Aimed at families on a budget, the economical line of baked goods came to include doughnuts, sheet cakes, and bread. A logo was created for the line which featured two kissing Dutch children.

During the 1950s the company closed a number of its older outlets and opened many new ones, bringing the total number of locations to 160 by 1960, the year the firm celebrated its 50th anniversary. There were now 12 independent stores, 112 service counters, and 36 new "self-service" locations in supermarkets, the latter minimally-staffed outlets that had been introduced in 1957. Some 20 percent of the firm's sales also came from home deliveries through a fleet of 115 independently owned and operated trucks. At this time Thomas Awrey was the company's

Company Perspectives:

While our products are efficiently mass produced, we always start from scratch. Each recipe maintains that homemade taste which earned Awrey's the title of America's Hometown Bakery. Our tradition of old-fashioned value and delicious quality are still reflected in our modern, progressive company—progressive in our products, our service, our technology, and even our environmental awareness in making packaging decisions. Across the country, Awrey's really is 'America's Hometown Bakery'.

president, with Wilbur Awrey serving as vice-president, and Elton Awrey secretary and treasurer.

In 1967 the company opened a new baking plant in the Detroit suburb of Livonia, moving its offices there as well. The original facility on Tireman Avenue was closed two years later. During the 1960s and 1970s Awrey's delivery and concession businesses were declining, due to increased competition as well as supermarket consolidation and the demands of concession workers for better wages. The firm sought new areas in which to expand, and the decision was made to introduce a line of frozen baked goods, which were modeled on the successful products of Sara Lee. The results were less than spectacular, but a parallel line of frozen baked goods aimed at the food service market began to take off, and this category grew to represent a sizable portion of Awrey's business by the end of the 1970s.

In 1981 control of the firm passed to the third generation of family members when Robert Awrey was named chairman and CEO. By this time ownership of the company had broadened to include several family members as well as some of the firm's management team, many of whom had been with the company for decades. This generation of employees was now reaching retirement age, and during the late 1980s the firm lost ten of its top 11 managers. To maintain an orderly transition from these experienced executives to younger ones, Awrey developed a plan whereby successors were named six months to a year in advance and then trained by the outgoing executive until they were ready to take over. Two such new additions were president Richard Pedi, who joined the company in 1986 after running an institutional produce firm in Chicago, and vice-president of finance Dean Calvert, a former independent financial planner. At this time Awrey's annual revenues were an estimated $45 million.

As its leadership began passing to a new generation, Awrey also started to implement a business philosophy of "continuous improvement," which emphasized quality and customer satisfaction as primary objectives over simple quantitative measures. The philosophy (derived from the ideas of W. Edward Deming, who had worked with the Ford Motor Company) eschewed radical change in favor of small improvements in day-to-day operations.

Food Service Baking Dominates the 1990s

By 1990 Awrey's food service business had grown to account for 70 percent of total revenues, with retail sales contributing one-quarter and contract baking making up the remainder. The company had 700 food service distributors and a national network of brokers that distributed its products to institutional accounts such as hospitals, schools, and restaurants. The retail line, which included pies, cakes, bread, doughnuts, rolls, croissants, muffins, and Danish pastries, was distributed in southeastern Michigan to stores that ranged from major supermarket chains to small independent grocers. By now 76 percent of the firm was owned by members of its management team, with Robert Awrey holding a 17 percent stake.

The year 1990 saw Awrey add a new line of low-fat, low-cholesterol baked goods to its retail offerings in an attempt to compete with rival Entenmann's, which was having great success with similar products. The company spent eight months and $75,000 to get four coffee cakes, two muffins, and two pound cakes formulated and ready to market. Awrey was the second major baking concern in the country to introduce such a line of baked goods.

The new products did not bring the success the company had hoped for, and in May 1991 President Rick Pedi announced that the firm would stop baking goods for retail sale entirely, though the Awrey brand name would continue to appear on bread and buns baked under license by Veri-Best Baking Co. of Ferndale, Michigan. The company's line of frozen food service baked goods had become its primary area of business, and it was decided to concentrate on this exclusively. Awrey had already begun to move in this direction, discontinuing a number of retail products and laying off 95 truck drivers, production workers, and retail-related workers earlier in the year.

Less than six months after Pedi's announcement, however, he and Chief Financial Officer Dean Calvert left the firm, and CEO Robert Awrey and his son Thomas took control of day-to-day operations. The company immediately announced it would return its retail baked goods to store shelves, though the distribution would be handled by Veri-Best Baking Co., meaning that many of the laid-off workers would not be rehired. The Awrey line was returned to most of the former retail outlets, which included Detroit-area Kroger, Foodland, Hollywood Markets, and Farmer Jack supermarket chains, as well as several independent grocers.

In 1994 a new food-labeling law took effect, forcing Awrey to spend ten months and $100,000 on new labeling equipment and the modification of existing equipment. By now the firm was employing 500 and posting $52 million in annual sales.

In 1995 Awrey beat Sara Lee Corporation to win a multi-million dollar baking account with Baskin-Robbins USA Co. to make the chocolate-brownie crusts for its new Polar Pizza flavor, which was launched in the ice cream chain's 2,500 stores in August. Baskin-Robbins would join several other national baking accounts the firm held that included Burger King (for which Awrey supplied Danish pastries, doughnuts, and birthday cakes) and Wal-Mart (which bought the firm's Danish pastries). Awrey also spent nearly $200,000 to "kosherize" its plant in Livonia after winning the Baskin-Robbins contract. In addition to certifying that the firm's suppliers adhered to Jewish dietary laws, Awrey's 260,000-square-foot production facility was shut down for four days while it was steam-cleaned and sanitized from floor to ceiling. Awrey food service goods were already distributed throughout the United States, but the kosher certification was expected to increase its business on the East Coast.

Key Dates:

1910: The Awrey family begins selling baked goods in their Detroit neighborhood.

1914: Family opens first retail outlet and begins volume baking operations.

1920s: Firm, known as Awrey & Sons, expands to 32 stores.

1930s: Growth continues during Depression; 91 outlets open by end of decade.

1950: Supermarket "service counters" help drive number of locations to 120.

1960: With 160 outlets, Awrey celebrates 50th anniversary.

1967: Awrey moves to new baking plant and headquarters in Livonia, Michigan.

1970s: Sales of frozen food service baked goods begin to grow; retail outlets dwindle.

1990: Revenues top $50 million; 70 percent of sales are now derived from food service products.

1991: Awrey abandons retail sales, then reinstates them amid management shake-up.

1995: To service new Baskin-Robbins account, firm kosherizes its baking plant.

1998: $20 million, 5-year modernization program begins.

In April 1996 Demetri Preonas took over the jobs of president and chief operating officer from Tom Awrey, who moved to the position of vice-chairman. Preonas had been with the company since the preceding June, serving as general manager of operations. Prior to joining the firm, he had run a family-owned bakery in Dayton, Ohio.

By 1997 Awrey's annual revenues had grown to an estimated $60 million, with 90 percent of sales coming from the food service market. Awrey products were found in restaurants, hotels, schools, hospitals, airlines, and other institutional settings such as business cafeterias. The company's factory operated five production lines which made Danish, cakes, doughnuts, croissants, and biscuits, with the latter two lines used alternately as the basis for dinner rolls and cookies. The plant operated 24 hours a day, five or six days per week. In addition to its own products, a few items from other bakeries were offered to food service accounts through the company, including English muffins and bagels, though these were manufactured to Awrey's specifications.

To keep up with constantly-changing customer preferences, Awrey added many new products each year—as many as 100 or more. The company maintained a five-member research and development team to come up with the new offerings, the majority of which were intended for the food service market. Many were test-marketed to customers at the firm's sole remaining retail outlet, near its packaging facility in Livonia.

In 1998 Awrey installed robotic devices to remove sweet rolls from pans in the firm's baking plant, which produced significantly better results than a 20-year old system that required frequent maintenance and damaged an estimated 6 percent of product. This move was one of the first steps in a $20 million modernization effort, which over the next five years would expand the firm's plant to 348,000 square feet.

2000s and Beyond

In 2002 Awrey was one of the first companies in the United States to win a prestigious American Institute of Baking Bakers Quality Seal Award, which was given for both quality and safety of baking operations. The company went through several rigorous inspections and surprise visits before receiving the award. Nine Awrey family members were now involved with the company, and they could often be found in the plant, checking quality and assuring that the production line was running smoothly.

In the spring of 2003 Awrey began widely marketing a six-inch chocolate cake that had originally been offered at the recently-defunct Bill Knapp's restaurant chain. The cake, which had been baked for Knapp's by Awrey, had been hugely popular with the chain's customers, and after the restaurant's demise Awrey bought the recipe for $15,000. The cakes were sold through Meijer stores, in many of the areas where the restaurants had been located.

Approaching the century mark, Awrey Bakeries had evolved into one of the top food service baking companies in the United States. With a strong distribution system and contracts with many major customers, as well as the continued involvement of its founding family, Awrey Bakeries maintained the quality and sense of pride that had helped it grow and prosper over the years.

Principal Competitors

Sara Lee Corporation; General Mills, Inc.; Weston Foods; Koepplinger's Bakery Inc.; Quality Bakery Products, Inc.

Further Reading

"Awrey Bakeries Golden Anniversary," Detroit: Awrey Bakeries, Inc., 1960.

Esparza, Santiago, "Robots Help Bakery, Human Touch Keeps it Flourishing," *Associated Press Newswires*, May 5, 2003.

Knape, Chris, "Happy Re-Birthday: Knapp's Specialty Gets New Life," *Grand Rapids Press*, April 12, 2003, p. A1.

Krumrei, Doug, "Judge Not By Label Alone," *Bakery Production and Marketing*, March 15, 1997, p. 20.

Lahvic, Ray, "No Longer Just a Numbers Game," *Bakery Production and Marketing*, May 24, 1990, p. 36.

"Robots Deliver Tasty Benefits," *Food Engineering*, October 1, 1999, p. 20.

Roush, Matt, "Food Labels Hard to Swallow," *Crain's Detroit Business*, May 2, 1994, p. 3.

Smith, Carolyn, "Awrey's Packaging Changes Boost Retail Sales," *Crain's Detroit Business*, July 20, 1987, p. 13.

Stopa, Marsha, "Everything's Just Kosher: Awrey Gets to Crust of Baskin-Robbins Deal," *Crain's Detroit Business*, September 18, 1995, p. 1.

Wernle, Bradford, "Awrey Adds Low-Fat Artillery," *Crain's Detroit Business*, May 28, 1990, p. 3.

——, "Awrey Ends Retail Sales in Favor of Contract Baking," *Crain's Detroit Business*, May 6, 1991, p. 1.

——, "Awrey Revives Retail Operation," *Crain's Detroit Business*, October 28, 1991, p. 1.

—Frank Uhle

Barratt Developments plc

Wingrove House, Ponteland Road
Newcastle upon Tyne NE5 3DP
United Kingdom
Telephone: (191) 286-6811
Fax: (191) 271-2242
Web site: http://www.barratthomes.co.uk

Public Company
Incorporated: 1958
Employees: 3,555
Sales: £1.79 billion ($2.75 billion) (2002)
Stock Exchanges: London
Ticker Symbol: BDEV
NAIC: 233210 Single Family Housing Construction;
    233220 Multifamily Housing Construction

Barratt Developments plc operates as a leading homebuilder in the United Kingdom and offers a wide variety of living options, including studio apartments, single-family homes, and large mansions that range in price from £50,000 to £3 million. Established in 1958, the firm has constructed more than 250,000 new homes and has more than 350 developments in progress from northeast Scotland to southern England. The company's U.S. subsidiary builds homes in southern California.

Company Origins

The company was founded in Britain in 1958 by Sir Lawrie Barratt. Barratt's original intention was to provide private housing for first-time buyers. This strategy proved to be very lucrative: after a slow start, between 1977 and 1979 alone turnover increased from £99.3 million to £163.2 million. The impressive rise in sales propelled Barratt to the forefront of the British housing industry.

For years prior to Barratt's success, more than one-third of new construction activity in Britain had been subsidized by the government. By early 1980, however, this situation had changed; the Thatcher administration drastically reduced appropriations for all building programs, especially public housing.

Although the company was initially hurt by the decision, later it was compensated by Thatcher's tax incentives to private home-owners. By 1982 sales surpassed £300 million and the company had built over 1,000 units more than its closest competitor, Wimpey's plc.

By the mid-1980s, Barratt decided to expand its product line. After conducting an exhaustive review of the British housing market, Barratt developed a range of individually designed houses. This series, called the Premier Collection, offered more than 60 different house types from which to choose, including retirement and luxury residences.

Barratt management also decided to shift its marketing emphasis away from first-time customers in order to attract second- and third-time homeowners. Because of escalating land prices due to the lack of available residential space, Lawrie Barratt thought it too difficult for the company to meet the needs of first-time buyers. As a result, Barratt would concentrate on satisfying the growing consumer demand for larger homes.

New Strategies Fuel Growth in the 1980s

At the same time, however, that the company began building larger private residences, it also initiated a number of successful projects designed to rehabilitate existing urban properties. Joint ventures with city councils, organizations, and lending institutions led to affordable housing for urban residents while halting the deterioration of inner-city properties.

In addition to these renovation projects, Barratt participated in novel development programs for cities throughout Britain. One such plan included offering shared ownership of dwellings through housing associations and subsidized rents for low-income tenants. Another effort, the Charlotte square development in Newcastle upon Tyne, resulted in the construction of inexpensive and attractive modern housing within the city's ancient walls. This marked the first time an industry leader in building private homes committed such large resources to urban renewal.

In 1980, the company created Barratt American Inc., a California-based subsidiary. The United States was chosen as a

Key Dates:

1958: Sir Lawrie Barratt establishes the company.
1980: Subsidiary Barratt American Inc. is established.
1982: Sales surpass £300 million and the company builds over 1,000 units more than its closest competitor.
1991: The company reports losses during an industry downturn; Sir Lawrie Barratt comes out of retirement to take over as chairman.
1997: Barratt retires and Frank Eaton is named his successor.
2002: Chairman and CEO Frank Eaton dies in a traffic accident; David Pretty is named CEO and Charles Toner becomes chairman.

site for expansion because of its thriving housing market and economic stability. Through direct sales, identifiable market segmentation, and low prices, it quickly entered the highly competitive market. In a few years, Barratt successfully established itself as one of the leading firms in the U.S. housing industry.

One of the most innovating aspects of Barratt's U.S. marketing strategy was the package deal available to first-time buyers. The company offered everything from domestic furnishings to trade-in deals on old homes, and U.S. customers often needed only to make a small downpayment in order to become residents of a Barratt house.

Barratt sold its products through Sears, Roebuck & Company, where potential customers could browse through a fully furnished condominium display. By selling small, inexpensive units in this way, the company provided a new opportunity for consumers formerly excluded from purchasing a home. Whereas the average price of a California house hovered around $120,000 in the 1980s, a Barratt unit could be purchased for $50,000. With these marketing programs, Barratt hoped its trademark would become as recognizable as that of an American car manufacturer.

Yet, while Barratt's American subsidiary captured a significant portion of the housing market in southern California, it began to experience difficult times. Rising unemployment, high interest rates, low housing starts, and the lengthy approval process to secure planning permission to sell some of its units all contributed to a decrease in sales. Nonetheless, Barratt remained confident that California's rising population and its growing affluence would work in favor of the company's U.S. investment.

In addition to its U.S. subsidiary, Barratt had home-building operations in 40 locations around Scotland and England in the late 1980s. In addition to these holdings, Barratt exhibited a talent for the development of leisure properties. Seven luxury resorts, constructed by Barratt Multi-Ownership and Hotels Limited, were located in attractive settings of the Scottish Highlands, Snowdonia, and the New Forest. Furthermore, Barratt's timeshare apartments in Costa Del Sol, Spain, had an impressive market reception. This led the company to construct two new resorts on the Mediterranean coast. These developments offered vacationers attractive dwellings in addition to generous amenities and afforded Barratt the position of Europe's market leader in timeshare apartments.

Barratt also participated in an area within the industry known as property investment and construction. By concentrating on specialist building contracts in the industrial and commercial sectors, the company gained a large financial return. Successful projects included the construction of an office building of bronze tinted glass and natural stone in Glasgow and the completion of factory units at the Stoneywood Industrial Park in Aberdeen.

Although the company had a long way to go in achieving its goal of ranking first in the U.S. homebuilding market, Barratt continued to perform well overall during the 1980s. Having grown in just less than 30 years from a small operation into a network of subsidiaries both in the United Kingdom and California, Barratt appeared to have a very promising future in the worldwide construction industry.

Overcoming Challenges: 1990s and Beyond

The early 1990s, however, were marked by faltering residential property markets in both California and in southern England. Having extended itself in both of these areas, Barratt found itself in a vulnerable position and began to post losses. During 1991, Chairman John Swanson made a hasty departure and founder Sir Lawrie Barratt was called out of retirement to rekindle the company's fortunes. He then tapped longtime company executive Frank Eaton to fill the CEO role.

Under the leadership of Sir Lawrie and Eaton, the company began to see a turnaround. Barratt shuttered unprofitable ventures, and soon the U.K. housing market began to rebound. In 1996, the firm announced plans to increase its housing output from 7,000 to 11,000 units per year by 2000. That year the company outperformed the U.K. housing industry in terms of pretax profits and earnings per share as well as housing completions. Success continued in 1997 as Barratt reported a 35 percent increase in pretax profits.

Sir Lawrie—confident Barratt was on the right track—retired for good in 1997. With Eaton at the helm, the firm's good fortunes carried on into the new millennium. During this time period, merger activity in the U.K. industry began to intensify. In fact, seven of the industry's top 12 firms had teamed up. Barratt, however, had significant land holdings and maintained that it would remain out of the acquisition arena. The company's financial statements continued to boast positive results and during 2002 the company achieved record sales and profits. Sales rose by 19 percent that year, reaching £1.79 billion. Market conditions—including strong demand, low interest rates, and short supply—continued to bode well for Barratt.

As the company celebrated its good fortune, it was blindsided by a sudden loss. In October 2002, Eaton was killed in a traffic accident. David Pretty, the firm's managing director, was named CEO and Charles Toner became a non-executive chairman. As the industry mourned the loss of one of its top executives, Barratt's new management team was confident it would continue Eaton's record of success in the years to come. During 2003, the company's financial position was solid and it had little debt. As it stood to record its 11th year of successive growth, Barratt Developments appeared to be well positioned as a leader in the U.K. homebuilding industry.

Principal Subsidiaries

Barratt Scotland Ltd.; Barratt Northern Ltd.; Barratt Midlands Ltd.; Barratt Southern Ltd.; Barratt South East Ltd.; Barratt American Inc.

Principal Competitors

The Berkeley Group plc; George Wimpey Plc; Persimmon plc.

Further Reading

"Barratt Bungle Bemuses Both Bulls and Bears," *Investors Chronicle,* August 2, 1991, p. 8.

"Barratt Developments," *Financial Times London,* March 28, 1996, p. 20.

"Barratt Developments," *Investors Chronicle,* March 28, 2003.

"Barratt Developments Says Can Outperform Rest of Industry This Year," *Extel Examiner,* November 21, 1996.

"Lawrie Barratt 'Extremely Positive' on Barratt Developments Outlook," *Extel Examiner,* September 24, 1997.

Waller, Martin, "Profits and Payout Double at Barratt Developments," *Times,* March 24, 1994.

—update: Christina M. Stansell

Blue Rhino Corporation

104 Cambridge Plaza Drive
Winston-Salem, North Carolina 27104
U.S.A.
Telephone: (336) 659-6900
Fax: (336) 659-6750
Web site: http://www.bluerhino.com

Public Company
Incorporated: 1994
Employees: 136
Sales: $205.6 million (2002)
Stock Exchanges: NASDAQ
Ticker Symbol: RINO
NAIC: 454312 Liquefied Petroleum Gas (Bottled Gas) Dealers

Based in Winston-Salem, North Carolina, Blue Rhino Corporation runs America's largest propane tank cylinder exchange service, mostly geared toward gas barbecue grills. Customers can either exchange like-for-like cylinders, upgrade to cylinders with additional safety features, or buy entirely new cylinders. The company essentially links local propane distributors with four types of retailers. Blue Rhino displays are found outside such home centers and hardware stores as Home Depot and Lowe's. Mass merchants include the likes of Sears, Wal-Mart, and Kmart. Major regional supermarket chains carrying Blue Rhino propane tanks include Kroger, Food Lion, and Winn Dixie. Blue Rhino also targets such convenience store chains as SuperAmerica, Emro-Speedway, and Minit Mart Foods. Founded in 1994, Blue Rhino has expanded rapidly beyond its initial South and Southeastern coverage. In recent years it has also begun to diversify its business by selling other products, in particular patio heaters, which use the same 20-pound propane tanks as gas grills and provide additional cylinder sales during the cooler months when customers tend to do less outdoor barbecuing. In addition, Blue Rhino has taken steps to offer products not associated with propane, such as fireplace accessories and garden products.

The Rise of the Gas Grill

Interest in outdoor grilling in America accelerated after World War II with the growth of suburbs and the raising of the baby boomer generation. Two major causes were the invention of charcoal briquettes and the introduction of the Weber Kettle Grill. The former is attributed to legendary automaker Henry Ford, who wanted to make use of wood and sawdust left over from the manufacture of his Model T. He had the excess wood burned in order to form charcoal, which was then ground into powder, mixed with a starch binder, and compressed into briquettes. The Ford Charcoal Company was located in the Michigan town of Kingsford, which would eventually bear the name of Ford's charcoal business.

Chicago native George Stephen invented the kettle grill in 1951 in the Weber Brothers Metal Works by welding together two half-spheres that were originally intended to make buoys to be placed in Lake Michigan. Once refined, "George's Barbecue Kettle" featured a domed lid, to ward off wind and rain, and venting that allowed better temperature control for cooking. Gas grills began to appear around 1960, but they were tied to natural gas lines and anchored in place. In the early 1970s propane tanks were introduced, making gas grills portable and able to winter in the garage.

By the mid-1980s gas was beginning to seriously challenge charcoal as the preferred outdoor cooking fuel, and even charcoal stalwarts like Weber took notice and began manufacturing gas units. Clearly, the trend was moving toward gas, and it would only be a matter of time before gas grills outstripped charcoal grills. Moreover, Americans were increasing their reliance on the outdoor grill, in many cases using one all year round.

The Rise of the Propane Tank Exchange System

A major problem for people with gas grills, however, was refilling the propane tank, especially on weekends when most grilling took place. Thus, when the tank was most likely to run out, the local propane supplier would be closed. Overall, refilling the cylinders was a messy and time-consuming chore. Cylinder exchange services were already fairly advanced in Europe, where many homes relied on cabinet heaters, portable

Company Perspectives:

The company intends to leverage its name, reputation and distribution networks to build Blue Rhino brand into a multidimensional franchise.

units that were fueled by small propane tanks. Advanced re-filling plants were also being built overseas. In the meantime, only small local cylinder exchange programs were becoming available in America. The principal founder of Blue Rhino, Billy D. Prim, became involved in the exchange business in 1993 when an Elkin, North Carolina, Wal-Mart manager asked if his heating oil business could set up a national cylinder exchange program to service customers who bought gas grills from the mass merchandiser. Prim quickly recognized he had an opportunity to dominate a fledgling industry.

Prim became a businessman earlier than he had planned, dropping out as a freshman at North Carolina State University in 1975 when his father died. He took over the family farm-supply business, Moxley Store & Oil Co., but with the farm economy flagging, he soon changed the emphasis of the business to fuel. He bought a Booneville, North Carolina, heating-oil company, Quality Oil, then with the help of investors added other oil distributorships, which he combined under a holding company, American Oil & Gas Inc. He also bought a chain of Quik-Pik Food Marts convenience stores and an interstate trucking company. When the chance arose to establish a major propane cylinder exchange business, he turned to a friend, Andrew J. Filipowski, who was also married to his wife's sister. They were already involved together in Filipowski's venture-capital firm, Venture Partners LLP.

Like Prim, Filopowski was an aggressive entrepreneur. He grew up in Chicago, the son of Polish immigrants, and did not learn to speak English until he started school. He dropped out of college after a year and went to work as a computer operator at Time-Life, and also worked at Motorola before taking a job at Cullinet Software, a data firm where he excelled. Striking out on his own, he started up a company similar to Cullinet, which did not proved successful. Then in 1987 he established Platinum Technology, developing software for business and information technology clients. Platinum would grow into one of the largest software companies in the world. (In 1999 Filipowski would sell the business for $3.5 billion, pocketing almost $300 million for himself.) Filipowski would create a number of separate businesses under the Platinum banner. His ties to North Carolina resulted from a golfing trip to Myrtle Beach in the late 1980s, when he met his future wife, Veronica Long, the sister of Prim's wife.

Blue Rhino Emerges in the Early 1990s

Prim developed a business plan for a cylinder exchange program, doing much of the work on a photo safari in Africa during February 1994. He was searching for a recognizable symbol for the company that could incorporate propane's distinct blue flame. He returned home with the Blue Rhino concept, influenced in part by Owens-Corning's use of the Pink Panther. In March 1994, he incorporated Blue Rhino in North Carolina, and later in the year reincorporated in Delaware. He raised $20 million from friends and family, including Filipowski who became vice-chairman of the board in May 1994.

The business originally set up shop in Prim's Booneville American Oil & Gas facility and quickly lined up five major retail customers. Calls from retailers asking when Blue Rhino would become available in their part of the country reinforced Prim's belief that the time was ripe for a national cylinder exchange business. His original plan called for a vertically integrated operation, which would require Blue Rhino to build and maintain an extensive operation—from the purchase of cylinders, refilling facilities, and delivery trucks, to the establishment of a sales, marketing, and MIS infrastructure. In March 1996 Blue Rhino began to switch to a business model that used independent distributors. Not only would this require less capital, it would allow Blue Rhino to spread its concept more quickly and claim a major market share. As a result, Blue Rhino hoped to become the dominant player in the inevitable consolidation of this new and highly fragmented business.

Federal laws prohibiting the indoor display of propane tanks also served to grow Blue Rhino's business and name recognition. Because retailers did not have to give up valuable indoor retail space, the decision to set up a Blue Rhino display outside the store in unutilized space was generally an easy one. Moreover, the Blue Rhino display was prominently located near entrances, serving as a free but extremely valuable billboard for the company.

In the two years after abandoning the vertically integrated model, Blue Rhino had signed up 51 major distributors delivering to more than 6,500 locations in 41 states. A year later the company would be serving 12,000 locations in 47 states and Puerto Rico. Net sales, as a result, increased at a fast pace, growing from $2.7 million in fiscal 1995 to $8.2 million in 1996, and $14.2 million in 1997. Although Blue Rhino was not yet profitable, Prim took the company public in June 1998, raising enough money to pay off $29 million in debt and keep some $7.5 million available for general purposes and acquisitions.

Blue Rhino also began to test a line of propane-powered patio heaters in 1998. One of its distributors in San Diego, Mr. Propane, had been active in the patio heater business since 1992 and proved how potentially lucrative it could be. Mr. Propane's founder, Chuck Dilts, had run a forklift cylinder exchange business, but when it failed he was forced to live on the streets for a spell. To feed himself he did odd jobs, one of which was to refill a restaurant's patio heater. It sparked the inspiration for a cylinder exchange and patio heater service business. Taken in by a friend in the oil business who provided some financial backing, Dilts began Mr. Propane with a single contract with a pancake house. Word of mouth brought more customers and eventually he had a thriving business. California's non-smoking legislation for public places added to the growth of patio heaters, as restaurants were eager to keep their smoking customers comfortable outside. With other areas of the country following California's lead on smoking regulations, Blue Rhino recognized patio heaters as a complementary business with tremendous potential, both in cylinder service and heater sales. The company would later develop mosquito magnets, which could be used near restaurants or on golf courses, powered by propane with the capacity of clearing as much as an acre of space.

In 1998 Blue Rhino's closest competitor, Amerigas Partners LP, lagged well behind with just 3,500 locations, and Prim was eager to press his advantage. His goal was to become a $500 million company by 2003, and in October 1998 he announced that Blue Rhino might issue another one million shares of stock to be used to acquire existing propane gas distributors. Blue Rhino's momentum, however, was soon blunted when the company came into conflict with its auditor, Pricewaterhouse-Coopers. At issue was Blue Rhino's connection to two companies. Blue Rhino paid $635,000 to Bison Valve LLC, which was developing an environmentally-sound safe valve for propane tanks. The accounting firm's Greensboro office treated the money as a loan on the balance sheet, only to be later overruled by the national office that insisted the money be considered an equity investment. A second company, USA Leasing LLC, proved even more troubling, because Prim and Filipowski and another board member owned 74 percent of it. Formed in October 1998, USA Leasing purchased $6.5 million of Blue Rhino's inventory of cylinders, with Blue Rhino guaranteeing 80 percent of the debt. Again the national office of Pricewater-houseCoopers overruled the local office, maintaining that USA Leasing's financial statements should be consolidated into Blue Rhino's.

Auditing Conflict Leads to Investor Concerns in 1999

Blue Rhino followed its auditor's instructions and revised its earnings. Subsequently, a January 11, 1999, *Wall Street Journal* article questioned the company's business practices. Robert Mc-Gough wrote that because of Blue Rhino's sale of cylinders to USA Leasing, "skeptics argue that Blue Rhino is thereby moving some of the burden of growing its business off its balance sheet, and contend the stock is overpriced at 50 times projected earnings of 49 cents a share for the year ending July 1999." The article also questioned the propriety of Prim and Filipowksi owning major stakes in distributorships. The controversy served to steadily drive down the price of Blue Rhino stock, which had been trading in the neighborhood of $25 per share, and resulted in Prim canceling a secondary stock offering.

Blue Rhino soon fired PricewaterhouseCoopers and sued, contending that the auditor's action led to the collapse of Blue Rhino stock and the cancellation of a $42 million stock offering. Blue Rhino would eventually drop the suit in December 2000. In the meantime, as its stock bottomed out at the $2 level, the company took steps to reassure investors while continuing to grow its business despite the cloud cast over it. Blue Rhino took USA Leasing in-house by purchasing it, and then Prim and Filipowski sold their interests in distributorships.

Unlike investors, however, retailers were not scared off, as Blue Rhino continued to add customers at a fast clip. In particular it bolstered its representation at supermarkets, not only expanding on relationships with Kroger and Food Lion, but adding Lucky Stores and Bruno's as well. On the product side, Blue Rhino introduced FuelCheck gas cylinders with a built-in gauge that indicated when a tank had less than two hours of fuel. Blue Rhino also announced a joint venture with Manchester Tank and Equipment Company to create an automated bottling plant, drawing on the experience of similar European efforts.

Blue Rhino had first-hand experience with the need for safe refilling facilities. At its Booneville facility in July 1995 a replenished cylinder fell off a conveyor belt, resulting in a leak that then ignited, causing considerable damage to the plant. When the automated plant eventually opened it would provide a consistent product at incredible speed. At Booneville the company had only been able to turn around 350 to 400 cylinders a day. The new facility was able to purge, fix, paint, fill, and test for leaks almost 10,000 cylinders each day.

Looking to diversify, in April 2000 Blue Rhino acquired two import and design companies. It paid $2.9 million in cash plus stock worth $1.1 million for International Propane Products, makers of patio heaters that Blue Rhino had exclusive North American rights to distribute. Prim hoped that the move would enable Blue Rhino to lower the price of patio heaters, thereby increasing the demand and creating a larger market for the company's propane services. A day later, Blue Rhino acquired Uniflame, Inc. in a $13.3 million deal that included approximately $4.3 million in cash, $6.7 million in stock, and another $2.3 million in deferred cash payments. Uniflame products included barbecue grills, garden art, and fireplace accessories, sold by such major retailers as Home Depot, Lowes, Wal-Mart, and Sears. Uniflame's import infrastructure would support Blue Rhino's patio heater sales, especially to the Far East. In October 2000, Blue Rhino acquired QuickShip Inc. in an $8 million deal that included approximately $1.2 million in cash and deferred payments and the balance in stock. An in-store, retail shipping service company, QuickShip was available at 200 retail locations in 16 states. Because the business operated out of retail bases in a manner similar to Blue Rhino's cylinder exchange service, Prim hoped to take advantage of his already existing infrastructure and retailer relationships to greatly expand upon the QuickShip concept.

Blue Rhino took a hit from high propane prices in late 2000, prompting the company to establish a hedging plan in order to protect it against future commodity price swings. Although the company was just reaching the break-even point, it was the unquestioned leader in its field, with the capacity to reach 90 percent of all gas grills in America and a patio heater business that also looked promising. In 2002, the company was able to report an increase in annual sales of some 47 percent, to $205.6 million, due in part to the acquisition of USA Cylinder Exchange from Suburban Propane. There was every reason to believe that Blue Rhino would continue to achieve profitability and expand its business.

Principal Subsidiaries

USA Leasing; Uniflame Corporation; Rhino Services; CPD Associates; Uni-Asia, Ltd.; QuickShip, Inc.

Principal Competitors

Amerigas Partners LP; Cornerstone Propane; Ferrellgas Partners LP.

Further Reading

Buchanan, Lee, ''Grilled Stakes: Blue Rhino was Red-Hot, Cooking on all Burners Until a Dispute with its Auditor Skewered its Stock Price,'' *Business North Carolina,* October 1999, p. 28.

Campbell, Doug, ''Blue Rhino Blazes New Trail with Patio Heater,'' *Business Journal Serving the Greater Triad Area,* December 3, 1999.

Downey, John, ''Fast-Growing Blue Rhino Plans to Pick up the Pace,'' *Business Journal Serving the Greater Triad Area,* October 9, 1998.

——, ''Out of Gas? Finances Cloud Blue Rhino's Outlook,'' *Business Journal Serving the Greater Triad Area,* March 12, 1999.

McGough, Robert, ''Blue Rhino's Complex Business Maneuvers May Put a Damper on the Red-Hot Shares,'' *Wall Street Journal,* January 11, 1999, p. B2.

Webb, Jennifer A., ''A Need for Speed: Fully Automated North Carolina Plant Revolutionizes Cylinder Processing,'' *LP/Gas,* February 2001, p. 20.

—Ed Dinger

Bradley Air Services Ltd.

3257 Carp Road
Carp, Ontario
K0A 1L0
Canada
Telephone: (613) 839-3340
Toll Free: (800) 267-1247
Fax: (613) 839-5690
Web site: http://www.firstair.ca

Wholly Owned Subsidiary of Makivik Corporation
Incorporated: 1946 as Bradley Flying School
Employees: 1,100
Sales: C$190 million ($299.5 million) (2002)
NAIC: 481111 Scheduled Passenger Air Transportation;
481112 Scheduled Freight Air Transportation; 481211
Nonscheduled Chartered Passenger Air
Transportation; 481212 Nonscheduled Chartered
Freight Air Transportation; 487990 Other Scenic and
Sightseeing Transportation; 488190 Other Support
Activities for Air Transportation

Bradley Air Services Ltd. operates First Air, Canada's largest northern airline. Its scheduled passenger and cargo services link 24 northern communities, some of them very small, to Ottawa, Montreal, Winnipeg, and Edmonton. The fleet of 34 aircraft ranges in size from prop planes to Boeing 727 and 737 airliners. First Air uses the Boeing 727s to fly charters all over the Western Hemisphere and beyond; two of these are stationed in Copenhagen for European freight jobs. The company carries 200,000 passengers and 20 million kilograms of freight a year. Passenger traffic accounts for about half of revenues, with the remainder divided between cargo and charter sales. About 450 of the company's 1,100 employees are based in the North; it is the region's largest private sector employer as well as its lifeline. Parent company Makivik Corporation also owns a smaller airline, Air Inuit.

Origins

Russell (Russ) Bradley formed Bradley Flying School at Ottawa International Airport in 1946. It began as a one-man operation. The first plane used was the Super Cub, a very small, simple, and forgiving airplane. Bradley moved to Carp Airport on the outskirts of Ottawa in 1950.

In 1954, Bradley began flying charter and survey missions to support construction of the DEW (Distant Early Warning) line of radar installations in the Northwest Territories. This work occupied four Cessna 180 aircraft. Even smaller planes, Piper Super Cubs, were used to support the Geological Survey of Canada in 1958. These planes were outfitted with special balloonlike, low-pressure tundra tires developed by Russ Bradley and his partner, Weldy Phipps.

The charter business continued to expand in the next ten years. Larger aircraft types, such as the de Havilland Beaver and Otter, were brought in. The Canadian government's long-running Polar Continental Shelf Project began in 1968 and was still producing a demand for air support more than 30 years later.

Flying in the arctic meant dealing with unusual and extreme conditions, noted the *Wall Street Journal*. The cold was world-class, often reaching 40 degrees below zero Fahrenheit. Darkness extended throughout most of the day during the winter. Wildlife like arctic hares sometimes occupied the runways. Sunspots could disrupt radio communications and the North Pole skews magnetic compass readings. The possibility of being stranded for days in winter storms prompts crews to carry tents on every flight.

Frozen Firsts in the 1970s

John G. Jamieson acquired Bradley Air Services in 1970 after the death of its founder. Jamieson subsequently served as president of the airline.

In 1971, Bradley opened the world's northernmost commercial air service base at Eureka, Ellesmere Island, only 600 miles

Company Perspectives:

In a few short decades, Bradley Air Services Ltd. has evolved to become Canada's foremost Arctic and remote region air carrier, operating under the trademark name— FIRST AIR. Today, First Air, The Airline of the North, is owned by Makivik Corporation, the body responsible for administering the land claim settlement of the Inuit of northern Quebec. Through a series of prudent acquisitions in recent years (Ptarmigan Airways and NWT Air), First Air has expanded its fleet, its route system, and already extensive range of air carrier capability. We are proud to say that throughout First Air's evolution and growth, Russ's legacy lives on. The First Air name is recognized around the world, more synonymous today than ever, with innovation and operational expertise for remote regions and unusual or especially taxing environments. Our service-based attitude and extensive northern experience are two of the main reasons why First Air planes and crews are a natural 'first choice,' when it comes to choosing an airline in Canada's Arctic.

from the North Pole. De Havilland's Twin Otter was added to the fleet in the same year, and in 1972 two DC-3s were acquired.

In 1973, a new base at Resolute Bay in the Northwest Territories became Bradley's major staging point for High Arctic charters. The trade name "First Air" was introduced in 1973 as the company began scheduled services between Ottawa and North Bay using a single eight-passenger plane. Bradley began the first commercial air operation on Antarctica in 1974, using a Twin Otter to fly in support of the U.S. Navy's Ross Ice Shelf Project. Bradley opened two more bases in the Northwest Territory. A base at Iqaluit opened in December 1975, followed by another one at Hall Beach in June 1978.

Jets in the 1980s

Revenues were about C$20 million in 1985. First Air acquired a Boeing 727 in 1986, allowing it to introduce chartered and scheduled jet operations to the North and throughout the Western Hemisphere. This plane was capable of carrying a variety of configurations of cargo and passengers. A newer model 727 was acquired in 1993; within a few years, the company was flying half a dozen 727s in all.

Also in 1986, First Air began operating a single, specially equipped Dash 7 aircraft on ice patrols for the government. In the late 1980s, First Air began acquiring Hawker Siddeley 748 aircraft, a turboprop-powered type that could carry 44 passengers. It would build up a fleet of eight of these over the next decade.

Inuit Ownership in 1990

Bradley was growing quickly, but debt made it seek out a partner for a capital infusion. The company was acquired by Makivik Corporation in 1990 for C$13 million. This was the corporate entity created to receive and invest more than C$100 million compensation funds for the Inuit of Northern Quebec

from the James Bay and Northern Quebec Agreement signed in 1975.

Makivik already owned Air Inuit; the combined operation had a fleet of 20 aircraft and more than 650 employees. Bradley was the largest independent regional airline in Canada, and its scheduled network connected 23 points in Canada, the United States, and Greenland. Revenues reached C$100 million in 1990, when First Air was carrying 23,000 metric tons of freight a year.

The airline scaled back scheduled services to Montreal and Boston in the early 1990s due to competition and a slow economy. The grounding of Nationair Canada diverted an additional thousand passengers a week to First Air's charter flights. In a striking change of scenery, in 1994 First Air dedicated one of its Twin Otters and crew to another airline in the Caribbean, flying between the Turks and Caicos Islands.

Growth by Acquisition in 1995 and 1997

First Air acquired Yellowknife-based Ptarmigan Airways Ltd. in 1995. Ptarmigan had been serving the western part of the Northwest Territories since the mid-1960s. It, too, operated a range of aircraft types, from the Cessna 185 to the Gulfstream 1 business jet.

First Air acquired NWT Air in June 1997, adding two Boeing 737s and one Hercules freighter to its fleet. NWT had been active in the North since the 1960s and had a more westerly orientation, with bases in Winnipeg, Manitoba, and Edmonton, Alberta. It had been bought out by Air Canada in October 1989. A marketing agreement provided Air Canada with access to NWT's feeder traffic after the sale.

Bob Davis became First Air president in 1998 after joining the company as a mechanic and rising through the ranks. Revenues were about C$165 million ($113 million) for 1998. During the year, First Air signed a code-sharing alliance with Air Canada.

A new Canadian territory, Nunavut, was fashioned from the Northwest Territories in 1999. It had a population of only 25,000 spread across one-fifth of Canada's land mass. Air transportation was central to the region's trade, and landing fees were heavily subsidized by the Canadian government. Adding to the expense, many of First Air flights were empty on the return trip.

Another Inuit-controlled airline, Air NorTerra Inc., was expanding its Northwest Territories services to compete directly with First Air on the Ottawa-to-Iqaluit corridor. NorTerra's service, launched in cooperation with Canadian Airlines, was marketed under the Canadian North name.

First Air was cooperating with tourism boards to promote Nunavut as a leisure destination. Activities such as hiking and kayaking, however, were mostly limited to the summer.

2001 and Beyond

In 2001, First Air began to replace its fleet of aging Hawker Siddeley 748s with 40-passenger ATR 42 turboprop aircraft.

Key Dates:

1946: Bradley Flying School is established at Ottawa International.
1950: Bradley relocates to Carp Airport on the outskirts of Ottawa.
1954: Construction of the DEW Line leads to arctic charter and survey work.
1971: The northernmost commercial air base opens at Eureka.
1973: First Air brand is created; Resolute Bay base is opened.
1986: The acquisition of a Boeing 727 allows for jet service to the North.
1990: Makivik Corporation acquires Bradley.
1995: First Air acquires Yellowknife-based Ptarmigan Airways.
1997: NWT Air is acquired.
1998: A marketing alliance is signed with Air Canada.
2001: The HS748 turboprop fleet is replaced with ATR42 aircraft.

Lower aircraft prices in the wake of the September 11 attacks allowed First Air to accelerate its fleet replacement. The company used mid-sized Boeing 737 jet airliners to launch Yellowknife-Vancouver service.

Although First Air's business was not affected by post-9/11 events to the same extent as other airlines, the company had started to diversify in order to weather an economy that had already been slowing. It had based a pair of Boeing 727s in Copenhagen for European cargo charters and was performing maintenance for other airlines.

Planning for the worst—reducing debt and cutting spending—helped First Air avoid the bankruptcy threats that faced other airlines in 2002, wrote the *Ottawa Citizen*. The *National Post* named it one of Canada's 50 best-managed companies.

Principal Competitors

Air NorTerra Inc. (Canadian North).

Further Reading

Bartlett, Ellen J., "An Unusual Hub—The Arctic," *Boston Globe,* November 19, 1989, p. B1.

Brean, Joseph, "Airline of the North: For First Air, the Inuit-Owned Airline, the Harshness of the Arctic Is Its Main Advantage," *National Post,* April 5, 2003, p. PT6.
Chianello, Joanne, "Tour Operators Scramble: Summer Rescheduling Expected to Be Cleared Up by Next Week," *Financial Post* (Toronto), Sec. 1, News, April 2, 1993, p. 5.
De Santis, Solange, "Destination Nanisivik—First Air Prospers Linking Tiny Arctic Villages," *Wall Street Journal,* May 25, 1999, p. B1.
Enman, Charles, "First Air: 'No Ordinary Airline'," *Ottawa Citizen,* June 15, 1999, p. C3.
"First Air Flight Attendants Sign First Contract After Four Years," *Ottawa Citizen,* June 24, 1994, p. F6.
"First Air Provides Unique Charter Service to Canada's Wilderness," *AirCommerce,* August 26, 1996, p. 37.
Fitzpatrick, Peter, "Air Canada Sells Regional Carrier," *Financial Post* (Toronto), Sec. 1, June 20, 1997, p. 4.
——, "Industry High Flyer in Group Planning Zoom Airlines," *National Post,* July 3, 2002, p. FP3.
Fowlie, Laura, "Smaller Lines Play Vital Role in Keeping Freight Moving," *Financial Post* (Toronto), Sec. 1, Focus on Air Freight, October 2, 1990, p. 17.
Hill, Bert, "Air Proposal Would Cripple North, Critics Say," *Ottawa Citizen,* November 21, 1992, p. C6.
——, "Flight Attendants Target Senator in Lengthy Fight for First Contract," *Ottawa Citizen,* September 23, 1993, p. D3.
——, "Northern Stops Land First Air Flight Crews with Payroll Tax," *Ottawa Citizen,* June 18, 1994, p. H2.
Jack, Ian, "First Air Fears Drop in Business: Needs Code-Sharing," *National Post,* October 9, 1999, p. D8.
Lofaro, Tony, "Destination Unknown: First Air Holidays Abandons Ottawa," *Ottawa Citizen,* December 8, 1995, p. B8.
"Northern Airline's Control Sold," *Financial Post* (Toronto), Sec. 1, May 9, 1990, p. 4.
Pilieci, Vito, "First Air Adds to Fleet," *Ottawa Citizen,* December 15, 2001, p. D3.
——, "First Air Flies Smoothly Through Turbulent Times: Three Years Ago, Managers Planned for the Worst," *Ottawa Citizen,* December 18, 2001, p. B3.
Quinn, Philip, "Nickels and Dimes Add Up," *National Post,* Canada's 50 Best Managed Companies, December 12, 2001, p. SR6.
Scanlan, David, "First Air to Cut 20 Jobs, Three Flights," *Ottawa Citizen,* February 26, 1992, p. C4.
Smyka, Mark, "First Air Braces for Competition," *Strategy,* May 10, 1999, p. 1.
Standen, Karyn, "First Air Demands Government Block Merger Attempt," *Ottawa Citizen,* October 9, 1999, p. D1.
Tower, Courtney, "Cold Fact About Arctic Flights: High-Tech Not Always Feasible," *Journal of Commerce,* May 21, 1998, p. 11A.

—Frederick C. Ingram

Buffalo Wild Wings, Inc.

1600 Utica Avenue South, Suite 700
Minneapolis, Minnesota 55416
U.S.A.
Telephone: (952) 593-9943
Fax: (952) 593-9787
Web site: http://www.buffalowildwings.com

Private Company
Incorporated: 1982 as Buffalo Wild Wings & Weck
Employees: 2,900
Sales: $96 million (2002 est.)
NAIC: 722211 Limited Service Restaurants; 722410
Drinking Places (Alcoholic Beverages)

Buffalo Wild Wings, Inc., runs a chain of more than 200 chicken wing restaurants, which are located around the United States. The company's concept of spicy wings and a sports-bar atmosphere is popular with a 20-something, mostly male crowd as well as with families, and many of the restaurants are located near college campuses or in growing residential areas. Most of the company's outlets are owned by franchisees.

1980s Beginnings

Buffalo Wild Wings was founded in 1982 by two longtime friends, Jim Disbrow and Scott Lowery. Disbrow was born in Kentucky, and had moved to Cincinnati at the age of 11 to live with figure-skating coaches David and Rita Lowery, who later became his legal guardians. Their son Scott, ten years younger, grew up regarding him as a brother. Disbrow was a talented skater, and was named an alternate to the 1968 U.S. Olympic team, later touring with the show Holiday on Ice. In 1974 he moved to Buffalo, New York, and it was there that he first experienced a spicy local version of barbecued chicken wings that had originated in 1961 at a place called the Anchor Bar.

One day in 1981, while judging a figure skating competition at Kent State University in Ohio, Disbrow met up with Scott Lowery and the pair decided to get themselves some Buffalo-style chicken wings. They looked everywhere in town and couldn't find any, and out of their frustration came the idea to open a restaurant of their own. They decided to locate it in Columbus, the home of the Ohio State University, because of its large student population. In 1982 the new restaurant was set up in an empty storeroom space near the campus, and christened Buffalo Wild Wings and Weck. The latter term was a reference to kimmelweck, a German roll covered with caraway seeds and kosher salt that was also popular in upstate New York. (The somewhat unwieldy name was soon shortened to ''bw-3'' by customers.) The menu featured barbecued chicken wings with a choice of a dozen sauces and beef sandwiches served on kimmelweck buns, all at moderate prices.

Six months after opening, Disbrow and Lowery added a third partner, Mark Lutz. Though they had no restaurant experience, they provided the college crowd with food they liked, and the trio found themselves deciding to stay in the food service business. During its early years the operation was run in a haphazard manner, with minimal attention paid to financial matters. When times were bad the partners would try to placate their creditors, and when times were good, they used the extra cash to open new restaurants. Over the next decade six more locations were added in Ohio, Indiana, and Steamboat Springs, Colorado, where the partners liked to ski.

In 1991 the company developed a plan to franchise its concept with Francorp, a Chicago-based law firm. Buffalo Wild Wings would charge a $15,000 to $20,000 fee plus a percentage of sales, and required use of its bottled wings sauces, which were manufactured by Wilsey, Inc., of Atlanta. Within two years the chain had grown to 14 locations, mainly in Ohio.

The niche the company had staked out was somewhere between a McDonald's and an Applebee's—unpretentious dining with an average meal check of between $5 and $6. Reflecting the company's largely college-age clientele, the motif was a sports bar, and the restaurants featured many wall-mounted televisions tuned to sporting events as well as computerized interactive sports trivia games and memorabilia displays. The dozen sauces that were offered ranged from mild to extremely spicy, and when ''Better-Be-Ready-Blazin' '' was ordered, it was delivered by a staff member wearing a fireman's outfit accompanied by the wail of a siren. Customers ordered their food from a central location while drink orders were taken by waiters. Food was served on disposable plates, so that there was less clean-up involved and the outlets could operate with smaller staffs, keeping expenses down. The back of each restaurant featured a bar where 50 different beers, many on draught, were served; sales of alcohol contributed as much as 30 percent of revenues.

Mid-1990s: Expansion and a Move

In late 1994 Buffalo Wild Wings hired Sally Smith to serve as chief financial officer, initially on a part-time basis. Disbrow had met Smith through his new father-in-law, who employed Smith as his CFO at a hearing-aid company, Dahlberg, Inc. He was impressed by her intelligence and unflappable personality. Smith wanted to remain in the Minneapolis/Saint Paul area, however, so Disbrow made the bold decision to move the firm's headquarters there from Cincinnati to win her services. Disbrow himself had been commuting weekly to the Minneapolis region from the company's home base since 1992, as his new wife preferred to live there to raise her two children from a previous marriage.

Upon joining Buffalo Wild Wings, Smith undertook a complete overhaul of its finances, which were in a state of chaos. The company was in trouble with both its lenders and the Internal Revenue Service, and was edging close to bankruptcy. Smith spent nearly a year working out a tax payment agreement with the IRS, updating the software systems used to pay vendors, and closing several money-losing restaurants. After getting the situation under control, she was able to secure several million dollars in loans to fund renewed expansion.

Anticipating more growth, in 1995 the company unveiled a prototype free-standing outlet that had 190 seats in a 5,000- to 7,500-square-foot space. The bar and dining areas were more clearly separated in this version than in the company's past restaurants, an indication of the firm's new strategy of moving from the college sports-bar mode toward the casual dining restaurant concept. The company also became more particular about the qualifications of new franchisees and encouraged development of more outlets by existing owners. A number of

new company-owned stores were planned as well. Buffalo Wild Wings now had nearly four dozen restaurants, three-quarters of which were owned by franchisees. Though Smith had literally been unable to determine the company's annual profit/loss figures prior to 1995, she tallied up losses of $1.6 million on revenues of more than $12 million for the year, while predicting a profit for 1996. System-wide revenues were approximately $80 million at this time.

In August 1996 Smith's resolution of the firm's financial problems was recognized with her appointment to the positions of president and CEO. Disbrow took the title of chairman of the board. By the end of the year Buffalo Wild Wings had 75 restaurants, 65 of which were franchisee-owned.

Late 1990s: Going National But Not Public

In 1998 Buffalo Wild Wings began preparing for an initial public stock offering of 1.5 million shares, but the idea was quickly abandoned due to unfavorable market conditions. The firm had launched its first national advertising campaign in the spring with such slogans as "Eat, drink and be messy," and "Be on a first-name basis with your dry cleaner." The company initially made several different versions of ads that used the name variations found in different markets, bw-3 or Buffalo Wild Wings, but the decision was soon made to standardize the name throughout the system to the latter format, and future ads reflected this. At the same time the company also upgraded the packaging of its bottled wing sauces in an attempt to increase their sales for home use. The firm was targeting a mix of young and/or sports-loving types and families, and ran irreverently humorous television spots on such cable networks as ESPN and Fox Sports, as well as on MTV, VH-1, Lifetime, and CNN.

October 1999 saw Buffalo Wild Wings open its 100th restaurant, in Apple Valley, Minnesota, only a few miles from its corporate headquarters. The company now owned 23 locations. In December the firm completed an $8.5 million private placement of stock to fund further expansion, with more than 260 sites projected by the end of 2003. The funding came mainly from three venture capital firms, which would afterwards own a majority stake. During 2000 Buffalo Wild Wings also began testing a variety of new sauces, including Cajun, Thai, and Caribbean Jerk-style. The latter two were subsequently added to the menu, as was the company's first dessert offering, a chocolate peanut-butter cookie wedge. During the year the company, which now had restaurants in 19 states, opened its first location in the home of its signature menu item, Buffalo, New York. The company was now calling its outlets Buffalo Wild Wings Grill & Bar.

At the beginning of 2001 the chain had a total of 140 locations, which generated system-wide sales of $150 million. Same-store revenue growth averaged 8 percent per year, which was attributed to improvements in the menu and the chain's tactic of locating new sites near growing residential areas. A new ad campaign was launched during the summer that was intended to enhance the chain's brand identity. "Wings, Beer, Sports. All the essentials" was the tagline. The campaign was budgeted at $3 million, and the television spots were made with higher production values than before, in an attempt to reach beyond the core market of 21–34 year old males. Takeout sales, which now accounted for 17 percent of sales, were also emphasized.

Key Dates:

1982: Jim Disbrow and Scott Lowery open a chicken wing restaurant in Ohio.
1991: Buffalo Wild Wings & Weck, with seven outlets, starts to franchise concept.
1994: Sally Smith joins company as CFO and begins to untangle the financial problems.
1996: Firm expands to 60 outlets; Smith named president and CEO.
1998: First national advertising campaign launched.
1999: 100th restaurant opened; company obtains $8.5 million in private funding.
2001: Buffalo Wild Wings-inspired potato chips introduced by Frito-Lay.

At the end of the year Buffalo Wild Wings announced plans to distribute branded potato chips to retail stores in conjunction with Frito-Lay. Wider distribution of the firm's sauces was also being contemplated. In the summer of 2002 the company rolled out new Turkey and Chicken Tender Wrappers, soft flour tortillas which were wrapped around chunks of meat, vegetables, and pineapple.

The Future

On October 16, 2002, cofounder and board chairman Jim Disbrow died of a brain tumor at the age of 54. In addition to his work with the company, he had remained involved with the sport of figure skating, acting as team manager of the 1998 U.S. Olympic team and serving from 1998 to 2000 as president of the U.S. Figure Skating Association. Company leadership remained with Sally Smith, while Scott Lowery served as vice-president of franchise construction.

In 2003 the company's advertising was updated again, this time focusing on the menu's finger foods. "Twelve tasty appetizers. Go crazy" was the theme of the $8 million promotional campaign. By summer there were 211 stores in 27 states, and Buffalo Wild Wings was now ranked the eighth largest restaurant chain in the United States by Technomic, Inc. For the most recent fiscal year system-wide sales had reached $286 million. The firm was now planning to ramp up its expansion, with a total of 400 locations anticipated by 2005.

After more than 20 years in business, Buffalo Wild Wings had opened restaurants in more than half of the country's states, and the it was preparing to double its number of outlets in the near future. The appeal of tasty, inexpensive fare served in a lively environment was strong, and the company's core clientele kept coming back for more. As additional Americans were introduced to the the company's offerings, its growth looked certain to continue for some time to come.

Principal Competitors

Champps Entertainment, Inc.; Jillian's Entertainment Corp.; Wingstop Restaurants, Inc.; Slaymaker Group, Inc.; Hooters of America, Inc.

Further Reading

Cebrzynski, Gregg, "Buffalo Wild Wings Puts the Finger on New Promo, Preps TV Spots," *Nation's Restaurant News*, March 10, 2003, p. 14.
——, "Buffalo Wild Wings Touts Takeout, Signs 'Chipper' Deal With Frito-Lay," *Nation's Restaurant News*, October 22, 2001, p. 14.
——, "Former Ad Agency Sues BW-3 Amid Launch of New Campaign," *Nation's Restaurant News*, October 12, 1998.
Cebulski, Cathy, "Franchising Takes Wing at BW-3," *Greater Cincinnati Business Record*, August 19, 1991, p. 1.
Hahn, Trudi, "Skating Authority Jim Disbrow Dies," *Star Tribune* (Minneapolis), October 18, 2002, p. 6B.
Kincaid, Valerie Bott, "Area Eatery Chain May Go Public," *Greater Cincinnati Business Record*, March 11, 1996, p. 2.
Linstedt, Sharon, "Minnesota Firm Tries to Shoulder Into Buffalo Wing Market, Upstate," *Associated Press Newswires*, May 21, 2000.
Lohmeyer, Lori, "Buffalo Wild Wings Co-Founder Disbrow Dead at 54," *Nation's Restaurant News*, November 4, 2002, p. 8.
MacArthur, Kate, "Wild Wings Takes Off: Chain Launches Branding Effort as Demand Rises," *Advertising Age*, July 9, 2001, p. 8.
McDowell, Bill, "Buffalo Wild Wings & Weck: Initially a College Hangout, BW-3 Aims to Cultivate its Image as a Casual-Dining Concept," *Restaurants & Institutions*, August 15, 1995, p. 26.
Merrill, Ann, "Hot Prospects: After a Faltering Start Buffalo Wild Wings is Finding its Stride," *Star Tribune* (Minneapolis), February 5, 2002.
Rugless, Ron, "Chicken-Wing Popularity Soars; Concepts Take Flight," *Nation's Restaurant News*, May 8, 2000, p. 5.
Walkup, Carolyn, "Buffalo Wild Wings Flies Further From the Nest, Sails Into New Territories," *Nation's Restaurant News*, January 8, 2001, p. 24.
Youngblood, Dick, "A Woman Worth Moving a Restaurant Chain For," *Star Tribune* (Minneapolis), December 22, 1996, p. 3D.

—Frank Uhle

Burger King Corporation

5505 Blue Lagoon Drive
Miami, Florida 33126
U.S.A.
Telephone: (305) 378-3000
Fax: (305) 378-7262
Web site: http://www.burgerking.com

Private Company
Incorporated: 1954
Employees: 340,000
Sales: $1.7 billion (2002)
NAIC: 722211 Limited Service Restaurants

Burger King Corporation is the second largest fast-food chain in the United States, trailing only McDonald's. The company franchises more than 10,400 restaurants and owns about 1,000 for a chainwide total exceeding 11,455, with locations in all 50 states and 56 countries. The company serves 15.7 million customers each day and over 2.4 billion Burger King hamburgers are sold each year across the globe. In the late 1990s and into the new millennium, Burger King was plagued by falling sales and deteriorating franchisee relationships. Burger King's parent, Diageo plc, sold the company to a group of investors led by Texas Pacific Group in late 2002.

Rapid Growth under Company Founders: 1954–67

Miami entrepreneurs James McLamore and David Edgerton founded Burger King Corporation in 1954. Five years later, they were ready to expand their five Florida Burger Kings into a nationwide chain. By the time they sold their company to Pillsbury in 1967, Burger King had become the third largest fast-food chain in the country and was on its way to second place, after industry leader McDonald's.

The story of Burger King's growth is the story of how franchising and advertising developed the fast-food industry. McLamore and Edgerton began in 1954 with a simple concept: to attract the burgeoning numbers of postwar baby boom families with reasonably-priced, broiled burgers served quickly. The

idea was not unique: drive-ins offering cheap fast food were springing up all across America in the early 1950s. In fact, 1954 was the same year Ray Kroc made his deal with the McDonald brothers, whose original southern California drive-in started the McDonald's empire.

McLamore and Edgerton tried to give their Burger King restaurants a special edge. Burger King became the first chain to offer dining rooms (albeit uncomfortable plastic ones). In 1957 they expanded their menu with the Whopper, a burger with sauce, cheese, lettuce, pickles, and tomato, for big appetites. But prices were kept low: a hamburger cost 18 cents and the Whopper 37 cents. (McDonald's burgers at the same time, however, cost only 15 cents.) In 1958 they took advantage of an increasingly popular medium, television: the first Burger King television commercial appeared on Miami's VHF station that year.

By 1959 McLamore and Edgerton were ready to expand beyond Florida, and franchising seemed to be the best way to take their concept to a broader market. Franchising was booming in the late 1950s because it allowed companies to expand with minimal investment. Like many other franchisers, McLamore and Edgerton attracted their investors by selling exclusive rights to large territories throughout the country. The buyers of these territorial rights, many of them large businesses themselves, could do what they wanted to in their territory: buy land, build as many stores as they liked, sell part of the territory to other investors, or diversify. McLamore and Edgerton took their initial payments (which varied with the territory) and their cut (as little as 1 percent of sales) and left their franchisees pretty much on their own.

The system worked well, allowing Burger King to expand rapidly. By 1967, when the partners decided to sell the company they had founded, the chain included 274 stores and was worth $18 million to its buyer, prepared-foods giant Pillsbury.

Difficulties with Franchisees
Under Pillsbury: 1967–77

The Burger King franchising system also worked well for the franchisees. Under the early Burger King system, some of the company's large investors expanded at a rate rivaling that of the parent company. Where this loosely knit franchising system

Company Perspectives:

Burger King is flamed-broiled burgers, fries and soft drinks at a good value, served quickly and consistently by friendly people in clean surroundings.

failed, however, was in providing a consistent company image. Because McLamore and Edgerton didn't check on their franchises and used only a small field staff for franchise support, the chain was noted for inconsistency in both food and service from franchise to franchise, a major flaw in a chain that aimed to attract customers by assuring them of what to expect in every Burger King they visited.

It was up to the new owner, Pillsbury, to crack down on franchise owners. But some large franchisees thought they could run their Burger King outlets better than a packaged-goods company. Wealthy Louisianans Billy and Jimmy Trotter bought their first Burger King outlet in 1963. By 1969, they controlled almost two dozen Burger King restaurants and went public under the name Self Service Restaurants Inc. In 1970, when the franchisees in control of the lucrative Chicago market decided to sell out, Billy Trotter flew to Chicago in a snowstorm to buy the territory for $8 million. By the time Pillsbury executives got to town the next day, they found they had been bested by their own franchisee.

The Trotters didn't stop there. By 1971 they owned 351 stores with sales of $32 million. They bought out two steak house chains (taking the name of one of them, Chart House), established their own training and inspection programs, and decided on their own food suppliers. By 1972 they were ready to take over altogether; the Trotters made Pillsbury a $100 million offer for Burger King. When that initiative failed, they suggested that both Pillsbury and Chart House spin off their Burger King holdings into a separate company. When that also failed, they continued to acquire Burger King piecemeal, buying nine stores in Boston and 13 in Houston.

However, Pillsbury wasn't about to allow Chart House to gain other valuable territories. They sued the Boston franchisees who had sold to Chart House, citing Pillsbury's contractual right of first refusal to any sale. Eventually Chart House compromised, agreeing to give up its Boston holdings in exchange for the right to keep its Houston properties.

New Leadership: 1977–80

Pillsbury's suit was proof of a new management attitude that involved more central control over powerful franchisees. However, it wasn't until Pillsbury brought in a hard-hitting executive from McDonald's that Burger King began to exert real control over its franchisees. Donald Smith was third in line for the top spot at McDonald's when Pillsbury lured him away in 1977 with a promise of full autonomy in the top position at Burger King. Smith used it to "McDonaldize" the company, a process that was especially felt among the franchise holders.

While Burger King had grown by selling wide territorial rights, McDonald's had taken a different approach from the very beginning, leasing stores to franchisees and demanding a high degree of uniformity in return. When Smith came on board at Burger King in 1977, the company owned only 34 percent of the land and buildings in which its products were sold. Land ownership is advantageous because land is an appreciating asset and a source of tax deductions, but more importantly it gives the parent company a landlord's power over recalcitrant franchisees.

Smith began by introducing a more demanding franchise contract. Awarded only to individuals, not partnerships or companies, it stipulated that franchisees may not own other restaurants and must live within an hour's drive of their franchise, effectively stopping franchisees from getting too big. He also created ten regional offices to manage franchises.

Smith's new franchise regulations were soon put to the test. Barry W. Florescue, chairman of Horn & Hardart, the creator of New York City's famous Automat restaurants, had recognized that nostalgia alone couldn't keep the original fast-food outlets alive and had decided to turn them into Burger Kings. Smith limited Florescue to building four new stores a year in New York and insisted that he could not expand elsewhere. When Florescue bought eight units in California anyway, Smith sued successfully. Florescue then signed with Arby's, and Smith again effectively asserted Burger King's control in court, based on the franchise contract. His strong response to the upstart franchisee kept Horn & Hardart from becoming too strong a force within Burger King.

Increasing control over franchisees was not the only change Pillsbury instituted at Burger King during the 1970s. Like many other chains, Burger King began to expand abroad early in the decade. Fast food and franchising were unfamiliar outside the United States, making international expansion a challenge. Burger King's international operations never became as profitable as anticipated, but within a decade the company was represented in 30 foreign countries.

At home the company focused on attracting new customers. In 1974 management required franchisees to use the "hospitality system," or multiple lines, to speed up service. In 1975 Burger King reintroduced drive-through windows. While original stands had offered this convenience, it had gradually been eliminated as Burger King restaurants added dining rooms. Drive-throughs proved to be a profitable element, accounting for 60 percent of fast food sales throughout the industry by 1987.

Smith also revamped the corporate structure, replacing eight of ten managers with McDonald's people. To attack Burger King's inconsistency problem, Smith mandated a yearly two-day check of each franchise and frequent unscheduled visits. He also decided that the company should own its outlets whenever possible, and by 1979 had brought the company's share of outlet ownership from 34 percent to 42 percent.

Smith also turned his hand to the food served in his restaurants. He introduced the french fry technique that produced the more popular McDonald's-type fry. In 1978, primarily in response to the appeal that newcomer Wendy's had for adults, he introduced specialty sandwiches—fish, chicken, ham and cheese, and steak—to increase Burger King's dinner trade. Offering the broadest menu in fast food did the trick, boosting traffic 15 percent. A more radical expansion for the Burger King menu came next. After McDonald's proved that breakfast could be a profitable fast-food addition (offering a morning meal spread fixed costs over longer hours of operation) Smith began planning a breakfast menu in 1979. But Burger King had a problem with breakfast: its flame broilers could not be adapted as easily to breakfast entrees as McDonald's grills could. Smith urged development of entrees that could be prepared on existing equipment instead of requiring special grills. He began testing breakfast foods in 1978, but it wasn't until the Croissan'wich in 1983 and French Toast sticks in 1985 that Burger King had winning entries in the increasingly competitive breakfast market.

Troubled Times in the 1980s

Smith left Burger King in June 1980 to try to introduce the same kind of fast-food management techniques at Pizza Hut. (Ironically, when he left Pizza Hut in 1983 he moved into the chief executive position at the franchisee that had given Burger King so much trouble, Chart House.) By following in Smith's general direction, Burger King reached its number-two position within two years of his departure, but frequent changes at the top for the next several years meant inconsistent management for the company. Louis P. Neeb succeeded Smith, to be followed less than two years later by Jerry Ruenheck. Ruenheck resigned to become a Burger King franchise owner in Florida less than two years after that, and his successor, Jay Darling, resigned a little over a year later to take on a Burger King franchise himself. Charles Olcott, a conservative former chief financial officer, took over in 1987.

Burger King did not stand still under its succession of heads, though. The company continued to expand abroad, opening a training center in London to serve its European franchisees and employees in 1985. Besides developing successful breakfast entries, Burger King added salad bars and a ''light'' menu to meet the demand for foods with a healthier, less fatty image. In 1985 the firm began a $100 million program to remodel most of its restaurants to include more natural materials, such as wood and plants, and less plastic. Burger King also completely computerized its cooking and cash register operations so even the

least skilled teenager could do the job. Average sales per restaurant reached the $1 million mark in 1985.

Even some of Burger King's post-Smith successes caused problems, though. The company introduced another successful new entree, Chicken Tenders, in 1986, only to find it that it could not obtain enough chicken to meet demand. Burger King was forced to pull its $30 million introductory ad campaign.

Burger King was still bedeviled by the old complaint that its service and food were inconsistent. The company played out its identity crisis in public, changing ad styles with almost the same frequency that it changed managers. After Smith's departure in 1980, Burger King's old ''Have it your way'' campaign (''Hold the pickles, hold the lettuce. Special orders don't upset us.'') was no longer appropriate. That ad campaign emphasized as a selling point what many saw as a drawback at Burger King: longer waiting times. However, under Smith's emphasis on speed and efficiency, special orders did upset store owners. So the company turned to the harder sell ''Aren't you hungry for Burger King now?'' campaign. The hard sell approach moved the chain into second place, and Burger King took an even more aggressive advertising line. In 1982 Burger King directly attacked its competitors, alleging that Burger King's grilled burgers were better than McDonald's and Wendy's fried burgers. Both competitors sued over the ads, and Wendy's challenged Burger King to a taste test (a challenge that was pointedly ignored). In return for dropping the suits, Burger King agreed to phase out the offending ads gradually, but Burger King came out the winner in its $25 million ''Battle of the Burgers'': the average volume of its 3,500 stores rose from $750,000 to $840,000 in 1982, sales were up 19 percent, and pretax profits rose 9 percent.

Burger King's subsequent ad campaigns were not as successful. In 1985 the company added just over half an ounce of meat to its Whopper, making the 4.2 ounce sandwich slightly larger than the quarter-pound burgers of its competitors. The meatier Whopper and the $30 million ad campaign using celebrities to promote it failed to bring in new business. All three of the major campaigns that followed (''Herb the Nerd,'' ''This is a Burger King town,'' and ''Fast food for fast times'') were costly flops. ''We do it like you'd do it'' followed in 1988, with little more success.

In 1988, the company faced another kind of threat. Parent Pillsbury, the target of a hostile takeover attempt by the British company Grand Metropolitan plc, devised a counterplan that included spinning off the troubled Burger King chain to shareholders, but at the cost of new debt that would lower the price of both Pillsbury and the new Burger King shares. Such a plan would have made it highly unlikely that Burger King could ever have overcome its ongoing problems of quality and consistent marketing.

Pillsbury's plan didn't work, and Grand Met bought Pillsbury in January 1989 for $66 a share, or approximately $5.7 billion. Pillsbury became part of Grand Met's worldwide system of food and retailing businesses with well-known brand names. In Burger King, Grand Met got a company with some problems but whose 5,500 restaurants in all 50 states and 30 foreign countries gave it a strong presence.

Turnaround under Grand Met in the 1990s

Grand Met's first move was to place Barry Gibbons, a successful manager of pubs and restaurants in the United Kingdom, into the CEO slot. Soon thereafter, in September 1989, Grand Met acquired several restaurant properties from United Biscuits (Holdings) plc, including the Wimpey hamburger chain, which included 381 U.K. outlets and 148 in other countries. By the summer of 1990, 200 Wimpeys had been converted to Burger Kings, bolstering the company's foreign operations, a traditional area of weakness. Over the next several years, Burger King was much more aggressive with its international expansion, with restaurants opening for the first time in Hungary and Mexico (1991); Poland (1992); Saudi Arabia (1993); Israel, Oman, the Dominican Republic, El Salvador, Peru, and New Zealand (1994); and Paraguay (1995). By 1996, Burger King had outlets in 56 countries, a dramatic increase from the 30 of just seven years earlier.

While Gibbons was successful in accelerating the company's international growth, overall his tenure as CEO (which lasted until 1993) brought a mixture of successes and failures. In the new product area, the hamburger chain hit it big with the 1990 introduction of the BK Broiler, a broiled chicken sandwich aimed at fast-food eaters seeking a somewhat more healthful meal; soon after introduction, more than one million were being sold each day. Also successful were promotions aimed at children. In 1990 the Burger King Kids Club program was launched nationwide, and more than one million kids signed up in the first two months. The program continued to grow thereafter; by 1996 membership stood at five million and the number of Kids Club meals sold each month had increased from 6.1 million in 1990 to nearly 12 million.

Also hugely successful was the long-term deal with Disney for motion picture tie-ins signed in 1992. Through 1996 (when Disney broke with Burger King to sign a deal with arch-rival McDonald's), the partnership had involved such Disney smashes as Beauty and the Beast, The Lion King, and Toy Story. In 1996 Burger King signed a new Hollywood deal with DreamWorks SKG.

Gibbons also worked to improve Burger King's profitability, under a mandate from Grand Met. Soon after taking over as CEO, Gibbons cut more than 500 jobs, mainly field staff positions. He also began to divest company-owned stores in areas where the company did not have critical mass, particularly west of the Mississippi. Doing so helped increase profitability, although some observers charged that Gibbons was selling off valuable assets just to improve the company numbers. In any case, during Gibbons's last two years as CEO, profits were about $250 million each year, compared to at most $175 million a year under Pillsbury.

Where Gibbons certainly failed, however, was in addressing Burger King's longstanding problem with image. The advertising program was still in disarray as the firm hired in 1989, D'Arcy Masius Benton & Bowles, created still more short-lived campaigns: "Sometimes you've gotta break the rules" (1989–91), "Your way right away" (1991), and "BK Tee Vee" (1992–93). Neither franchisees nor customers were endeared to any of these. In the face of the improving profitability of the corporation, such marketing blunders led to abysmal chainwide sales increases, such as a 3.6 percent increase for fiscal years 1991 and 1992 combined.

In mid-1993, James Adamson succeeded Gibbons as CEO, a position for which he had been groomed since joining Burger King as COO in 1991. Adamson, who actively sought out the advice of company co-founder James W. McLamore, moved to build on Gibbons's successes as well as rectify the failures. Adamson's most important initiatives addressed key areas: quality, value, and image. He improved the quality of products, such as in 1994 when the size of the BK Broiler, the BK Big Fish, and the hamburger were increased by more than 50 percent. He belatedly added a "value menu" after most other fast feeders had already done so, as well as offering special promotions, such as the 99¢ Whopper. Related to both value and image was the long-awaited successful ad campaign, "Get your burger's worth," created by Ammirati Puris Lintas, and emphasizing a back-to-basics approach and good value. The focus on the basics also led to a simplification of what had become an unwieldy menu—40 items were eliminated. The new focus was on burgers—with an emphasis on flame broiling—fries, and drinks. By early 1995, Adamson's program was paying off as same-store sales increased 6.6 percent for the fiscal year ending March 31, 1995. Morale among the franchisees had improved dramatically as well.

Adamson resigned suddenly in early 1995 to head Flagstar Cos. of Spartanburg, South Carolina. In July, Robert C. Lowes, who had been chief officer for Grand Met Foods Europe, was named CEO. Later that same year he became chairman of Burger King and gained a position on the Grand Met executive committee, a move that signaled Grand Met's commitment to Burger King and the strength of the company's resurgence. Lowes soon set some lofty goals for Burger King, including $10 billion in systemwide sales by 1997 (from $8.4 billion in 1995) and 10,000 outlets by the year 2000 (there were 8,455 in mid-1996). Management changes continued however, and in 1997 Dennis Malamatinas, an executive from Grand Met's Asian beverage division, was named CEO. Later that year, Grand Met merged with Guinness, creating Diageo plc. The new company's main focus was on its beverage and spirits business, leaving many analysts speculating that Diageo would eventually sell or spin off Burger King.

Despite the changes in ownership and management, Burger King remained dedicated to beating out its main competition, McDonald's. It introduced the new Big King burger to compete with McDonald's Big Mac and also launched a $70 million french fry advertising campaign that included a free fryday give-away at its restaurants. By 1998 both domestic and international sales were increasing, along with market share.

Bolstered by its recent success, Burger King launched an aggressive restructuring campaign that included adopting a new logo; store remodeling with cobalt blue, red, and yellow décor; new packaging; drive-thru lane upgrades; and a new cooking system. The firm also began to turnaround its European operations, exiting the highly competitive French region and focusing on growth in the UK, Germany, and Spain. The company's Latin America, Mexico, and Caribbean operations also experienced modest growth.

Problems Lead to a Sale: 1999 and Beyond

Burger King's success however, proved to be short-lived. In 1999, the company was forced to recall a promotional toy, the Pokemon ball, after it was discovered to be potentially dangerous for children. A class-action suit followed, claiming the company acted in a negligent fashion when it distributed the toy in its kids' meals. The firm's relationship with its franchisees was also deteriorating, marked by a highly publicized lawsuit with franchisee La Van Hawkins. The Detroit-based entrepreneur claimed Burger King failed to help him develop and purchase restaurants as promised. The firm counter-sued claiming that Hawkins owed the company $16 million. Civil rights activist Al Sharpton threatened to boycott Burger King as a result. To top it off, sales were falling, and the company experienced yet another change in management. Malamatinas left the firm in 2000, and Colin Storm was named interim CEO.

By this time, Burger King's parent company had announced plans to exit the fast food industry. Many franchisees were experiencing financial difficulties—including bankruptcy—and had long since complained that Diageo had neglected Burger King in favor of its premium liquor business. These franchisees adopted an internal program entitled "Project Champion" aimed at forcing a sale of Burger King. They approached J.P. Morgan Chase & Co. to orchestrate the deal, and, eventually, Diageo agreed to sell Burger King. Texas Pacific Group along with Bain Capital and Goldman Sachs Capital Partners purchased the fast food chain for $1.5 billion in late 2002.

According to a 2003 *Feedstuffs* article, Burger King's franchisee association claimed that the new ownership marked "the first day of a new era" for Burger King. CEO John Dasburg—elected in 2001—also felt the acquisition had significant benefits. In the aforementioned article Dasburg remarked that it would "better position Burger King as a healthy, independent company for the first time in more than 30 years."

While company management appeared optimistic about its future, Burger King remained embroiled in intense competition. The firm continued to launch new advertising campaigns and in 2002 introduced the BK Veggie, the first fast food veggie burger to be offered in the United States. Also in 2002, Burger King revamped the BK Broiler, making a new product they called the Chicken Whopper. The firm also moved into its new world headquarters in Miami, dedicating the building to founders Edgerton and McLamore. Management focused on capturing a larger portion of the fast food market. However, only time would tell if Burger King's new independence would help realize its goals.

Principal Competitors

McDonalds Corporation; Wendy's International Inc.; Yum! Brands Inc.

Further Reading

Alva, Marilyn, "Can They Save the King?," *Restaurant Business*, May 1, 1994, p. 104.

"Burger King Sale as Much Hot Temper as Cool Cash," *Houston Chronicle*, December 29, 2002, p. 1.

Collins, Glenn, "Grand Met Names a Chief for Burger King Subsidiary: Turnaround Is Seen at Fast Food Chain," *New York Times*, July 12, 1995, p. C2.

DeGeorge, Gail, "Turning Up the Gas at Burger King: It's Discounting Burgers and Dumping Yet Another Ad Campaign," *Business Week*, November 15, 1993, pp. 62–67.

Emerson, Robert L., *Fast Food: The Endless Shakeout,* New York: Lebhar-Friedman Books, 1979.

——, *The New Economics of Fast Food,* New York: Van Nostrand Reinhold, 1990.

Farrell, Greg, "Burger King: Whopper on the Rebound?," *Brandweek*, February 7, 1994, p. 22.

Gibson, Richard, "Burger King Overhaul Includes Refocus on Whopper," *Wall Street Journal*, December 15, 1993, p. B4.

Harrington, Jeff, "Burger King Executives Struggle to Turn Around Company," *St. Petersburg Times*, October 16, 2000.

Hays, Constance L., "Burger King Campaign Is Promoting New Fries," *New York Times*, December 11, 1997, p. D12.

Howard, Theresa, "BK Looks toward Recovery under New Chief Adamson," *Nation's Restaurant News*, August 2, 1993, p. 5.

Kramer, Louise, "Burger King Gets Back to Basics in Latest Ad Blitz," *Nation's Restaurant News*, April 29, 1996, p. 14.

Luxenberg, Stan, *Roadside Empires: How the Chains Franchised America,* New York: Viking, 1985.

Maremont, Mark, Pete Engardio, and Brian Bremner, "Trying to Get Burger King Out of the Flames: It's a Tall Order, Even for Grand Met Hotshot Gibbons," *Business Week*, January 30, 1989, p. 29.

Pollack, Judann, "Burger King Sizzles in Wake of Arch Deluxe," *Advertising Age*, June 17, 1996, p. 3.

Thomson, Richard, "GrandMet Fails to Stop Rumour Mill Biting Into Burger King," *Times*, November 10, 1995.

Smith, Rod, "Burger King's Sale Readies System for Growth," *Feedstuffs*, January 6, 2003, p. 7.

Walker, Elaine, "Burger King Takes Aim at First Place in Fast-Food Battle," *Miami Herald*, May 10, 1999.

—Ginger G. Rodriguez
—updates: David E. Salamie and
Christina M. Stansell

California Sports, Inc.

555 North Nash Street
El Segunda, California 90245
U.S.A.
Telephone: (310) 426-6000
Fax: (310) 426-6106
Web site: http://www.nba.com/lakers

Private Company
Founded: 1947
Employees: Not Available.
Sales: $152 million (2002)
NAIC: 711310 Promoters of Performing Arts, Sports, and
Similar Events with Facilities

California Sports, Inc. is the majority owner of the Los Angeles Lakers basketball team of the National Basketball Association (NBA), one of the most successful and valuable properties in professional sports. Since their inception as the Minnesota Lakers in the late 1940s, the team has won 14 titles. Its games at its home court at Los Angeles's Staples Center are consistently sold-out; the team is also one of the most popular draws in other NBA cities. Thanks to its regular appearances in the NBA playoffs and a history of such star players including Wilt Chamberlain, Kareem Abdul-Jabbar, Magic Johnson, and Shaquille O'Neal, the Lakers franchise is also a leader in sales of licensed NBA merchandise. California Sports also owns the Los Angeles Sparks of the Women's National Basketball Association. Between 1994 and 2001 the company's sales more than doubled, increasing from $68.7 million to $144 million.

Creating Professional Basketball in the 1940s

The Los Angeles Lakers basketball team was born at a time when professional basketball did not even enjoy a shadow of its century-end popularity. In 1947 Max Winter, Ben Berger, Maurice Chalfen and a group of other investors paid $15,000 for the Detroit Gems and moved that team to Minneapolis, where it became the Minneapolis Lakers of the National Basketball League (NBL). Anchored by center George Mikan, who would soon become basketball's first star, the Lakers quickly proved themselves the dominant team of the early days of the pro game. Its first year in the league, the team won the NBL championship. When it jumped to the Basketball Association of America (BAA) for the 1948 season, the Lakers became the BAA champs; and, when one year later the NBL and BAA merged to form the National Basketball Association, the Lakers were that league's first title winners as well, going on to win more titles in 1950, 1952, 1953, and 1954. Most fans believed that only George Mikan's injured ankle kept them from the championship in 1951.

The Lakers were the team to beat in the late 1940s and early 1950s. With players like Mikan, Slater Martin, and Vern Mikkelsen, Minneapolis brought pro basketball its first widespread public recognition. However, basketball was still a long ways from the spectacle sport and big business it would become in the 1980s. In 1947 salaries for the entire Lakers team totaled $70,000, of which George Mikan's alone salary accounted for $25,000. In 2003, NBA teams had an annual salary cap of approximately $40 million a year.

By the latter half of the 1950s, Mikan and his teammates had either retired or were showing signs of age. In February 1957, Berger and Chalfen put the team up for sale. A St. Louis group expressed interest and it looked like the team would be changing cities again. At the last minute a local trucking and hotel magnate, Bob Short, put together a consortium that purchased the Lakers for $150,000. Once Short owned the team he had to contend with various problems. With Mikan gone, the Lakers were in the middle of a transitional period, which led, in turn, to falling attendance. Most problematic, the team did not have a regular court for its home games, dividing its home appearances among as many as six sites. While the Minneapolis Auditorium was its main venue (whenever other events were not scheduled), some of the Lakers' other home courts were not even in the Twin Cities. The playoffs, which could not be penciled in on a calendar more than a few weeks in advance, were a particularly uncertain time of year.

Making Los Angeles Home in the 1960s

Citing the Lakers' arena problems, in 1960 Short negotiated a move to Los Angeles. Although Minneapolis fans would later

---

Key Dates:

1947: A group of Minnesota investors purchases the Detroit Gems and renames the team the Minneapolis Lakers.

1948: Lakers jump from National Basketball League to Basketball Association of America (BAA), winning BAA title.

1949: Lakers join the National Basketball Association (NBA) and win the league's first championship.

1957: Lakers are sold for $150,000 to group led by Bob Short.

1960: The Lakers move to Los Angeles.

1965: Bob Short sells the Lakers to Jack Kent Cooke for $5.2 million.

1967: Construction of the Los Angeles Forum is completed.

1979: Lakers sold to Jerry Buss for $67.5 million.

1982: Jerry West becomes Lakers' general manager.

1989: Last holdings in Los Angeles Kings hockey team are sold to Bruce McCall.

2000: Lakers' home court moves from Great Western Forum to Staples Center; Jerry West retires as general manager; Jeanie Buss takes over operations from her father, Jerry Buss.

---

complain that Short had only moved the team in order to push its market value up, at the time the move occasioned next to no reaction in the Twin Cities. On the other hand, NBA owners vehemently opposed the move to Los Angeles. With most teams located east of the Mississippi, they were concerned that it would lead to exorbitant travel costs. They only changed their minds and gave their unanimous approval for the move when it was announced that the owner of the Harlem Globetrotters was about to launch a rival league, and install a team on the West Coast.

The Lakers' first season in Los Angeles began in autumn 1960. Despite the incongruity of a Southern California team situated on the Pacific Ocean being called the Lakers, no thought was given to a new name. The team had more pressing issues to contend with. Interest in basketball in Los Angeles was so low that no radio stations were even interested in broadcasting games until the *end* of the first season when a new star, Elgin Baylor, led the Lakers in an exciting playoff match-up against the St. Louis Hawks. Baylor, with his driving, leaping acrobatic style, which was about to revolutionize play in the NBA, would draw fans to Lakers games throughout much of the 1960s. By the time Jerry West, another future Hall of Famer, joined the team, the Lakers were once again among the finest teams in professional basketball.

As the Lakers' play improved, their market value shot upwards. When Bob Short decided to sell the team in 1965, he asked $5.175 million. He found an eager buyer in Jack Kent Cooke. Cooke, born in Canada and a naturalized American citizen since 1960, was a passionate sports fan. He owned the National Football League's Washington Redskins and had tried unsuccessfully to obtain the California Angels baseball team when the American League expanded in 1960.

In 1967 Cooke would add the expansion Los Angeles Kings hockey franchise to his portfolio. It was Cooke's desire for a hockey club that led, in part, to his decision to build the Los Angeles Forum, which would be the home of the Lakers for more than 30 years. The Los Angeles Coliseum refused to allow Cooke's prospective hockey team to play in the arena, holding Cooke to a contract that Bob Short had signed on behalf of the Lakers. In frustration Cooke built a new home for the Lakers. Modeled on the architecture of ancient Rome, the Forum cost Cooke $12.5 million. The Kings played the first game in the structure on December 30, 1967, and a day later the Lakers followed suit. Once the arena had opened, Cooke stamped it with the mark of his flamboyant personality. He removed the press from courtside and gave the seats over to Hollywood stars and other glitterati.

Cooke desperately wanted a title for his Lakers and spared no expense in its pursuit. In summer 1968 he obtained Wilt Chamberlain, signing the former Philadelphia superstar to a $4 million, four-year contract. In the NBA finals the Lakers battled their nemesis, the Boston Celtics, to a three game tie before returning home for deciding game seven. So certain was Cooke that his team would win the championship that he readied thousands of balloons in the rafters for the post-game celebration—a fact that did not escape the notice of Celtics' coach Red Auerbach. In the fourth quarter, Chamberlain injured his knee and had to leave the game. Boston won 108–106. The balloons remained in the rafters. Laker glory days were still more than a decade away.

New Players and a New Owner in the 1970s

It would be 1972 before the Lakers won another NBA championship, in what would be the swansong of the Baylor, West, and Chamberlain era. Baylor left during the 1971–72 season, Chamberlain hung up his sneakers a year later, and West retired in summer 1975. The Lakers went into an almost inevitable decline. In 1975 they missed the playoffs for the first time since 1960. After that debacle, Cooke took the first steps towards the next Laker dynasty, trading three players to acquire Kareem Abdul-Jabbar from the Milwaukee Bucks. The foundation was completed in 1979 when Cooke selected Earvin "Magic" Johnson in the NBA draft. With Abdul-Jabbar, Johnson, and other players like James Worthy on the team, the Lakers would go on an impressive run, winning conference titles every year of the 1980s, and NBA titles in 1979–80, 1981–82, 1984–85, 1986–87, and 1987–88.

At the end of the 1979 season, the Lakers were once again on the sales block. Reasons for the sale were varied. Cooke was concerned about his health, and he had also lost a sizable chunk of his fortune when his wife was awarded nearly half of his net worth—some $100 million—in a divorce settlement. Most importantly, however, as owner of the Washington Redskins, Cooke was also confronted with an NFL rule obliging him to divest himself of any interests in other professional sporting teams.

On May 18, 1979, Cooke sold the team to Jerry Buss, a chemist turned real estate tycoon. The deal, characterized by the *New York Times* as "the largest single financial transaction in the history of professional sports" and "the most confusing, complex transaction in the history of sports," was valued at

$67.5 million and included not only the Lakers but also the L.A. Kings hockey franchise, the Forum, and, reportedly, a lease on New York City's Chrysler Building. The deal almost fell apart the day before it was to close when Buss realized that he was $2.7 million short of funds. The money was raised through last minute phone calls to Donald Sterling, the owner of the Los Angeles Clippers, and Sam Nassi, who would later purchase the Indiana Pacers.

Like Cooke, Buss was a sports nut who happened to be rich. He bought the Los Angeles Strings, a World Team Tennis franchise, in the late 1970s, and as owner of the Lakers would add to his holdings the L.A. Lazers indoor soccer team and the L.A. Sparks of the Women's National Basketball Association (WNBA). Buss also had a reputation as a high-living playboy, and he made the Lakers into an extension of his lifestyle. "A person doesn't go into sports to make money," Buss told the *Boston Globe*, "but it's still a business. I decided that I wanted the Lakers to play a certain style of basketball and I wanted certain people to come to the games." He introduced the Laker Girls, a squad of sexy cheerleaders. He brought the idea of "Showtime" to the Forum, inviting a select list of movie and television stars to Laker games.

Under Buss, courtside seats became highly coveted items. Going for $15 apiece when he bought the team, the ticket price was bumped to $45 the following year. Buss kept increasing the price until by 2001 a seat at courtside cost $1,500. In 1982 Buss hired former Lakers star Jerry West as general manager and gave him full authority in making player decisions. That same year, Buss brought in a new coach, Pat Riley, whose slicked-back hair and designer suits would become as synonymous with the Laker dynasty as Magic Johnson's smile.

Once he was firmly ensconced in the business he loved best—professional sports—Buss started selling off his real estate businesses to concentrate on the Lakers. That, along with his free spending on players, led to a minor financial crisis in his company, California Sports, Inc. In February 1985 a Los Angeles television station reported that the company's banks were considering a seizure of the Kings and Lakers, which were held as collateral on unpaid loans. Without explicitly denying the charges, Buss managed to avoid foreclosure, and the banks were not exactly anxious to foreclose, fearing such a move could force their market value down. Buss' marketing innovations, such as the Showtime concept, helped offset the crises. In 1988 he put together one of the first corporate licensing deals in professional sports with the great Western Financial Corporation worth $17.8 million after which the Forum was renamed the Great Western Forum. Buss sold off his holdings in the unsuccessful L.A. Kings hockey team piecemeal between 1986 and 1989 to Bruce McCall, an antique coin dealer, and in 1989 was trying—unsuccessfully—to purchase a Major League Baseball team.

Turmoil and Change in the 1990s

In November 1991, the Lakers organization, indeed professional basketball as a whole, was shaken by the revelation that Earvin "Magic" Johnson, arguably the most popular in the NBA and the Lakers' most important player, had been infected with the HIV virus. Uncertain of his personal future, Johnson announced his retirement from the team, a decision which threw the immediate future of the Lakers into doubt as well. A comeback by Johnson the following year was canceled when opposing players expressed concern about the possibility of becoming infected themselves perhaps through an open cut during a game. Johnson did finally return to the Forum as the Lakers' coach for part of the 1993–94 season, without particular success; it was one of the few seasons in Lakers history in which they failed to make the playoffs. Magic Johnson returned as a player for the 1995–96 season and retired again for good after the team's defeat in the playoffs that year, remaining affiliated with the team as a 5 percent owner.

A large part of the Lakers' success as a team in the 1980s and 1990s was attributable to the savvy of its long-time general manager, Jerry West, as well as to owner Jerry Buss' willingness to give West virtually free rein in player selection. Not only did West bring the Lakers superstar players such as Vlade Divac, Kobe Bryant, and Shaquille O'Neal (players that brought the Lakers back into contention in the 1990s), he was also able to construct teams that functioned well with the Lakers' star talent.

At the end of the 1990s the Lakers made a controversial decision to leave their long-time home in the Great Western Forum. The decision was based largely on the building's age. It had been built in another era of sports, one in which arenas did not include luxury suites or corporate boxes. Remarkably, after two decades of being his own landlord, Buss decided not to build a new arena of his own, but to become instead a tenant of the new Staples Center in downtown Los Angeles. The move was a financial masterstroke. Under the terms of the contract, Buss received 25 percent of the luxury suite revenue at the Staples Center, which were reported to lease for a total of about $300,000 a year. In all, the move increased the value of the Lakers franchise by about $100,000. With the move, Philip Anschutz and Edward Roski, the owners of the L.A. Kings hockey team who built the Staples Center, were able to acquire a 25 percent share of the Lakers franchise.

Throughout his ownership of the Lakers, Jerry Buss gave responsibility for various California Sports operations to his children. For three seasons in the 1980s, his son Jim ran the Los Angeles Lazers, an indoor soccer team which later went broke. In 1998 Jim Buss was made an assistant to Jerry West, prompting speculation that he would eventually take over the company when his father retired or passed away. In 1998 son John Buss was president of the Lakers' sister team, the Los Angeles Sparks of the Women's National Basketball Association. This team had mixed success in Los Angeles, and its failures were frequently attributed to the unwillingness of John Buss to market the franchise imaginatively. By far the most promising of the Buss clan was daughter Jeanie. With a degree in business from the University of Southern California, she proved her ability as the president of the L.A. Forum. In 2000, after the Lakers moved to the Staples Center, Jerry Buss turned over much of the responsibility for the running of the team to Jeanie, making her one of the most powerful, influential women in professional sports.

Other major changes were taking place within the franchise as the decade ended. In 2000 Jerry West resigned as Laker general manager, citing health problems. That same year the team signed Shaquille O'Neal to a blockbuster contract worth $88.4 million over three years. A major problem during this time for the Lakers was finding a coach who could win the respect of multimillionaire superstars like O'Neal and Kobe Bryant. During the 1998–99 season the team went through two coaches, Del Harris and Kurt Rambis, neither of whom had been able to make his mark on the team. In June 1999 Buss took the bull by the horn and gave a five-year contract worth a reported $6 million to Phil Jackson, the coach who had not only led the Chicago Bulls to multiple NBA championships in the 1990s, but who had proved himself capable of coaching Michael Jordan, one of the five greatest players in NBA history. Jackson got off on the right foot almost immediately when Shaquille O'Neal called him "a white version of my father" and said he would only play for the Lakers so long as Jackson was the team's coach. When Jackson arrived, he brought with him many of his assistants who had helped him build the dynasty in Chicago, including 77-year-old Tex Winter, the creator of the Bulls fabled "triangle offense." Jackson proved his value over the coming three years, leading the Lakers to three consecutive NBA championships in 2000, 2001, and 2003.

Principal Divisions

Los Angeles Lakers; Los Angeles Sparks.

Principal Competitors

L.A. Kings Hockey Club; L.A. Clippers; Mighty Ducks of Anaheim.

Further Reading

Adande, J.A., and Steve Springer, "They're No Longer Staples," *Los Angeles Times*, May 5, 1999, p. D1.

Aschburner, Steve, "The Era of Elgin," *Star Tribune* (Minneapolis), February 11, 1994, p. 3S.

Barnes, Bart, "A Washington Monument—The Master Salesman's Biggest Success Was Himself," *Washington Post*, April 7, 1997, p. A1.

Bechtel, Mark, "From Their Winning Beginnings in Minneapolis, the Lakers Have Cast Big Men in Starring Roles," *Sports Illustrated*, July 27, 2001, p. 10.

"Cooke Set to Sell," *Washington Post,* May 29, 1979, p. D1.

Gergen Joe, "Mikkelsen Was At Center Of Big Change In The NBA," *St. Louis Post-Dispatch*, February 12, 1995.

Greenberg, Dan, "An Interview With Jerry Buss," *Register,* December 4, 1989, p. D1.

Hartman, Sid, "Minneapolis Lakers were Genuine Article," *Star Tribune* (Minneapolis), June 22, 1993, p. 2C.

Heisler, Mark, "A Road Well Traveled," *Los Angeles Times,* November 16, 1997.

——, "Jackson Adds Final Side of Triangle to Coaching Staff by Hiring Winter," *Los Angeles Times*, July 17, 1999, p. D4.

Hoffer, Richard, "Mister Clutch, Master Builder," *Sports Illustrated*, April 4, 1990.

Howard-Cooper, Scott, "Team Owner Jerry Buss Does It His Way—Casually," *Seattle Times,* May 18, 1997, p. D5.

"Jerry Buss Buys Cooke Sports Empire," *Globe and Mail,* May 28, 1979, p. S4.

Kawakami, Tim, "Buss' Son Will Join the Lakers," *Los Angeles Times*, October 7, 1998.

Lidz, Franz, "She's Got Balls," *Sports Illustrated*, November 2, 1998.

Reilly, Rick, "The Day Jack Kent Cooke Dies, Nobody Will Be More Surprised Than Him," *Sports Illustrated*, December 16, 1991.

Reusse, Patrick, "Green's Move Repeats History," *Star Tribune* (Minneapolis), March 14, 1993, p. 1C.

Saxon, Wolfgang, "Robert E. Short, Businessman, Dies," *New York Times*, November 22, 1982, p. B16.

Springer, Steve, "Buss—The Next Generation." *Los Angeles Times Magazine*, November 24, 2002, Sec. 9, p. 16.

Springer, Steve, and Larry Stewart, "L.A.'s Leading Man," *Los Angeles Times*, June 15, 2001, p. D1.

Uchiyama, David, "Fantastic Franchise," *Star Tribune* (Minneapolis), June 14, 2000.

Visser, Lesley, "All That Glitters: Jerry Buss Gives LA Purple-And-Gold Star Treatment," *Boston Globe*, June 2, 1987.

Weiskopf, Chris, "Uh-Oh, It's Magic," *National Review*, April 22, 1996.

—Gerald E. Brennan

Canadian Utilities Limited

1500, 909 11th Avenue South West
Calgary, Alberta T2R 1N6
Canada
Telephone: (403) 292-7500
Fax: (403) 292-7532
Web site: http://www.canadian-utilities.com

Public Subsidiary of ATCO Ltd.
Incorporated: 1911 as the Canadian Western Natural
    Gas, Light, Heat, and Power Company Limited
Employees: 5,000
Sales: $2.97 billion (2002)
Stock Exchanges: Montreal Toronto
Ticker Symbol: CU
NAIC: 221122 Electric Power Distribution; 486210
    Pipeline Transportation of Natural Gas; 221112 Fossil
    Fuel Electric Power Generation; 211112 Natural Gas
    Liquid Extraction

Company Origins: 1900–25

The earliest enterprise of Canadian Utilities Limited was Canadian Western Natural Gas Company, Ltd., which was founded in the early 1900s by geological engineer Eugene Coste. According to company historian Len Stahl, Coste had become known as ''the father of the natural gas industry in Canada, having . . . brought in the first commercial discovery of natural gas in Ontario in 1889.'' While employed by the Canadian Pacific Railway (CPR) in 1909, Coste discovered a large natural gas reserve on a bank of the South Saskatchewan River in southern Alberta. He acquired rights to this field, dubbed Bow Island field, from the CPR and then went to England to raise capital, selling $4.5 million worth of stock slated for building a pipeline from the Bow Island site to the cities of Calgary and Lethbridge.

On July 19, 1911, Coste incorporated his company under the name Canadian Western Natural Gas, Light, Heat, and Power Company Limited. In addition to planning the construction of the

Bow Island pipeline, the company acquired two established Calgary franchises: a coal gas plant consisting of 30 miles of pipe serving 2,200 customers and a pipeline serving about 50 customers, including the Calgary Brewing & Malting Company. On April 12, 1912, the company began construction of its 170-mile Bow Island pipeline. Eighty-six days later, the completed pipeline was the third largest gas pipeline in North America and the most northerly gas transmission line in the world.

Although the public initially greeted the transition from coal to gas fuel with some skepticism, residents of Lethbridge began using Canadian Western gas for lighting purposes by the fall of 1912, and thereafter the demand for gas increased dramatically. Soon the nearby towns of Nanton, Okotoks, and Brooks were linked to the system, and in 1913 Fort Macleod, Granum, and Claresholm also gained the option of gas lighting. Over the year, Canadian Western gained a client base of 3,400, whom it served from 20 wells yielding gas in the Bow Island field. By 1914 Canadian Western's revenues topped $1 million.

Although the years immediately following its establishment presented some challenges for the company, Canadian Western continued to gain customers. The company suffered a temporary setback in 1915, when torrential rainfall wiped out its main pipeline to Calgary. The city was without gas service for two days while the company's repair crew worked to get supplies and repair the break in the face of severe weather conditions that had washed out railroad tracks and bridges. This time also marked the beginning of a legal dispute between the company and the city of Calgary, whose officials maintained that the company's franchise did not cover the entire city of Calgary. Canadian Western prevailed in 1917, when the Supreme Court of Alberta ruled that it did have the right to provide gas to all parts of the city.

By 1920, supplies of gas in Canadian Western's Bow Island field had begun to wane. Because of the shortage of gas, the company was forced to limit its service to some industrial customers, in order to supply residential sites. Operators at regulator stations in the city communicated by phone in order to move supplies of gas around quickly and maintain high pressure in the lines. As a result of these measures, Canadian Western's revenues dropped by 10 percent.

To alleviate this shortage, Canadian Western began an effort to develop new supplies of gas. The company expanded its gas supply beyond Bow Island in 1921, when it opened the Chin Coulee well 40 miles east of Lethbridge. To cover the costs of this expansion, the company requested its first rate increase from its customers. This increase was grudgingly granted by the city, on the conditions that the company also construct a second ten-inch gas line from a site in the Turner Valley, as well as begin a drilling program at two other sites.

Two years later, in 1923, another gas company, called Northwestern Utilities Limited, was established in Edmonton. This company was a successor to a corporation formed in 1914 to develop the resources of the Viking Field, a deposit of natural gas in northern Alberta. During the summer and fall of 1923, a pipeline was constructed from the Viking Field to Edmonton under tense conditions, as the company raced to beat the winter freeze.

During this time, a controlling interest in Northwestern Utilities was held by the International Utilities Corporation, a company based in the United States, which financed, engineered, and managed a variety of public utilities. In 1925, this company also began to buy up shares in Alberta's Canadian Western, and the two utilities became sister companies, linked by ownership and shared expertise in management.

In the late 1920s, other non-gas utilities companies were established in Canada, which would later become linked to Northwestern and Canadian Western. These included Northern Power and Light, Ltd. and Mid-West Utilities, Limited, which in turn owned Vegreville Utilities, Ltd. During this time, Mid-West Utilities changed its name to Canadian Utilities, Limited, hoping to avoid confusion with another American utility company of the same name.

Northwestern suffered a major setback in January 1928, when shifting ice in a farmer's ditch broke the Viking pipeline, cutting off gas to Edmonton in −20 degree weather. Although gas was restored as quickly as possible, this event, and other concerns, prompted the company to begin an effort to duplicate this pipeline, increasing its capacity. Other safety measures were installed as well.

At the same time, Canadian Utilities was working to set up an electrical grid system in the areas where it served customers.

The company purchased additional power plants in key locations, and then ran transmission lines between them. In this way, new communities were brought into the system, and antiquated equipment was gradually retired. In 1930, the network of Canadian Utilities companies was purchased by the Dominion Gas and Electric Company, a subsidiary of the American Commonwealths Power Corporation.

Weathering the Great Depression and World War II

With the advent of the Great Depression in 1929, Northwestern found that demand for its products dropped significantly, as many industrial customers went out of business and residential customers were forced to resume use of coal. Northwestern Utilities also faced a spectacular misfortune in 1932, when the leak of a Northwestern gas main in downtown Edmonton caused the destruction of a leading hotel in the city and several surrounding structures. The fire broke out in the basement of the Corona Hotel on a February evening, and firemen fought it throughout the night before they were able to bring it under control. The resulting lawsuits from this event threatened to put Northwestern into bankruptcy. In an effort to ensure that no such conflagration ever took place again, the company instituted a program of odorization of its gas for safety purposes. In 1934, Northwestern was handed a legal defeat in cases resulting from the hotel fire. This blow came on top of the generally bleak economic picture in Alberta at that time.

Northwestern's sister company, Canadian Western, fared better during the 1930s, adding customers in new communities and new features to its gas distribution system. One innovation involved the storing of excess gas resulting from oil extraction at Turner Valley, gas that had previously been burned off as a waste product. P.D. Mellon, Canadian Western's vice-president, worked with geologists on his idea for storing the gas via pipes at the Bow Island site. The resulting piping system was reversible and could therefore accept gas for storage in the summer and make it available again during peak winter months.

In the mid-1930s, the electric utility company, Canadian Utilities, was merged with the Union Power Company in an effort to stem the tide of losses that Canadian Utilities had suffered every year since 1928. Canadian Utilities was thereafter able to benefit from the proceeds of Union Power's coal holdings.

After Britain declared war on Germany in 1939, Canada, as part of the British Empire, became embroiled in World War II. Many employees of the gas and electric utilities of Alberta left their jobs to join the armed forces, and materials and supplies were also diverted to the war effort. In 1940, Northwestern installed heating, cooking, and water heating equipment at two air training schools being constructed in the area. Canadian Western also began serving air force training centers.

The wartime economy provided opportunities for some utilities and challenges for others. For example, Canadian Utilities was able to expand into the far northern territories of Canada, via the newly constructed Alaska Highway, and began supplying electric power to the booming town of Fort St. John, British Columbia. While Canadian Western was reporting record sales, Northwestern's efforts to meet increasing demand for gas were

Key Dates:

1911: Canadian Western Natural Gas, Light, Heat, and Power Company Limited is founded by Eugene Coste.

1925: Canadian Western becomes a sister company to Edmonton-based Northwestern Utilities Limited under International Utilities Corporation, a U.S.-based holding company.

1930: The network of Canadian Utilities companies is purchased by the Dominion Gas and Electric Company, a subsidiary of the American Commonwealths Power Corporation.

1944: Dominion Gas and Electric Company merges with the International Utilities Company.

1961: International Utilities, the corporate owner of the three linked Alberta companies, also purchases Northland Utilities, Limited.

1980: Majority ownership of Canadian Utilities (CU) is transferred from International Utilities to ATCO Ltd., a Canadian-based conglomerate.

1999: CU moves to separate its regulated utility businesses from its non-regulated businesses, forming a new subsidiary, known as CU Inc., to acquire all of the common shares and debt of its regulated subsidiaries.

thwarted by the rationing of steel, which was needed to lay additional pipe.

In 1944, the Dominion Gas and Electric Company merged with the International Utilities Company, the old American partner of the Alberta companies. In doing so, International Utilities provided additional capital to the Canadian operations. The company used a portion of these funds to push forward with efforts at rural electrification. Test lines were run out to Vegreville in February 1945 and to Melfort, Saskatchewan. Moreover, International began investing in Northwestern and Canadian Utilities.

After the war's end in 1945, the utility companies resumed their normal operations and rate of growth. Alberta saw the formation of another new gas and electric company, Northland Utilities, Limited, which served customers in the Peace River area. Moreover, Canadian Utilities' operations were soon focused solely in Alberta, when the Saskatchewan Power Commission began buying up all the smaller utilities with a vision of nationalizing the industry in that province. A similar trend soon took Canadian Utilities out of British Columbia as well.

In 1947, Alberta's demand for gas began increasing rapidly due to a population boom and an accident at an oil well. Canada's oil boom began in February of that year with the discovery of oil near the town of Leduc, Alberta, and increasing numbers of people began moving to the area to share in the wealth. One year later, another well at this site, the Atlantic No. 3, went out of control, spilling oil onto the countryside for six months before igniting in September, and finally being subdued. Northwestern was soon struggling to meet the demand for gas.

Unifying Gas and Electric in the 1950s and 1960s

In 1954 the first step to uniting Alberta's gas and electric companies was taken, when one man, F. Austin Brownie, president of Northwestern and Canadian Western, was also appointed head of Canadian Utilities. Under Brownie, Canadian Utilities began expanding its Alberta holdings, purchasing the McMurray Light and Power Company, Limited, and Slave Lake Utilities.

In 1961, International Utilities, the corporate owner of the three linked Alberta companies, also purchased Northland Utilities, Limited, and merged this company into the group. At that time, due to changes in the Canadian tax structure, International Utilities also established itself as a U.S. corporation resident in Canada, hoping to blunt criticism of foreign ownership of the Alberta properties.

Later in the 1960s, International Utilities nearly doubled in size through the purchase of the General Waterworks Corporation. This move helped to pave the way for a major restructuring of the companies in the early 1970s, when Canadian Utilities became the corporate parent of Canadian Western, Northwestern, Northland, and Alberta Power, Limited, which was formed to take over the electrical operations previously run by Canadian Utilities. Northland was then merged into Northwestern. The resulting company, known as CU, became one of the largest investor-owned utilities in Canada. At this time, International Utilities also returned to residence in the United States.

Expansion and Diversification in the 1970s and 80s

In the early 1970s, a unified CU began to devote more of its attention to conservation and environmental awareness. In addition, the company began to branch out to other areas related to the utilities industry. In 1973, CU Engineering Limited was formed to provide consulting services; in 1975, CU Ethane Limited was formed to build and operate an ethane extraction plant in Edmonton as a joint venture; and, in 1976, CU Resources Limited was created to develop non-utility resource properties.

One of CU's missions during the 1970s was to respond to environmental issues. Canadians were becoming increasingly aware of the need to conserve energy, and also sought to enact laws for keeping their air and waters clean and protecting wildlife. Toward that end, the company formed an environmental planning commission, headed by Gordon R. Cameron, which worked to ensure that CU was respecting the environment by modernizing facilities to emit fewer pollutants. Moreover, the company investigated such novel ideas as using natural gas to power automobiles.

At the start of the 1980s, majority ownership of CU was transferred from International Utilities to ATCO, Ltd., a Canadian-based conglomerate that had started as a vendor of trailer homes in 1946. In the spring of 1980, ATCO paid $325 million for International's 58 percent share in the company, and installed its chairman as the chief executive officer of CU. In the wake of this purchase, the Calgary Power Company (which then changed its name to the TransAlta Utilities Corporation) offered to buy up the 42 percent of CU's shares that ATCO did not own. This offer led to a standoff between CU and TransAlta, with legal entanglements that reached all the way to the Canadian Supreme Court. In 1982, the two companies agreed to withdraw from the dispute and gradually dispose of each other's shares.

In the early 1980s, CU also suffered from the effects of a recession that hit Alberta. The company attempted to reduce operating costs and also applied for a rate increase to offset the financial downturn. In the spring of 1982, CU also restructured its subsidiaries, creating ATCOR Resources, Limited. This group was formed from the ATCO Gas & Oil operations and the non-utility branches of CU. Shortly after this merger, CU discontinued the engineering consulting branch, after demand for these services dropped.

In the mid-1980s, ATCOR became increasingly involved in frontier exploration. In 1986, the division was reorganized again, taking the name CU Enterprises, Inc. This entity specialized in oil and gas exploration and production, and the processing and marketing of natural gas. By 1987, it had become the largest direct marketer of natural gas to final users in Canada.

By the late 1980s, CU served more than 600,000 natural gas customers and 150,000 electric customers. The company continued to turn a profit, despite a sharp drop in growth for its main area of operation, Alberta. These earnings continued throughout the early 1990s. By the end of 1994, CU was servicing nearly 900,000 utility customers. Under the leadership of R.D. Southern, chairman and CEO, and J.D. Wood, president and CEO, the company also became involved in some new complementary operations, including the acquisition from ATCO of Frontec, a leading Canadian contractor of technical services with over $3 billion in assets and facilities. CU was also pursuing acquisitions of independent power plants in Western Europe, Australia, and the United States.

Gearing Up for Deregulation in the 1990s

In the late 1990s CU began to address the challenges associated with dramatic changes in the competitive landscape that would come from utilities deregulation. In anticipation of the new competitive environment, CU initiated various streamlining programs aimed at cutting costs and improving efficiency. In 1997, ATCO and CU consolidated their corporate headquarters, creating a single ATCO Group Corporate Office in Edmonton. In addition to eliminating duplicate office work and staff redundancies, the reorganization improved efficiency by shifting support services previously handled by CU directly into the operating companies that required them. The shift was also aimed at reinforcing the autonomy of the operating companies. Further belt-tightening was implemented in 1997 with the reduction of about 350 jobs from CU's utility companies, Canadian Western Natural Gas, Northwestern Utilities, and Alberta Power.

Another push for efficiency was made in 1998 when CU decided to merge its natural gas subsidiaries, Canadian Western Natural Gas Company Limited and Northwestern Utilities Limited, and to create an intra-Alberta transmission company and a province-wide distribution company. The new transmission company transported gas through high-pressure pipelines beyond urban areas within Alberta, while the new distribution company continued to deliver gas from the transmission systems to customers. CU anticipated that the establishment of separate transmission and distribution businesses would bring significant savings to customers and further position the company to become a major player in the newly deregulated Alberta energy market.

Principal Subsidiaries

Alberta Power Ltd.; ATCO Power Ltd.; ATCO Electric Ltd.; ATCO Gas and Pipelines Ltd.; CU Water Ltd.; ATCO Frontec Corp.; ATCO Midstream Ltd.; ATCO I-Tek Business Services Ltd.; ATCO Travel Ltd.; ASHCOR Technologies Ltd.; Genics Inc.

Principal Competitors

BC Gas Inc.; EPCOR Utilities Inc.; TransAlta Corporation.

Further Reading

"ATCO Group Announces Reorganization of the ATCO Ltd. and Canadian Utilities Limited Head Offices," *Canada NewsWire,* March 7, 1997.

Atkinson, Pat, "Ten Top Shops: Canadian Utilities Automates Computer Operations," *Canadian Datasystems,* September 1990, pp. 40, 42.

"Canadian Utilities Limited Announces a Streamlining of Operations," *Canada NewsWire,* November 21, 1997.

"Canadian Utilities Limited Announces Purchases," *Canada NewsWire,* January 31, 1995.

"Canadian Utilities Reports 2002 Results," *Canada NewsWire,* February 26, 2003.

Sherman, Kevin, "Local-Area Networks: The Canadian Utilities Experience," *Computing Canada,* March 16, 1989, p. 40.

Stahl, Len, *A Record of Service: The History of Western Canada's Pioneer Gas and Electric Utilities,* Edmonton: Canadian Utilities Limited, 1987.

—Elizabeth Rourke
—update: Erin Brown

CarrAmerica Realty Corporation

1850 K Street Northwest, Suite 500
Washington, D.C. 20006
U.S.A.
Telephone: (202) 729-7500
Toll Free: (800) 417-2277
Fax: (202) 729-1150
Web site: http://www.carramerica.com

Public Company
Incorporated: 1992
Employees: 780
Operating Revenues: $527.72 million (2002)
Stock Exchanges: New York
Ticker Symbol: CRE
NAIC: 525930 Real Estate Investment Trusts; 531210
Offices of Real Estate Agents and Brokers

CarrAmerica Realty Corporation operates as a real estate investment trust (REIT) focusing on the acquisition, development, ownership, and management of office properties in more than a dozen markets in the United States. CarrAmerica is distinguished as the first REIT to specialize in office buildings on a national scale. The company owns greater than 50 percent interest in 260 office buildings, which contain roughly 20 million square feet of net rentable area. CarrAmerica's properties are located in Washington, D.C.; Seattle, Washington; Phoenix, Arizona; Austin and Dallas, Texas; Chicago, Illinois; Atlanta, Georgia; south Florida; Denver, Colorado; and throughout California.

19th-Century Origins

CarrAmerica, as it stood at the beginning of the 21st century, represented the culmination of assets, interests, and companies whose origins stretched back to the late 19th century, to the arrival in the United States of the Carr family. In 1885, Solomon Carr emigrated from Leicester, England, taking his six children to Washington, D.C. Shortly after his arrival, Solomon Carr established himself as a homebuilder, developing a successful business in an area west of the Capitol building.

Generation by generation, Solomon Carr's progeny established themselves as prominent entrepreneurs in Washington, forging a family enterprise whose scope of operations broadened beyond home construction and the nation's capital. Solomon Carr's son, Arthur Carr, led the second generation of the family, guiding the company into its principal area of business for much of the 20th century. Arthur Carr managed office buildings in Washington, most notably the original Mills building. Arthur Carr's management of the Mills Building—a property that would be long affiliated with the Carr family—led to his collaboration with General Anson Mills. Together, they began building office buildings in Washington, D.C., and Houston, Texas.

The next generation of the family was headed by Arthur Carr's son, Oliver T. Carr, who took over the management of the Mills Building in 1922. His son, Oliver T. Carr, Jr., formed Oliver T. Carr, Jr., Inc., a homebuilding company founded in 1955. Through this entity, Oliver T. Carr, Jr., began building houses in Montgomery County, Maryland, a suburban region outside the Washington metropolitan area. It was through Oliver T. Carr, Jr., that the Carr collection of assets took on the characteristics that later described CarrAmerica. Specifically, the real estate service company that existed at the beginning of the 21st century drew its most direct ancestral line from Oliver T. Carr Management, Inc. Founded in 1962, Oliver T. Carr Management, Inc. operated as an office and apartment building management and development company. The company's first project was the development of the Jefferson House, a high-rise apartment building in Washington. Following the development of the Jefferson House, the company began focusing primarily on building and managing properties.

Emergence of a Development Company: 1960s

As the management and development company matured, it became the heart of the Carr family enterprise, a business recast as The Oliver Carr Company that focused nearly exclusively on the development of office properties. After redeveloping the Mills Building in 1966, the company began developing several office properties in the center of Washington, including 1800 M Street and 1730 Pennsylvania Avenue. Next, the company fo-

Company Perspectives:

"We are committed to building a company that will be a great place to work, that will make a difference in our industry, and, most important, that will make a difference for our customers. By focusing on these objectives, CarrAmerica is building a great future."

—Tom Carr, president and CEO

cused its attention on the western reaches of Washington. After purchasing the Sealtest Dairy site at 26th Street in what was known as Washington's West End, the company formed West End Planning, Inc., a nonprofit company created to assist in the planning of a community on the Sealtest Dairy site.

Success in Washington's West End encouraged the company to expand its presence in the city's eastern markets. Throughout the 1970s and into the 1980s, The Oliver Carr Company established itself in several of Washington's fast-growing suburban markets. At the same time, the company also forged relationships with numerous corporate denizens, developing office complexes according to customer specifications. The Oliver Carr Company developed headquarter facilities for organizations such as the American Association of Retired Persons, telecommunications giant MCI, and The American Automobile Association. During this period of expansion, a new generation of Carr leadership joined the company. In 1973, Oliver T. Carr, Jr.'s son, Robert O. Carr, joined the company as a development project manager, the first step in his climb toward becoming president and chief executive officer of The Oliver Carr Company. In 1985, Robert Carr's brother, Thomas A. Carr, joined the company, starting as vice-president of suburban development and eventually becoming president of The Oliver Carr Company's successor.

By the end of the 1980s, The Oliver Carr Company ranked as the largest office property owner and management-services provider in the greater Washington area. Although the company's stature by the end of the decade was impressive, a period of unprecedented growth was set to follow, its arrival signaled by several important changes implemented by The Oliver Carr Company's management. The first of the significant changes to occur during the 1990s happened in February 1993, when the company changed its name to Carr Realty Corp. and converted to public ownership. The public offering raised $147.4 million, but equally as important as the infusion of capital was the new corporate designation under which Carr Realty went public. Management decided to convert to a real estate investment trust, more commonly known as a REIT. The reorganization into a self-administered and self-managed, publicly traded REIT greatly increased the company's ability to raise capital, fueling its evolution into a nationally oriented enterprise.

Although there were many requirements for a company to qualify as a REIT—some quite technical—several conditions described the rough framework of Carr Realty's new status. According to requirements mandated by the Internal Revenue Service (IRS), Carr Realty was forced to distribute at least 90 percent of its taxable income to shareholders. Further, at least

95 percent of the company's gross income needed to be derived from passive sources, such as rent. In return for conforming to these conditions and others, Carr Realty enjoyed greater ease in raising capital to finance its growth. Generally, REITs were able to build new projects more economically than traditional developers because they paid no development fees or interest on loans. Instead, REITs raised capital through the sale of stock and debt, freeing them from securing investment partners for individual projects. Able to develop projects more quickly and under more salubrious financial conditions because of its status as a REIT, Carr Realty stood poised to eclipse the efforts of its conventionally structured rivals. "We're delivering more bricks and sticks for the money than a traditional developer," remarked a Carr Realty vice-president in a November 17, 1996 interview with the *Austin American-Statesman.*

National Expansion in the 1990s

With its qualification as a REIT, Carr Realty pursued a new strategy. Beginning in February 1993, the company sought to increase the value of its portfolio and to increase its cash flow by expanding its management and leasing business and by acquiring properties in the greater Washington metropolitan market. Toward this end, the company increased the size of its portfolio by 700,000 square feet in 1994. During the year, the company also commenced development of projects representing 400,000 square feet. In 1995, Carr Realty acquired two office buildings, one in Tysons Corner, Virginia, and another in Bethesda, Maryland. The purchase of the two office buildings, which contained 620,000 square feet, marked the beginning of the company's emphasis on suburban office buildings. Before the end of the year, a new, much broader and more ambitious strategy was hatched. The implementation of the company's new strategic focus spawned a new era of growth and distinguished Carr Realty as an industry pioneer.

In a December 1997 interview with *National Real Estate Investor,* Oliver T. Carr, Jr.'s son, Thomas A. Carr, Carr Realty's president and chief executive officer, explained the major shift in the company's focus. "While we came public as a very tightly focused regional company with every square foot of office space we owned being located in downtown Washington, we saw the opportunity in the broader national markets." Carr continued, "So, in November 1995, we announced our new national strategy, which was concurrent with our announcement of a major strategic investment of Security Capital U.S. Realty." Security Capital U.S. Realty was a component of one of the most successful REITs in the United States, the Security Capital Group of Santa Fe, New Mexico.

The deal struck between Carr Realty and Security Capital in November 1995 was consummated in April 1996, when Security Capital invested $250 million in Carr Realty in exchange for a 39 percent interest in the Washington-based REIT. With the infusion of capital, Carr began to expand nationally for the first time, a shift in strategy reflected in the change of the company's name to CarrAmerica Realty Corporation, effected in April 1996 as well. Expansion came quickly, with decided vigor, as CarrAmerica spread its presence across the country. The company entered suburban markets in Austin, Denver, Seattle, Chicago, and Atlanta during its first wave of expansion, distinguishing itself as one of the most active REITs in the nation. By November 1996, CarrAmerica had purchased, or agreed to purchase, more than $840 million worth of real estate in nine suburban markets, giving it an interest in 147 office properties containing more than 12 million square feet of office space. By the end of 1996, the company had spent no less than $1 billion on new properties, closing 27 transactions. "Our game plan," a CarrAmerica vice-president explained in the November 17, 1996 issue of the *Austin American-Statesman,* "is to come into a market and quickly develop a critical mass. We've found that's the most efficient way to come into a market."

As CarrAmerica prepared for its first full year of expansion following its signal partnership with Security Capital, the company hoped to duplicate the achievements of 1996. Among the purchases completed during the year was a significant investment in the executive suites business, a new market niche entered into through an investment in OmniOffices, Inc., completed in August 1997. More traditional purchases of land, development properties, and office buildings ensued throughout the year, enabling CarrAmerica to meet its goal of investing $1 billion during the year. From there, however, the company's pace of expansion decelerated, as CarrAmerica management responded to changing market conditions, a common occurrence in the cyclical real estate business. In 1998, the company cut its investments in half, spending $500 million on new properties. During the year, the company also sold $180 million worth of assets.

By the end of the 1990s, CarrAmerica exuded impressive strength, despite the reductions in spending. The company owned a controlling interest in a portfolio of roughly 255 office properties. By the end of 1999, CarrAmerica also was involved in the development of 40 office properties, development projects that were located in more than a dozen fast-growing markets. In the years ahead, the company continued to exert its might, albeit in slightly different fashion than during the mid-1990s.

As CarrAmerica entered the 21st century, the company adapted to the anemic economic conditions, making subtle yet significant changes to the way in which it conducted business.

CarrAmerica began to focus on developing office buildings rather than purchasing them, a change in strategy adopted by many REITs. The harsher economic climate also forced management to take a second look at where company properties were being developed. In this process, decisions were made to reduce or to exit some markets and re-deploy the resources in other markets. In 2000, for instance, the company decided to exit the south Florida market, "a national decision," according to a CarrAmerica executive in the April 14, 2000 issue of the *South Florida Business Journal,* "not a reflection on the South Florida office market at all." In November 2001, the company made another move to bolster its financial position when it agreed to purchase more than nine million shares of its stock from Security Capital. The following month, Security Capital divested the remainder of its holdings in CarrAmerica, completing what was referred to as a "quick and uncomplicated exit" of the relationship between CarrAmerica and Security Capital, according to the CarrAmerica corporate web site.

Principal Subsidiaries

Carr Real Estate Services, Inc.; CarrAmerica Development, Inc.

Principal Competitors

Jones Lang LaSalle Incorporated; Shorenstein Company, L.P.; Trizec Properties, Inc.

Further Reading

Berton, Brad, "Voit Sells Last of His Warner Center Holdings to CarrAmerica Realty," *Los Angeles Business Journal,* July 22, 1996, p. 23.
Breyer, R. Michelle, "CarrAmerica of Washington D.C., Buys 10 Buildings in Austin, Texas," *Knight Ridder/Tribune Business News,* July 19, 1996.
——, "CarrAmerica's Growth Shows Dramatic Power of REITs," *Austin American-Statesman,* November 17, 1996, p. K1.
"CarrAmerica's Realty Corp.," *National Real Estate Investor,* September 1, 1999, p. R20.
Feuerstein, Adam, "CarrAmerica Revs Engine; REIT Accelerates Bay Area Buying Binge," *San Francisco Business Times,* July 11, 1997, p. 1.
Garrison, Trey, "Aggressive REIT Will Buy Another Dallas Office Building," *Dallas Business Journal,* April 11, 1997, p. 4.
Heath, Tracy, "CarrAmerica Customizes a Plan for Future Growth," *National Real Estate Investor,* December 1997, p. 34.
Moore, Paula, "CarrAmerica Emerging As Big Player in Denver," *Denver Business Journal,* May 30, 1997, p. 6A.
Raiford, Regina, "Building Blocks," *Buildings,* September 1999, p. 34.
Robson, Douglas, "S.F. Deal Comes Up Golden for Shorenstein," *San Francisco Business Times,* April 3, 1998, p. 1.
Rutledge, Tanya, "CarrAmerica Hopes Third Time Is the Charm to Find Tenant," *Business Journal,* May 11, 1998, p. 5.
Welch, David, "CarrAmerica to Close on Search Plaza," *Dallas Business Journal,* December 6, 1996, p. 1.
White, Suzanne, "CarrAmerica Realty," *Washington Business Journal,* July 27, 2001, p. 25.

—Jeffrey L. Covell

CHESAPEAKE
UTILITIES CORPORATION

Chesapeake Utilities Corporation

909 Silver Lake Boulevard
Dover, Delaware, 19904
U.S.A.
Telephone: (302) 734-6799
Fax: (302) 734-6750
Web site: http://www.chpk.com

Public Company
Incorporated: 1947
Employees: 582
Sales: $142.2 million (2002)
Stock Exchanges: New York
Ticker Symbol: CPK
NAIC: 221210 Natural Gas Distribution

Chesapeake Utilities Corporation, based in Dover, Delaware, is a small, diversified utility company involved in four areas: natural gas distribution and transmission, propane gas distribution and wholesale marketing, advanced information services, and water services. Distribution and transmission of natural gas is the company's primary business, serving more than 45,000 residential, commercial, and industrial customers through three divisions. On the gas distribution side, in central and southern Delaware and Maryland's Eastern Shore, the company does business under its own name, while in Florida, primarily in the corridor between Orlando and Tampa, it operates as Central Florida Gas Company. Natural gas transmission is conducted by a subsidiary, Eastern Shore Natural Gas Company, owner and operator of the only natural gas transmission system south of the Chesapeake and Delaware Canal. Chesapeake's propane distribution and marketing segment is handled by two subsidiaries: Sharp Energy, Inc., which serves some 35,000 customers in central and southern Delaware, and the Eastern Shore of Maryland and Virginia. In recent years, Chesapeake has taken steps to extend its propane operations to its Florida markets. In addition, another Chesapeake subsidiary, Houston-based Xeron, markets propane to major independent oil and petrochemical companies as well as retail propane companies and provides pricing flexibility for Sharp customers. The

Advance Information Services segment is conducted by Brave-Point, Inc., providing information technology consulting services, custom programming, and training to corporate clients around the world. Finally, Chesapeake's Water Services segment offers water conditioning and treatment services through seven EcoWater dealerships operating in Delaware, Florida, Idaho, Maryland, Michigan, and Minnesota. Beyond its four core businesses, Chesapeake also owns two real estate companies, Skipjack Inc. and Eastern Shore Real Estate, whose primary functions to lease property to Chesapeake affiliates.

Origins of Company Date Back to Mid-1800s

Chesapeake Utilities Corporation was formed in Delaware on November 12, 1947, and was soon comprised of three operating subsidiaries: Dover Gas Light Company, Citizens Gas Company, and Sussex Gas Company. The oldest of these entities was Dover Gas Light Company, chartered in 1850 but not operational until 1859. The company was owned by a Philadelphia businessman named Daniel Trump, who in October 1859 bought a 12,000-square-foot facility in Dover, Delaware, where he established the headquarters of Dover Gas Light. Like many gas companies of the era, it was established to provide street lighting, which was just starting to become widespread. Scientists had experimented throughout the 1700s with the concept of creating an illuminant from gas distilled from coal that had the potential to replace candles and oil lamps, but it was not until 1798 that the technology applied in a commercial way, when William Murdock distributed coal gas through pipes in the Boulton and Watt Soho Works in Birmingham, England. In 1807, Frederick Winsor used gas to light the Pall Mall section of London, and in 1812 he was granted a charter from Parliament to create The London and Westminster Chartered Gas Light and Coke Company. Paris had gas lights in 1816, and Vienna in 1818. The first gas streetlight company to be chartered in America was located in Baltimore in 1817, followed by Boston in 1822 and New York a year later. Dover Gas was one of the earlier gas light companies organized in the country.

At first Trump manufactured his gas using resin, which cost around $1.50 a barrel. A few years later, because of the Civil War, the price of resin reached an astounding $60 a barrel, forcing Trump to turn to coal-oil and wood as a substitute. He sold the business to Richardson and Robbins, a canning company, which resumed the use of resin before opting to employ the more popular method of coal gas. At this time in America, gas was still distributed by a multitude of small operators like Dover Gas, which manufactured their own product in local plants. Typically, coal gas was produced by reducing coal to coke in a retort house, then piping the product to another facility where it was purified by lime. The gas was then piped to a massive tank called a gasholder or "gasometer." This method of providing commercial gas would remain essentially unchanged until the 1930s, when advances in pipeline technologies began to make the use of natural gas practical. Dover Gas, in fact, would use its coal gas plant until the post-World War II era.

From 1947 Incorporation to 1970s Gas Shortages

Dover Gas was incorporated in 1881. Harry A. Richardson was named president, his family owning a controlling interest in the business. Several years later Dover Gas became a subsidiary of a holding company, General Gas and Electric Corporation. It remained a part of General Gas and Electric until 1942, when it was sold to the Philadelphia investment banking firm of Harrison and Company, which already owned a Maryland utility, Hagerstown Gas Company. A key element of this transaction that would affect the future of Chesapeake Utilities Corporation was the decision of Edward C. Burton, Sr., manager of Dover Gas and another gas subsidiary, to cast his lot with Harrison and Company and take over the management of Dover Gas and Hagerstown Gas. In November 1947, Harrison and Company incorporated Chesapeake Utilities Corporation to serve as the parent company for its Dover Gas and Hagerstown Gas assets. Only a few months later, in March 1948, Chesapeake acquired Citizens Gas and Sussex Gas, the other companies that would form the bulk of its present holdings.

The history of Citizens Gas can be traced back to 1907 with the creation of Salisbury, Maryland-based Home Gas company, financed by a group of wealthy local investors. It became known as Citizens Gas Company in 1914 after it was acquired by William J. Downing. The business then changed hands twice in a short period of time, first acquired by Southern Cities Utilities and later becoming a subsidiary of Consolidated Electric and Gas Company, which at the same time acquired Sussex Gas Company, the third of the three principal subsidiaries of Chesapeake Utilities. Sussex Gas was started in 1910 to serve Seaford, Delaware. Beyond that fact, little is known about the roots of the business. Consolidated Electric and Gas looked to divest its gas interests in the late 1930s, and in 1939 Citizens Gas and Sussex Gas were sold to a partnership doing business as C.M. Lucas Co. and James Piper. They remained under

management of this firm until 1948, when the companies were sold to Chesapeake Utilities.

Burton was named vice-president of the merged company and for the next 23 years acted essentially as its chief operating officer and was responsible in large measure for the success of the enterprise. One of the first areas of change for the business was the switch from manufactured gas to propane-air, a change which had already been undertaken by Sussex Gas a short time before the merger. Dover Gas converted later in 1948, followed by Citizens Gas two years later. It was also in 1948 that Burton's son, Edward C. Burton, Jr. started his business career by becoming manager of the Eastern Shore Public Service Company, bought by the Burton family in that year. In 1950, he became president of the company, which in 1955 became a subsidiary of Chesapeake Utilities.

The major thrust of Chesapeake Utilities in the 1950s was to create a consolidated system and to expand upon it. A key element was put in place in 1956 when Eastern Shore Natural Gas Company was incorporated as a subsidiary and a year later began to construct a natural gas pipeline to connect with the network of Transcontinental Gas Pipeline Corporation in order to supply Dover, Citizens, and Sussex, as well as other users in Maryland and Delaware. In recent years, natural gas provided by wells in the southwestern United States had begun to be distributed throughout the country by thousands of miles of pipeline, making gas a popular choice for heating and cooking in the new housing developments that sprung up during the boom years of the post-war era. With the completion of the Eastern Shore pipeline, Chesapeake Utility's three operating gas companies in 1959 converted from propane-air to natural gas. As a result, customers' rates were reduced by as much as 20 percent.

In January 1960, due to changes in federal legislation governing utilities, Chesapeake was able to merge its three gas subsidiaries and begin to do business as a single company. Eastern Shore, because it was not a utility, remained a subsidiary. With the industrialization of the Delmarva Peninsula in 1960s, Chesapeake underwent significant expansion to keep pace with rising demand for gas in its market, completing a number of extensions to its distribution network. This effort continued into the 1970s, but Chesapeake now faced a different challenge: a gas shortage.

In 1971, Transcontinental Gas Pipeline Corporation cut back on the supply of gas it delivered to Chesapeake by 4 percent. Even as Chesapeake continued to expand its distribution network, cutbacks in gas mounted over the next several years, resulting in a 19 percent decrease in net income between 1972 and 1977. The gas shortage grew so severe that in 1977 some of Chesapeake's industrial customers were cut off completely for weeks at a time. Nevertheless, Chesapeake was able to find and deliver alternative sources of fuel, and as a result no businesses were closed or jobs lost, occurrences that were commonplace elsewhere in the eastern United States. To help alleviate the shortage, Chesapeake, through an Eastern Shore subsidiary, Dover Exploration Company, began in the mid-1970s to invest in exploration. Within a few years, gas drawn from successful wells began to flow through the natural gas system and reach Chesapeake customers. As gas supplies improved, Dover Exploration changed its focus from drilling to the development of existing wells.

New Leadership and Growth: 1980s–90s

Edward C. Burton, Sr. died in February 1974. His son took over a position of leadership, becoming president of the company, then in June 1980 was named chief executive officer and chairman of the board of directors. He oversaw the start of a diversification effort in the 1980s, including involvement in propane. (Piped propane was a viable alternative to natural gas for residential subdivisions, either delivered by a community gas system that served an entire development from a central site or by a cluster tank system that relied on a number of smaller storage facilities.) In 1980, the company acquired Mitchell's Gas Service, a Laurel, Delaware, propane distribution company, then in 1981 purchased the Clarence E. Sharp Company, a Georgetown, Delaware, propane company. They would be consolidated as Sharpgas, Inc. and form the basis of today's Sharp Energy, Inc. These propane assets were augmented a year later with the acquisition of a division of Northern Propane Gas Company, which doubled the size of Sharp.

Edward C. Burton, Jr. retired as CEO in July 1983, ending the long tenure of active service by the Burton family. Under new leadership the company continued to diversify in the 1980s. In order to help fund these efforts, Chesapeake went public in 1985 and began trading on the NASDAQ. (In 1993 it would move to the New York Stock Exchange.) To offset the dependence of its gas distribution business on the temperature-sensitive Delmarva region, Chesapeake looked to Florida. In 1985, it paid $3 million to acquire Central Florida Gas Company, a Winter Haven, Florida, natural gas distribution company that served the rapidly growing area surrounding Walt Disney World. The company in 1988 used stock to acquire the Plant City Natural Gas Company and Saf-T-Gas Co., a propane business, both located in Plant City, Florida. In the meantime, Chesapeake also looked to expand on its home territory. In 1986, it bought Cambridge Gas Company, a Cambridge, Maryland, gas company, then in 1987 acquired Georgetown Service and Gas Company, a propane distribution business located in Georgetown, Delaware. Chesapeake next paid more than $13.5 million in 1988 to acquire the propane and oil products distribution assets of Kellam Energy, Inc., based in Belle Haven, Virginia.

It was also in the 1980s that Chesapeake laid the foundation for its Advance Information Services segment of its business. In 1988, it bought Capital Data Systems, Inc. to develop in-house financial and energy billing systems as well as serve outside clients. In 1991, Chesapeake hired Atlanta-based United Systems, Inc. to act as a consultant to the struggling subsidiary, and management was so pleased with its relationship that later in 1991 it acquired United Systems. These two information technology purchases would evolve into Bravepoint, Inc.

In the 1990s, Chesapeake continued to adjust its business mix. It sold its Florida propane business and opted to exit the fuel oil and motor fuels delivery business in Maryland and Virginia. In 1998, Chesapeake established its water services segment by acquiring Salisbury, Maryland-based Tolan Water Service, an EcoWater dealership and water conditioning and treatment business. A year later, the company acquired EcoWater Systems of Michigan, Inc., a Detroit-area company doing business as Douglas Water Conditioning. In 2000, Carroll Water Systems, Inc. of Westminster, Maryland, another EcoWater dealership, was brought into the fold. Then in 2001 the Chesapeake water services segment acquired water conditioning and treatment assets from Absolute Water Care, Inc., serving Sarasota, Charlotte, and Manatee counties in Florida; Aquarius Systems, Inc., serving Fort Pierce and Port St. Lucie, Florida; Automatic Water Conditioning Inc, another company serving Port St. Lucie; EcoWater Systems of Rochester, serving Rochester, Minnesota; and Intermountain Water Inc./Blue Springs Water, serving Boise, Idaho.

Other acquisitions in the 1990s that filled out Chesapeake's slate of businesses included the 1997 acquisition of Eastern Shore Real Estate and the 1998 purchase of Xeron, a propane marketing company. In its core gas distribution segment, Chesapeake faced the challenge of deregulation, first in Florida and later in its main markets. Increasingly, the future of the company lay with the unregulated portions of its business. As Chesapeake entered a new century, it looked to continue investing in its traditional gas distribution business while at the same time seeking opportunities in other areas in an effort to establish a stable base of earnings and generate higher returns that a traditional utility.

Principal Subsidiaries

Eastern Shore Natural Gas Company; Chesapeake Service Company; Xeron, Inc; Sharp Water, Inc.

Principal Competitors

Heritage Propane Partners L.P.; NUI Corporation; Suburban Propane Partners, L.P.

Further Reading

Chesapeake Utilities Corporation, *2002 Annual Report*.
Chesapeake Utilities Corporation, *Historical Journal 1983*, Dover, Delaware: Chesapeake Utilities Corporation, 1983.
Rainey, Doug, "Chesapeake Plans to Tap into Growth on Delmarva," *Delaware Business Review*, May 18, 1992, p. 1.

—Ed Dinger

Compañia Española de Petróleos S.A. (Cepsa)

Campo de las Naciones, Avenida del Partenón 12
28042 Madrid
Spain
Telephone: (91) 337-60-00
Fax: (91) 337-41-46
Web site: http://www.cepsa.es

Public Company
Incorporated: 1929
Employees: 9,708
Sales: EUR 11.6 billion ($10.4 billion) (2001)
Stock Exchanges: Mercado Continuo
Ticker Symbol: CEP
NAIC: 211111 Crude Petroleum and Natural Gas
Extraction; 324110 Petroleum Refineries

Compañia Española de Petróleos S.A. (CEPSA) stands as Spain's second largest integrated oil and gas concern just behind Repsol YPF S.A. The group's core activity is refining—its three main refineries include Gibraltar, La Rabida, and Tenerife—and it is also involved in exploration and oil production, petrochemicals, as well as having its own service station network. CEPSA operates on a global scale and maintains a strong presence throughout Spain, Portugal, Panama, Morocco, Algeria, Columbia, Canada, Brazil, Italy, and the United Kingdom. TOTAL FINA ELF S.A. owns nearly 44 percent of the company.

Early History: Late 1920s

In 1927 the Spanish dictator Primo de Rivera issued a decree expropriating all foreign and domestic oil companies and placing them under the control of a state agency. Administration was entrusted to Compañia Arrendataria del Monopolio de Petróleos Sociedad Anónima (CAMPSA), which until the 1980s had sole rights to purchase oil from producers at state-controlled prices.

The Canary Islands and the Spanish Moroccan territories of Ceuta and Melilla were exempted from the decree, in part because they were already exempted from a number of customs regulations and had long served as important trade intermediaries between Spain and the rest of the world. The exemption also would provide a golden opportunity for CEPSA.

Spain's lack of refineries posed a severe barrier to industrialization, but there was no domestic crude to refine. The few attempts at exploration had failed to find a commercial Spanish field. Spain was heavily dependent on imported foreign oil, supplied by Shell and other foreign multinationals at international prices. Political and economic problems made it difficult for the government to build a refinery.

These problems ensured that when the financier Francisco Recasens and a group of investors incorporated CEPSA in Madrid on September 26, 1929, the Spanish government did not oppose them. Recasens, whose brother was an adviser to CAMPSA, the newly organized state monopoly, convinced government officials that a private concern would have more freedom to acquire crude for Spain abroad.

Recasens had already acquired important concessions in Venezuela and Texas, previously owned by the American Falcon Oil Company. These were transferred to CEPSA. From these early days, the company maintained an international identity and special role. By this means, the company helped preserve its independence from CAMPSA.

By building a refinery in Tenerife, Canary Islands, CEPSA was officially outside the state monopoly, but in practice, it was dependent on a close relationship with the Spanish government. CEPSA could not sell oil in Spain to anyone other than the government. In effect, the government had a de facto veto over CEPSA's sales to non-Spanish customers because it could simply extend its mainland monopoly to the Canaries. The company had more freedom, however, to trade abroad and to supply ships and international trade in Tenerife.

The Tenerife refinery opened as Spain's first refinery in November 1930. It remained so until 1949 and supplied 50 percent of the country's needs with an initial capacity of 5,000 barrels a day or 250 billion tons annually.

Surviving Political Unrest: Late 1930s–40s

The Canary Islands location may have helped secure the company's future in another way. It was from this island base that General Francisco Franco, then their military commander, began his campaign against the Spanish Republic. In 1936 he flew from Tenerife to Spanish Morocco and raised an invasion force that attacked the mainland and started a bloody civil war that lasted until he finally triumphed over Republican forces in 1939.

During the civil war, the Canary Islands remained firmly in the Nationalist camp, and CEPSA's refinery became an asset of significance to Franco's Nationalist cause. Refinery production, denied to Madrid and out of bombing range of the Republic's mostly Loyalist air force, helped earn foreign exchange and fuel Franco's success.

The monopoly law prohibited CEPSA from exploration on the Spanish mainland and from 1936 the civil war made exploration practically impossible. CEPSA began to produce oil in Venezuela in 1930, however, and the country remained an important source for decades to come.

In 1939, Franco's newly established dictatorship announced a policy of industrial self-sufficiency and independence from foreign control. During the civil war, support for the republic from the Soviet Union and international communist movement helped ensure that Spain's small group of capitalists and industrialists lined up, sometimes reluctantly, behind Franco.

The Nationalists were not interested in free market solutions for a devastated economy with little industry and scarce domestic capital. By the time the civil war ended in September 1939, World War II had begun. There was little prospect of foreign investment.

The Franco dictatorship's main pillars of support were not the capitalists, but the Catholic church, the traditional land-owning classes, and the Falange, a political movement resembling the Italian Fascist Party. The chosen means of implementing self-sufficiency was nationalization of the main industrial sectors. State companies were placed under the direction of a state agency, the Instituto Nacional de Industria (INI).

CEPSA remained under ultimate state control as a privately owned Spanish company engaged in supplying petroleum to the state company CAMPSA, its price-setting major customer. During World War II, Franco maintained a state of nonbelligerency. Effectively, the Spanish government sympathized with its former German and Italian patrons while maintaining a diplomatic stance to stay out of the war. Spain was isolated. CEPSA, though privately owned, took its orders from the government but it retained its independence in order to acquire crude abroad.

Spain's need for self-sufficiency inspired intensified exploration for oil by CAMPSA, which finally discovered a strike of limited value during the Tudanca survey of 1941. From 1942, CEPSA was allowed to explore on the mainland. A subsidiary, Compañia de Investigacion y Exploitaciones Petrolifera (CIEPSA), was formed as a separate exploration and production concern, but CEPSA was to be much more successful as a refinery and petrochemical concern than as an exploration and production company.

No important Spanish fields were discovered until state-controlled companies made important finds off the Mediterranean coast in the mid-1960s. In the 1990s, most of CEPSA's Spanish production was concentrated in one of these areas, the Casablanca field.

With the end of World War II in 1945, Spain was in a difficult international position. Nazi Germany and Fascist Italy were defeated. A need to become friendlier with the United States and Britain—who were increasingly the opponents, rather than the allies, of the Soviet Union—and the desire for foreign investment capital led Franco to abandon strict self-sufficiency in favor of controlled foreign investment and private sector participation.

Liberalization Leading to Diversification: 1947–60s

In a 1947 decree, the Spanish government relaxed its oil monopoly. CAMPSA was left in control of marketing and distribution, but this new law enabled the government to authorize private and public companies to develop a wide range of activities: trade; industrial handling, especially refining; storage; research; and the exploration for and production of oil and gas fields. In practice, the government usually required foreign companies, such as Caltex and Esso, to work under joint participation schemes with CAMPSA.

The requirement that both private and public refineries sell to CAMPSA continued, and in 1957 it was extended to gasified petroleum products. After 1950 two new mainland refineries were built by small Spanish companies heavily reliant on foreign participation, and three new state refineries were built. CEPSA's Spanish refining activities faced new competition.

One of CEPSA's solutions was diversification, and the company used the 1947 law to look for foreign partners. CEPSA began to diversify into lubricants in 1950 and launched its own CEPSA brand name for industrial and motor oils, but these are sold, in large part, within the Iberian world. By 1989, 87 percent of its lubricants market was still within Spain and Portugal.

Petrochemical production started in 1955 when the Tenerife refinery built an aromatics extraction plant utilizing the Udex

<table>
<tr><td colspan="2">Key Dates:</td></tr>
<tr><td>1929:</td><td>Financier Francisco Recasens and a group of investors establish CEPSA.</td></tr>
<tr><td>1930:</td><td>The Tenerife refinery opens as Spain's first refinery.</td></tr>
<tr><td>1950:</td><td>CEPSA diversifies into lubricants.</td></tr>
<tr><td>1955:</td><td>The company begins petrochemical production.</td></tr>
<tr><td>1969:</td><td>The Gibraltar refinery is established.</td></tr>
<tr><td>1990:</td><td>Elf Aquitaine acquires an interest in CEPSA.</td></tr>
<tr><td>1992:</td><td>The firm acquires 25 percent of CAMPSA's commercial assets.</td></tr>
<tr><td>1998:</td><td>CEPSA enters the butane cylinder market.</td></tr>
<tr><td>2002:</td><td>The company begins exploration at the Ourhoud field in Algeria.</td></tr>
</table>

process. The first of its kind in Europe, it involved the separation of high purity aromatics from mixtures with other hydrocarbons using an efficient multistage extraction column. During the 1950s and 1960s, CEPSA cooperated with multinationals in joint ventures to set up a number of derivative production plants. By 1989, CEPSA had signed agreements with the Japanese company Dainippon Ink and Chemicals (DIC) to expand its presence in European markets.

After a series of unsuccessful attempts, CEPSA finally secured government authorization to build a second refinery on the Spanish mainland at Cadiz in 1964. The plant opened in 1969 as the Gibraltar refinery and became the stimulus for one of the largest new industrial complexes in Spain.

In 1964, CEPSA Compañía Portugesa, a new subsidiary, began to sell petroleum and petrochemical products in Portugal. It also operated an extensive service station network. In 1975, CEPSA established its own research center at San Fernando de Henares. Even so, CEPSA's share of the Spanish market for most petroleum products remained small in relation to the state-owned companies, including CAMPSA, controlled by the state through the Instituto Nacional de Hidrocarburos (INH).

Changes in the 1980s

In 1987, most state monopoly interests were reorganized into the Spanish multinational Repsol which, in 1989, was partially privatized. Throughout the 1980s, government policy increasingly favored the growth of Repsol as a major Spanish institution, capable of keeping the Spanish oil industry in Spanish hands, rather than opening up the market to smaller private companies.

This policy brought increased criticism from the European Community, which required Spain, as a condition of membership, to restrict the monopoly role of CAMPSA and Repsol. In June 1983 CEPSA, the government, CAMPSA, and other private refineries reached an agreement known as the Protocol, which attempted to protect the domestic oil industry without a formal monopoly.

CAMPSA shares were split among the refineries, with the Spanish government holding the majority of the shares, but the refineries agreed to sell products destined for the domestic

market to CAMPSA. Refineries soon began to ignore the Protocol, however.

Under pressure from the European Community (EC) commission, Spain agreed to change a restrictive law by halving the distance required between service stations and making it easier for independents to use CAMPSA's distribution network. In 1989, Repsol, by then holding the Spanish government's majority shares, CEPSA, and other minority shareholders in CAMPSA decided that CAMPSA's service stations and some other retail assets would be divided among them by mid-1991. CAMPSA would continue as a distribution and transportation company, under Repsol's control. This process was completed in 1992—Repsol gained slightly more than a 66 percent interest while CEPSA acquired nearly 25 percent of CAMPSA's assets.

CEPSA, as a relatively small company, was unable to fully exploit its excellent position within a liberalized market in which most analysts expected to see rapid growth during the 1990s. CEPSA's investment potential, however, attracted the attention of several large foreign investors. In May 1988, the Abu Dhabi Investment Corporation acquired 10 percent of CEPSA.

In November of that year, the company announced a one-for-five rights issue. In a complex series of transactions, the French multinational Elf Aquitaine—now known as TOTAL FINA ELF—acquired 20 percent of the company's equity and later acquired additional stock through a deal with another major shareholder, the Banco Central. CEPSA went public on the Spanish Continuous Market on September 18, 1989. The company's stock could be purchased or sold by any authorized trader anywhere in Spain by means of a computerized communications network with a single quote given at the end of each session.

By 1989, CEPSA was less active in exploration but held domestic mining rights over 5,000 square kilometers in exploration permits in Spanish territory and 1,385 kilometers outside Spain. Production came mainly from the Casablanca field, in which it had a 7.4 percent interest in exploitation rights. CEPSA entered into a natural gas exploration agreement with the Algerian government.

During the late 1980s, the two modernized CEPSA refineries processed about 20 percent of the petroleum refined in Spain, but the Tenerife refinery produced mainly for the local market and ships passing through its ports. CEPSA restructured its commercial division and reinforced its distribution network. It also expanded its network of service stations in Spain and bought a distribution network in the north of France.

The influence of Elf, which owned 25 percent of CEPSA's equity in the late 1980s, was growing and it was rumored that the company would eventually fall under Elf's direct control. Regardless of this possibility, the unique environment in which CEPSA operated as the most important and diversified private Spanish oil company was changed forever by Spain's entry into the EC, the dismantling of the state monopoly, the emergence of Repsol, and competition.

Creating a Diversified Company: 1990s and Beyond

As certain facets of the Spanish oil and gas sectors were liberalized during the 1990s, CEPSA's operating environment became increasingly challenging. As such, the company made several key moves during the 1990s to position itself as a diversified oil and gas concern. During 1994, it made an important discovery of crude oil at the Ourhoud field in Algeria, the country's second largest field. By the late 1990s, the company was heavily focused on its exploration and production business, mainly due to Ourhoud's promising reserves and those of the RKF field, which had been discovered in 1992. By 2003, Ourhoud was at full capacity, producing 230,000 barrels per day.

During this time, CEPSA also was focused on strengthening its presence in the petrochemicals industry. The company acquired petrochemicals firm ERTISA in 1994. The following year, the firm opened its first North American plant in Canada, where it began petrochemical-related operations. In 1999, CEPSA acquired a 72 percent interest in Brazil-based Deten, a manufacturer of raw materials used to make detergents.

In September 1998, Spain passed a new hydrocarbons law that enabled CEPSA to enter the liquefied petroleum gas (LPG) market over which Repsol had monopolistic control. In December of that year, the firm introduced new butane cylinders made of stainless steel and, in just one week, landed more than 200 contracts in southern Spain. By 2000, the company was distributing butane cylinders through its network of service stations. The company also made additional diversification efforts that year when it began importing liquefied natural gas from Algeria.

CEPSA entered the new millennium on solid ground despite a challenging economy and falling refining margins. During 2001, seven million barrels of oil were extracted from the firm's RKF field, the firm processed 20 million tons of crude oil, and it sold more than 25 million tons of oil and chemical products. In 2002, crude oil prices continued to rise while refining margins fell by 43 percent over the previous year to one of the lowest levels in nearly 12 years. Nevertheless, CEPSA posted a net income of EUR 460.9 million, a 6 percent rise over 2001 results.

Company management remained optimistic about CEPSA's future and focused on expanding its retail operations into Portugal, increasing butane sales to residential customers, and developing new products and services. The firm also eyed strengthening its petrochemical operations and gaining a significant foothold in the natural gas market as key to future success. Although CEPSA's operating environment had indeed changed dramatically over the past 20 years, the diversified company appeared to be well positioned to take on any new challenges that would cross its path in the years to come.

Principal Subsidiaries

Deten Química S.A. (Brazil); CEPSA International B.V. (Holland); CEPSA Italia SpA; CEPSA UK Ltd.; ETERSA Great Britain Ltd.; ETERSA Netherland B.V.; ETERSA S.A.; INTERQUISA Canada; Intercontinental Química, S.A.; Petresa Canada Inc.; Petresa Internacional N.V. (Belgium); Petroquímica Española, S.A.; Plastificantes de Lutxana, S.A.; Asfaltos Españoles, S.A.; CEPSA Card, S.A.; CEPSA Elf Gas, S.A.; CEPSA Estaciones de Servicio, S.A.; CEPSA Lubricantes, S.A.; CEPSA Maghreb (Morocco); CEPSA Panama S.A.; CEPSA Portuguesa Petróleos, S.A.; Compañía Logística de Hidrocarburos C.L.H., S.A.; Compañía de Investigación y Explotaciones Petrolíferas, S.A.; Lubricantes del sur, S.A.; Productos Asfálticos, S.A.; Refinería Gibraltar; Refinería La Rábida; Refinería de Santa Cruz de Tenerife; Societat Catalana de Petrólis, S.A.

Principal Competitors

BP plc; Repsol YPF S.A.; Royal Dutch/Shell Group.

Further Reading

''CEPSA Breaks Butane Monopoly,'' *El Mundo,* December 13, 1998, p. 47.

''CEPSA Buys ERTOIL from Elf,'' *Platt's Oilgram News,* April 23, 1991, p. 4.

''CEPSA Charts Rising Profits,'' *Oil Daily,* December 12, 2001.

''CEPSA Prepares to Assume Mantle of Leading Private Oil Firm in Spain,'' *European Energy Report,* July 26, 1991, p. 3.

Correlje, Dr. A.F., *The Liberalisation of the Spanish State Oil Sector: Strategies for a Competitive Future,* Rotterdam: Centre for Policy Studies Erasmus University, 1990.

McBride, Tom, ''CEPSA Broadens Its Base,'' *Petroleum Economist,* April 2000, p. 51.

''Oil Company Says Net Rose, Beating Analysts' Estimates,'' *Wall Street Journal* (Europe), February 7, 2003, p. A4.

''REPSOL/CEPSA Square Off,'' *International Gas Report,* October 16, 1998, p. 8.

Santamaria, Javier, *El Petroleo en Espana del Monopolio a La Libertad,* Madrid: Espasa Calpe, 1988.

''Spanish Bank Deal Leaves Elf as Leading CEPSA Shareholder,'' *European Energy Report,* August 5, 1994, p. 8.

''Spanish Petrol Station Liberalization Sparks Fierce Battle,'' *European Energy Report,* July 22, 1994, p. 2.

—Clark Siewert
—update: Christina M. Stansell

Continental AG

Vahrenwalder Strasse 9
D-30165 Hanover
Germany
Telephone: +49-0511-938-01
Fax: +49-0511-938-81-770
Web site: http://www.conti-online.com

Public Company
Incorporated: 1871 as Continental-Caoutchouc und
    Gutta-Percha Compagnie
Employees: 64,379
Sales: $11.95 billion (2002)
Stock Exchanges: Hanover OTC
Ticker Symbols: CON; CTTAY (ADR)
NAIC: 326211 Motor Vehicle Tires Manufacturing;
    336322 Other Motor Vehicle Electrical and Electronic
    Equipment Manufacturing

Long established as the leading tire producer in Germany, Continental AG attained international prominence through a series of major acquisitions in Europe and in the United States starting in 1979. By 1991 Continental was the fourth largest tire producer in the world. After weathering considerable economic pressures in the early 1990s, the company began making significant strides to secure a competitive position in the more lucrative arena of auto components. One of its most significant acquisitions came in 2001 when it bought a controlling interest in DaimlerChrysler's Temic auto-electronics business.

Continental Originates As a Rubber Goods Manufacturer: 1871

The Continental-Caoutchouc und Gutta-Percha Compagnie (Continental) was established in Hanover in 1871, and the city remained the center of the firm's operations. It was by no means the first German rubber company; several small firms had been active in Hanover in the previous decade. Continental was promoted by a group of financiers and industrialists with established interests in the rubber business. The initial capital was 900,000 marks. The firm's product range consisted of waterproofed fabrics, footwear, and solid tires, but soon a general line of industrial rubber goods, medical supplies, and sundry consumer goods, such as balls and toys, was added.

During the 1870s Continental developed slowly; dividends were first paid in 1875 when additional capital was raised. In the following decade, however, the firm became highly prosperous and dividends increased from 7 percent of nominal ordinary share values in 1880 to a constant 27 percent between 1884 and 1892.

An expanding demand for industrial rubber goods was accompanied by the introduction of cushion tires under a patent from the British firm Macintosh. More significantly, in 1892 Continental commenced the manufacture of pneumatic tires for bicycles to cater to the growing interest in cycling. Although less innovative than Dunlop or Michelin, in the 1890s Continental was the first German producer of pneumatic tires. The 1890s proved more profitable than the previous decade. Continental's gross profit rose from 485,821 marks in 1891 to 1.8 million marks by 1898, and dividends were 55 percent annually between 1896 and 1898. The firm's capitalization was increased in 1897, doubled again two years later, and totaled 3 million marks by 1901. The workforce expanded from 600 to 2,200 between 1893 and 1903. This growth was primarily domestic and was supported by the development of agencies throughout Germany. Continental's leading position was suggested by its 65 percent share of a market-sharing agreement for cycle tires with Hannoverische Gummi-Kamm in 1894. The establishment of a German factory by Dunlop in 1892, however, provided a potent rival.

Responding to Increased Demand for Automobile Tires: 1890s to 1900s

The next phase was the development of the automobile tire business. During the late 19th century the prominence of German engineers in the early car industry created an additional market for solid tires, and there was also a growing demand for motorcycle tires. In 1898 Continental designed and began to manufacture a pneumatic tire, a significant technical accomplishment given the larger tires and greater weight and forces involved in automobiles. In 1904 a patterned tread was added to the previously smooth tires, an innovation in which Continental was slightly ahead of the U.S. tire industry. Four years later the detachable rim was adopted to simplify the mounting of tires. This sequence of product innovations completed the fundamental advances in motor tire design, although Continental continued to refine and improve its tires to 1914.

The effectiveness of Continental's response to the demand for car tires confirmed its leading status in Germany, particularly as Dunlop's German subsidiary failed to move into the new sector. Continental's workforce expanded to 12,000 by 1913. In the same year capitalization was raised to 12 million marks while dividends averaged 43 percent from 1900 to 1913. Such profitable growth also encouraged regular extensions of the factory and new investment. An export trade was built up with the establishment of marketing subsidiaries in Britain, Denmark, Sweden, Romania, Italy, Norway, and Australia between 1905 and 1913. Nonetheless the firm lagged behind Dunlop, Michelin, Pirelli, and U.S. Rubber in the establishment of overseas factories and, in some cases, rubber plantations. The outbreak of World War I forced a concentration on supplying military requirements and led to the dissipation of the overseas sales network. At the same time shortages of natural rubber compelled rationing of supplies, use of reclaimed rubber, and experiments with synthetic rubber. In 1909 Continental had produced a few tires using synthetic rubber supplied by the Bayer laboratories. Overall the war severely disrupted the firm's prewar expansion and prosperity.

Civilian production began again in 1919, but despite the underlying civilian demand for tires Continental faced difficulties. Although exports resumed, the earlier momentum had been lost. Moreover, the German car industry grew relatively slowly in the 1920s, and the general economic instability was a further constraint. Continental's response was imaginative. Goodrich, then the fourth-ranking U.S. tire firm, seeking overseas connections, took a 25 percent financial stake in the German firm in 1920. Bertram G. Work, a prominent Goodrich executive, was a director of Continental in the mid-1920s. The relationship provided access to superior technology for tire designs, rubber chemistry, and manufacturing.

In 1921 Continental introduced the cord tire, a lower pressure tire already coming into vogue in the United States, and three years later added the balloon cord tire, a design first adopted in France. The Goodrich connection may also explain

Continental's use of carbon black—a filler used to improve the durability of tires, especially aging, and a standard additive in the United States—in its tires from 1924. In addition, Continental endeavored to modernize its production processes, adopting U.S. tire-making machinery, with a subsequent rise in productivity. Generally the relationship with Goodrich appears to have been highly valuable for Continental. Nonetheless, the unfavorable business environment ensured that the firm's workforce barely increased during the 1920s. Returns were poor compared to the heady prewar levels, and no dividends were paid in 1922, 1923, or 1926. The resulting competitive and financial pressures led to the amalgamation of several German rubber firms to create a new and larger Continental company.

In 1928 Continental took effective control of the neighboring Hannoverische Gummiwerke ''Excelsior,'' and the Goodrich shareholding was terminated at this point. In the following year, four further companies were added to the amalgamation: Peters Union of Frankfurt, Gummiwerke Titan B. Polack of Waltershausen, Liga-Gummiwerke of Frankfurt, and Mitelland-Gummiwerke of Hanover. Negotiations to add the Phoenix Gummiwerke AG company failed, but the expanded Continental firm was by far the largest German tire company. In April 1929 it became known as Continental Gummi-Werke Aktiengesellschaft. During the amalgamation, the Opel family, which had recently sold its car business to General Motors, acquired a substantial shareholding in Continental. Fritz Opel was a director between 1932 and 1938, and the family representation on the supervisory board continued with Wilhelm von Opel from 1939 to 1946 and Georg Opel from 1939 to 1971.

The Influence and Implications of the Nazi Government in the 1930s and 40s

At first the new combine had to retrench in the face of the Depression: Continental's workforce declined from 16,765 to 10,602 between 1929 and 1932 as demand, prices, and profits all slumped. From 1932 the economic upturn and, in particular, the impact of the Nazi government's program to motorize the German economy and use the construction proceeds as a contribution to reducing unemployment produced a new phase of rapid expansion in car-tire demand. Total German tire output doubled between 1934 and 1938, and Continental's workforce rose to 15,254 by 1937. Output and sales expanded rapidly, although dividends rose rather modestly. At the same time the strengthening of state controls resulted in trade agreements covering rubber products so that production and pricing decisions were subject to central direction. In 1938 a new factory was opened at Stocken, Hanover. Buoyant domestic demand made Germany the principal market, but there was a revival of exports within the framework of Nazi trade policies, including expansion in Spain, where Continental established a sales subsidiary in 1934.

The rearmament program of the late 1930s increased state influence, especially given the interest in synthetic rubber development. In World War II tire and rubber output was regulated closely to meet military requirements, especially for truck and aircraft tires and the manufacture of clothing, footwear, and other supplies. With the severe shortage of natural rubber, Continental cooperated with the major German chemical firms in the development and, especially, the utilization of new synthetic rubbers.

Key Dates:

1871: The Continental-Caoutchouc und Gutta-Percha Compagnie (Continental) is established in Hanover, Germany.

1898: Continental designs and begins to manufacture a pneumatic tire for the automobile, a significant technical accomplishment.

1929: Company becomes known as Continental Gummi-Werke Aktiengesellschaft.

1951: Continental initiates a concentrated program of product innovation.

1979: Continental pursues strategic acquisitions, beginning with the purchase of the European tire factories of Uniroyal.

1987: With the purchase of General Tire, Continental transforms itself into a major international producer; the firm's name is shortened to Continental Aktiengesellschaft.

1991: The operations of Industrial Products are reorganized under the brand name ContiTech.

1995: Continental establishes an Automotive Systems division to pursue research and technology in automotive electronics.

2001: Company spends $570 million to purchase a controlling interest in DaimlerChrysler's Temic auto-electronics business.

Overall, with the reduction of civilian business and conscription, sales and employment actually declined during the war.

In the immediate postwar years Continental struggled to resume civilian production amid the physical damage of war and the uncertainties of occupation and reconstruction. Factory employment, down to 6,733 in 1945, rose gradually to 11,891 four years later and dividends resumed in 1948. In a strategy reminiscent of the 1920s, Continental turned to the United States. From 1948 to 1954 Continental had a technical assistance agreement with General Tire. More indirect technical guidance was obtained through a contract to manufacture Goodyear tires for the leading U.S. firm's German marketing operation. Again, the U.S. link provided advice on modern machinery and manufacturing methods, but the necessary new investment was financed by Continental itself.

Deutsche Bank had a major influence on the company's affairs, with representatives on the board from 1953; the Opel family remained the largest single shareholder, with Georg Opel serving as chairman of the supervisory board between 1946 and 1969. The Deutsche Bank was the major financial institution involved with Continental.

Product Innovation and Diversification in the 1950s and 60s

Continental, like tire producers everywhere, undertook considerable product innovation. A line of mud tires and snow tires was introduced in 1951, tubeless tires in 1955, and radial tires appeared in 1960. These products kept the firm abreast of general developments, although Continental lagged behind Michelin and Pirelli with radials. Over the same period, there were successive changes in the materials used in tire construction with the advent of synthetic fibers. The technical challenges and the increasing sophistication of rubber and tire science required the development of research facilities, including in 1967 the opening of the Contidrom tire testing track. Continental remained the largest German tire producer and competed primarily with the subsidiaries of multinational companies.

Between 1950 and 1965 Continental enjoyed a rapid expansion due to the strong growth of the German car industry. The firm supplied original equipment tires—tires installed on new cars—to leading German carmakers and also benefited from the spread of motoring in the increasingly prosperous domestic economy. By 1965 employment totaled 27,447, more than double its 1950 level, and capitalization stood at DM 210 million.

The firm also followed the carmakers, notably Volkswagen, overseas with increased export sales. This expansion was supported by investment in a tire factory in northeastern France in 1964 and the acquisition of marketing subsidiaries in Italy, Portugal, and the United Kingdom. Foreign subsidiaries were also acquired in Spain, South Africa, and Brazil. The firm promoted its tires, often on German cars, in various forms of motor sport in the 1950s. The industrial rubber goods business, much of it also related to the automotive sector, also expanded.

In the early 1960s Continental opened a new plant to produce plastic components for cars and established a new industrial goods plant. Acquisitions of smaller, specialist rubber firms in Germany achieved further expansion of the nontire sector, including footwear, foam, rubber boots, and plastics. Continental usually purchased a full shareholding or a majority stake; later this domestic strategy of acquisitions was to be transferred to a global stage.

Increased Competition Leading to International Expansion: 1970s–80s

Continental's sales and profits remained good in the late 1960s, but as the rate of growth slackened competition increased. In the 1970s these tendencies were aggravated by the effects of recessions and higher oil prices in the car sector. There was a swift transition to radial tires, whose greater durability further dampened sales, while new investment was required to produce radials. Similar influences and the resulting financial problems affected all European and U.S. tire markets. The leading international tire companies now competed aggressively in all markets, with the Japanese industry emerging as a potent force. The consequence was a restructuring of the global industry through companies leaving the industry, acquisitions, and new foreign investments. Continental experienced financial difficulties; there were no profits between 1972 and 1974 and no dividends between 1971 and 1979.

Chairman Carl Hahn directed Continental's initial retrenchment, and reports of merger negotiations with Phoenix came to nothing. There was a degree of diversification with the expansion of the automotive products division including the addition of fan belt manufacture in 1975 and investment in a massive facility for conveyor belt production. Nonetheless, tires remained the principal product and the intensifying oligopolistic rivalries resulted in more potent competition from subsidiaries, notably Michelin, in Germany.

By world standards Continental was relatively small and exposed to the threats of takeover, isolation in a few markets, and inability to sustain investment in new technology and research. In this context Hahn settled on a bold strategy of international expansion through acquisition. Continental's approach was not unique. Pirelli, Bridgestone, and Sumitomo all pursued a similar course and many smaller firms merged defensively. By contrast, Michelin invested directly in its own foreign factories, notably in the United States. In 1979 Continental purchased the European tire factories of Uniroyal, the U.S. firm that was beginning its retreat from the tire business. As a result Continental obtained a second French factory and another German plant plus factories in Belgium and Scotland. The other gain was the established marketing position of the Uniroyal brand. The acquisition of Kleber-Colombes, a financially troubled French firm in which Michelin held a major stake, was discussed, but not pursued in 1980.

The firm's penetration of two important markets was increased by production contracts. In 1981 a contract was signed for Toyo Rubber Industry Co., Ltd. to manufacture Continental tires in Japan, and there was a similar agreement with General Tire in the United States in the following year. In 1982 Hahn was succeeded by Helmut Werner who had been with Englebert, Uniroyal's Belgian subsidiary.

In 1985 Continental purchased the tire division of Semperit, the largest Austrian rubber firm, for DM 47 million. The expansion and diversification coupled with an economic upturn contributed to an improvement in the firm's finances. Dividends were resumed in 1983, and in 1986 Continental's profits totaled DM 114.4 million on a total turnover of DM 4.97 billion. The most remarkable step in Continental's transition, via acquisition, to major international producer came in 1987 with the purchase of General Tire for US$650 million from GenCorp. Continental obtained the four factories, the brands, the original equipment contracts, and the marketing network of the fifth largest U.S. tire manufacturer. In addition, General Tire had owned Mexican and Canadian factories. As a result, Continental then accounted for 6.6 percent of the world tire market in 1988 and 8.1 percent in 1989, making it the fourth largest producer, with more than double its market share at the beginning of the decade. Even so, Continental's market share remained less than half that of Michelin, Goodyear, and Bridgestone. The expansion raised Continental's market share and its profile in the business, but also substantially raised its managerial tasks in directing a large, global, and diverse business, particularly one in which the various national units often had their own traditions.

In 1990 Continental purchased a 49 percent stake in Nivis, a tire firm created by the earlier merger of the two leading domestic tire firms in Sweden and Norway; a share in Mabor of Portugal; and a British tire distribution business. Continental also entered several technical agreements with overseas producers. The political changes in Eastern Europe prompted further developments in the form of cooperative relationships and continuing discussions of other possible ventures as Continental followed the German car manufacturers' lead.

In 1987 the firm's name was shortened to Continental Aktiengesellschaft (AG). During the 1980s Continental appeared in a strong position with solid finances, persistent expansion in the passenger tire and truck tire markets, and innovative tire development and research. The earlier dependence on the German market had been successfully reduced; foreign markets accounted for 62 percent of the group's sales in 1990 compared to 38 percent a decade earlier. Nonetheless, tires accounted for around three-quarters of company sales, and the competitive forces that had inspired Continental's acquisition policy remained powerful as tire capacity outstripped demand once again in 1989 and the early 1990s. The tire business, notably the General Tire subsidiaries in North America, recorded substantial losses in 1990: DM 48.63 million in the United States and DM 36.15 million in Canada. Despite increasing total sales, Continental's net income declined from DM 227.8 million in 1989 to DM 93.4 million a year later. Further restructuring plus the effort to implement improvements in quality posed new challenges.

Werner, a leading figure in the achievements of the 1980s, resigned to move to Daimler-Benz in 1987. In September 1990 Pirelli, fifth in the world tire industry and also experiencing losses on its tire business, proposed that Continental purchase Pirelli's tire division to form a combined business, in which Pirelli would hold the controlling interest and thus managerial control. Such a merged business would be virtually on a par with the largest producers in terms of market share. After negotiations Continental rejected the scheme, but Pirelli and several supporters bought a stake in Continental and claimed the backing of a majority of shareholders. In May 1991 Horst Urban, Continental's chairman and an opponent of the Pirelli proposal, resigned—an apparent indication of a softening in Continental's attitude.

Apart from Deutsche Bank, other important German shareholders were Bayer, Volkswagen, Daimler-Benz, and BMW. Discussions of possible forms of cooperation, such as research-and-development work, continued, although an immediate merger appeared less probable. The persistent trend toward the domination by Goodyear, Michelin, and Bridgestone of the world tire industry suggested that Continental would move into some form of merger sooner or later, but would seek to maintain its independence.

Relentless Cost-Cutting in the 1990s

When Hubertus von Grunberg took over as CEO of Continental in 1991 the company was, in his words, "bleeding like a stuck pig." Fierce competition persisted in the worldwide tire market, and Continental recorded losses of 128 million marks, or US$78 million, for the year. After signs of recovery in the first half of 1992, market conditions deteriorated again, and von Grunberg characterized the early months of 1993 as "miserable."

During this period, Continental committed itself to rigorous cost-cutting and company-wide restructuring. Central to these initiatives was the effort to reduce labor costs. Hence Continental laid off 10,168 workers, or 20 percent of its labor force, between 1991 and 1993. In 1994, the company announced plans to trim another 1,500 to 2,000 employees from its ranks.

Continental also made aggressive strides to improve returns by shifting production away from Germany, with its high labor costs and highly regulated work practices, to less expensive locations in Eastern Europe, Central and South America, and Southeast Asia. In 1993 Continental and General Tire entered a joint venture with Mexican manufacturer Carso to oversee the operations of four manufacturing plants and 1,000 sales outlets in that country. Under the brand name Euzkadi, the venture would account for the majority of tire distribution in Mexico. Also in 1993, Continental gained a majority interest in Barum, a Czech company whose assets included a commercial vehicle tire plant in Otrokovice. By 1998, the Czech Republic plant was Continental's highest producing car tire manufacturer. In 1995, Continental completed construction of a new DM 180 million manufacturing plant in Lousado, Portugal. Heralded by Grunberg as the company's "most modern plant in Europe," the factory was expected to yield labor costs one-third lower than those in Germany. In 1997, Von Grunberg's goal was to realize 40 percent of Continental's tire production from such low-cost sites.

Technical innovation was another key component of Continental's cost-cutting program. To further facilitate the globalization of tire production, the company developed something called the modular manufacturing process (MMP), whereby basic tire parts, or modules, were produced at low-cost sites and subsequently shipped to plants in other markets for assembly. In 1998, Continental was building plants in Russia and Brazil where MMP would be implemented. Von Grunberg estimated that MMP plants would be six times more cost efficient than standard conventional plants.

By the late 1990s, Continental's dogged determination to cut costs had begun to pay off. Even while 1997 tire prices averaged lower than in 1996, the company realized a 67 percent increase in net income to $176 million during 1997, marking the return to profitability of U.S. subsidiary General Tire, as well as Continental's beleaguered truck tire division.

Diversification for the 21st Century

Von Grunberg was cautiously optimistic about Continental's recovery, but he was by no means content to leave his company at the mercy of the fiercely competitive, low-margin tire business. According to von Grunberg's vision, diversification was essential to Continental's long-term success. Throughout the 1990s, the company had invested heavily in technology, and the sales of Contitech, the company's diversified rubber products division, had contributed significantly to stabilizing the company's profits.

In 1995, von Grunberg established Continental's Automotive Systems division to pursue research and technology in automotive electronics, which promised much higher profit margins than tires. One of the key innovations of this group, introduced in 1997, was an electromechanical brake system called the Integrated Starter Alternator Damper (ISAD).

The ISAD received widespread praise and garnered the German Industry's Innovation Award. In 1998 Continental broadened its investment in auto components with the $1.93 billion purchase of ITT Industries' brake and chassis business.

In 1999, Continental forged even further ahead with its investment in electronic safety systems. In 2001 the company spent $570 million to purchase a controlling interest in Daimler-Chrysler's Temic auto-electronics business. The objective was to gain strong competitive position in the fast-growing market for electronic stability programs (ESPs). ESPs, which evolved from antilock braking systems, were electronic sensors that helped to detect and correct the instability responsible for vehicle rollovers, an increasingly high-profile safety problem in the era of SUVs.

In 2002, weathering continued instability in the economic climate, Continental resumed broad restructuring, including widespread job cuts and plant closures. While the cutthroat competition and price pressures of the world tire market posed ongoing challenges, the company's demonstrated determination to contain costs and its shrewd ability to innovate would likely continue to serve it well.

Principal Subsidiaries

Benecke-Kaliko AG; Continental Teves AG & Co. oHG; ContiTech Antriebssysteme GmbH; ContiTech Vibration Control GmbH; ContiTech Luftfedersysteme GmbH; ContiTech Kühner GmbH & Co. KG (86%); ContiTech Schlauch GmbH; ContiTech Transportbandsysteme GmbH; ContiTech Techno-Chemie GmbH; Conti Temic Microelectric GmbH; Vergolst GmbH (87.5%); Barum Continental Spol. s.r.o. (Czech Republic; 85%); Continental Automotive Products s.r.l. (Romania); Continental Benelux S.A. (Belgium); Continental France SNC; Continental Gislaved Dack AB (Sweden); Continental Industrias del Caucho (Spain); Continental Mabor Industria de Pneus (Portugal); Continental Matador s.r.o. (Slovac Republic; 76%); Continental Teves Czech Republic, s.r.o.; Continental Teves UK Ltd. (U.K.); Continental Tyre Group Ltd. (U.K.); ContiTech AGES S.p.A. (Italy); ContiTech Anoflex SNC (France); Semperit Reifen Ges.m.b.H. (Austria); Temic Telefunken Microelectronic Hungary Kft. (60%); Continental Automotive Mexicana de C.V. (Mexico) Continental do Brasil Produtos Automotivos Lda; Continental Teves Corporation Japan K.K. (51%); Continental Teves Inc. (U.S.A.); Continental Tire de Mexico, S.A. de C.V. (80.6%); Continental Tire North America Inc. (U.S.A.; 80.6%); Continental Tyre South Africa (Pty) Ltd (60%); Compañia Ecuatoriana del Caucho (Ecuador; 38.6%); Drahtcord Saar GmbH & Co. KG (Germany; 50%); KG Deutsche Gasrusswerke GmbH & Co. (Germany; 32.1%).

Principal Competitors

Bridgestone Corporation; The Goodyear Tire and Rubber Company; Compagnie Générale des Établissements Michelin.

Further Reading

Bowley, Graham, "Continental Chairman Follows Cost-Cutting Route to Recovery: German Tyre Group Is Reaping the Rewards of Its Tough Programme," *Financial Times (London)*, March 25, 1998, p.43.

——, "Continental in Move to Open Plant in Russia; Tyres Facility Will Service Growing Market," *Financial Times (London)*, March 25, 1998, p.31.

Chandler, Alfred D., *Scale and Scope: The Dynamics of Industrial Capitalism*, Cambridge: Harvard University Press/Belknap, 1990.

French, Michael J., *The US Tire Industry: A History*, Boston: Twayne, 1991.

Hicks, Jonathan P., "United Front May Make Higher Tire Prices Stick," *New York Times*, September 9, 1991, p. D3.

Jones, Geoffrey, ed., *British Multinationals: Origins, Management, and Performance*, Aldershot, England: Gower, 1986.

Munchau, Wolfgang, "Survey of World Tyre Industry," *Financial Times (London)*, January 29, 1996, p. 14.

Overy, R.J., "Cars, Roads, and Economic Recovery in Germany, 1932–8," *Economic History Review*, August 1975.

Schmidt, H. Th., *Continental: Ein Jahrhundert Fortschritt und Leistung*, Hanover: Continental Aktiengesellschaft, 1971.

Tierney, Christine, "Continental: From Tires to High-Tech Titan?," *Business Week*, April 23, 2001, p. 21.

West, Peter J., *Foreign Investment and Technology Transfer: The Tire Industry in Latin America*, Greenwich, Conn.: Jai Press, 1984.

—Michael John French
—update: Erin Brown

Cygnus Business Media, Inc.

830 Post Road East
Westport, Connecticut 06880
U.S.A.
Telephone: (203) 227-4037
Fax: (203) 227-4245
Web site: http://www.cygnusb2b.com.

Wholly Owned Subsidiary CommerceConnect Media LLC
Incorporated: 1996 as Cygnus Publishing, Inc.
Employees: 640
Sales: $75 million (2002 est.)
NAIC: 511120 Periodical Publishers; 511140 Database
and Directory Publishers; 561920 Convention and
Trade Show Organizers

As of mid-2003, Cygnus Business Media, Inc. published 80 business-to-business (B2B) publications consisting of trade magazines, directories, and card decks. The company also produced 47 trade shows, many of them related to its print publications. In addition, its B2B Web sites had more than 90 million page views in 2002, with nearly one million unique visitors.

Cygnus Business Media is organized into four divisions: Cygnus Publishing, which produces 51 B2B magazines with a combined circulation of nearly three million and covering 15 major markets; Cygnus Interactive, which manages the company's 68 Web sites; Cygnus Custom Marketing, which publishes custom publications to meet specific client objectives; and Cygnus Expositions, which runs the company's nearly 50 trade shows and expositions.

Formed in 1996, Cygnus Business Media became a player in B2B publishing with the 1997 acquisition of PTN Publishing, Inc. The acquisition brought to Cygnus more than 50 B2B publications serving 14 markets as well as several custom publications and related trade shows. From 1997 through 1999, Cygnus acquired new publications and trade shows and also divested some of its periodicals. In 2000, Cygnus was acquired for $275 million by CommerceConnect LLC, a company formed by Paul Mackler and ABRY Partners, LLP for the purpose of acquiring media properties. As a subsidiary of CommerceConnect, Cygnus embarked on an aggressive growth strategy, including acquisitions and new product launches, which it carried out over the next several years.

Publisher of Business-to-Business Magazines: 1996–99

Cygnus Business Media, Inc. was organized in March 1996 under the name Cygnus Publishing, Inc. The company was headquartered in St. Petersburg, Florida, and founded by two media veterans, Gerry Hogan and Blair Schmidt-Fellner. Hogan was formerly the CEO of the Home Shopping Network and previously was an executive at Turner Entertainment Networks and Whittle Communications. Hogan teamed with fellow former Turner executive Schmidt-Fellner in 1996 to form Cygnus Publishing, with Hogan as chairman and CEO and Schmidt-Fellner as COO. The company was established with financial backing from New York investment banking firm Kelso & Company.

Cygnus's mission was to acquire media properties. Although Hogan and Schmidt-Fellner were more familiar with electronic media, they were also interested in publishing. They were especially interested in business-to-business (B2B) publishing. As Hogan told *Folio: The Magazine for Magazine Management* in 1997, "We think business-to-business publishing is undervalued. The need for information among business people in America is skyrocketing."

After looking at various media properties for about a year, Cygnus acquired PTN Publishing, Inc. in mid-1997 for about $100 million. Based in Melville, New York, PTN was a major publisher in the B2B market. The company had 52 trade magazines and also published custom publications for clients such as Goodyear Tire and Rubber and Caterpillar. PTN also conducted trade shows and expositions in connection with some of its publications, including the annual Firehouse Expo and the National Pavement Maintenance Expo. CEO Gerry Hogan said of the acquisition in the *St. Petersburg Times*, "We intend to use this acquisition as a platform to begin building a serious media company."

PTN, which stands for *Photographic Trade News,* began as a publisher of trade magazines for the photographic trade in 1937.

Although its first publication was *Photographic Trade News,* the company later acquired the printing industry periodical *Printing News,* which began publication in 1928, and *Ink Maker,* a publication for manufacturers of printing inks and related graphic arts specialty colors that began publication in 1922 as *American Inkmaker.* Other printing industry magazines published by PTN at the time it was acquired by Cygnus included *Modern Reprographics Magazine* (founded 1993), *Print Business Register* (1986), *Print on Demand,* and *Quick Printing* (1977).

In 1994, PTN acquired Johnson Hill Press of Fort Atkinson, Wisconsin. At the time PTN published nearly 30 trade publications. The acquisition of Johnson Hill added another 13 noncompeting B2B magazines serving industries such as agriculture and food, aviation and transportation, building and home products, and construction equipment. Among the Johnson Hill titles that PTN acquired were *Farm Equipment Magazine* and *Feed & Grain* (both established in 1969), *Aircraft Maintenance Technology Magazine* (1989), *Airport Business* (1993), *Fleet Maintenance, Ground Support Magazine* (1993), *Mass Transit Magazine* (1974), *Qualified Remodeler* (1975), *Wood Digest Magazine* (1984), *Construction Distribution* and *Equipment Today* (1966), *Pavement Magazine* (1985), and *Rental Product News* (1978). Following the acquisition of Johnson Hill by PTN, these and other Johnson Hill publications continued to be published at the Fort Atkinson office. In 1996, *Laminating Design & Technology* and *Sport Truck & SUV Accessory Business* were launched from Fort Atkinson.

The acquisition of Johnson Hill was part of PTN's growth strategy being conducted by CEO Stanley Sills, who became head of PTN in 1987 when he acquired the firm along with Chase Venture Partners and Chicago-based investment banker Golder, Thoma, Cressey, Rauner, Inc. In 1992, PTN gained an additional $20 million worth of equity financing from Golder, Thoma. While the price of Johnson Hill was not made public, *Folio* estimated the cost at $25 million. By 1995, the owners of PTN were searching for an exit strategy. The company had annual revenue of about $70 million, according to estimates published in *Folio.* Among the new partners it was considering were Penton Publishing in 1995 and then Prudential Insurance Co. of America in 1996. However, negotiations with Penton did not get past the preliminary stages, and Prudential's offer of $120 million was rejected. At the time PTN was owned by a partnership between CEO Stanley Sills, Chemical Capital Ventures, and Golder, Thoma.

After acquiring PTN in mid-1997, Cygnus fine-tuned its B2B media empire over the next three years through acquisitions and divestitures involving publications as well as trade

shows. In 1998, it entered into a partnership agreement with Maryland-based Spencer Communications, which published four regional graphics arts periodicals. The partnership created the Spencer/Cygnus Regional Print Network and gave Cygnus 49 percent ownership of the four regional publications: *Southern Graphics Magazine,* founded in 1924; *Printing Journal* (1974) for the West Coast; *Print & Graphics Magazine* (1980) for the Northeast and mid-Atlantic states; and *Printing Views,* which covered the Midwest.

In January 1999, Cygnus acquired the Fire-Rescue West Conference and Exposition from the California Fire Instructors Workshop, which had run the trade show since its inception in 1978. The acquisition complemented Cygnus's Firehouse Emergency Services Expo and its fire rescue and emergency medical services (EMS) magazines *Firehouse* and *Public Safety Product News.*

In May 1999, Cygnus acquired three trade publications from Laguna Beach, California-based publisher Rudy Wolf. The titles were *Professional Tool & Equipment News, Body Tool & Equipment News*—subsequently renamed *Body Shop Expo*—and *Fleet Maintenance Tool & Equipment News,* which was renamed *Fleet Maintenance Supervisor.* All three titles began publication in the early 1990s. Following the acquisition, Wolf continued to serve as publisher of these magazines from Cygnus's office in Laguna Beach. Around this time Cygnus also acquired the *Journal of the Solid Surface Industry* from Joanna and Michael Duggan of Las Vegas, Nevada, who founded the periodical in 1995. Following the acquisition, the journal was renamed *Solidsurface,* and editorial operations were relocated to Fort Atkinson, where Joanna Duggan continued to serve as the periodical's publisher.

Micro Publishing News was also acquired in 1999. Founded in 1989, the periodical served the desktop publishing market. In 2001, Cygnus stopped publishing *Micro Publishing News* and integrated its editorial and circulation operations with *Digital Imaging.* In mid-1999 Cygnus divested two of its Atlanta, Georgia-based publications, *Modern Paint & Coatings* and *Soap & Cosmetics.* The periodicals, part of Cygnus's Shelter & Interiors Group, were sold to Chemical Week Associates.

Before the end of 1999, Cygnus Publishing changed its name to Cygnus Business Media, Inc. to better represent its media properties and business vision. At the time, Cygnus published more than 50 magazines, produced 18 expositions, operated 55 Web sites, produced a variety of custom media publications, and was involved in electronic commerce. In December, the company expanded its trade show and exposition operations by acquiring Champion Productions. Based in Minneapolis, Minnesota, Champion produced 13 trade shows for industries that included information technology, engineering, damage prevention, and the farm, ranch, and agricultural industry. These shows included the Strictly Business Expo, which featured computer-related equipment and software; Damage Prevention Convention for the construction industry; six ranch and farm expositions; ELAXACON for designers, engineers, and manufacturing professionals; and Digital Media Expo for the high-technology sector of the printing industry. Following the acquisition, Minneapolis became the headquarters of Cygnus Expositions, the company's trade show division.

Key Dates:

1996: Cygnus Publishing, Inc. is established in St. Petersburg, Florida, by former media executives Gerry Hogan and Blair Schmidt-Fellner.

1997: Cygnus acquires PTN Publishing, Inc. and moves its headquarters to Melville, New York.

1999: Champion Productions is acquired.

2000: Cygnus is acquired by CommerceConnect Media LLC.

2001: *Design/Build Magazine, GSE Today* magazine, *Professional Tool and Equipment Distributor* magazine, and related trade shows and Web sites are acquired.

2002: Cygnus acquires *Frozen Food Age* and *Food Logistics* from VNU Business Media, eight leading construction and industrial magazines from Vulcan Publications, aviation trade show AS3, and the Fire-EMS Information Network.

2003: Cygnus acquires more than 25 trade shows from Penton Media, Inc.

Aggressive Acquisition Plan: 2000 and Beyond

In mid-2000, Cygnus agreed to be acquired by CommerceConnect Media LLC for about $275 million. At the time of the acquisition Cygnus published 48 trade magazines, produced 16 trade shows and conferences, published 17 custom publications, and operated 60 Web sites. The company projected 2000 revenue of $96 million, up from $82 million the previous year and $66 million in 1997. Owners Gerry Hogan and Blair Schmidt-Fellner left the company following its acquisition by CommerceConnect Media.

CommerceConnect Media was formed in October 1999 for the purpose of acquiring media properties. It was a partnership between CEO Paul Mackler and Boston-based investment firm ABRY Partners, LLP. Mackler was formerly president of Reed Exhibition Companies, North America, a division of media conglomerate Reed Elsevier. Before that he was a principal and CEO of CMC, a company that developed trade shows and expositions in association with a variety of publishers. Following the acquisition of Cygnus, Mackler became its president and CEO. Otherwise, Mackler told *Tradeshow Week,* "We intend to operate the company as it is now being operated and will keep all management and staff in place."

Mackler also spelled out his vision for Cygnus's future. "The strategy for Cygnus is to offer a variety of media solutions to customers and clients in every market served, including print media, live media, and interactive media. We're going to be very strategic about our acquisitions and our organic growth."

Cygnus's first major acquisition under new ownership took place in December 2000, when the company acquired Locksmith Publishing Corp. The purchase included two print media publications, *Locksmith Ledger International* (established 1939) and *Security Technology & Design* (launched in 1991); two Web sites—LLedger.com, serving the locksmith industry, and SIMON-NET.com, a security industry portal; and the

LedgerWorld trade show and conference, serving the locksmith market. Steve Lasky, publisher of *Locksmith Ledger International* and *Security Technology & Design,* joined Cygnus as group publisher of its Residential, Commercial, and Industrial Security Industry Group while remaining as publisher and editorial director of the two acquired periodicals. All of the properties acquired from Locksmith Publishing bolstered Cygnus's presence in the security industry and complemented the company's own *Security Dealer Magazine,* which was launched in 1977 as *Security Information and Product News,* and its online counterpart.

During the second half of 2000, Cygnus also developed a stronger presence online by making Firehouse.com, a wholly-owned subsidiary and launching a new industry portal, WoodWorkingPro.com, for the woodworking industry. The new portal complemented the company's *Wood Digest Magazine,* which reached more than 50,000 subscribers every month. Firehouse.com, with nearly 20,000 daily visitors, was part of Cygnus's Fire Rescue and Emergency Medical Services Group that included *Firehouse Magazine,* the industry's leading publication with a circulation of 100,000, and several trade shows.

Cygnus made several acquisitions in 2001. At the beginning of the year it was able to purchase complete ownership of the Spencer/Cygnus Regional Print Network from Spencer Communications. In mid-2001, Cygnus acquired *Design/Build Business* magazine and Web site, which became part of the company's Building and Home Products Group. The group also published *Kitchen & Bath Design News, Qualified Remodeler, Solid Surface, Laminating Design & Technology,* and *Wood Digest,* and it operated five Web sites.

Cygnus expanded its Aviation and Transportation Group with the acquisition of *GSE Today* magazine, Web site, and trade show in October 2001. The three properties served the ground support equipment (GSE) segment of the aviation industry and complemented the group's other publications, including *Airport Business, Aircraft Maintenance Technology, Fleet Maintenance, Ground Support, Mass Transit, Professional Tool & Equipment News,* and related Web sites. In November 2001, Cygnus added *Professional Tool & Equipment Distributor,* which it acquired from Marketing Advertising Communication Services, Inc. of Illinois. The periodical's circulation went to 10,000 tool distributors in the automotive industry. It complemented *Professional Tool & Equipment News,* which went to more than 110,000 qualified automotive repair professionals.

Cygnus's aggressive acquisitions strategy continued in 2002, when the company purchased several periodicals and trade shows. In May, Cygnus acquired two food-related titles from VNU Business Media: *Frozen Food Age,* the leading magazine in the retail frozen food industry with a circulation of 17,000, and *Food Logistics,* the leading periodical for the food logistics and supply chain industry, with a circulation of 27,000. The publications were integrated into Cygnus's group serving the agriculture and food markets, which also included *Farm Equipment, Feed & Grain,* and *Health Products Business.*

In June 2002, Cygnus added half a million targeted professionals to its circulation base when it acquired several constructions and industrial magazines, card decks, and related Web sites from Alabama-based Vulcan Publications. The magazines, which had a combined circulation of more than 300,000, were *Construction Site News, Electrical Contracting & Engineering News, Fabricating & Metalworking, Heavy Equipment News, Industrial Machinery Digest, iSource Business, Plant Safety & Maintenance,* and *Transportation Equipment News.* The acquired card decks reached an additional 200,000 professionals and included the National Equipment Card Deck, Plant Safety & Maintenance Card Deck, and Total Outdoor Equipment Card Deck. In addition, four Web sites were included in the purchase: NDX.com, a manufacturing portal; concretepaving.com, which served the concrete and asphalt market; Heavyequipmentnews.com, which served contractors in the highway, heavy construction, building, mining, and other specialized construction industries; and iSourceonline.com, a source of information on Internet-based B2B commerce and procurement. The Vulcan acquisition established a third major publishing operation for Cygnus in Birmingham, Alabama, in addition to its operations in Melville and Fort Atkinson.

In the second half of 2002 and first half of 2003, Cygnus made several acquisitions on behalf of its trade show division, Cygnus Expositions. In August, the company acquired another aviation trade show, AS3: The Aviation Services and Suppliers Super Show, from the National Air Transportation Association (NATA) and the Professional Aviation Maintenance Association (PAMA). NATA and PAMA continued to sponsor the trade show, which was co-located with the GSE International Expo in spring 2003. In January 2003, Cygnus more than doubled its portfolio of trade shows when it purchased Penton Media, Inc.'s Professional Trade Shows (PTS) operation for an estimated $3.8 million. PTS was considered the leading producer of regional industrial trade shows, staging more than 25 shows in 22 states for four principal markets: plant engineering and maintenance, building and facilities, materials handling, and machine tools. The acquisition of PTS, which was integrated into Cygnus Expositions, made Cygnus one of the ten largest trade show organizers in the United States based on the number of shows it produced. In other trade show developments, Cygnus staged its first Firehouse World Exposition and Conference in San Diego in February. The company also acquired the Solid Surface International Trade Show and Exposition from Nevada-based International Solid Surface Fabricator's Association in February. Solid surface materials were most commonly used in kitchen and bathroom countertops and were also used commercially in food courts, banks, airports, and malls. In addition, the company announced it would launch two new trade shows in 2003, the Iowa Farm Show in August and the Mid-Atlantic Print Expo in spring 2003.

Cygnus also bolstered its online division, Cygnus Interactive, with the purchase of the Fire-EMS Information Network in November 2002 from Illinois-based Cambert Ltd. The online portal was one of the first to serve the emergency services industry. It hosted thousands of home pages at no cost for EMS departments worldwide. Cygnus relaunched the network in December as the Firehouse Network and made it part of its highly successful Firehouse.com portal.

New periodicals added to Cygnus's group of publications included *VDV World,* which was launched in September 2002 to serve the commercial voice, data, and video electrical con-

tractor market. In May 2003, Cygnus acquired *Finishing & Restoration* magazine from Woodland Hills, California-based McCloskey Communications. The periodical became part of Cygnus's Building and Home Products Group. With the acquisition, Cygnus published a total of 80 B2B media products, including trade magazines, directories, and card decks. The company also produced 47 trade shows serving 15 major markets. Including its Web sites, Cygnus boasted a portfolio of more than 200 separate media products reaching five million professionals annually. Its diversity in serving 15 different market combined with its presence in high-interest industries such as security, fire and rescue, emergency services, and construction helped the company maintain revenue growth in the midst of a general downturn in B2B advertising during 2002, 2003, and the foreseeable future.

Principal Divisions

Cygnus Publishing; Cygnus Expositions; Cygnus Custom Marketing; Cygnus Interactive.

Principal Competitors

Bobit Publishing Co.; Hanley-Wood, LLC; Lebhar-Friedman, Inc.; North American Publishing Co.; Penton Media, Inc.; Primedia Business Magazines & Media, Inc.; Randall Publishing Co.; Vance Publishing Corp.

Further Reading

Albright, Mark, "Florida-based Publishing Company Buys Trade Magazines," *Knight Ridder/Tribune Business News,* June 10, 1997.
"As Cygnus CEO Mackler Touts Aviation Tradeshow Buy, Denies Penton Pairing," *Min's B to B,* August 26, 2002.
Case, Tony, and Karen Hudes, "June Yields Half-Billion in Trade Deals," *Folio: the Magazine for Magazine Management,* July 1, 1997, p. 17.
"CommerceConnect Media to Acquire Cygnus Business Media," *Business Publisher,* May 31, 2000, p. 1.
"Cygnus Acquires 'Design/Build Business' from McKellar Publications," *Business Publisher,* June 16, 2001, p. 1.
"Cygnus Acquires Four Magazines in Two Deals," *Business Publisher,* May 31, 1999, p. 1.
"Cygnus Acquires 'GSE Today' Magazine and Related Expo & Web Site," *Business Publisher,* October 17, 2001, p. 3.
"Cygnus Acquires West Coast Fire/Rescue Conference," *Business Publisher,* January 18, 1999, p. 6.
"Cygnus Bulks up on Trade Shows with $5m Purchase from Penton," *Min's B to B,* February 4, 2003.
"Cygnus Bus. Purchases Construction and Industrial Mags from Vulcan," *Business Publisher,* May 30, 2002, p. 1.
"Cygnus Business Media Acquires Locksmith Publishing," *Business Publisher,* December 22, 2000, p. 5.
"Cygnus Business Media Launches Second Industry Portal," *Business Publisher,* September 30, 2000, p. 7.
"Cygnus Business Media's *Security Dealer* Still Ticking after 25 Years," *Min's B to B,* January 27, 2003.
"Cygnus CEO Mackler Builds Bigger with Vulcan Construction Books," *Min's B to B,* June 10, 2002.
"Cygnus Expo's Price Is Bullish on Trade Shows in Bear Market," *Min's B to B,* December 9, 2002.
"Cygnus Purchases Champion Productions from 1st Communications," *Business Publisher,* October 31, 1999, p. 2.
Garigliano, Jeff, "PTN Left at the Altar," *Folio: the Magazine for Magazine Management,* November 15, 1996, p. 18.

Manly, Lorne, "PTN Acquires Johnson Hill Press," *Folio: the Magazine for Magazine Management*, September 1, 1994, p. 18.

——, "PTN Negotiates with New Suitor," *Folio: the Magazine for Magazine Management*, June 1, 1996, p. 16.

Mather, Joan, "CommerceConnect Media to Acquire Cygnus Business Media," *Tradeshow Week*, June 5, 2000, p. 1.

Moseley, Bob, "Focusing on Core Products with a Eye on Expansion," *Folio: the Magazine for Magazine Management*, July 15, 2000, p. 12.

"Penton and PTN Talk Alliance," *Folio: the Magazine for Magazine Management*, May 15, 1995, p. 14

Silber, Tony, "Does High Price for Cygnus Bode Well for Other B-to-B Deals on the Horizon?," *Folio: the Magazine for Magazine Management*, July 1, 2000, p. 17.

"Steve Smith's New Media Strategies: Cygnus Looks to Build the Next Firehouse," *Min's B to B*, November 4, 2002.

—David P. Bianco

Dearborn Mid-West Conveyor Company

20334 Superior Road
Taylor, Michigan 48180-6031
U.S.A.
Telephone: (734) 288-4400
Fax: (734) 288-1914
Web site: http://www.dmwcc.com

Wholly Owned Subsidiary of Tomkins Plc
Incorporated: 1995
Employees: 150 (est.)
Sales: $90 million (2003 est.)
NAIC: 333922 Conveyor and Conveying Equipment
   Manufacturing; 333923 Overhead Traveling Crane,
   Hoist, and Monorail System Manufacturing

Dearborn Mid-West Conveyor Company is a leading maker of conveyor systems. The company's products are sold primarily to the auto industry, the U.S. Postal Service, and bulk materials handling firms. Dearborn Mid-West was created in 1995 by the merger of two established conveyor makers, Dearborn Fabricating and Engineering Corp. and Mid-West Conveyor Co., both of which had been acquired by the British conglomerate Tomkins plc. DMW was forced to downsize following the U.S. economic recession that began in late 2000 and in 2002 closed one of its two manufacturing plants.

Origins

The roots of Dearborn Mid-West Conveyor Co. date to 1947, when the Dearborn Fabricating and Engineering Corp. was founded by members of the Dunville and Wells families. The firm's original location was a 10,000-square-foot site in Dearborn, Michigan, but operations were soon moved to larger quarters in the nearby city of Detroit. The company's primary work was fabricating parts for conveyors, such as platforms, chutes and housings, as well as supplying and installing crane systems. In 1956, the firm bought the American Cable Company, a conveyor maker.

The 1960s saw the major automakers switch from buying parts to build their own conveyors to purchasing entire conveyor subassemblies, and manufacturing of the latter became the focus of Dearborn Fabricating and Engineering. The company grew into one of the leading conveyor makers in the Detroit area, which was home to a number of such firms. Dearborn Fabricating got much of its work from the Chrysler Corp. and was eventually recognized by Chrysler as its primary conveyor contractor.

In the 1980s, conveyor makers began to add computers to their systems with programmable controls that could monitor fault conditions and downtime. Dearborn Fabricating and Engineering kept pace with the industry and added these features to its products. During the early and mid-1980s, automakers retooled their factories to install the new computerized manufacturing equipment, which brought considerable business to the Dearborn Fabricating. The firm's conveyors were used for purposes such as transporting parts and subassemblies along the assembly line to be received or modified by workers. They could handle such items as doors, engines, or entire vehicle bodies, running in an endless loop which kept the line going non-stop. Reliability was an important factor, as any downtime would reduce the number of vehicles completed.

In 1983, the owners of Dearborn Fabricating put the company up for sale, and the following year it was purchased by a group consisting of management and a small number of employees. During this period the company was growing, and by 1986 it had a staff of 120 and revenues of $54 million. The firm was run by 37-year-old President and CEO Wes Paisley.

Detroit was a particularly competitive market for conveyor makers, with nearly three dozen such firms located in the area by this time. When orders from automakers dropped off in the latter half of the 1980s, many companies consolidated or sold facilities to cut costs. In October 1987, Dearborn Fabricating was purchased by Philips Industries of Dayton, Ohio, a company that primarily supplied components for building contractors and recreational vehicle makers.

With Philips' backing, in 1988 Dearborn Fabricating acquired Unified Industries of Howell, Michigan, and the con-

Company Perspectives:

The DMW mission is to provide our customers with people, business practices, and conveyor systems of the highest integrity.

veyor division of Detroit-area firm Taylor and Gaskin, Inc. The company now had a total of 170 employees, with its work still largely drawn from the auto industry. Annual earnings had declined to approximately $40 million. The firm was building systems for Chrysler Corp.'s St. Louis assembly plant, Ford's Wixom, Michigan, plant, and General Motors' Lansing, Michigan, Buick-Oldsmobile-Cadillac plant, at budgets of between $2 million and $5 million per project.

A year after it had acquired Dearborn Fabricating, Philips Industries bought a second large conveyor maker, Mid-West Conveyor Co. of Kansas City, Kansas. Like Dearborn Fabricating, Mid-West had been founded just after World War II, beginning its operations on January 1, 1947. The firm's founders, Harlan and Omer Potter and Vernon Street, grew Mid-West over the years into a full-system conveyor supplier until the company was purchased by Conergics Co. in 1970. Conergics was acquired by Foster Wheeler Corp. in 1984 before winding up in the portfolio of Philips four years later. At this time, Mid-West had 320 employees at a plant in Kansas City, Kansas, and specialized in making undercarriage conveyors for use by the mining and automotive industries. The firm's work included such projects as designing and building a $12 million overland conveyor system to transport coal from a mine in Wyoming to a nearby power plant, as well as designing and installing the materials handling systems for the Mack Truck plant at Winnsboro, South Carolina. Philips' two new conveyor firms accounted for approximately $135 million of its $962 million in revenues for fiscal 1989.

In 1990, Philips' management decided to spin off its materials handling operations over concerns about their profitability. Observers cited the intensely competitive conveyor marketplace, Philips' inexperience in bidding on such work, and several money-losing projects that had been underbid by Mid-West as reasons for the move. Another Philips auto industry unit, wheel maker Shelby Advanced Automotive Technology Inc., was also put up for sale at this time.

Sale to Tomkins Plc in 1990

In June 1990, an agreement was reached to sell Philips Industries to Tomkins Plc of London, England, for $550 million. Tomkins was a large manufacturing conglomerate that controlled a number of different businesses, many of which were located in the U.S. Tomkins soon announced that it would continue seeking to sell the conveyor firms, but in the absence of a substantive offer made the decision to keep them.

Under Tompkins, Dearborn Fabricating and Mid-West Conveyor's operations were gradually combined, and in the fall of 1995 the merged companies took the new name of Dearborn Mid-West Conveyor Co., or DMW. Dearborn Fabricating head Wes Paisley was named president. Initially the firm was head-

quartered in Detroit, but several years later ground was broken in nearby Taylor, Michigan, for construction of new administrative offices. The 23,000-square-foot, $2.9 million headquarters was opened in 1998, replacing offices that had been occupied since shortly after the company's founding in 1947. A new $8 million, 105,000-square-foot plant next door was completed two years later. A second factory and several other operations remained in Kansas City. At this time, the firm's assignments were largely drawn from the automotive, postal, and bulk materials handling industries.

In March 2000, DMW announced it would begin manufacturing and selling an automated electrified monorail system (AEM) licensed from Fredenhagen GmbH of Germany. The AEM fixed-path system was designed with speed, ergonomics, and noise reduction in mind, and could be used in place of conventional overhead conveyor systems.

The U.S. economy was now booming, and DMW was enjoying a period of growth. Revenues for 2000 topped out at approximately $250 million, and the firm had a backlog of work during most of the year. The company was now ranked 16th on *Modern Materials Handling* magazine's list of the top 20 materials handling systems suppliers in the world. The year also saw DMW win DaimlerChrysler's Gold Award for quality, one of many such honors it had received from the auto industry. The firm had recently supplied the first automotive production "skillet system" to DaimlerChrysler's Sterling Heights, Michigan, Trim Shop. The skillet design used scissors lifts to raise an item being assembled to a comfortable height for workers, yielding greater operator flexibility and improved ergonomics.

Materials handling equipment was becoming increasingly sophisticated, and the offerings of DMW were no exception. Electric systems were now replacing pneumatic and hydraulic ones, resulting in lower costs and reduced maintenance requirements, as well as better compatibility with the software-based control equipment that was now in vogue. The new systems were also quieter and more easily adaptable to the individual needs of employees, which improved worker comfort and sped up production. In addition to these benefits, the more flexible systems allowed manufacturers to respond more quickly to changing market conditions, which was a necessity in the era of "Just-In-Time" ordering and shipping practices, which had become a standard way of doing business.

A plant where much of the new equipment had been installed was DaimlerChrysler's Toledo North Assembly Plant in Toledo, Ohio, where the Jeep Liberty sport-utility vehicle was built. Among the devices installed there by DMW were skillet, power and free, and belt conveyor systems, as well as Just-In-Time slug delivery systems for seats and instrument panels. A total of 3.75 miles of conveyor systems were situated within the 2.1 million-square-foot plant.

Orders Drop Following Cutbacks at DaimlerChrysler in 2000

When the U.S. economy began to slip at the end of 2000, DMW was hit hard. Leading customer DaimlerChrysler reported a disastrous fourth quarter and cancelled conveyor orders and factory improvements almost immediately, with the other

Key Dates:

1947: Dearborn Fabricating and Engineering Corporation is founded near Detroit.

1947: Mid-West Conveyor Company is founded in Kansas City, Kansas.

1956: Dearborn Fabricating acquires American Cable Company.

1960s: Dearborn Fabricating focuses on building conveyor systems for the auto industry.

1970: Conergics Co. buys Mid-West Conveyor.

1984: Management-led group buys Dearborn; Conergics is sold to Foster Wheeler.

1987: Philips Industries purchases Dearborn Fabricating.

1988: Philips buys Mid-West; Dearborn Fabricating acquires two other conveyor businesses.

1990: Philips is sold to Tomkins plc of England.

1995: Dearborn Fabricating and Mid-West Conveyor merge to form Dearborn Mid-West Conveyor Co.

1998: Dearborn Mid-West moves to new headquarters in Taylor, Michigan.

2002: Auto firms make cutbacks; Dearborn Mid-West closes its Kansas plant and lays off 160 employees.

service was a $61 million installation of sorting and conveyor systems at all 21 bulk mail centers around the United States, as well as at many of the agency's parcel and distribution centers.

Despite its ongoing financial woes, the firm was showing a strong commitment to the environment and its workers, and DMW was named a Clean Corporate Citizen by Michigan Governor John Engler in 2002. The company had already met the ISO 140001 environmental standard, and its new plant incorporated such features as welding and paint fume extractors and ergonomically-designed work stations.

Though it was struggling with a downturn in business, Dearborn Mid-West Conveyor Co. was a survivor in a field in which several of its competitors had recently gone under. The company's dependence on the auto industry placed its fate, to a certain extent, in the hands of the big three carmakers, but it was also seeking work in other areas, and its experienced management had successfully guided the firm back to health during other lean periods.

Principal Competitors

Jervis B. Webb Co.; Peak Industries, Inc.

Further Reading

Barkholz, David, "Big 3 Cuts Hit Conveyor Companies," *Crain's Detroit Business*, February 20, 1989, p. 1.

"DMW Contracts with German Manufacturer," *Modern Materials Handling*, March 31, 2000, p. 20.

Feare, Tom, "Shifting into High Gear," *Modern Materials Handling*, August 1, 2001, p. 28.

Jenke, Anita C., "Philips Aborts High-Tech Auto Push; Wheel, Conveyor Units Put On Block," *Metalworking News*, April 9, 1990, p. 1.

King, Angela, "Fate of Dearborn Fabricating Is Unclear," *Crain's Detroit Business*, July 23, 1990, p. 15.

Mazurkiewicz, Greg, "Material Delivery Glitches? Mack Trucks Has the Answer and It Cuts Inventory Levels," *Industrial Engineering*, February 1, 1991, p. 28.

Strong, Michael, "Slowdown Puts Brakes on Conveyor Industry," *Crain's Detroit Business*, September 23, 2002, p. 18.

White, Jane, " 'Factory of Future' Hikes Sales Right Now," *Crain's Detroit Business*, May 5, 1986, p. 3.

—Frank Uhle

automakers soon following suit. DMW's workload was cut in half, and revenues dropped to just $120 million during fiscal 2001. In September 2002, president Wes Paisley told *Crain's Detroit Business* that the company would be happy to realize even $90 million in sales for that year. To reduce operating costs, DMW began making layoffs in early 2001, and in July 2002 closed its Kansas City plant, which employed 160. The firm's Kansas City-based project management and engineering division was not affected. During this period several of the company's Detroit-area competitors closed major facilities or went out of business entirely.

As DMW's contracts with the auto industry dropped off, it continued to build conveyor systems for other customers. These included the U.S. Postal Service, for which the company had been working since the mid-1970s. Products in this area included bulk mail, tray mail, and loose mail sorting systems. Among the projects the firm had completed for the postal

Deltec

Deltec, Inc.

1265 Grey Fox Road
Saint Paul, Minnesota 55112-6929
U.S.A.
Telephone: (651) 633-2556
Toll Free: (800) 426-2448
Fax: (651) 628-7485
Web site: http://www.deltec.com

Wholly Owned Subsidiary of Smiths Group plc
Incorporated: 1984 as Deltec Systems
Employees: 450 (est.)
Sales: $150 million (2002 est.)
NAIC: 339112 Surgical and Medical Instrument
    Manufacturing

A subsidiary of the British firm Smiths Group plc, Deltec, Inc. designs, manufactures, and distributes medical devices used in ambulatory infusion therapy, including ambulatory infusion pumps, large volume infusion pumps, implantable access systems, dialysis and infusion catheters, needles, and insulin delivery systems. The company's headquarters is located in Saint Paul, Minnesota. Products include PORT-A-CATH devices that help in the administration of chemotherapy, lowering the risk that chemotherapy drugs will damage tissues surrounding veins, and CADD Pumps, which help in the delivery of drugs such as insulin. In addition, Deltec offers ancillary products: specialized needles, catheters, a subcutaneous tunneling device, communication devices, reservoirs, tubing extension sets, and IV stands.

Three Companies Merge in 1986 to Form Deltec, Inc.

Deltec was created in 1986 when three medical companies felt it was in their best interest to pool technologies and personnel. They were Deltec Systems, Inc. located in Saint Paul, Minnesota; Pharmacia NuTech, in Walpole, Massachusetts; and Pharmacia Hospital Products of Piscataway, New Jersey. The man behind the creation of Deltec Systems was Clark Adams, a marketing manager for Minnesota-based Cardia Pacemakers Inc. In addition to pacemakers, CPI sold insulin pumps con-

trolled by microprocessors, which was the inspiration behind Adams' idea to develop a light-weight, programmable infusion pump for the safe delivery of drugs over an extended period of time. The pump would be the size and weight of a paperback book, easily transportable by patients. When his employer declined to pursue his idea, Adams resigned in February 1983 to launch his own company to produce a Computerized Ambulatory Drug Delivery System device, or CADD pump. Several months later, Adams was able to convince CPI's former vice-president for operations, Manuel F. Cabezas, to come out of retirement to serve as CEO of the start-up. They then brought in three more CPI employees, the five of them contributing a total of $385,000 in seed money. By March 1984, Cabezas and Adams had lined up enough outside investors to have $2 million in commitments. For the name of the company they chose Deltec Systems, playing on the term "Delivery Technologies." The site of their headquarters was the Minneapolis, Minnesota, suburb of Arden Hill. Just starting out, Deltec Systems was also the major beneficiary of a front-page story in the *Wall Street Journal* concerning patient-controlled devices for delivering painkilling medication, in which the author noted that the company was developing a drug pump for home use by terminally ill cancer patients. A number of major pharmaceutical companies quickly contacted Cabezas. One of the people who called was Frank Brown of Pharmacia, Inc., a North American subsidiary of a $1 billion Swedish conglomerate, Pharmacia AB. Pharmacia also owned Walpole, Massachusetts-based Pharmacia NuTech, which made the PORT-A-CATII, an implantable drug port, and catheters used by cancer patients.

Brown recognized that the infusion pump Deltec Systems was creating could be combined with NuTech's products to create a total ambulatory drug delivery system. Although Cabezas and Adams, still in the hunt for further funding, met with Brown, at this stage they could not come to terms on a deal. In December 1984, however, another Massachusetts-based Pharmacia subsidiary, Pharmacia Hospital Products Inc., reached an agreement to market the first two models of the Deltec pump: the CADD-VT to administer antibiotics and the CADD-LD, which delivered small dosages of medications. Marketing proceeded well, but by the end of 1985 Deltec Systems was in need of another $5 million to market two later versions of the

CADD pump. Because the company was unable to raise the kind of money it expected in a private equity placement, it now became open to a merger with NuTech, which was having its own problems. Because the margin on its products was so slim, the company could not afford to adequately fund its research and development. It became apparent to Brown and the founders at Deltec Systems that all concerned would be better off by consolidating their efforts. Thus, in December 1986 Phamacia merged NuTech and Hospital Products with Deltec Systems, gaining an 81 percent stake in the combined enterprise called Pharmacia Deltec. In addition, Pharmacia contributed $10 million for working capital. Deltec shareholders were given the choice of either selling half or all of their shares for $8.20—a tidy profit on the $2 per share they paid in March 1984—or receiving a proportionate share of the new company.

All Operations Move to Minnesota in 1987

Cabezas became chairman of the board of directors, while Clark Adams resigned, although he later rejoined the company to head business development. Brown took over as the CEO of Pharmacia Deltec and immediately had to decide where to locate the business. For such a small company, it was out of the question to have research and development taking place in both Massachusetts and Minnesota, with administration and marketing conducted in New Jersey. Because the engineers located in Massachusetts and Minnesota were key to the success of the enterprise, Brown knew that he had to choose between Arden Hill and Walpole. Because the pumps were more technically demanding, placing a premium on the talents of Deltec Systems' engineers, he decided on Minnesota as the home for Pharmacia Deltec to prevent the loss of engineers who might not want to relocate to Massachusetts. Within six months, the marketing and administrative people moved from New Jersey to Minnesota, and by the beginning of 1988 the company was shipping products.

In 1987, Pharmacia Deltec generated revenues of $28 million and the prospects for the company appeared bright. In 1983, Cabezas guessed that the market for drug infusion pumps was in the $500 million range, and only two years later he revised his estimate to $1 billion. What was more easily determined was Pharmacia Deltec's dominant position in the marketplace, soon controlling about half of the portable drug infusion pump business and 60 percent of the overall market for ports. Management's greatest fear was that another company might achieve a breakthrough in technology, making obsolete the products of Pharmacia Deltec, which relied on developments from the early 1980s. With its Swedish corporate parent providing financial backing, however, the company seemed to be well positioned to maintain its edge in research and development.

Sales improved to $40 million in 1988 and approximately $60 million in 1989, as Pharmacia Deltec added hundreds of jobs to keep pace with growth. In 1989, the company introduced the P.A.S. Port System, the first peripheral implantable venous access system. In 1991, it brought out the CADD-TPN (Total ParenteralNutrition) pump to address the nutritional needs of patients. In 1993, the company introduced the CADD-Micro pump for intravenous, intra-arterial, subcutaneous, intraperitoneal (abdominal), and epidural (spinal) microinfusions. By now, the pain-control product (patient-controlled analgesia, or PCA) market was gaining strength as doctors became more comfortable with the patient's ability under certain circumstances to control the flow of drugs into their bodies. Most of the business came from hospitals, where Pharmacia Deltec had the third largest market share with 13 percent. In the home care market, however, the company controlled more than 65 percent of the ambulatory pump business and 85 percent of PCA pumps. In 1993, the company posted sales in the $110 million range.

Changes in the health care field in the early 1990s altered the course of Pharmacia Deltec. In an effort to cut costs, an increasing number of hospitals were opting to do business only with companies that offered a wide range of products. Brown and the management team at Pharmacia Deltec believed that developing new product lines was simply not practical, given how long it took to receive approval from the Food and Drug Administration. Instead, they wanted to expand by acquiring companies with products already on the market. Because of a lack of ready money, Brown claimed that the company lost four acquisition possibilities. Moreover, the company wanted more cash in order to grow the business outside of the United States. Already overseas sales accounted for some 30 percent of all revenues, and management believed it could improve that number to 40 percent given the proper backing. Pharmacia AB was unwilling to invest the kind of money the subsidiary needed, opting instead to concentrate on its European pharmaceutical operations. The Minnesota operation was just a very small part of a large concern, one involved in any number of medical fields, including therapeutic drugs, chemicals for cataract surgery, and growth hormones in addition to medical devices. As Brown explained to the press, ''We are not a core business of theirs. So we said if they could not afford to invest in us then we should be divested.'' The corporate parent agreed, and rather than attempt a spin-off and go public the subsidiary hired Lehman Brothers in 1994 to find a buyer. According to the *Star-Tribune*, ''Brown said he's looking for a new parent company that has $50 million to $75 million to invest in Pharmacia, plus a complementary business that could be combined with Pharmacia. Alternately, he's looking for a company with no complementary business but $100 million to invest in his firm.'' It was not the best of times to put the business on the block, with a number of medical stocks underperforming in the stock market and other medical device companies, such as the Cardiac Pacemakers unit of Eli Lilly, also up for sale.

Business Sold to Smith Industries in 1994

Some four months after Pharmacia AB agreed to sell off Pharmacia Deltec, the United Kingdom's Smiths Industries plc agreed to pay $150 million for the business, including the assumption of debt. Smiths Industries, a $4.6 billion company

Key Dates:

1984: Deltec Systems is incorporated.
1986: Deltec Systems merges with Pharmacia NuTech and Pharmacia Hospital Products to form Pharmacia Deltec.
1994: Smith Industries acquires the company, which is renamed SIMS Deltec.
2001: Company is renamed Deltec, Inc.
2002: Insulin pump is introduced.

founded by watchmaker Samuel Smith in 1851, was an engineer-focused company looking to become less dependent on its aerospace segment. Today, it is dedicated to four areas of specialization: Aerospace (avionic systems and equipment), Sealing Solutions (mechanical and polymer seals), Industrial (electrical interconnect systems), and Medical (devices and equipment). Once the purchase of Pharmacia Deltec was completed, the company was renamed SIMS Deltec, Inc.

Although it had a new corporate parent with deep pockets, SIMS Deltec did not pursue the acquisition strategy that Brown had been so keen about. Not until 1998 did the company grow by external means when Smiths bought Graseby plc and folded the Graseby Medical, Inc. unit into SIMS Deltec. Instead, the Minnesota company continued to focus on its narrow range of products, yet still managed to maintain a sizeable market share in its core businesses. As before, the key was the ongoing development of new models and related products. After receiving FDA approval in 1996, SIMS Deltec introduced a new ambulatory infusion pump, the CADD-Prizm PCS (Pain Control System), intended for the management of acute, postoperative, and chronic pain in both the hospital and home market. Also in 1996, the company introduced the CADD-PRIZM VIP pump, which was able to provide a number of therapies in addition to pain management. On the ports and catheters side of the business, in 1999 SIMS Deltec brought out the P.A.S. Port T2, an implantable peripheral venous access system.

Smiths underwent some organizational changes in 2001, in the process changing its name to Smiths Group plc and creating the Smiths Medical division. SIMS Deltec's name was shortened to Deltec, Inc. and it was tucked into this new division.

The subsidiary continued to market improved versions of its established product lines. A major shift in strategy came in 2002 when the company announced that it was about to enter the potentially lucrative diabetes market and was seeking FDA approval on a new insulin pump, one that would deliver a continuous flow of insulin, both day and night, to better help people manage their diabetes. The advantage to such a system was that it allowed blood glucose levels to remain normal or near normal, reducing significantly the risks of a patient suffering diabetes complications. The insulin pump was the result of years of effort, including gathering input from patients and doctors on an ideal way to deliver insulin. The product, named the Deltec Cozmo pump, was lightweight and as small as a cell phone. It was also easily maintained, powered by a single AAA battery and merely requiring that a short section of plastic tube, inserted just under the skin, be replaced every few days. In addition, the device contained a number of safety features to ensure proper usage. Later in 2002, the company received FDA clearance and began to ship the Deltec Cozmo insulin pump. The company estimated that the world market for insulin pumps would be worth $1.5 billion within five years. If that estimate proved correct, Deltec was on the verge of becoming very much a cash cow for its corporate parent.

Principal Operating Units

Clinical Research; R & D Product Development.

Principal Competitors

Abbott Laboratories; C.R. Bard, Inc.

Further Reading

Alexander, Steve, "Pharmacia Deltec Seeks Well-Off Buyer to Provide It With Cash for Acquisitions," *Star-Tribune*, February 15, 1994, p. 1D.

Phillips, Carolyn, "Patient-Controlled Device for Painkillers Meets Some Resistance on Hospital Staffs," *Wall Street Journal*, February 8, 1984, p. 1.

Rosenbaum, Sharyn, "Pain Control Devices Gaining Acceptance, Will Expand," *Health Industry Today*, May 1992, p. 1.

Schafer, Lee, "Growing, Growing, Gone," *Corporate Report–Minnesota*, February 1989, p. 24.

—Ed Dinger

Dippin' Dots, Inc.

5101 Charter Oak Drive
Paducah, Kentucky 42001
U.S.A.
Telephone: (270) 443-8994
Fax: (270) 443-8997
Web site: http://www.dippindots.com

Private Company
Incorporated: 1988
Employees: 160
Sales: $34 million (2002 est.)
NAIC: 311520 Ice Cream and Frozen Dessert
    Manufacturing

Dippin' Dots, Inc. makes a unique form of ice cream which consists of tiny beads that have been flash-frozen at an extremely low temperature. The patented process, which was invented by company founder and owner Curt Jones, virtually eliminates the presence of trapped ice and air and gives the ice cream a fresh flavor and a hard texture. The company sells its ice cream—as well as beaded versions of frozen yogurt, flavored ices, and sherbet—at more than 2,000 locations in North America, Europe, and Asia, many of which are owned by franchisees. Dippin' Dots outlets are found at shopping malls, amusement parks, stadiums, movie theaters, and special events, and the firm has recently begun marketing its products through McDonald's restaurants on the West Coast. The company is ranked third in the United States in number of ice cream franchise locations behind Baskin Robbins and Dairy Queen.

Beginnings

Dippin' Dots was founded by Curt Jones, a former vocational education teacher turned research microbiologist. In the mid-1980s, while working in Lexington, Kentucky, for Alltech Biotechnology Center, he developed a process for making cattle feed by freezing it in pellet-size chunks at 350 degrees below zero, which better preserved the nutritional content. One weekend in 1987, when he was making ice cream at home with a neighbor, he was struck by the idea of using the same technique

to make the frozen dessert. He began to experiment, and after six months of trial and error arrived at a method of flash-freezing a stream of raw ingredients with liquid nitrogen vapor. The result was a product which contained virtually no ice crystals or air and had the appearance of tiny, hard beads that were between the size of a BB and a small pea. When a spoonful of them was eaten, it would slowly melt to release an intense, fresh flavor. Different varieties of beads could also be mixed together to create new flavors. Though the first experimental versions had been consumed at such a low temperature that Jones later recalled, ''They welded our tongues to our jaws,'' the firm established a shipping and storage standard of 40 degrees below zero and a serving temperature of 20 degrees below. After being served, the beads could retain their shape for more than ten minutes, even on a warm day.

Once Jones had perfected the process, he patented it, then quit his job, bought production equipment, and opened a retail outlet for the ice cream with his wife Kay. The operation, which was christened Dippin' Dots, was based in their home town of Grand Chain, Illinois, though the first store was located at a shopping center in nearby Lexington, Kentucky. The location was not a busy one, however, and the Joneses found themselves struggling to keep the business afloat. After using up most of their savings, selling a car, and running up the balance on six credit cards, they decided to try a new tack and took out a loan to fund distribution to fairs and amusement parks, using their farm as collateral. In late 1989, by the time the Joneses had decided to close down their store, Dippin' Dots was already being sold at such places as Opryland USA in Nashville, Tennessee, and at events like the Tulsa, Oklahoma, State Fair. Though it was slightly more expensive than regular ice cream, small samples handed out to passers-by proved irresistible to many of them, especially children, and sales began to take off. A small pouch-size container of the beads cost $1.25, and flavors included vanilla, strawberry, or a combination of the two. Several varieties of frozen yogurt were also offered.

In 1990, production was moved to a new site in Paducah, Kentucky, and the following year a formal dealer network was established for distribution to fairs, festivals, and retail locations. The treat was especially popular at outdoor venues, where it was often sold alongside carnival fare such as corn dogs and elephant ears. The company promoted Dippin' Dots as "the world's coldest ice cream" and "the ice cream of the future." More than a dozen flavors such as mint chocolate, banana split, and blue bubblegum were added, and frozen sherbet and flavored-ice beads were offered as well. Because of its unusually low serving temperature, selling Dippin' Dots as a packaged product through food stores was avoided. Although grocers could maintain the necessary storage temperature, not all home freezers could, and in some cases the beads would clump together before use.

Expansion in the 1990s

Dippin' Dots was now growing rapidly, and sales shot up by 1,385 percent during the first half of the 1990s. Outlets were being opened in shopping malls as well as at amusement parks, fairs, and other seasonal sites, and by 1995 numbered more than 150 in 33 states across the United States. Some were owned by the company, while others were run by independent dealerships. The product was typically distributed from a free-standing cart or kiosk, rather than a full-scale store.

With domestic sales growing by leaps and bounds, Jones began eyeing foreign markets, and in 1994 plans were drawn up to begin distribution to Mexico, Canada, and Japan. In the last-named country, a licensing agreement was signed with the firm Itochu, which began testing Dippin' Dots at an amusement park, a shopping center, and a movie/arcade complex in November 1994. The ice cream was a hit, and the number of Japanese outlets quickly expanded. To keep up with demand, the firm constructed a new 32,000-square-foot processing plant in Paducah, which opened in the spring of 1995.

Following Dippin' Dots' enthusiastic reception in Japan, sales were expanded to Korea, the Philippines, and other Asian countries. By 1997, Japan alone accounted for one-fifth of the firm's total sales. The company was also successfully exporting to Europe by this time, and Dippin' Dots could be found in England, Ireland, France, Germany, Belgium, and Holland at sites operated by licensee Dots Distribution. Cultural differences sometimes caused minor problems, as when Europeans rejected the relatively unfamiliar flavor of peanut butter. When its name was changed to "walnut," it became one of the most popular varieties.

Dippin' Dots' products continued to be manufactured only in Paducah, and because of their low storage temperature had to be shipped in special containers surrounded by liquid nitrogen. The beads could last up to 15 days in this form, though they typically reached their destination within five days. Import tariffs and shipping were not inexpensive, and as a result the ice cream was sold at a premium price. Nevertheless, the unique-

ness of Dippin' Dots helped the brand take hold wherever it was offered.

With growth still surging, in 1997 the company added another 20,000 square feet of production capacity. By the fall of 1998, Dippin' Dots products were being sold in 42 states and 13 countries by 110 dealers at 350 different locations. These now included some frozen-food vending machines as well as movie theaters, sports stadiums, and such popular tourist sites as the Kennedy Space Center in Florida, where they were dubbed "Space Dots." A deal was also reportedly in the works for the ice cream to be offered to airline passengers. Annual sales now stood at approximately $18 million.

In 2000, the company formed a subsidiary, Dippin' Dots Franchising Inc., to further expand its reach. The year also saw Japanese distributor Itochu sell its rights to Gradco Systems, Inc. for $175,000 and three years of royalties on sales.

McDonald's Adds Dippin' Dots in 2002

Although 2001 started on a bad note with the layoff of 13 of the firm's 160 workers due to a sales slump, the year also brought good news when plans were made to test-market Dippin' Dots at more than 250 McDonald's restaurants in the San Francisco Bay area. The trial was a success, and an official rollout was begun in May of 2002. McDonald's spent $1.2 million to promote the ice cream, which was offered in vanilla, chocolate, and banana split flavors. Soon, other McDonald's in California and Nevada signed on, with additional locations expected to follow suit. To supply the restaurants, Dippin' Dots set up a special distribution system. Although concerns were expressed about a possible negative impact on sales at established outlets, it was felt that the increased availability would boost public awareness of the products across the board. In addition to the McDonald's restaurants, Dippin' Dots were available around the United States at 800 sites, including theme parks, stadiums, movie theaters, and travel plazas, as well as in 250 shopping malls and at 300 special events. The company was now ranked the third largest ice cream franchiser in the country behind Baskin Robbins and Dairy Queen.

Dippin' Dots' core customer group were children and teenagers, and during the summer of 2002 the company's first national advertising campaign was launched with ads in *Seventeen* and *Nickelodeon* magazines. A firm was also hired to place Dippin' Dots in movie and television programs to gain exposure through so-called "product placement." At the same time, a new freezer which almost doubled the firm's storage capacity was added to the Paducah plant.

The company was also now beginning the process of fighting a patent infringement lawsuit that had been brought against it by a Canadian firm, IQF, Inc., which alleged that Dippin' Dots' patent for freezing ice cream infringed on an earlier one held by IQF. Several years before this, Dippin' Dots itself had filed suit against a company called Mini Melts of Mystic, Connecticut, for alleged trademark, patent, and trade dress infringements, as well as against the makers of Frosty Bites, a knock-off product created by a former Dippin' Dots distributor and marketed in several cities in the South.

Key Dates:

1988: Inventor Curt Jones forms Dippin' Dots, Inc. to sell beaded ice cream.
1989: Jones closes his initial store but sales to fairs and Opryland USA take off.
1990: The company's production facilities are moved from Illinois to Paducah, Kentucky.
1991: The firm establishes a dealer network for sale to fairs, festivals, and other sites.
1994: International sales begin through licensee in Japan.
1995: The company opens a new 32,000-square-foot production facility.
1997: The company's plant is expanded by an additional 20,000 square feet.
2002: Dippin' Dots are added to the menus of more than 250 West Coast McDonald's.
2003: An Asian licensee opens a new manufacturing plant in South Korea.

In early 2003, a second manufacturing plant was opened in Ansong, South Korea, which was owned by Dippin' Dots Korea, an independent licensee. It would supply the firm's products to Southeast Asian countries, including Korea, Japan, Singapore, and the Philippines. Dippin' Dots now came in more than 23 flavors, including the recently added chocolate-covered cherry, cotton candy, and chocolate chip cookie dough. Some varieties were low-fat and fat-free. Serving sizes were four, five, and eight-ounce cups, as well as special foil pouches sold in vending machines.

In the spring of 2003, Dippin' Dots celebrated its 15th anniversary by launching a sweepstakes in conjunction with Universal Studios. The prizes included four trips to the Universal Studios and Islands of Adventure theme parks in Florida, where Dippin' Dots was sold. The contest was advertised on the company's Web site and on Nickelodeon cable television, which broadcast a cartoon that was the basis for a new ride.

Dippin' Dots was now ranked 144th on *Entrepreneur* magazine's list of the top 500 franchises in North America, and 4th on its list of new franchise opportunities. It was the highest-placing food vendor in the latter category. The initial franchise fee charged by the company was $12,500, with startup costs estimated at between $46,000 and $190,000.

With its expansion still in high gear, Dippin' Dots, Inc. was celebrating 15 years in business with an eye toward greater triumphs ahead. The firm's unique bead-sized frozen treats were irresistible to many, and with further markets left to conquer the company's growth looked assured for some time to come.

Principal Subsidiaries

Dippin' Dots Franchising Inc.

Principal Competitors

Baskin-Robbins Ice Cream Co.; International Dairy Queen, Inc.; Allied Domecq PLC; CoolBrands International, Inc.

Further Reading

Aldrich, Martha, ''Flash-Frozen Ice Cream Market Wars Get Chillier,'' *Plain Dealer* (Cleveland), September 17, 2000, p. 3H.
Autman, Samuel, ''Fairgoers Find Fun in Latest Frozen Treat,'' *Tulsa World*, October 2, 1989, p. A2.
''Dippin' Dots in McDonald's,'' *Ice Cream Reporter*, May 20, 2002, p. 1.
''Dippin' Dots Plant Opens in Korea,'' *Ice Cream Reporter*, February 20, 2003, p. 2.
''Dippin' Dots to Japan,'' *Ice Cream Reporter*, September 20, 1994, p. 2.
''Fazoli's, Dippin' Dots Form Partnership with McDonald's,'' *Lane Report*, June 1, 2002, p. 6.
''Ice Cream Novelty Big in Asia—Japanese in Love With Dippin' Dots,'' *Cincinnati Post*, November 28, 1997, p. 7B.
''Ice Cream Pellets? Yep, and They're Good,'' *Capital Times* (Madison, Wisconsin), March 19, 1998, p. 1B.
Jaeger, Lauren, ''Mini Melts Opens New Location; Dippin' Dots Has Lawsuit Pending,'' *Amusement Business*, September 22, 1997, p. 16.
Jones, Norah, ''Venue Change Granted in Patent Infringement Suit,'' *Daily Record of Rochester*, June 21, 2002.
''Judge Says Miami Man Violated Contract with Paducah, Kentucky Company,'' *Paducah Sun*, December 15, 2000.
Mabin, Connie, ''Ice Cream Dots Lure Kids, Adults,'' *Associated Press State & Local Wire*, December 20, 1998.
Rodriguez, Geraldine, ''On the Dot,'' *Business Daily*, March 6, 1997.
Selz, Michael, ''The Entrepreneurial Life—Straight and Narrow: Many Entrepreneurs Dream of Finding Just the Right Niche Product,'' *Wall Street Journal*, September 28, 1998, p. 24.
Walker, Joe, ''Paducah, Ky.-Based Ice Cream Firm Continues Growth Worldwide,'' *Paducah Sun*, December 29, 2002.

—Frank Uhle

Dominick's Finer Foods, Inc.

711 Jorie Boulevard
Oak Brook, Illinois 60523
U.S.A.
Telephone: (603) 891-5000
Fax: (630) 891-5210
Web site: http://www.dominicks.com

Wholly Owned Subsidiary of Safeway Inc.
Founded: 1918
Employees: 20,000 (est.)
Sales: $2.4 billion (2002)
NAIC: 445110 Supermarkets and Other Grocery (Except Convenience) Stores

A subsidiary of Safeway Inc., Dominick's Finer Foods, Inc. is Chicago's second-largest supermarket operation, trailing only the Jewel chain. Most of the company's 116 outlets combine food stores and drugstores, many under the Dominick's Fresh Store banner, which offers in-store cafés, floral departments, and expanded produce sections. To provide prepared foods sold in its stores, Dominick's also operates a commissary. Dominick's has proven to be a poor fit for Safeway, which purchased the chain in 1998. As part of a temporary agreement to settle contentious contract negotiations in 2002, Safeway has promised to make a good faith effort at selling Dominick's.

Dominick's Established in 1918

The roots of Dominick's reach back to 1909 when Sicilian-born Dominick di Matteo immigrated to America, settling in Chicago. In 1918, he established a small deli, squeezed into a 20-by-50 foot location on Chicago's west side. In that same year, Dominick di Matteo, Jr. was born. As soon as he was old enough, the young Di Matteo began helping out with the business. He was only 16 years old when he took over the management of a second store, launched in 1934. It was a time of transition in the grocery business, which was making the switch from orders being filled by clerks to self-service, a concept pioneered by Clarence Saunders and his Piggly Wiggly stores. Next came the supermarket concept that flourished in the years following World War II. In 1950, the Di Matteos opened their first supermarket. The facility

was 14,000 square feet in size and inaugurated the rise of a major Chicago-area chain of large format stores. It was also one of the first of the new supermarkets to introduce in-store delicatessens and a frozen foods section.

By 1968, the Dominick's chain totaled 19 stores, at which point the Di Matteos elected to sell the business to Fisher Foods Inc., a Cleveland company run by John and Carl Fazio, who in a short period of time had transformed a six-store chain into a 74-store operation. The Di Matteo family continued to run the Chicago stores, and although Fisher Foods had the financial resources to grow the chain to 71 units, the Di Matteos were not happy with the arrangement. In 1981, the family bought back the chain for $100 million, the same year that Dominick di Matteo, Sr. died.

Dominick's continued to expand during the early 1980s through new store openings, the remodeling of older units, and the acquisition of Kohl and Eagle stores. As a result, it made serious inroads on the market share of Chicago's leading supermarket chain, Jewel, whose own growth had been curtailed since it had been acquired in 1984 by Salt-Lake City-based American Stores Co., now undergoing internal problems. At the time, Jewel had a 35 percent share of Chicago's $6 billion market, while Dominick's controlled just 13 percent, according to *Supermarket News*. Two years later, however, Jewel saw its share slip to 34 percent while Dominick's had improved to 22 percent, prompting some observers to speculate that within five years Dominick's might actually passed Jewel in marketshare. Also impressive was the fact that with only half as many stores as Jewel, 88 compare to 175, Dominick's was able to achieve two-thirds of its competitors' marketshare. Dominick's was especially successful in its remodeling program, which both improved the shopping experience and added selling space. It also introduced floral and cosmetic boutiques, as well as expanded deli and seafood sections. Jewel countered by offering similar features but lacked Dominick's flair.

James di Matteo Replaces Father as CEO in 1985

In 1985, Dominck di Matteo, Jr. stepped down as chief executive officer, replaced by his son James, although as chairman he continued to hold sway over the business. While Do-

---

Company Perspectives:

A third generation of Di Matteos is carrying on the traditions of Dominick's Finer Foods. And despite its size and success, Dominick's fundamental business model remains intact. Now as part of Safeway Inc., it continues its original focus: primary attention to the needs of shoppers partnered with the highest standards for all of its merchandise. It is a positioning that is basically identical to the one expressed by the legendary 'Mr. D,' Dominick Di Matteo, in 1918 in his 20x50 foot deli: 'Dominick's belongs to the customers.'

---

minick's remained the trendsetter among the Chicago supermarket chains during the rest of decade, but it did not close the gap on marketshare with Jewel, which was especially well established in city neighborhoods. Dominick's was primarily making its mark in the suburbs, which were now receptive to some of the chain's innovations, such as prepared foods. It even joined forces with Starbucks Coffee to install coffee bars in several of the suburban stores. In 1990, well before the Internet had become a major force, Dominick teamed with the Prodigy online service to provide a way for customers to order groceries from their personal computers. Moreover, it was well ahead of the curve when it began testing a shopping cart that included a computer screen, which not only displayed a store directory but also recipes and advertisements. On the other end of the grocery business, Dominick's took steps to counter the rise of warehouse stores, in 1987 introducing Omni Superstores, massive stores (more than 85,000 square feet) that sold both food and non-food items 24 hours a day.

In 1993, Dominick di Matteo died, leading to speculation that his heirs would soon sell the business. Although James di Matteo vowed to keep running the family-owned operation, the local press reported that he and his four sisters did not appear to share their father's passion for the supermarket business. At the time of James di Matteo's death, Dominick's, with an estimated 26 percent share of the Chicago market, operated 86 Dominick's stores and 16 Omni Superstores, altogether generating around $2 billion in annual sales. Although there was no shortage of suitors, more than a year passed before the family did indeed decide to sell the business. As Goldman Sachs & Co shopped the company, prospective buyers included Kohlberg Kravis Roberts & Co., Kroger Co., Albertson's Inc., Super Valu Inc., as well as European supermarket heavyweights Sainsbury Plc of Great Britain and Koninklijke Ahold N.V. of the Netherlands. In the end, the Di Matteo family sold the chain to an investment partnership headed by Yucaipa Co., a rapidly growing Los-Angeles-based supermarket holding company. The purchase price was $692.9 million, of which $420.9 million bought the stock, which was mostly held by the Di Matteo family, and $272 million covered debt. Also involved in the deal was the New York investment firm Apollo Advisors L.P. For Yucaipa and its head, Ronald W. Burkle, it was a crafty deal. The firm put up only $20 million of the funds and immediately received $14 in handling fees, as well as arranging to be on the receiving end of an annual management fee of 2 percent of cash flow. The Di Matteo family as well as senior management also retained a small stake in the business.

Burkle had roots in the grocery industry; his father managed a Claremont, California, supermarket, part of the Stater Bros. chain. From the age of five, Burkle spent time with his father at the store, sweeping up and stacking shelves. As a teenager and college student, he worked part-time at the store, saving up some $3,000, which he successfully invested in the stock market. As an adult, Burkle maintained a dual interest in investing and the grocery industry. Although he intended to study dentistry at the California State Polytechnic College, he dropped out in 1973 and went to work full-time for the Stater chain. In 1981, Stater's corporate parent, the energy firm of Petrolane, decided to sell the chain. Burkle and his father, who was now Stater's president, assembled a buyout group which through a series of fortuitous circumstances grew to include Warren Buffet's partner, Charles Munger. Although the Burkles' bid had the support of Petrolane's president, the father and son team failed to vet their interest with the chairman of the board. When they made their pitch to the board of directors, they were promptly sacked.

Ron Burkle busied himself with his investments until 1986, when he decided to form a holding company with two former Stater colleagues to invest in supermarkets. He named the new company Yucaipa after the town he lived in west of Los Angeles. The firm's first deal came in 1987 when it acquired the Kansas-based Falley's chain. A series of other acquisitions followed, all with a similar pattern: the deals were highly leveraged, with Yucaipa contributing a modest amount of the funds and taking back a portion in cash fees. It was often a high-wire act but one that Ron Burkle performed skillfully.

Fresh Store Concept Flourishes in Mid-1990s

Yucapia planned to continue Dominick's expansion program, which included rolling out more stores adopting the chain's new European-style, open market "Fresh Store" concept that featured in-store dining, restaurant quality take-out food, upscale meat and produce departments, specialty bakeries, and floral shops. Not only did consumers like the Fresh Stores, these units produced higher grosses and stronger profit margins than conventional supermarkets. In fiscal 1996, Dominick's opened eight Fresh Store outlets, followed by another 15 the following year. The Omni warehouse format, on the other hand, had fallen out of favor with consumers, and management opted not to open any news units. Another improvement to the bottom line was expected to come from the introduction of upscale products carrying a new private label called Private Selection, replacing the tired Heritage House brand Dominick's had been carrying. Another initiative the chain was pursuing during this period was the introduction of in-store banking branches, in partnership with First Chicago NBD Corp., the first opening in 1995. To help fund the chain's growth, Yucapia also looked to cut operating costs, realizing some savings through administrative efficiencies and even more by closing down less profitable stores. Although it opened more Fresh Store units, Dominick's remained essentially the same size and even lost some market share. Moreover, sales were flat, in the $2.5 billion range, but a $7.5 million profit in 1995 turned into a $10.6 million loss a year later, the result of servicing the debt taken on by Yucaipa in buying the chain. While Dominick's was losing marketshare in Chicago, Jewel edged over 31 percent and other competitors entered the fight. To gain

Key Dates:

1918: Dominick di Matteo opens his first store.
1934: A second store is opened.
1950: The company's first supermarket opens.
1968: The Dominick's chain is sold to Fisher Foods Inc.
1981: The Di Matteo family reacquires the chain.
1995: Yucaipa Cos. buys the company.
1998: Safeway Inc. acquires the chain.

some much needed cash, Yucapia took Dominick's Finer Foods public through a parent entity known as Dominick's Supermarkets. In October 1996, the offering was completed, raising $144 million on the sale of eight million shares of common stock priced at $18 per share. Most of the money was used to pay down bank debt.

Following its initial public offering, Dominick's launched another expansion and remodeling effort, and once again made gains in marketshare. In 1997, the chain acquired two area Byerly's Inc. grocery stores and also decided to convert its 17 Omni stores to the more profitable Fresh Store format. It appeared once again that Dominick's was on an upward trajectory, as reflected by the company's rising stock price. At this point Burkle elected to sell the chain, considered a prize catch in the rapidly consolidating grocery industry, which was becoming national if not global in scale. For any of the major supermarket holding companies that wanted to gain an immediate presence in the desirable Chicago market, acquiring Dominick's was a quick fix. The early favorite in the spring of 1998 was the Dutch giant Ahold, but by the autumn of the year it was California-based Safeway Inc. that succeeded in buying Dominick's at a price tag of $1.2 billion, as well as the assumption of $646.2 million in debt. For Burkle and his partners, their ownership of Dominick's, which lasted less than four years, resulted in a tidy profit, an estimated sevenfold return. Safeway, on the other hand, gained a major stake in the Midwest, augmenting the stores it already owned in Indiana.

Safeway brought in their own man to run Dominick's, Tim Hakin, and instituted a number of changes to bring the chain in line with the way the corporate parent did business. Most of those steps proved to have adverse, and in some cases disastrous, consequences that resulted in the steady erosion of marketshare. Safeway tried to save money by having the California office handle buying, in the process eliminating a host of middle managers who knew the tastes of local consumers. While pricing and marketing executives were lopped off, other significant members of management quit on their own, resulting in Dominick's losing touch with its market. Familiar products were replaced by the higher-margin Safeway Select house brand of products, foreign to Chicago consumers. For years Dominick's had carried a wide selection of products. But now, as the *Wall Street Journal* explained, "a chain with a 'reputation for having truffle oil and four different kinds of sun-dried tomatoes' had shelves filled with unfamiliar products." Moreover, Safeway ended a longstanding practice of Dominick's filling customers' special order requests, indicative of Dominick's di Matteo's formula of offering personalized neighborhood service that had

made the chain a success in the first place. Customers did not like the changes and showed their displeasure by shopping elsewhere, resulting in Dominick's marketshare dropping to 22.8 percent by the end of 2001. It was a perilous time to be losing a grip on customers, as several major players prepared to enter the Chicago market, including Target Corp., Kroger Co., and Wal-Mart Stores Inc.

In 2002, Dominick's faced new difficulties, this time from a labor negotiation. Management insisted the leaders of the United Food and Commercial Workers union, representing nearly 9,000 Dominick's employees, accept a cut in wages, putting them in line with non-union Jewel, as well as sharing costs in health care. Should the union strike, Safeway maintained that it would not attempt to operate any of the Dominick's stores and would simply shut down the subsidiary. When workers voted to reject management's offer and authorized a strike, management attacked the credibility of the vote, claiming that some employees were intimidated or given misleading information about the offer and demanding that the union conduct a revote. The two sides had clearly reached a stage where neither side trusted the other. Ultimately, a short-term deal was reached that allowed Safeway enough time to find a buyer for the Dominick's chain. The agreement was set to expire by the end of July 2003.

Once again Dominick's was on the block, with Safeway expected to only receive a fraction of what it paid for the chain just four years earlier. Ironically, Burkle and Yucaipa, which had profited nicely from their involvement with Dominick's, emerged as a leading candidate to buy the company. The union had enjoyed good relations with Yucaipa management and reportedly approached the company about reacquiring Dominick's during the recent labor fight. If Yucaipa indeed reacquired Dominick's, unlike the first time around, it would be taking on a chain in need of a turnaround rather than a business that was in the midst of an expansion program. It was likely, however, that the union would be more receptive to granting givebacks to Yucaipa than it was with Safeway, although in return the workers might gain an ownership stake.

Principal Competitors

Jewel Foods Stores; Eagle Food Centers, Inc.; SUPERVALU Inc.

Further Reading

Arndorfer, James B., "Dominick's : No Safe Way," *Crain's Chicago Business*, November 11, 2002, p. 3.
Berner, Robert, "Safeway to Acquire Dominick's for $1.2 Billion," *Wall Street Journal*, October 14, 1998, p. A4.
Crown, Judith, "Nimble Dominick's Ringing up Big Gains," *Crain's Chicago Business*, October 1, 1990. p. 1.
Merrion, Paul, "Cha-ching! Dominick's Money Machine," *Crain's Chicago Business*, October 19, 1998, p. 1.
Picker, Ida, "From Bags to Riches," *Institutional Investor*, May 1998, pp. 60–66.
Snyder, David, "Feisty Dominick's Eats into Jewel Lead," *Crain's Chicago Business*, November 3, 1986, p. 1.
Waters, Jennifer, "Time for Dominick's to Produce," *Crain's Chicago Business*, September 9, 1996, p. 1.

—Ed Dinger

Donna Karan International Inc.

550 Seventh Avenue
New York, New York 10018
U.S.A.
Telephone: (212) 768-5800
Fax: (212) 354-5215
Web site: http://www.donnakaran.com

Wholly Owned Subsidiary of LVMH
Incorporated: 1984
Employees: 2,000
Sales: $650 million (2001 est.)
NAIC: 315233 Women's and Girls' Cut and Sew Dress
Manufacturing; 315299 All Other Cut and Sew
Apparel Manufacturing; 315999 Other Apparel
Accessories and Other Apparel Manufacturing;
316214 Women's Footwear (Except Athletic)
Manufacturing; 316992 Women's Handbag and Purse
Manufacturing; 316999 All Other Leather Good
Manufacturing; 339911 Jewelry (Except Costume)
Manufacturing; 448120 Women's Clothing Stores

Donna Karan International Inc. is a leading American clothing designer and a powerhouse in the international fashion industry. Though founder Donna Karan began her career designing for women, she also designs full clothing lines for men, teens, children, and infants, as well as an extensive line of accessories, beauty products, and home furnishings. Donna Karan International (DKI) also owns and operates freestanding stores in fashion meccas around the world, including New York, Beverly Hills, Las Vegas, and London, with new stores dotting the globe in Japan, Singapore, Switzerland, Saudi Arabia, Taiwan, and the United Arab Emirates. While DKI was acquired by French fashion titan LVMH in 2001, Karan continues as chief designer for the renowned fashion labels bearing her name.

Founding an Empire: 1970s to 1984

Donna Karan New York was created by designer and entrepreneur Donna Karan and her husband Stephan Weiss in 1984.

With help from outside investors, Karan and Weiss developed the company into a half-billion-dollar-plus empire in little more than a decade. Karan's quick success, though, was the result of a youth spent in and around the design and fashion industries. Her father, who died when Karan was three years old, was a custom tailor, and her mother was a showroom model and sales representative. Even Karan's stepfather was in the business—he sold women's apparel.

Inspired by her parents and endowed with an innate knack for design, the then Donna Faske enrolled in New York City's Parsons School of Design. At the age of 20, she took a job with fashion industry legend Anne Klein. Her rise at Anne Klein was phenomenal. She instantly found her niche and was able to thrive in the Klein organization. Her energy, determination, and perfectionism helped her to succeed at Klein and later to prosper in her own design business when the industry was largely dominated by men. Anne Klein, who became a sort of idol to Karan, was known as extremely demanding and a perfectionist. It was those common qualities that drew the two women together; after only four years of working together, Karan had become Klein's successor.

While at Klein, Donna Faske married Mark Karan, a clothing boutique owner. In 1974, at the age of 26, she gave birth to her daughter, Gabby. Tragically, just one week after Gabby's birth, Anne Klein died. As Klein's respected protege, Karan was her natural successor. Karan was elevated to head of design and credited with preserving the Klein name and building up the company during the next ten years. During these years Karan worked with a friend from Parsons School of Design, Louis Dell'Olio, to sustain the Anne Klein legacy and branch into new markets. In 1982 the two designers launched a successful line of clothes for working women (dubbed ''Anne Klein II''), targeted at the lower-priced market.

With the Anne Klein II line, Karan had designed an entire new collection of clothing. This success, along with the desire to have more creative control, influenced her decision to start her own company. Anne Klein was owned at the time by Japanese textile conglomerate Takihyo. Takihyo's executives were open to the idea of Karan branching out, but she was hesitant to leave the security of Klein. To force her to take the next step, Karan's boss, Frank Mori, fired her in 1984. Takihyo

Key Dates:

1984: Karan, with the help of husband Stephan Weiss, forms Donna Karan New York.

1985: The first Donna Karan New York collection is introduced; Karan is named Designer of the Year by the CFDA (Council of Fashion Designers of America).

1989: DKNY is launched.

1990: DKNY Jeans hit stores; Karan's earns second CFDA Designer of the Year award.

1992: Karan's first menswear collection, signature fragrance, and DKNY Kids are introduced.

1993: DKNY Men, a more casual line of menswear, is introduced.

1994: The first DKNY store opens in London.

1996: Donna Karan International goes public on the New York Stock Exchange; a DKNY store opens in Manchester, England.

1998: DKNY stores open in Beverly Hills, Las Vegas, Manhasset (New York), and Short Hills (New Jersey).

1999: Two DKNY fragrances are launched through Estée Lauder; five more stores open across the United States.

2000: Four more DKNY stores open, and several new products are rolled out including DKNY jeans for juniors, DKNY watches through Swatch and Fossil, and scarves through Mantero.

2001: Fashion group LVMH acquires the company.

2002: DKNY Kids is relaunched through a deal with CWF.

offered her $3 million in capital to launch her own venture, with a 50 percent equity stake.

By 1984 Karan had divorced her first husband and was married to sculptor Stephan Weiss, and the two teamed up as co-chief executives of the new design company. Karan showed her first collection at her own fashion show in 1985, just six months after leaving her post at Klein. The crowd greeted the line with wild applause, whistles, and a standing ovation. The market reacted similarly, generating a huge early demand for Karan's apparel. The major appeal of the clothing was offering working women an elegant, classic alternative to the often quixotic, fanciful, and sometimes uncomfortable designs of the day. For her efforts, Karan was awarded the Council of Fashion Designers of America (CFDA)'s Designer of the Year award.

Taking the Fashion Industry by Storm: 1986–89

Throughout the middle and late 1980s Karan was a savvy risk-taker: breaking new ground by designing practical, comfortable, refined clothing that made women look good, and shying away from bizarre, jaw-dropping fashions and tacky frills. Signature designs included easy-fitting jackets, wrap skirts, and one-piece silk bodysuits. Karan became increasingly known for her ability to create skirts, pants, and other clothing to complement a woman's figure, even if she was not as thin as a

model. The down-to-earth approach was well received in the market, where Karan's style was considered refreshing.

By the later years of the decade Karan relied primarily on her Donna Karan New York collection of upscale clothing, originally launched in 1985. The apparel included blazers and blouses ranging in price from $500 to $1,000 or more. In 1987 Karan jumped into the very competitive hosiery business, convinced women would be willing to spend more money for better quality hosiery. Critics balked, but Karan and partner Hanes developed a hosiery that was twice as thick and twice as expensive as what was currently available. Customers were indeed willing to pay for the quality and Karan's hosiery products were well received. Within five years the company was selling more than $30 million in hosiery to wholesalers.

Karan drew on the recognition of her Donna Karan New York collection to launch a second line dubbed "DKNY" in 1989. The DKNY line was designed to provide stylish, casual, and affordable clothing for a less elite market segment. The apparel was still relatively expensive but it brought an entirely new and much broader range of buyers to Karan designs. The line, which was craftily marketed on a background of black-and-white cityscapes that enhanced its urban nature, was one of the most successful launches in fashion history. DKNY helped the fashion firm generate about $115 million in sales for 1989.

Karan's increasing influence on the fashion scene had earned her the title "The Queen of Seventh Avenue" with the press, and the Donna Karan name was considered "red hot" in the apparel retailing industry. Encouraged by the gains, Karan and Weiss pushed ahead with plans for new products ranging from fragrance and accessories to children's clothing. Karan also hoped for further international expansion, since the company had started selling clothes in Germany and Japan as early as 1986, and had opened a chic London boutique in 1989.

Licensing and International Expansion: 1990s

To help make the transition from a family-owned business to a more conventional corporate entity, Karan brought in apparel industry pro Stephen Ruzow, a former Warnaco executive. Among other tasks, Ruzow was hired to eliminate production problems and increase quality control. As the company continued to grow, so did Karan's reputation within the industry and she was once again awarded CFDA's prestigious Designer of the Year award in 1990. Karan and Weiss extended the design house's reach further with the 1992 introduction of men's clothing under Donna Karan New York, then another line under the DKNY label the following year. Critics scoffed at the lines, claiming men would never wear clothes designed by a woman—and yet again they were proved wrong.

DKI began licensing its name for products ranging from intimate apparel and furs to shoes and eyeglasses. The company also launched a more aggressive overseas initiative, started Donna Karan Beauty Company, and tried to market its own fragrance rather than hire an outside marketing firm. Early results from the sales campaign were disappointing and the project was temporarily shelved. The slow start for Karan's fragrance venture was a precursor to a spate of setbacks that plagued the company beginning in 1992. The problems showed up on DKI's bottom line as financial losses and in the organization as late deliveries and insufficient cash flow. Part of the problem was traced to the addition of the men's lines and beauty business, both expensive efforts, which when combined with other initiatives loaded the company with debt. Karan and Weiss were also criticized for their unconventional licensing program, particularly related to the fragrance endeavor. Although sales continued to rise to $260 million in 1992 and well over $300 million in 1993, DKI was bleeding losses and buckling under its debt load.

Confident of Karan's core business strategy, investors stepped in to buoy the enterprise. A group of banks led by Citicorp infused $125 million into the company, while a Singapore-based company invested $21 million in Donna Karan Japan, the company's Japanese subsidiary. DKI scrambled to restructure its debt, cut unnecessary costs, and shuffle its management team. To this end, Karan's husband eventually announced his intent to relinquish his co-CEO position and return to sculpting, although he continued to be active as a legal adviser and in various product developments.

As the company's finances stabilized, sales growth continued at a rampant pace. Annual revenues rose to more than $450 million in 1994, helped by the opening of a London flagship store, and to $550 million in 1995, the year Karan launched *Woman to Woman,* her in-house magazine. Substantial gains came from several DKI operations, including the DKNY lines and the once-lagging beauty business. The international businesses were also taking off—with distribution centers in Hong Kong, Amsterdam, and Japan, and 15 freestanding stores in Europe, Asia, and the Middle East. Overseas operations were generating about $140 million in revenue by 1995.

In 1996 Donna Karan International went public on the New York Stock Exchange, a crowning achievement for Karan, Weiss, and the designer was hailed once more as CFDA's Designer of the Year and was also honored with the Parsons School of Design Critics Award. The next three years saw the opening of stores in London and Manchester, England; Las Vegas and Beverly Hills; and Short Hills, New Jersey; the introduction of DKNY jeans; the sale of Donna Karan Beauty to Estée Lauder and Donna Karan Japan to Onward Kashiyama; the launch of men's dress shirts with Van Heusen Corporation; a new infants and toddlers line through Esprit de Corp; DKNY underwear and coat collections; a home furnishings line; and a successful fragrance with Estée Lauder. Two scents, DKNY Men and DKNY Women, debuted in 1999; the latter with a bottle designed by Weiss, reminiscent of a woman's (presumably Donna's) back. While the Donna Karan name seemed to be everywhere, with licensing deals on everything from jeans, beauty products, footwear, watches, and furniture—sales and earnings seesawed from 1997 through 1999. Happily, after a slew of losses, DKI ended the century with an upswing in sales to $662 million.

Major Changes in the New Millennium: 2000 Onward

In 2000 rumors began circulating that French luxury group LVMH Moët Hennessey Louis Vuitton, which had been gobbling up major players in the fashion industry, was interested in DKI. The official offer came in December, with LVMH offering Karan and Weiss $450 million for Gabrielle Studio, Inc. (named for Karan's daughter Gabby), which held all of the Karan trademarks. Karan and Weiss counteroffered, slashing $50 million off the price if the deal could be done quickly. LVMH agreed and the purchase was completed in early 2001, so Karan and an ailing Weiss, who was dying of lung cancer, could spend their time outside the boardroom. Weiss died in June and while Karan was devastated by the loss, she went on designing for her next New York show, scheduled for September 11. Due to the World Trade Center tragedy, the show was canceled. Karan met privately with buyers the following week, then traveled to Milan to promote her new designs under the aegis of LVMH.

In November 2001 Karan sold the remainder of her company—the manufacturing and distribution units of DKI—to LVMH for $243 million. She remained chief designer and chief creative officer, while Giuseppe Brusone of Armani came on board as CEO. Karan then stepped back a bit and reshaped her life, spending more time away from New York with her children and grandchildren in the Hamptons. While DKI seemed stable, the firm continued to waver in a weak fashion market. Sales rose and fell, but income remained considerably less than projected. In 2002 Brusone moved up to chairman and LVMH insider Fred Wilson was appointed CEO. Karan herself was rumored to be clashing with LVMH over control of her collections, while the conglomerate reportedly sought new designers to work within DKI's divisions.

Though Donna Karan was still considered one of the Big Three designers in New York, the 2000s were difficult years for DKI and Karan personally. Nevertheless, she had weathered the ups and downs and continued to do what she did best—design sensual, stylish, and comfortable apparel that attracted a wide following.

Principal Divisions

DKNY; DKNY Active; DKNY Baby; DKNY Jeans; DKNY Jeans Juniors; DKNY Kids; DKNY Men; Donna Karan Home; Donna Karan Intimates; Donna Karan Menswear; Donna Karan Studio.

Principal Competitors

AnnTaylor Inc.; Calvin Klein Inc.; Liz Claiborne Inc.; Polo Ralph Lauren.

Further Reading

Benbow-Pfalzgraf, Taryn, ed., *Contemporary Fashion,* 2nd ed., Farmington, Mich: St. James Press, 2002.

Donovan, Carrie, "The Last Word," *New York Times Magazine,* December 2, 2001, pp. 95–99.

Foley, Bridget, "Donna's Quest," *W,* August 1995, p. 96.

Gault, Ylonda, "Donna Karan Sells Her New York Style," *Crain's New York Business,* May 1, 1995, p. 24.

Goldstein, Lauren, "Can Donna Karan Get Back into Black?," *Fortune,* April 12, 1999, p. 31.

Greene, Richard, and Katherine Greene, "The 20 Best-Paid Women in Corporate America: Executive Privilege," *Working Woman,* January 1997, p. 26.

Horyn, Cathy, "From Karan, Sensuality and Steel," *New York Times,* February 18, 2003, p. A22.

Karan, Donna, and Ingrid Sischy, *Donna Karan: New York,* New York: Universe, 1998.

Lipke, David, "DKNY Revamps, Prices Kept Stable," *DNR,* January 27, 2003, p. 1.

Lockwood, Lisa, "DKI, LVMH Ready for Deal?," *WWD,* April 2, 2001, p. 2.

Ozzard, Janet, "Getting Down with DKNY," *WWD,* August 13, 2001, p. 15.

Rubenstein, Hal, "A Separate Peace," *InStyle,* November 1, 2002, p. 468.

Rubin, Bonnie Miller, *Fifty on Fifty: Wisdom, Reflection, and Inspiration on Women's Lives Well Lived,* New York: Warner Books, 1998.

Rudolph, Barbara, "Donna Inc.," *Time,* December 21, 1992, p. 54.

Ryan, Thomas J., "Karan Loss Widens; Hopes Still High," *WWD,* August 11, 1999, p. 8.

——, "Women's Still Lags, But Donna Moves Further into Black," *WWD,* March 22, 2000, p. 1.

Seider, Jill Jordan, "Donna Karan's Chic Design for Success," *U.S. News & World Report,* December 18, 1995, pp. 59–60.

Singer, Sally, "Love Story," *Vogue,* August 2001, pp. 280–84.

Socha, Miles, "Karan Slashes Loss for Quarter," *WWD,* August 7, 1998, p. 2.

Steinhauer, Jennifer, "New Chief at Donna Karan and Wall Street Is Pleased," *New York Times,* July 29, 1997, p. C1.

Tippins, Sherill, *Donna Karan,* Ada, Okla.: Garrett Educational Corp., 1991.

Wilson, Eric, "Donna Now," *New York,* November 2001, pp. 72–73.

——, "A New Combo at DKI: Wilson Is CEO and Brusone Is Chairman," *WWD,* October 1, 2002, p. 1.

—Dave Mote
—update: Nelson Rhodes

DSM 🔆

DSM N.V.

Het Overloon 1
6411 TE Heerlen
The Netherlands
Telephone: (45) 578-8111
Fax: (45) 571-3741
Web site: http://www.dsm.nl

Public Company
Incorporated: 1902
Employees: 21,504
Sales: EUR 6.6 billion (2002)
Stock Exchanges: Euronext Amsterdam Swiss SEAQ
    International
Ticker Symbol: DSM
NAIC: 325412 Pharmaceutical Preparation Manufacturing;
    325320 Pesticide and Other Agricultural Chemical
    Manufacturing; 325211 Plastics Material and Resin
    Manufacturing; 325998 All Other Miscellaneous
    Chemical Product and Preparation Manufacturing

DSM N.V. operates as an integrated specialty chemicals group with operations in more than 40 countries. Originally established as a state-owned coal company, DSM has evolved into a manufacturer of life science products, performance materials, and industrial chemicals that are used in the pharmaceutical, food and feed, automotive, and electronics industries. The company sold off its petrochemicals business in 2002 as part of its strategy to become a leading force in the specialty chemicals industry.

Operating as a State-Owned Coal Company: Early 1900s

Near the turn of the century many Dutch companies had tried and failed to establish operations, or even purchase an interest in Holland's energy supply. All coal production, including that within the country and that imported, was held entirely by foreigners. Not only did this leave Holland vulnerable to political and economic changes in other countries, but there was the fear in Holland itself that the continuing exploitation of the coal mining concessions by foreigners would lead to destruction of the local agrarian communities. More experienced in trade than in production and mining, Dutch businesses repeatedly failed to form their own energy companies. For this reason, the government decided to take measures to rectify the situation.

In 1902 the government established Dutch State Mines, a government owned but competitively operated company. The company was run by a politically independent managing board of directors and given full authority to create company objectives based on economic and competitive principles rather than on any state ideology. The company staff was not comprised of civil servants, but was given separate status and pay competitive with that in private industry, enabling the company to attract talented businessmen. The Ministry of Finance was responsible for the overall expenditures of the company, but profits could be retained by the company to finance its own operations. Since 1939 the company has paid taxes on those profits, as well as dividends to the state, the sole shareholder. DSM increased its holdings to include four large mines and two coking plants operated in Dutch Limburg. Soon afterward, the company's production of anthracite and bituminous coal grew to 12 million tons per year, about two-thirds of all Dutch output.

The company later formed its own coke and gas production business. When coke oven gas was no longer used exclusively for the public gas supply, however, DSM moved into other areas. In 1929 the company's nitrogen works, utilizing the coke oven gas, were established to produce fertilizers. Gradually, DSM began to produce other chemicals. Yet it was the postwar energy shortage that stimulated significant growth for the company through the coal and coke production facilities. After 1945 a large corporate research laboratory was established and the chemical works expanded to include the production of plastics. Up to 1960 DSM remained small internationally, occasionally adding to its production line items such as yarn and fiber feedstocks.

Opportunity Outside the Coal Industry: 1960s–80s

In the 1960s Holland's national government, like many other European governments, was forced to accept the fact that coal was an outmoded energy source, and that it was time to

Company Perspectives:

"Vision 2005: Focus and Value" is the company strategy that will carry DSM to a turnover level of EUR 10 billion by 2005. About 80 percent of this will come from specialties such as high-quality biotech and chemical products and materials. These, in turn, make their way to the pharmaceutical industry, food sectors, the automotive market, and to manufacturers of electrical equipment and electronics. With *"Vision 2005,"* DSM is continuing its focus to take a leading worldwide position in activities with greater added value, strong growth, and stable results.

close the country's collieries and coking plants. The coal and coke operations had given DSM nearly two-thirds of its total sales and profits. With this source of its profits gone, however, the company had to expand its chemical works simply to survive. Therefore, from 1965 to 1979 a major investment program was carried out with two objectives—continuity of the company and profitability. In 1967 DSM became a Naamloze Vennootschap (an unquoted public limited company). The company was no longer dependent upon the Ministry of Finance, but would have to continue operations on investments from the capital markets. DSM also hoped to enter into joint ventures with other companies, which would not have been easily done if it remained under the Ministry of Finance. The state's control was reduced to the appointments of the Board of Supervisory Directors, and to the final approval of company policy.

By 1970 all coal mining operations in The Netherlands had been phased out. During this time, the gas distribution operations were transferred from DSM to N.V. Nederlandse Gasunie. The company's use of coke oven gas was replaced by natural gas and petroleum products for chemical production. In the northern part of Holland there was a supply of naphta gas, and pipelines were constructed to transport this gas inland from Antwerp and Rotterdam on the coast. More pipelines were built to exchange ethylene, an important chemical intermediate, with other companies. In cooperation with a number of Dutch companies, DSM moved into the production of industrial chemicals, plastics, and resins, while spinning off its European fertilizer businesses into a wholly owned subsidiary called Unie van Kunstmestfabrieken (UKF).

With European chemical production becoming extremely competitive during the 1960s and 1970s, particularly in West Germany, DSM concentrated not only on expanding its market share, but on what it could produce from the basic materials obtained from its own cracking installations. DSM also improved its marketing organization by acquiring controlling interests in companies that already had captive markets and by creating a worldwide sales organization. To market its own discoveries from company research laboratories, DSM established another subsidiary called Stamicarbon. Much of DSM's early expansion occurred in the United Kingdom, the United States, Mexico, Brazil, Belgium, and West Germany. By 1976 DSM ranked 61st in the *Fortune* 500 list of non-U.S. firms, employed 32,000 people, and had achieved sales of nearly 10 billion guilders.

In the 1980s DSM handled the state's 40 percent interest in the distribution operations of the Dutch natural gas reserves through its subsidiary DSM-Aardgas B.V. Nevertheless, the national government still had direct control over the sale and pricing policy of the gas and retained final power of approval on all export contracts.

During this time period, management at DSM considered that its major investment and expansion programs were completed and felt that work must begin on streamlining company operations. While continuing to emphasize the production of bulk chemicals, DSM recognized that sales for these products would grow more slowly in the future and that the company must increase the number of special and fine chemicals in its product line. With the fall in oil prices and the low dollar, profits in the mid-1980s were unimpressive but steady. In 1986 sales dropped by 34 percent in fertilizers, by 25 percent in chemical products, and by 32 percent in plastics. Resins sales did rise by 8 percent, however. DSM's operating profits for the year were Dfl 727 million. With this decline in sales, DSM increased funds for its research and development division. Quite a number of new polymer blends were developed, as well as new production techniques. In 1989 DSM began its privatization in one of the largest listings of state-owned shares. The offering was extremely successful, with shares selling at Dfl 116.

Focusing on Specialty Chemicals: 1990s and Beyond

As a publicly listed company, DSM spent the majority of the 1990s focused on growth and developing products for the pharmaceutical, food, and automotive industries. The company's strategy continued to bend toward the specialty and fine chemicals sector—these chemicals generally had profit margins higher than those for petrochemicals. As such, the firm made several key acquisitions. During 1996 DSM purchased chemical manufacturers Chemie Linz of Austria and Deretil of Spain. Two years later the firm made a $1.3 billion play for Royal Gistbrocades NV, a chemicals manufacturer catering to the pharmaceutical and food sectors. As a result of the deal, DSM gained a leading position in the global antibiotics market and also strengthened its position as a supplier of ingredients for flavors, beverages, and dairy products. DSM chairman Simon de Bree commented on the lucrative nature of the union in a 1998 *Chemical Market Reporter* article: "There are no other companies which are spread across such a range of clearly-defined technologies, pooled into a single source. We have the most complete tool box of any company in our target markets of pharma and food industry."

A third major acquisition took place in 2000 when DSM purchased California-based Catalytica Pharmaceuticals Inc. for approximately $800 million. The deal gave DSM a foothold in the U.S. fine chemicals manufacturing market and bolstered its specialty chemicals sales by 31 percent. DSM also gained access to Catalytica's pipeline of 35 new drugs that were in developmental stages. During this time period, DSM launched its "Vision 2005: Focus and Value" strategy, which was centered on transforming the company into a leading specialty chemicals firm focused on life science products and performance materials. The company appeared to be moving in a positive direction. In 2000 DSM reported record financial results—sales of EUR 8 billion and net profit of EUR 580 million.

Key Dates:

1902: The Dutch government forms the Dutch States Mines.
1929: The firm's nitrogen works, utilizing coke gas ovens, are established to produce fertilizers.
1967: DSM becomes an unquoted public limited company.
1970: By now, all coal mining operations in The Netherlands have been phased out.
1989: The company is privatized through a public listing.
1998: Royal Gist-brocades NV is acquired.
2000: The firm purchases Catalytica Pharmaceuticals Inc.
2002: DSM sells its petrochemicals business to SABIC.

DSM's 100th anniversary celebration in 2002 was marked by the sale of its petrochemicals business. The move—part of the company's Vision 2005 strategy—proved to be a significant milestone in the company's quest to become a major specialty chemicals concern. The company sold the business to Saudi Basic Industries Corporation, the largest petrochemical producer in the Middle East, for nearly $2 billion and planned to use the proceeds to make further investments in its Vision 2005 strategy. In fact, the firm's next move came in late 2002 when it announced that it planned to purchase Roche Holdings Ltd.'s vitamin and fine chemicals division for EUR 1.95 billion in order to bolster its life science unit. When complete, the deal would secure DSM as the leader in the global vitamin market.

Principal Operating Units

Life Science Products; Performance Materials; Industrial Chemicals.

Principal Competitors

BASF AF; Bayer AG; E.I. du Pont de Nemours and Company.

Further Reading

"DSM Has Formally Signed the Contract to Buy Roche's Vitamins, Carotenoids and Fine Chemicals Business," *European Cosmetic Markets,* March 2003, p. 78.
"DSM Sees Fine Chemical Sales Over 1 Bln Nfl in 1996," *AFX News,* January 18, 1996.
Firn, David, "DSM Bucks Sector Trend," *Financial Times London,* April 29, 2003, p. 29.
Milmo, Sean, "DSM to Acquire Gist-brocades in Pharma Move," *Chemical Market Reporter,* March 2, 1998, p. 1.
"Overselling, Oversold—The Privatisation of Chemicals Conglomerate DSM Required Plenty of Hype to Interest Punters," *Banker,* April 1, 1989.
Sinclair, Neil, "DSM in Record '00 Pfts But Warns of Economic Slowdown," *Chemical News & Intelligence,* February 7, 2001.
Walsh, Kerri, "DSM Swallows Catalytica's Pharmaceuticals Business," *Chemical Week,* August 9, 2000, p. 8.

—update: Christina M. Stansell

THE PAINT THAT PROTECTS.®

Dunn-Edwards Corporation

4885 52nd Place
Los Angeles, California 90040
U.S.A.
Telephone: (323) 771-3330
Toll Free: (800) 733-3866
Fax: (323) 826-2650
Web site: http://www.dunnedwards.com

Employee-Owned Company
Incorporated: 1925 as the Consolidated Wallpaper
   Corporation
Employees: 1,500
Sales: $250 million (2002)
NAIC: 325510 Paint and Coating Manufacturing

Dunn-Edwards Corporation is an employee-owned, Los Angeles-based manufacturer and distributor of paints and painting supplies (as well as wall coverings), catering mostly to painting contractors, who provide 90 percent of all sales. Dunn-Edwards supports the contractor customer in a variety of ways. It offers seminars that teach business techniques as well as offer training on how to best apply Dunn-Edwards paints. Because the product is made to certain specifications it often requires the use of certain application tools and procedures. In addition, the company provides paint contractors with customer marketing materials such as yard signs and door hangers. Dunn-Edwards also maintains a web site that provides customers with other business tools for developing job proposals, even a program to design professional-looking logos and letterhead. Geared more to the do-it-yourself customer, Dunn-Edwards stores offer many "how-to" brochures, providing useful hints about tackling a project and tips on how to determine the right kind of coating to use and the best way to apply it. Dunn-Edwards operates 75 stores in California, Arizona, Nevada, New Mexico, and Texas, with its paints formulated to withstand the climate of the Southwest. Dunn-Edwards coatings also are sold through independent dealerships. In addition to a manufacturing plant at its main Los Angeles complex, the company maintains production facilities in Tempe, Arizona, and Albuquerque, New Mex-

ico. Dunn-Edwards is one of the few paint companies to employ a computer-automated manufacturing process, the "slurry system." Rather than have workers add ingredients into paint mixing tanks by hand, this method relies on a dual computer network to ensure that a precise amount of raw materials are used, resulting in a highly consistent product. Dunn-Edwards paint has been used in many recognizable sites in the West and Southwest, including the famous HOLLYWOOD sign.

1925 Origins

According to an unproduced video script commissioned by the company, the Dunn of Dunn-Edwards was Frank "Buddy" Dunn, a wallpaper salesman who along with a colleague named Charles Smith founded what would become Dunn-Edwards in August 1925, when they bought a Los Angeles wallpaper business, the Garman and Woodson Company. Initially known as the Consolidated Wallpaper Corporation, the new company did not offer paint until 1927, prompting a change of name to Consolidated Wallpaper and Paint Corporation. The paints were supplied by Pittsburgh Plate Glass Company and sold under the Sunset Paint Company label. Consolidated later sold a paint under its own label, manufactured by the Premier Company. In 1930 Smith sold his interest in the business to a man named Robert Evans, the same year that Dunn contracted tuberculosis, forcing him to take a leave of absence. His wife, her father, and some employees struggled to keep the business afloat while he recovered, with the situation exacerbated by the effects of the Great Depression. The fortunes of the company reached their nadir in 1933 when sales plunged to just $57,000 and most of the workers gave up hope and quit to look for other employment. Both Dunn and the company he cofounded recovered, however, and in 1934 a second store was opened. Because an area competitor was doing business as the Consolidated Paint Company, the business changed its name to Dunn's Inc. in 1936. It was also during this period that paint sales surpassed wallpaper sales, a reflection of a wider cultural change, and the company took steps to establish its own paint factory, which opened in 1937. At first it was just a one-man operation, with the equipment limited to two used stone mills, an agitator, and a cooking kettle.

A friend of Dunn, Arthur C. Edwards, who would one day contribute the second half of the Dunn-Edwards name, joined

Company Perspectives:

The cornerstone of our business philosophy is a commitment to research, formulation technology, and unmatched service and support for each of our customer divisions.

the company in 1938. Born in San Francisco in 1904, Edwards came from a family familiar with the paint business. Both his father and his mother's brothers were contract painters. Edwards dropped out of school and went to work himself as a house painter at the age of 13. In his early 20s he left the contract business to work as a salesman for National Lead Co., which later became Dutch Boy Paints and was well known to major paint contractors. He became the firm's leading salesman and transferred to southern California. He was 35 when he bought Robert Evans's interest in Dunn's Inc., which at this stage consisted of just two stores and a small factory. His impact was quickly felt, as a new emphasis was placed on producing quality paints at a fair price and offering superior customer service, an approach that over the course of the next few years won over many contract painters. Having worked as a painter, Edwards knew his customer and personally tested the company's paints. Only when he was satisfied would a product be ready to market. In addition to selling a high-quality paint, he also believed in operating high-quality stores, offering excellent customer service by top-notch personnel. With the basic formula for success in place, annual sales topped $200,000 by the end of 1940. With America's entry into World War II and the resulting shortage of raw materials, the company faced a new challenge, but because Dunn's was contracted to produce government specification paint it was able to procure enough ingredients to meet the needs of its regular customers as well. Before the war was over, in 1944, the company changed its name once again, now becoming the Dunn-Edwards Corporation.

In the final year of the war, Dunn-Edwards generated more than $700,000 in revenues, but because of a postwar housing boom this level was quickly exceeded. A Glendale store was opened, and in 1947 the company topped the $1 million mark in sales. In the 1950s Dunn-Edwards adjusted to the introduction of water-based vinyl paints into the market by selling such products made for them by third-party manufacturers, before eventually manufacturing water vinyls itself. Also during this decade, the paint industry witnessed the introduction of rollers. After assigning someone to work for the Purdy Brush Company to learn both the roller and brush business, Dunn-Edwards was able to expand beyond paint and wallpaper to offer professional brushes and rollers and, later, spray equipment. During the first half of the 1950s the company also moved into the Arizona market. In 1955 annual revenues approached the $5 million level.

Changes at Mid-Century

Frank Dunn died suddenly in 1956 and several top employees were afforded a chance to purchase his stock from his widow. Only Edwards was interested, and on January 8, 1957, he became the sole owner of the business, although he continued to carry the Dunn name. In the second half of the 1950s, Dunn-Edwards opened several more stores: San Jose in 1956, Van Nuys in 1957,

and San Diego in 1959. During this time, Edwards's oldest son, Ken, a trained chemist, joined the company.

In the 1960s Dunn-Edwards became a family-owned company when 30 shares were distributed to each of the sons of Arthur Edwards. In addition to Ken Edwards, the second eldest child, Ed Edwards, who had been working as a junior high teacher, went to work for Dunn-Edwards in 1962. He was followed in 1968 by the youngest son, Jim Edwards, who joined the firm upon graduation from high school. By the middle of the 1960s the company was closing in on the $12 million mark in total revenues. During this period Dunn-Edwards moved into the northern California market with the opening of a store in Daly City in 1969. All told, the company enjoyed significant expansion during the 1960s, opening ten other stores, including Long Beach in 1961; Anaheim in 1962; Tucson, Arizona, in 1963; Phoenix, West Covina, Hollywood, and San Jose in 1965; another Tucson outlet in 1967; Colton in 1968; and Maywood in 1969.

As the 1970s began annual sales reached the $20 million level and growth in the balance sheet was further fueled by several more store openings: Tempe in 1974, Pasadena in 1975, Ventura in 1977, and Mission Hills in 1979. By the end of the decade revenues had soared past $60 million. Steady expansion continued into the 1980s, both from internal start-ups as well as by acquisition. New Dunn-Edwards store openings included: Laguna Hills in 1980; Bakersfield in 1981; Bell Road in 1983; Escondido, Cathedral City, and Huntington Beach in 1985; Modesto, Las Vegas, and El Cajon in 1986; Culver City and Salinas in 1987; Cotati in 1988; and Herperia in 1989. Dunn-Edwards moved into the markets of New Mexico and Texas in 1985 when it acquired the Wellborn Paint Manufacturing Company, based in Albuquerque, New Mexico, adding a dozen stores bearing the Wellborn name. As a result, Dunn-Edwards became a major regional paint company. In a matter of just ten years the company witnessed a tripling of its annual sales and employment topped 1,000. To support this constant growth over the years, the company's main plant in Los Angeles expanded in stages, so that by the mid-1980s it covered some 100,000 square feet. Because all the surrounding land was occupied, the company focused on being efficient in order to increase productivity and began to computerize its manufacturing operations. Also during this decade, in 1988, 50 years after buying out Robert Evans, Art Edwards died at the age of 85 following a stroke and a long battle with cancer. Control of Dunn-Edwards was now entrusted to his three sons, Ken, Ed, and Jim. In addition to coping with a change at the top, the company faced regulatory challenges when California instituted tough volatile organic compounds (VOC) standards, forcing Dunn-Edwards and other paint companies doing business in the state to reformulate their products. In the ensuing years, Dunn-Edwards took the lead among small and regional paint manufacturers to fight against overly stringent VOC-reduction legislation at both the federal and state level. Nevertheless, Dunn-Edwards maintained a record for being an environmentally responsible manufacturer, often adhering to standards that exceeded federal, state, or local regulations. It became the first major paint company to voluntarily discontinue the use of the latex paint additive ethylene glycol, which was deemed a hazardous and toxic substance in some state and federal regulations. Dunn-Edwards replaced the ingredient with the more costly propylene glycol, a nontoxic substance that had FDA approval for use in foods, beverages, medicines, and cosmetics. Dunn-Edwards also became involved in the environmentally friendly recycled paint business. In 2000 it formed a joint venture with Amazon Environmental Inc. to sell recycled latex paint in the southwestern United States.

Dunn-Edwards chemists achieved other successes in the 1990s, developing new high-quality coatings, including Endurawall, Enduraseal, and W 704 Acri-Flat. The company started off the decade with annual sales in excess of $155 million. By the end of the 1990s revenues reached the vicinity of $300 million. Traditionally highly fragmented, the paint industry experienced a wave of consolidation as the century came to a close, prompting Dunn-Edwards to take a number of measures in order to maintain its position as a major, independent regional paint company.

2000 and Beyond

In 2000, after 75 years in business, the company for the first time hired an ad agency to help it grow the business and make Dunn-Edwards into a super regional brand. Also in that year, Dunn-Edwards joined Paint America, an alliance of regional coatings manufacturers of similar size. It had been founded a year earlier by Pennsylvania-based M.A. Bruder & Sons, makers of M.A.B. Paints, and San Carlos, California-based Kelly-Moore Paint Company The alliance helped them to transcend their size and maintain their independence while gaining a national presence and the ability to bid on national jobs. Under the agreement M.A.B. would provide paint for East Coast jobs and Kelly-Moore would supply the West Coast. Soon a mid-

western paint company joined the alliance, Diamond Vogel Paints, located in Orange City, Iowa. With the subsequent addition of Dunn-Edwards, which agreed to share business in the West with Kelly-Moore, the alliance consisted of 16 manufacturing facilities and 525 stores. National customers of the alliance could now obtain high-quality coatings, made to specifically suit a region's environment, receive local support, and still enjoy the benefits of centralized ordering and bookkeeping.

In 2001 the ownership arrangement changed at Dunn-Edwards. The two younger sons of Arthur Edwards decided they wanted to sell their interest in the business. Ken Edwards, wanting to continue running the company, arranged for an employee stock ownership plan (ESOP) to raise the necessary amount of money, in excess of $100 million, needed to buy out the brothers. Almost 800 of the company's 1,500 workers invested $12.3 million and the ESOP borrowed nearly $100 million to meet the price. According to company officials the change to employee ownership had an energizing effect, as evidenced by the spike in the number of money-saving ideas that were now suggested. With a troubled national economy and even worse business conditions in California having an adverse impact on the balance sheet, Dunn-Edwards nevertheless remained well positioned for the future. It had decades of tradition and expertise to draw on, as well as the positive spirit of a workforce that now owned the business.

Principal Subsidiaries

DE Brush and Roller Company; Wellborn Paint Manufacturing Company.

Principal Competitors

Benjamin Moore and Co.; Kelly-Moore Paint Company, Inc.; The Sherwin-Williams Company.

Further Reading

"Arthur Edwards; Was Dunn-Edwards Corp. Owner (Obituary)," *American Paint & Coatings Journal,* November 21, 1988, p. 45.

Bailey, Jeff, "Tight Buyout Financing May Boost Use of Employee Stock Plans," *Wall Street Journal,* April 30, 2002, p. B6.

Reitter, Chuck, "Quality, Service and Fairness: That's Dunn-Edwards' Recipe," *American Paint & Coatings Journal,* October 10, 1988, p. 150.

—Ed Dinger

Eckes AG

Ludwig-Eckes-Allee 6
D-55268 Nieder-Olm
Germany
Telephone: (49) (6136) 35-0
Fax: (49) (6136) 35-1400
Web site: http://www.eckes-ag.de

Private Company
Incorporated: 1922 as Eckes & Co. OHG
Employees: 2,389
Sales: EUR 1.35 billion ($1.41 billion) (2002)
NAIC: 312111 Soft Drink Manufacturing; 312140
   Distilleries; 312130 Wineries

German-based Eckes AG is Europe's top manufacturer of fruit juices and the fourth ranked maker of spirits. The company's non-alcoholic beverage division produces the major brands Hohes C, Granini, and Joker, among other fruit and soft drinks. The company's brand-name liquors include Germany's leading brandies Mariacron and Chantré, and other well-known liquors such as Eckes Edelkirsch and Echter Nordhäuser, as well as the international brands Stock and Stroh. The company's alcoholic beverage division, which also markets wine and sparkling wine, is organized under the umbrella of Eckes & Stock International GmbH (ESI), which is the leading supplier of spirits in Germany, Italy, the Czech Republic, and Austria. Roughly half of the company's total sales come from alcoholic beverages and about half of all revenues are generated abroad. Eckes AG is owned and controlled by descendants of company founder Peter Eckes.

Origins as a Distillery in 1857

The history of the Eckes family firm may be traced to the middle of the 19th century. In 1857 farmer Peter Eckes I, who ran a small transportation business in the German town Nieder-Olm, near Mainz, began distilling liquor from fruit and the byproducts of wine-making (pressed grapes and wine yeast). By the early 1870s, with the construction of the first railway service between Mainz and Alzey, the company exited the transport business to focus on beverage production.

When Peter Eckes I died, he was succeeded by his son Peter Eckes II, who expanded the distillery and added a new product—precious grape oil—which he sold to manufacturers of essential oils. The younger Eckes began purchasing raw materials from wineries all over the traditional German wine country of Rhein-Hesse. During the wine-making season, Eckes employed a staff of four to work day and night, seven days a week, at the distillery.

In 1883 the Eckes facility was expanded, allowing its output of grape oil and liquor to double in volume. This facility sufficed until 1906, when Eckes acquired larger property and built a new plant, which featured Nieder-Olm's first 66-foot-tall chimney. The year before his death at age 61 in 1908, Peter Eckes II turned the business over to sons Heinrich and Jakob, who became co-owners. A third son, Richard, joined the Eckes business in 1913 but died two years later.

During World War I, German troops came though the small town, requiring food and shelter; Eckes helped supply the liquor. After the war, Jakob Eckes emerged as the driving force behind further expansion and modernization of the distillery. The Eckes brothers managed to expand the property the factory was built on through acquisitions and land swaps. A new boiler facility with an even taller chimney was erected and the factory further expanded.

A new Eckes enterprise, Eckes & Co. OHG, was founded in 1922 and was merged with the original family firm. The focus of the new company was on making consumer products, such as wine and high-quality brandy. The company hired master distiller Josef Kern, who developed the first range of Eckes brandies and other spirits. The new venture took off right away. Only two years later, alcoholic beverages, which were sold in barrels and jugs, accounted for almost two-thirds of total sales. In 1930 the company launched the first line of bottled alcoholic beverages under the Eckes brand name, which would become the cornerstone of the company's brand strategy.

The year 1931 saw Eckes's introduction of non-alcoholic beverages to its product line. When Ludwig Eckes, a son of Jakob Eckes, joined the company in October of that year, his first job was to market the company's new line of apple and grape juices. While production facilities were modernized, the company made efforts to publicize the Eckes brand among

100

Company Perspectives:

With subsidiaries in 12 European countries, and with the majority of its workforce active outside of Germany, the Eckes-Group is a European enterprise. With our ''multi-domestic'' concept in our structure and management of the group, we tap into the diversity and individual strength of Europe's countries as our potential for growth and success.

consumers. Toward that end, in 1935 Eckes participated for the first time in a trade show in Berlin's Kroll Opera, and Eckes beverages were well received. One year later, Heinrich Eckes retired and was succeeded by his son Peter. In 1939 the two juniors Ludwig and Peter Eckes became shareholders in the family enterprise. By then the company offered about 50 different alcoholic beverages for sale and employed about 70 people.

New Brands Bring Success after World War II

The year that Ludwig and Peter Eckes became company shareholders was also the year in which Hitler-led Germany marched into Poland. When Ludwig Eckes was drafted into the army, his sister Gertrud took over at the company for him. Already retired, Heinrich Eckes came back to manage the main production facilities once again. Despite all difficulties brought about by the war, the company managed to survive with employment at a minimum level. Eckes manufactured a dozen or so liquors and half a dozen other alcoholic beverages for the *Versorgungsämter*, the German government agencies that administered civilian food supplies, aw well as wine-related chemicals for the armaments industry. Since the production of spirits from wine yeast, called *Olmer Pitt*, was not restricted, the company continued to make it and distributed it among its customers at no cost. The company also continued to make limited quantities of grape and apple juice. Many male Eckes employees did not come back from the war, including Heinrich Eckes's son Richard and Jakob Eckes's son Hugo. Peter Eckes returned in 1948 and Ludwig Eckes the year after. After rationing was ended with the introduction of a new currency, the *Deutsche Mark*, in June 1948, it took about a year for the German beverage industry to return to normal operations. Eckes's production facilities were relatively unharmed by the war. However, the purchasing of raw material was difficult. By 1949, there were 50 people working for Eckes again.

The 1950s became one of the most successful chapters in the company's history. After Jakob Eckes' death, Peter and Ludwig Eckes became the sole owners and personally liable shareholders of the family business. Their first venture was the launch of a new kind of brandy. Most of the brandies sold in Germany, including the French Cognacs, had a ''hard'' taste. What was missing in the market was a mild counterpart. The new mild creation Eckes launched in 1952 was labeled Chantré—the maiden name of Ludwig Eckes's wife—and sold at a very affordable price in order to quickly gain a considerable share in the market. The strategy worked. The soft brandy became a best-seller immediately.

Beginning in 1953, Eckes's annual sales tripled for three years in a row, reaching DM 81 million in 1956. The company

had a hard time catching up with the exploding demand and was only able to satisfy it by subcontracting with other distilleries. Warehouse capacity was greatly expanded, a brand-new distillery built, and a fully automated bottling facility installed. However, the company's premises remained a construction site until the early 1960s. By 1957 Chantré was the German market leader in the brandy segment with a 30-percent market share.

As a response to the overwhelming success of just one brand product, Eckes management decided to radically reduce the company's remaining line of alcoholic beverages. Only four out of 13 products survived: the cherry liquor called Eckes Edelkirsch; a herb liquor known as 1857er Laurentiner-Klosterlikör; and two products under the Eckes label, apricot fruit liquor and Curacao. At the same time, the company invested in the expansion of its non-alcoholic beverages branch. Ludwig Eckes was the driving force behind the introduction of the company's first orange juice in 1958. It was named Hohes C (High C), indicating the high levels of vitamin C it contained. Hohes C, positioned as the orange juice that supplied natural vitamin C to the whole family, turned out to be another instant success. In 1959 the company launched a new ''naturally cloudy'' apple juice called Dr. Koch's and named after professor Julius Koch, a fruit juice expert who was hired to head Eckes' newly-founded Institute for Beverage Research. The launch of the two new brand products was backed by a massive advertising campaign, which focused on the health benefits of drinking these fruit juices.

In 1961 Eckes was able to take over a small regional brandy manufacturer: Oppenheim-based Klosterbrennerei Mariacron. The brand Mariacron was launched nationally the following year. Ten years later, annual sales of Mariacron would surpass those generated by Chantré for the first time. Another successful product launch of the time was ZINN 40, a clear spirit made from wine, which competed successfully in the German market for many decades. On the soft liquor front, Eckes Edelkirsch became Germany's number one fruit liquor in the mid-1960s.

To secure raw material supplies for the new consumer brands, the company established its own import organization and acquired shares in manufacturers of fruit juice concentrates and wine distillates, some in the United States and Italy. In addition, Eckes set up new operations, such as a plantation to grow varieties of tropical fruit in Brazil, and a plant for making apple juice in Argentina.

New Company Structure in the 1960s–70s

In 1963 the next generation of the Eckes family—Ludwig's daughter Heidrun and son Harald, and Peter's sons Michael and Peter Eugen—became shareholders in the company. The company's legal form was changed into Eckes & Co. KG. Ten years later, the seniors stepped back from their leading roles in executive management. However, in order to protect the company from the seemingly inescapable fate of many family enterprises—weakness in leadership because of family disputes, a diminished capital base, or even disintegration of profits because of financial demands of family members—they established a new legal structure. Their main goal was to secure the company's future growth by strictly limiting the family's share in profits that could be taken out of the business.

Ludwig and Peter Eckes themselves had followed such a rule, never taking more than 10 percent of the company's

Key Dates:

1857: Peter Eckes I starts distilling brandy from the by-products of wine-making.
1922: Eckes & Co. OHG is established.
1930: The company launches the first bottled brandy under the Eckes brand name.
1952: The soft brandy Chantré is launched in Germany.
1958: Eckes introduces the orange juice Hohes C.
1962: Another national brandy is launched under the Mariacron label.
1973: The Eckes family trusts take over 30 percent in the company.
1991: The company is transformed into the family-owned joint-stock corporation Eckes AG; acquisition spree ensues.
2001: Eckes takes over the French Joker group and the Finnish Oy Marli AB.

profits, plus a sum to cover their taxes. As a result, the Eckes-enterprise was well-funded. The company's own financial assets accounted for roughly half of the total assets on the Eckes balance sheet. In the summer of 1973 the two senior partners transferred 30 percent of the Eckes parent company, Eckes & Co. KG, into family trusts, kept a small amount of shares for themselves, and distributed the rest among family members. The company's legal form was changed again to Eckes & Co. KGmbH. However, to give every family member an opportunity to learn through their own entrepreneurial activity, a number of Eckes subsidiaries, many of them abroad, were entrusted to younger family members, who were then solely responsible for their management.

The second step was the establishment of a governing body to oversee the management of the Eckes family enterprise. The newly established *Stiftungsbeirat,* the advisory board for the family foundations, was comprised of members of the Eckes family as well as some non-family members. This group then elected the executive management board. The number of Eckes family members was limited to half of the members of each body. The two senior partners Ludwig and Peter Eckes became members of the *Stiftungsbeirat,* while the juniors Harald Eckes-Chantré, and Michael and Peter Eugen Eckes became the first members of the company's executive management board. The Swiss manager Max Rüegger became the board's first chairman. Ludwig and Peter Eckes stayed actively involved in the family business after they officially retired. Besides being members of the *Stiftungsbeirat,* Ludwig Eckes lobbied for the company and the German spirits industry as the president of the Bundesverband der Deutschen Spirituosen-Industrie, the national trade association of German distillers, while Peter Eckes represented the company in Germany's trade association for fruit juice manufacturers. Ludwig Eckes died in 1984, Peter Eckes in 1987.

Diversification and Acquisitions in the 1980s–90s

By the beginning of the 1980s, Eckes was one of Germany's leading manufacturers of alcoholic and non-alcoholic bever-

ages. The next two decades were characterized by the diversification of the company's product lines and later by international expansion, mainly through acquisitions. Diversification began in the late 1970s, when Eckes acquired shares in a German sparkling wine maker and a Californian vineyard, and ventured into beverage vending machines with a manufacturer of coffee concentrate as a business partner. In the 1980s the company acquired Lorenz + Lihn Obst-Edelerzeugnisse GmbH, the leading German manufacturer of fruit jams for diabetics, and Schneekoppe GmbH, a manufacturer of a line of health food products. However, none of these activities became a major priority and would be discontinued in the mid-1990s. Rather, the company took the strategic path of capitalizing on their major brand names by extending the respective product lines.

The Hohes C orange juice was also sold in two other versions—one with pulp and one with calcium. Later the Hohes C range was further expanded to include apple and multivitamin juice, as well as a number of fruit juice blends. Dr. Koch's apple juice was complemented by the launch of several variations, including Dr. Koch's Trink 10, a multivitamin fruit juice; Dr. Koch's Plus E, a vitamin E-enriched fruit juice; Dr. Koch's Minikal, a line of six different dietary fruit nectars; Dr. Koch's Goldklarer Apfelsaft, a clear apple juice; Dr. Koch's Trink 10 junior, a multivitamin juice for kids; and Dr. Koch's Vital, a fruit beverage for people age 50 and older.

Line extensions within the company's major alcoholic beverage brands included Eckes Edelkirsch Cream, Mariacron Premium, and Cognac Chantré, among others. Besides the extension of major brands, Eckes launched a number of other products under different names, including several fruit juices, non-alcoholic soft drinks, liquors and alcoholic drinks, some of them especially designed for the needs of the restaurant and catering industry.

During the 1980s, Eckes had already acquired a number of distilleries, such as the German Weinbrennerei Stromburg, Siegert & Co. and the Italian Distillerie Sanley DI. SA. After the two German states were reunited in 1990, and after two independent divisions for alcoholic and non-alcoholic beverages had been founded in the year after, the company bought East Germany's largest distiller Nordbrand Nordhausen in the state of Thuringia in 1991. With a hefty investment in the new subsidiary and its major brand, the clear liquor Nordhäuser Doppelkorn soon became Germany's market leader in its niche market for *Korn,* a popular clear spirit. In 1995 Eckes acquired two internationally renowned distillers, Italian Stock S.p.A. and Austrian Sebastian Stroh Ges. m.b.H. In addition, the company established distribution partnerships to market its alcoholic beverages in France, Luxembourg, Austria, Hungary, the Czech Republic, the Baltic, and Russia. On the other hand, Eckes also took on the distribution of manufacturers' brands, such the international sparkling wine brand Freixenet. However, the market for liquors began stagnating in the 1990s. Consequently, the company refocused its growth strategy on non-alcoholic beverages.

Major opportunities for growth in that market were mainly seen beyond Germany's borders. Therefore, a series of international acquisitions began in 1993, when Eckes took over the Hungarian fruit beverage maker Sió Nektar Kft. One year later the company was able to acquire a majority stake in its top German competitor, Granini, which was merged with Eckes' non-alcoholic beverage division. The new company—in which Eckes held a 74-percent stake, while the previous owner, the German Melitta group, kept the remaining share—was named Eckes-Granini GmbH & Co. KG. In 1995 Eckes formed Eckes-Granini (Suisse) S.A., a joint venture with the Swiss Henniez S.A. to manufacture and market brand-name fruit juices in Switzerland. Three years later Eckes took over Les Vergers d'Alsace SA, a major manufacturer of fruit juices in France.

Two more major acquisitions made Eckes Europe's leading manufacturer of fruit juices. In 2001 the company took over the French Joker group, the country's leading producer of branded fruit juices. In the same year Eckes bought Finnish beverage manufacturer Oy Marli AB. In order to mobilize the necessary cash for additional acquisitions in the European non-alcoholic beverage market, Eckes put its alcoholic beverage division up for sale in October 2002. However, when it became clear that the package deal would not bring the intended results, Eckes abandoned the idea. Looking ahead, the company was planning to revive domestic sales of its Chantré brand and to further expand the company's non-beverage arm into other parts of Europe, such as the Mediterranean, Scandinavia, the Baltic states, and Russia. When confronted with the management decision to sell off Eckes AG's alcoholic beverage division in late 2002, the chairman of the company's employee council at company headquarters reportedly shouted: "Eckes without 'Eckes Edelkirsch,' without 'Chantré' and without 'Mariacron'—that is like Volkswagen without cars!"

Principal Subsidiaries

Eckes-Granini GmbH & Co. KG; Eckes-Granini Deutschland GmbH; Eckes-Granini France S.A. (France); Joker S.A. (France); Les Vergers d'Alsace S.A. (France); Oy Marli Ab (Finland); Eckes-Granini Nordic Oy Ab (Finland); Eckes-Granini Ibérica S.A. (Spain); Sió-Eckes Kft. (Hungary); Eckes-Granini Austria GmbH (Austria); Eckes-Granini (Suisse) S.A. (Switzerland); Aronia S.A. (Poland); OOO Eckes-Granini Rus (Russia); Eckes & Stock International GmbH; Eckes Spirituosen & Wein GmbH; Nordbrand Nordhausen GmbH; Stock Plzen a.s. (Czech Republic); Stock S.p.A. (Italy); Stock Austria Gesellschaft m.b.H. (Austria); Stock Trade d.o.o. (Slovakia).

Principal Competitors

PepsiCo, Inc.; The Coca-Cola Company; Cadbury Schweppes plc; The Procter & Gamble Company; Rauch Group; Allied Domecq PLC; Bacardi Limited; Diageo plc; Pernod Ricard; Henkell&Soehnlein Sektkellereien KG; Berentzen Group.

Further Reading

Dohm, Horst, "Ausgegliederte Gesellschaften dienen als unternehmerisches Erprobungsfeld," *Frankfurter Allgemeine Zeitung*, August 11, 1995, p. 17.
"Eckes: Das Wachstum schwächt sich ab," *Frankfurter Allgemeine Zeitung*, July 2, 1993, p. 18.
"Eckes stemmt sich gegen den Trend," *Lebensmittel Zeitung*, May 17, 1996, p. 18.
Giersberg, Georg, "Eckes wird abstinent," *Frankfurter Allgemeine Sonntagszeitung*, October 13, 2002, p. 39.
Pilar, Gabriel v., "Hoffnung auf Frechling und Co.," *Lebensmittel Zeitung*, October 27, 2000, p. 52.
Vossen, Manfred, "Eckes-Granini treibt Europageschäft massiv voran," *Lebensmittel Zeitung*, November 30, 2001, p. 14.
Vossen, Manfred, "Für Eckes haben Fruchtgetränke weiter Priorität," *Lebensmittel Zeitung*, May 16, 2003, p. 14.

—Evelyn Hauser

SOUTHERN CALIFORNIA
EDISON®

An *EDISON INTERNATIONAL®* Company

Edison International

2244 Walnut Grove Avenue
Rosemead, California 91770
U.S.A.
Telephone: (626) 302-1212
Toll Free: (800) 302-2517
Fax: (626) 302-2517
Web site: http://www.edison.com

Public Company
Incorporated: 1909 as Southern California Edison
    Company
Employees: 15,038
Sales: $11.4 billion
Stock Exchanges: New York
Ticker Symbol: EIX
NAIC: 22111 Hydroelectric Power Generation; 221112
    Fossil Fuel Electric Power Generation; 221113
    Nuclear Electric Power Generation; 221119 Other
    Electric Power Generation; 221121 Electric Bulk
    Power Transmission and Control; 221122 Electric
    Power Distribution; 551112 Offices of Other Holding
    Companies

Edison International, formerly known as SCEcorp, acts as a
holding company for Southern California Edison, one of the
largest public utilities in the United States. Edison's other
subsidiaries include: Edison Mission Energy, an independent
power producer; Edison Capital, a unit that provides financing
for energy-related projects and affordable housing; Edison Enterprises, a firm that oversees Edison's International's retail
companies; and Edison O&M Services, a company that offers
services related to increasing power plant efficiency. With operations in nine countries, Edison International maintains a power
generation portfolio of over 28,000 megawatts and has assets
exceeding $33 billion. California's deregulation and subsequent
energy crisis nearly forced the company into bankruptcy in
2001. Edison International avoided insolvency by focusing on
paying off debt and recovering costs related to the crisis.

Regional Growth Sparks the Need for Power

In the first three decades of the 20th century, the population
of California grew four-and-a-half times as quickly as the total
population of the United States. This growth meant a giant leap
in the area's need for power, a need that was reflected in the
expansion of public utilities there. By 1909 Edison Electric
Company of Los Angeles was already a sizable utility concern.
Over several years, Los Angeles Edison had acquired and
consolidated the generating and distributing capabilities of 13
pioneer utility companies in and around Los Angeles. Southern
California Edison was organized in August 1909 to acquire all
of Edison's properties. In the next several years, Edison made
only one minor acquisition, the Downey Light, Power and
Water Company in 1914, and rather than expanding, it concentrated primarily on developing the existing electric properties
and eliminating its gas properties, which were bringing in only
about 6 percent of the company's gross revenues.

The most important expansion in Edison's early years occurred in 1917, when the company acquired all of the assets and
business of Pacific Light & Power Corporation and a controlling interest in Mount Whitney Power & Electric Company.
Pacific was a rapidly growing power company controlled by
H.E. Huntington and Los Angeles Railway Company and operating in the same service area as Edison. Mount Whitney was
operating in the nearby agricultural area of Tulare County and
had no competitors there. These acquisitions left Edison firmly
in control of the electricity business in the region. Also in 1917,
the city of Los Angeles purchased Edison's distribution system
inside the city, and began to buy power wholesale from Edison
for its municipal plant.

By adding the facilities formerly belonging to Pacific, Edison more than doubled its generating capacity. Shortly after the
acquisition, Edison embarked on a decade-long construction
project in the area of Pacific's Big Creek hydroelectric station,
transforming it from a plant capable of generating about 63,700
kilowatts of power to a huge system that included 3 reservoirs, 8
concrete dams, and 41 miles of tunnels, and that could generate
more than 373,000 kilowatts of power. Through 1928, the
area's population was growing so rapidly that Edison had no
problem using this greatly increased capacity. Because overall

Company Perspectives:

Moving beyond the basics, while never losing focus of our core strengths. That's a key business value for Edison International. And because nothing in today's energy, financing, and retail service markets remains static, Edison International pursues opportunity wherever it can. Change can be good. Progress is better.

use of electricity was accelerating, especially in industry and agriculture, Edison found no need to seek new business.

Edison's gross revenues grew each year during the 1920s, and as the 1930s began the company continued to do well in spite of a general downturn in industry. By the end of 1930, revenues had reached $41 million, and the balance Edison had achieved between hydroelectric and steam generation helped protect the company against fluctuating earnings due to weather problems or fuel-price hikes. For instance, when low-water conditions hindered hydroelectric generation, emphasis could be shifted to steam. In addition, Edison's steam plants were capable or running on either oil or natural gas, so costs could be minimized by taking advantage of price fluctuations between the two types of fuel. The drop in industrial power use was largely offset by great increases in residential use. More households during this period were beginning to use electric appliances such as washers, refrigerators, space heaters, and water heaters. Agricultural use of electricity also was rising quickly. Pumping plants for irrigation, previously powered by other means, were converted to electricity, and by 1930 these irrigation plants accounted for roughly one-eighth of Edison's total connected load. In 1930 the company changed its name to Southern California Edison Company Ltd. The "Ltd." was dropped in 1947.

Edison's output, revenues, and service area continued to expand through the 1930s. In 1930 construction began on the Boulder Dam—later renamed Hoover Dam—project. Built on the Colorado River about 300 miles northeast of Los Angeles, the dam's power stations initially were capable of generating nearly 750,000 kilowatts of electricity. The dam was constructed and run by the U.S. government, and contractual agreements were made with several power companies and municipal systems concerning the use of the power it generated. Edison's share of the power was to be 7.2 percent of the total output, although the company was obligated to absorb up to 14.4 percent more of the total if the states of Nevada and Arizona did not use their shares. The company spent more to purchase Boulder Dam power than it did to generate power at its most efficient steam plant.

Postwar Expansion

Population growth of Edison's service area continued to outpace by far that of the United States as a whole in the 1940s, increasing by 80 percent compared to the national rate of 15 percent. This statistic was reflected in the growth of company revenues. While the national average during this decade for privately owned electric utilities was an 83 percent increase in gross operating revenues, Edison's figure was 135 percent.

While Edison's rates continued to be significantly lower than the national average through the first half of the decade, this situation began to change over the next several years as the national average began to drop rapidly. One reason for the company's increase in electric rates relative to the national average was an increasing emphasis in the post-World War II years on steam-generated power, which cost the company up to twice as much to produce as hydroelectric.

By the early 1950s Edison was the fifth-largest investor-owned power company in the United States. Its service area covered 18,500 square miles and contained about 225 communities with a combined population of almost three million. The company's customers numbered more than one million by 1952, twice the count for 1940, and were very diverse in nature. Of the power sales in its territory, 25 percent was to industrial concerns, 34 percent to residential, 10 percent to agricultural, and 21 percent to commercial. The region had proven in many ways to be nearly ideal for a utility company: the climate was excellent, agriculture was widespread and booming, and industries were thriving and greatly varied. The only major drawback of the area seemed to be the competition provided by cheap and readily available natural gas, which could be used for many appliances.

From the end of World War II through 1953, Edison spent about $500 million on construction, and by 1954 the company's 24 hydroelectric plants and five steam stations had a capacity of 1.6 million kilowatts. Most of the postwar expansion went toward steam generating which, while more expensive than hydroelectricity, was not hampered by water shortages. The largest cost increases the company experienced during this period were due to jumps in the prices of gas and oil—required to run the steam plants—that occurred during the Korean War. Still, Edison's sources of power were both diverse and geographically separated, thereby spreading the risk of property damage and offering protection from droughts. Half of the company power came from its steam plants in the Los Angeles area; 35 percent came from its own hydroelectric properties fed by the western slopes of the Sierra Nevadas; and 15 percent was purchased, mainly from the Hoover Dam.

Edison's revenues nearly doubled during the 1960s, rising gradually from $369 million in 1960 to $721 million in 1970. The company continued to stay ahead of most others within its industry in such statistics as net income, revenues, and kilowatt-hour sales, largely due to the fact that California's population continued to grow faster than any other state's. Jack K. Horton, an important figure at Edison during this decade, became president in 1959, chief executive officer in 1965, and chairman of the board in 1968.

New Trends in the 1960s–70s

The period from 1960 to 1968 was defined by three trends: the acquisition of several smaller utilities, a shift from oil to natural gas to fuel the steam plants, and a gradual decrease of electricity rates. All three of these trends ceased after 1968. Edison's minor burst of expansion during the period included the 1962 acquisition of all the utilities—gas, electric, and fresh-water services—on Santa Catalina, an island about 25 miles off the coast of southern California; the 1963 acquisition of California Electric Power Company; the purchase in 1965 of Desert

Key Dates:

1909: Southern California Edison is organized to acquire all of Edison Electric Company's properties.

1917: The firm acquires Pacific Light & Power Corporation and a controlling interest in Mount Whitney Power & Electric Company.

1930: The company changes its name to Southern California Edison Company Ltd.

1980: Edison begins to focus on alternative and renewable energy.

1988: SCEcorp is formed as a holding company for Edison and new subsidiary The Mission Group.

1996: SCEcorp changes its name to Edison International; deregulation begins in California's energy sector.

2001: Edison faces bankruptcy during its home state's energy crisis.

Electric Cooperative, Inc., which involved 2,600 customers and 600 miles of distribution line near Twentynine Palms, California; and the 1966 purchase of most of the physical assets belonging to Valley Power Company, which served a small number of Nevada customers.

The shift from oil to natural gas is reflected in the following fuel-mix statistics. In 1960 almost half of Edison's power output was fueled by natural gas, more than one-third by oil, and the rest primarily hydroelectric. By 1968 the balance was 74 percent gas and only 12 percent oil. This trend began to reverse itself in the next couple of years, however, as the availability of natural gas decreased. By 1970 when the share fueled by natural gas was down to 56 percent, the company began to enter long-term oil supply contracts in anticipation of this reversal continuing.

Utility costs per unit of power generally declined well into the 1960s, and accordingly Edison's rates dropped by 16 percent from 1960 to 1968. In the late 1960s and early 1970s, however, the company saw huge jumps in the costs of fuel, construction, and interest. Also, around this time both public and government agencies started to become more concerned about the environment, and utility companies faced greater difficulties getting approval for the construction of new power plants. This was especially true for Edison because of its location in the southern California "smog belt." By the early 1970s approval from roughly 30 different agencies was required before a new plant could be built; and in 1972 a referendum was overwhelmingly passed requiring any who wanted to undertake major development along the California coastline to first seek approval from the California Coastal Zone Construction Commission. One way in which Edison dealt with California's environmental regulation was to build out of state. Two coal-burning plants were started in joint ventures with other companies. The two plants, located in New Mexico and southern Nevada, accounted for 12 percent of the company's total capacity in 1973. By 1973 Edison ranked behind only New York's Consolidated Edison, Chicago's Commonwealth Edison, and the Southern Company of Atlanta, Georgia in gross revenues for electric companies, bringing in nearly $1 billion. The com-

pany had 7.5 million customers in a 50,000 square-mile area, and more than $3 billion in assets.

The oil embargo of 1973 created difficulties for many utility companies, including Edison, and the price of electricity increased throughout the United States. Excluding increases in the cost of fuel, however, Edison's rates rose more slowly than the industry average through the remainder of the 1970s. Edison's electricity prices went up about 6.7 percent annually, while prices nationally grew at the rate of about 9 percent per year.

Alternative and Renewable Energy Sources: 1980s

In 1980 William R. Gould became chairman and chief executive officer of Edison, marking an important change in approach for the company. Gould had joined Edison in 1948 as a mechanical engineer, working his way up to vice-president in 1963, senior vice-president in 1973, and president in 1978. Within a few months of being named chairman in 1980, Gould unveiled a plan calling for a major commitment to alternative and renewable energy sources in the coming years. In 1981 oil, gas, and coal supplied the fuel for 70 percent of the company's 15.5-million kilowatt capacity. Under Gould's plan, however, one-third of the company's new power needs during the 1980s would come from nontraditional sources such as solar, geothermal, and wind power. The plan also entailed increasing the purchase of alternative forms of power from third-party sources, thereby decreasing the company's reliance on power from large, centralized generating stations, which were no longer as economical to run as they once were. In 1980 Edison began generating 3,000 kilowatts with a wind-powered turbine at San Gorgino Pass near Palm Springs, California. In 1981 it purchased the steam required to produce about 10,000 kilowatts of power from a geothermal well operated by Union Oil Company of California. Construction on a pilot solar facility was begun in the Mojave Desert that year as well.

In 1984 Howard P. Allen became chief executive officer of Edison, inheriting Gould's expansive network of energy suppliers, which together represented nine different sources of power. Although not all of these sources were as cost-efficient as oil, this diversified approach made the company less vulnerable to the volatile world oil market. By 1985 oil accounted for only 2 percent of the company's fuel needs, down from 60 percent ten years earlier. In the mid-1980s, the emergence of cogeneration by nonutility companies began to erode the earnings of some electric utilities, including Edison.

One way that Allen and Edison battled this trend was by reducing the rates charged to large industry, which accounted for about one-fifth of Edison's revenues, in order to encourage them to stay within Edison's system. Another strategy employed by the company was to start its own cogenerating subsidiary, Mission Energy.

By 1987 Edison was the second-largest electric-generating company in the United States, earning a company record $789 million that year. One-tenth of its power came from cogeneration and alternative sources, and 20 percent came from the San Onofre nuclear facility.

In 1988 SCEcorp was formed as the holding company for Edison, and a newly formed subsidiary called The Mission

Group. The Mission Group—eventually known as Edison Mission Energy—in turn became a holding company for SCEcorp's nonutility subsidiaries. Edison stockholders received shares of SCEcorp stock, and operations continued essentially as before. Also in 1988 a merger was proposed between SCEcorp and San Diego Gas & Electric Company. The merger was approved by the shareholders of both companies the following year, but after two years of review it was rejected by the California Public Utilities Commission (CPUC).

Howard Allen retired in 1990, and was replaced as chairman and chief executive of both SCEcorp and Edison by John Bryson. Bryson, a former head of the CPUC, had joined Edison in 1984 as chief financial officer. Company records were set in 1990 in both earnings and revenue. Two trends that had begun in the 1980s had continued into the 1990s: the movement toward cogeneration continued to the degree that 57 percent of the new generating capacity built in the United States in 1990 was built by nonutility companies; and the trend toward zero consumption of oil as a generating fuel reduced SCEcorp's oil use to three million barrels in 1990 from a peak of 58 million barrels in 1977.

Deregulation Leads to Crisis: Mid-1990s and Beyond

SCEcorp and Southern California Edison traditionally benefited from the advantages of their location; advantages that were grounded in demographic, economic, and environmental factors. Although California's rate of growth did not assure the health of its utility companies forever, SCEcorp's willingness to adapt to the demands of the global economy and the global environment appeared to put it in an envied position. This would soon change however, as future deregulation promised to significantly change the utility landscape in California.

Before deregulation took place, Edison and its subsidiaries were focused on expanding business. The company's financing arm, Edison Capital, began investing in affordable housing projects and in 1993 started to provide financing to the Dutch national rail authority. Edison Mission Energy entered the international scene when it became involved in the Roosecote project in England. This unit also branched out into Australia and Northern Wales and by 1997 had interests in Indonesia, Italy, Turkey, the Philippines, and Thailand.

To prepare for deregulation, Edison began to sell off its oil and gas power plants in 1996 due to changes in laws that made it illegal for utilities to own both power generation and distribution operations. That year the company adopted Edison International as its new corporate moniker and with a new name in place, continued to restructure its operations successfully.

California's market opened up to competition in 1998, which marked the beginning of a chaotic period for California's citizens, the state's utilities companies, the government, and investors around the world. Rates were frozen that year, which proved to be problematic for Edison. From December 1999 into 2001, the company experienced a 900 percent rise in its power purchasing costs as demand increased. According to an August 2000 *Los Angeles Business Journal* article, there had been excess capacity in the industry during the mid-1990s. "Utilities were wary about adding capacity because of uncertainty about deregulation," the article claimed. "That didn't matter during

the recession of the early to mid-1990s. But since the economy has come roaring back, demand has soared." This demand eventually began to outweigh supply, leaving many California residents in the dark.

Edison and its competitors stood in an unfavorable position. The public utilities had to purchase additional power, but were unable to pass on those costs to customers due to the rate freeze. From May 2000 to June 2001, the cost of unregulated wholesale power greatly exceeded what Southern California Edison collected from its customers. By 2001, costs had risen to $4.7 billion, and the company faced impending bankruptcy. In January of that year, the state began purchasing power for Southern California Edison so it could continue to supply its customers.

In October 2001, Edison reached an agreement with the CPUC in which it was allowed to recover $3.6 billion in costs by passing along a surcharge to its power customers. The plan was highly controversial and met with opposition from The Utility Reform Network (TURN), a consumer group that claimed the surcharge violated California's deregulation laws. The case was slated to go before the California Supreme Court in the summer of 2003.

During 2002, Edison focused on reducing debt and recovering costs related to the energy crisis. Meanwhile, the CPUC continued to revamp certain aspects of California's utilities industry to encourage infrastructure investment in an attempt to head off any future crises. Southern California Edison resumed its purchasing function in early 2003 and Edison planned to restore its dividend payment to shareholders—a payment it had made from the start of its history until it was suspended in 2000—by year end. Edison's financial turnaround however, was contingent upon success in the aforementioned case.

Principal Subsidiaries

Southern California Edison; Edison Mission Energy; Edison Capital; Edison Enterprises; Edison O&M Services.

Principal Competitors

Mirant Corporation; PG&E Corporation; Sempra Energy.

Further Reading

Brower, Derek, "Power Meltdown," *Petroleum Economist*, April 2001, p. 49

"Edison International," *Institutional Investor*, May 1998, p. 2.

Hayes, Elizabeth, "Edison Can't Cash in on Increased Demand for Power," *Los Angeles Business Journal*, August 21, 2000, p. 7.

"One of California's Leading Utilities," *Barron's*, May 23, 1932.

"Outages Loom as Edison Says 'Can't Pay'," *United Press International*, January 16, 2001.

Palazzo, Anthony, "Reinvigorated Edison Planning to Resume Dividend Payments," *Los Angeles Business Journal*, January 27, 2003, p. 26.

Palmeri, Christopher, "Time to Cut This Utility's Cord?," *Business Week*, July 9, 2001.

"Southern California's Edison," *Barron's*, March 10, 1952.

—Robert R. Jacobson
—update: Christina M. Stansell

Electricity Generating Authority of Thailand (EGAT)

53 Charan Sanitwong Road, Bang Kruai
Nonthaburi 11130
Thailand
Telephone: (2) 436-0000
Fax: (2) 436-4723
Web site: http://www.egat.co.th

State-Owned Company
Founded: 1969
Employees: 28,543
Sales: $629 million (2002)
NAIC: 221111 Hydroelectric Power Generation; 221112 Fossil Fuel Electric Power Generation; 221119 Other Electric Power Generation

The Electricity Generating Authority of Thailand (EGAT) operates as a state-owned enterprise involved in the generation and transmission of energy throughout Thailand, selling wholesale power to both the Metropolitan Electricity Authority and the Provincial Electricity Authority. The group produces over 15,000 megawatts (MW) of electricity each year and purchases additional power from independent power producers and small power producers. EGAT maintains a number of hydroelectric, thermal, and alternative energy facilities and offers a variety of energy-related services. Controversy and debate have surrounded the state-owned entity as it works to restructure in preparation for its privatization. The Thai government plans to launch a public offering for EGAT, tentatively slated for 2004.

Background

Thailand's use of electricity dates back to 1887 with the creation of the Siam Electric Company. The firm used steam from burning rice husks to provide power to its customers, a method used through the 1950s. The Thai region proved to have abundant natural resources that could be used for fuel, including rice husks, wood, and bagasse, the dry pulp that remains after sugar cane has been harvested. Hydroelectric resources, lignite, oil, and natural gas were also available in the region but were not utilized until later in the 20th century.

The energy industry in Thailand did not experience much growth until after World War II, when demand for electricity began to rise. The nation's supply during the 1940s and into the 1950s was unreliable at best, prompting the government to take action. In 1958, the Thai Ministry of the Interior enacted the Metropolitan Electricity Authority Act, which in effect established the Metropolitan Electricity Authority (MEA), an amalgamation of the Bangkok Electricity Authority and the Samsen Royal Electricity Authority. The MEA generated and sold electric power until 1961, when its generation capabilities were taken over by the Yanhee Electricity Authority, which had been created in 1959 to exploit hydroelectric power in the area.

During the 1960s, the need for power increased significantly in the Thailand. The region's first major oil-fired plant—the North Bangkok Power Station—was developed in 1961. This was followed by the creation of the Phumiphon Dam, a hydroelectric generating facility that began operation in 1964. Regional power companies struggled to keep pace with demand and it soon became apparent that major expansion was necessary to avoid a collapse in Thailand's energy sector.

Keeping Pace with Demand: 1960s–80s

Power shortages prompted the government to act, and on May 1, 1969, the Electricity Generating Authority of Thailand (EGAT) was created. This state-owned entity was formed by combining the assets of Yanhee Electricity and two other regional concerns, Lignite Authority and Northeastern Electricity Authority. During the 1970s, EGAT used fuel oil and hydro power to supply the region. It added several new facilities to its holdings including the oil-fired South Bangkok Thermal Power Plant in 1970 and the country's second hydroelectric plant at the Sirikit Dam on the Mae Nam Nan tributary in 1974. The company also began to rely on lignite as oil prices started to rise.

Acting under the 1978–85 power generation development plan, EGAT continued to construct new power plants. Thailand's third hydroelectric plant at Ban Pho was launched during this time and was used not only for power, but for irrigation and flood control. A lignite-fueled plant also began operation at Mae Mo and was generating 825 MW by 1987. By this time, Thai-

Company Perspectives:

EGAT's main mission is to run efficient electricity business by providing and transmitting an efficient, reliable, and reasonably priced electric power supply to meet the country's demand in an environmentally responsible way. In light of the country's electricity industry reform, EGAT's immediate mission is also to restructure its organization to further improve efficiency and be prepared for its new role as the center that manages and controls the national grid in a more competitive market.

land's power industry was made up of three government-owned concerns: EGAT; MEA, which distributed power to Bangkok and the surrounding areas; and the Provincial Electricity Authority (PEA), which distributed power outside of Bangkok.

During the 1980s, the Thai economy and electricity consumption grew at a rapid clip. EGAT continued to push for the development of new hydro-electric facilities but opposition from environmental groups threatened to thwart the company's plans and tarnish its image. In 1988, EGAT's Nam Choan dam project was terminated by the government, marking the first time that a major EGAT project failed to reach fruition. That year proved disastrous for the firm. A drought during the first part of the year took its toll on hydrogeneration, cutting production by nearly 25 percent. Then, typhoon Gay wreaked havoc on Thailand in November and floods caused significant damage to country's southern provinces and to the dams there. The storm was the worst to hit the region in 35 years, killing 650 residents and injuring thousands. To make matters worse for EGAT, the flooding of its hydro systems caused dangerous mudslides and sent thousands of logs—cut by loggers—careening into villages. In September 1989, EGAT announced it would curtail domestic hydroelectric power development but set plans in motion to expand capacity in Laos along the Nam Theun River. This decision drew further criticism from environmentalists, who claimed the dams would destroy crucial tropical evergreen forests and have devastating environmental effects on Laos.

Changes in the 1990s

The landscape of Thailand's energy sector began to change in the 1990s. Thailand began entertaining the idea of privatizing a large portion of its state-owned entities, including those in its energy sector. In 1992, the government created the National Energy Policy Council (NEPC). This council amended the EGAT Act of 1968 in order to end EGAT's longstanding monopoly on power generation, which in turn allowed for the private production and sale of electricity. The NEPC also laid the groundwork to allow independent power producers (IPPs) and small power producers (SPPs) into the Thai market.

In response to these actions, EGAT created the Electricity Generating Public Company Ltd. (EGCO) in 1992. This subsidiary generated power and then sold it to EGAT. In 1994, EGAT gained partial independence from the government and was able to sell electricity, purchase fuel, and purchase electricity from IPPs and other countries for the first time. By 1996, the govern-

ment was convinced that privatization would be necessary for energy sector reform, for the stability of the Thai economy, and for overall success in the new millennium. Certain members of EGAT management and its trade union—comfortable with the status quo—were not as optimistic about the changes and fought against placing EGAT in the hands of foreign investors.

Driving the government's desire for reform were several factors. Not only would it reduce its role in the energy industry and provide a new source of state revenues, privatization had the potential to increase overall efficiency of the energy sector as well as promote competition. Thailand also believed that making EGAT a public company would ensure future energy availability, encourage private investment, and lead to a greater focus on energy conservation and environmental issues. The downturn in the Asian economy during the late 1990s also forced the issue of privatization. Thailand's economic growth slowed dramatically and energy consumption dropped. The government was forced to launch a major cost restructuring effort which in turn put pressure on EGAT to restructure and adopt cost efficient business practices.

An Uncertain Future

The process of privatization along with opening the energy sector to competition continued in the early years of the new millennium. During 2000, the Ratchaburi Electricity Generating Holding Company Ltd. (RATCH) was created as part of EGAT's privatization plan. Ratchaburi used funds from its public offering—EGAT retained a majority interest—to purchase the Ratchaburi power plant. In 2002, EGAT transferred full control of the plant to RATCH, making it the largest IPP in Thailand.

EGAT dealt with higher oil prices and oversupply in 2000 and 2001, which threatened to prolong its transition into a public entity. The downturn forced EGAT to put off purchasing electricity from several IPPs. During 2002, however, the Thai economy and electricity demand began to rebound. In October of that year, Sitthiporn Ratanopas took over as governor of EGAT. At the same time, Prime Minister Thaksin Shinawatra created the Ministry of Energy to oversee the country's energy holdings. EGAT had spent its history under control of the Prime Minister and anticipated that creation of this new office would greatly reduce the amount of time it took to gain approval for certain actions including the application process for new power facilities.

Under the leadership of Sitthiporn, EGAT continued to work towards its foray into public ownership. In a November 2002 interview with *Asiamoney* magazine, the governor explained his overall strategy for EGAT, claiming, "the power resources in Thailand are very limited. If we need more power to develop the economy in the future, we will have to import the resources." He went on to state, "my vision is to make Thailand the hub of the Asean power grid through co-operation with neighbouring countries. As you know, this region has a wealth of natural energy resources, such as the immense hydropower potential in Myanmar, upper Laos and southern China, as well as the fossil fuel resources including coal and natural gas in the south. We can help these countries which are less developed to bring their resources on stream. If we can do that, it is good for each country and good for the region as a whole." Sitthiporn concluded,

Key Dates:

1958: Metropolitan Electricity Authority is established.
1959: The Yanhee Electricity Authority begins operation.
1969: The Electricity Authority of Thailand (EGAT) is formed by the merger of Yanhee Electricity Authority, Lignite Authority, and Northeastern Electricity Authority.
1992: The Electricity Generating Public Company Ltd. is established.
1994: Deregulation continues in Thailand's energy sector.
1996: Plans are set in motion to privatize EGAT.
2002: The Ministry of Energy is created in Thailand.

"we should bring all the power plants into one single grid to be called the Asean [Association of Southeast Asian Nations] grid."

While EGAT's initial public offering (IPO) was postponed several times, the Thai government appeared set to go public in 2004. Slated to be the largest offering in Thailand's history, the original plan called for EGAT to be divided into three separate entities: electricity generation, power transmission, and maintenance services. EGAT management argued vehemently against a breakup and in March 2003, Prime Minister Thaksin agreed to offer the company as a whole unit. The size of the IPO remained in debate in the summer of 2003 but officials anticipated that the Thai government would retain a majority interest.

As one of the most profitable state-owned companies in Thailand, the future of EGAT remained very much up in the air and in the public eye. While privatization threatened to unsettle the balance in the country's energy industry and possibility undermine EGAT's bottom line, government officials were determined to see it through believing its completion was crucial to future economic growth. The last decade of the company's history had brought with it much change—the coming years would no doubt bring even more.

Principal Subsidiaries

Electricity Generating Public Company Ltd.; Ratchaburi Electricity Generating Holding Public Company Ltd.

Principal Competitors

CLP Holdings Ltd.; International Power plc; Thai Oil Company Ltd.

Further Reading

"Country Focus; EGAT; Rough Road to Privatization," *Power Economics*, June 30, 1998, p. 34.

Davies, Ben, "Can EGAT's New Governor Get it Right?," *Asiamoney*, November 2002, p. 20.

"EGAT," *Daily Deal*, July 9, 2003.

"EGAT Privatization Faces Grass-Roots Resistance," *Power Asia*, April 24, 1997, p. 1.

"EGAT Privatization for the Good of the Nation," *Bangkok Post*, June 23, 2003.

"EGAT's Belt Tightened, Share Sell Off Likely," *Power in Asia*, October 6, 1997.

"EGAT Union Blinks First As Decks Cleared for Private Sector," *Power Asia*, February 25, 1991, p. 1.

"For First Time, Thailand Has Energy Ministry," *Platts Oilgram News*, October 7, 2002, p. 2.

"Greens Play Havoc With EGAT," *Power Asia*, November 20, 1989, p. 1.

"Storm Damage and Lawsuits Leave EGAT Fit to Be Tied," *Power Asia*, December 19, 1988, p. 16.

"Supply From IPPs to Be Postponed," *Business Thailand Magazine*, February 2001.

"Thailand Reviews Long Term Power Plan," *Energy Economist*, August 1, 1988.

—Christina M. Stansell

EPIQ Systems, Inc.

501 Kansas Avenue
Kansas City, Kansas 66105-1309
U.S.A.
Telephone: (913) 621-9500
Fax: (913) 321-1243
Web site: http://www.epiqsystems.com

Public Company
Incorporated: 1964
Employees: 170
Sales: $38.28 million (2002)
Stock Exchanges: NASDAQ
Ticker Symbol: EPIQ
NAIC: 511210 Software Publishers; 541512 Computer
  Systems Design Services

EPIQ Systems, Inc. supplies specialized software to help trustees manage the bankruptcy process. Its Trustee Case Management System (TCMS) handles Chapter 7 filings, which liquidate a debtor's assets in exchange for a clean slate. Chapter 13 reorganizations, which involve a scheduled repayment of part of an individual's or a business's debt, are managed with CasePower software.

EPIQ (pronounced "epoch") products also have some involvement with Chapter 11 corporate reorganizations and farm-related Chapter 12 bankruptcies. In the case of Chapter 7 filings, rather than simply licensing the software, EPIQ generates fees based on the amount of money in trustees' accounts. The number of cases in a clients' database determines the fees for Chapter 13 software. EPIQ's financial services division, which accounts for about 15 percent of revenues, provides secure e-business communications software for handling data using various protocols.

EPIQ has become a regular on *Forbes* magazine's annual listing of the best small companies in the United States. It has grown rapidly both through acquisitions and organically, and the company prides itself on staying ahead of the competition in terms of technology. The rising number of bankruptcy filings in the United States—there were 1.58 million in 2002—did not hurt business. In 2003, *FSB: Fortune Small Business* found EPIQ to be the fifth-fastest growing small company in the United States. In its market, it was second only to financial services giant J.P. Morgan Chase & Co.

Kansas City Origins

Kansas City attorney Claude Rice, one of the founders of the law firm McDowell Rice Smith & Gaar, started what would become EPIQ systems in 1964. Rice was a Chapter 13 bankruptcy trustee and realized that computers could make tracking assets, collections, and payments to creditors, as well as court filings, more manageable for fellow trustees. In Chapter 13 bankruptcies, individuals or businesses set up installment plans to pay back all or a portion of their debts.

The business was then known as Electronic Processing Inc. (EPI). One of Rice's employees at his law firm and at EPI, R. Pete Smith, eventually acquired a 25 percent holding in EPI. Universal Money Centers Inc. (UMC) bought the company in 1984 in a deal worth about $4.5 million. UMC, founded in 1981, operated a data switch for ATMs (automated teller machines) in three states.

Olofson Acquires EPI in 1988

An investment group led by former Marion Laboratories Inc. and Xerox executive Tom W. Olofson acquired EPI in July 1988 after UMC defaulted on its financing. Olofson served as chairman and chief executive officer, while his son, Christopher E. Olofson, a Fulbright scholar via Princeton University, became chief operating officer and president in 1993.

EPI was not profitable under UMC, but this changed under the Olofsons' management. The company posted revenues of $5.23 million in 1995, producing net income of $83,000. The next year, sales were up 21 percent to $6.32 million, with net income rising to $190,000.

1997 IPO

In spite of a long-running bull market, bankruptcy filings reached record levels in the late 1990s. As Tom Olofson told

---

Company Perspectives:

More than any other single concept, we value the golden rule throughout EPIQ Systems. In each personal interaction we have—whether with a coworker, customer, vendor, investor, or business partner—we strive to treat that person the same way that we would want to be treated in a similar circumstance. While in many ways EPIQ Systems offers the feel of a start-up (quick times-to-market, entrepreneurial spirit, and high growth), we back up our agility with seasoned, professional managers. The senior managers at EPIQ Systems have years of experience in their fields and lead our growth in a highly planned, organized fashion. Best of all, we produce high-quality products and services with pride. The level of commitment our associates feel to our success comes from within—is not management-driven, but comes from each person individually.

The Wall Street Transcript, bankruptcy filings were tied to debt levels, rather than to the general health of the economy. Debt levels showed no signs of slowing. According to the *Kansas City Business Journal,* EPI estimated there were more than half a million pending Chapter 13 cases managed by just 180 trustees across the country, while 1,200 Chapter 7 trustees held $2 billion on deposit. Without software, it would have been impossible for the trustees to handle thousands of cases each.

This produced an ideal environment for EPI's initial public offering on February 4, 1997. The offering raised $5.6 million. A secondary offering in 1998 raised another $11 million. EPI had sixty employees at the time of the IPO. The company chose the ticker symbol "EPIQ" for its listing on the NASDAQ exchange. The letter "Q" was used to flag companies in bankruptcy, and investors were already referring to the company as EPIQ.

EPI acquired a Chapter 13 software product from its founder, Claude Rice, in April 1998. It was the second largest bankruptcy software company in the late 1990s and acquired the third largest, DCI Chapter 7 Solutions, Inc., for $10.2 million in cash in November 1999. DCI was a subsidiary of Union Bank of California and specialized in Chapter 7 bankruptcy software. The purchase of DCI intensified EPIQ's rivalry with Chase Manhattan Bank (later part of J.P. Morgan Chase & Co.), whose affiliate in the bankruptcy software business was the market leader. A licensing agreement with Bank of America provided most of EPIQ's revenues.

New Name in 2000

EPI changed is name to EPIQ Systems, Inc. in March 2000. In the same month, the company acquired Phitech, Inc., a San Francisco developer of business-to-business e-commerce software, for $6.25 million in cash. Phitech's main product, Data Express, allowed businesses to acquire and route data over the Web using different protocols. For example, it was used to handle credit card transactions. Phitech's 1999 revenues of $2.1 million were up 60 percent over the previous year. A new Java-based product was expected to double revenues each year for

three years. The company had 20 employees. Phitech had been founded in 1985 by its president and CEO, Hinda Gilbert.

In 2000, EPIQ began appearing on *Forbes* magazine's annual listing of the 200 best small companies in the United States. In March 2001, EPIQ would top *Investor's Business Daily's* ranking of financial services software companies.

Although business was strong in the bull market of the late 1990s, the weakening economy in 2001 enhanced EPIQ's prospects even more. Its stock reached record highs in May 2001, passing $30 a share for the first time. The company's performance was just beginning to get analysts' attention. As a "micro cap" stock with a market capitalization of less than $250 million, EPIQ had been considered small even among small-company funds, reported the *Kansas City Star.* Yet its main competitor, according to *Investor's Business Daily,* was the behemoth full-service financial firm J.P. Morgan Chase & Co.

Investor's Business Daily described some of EPIQ's market-leading statistics of the time. Among the most compelling stats, about a third of the country's 1,700 Chapter 7 trustees used the company's software. The Trustee Case Management System (TCMS) unit responsible for the Chapter 7 and Chapter 11 product accounted for three-quarters of EPIQ's business. The total amount its client trustees held in Bank of America accounts—the basis for EPIQ's Chapter 7 fees—had more than tripled to $800 million in three years.

Most of EPIQ's competition came from banks that had developed in-house software for administering bankruptcy cases. The company began to acquire its competition. It bought the relevant unit of Comerica Inc. in October 2001. The company paid $12 million for ROC Technologies, Inc., the Chapter 7 software subsidiary of Comerica's Imperial Bank unit. ROC had 100 trustee customers.

EPIQ acquired the Chapter 7 trustee business of Orange County, California's CPT Group, Inc. in July 2002. California had the greatest volume of bankruptcy filings and the highest values of liquidated assets. Later in the year, EPIQ announced a plan to buy Trumbull Bankruptcy Services LLC from The Hartford Financial Services Group for $31 million in cash. This would have greatly expanded EPIQ into the market for Chapter 11 services, which involved the high-growth area of corporate reorganizations. However, EPIQ soon canceled the deal. EPIQ did have a limited involvement with Chapter 11 management and continued to look for acquisitions in this area.

Record levels of debt and bankruptcy filings in 2002 were a boost for EPIQ's revenues. Bankruptcy filings rose 6 percent to 1.6 million. Sales for 2002 rose 27 percent to $38.3 million over 2001's record results. The company logged a net profit of $8.2 million. Chapter 7 bankruptcies accounted for 70 percent of filings in 2002. While bankruptcy services led growth, EPIQ's Phitech unit had high hopes for its new DataXpress Open Platform package, a Java-based product that made it simple for different computer systems to communicate online in e-commerce transactions.

Chapter 11 case management specialist Bankruptcy Services LLC (BSI) was acquired in January 2003. EPIQ paid $66 million in cash and stock for BSI, whose software was being

Key Dates:

1964: Attorney Claude Rice forms EPI to provide Chapter 13 case management software.
1984: Universal Money Centers Inc. buys EPI.
1988: EPI is acquired by Tom Olofson-led investment group.
1997: EPI has the most successful IPO of the year.
1999: DCI Chapter 7 Solutions is acquired.
2000: The company's name is changed to EPIQ Systems; Phitech is acquired.
2003: Chapter 11 specialist BSI is acquired.

used to handle such high profile bankruptcies as Enron Corporation and Global Crossing Ltd. CEO Tom Olofson relayed to *The Wall Street Transcript* the company's goal of raising its market share from 30 percent to 50 percent within several years.

Principal Subsidiaries

EPIQ Systems Acquisition, Inc.

Principal Divisions

Bankruptcy Management; Infrastructure Software.

Principal Competitors

J.P. Morgan Chase & Co.

Further Reading

Alm, Rick, "Kansas-Based Software Firm Walks Away from Purchase of Connecticut Company," *Kansas City Star*, September 6, 2002.

"Bankruptcy Services Co. to Issue Stock," *Corporate Financing Week*, August 11, 2002.

Biswas, Soma, "EPIQ Rounds out Software Line," *Daily Deal*, August 3, 2002.

Brennan, Terry, "EPIQ Buys Bankruptcy Software Rival," *Daily Deal*, October 11, 2001.

Brockhoff, Anne, "Romance, Intrigue of IPOs Intoxicate Some Executives," *Kansas City Business Journal*, December 12, 1997, pp. 22f.

Butcher, Lola, "Universal's Honeymoon Ends as Tough Year Comes to a Close," *Kansas City Business Journal*, January 14, 1985.

——, "Universal Money Centers Adopts a New Low Profile," *Kansas City Business Journal*, May 6, 1985.

Davis, Mark, "Weaker Economy Bodes Well for Kansas-Based Bankruptcy Software Company," *Kansas City Star*, January 30, 2001.

——, "Buyers Take Notice of Kansas City, Kan.-Based Bankruptcy Software Firm," *Kansas City Star*, May 15, 2001.

"Electronic Processing Inc.," *IPO Reporter*, May 19, 1997.

"EPIQ Systems, Inc. (EPIQ)," *Wall Street Transcript*, January 2003.

Gajilan, Arlyn Tobias, "The Tech Holdout," *FSB: Fortune Small Business*, July/August 2003, pp. 58–59.

Mann, Jennifer, "Kansas-Based Systems Developer Reports Higher Earnings for Fourth Quarter," *Kansas City Star*, February 20, 2003.

Margolies, Dan, "Bankruptcy Software Firm Going Public," *Kansas City Business Journal*, January 17, 1997, pp. 1f.

——, "EPI Heads Back to Market Seeking Funds for Expansion," *Kansas City Business Journal*, May 22, 1998, p. 7.

——, "EPI Buys Closest Bankruptcy Software Competitor," *Kansas City Business Journal*, December 3, 1999, p. 3.

——, "Kansas-Based Bankruptcy Software Firm Completes Private Placement of Shares," *Kansas City Star*, November 9, 2002.

Schaff, William, "Taking Stock—When Bankruptcies Are Good for a Company's Bottom Line," *InformationWeek*, October 29, 2001.

Sleeper, Sarah Z., "Software Firm Likes Bankruptcy; Kansas-Based EPIQ's Products Have Admirers among Chapter 7 Trustees," *Investor's Business Daily*, May 9, 2001, p. A6.

—Frederick C. Ingram

Ernie Ball, Inc.

151 Suburban Road
San Luis Obispo, California 93401
P.O. Box 4117
U.S.A.
Telephone: (805) 544-7726
Toll Free: (800) 543-2255
Fax: (805) 544-7275
Web site: http://www.ernieball.com

Private Company
Incorporated: 1958 as the Ernie Ball Company
Employees: 240
Sales: $37 million (2001)
NAIC: 339992 Musical Instrument Manufacturing

Ernie Ball, Inc. produces guitar strings and custom-built guitars and basses, as well as numerous guitar accessories, such as picks, cables, and straps. Owned and operated by the Ball family, the company sells its products to more than 5,500 music shops in the United States. Ernie Ball's foreign business is maintained by 68 distributors who sell the company's products in more than 75 countries. The company pioneered the development of guitar strings for rock-and-roll guitarists.

Origins

The son of a car salesman, Ernie Ball grew up in Santa Monica, California. His father, who supplemented his income by teaching people to play the Hawaiian steel guitar, encouraged his nine-year-old son to learn the instrument, a pursuit that the younger Ball quickly tired of. When he was a teenager, however, Ball became strongly interest in music and began practicing the Hawaiian steel guitar between two and three hours a day. Ball joined the Musicians' Union and got his first job, playing six nights a week in a south central Los Angeles tavern. When he was 19, he joined the Tommy Duncan band as a pedal guitarist. He toured the southwestern United States with the Tommy Duncan band for a year, ending his stint when the Korean War broke out. Ball joined the U.S. Air Force Band, formed a five-member band on the side, and played four nights a week on the air base. During his three-year tour, during which

he learned to play the standard guitar, Ball fleshed out his repertoire through exposure to a variety of musical genres such as Dixieland, concert band, classical, big band, and jazz.

When Ball left the military, he returned to the haunts of his youth in Los Angeles. He began playing in bars again, but his $53-per-week paychecks were not enough to support his wife and children. Like his father, Ball supplemented his income by giving music lessons. Ball's financial situation improved considerably when the bandleader of a weekly television program, *Western Varieties,* heard him play. Ball was offered a seat on the staff band and the opportunity to feature in two solo parts, which greatly increased his recognition in the Los Angeles music community. Ball's income swelled by a factor of three once he began appearing weekly on *Western Varieties.* Perhaps equally as important, his rising reputation in the Los Angeles music community led to steady offers for studio work and dramatically increased the number of students seeking his expertise. Not long after joining *Western Varieties,* Ball was giving music lessons to more than 80 students.

The First Guitar-Only Shop Opens in 1958

Ball achieved fair success as a musician, but his greatest accomplishments were achieved without an instrument in his hand. In 1958, he opened a small music shop in Tarzana, not far from Hollywood. The store was unique because inside there were only guitars and guitar accessories for sale. The store's inventory flew in the face of convention, representing the only retail establishment in the United States to sell only guitars. From the start, Ball faced criticism and pressure to broaden the selection of products stocked in his stores. On the company's corporate Web site, Ball remembered the reaction of industry insiders to his novel retail concept. He wrote, ''Sales reps would come in and say, 'Ern, you've got to sell clarinet reeds, drum sticks, valve oil, blah, blah, blah,' and I'd tell them, 'I just want to sell guitars,' and they'd argue, 'There's no such thing as a guitar store, you'll never make it.' '' Ball brushed aside the resistance to his business approach and kept his eyes focused exclusively on guitars. Before long, customers were traveling from miles away to frequent Ball's music shop, and the store became a haven for guitar enthusiasts throughout the greater Los Angeles area.

Company Perspectives:

Ernie Ball was the first to offer rock strings with the creation of Slinkys, and further revolutionized the market by offering guitarists Custom-Gauge single strings. The Ernie Ball company also produces Music Man guitars and basses, volume pedals, and other accessories.

As it turned out, Ball's music shop provided a venue for him to display his greatest talent. Ball did not achieve his success as a retailer; a chain of Ernie Ball music shops did not spring from the original Tarzana store. Instead, Ball made a name for himself as problem-solver, thriving as a designer attuned to the particular needs of guitarists. He began developing his renown in this area because of his time spent giving music lessons. He noticed that his beginning students were experiencing difficulties with the most popular electric guitar strings of the day, the Fender #100 medium-gauge set. Specifically, his young students were struggling to press down the third string. On the company's Web site, Ball explained, "The third string was a 29 gauge, like a giant cable, and the poor kids were getting finger blisters." Ball reported the problem to Fender, asking one of the company's sales representatives to talk to Leo Fender. The sales representative returned with the news that Leo Fender was not interested in making lighter gauge strings because the lighter strings would force him to re-engineer his guitars to compensate for the different tension. Undeterred, Ball contacted a string manufacturer and had custom gauge sets produced with a lighter, 24-gauge third string.

At the time, Ball was delving into custom manufacturing, a new, powerful musical style was sweeping across the country. The early 1960s witnessed rise of rock and roll and the attendant explosive growth in the popularity of electric guitars. Rock-and-roll guitarists needed lighter, more flexible guitars strings, qualities that made bending the strings much easier. As a retailer, Ball witnessed his customers tailoring existing products to meet their needs. The string manufacturing industry had yet to address the needs of rock-and-roll oriented, electric guitar players. Many rock guitarists would buy a set of guitar strings, throw away the sixth string, and replace it with a banjo first string. Ball believed there should be a set of lighter gauge strings designed specifically for playing rock and roll. Again, he approached the established manufacturers in the industry, contacting the same Fender sales representative that had served as his go-between with Leo Fender. The sales representative reported back that Leo Fender was unwilling to discuss the matter. Ball contacted another veteran guitar company, Gibson, and received a similar response. Ball decided to do it himself, which led to the introduction of Slinky strings in 1962. At first, Slinky strings were available only at Ball's retail store, but the popularity of the custom strings soon carried the Ernie Ball name toward global recognition.

A String Manufacturer Blossoms in the 1960s

Slinky strings confirmed a place for the Ernie Ball name in the music industry. The Tarzana shop began to attract the legends of the day, including artists such as Merle Travis and the Ventures, who became frequent visitors to the store. Established musicians became emissaries for Ball's strings, taking them on tour and replying "Ernie Ball" when asked which type of strings they used. (Ball's third son, Sterling Ball, once remarked that magazine interviewers had little idea what to ask the guitarists, so they asked them which type of strings they used.) Word-of-mouth advertising of Slinky strings propelled Ball's company forward in directions he had not anticipated. Ball's enterprise was tugged and pulled by interest in Slinky strings, gradually expanding the company's geographic reach and transforming its focus. Mail orders started to arrive, first from guitarists who lived far away from the Tarzana shop and next from other retail establishments. "We weren't a string company yet," Ball wrote on the company Web site. "We were just a little store that had some strings people wanted to buy."

The turning point in the company's evolution from a retail operation into a manufacturing operation occurred in 1967. That year Ball sold his Tarzana shop and moved his rapidly growing string business to Newport Beach. At first blush, the move suggested the emergence of a more ambitious business venture, but according to Ball's reflections on his company's Web site, the transition was made for opposite reasons. "I wanted to change my lifestyle and work shorter days," he wrote. "[I wanted to] learn to surf, learn to fly a plane, and grow a beard." Ball made the move, settling into his new operation with only a staff of two. His dream of a bohemian lifestyle was never realized, however. Interest in Slinky strings and the Ernie Ball name did not allow any time for his lifestyle changes save growing a beard.

Overwhelmed by the demands of his new manufacturing operation, which ranged from laying out artwork to packaging string sets, Ball enlisted the help of his sons—Sterling, David, and Sherwood—who helped out in the warehouse after school. Sterling, in particular, was a pivotal addition to the company, serving as an adept salesman, an orchestrator of artist and dealer relations, and eventually as the company's leader.

Once Ball was able to settle into his new operation, he began pursuing a long-held dream. For years, he had wanted to make an acoustic bass guitar, a yet-to-be-developed instrument whose only close relative was the Mexican guitarron, common in mariachi bands. Ball took a trip south to Tijuana and bought a guitarron, but his efforts at retrofitting the instrument into his vision of an acoustic bass failed. Later, he teamed with a former Fender employee, George Fullerton, and realized success in making an all-wood acoustic bass. The partnership resulted in the 1972 introduction of Earthwood guitars, basses, and strings. Although the Earthwood operation experienced production and personnel problems early on, the venture ultimately produced roughly 2,000 prized Earthwood basses, guitars, mandolas, and baby guitars before shuttering production in 1985.

While Ball was developing his concept of an acoustic bass, his son, Sterling, came to the fore in the company's growth and expansion. Sterling Ball figured prominently in the Ernie Ball Company's expansion overseas, spearheading the company's export activities. By 1977, as the Earthwood operation wrestled with its own maturation, the Ernie Ball Company was exporting its products to 14 countries. Sterling Ball, surreptitiously, aggrandized the company's international operations. In a May 2002 interview with *World Trade*, Sterling Ball recalled his actions. "We had a sales manager who thought we had done all we could in export. I was a young upstart. I had a friend who was working in another company who was a very good export manager. I said, 'Hey, could you send me some names, but don't tell the sales manager that I got these names.' I sent a mailing behind his back. I think I opened 21 new markets that way. It was then when we became a pretty serious exporter.''

In the music industry, Ernie Ball established a precedent for exporting merchandise. Instead of using foreign markets as a dumping ground for outdated products that had outlived their retail appeal in the United States, the company applied the same degree of commitment to overseas sales as it did to domestic sales. The attention to foreign markets paid dividends, helping the company to turn into a highly successful exporter.

While the company was making its indelible imprint overseas, it also aggrandized its stature domestically. In the early 1980s, Ernie and Sterling Ball readied themselves for their next achievement. They felt business conditions were ripe for the production of a highly crafted, U.S.—manufactured electric guitar, a domestically made instrument that could compete with the inexpensive guitars produced in Japan, Korea, and Mexico. The father-and-son team sought to enter the new business realm via acquisition.

The target found in the Balls' acquisitive search was a company known for producing high-quality electric basses and amplifiers. The company was called Music Man, and in 1984 the operation was up for sale. The Ernie Ball Company's ties to Music Man were intimate. Leo Fender had manufactured the company's instruments. The Fender sales representative that Ernie Ball had talked to about string manufacture during the early 1960s built Music Man's amplifiers. Sterling Ball had been involved in the design of the company most successful instrument, the StingRay bass, introduced in 1976.

The Ernie Ball Company acquired Music Man in the fall of 1984. Once the acquisition was completed, Sterling Ball gathered a team of musicians, designers, and production specialists to develop a new product line marketed under the Music Man banner. Meanwhile, his father oversaw the construction of a new facility in San Luis Obispo to house the operations of both the Ernie Ball Company and Music Man. In 1985, the San Luis Obispo facility was occupied. One year later, the first bass designed at the San Luis Obispo facility was introduced, the Stingray 5.

A steady stream of new product introductions and Sterling Ball's efforts to affiliate the company with the stars of rock and roll galvanized the company's reputation across the globe. The list of musicians who used Ernie Ball instruments, strings, and accessories included the icons of the industry. Members of bands such as The Rolling Stones, The Eagles, The Pretenders, U2, AC/DC, and Fleetwood Mac relied on Ernie Ball for their equipment. During the 1990s, a new generation of guitarists embraced the slew of products made in San Luis Obispo, ensuring that the legacy of the Ernie Ball name would continue into the 21st century. Guitarists such as Mike McReady and Stone Gossard of Pearl Jam, Chris Cornell of Soundgarden, and Jerry Cantrell of Alice in Chains, as well as members of 311, Nine Inch Nails, Smashing Pumpkins, and Social Distortion used Ernie Ball products.

As Ernie Ball neared the end of its first half-century of existence, the company enjoyed an entrenched market position and the esteem of musicians throughout the world. By 2002, the company's product line had expanded to include Music Man guitars and basses, volume pedals, and other accessories. Ernie Ball strings and accessories were sold in more than 5,500 music stores scattered throughout the United States. The company's international business was substantial, conducted through long-term relationships with 68 distributors who exported Ernie Ball products to more than 75 countries. Under the astute leadership of Sterling Ball, who served as chief executive officer and president, the company promised to figure prominently in its industry well into the future.

In 2002, the company ended its 17-year stay in San Luis Obispo, citing high housing costs and the city's low unemployment rate as the reasons for the move. In a June 20, 2002 interview with *The Tribune,* Sterling Ball remarked, ''It's really hard doing business in San Luis Obispo and it isn't getting any easier. For the past seven years, I've looked at other places.'' In October 2002, the company announced it was leaving San Luis Obispo. Ernie Ball planned to build a 100,000-square-foot office and manufacturing facility in Coachella, California, west of Palm Springs. The company planned to complete the move into its new string instrument plant during the first fiscal quarter of 2004.

Principal Subsidiaries

Music Man Co.; Paladar.

Principal Competitors

Fender Musical Instruments Corporation; Gibson Guitar Corp.; J. D'Addario & Company, Inc.

Further Reading

''Ernie Ball, Inc.,'' *Knight Ridder/Tribune Business News,* June 20, 2002.
''Firm to Move Instrument String Unit from San Luis Obispo, Calif.,'' *Knight Ridder/Tribune Business News,* October 22, 2002.
Sowinski, Lara L., ''Ernie Ball's Breaking All the Rules,'' *World Trade,* May 2002, p. 16.
Villagran, Nadia T., ''Guitar-String Maker Moving to Coachella,'' *Desert Sun,* October 23, 2002, p. E1.

—Jeffrey L. Covell

ESPN, Inc.

935 Middle Street
Bristol, Connecticut 06010
U.S.A.
Telephone: (860) 766-2000
Fax: (860) 766-2213
Web site: http://www.espn.go.com

Joint Venture (80% Walt Disney Company; 20% Hearst Corporation)
Incorporated: 1978 as Entertainment Sports Programming Network, Inc.
Employees: 2,600 (est.)
Sales: $2.12 billion (2002)
NAIC: 513210 Cable Television Networks; 512110 Video Production; 511120 Magazine Publishers

ESPN, Inc. is a pioneer among basic cable television networks, devoting its entire programming to a single subject: sports. By 2002 the company's flagship network, ESPN, reached more than 87 million households and televised all of the major professional leagues: baseball, football, hockey, and basketball. According to the 2002 annual report of ESPN's parent company, Walt Disney, ESPN was the number one basic cable network in terms of affiliate, national, and local advertising revenue. Considered by many to be the most successful basic cable network, ESPN delivered the hard-to-capture audience of young males to a wide range of advertisers. Cable system operators consistently selected ESPN as the number one cable network in perceived value.

Early History: 1978–80

ESPN, Inc. was the brainchild of Bill Rasmussen, an unemployed sports announcer. In the spring of 1978 Rasmussen was fired by the New England Whalers of the World Hockey Association as its communications director and play-by-play announcer. He began looking for a way to broadcast University of Connecticut basketball games through cable television operators in the state. At the time, satellite technology was a rela-

tively new way of transmitting programming to cable operators. RCA had an underused satellite on which Rasmussen could lease time. With six of 23 active transponder sites fully available, RCA was eager for customers.

After discovering that it was cheaper to rent satellite time from RCA for 24 hours rather than for five hours, Rasmussen decided to offer 24-hour sports programming on a national basis. RCA offered Rasmussen an easy payment program, so he used his credit card to lease space on RCA's Satcom 1 in July 1978. He called his company Entertainment Sports Programming Network, Inc., or ESP Network for short. According to company legend, it became ESPN when the company's letterhead came back that way from the printer.

ESPN began broadcasting in September 1979 with limited airtime during the week and 24-hour coverage on the weekends. The company had signed up 625 cable system affiliates, reaching more than one million of a total of 20 million households that had cable at that time. Its first televised event was a slow-pitch world series softball game between the Milwaukee Schlitzes and the Kentucky Bourbons. ESPN's first sponsor was Anheuser-Busch, which purchased $1.4 million worth of advertising—a record for cable television. Through a deal with the NCAA, ESPN broadcast college football games as well as other sports. To fill airtime, ESPN would often broadcast the same games more than once. In March 1980 ESPN covered early rounds of the NCAA basketball tournament, which featured future NBA stars Larry Byrd and Earvin "Magic" Johnson. In September 1980 ESPN began broadcasting on a full, 24-hour basis. New programming included weekly boxing matches.

Becoming an Established Sports Network: 1980s

ESPN's early financing came from Getty Oil, which invested $10 million in the company in 1979 for a controlling interest. Getty hired Chet Simmons, president of NBC Sports, to run ESPN. After seeing its financing rise to $25 million with no profits in sight, Getty hired management consultant McKinsey & Co. to assess ESPN's future. McKinsey's lead consultant on the project was Roger Werner, who forecast that ESPN would become profitable in five years with another $120 mil-

Company Perspectives:

ESPN, Inc., the leading destination for American sports fans, continued its growth in 2002, led by major programming acquisitions and original programs, increased viewership, greater distribution of its domestic networks, and international network launches.

lion investment. Werner joined ESPN as its vice-president of finance, administration, and planning, and developed a new business plan. Up to this time ESPN's only revenue stream came from advertising. Werner proposed charging cable operators, who had been receiving ESPN programming for free, small monthly fees, starting at six cents per subscriber and gradually increasing to 10 cents by 1985. While this innovative system of affiliate fees eventually became standard practice among cable programmers, cable operators were not interested at first. Werner received help in convincing cable operators of the need to support ESPN from the company's new CEO, Bill Grimes, who replaced Chet Simmons in June 1982. Meanwhile, Werner was promoted to senior vice-president. When CBS Cable folded in October 1982, Grimes and Werner convinced major cable companies that ESPN could not survive without subscriber fees. About half of the major cable companies agreed to ESPN's rates.

By the end of 1983 ESPN was cable's largest network, with a reach of 28.5 million households. In January 1984 ABC, Inc. bought a 15 percent stake in the company, then acquired control of the company six months later. The acquisition of ESPN by ABC put the sports network on firmer financial footing and provided a foundation for its phenomenal growth in the coming years.

When college football on television was deregulated through a court decision in 1984, ESPN began broadcasting Thursday and Saturday night games. These college football broadcasts helped improve the image of ESPN's audience with advertisers, who began noticing upscale demographics among ESPN's viewers. When ESPN announced it would cover the 1986–87 America's Cup competition, advertisers quickly bought up all of the advertising time for the network's 70 hours of coverage of yachting's premiere event.

Following its acquisition by ABC, which was acquired by Capital Cities Communications, Inc. at the beginning of 1986 to form Capital Cities/ABC Inc., ESPN landed major broadcasting contracts from the National Hockey League (1985), the National Football League (1987), and Major League Baseball (1989). According to *Cablevision*, ESPN became part of the American consciousness when it broadcast the finals of yachting's America's Cup live from Australia in January 1987. The *New York Times* devoted a front-page story to the coverage, noting how people were hosting late-night and early-morning parties to watch the races, or gathering in bars to cheer on the American team. Two months later the National Football League awarded ESPN its first-ever package of games to be broadcast on cable television, which began in August 1987 with the televised broadcast of the inaugural game at the Miami Dol-

phins' Joe Robbie Stadium against the Chicago Bears. The four-year contract was renewed for 1990–93 at a cost of about $450 million to ESPN. In addition, ABC-TV paid about $900 million for its package of Monday night and weekend games.

ESPN also expanded internationally in the 1980s. The company began distributing programming overseas in 1983, and in 1988 it formally created ESPN International to launch networks in other countries. In March 1989 ESPN Latin America was introduced, followed by ESPN Asia in 1992. ESPN gained a foothold in Europe in 1993 with the launch of a redesigned Eurosport in partnership with European broadcasters TF1 and Canal Plus.

Expanding Its Brand: 1990–95

ESPN began the 1990s with a new president and CEO, when Steve Bornstein replaced Roger Werner. Werner, the former McKinsey & Co. consultant, was ESPN's president and CEO from 1988 to 1999. He left ESPN to become president and CEO of Daniels & Associates Inc., which owned a wide range of sports properties. Bornstein was formerly ESPN's executive vice-president in charge of programming and production and the network's second in command. He first joined ESPN in 1980 as a program coordinator.

Under Bornstein's leadership, ESPN extended its brand name in the 1990s by launching new networks, expanding globally, and signing contracts to broadcast games of major sports leagues. The brand expansion began in 1991 with the launch of ESPN Radio Network in conjunction with the ABC Radio Network. ESPN Radio began with 16 hours of programming per week and was offered to 200 radio stations. In 1993 ESPN introduced a second cable network, ESPN2, which began transmission on October 1, 1993. Billed as an alternative sports network, ESPN2 was expected to reach a younger demographic than ESPN. Its initial programming included college basketball games, arena football, volleyball, motor racing events, fitness programs, soccer, karate, kickboxing, and other sports, as well as two sports and talk shows. When ESPN2 was launched, it reached about nine million homes, compared to 61.7 million for ESPN. ESPN2 had agreements in place with 15 of the top 20 multiple cable system operators (MSOs) and was expected to reach 30 million homes within a couple of years.

ESPN's first contract with Major League Baseball was a four-year, $400 million package that was signed in January 1989 and began in 1990. It called for ESPN to broadcast 175 games, six games a week. The contract was baseball's first cable package since 1983. At the time ESPN reached more than 50 million households. After sustaining losses of more than $200 million on its baseball broadcasts, ESPN announced at the end of the 1992 season that it would not renew its contract with Major League Baseball, which expired at the end of the 1993 season. At the end of the 1993 season, however, the two sides reached an agreement for a scaled-back six-year contract to begin with the 1994 baseball season.

In March 1993 ESPN acquired the sports programming division of Ohlmeyer Communications Inc. Donald Ohlmeyer, the company's founder and CEO, had recently been named president of NBC West Coast. His company was known for

Key Dates:

1978: Bill Rasmussen forms Entertainment Sports Programming Network, Inc. (ESPN) to broadcast sporting events to cable television operators via satellite.
1979: ESPN begins broadcasting on a limited-time basis.
1980: ESPN begins broadcasting 24 hours a day, seven days a week.
1984: ABC, Inc. acquires ESPN.
1986: Capital Cities Communications, Inc. acquires ABC and becomes Capital Cities/ABC, Inc.
1987: ESPN begins broadcasting National Football League games.
1988: ESPN International is created.
1989: ESPN begins broadcasting Major League Baseball games.
1990: The Hearst Corporation acquires a 20 percent interest in ESPN from RJR Nabisco Inc.
1991: ESPN Radio Network is launched in conjunction with the ABC Radio Network.
1993: ESPN2 begins transmission.
1995: Walt Disney Company acquires Capital Cities/ABC, Inc. and becomes ESPN's parent company.
1997: ESPN purchases the Classic Sports Network and launches ESPN Classic.
1998: *ESPN: The Magazine* is launched.
2003: ESPN HD, a high-definition television sports network, is introduced.

developing professional golf's Skins Game, among other sports programs. It also produced the television coverage of the Indianapolis 500 auto race.

Another acquisition took place in 1994, when ESPN acquired an 80 percent interest in SportsTicker from Dow Jones. SportsTicker was a sports news information service. ESPN planned to use its sports feed to supplement other information sources for its recently launched online service, ESPNET, which was available at the time through Prodigy.

ESPN began developing its Extreme Games competition in 1994, and the first annual Extreme Games were held in June-July 1995. ESPN and ESPN2 broadcast more than 60 hours of Extreme Games, which included nine extreme sports such as in-line skating, mountain biking, skateboarding, sky surfing, and street luge racing. Television coverage also included a beach party and concert. In 1996 the name of the competition was changed to X Games, with more than 400 athletes competing in events that included bungee jumping and bicycle stunt riding. ESPN and ESPN2 carried about 35 hours of X Games programming in 1996. By 1997 the X Games enjoyed a range of merchandising tie-ins that included sporting apparel, music CDs, videotapes, and video games. Advertising for the annual event was sold out each year. The EXPN web site provided online coverage of a variety of extreme sports.

It was during the first half of the 1990s that ESPN began facing serious competition from Fox Sports. In 1994 a new

contract with the National Hockey League, whose games ESPN had been broadcasting since 1992, split coverage of the 1995 Stanley Cup playoffs between ESPN and Fox Sports and gave Fox Sports the right to broadcast the 1995 All-Star game.

New Parent, Walt Disney: 1995–99

In mid-1995 Walt Disney Company acquired ESPN's parent company, Capital Cities/ABC, giving Disney an 80 percent interest in ESPN and full control of its operations. The Hearst Corporation, a passive investor in ESPN, retained the 20 percent interest in ESPN it had purchased from RJR Nabisco Inc. in 1990 for an estimated $170 million. In April 1996 Disney announced plans to combine ESPN and ABC Sports into a single operating unit under the control of Steve Bornstein. Although Bornstein became president of both ESPN and ABC Sports, he made it clear that the two would remain separate and distinct businesses.

ESPN gained another cable sports network in September 1997 with the purchase of the Classic Sports Network (CSN), an independently owned cable service that broadcast classic sporting events from the past. While financial terms were not disclosed, it was reported that Disney paid between $150 million and $200 million. At the time of the acquisition CSN had about 11 million subscribers and was expected to gain another four million in November when Time Warner Cable in New York City began carrying it. Analysts agreed that CSN would provide a good cable outlet for ESPN's and ABC Sports' extensive sports libraries. CSN was ESPN's fourth network. At the time ESPN reached about 71 million homes, ESPN2 was available in 52 million homes, and ESPNews reached five million households.

In 1998 ESPN committed to new long-term contracts with the National Football League and the National Hockey League. An eight-year, $18 billion television package with the NFL was announced at the beginning of the year that included ABC, CBS, and ESPN. NBC and TNT (Turner Network Television) dropped out of the package. ESPN's and ABC's parent, Walt Disney, paid more than half of the total package, or $9.2 billion. ABC retained its Monday Night Football package and ESPN expanded its Sunday night coverage for the full season. Annually, ABC would pay about $550 million a year and ESPN $600 million a year to broadcast NFL football games for the next eight years. Later in the year, in spite of ratings declines, ABC and ESPN agreed to a five-year, $600 million contract with the NHL to start with the 1998–99 season. The contract gave ABC exclusive national broadcast TV rights and ESPN exclusive national cable TV rights for NHL games.

ESPN launched *ESPN: The Magazine* in 1998 under the direction of John Skipper, president of Disney Publishing. Previously ESPN's only presence in print was *Total Sports,* an irregularly published magazine produced in association with Hearst. In its first year of existence, *ESPN: The Magazine* achieved a circulation of 400,000 and ranked second behind *Sports Illustrated* in number of advertising pages. Its target audience was males in their 20s.

In 1998 Fox Sports' regional programming approach was giving ESPN significant competition for advertising dollars.

Fox customized its "Fox Sports News Primetime" broadcasts for each local market. Its regional approach to baseball resulted in larger audiences nationwide than ESPN, even though ESPN reached 12 million more households that Fox/Liberty's 22 networks combined. Fox/Liberty, Fox Sports Net's parent, was a 50–50 joint venture between Rupert Murdoch's Fox Sports and TCI Chairman and CEO John Malone's Liberty Media.

Toward the end of 1998 Steve Bornstein was named to the newly created position of chairman of ESPN. George Bodenheimer, who had been with ESPN since shortly after its launch in 1979, became ESPN's president. Bornstein retained the presidency of ABC Sports. Further management changes took place in March 1999, when Bornstein was promoted to president of ABC Inc. Howard Katz, ESPN's head of production, was named president of ABC Sports.

During most of the 1999 baseball season ESPN was involved in a dispute with Major League Baseball. Seeds of the disagreement began in 1998 when ESPN preempted three Sunday night baseball games with football broadcasts. ESPN chose to move the baseball games to ESPN2 and broadcast the football games on ESPN. At issue was whether or not MLB had the right to reject any proposed preemption. Under its contract with MLB, ESPN had the right to preempt up to ten games per season for events of "significant viewer interest." At the beginning of the 1999 season, MLB announced it would terminate its six-year contract with ESPN at the end of the season. ESPN responded by filing a lawsuit against MLB to enforce its contract. After much squabbling, the two sides reached a compromise agreement in December 1999. A new six-year agreement valued at $815 million extended ESPN's right to cover Major League Baseball through 2005. ESPN agreed to increase the number of regular games it broadcast from 90 to 108 on both ESPN and ESPN2 and to increase its studio coverage of baseball. ESPN Radio would continue to have regular and postseason broadcast rights. ESPN.com would be able to show daily four-minute video highlight packages, and the company's video games division was granted interactive rights.

ESPN's combination of Sunday night football and the Major League Baseball playoffs pushed the sports network to the number one ranking in prime time among cable networks in October 1999. Its NFL games were the top three rated cable shows for the month, with one game achieving a 9.5 rating and viewership of 7.3 million households.

Mixed Blessing for Disney: 2000–03

In Walt Disney's annual report for 2000, CEO Michael Eisner praised ESPN as "in a class of its own." Dubbed the "worldwide leader in sports," ESPN contributed $2.6 billion in revenue in 2000 and $824 million in operating income. ESPN was worth $20 billion, or 25 percent of Disney's market value, but it only provided 10 percent of Disney's total revenue, according to one estimate published in *Forbes*. ESPN reached 82 million cable households, and cable system operators paid ESPN 70 cents per subscriber to carry it. ESPN's fees were double those of CNN and four times those of MTV. By 2002 *Business Week* reported that ESPN's fees averaged $1.50 per subscriber, more than double those of CNN, with contracts calling for annual 20 percent increases.

Nevertheless, ESPN was facing significant competition from Fox Sports as well as regional cable networks and numerous web sites. For the period from October 2000 to March 2001 ESPN's ratings declined 19 percent from the previous year, reaching their lowest point in three years. ESPN's ad revenue in 2000 increased by 3.5 percent to top $1 billion, while ESPN2's ad revenue increased 15 percent. For 2001 ESPN's ratings in the 18- to 49-year-old male group sank by 14 percent from the previous year, while Fox Sports' ratings increased by 12 percent in the same group.

Adding to ESPN's woes was the high cost of its premiere sports contracts with the NFL and Major League Baseball. To offset some of its costs, ESPN dropped some high-priced contracts, letting NASCAR jump to other networks in 1999 with a $2.4 billion six-year deal. In January 2001 ESPN declined to sign up golf's Senior PGA Tour, which went to CNBC. In an effort to buy some low-cost viewers, ESPN acquired B.A.S.S., the largest fishing organization in the United States with more than 600,000 members, in April 2001. B.A.S.S. ran two fishing tournament series, both of which already aired on ESPN2, and published three magazines. ESPN also hoped to attract viewers with original programming, including a movie about controversial basketball coach Bobby Knight that aired in March 2002, and a new late-night sports variety show that launched in April 2002. A large-format movie produced with Touchstone Pictures called *ESPN's Ultimate X Games* was released in May 2002. Other revenue sources included eight Zone restaurants and a new interactive channel on DirecTV. In addition, ESPN's wireless unit delivered scores and sports news to cell phones and personal digital assistants for a fee.

New contracts signed in 2002 included a blockbuster six-year contract with the National Basketball Association for $4.6 billion. The contract began with the 2002–03 season, with ABC and ESPN paying $2.4 billion and AOL Time Warner's TNT paying about $2.2 billion. NBC, which held the NBA contract for the past 12 years, dropped out of the bidding. ABC and ESPN also signed a six-year contract with the Women's NBA in June that called for sharing expenses and revenue without having to pay a rights fee. Under another contract with Major League Soccer to broadcast the 2002 and 2006 men's World Cup soccer tournaments and the 2003 women's World Cup, Major League Soccer agreed to buy time on ABC and ESPN to air the World Cup matches. As part of the deal ESPN2 agreed to broadcast 26 MLS matches on Saturdays, with ABC carrying at least three MLS games including the MLS Cup and MLS All-Star game.

In an interview published in *Multichannel News* in mid-2002, ESPN President George Bodenheimer identified three programming areas of growth outside of ESPN's major sports franchises. They were the X Games, with ESPN introducing the X Games Global Championship in the spring of 2003; outdoor programming, including the Great Outdoors Games and programming from B.A.S.S.; and NCAA national championships in 15 different sports. He also cited SportsCenter as a solid piece of programming for the network; it aired its 25,000th live edition in August 2002, more shows than any other television series. In March 2003 Bodenheimer added the presidency of ABC Sports to his duties following the resignation of Howard Katz.

In the final quarter of 2002 ESPN continued to enjoy a high position in the cable TV ratings. It jockeyed with Lifetime Television for the primetime ratings crown, losing the top overall rating spot in October but gaining the number one position among adults in the 18–34 and 18–49 age groups. It beat out MTV in the 18–34 age group and USA Network in the 18–49 age group. For the year 2002, ESPN led 13 other cable networks in double-digit increases in primetime ratings. ESPN's pro football games led the way, capturing 9 of the 10 highest-rated positions for individual programs. As a result, ESPN was up 15 percent in households, 20 percent among adults 25–54, and 24 percent among adults 18–49 for the year.

Looking to expand its brand and gain additional revenue sources, ESPN began broadcasting in high definition (HD) in March with a live cablecast of an opening game of Major League Baseball. Its new spinoff network, ESPN HD, was a clone of ESPN and provided an exact replica of ESPN's 24-hour programming. At first only select events were broadcast in HD, giving ESPN HD subscribers higher quality sound and image. What more could a sports fan want?

Principal Operating Units

ESPN; ESPN2; ESPN Classic; ESPNews; ESPN HD; ESPN Interactive; ESPN International; ESPN Original Entertainment; ESPN Outdoors; ESPN The Magazine; ESPN Radio; ESPN.com; ESPN ABC Sports Customer Marketing and Sales.

Principal Competitors

AOL Time Warner Inc.; Fox Sports Networks, LLC; National Broadcasting Company, Inc.; Universal Television Group.

Further Reading

"ABC and ESPN Retain $1.35 Billion Pieces of NFL Pie," *Broadcasting,* March 5, 1990, p. 33.

"ABC, ESPN Agree to WNBA Pact," *Mediaweek,* June 17, 2002, p. 40.

Adalian, Josef, and Jenny Hontz, "Iger and Bornstein Climb up Alphabet," *Variety,* March 1, 1999, p. 65.

Battaglio, Stephen, "Bornstein: ESPN's New Captain," *AdWeek Western Edition,* September 24, 1990, p. 27.

Berman, Chris, "Sportscaster Relives His 15 Years with ESPN," *Sport,* October 1994, p. 86.

Berniker, Mark, "ESPN Buys 80% of SportsTicker," *Broadcasting & Cable,* November 14, 1994, p. 47.

Brown, Rich, "ESPN on Course in Merger's Wake," *Broadcasting & Cable,* August 7, 1995, p. 21.

Carvell, Tim, "Prime-Time Player," *Fortune,* March 2, 1998, p. 134.

Chunovic, Louis, "ESPN Wins Cable's Young Demo Crowns," *Electronic Media,* November 4, 2002, p. 8.

Consoli, John, "ABC, ESPN Kick up '02 Cup," *Mediaweek,* January 7, 2002, p. 5.

Dempsey, John, "ESPN HD Sports High-Def TV," *Daily Variety,* March 28, 2003.

——, "ESPN Pitches Suit at Baseball," *Variety,* May 10, 1999, p. 135.

——, "NFL Gains Yardage for ESPN," *Daily Variety,* January 2, 2003, p. 1.

Dolliver, Mark, "Let the Extreme Games, Like, Man, Begin," *AdWeek Eastern Edition,* June 24, 1996, p. 22.

Donohue, Steve, "ESPN, Baseball Make up with 6-Year, $815M Kiss," *Multichannel News,* December 13, 1999, p. 6.

——, "ESPN Throws the Heat at MLB," *Electronic Media,* May 10, 1999, p. 2.

Dunnavant, Keith, "Wider World of Sports," *AdWeek Western Edition,* January 20, 1992, p. 40.

Dupree, Scotty, "ABC Sports to Go to ESPN?," *Mediaweek,* April 1, 1996, p. 6.

"ESPN Combines Internet, Publishing Units," *Multichannel News,* November 19, 2001, p. 5.

"ESPN Gets to 'Play Ball' for $400 million," *Broadcasting,* January 9, 1989, p. 43.

"ESPN Hooks B.A.S.S.," *Mediaweek,* April 9, 2001, p. 22.

"ESPN's Bodenheimer: From Field to Field General," *Multichannel News,* June 3, 2002, p. 9.

"ESPN Sees Change at Top," *Multichannel News,* November 23, 1998, p. 5.

"ESPN's Full-Court Press," *Business Week,* February 11, 2002, p. 60.

Fink, James, "Cable Companies Hope to Add ESPN2 Network to Their Rosters," *Business First of Buffalo,* October 4, 1993, p. 13.

Frankel, Daniel, "ESPN, MLB Reconcile," *Electronic Media,* December 13, 1999, p. 8.

Fry, Andy, "On Top of Their Game," *Variety,* January 19, 1998, p. A1.

Goldsand, Alan, "Buyers Lukewarm on ESPN Sports News Radio Plan," *Mediaweek,* September 9, 1991, p. 4.

Grossman, Andrew, "Bornstein Succeeds Werner As ESPN President, CEO," *Multichannel News,* September 17, 1990, p. 3.

Haley, Kathy, "Blazing a Trail," *Cablevision,* September 13, 1999, p. 6A.

——, "Breaking Through," *Cablevision,* September 13, 1999, p. 3A.

"Hearst Spends $170 Million for ESPN Stake," *Multichannel News,* November 12, 1990, p. 49.

Higgins, John M., "Bodenheimer to Lead ESPN," *Broadcasting & Cable,* March 8, 1999, p. 18.

——, "ESPN Snags a Classic," *Broadcasting & Cable,* September 8, 1997, p. 1.

Hoffer, Richard, "Bill Rasmussen," *Sports Illustrated,* September 19, 1994, p. 120.

Katz, Richard, "ESPN Creates Extreme Games Tourney for Summer '95," *Multichannel News,* April 18, 1994, p. 23.

Kelly, Keith J., "ESPN Buys Classic Sports Network," *Knight Ridder/ Tribune Business News,* September 4, 1997.

Larson, Megan, "ESPN in the Cross Hairs," *AdWeek Eastern Edition,* June 11, 2001, p. SR22.

Maurer, Rolf, "John Skipper," *Folio: The Magazine for Magazine Management,* April 15, 1999, p. 56.

McClellan, Steve, "The New NFL Ticket Price: $18 Billion," *Broadcasting & Cable,* January 19, 1998, p. 4.

McConville, Jim, "ABC Combines Sports with ESPN Under Bornstein," *Broadcasting & Cable,* April 15, 1996, p. 18.

——, "ESPN Extends Brand with Classic Sports," *Electronic Media,* September 8, 1997, p. 3.

——, "ESPN Leads Race for Classic Sports," *Electronic Media,* September 1, 1997, p. 8.

——, "ESPN's X Games a High Flying Success," *Broadcasting & Cable,* June 23, 1997, p. 3.

——, "ESPN Tops in Cable," *Electronic Media,* November 8, 1999, p. 40.

——, "Fox Heats up Cable Sports Competition," *Electronic Media,* August 17, 1998, p. 1.

Mitchell, Kim, "MLB Approves New ESPN Pact," *Multichannel News,* September 13, 1993, p. 2.

Moss, Linda, "ESPN2, Fox Take Dead Aim at MTV Generation," *Multichannel News,* July 19, 1993, p. 60.

——, "ESPN2 Wins over Many Operators with Local Avails," *Multichannel News,* December 20, 1993, p. 31.

"Ohlmeyer Deals Sports to ESPN," *Broadcasting & Cable,* March 22, 1993, p. 24.

"Out of the Lineup," *Sports Illustrated,* August 31, 1998, p. 18.

Pomerantz, Dorothy, "Seventh-Inning Slump," *Forbes,* May 14, 2001, p. 54.

Reynolds, Mike, "Bodenheimer Adds ABC Sports Gig," *Multichannel News,* March 10, 2003, p. 14.

"Roger Werner and the Sporting Life," *Broadcasting,* January 23, 1989, p. 175.

Romano, Allison, "Pay It Forward," *Broadcasting & Cable,* January 28, 2002, p. 16.

Ross, Dalton, "First . . . and Long," *Entertainment Weekly,* September 8, 2000, p. 94.

Schlosser, Joe, "Disney Grabs the Puck," *Broadcasting & Cable,* August 24, 1998, p. 1.

Taaffe, William, "ESPN Shoots and Scores," *Sports Illustrated,* May 5, 1986, p. 48.

Umstead, R. Thomas, "ESPN, Fox to Carry National Hockey League Games," *Multichannel News,* September 19, 1994, p. 24.

——, "ESPN Walks from Baseball Package," *Multichannel News,* November 2, 1992, p. 1.

——, "Lifetime Leads, but Broadcast Rules," *Multichannel News,* November 4, 2002, p. 57.

——, "MLB Plays Hardball, Terminates ESPN," *Multichannel News,* May 10, 1999, p. 1.

——, "Werner Resigns Post at ESPN," *Multichannel News,* September 3, 1990, p. 1.

"The Walt Disney Co. Reached over to ESPN for Its New President of ABC Sports," *Broadcasting & Cable,* March 29, 1999, p. 76.

Zahradnik, Rich, "ESPN's Cup of Cheer," *Marketing & Media Decisions,* November 1986, p. 20.

Zoglin, Richard, "Tightening the Belts at ABC," *Time,* May 5, 1986.

—David P. Bianco

Ferro Corporation

1000 Lakeside Avenue
Cleveland, Ohio 44114-7000
U.S.A.
Telephone: (216) 641-8580
Fax: (216) 875-2705
Web site: http://www.ferro.com

Public Company
Incorporated: 1919 as Ferro Enameling Company
Employees: 7,481
Sales: $1.5 billion (2002)
Stock Exchanges: New York
Ticker Symbol: FOE
NAIC: 325131 Inorganic Dye and Pigment
    Manufacturing; 325998 All Other Miscellaneous
    Chemical Product and Preparation Manufacturing;
    325510 Paint and Coating Manufacturing; 325910
    Printing Ink Manufacturing

Ferro Corporation is a leading worldwide producer of coatings and performance chemicals used in the electronics, transportation, appliance, building and renovation, and household furnishing industries. The company has utilized an acquisition strategy for much of its history to promote growth and has operations in over 20 countries—its products are sold in over 100 countries across the globe. Established in 1919, Ferro operates as the largest supplier of ceramic glaze and porcelain enamel coatings.

Early History: 1920s

Ferro was founded in 1919 by Harry D. Cushman as the Ferro Enameling Company. Cushman had worked for the American Rolling Mill Co. (Armco) of Cleveland since the early 1900s when he and fellow employee Raymond L. Williams decided to strike out on their own with a porcelain enamel shop, making themselves president and vice-president, respectively.

In the early 1920s, enameling was based on the manufacture of frit, a glass compound. The business commenced in 1920 with an investment of $1,000. As a subcontractor, Ferro Enameling Company applied porcelain enamel finishes to component parts, then returned the parts to the client for assembly. In its first year of operation, Ferro produced 59,000 pounds of porcelain enamel.

During that first year, salesman Robert A. Weaver approached Harry Cushman with an unusual proposal. Weaver offered to provide marketing and other services through a separate company and leave the technical aspects of the business to the original enterprise. He had been involved in sales and advertising with several porcelain enameling companies in the 1910s and, like his prospective clients, hoped to go into business for himself.

Cushman and Williams agreed to Weaver's proposition, and in 1920 Weaver founded the Ferro Enamel & Supply Co. to sell and service Ferro Enameling Co. products. The two companies endured early financial problems but soon grew in the favorable economic climate of the 1920s.

By passing marketing responsibilities on to Weaver, Cushman was given more time to concentrate on the technical aspect of the enameling business. His early emphasis on technical research and development started a tradition of scientific inquiry at Ferro that would continue throughout the company's history and drive its growth and expansion. Cushman's emphasis on quality control gave birth to the company's logo in 1921. The "Check-Mark-Within-a-Circle" has evolved over the decades but remained the trademark into the new century.

While Cushman concentrated on the technical aspects of the business, Robert Weaver formulated a new marketing plan that later would be known as "systems marketing." He proposed that the company not limit its products to porcelain enamel frit, but also produce the tools customers needed to complete the enameling process.

Soon Ferro Enamel & Supply Co. was in the business of designing and manufacturing complete equipment for enameling, from furnaces to finishing. In 1926, the company formed an engineering division to handle this burgeoning business that grew with the expanding appliance industry. The division's first technical achievement came in 1928 when Ferro patented the "U-type" continuous furnace, which soon became an industry standard.

In 1923, Weaver came up with another innovative marketing tool. He founded the industry's first trade journal, *The Enamelist,* to foster use of enamel coatings. The periodical featured advertising, news, and semi-technical pieces. It was emulated by competitors and eventually evolved into *The International Enamelist,* reflecting Ferro's global scope.

The company's first international expansion came in 1927 after a Ferro executive from Canada suggested that the company build a plant in his adopted homeland. In its first three years of operation, Ferro Enamels (Canada) Limited, Canada's first porcelain enamel supplier, imported the product from the United States. By the end of the decade, the company opened a modest plant in Ottawa.

Ferro ventured across the Atlantic Ocean before the decade's end, but the company took many factors into account before deciding on its overseas locations. At the time, long-distance communications still posed a problem. Political and currency stability and the initial investment were also considered before Ferro settled on England and Holland as subsidiary locations.

Despite the relatively high shipping costs associated with exporting, The Ferro Enameling Company (England) Limited was undertaken as strictly a marketing business in 1929. The company was established in a Wombourne warehouse about 120 miles from London. Ferro chose Rotterdam as its Holland site for production and distribution because of its access to fuel and raw materials, and for its situation on the largest port in continental Europe.

This first decade of growth ended with three events that shaped Ferro's future: the decision to sell shares in Ferro Enameling Company on the American Stock Exchange, the October 1929 stock market crash, and the worldwide economic depression of the 1930s. The onslaught of the Great Depression motivated Ferro Enamel & Supply to merge with Ferro Enameling to form the Ferro Enameling Corporation in the spring of 1930. The company was struck another blow when Harry Cushman, recently named chairman of the new entity, died in May. Cofounder Raymond Williams replaced Cushman as chairman, and Robert Weaver was elected president.

Expansion in the 1930s

In Weaver's continuing quest to promote Ferro's porcelain enameled products, he advanced the idea of an all-porcelain house in 1932. The company's first attempt at the concept featured porcelain enameled steel shingles on the outside and porcelain amenities inside. A second model, opened that same year, was subjected to various strength tests to illustrate the durability of Ferro's products. Although the company would make forays into the residential building materials market in the 1940s and 1970s, the products did not catch on.

Despite the deepening recession, Ferro continued to expand in the 1930s. In 1933, the company acquired Allied Engineering Co. of Columbus, Ohio, and made it a second engineering division. Allied was a recognized leader in the design and manufacture of china, pottery, and tile kilns, having created the industry's first circular kiln.

Ferro dramatically expanded its international influence in the 1930s, establishing businesses in four countries within just two years. Ferro France, founded in 1934 about 150 miles from Paris, imported porcelain enamel frit from Ferro Holland for its first year in operation, then inaugurated a smelting facility the following year. Ferro Enamels (Australia) Ltd. in Victoria, Ferro Brazil in Sao Paulo, and Ferro Enamel S.A. (Argentina) were created in 1935 with the cooperation of American Rolling Mills Co., former employer of Ferro's two founders.

As the world emerged from the Great Depression, Ferro expanded its operations in Britain and Holland with manufacturing facilities in England and enlargement of the Holland business. Ferro achieved 100 percent ownership of both the Holland and Canada enterprises in 1937, making the operations full-fledged subsidiaries.

Ferro augmented its product line and improved its original products near the end of the 1930s. The corporation purchased the Ceramic Supply Company (Cesco) in 1936 to supply kiln furniture and complement its Allied Engineering Division's kiln business. Ferro's sales more than doubled over the course of this difficult decade, but net income grew by only 15 percent, from $390,000 to $457,500.

Ferro penetrated the paint industry in 1940 with the purchase of the Chase Drier & Chemical Co. in Bedford, just outside Cleveland. Later renamed Bedford Chemical, the company made metallic soaps that promoted the paint drying process. This timely acquisition initiated Ferro's Chemical Division and provided inroads for wartime contracts.

Finding Opportunities in the 1940s and 1950s

As the United States' entry into World War II grew imminent, the federal War Production Board prohibited all industrial production except "war work." The ban included a Ferro mainstay, appliance manufacture, thereby threatening the company's future. Sales manager Dud Clawson earned the gratitude of his co-workers (and the presidency of Ferro in 1947) when he negotiated U.S. government contracts to manufacture incendiary products like thermit, an iron oxide-aluminum metal powder, and the newly-developed napalm, a liquid explosive. Over the course of the war, Ferro produced more than 61 million

Key Dates:

1919: Harry D. Cushman establishes the Ferro Enameling Company.
1920: Robert A. Weaver creates the Ferro Enamel & Supply Co.
1930: The two companies merge to form Ferro Enameling Corp.
1940: Ferro enters the paint industry with the purchase of Chase Drier & Chemical Co.
1951: The firm changes its name to Ferro Corporation.
1957: The company merges Cesco, Louthan Manufacturing Co., and American Clay Forming Co. to create its Refractories Division.
1979: Ferro buys five plastic color businesses; the Thermoplastic Colors and Compounds Division is established.
1982: The company fends off a takeover attempt by Crane Co.
1995: Synthetic Products Company is added to Ferro's arsenal.
2001: Ferro buys dmc2's electronics materials, ceramics, glass, and pigments business segments.

pounds of thermit and more than eight million pounds of napalm. The government even asked Ferro to take over a munitions plant in Marion, Ohio. Ferro's unanticipated involvement in the war effort earned it five Army-Navy "E" awards.

The company's overseas outposts were more directly affected by the war. In Holland, Rotterdam was unmercifully shelled for four days in 1940. The city was occupied by Germany throughout most of the war, and inhabitants concerned themselves more with day-to-day survival than with frit. Similar conditions prevailed in occupied France. Ferro England supplied hospital ware and military canteens for the government.

After the war, Ferro concentrated on reconstruction of war-damaged plants in Europe and expansion of other international interests. Canadian facilities were moved to Oakville, Ontario, and expanded by 1947. A new South African subsidiary, Ferro Enamels (Pty.) Ltd., imported ceramic products from Ferro's England subsidiary.

Ferro also focused on meeting postwar demand for appliances in the United States. The company built two new frit manufacturing facilities in Nashville, Tennessee, and Los Angeles, California, to meet market requirements. In 1946, Ferro research perfected a new frit composition that soon became an industry standard.

Ferro's Color Division grew rapidly in the postwar era. It had been established in 1939, but the work had been suspended during the war. The company's line of porcelain enamel was soon complemented with a series of ceramics pigments that catapulted Ferro to international leadership in the field. Recognizing the ascendancy of plastics, the company developed a third line of coloring agents engineered for that market. By 1947, the Color Division produced almost 5,000 different colors for the enamel, clayware, and plastics fields.

Ferro focused on expanding its product base through technological research and acquisitions in the 1950s and changed its name to Ferro Corporation in 1951 to reflect these new aspirations. When the U.S. Supreme Court eliminated the Owens-Corning Fiberglas Company's monopoly on the fiber glass industry that year, Ferro invested heavily in five domestic fiber glass plants. However, the company's profit margins never met industry standards, and the operations were eventually divested in the late 1970s.

Ferro's gel coat business fared much better than its fiber glass enterprise. This durable plastic coating developed at Ferro's Los Angeles plant in 1953 was used to coat fiber glass boats and soon became an important product line for the company.

Ferro applied two criteria to new acquisitions: each must have the potential for growth and competent management in place. During the 1950s, two specialty ceramics companies were purchased that contributed to Ferro's diversification goals: the Louthan Manufacturing Company in East Liverpool, Ohio (1954) and the American Clay Forming Company of Tyler, Texas (1957). In 1957, these two companies were organized with the Cesco Company as members of the Refractories Division.

Technological developments in the 1950s revolutionized Ferro's primary business, porcelain enameling. After observing a customer's experimental frit cooling process, Ferro engineers spent several years developing a procedure that used water-cooled steel rolls to cool molten frit. The new process was cheaper and cleaner than the centuries-old water cooling technique and gave Ferro an advantage in the industry.

The Korean War precipitated another major development for Ferro when the company was asked to develop camouflage colors for the U.S. Army Engineer Corps. The Color Division maintained sole rights to produce camouflage colors for many years and continued to hold more than three fourths of the market through the 1980s.

Ferro expanded its international presence in the 1950s with the launch of international businesses in Japan (1950), Mexico and West Germany (both 1951), Hong Kong (1953), and Italy (1958). After postwar reconstruction, Ferro Holland grew quickly, subsuming many competitors and launching many foreign subsidiaries. Ferro Holland also developed a technical advance in ceramic tile glaze that cut production costs in half. Ferro England and Ferro France expanded research facilities, entered the plastics field, and brought modern equipment on line.

The end of the decade was marked by the untimely death of president Dud Clawson. Over the course of the 1950s, Clawson had managed dramatic growth and expansion at Ferro: sales rose from $17 million to almost $64 million during that time. He was succeeded by Harry Marks, a 25-year Ferro veteran who would serve 17 more years as president, chairman, and CEO.

Acquisitions and International Growth Continue: 1960s–1970s

The company continued its acquisitions spree in the 1960s, adding nine domestic companies in the chemical and ceramics fields and making the largest purchase in its then 48-year history. Although some of the purchases were short-lived, others further expanded Ferro's product line. The addition of Pittsburgh's Vitro Company at the beginning of the decade eventually propelled Ferro to leadership in the glass color industry. Other acquisitions added coated fabrics, porous ceramic components, and specialty organic and inorganic chemicals to the conglomerate's list of products.

In 1967, Ferro purchased the Electro Refractories and Abrasives Company and thereby entered the high-temperature ceramics industry. The massive acquisition took several months to negotiate and brought such specialty products as cements, diffusing plates, and silicon carbide under Ferro's growing product umbrella.

Technological developments in the 1960s were encouraged and consolidated with the construction of a Central Research Division where research on porcelain enamel, glaze, and pigments was undertaken. One of the center's innovations was the development of "self-cleaning" coating for household ovens, which was instantly popular.

Ferro's international businesses in Japan, Holland, Canada, and Australia grew during the 1960s, and new extensions in Spain and India spread the company's global influence. The Holland subsidiary's reorganization of Ferro's French business raised that operating unit to full ownership.

Ferro's dramatic growth in the 1960s required a move into larger headquarters, and in 1969 the company moved to Cleveland's new trade center at Erieview Plaza. Driven by acquisitions, the conglomerate's sales more than doubled over the decade from $64 million to $148 million; net income kept up with that pace.

Despite economic fluctuations, a worldwide oil crisis, new environmental regulations, and shifts in top management, Ferro managed to record several accomplishments in the 1970s. Cliff Andrews was elected president and chief operating officer in 1972; he added CEO and chairman to his list of titles in 1975 and 1976. However, within just six months of those promotions, Andrews was obliged to leave his post because of poor health. Ad Posnick ascended to the presidency and chief executive officership in 1976 and led the company throughout the 1980s and into the 1990s.

Ferro established manufacturing facilities in Portugal and Venezuela and expanded operations in Spain, West Germany, Japan, and Brazil. Ferro Canada reached $10 million in sales in 1973, and Ferro Holland grew so large and complex that a holding company, Ferro (Holland) B.V., was organized to manage those businesses. Political instability and anti-American terrorism plagued Ferro's Argentinian subsidiary in the 1970s and forced the company to take extraordinary measures to protect its employees.

Technological developments were facilitated by a new corporate Technical Center that replaced the Central Research Division in 1970. Ferro's Frit Division developed forehearth colors, enabling the company to produce small runs of colored glass by the early 1970s. VEDOC organic powder coatings developed in the 1970s helped Ferro capture a vital share of the paint and enamel market. VEDOC stood for "versatile, everlasting, durable organic coating": the product line was used to finish appliances, automotive parts, and outdoor furniture.

Ferro's Refractories Division grew in the 1970s with the acquisition of the Gem Manufacturing Company, and Ferro began manufacturing vacuum-formed products like catalytic converters, insulation, and refractories for the steel industry following the purchase of the Gemcolite and Therm-X companies. The acquisition of the Keil Chemical Company in 1974 expanded Ferro's Chemical Group. At the end of the decade, Ferro purchased Transelco, Inc., a manufacturer of extremely specialized ceramic materials for the optical and electronics fields.

Having entered the plastics field just after World War II, Ferro expanded those operations into a full-fledged division in 1979 with the purchase of five plastic color businesses. The new Thermoplastic Colors and Compounds Division manufactured and marketed a comprehensive line of thermoplastic colorants.

Reorganizing in the 1980s and Early 1990s

By the end of the decade, Ferro had evolved into a highly diversified worldwide conglomerate with sales of almost $600 million. However, a deep recession in the early 1980s forced divestments and a mid-decade reorganization. The company identified thermoplastics as its new core business early in the decade and worked to bring those new operations to profitability. The new kid on the block, Ferro had competition in the industry that included established companies like General Electric, Imperial Chemical, Hercules, and Rhone-Poulenc. Occupied by the competition, Ferro was threatened with takeover by Crane Company, which acquired 22.4 percent of Ferro's stock between 1980 and 1982. Ferro blocked the hostile action by repurchasing 1.73 million shares from Crane in late 1982.

In the latter half of the decade, plastics became Ferro's fastest-growing business, providing up to a third of revenues. The company acquired plastics manufacturers in France, Portugal, and Great Britain and established or expanded plastics operations in Holland, Canada, Spain, South Africa, and Brazil. Ferro added a plastics lab to its corporate Technical Center and focused on the food packaging industry as a growth vehicle.

Ferro's reorganization started with the development of a new mission statement to establish general goals for the corporation but soon progressed to more concrete changes. Over the course of the decade, the corporation pared down its specialty ceramics division to concentrate on high-margin niche markets and sold its Allied Division and coated fabric business. In an effort to streamline operations, Ferro Europe was reorganized to include three core product lines: frit, pigments, and plastics.

Ferro Corporation moved into a new headquarters in time for its 70th anniversary in 1989. The renovated building featured Ferro architectural products, including ceramic tiles, engineered plastic materials, and powder coatings. The company entered the 1990s with a strong earnings growth of 24 percent annually from 1985 to 1989, surpassing $1 billion in worldwide sales by 1988.

Nevertheless, Ferro was not without problems. As the corporation's share price plummeted from over $40 in 1989 to under $20 in 1990, takeover threats came from four directions. Scarce raw materials and low profit margins kept the plastics division hamstrung, and both sales and earnings dropped from 1990 to 1991.

That year, Albert C. Bersticker succeeded Ad Posnick as president and CEO. Even before advancing to Ferro leadership, Bersticker set out to enhance the company's positives and eliminate the negatives. His plan to restructure the company featured three primary parts: an emphasis on income over sales growth, concentration on core businesses, and reliance on Ferro's long history of global, technological, and customer service advantages. The strategy equated into $60 million in capital investments, the elimination of 12 percent of the company's U.S., European, and Latin American salaried workforce, and increased corporate debt from about 20 percent up to 40 percent.

A number of changes occurred in the early 1990s. In March 1992, Ferro sold its steel mill products business in Tyler, Texas, to Vesuvius USA Corporation. In 1993, Ferro's Plastic Colorants and Dispersions Division acquired Imperial Chemical Industries' North American and European power coatings business, which produced polyester, epoxy, and urethane dispersions. That same year, Ferro purchased Bayer S.p.A.'s ceramic frit and color operations in Milan, Italy.

As the 1990s progressed, Ferro Corporation continued to find strength in its core businesses and international companies. The company continued to hold about 40 percent of the world's steel and porcelain enamel markets. Foreign sales, which had profit margins of 5 percent, brought in more than half of the company's revenues and 75 percent of net earnings.

Growing the Business: Mid-1990s and Beyond

After losing much of its focus on specialty ceramics in the late 1980s, Ferro made a resurgence in this sector during 1994 when in bought Diamonite Products, a unit owned by W.R. Grace & Company. The custom ceramic manufacturer added to Ferro's growing line of high-performance specialty ceramics and fit nicely into the company's strategy of gaining a stronger foothold in that segment of the market. Ferro topped off its acquisition plan with the 1995 purchase of Synthetic Products Company. The deal—one of the largest in its history—nearly doubled of the size of its polymer additives product line. Three years later, the company secured a majority interest in a powder coatings manufacturer based in China.

During the latter half of the decade, Ferro launched another restructuring effort designed to secure profit growth and shore up sales. By this time, the specialty chemicals industry had become increasingly competitive due to a flurry of merger activity. Speculation arose the Ferro could become the target for another takeover attempt and company management acknowledged the difficult road that lie ahead for the company. "I really think Ferro has a major challenge, and that is to grow the business," claimed Bersticker's successor Hector R. Ortino in a 1999 *Chemical Week* article. The CEO pointed to the importance of Ferro's restructuring, stating that it was "a matter of survival."

Indeed, as Ferro's sales remained lackluster, Ortino set plans in motion to revitalize Ferro's holdings. In 1999, the firm added electronics materials supplier Tam Ceramics Inc. and Advanced Polymer Compounding to its arsenal. Additional acquisitions followed during the early years of the new millennium. In 2000, the company snatched up the polymer modifiers business of

Solutia Inc. and National Starch and Chemical Co.'s EMCA-Remex Products division. Ferro then made a $525 million play for certain assets of OM Group Inc.'s dmc2 division the following year. The deal included dmc2's electronics materials, ceramics, glass, and pigments business segments, all of which were deemed high growth areas by Ferro management.

By 2002, the company had strengthened its international position, revamped its production facilities, and bolstered its research and technology activities. Ferro sold off its powder coatings business unit that year and announced plans to divest its specialty ceramics business in May 2003 in an attempt to focus on three core segments—Electronic Material Systems, Color and Glass Performance Materials, and Tile Coating Systems. While competition and faltering economies continued to challenge Ferro's financial performance, the company appeared to be on the right track for future success.

Principal Subsidiaries

Ferro Electronic Materials Inc.; Ferro Pfanstiehl Laboratories Inc.; Ferro Pfanstiehl (Europe) Ltd. (United Kingdom); Ferro Glass & Color Corporation; Ferro Graphics Inc.; Ferro Colores S.A. de C.V. (Mexico); Ferro EM L.P.; Ferro Industrial Products Ltd. (Canada); Ferro B.V. (The Netherlands); Ferro (Belgium) S.p.r.l.; Ferro (Holland) B.V.; Ferro France S.a.R.L.; Ferro (Italia) S.R.L.; Ferro Industrias Quimicas (Portugal) S.A.; Ferro Investments BV (The Netherlands); Ferro Toyo Co., Ltd. (China; 60%); Ferro Electronic Materials B.V. (The Netherlands); Ferro Holdings GmbH (Germany); Ferro Couleurs France S.A.; PT Ferro Ceramic Colors Indonesia (59%); Ferro Additives Asia (75.4%); dmc2 Italia SrL; Cerpart SrL (Italy); Cerdec Ceramics Italia SpA; Smaltochimica SrL (Italy; 40%); Degussa-Metais, Catalisadores e Ceramica, Lda (Portugal); Ferro Spain S.A.; Chilches Materials S.A. (Spain; 20%); Gardenia-Quimica S.A. (Spain; 48%); Kerajet S.A. (Spain; 25%); Ferro (Great Britain) Ltd.; Ferro Argentina S.A.; Minera Loma Blanca S.A. (Argentina); Procesadora de Boratos Argentinos S.A. (Argentina); Ferro Enamel do Brasil, Industria e Comercio Ltda; Ferro Mexicana S.A. de C.V.; Ferro de Venezuela C.A. (51%); Ferro Corporation (Australia) Pty. Ltd.; Ferro Far East, Ltd. (China); Ferro Suzhou Ceramic Color & Glaze Co. Ltd. (China); Ferro Taiwan Co. Ltd.; Ferro EMS Taiwan Ltd.; Ferro (Thailand) Co., Ltd. (49%); Ferro Cerdec (Thailand) Company Limited (49%); Ferro Ceramic Colors (Thailand) Co. Ltd. (51%); Ferro Electronic Materials Japan Co., Inc.; Ferro Japan K.K.; Ferro Performance Chemicals K.K. (Japan); DC-Ferro Co., Ltd. (Korea; 50%); PT Ferro Mas Dinamika (Indonesia; 95%); Ferro Enamels (Japan) Ltd. (10%); ESFEL Ecuatoriana S.A. (Ecuador; 19%).

Principal Competitors

Great Lakes Chemical Corporation; PPG Industries Inc.; Spartech Corporation.

Further Reading

Bozsin, Michael A., Harold P. Connare, and Catherine N. Scott, *Ferro: The First Seventy Years, 1919–1989*, Cleveland: Ferro Corporation, 1990.

"Ferro Completes dmc2 Buy," *Chemical Market Reporter*, September 24, 2001, p. 30.

"Ferro Corp. of Cleveland Has Completed the Sale of Its Powder Coatings Business Unit in Two Separate Transactions," *Plastics Engineering*, December 2002, p. 59.

"Ferro Moves Forward in the Electronic Materials Market," *Ceramic Industry*, April 2001, p. 24.

"Ferro Moves Forward with Geographic and Product Expansion," *Chemical Market Reporter*, December 11, 2000, p. 26.

"Financial Group Buys Ferro's Ceramics," *Chemical Week*, May 14, 2003, p. 10.

Kiesche, Elizabeth S. and Debbie Jackson, "JV Talks Falter," *Chemicalweek*, January 29, 1992.

Lappen, Alyssa A., "Someone Else's Turn?," *Forbes*, February 4, 1991, p. 94.

Marcial, Gene G., "At Ferro, It's 'Move Over, Mario,' " *Business Week*, October 29, 1990, p. 92.

McConville, Daniel J., "Despite a Trying Year, Ferro Keeps a Confident Outlook," *Chemical Week*, November 21, 1990, pp. 36–37.

Moskal, Brian S., "The Buck Doesn't Stop Here," *Industry Week*, July 15, 1991, pp. 29–30.

Schmitt, Bill, "Ferro's Challenge Pulling Out All the Stops for Growth," *Chemical Week*, June 16, 1999, p. 23.

—April S. Dougal
—update: Christina M. Stansell

First International Computer, Inc.

6F, Formosa Plastics Rear Building
201-24 Tun Hwa North Road
Taipei
Taiwan
Telephone: (+886) 2-2717-4500
Fax: (+886) 2-2718-2782
Web site: http://www.fic.com.tw

Public Company
Incorporated: 1980
Employees: 4,500
Sales: $2.7 billion (2002)
Stock Exchanges: Taiwan
Ticker Symbol: FIC
NAIC: 334111 Electronic Computer Manufacturing

Taiwan-based First International Computer, Inc. (FIC) is one of the world's leading suppliers of motherboards and other computer peripherals, as well as integrated desktop computers, notebook computers, and handheld and tablet personal computers. Motherboards remain one of the company's most important business segments, with shipments of nearly five million motherboards each year. The maturity of that market, however, has led FIC to tap into new markets for growth, such as a new line of graphic cards in 2003. The company's original equipment manufacturer (OEM) operations construct desktop and notebook computers for many of the world's top brands, including Hewlett Packard, Compaq, NEC, Packard Bell, Dell and IBM. The company is one of the top five Taiwanese notebook makers, with shipments expected to top 1.8 million units in 2003. Yet, with the shift in the notebook market to low-priced, low-margin products, FIC has begun repositioning itself as maker of "3C" (Computer, Communication, and Consumer Electronics) products, specifically with a push into the growing handheld and tablet personal computer (PC) markets, and a complementary investment into wireless technology. FIC, which posted sales of $2.7 billion in 2002, has manufacturing and assembly operations in Taiwan, mainland China, the United States, Mexico, the Czech Republic, and the Netherlands. The company is listed on the Taiwanese Stock Exchange and is linked to Taiwan's industrial powerhouse Formosa Plastics Group through cofounder Charlene Wang. Her husband, Ming Chien, remains company chairman, seconded by CEO Horace Tsiang.

Taiwanese High-Tech Pioneer in the 1980s

Founded in 1980 by the husband and wife team of Ming Chien and Charlene Wang, First International Computer brought together two opposite sides of Taiwan's political and economic history. Chien's father, Ji Chien, had been a poor farmer in pre-war Taiwan who had become a political figure protesting the industrialization policies of the new Nationalist government that had fled to Taiwan from the communist mainland. Ji Chien was thrown in jail and later executed. Ming Chien, who never knew his father, went on to study at the University of California at Berkeley, ultimately receiving a Ph.D. in electrical engineering in 1975 and marrying classmate and fellow Taiwanese Charlene Wang.

Wang's background could not have been more different from Chien's. Wang was the daughter of Wang Yung-ching, chairman of the Formosa group, who became the country's leading industrialist and one of the wealthiest people in the world—in part through support from the Nationalist government, which held Wang, who had been born into poverty himself, as an example of Taiwanese industrial and economic prowess. Yet the famously frugal Wang insisted that his children live frugally as well. As daughter Cher Wang, who became chairman of dominant Taiwanese semiconductor company VIA Technologies, told *Business Week:* "My father felt we should know the value of everyday life and how to live independently."

Like many Taiwanese in the Cold War era, Charlene came to the United States to study in the 1970s, earning a master's degree in statistics in 1973. Following their marriage, Wang and Chien went to work for Rockwell International and Bell Labs, respectively, in order to gain first-hand international work experience before returning to Taiwan in the late 1970s.

Taiwan by then had started to make its historic transition from an economy based on low-cost manufacturing and subsistence farming into one of the world's most vibrant high technology-

Company Perspectives:

First International Computer, Inc. was formed by Dr. Ming J. Chien in 1980 and has enjoyed considerable success year after year. FIC is now a dominant force in the technology market both in research and development and manufacturing fields. As Computer, Communication and Consumer Electronics (3C) markets have converged, FIC has adapted and developed to become a respected producer of 3C related products. Many new and innovative products have joined the FIC range and the company is no longer simply known for its award winning range of motherboards. Now firmly established at the top of the 3C market, FIC is determined to continue achieving excellence in the field of engineering and manufacturing services.

driven economies. Wang and Chien were to play an important part in that transition. In 1980, the couple put up their savings to establish their own business, called First International Computer. The company initially acted as a Taiwanese sales agent for international micro computer mainframe computer manufacturers. FIC quickly established itself as a major player in that market, in part because the couple's international experience helped it in its negotiations with foreign business. Yet the strength of the Formosa group, which became a major customer, also played a role, despite Wang and Chien's insistence on building their company without help from Wang's father.

Indeed, a factor in Wang and Chien's choice of business lay in the fact that electronics was an area that the elder Wang had refused to enter. As Charlene Wang told *Business Times:* "The safest thing was to go into something he knew nothing about." As it began to expand, notably into computer manufacturing, in the early 1980s, the company went to Taiwan's banks, rather than to Wang Yung-ching. Nonetheless, the willingness of banks to lend to the young company was encouraged by its relationship to Formosa.

In 1983, FIC launched its own computer brand, Leo, and by 1986 had established its own computer assembly and sales unit, Leo Systems Inc. FIC quickly recognized the potential of the nascent personal computer market, and especially the importance of one of the new computer design's primary components, the motherboard, which provided housing for the processor and other chipsets and connectivity to a computer's other components. FIC recognized that Taiwan's relatively low labor costs, a large pool of well-trained computer engineers and designers, coupled with the company's access to Formosa Group's plastics and other materials, would give it an edge in gaining a major share of the worldwide motherboard market.

Motherboard Leader in the 1990s

FIC launched motherboard production in 1987. The company continued operating as an assembler for third-party PCs as well, building a new large-scale factory in Hsien-Tien, Taiwan. This new capacity enabled the company begin distributing internationally, and for a time the Leo brand became one of Asia's top computer brand.

In 1989, the company launched its first Intel-based motherboard, gaining an early spot in a market set to explode in the 1990s. The company's fast-growing manufacturing capacity, as well as its circuit board supply relationship with Formosa's Nan Ya Plastics unit, placed it in a strong position as the PC market underwent its first price war at the beginning of the new decade. PC manufacturers suddenly shifted component sourcing to the Far East, especially Taiwan, which quickly established itself as one of the world's centers for a number of primary computer components—including motherboards.

At the beginning of the 1990s, Taiwan boasted more than 400 motherboard manufacturers. Yet FIC's superior manufacturing capacity, and its access to capital funding, enabled it to fight off the competition. In 1991, after going public on the Taiwan Stock Exchange, the company opened a new factory in Linkou, Taiwan, dedicated to motherboard production, boosting its total capacity to some 2.4 million units per year. By then, the company had set up subsidiaries in the United States and Europe in order to bring the company closer to its important U.S. and European computer clients.

FIC, which had been selling computers based on third-party designs, launched its first in-house PC computer system in 1990. In 1992, FIC set up a new production plant in Linou and established a new business unit, the Portable Computing Group, as it entered production of notebook computers as well.

By 1993, fewer than 30 motherboard manufacturers remained, and FIC itself claimed the worldwide number one position. The company's notebook production was also building steam and by the end of 1994 approached a production capacity of 10,000 per month. That year, the company opened a European configuration center in the Netherlands. At this time, the company's sales had swelled to $600 million.

FIC began to migrate its production to mainland China in the mid-1990s in order to take advantage of that market's lower wages. The company was joined by other members of the growing Wang family of high-tech companies, which included California's Everex Systems, acquired in 1993 and led by Cher Wang, and Nan Ya, led by Winston Wang, which had expanded into production of various computer components, including LCD screens. Meanwhile, FIC expanded its own production range in 1995, opening a factory in Pingzhen, Taiwan, in order to produce monitors and scanners, as well as notebook and desktop computer systems.

3C Champion for the New Century

FIC established a new factory and configuration center in Austin, Texas, in 1996. That subsidiary soon expanded, opening a second production plant in Mexico. In the meantime, FIC recognized the growth of a new type of computer user, one more willing to build their own systems and exchange components in their existing systems. To reach this new consumer market, FIC launched its own line of FIC-branded motherboards in 1996.

As the company continued to transfer its main production from Taiwan to the Chinese mainland, FIC also expanded its overseas facilities elsewhere. At the end of 1997, the company began construction of a $100 million assembly and configuration facility in the Czech Republic that was capable of produc-

Key Dates:

1980: Charlene Wang and Ming Chien found company as a sales agent for main frame and micro computers.
1983: The company begins assembling its first PC computer systems under the Leo brand.
1987: The company enters motherboard manufacturing with large-scale production facility in Hsien-Tien.
1989: First International begins assembling PCs with Intel processors.
1991: U.S. and European subsidiaries are opened and production of the first in-house personal computer design begins.
1994: A configuration plant is opened in the Netherlands.
1996: A manufacturing and configuration plant is opened in Austin, Texas.
1997: A plant is opened in the Czech Republic.
1998: A plant is opened in Brazil.
1999: A large scale production facility is opened in Guanzhou, in mainland China.
2002: A new manufacturing headquarters is set up in China.
2003: A new generation Digital Home personal computer is launched.

ing 50,000 computers per month. Production began at the Czech plant in 1998. That same year, FIC expanded again, setting up a production and configuration plant in Brazil in order to be closer to the growing South American market.

FIC's early entry in the notebook computer market gave it a strong position as that market began to take off at the end of the 1990s. As configurations approached the power of desktop computers, and prices began to fall, notebooks computers became one of the fastest-growing—and highest-margin—computer segments. FIC's own production grew strongly, particularly after it gained OEM contracts with such major PC brands as Hewlett Packard, Compaq, and, in 1998, Japan's NEC, which helped the company to double its notebook production that year to more than 350,000 units.

By the beginning of the 2000s, FIC's notebook production had topped 1.2 billion computers per year, helping it crack into the top five of Taiwan's notebook computer makers, and had come to account for a major portion of the company's more than $2 million in revenues. Yet FIC had already begun to prepare for the post-notebook market. In 1999, the company opened a new, large-scale production facility the Guanzhou free trade zone in mainland China.

The new facility was targeted at what the company called the "3C" market—for Computer, Communication, and Consumer Electronics. FIC now began developing a new generation of portable computing products, including personal digital assistants (PDAs) and, especially, a new breed of computer, launched in 2001 and backed by Microsoft, called the Tablet

PC. FIC also began developing its own wireless technologies, another market set to boom in the new decade.

FIC's transition to the Chinese mainland appeared to be reaching its logical conclusion at the end of 2002, when the company announced that it was establishing its new manufacturing headquarters on the mainland, while moving its corporate home, as well as the base for its research and development operations, to new quarters in Taipei. Nonetheless, for many industry observers, the move of these operations as well to the mainland appeared inevitable.

In the meantime, FIC continued to enjoy rising sales of its core motherboard, desktop, and notebook PC lines. The latter range was boosted in 2003 with a cooperation agreement to launch a new line of notebooks based around the wireless-capable Centrino processor from Intel into mainland China. The company also entered the computer peripherals market that year, launching its own line of graphics cards based on ATI components.

At the same time, FIC continued to pursue its 3C strategy. In June 2003, the company prepared to unveil what it considered to be the next generation in personal computing, the so-called Digital Home PC, developed jointly with Intel and Microsoft. The new system, which incorporated wireless technology into a computer design midway between a desktop and notebook configuration, had already achieved strong pre-orders from computer manufacturers as the company prepared an initial launch in Japan for October 2003. FIC now prepared to lead the computer market into its vision of a 3C future.

Principal Subsidiaries

First International Computer of America, Inc.; FIC Sales Corp. (Japan); FIC Europe; FIC Brazil.

Principal Competitors

Quanta Computer Inc.; Acer Inc.; Asustek Computer Inc.; Compal Electronics Inc.; Tatung Co.; Lite-On Technology Corp.; Synnex Technology International; VIA Technologies Inc.; Elite Group Computer Systems Company Ltd.; Gigabyte Technology Company Ltd.

Further Reading

Engardio, Pete, "A New Asian Dynasty?," *Businessweek International*, August 15, 1994.
"FIC to Expand Mainland Production," *Taiwan Economic News*, March 27, 2002.
"FIC Quick to Reap Dividends of Boost by Gates," *South China Morning Post*, November 19, 2001.
"Minds Over Matter," *Business Week*, November 27, 2000, p. 142.
"Motherboard Makers Edge into Graphics Card Business," *Taiwan Economic News*, December 19, 2002.
Savitt, Scott, "A Tale of Two Extremes," *California Monthly*, April 2001.

—M.L. Cohen

Flow International Corporation

23500 64th Avenue South
Kent, Washington 98032
U.S.A.
Telephone: (253) 850-3500
Toll Free: (800) 446-3569
Fax: (253) 813-3285
Web site: http://www.flowcorp.com

Public Company
Incorporated: 1980
Employees: 895
Sales: $179.2 million (2002)
Stock Exchanges: NASDAQ
Ticker Symbol: FLOW
NAIC: 333999 All Other General Purpose Machinery
    Manufacturing; 333298 All Other Industrial
    Machinery Manufacturing; 333319 Other Commercial
    and Service Industry Machinery Manufacturing;
    333512 Other Commercial and Service Industry
    Machinery Manufacturing

Flow International Corporation, an industry pioneer, designs and manufactures cutting and cleaning systems that use ultra-high-pressure water to perform their tasks. Flow's waterjet machines are used in a variety of applications by the aerospace, automotive, and food industries, where their ability to precisely cut everything from metal to baby diapers has won many converts to waterjet cutting technology. Flow is also a leading provider of robotics and assembly equipment. The company sells its products in more than 45 countries. In addition to its global headquarters in Kent, Washington, the company maintains a physical presence in Indiana, Michigan, Ohio, Louisiana, Canada, France, Italy, Germany, Spain, Sweden, Switzerland, the United Kingdom, Argentina, Brazil, Taiwan, China, Korea, and Japan.

Origins

The pioneering work predicating Flow's success began in the basement of Y.H. Michael Pao, a former research scientist at aerospace giant Boeing Co. During the early 1970s, Pao began working on developing new businesses based on an advanced technology, specifically the use of ultra-high-pressure (UHP) as a cutting tool for industrial applications. Once Pao had developed a workable product, he formed Flow in 1974, organizing it at first as a division of Flow Industries. The division was spun off in March 1983, when it completed its initial public offering of stock. At the end of the 1980s, Flow acquired and retired Flow Industries' interest in the Kent, Washington-based company.

Flow's debut as an enterprise coincided with the commercialization of UHP technology. The innovative technology found in the company's first product, as it was in later generations of Flow products, was found in the pump. The industrial cutting and cleaning pumps developed by Pao pressurized water as greatly as 100,000 pounds per square inch. The water then was directed through special plumbing to a "cutting head," a small nozzle that directed the water at its targeted surface. Powered by the pump, the water emerged from the cutting head at three times the speed of sound. The force was sufficient enough to cut through material without getting it wet, a stunning display of the power of water. Pao later invented and patented the world's first abrasive waterjet system, further expanding upon the capabilities of pressurized water in industrial settings. By mixing abrasive particles, such as garnet, into the waterjet stream, Pao's systems could perform astounding feats, cutting through stone or metal measuring ten inches thick.

The potential for Pao's invention clearly was promising. As the technology evolved and its market acceptance widened, Flow's systems found many uses. The company's products were used to fillet fish, make airplane wings, cut baby diapers, and shape automobile doors, among a of host of other tasks that involved cutting food, paper, rubber, foam, metal, stone, and glass. Pao's innovation joined the ranks of other cutting technologies old and new, competing against laser, plasma, and conventional saw methods. When compared against such technologies, UHP revealed several advantages. The technology created no heat in the cutting process, removing the fear of distorting materials due to high temperatures. The technology was more hygienic in food settings than conventional saws. Further, Flow's systems sold for roughly half the price of advanced cutting technologies such as laser-based systems. Flow's water-based processes were also more environmentally

Company Perspectives:

Flow's global preeminence can be attributed to its focus on four key areas: technology leadership, providing total system solutions, new product development, and expanding applications within core markets.

sound than toxic chemical and mechanical methods of cutting and cleaning. As Pao set out, it was not hard to imagine a future in which waterjet systems were ubiquitous industrial tools.

By the time Flow's fifth anniversary as a publicly traded concern occurred, the company could be described as an impressive but not overwhelming success. In 1988, when Flow's assets amounted to nearly $40 million, annual sales eclipsed $30 million, but for the previous two years the company had averaged an annual loss of $13.2 million. Flow turned the losing streak around in 1989 and 1990, averaging more than $5.5 million in annual profit during the two-year period, but in 1991 the company reported a loss of $500,000. Although the loss recorded in 1991 was not devastating, the pattern of financial instability was cause for concern. Moreover, there were worrisome events at the company's headquarters in Kent that pointed to a crisis.

Undoubtedly, Flow's strength was its technology. Effectively expressing the promise of UHP technology in the marketplace was a problem, however. Perhaps because the technology promised so much, its developers—Flow's engineers—were seduced by the possibilities of invention and failed to demonstrate the precise focus of the pressurized water streams that underpinned the company. With Pao as their steward, Flow's engineers delved into developing products that sometimes ignored what the market needed, one of the chief contributors to the company's lackluster financial performance. In reference to the freewheeling development conducted by the company's engineers, a senior executive remarked in a March 13, 1992 interview with the *Puget Sound Business Journal*, "They fragmented their efforts through these things, but nobody went out to see if anyone in the United States wanted to cut that substance."

At the beginning of the 1990s, Flow's troubles ran deeper than wayward product development, although the exact cause of the problems was hidden from those outside the company. The evidence that something was wrong was apparent to all who chose to look, however. In the spring of 1990, six Flow managers resigned *en masse*, citing differences in policies and strategy with Pao as the motivation for their exodus. Against the backdrop of the clash involving personalities and policies, Pao was looking to sell the company. In an August 27, 1990 interview with the *Puget Sound Business Journal*, Pao stated that "serious discussion with potential buyers" would be underway the following month, adding, "I don't think I want to continue to run this company." Pao's desire was soon fulfilled.

A New Era Begins in 1991

In 1991, Flow's board of directors made their move. After Pao resigned, the board appointed Ronald Turrant as president and chief executive officer and Thomas Cross as chief financial officer. The pair arrived in May 1991, recruited as a team from Augat Inc., a Massachusetts-based telecommunications firm.

Together, they headed up Augat's profitable telecommunications division, spending seven years at Augat before being tapped for their managerial expertise by Flow's board.

Pao's legacy of success was in invention, not in management. The Turrant-led era became known for its managerial prowess, something Flow sorely needed to eradicate its reputation as a company with brilliant technology but hobbled by a murky marketing focus. Turrant's challenge was to create financial stability by reining in Flow's research and development efforts without stifling the creativity of its engineers. To achieve his goal, Turrant looked to the market for what it wanted and, subsequently, focused on three sectors: aerospace, automotive, and food and forest industries. Turrant also altered the company's product mix to include less expensive waterjets and complete cutting systems that included waterjets. Additionally, the company announced plans to introduce three new pumps within the coming year, a move designed to move Flow into new market segments.

Turrant's restorative touch worked wonders, lending a focused and ambitious air to Flow's operations. In 1992, he set of goal of turning Flow into a $100 million-in-sales company in five years, an objective the new chief executive officer easily met. Acquisitions played a part in Flow's turnaround, beginning with the January 1992 purchase of Rampart Waterblast Inc., a $4 million-in-sales company that used Flow's technology to remove rubber and paint from airport runways. The following month, the company forged a global sales and distribution agreement with Emerald Creek Garnet Co. In September 1992, Flow acquired Spider Staging Corp., the first of two acquisitions that added a new facet to the company's structure. Spider Staging produced power-driven scaffolding and exterior building maintenance systems. In March 1993, Flow acquired Power Climber Inc., a maker of power hoists and other power scaffolding equipment. During the first two years of his reign, Turrant also consolidated Flow's operations into a new headquarters building. The affect the Turrant-led additions and changes had on Flow were clearly evident, turning the money-losing, $41 million-in-sales company he inherited into a $79 million-in-sales company with a profit of $4.6 million in 1993.

Turrant's initial success in transforming a technical company into a marketer was followed by an ill-fated attempt at greatly aggrandizing the company's operations. Flow became embroiled in a fight with the U.S. Department of Justice (DOJ) in the spring of 1994 after Turrant proposed to acquire its largest rival, the Waterjet Cutting Systems Division of Ingersoll-Rand Co. Flow incurred $400,000 in expenses pleading its cause, but eventually abandoned the proposed acquisition. The DOJ alleged Flow and Waterjet constituted the only two significant competitors in the industry, declaring their union would create a "near total monopoly," as reported in the January 27, 1995 issue of the *Puget Sound Business Journal*. Forced to look elsewhere for a way to grow, Turrant set his acquisitive sights on two other companies. In December 1994, the company acquired Dynovation Machine Systems, Inc., an Ontario, Canada-based robotics manufacturer. The following month, Flow purchased ASI Robotics Systems, a designer and manufacturer of robots and related systems used in waterjet applications. Together, the acquisitions added $20 million to Flow's revenue volume and enabled the company to sell complete precision cutting systems. Previously, customers were forced to purchase waterjets and robotics separately.

By the mid-1990s, Flow stood as the preeminent leader in its field. The company's product line, encompassing models that sold for between $80,000 and $3 million, controlled between 40 percent and 60 percent of the waterjet market, according to industry observers. By 1995, annual sales reached $110 million, well ahead of the growth projections articulated at the beginning of the Turrant era. Encouraged by the progress, Turrant entered the latter half of the 1990s pursuing another financial goal. By 2008, he intended to reach $208 million in sales.

Flow Falters in the Late 1990s

During the late 1990s, much of Flow's attention and hope was placed on a new application for the company's technology. Trademarked as "Fresher Under Pressure," Flow's new business line focused on the food industry, the single largest manufacturing industry in the world. Using its UHP technology, the company developed a process that pasteurized food without heat, a capability that caused a stir of excitement within both the food and waterjet industries. The uses of Fresher Under Pressure were numerous, applicable to products such as wine, juice, eggs, guacamole, baby food, and dozens more. One model, a $500,000 Flow machine, was eagerly embraced by the shellfish industry for its ability to cleanly shuck oysters and eradicate any pathogens present.

As Flow exited the 1990s and entered the 21st century, all eyes were focused on the market success of Fresher Under Pressure. In March 1999, the company purchased ABB Pressure Systems, a subsidiary of Swedish industrial giant Asea Brown Boveri AB, to help bolster its reach into the developing business of treating food with UHP. ABB Pressure Systems ranked as the world's leading supplier of large, bulk UHP systems to the food industry, as well as the global leader in isostatic and flexform press systems for the aerospace and automotive industries.

By 2001, Flow's Fresher Under Pressure business had yet to fulfill its promise. The company had invested nearly $70 million in its food safety business, but the business, operating as a subsidiary named Avure Technologies, was consistently losing money. Turrant remained optimistic, however. In an August 29, 2001 interview with *The Seattle Times,* Turrant declared, "Fresher Under Pressure will be at least as big as our core business in five years." As it happened, Turrant would never see if his prediction came true, at least not as Flow's chief executive officer.

For the company's fiscal 2002, it reported a $6 million loss on a 13 percent drop in sales to $179.2 million. In August 2002,

several months after the financial figures were announced, Turrant announced his departure from Flow. In December 2002, he stepped down as chairman and chief executive officer, retaining his position as president until a new president and chief executive officer joined the company. In January 2003, Turrant's replacement arrived, a corporate turnaround specialist named Stephen Light. Previously, Light had served as the president and chief executive officer of Wisconsin-based OmniQuip, a Textron subsidiary that manufactured light construction equipment.

As Light plotted Flow's future course, his challenge was to return the company to financial growth and resolve the difficulties experienced by Avure Technologies. Early in 2003, Light reduced the company's workforce and launched a two-year restructuring program. Light also hinted that Flow might sell Avure Technologies. Looking ahead, Flow's technology held it in good stead—as it had throughout the company's history. The general problem was in effectively applying the technology to the marketplace, the chief concern at the beginning of the Turrant era and the chief concern at the beginning of the Light era. Whatever the outcome of Light's attempts to restore financial growth, Flow's place in industry history was secure. The company was a pioneer, responsible for bringing a promising new technology to manufacturing firms throughout the world.

Principal Subsidiaries

Flow International Sales Corporation (Guam); Flow Europe, GmbH (Germany); Flow Asia Corporation (Taiwan); Flow Asia International Corporation (Mauritius); Flow Japan Corporation; Foracon Maschinen und Anlagenbau GmbH & Co. (Germany); CIS Acquisition Corporation; Robotic Simulations Limited (United Kingdom); Hydrodynamic Cutting Services; Flow Automation Systems Corporation; Flow Autoclave Systems, Inc.; Flow Holdings GmbH (SAGL) Limited Liability Company (Switzerland); Flow Pressure Systems Vasteras AB (Sweden).

Principal Competitors

Giddings & Lewis, Inc.

Further Reading

Baker, M. Sharon, "Redirecting Flow Pays Off with Stream of Profits," *Puget Sound Business Journal*, August 27, 1993, p. 7
"CEO Announces Retirement," *Stone World*, December 2002, p. 32.
"Flow International Posts Losses in 4th Quarter and Fiscal Year," *Seattle Post-Intelligencer*, June 6, 2002, p. D2.
Fryer, Alex P., "Analysts Going with Flow Despite CFO's Departure," *Puget Sound Business Journal*, June 7, 1996, p. 6.
Karuza, Jennifer, "A Pasteurizing Shucker Extends Oyster Shelf Life," *National Fisherman*, July 2002, p. 10.
Peterson, Kim, "Slump Causes Retooling at Flow; Layoffs Expected Soon," *Seattle Times*, February 20, 2003, p. E1.
Virgin, Bill, "Flow Sizes Up Losses, Maps Out Strategy," *Seattle Post-Intelligencer*, March 18, 2003, p. D7.
Wilhelm, Steve, "If Flow Has Its Way, It'll Be Getting New Owners," *Puget Sound Business Journal*, August 27, 1990, p. 3.
——, "Flow Puts Fresh Bounce in Its Achilles' Heel," *Puget Sound Business Journal*, March 13, 1992, p. 5.
——, "Flow Turns Up Pressure in Promising Markets," *Puget Sound Business Journal*, June 19, 1998, p. 4.

—Jeffrey L. Covell

Flying Boat, Inc. (Chalk's Ocean Airways)

704 S.W. 34th Street
Fort Lauderdale, Florida 33315
U.S.A.
Telephone: (954) 359-0329
Toll Free: (800) 4 CHALKS
Web site: http://www.chalksoceanairways.com

Private Company
Incorporated: 1919 as Chalk's Flying Service
Employees: 130
Sales: $6 million (1999 est.)
NAIC: 481111 Scheduled Passenger Air Transportation;
481211 Nonscheduled Chartered Passenger Air
Transportation; 487990 Scenic and Sightseeing
Transportation, Other; 488190 Other Support
Activities for Air Transportation

Flying Boat, Inc., which does business under the trade name Chalk's Ocean Airways, is the world's top seaplane airline. The mode of travel is a unique mixture of convenience and sightseeing, as the planes fly closer to the turquoise Caribbean water than conventional land-based craft and are able to land directly next to some Bahamian resorts. Its seaplanes have become something of a visual icon for Miami; the company also flies from Fort Lauderdale, where it maintains its headquarters. Chalk's has changed ownership and names several times. The undeniable glamour and excitement of flying boats often forms some part of the attraction for buyers, though the economics of these high-maintenance craft provides a considerable challenge. Chalk's also lays claim to being the world's oldest scheduled airline, beating KLM Royal Dutch Airlines and Avianca Venezuela Airlines by some months.

Origins

Arthur Burns ''Pappy'' Chalk founded Chalk's Flying Service in 1919, two years after moving to Miami from Paducah, Kentucky. His story is linked with that of aviation legend Tony Jannus, who pioneered the scheduled airline by launching a regular hop from St. Petersburg to Tampa in 1914.

Chalk met Jannus after he made an unscheduled landing in the Ohio River in 1911. Chalk traded his skills as a mechanic at the Kentucky Auto Mechanic Co. for flying lessons. He then spent a few years barnstorming around the South before serving with the U.S. military in World War I. After the war, Chalk started his own flying service in Miami, then largely undeveloped, with a single Stinson Voyager seaplane. He charged $5 for sightseeing flights and $15 for flying lessons.

The operation's first terminal was a beach umbrella next to the dock of the Royal Palm Hotel. Bimini was the first destination. In the early days, Chalk hired Bahama natives to carry passengers ashore piggyback. Pappy Chalk himself was flying up to 12 hours a day. Aircraft used included a pair of S-29 Sikorsky seaplanes.

In the prohibition era, rumrunners and their pursuing lawmen formed much of Chalk's clientele. In 1926, Chalk's began using Watson Island, a newly created landfill, as an operating base. The airline developed a storied charter business, at one point rescuing deposed Cuban President Gerardo Machado amid of volley of bullets.

Wealthy big game hunters and fisherman, typified by Ernest Hemingway, became regular customers after the repeal of prohibition in 1933. The first terminal structure of any substance on Watson Island was built out of coral in 1936.

During World War II, Chalk operated a Fairchild aircraft on submarine patrols. In the postwar period, the nine-passenger Grumman Goose was the workhorse of the fleet.

Pappy Chalk retired in 1964 after the death of his wife, Lillie Mae Chalk, who had helped run the operation since their marriage in 1932. Dean Franklin, Chalk's long-time friend, bought the airline in 1966, adding service to Key West and Fort Jefferson the following year.

Businessman Edward Dixon was the next to acquire Chalk's in 1973, and he sold it to Resorts International, a developer of hotels in the Bahamas, the next year. Chalk remained chairman of the airline until his death in 1977.

Company Perspectives:

New ownership, new identity, new destinations, and a bold outlook will ensure that Chalk's Ocean Airways remains the world's premier seaplane airline.

New Planes in the 1970s–80s

In the late 1970s, Chalk's began using 30-passenger G-111 Albatross seaplanes, a modification of the venerable HU-16, which had been produced as a military aircraft between 1949 and the mid-1960s. At the time, Chalk's was flying about 45,000 passengers a year, and demand was increasing. No aircraft companies were then making commercial amphibious airplanes, so Chalk's upgraded its own. Antilles Air Boats was acquired in 1979.

Service between Miami, Paradise Island, and West Palm Beach began in 1981. The company upgraded the fleet of five 13-place Grumman G-73 Mallard aircraft to turboprop engines in the early 1980s, at a cost of $4 million.

The television show *Miami Vice,* a symbol of both Miami and the 1980s, featured a Chalk's seaplane in its opening credits. Chalk's fleet was as high-maintenance as it was glamorous. It was a unique carrier, its Watson Island base being the smallest port of entry in the United States. Chalk's revenues were about $7.5 million in 1986, when it carried 130,000 passengers. Most were staying at Resorts International properties, although island residents used the airline for shopping trips to Miami.

Resorts International owner Jim Crosby was an enthusiastic supporter of the airline and began to expand its fleet with 13 thoroughly upgraded, 30-passenger Grumman G-111 seaplanes. After Crosby's death, these planes went into storage in Arizona. Donald Trump acquired Resorts International in 1987. He owned it for a year before selling it to Merv Griffin Enterprises.

Chalk's signature seaplanes were restricted to daylight operations due to the difficulty of ascertaining landing conditions on water at night. In March 1989, Resorts launched another airline, Paradise Island Airways, to handle increased vacation traffic from Florida to the Bahamas. Its three 50-seat, STOL (short take-off and landing) Dash-7 planes were operated by Chalk's personnel to land-based airstrips. The two brands were carrying more than 60,000 passengers a year, only a quarter of them on Chalk's seaplanes. A handful of other small South Florida airlines, like Aero Coach, plied the skies between Miami or Fort Lauderdale and Nassau or Freeport.

Crossing Stormy Seas in the 1990s

The 1990s began with the near-closing of the airline and its sale in early 1991 to United Capital Corporation of Rockford, Illinois. This venture capital group was owned by Seth and Connie Atwood, two seaplane enthusiasts. The legal entity was called Flying Boat, Inc., but the airline continued to do business under the Chalk's name.

Chalk's passed an interesting milestone on June 28, 1991, when it flew its first scheduled domestic flight, connecting Miami directly to the Florida Keys. The company had nearly 30,000 passengers in 1991. Chalk's became licensed to perform maintenance for other seaplane operators in 1993.

After 75 years of flying, Chalk's experienced its first fatal accident in March 1994 when one of its seaplanes crashed upon take-off from the Florida Keys. Two crewmembers were killed.

A group of investors then acquired Chalk's—known as Chalk's International Airlines at the time—for about $5 million in January 1996. The partners included Miami developer Craig Robins; Chuck Slagle, owner of Alaska's Seaborne Aviation; and Chuck Cobb, who held rights to the Pan Am name.

Chalk's began operating as Pan Am Air Bridge on March 1, 1996. However, the airline was not a feeder airline for the new Pan Am, which had returned to operations along the East Coast. The legendary trademark evoked the massive Clipper flying boats that the original Pan American had flown to exotic destinations. Pan Am Air Bridge was then operating a fleet of five Grumman seaplanes.

The former Chalk's was up for sale again by September 1997. By this time, it was breaking even. Aircraft leasing company Air Alaska acquired a 70 percent share in the company from Craig Robins in January 1998 for $2 million, at the same time signing notes for another $8 million for five of the company's planes. Pan Am Corp., through its Pan American World Airways unit, retained a 30 percent holding in Pan Am Air Bridge. Air Alaska also acquired land rights to its Watson Island base. A few months later, Guilford Transportation Industries acquired a 30 percent holding in Pan Am Air Bridge via its purchase of Pan American World Airways.

An involuntary bankruptcy temporarily grounded Pan Am Air Bridge in February 1999. It soon restarted operations under its former name, Chalk's International Airlines. Chalk's was rebranded again in December 1999, as Chalk's Ocean Airways. That month, the company relaunched service, opening a new route to Paradise Island, in the Bahamas, whose airport had been closed and was directly accessible only by seaplane. Chalk's planes were refurbished and repainted for the opening; the company's terminals were also being upgraded. Paradise Island Airways, Chalk's land-based air service, closed in May 1999.

Miami entrepreneur and former Eastern Airlines pilot Jim Confalone acquired Chalk's out of bankruptcy on August 2, 1999, for $925,000. By this time, it was operating just two leased aircraft and had only 35 employees. After buying the airline, Confalone agreed to buy 14 30-seat Grumman G-111 seaplanes from Chalk's former owner, Seth Atwood of Chicago.

Hope on the Horizon in 2000 and Beyond

The tremendous growth of the Bahamas as a tourist destination, particularly among the affluent, boded well for Chalk's niche, a blend of transportation, convenience, and entertainment. In 2000, Chalk's began flying from Fort Lauderdale to a Freeport resort, called "Our Lucaya," which was being overhauled by Hong Hong developer Hutchinson & Whampoa Ltd.

Like most airlines, Chalk's was affected by the September 11, 2001, terrorist attacks on the United States. It cut schedules

Key Dates:

1919: Chalk's founded in Miami by Arthur B. "Pappy" Chalk.
1926: Watson Island base established.
1964: Arthur Chalk retires from Chalk's daily operations.
1966: Chalk's friend Dean Franklin buys airline.
1974: Resorts International acquires Chalk's.
1987: Donald Trump acquires Resorts International.
1988: Trump sells Resorts to Merv Griffin Enterprises; Chalk's files bankruptcy.
1991: Resorts sells Chalk's to United Capital Corporation; company's legal name changed to Flying Boat, Inc.
1996: Investment group buys Chalk's, operates it as Pan Am Air Bridge.
1999: Jim Confalone acquires Chalk's; refurbishes fleet, terminal.
2003: Chalk's continues to grow despite three challenging years for the aviation industry.

by up to 25 percent, and reduced its operations from four full-time aircraft to three flying part-time. The schedule was soon restored, however. While major carriers such as United and American Airlines were dealing with bankruptcy issues, Chalk's was beginning to grow again, though the 2003 war in Iraq prompted another temporary slowdown.

Confalone described his "CEO" business model to the *Miami Herald:* "Customer is first, the Employee is second, and the Owner is last." To ensure the promptest service, employees were discouraged from talking to each other on duty, a practice Confalone borrowed from The Car Wash, one of his successful service-driven enterprises.

In 2003, some industry analysts speculated that Chalk's might return to profitability in the coming year. With its long history of weathering financial turbulence, Flying Boat and Chalk's seemed likely to remain a leader in its niche market.

Principal Divisions

Bimini Landing.

Principal Competitors

American Eagle; Bahamasair Holdings Limited; Continental Airlines.

Further Reading

Bell, Maya, "Land Feud Threatens Miami's Flying Legend," *Orlando Sentinel,* February 20, 1989, p. B1.

Bellido, Susana, "A New Pan Am in the Air," *Miami Herald,* March 2, 1996, p. B5.

Blackerby, Cheryl, "It's Not Splashy, But Seaplane Airline Keeps Floridians Flying," *Orange County Register,* August 22, 1993, p. D7.

"Chalk One Up for Miami Businessman," *Press Journal* (Vero Beach), August 13, 1999, p. D1.

"Chalk's International: 75 Years of Uninterrupted Service," *Business & Commercial Aviation,* July 1, 1994.

"Chalk's International Becomes Pan Am Air Bridge; No Feeder Plans Yet," *Commuter/Regional Airline News,* February 19, 1996.

"A Chalk's Outline—How the Carrier Went from Grounding to Growth," *Commuter/Regional Airline News,* August 30, 1999.

Chandler, Michele, "Beach Developer Wants Chalk's," *Miami Herald,* December 22, 1995, p. C1.

Clary, Mike, "Passengers Still Get a Rush from Chalk's Adventure Flights," *Miami Herald,* August 23, 1992, p. F5.

Cordle, Ina Paiva, "Entrepreneur Moves to Buy Miami's Historic Seaplane Venture," *Miami Herald,* May 5, 1999.

——, "Nonstop Flight Service Between Miami and Anchorage Planned," *Miami Herald,* January 31, 1998.

——, "Pan Am Air Bridge in Miami May Have to Change Its Name," *Miami Herald,* June 30, 1998.

——, "Trustee Weighs Offers for Miami Seaplane Business; Judge to Decide," *Miami Herald,* April 27, 1999.

Doris, Tony, "Former Chalk's for Sale," *Broward Daily Business Review,* September 18, 1997, p. A1.

Fields, Gregg, "Miami Seaplane Service Sees Sunny Skies Ahead After Years of Turbulence," *Miami Herald,* April 11, 2003.

——, "Trump Bid Leaves Chalk's Up in the Air," *Miami Herald,* March 11, 1987, p. 4.

Gonzales, Aminda, "Seaplanes Chalk Up 75 Colorful Years," *Miami Herald,* June 18, 1994, p. B1.

Hagstrom, Suzy, "Rough Skies for Commuters; Arriving at Profits Not Easy for Regional Airlines Serving Florida," *Orlando Sentinel,* July 1, 1985.

Jaffe, Charles A., "Pioneer Tony Jannus Played a Part in Chalk's Colorful Past," *St. Petersburg Times,* Bus. Sec., June 7, 1987, p. 31.

——, "Turbulent Times for Romance," *St. Petersburg Times,* June 7, 1987, Bus. Sec.

Keating, Dan, "Chalk's Spreads Its Wings, Adds Flights to Key West," *Miami Herald,* June 13, 1991, p. B5.

Kleinberg, Howard, "Beloved Chalk's the Oldest Airline? Maybe, Maybe Not," *Miami Herald,* February 13, 1996, p. A9.

Magnotta, Ann and Vince, "New Planes Help Deliver Visitors to Paradise Island," *Sun Sentinel,* March 12, 1989, p. 8J.

Matas, Alina, "Chalk's New Chapter," *Broward Daily Business Review,* October 26, 2001, p. A1.

Nesbitt, Jim, "Flying Closer to a Last Splash in the Bahamas," *Newsday,* November 5, 1989, p. 21.

"New Chalk's Owners Plan Gradual Growth in Seaplane Service," *Regional Aviation Weekly,* February 15, 1991, p. 60.

North, David M., "Albatross Refurbished for Commuter," *Aviation Week & Space Technology,* April 9, 1979, p. 32.

"One-on-One with Chalk International's Jim Confalone," *Commuter/Regional Airline News,* August 23, 1999.

Reed, Ted, "Chalk's Gets New Owner, New Name," *Miami Herald,* January 30, 1996, p. B7.

"Resorts International Sells Chalk's to United Capital," *Aviation Daily,* February 19, 1991.

Rimmer, David, "Chalk's Responds to Terror," *Business & Commercial Aviation,* November 1, 2001, p. 30.

Staletovich, Jenny, "Two Men Die When Seaplane Crashes in Waters Off Key West," *Palm Beach Post,* March 19, 1994, p. 2B.

Stieghorst, Tom, "Chalk Up 3 New Flights to Freeport; Seaplane Service Starts in December," *Sun Sentinel* (Fort Lauderdale), September 27, 2000, p. 1D.

——, "Small Airlines Stay Aloft on Service to Islands," *Sun Sentinel* (Ford Lauderdale), August 15, 1988, p. 3.

Stiteler, Rowland, "Sea Shuttle," *Orlando Sentinel,* October 23, 1988, p. 8.

Weller, Steve, "Chalk's Venerable Seaplanes Downed by High-Roller with Low Bank Balance," *Sun Sentinel* (Fort Lauderdale), November 21, 1989, p. 12A.

—Frederick C. Ingram

Fresenius

Fresenius AG

Else-Kröner-Strasse 1
D-61352 Bad Homburg
Germany
Telephone: (49) 6172 608-0
Fax: (49) 6172 608-2488
Web site: http://www.fresenius-ag.com

Public Company
Incorporated: 1912 as Dr. E. Fresenius KG
Employees: 63,638
Sales: EUR 7.5 billion ($7.9 billion)(2002)
Stock Exchanges: Frankfurt Dusseldorf Munich
Ticker Symbol: FRE
NAIC: 621492 Kidney Dialysis Centers; 325412
  Pharmaceutical Preparation Manufacturing; 339112
  Surgical and Medical Instrument Manufacturing;
  334510 Electromedical and Electrotherapeutic
  Apparatus Manufacturing; 622310 Specialty (Except
  Psychiatric and Substance Abuse) Hospitals

Fresenius AG is a global, diversified manufacturer of health care products and provider of health care services with headquarters in Bad Homburg, Germany. The company's largest subsidiary, Fresenius Medical Care AG (FMC AG), in which Fresenius AG holds a majority stake in the voting capital, is the world's largest provider of services for patients with chronic kidney failure and is listed on the New York Stock Exchange. Over 100,000 patients are treated in FMC AG's more than 1,500 dialysis centers around the world. Another subsidiary, Fresenius Kabi, makes machines and special solutions used in infusion therapy as well as products for clinical nutrition with a leading position in China and South Korea and a strong foothold in Western Europe. The company's third area of activity is project and facility management for hospitals, including staff recruitment and training, which is organized under the umbrella of Fresenius ProServe. Fresenius ProServe owns Wittgensteiner Kliniken AG, a chain of clinics with 4,600 employees and facilities in Germany, the Czech Republic, and Finland. Fresenius ProServe also builds and manages clinics in Malaysia

and the Philippines. In addition, Fresenius makes medical technology for blood treatment. Fresenius AG generates about nine-tenths of all revenues outside of Germany, with FMC AG contributing 71 percent of total sales. North America is the most important market for the company, followed by Western Europe. Fresenius AG is also active in South America, Asia, and Eastern Europe. The not-for-profit Else Kröner Fresenius-Foundation owns a majority stake in the company.

Pharmacist Becomes Entrepreneur in 1912

The roots of Fresenius AG go back to the 18th century. At that time, the Fresenius family took over one of Frankfurt's oldest pharmacies—the Hirsch Apotheke. Founded in 1462, the pharmacy was located on the Zeil, a busy market street in the city center of Frankfurt am Main. In 1911, pharmacist Dr. Eduard Fresenius became the new owner of the long-established store. Fresenius, however, was not only a skilled pharmacist but also an ambitious businessman. In his pharmacy, Dr. Fresenius had a small laboratory where he soon started experimenting with pills, salves, and solutions. Only one year after he had taken over the pharmacy, Fresenius established his own pharmaceutical company, Dr. E. Fresenius KG.

Right from the beginning, Fresenius paid close attention to the practical needs of doctors and patients and developed a sense for promising niche markets. The first product of the Fresenius manufacturing operation was a nasal ointment based on a recipe developed by an otolaryngologist—an ear, eye, nose, and throat doctor—which was called "Bormelin." Dr. Fresenius began a fruitful cooperation with professors from Frankfurt University's Medical School, which resulted in the development of pharmaceutical specialties such as injection solutions and serologic reagents.

In the 1920s, Dr. Fresenius took his business venture to new heights when he entered the pharmaceutical wholesale trade. Fresenius was among the first German firms to import insulin from England. Until the early 1930s, all three business branches—manufacturing, wholesale trade, and pharmacy—were organized under the umbrella of the Dr. Fresenius company. However, when the National Socialists came into power in 1933, new laws were passed that called for a clear separation of the pharmacy from the rest of the business. Consequently, Dr. Fresenius moved his manufacturing operation to Bad Homburg, a city North of Frankfurt, in 1934, where it was greatly expanded. At the height of the company's success, Dr. Fresenius employed up to 400 people. However, the growing anti-Semitism of the Nazi regime took its toll. More and more of Dr. Fresenius' partners from clinics and universities—leading doctors and scientists of Jewish origin—left the country. In 1939, Adolf Hitler led Germany into a devastating war which ended with the country in ruins in the spring of 1945. The Hirsch Apotheke was completely destroyed during the war. Company founder Dr. Eduard Fresenius died in 1946.

A New Beginning After World War II

In his will, the company founder had determined Else Fernau, a young woman who grew up in Dr. Fresenius's house, as the heir of his enterprise. The inheritance was more of a challenge than a blessing to the 26-year-old. The Hirsch pharmacy lay in rubble. The manufacturing company was deeply in debt. The number of employees had dropped to a meager 30. Like the rest of the country, it was a new beginning for the company. While Else Fernau finished her studies in pharmacology, Fresenius resumed the production of the nasal ointment Bormelin. Another popular product during the postwar reconstruction years were "Terpinol" cough drops. The drops contained high levels of sugar and malt—therefore people bought them not only to cure their colds but also as a substitute for candy, which was still a rare commodity in Germany at the time. In 1951, Else Fernau took over the leadership of the company. Later she married legal expert Hans Kröner, and under their joint leadership Fresenius introduced a range of new products in the 1950s which laid the groundwork for a new period of growth. With the number of serious traffic accidents in Germany on the rise, leading to an increase in major surgeries, the demand for various injection solutions began to grow. Another new product area was that of special nutrition solutions for infusion therapy. The range of products in this niche market was expanded further in the 1960s and 1970s. In 1974, a new manufacturing facility for infusion solutions and medical disposables started operations in St. Wendel, a city in the Saar. Fresenius also started selling the equipment used in infusion therapy—at first from other manufacturers, then later produced by them—and added a number of products for artificial nutrition. Among them were special dietary products which were based on the food developed for astronauts and given through a tube into the stomach or intestines. Beginning in the 1970s, the company began to expand abroad, starting out with subsidiaries in France and Switzerland.

A turning point in the company's history came in 1966, when Fresenius entered the new market of supplying equipment used in dialysis therapy on patients suffering from chronic kidney failure. At first the company traded dialysis machines and dialysers—artificial kidneys—made by other manufacturers from abroad, such as the American manufacturer Drake Willock. Dialysis machines were used to pump the blood through the dialyser, where the blood was then cleaned from toxic substances. Over the course of only a few years, Fresenius was able to gain a significant share in the German market. However, mechanical engineer Gerd Krick, the company's new director of research and development, saw trading equipment from other manufacturers only as a first step. In the late 1970s, Fresenius developed their own dialysers and dialysis machines under Krick's leadership. With an enormous input of energy and resources, Krick succeeded despite the strong resistance of many people inside the company who believed this path to be too risky. One of the new products, the "A2008" dialysis machine, was awarded a gold medal at the Leipzig Trade Fair. In 1978, the company opened a production line for capillary dialysers in St. Wendel. One year later, another production line at a new site in Schweinfurt started putting out the A2008. By the onset of the 1980s, Fresenius had achieved a leading position among dialysis technology manufacturers in Germany. In 1983, the company started making synthetic polysulfone fiber membranes, which over time became a standard component used in blood purification. By 1986, every other dialysis machine purchased in Germany was made by Fresenius.

A Decade of Management Changes and Reorganization: 1980s

In 1981, Dr. E. Fresenius KG was transformed into a joint stock company and renamed Fresenius Aktiengesellschaft—in short Fresenius AG. Hans Kröner became the company's CEO, while Else Kröner left the executive management team and became the president of the board of directors. Else Kröner held 95 percent of the company's shares and Hans Kröner the remaining 5 percent. Five years later, the company opened up somewhat to outside investors. In December 1986, Fresenius AG offered 15 million preferred shares without any voting rights on the Frankfurt Stock Exchange. When Else Kröner died in June 1988, Hans Kröner passed on an option to inherit the company which had been laid out in her will. Consequently, Else Kröner's estate, including a majority of 66.99 percent of Fresenius common shares, were transferred into a not-for-profit foundation. According to Else Kröner's will, the Else Kröner Fresenius-Foundation channels profits from Fresenius AG into medical research and other humanitarian projects.

By 1990, Fresenius AG had grown into a large corporation. The number of people working for Fresenius AG had risen to 5,200. In that year, the company passed the DM1 billion sales mark for the first time. Two years later, Fresenius went through a major management change. When Hans Kröner retired in 1992, research and development director Gerd Krick became the company's new CEO. By that time, there were 14 major companies in Europe competing in the dialysis segment, another five in the United States, and eight in Japan. In Krick's view, consolidation was inevitable. A combination of pressures to cut health care cost, limited market volumes, and the constant drive for product innovation had made competition among these players fierce. His vision was to be among the four or so surviving companies in the global market for dialysis products. The new man at the top initiated a number of changes which resulted in a new corporate culture. Krick was mainly responsible for the company's success in the market for dialysis products. Kröner had avoided any media attention to protect crucial information from competitors. Krick opened communication channels—within the company as well as with the media.

Finally, Krick initiated a reorganization of the whole company. However, instead of streamlining the existing organization, as various studies had suggested, the company was re-created from the ground up. First, the whole business was divided into 17 units—the new profit centers within the company. Second, 17 leaders were chosen to manage the 17 units, each an entrepreneur within an enterprise. Third, all of the 17 new leaders were free to reorganize their individual units according to their own ideas and preferences. From then on, the company's executive management board issued only general guidelines and targets, leaving the execution to the respective "entrepreneur within the company." The strategy paid off. In the following years, costs started growing slower than profits. In the business year 1993, profits almost doubled compared with the year before. They grew by 57.8 percent in the following year, reaching DM71 million in 1994.

A Global Player in the 1990s

Beginning with the change in management in 1992, Fresenius entered an era of expansive growth, which was mainly driven by a long series of acquisitions. In the spring of 1992, the company acquired the infusion and dialysis solutions division IDM from Knoll AG, a subsidiary of chemical giant BASF. The acquisition of the 956-employee and DM188-million-sales operation considerably strengthened Fresenius's pharmaceuticals division and resulted in a more than 20 percent jump in total revenues. After the first offering of common shares in July had brought in a fresh supply of capital, the company bought the dialysis business from American chemicals and pharmaceuticals manufacturer Abbott Laboratories in February 1993. One year later, Fresenius took the chance to venture into a new market when the company purchased the hospital construction and equipment business, Hospitalia, from the German Siemens group. These transactions and a number of smaller acquisitions resulted in another significant increase in sales, which roughly doubled from the DM1.1 billion right before the IDM acquisition to about DM2.2 billion at the end of 1995. In the same time period, the number of employees went up from roughly 5,700 before the IDM acquisition to 6,970 afterwards and passed the 9,000 mark by the end of the 1995 business year.

However, compared to the second half of the 1990s, this was just a warm-up exercise. When the American specialty chemicals manufacturer W.R. Grace & Co. put the dialysis division of their subsidiary National Medical Care Inc. (NMC) in Waltham, Massachusetts, up for sale, Fresenius was among the bidders. Major American competitor Baxter International Inc. offered $3.8 billion in cash—a figure that seemed way out of Fresenius's league. On February 6, 1996, the company surprised the public, announcing that Fresenius was going to spin off their own dialysis division and merge it with its U.S. subsidiary Fresenius USA Inc. and NMC to create a new company, Fresenius Medical Care AG (FMC AG), under German law and with headquarters in Germany. The deal went through as planned. On October 1, 1996, the new company was listed at the New York Stock Exchange. The shares were traded as American Depository Shares (ADS). W.R. Grace and Fresenius USA Inc. together received 49.7 percent of FMC AG's share capital, while Fresenius AG retained a majority stake of 50.3 percent and consolidated FMC as a subsidiary. Just before the share-swap was carried out, NMC paid $2.3 billion, a sum which included the company's bank liabilities, to the parent company, which was financed through a loan by an American consortium of banks. The transaction instantly created the world's largest vertically integrated enterprise in the dialysis market with 25,000 employees generating annual sales of about $3.2 billion. The two partners were a perfect match. Fresenius provided the products needed to treat some 43,000 patients in NMC's roughly 600 dialysis centers across the United States. Before the deal, Fresenius AG had provided only one-third of NMC's dialysis products purchases.

In 1994, Fresenius' top management started working on another major deal. Four years later, the company acquired the international nutrition business, the so-called Kabi branch, from Pharmacia & Upjohn AB for an estimated DM700 to DM970 million. The manufacturer of infusion solutions was merged with the company's pharmaceutical branch, which had just expanded its own production capacity by building a brand new, high-tech plant for turning out infusion solutions in nearby Friedberg. The new Fresenius Kabi AG, with annual sales of approximately DM1.6 billion and about 7,500 employees worldwide, became the market leader in Western Europe and was headquartered in Bad Homburg, Germany, as well as in Uppsala, Sweden. Kabi especially strengthened Fresenius's position in the market for artificial nutrition infusion solutions, which at that time accounted for only 14 percent of the company's sales. Through a couple of joint ventures with plants near Peking and Shanghai, Kabi also expanded Fresenius's reach into China, one of the most promising markets for infusion solutions. In the mid-1980s, there were only 15,000 infusion bags consumed per year in China. By 1999, the country's demand had gone up to six million annually—twice the amount consumed in Europe.

Finally, in 2001 Fresenius took over Wittgensteiner Kliniken AG, a chain of 28 clinics with 4,600 employees and facilities in Germany, the Czech Republic, and Finland. This transaction was a step towards the company's strategic goal of becoming a leading international provider of project and facility management services for general hospitals, specialty clinics, and health care facilities.

Unexpected Challenges in the New Century

By the late 1990s, Fresenius had truly become a global player. In 1992, over half of the company's revenues came from abroad. After the FMC transaction, that number had jumped to 87 percent, reaching almost 90 percent in 2001. However, the rush for world leadership in the areas of dialysis and infusion solutions involved intense competition that proved especially challenging for Fresenius. In 2001, the company was still struggling to integrate Kabi. For a number of years the division had been striving to cut cost and failed to meet the projected profit expectations. Kabi subsidiary ProReha, which had been acquired in 2000, failed to get out of the red and was finally sold off in 2002.

In addition, a number of legal problems in the United States was putting a strain on Fresenius's resources. On one hand, FMC AG was not getting paid for certain laboratory and infusion therapy services provided to dialysis patients it claimed had life-threatening conditions. Two U.S. health insurers claimed that these services were not covered under their agreement with NMC. On the other hand, W.R. Grace was confronted with a swelling number of lawsuits for using asbestos in some of its fire protection products, a practice which the company had stopped in 1973. When the number of claims reached untenable proportions in 2000, the company filed for bankruptcy the following spring. As a consequence, the people who had sued W.R. Grace now threatened Fresenius AG with legal action, claiming that Fresenius AG had paid too little for NMC, which had resulted in lower capital assets for W.R. Grace, out of which the asbestos claims could be satisfied. The conflict was finally settled in November 2002 and cost Fresenius some $200 million.

The problems Fresenius was struggling with did not go unnoticed by the stock market. As a result, in May 2003 the share capital of Fresenius AG was worth less than the company's shareholdings in FMC. However, Gerd Krick, who had handed the tiller over to FMC's CFO Ulf Schneider at the company's annual shareholder meeting in May 2003, believed that the Fresenius shares were undervalued and saw the com-

pany moving towards a brighter future. In his opinion, FMC was well positioned as the leader in a market with a solid long-term growth potential due to an ever-increasing world population, the rise of life expectancy, and the expanding health care budgets of the Asian "tiger economies." Krick also saw promising opportunities for growth in the area of management services for hospitals. In Germany, the company was planning to establish regional networks of specialized clinics and nursing homes.

Principal Subsidiaries

Fresenius Medical Care AG (36.94%); Fresenius Kabi Deutschland GmbH; Wittgensteiner Kliniken Gruppe (93%); Pharmaplan Gruppe; VAMED Gruppe (Austria; 77%); Fresenius Kabi AB (Sweden); Fresenius Kabi Austria GmbH; Fresenius Kabi France S.A.S.; Fresenius Kabi Ltd. (United Kingdom); NPBI International B.V. (Netherlands); Sino-Swed Pharmaceutical Corporation Ltd. (China; 51%); Fresenius Kabi Compounding GmbH (Germany); Fresenius Kabi Italia S.p.A.; Fresenius Kabi Norge A.S. (Norway); Fresenius Kabi España S.A. (Spain); Grupo Fresenius México S.A. de C.V.; Calea Ltd. (Canada); Fresenius Kabi South Africa Ltd.; Beijing Fresenius Kabi Pharmaceutical Co., Ltd. (China; 65%); Calea France S.A.S.; Fresenius Vial S.A. (France); Fresenius HemoCare Italia S.r.l. (Italy); Fresenius Kabi N.V. (Belgium); Fresenius Kabi Clayton L.P. (United States); Hospitalia Care Gruppe (Germany; 93%); MC Medizintechnik GmbH; Fresenius HemoCare Deutschland GmbH; Fresenius Kabi Polzka Sp.Z.o.o. (Poland); Hospitalia Kliniken GmbH (Germany); Fresenius Kabi (Schweiz) AG (Switzerland); Fresenius Kabi India Private Ltd. (India); Fresenius Kabi Nederland B.V. (Netherlands); Fresenius Kabi Green Cross Ltd. (South Korea); Fresenius Kabi Brasil Ltda. (Brazil).

Principal Competitors

Baxter International Inc.; Abbott Laboratories, Inc.; DaVita Inc.; Gambro AB.

Further Reading

"Aktie im Blick: Fresenius AG," *Frankfurter Allgemeine Zeitung*, July 26, 2002, p. 22.

Aschenbrenner, Norbert, "Fresenius; Schöne Töchter," *Focus Magazin*, March 1, 2001, p. 30.

"Aktionäre erteilen Fresenius Zustimmung zum Geschäft mit Grace," *Frankfurter Allgemeine Zeitung*, April 12, 1996, p. 25.

"Die Fresenius-Aktienstruktur soll unverändert bleiben," *Frankfurter Allgemeine Zeitung*, May 30, 2003, p. 20.

"FMC belastet Fresenius-Ergebnis," *Frankfurter Allgemeine Zeitung*, October 31, 2001, p. 23.

"FMC bremst Fresenius auch in diesem Jahr," *Frankfurter Allgemeine Zeitung*, July 31, 2002, p. 14.

"FMC drückt das Ergebniswachstum im Fresenius-Konzern," *Börsen-Zeitung*, October 31, 2001, p. 12.

"Fresenius-Aktionäre billigen Kauf der Wittgensteiner Kliniken," *dpa*, May 31, 2001.

"Fresenius erwirbt die Mehrheit an Laevosan," *Frankfurter Allgemeine Zeitung*, October 26, 1996, p. 16.

"Fresenius Medical Care an der Börse gestartet," *Frankfurter Allgemeine Zeitung*, October 4, 1996, p. 25.

"Fresenius Medical Care bereinigt Asbest-Probleme in Amerika," *Frankfurter Allgemeine Zeitung*, November 30, 2002, p. 15.

"Fresenius übernimmt Infusionsgeschäft von Pharmacia & Upjohn," *Frankfurter Allgemeine Zeitung*, June 9, 1998, p. 22.

Lill, Uwe, "Fresenius hat von langer Hand den Aufstieg an die Weltspitze geplant," *Frankfurter Allgemeine Zeitung*, July 18, 1998, p. 18.

"Pharmawerk Fresenius wächst zweistellig," *Süddeutsche Zeitung*, November 28, 1992.

Wadewitz, Sabine, "Zäsur bei Fresenius," *Börsen-Zeitung*, May 24, 2003, p. 8.

—Evelyn Hauser

Grévin & Compagnie SA

BP 8
60128 Plailly
France
Telephone: (+33) 3-44-62-37-37
Fax: (+33) 3-44-62-34-40
Web site: http://www.grevinetcie.com

Wholly Owned Subsidiary of Compagnie des Alpes
Incorporated: 1989 as Parc Asterix SA
Employees: 1,382
Sales: EUR 125 million ($120 million) (2002 est.)
NAIC: 713110 Amusement and Theme Parks

Grévin & Compagnie SA is France's leading operator of amusement parks and tourist attractions (in terms of attendance figures) and one of the fastest growing in the European market. Grévin intends to be a motor in the consolidation of the highly fragmented European attractions industry. The company's portfolio of attractions in France, The Netherlands, Germany, and Switzerland attracts more than five million visitors per year, with an emphasis on a local, family-oriented clientele. The company's core holding remains the Parc Asterix theme park, based on the famed Asterix comic book character created by Rene Goscinny and Albert Uderzo, which accounts for approximately 55 percent of the group's ticket revenues. Grévin also owns the world-renowned Musée Grévin in Paris, that city's second largest privately held tourist attraction (the first is the Eiffel Tower), which gave the company its name in 1999 and forms the core of the company's tourist attractions segment, also including France Miniature in the Paris region and Mini-Chateaux in the Loire Valley region. The company's grouping of amusement parks includes Bagatelle in the north of France, Avonturenpark Hellendoorn, near Amsterdam, in The Netherlands, Fort Fun in Germany's Hochsauerland, and Aquaparc, a water-themed park on Switzerland's Lac Léman. Grévin's third pole of activity revolves around nature and animals, and includes the Grand Aquarium-Saint Malo, in the Brittany region; the Dolfinarium in The Netherlands' Hardewijk; and the Aquarium du Val de Loire. The company is currently constructing a new nature and health-themed park, called Bioscope, in

France's Alsace region. Led by CEO Olivier De Bosredon, Grévin is a wholly owned subsidiary of French ski lift operator Compagnie des Alpes.

French Theme Park Pioneer in the 1980s

The Asterix the Gaul comic books first appeared in 1961 (the characters had originated two years earlier), and by the 1960s had become an international success. Creators Goscinny and Uderzo quickly realized the potential for extending the popular series—based around the adventures of the Gallic Asterix and Obelix and their resistance to Roman occupation—into other formats. Among the authors' ideas was that of a theme park, patterned after the Disney model. Although Goscinny died in 1977, Uderzo kept both the Asterix series and the theme park idea alive. Yet the French market, where amusement parks were more readily associated with small, often shoddy traveling carnivals, appeared unready for a theme park.

Disney's announcement that it intended to open a Disneyland in France created a new interest in the sector. A number of new projects came into being during the period, including Big Bang Smurf, based on the popular comic book characters, located in Metz near the German border; the Zygofolis in Nice; and Mirapolis, featuring Rabellais' Gargantua character, near Paris. While the Smurf park opened only in 1987, both Zygofolis and Mirapolis were operational by 1987.

In 1984, Uderzo brought the theme park idea to Barclays bank, which brought in conglomerate Genérale des Eaux and the fast-growing hotel group Accor as investment partners in the project. Planning began soon after, and construction, on a 500-acre site just north of Paris, began in 1987. The opening of the park, in April 1989, was accompanied by the creation of a company to operate it, Parc Asterix SA. Included on the management team of the new company was Olivier de Bosredon, formerly with Accor, who initially served as managing director.

Extensive media coverage helped ensure early interest in the park—opening day boasted a sellout crowd—and by the end of its first year, Parc Asterix had succeeded in attracting nearly 1.4 million visitors. The company's emphasis on family entertainment—which was to remain a company hallmark—and the

143

Company Perspectives:

Grévin & Cie's success with developing and managing family entertainment facilities derives from its adherence to set management principles: offering attractions that are anchored in local heritage and traditions; developing and retaining highly creative teams of employees; a management approach that respects the particularities of each facility; and, a senior management team with a solid track record of international development.

park's accessibility to the vast Parisian market, gave it a strong returning clientele rate as well.

Yet the park was to remain a money-loser into the early 1990s, despite its success. Construction costs, which reached some $155 million, a heavy debt load, and high operating costs combined to plunge Parc Asterix into losses. Parc Asterix, like its rivals, suffered from a combination of factors, combining French inexperience in theme park creation and operation with a lack of understanding of culture-specific client habits.

While Asterix and its competitors found themselves overspending to attract customers—ranging up to $200 and more per customer, compared to an average of $70 per attendee in the United States—the company also misjudged certain French particularities. For one thing, the French, whose children attended school on Saturday mornings, tended to reserve family outings for Sundays. As opposed to U.S. customers, who tended toward informal meals taken at no set time throughout the day, French customers preferred sit-down meals at fixed times; Asterix quickly found its restaurants overwhelmed at mealtimes. Yet French customers were also much less patient with long waiting times, exposing another shortcoming at Parc Asterix, which had not included enough thrill rides in initial planning. These oversights forced the company to close the park to new entries on certain days.

Worse for the company was the impending arrival of a new heavyweight to the French attractions market: Disney. The 1992 opening of the new $3 billion Euro Disney (later Disneyland Paris), situated like Parc Asterix near the French capital, proved irresistible to the company's French clientele, despite the country's much-trumpeted disdain for American culture. By the end of that year, Parc Asterix's attendance rates were down by more than 30 percent and the company appeared headed for disaster. Meanwhile, two of the company's early competitors, Mirapolis and Zygofolis, had already gone bankrupt, while the third, the Smurf park, was struggling along backed by government subsidies.

Asterix began fighting back, however, as Bosredon took over the CEO spot in 1992. The company restructured its debt and also took steps to reduce its costs, shedding about one-third of its employees and adopting a winter closing schedule—the park now remained open only from April to November. The company also took steps to reduce waiting times, as well as adapt its restaurant offerings to its French family market— notably by allowing families to bring their own picnic lunches.

Although draining Parc Asterix initially, Euro Disney proved to have certain beneficial side effects for the company.

For one, Disney's heavy marketing helped educate the French public about theme parks and amusement parks in general, helping to overcome reluctance from many potential Asterix customers as well. For another, French backlash against the "invading Americans" played into Parc Asterix's French-dominated culture, in particular given the ready parallels between the Americans and Asterix's Roman foes. Not least, Disney's "artificial" culture—where employees are forced to smile all the time—contrasted sharply with Asterix's more "natural" employees, who, if grumpy at times, remained recognizable for the French customer.

Meantime, Disney itself was hampered by many of the same oversights as Asterix and the other French theme parks, slipping into losses. Attendance began to pick up again at Parc Asterix. By the end of the 1993, the company had entered into profitability for the first time. The company then began expanding its amusement offerings, spending FFr 20 million ($3.5 million) to build a new, Greek-themed village, based around the Icarus myth, for the 1994 season. Also helping the company was the creation of the "Great European Theme Parks" grouping, with England's Alton Towers, Germany's Europa-Park, The Netherlands' Efteling, and Liseberg in Sweden, formed to counter Disney's marketing muscle with agreements to exchange discounted ticket offerings and increased marketing among Europe's travel agencies.

By the end of the 1994 season, Parc Asterix could claim that it had been "adopted" by its core French public, as attendance topped 1.5 million, and sales jumped some 32 percent, to nearly FFr 270 million ($50 million). In that year, too, the company's backers—by then Accor had gained a majority share—agreed to a new restructuring of its debt.

Attendance and profits continued to grow into the mid-1990s and the company began preparing a public offering for 1996. Poor market conditions forced it to put off that move, however. But by 1997, Parc Asterix had successfully listed its shares on the Paris exchange's Secondary Market. In that year, attendance at the park neared two million for the first time.

European Expansion for the New Century

The company's public offering set the stage for the next phase in its growth—that of expansion through the acquisition of other attractions. In 1998, the company paid FFr 37 million for its first acquisition, that of the Saint-Malo Aquarium in the Brittany region. Opened in 1996, the aquarium was not only popular, but profitable. Originally designed on a pedagogic basis, Parc Asterix launched a redesign of the site to emphasize an entertainment aspect. That year, also, the company received the contract to manage the government-backed Maison de la Magie in the Loire Valley.

The company found its next acquisition target in 1999, when it acquired the famed Musée Grévin, along with that company's France Miniature attraction. Grévin had been founded in the early 1880s, when noted French journalist Arthur Meyer came up with the idea of providing three-dimensional displays of noted current and historical events. Meyer turned to sculptor, costume designer, and caricaturist Albert Grévin, who created a series of wax figures, and the Musée Grévin opened in 1882.

Key Dates:

1961: The first edition of *Asterix the Gaul* comic book is released.

1984: Albert Uderzo, co-creator of Asterix, approaches Barclays Bank with an idea for a theme park based on the Asterix characters.

1987: Construction begins on Parc Asterix, backed by Barclays, Accor, and Genérale des Eaux.

1989: Parc Asterix opens to the public, attracting 1.3 million visitors in its first year.

1993: Parc Asterix expands, opening a new Greek-themed area, which helps boost attendance, as the company becomes profitable.

1997: Parc Asterix SA goes public on the Paris stock exchange.

1999: The company acquires Musée Grévin and Paris Miniature in Paris and changes the company name to Grévin & Cie.

The acquisition of Musée Grévin led the company to change its name, to Grévin & Compagnie, that year. The company then began plans for a major upgrade to the wax museum, which was unveiled in 2001. In the meantime, Grévin continued making acquisitions. In 2000, the company added the amusement park Bagatelle, which, founded in 1955, was considered the country's first theme park.

Grévin's insistence on appealing to local culture became one of the company's strongest points in its continued expansion, as it sought attractions with strong local, family-oriented appeal—contrasting with its competitors' attempts to woo the tourist market. Grévin sought to apply this formula beyond France, and in 2001, the company made its first foreign acquisition, that of the Dolfinarium in The Netherlands' Hardewijk, the largest marine animal park in Europe.

The Loire Valley region, France's fourth largest tourist market, became the company's next expansion target in 2002, when it acquired the Aquarium de Touraine and the Mini-Chateaux sites from the failed Durand Allizé group. The company then renamed the aquarium site as Aquarium du Val de Loire, to emphasize its regional roots, and began an investment program in both sites expected to cost as much as EUR 3.5 million. By then, the company's expansion had successfully reduced its reliance on Parc Asterix, which now accounted for just 55 percent of annual sales. The company also had become a year-round operator, boosting its annual attendance totals from just two million at the beginning of the decade to more than five million by the end of 2002.

Grévin continued to look beyond France, however, and in 2002 acquired a new Dutch site, the family park Avonturenpark Hellendoorn, near Amsterdam, founded in 1936. That year, the company moved into new territory, acquiring Ruhr Valley-based Fort Fun, bringing the company into the German market for the first time.

Meanwhile, Grévin itself had become a takeover target. In early 2002, Compagnie des Alpes, the country's leading ski lift operator, announced its interest in acquiring Grévin & Cie. CDA, which had reached the limits of its own expansion, and which remained active primarily during the winter season, was particularly attracted to the potential of extending its cash flow year round. The two companies also shared a major shareholder, C3D, part of the Caisse des Depots et Consignations, which held nearly 54 percent of CDA and more than 30 percent of Grévin.

Despite Grévin's refusal of CDA's initial offer, the two sides reached agreement by May 2002, in part because of CDA's promise not only to keep Bosregon on as CEO of Grévin, but also to inject much needed capital for further expansion of the theme park and attractions business.

CDA proved true to its word, and with its new financial backing, Grévin began a number of new projects, including a EUR 9 million revamp of the Dolfinarium site, expected to be completed in 2005; a complete revamp of Bagatelle, converting it from its somewhat faded Wild West theme to a more locally rooted seaside theme; a EUR 1 million renovation of the Val de Loire aquarium; a number of new attractions at Avonturenpark; and the launch of a new thrill ride, Transdemonium, at Parc Asterix, which opened in 2003 at a cost of EUR 6 million.

Grévin had not merely contented itself with expanding its existing sites. In early 2003, the company announced its acquisition of its first site in Switzerland, that of Aquaparc on that country's Lac Leman. Grévin now boasted operations in four countries and was also able to present itself as a unique entertainment company. Whereas its main competitors, including the Tussauds Group, Disney, Busch Garden, Universal, and others, targeted the international, vacation-based customer, Grévin focused on its local markets, emphasizing local cultural roots, allowing it to offer attractions with strong individual identities. Grévin, backed by CDA, counted on this strategy to help it lead what many observers saw as a coming consolidation among Europe's highly fragmented amusement park and tourist attractions market.

Principal Subsidiaries

Grévin Developpement SA.

Principal Competitors

Busch Entertainment Corporation; Universal Studios Inc.; Lego A/S; Euro Disney SCA; The Tussauds Group; Recreatiepark De Efteling BV; Liseberg AB.

Further Reading

"Grévin se rende à la Compagnie des Alpes," *Le Monde,* June 7, 2002, p. 22.

Koranteng, Juliana, "Cash Infusion Propels Grévin Expansion," *Amusement Business,* April 7, 2003, p. 3.

——, "Grévin & Co.," *Amusement Business,* January 27, 2003, p. 3.

——, "Grévin Group Continues to Acquire Attractions in European Markets," *Amusement Business,* March 4, 2002, p. 10.

——, "Grévin's CEO Eyes European Sector's Future," *Amusement Business,* November 4, 2002, p. 6.

Lewis, Leo, "What Gaul!," *Independent,* April 29, 2001, p. 1.

—M.L. Cohen

طيــران الخليــج
GULF AIR

Gulf Air Company

P.O. Box 138
Manama
Bahrain
Telephone: (971) 2 633 1700
Fax: (971) 2 632 9721
Web site: http://www.gulfairco.com

State-Owned Company
Incorporated: 1950 as Gulf Aviation Company
Employees: 5,000
Sales: BD 340 million ($902 million)(2002)
NAIC: 481111 Scheduled Passenger Air Transportation;
481112 Scheduled Freight Air Transportation; 488190
Other Support Activities for Air Transportation;
561520 Tour Operators

Gulf Air Company is the national airline of Bahrain, Oman, and the United Arab Emirates (UAE). It operates a fleet of 30 aircraft to 43 cities in 32 countries from Europe to Asia. The company has developed a reputation for outstanding cabin service and takes pride in its history as a pioneer in the Gulf airline industry and as an example of cooperation between governments.

Origins

Gulf Air traces its origins to Gulf Aviation Company, which was established in Bahrain by a young British aviator, Freddy Bosworth. Bosworth had captured the local community's interest in flying via sightseeing trips and soon set up a commuter service between Bahrain, Doha, and Dhahran with his single airplane.

Bosworth secured backing from a group of local businessmen and registered Gulf Aviation Company on March 24, 1950. Operations started on July 5. British Overseas Airways Corp. (BOAC) acquired a 55.5 percent interest the next year.

Most of the airline's business was charter work for oil companies. The company started out operating rather small aircraft. Its first plane, the Avro Anson Mark 1, seated seven

people. It was replaced in 1951 by the de Havilland Dove, which had room for one more person. The Dove flew for Gulf Air until the 1960s. Gulf Air was also using four-engine de Havilland Herons, which could carry more people and cargo and fly them farther.

The scheduled network grew. Abu Dhabi, Al-Ain, Kuwait, Muscat, and Sharjah were connected in the 1950s. In the 1960s, Bandar Abbas, Bombay, Dubai, Karachi, Salalah, and Shiraz were added, while Fokker F27 turboprops replaced older model aircraft in 1968. This was an especially significant year because it marked the beginning of in-flight service for Gulf Air, an area that would become one of the pillars of the company's reputation.

Foundation Treaty of 1974

In 1973, BOAC's controlling shareholding was bought by four Arab governments: Bahrain, Qatar, the Sultanate of Oman, and Abu Dhabi (on behalf of the United Arab Emirates). The airline was named the official flag carrier of each of the four countries in the Foundation Treaty of January 1, 1974. Gulf Air linked these member states with other Middle Eastern countries. It also built hotels in each of the four to accommodate business travelers.

Gulf Air used VC-10 airliners made by British Aircraft Corp. to launch service to London in April 1970. (The BAC 1-11 had been the airline's first jet.) The acquisition of the VC-10s was accompanied by a technical assistance and training agreement with British Airways. BA was also something of a competitor and launched a London-Bahrain service via Concorde two years later. As successor to BOAC, British Airways inherited a strong presence throughout the Gulf.

The narrowbody VC-10 aircraft were intended only as an interim means to start intercontinental service. In 1976, Gulf Air began receiving deliveries of its replacement, the widebody Lockheed L-1011 TriStars, as well as mid-sized Boeing 737 airliners. The VC-10s were shifted to less established international routes. (Service between the four partner countries was considered domestic.)

The growth of international business led to a four-fold increase in the number of employees. Gulf Air had 800 employees in mid-1974, reported *Aviation Week & Space Technology,* and about 3,300 at the start of 1976. The L-1011 operation was initially based on crews hired from the defunct British charter carrier Court Line Aviation, Ltd., but Gulf Air was working towards having a 100 percent Arab staff.

Gulf Air posted a record profit of $51.8 million in 1983 when it carried 2.6 million passengers. (The year was marred by the loss of an airliner to a bomb.) By 1986, unfortunately, Gulf Air was posting its first loss of the decade ($5.5 million) as the region's oil revenues declined while the international market remained competitive. Emirates Airlines, a new carrier in the UAE, would make it more so, though its activities were coordinated with that of Gulf Air and Kuwait Airways by the Gulf Cooperation Council.

Maintenance Unit Opened in 1987

Gulf Air continued to become more independent. It opened its Gulf Aircraft Maintenance Company (GAMCO) unit in Abu Dhabi in 1987. It owned interests in hotels; Bahrain Airport Services; Gulf Helicopters; and GCC Aviation Services, a caterer.

Boeing 767 airliners were added to the fleet in 1988, improving the company's on-time performance. Airbus A320s were added in 1992 to phase out the fleet of ten Boeing 737s. Two years later saw the arrival of Airbus A340s.

Smiling in the Early 1990s

Gulf Air retrenched during the downturn in business precipitated by the Iraqi invasion of Kuwait, laying off 350 employees in 1990 en route to a loss of $95 million. However, by the end of 1991 a recovery was already in evidence, and the airline rapidly rolled out expansion plans. New routes (Singapore, Sydney, Thiruvananthapuram) and new planes were added. Gulf Air achieved net profits of $48 million in 1991 and 1992; it was one of the few airlines to make money in the early 1990s.

In 1993, Gulf Air unveiled a $10 million ad campaign pitching the carrier as "The International Smile of the Gulf." Routes extended as far as Australia, Hong Kong, and Johannesburg, and the company was carrying nearly four million passengers a year. By the end of 1993, Gulf Air was planning an initial public offering to offset the cost of a $2.2 billion expansion, which made the airline the largest in the Middle East, flying about 40 aircraft to 50 destinations. Tentative plans for a stock offering dated back to 1984. At the time, Gulf Air had 5,000

employees, more than half of them Gulf nationals. The airline opened an aviation college in Doha that year, led by former CEO Ali Ibrahim Al-Malki.

Significant passenger perks were introduced in 1994, including an in-flight entertainment system on long-haul planes and the new FALCON Frequent Flyer Program.

After making money for four years, Gulf Air posted a $159 million loss in 1995. Contributing factors were a downturn in the regional economy and very high levels of competition, according its new president and CEO, Sheikh Ahmed bin Saif al-Nahyan.

By 1997, Gulf Air was more than $1 billion in debt, leading to more route cutbacks (including services to New York, Geneva, and Johannesburg) and the sale of 17 aircraft worth $850 million. This left a fleet of 28, six of them leased.

The staff had become almost entirely made up of Arabs by the mid-1990s; most of the 3,000 employees were from Bahrain. However, during the late-1990s crisis, a couple of former British Airways executives were brought in.

Shareholder states Qatar and Oman were developing their own airlines, Qatar Airways and Oman Aviation, complicating decisions on how to re-capitalize Gulf Air as well as diluting its business. In addition, Emirates Airlines had been operating out of Abu Dhabi for more than a decade, though that government was aiming to infuse more capital into Gulf Air in exchange for a higher ownership stake. After considerable losses in 1995 ($159 million) and 1996, Gulf Air was again able to post an operating profit ($48 million) in 1997.

50th Anniversary in 2000

New uniforms in gray, blue, and peach were introduced in Gulf Air's 50th anniversary year. As part of the celebration, Gulf Air hired two vintage aircraft—an Avro Anson and a de Havilland Dove—to recreate the company's first flights. Sadly, in August 2000 Gulf Air also experienced its second fatal crash ever and the loss of an Airbus A320.

Passenger numbers were falling worldwide, exacerbating Gulf Air's struggle with a heavy debt load. Gulf Air posted a $98.1 million loss for 2000 and a $132.3 million one for 2001. The partners invested $159.2 million in a restructuring package in May 2001. A year later, Qatar announced it was withdrawing its 25 percent stake, preferring to focus its resources on Qatar Airways. The remaining partners provided another $81 million capital injection.

For the first time, the airline hired an airline professional as CEO: James Hogan, who formerly held top jobs at Ansett Airlines and British Midland International. While cutting costs, Hogan also sought to develop the partnership with tourism sections of the three shareholding partners.

In November 2002, Gulf Air rolled out a new first class service. On flights to London, Paris, and Frankfurt, this featured chefs from elite European restaurants preparing food to order— the "Restaurant in the Sky" concept. A holiday package focusing on Oman, Abu Dhabi, and Bahrain was introduced at the

Key Dates:

1950: Gulf Aviation Company is created.
1951: BOAC acquires a majority control in the company.
1968: Cabin service is introduced.
1970: Service to London is launched with a VC-10.
1973: Bahrain, Qatar, Oman, and UAE acquire control of the airline.
1974: Gulf Air becomes the official airline of four shareholding states.
1987: GAMCO maintenance unit is opened.
1993: Major expansion takes places and a fleet renewal program is launched.
2000: Gulf Air's 50th anniversary is celebrated with flights of vintage aircraft.
2003: A recovery plan is launched.

same time with the aim of attracting tourists to the region despite the impending war with Iraq.

The next month, the three remaining partners injected 90 million dinars ($238 million) in a demonstration of their commitment to Gulf Air, which lost BD52 million in 2001. Early signs of a turnaround were in evidence; the 2002 loss of just under BD41 million ($110 million) was about BD8 million less than had been predicted.

A New Course in 2003

A new three-year recovery plan officially began on January 1, 2003. The company was planning to expand its route network and increase its fleet. In May, Gulf Air launched its Gulf Traveller subsidiary, "the region's first full service all-economy airline." Gulf Traveller, which was started with six of Gulf Air's Boeing 767s, flew short and medium haul routes around the Gulf and to the Indian subcontinent. These were already served by Gulf Air's main line; the new operation offered additional frequency of flights for leisure travelers and expatriate employees. Business travelers were to be wooed by replacing once or twice daily service on full size airliners with more frequent smaller regional jet flights.

New livery featuring a restyled falcon was unfurled in April 2003, underscoring Gulf Air's commitment to improvement. The company perched an 11-meter tall neon golden falcon atop the Falcon Tower in Manama, Bahrain. Gulf Air's six-year-old Web site was revamped in the same month.

The airline was also planning to establish a reservations center in Muscat that would employ 300 Omani nationals. Gulf Air aimed to reduce its losses to BD20 million in 2003 and to break even by 2004. To bring in traffic from the rest of the world, Gulf Air was planning to join a global airline alliance. It was also discussing potential areas of cooperation with KLM Royal Dutch Airlines and Oman Air.

Principal Subsidiaries

Alzouman Aviation; Gulf Air; Gulf Air Cargo; Gulf Air Holidays; Gulf Traveller.

Principal Competitors

Emirates Airlines; Oman Aviation; Qatar Airways.

Further Reading

Ahmed, Ashfaq, "Vintage Aircraft Recreate Gulf Air Flights," *Gulf News*, April 12, 2000.

Allen, Robin, "Abu Dhabi Flies to Gulf Air's Rescue: Regional Stability Behind Move to Bolster Carrier with Debts Exceeding $1bn," *Financial Times* (London), January 2, 1997, p. 4.

——, "Gulf Air Returns to Profitability," *Financial Times* (London), March 16, 1998, p. 27.

——, "Gulf Air Expects Bigger Loss for 1987," *Financial Times* (London), June 2, 1988, p. 32.

Almezel, Mohammed, "Gulf Air May Break Even in 2004; Qatar Pulls Out," *Gulf News*, December 20, 2002.

Baby, Soman, "Gulf Air Needs 'Fresh Start to Stay Airborne'— Bahrain Should Consider Starting Own Airline, Says Expert," *Egyptian Gazette*, May 9, 2002.

Cameron, Doug, "Gulf Air Split Put on Hold," *Airline Business*, February 1997.

Critchlow, Andy, "Last Chance Saloon," *Middle East Economic Digest*, June 21, 2002, p. 4.

Endres, Gunter, "Gulf Air Boss Calls for Action," *Flight International*, April 3, 1996.

Field, Michael, "Gulf Air Loses Its Eastern Glamour," *Financial Times* (London), Sec. I, May 14, 1987, p. 36

Fink, Donald E., "Gulf Air Seeks Bigger Share of Market," *Aviation Week & Space Technology*, February 23, 1976, p. 37.

Frings, Mary, "Privatisation for Gulf Air to Go Ahead by 1986," *Financial Times* (London), February 7, 1985, p. 26.

"Gulf Air Board Approves Improved Financial Figures," *Middle East Company News*, May 1, 2003.

"Gulf Air Major Expansion Plan Lifts Off," *Flight International*, July 10, 1991.

"Gulf Air and Oman Air Explore Areas of Cooperation," *Al-Bawaba News*, April 21, 2003.

"Gulf Air Pilots 'Among Best in World,' " *Gulf Daily News*, August 31, 2000.

"Gulf Air Spreads Wings to Meet New Challenges," *Gulf Daily News*, February 15, 2000, p. 1.

"Historic Landmarks—Soaring to Success," *The Independent*, January 20, 2000.

"Keen Competition Knocks Gulf Air Into the Red," *Financial Times* (London), Sec. I, June 30, 1987, p. 33.

Kj, Max, "Gulf Air Restructures Fleet and Network," *Flight International*, January 22, 1997, p. 8.

Madhavan, Adarsh, "Gulf Air to Launch All-Economy Airline," *Times of Oman*, February 18, 2003.

Muqbil, Imtiaz, "Gulf Air Breaks Ground with All-Economy Carrier," *Bangkok Post*, May 19, 2003.

Nair, Manoj, "Piloting Gulf Air's Return to Profitability," *Gulf News*, February 15, 2003.

Pinkham, Richard, "Gulf Challenge," *Airline Business*, March 1, 2003, p. 36.

——, "Hogan Works on Restoring Ailing Gulf Air's Fortunes," *Airline Business*, November 1, 2002, p. 28.

Poole, Anthony, "Gulf Air Plans Public Share Launch," *Lloyd's List*, November 10, 1993, p. 10.

Rahman, Saifur, "Gulf Air Launches Economy Airline," *Gulf News*, May 8, 2003.

Vandyk, Anthony, "Four Flags Over the Gulf," *Air Transport World*, April 1, 1993.

—Frederick C. Ingram

hansgrohe

AXOR | PHÂRO

Hansgrohe AG

Auestrasse 5-9
D-77761 Schiltach
Germany
Telephone: (49) 7836 51-0
Fax: (49) 7836 51-1300
Web site: http://www.hansgrohe.com

Private Company
Incorporated: 1905 as Hans Grohe, Schiltach
Employees: 2,325
Sales: EUR360 million ($360 million) (2002)
NAIC: 332998 Enameled Iron and Metal Sanitary Ware
    Manufacturing; 332913 Plumbing Fixture Fitting and
    Trim Manufacturing

Hansgrohe AG is one of the world's leading manufacturers of upscale bathroom fixtures. The company markets its stylish designer line of bathroom fixtures under the ''Axor'' brand name and its state-of-the-art shower systems, including shower temples, whirlpools, and steam cabins, under the ''Pharo'' brand. Hansgrohe also makes plumbing fixtures and water recycling systems. Based in the German Black Forest, the company manufactures its products in five countries, including Germany, the United States, France, the Netherlands, and China. More than 70 percent of Hansgrohe's total output is sold outside of Germany, with the United States being the largest market abroad. The American Masco Corporation owns a majority stake of 64.35 percent in Hansgrohe, while the company founder's son Klaus Grohe and his family own most of the other shares in the company.

Small Metal Workshop Established in 1901

Hansgrohe has its roots in a small family enterprise set up by Hans Grohe in Schiltach, a small German town in the Black Forest. The sixth child of cloth maker Karl Grohe, Hans Grohe, grew up near Berlin and learned the weaving craft himself. In 1890, the 19-year-old Hans hit the road and spent three years working in different places as a traveling journeyman. In the following seven years, Hans Grohe worked as a master weaver

in his hometown Luckenwalde, while starting his own family. In May 1899, he and his wife, two daughters, and one son, Hans, moved to Schiltach in the Black Forest. After working as a master weaver at a local textile factory for a few months, Hans Grohe started working at the Schwab & Voigt metal pressing plant, where he acquired the skills and knowledge of the metal pressing trade. Soon after, Grohe, together with Wilhelm Schwab, one of his coworkers, rented a workshop space and launched a small enterprise. In their metal pressing workshop, Grohe and Schwab started making casings for alarm clocks. However, in March 1901, a fire destroyed the small plant and all the machinery. Two months later, Grohe and Schwab ended their business partnership.

In the same year, Hans Grohe started his own metal pressing business. He acquired a wooden shed that used to belong to a metal pressing plant and hired two workers who operated the water-powered machinery. At first, they made metal casings for alarm clocks for the German firm Junghans—at the time the largest watchmaker in the world—followed by stovepipe rings, metal parts for lamps and lanterns, galvanized roofing tips, and other pattern-based metal parts. Soon they also started making metal parts for household plumbing fixtures. In the meantime, Grohe traveled through the Black Forest on his bicycle, drumming up business from plumbers and pipe layers. The growing number of orders enabled Grohe to hire two more workers.

On June 14, 1905, Hans Grohe's new enterprise was officially registered. Over the next decade, the company founder focused on establishing himself as a supplier of plumbing fixtures and expanded his reach beyond Germany's borders. While still participating in the manufacturing process, Grohe oversaw the operations, took care of the bookkeeping, and traveled widely to win over new customers. His wife and oldest daughter packaged the finished goods. New, larger orders rolled in from wholesalers all around Germany, as well as from the Netherlands, Switzerland, and Italy. In 1908, Hans Grohe put out his first catalogue of products, and the following year built a new two-story factory, including a warehouse and shipping department, next to the new family residence. By 1910, Hans Grohe employed twelve workers and one office clerk. Within the next four years, the company's work force doubled.

International Growth Between Two World Wars

With the beginning of World War I, Hansgrohe entered an era of unpredictability and economic volatility that lasted almost four decades. In 1914, half the company's work force was drafted into the military. All of the company's reserves in raw materials and semi-finished and finished goods were seized by the German government. As more valuable metals such as copper and brass became scarce, the company was forced to use less precious materials such as iron and zinc. Finally, the company was required to actively contribute to the war economy and began manufacturing parts for fuses. Luckily, Hansgrohe survived the war without any damage and—after the war ended in late 1918—resumed pre-war operations. Furthermore, just a year later there were almost twice as many workers employed by the company.

However, with the onset of the 1920s, the German market was down and Hans Grohe decided to push exports. He took long sales trips to northern European countries, including Denmark, Sweden, Norway, and Finland, and established new business relationships. He also connected with potential clients in Switzerland and the Netherlands. Rising exports saved the company from severe financial trouble during the galloping inflation years 1922 and 1923. In 1926, Hans Grohe hired a traveling salesman who also became the company's export agent. Between 1924 and 1927, export sales grew by 160 percent. In 1933, the company's catalogue was published in English, French, Italian, and Spanish for the first time. One year later, several sales offices were set up abroad and new business contacts made in North Africa, Palestine, and Syria. By November 1938, there were 21 sales agents drumming up business for Hansgrohe in and outside of Germany.

While business was soaring, production capacity had to be expanded constantly. In 1921, a brass foundry was set up at a new site in nearby Alpirsbach. Seven years later, Hansgrohe moved into a newly built three-story factory. The company manufactured such bathroom fixtures as shower heads, spigots, and faucets, along with other metal products, and employed about 100 people.

The beginning of World War II in September 1939 disrupted the company's development for a second time. Once again, zinc, iron, and other materials had to substitute for copper and brass. Once again, Hans Grohe lost his reserve stockpiles of raw material to the government. Once again, the company started

manufacturing fuses. However, rather than losing half its employees to the military, as happened during World War I, the company's work force grew significantly. Male workers lost to military service were replaced by their wives and daughters. In addition, the German military administration assigned foreign slave workers to work at Hansgrohe. By 1944, the company's work force had reached 466. After the war ended in 1945, the French military government ordered the dismantling of half the company's machinery. Remaining reserves of zinc and aluminum were also taken away. At the same time, businesses in the French occupation zone had no access to copper and brass imports. Hansgrohe survived the postwar period that ended with the currency reform in 1948 with only a modest collection of simple kitchenwares such as aluminum cans, bowls, milk containers, ladles, and strainers.

Postwar Boom

In the 1920s, Hans Grohe's two sons joined the family business. In 1921, Hans Grohe, Jr. took over the management of the new facility in Alpirsbach with over 30 workers until it was closed down in 1932. Friedrich Grohe, the company founder's second son from his second marriage, also joined his father's company and introduced new brass die casting technology. However, in 1934, Friedrich left the family business to strike out on his own. Two years later, he took over a business in the Westphalian town Hemer and developed it into another major manufacturer of plumbing fixtures. In August 1934, after Friedrich had left the family business, Hans Grohe, Jr. took over the management of the facilities in Schiltach. At the end of 1936, the company was transformed from a sole proprietorship into a general partnership, with Hans Grohe, Sr. and Hans Grohe, Jr. as general partners. One year later, the legal form was changed into a limited partnership, with Hans Grohe's daughters Helene and Liesel as limited partners. In 1953, Hans Grohe, Jr. took over as Hansgrohe's CEO. Two years later, company founder Hans Grohe, Sr. died.

Both Grohe companies greatly benefited from the postwar construction boom, which significantly increased the demand for kitchen and bathroom fixtures. Since the only problem was how to satisfy the ever-growing demand, the two companies remained on friendly terms. Friedrich Grohe, who had named his company after himself in 1948, and Hans Grohe, Sr.'s third wife, Friedel Grohe, Klaus Grohe's mother, became limited partners in the Hans Grohe company in 1956. Two years later, the two Grohe families and some 2,000 employees celebrated together at a company party in Schiltach. They even began to jointly exhibit their products at major trade shows. However, the sudden death of Hans Grohe, Jr. from a heart attack in September 1960 caused a major change for the original family business.

A few months after Hans Grohe, Jr.'s death, the company was transformed into a limited liability company and partnership. The company was named Hans Grohe GmbH & Co. KG. Friedrich Grohe became CEO of Hans Grohe, while still managing his own company. To prevent potential problems in the future, the product lines of the two firms were adjusted to minimize direct competition. Hans Grohe focused on drains, shower heads, and shower-handrails; Friedrich Grohe on faucets and hot-and-cold-water mixers. In 1968, Hans Grohe's

Key Dates:

1901: Hans Grohe establishes a metal pressing workshop in Schiltach.
1905: Grohe's business is officially registered.
1905: The small plant starts making shower heads.
1938: The company is transformed into a limited partnership.
1953: Hans Grohe, Jr. becomes CEO.
1953: The wall-mounted shower holder is introduced.
1969: Klaus Grohe joins the top management team.
1973: The company's plastic molding plant starts operations.
1973: Hans Grohe's first foreign subsidiary opens in Spain.
1975: Klaus Grohe becomes second CEO.
1985: American Masco Corporation becomes a major shareholder in the company.
1995: Hansgrohe's production plant in Atlanta, Georgia, goes into operation.
1999: Hansgrohe is transformed into a family-owned public stock corporation.
2003: Masco Corporation becomes majority shareholder in Hansgrohe.

third son from his third marriage, Klaus Grohe, entered the older Grohe family enterprise. He played a major part in introducing electronic data processing into his father's company. In 1969, he became sales manager and chief clerk.

Although merging the two family businesses seemed to be an obvious solution, it did not happen. Instead, Friedrich Grohe sold a 51 percent majority stake in his company to the American telephone giant International Telephone & Telegraph (ITT) in 1968. Despite the fact that Friedrich Grohe kept a 27 percent stake in his brother's firm, the two companies started drifting apart and over time even became competitors. Following Friedrich Grohe's death in 1983, his heirs bought back ITT's majority stake in Friedrich Grohe and sold their 26 percent stake in Hans Grohe to the American Masco Corporation of Indianapolis, an offspring of American faucet maker Delta Faucet. Due to growing competitive pressures, the two companies fought over the rights to the ''Grohe'' brand for a number of years. The conflict was settled in the early 1990s when Friedrich Grohe agreed to use the brand name ''Grohe'' while Hansgrohe marketed its products under the ''Hansgrohe'' label. The company's name had already been changed from Hans Grohe GmbH & Co. KG to Hansgrohe GmbH & Co. KG in 1977.

Redesigning the Shower in the 1970 and 1980s

From 1961 until 1975, Friedrich Grohe functioned as Hans Grohe's CEO, with Klaus Grohe taking on more and more top management responsibilities. In January 1975, Heinz Mathauer, Klaus Grohe's uncle, took over as executive director. Six months later, he was joined by Klaus Grohe, and the two managed the company until Mathauer resigned in mid-1977. During the 1970s and 1980s, Hans Grohe introduced a number of innovations and paid special attention to more cutting-edge

designs. At the same time, the company's international distribution network was strengthened.

Since the company had started manufacturing shower heads in 1905, Hans Grohe kept putting out a stream of technical and design innovations in that market segment. In 1928, the company had introduced the first shower head—which in Europe are generally popular in the form of hand-held models—with a handle made from white porcelain. Forty years later, Hans Grohe revolutionized the shower experience by introducing the first hand-held shower with an adjustable spray. In 1970, the company brought more color into the bathroom. Its new SIXTY shower set was available in black, white, and orange. The introduction of plastic molding allowed the launch of even more colorful collections later in the decade. In 1971, the company began to make gold-coated bathroom fixtures upon request. In 1974, the company launched the first hand-held shower with three different spray modes, for which Hans Grohe won its first design prize—later followed by many more, both national and international. Other innovations included the ''Mistral'' hand shower with a rotor-massage spray, introduced in 1976, and the ''Aktiva'' hand shower with a ''Quickclean'' function that prevented the buildup of lime. The company's product range was further extended to include mirrored bathroom cabinets and other bathroom accessories, as well as faucets.

Although exports had been thriving for many decades, the already existing export infrastructure was expanded even more in the 1970s and 1980s. In 1973, Hans Grohe's first foreign subsidiary was established in Spain. Two years later, Interbath, a marketing company, was set up in the United States with another business partner. A French subsidiary was founded in 1979, followed by one in Italy in 1982, in Austria in 1986, and in Denmark in 1987. A second sales office in the United States was set up in California in 1988 to handle customers on the West Coast. One year later, an information center was established in Belgium.

Another major factor in Hans Grohe's success was the company's concerted marketing effort. Intent on forming close relationships with its customers, the company focused on practical demonstrations at national and international trade shows, as well as at customers' locations and on its own premises. As early as in the mid-1960s, the company flew in plumbers from Belgium and France to educate them about Hans Grohe products. In 1971, the company started advertising directly to its clientele, including wholesalers, architects, and plumbing contractors. In 1974, Hans Grohe remodeled a former movie theater in Schiltach into a training center for plumbers. Beginning in 1972, the company took its products on the road, at first with a Volkswagen van with an exhibit of the company's new mirrored bathroom cabinet line. Two years later, a large Mercedes van was converted into a mobile demonstration booth. In 1983, there were three exhibition vans traveling all over Germany. By 1989, 28 such vehicles were visiting Hans Grohe customers in 13 countries. The ''Hansgrohe'' brand was created in 1977, and the corporate design modernized in 1984.

The results of these combined efforts were impressive. In 1967, Hans Grohe already shipped to 40 countries around the world. By 1978, the company exported its products to 50 countries, with exports accounting for over 40 percent of total sales. The company's work force grew from 441 in 1965 to 700 in 1976, reaching 1,000 in 1989. In 1976, sales passed the DM100 million mark for the first time and more than doubled in the following decade, reaching DM239 million in 1989. In that year, the company acquired a large property in Offenburg, another city in the Black Forest, which provided the basis for further production expansion in the 1990s.

Innovation and Global Focus in the 1990s and Beyond

The reunification of Germany in the early 1990s spurred a construction boom that lasted a few years but dried up towards the middle of the decade. After that, the German market stagnated and even shrunk during the late 1990s. Some export markets had become more unpredictable through volatile exchange rates. In the mid-1990s, cheap plumbing fixtures from Asia flooded the European markets, putting established manufacturers under growing price pressure. Hansgrohe countered by focusing on high-quality, upscale product lines marketed under a new branding strategy, improved customer service, and intensified efforts to break into the eastern European and U.S. markets. In the first half of the 1990s, Hansgrohe introduced the "Axor" and "Pharo" brands. Axor unified an upscale, design-oriented line of bathroom-related "lifestyle products" under its brand name. Pharo stood for pre-assembled shower systems with high design standards and a luxury appeal. The new product strategy was successful. Axor and Pharo products were installed in large and prestigious construction projects, such as the remodeled German Reichstag in Berlin and the Grand Hyatt hotel in Shanghai. Hundreds of Ramada hotel rooms and British Airways lounges were equipped with Hansgrohe bathroom fixtures and shower systems.

Despite stagnating domestic sales, Hansgrohe committed to its German production locations but also established new sales and production subsidiaries abroad. New sales offices were set up in Belgium, the United Kingdom, Switzerland, Hungary, Sweden, Poland, and the Czech Republic. At the same time, the company intensified trade show presentations in other parts of the world, including Asia, the Middle East, Australia, and South America. In mid-1995, Hans Grohe started a production of showers and other products designed for the U.S. market at a leased facility in Atlanta, Georgia. A few months later, the company received a $20 million purchase order for a complete line of shower heads from Delta-Faucet. By mid-1997, a new manufacturing plant in Atlanta with a daily output of 5,000 shower heads accomplished the job. In addition to the acquisitions of Zenio S.A., a French manufacturer of sanitary products, and the Dutch C.P.T. Holding BV, a manufacturer of steam rooms and whirlpools, a production plant was set up in China.

CEO Klaus Grohe not only led the company to renewed growth in an increasingly global market, but also made Hansgrohe into a environmentally friendly manufacturer—from solar-powered, low-pollution production facilities to 100 percent recycling policies to water-saving faucets. At the same time, it became clear that in order to sustain a competitive edge on a global scale the company had to adjust its organizational structure and financial basis to the new environment. Effective with the beginning of 1999, Hansgrohe was transformed into Hansgrohe AG, a family-owned public stock corporation, with the ultimate goal of taking the company public. In 2001, Klaus Grohe, the new chairman of the board, summed up his view on the history of his family's enterprise in *A Company Makes History:* "There were ups and downs on our road to becoming a leading bathroom amenity supplier. Our focus never faltered—it remained on the goal of manufacturing innovative designer products that are gentle on the environment. Hansgrohe is proud of having played a vital part in turning the bathroom, once regarded a mere utility room, into the center of well-being and relaxation in so many homes." With the approval of the company's shareholders, Masco Corporation bought shares from Grohe family members and raised its stake in Hansgrohe to 64.35 percent. Klaus Grohe, who kept most of the rest of the shares and continued his involvement as the company leader, commented on this step as a necessary measure to ensure Hansgrohe's future. By 2003, the company generated almost three-fourths of its sales outside of Germany.

Principal Subsidiaries

Hansgrohe Deutschland Vertriebs GmbH (Germany); Pontos GmbH (Germany); Hansgrohe International GmbH (Germany); Hansgrohe Inc. (United States); Hansgrohe Sanit'Air L.L.C. (United States); Hansgrohe Ltd. (China); Hansgrohe Wasselonne S.A. (France); Hansgrohe S.A.R.L. (France); Hans Grohe Hdl. Ges. mbH (Austria); Hans Grohe B.V. (Netherlands); C.P.T. Holding B.V. (Netherlands); Hans Grohe AG (Switzerland); Hansgrohe A/S (Denmark); Hansgrohe A.B. (Sweden); Hans Grohe Ltd. (United Kingdom); Hans Grohe S.A. (Belgium); Hansgrohe S.R.L. (Italy); Hansgrohe S.A. (Spain); Hans Grohe Kft (Hungary); Hans Grohe CS s.r.o. (Czech Republic); Hans Grohe Sp. Zo.o. (Poland); Hansgrohe Geberit SAS (France; 50%); Hans Grohe Pte. Ltd. (Singapore).

Principal Competitors

Friedrich Grohe AG & Co. KG; Hansa Metallwerke AG; American Standard Companies Inc.; Kohler Co.; Moen Incorporated; TOTO LTD.

Further Reading

A Company Makes History: Hansgrohe 1901–2001, Schiltach, Germany: Hansgrohe AG, 2001, 92 p.

"Grohe hat ehrgeizige Pläne im Ausland," *Frankfurter Allgemeine Zeitung,* October 6, 1997, p. 24.

"Hansgrohe wächst im Ausland," *Frankfurter Allgemeine Zeitung,* March 19, 2003, p. 18.

"Masco übernimmt Mehrheit bei Hansgrohe," *Frankfurter Allgemeine Zeitung,* January 11, 2003, p. 14.

Spies, Felix, "Lifestyle für das Badezimmer," *Süddeutsche Zeitung,* March 1, 1997.

"Das Unternehmergespräch," *Frankfurter Allgemeine Zeitung,* October 1, 2001, p. 20.

Wai, Cheong Suk, "Haute Water," Straits Times (Singapore), April 21, 2001.

—Evelyn Hauser

Harvey Norman Holdings Ltd.

A1 Richmond Road
Homebush West
New South Wales 2140
Australia
Telephone: (+61) 2-9201-6111
Fax: (+61) 2-9201-6250
Web site: http://www.harveynorman.com.au

Public Company
Incorporated: 1982 as Caviton Ltd.
Employees: 2,228
Sales: A$1.16 billion ($653.3 billion)(2002)
Stock Exchanges: Australia
Ticker Symbol: HVN
NAIC: 533110 Owners and Lessors of Other Non-
    Financial Assets; 237210 Land Subdivision; 452111
    Department Stores (Except Discount Department
    Stores); 522291 Consumer Lending

Harvey Norman Holdings Ltd. is one of Australia's most successful retail groups, controlling an empire of more than 150 department stores. Nearly all of these stores, which emphasize computers, home entertainment equipment, and home appliances are operated on a unique franchise model, wherein Harvey Norman owns and leases the property and tightly controls the retail operations, taking licensing fees. The company operates under its main Harvey Norman store format and three newer formats: Space, a furniture store format patterned after Ikea stores; Domayne, an upscale store; and the fast-growing Rebel Sport chain, acquired in 2001. Most of the company's stores are located in its Australian base; however, with its coverage of the country more or less complete, the company has begun looking towards international expansion to drive its growth in the new century. As such, Harvey Norman has established a strong presence in New Zealand, with some 20 stores, and in South Africa, with five stores. The company has especially targeted the nearby Southeast Asian market, with its initial launch in Singapore, through its acquisition of control of that country's Pertama retail group in 2000, giving it 14 stores

there. The company also plans to move into Malaysia in 2003. At the same time, Harvey Norman has targeted growth in both Eastern and Western Europe, beginning with Slovenia and Ireland, opening stores in both countries in 2002. Harvey Norman is controlled by chairman Gerald Harvey, Australia's first "retail billionaire," who co-founded the company in 2002.

Second-Time Retail Success in the 1980s

Harvey Norman was not the first retail success for company co-founders Gerald Harvey and Ian Norman. The pair had met up in the early 1960s, launching the Norman Ross retail chain in 1961. Harvey, the motor for the later Harvey Norman retail empire, had originally intended to go into farming and had attended agricultural college on a scholarship in the 1950s. However, when his family ran into financial difficulties, Norman switched schools to study economics and accountancy at the University of New South Wales, which enabled him to work part-time.

After leaving school, Harvey took a job selling vacuum cleaners door-to-door and discovered that he had a talent for sales, quickly becoming the top seller in the company he worked for. Harvey decided to go into the retail business for himself and turned to his friend Ian Norman, who had inherited some £700 after his father's death. The pair opened their first store, called Harvey Norman, in 1961.

The store specialized in electrical goods and appliances, and by 1962 Harvey and Norman began looking to expand. The pair came in contact with retailer Keith Lord, who was looking to expand his own retail group, and opened a second store. Yet Lord did not want the new store to be named after Harvey—and Harvey did not want the store to be named after Lord. Instead, the group kept Norman's name and added that of its store manager, forming the basis of the Norman Ross retail group.

By the end of the 1970s, Norman Ross had grown into one of the largest appliance retail chains in the New South Wales and Queensland regions, with 42 stores and sales of more than A$240 million. At the beginning of the 1980s, however, Norman Ross caught the attention of two suitors, Grace Bros. and Alan Bond, the latter in the process of building his highly diversified—and ultimately unstable—business empire. A bidding war ensued and resulted in Harvey and Norman selling their stake, a combined 40 percent of the company, to Grace Bros. in 1982.

Harvey and Norman remained with Norman Ross, directing the company in exchange for a share of the profits. However, the angered Bond turned to Grace Bros. and succeeded in convincing company head Michael Grace to sell him Norman Ross just three weeks after Grace had bought the retailer. Not long after that purchase, Harvey gave an interview on the radio during which he told the *Daily Telegraph:* "I said I wished Bond would pack up his marbles and go back to Perth. Then I got a telegram telling me I was sacked."

Both Harvey and Norman were given notice and a six-month pay parachute. Yet neither had lost the taste for retailing, and one day Harvey noticed a newly built shopping center for sale in Auburn, outside of Sydney. Harvey and Norman decided to buy the complex, paying A$3 million, and launched a new store they named Harvey Norman. The partners formed a new company, called Caviton Ltd., for the venture.

Initially, Harvey and Norman had planned to open just a single store, with Harvey taking the active role and Norman acting more or less as the company's silent partner. Yet the success of the store's discount formula led the company to open a new store and then a number of others. By 1987, the company had grown sufficiently to make its public offering. The newly listed company changed its name, to Harvey Norman, that year. Not long after that, the empire built up by Alan Bond during the 1980s collapsed, and the Norman Ross chain was shut down.

Category Killer to Retail Leader in the 1990s

Harvey Norman's growth was to take off in the 1990s, when the company introduced a new retail "category killer" concept brought over from the United States—the superstore. In initiat-

ing its new retail formula, Harvey Norman took the risk on a relatively small market, that of computer sales.

The risk paid off, and the company's computer superstores soon dominated that retail market. Meanwhile the company's main Harvey Norman stores continued to broaden their product range, adopting a department store formula based on home appliances and furnishings.

Another strong factor in the company's success was its unique—and tightly controlled—franchise formula. Harvey Norman owned the properties for their franchised store locations, enabling the company to generate multiple revenue streams—through site leases, licensing fees, as well as department-by-department purchasing fees—from a single store. The franchise concept worked so well for the company that it owned only one store of its growing retail group.

Harvey attempted to replicate his success in computers with a venture into another retail branch, that of toys and nursery products, in 1993. Yet the format never took off, and after suffering three years of losses, the company shut down that operation.

In the meantime, the boom in computer sales in the early to mid-1990s placed Harvey Norman and its early commitment to that market ahead of the pack. By the mid-1990s, the company's revenues had shot beyond the A$1 billion mark. The company continued its growth drive into the second half of the decade, reaching 60 stores—including 59 franchises—by 1997, for A$1.2 billion in revenues. In that year, Harvey Norman made its first international move, opening its first store in New Zealand. The success of that site led the company to step up its ambitions in that country, with plans to open as many as 12 stores there by decade's end. At the same time, the company set a goal of reaching 100 stores for its entire retail network by 2000.

Until late in the decade, most of the company's growth had come organically, through property purchases and new franchise developments. As Gerry Harvey told the *Daily Telegraph,* "Usually if we wanted a store somewhere we would just open one of our own." In 1998, however, Harvey Norman made its first acquisition, buying up the Joyce Mayne chain of furniture and appliance stores. The purchase, at a cost of A$45 million, added annual sales of A$70 million from seven stores in Sydney, Newcastle, and along Australia's central coast. By the end of that year, the Harvey Norman network had topped 70 stores.

The ebullient Harvey, who had by now entered Australian history as the nation's first retail billionaire, continued to seek expansion outlets for the company. In 1999, it launched a new phone-order wine club, putting it in direct competition with that market's leaders, Foster's and Coles Myers.

The company also kept an eye out for new expansion opportunities for its core retail network. In 1998, it had acquired seven Archie Martin Vox stores, based in Western Australia, paying A$4 million. By 2000, the company's network had topped 100 stores. In that year, the company returned to the Vox network, which had lost money through most of the 1990s, picking up a further 22 stores from owner Brierly Investments (later BIL). The company began converting its new stores to the Harvey Norman format, boosting its total store network to 125 stores.

Going Overseas for Growth in the New Century

Harvey Norman expected to added as many as 40 more stores in Australia and an additional 15 new stores in New Zealand in the early years of the new century. The company also broadened its retail offering, launching a new Space furniture store format, patterned after Ikea stores, and the upscale Domayne store format, which opened in Sydney. Yet by the beginning of the 2000s, the company had already recognized that its future growth in Australia was limited and achieving the kind of double-digit growth that had marked the 1990s would not be possible.

Instead, the company began to look abroad, casting its eyes on both the nearby Southeast Asian market and on more distant Eastern and Western European markets. In Eastern Europe, the company targeted Slovenia, in part as a testing ground for further development in the region but also for that country's proximity to Italy and Austria, expecting to attract shoppers from both countries looking for the lower prices available in Slovenia.

In the west, the company naturally looked toward England and began plans to open a flagship store in London in 2000. Meanwhile, the company, which had earmarked some £190 ($300 million) for its international expansion effort, also looked toward an entry into Singapore, which would then give it access to neighboring Malaysia. The company's entry into Singapore came in 1999, through a 60–40 joint venture with that country's Ossia International. The joint venture, Harvey Norman Singapore, then acquired a 50.6 percent stake in retail chain Pertama in October 1999.

Singapore quickly became the company's fastest-growing international market. In 2001, the company acquired the Electric City chain, which, together with its existing stores, were rebranded under the Harvey Norman name that year. The company pinned much of its future growth hopes on its Asian entry, with expectations that Asian revenues would top its domestic revenues in the new century. In 2003, the company began plans to open its first store in Malaysia, which was expected to open by that year.

Back home, the company found another growth target when it moved to acquire control of struggling sporting goods chain Rebel Sport Ltd. With new management in place, the publicly listed Rebel Sport soon resumed its growth, regaining profitability by 2002. That year marked the long-postponed opening of the company's first Slovenia store. Despite losses continuing into 2003, the company remained committed to testing its retail format in the Eastern European region. In the meantime, the company prepared its entry into a new market, that of Ireland, where it scheduled two store openings for mid 2003.

Despite a sagging stock price, due in part to the uncertain international retail climate, Harvey Norman remained a true Australian success story and one of its strongest growing companies in the previous two decades. Gerry Harvey, who vowed to remain at the head of the company for the rest of his life, was himself widely regarded as Australia's greatest retailer. With plans to duplicate its success on an international scale, including a possible entry into the United States in the 2000s, Harvey Norman looked forward to future expansion.

Principal Subsidiaries

Achiever Computers Pty Ltd; Bundall Computers Pty Limited; Cairncom Pty Limited; Calardu Pty Limited; Cannapp Pty Limited; Cropp Pty Limited; Daldere Pty Limited; Geraldcom Pty Limited; Hardly Normal Limited; Hardly Normal Pty Limited; Harvey Cellars Pty Limited; Harvey Liquor Pty Limited; Harvey Norman Europe d.o.o.; Harvey Norman Gamezone Pty Limited; Harvey Norman Singapore Pte Limited; Harvey Norman Stores (N.Z.) Pty Limited; Home Mart Furniture Pty Limited; J.M. Plant & Equipment Hire Pty Limited; Joyce Mayne Penrith Pty Limited; Lesandu Pty Limited; Network Consumer Finance (N.Z.) Limited; Network Consumer Finance Pty Limited; P & E Sale Pty Limited; Space Furniture Limited; Tisara Pty Limited.

Principal Competitors

Westel Group Ltd.; Coles Myer Ltd.; Woolworths Ltd.; David Jones Ltd.; James Richardson Corporation Proprietory Ltd.; Strathfield Group Ltd.

Further Reading

Barlow, Robert, "Case Study: Harvey Norman," *Business Studies Network*, 2002.
Bawden, Tania, "Harvey Hunts Offshore for Retail Expansion," *The Advertiser*, September 14, 2002, p. 54.
"Gerry Harvey Admits Slovenia Is Quite a Risk," *Sydney Morning Herald*, October 10, 2002.
Gosnell, Peter, "Reaping Success," *Advertiser*, April 10, 2002, p. 34.
Koch, David, "Interview: Gerry Harvey," *Sunday Sunrise*, October 13, 2002.
Lovett, Ian, "The Golden Touch Extends to a Rebel," *Daily Telegraph*, Marchb 13, 2003, p. 43.
"Maverick Buys $4m of Battered Own Stock," *Courier-Mail*, March 15, 2003, p. 74.

—M.L. Cohen

Hastings Manufacturing Company

325 North Hanover Street
Hastings, Michigan 49058
U.S.A.
Telephone: (269) 945-2491
Fax: (269) 945-4667
Web site: http://www.hastingsmanufacturing.com

Public Company
Incorporated: 1915
Employees: 345
Sales: $34.79 million (2002)
Stock Exchanges: American
Ticker Symbol: HMF
NAIC: 336312 Gasoline Engine and Engine Parts Manufacturing

Hastings Manufacturing Company makes piston rings, auto mechanic service tools, and, through a joint venture, engine additives and other automotive chemical products. The company's goods are primarily sold in the United States and Canada, though they are also distributed internationally. Hastings products include Flex-Vent Oil Rings, PowerFLEX Precision Racing Rings, and Motor Honey Oil Treatment, which is produced by the 50 percent-owned Casite Intraco LLC. Most Hastings products are sold on the aftermarket, but the company also makes original equipment piston rings for the likes of DaimlerChrysler AG. A sizable minority of Hastings' stock is owned by descendants of the firm's founder Aben Johnson, and the company is run by his grandsons Mark Johnson (CEO) and Alex Johnson (president).

Beginnings

Hastings Manufacturing was founded in 1915 in Hastings, Michigan by Aben Johnson. The firm was created to manufacture so-called "aftermarket" products, which car owners could buy to enhance or upgrade their vehicles. Early offerings included a luggage carrier, a tire carrier, a bumper, a steering stabilizer, a water pump, an oil engine, and a curtain light.

In 1923 Hastings introduced its first piston rings, cast-iron metal semicircles that fit around an engine's pistons to protect them as they cycled up and down to generate power. Piston rings, especially in early combustion engines, had a relatively short lifespan and needed to be replaced when worn to avoid causing damage to the engine. Buying "original equipment" replacement rings from a dealer could be somewhat costly, and substitute versions made by companies such as Hastings provided consumers with a less expensive alternative.

During the automobile's early years most carmakers used low compression engines that required minimal oil-sealing ability from piston rings. In 1932, however, the Ford Motor Co. made the V-8 engine standard on its vehicles, and the new "flathead" motor utilized a high-compression design. The popularity of the reasonably priced, higher-power vehicles soon led to problems for mechanics who had to find a new type of replacement ring that could control the greater oil compression ratios involved.

To address this issue, in 1935 Hastings introduced its "Steel-Vent" oil control piston ring, the first multiple-piece ring, which was a vast improvement over the cast iron versions heretofore used. To advertise the new product, the company created the Hastings Tough Guy, a cartoon character who touted the product in print ads. The new ring design was a huge success, and Hastings Manufacturing soon grew from a minor aftermarket parts maker into one of the world's leading manufacturers of replacement piston rings.

Expanding the Product Line in the 1940s

In 1941 the growing company formed a Canadian subsidiary, Hastings, Limited, to do business north of the border. The firm also added a line of oil filters in 1944. Hastings' "Densite" filtering media, which was composed of short cotton fibers, worked well, and demand for the company's filters grew steadily over the years.

Following World War II Hastings again expanded its product offerings, adding spark plugs and auto service tools. In 1947 the company acquired the Casite brand of automotive chemical products, which had been introduced in 1939. Casite's offerings included Motor Honey Oil Treatment, an engine additive. Advertisements for Casite from this era emphasized the product's ability to free sticky valves, retard congealing of oil, and eradicate engine sludge, and guaranteed "Better and Smoother Motor Performance or Double-Your-Money-Back." During the 1940s founder Aben Johnson's son Stephen also began working for Hastings. He would later take control of the firm from his father.

In 1950, following six years of design and testing, Hastings added a line of oil filter cartridges. The firm began manufacturing safety belts in 1956 and introduced the new Flex-Vent three-piece oil control ring the same year.

In 1957 Hastings began construction of a foundry, which became operational in October. The year 1958 saw the company purchase its first computer and also start construction of a new filter manufacturing facility, which was completed the following spring. The "state-of-the-art" plant was highly automated. In 1963 Hastings discontinued its spark plug line, which had not proven to be profitable.

In the early 1970s company head Stephen Johnson's sons Mark and Andrew began working for the firm in its marketing and financial departments. By 1980 Hastings, whose stock was now trading on the Amex exchange, was reporting annual sales of more than $47 million. Earnings for that year topped $1.4 million.

Increasing Filter Manufacturing in 1985

In 1985 Hastings enlarged its filter manufacturing operations by creating a new assembly division in Yankton, South Dakota. The unit was charged with making filters for sale through mass merchandisers, which the company was targeting to increase sales. In 1986 Hastings' Canadian subsidiary, now known as Hastings, Inc., built a new facility in Barrie, Ontario to accommodate sales growth expected in that country.

In 1987 the company opened a new distribution warehouse in Knoxville, Tennessee. The 150,000-square-foot facility gave Hastings better inventory handling capability and also improved the company's ability to ship to customers in a timely fashion, given its more central location. That year the company's sales topped $65.5 million and its net earnings totaled slightly less than $1.5 million.

In November of 1991 a former Hastings employee and an alleged accomplice were arrested and charged with stealing company plans for an oil-control ring system and offering them for sale. An undercover police officer had reportedly arranged to buy the plans from them for $300,000. The company had discovered that the documents were missing during the summer.

In the spring of 1994 Hastings president Stephen Johnson stepped down and his sons Mark and Andrew were named

co-CEOs and co-presidents of the company. Stephen Johnson continued to serve as board chairman.

Hastings sold its filter-making operations in the fall of 1995 to Clarcor, Inc. of Rockford, Illinois for $13.9 million. The deal included the company's Yankton and Knoxville facilities. After the sale was finalized, Clarcor would continue to make filters under the Hastings and Casite names, joining its own Baldwin, Clair, and Airguard brands. Hastings' decision to sell had been motivated by a desire to concentrate the company's efforts on its core product line of piston rings. A total of 250 employees who were involved with the filter operation were transferred to Clarcor, leaving Hastings with a total of 624.

In December of 1996 the company restructured its operations, reducing staffing levels and phasing out piston ring manufacturing in Canada. During this time period the firm also was gaining QS-9000, ISO-9002, and ISO-9001 certification of its manufacturing procedures.

In 1997 Hastings began exporting its own products abroad, following the termination of an international distribution contract with an outside firm on December 31, 1996. The new "country-direct" method of distribution involved working with subdistributors in each country, rather than a master distributor for all foreign sales. In May of 1997 Hastings also introduced a new product line, PowerFLEX Precision Racing Rings, which were marketed to the auto racing industry. Sales for the year reached $35.7 million, with net earnings of $955,000.

In 1998 Hastings began to adopt lean manufacturing practices, for which the company's factory was reconfigured to minimize waste in materials and labor. This was done primarily to address a problem with manufacturing capacity that had caused product shortages during the latter half of the year.

Starting a Joint Casite Venture in 1999

In the fall of 1999 the company formed a joint venture with Intraco Corp. called Casite Intraco LLC, or The Casite Company, to develop, market, and sell Casite vehicle chemicals worldwide. The 50–50 jointly owned venture would be headquartered in Hastings. The Troy, Michigan-based Intraco was an international building, industrial, and automotive products distributor, which had earlier distributed Hastings piston rings abroad. Hastings would transfer all trademarks for Casite products to the new entity, but would continue to market the line in the United States for the first two years of the agreement. In conjunction with the joint venture, Hastings announced plans to increase the offerings in the Casite line from six to nearly two dozen products. In addition to established items like the Motor Honey and Tranny Honey additives, new fuel, maintenance, and aerosol products were planned. The Casite line was already distributed widely in the United States through Kmart, Meijer, and Murray's stores.

The year 1999 also saw Hastings' Canadian subsidiary begin to distribute the products of other U.S. automotive aftermarket goods makers through a new distribution, administration, and sales program in that country. The Canadian unit took on all packaging and distribution of the firm's mechanics specialty tool line, as well.

Key Dates:

1915: Hastings Manufacturing Co. is formed to make auto accessories.
1923: The company introduces a line of cast-iron piston rings.
1935: New Steel-Vent oil control rings debut.
1941: A Canadian subsidiary, Hastings Ltd., is created.
1947: The company acquires the Casite automotive chemical product line.
1950: The company introduces oil filter cartridges.
1963: Spark plugs are discontinued.
1985: A new filter making division is formed in South Dakota.
1987: A distribution center opens in Knoxville, Tennessee.
1994: Mark and Andrew Johnson are named co-presidents, co-CEOs of the firm.
1995: The filter operations are sold to Clarcor, Inc.
1999: The Casite Intraco LLC joint venture is formed to market the Casite line.
2001: The company undergoes a restructuring; Hastings begins distributing products of other firms in the United States.

A slowdown in demand for the company's products led to new cost-cutting measures in 2000 and 2001, including suspension of stock dividend payments and the layoff of 11 percent of the company's workforce of 345 in February 2001. March of that year saw the company sign an agreement with Karl Schmidt Unisia, Inc. (KUS), to distribute its Zollner brand pistons in the United States and Mexico. KUS, an affiliate of the German-based Kolbenschmidt Pierburg AG, would make the pistons at a plant in Wisconsin. Zollner, originally located in Fort Wayne, Indiana, had been acquired in 1999 by KUS. By the summer of 2001 business had begun to rebound, and Hastings was able to offer most of its laid-off workers their jobs back and also hire ten additional employees.

Another marketing agreement was signed in November of 2001 with Norcross, Georgia-based Automotive Components Limited (ACL), a maker of engine parts including bearings, gaskets, and pistons. Hastings would distribute that company's products along with its own in the United States and Mexico. Shortly afterward, Hastings created a new Global Automotive Aftermarket unit, which would be run by two former ACL executives to help position Hastings as a single-source supplier of engine components worldwide. Creation of the new unit was part of a restructuring in which the company's Michigan operations were split into two parts, the other of which would be responsible for piston ring production and distribution. At the same time the company made changes at the top, naming Andrew Johnson president and giving Mark Johnson the titles of CEO and board chairman.

After several years of losses, Hastings reported net earnings of more than $1 million for fiscal 2001 on sales of $34.8 million. The profits were due in part to $714,000 received from the company's sale of a 120-acre fishing lodge it owned near Baldwin, Michigan.

In the spring of 2002 Hastings reached an agreement with Intraco for the latter to market Hastings piston rings and other products in Central America, South America, and the Middle East. At year's end the firm also resolved a two-year-old lawsuit that had been filed by company retirees, who charged that Hastings had improperly reduced their healthcare benefits. The settlement would cost the company approximately $4 million over a 12-year period.

More than 85 years after its founding, the Hastings Manufacturing Company continued to produce quality automotive piston rings and other aftermarket products. Recent agreements to expand distribution of goods worldwide and to distribute other manufacturers' engine components in North America, as well as a refinement of the company's manufacturing process, had returned it to profitability after a period of losses in the late 1990s.

Principal Subsidiaries

Hastings, Inc. (Canada); HMC, Inc.; Casite Intraco, LLC (50%).

Principal Competitors

Dana Corporation; Federal-Mogul Corporation; Robert Bosch GmbH; TRW Automotive, Inc.; Nippon Piston Ring Co., Ltd.

Further Reading

"Barry Company to Distribute Pistons," *Grand Rapids Press*, March 28, 2001, p. A9.
Bodipo-Memba, Alejandro, "Two Car-Parts Suppliers in Michigan Lay Off Workers," *Detroit Free Press*, February 23, 2001.
"Hastings Agrees to Pay More for Retiree Health Care," *Grand Rapids Press*, December 5, 2002, p. A15.
"Hastings Firm Makes Changes in Top Echelon," *Grand Rapids Press*, May 12, 1994, p. B6.
"Hastings Firm Plans World Sales," *Grand Rapids Press*, October 8, 1999, p. A11.
"Hastings, Intraco in Piston Rings Marketing Venture," *Autoparts Report*, June 21, 2002.
McCarthy, Tom, "Drop in Sales Brings Reduction in Jobs at Hastings Firm," *Grand Rapids Press*, February 24, 1992, p. B4.
"Pair Accused in Sale of Company Plans," *Grand Rapids Press*, November 11, 1991, p. B3.
Sabo, Mary Ann, "Hastings to Sell Filter Production," *Grand Rapids Press*, September 5, 1995, p. B7.
"Slowdown Brings Loss at Hastings Manufacturing," *Grand Rapids Press*, March 13, 2001, p. A5.
Wieland, Barbara, "Automotive Parts Firm Turns Loss into Gain," *Grand Rapids Press*, March 13, 2002, p. D3.
——, "Cutting Expenses Pays Off for Hastings Manufacturing," *Grand Rapids Press*, August 8, 2001, p. A8.
——, "Hastings Manufacturing Realigns Its Business," *Grand Rapids Press*, December 4, 2001, p. A15.
——, "Hastings Plant Cuts 10 Percent of Jobs," *Grand Rapids Press*, February 23, 2001, p. A6.
——, "Plant Renovations Drag Down Hastings Manufacturing's Profits," *Grand Rapids Press*, March 16, 2000, p. B5.

—Frank Uhle

Headwaters Incorporated

10653 South Riverfront Parkway, Suite 300
South Jordan, Utah 84095
U.S.A.
Telephone: (801) 984-9400
Fax: (801) 984-9410
Web site: http://www.hdwtrs.com

Public Company
Incorporated: 1987 as Cynsulo Inc.
Employees: 840
Sales: $119.35 million (2002)
Stock Exchanges: NASDAQ
Ticker Symbol: HDWR
NAIC: 324199 All Other Petroleum and Coal Products
   Manufacturing

Through its subsidiaries, Headwaters Incorporated is a leader in both the pre-combustion treatment and the post-combustion treatment of coal. It manages and markets coal combustion products (CCP), or the by-products of burning coal for electricity, on behalf of power plants. The only CCP manager in the United States with national coverage, Headwater makes its revenues by licensing its technology, selling interests in synfuel plants it has developed alone or with partners, and by supplying plants with chemical reagents. It sold more than 59 million pounds of reagents in fiscal 2002.

Origins

Headwaters Incorporated can trace its source to Cynsulo Inc., which was incorporated in Nevada in 1987. Cynsulo had a small initial public offering in 1988. Cynsulo changed its name to McParkland Properties Inc. after acquiring McParkland Corp. in December 1988. However, this purchase was rescinded in February 1990. In August of that year, the company became known as Riverbed Enterprises, Inc. At the same time, it shifted its focus to growing alfalfa and other agricultural products.

In July 1991, the company changed its name to Enviro-Fuels Technology, Inc. It had acquired technology for making briquettes

from waste particles using binding agents. The company spent the next four years researching briquetting of iron, coal, and coke waste. In 1992, it built a prototype briquetting plant in Price, Utah. To generate cash flow, Enviro-Fuels acquired three construction companies in 1993: Industrial Management and Engineering, Inc., State Incorporated, and Central Industrial Construction, Inc.

The company was known for a time in 1994 as Environmental Technologies Group International. By this time, it was based in Lehi, Utah, south of Salt Lake City. Environmental Technologies acquired Utah's Larson Limestone Co. in October 1994. Larson was valuable for its rock-pulverizing equipment, which was expected to increase Environmental Technologies' revenues by as much as $4 million a year.

Environmental Technologies entered an agreement with Geneva Steel Company in May 1995 to build a commercial briquetting plant in Vineyard, Utah. In July 1995, the company licensed its coke-breeze technology to Greystone Environmental Technologies Inc. of Birmingham, Alabama. This process allowed a waste product of coke to be bonded into a solid, useable substitute for coke.

Due to a similarity with another public company's name, Environmental Technologies changed its name to Covol Technologies Inc. in August 23, 1995, at the same time changing its state of incorporation to Delaware. Concurrent with the decision to focus on commercializing the synfuel technology, Covol began divesting its construction subsidiaries.

Focusing on Coal After 1995

Covol believed developing synthetic fuel from coal fines was its best bet for commercializing this technology. One reason for this strategy was the fact that it enabled the company to take advantage of significant tax benefits. After two Arab oil embargos in a single decade, Congress created a federal synthetic fuels tax credit (Section 29) in 1979 to promote alternative energy production within the United States. This included producing methane from coalbeds and extracting oil from shale or tar sands.

Coal particles less than one-quarter inch in diameter are called "fines." Covol Technologies developed a process for turning this waste product into solid briquettes or pellets of useable fuel by blending it with low-sulfur coal and baking the moisture out of it (30 minutes at 450 degrees).

Covol agreed to acquire the Wellington Loadout in Carbon County, Utah, from Nevada Electric Investment Co. in November 1995. At least five million tons of low-sulfur coal fines suitable for conversion to briquettes remained at the site.

NASDAQ in 1998

Covol began trading on the NASDAQ exchange in May 1998. By this time, the company had completed 24 synthetic fuel facilities, mostly in Appalachia, Alabama, and the Great Basin area. All were in partnerships, joint ventures, and alliances, rather than outright ownership. This completed the first phase of its business plan.

In July 1998, Brent M. Cook replaced Ray Weller as chairman of the board. Cook, formerly director of strategic accounts at PacifiCorp Inc., had first joined Covol in June 1996 as chief financial officer and was named president and CEO four months later. After becoming chairman, he remained company CEO but stepped down as president. Kirk Benson became CEO of Covol in April 1999.

Covol reported losses of $74 million between 1987 and 1999. Shares fell by 91 percent in 1999. It faced another difficult year in 2000. A stellar climb was just around the corner, however. Covol had about 50 employees at the time, most of them in research and development.

A New Name in 2000

In 2000, royalty growth increased fivefold as Covol achieved profitability for the first time in its history. Revenues for Covol's fiscal year, which ended September 30, 2000, were $45.8 million, up from $6.7 million. Most of this came from selling synfuel plants. Recurring revenues were $27.9 million. The company was able to pay down its debt by more than 95 percent. These results, said Covol, validated its technology-to-market business model.

Since synfuel plants had to be in operation by mid-1998 to be eligible for the Section 29 tax credit, their numbers were limited to about 55. The tax credits had become an important commodity in themselves—more valuable than coal itself. Both of these factors drove up the price of Covol's plants.

Synfuels competed directly with coal. Some of Covol's competitors drew criticism for secretive and dubious processes of converting coal waste into synfuels. One company was said to merely spray useable coal with a diesel fuel mixture. However, Covol openly described its process in trade journals. Covol sold its proprietary chemical reagent to plants that licensed its technology, a process that involved treating coal

wastes with various bonding agents, which, when heated under pressure, changed the molecular structure of the coal—a key requirement of the tax credit legislation.

Covol Technologies, Inc. changed its name to Headwaters Incorporated in September 2000. The name reflected an expanded focus beyond the core synthetic fuels business. Covol used a venture capital approach to acquire minority holdings in new business, which it aimed to integrate with other Covol affiliates.

Around the same time as its name change, Headwaters created a new unit, Kwai Financial Inc., to provide bridge loans to new technology companies in the earliest stages of financing—between the seed capital provided by angels and the subsequent rounds of venture capital funding. Kwai's area of expertise was in application services, e-commerce, infrastructure services, and networking. Kwai was soon made part of Avintaquin Capital, LLC, which had Headwaters in its portfolio.

Later in 2000, Headwaters consolidated its business operations into a new facility in the Salt Lake City suburb of Draper, Utah. Revenue for the 2001 fiscal year rose 63 percent to $45.5 million. Net income was $21.5 million. Headwaters' share price rose 383 percent during the 2001 calendar year, reported the *Salt Lake Tribune,* making it the best-performing stock among Utah's publicly held companies.

HTI bought in 2001

Headwaters acquired another company with extensive intellectual property rights in August 2001. Hydrocarbon Technologies Inc. (HTI) of Lawrenceville, New Jersey, had developed technology to produce diesel fuel from coal and heavy oil and to make carbon products from used tires and oil. HTI had been owned by its 49 employees and was founded in 1943 as Hydrocarbon Research. The acquisition was potentially worth about $17 million in cash ($1.5 million), stock, and assumption of debt ($1.5 million).

HTI was involved in ventures in China and elsewhere in the world. It was developing leading-edge nano-catalysis technology to reduce the use of precious metals in such applications as catalytic converters for automobiles.

In May 2002, HTI acquired a worldwide license to develop and market a catalytic heavy oil upgrading technology called (HC)3. This helped produce synthetic crude or liquid fuels from bottom of the barrel, bitumen, or heavy oil. It had been developed by the Alberta Research Council Inc. in cooperation with two HTI executives.

In June 2002, HTI agreed to license technology for a $2 billion direct coal liquefaction plant to be built by China's largest coal company, Shenhua Group Corporation Ltd., in Inner Mongolia. This would make up to 50,000 barrels a day of ultra-clean liquid fuels such as diesel fuel and gasoline from indigenous coal.

This deal had been years in the making. The technology was developed under the auspices of the U.S. Department of Energy (DOE) following the 1970s oil crisis. The DOE and other

Key Dates:

1987: Cynsulo Inc. is incorporated in Nevada.
1989: The company is renamed Riverbed Enterprises.
1991: Riverbed acquires briquette-making technology.
1995: Riverbed renamed Covol Technologies Inc.
1998: Covol stock migrates to the NASDAQ Stock Exchange.
2000: Covol is renamed Headwaters Inc.
2001: Headwaters acquires HTI.
2002: Headwaters acquires ISG.

federal agencies helped HTI work out a licensing deal with the Chinese beginning in 1996.

ISG Acquired in 2002

Headwaters' high stock value helped it make acquisitions during 2001 and 2002, while its acquisition were helping maintain its share price. In July 2002, the company acquired another Salt Lake area business, Industrial Services Group Inc. (ISG), in a deal worth $227 million, including $181 million of debt. ISG was the parent company of ISG Resources, Inc., which marketed the fly ash, bottom ash, and scrubber sludge that were the by-products of coal combustion. Fly ash was being increasingly used as a substitute for cement in concrete and stucco. In *Investors Business Daily*, Headwaters CEO Kirk Benson compared it to the volcanic ash used by builders in ancient Rome. However, it was only found in 10 percent of U.S. concrete, while it was used in 25 percent of concrete in Europe.

ISG had been formed in 1997 by Steve Creamer and Chip Everest, who acquired a number of coal combustion residue companies after selling their interest in an eastern Utah landfill. Its 2001 revenues were $216 million—four times that of Headwaters—but it had been losing money since 1999. ISG employed about 760 people at dozens of sites across the United States. Its fleet included more than 400 trucks and 1,200 railcars. The company had long-term contracts with more than 115 power plants in 35 states.

The ISG buy combined the leader in pre-combustion treatment of coal with the leader in post-combustion treatment. HTI was also experimenting with converting paper, plastics, and wood from municipal landfill waste into fuel.

HTI acquired the license to a new technology for heating or mixing liquids in July 2002. The Shockwave Power Generator (SPG) used controlled cavitation to improve the dispersion of gases in liquids and to increase chemical reaction rates. For HTI, it had applications in heavy oil upgrading and coal liquefaction.

Total Headwaters revenue increased 163 percent in fiscal 2002 to $119.3 million, another record. Income taxes kept the net income down to $24.3 million. The largest growth came in the sales of chemical reagents, which more than tripled to $74.4 million.

Headwaters relocated its headquarters to South Jordan, Utah—another Salt Lake suburb—in January 2003. The company planned to continue to acquire small fly ash companies to enhance its position as the national leader in coal combustion product management. Headwaters controlled about half of the 24 million tons of fly ash that were produced annually in the United States. This reduced the company's dependence on synfuels. The Section 29 tax credit for synfuels was scheduled to expire in 2007, which would likely make this side of the business unprofitable. However, Congress had extended the program several times since its inception in 1979.

Headwaters also owned proprietary technologies for a number of building products related to fly ash, including aerated concrete, rapid setting concrete, mortars, and stuccos. Some of these uses originated in Europe, which had a much higher utilization of fly ash. Headwaters was aiming to increase its acceptance in the U.S. market through an aggressive sales, marketing, and lobbying program.

Principal Subsidiaries

Environmental Technologies Group, LLC (50%); Hydrocarbon Technologies, Inc.; Industrial Services Group, Inc.

Principal Divisions

Covol Fuels.

Principal Competitors

Progress Energy, Inc.; Lafarge North America, Inc.; Ondeo Nalco Company.

Further Reading

Alva, Marilyn, ''A Fortune in Fly Ash? This Company Says So,'' *Investor's Business Daily*, November 19, 2002, p. 10.

Boehme, Natalie, ''Fuel Pellets Are an Energy Find for Company,'' *State Journal Register* (Springfield, Ill.), July 14, 1998, p. 16.

''China: Joint Venture Construction Start-Up on Planned $2,000,000,000 Coal Liquefaction Plant Is Tentatively Scheduled to Begin in Early 2003,'' *WWP—Report on Oil, Gas & Petrochemicals in the Developing World*, July 1, 2002.

''Covol in Talks to Sell Fuel Business and Possibly Merge,'' *New York Times*, June 24, 1999.

''Covol Sells Briquette Plant; Gallagher to Finance Utah Unit,'' *Coal Week*, November 25, 1996, p. 3.

''Draper Company Is Focusing on Converting Fuels,'' *Deseret News* (Salt Lake City), June 9, 2002, p. M5.

''Draper Firm Makes $14.5 Million Acquisition,'' *The Enterprise* (Salt Lake City), May 7, 2001, p. 7.

''Environmental Tech Buys Utah Limestone Firm,'' *Dow Jones News Service*, October 26, 1994.

Goodwin, Morgan, ''Dealing with the Very Dregs of Steelmaking,'' *American Metal Market*, August 24, 1995, p. 5A.

''Headwaters Inc. Delivering to 2 Relocated Facilities,'' *Deseret News* (Salt Lake City), March 15, 2002, p. B7.

''Headwaters Sells Interest in Original Synfuel Facility,'' *Deseret News* (Salt Lake City), January 8, 2002, p. B6.

''Kenneth Fraily Is Covol Fuels' New President,'' *The Enterprise* (Salt Lake City), March 10, 2003, p. 3.

Mitchell, Lesley, ''China Will Change Coal Into Gasoline Using Draper Company's Technology,'' *Salt Lake Tribune*, June 19, 2002, p. B4.

Nyden, Paul J., ''Tax Break Helps Synthetic Fuels Cut into Market,'' *Charleston Gazette* (WV), February 2000, p. 2B.

——, "Synfuel Tax Credits Continuing to Grow: Although Credits Disrupt Coal Prices, Public Officials Not Stirred to Action," *Charleston Gazette* (WV), September 24, 2000, p. 1A.

——, "IRS Seeks Public Comments on Synfuel Tax Credits," *Charleston Gazette* (WV), November 22, 2000, p. 3A.

——, "Synfuels' Legitimacy at Heart of Probe," *Charleston Gazette* (WV), November 26, 2000, p. 1A.

——, "Plants Petition to Keep Tax Credits: Stricter Synfuel Rules Opposed," *Charleston Gazette* (WV), December 8, 2000, p. 6A.

——, "West Virginia Synthetic Fuels Firm Outlines Future Risks in Report to SEC," *Charleston Gazette* (WV), December 27, 2000.

Oberbeck, Steven, "Utah Publicly Held Stocks Stood Up Well in 2001," *Salt Lake Tribune,* January 1, 2002, p. B4.

——, "Headwaters to Buy ISG for $227M," *Salt Lake Tribune*, July 17, 2002, p. B4.

Ondrey, Gerald, "Waste-to-Fuel," *Chemical Engineering*, October 1, 2001, p. 21.

"Tax Credits Put Fire Under Briquettes; Covol Targets Utilities, Steel Mills," *Coal Week*, January 1, 1996, p. 1.

"$216 Million ISG Resources Sold for Cash and Stock to Draper-Based Headwaters," *The Enterprise*, July 22, 2002, p. 1.

—Frederick C. Ingram

Health Management Associates, Inc.

5811 Pelican Bay, Suite 500
Naples, Florida 34108-2710
U.S.A.
Telephone: (239) 598-3131
Fax: (239) 598-2705
Web site: http://www.hma-corp.com

Public Company
Incorporated: 1977 as Hospital Management Associates,
    Inc.
Employees: 23,000
Sales: $2.3 billion (2002)
Stock Exchanges: New York
Ticker Symbol: HMA
NAIC: 622110 General Medical and Surgical Hospitals

Health Management Associates, Inc. is a highly successful operator of more than 40 general acute care hospitals and two psychiatric-only hospitals. The facilities are located in what management calls ''non-urban'' communities, with populations between 30,000 and 400,000, primarily in the southeastern and southwestern United States. HMA operates the only hospital in most of its markets, granting it greater leverage in negotiating prices with health providers. For nearly 20 years, HMA has been successful in acquiring small hospitals, generally 100 to 300-bed facilities, at reasonable prices. The company then invests money to significantly upgrade the institution, prompting area residents to turn to the local hospital rather than travel to a larger facility in a bigger city. Moreover HMA is proficient at instituting popular hospital management practices, such as ensuring that the first person a patient meets is a nurse. While the hospitals take advantage of HMA's size when it comes to buying power and operating systems, they are essentially managed at the local level. The company maintains a lean headquarters in Naples, Florida.

Late 1970s Origins

HMA, which was originally called Hospital Management Associates, Inc., was formed in 1977 in Naples, Florida, by Joseph Greene. He was helped in running the hospital management

company by his brother Charles, while his son, Joseph Greene, Jr., headed the company's Florida hospitals. The original plan was to manage hospitals throughout the country, but the company had difficulty competing in urban areas like Atlanta, resulting in a steady erosion in profits. Hospital Management Associates became Health Management Associates in 1979, but the change in name did nothing to correct the company's dwindling fortunes, and by 1983 HMA was in desperate need of an infusion of fresh cash. Enlisted to help was a Naples resident, William J. Schroen, a semi-retired executive with strong Wall Street credentials and experience in turnarounds, albeit in the beer industry. Approached by a First Chicago venture capital banker named Kent Dauten, Schoen agreed to join HMA's board of directors to both raise money and help work a turnaround.

Schoen earned a degree from the University of Southern California but received a practical education working for Pierce Glass, a subsidiary of Indian Head, Inc.,which in turn was a spinoff of Textron, the first modern conglomerate founded by the legendary Royal Little. Schoen served as president of Pierce from 1971 to 1973, forging a solid reputation by moving the company into specialty packing that resulted in a significant improvement in sales. He then spent the next several years in New York City turning around F&M Schaefer Corporation, managing to prosper by making Schaefer the premium beer in Puerto Rico. Schoen was in his mid-40s when he sold Schaefer to Stroh Brewery Co. and moved to Naples, where in semi-retirement he started up a small bank, Commerce National Bank.

When Schoen was elected to the board of directors in February 1983, HMA had reported a meager profit of $251,000 on revenues of $25 million in its latest annual results. Serving initially as a consultant to the company, he was soon named president and chief operating officer in December 1983 despite his lack of knowledge of the health care field. Over the course of two years, he helped shift the company's focus to non-urban hospitals and brought in $7 million in outside investments, which led to Schoen being named co-CEO with Greene in December 1985. According to *Florida Trend,* ''In no time, Schoen was butting heads with co-Chief Executive Joseph Greene, who wanted to keep control totally centralized.'' Within months, in April 1986, Greene retired, leaving Schoen HMA's sole CEO.

Company Perspectives:

Health Management Associates, Inc. is the premier operator of acute care hospitals in the southeast and southwest areas of non-urban America.

New Leadership in the 1980s

Free now to make changes that he deemed necessary, Schoen divested ten of HMA's dozen hospitals, all deep in debt and losing money, and retained only two facilities. He swore off urban hospitals and began to carve out a healthcare niche by focusing on the acquisition of smaller nonprofit hospitals in southern cities with populations under 75,000 and no local competition. Moreover, he slashed the head count at corporate headquarters, terminating 50 of 82 managers and executives as part of an effort to decentralize the operation. He then established competitive performance goals, developed a profit plan for each hospital, and instituted regular evaluations. The rankings of all the hospitals were shared throughout the chain. By the end of 1986, HMA added three hospitals to the fold, leasing hospitals in Biloxi, Mississippi, and Marathon, Florida, and buying another in Louisbourgh, North Carolina. To help support this expansion, Schoen took HMA public at $10 per share in 1986. However, even though the company went on to post solid results, the price of its stock languished, tainted by the problems of other hospital chains of comparable size. American Healthcare Management and Westworld Community Healthcare filed for bankruptcy, while National Healthcare defaulted on some $100 million as part of a restructuring. HMA added three more hospitals in 1987, leasing a facility in Van Buren, Arkansas, and buying hospitals in Durant, Oklahoma, and Hamlet, North Carolina. Another hospital, located in Gaffney, South Carolina, was purchased in March 1988. At this point, Schoen believed that HMA was severely undervalued by Wall Street, and he mounted a drive to take the business private once again, enlisting the help of board members from First Chicago and Prudential Ventures. In August 1988, a management-led investment group paid $14.75 for each share of stock, nearly $85 million in all, and removed HMA and its chain of a dozen hospitals from public ownership. Just as important, the company took on no debt to finance the buyout.

By now, the HMA model for acquiring hospitals and integrating them into the chain was well established. First, management targeted financially troubled non-profit medical facilities located in small markets that could be bought well below the industry standard. In this regard, Schoen was able to take advantage of changes in the health care industry. With the federal government instituting tighter controls on Medicare payments in the early 1980s, moving toward fixed prices, a number of inefficiently run, smaller hospitals, were put up for sale in a market with few buyers. As a result, facilities that just a few years earlier had fetched as much as $250,000 a bed to acquire now cost in the range of $150,000 per bed. In contrast to more experienced health care executives, Schoen actually saw fixed prices as a guaranteed profit, provided that HMA cut costs below the Medicare rate. Part of those savings were the result of group purchasing, a process that became highly organized and progressively easier to apply to new hospitals in the system. HMA was also successful in using computers to speed up bill

collections, and even saved money by buying used equipment that technicians beefed up on the cheap. HMA was able to shave off a considerable amount of time needed to collect bills, just 49 days, compared to the industry standard of 75 days. Aside from organizational changes, HMA made efforts to earn the good will of residents, who were naturally skeptical about an outside company taking over a local institution.

HMA acquisitions were upgraded, which involved remodeling as well as the purchase of new equipment, and specialists were recruited at great cost. The expansion of services and the availability of specialized equipment paid off in a number of ways for HMA. Not only did these additions generate greater revenues, they persuaded residents that they did not need to travel 50 miles to a big city hospital. To keep the economics in line, HMA rotated the most expensive equipment among its hospitals on a set schedule. Another effective step that HMA took with a new acquisition was to simply survey patients and address basic concerns. The hospital and its new management also sought to be good corporate citizens, sponsoring local events and offering cafeteria discounts to senior citizens, a key constituency. One popular program that HMA developed was Med-Key, a plastic identification card that contained basic information about a resident, the use of which cut down on the amount of time people had to spend on completing medical forms when visiting the local hospital. As an inducement to use Med-Key, residents also received discounts from participating merchants.

In January 1989, HMA purchased an Orlando psychiatric hospital and a year later added the second of the company's two psychiatric hospitals by acquiring a Tesquesta, Florida, facility. With HMA thriving, posting a string of increasing profitable quarters, Schoen now deemed it advantageous to once again take HMA public. In February 1991, the company conducted an offering priced at $16 per share. The years HMA spent as a private concern proved advantageous to its backers, who made handsome returns on their investments as the company's value virtually doubled.

Acquisitions in the 1990s

In the early 1990s, HMA continued to add to its holdings at a steady pace. In 1991, it bought 281-bed Riverview Regional Medical Center, located in Gadsden, Alabama, the company's largest facility to date. In 1993, HMA acquired hospitals in Greater Haines City, Florida, and Natchez, Mississippi. The company added one hospital in 1994, the Charlotte Regional Medical Center, located in Punta Gorda, Florida. Starting in the winter of 1993, there was a run-up on the price of HMA stock, prompting a 3-for-2 split in June 1994, at which point the price fell precipitously, perhaps caused by the large amount of shares unloaded by insiders in recent months and a June 1994 *Forbes* article that expressed skepticism about the company's rationale that executives were merely diversifying their personal portfolios, the writer commenting, "Maybe so, but we suspect the bloom is off this one." Regardless of the reasons for the loss of investor confidence, HMA attempted to address the problem by announcing a major stock buyback program, the board authorizing the purchase of 2.5 million shares.

The price of HMA stock soon rebounded as the underlying financial strength of the company ultimately overcame investor

---

Key Dates:

1977: Hospital Management Associates, Inc. is founded by Joseph Greene.
1979: The company name is changed to Health Management Associates.
1983: William Schoen is named director
1986: The company goes public.
1988: Company is taken private.
1991: HMA returns to public ownership.
2001: Joseph Vumbacco replaces Schoen as CEO.

---

doubts, and Schoen and his team were able to return their focus to growing the business. In 1995, they added two hospitals, one in Hartsville, South Carolina, and another in Statesboro, Georgia. A year later facilities in Clarksdale, Mississippi, and Midwest City, Oklahoma, were acquired. HMA added three hospitals to its system in 1997, agreeing to manage a hospital in Anniston, Alabama, leasing one in Brandon, Mississippi, and buying yet another in Little Rock, Arkansas, a market larger than the norm for the company.

In late 1996, Schoen brought in a new executive, Joseph V. Vumbacco, with the goal of grooming him to one day succeed him as HMA's CEO. While Schoen headed Schaefer in the 1970s, Vumbacco served as its senior vice-president, secretary, and general counsel following a stint as an attorney with a New York law firm. He came to HMA after being employed for 14 years with a construction and real estate firm, The Turner Corporation, where he served as an executive vice-president. In April 1997, he was named HMA's president as well as chief administrative officer and chief operating officer.

HMA picked up the acquisition pace in 1998, adding five hospitals to the chain, leasing facilities in Brooksville, Florida, and Spring Hill, Florida, and buying two hospitals in Flowood and another in Meridian, Mississippi. In 1999, HMA arranged to lease two more hospitals, located in Jackson, Mississippi, and Key West, Florida, and bought a third in Lancaster, Pennsylvania. The move into Lancaster was out of character for HMA because the city had two other larger hospitals. Nevertheless, Schoen felt confident that once HMA instituted changes it would become the hospital of choice in the community. A year later, HMA significantly increased its marketshare in Lancaster by acquiring St. Joseph Hospital, a 268-bed acute care hospital. Also in 2000, HMA added hospitals in Dade City, Florida, and Statesville, North Carolina.

The 2000s and Beyond

In January 2001, Schoen, at 65 years of age, stepped down as CEO in favor of Vumbacco, some ten years younger, although he stayed on as chairman. In truth, it was more a change in titles than workloads, because two years earlier Schoen had stepped back from the day-to-day operations of the company. The company was well positioned for the change, its finances so strong that later in 2001 HMA was added to the S&P 500 Index, joining the ranks of other notable large-capitalization stocks. HMA faced competition from two Tennessee-based companies, Community Health Systems, operating 57 hospitals, and Providence Healthcare with 19 hospitals, but the future continued to look bright for HMA. For the past decade the company achieved an eight-fold increase in revenues, which total $2.26 billion in fiscal 2002, with net income of $246.4. There also appeared to be plenty of hospitals in America's heartland that management might acquire to fuel further growth. Moreover, the greying of America bade well for HMA's future. While 97 million American were over the age of 45 in 2000, the number was estimated to increase to 120 million by 2020. Already HMA was preparing for that time, making considerable investments in specialty cardiac and MRI units. In addition, another trend favored the company's prospects: an increasing number of aging Americans were opting to live in the kind of non-urban markets in which HMA specialized.

Principal Subsidiaries

Health Management Investments, Inc.; Insurance Company of the Southeast, Ltd.

Principal Competitors

Community Health Systems, Inc.; Providence Healthcare Group Inc.; Triad Hospitals, Inc.

Further Reading

Byrne, Harlan S., "Health Management Associates: Small-town Caregiver," *Barron's*, August 26, 2002, p. 16.
Cooper, Helene, "Health Management Thrives as Others Falter," *Wall Street Journal*, May 4, 1993, p. A4.
Flint, Jerry, "Legal Monopolies," *Forbes*, August 28, 1995, p. 90.
Fritz, Michael, "Healthy Profits," *Forbes*, July 13, 1987, p. 454.
Gallagher, Leigh, "The Forbes Platinum List: Health Care Services: The Big Money Is in Small Towns," *Forbes*, January 11, 1999, pp. 182–83.
Jaspen, Bruce, "Investor-Owned Chains Seek Rich Rural Harvest," *Modern Healthcare*, July 1, 1996, p. 32.
Jereski, Laura, "Healthy, Wealthy and Wise," *Florida Trend*, August 1992, p. 32.
Lutz, Sandy, "Hospital Chain's LBO Reads Like Textbook Case," *Modern Healthcare*, February 18, 1991, p. 33.

—Ed Dinger

Hospital Central Services, Inc.

2171 28th Street South West
Allentown, Pennsylvania 18103-7073
U.S.A.
Telephone: (610) 791-2222
Toll Free: (800) 444-HCSC
Fax: (610) 791-2919
Web site: http://www.hcsc.org

Not-for-Profit Company
Incorporated: 1970
Employees: 1,200
Sales: $71.6 million (2002)
NAIC: 561110 Office Administrative Services ; 621991
Blood and Organ Banks; 812310 Linen Supply;
812320 Drycleaning and Laundry Services (Except
Coin-Operated)

Working through a group of separately incorporated affiliates, Allentown, Pennsylvania-based Hospital Central Services, Inc. offers an array of programs and services to healthcare providers in Pennsylvania and New Jersey. Included are HCSC-Laundry, the nation's largest not-for-profit linen rental service; HCSC-Purchasing, which contracts bulk purchasing of supplies for its members' facilities; HCSC-Financial Services, which offers a fee collection service for its members; and the HCSC-Blood Center, which operates the Miller Memorial Blood Center and the Keystone Community Blood Bank. The organization is also a member affiliate of the Mid-Atlantic Group Network of Shared Services (MAGNET), founded in 1979, which provides HCSC and other member affiliates with contract portfolios of cost-reducing services, equipment, and other commodities. Operating through four corporate boards and a variety of divisional committees, HCSC is structured as a cooperative, not-for-profit organization. While maintaining that status, the cooperative has awarded grants to a variety of community and educational organizations.

1964–71: A Cooperative Is Formed

The evolution of Hospital Central Services, Inc. began in 1964, when a group of Lehigh Valley, Pennsylvania, business

leaders created the Greater Lehigh Valley Hospital and Health Planning Council. Its aim was to plan for providing adequate hospital and other medical support facilities in the Lehigh Valley area, for improving patient care and education at these facilities, and for coordinating the development of them in order to avoid unnecessary and costly duplication of services and programs.

Three years later, in 1967, the Council incorporated Hospital Central Services Corporation (HCSC). Its first aim was to provide linen rental and laundry services to the non-profit, tax-exempt hospitals in the Lehigh Valley area, but it quickly added other goals. In 1969, it incorporated HCSC-Group Purchasing and HCSC-Credit and Collections. The former affiliate's purpose was to provide centralized purchasing services for area healthcare facilities; the latter's purpose was to provide collection services for those same agencies. Another affiliate, HCSC-Blood Center, was also incorporated in 1969. In 1970, to oversee the operations of these affiliates, the Council incorporated Hospital Central Services, Inc.

The first HCSC-Laundry went into operation in June 1970, in Allentown, Pennsylvania. It immediately began servicing the linen supply and laundry needs of ten founding hospitals, which signed 15-year contracts with HCSC, allowing the company to finance the start-up. In the next year, the HCSC-Blood Center began operating at the Samuel B. Miller Memorial Blood Center, providing the Lehigh Valley area with its first centralized site for the collection, processing, and storage of whole blood, plasma, and other blood components. The idea behind the community blood bank had evolved from many gifts given in memory of the late Samuel W. Miller, the popular and esteemed editor and publisher of *The Morning Call*, Allentown's chief newspaper. The center was built on the grounds of the Muhlenberg Hospital Center in Bethlehem, Pennsylvania. Initially, the Miller Memorial Blood Center began providing the blood needs and services for six area hospitals.

Soon after HCSC-Group Purchasing was incorporated, it started offering primary vendor contracts to all of the hospitals represented by the Greater Lehigh Valley Hospital and Health Planning Council. Contracts, which covered medical, surgical, pharmaceutical, nutritional, laboratory, and office products, provided a cost-saving and efficient means of supplying each hospital's needs. Meanwhile, in 1970, HCSC-Credit & Collections started its bad-debt recovery service for these same hospitals. Its primary aim was to protect their image and at the same time provide an efficient means of recovering funds lost through patients' non-payment for services rendered them.

1972–91: Expansion and New Services

Over the next decade, the number of hospitals and other health care units in some way dependent on HCSC continued to grow. By 1981, more than 70 hospitals were using one or more of its services. While only a few hospital subscribed to the whole range of HCSC services, each of the company's divisions had increased the number of its clients. For example, by 1981 the HCSC-Laundry was servicing 19 hospitals in Pennsylvania and New Jersey, nine more than it had initially serviced. Through the 1980s and into the 1990s, the growth in its client base and the geographical range that it covered figured importantly in HCSC's expansion in both some of its services and its facilities.

In the 1980s, HCSC enhanced its range of services by creating a couple of new corporations. The first of these, HCSC-Enterprises, Inc., created as a for-profit, taxable entity, was formed in 1982 to permit HCSC Credit Services to provide healthcare collection services in the for-profit marketplace, extending such services to individual physicians, emergency medical services (EMS), and other healthcare providers. Two years later, in 1984, HCSC introduced Healthcare Financial Systems as a billing service for hospitals and physicians, and, somewhat later, for non-profit EMS providers, including municipally owned or operated ambulance and fire departments.

Meanwhile, HCSC's established divisions were rapidly expanding. Laundries, in particular, grew quickly. Although it was not until 1986 that HCSC-Laundry opened its second laundry plant, located in Greensburg, Pennsylvania, some 50 miles southeast of Pittsburgh, others soon appeared, including two in 1989. One of these was located in Kingston, Pennsylvania, just north of Wilkes-Barre, while the other one, formerly the Mid-Atlantic Laundry Plant, opened up in Camden, New Jersey.

Meanwhile, the Samuel W. Miller Memorial Blood Center (MMBC) was both attracting an increasing number of donors and expanding its services. In 1981, when it celebrated its tenth anniversary, MMBC collected 22,431 units of blood. The next year, using a new blood bag preservative, it was able to extend the shelf life of blood from 21 to 35 days. By 1986, the year

after it first started donor scanning for the HIV antibody, MMBC surpassed the 100,000 blood-unit donation mark, and in that year alone recorded over 35,000 donations. With the increase in volume, in 1987, HCSC-Blood Center opened its first branch, located on Cedar Crest Boulevard in Allentown, and its first satellite location at Slate Medical Center in Bangor, Pennsylvania. The following year, HCSC-Blood Center established a second satellite, at Quakertown Community Hospital; it also began using a new blood bag preservative with a 42-day storage capability and broke ground at the site of a new MMBC at the Lehigh Valley Corporate Center. That new 29,000 square-foot facility opened in 1990.

The number of hospitals and healthcare organizations in a partnership relationship with HCSC had risen to over 100 by 1991. That year, the HCSC-Group Purchasing members contracted for over $135 million in purchases through that agency, while HCSC-Financial Services realized over $21 million in placements and $5 million in collections and Miller Memorial Blood Center processed over 74,000 blood components used by the ten hospitals affiliated with the program.

1992–99: Restructuring and Continued Expansion

In 1992, HCSC underwent a restructuring when the boards of HCSC-Group Purchasing and HCSC-Laundry opted to elect a subchapter T tax status. Its aim was to reward its clients. In accordance with subchapter T of the Internal Revenue Code, HCSC-Laundry, HCSC-Group Purchasing, and HCSC-Credit & Collections merged as Hospital Central Services Cooperative, Inc., a Pennsylvania, non-profit corporation. HCSC, Inc. was then able to offer participating hospitals patronage dividends, paid in cash and scrip, while realizing tax savings for itself.

Several other new developments marked the 1990s. In 1993, HCSC purchased a self-contained bloodmobile coach to collect donated blood at sites unable to accommodate bloodmobiles because of restricted space or an excessive number of donors. Also, for the first time, MMBC was licensed for collecting blood in New Jersey when the Hackettstown Community Hospital became its ninth affiliate.

A new spurt in the growth of HCSC-Laundry's operations began in 1997, when it purchased its fifth laundry plant, a previously owned laundry cooperative in Pittsburgh. The size of the acquired facility allowed HCSC to phase out its Greensburg operation early the next year, when it transferred it linen service to the Pittsburgh plant. However, it was again operating five laundries when, later in that same year, 1998, it acquired one more laundry processing plant, this time in Scranton, Pennsylvania.

In 1999, the HCSC-Blood Center entered an agreement with two other Pennsylvania blood banks: the Central PA Blood Center in Hummelstown and the Keystone Community Blood Bank in Reading. Their purpose was to explore a possible affiliation and the potential for sharing services for achieving increased blood recruitment and more efficient use of the region's existing supply of blood.

2000 and Beyond: Poised for Continued Growth

The new decade started well for the cooperative. By the end of June 2000, HCSC-Group Purchasing's contracts had gone

Key Dates:

1964: Lehigh Valley, Pennsylvania, business associates incorporate the Greater Lehigh Hospital and Health Planning Council.

1967: Hospital Central Services Corporation (HCSC) is incorporated.

1969: HCSC-Group Purchasing, HCSC-Credit and Collections, and HCSC-Blood Center are incorporated.

1970: HCSC-Laundry goes into operation in Allentown, Pennsylvania, and Hospital Central Services, Inc. is incorporated to promote education and provide a centralized oversight for the various HCSC affiliates.

1971: HCSC-Blood Center (Miller Memorial Blood Center) opens.

1982: HCSC-Enterprises, Inc. is formed to permit HCSC Credit Services to offer healthcare collection services in the commercial (for-profit) marketplace.

1984: Health Care Financial Systems is created as a collection service for hospitals and physicians.

1992: HCSC-Group Purchasing and HCSC-Laundry become Hospital Central Services Cooperative, Inc.

2001: Keystone Community Blood Bank is merged with HCSC operations.

beyond the $2 billion mark in the purchase of various goods and services, and through the beginning of 2001, HCSC was still successfully maintaining operations at its five laundries located in Camden, New Jersey, and in Pennsylvania sites in Allentown, Kingston, Pittsburgh, and Scranton. Also, during 2001, HCSC's Group Purchasing Division introduced its contract catalog on CD-ROM, and its Pharmacy Program, in an affiliation with Shared Services Healthcare in Atlanta, first made its contract portfolio accessible on the Internet. The cooperative also added 43 new contracts to that portfolio during the year.

The Miller Memorial Blood Center, meanwhile, was providing whole or partial blood products to 21 hospitals and healthcare providers in eight countries, and was, by 2001, manufacturing over 80,000 blood components per year. Also, in addition to its main facility in the Lehigh Valley Corporate Center, the Blood Center had in operation three blood-donor satellite facilities, located in Allentown and Bangor, Pennsylvania, and Newton, New Jersey. In March 2001, MMBC achieved a much coveted ISO 9002 certification, becoming only the fourth not-for-profit community blood service to attain that distinction. Also, a month later, HCSC announced the imminent merger of the Keystone Community Blood Bank of Reading into its operations. Keystone, established in 1966, was providing blood and blood products to hospitals in Berks County, Pennsylvania, and at the time of the merger was garnering over 11,000 blood donations per year.

All in all, over HCSC's 2001 fiscal year, the cooperative provided services to more than 400 healthcare organizations throughout the Mid-Atlantic region, increasing the organization's revenues to $67.3 million, a 1 percent growth over the previous year. On the cooperative's drawing board were plans for many new developments, including additional laundry sites, more commitments to educating the public through additional awards to community organizations, and a growth in it contract portfolio affiliations. Some of these goals were realized in 2002, as another laundry facility was established in Baltimore and grants were awarded to a variety of community organizations. Demand for blood and blood products peaked at MMBC following the terrorist attacks of September 11, 2001, as the HCSC affiliate was tapped to provide blood products for victims of the tragedy. Extensive costs incurred for staffing and supplies during this chaotic time were offset by a grant. As it looked to the future, HCSC, led by President and CEO J. Michael Lee, remained committed to focusing on good customer relations, because, as the company's annual report for 2002 noted "The bottom line for our customers may be profitability, but they continue to find great value in HCSC flexibility, responsiveness and dependability."

Principal Divisions

HCSC-Laundry; HCSC-Group Purchasing; HCSC-Financial Services; Samuel W. Miller Memorial Blood Center.

Further Reading

Csencsits, Sonia, "Miller Memorial, Berks Blood Center Merge," *Allentown Morning Call*, May 2, 2001.

"Imation Corp. Signs Agreement with Magnet, Inc.," *PR Newswire*, July 16, 1998.

"Instrumentation Laboratory Secures Primary Supplier Agreement with MAGNET," *PR Newswire*, January 4, 1999.

"Mid Atlantic Group Network of Shared Services, Inc. Signs Agreement with Trek Diagnostic Systems, Inc.," *PR Newswire*, April 28, 2000.

Rohland, Pamela, "Nonprofit Supports Hospitals with Plethora of Services," *Eastern Pennsylvania Business Journal*, January 1, 1998, p. 18.

"Stealing Surgical Garb and Picking Up a Bridge, Cheap," *New York Times*, January 26, 1986, p. 57.

"Wave of Thefts of Surgical Suits," *New York Times*, September 7, 1986, p. 26.

—John W. Fiero

Hyundai Group

140-142, kye-dong, Chongno-gu
Seoul 110-793
South Korea
Telephone: (02) 746-1114
Fax: (02) 741-2341
Web site: http://www.hyundaicorp.com

Public Company
Incorporated: 1947 as Hyundai Engineering &
    Construction Company
Employees: 359
Sales: $75 billion (Hyundai Group 2000); $20.4 billion
    (Hyundai Corp. 2001)
Stock Exchanges: Korea
Ticker Symbol: 11760
NAIC: 423390 Other Construction Material Merchant
    Wholesalers; 423510 Metals Service Centers and
    Other Metal Merchant Wholesalers; 423620 Electrical
    and Electronic Appliance, Television, and Radio Set
    Merchant Wholesalers; 423810 Construction and
    Mining (Except Petroleum) Machinery and Equipment
    Merchant Wholesalers; 423820 Farm and Garden
    Machinery and Equipment Merchant Wholesalers;
    423830 Industrial Machinery and Equipment
    Merchant Wholesalers

The Hyundai Group spent most of its history operating as one of South Korea's largest chaebols, or conglomerates. The group displayed spectacular growth since its founding in 1947 and its rapid expansion—to a point where its interests included car manufacturing, construction, shipbuilding, electronics, and financial services—reflected the achievements attained during South Korea's economic miracle. The South Korean economy took a turn for the worse during the late 1990s, however, which prompted President Kim Dae Jung to launch a series of reforms aimed at dismantled large, often corrupt, chaebols. By 2001, much of the Hyundai Group had been dismantled. Roh Moo

Hyun, elected President in 2002, continues to reform the South Korean business sector.

Hyundai's growth was linked inextricably to South Korea's reconstruction programs following World War II and the Korean War as well as to the state-led capitalism that resulted in a polarization of the country's corporate structure and the domination of the economy by a number of conglomerates. World War II left the country devastated, and the small recovery Korea had been able to make following this conflict was reversed during the Korean War, which lasted from 1950 to 1953. The chaebols, which are similar to Japan's zaibatsu, worked with the government in rebuilding the economy and formed an integral part of Korea's economic strategy and its drive to build up its industrial base.

One man, Chung Ju Yung, stood at the center of Hyundai's progress from 1950 until he died in 2001. Chung, considered a founding father of the Korean chaebol structure, left school at an early age and developed what has been described as an autocratic and unconventional management style. He noted those areas of industry that the government had selected as crucial to economic development and structured the group accordingly.

Explosive Postwar Growth

The foundation of Hyundai was laid before the Korean War, in 1947, when Chung set up Hyundai Engineering & Construction Company. The company was involved in the early stages of the country's recovery following World War II. After the Korean conflict, development intensified, and Hyundai was quick to take on a key role, working on civil and industrial projects as well as housing programs. In 1958, it set up Keumkang Company to make construction materials; four years later, when the first of Korea's five-year development plans was launched, Hyundai was well placed to win a range of infrastructure contracts. This plan and its successors aimed to lay the foundations for an independent economy by targeting sectors of industry for expansion.

Against this background, Hyundai expanded its construction and engineering operations as the economy's momentum increased. In 1964, it completed the Danyang Cement plant,

Company Perspectives:

Hyundai Corp. is preparing to leap over the world's top-ranking companies through the utilization of business network experience and know-how to create a new business model for the 21st digital era.

which in 1990 produced well over one million tons of cement. In 1965, the company undertook its first overseas venture with a highway-construction project in Thailand. Hyundai expanded rapidly overseas, developing a market with particular success in the Middle East. Its projects in this region included the $931 million Jubail industrial harbor project in Saudi Arabia.

In 1967, the group took one of its most significant steps, setting up the Hyundai Motor Company and thus sowing the seed for what was to become the country's leading domestic car manufacturer. Initially the company assembled Ford Cortina cars and Ford trucks. Two years later, Hyundai took another step abroad with the establishment of Hyundai America, incorporated in Los Angeles, to work on housing complexes and other civil projects. In 1970, it further enhanced its position in the construction sector by setting up Hyundai Cement Company to deal with increased demand at home and overseas.

Toward the end of the 1960s, the government had begun to promote the heavy and chemical industries. Oil and steel were both targeted. The planners then turned their attention to the consumption of indigenous steel and focused on shipbuilding, which was then relatively backward (producing only coastal and fishing vessels), and on the automotive industry. The ambitious plans for these industries were to be of great significance both to Hyundai and the nation as a whole, and the 1970s proved to be a period of rapid development.

Expansion into Shipbuilding: Early 1970s

Hyundai's entry into shipbuilding would eventually take Korea's shipbuilding industry to second position in the world, behind Japan. In 1971, Chung decided to begin shipbuilding, and by the following year the company's shipyard had held its ground-breaking ceremony in Mipo Bay, Ulsan, on the southeastern tip of the Korean peninsula. In the following year the yard was incorporated as Hyundai Shipbuilding and Heavy Industries Company.

The Ulsan yard was still at the planning stage when Hyundai won its first contract, for two oil tankers, from Livanos, a Greek shipowner. The order paved the way to a loan from Barclays Bank of the United Kingdom. Chung had to borrow capital from foreign banks to build the yard, which was opened in 1974. In the following year, the Hyundai Mipo Dockyard Company was set up to do conversions and repairs.

This sector developed rapidly throughout the 1970s, but the group was hit by the first oil crisis and the consequent decline in demand for large tankers. Hyundai, however, quickly won four orders for large tankers from the Japanese, its main competitors, and concluded technical cooperation deals with Kawasaki Heavy Industries of Japan and Scott Lithgow of the United

Kingdom. Before the market collapsed, 12 large tankers were built at the yards.

This collapse forced Hyundai to turn to the building of medium-sized vessels. It also took steps to remain abreast of technological developments in the industry and to develop spin-offs. In 1975, Hyundai Shipbuilding and Heavy Industries created an industrial-plant and steel-fabrication division, and in the following year began to produce marine engines carrying famous names such as Sulzer and B&W.

A further collaboration was clinched in 1977 with Siemens, of West Germany, which led to the creation of the electrical-engineering division. In the following year the company changed its name to Hyundai Heavy Industries Company (HHI) to reflect its diverse operations. At the same time it incorporated its engine and electrical engineering divisions into Hyundai Engine and Machinery Company and Hyundai Electrical Engineering Company, respectively.

Focusing on Auto Production: Mid-1970s

One of the most significant moves in Hyundai's relatively short history was made in 1975, when the group began constructing an integrated car factory adjacent to its heavy-industry complex at Ulsan. It was to be the foundation of Korea's largest auto company, one that was to dominate Korea's home and export markets. By the late 1980s, UBS Phillips and Drew Global Research Group ranked Hyundai 13th in the world auto industry, with the production of 819,000 vehicles and 1.9 percent of the world retail market.

The aim of this ambitious project was to move away from car assembly only and to produce, with government backing, a Korean car, a four-seat sedan called the Hyundai Pony. To this end, it called on overseas expertise and finance, a policy used not only by Hyundai but by other Korean industrial groups as well. George Turnbull, a former managing director of British Leyland, who was then vice-president of Hyundai Motors, was in charge of the project. The car was styled by the well-known Italian designer Giorgetto Giugiaro, was powered by a Mitsubishi Motor engine, and used U.K. components. The project was financed largely by U.K. and Japanese sources.

The vehicle was launched in 1975. By the following year, Hyundai was producing 30,000 cars, and by 1979 the total had risen to 110,000. Although Hyundai could sell every vehicle it produced in the protected home market, it soon sought to attack export markets by reserving approximately one-fifth of its production for overseas sale. The company first tested the European market, and its potential for sophisticated markets, by setting up a network of dealers in the Benelux countries, where there were no dominant local manufacturers.

Other areas of the group saw intense activity throughout the 1970s. In 1975, Dongsu Industrial Company, a construction-material manufacturer, was created, followed in the same year by Seohan Development Company, a welding and electrode carbide maker. Since it was so heavily reliant upon exports and several essential imports, the group in 1976 set up Hyundai Corporation, its trading arm. The corporation integrated the group's sales and marketing strategies, imported natural resources through overseas investment and joint ventures, and

Key Dates:

1947: Chung Ju Yung forms Hyundai Engineering & Construction Company.
1958: The company sets up the Keumkang Company to make construction materials.
1965: Hyundai Engineering & Construction begins its first overseas venture—a highway project in Thailand.
1967: The Hyundai Motor Company is formed.
1973: The group's shipyard is incorporated as Hyundai Shipbuilding and Heavy Industries Company.
1975: The group begins construction on an integrated car factory and launches a new Korean vehicle.
1976: Hyundai Corp. is established as a trading arm.
1978: Hyundai Shipbuilding changes its name to Hyundai Heavy Industries Company (HHI).
1983: Hyundai Electronics is formed.
1998: Korea's economic crisis forces the group to begin restructuring efforts, which include selling off subsidiaries and focusing on five core business areas.
2001: The Hyundai Group conglomerate continues to be dismantled.

provided assistance to overseas operations. The corporation eventually led the numerous member companies of the group in sales. At the same time, it created Hyundai Merchant Marine Company, which concentrated on cargo services, chartering, brokerage, and related services. The trading arm proved to be an important source of revenue and quickly grew into one of the country's top exporters.

In the same year, on the construction side, Hyundai formed Koryeo Industrial Development Company and Hyundai Housing and Industrial Development Company, whose operations included construction design and property development. Hyundai Precision and Industry Company was created in 1977. Its activities included auto parts, container manufacture, and locomotive parts.

A year later the group turned its attention to the timber industry with the formation of Hyundai Wood Industries Company, which made wood products and furniture. In 1978, the group expanded its heavy and chemical industries to include iron and steel manufacturing when it absorbed Incheon Iron & Steel Company and Aluminum of Korea.

Tough Times for HHI: 1980s

The 1980s brought problems for HHI. Two of its key businesses, shipbuilding and overseas construction (the development of which had been actively encouraged by the government in the 1970s), encountered worldwide decline during the decade. Korean shipbuilders saw new export orders in 1985 slump to only $522 million, compared with $2.3 billion the year before, while profits plummeted. Overseas construction orders also fell away quickly after reaching a peak of more than $13 billion in 1981 and 1982.

In both cases, Korean industry had to discard its policy of growth at any price. There were job cuts and a move toward more sophisticated projects such as industrial plant construction and improved technology. In addition, the company had to contend with damaging labor strikes, which hit its shipyards and other parts of the group, notably the car factories. HHI instituted major productivity improvements at the beginning of the decade and stepped up its diversification with the creation of the Offshore & Steel Structure Division in 1980. Through this division it launched a major drive into the offshore market, into which it had broken in the late 1970s with orders for the Jubail project in Saudi Arabia. The division initially operated one yard, but, as demand increased, a second was added in 1983.

In 1982, HHI took over three dry docks from Hyundai Mipo Dockyard Company, which brought the total it operated to seven. Hyundai Mipo, which looked after the company's ship repair and conversion business, was reorganized and moved to a new repair yard two kilometers away from HHI. A year later HHI undertook further reorganization by turning its maritime-engineering division into the special and naval shipbuilding division, which now concentrates on building naval craft such as destroyers, frigates, and patrol boats.

The increased emphasis on new technology and innovation was reflected in the setting up of Hyundai Welding Research Institute in 1983—whose work has since been extended to take in factory automation—and the creation of a research-and-development center, the Hyundai Maritime Research Institute, a year later. Work continued on developing products such as the new generation of very large crude carriers, the world's first semi-submersible drilling rig, delivered in 1987, and a mixed container-passenger vessel for a Norwegian operator in 1988. The company also broke into the gas-carrier market in 1986.

The latter part of the decade was clouded by strikes that were to tarnish the Korean shipbuilding industry's image. In addition, the company had to contend with higher wage costs that blunted the competitive edge it had over its Japanese rivals. HHI also became embroiled in a legal wrangle with Sir Yue-Kong Pao's World-Wide Shipping Group in 1988. The dispute was over an order for very large crude carriers, which it had agreed to build in 1986 when the market was in a trough.

The strikes that affected the Ulsan yard in the latter part of the 1980s hit production and sales, and in 1988 HHI was to record its first-ever loss, that of W29 billion on sales that declined slightly to W945 billion; this came after breaking even the previous year. In 1990, the yard was hit by further strikes, although it managed to land a $600 million order for ten combination vessels from a Norwegian shipping group.

Challenges for Hyundai Motor in the 1980s

The 1980s were to prove equally eventful for Hyundai Motor Company. After the oil shock of 1979, the government took steps to protect the industry, which had by then made large investments in plants and equipment. It kept a tight grip on the development of this sector and in 1981 divided the market, restricting Hyundai to car and large commercial vehicle manufacture. These regulations were revised in 1986 following the recovery of the market, and Hyundai was able to resume manufacture of light commercial vehicles.

By the middle of the decade, Hyundai had taken Canada by storm. Its Pony subcompact vehicle became Canada's top-selling car less than two years after entering the market. Hyundai's sales in Canada, where it was also selling the Stellar, shot from none in December of 1983 to 57,500 units in the first nine months of 1985, topping those of Honda and Nissan combined. Total production in 1985 had risen to 450,000.

In 1985, the company announced plans to build a car assembly plant at Bromont, near Montreal, and at the same time decided to enter the U.S. market. The entry into the U.S. market, begun in 1986, proved an immediate success. Its low-priced Excel model was well received, and of the 302,000 cars exported in that year, 168,000 were sold in the United States, where sales were to increase to 263,000 the following year. Hyundai's initial success in the United States, though, faded before the end of the decade when sales began to flag. Problems in the company's key overseas market were attributed to the lack of new models, increasing competition in the weakened U.S. car market, and the severe strikes that hit the company in the latter part of the 1980s and in 1990.

Hyundai decided to move up market with the introduction of the Sonata, a four-door sedan, in late 1988; initial sales, though, proved disappointing. A year later, this car was being manufactured at the Bromont plant, following the opening of the factory in 1989. In the same year, Hyundai signed a deal with Chrysler Corp. to build 30,000 midsize, four-door cars for the U.S. company, starting in 1991. Chrysler was linked to Mitsubishi Corporation, which in turn was affiliated with Hyundai, in which it held a 15 percent stake.

Hyundai planned to increase production at the Canadian plant to 100,000 by the time the Chrysler deal came into effect. Export sales, which were also hit by the appreciation of the won and the depreciation of the yen, remained sluggish. Increased wage costs also affected the group but had the advantage of boosting domestic sales that, for the industry as a whole, increased 50 percent to 356,000 units in 1989.

Hyundai in the Early 1990s

The group became intent on reducing its dependence on the U.S. markets. By 1990, the domestic market was proving increasingly important to the essentially export-oriented group. Both the car and construction markets were enjoying strong demand at the end of the decade. This situation helped Hyundai Engineering & Construction, like the vehicle operations, to take up the slack created by declining markets abroad, particularly in the Middle East. The group had accumulated experience in a broad range of plant construction, including Korea's first nuclear power plant. Meanwhile exports in the shipbuilding sector were showing a marked improvement.

Following the creation in 1983 of Hyundai Electronics, Hyundai stepped up its presence in the electronics field and produced semiconductors, telecommunication equipment, and industrial electronic systems. The company, which focused on industrial markets, sought to increase its presence in consumer electronics, despite formidable competition from domestic companies such as Samsung and Goldstar.

The group as a whole had proved itself capable of taking diverse markets by storm and was determined to maintain and expand its markets by stepping up research-and-development spending. However, the country's drive towards democracy brought new uncertainties. In the changing economic and political environment, the group faced a labor force seeking higher wages, a less competitive currency, and increasing competition in the all-important overseas markets.

Faced with this changing political scene and a less favorable international rate of exchange, Hyundai shifted gears in the early 1990s. In automaking, its largest enterprise, it worked to regain lost ground in the United States, where demand for its low-priced Excel and somewhat higher-priced Sonata models slumped in the wake of widespread consumer complaints and a depressed entry-level market. Hyundai's new Elantra sedan, selling for $9,000, was to be its lead item in the U.S. market. The group's chairman at that time, Chung Ju Yung's younger brother, Chung Se-yung, was expecting a new day for the group, as Korea itself matured with new labor and political freedoms.

As Korea's second-largest conglomerate, with 1990 revenues estimated at $35 billion, Hyundai Group was clearly to play an important role in the new Korea. Indeed, the Hyundai founder and chairman, Chung Ju Yung, chose personally to play a new, political role in that development, founding a new political party early in 1992 with a view to promoting open-market policies. Chung's Unification National Party (UNP) promptly won 10 percent of National Assembly seats; Chung himself then retired from his Hyundai chairmanship to set his sights on the Korean presidency. The Hyundai conglomerate, already forced by the government to pay billions in back taxes, came under even more severe government pressures after Chung formed his party. Regulators charged illegal political contributions by one Hyundai company and accused others of tax evasion. In addition, Hyundai's ability to finance its operations was threatened by other government actions. In return, Hyundai, at this time headed by Chung Se Yung, threatened to withhold huge investments planned for the coming year. In 1993, having finished third in South Korea's presidential election, Chung Ju Yung reportedly said that he would resume chairmanship of the Hyundai Group and would reorganize the corporation into many specialized, independently run companies. In 1995, his second-eldest son, Chung Mong Koo, was named chairman of the group while Chung remained honorary chairman.

In auto and personal-computer sales, Hyundai companies moved aggressively. In mid-1992, Hyundai's new Motor America president, Dal Ok Chung, took over in the Fountain Valley, California, headquarters. Among other marketing devices, Hyundai offered generous rebates and free two-year service warranties that covered even windshield wiper blades. By early 1993, Hyundai was offering the first auto engine it had designed and made itself, as opposed to the Japanese-made Mitsubishi engines that were used in its earlier models. More than ever committed to the smaller vehicle, Hyundai was selling autos in more than 100 countries.

In personal computers, Hyundai in mid-1992 took a drastic step when it moved its entire electronics operation to the United States, the world's largest computer market. Hyundai Information Systems had already entered the direct personal-computer market, cutting prices and offering toll-free telephone support and sales. The new operation, based in San Jose, California, had entirely American leadership, headed by IBM veteran and former CompuAdd president Edward Thomas. The California advantage was mainly proximity to the market, which meant lessened inventory requirements. These developments showed the Hyundai Group to have the same innovative and energetic approach that had characterized its earlier ventures.

The Dismantling of Hyundai

The latter years of the 1990s brought with them economic turmoil for South Korea. In order to restore the nation's financial health, President Kim Dae Jung, who took office in 1998, launched a series of restructuring programs designed to reform the chaebols, many of which had become heavily debt-burdened. His reforms included changing the ownership, business, and financial structures of the region's large conglomerates. By this time, the Hyundai Group was responsible for approximately 20 percent of Korea's GDP. As such, its financial health was directly related to South Korea's overall economic condition.

As a result of government pressures, Hyundai and other South Korean chaebols, including the Daewoo Group, set plans in motion to sell off many of their businesses in order to pay down debt and shore up profits. Hyundai's concentration remained on autos, electronics, heavy industry, construction, and finance. Even as the group struggled under its debt load, it strengthened its holdings with the purchase of Kia Motors Co. Ltd. and LG Semiconductor.

Despite the government's involvement, Hyundai was slow to comply with restructuring demands. Its questionable accounting practices often made it the target of negative publicity. Rivalries between members of the founder's family also led to bad press, leaving many investors anxious about the future of the group and its member companies. Indeed, many Hyundai affiliates, including Hyundai Engineering & Construction and Hyundai Electronics, were nearing bankruptcy as debt continued to spiral out of control. By 2001, total group debt reached W35.87 trillion ($25.59 billion).

Hyundai Motor Co., on the other hand, was prospering as Korea's largest car maker. The auto concern officially separated from the Hyundai Group in September 2000, signaling the start of sweeping changes that led to the eventual dismantling of what was once South Korea's largest conglomerate. In August 2001, nine core Hyundai companies, including Hyundai Engi-

neering & Construction and Hynix Semiconductor Inc. (formerly known as Hyundai Electronics Industries), left the chaebol. The separation cut Hyundai Group's assets to just $20.8 billion and left it in control of 18 member companies. Hyundai continued to be pared down the following year.

South Korea had bounced back from its economic crisis of 1997 and 1998 to become a leading global force in the technology sector. By 2003, foreign investors owned over a third of the shares of companies listed on Seoul's stock exchange. During 2002, Roh Moo Hyun was elected president of South Korea. Feeling the pressure from foreign investors, he maintained that harsh reform would continue within South Korea's chaebols. A May 2003 *Business Week* article supported the efforts of the new president, who stated that "slowly and steadily, good governance has been asserting itself in Korea." Indeed, it appeared as though the powerful, family-run Korean chaebols were a thing of the past. While this marked an end to the Hyundai Group's history, it pointed to a fresh start for many companies bearing the Hyundai name.

Principal Competitors

LG Group; Samsung Group; SK Group.

Further Reading

Bangsberg, P.T., "Hyundai Group Plans Drastic Downsizing," *Journal of Commerce*, April 26, 1999, p. 13A.

Burton, John, "Hyundai Group's Positive Trend," *Financial Times*, March 11, 1994, p. 28.

Hashimoto, Ryusuke, "Chaebol Breakup Shows South Korea's Commitment, But Hits Economy Hard," *The Nikkei Weekly*, September 3, 2001.

"Hyundai Group Picks Chung's Son as New Chairman," *Japan Economic Newswire*, December 28, 1995.

"Hyundai Motor Officially Severs Ties with Hyundai Group," *Korea Economic Weekly*, September 11, 2000.

Ihlwan, Moon, "Crackdown on Korea Inc.," *Business Week*, May 19, 2003.

——, "Is Hyundai About to Topple Too?," *Business Week*, November 27, 2000.

James, H., *Korea: An Introduction*, London: Kegan Paul International, 1988.

Kyoung-Sook, Park, "Hyundai After Chung Ju-Yung: Founder's Legacy Is Mixed Fortunes," *Business Korea*, April 2001, p. 8.

Woronoff, Jon, *Asia's "Miracle" Economies*, Seoul: Si-Sa-yong-o-sa Inc., 1986.

—Bob Vincent
—updates: Jim Bowman and Christina Stansell

James Hardie Industries N.V.

Level 7, 65 York Street
Sydney 2000
Australia
Telephone: (+61) 2-9638-9200
Fax: (+61) 2-9638-0833
Web site: http://www.jameshardie.com

Public Company
Incorporated:
Employees: 2,920
Sales: $803.7 million (2003)
Stock Exchanges: Australian
Ticker Symbol: JHX
NAIC: 327310 Cement Manufacturing; 332913 Plumbing
    Fixture Fitting and Trim Manufacturing

Australia-based, Netherlands-registered James Hardie Industries N.V. is one of the world's leading manufacturers of fiber-based cement products and technologies for the construction industry. The company is especially strong in the United States, where it is market leader and where it generates more than 85 percent of its total revenues. The company operates six production plants in the United States and continues to expand its production capacity in the booming U.S. housing market of the early 2000s. The company also operates plants in Australia, New Zealand, the Philippines, and Chile. Formerly a diversified conglomerate, James Hardie has slimmed down at the turn of the century, and, ultimately, after shedding its gypsum board and windows subsidiaries, has focused itself as a specialist fibro-cement company. In 2000, the company transferred its registration to Amsterdam, in the Netherlands, in order to take advantage of more lenient tax treaties between that country and the United States (under the Australian-U.S. tax treaty, nearly 75 percent of all shareholder profits were taken up by taxes). The company, which retains its listing on the Australian Stock Exchange, has been interested in seeking a full listing on the New York Stock Exchange as well.

Fibro-Cement Pioneer at the Turn of the Century

In 1888, when he was 36 years old, James Hardie traveled from Scotland to Australia, where he set up a trading company in Melbourne. Hardie's background in his family's tannery in Scotland led him initially to concentrate on importing animal oils and products for the tanning of animal hides. Hardie soon began to branch out, however, acquiring the import agencies for a variety of other products.

Hardie was joined by Andrew Reid, with whom he had become acquainted while working as a shipping agent in Scotland. Reid immigrated to Australia in 1892 and by 1895, at the age of 28, had become a full partner in Hardie's business.

The following year marked the invention of a new material that was to play an important role in the company's development—and indeed become its specialty more than one hundred years later. A composite of asbestos and cement that enabled the production of thin cement sheets, this material proved itself useful for a variety of purposes. The first imports of fiber cement into Australia began in 1903, and James Hardie quickly became a leading importer of "fibrolite," as the French variant of the material was called. Fibrolite's flexibility and ability to withstand high pressure made it a popular material for the production of pipes.

James Hardie retired in 1911, selling his half of the company to Andrew Reid, who nonetheless retained the company's original name. Until the outbreak of World War I, James Hardie contented itself with its rising sales of imported fiber cement products. Imports became impossible during the war, however. Instead, the company imported the machinery to produce fiber cement itself. James Hardie's first fiber cement production started up in 1917.

Originally, James Hardie produced its own fibrolite. By 1920, however, the company began to develop its own fiber cement formulas and production processes. In 1923, the company debuted its Sutton process, named after the company employee that developed it, and by 1926 had perfected the process. The company was now able to produce pipes measuring up to 3.6 meters in length. The process also provided a low-cost alternative to the traditional pipe-production process.

Following the successful development of the Sutton process, James Hardie split off its import agency operations into a separate company in order to concentrate on building its fiber cement business. By the end of the 1930s, the company had succeeded in establishing itself as a technology leader. The company had also expanded throughout much of Australia, setting up production plants in Sydney, Victoria, Western Australia, Newstead, and Riverdale.

North American Entry in the 1980s

James Hardie continued to invest in technology development, adding new, more modern equipment in 1937. The company also became involved in asbestos mining, forming Asbestos Mines Pty Ltd. in conjunction with CSR company Wunderlich in 1944. Aiding the company's further expansion was a public listing on the Australian Stock Exchange, made in 1951. James Hardie had in the meantime been developing a new production process, the autoclave, or steam-curing, process, which was launched in 1959.

James Hardie had already begun to diversify, adapting its expertise in working with asbestos to a variety of areas, including automobile products and railroad brake components. In 1962, the company set up a joint-venture with Turner & Newell, the leading manufacturer of asbestos products in the United Kingdom. James Hardie had also expanded into other international markets, especially in the Pacific Southeast, including shares in fiber cement production plants in Malaysia and elsewhere.

In the late 1970s, James Hardie, under the leadership of Andrew Reid's grandson John Reid, began a diversification drive. Through the 1980s, the company repositioned itself as a full-scale building products group, particularly as the long-time health concerns over asbestos exposure had at last resulted in bans on its use around the world. Yet the company expanded into other areas as well, particularly with the A$52 million purchase of the Australian publishing and paper operations of Reed International.

Following the acquisition, the company restructured into three primary business units: Building Products, Paper Merchanting and Converting, and Technology and Services. Over the next decade, the company worked to replace the asbestos component of its products, especially its flagship fiber cement products. By the middle of the 1980s, the company had succeeded in developing a new, cellulose-based fiber cement. At the same time, the company succeeded in introducing new insulation materials based on magnesia, allowing it to exit the asbestos market entirely.

Backed by its new product, the company stepped up its export efforts, particularly with an eye to the U.S. market. The company set up a U.S. subsidiary in 1988 and began marketing its fiber cement siding and other products to the building industry in the United States. Originally the company supplied its U.S. sales with product imported from Australia; in 1989, however, James Hardie set up its first fiber cement production facility in the United States.

Yet the company found it hard going in its attempt to persuade builders to switch to its product from the traditional vinyl and treated hardwood materials. The U.S. subsidiary quickly began losing money. In 1991, a review of the company's operations by management consultants encouraged the company to shut down the U.S. plant and exit the North American market. Instead, James Hardie decided to stick it out. That decision was to play an important part in redefining the company as it approached its centenary celebration.

Fiber Cement Specialist in the 21st Century

The revitalization of the U.S. building market, after several years of economic recession, coupled with increasing industry interest in the strength and versatility of fiber cement, enabled James Hardie's U.S. subsidiary to turn its first profit by 1994. Fiber cement quickly became the company's fastest-growing segment, and the U.S. market was easily its fastest-growing and most profitable market. By 1998, the United States accounted for more than 45 percent of the company's sales and 61 percent of its profits. Just two years later, the United States represented 60 percent of its annual revenues and 90 percent of its profits.

John Reid was forced to step down from the company's lead in 1995, in part because of a costly loan guarantee made through James Hardie in the late 1980s. Reid's place was filled by Keith Barton, who promptly launched the company on a streamlining drive that refocused the company on its building products segment and placed an emphasis on growth in the United States.

As part of that effort, the company made a push to enter U.S. gypsum wallboard market—representing 50 percent of the worldwide market—building and buying plants in Nevada, Georgia, Louisiana, and Texas. The company's gypsum operation also included its own gypsum mine. In 1997, James Hardie expanded again, paying A$121 million to Australian Boral Ltd. for its Briar Gypsum plasterboard operation in Arkansas. The purchase gave James Hardie a production capacity of nearly 2,000 million square feet, making it the fourth-largest producer in the United States.

In 1999, James Hardie, which faced compensation fines for its former asbestos operations, split the company into two components, creating a new company, James Hardie Industries N.V. to take over its gypsum and fiber cement business. At the same time, the company shifted its corporate legislation to the Netherlands. Initially, James Hardie had considered moving its corporate headquarters to California and listing on the New York Stock Exchange, but the unfavorable climate for "old-fashioned" sectors, such as the building market, led it to Amsterdam instead.

Key Dates:

1888: James Hardie emigrates from Scotland and establishes a trading company for imports of animal oils and tanning agents.

1882: Hardie is joined by fellow Scot Andrew Reid, who becomes a partner in the company three years later.

1903: The company begins importing fiber cement products.

1911: James Hardie retires and Andrew Reid takes over the business.

1917: Production of fiber cement begins after imports are blocked during World War I.

1951: James Hardie goes public on the Australian Stock Exchange.

1959: The company-developed autoclave production process debuts.

1978: As part of a diversification drive, the company acquires the Australian publishing and paper operations of Reed International.

1988: A U.S. subsidiary is set up in order to introduce fiber cement to American building market.

1997: After exiting most of its non-building products operations, the company acquires Briar Gypsum as part of expansion into the U.S. wallboard and gypsum mining market.

1999: The company shifts corporate registration to Amsterdam in order to reduce its taxes.

2001: James Hardie begins to sell-off of its gypsum business and refocuses as a fiber cement specialist.

2003: The company posts net profits of $170 million.

The new legislation enabled the company and its shareholders to escape the double tax that resulted from the then-current Australian and U.S. tax treaty, which in effect captured nearly 75 percent of share benefits as tax. The move to Amsterdam also promised to save the company some A$30 million per year in taxes. In the meantime, the company maintained its core Australian shareholders group and its listing on the Australian Stock Exchange.

James Hardie continued to expand its fiber cement operation in the new decade. In 2000, the company boosted its number of U.S. fiber cement plants to six with the opening of a new facility in Texas. The company also began enlarging its existing plant in order to meet soaring demand. By then, the company's fiber cement products had become a new industry standard. At the same time, with mortgage rates dropping to their lowest levels in decade, the United States was experiencing a huge construction boom.

Fiber Cement was also imposing itself elsewhere in the world, and at the end of 2000 James Hardie targeted entry into the promising South American market, buying a factory in Chile for A$12.8 million. By then, the company had also expanded its production capacity in Asia, notably through a plant in the Philippines.

As fiber cement sales continued rising, wallboard sales were sinking as prices dropped in the market. The division began losing money, and in 2001 new CEO Peter MacDonald, former head of the James Hardie's U.S. division, moved to exit the gypsum business. In July of that year, the company sold off its Nevada gypsum mine to developer WL Holmes for A$98 million. By 2002, the company had succeeded in finding a buyer for the rest of its gypsum operations, which was acquired by BPB Plc for $345 million. At the same time, the company moved to exit another remaining building products unit, that of manufacturing windows, which was spun off in a management buyout led by Crescent Partners at the end of 2001.

By May 2003, the end of its fiscal year, James Hardie's streamlining effort appeared to be paying off as the company posted profits of $170 million on sales of more than $800 million. The company was also the out and out leader of the fiber cement market in the United States, which by then had risen to more than 85 percent of the group's annual sales. At that time, James Hardie did not rule out an eventual transfer of its headquarters and stock listing to the United States. For the near future, however, the company prepared to continue its international expansion, now targeting the European market. One hundred years after its "discovery" of fiber cement, James Hardie seemed to have come full circle as a focused fiber cement products specialist.

Principal Subsidiaries

James Hardie Building Products Inc (United States); James Hardie Building Products Ltd.; James Hardie Export; James Hardie Industries USA; James Hardie Irrigation Inc. (United States); James Hardie New Zealand Ltd.

Principal Competitors

Georgia-Pacific Corporation; CertainTeed Corporation; Maxi-Tile Inc.; Cemplank Inc.

Further Reading

"Australia's James Hardie to Move Head Office to Netherlands," *AsiaPulse News*, October 12, 2001.

"Australia's James Hardie to Sell Windows Business," *AsiaPulse News*, November 7, 2001.

Baynes, Jim, "Hardie Sells off US Gypsum Mine," *Courier-Mail*, July 3, 2001, p. 25.

Carroll, B. *"A Very Good Business": One Hundred Years of James Hardie Industries Limited, 1888–1988*, Sydney: James Hardie Industries.

"Hardie Soars in US," *Daily Telegraph*, October 23, 20002, p. 50.

History of James Hardie & Co Pty Ltd. 1888–1966, Sydney: James Hardie & Co Pty Ltd, 84 pp.

"James Hardie Retires $60 million in Debt," *Home Channel News*, January 6, 2003, p. 1.

Roberts, Jeremy, "Hardie Rides Housing Boom to $264m," *Australian*, May 16, 2003, p. 22.

—M.L. Cohen

"K" LINE

Kawasaki Kisen Kaisha, Ltd.

Hibiya Central Building
2-9 Nishi-Shinbashi
1-chome, Minato-ku
Tokyo 105-8421
Japan
Telephone: (3) 3595-5000
Fax: (3) 595-5001
Web site: http://www.kline.co.jp

Public Company
Incorporated: 1919
Employees: 6,058
Sales: ¥632.7 billion ($4.3 billion) (2002)
Stock Exchanges: Tokyo Osaka Nagoya Fukuoka
    Frankfurt Brussels
Ticker Symbol: 9107
NAIC: 483111 Deep Sea Freight Transportation

Kawasaki Kisen Kaisha, Ltd. ("K" Line) is one of the largest shipping companies in Japan, operating a fleet of approximately 320 vessels totaling 16.3 million deadweight tons. The company transports coal, grain, iron ore, lumber, automobiles, crude oil, and liquefied natural gas (LNG) across the globe. Along with marine transportation, "K" Line is involved in insurance, warehousing, and land and air transport services.

Beginnings: 1919 to the Early 1930s

"K" Line was established on April 10, 1919, in Kobe, a major shipping center in Japan. After World War I, the world maritime industries were hit by a severe depression, which was felt strongly by the Japanese shipping and shipbuilding industries. This situation was in contrast to their enormous expansion during World War I, when they had taken advantage of their favorable geographical position far away from the main battlefield in Europe, although Japan was a member of the Allied Forces.

Kawasaki Zosenjo (Kawasaki Shipbuilding Co., established in 1886), the second largest and oldest shipbuilder in Japan after

Mitsubishi Zosen, was left after World War I with a large fleet of unsold ships. This fleet continued to increase for some time after the war because Kawasaki Zosenjo was forced to go on building ships due to the continued supply of steel plates from America under the Ship-Steel Exchange Agreement (Sen-Tetsu Kokan Keiyaku). The agreement had been concluded in 1918 between the U.S. government and individual Japanese shipbuilders, as well as several shipowners.

In order to deal with these unwanted stock boats, Kawasaki Zosenjo invested 11 ships of a total 100 thousand deadweight tons in setting up Kawasaki Kisen ("K" Line) in Kobe in 1919. The remainder of the unsold stock boats—16 ships totaling 139 thousand deadweight tons—was kept under the management of the Sempaku-bu, created in 1918 as a ship operation division within Kawasaki Zosenjo. The actual operation of these ships was, however, entrusted to "K" Line on a commission basis. Thus "K" Line entered the shipping business with a total of 27 ships of 239 thousand deadweight tons. The ships were initially chartered out to NYK (Nippon Yusen Kaisha), the biggest liner company in Japan, Suzuki Shoten, and other shipping companies. Among these, the most closely connected customer was Suzuki Shoten, a trading corporation that had achieved rapid growth during the war and was almost as large as Mitsui Bussan, the largest trading corporation at the time. In the latter half of 1920, however, "K" Line started to carry cargoes on its own account, due to the depressed chartering market.

In the meantime, an independent shipping company named Kokusai Kisen was established in Kobe in 1919, with an investment-in-kind of ships amounting to some 500 thousand deadweight tons, mainly from the shipbuilders and their subsidiary shipping companies. Although the process of establishment was complicated, the aim was to form, with some financial assistance from the government, a shipping company to operate unsold stock boats on a larger scale. Here again the majority of the investment, ships of 275 thousand deadweight tons, came from the Kawasaki group—Kawasaki Zosenjo and "K" Line. This meant that Kokusai Kisen became part of the Kawasaki group, although Suzuki Shoten and others also contributed some tonnage. Kokusai Kisen's ships sailed under A1 flags, which indicated that they were superior vessels qualified as A1

Company Perspectives:

Amid intensifying international competition, truly customer-oriented service is growing in importance. To fulfill its mission as an international integrated distribution enterprise, "K" Line is greatly expanding its domestic and overseas networks, thus further increasing the overall strength of the "K" Line group.

class by Lloyd's Register, and were deployed mainly on cross trades in order to reduce competition among Japanese shipping firms on the routes to and from Japan. Kokusai Kisen's business, however, was not particularly successful.

In August 1920, several months after the formation of Kokusai Kisen, Kojiro Matsukata was nominated as president of Kokusai Kisen and as a result assumed three presidential positions, including those of Kawasaki Zosenjo and "K" Line, which he already possessed. He planned to incorporate the tonnage owned by the three companies into a single operation to achieve efficiency, and in 1921 organized a joint service named K Line, with its head office in Kobe.

K Line must be distinguished from "K" Line. It took the initial letter K, common to the names of the three participants. Nominating Suzuki Shoten as its sole agent, K Line started tramp shipping—taking cargo as the opportunity arose—largely on the cross trades in the Atlantic region. It entered the liner trade as the tramp market became depressed and gradually expanded the business to include Japan Australia Line (JAL), a joint liner service with Yamashita Kisen between Japan and Australia. In 1923, a pooling agreement on revenue, cargo, and chartering was concluded among the participants to rationalize operations to meet the depressed market. Thus K Line came to operate 103 ships of 7.91 million deadweight tons in 1926, its peak year. With the establishment of K Line, "K" Line transferred most of the trade in the distant sea region to K Line and mainly concentrated on trade in the near sea region.

The Great Kanto Earthquake of 1923 resulted in an enormous demand for tonnage to carry relief and reconstruction goods. Taking advantage of this opportunity, "K" Line entered into near-sea liner services and opened new services successively: Japan-Korea and Japan-Taiwan in 1924, Japan-Vladivostok in 1925, and Japan-Shanghai and Japan-Sakhalin in 1926. These services developed further after around 1931 when Japan invaded China.

In 1927, the Japanese economy was hit by the so-called *Kinyu Kyoko*—financial crisis—and entered a severe depression, which was to be aggravated by the impending worldwide Depression that started in 1929. Under the direct impact of the crisis, Suzuki Shoten went bankrupt in 1927 and was no longer able to act as sole agent for K Line. Kawasaki Zosenjo was also a victim of the crisis and went into liquidation in the same year. As a result, Kojiro Matsukata was forced to resign as president and thus relinquished his position as president of "K" Line. Kokusai Kisen could not remain untouched by the crisis and soon experienced difficulties of its own.

These events had completely changed the situation for "K" Line. With the liquidation of Kawasaki Zosenjo and the resignation of President Matsukata, Kokusai Kisen broke away from the Kawasaki group and entered the control of the banks which had lent it money. The movement led to the withdrawal of Kokusai Kisen from K Line. This meant that K Line virtually disappeared, and "K" Line had to carry on its shipping business in distant seas independently, operating in 1928 a fleet of 41 ships totaling 265 thousand tons, probably including the tonnage of Kawasaki Zosenjo, which "K" Line had undertaken to operate. At this time, "K" Line was a fully owned subsidiary of Kawasaki Zosenjo and does not seem to have achieved complete independence until 1934, when "K" Line bought 11 ships from Kawasaki Zosenjo.

"K" Line's Independence Begins in 1934

During the period from "K" Line's fresh start to the end of World War II, world shipping as well as Japanese shipping experienced frequent changes: a severe depression until around 1935, then a brief period of prosperity due to heightened international political tension which led to increased shipping of war supplies, and finally chaos with the outbreak of World War II. "K" Line was, as a matter of course, exposed to these changes.

For some time after its fresh start, "K" Line concentrated, in the liner sector, on the Japan-North American Pacific Coast route in addition to the JAL, giving up the other businesses shared with Kokusai Kisen due to the shortage of tonnage. The main cargo on this trade was silk. In 1932, the company opened the Japan-New York service, following the change in silk transport from the Pacific Coast route to the direct service to New York.

From the middle of the 1930s, new services were opened, assisted by favorable trade conditions and various government schemes to promote new shipbuilding, such as the Yushusempaku Kenzo Josei Shisetsu (the Superior Ship Building Promotion Scheme) in 1937, and the Interest Subsidy to Shipbuilding Finance in 1940. This marked the "K" Line's entry to genuine liner trade on the distant sea routes. Prior to this change, "K" Line provided a semi-liner service (*han-teiki*), whereby it carried tramp cargoes at least on return voyages. Thus "K" Line opened the Japan-African East Coast service in 1934, reopened the Japan-Bombay service in 1935—it had been closed owing to the overall shortage of ships in 1928—the Japan-Middle and South American West Coast service in 1936, and the Round the World westbound service in 1937. "K" Line also strengthened services on the existing routes such as the New York route, the North American Pacific Coast route, and the JAL. However, it was forced to terminate these new and strengthened services with the approaching Pacific War in 1941.

"K" Line was active in the liner business, but its main business line had originally been tramp shipping, following the K Line tradition, and continued to be so until 1941. Moreover, even when liner services began, the ships took tramp cargoes as return cargoes. Tramp activities were carried out with changes to routes and cargoes according to circumstances. This procedure differed from the K Line period when the main field was in cross trades. In 1935, Malaysian iron ore was added to the main cargoes. Most important for "K" Line in the nonliner sector was the entry into tanker trade in 1933, with two chartered

Key Dates:

1919: "K" Line and Kokusai Kisen are established.
1921: The tonnage owned by Kokusai Kisen, Kawasaki Zosenjo, and "K" Line are organized into a joint service named K Line.
1928: The K Line collapses due to an economic depression; the "K" Line is left to carry on its distant seas shipping independently.
1934: "K" Line achieves complete independence after purchasing 11 ships from Kawasaki Zosenjo.
1945: The company's war losses amount to 60 ships of 271 thousand deadweight tons.
1952: Free activity in ocean-going shipping resumes.
1964: The Japanese government launches a major reorganization of the shipping industry.
1970: The Pure Car Carrier (PCC) is built for the first time in Japan.
1990: The firm enters the cruise market through subsidiary Seven Seas Cruise Line.
1998: The New K-21 strategy is adopted to prepare for business in the new century.

British tankers. This was a very early attempt among the common carriers in Japan to venture into tanker trade and was motivated by the increased oil consumption and the change in fuel transportation policy of the Japanese Navy in 1929, which up to that time had used its own tankers but thereafter relied on commercial tankers. "K" Line acquired a newly built tanker in 1935. Thereafter, "K" Line's tanker fleet grew to include 14 tankers in operation, totaling 193 thousand deadweight tons in 1937, the peak year in terms of fleet size.

To achieve the increase in the tonnage required due to expansion, "K" Line started to charter foreign ships in addition to domestic ships. Chartered tonnage continued to increase year after year up to 1938, when it amounted to 444 thousand deadweight tons and accounted for 65 percent of the total operating tonnage. In that year, chartered foreign tonnage accounted for 60 percent of total chartered tonnage.

Emphasis on tramp shipping, gradual expansion in liner trade, which accelerated after 1932, and reliance on chartered tonnage, which led to comparatively good business performance even in the depressed market, were the characteristics common to the so-called *Shagaisen* to which "K" Line belonged. The *Shagaisen*, which were originally tramp ship operators, together with the *Shasen*, the two large long-established liner companies, formed the Japanese shipping industry between the wars.

Surviving the War

In December 1941, the Pacific War began. As early as May 1942, all merchant ships above 100 gross tonnage and seamen were requisitioned by the state and were put under the unified control of a body called the *Sempaku Uneikai*. The war ended in August 1945, with heavy damage to the merchant fleet. "K" Line also suffered severely. At the start of the war, it owned 36 ships

with a total of 260 thousand deadweight tons, but only 12 ships totaling 31 thousand deadweight tons survived, notwithstanding additions during the war. Indeed, "K" Line's war loss amounted to 60 ships of 271 thousand deadweight tons, for which no compensation was made under the policy of the Allied Powers.

Commercial ocean-going shipping was not permitted by the Allied Powers until 1950, and free activity was permitted only after 1952, when the treaty signed at the San Francisco Peace Conference came into effect. From then onward, the Japanese shipping industry grew rapidly along with the Japanese economy as a whole, partly as a result of the 1947 state shipbuilding policy, the *Keikaku Zosen* (Programmed Shipbuilding Scheme). "K" Line resumed oceangoing shipping business based on expertise accumulated in the interwar period and began technological improvement of its ships. The first oceangoing ship was contracted in 1950 to transport rice from Thailand. In the following year, the first liner service was launched on the Japan-Bangkok route. "K" Line continued to open new liner services, following its pre-war policy of placing more emphasis upon liner trade. By 1957, all of "K" Line's major liner services had been opened. By this time, "K" Line succeeded in setting up a liner service network that extended over North and South America, Africa, Australia, and Asia, leaving the Japan-Europe and the Japan-India, Pakistan routes, among major ones, untouched. The Japan-India, Pakistan route was to be opened in 1964 when "K" Line merged the liner department of Iino Kaiun together with its sailing rights on this service. In the period between 1957 and 1964, existing services were developed while several new but minor services were added.

In the non-liner sector development also took place, extending the service area and carrying a greater variety of cargoes. Most important among these was the re-entry into the tanker trade in 1953 with a chartered foreign tanker, followed in 1957 by a tanker built for "K" Line. Another important development was the introduction of ore carrier trade in 1960. The tanker and ore-carrier trades were to expand year after year as the size of the respective ships increased.

In the period between 1957 and 1964, the Japanese shipping industry underwent remarkable expansion in terms of fleet size, but its performance deteriorated steadily. This decline, while partly attributable to the worldwide shipping depression, was largely due to the negative effect of the Programmed Shipbuilding Scheme, which caused excessive competition among Japanese firms, particularly in the liner sector. Finally, in 1964, a major reorganization took place—involving about 90 percent of Japan's deep sea fleet and with strong guidance from the government—in order to reduce excessive competition within the industry. This resulted in the formation of six groups. "K" Line formed one of these groups as a core company with 15 subsidiaries. This necessitated "K" Line's merger with the liner department of Iino Line.

Branching Out into Specialized Ships: 1960s–70s

A few years after the reorganization, "K" Line, along with the Japanese deep sea shipping industry as a whole, made a rapid recovery from the depression and thereafter enjoyed nearly ten years of prosperity for the first time in its history. During this period, "K" Line expanded its tonnage from 735 thousand gross tonnage in September 1964 to 2.5 million gross tonnage in March 1973, while greatly diversifying its business into the operation of specialized ships to meet the enormous increase in Japan's foreign trade. As a result, "K" Line's fleet composition by ship type underwent a fundamental change between 1964 and 1973, with cargo ships declining from 44.4 percent to 16 percent of the fleet, specialized ships increasing from 12.7 percent to 34.6 percent, and tankers from 42.5 percent to 49.6 percent.

The specialized ships introduced in this period included coal carriers, reefers, timber carriers, and LPG tankers. Most important among them was the introduction of a car-bulker in 1968 to carry Toyota cars to the United States. In 1970, a PCC (Pure Car Carrier—a ship which carried only cars) was built, the first ship of this type in Japan. Since then, particularly after the oil crisis in 1973, the car carrier trade experienced remarkable growth, and "K" Line ranked among the four biggest car carriers in the world.

In the liner sector, "K" Line ventured into container services, starting with the Japan-North American California route in 1967 and forming a consortium on a space charter basis with three other Japanese firms. Thereafter, "K" Line extended its container services and by 1979 had established a container network which included the main routes. In 1975 "K" Line opened a container service on the Far East-Europe route by organizing a container consortium, the ACE group, with several Scandinavian shipowners. Prior to this, "K" Line had been admitted to the Far Eastern Conference in 1968 through its participation in Kawasaki Maersk Line (KML), a joint service with the Danish shipowners Maersk Line. In 1973, when "K" Line was contemplating opening a container service on this route, the company succeeded in gaining membership independently and therefore dissolved KML. On the Japan-Australia route, "K" Line organized a container consortium, the Eastern Seaboard Service (ESS), with the Australian National Line (ANL) and started a container service in 1969 with roll-on/roll-off (RORO) container ships. As a result the Japan Australian Line (JAL), a long-established joint service with Yamashita Kisen, was dissolved. Another development in the liner sector was carriage of industrial equipment using ships with derricks of increasing capacity. The trade increased sharply after the oil crisis but declined in importance toward the mid-1980s.

Overcoming Hardships: 1980s and Beyond

The Oil Crisis of 1973 brought dramatic changes. The world shipping industry entered a depression which affected Japanese shipping particularly severely due to the sharp rise in the value of the yen. The depression, with only a brief intermission, lasted until 1988. Under these circumstances, "K" Line switched from an expansion policy to reduction in tonnage. Its main goal was to sell a large tonnage of its redundant large-size tankers and the smaller ships that had become uneconomical due to the high yen value and high labor costs. At the same time, "K" Line tried to rationalize its operations. This included an increasing use of flag of convenience (FOC) ships, often in the form of *Shikumisen* or "tie-in" ships, and reduction in the manning of Japanese flag ships.

"K" Line also tried to enter or develop a number of businesses that looked promising. In 1981, "K" Line launched its LNG tanker operation, building a new ship jointly with several other Japanese firms. The business has continued to grow. Car carrier business was another of the few sectors that flourished after the oil crisis.

In the liner sector, while extending or consolidating its network with container or conventional ships, "K" Line was attaching more importance to the Far East-North America route on which the company was a pioneer among Japanese firms. To develop the intermodal service on this route and to gain advantage over competitors, in 1986 "K" Line began operation of its Double Stack Train (DST), originated by "K" Line for its own use, in the United States. This was followed by a door-to-door delivery service for small cargoes on this route in 1988. In 1990, "K" Line ventured into the cruise business via a subsidiary, Seven Seas Cruise Line.

The 1990s proved to be just as turbulent as the previous decade. While the company focused on broadening its global reach, changing economies and fluctuations in the value of Japanese currency forced it adopt a reorganization plan, and in 1993 the "K" Line re-engineering program was launched. Designed to position the company as a leading global concern, the new strategy focused on cutting costs, moving employment outside of Japan, and trimming expenses in order to bolster profits. The company also eyed partnerships as crucial to expansion. In 1993, "K" Line teamed up with Mitsui O.S.K. Lines, Nippon Yusen, Showa Line, and Iino Kaiun to transport Qatar Liquefied Gas Co.'s LNG from Qatar to Japan. That year, the Corona Ace, "K" Line's first coal carrier serving the electric power industry, made its debut. In 1994, the firm joined forces with Yang Ming Marine Transport Corp. and Hyundai to provide service between North America and Europe. In October of that year, K-S Shipping Ltd. was created as a joint venture with Sinotrans Liaoning. Two years later, the Trans-Atlantic Container Service was established.

"K" Line began to prepare for its entrance into the new century just as Asia began to experience a financial crisis. The company, however, was determined to restore profits—especially in its container business where its market share had tumbled—and increase shareholder value. Phase two of its re-engineering program was introduced in 1996 and was followed by a five-year management plan adopted in 1998. Entitled New "K" Line Spirit for 21 (New K-21), the plan detailed the company's business approach for the new century. New K-21 emphasized several points, including a stable payment of dividends, a focus on the logistics market with shipping as a core business, pursing the growth of profits through expansion, bolstering customer service, and safety in navigation.

During 1999, the firm began new containership services from Asia to the East Coast, Asia to the Mediterranean, and from the Mediterranean to the East Coast. Upon entering the 21st century, the company began to realign several of its subsidiaries and created "K" Line Logistics Holdings Inc. as part of its New K-21 strategy. The firm pursued partnerships in 2001 and 2002, established a shipping business in Singapore, and continued to strengthen its logistics holdings. Despite "K" Line's efforts, profits languished as freight container shipments—responsible for nearly half of overall sales—fell due to sluggish worldwide economies and increased competition.

In 2002, the company adopted a new three-year management plan, KV-Plan, which management set in place to renew its efforts at restoring and maintaining profitability. While the company had endured hardships over the past few decades, "K" Line's tenacity left it well equipped to fend off and overcome future problems. As Japan's third-largest marine transportation concern, "K" Line appeared to be well positioned to battle any rough waters that lie ahead.

Principal Subsidiaries

Badak LNG Transport Inc.; Kawasaki Kinkai Kisen Kaisha Ltd.; Taiyo Nippon Kisen Co. Ltd.; "K" Line Ship Management Co. Ltd.; Rokko Warehouse & Transport Co. Ltd.; "K" Line Accounting and Finance Co. Ltd.; Intermodal Engineering Co. Ltd.; "K" Line Japan Ltd.; Tokyo Maritime Agency Ltd.; Shimizu Kawasaki Transportation Co. Ltd.; Daito Corporation; Hokkai Unyu Co. Ltd.; Naigai Unyu Co. Ltd.; Nitto Tugboat Co. Ltd.; Rinko Corp.; "K" Logistics Corporation; "K" Line Air Service Ltd.; "K" Line Travel Ltd.; Japan Express Transportation Co. Ltd.; Shinto Rikuun Kaisha Ltd.; Maizuru Kousoku Yusou Co. Ltd.; "K" Line Systems Ltd.

Principal Competitors

Evergreen Marine Corporation Ltd.; Mitsui O.S.K. Lines Ltd.; Nippon Yusen KK.

Further Reading

Chida, T., and P.N. Davies, *The Japanese Shipping and Shipbuilding Industries*, London: Athlone Press, 1990.
"Japanese Marine Carriers' Profits Sink on Lower Cargo Fees," *AsiaPulse News*, May 20, 2002.
"Japan's Kawasaki Kisen Books 61% Drop in Group PreTax Profit," *AsiaPulse News*, February 18, 2002.
"Japan's Kawasaki Kisen to Cooperate With Two Overseas Rivals," *AsiaPulse News*, September 26, 2001.
Kawasaki Kisen, *50-nen Shi*, Tokyo, 1969.
Nakagawa, Keiichiro, *Ryo-Taisen kan no Nippon Kaiun Gyo*, Tokyo: Nippon Keizai Shinbun Sha, 1980.
Richardson, Paul, " 'K' Line, Yang Ming Restructure Asia-Europe Runs," *Journal of Commerce and Commercial*, July 14, 1998, p. 12A.
"Shipping Lucrative Despite Drop in Exports," *Automotive Industries*, October 2002, p. 16.

—Tomohei Chida
—update: Christina M. Stansell

Keane, Inc.

100 City Square
Boston, Massachusetts 02129
U.S.A.
Telephone: (617) 241-9200
Toll Free: (800) 365-3263
Fax: (617) 241-9507
Web site: http://www.keane.com

Public Company
Incorporated: 1965
Employees: 7,331
Sales: $873.2 million (2002)
Stock Exchanges: American
Ticker Symbol: KEA
NAIC: 541511 Custom Computer Programming Services;
541512 Computer Systems Design Services; 541611
Administrative Management and General Management
Consulting Services

As a consulting firm offering customized software services, Keane, Inc. enjoyed phenomenal growth in the late 1990s by providing Y2K-related software solutions. Its annual revenue surpassed $1 billion in 1998 and 1999. Following the loss of Y2K-related business, Keane planned to achieve annual revenue of $3 billion by 2005 primarily through acquisitions. The company's diversified software services include outsourcing, application development and integration, and business consulting. Keane has more than 1,400 clients, with separate divisions devoted to serving the healthcare industry and government agencies as well as Global 2000 companies across every major industry. The company has implemented a global delivery strategy that includes offshore development centers in India and a near-shore development center in Canada. Although Keane is a public company, it has remained a family-run business since its inception in 1965.

Providing Software Services: 1965–85

Keane, Inc. was founded in December 1965 in a small office above Nichols Donut Shoppe in Hingham, Massachusetts, by John F. Keane, a former programmer at IBM. Keane established his software services company to help businesses better utilize the power of computer technology. He recognized that computers often have more processing power than businesses know how to use. Keane offered to provide custom software for a business's computer and improve its productivity.

Keane, Inc. went public in 1970. The following year saw the company experience several project overruns. After analyzing the problems associated with these cost overruns, Keane developed a new approach to project management called Productivity Management. This tool helped Keane survive in a highly competitive industry. It became the foundation for all of the company's application development and outsourcing methodologies. Productivity Management seminars were held over the years to train thousands of Keane's employees.

Keane established its Healthcare Services Division in 1975 under the name KeaMed Hospital Systems. This unit focused on marketing information services to hospitals and other healthcare clients and was soon offering turnkey software solutions.

Refocusing on Core Business: 1986–90

After enjoying steady growth for the first 20 years, Keane experienced its first quarterly operating loss in the second quarter of 1986. The loss was attributed to the company's diversification into packaged software and other software products. It served as a wake-up call; Keane dropped the software products and refocused its efforts on its core business of providing custom software services. The company returned to profitability in the next quarter. In 1989 *Forbes* named Keane one of "The Best Small Companies in America."

In 1987 Keane formed an alliance with Boston University that resulted in Keane's intensive Accelerated Software Development Program. The program combined Keane's business expertise with the university's technical training experience. The result of Keane's emphasis on internal training, begun earlier in the decade, the Accelerated Software Development Program provided important training for entry-level personnel in the company's software development and project management methodologies.

Company Perspectives:

Keane develops long-term client relationships and recurring revenues through its broad range of services, multi-year outsourcing contracts, and an unwavering commitment to customer satisfaction. Keane delivers its services with world-class processes, management disciplines, and performance metrics via an integrated network of branch offices in North America and the United Kingdom, and Advanced Development Centers (ADCs) in the United States, Canada, and India. This global service delivery model offers customers the flexibility and economic advantage of fluidly allocating work between a variety of delivery options including on-site at a client's facility, off-site at a remote location, near-shore in Halifax, Nova Scotia, and offshore in India. Branch offices work in conjunction with Keane Consulting Group, the Company's business consulting arm, and are supported by centralized Strategic Practices and Quality Assurance Groups.

In 1988 Keane developed its Application Management Methodology (AMM) to bring greater efficiency to the way the company managed its production systems. AMM was an application maintenance process that grew out of a contract that Keane had to support the system software of a major hardware vendor. AMM later became the basis of the company's Application Outsourcing solution.

By the end of the 1980s Keane had begun to standardize its approach to software development. Previously, the company had relied on areas of individual expertise to develop software solutions. With newer technology becoming more complex, Keane established frameworks to provide clear and disciplined guidelines for developing business application software.

Enjoying Growth During the 1990s

By 1990 Keane was known as a custom programmer of computer mainframes, minicomputers, and workstations. Its biggest client was IBM, which accounted for about 24 percent of its sales. For 1990 Keane reported net income of $5 million on sales of $93 million. Sales were up 20 percent over the previous year, while net income rose by 46 percent.

Keane made several acquisitions in the first half of the 1990s to fuel its growth. In 1992 it acquired Ferranti Healthcare Systems Corp. of Maryland, which was in Chapter 11 bankruptcy protection. In 1993 it purchased GE Consulting Services and Professional Healthcare Services (PHS). Keane's acquisitions helped boost the company's revenue from around $100 million to $350 million.

In early 1994 Keane acquired several software companies from Nynex Corp., which was in the process of divesting all of its software service businesses. The businesses that Keane acquired from Nynex included AGS Information Services and associated businesses, such as Tremblay & Associates of Canada, AGS Federal Systems, AGS Management Systems, and Lamarian Systems. These acquisitions gave Keane a presence in such cities as Seattle, Houston, Phoenix, and Columbus, Ohio. They also gave Keane a stronger foothold with government

clients, and the company established Keane Federal Systems to service public sector clients. Later in 1994 Keane was again named to *Forbes'* list of the 200 best small companies in the United States. The company reported net income of $16.2 million for the year.

By the end of 1995 Keane had 4,500 employees, 40 sites, and annual revenue approaching $400 million. Its software services included software application development, outsourcing, and integration services. A new contract with Microsoft called for providing a 500-person help-desk support center for Windows 95 customers. Keane provided similar support for IBM's AS/400, PC, and OS/2 Warp systems. Keane also had a $13.5 million contract with AT&T to support 25 human resources applications on AT&T's personal, midrange, and mainframe computers.

By 1996 companies were beginning to assess the extent of their possible problems with Y2K, or the millennium bug. By the second half of the year Keane was winning three to four Y2K contracts a week, including a $107 million contract from the U.S. Department of Justice. To address the Y2K concerns of potential clients, Keane developed a Year 2000 Compliance Methodology through a partnership with Viasoft, Inc. For 1996 Keane reported revenue of $467.1 million and net income of $25.4 million. In the first half of 1997 Keane hired an additional 1,000 employees because of Y2K contracts. Its workforce reached 7,500 people in 40 locations in North America, and the company planned to hire another 1,000 employees by the end of 1997. Revenue for 1997 rose to $654 million.

Largely as a result of its Y2K business, Keane's revenue soared above $1 billion in 1998 and 1999. The company was extremely profitable during those two years, reporting net income of $96.3 million in 1998 and $73.1 million in 1999. Keane also continued to expand through acquisitions. In 1998 it acquired GSE Erudite Software Inc., a software services company based in Salt Lake City, Utah, with revenue of $18 million. Keane also acquired Omega Systems, a Pittsburgh-based consulting firm with about 100 employees and annual revenue of $6 million. In August 1998 Keane made its first acquisition in the United Kingdom, when it purchased Icom Systems Ltd. of Birmingham, England. Icom provided IT services to U.K. corporations, especially financial services and utilities.

Another acquisition in 1998 gave Keane management consulting capabilities, when it purchased Chicago-based Bricker & Associates Inc. for $110 million. Bricker had annual revenue of $15 million in 1997 and was expected to post $26 million in revenue in 1998. The firm also enjoyed a healthy profit margin of 26 percent, compared to Keane's average operating margin of 9.1 percent. Toward the end of 1998 Keane acquired Fourth Tier Inc., a Los Angeles-based provider of front-office applications for customer service, sales and marketing, technical support, and product development, in an all-stock transaction valued at $26.7 million.

Investors in 1998 appeared pleased with Keane's performance and business strategy. *Wall Street Journal* named Keane the number one ten-year performer on its Shareholder Scoreboard, noting the firm's stock had risen some 1,500 percent during the previous ten years. Analysts were predicting 40 percent growth for Keane in 1998. In fact, the company exceeded

Key Dates:

1965:   John F. Keane founds his company to provide software services to businesses.

1970:   Keane's company goes public.

1971:   Keane develops a productivity management process to avoid project overruns.

1975:   Keane establishes its Healthcare Services Division under the name KeaMed Hospital Systems, to provide software services to hospitals and other healthcare facilities.

1986:   After experiencing its first-ever quarterly loss, the company refocuses on its core business of delivering software services.

1987:   Keane forms an educational alliance with Boston University and establishes an Accelerated Software Development Program for students there.

1988:   Keane develops its Application Management Methodology (AMM), an application maintenance process that evolves into the company's Application Outsourcing solution.

1996:   Keane begins offering Y2K solutions.

1997:   Keane launches its first Advanced Development Center (ADC) in Halifax, Nova Scotia, to provide near-shore outsourcing.

1998:   Company revenue surpasses $1 billion for the first time.

1999:   Strategic acquisitions include Jamison/Gold in Los Angeles, Parallax Solutions Ltd. in the United Kingdom, and ANSTEC, Inc. in Washington, D.C.

2000:   Keane consolidates its consulting subsidiaries and forms Keane Consulting Group; key acquisitions include Denver Management Group and Care Computer Systems.

2001:   Keane acquires Metro Information Services, Inc.

2002:   Keane acquires SignalTree Solutions Holding, Inc. and gains two ADCs in India.

those expectations by posting revenue of $1.07 billion for 1998, an increase of nearly 65 percent over 1997. An estimated 35 percent of Keane's revenue in 1998 came from Y2K-related work. In 1999 Keane was named Company of the Year by the *Boston Globe,* an honor it had achieved once before in 1990.

Developing Initiatives and Making Acquisitions to Replace Y2K Business: 1998–2000

As early as the final months of 1998, Keane was looking to increased applications outsourcing to replace lost Y2K business. Some new business came from companies for which Keane had performed Y2K work, which then gave Keane contracts for applications outsourcing. Keane's acquisitions in 1998 were also designed to give it entrée into higher-margin businesses, such as management consulting and front-office applications.

Keane continued to acquire companies in 1999 to broaden its expertise. In January it acquired Emergent Corp., a business consulting firm and systems integrator that specialized in pro-

viding scalable data warehousing solutions. Emergent, which had revenue of $4 million in 1998, was expected to strengthen Keane's enterprise relationship management (ERM) solutions. In March Keane acquired Advanced Solutions Inc., a New York-based IT solutions and applications development firm that specialized in electronic commerce and advanced technologies as well as enterprise resource planning and supply chain management. Keane acquired Boston-based Amherst Consulting Group, Inc. in May 1999 and merged it with Bricker & Associates. The acquisition strengthened Keane's management consulting business and added a Boston office to Bricker's practice. Also in May, Keane bolstered its presence in the United Kingdom by acquiring Parallax Solutions Ltd., a software services consulting firm based in Coventry, England. Parallax had about 150 employees and projected annual revenue of $14.7 million, and it had strong ties to large automotive companies, including BMW AG, Rover, and Ford Motor Co. Ltd., as well as to retail finance and capital market companies.

In June 1999 Keane acquired Jamison/Gold, LLC, an Internet consulting firm based in Marina del Rey, California. Company founders and principals Brian Jamison and Josh Gold were expected to assume management positions within Keane's e-Solutions practice. Together the two had written a well-known book on electronic commerce, *Electronic Selling: 23 Steps to E-Selling Profits.*

During 1999 Keane also signed new outsourcing contracts and developed new initiatives to diversify away from Y2K business. Among the new contracts was a five-year outsourcing agreement for application management and development with SuperValu Stores, Inc., worth more than $20 million, and a five-year, $10 million outsourcing contract with Dominion General Insurance Co. of Canada. In April 1999 Keane launched a new full-service customer relationship management (CRM) solution that helped clients plan, build, and manage a customer-oriented focus. Through a strategic partnership with CRM applications vendor Siebel Systems, Inc., Keane offered clients help in implementing Siebel's applications as part of its CRM solution. At the time its CRM solution was introduced, Keane announced it planned to generate $75 million in CRM-related revenue in 1999.

In spite of its efforts, Keane was forced to revise its revenue forecasts downward in mid-1999. Noting a softening in non-Y2K revenue that began in June, Chairman and CEO John F. Keane announced the company's year-over-year revenue growth would fall below the anticipated 30 to 35 percent range it had enjoyed in the past few quarters. For the next three to five years, Keane forecast that the company would post an average revenue growth of 20 to 25 percent.

In the second half of 1999 Keane made two more acquisitions and announced a change in management involving the next generation of Keanes. After receiving the Albert Einstein Technology Medal in conjunction with a senior-level high technology mission to Israel, company founder John F. Keane reported that his two sons, Brian and John Keane, Jr., would become CEO and president, respectively, of Keane, Inc. John F. Keane, Sr., retained his position as chairman. For the prior two years Brian, 38, and John, Jr., 39, had served in the office of president and were responsible for the company's operations and corporate functions. At the time of the announcement at the end of November 1999, Keane had 10,500 employees.

Keane completed two acquisitions before the end of 1999. One involved ANSTEC, Inc., an IT company based in McLean, Virginia. Keane announced it would combine ANSTEC's capabilities and client base with Keane Federal Systems, which allowed Keane to compete for larger government contracts. Some 90 percent of ANSTEC's client base consisted of federal agencies. The other acquisition involved First Coast Systems, Inc., a leading developer of integrated software solutions for the healthcare industry. Operations of the Jacksonville, Florida-based company would be combined with Keane's Healthcare Solutions Division.

Struggling to Remain Profitable: 2000–03

Celebrating its 35th year in business, Keane began the new millennium as a recognized leader in computer and software services. The company was active in several high-growth sectors, including electronic commerce, customer relationship management, data warehousing, and application management. In January 2000 *Forbes* recognized Keane by placing it on its Platinum 400 list of America's Best Big Companies. The selection was based on Keane's five-year performance, which included an average return on capital of 25 percent, sales growth of 37.6 percent, and net income growth of more than 54 percent.

At the beginning of 2000 Keane formed a new division, Keane Interactive, to provide Internet design and development services. The recently acquired Jamison/Gold, LLC was renamed Keane Interactive and formed the core of the new division. Keane Interactive's first contract was with 3M of St. Paul, Minnesota, to develop web sites for 3M's customer centers.

In April 2000 Keane consolidated two of its management consulting groups, Bricker & Associates and Amherst Consulting, to form Keane Consulting Group (KCG). KCG would help clients establish new business models, transform business processes to leverage the Internet, and identify e-business opportunities.

Another management change occurred at Keane in July 2000, when John F. Keane, Jr., left the company to pursue his interests in wireless technology. Upon his departure Brian Keane assumed the duties of president in addition to those of CEO.

Keane made two additional acquisitions in the second half of 2000. The first involved Denver Management Group, a Denver-based consulting firm specializing in supply chain management and integrated distribution for *Fortune* 1000 companies. The second acquisition involved Care Computer Systems, Inc., a leading provider of software solutions for the long-term care industry. Based in Bellevue, Washington, Care Computer Systems had 225 employees, annual sales of $17.6 million, and some 3,200 software installations in the United States. Its operations would be combined with Keane's Healthcare Solutions Division. As a result, Keane's Healthcare Solutions Division became the leading provider of software services to the long-term care industry with a 26 percent market share in the United States.

Keane expanded its off-site development and management capabilities at the end of October 2000 with the opening of a new Advanced Development Center (ADC) in Rochester, Minnesota. Similar to the ADC in Halifax that was launched in 1997, the ADC in Rochester enabled clients based anywhere in North America or Europe to speed delivery and improve the cost-efficiency of software application development and management.

Although Keane's revenue for 2000 declined to $872 million, the company remained profitable with net income of $20.4 million. The decline continued in 2001, when the company reported revenue of $779.2 million and net income of $17.4 million. In early 2001 Keane divested its help-desk business, which provided call center support for a wide range of software applications. Convergys Corp. paid $15.7 million for the technical support centers, which employed about 1,000 people and were located in Tucson, Arizona, and Kirkland, Washington. Around this time Keane also cut about 2 percent of its workforce.

Keane made one significant acquisition in 2001 went it acquired Metro Information Services, Inc. of Virginia Beach, Virginia, in a stock-for-stock transaction valued at $135 million. Founded in 1979, Metro Information Services provided a wide range of IT consulting services and solutions to Global 2000 companies. It employed nearly 2,000 consultants and had offices in 33 metropolitan markets, 26 of which overlapped with markets served by Keane. As a result, Keane anticipated increasing its average branch size from $22 million to $27 million in annual revenue. The acquisition significantly increased Keane's customer base. Metro had about 600 clients. Of the company's top 300 accounts, 236 were brand new to Keane. Keane expected the acquisition of Metro Information Services to increase its annual revenue by a factor of 10 percent. Following the acquisition, Metro Chairman and CEO John H. Fain became a member of Keane's board of directors.

Although Keane made only one acquisition in 2001, the company planned to achieve annual revenue of $3 billion in five years through a program of strategic acquisitions. In the first quarter of 2002 the company acquired SignalTree Solutions Holding, Inc., a U.S.-based corporation headquartered in Irvine, California. SignalTree had two software development facilities in India as well as operations in the United States. Founded in 1982, SignalTree had about $50 million in annual revenue in 2001; some 400 of its 750 employees worked at its software development facilities in Hyderabad and Delhi, India. Keane acquired SignalTree for $62 million. Following the acquisition Keane formed Keane India Ltd. and announced plans for additional investment there, including plans to open a third ADC, or software development center. By September 2002 Keane India Ltd. had hired 85 additional people and planned to expand its workforce there to 700 employees.

Although the acquisition of SignalTree did not affect Keane's 2002 revenue, its 2001 acquisition of Metro Information Service helped the company achieve a 12 percent growth in revenue for the year to $873.2 million. Net income for 2002 was $8.2 million, down from $17.4 million in 2001, due in part to costs associated with acquisitions.

In February 2003 Keane formed a strategic alliance with The Unilog Group, a European IT consulting firm with operations in Austria, France, Germany, Italy, Luxembourg, Spain, and Switzerland. Together, Keane and Unilog could offer clients the combined resources of more than 18,000 business and IT professionals. In addition, Keane planned to make its offshore ADC's in India available to Unilog clients and leverage India as part of its global delivery strategy.

Principal Subsidiaries

Keane Federal Systems, Inc.; Keane Ltd. (U.K.); Keane India Ltd.

Principal Divisions

Keane Consulting Group; Keane Healthcare Solutions; Project Management Services Group; Keane Interactive.

Principal Competitors

Accenture Ltd.; American Management Systems, Inc.; Computer Sciences Corp.; Electronic Data Systems (EDS); IBM Global Services; KPMG Consulting, Inc.; LogicaCMG plc; Sapient Corp.

Further Reading

Autry, Ret, "Keane," *Fortune,* July 1, 1991, p. 72.

Caldwell, Bruce, "Keane Acquisitions to Add Management Consulting," *InformationWeek,* April 27, 1998, p. 172.

Deck, Stewart, "Keane's 21st-Century Bridges," *Computerworld,* November 18, 1996, p. 155.

Doyle, T. C., "VARbusiness 500—Spotlight on Keane," *VARbusiness,* May 17, 1999, p. 14.

Frye, Colleen, "Keane Touts Business, Cultural Compatibilities of Near-Shore Development," *Software Magazine,* April 2001, p. 10.

Fugazy, Danielle, "Arlington Sells Stake in SignalTree," *Buyouts,* April 1, 2002.

Jaleshgari, Ramin P., "Selling at the Top—The New World Order," *VARbusiness,* June 14, 1999, p. 62.

"Keane Buys Care Computer," *Puget Sound Business Journal,* September 15, 2000, p. 69.

"Keane Cuts 176 Jobs, Agrees to Sell Its Help Desk Division," *Boston Business Journal,* February 9, 2001, p. 77.

"Keane India to Hire More," *Asia Africa Intelligence Wire,* September 10, 2002.

"Keane Moves in CRM Direction," *PC Week,* May 3, 1999, p. 72.

"Keane Names Keane President," *Providence Business News,* July 17, 2000, p. 14.

"Keane Plans Acquisitions," *InformationWeek,* April 20, 1998, p. 158.

"Keane Plans Third Centre," *Asia Africa Intelligence Wire,* February 28, 2003.

"Keane, Unilog Plan to Tap Europe Via India Development Centres," *Asia Africa Intelligence Wire,* February 28, 2003.

Lingblom, Marie, "Keane Banks on Acquisitions As It Aims to Become $3 Billion Company in Five Years," *Computer Reseller News,* September 10, 2001, p. 34.

Lyons, Daniel, "Keane: On Call to Help the Likes of IBM and Macintosh," *VARbusiness,* November 15, 1995, p. 73.

Mateyaschuk, Jennifer, "Keane to Buy Fourth Tier for App Expertise," *InformationWeek,* October 12, 1998, p. 179.

——, "Midtier Consultancies Acquire Expertise," *InformationWeek,* March 8, 1999, p. 99.

——, "Vendors Plan for Post-2000 Work," *InformationWeek,* November 16, 1998, p. 106.

——, "Y2K Vendors Change Strategies," *InformationWeek,* February 22, 1999, p. 36.

McHugh, Josh, "Keane, Geek-Free Software," *Forbes,* January 10, 2000, p. 112.

Panettieri, Joseph C., "Better Luck Next Year," *Sm@rt Partner,* December 18, 2000, p. 60.

Reidy, Chris, "Boston-Based Software Firm Plans Hiring Binge to Deal with Year 2000 Problem," *Knight Ridder/Tribune Business News,* September 18, 1997.

Rosa, Jerry, "Keane Looks for Growth by Focusing on Internet," *Computer Reseller News,* January 24, 2000, p. 3.

Schuman, Michael, et al., "Winners and Losers," *Forbes,* November 7, 1994, p. 228.

Slack, Shawna, "Keane," *Boston Business Journal,* February 10, 1992, p. 2.

Vaughan, Jack, "Nynex's Breakup," *Software Magazine,* February 1994, p. 35.

Vijayan, Jaikumar, "U.S. Firms Look North for Outsourcing Help," *Computerworld,* February 25, 2002, p. 8.

Violino, Bob, and Bruce Caldwell, "Customer-Relationship Services Expand," *InformationWeek,* May 3, 1999, p. 109.

—David P. Bianco

Kelly-Moore Paint Company, Inc.

987 Commercial Street
San Carlos, California 94070
U.S.A.
Telephone: (650) 592-8337
Fax: (650) 508-8563
Web site: http://www.kellymoore.com

Private Company
Incorporated: 1946
Employees: 2,300
Sales: $350 million (2002 est.)
NAIC: 325510 Paint and Coating Manufacturing

Kelly-Moore Paint Company, Inc. is an employee-owned regional paint manufacturer and retailer, with its headquarters located in San Carlos, California. The company concentrates its efforts on western and southwestern states, operating more than 160 stores in 11 states and Guam. Four manufacturing facilities, capable of producing 20 million gallons of more than 100 types of paints and finishes each year, are strategically located in Seattle, Washington; Hurst, Texas; Tempe, Arizona; and San Carlos, California. As has been the case for more than 50 years, Kelly-Moore mostly caters to professional contractors and the do-it-yourself market, building a reputation for selling high-quality products while providing strong service. Retail sales account for less than 15 percent of the company's business.

Founding Kelly-Moore in 1946

The driving force behind Kelly-Moore was the company's cofounder, William E. Moore, who was born in the small town of Hartford, Arkansas, the son of a barber. Ambitious from an early age, according to a video tribute produced by his alma mater, Georgia Tech, he started shining shoes at nine in order to fund his college education. More important, he learned how to play tennis on a makeshift court in front of his home. When he began his studies at Georgia Tech in 1934 he was accomplished enough at the game to win a scholarship as a walk-on. Nevertheless, he needed living expenses and to support himself through his college years he held eight odd jobs simultaneously, yet still main-

tained high grades and achieved an impressive athletic record. In the process Moore became something of a local legend. When he graduated in 1938 with a dual degree in Industrial Management and Chemical Engineering, America was still very much in the grips of the Great Depression and Moore was happy to find any job, accepting a position as a salesman for National Theatre Supply at a salary of $110 per month, a considerable falloff considering he had been able to cobble together $150 per month from his part-time college jobs. Moore soon found work at Glidden Paint as a salesman and lab technician. Starting with a $160 per month draw, Moore set a goal of earning $1,000 per month and launched a systematic approach to achieving that amount. After analyzing sales information he was able to determine that just 20 percent of his customers accounted for 80 percent of his sales. Rather than continue to spend the same amount of time on all of his customers, he decided to return his smaller accounts to the company in order to focus his efforts on the top 20 percent. As a result, he reached his target goal of $1,000 per month within the first year, and ultimately he became Glidden's top West Coast producer.

Moore's business career was interrupted by a stint in the Navy during World War II when he served on a destroyer in the Pacific, but his time at Glidden convinced him that his future lay in the paint business and he devoted much of his spare time in the service studying two books on paint making. Like many in his generation, the war had a profound effect on Moore. Having lost several years of his life to the service, he felt that he had fallen behind schedule in his life, a condition that served to fuel his already ambitious nature. In 1946, at the age of 29, in the same year that he married, Moore decided to strike out on his own in the paint business. He studied the southern California market and concluded that the ideal location for his enterprise was the city of San Carlos, located some 30 minutes north of San Jose, in the heart of what would one day become the Silicon Valley. At the time, it was home to a large number of orchards, some of which were being converted to tract-home communities. Seed money to establish a single store and manufacturing facility came from the funds he had saved during his stint at Glidden, which during the war he had then wisely invested in Tulsa, Oklahoma, real estate. All Moore needed now was someone experienced in mixing paint. He found the ideal part-

Company Perspectives:

Our Mission: To be a service-oriented paint company that provides a broad selection of high quality paint and paint related products at fair prices to Painting Contractors, Commercial and Maintenance Accounts and Do-It-Yourself Consumers through strategically located neighborhood paint stores.

ner in the form of William H. Kelly, a retired superintendent at Glidden who was tired of having free time and was now very much interested in starting a little factory. The plan was to mix paint in the mornings and Moore would make deliveries in the afternoons, with the hope that the start-up business would show a $500 profit each month. What Moore and Kelly failed to anticipate was the pent-up demand for housing caused by the privations of war that resulted in a dramatic building boom. In the first six months of existence, Kelly-Moore, instead of a $3,000 profit, made $30,000.

Kelly-Moore's success was more than a simple matter of fortuitous timing. Moore's decisions and innovations were of far greater importance to the future growth of the business. From the start, he decided to focus on the tract-home paint contractors, a market segment that was being overlooked by the national brands who were eagerly pursuing consumer sales. To win over contractors, Kelly-Moore developed the kind of high-quality paint required by them, one that could do the job with a single coat. The store also maintained the kind of high inventory levels that contractors required and could rely on. As the business grew the company opened stores larger than the norm in the industry, in effect serving as a warehouse for paint contractors, who mostly worked out of their homes and were unable to store large quantities of paint. In addition, Kelly-Moore was in the vanguard of making credit a function of sales, treating its customers like partners. Kelly-Moore further separated itself from the competition by offering innovative customer service. It opened early in the day and served free coffee, a small matter but one that meant a great deal to paint contractors who regularly put in long, tiring days of work. Kelly-Moore was also the first to own a fleet of its own trucks to provide delivery. In the end, Kelly-Moore's success was built on the character of Moore, whose dedication to honest business dealings and commitment to producing a high-quality product supported by superior customer service resulted in repeat business.

Buying Out Kelly in 1952

Moore bought out Kelly in 1952 but he continued to carry his partner's name as the business grew beyond northern California. There was no doubt, however, that the success of Kelly-Moore was very much dependent on the integrity, skills, and hands-on leadership of Bill Moore. He was deeply involved in every area of the business, instrumental in developing manufacturing techniques as well as designing the company-owned stores. Of key importance was his smart choice of real estate, establishing stores at locations with reasonable rental rates, which helped to produce high margins for the business. Able to operate larger stores and thereby act as a warehouse for cus-

tomers, Kelly-Moore had the ability to better plan its inventories, which also resulted in strong net margins. While industry giants Glidden and Sherwin-Williams netted profits in the range of 2.5 percent, Kelly-Moore by the mid-1980s generated a net profit of more than 10 percent of sales. It was also at Moore's insistence that the company never succumbed to the temptation of saving money by cutting back on the quality of its paint, relying on high-quality raw materials such as titanium in the formulation of all of its paints. Moreover, Kelly-Moore instituted tough quality control measures. In addition to the efforts of the production department, the sales department maintained its own quality control testing.

Over the years Kelly-Moore picked up some consumer sales, due to a large extent to contractors leaving behind touch-up cans, which served both as a product sample and a professional endorsement for Kelly-Moore. By 1974 consumer sales accounted for about one-quarter of total revenues. That amount would grow over the next decade to 37 percent, the result of a changing marketplace. An increasing number of homeowners were opting to do their own painting. Despite the rise of the do-it-yourself customer and an ever-changing housing market, Kelly-Moore was able to maintain a decade of growth averaging 13 percent each year. By the time Bill Moore began the process of retiring and turning over day-to-day responsibilities to a new chief executive in 1984, Kelly-Moore generated sales of 136 million and a profit of more than $11 million, with more than 80 stores located in California, Arizona, Colorado, Texas, Oklahoma, and the Pacific Northwest.

After building a successful business, Moore, approaching 70 years old, set about the task of making sure the company was in a position to carry on without him. (During the 1980s he also became involved in highly successful ventures in the diverse fields of life insurance in California and ranching in Montana, applying the same business principles he had used in the success of Kelly-Moore.) A 33-year-old daughter was in charge of advertising, but to find his replacement at the top of the organization, Moore recruited outside the company, finally hiring Joseph P. Cristiano, who was actually dispatched by his employer in an effort to acquire Kelly-Moore. Instead, Moore sold Cristiano on coming to work for him. For the first six months Cristiano was on the road with sales representatives learning firsthand how Kelly-Moore operated. In January 1985 Moore officially turned over the reins to Cristiano, although he continued to serve as the company's chairman of the board and retained about 97 percent of the stock.

Cristiano adhered to the formula established by Moore and the company continued its steady growth over the next ten years. Although Kelly-Moore primarily relied on internal growth, it used external means as well. In 1994 it acquired Seattle-based Preservative Paint Co., which now became a wholly owned subsidiary, adding two stores in Alaska and 15 in Washington, as well as a pump and compressor center. A year later Kelly-Moore bought K-M Universal, gaining a factory in Tempe, Arizona, as well as additional stores in Arizona and California. Kelly-Moore added to this new subsidiary in 1996 when it folded in another purchase, the Guam-based paint division of Island Equipment Co. Also during this period, Kelly-Moore experienced some internal growth by becoming involved in the recycling of paint. The effort started out on a small scale,

Key Dates:

1946: The company is founded by William E. Moore and William H. Kelly.
1952: Moore buys out Kelly.
1984: Joseph P. Cristiano replaces Moore as president and CEO.
1994: Preservative Paint Co. is acquired.
1998: An employee stock ownership program is instituted.
2002: Herb R. Giffins replaces Cristiano as president and CEO.

essentially a pet program that allowed paint contractors to return unused paint at no cost, a useful service because professionals were not permitted to use free public collection facilities. The company stockpiled a large amount of recycled paint and began to actively seek a market for it. In the summer of 1994 Kelly-Moore was able to land a contract for 50,000 gallons of recycled latex paint with the federal General Services Administration. The contract called for a product that contained at least a 50 percent post-consumer recycled content, which was packaged under the company's "e coat" brand name, to be used by military installations, U.S. forestry facilities, and other federal outlets. As a result, the "e coat" line became listed in the GSA catalog, which gave the company a leg up on future contracts for recycled paint. In addition, the company moved aggressively to sell its recycled paint product at the state and local levels, to schools and other facilities.

As Kelly-Moore reached its 50th year in business in 1996, it was generating some $240 million in annual sales, boasting 140 stores located in Guam and ten states: Alaska, Arizona, Arkansas, California, Colorado, Nevada, Oklahoma, Oregon, Texas, and Washington. The company employed more than 2,300 people. Its continued success remained based on a longtime formula of producing quality paints and offering superior service to the contract painter. Moreover, the company was able to adjust to changing circumstances in the marketplace. The state of California instituted tough volatile organic compounds (VOC) standards, forcing Kelly-Moore and other paint companies doing business in the state to reformulate their products. Kelly-Moore's efforts in new product development was now devoted to waterbourne products, as opposed to oil-based paints, with the challenge of maintaining the high quality of its architectural coatings and high gloss exteriors.

Establishing ESOP in 1998

Aside from keeping pace with regulatory changes, Kelly-Moore took other measures to remain competitive. In 1998 Moore and his wife established a combined retirement and employee stock ownership program (ESOP), which allowed qualifying employees to gain an ownership stake in the business. The plan was instrumental in helping the company retain personnel and instill an even greater degree of loyalty. To improve its position in the marketplace, in 1999 Kelly-Moore formed a marketing alliance with Pennsylvania-based M.A.

Bruder & Sons, a company of similar size and philosophy that operated primarily in the eastern states. Because their territories did not overlap, the two companies were able to serve national accounts, with M.A. Bruder responsible for East Coast projects and Kelly-Moore for West Coast projects. As a result of the venture, the companies were joint-listed in the American Institute of Ameritect's MasterSpec Finishes directory, used by some 5,500 architectural and construction firms and that included only a handful of other paint companies. The marketing alliance grew in 2000 with the addition of Diamond Vogel Paints, based in Orange City, Iowa. The resulting venture was named Paint America, a key component in the regional partners' efforts to resist industry consolidation and maintain independence while still being able to serve national chain retail and property management customers. West Coast paint company Dunn-Edwards soon joined Paint America as well. To a small degree Kelly-Moore took part in the consolidation of the paint industry in 2000 when it acquired Ponderosa Paint Manufacturing Inc., adding 15 stores in Oregon, Utah, and Idaho.

After almost 20 years at the helm, Cristiano stepped down as president and CEO of Kelly-Moore. Although his retirement was not official until January 2003, in November 2002 he was replaced by Herb R. Giffins, an executive with 24 years of experience in the paint industry. After starting out at Sherwin-Williams he joined Kelly-Moore in 1985, serving as general merchandise manager. He then became vice-president of store operations two years later and played a key role in the growth and development of company stores. Giffins was named president of Kelly-Moore's southwest division in 1996. He was taking charge of a company ranked No. 32 in Coatings Work's Top Companies Report, with estimated annual sales of $350 million, one that had made the successful transition from its founder to a second generation of management. Although still a small player compared with industry giants, Kelly-Moore remained a very successful business, well entrenched in its niche in the market and positioned to thrive for the foreseeable future.

Principal Subsidiaries

Preservative Paint Co.; K-M Universal.

Principal Competitors

Benjamin Moore and Co.; E.I. du Pont de Nemours & Company; The Sherwin-Williams Company.

Further Reading

Bjerklie, Steve, "Leading with Service," *Modern Paint and Coatings,* October 1, 2000, p. 40.
Dill, Larry, "Paint Recycling: Kelly-Moore Is Supplying the Federal Government and Looking for Other Markets," *Modern Paint and Coatings,* January 1, 1995, p. 19.
Neal, Roger, "Color It Profitable," *Forbes,* January 28, 1985, p. 76.
Reitter, Chuck, "There Are No Ivory Towers in San Carlos, California," *American Paint & Coatings Journal,* February 3, 1986, p. 42.
Valero, Greg, and Bill Schmitt, "Regional Paint Makers Link to Serve National Accounts," *Chemical Week,* May 17, 2000, p. 39.

—Ed Dinger

Kohlberg Kravis Roberts & Co.

9 West 57th Street
New York, New York 10019
U.S.A.
Telephone: (212) 750-8300
Fax: (212) 593-2430
Web site: http://www.kkr.com

Private Company
Founded: 1976
Employees: 100 (est.)
Sales: $1.2 billion (1996 est.)
NAIC: 523120 Security Brokerage

Kohlberg Kravis Roberts & Co. (KKR) is one of the largest investment and merchant banking houses in the United States. In early 2003, its portfolio of companies in the United States and Europe boasted aggregate revenues of more than $20 billion, and included such well-known names as Owens-Illinois, Inc., Borden, Inc., Spalding Holdings Corporation, and Evenflo Company, Inc. A pioneer of the leveraged buyouts (LBOs) that privatized many American corporations in the 1980s, KKR has a number of deal-making firsts to its credit. In 1979, the firm staged the first large public-to-private transaction. Five years later, it executed the first billion-dollar public-to-private buyout. And in the biggest LBO ever, KKR purchased RJR Nabisco Inc. for $30.6 billion in 1989. Over the course of its first quarter-century in business, KKR has completed more than 100 deals with total financing of more than $100 billion. Although KKR cast a lower profile in the 1990s, it has continued to chalk up firsts, becoming one of the foremost American firms to finance a buyout in Europe in 1997. By 2003, it had six European companies in its portfolio.

A Decade of Megabuck Deals: 1976–86

Jerome Kohlberg, Jr., was in charge of the corporate finance department at the Wall Street firm of Bear, Stearns & Co. when he devised or first utilized, in 1965, the technique later to be called the leveraged buyout. Kohlberg believed a company would be better managed if it were owned by a small group of highly motivated investors—often including the top company executives—rather than thousands of shareholders who rarely had the knowledge or time to make sure the business was being run effectively. It would remain a key principle of KKR's operations throughout the firm's history. To raise the money, the investors would borrow heavily—as much as ten times the cash they actually contributed—usually pledging as collateral the assets of the company they intended to acquire. They would reap their profit by later selling the company to new owners or issuing stock to the public.

George Roberts and his cousin Henry Kravis became protégés of Kohlberg at Bear, Stearns, although Roberts relocated to the company's San Francisco office. They conducted 14 buyouts between 1969 and 1975 with generally mediocre results in a time of recession and falling stock prices. One of the companies they bought for $27 million, Cobblers Industries, went bankrupt. However, investors in Vapor Corporation, purchased in 1972 for about $37 million, recovered their stake 12-fold when the company was sold in 1978. Industrial Components Groups, a division of Rockwell International purchased in 1975, yielded 22 times the original investment in five years.

Restive at Bear, Stearns, Kohlberg persuaded Kravis and Roberts to join him in the partnership that opened its doors in 1976. KKR created an equity fund that KKR, as general partner, used to purchase companies. Adding to the pool were major lenders entitled to fixed returns and, where law permitted, sweeteners like warrants or common stock free or at bargain prices. A favorite inducement for banks was preferred stock, which offered an 85 percent tax exemption on dividends. Because of the huge debt incurred in LBOs, a prospective target had to be able to generate the high cash flow needed to make interest payments. This excluded high-technology companies with heavy research and development expenditures. The most attractive prospects were businesses like supermarket operators, provided they had little prior debt and a market niche that protected them from severe competitive pressures.

In 1977 KKR bought three companies, but investors were hard to find and the firm made no deals the next year. In 1979, however, KKR bought Houdaille Industries for about $355 million—by far the largest LBO transaction to that time and KKR's first buyout of a major publicly held company. Prior to

Company Perspectives:

KKR's business philosophy reflects a deep-seated belief that value is created by focusing on a few unshakable fundamentals: solid management, operational excellence, optimal capital structures, and a sound, long-term investment program. We have been able to successfully put our money to work through a wide range of economic situations—regardless of fluctuations in equity markets, lending rates, or lending capacity—and achieve excellent returns on large amounts of invested capital.

then no LBO had been for much more than $100 million. For investing $12 million of its own money, KKR received 37 percent of the voting common stock. Investors, including big banks, now began to come on board. By the fall of 1980 the firm had paid nearly $800 million to acquire seven companies with combined annual sales totaling about $1.3 billion.

Another breakthrough for KKR came in 1981, when Roberts tapped a conservative investor—Oregon's public employees' pension fund—to contribute $178 million for the leveraged buyout of Fred Meyer Inc., one of the seven companies KKR acquired that year. Soon other state pension funds, looking for a better yield than what they were earning from bonds, were willing to sign on. By 1986 11 state pension funds were partners in KKR equity pools. When KKR initiated a $5.6 billion fund—its largest ever—in 1987, the 11 provided 53 percent of the money.

In addition to pension funds and other limited partners willing to provide equity (about 10 percent of an LBO) and banks willing to make loans (60 percent), KKR needed subordinated lenders (30 percent), who earned a higher fixed rate by taking more risk because they were the last to get paid. Historically, insurance companies tended to be the main source of subordinated debt. By the mid-1980s, however, firms such as Drexel Burnham Lambert Inc. had assembled big money by attracting private investors to high-yield junk-bond funds that would assume the necessary risk.

For its own part, KKR collected the standard investment banking fee of around 1 percent for making a deal, which it usually invested in the stock of the acquired company. It also collected annual consulting fees from the acquired company. KKR partners sat on the boards of these companies and collected directors' fees. KKR also received a 1.5 percent annual management fee on the money in an equity fund not yet invested. But the real payoff for the firm was, as general partner, its 20 percent share of the capital gains from the eventual resale of the acquired company. KKR even took a fee—1 percent—when it sold a company at a loss. Everybody in the firm, from the partners to the secretaries, had a stake in the rewards.

By 1983 KKR was claiming an average annual return of 63 percent to its equity partners. That year KKR's fourth equity fund accumulated $1 billion from investors, enabling its roster of companies to reach 18, acquired for a total of $3.5 billion. KKR was using this money for ever-bigger deals. In 1985 the firm acquired Storer Communications for a record $2.5 billion. When Storer was sold in 1988, KKR's partners achieved an annual

return of around 50 percent. Also in 1985, KKR conducted its first hostile takeover; previously it had made an acquisition only when management (which got a stake in the deal) agreed.

KKR launched a new $2 billion fund in 1986. The acquisition of Safeway Stores Inc. that year was the best transaction KKR ever made, according to a *Fortune* article that appeared ten years later. The firm paid $4.3 billion but put down only $130 million itself and reaped more than $5 billion in realized and paper profits. KKR's remaining one-third stake in the company was valued at more than $3.5 billion in early 1997 and more than $7.4 billion by 2001. Even bigger was KKR's 1986 takeover of Beatrice Cos. for about $6.2 billion. The firm put up $402 million in equity capital, while Drexel provided $2.5 billion in junk bond financing. According to KKR, when the final returns from this deal were realized in 1992, limited partners enjoyed an annual return of 43 percent.

The Going Gets Tougher: 1987–89

By this time, however, Kohlberg was now on his way out. After spending 1984 recovering from a serious illness, he returned to find that he was not needed or wanted by his younger partners. Kohlberg was disturbed by KKR's ever more aggressive search for deals that disturbingly echoed the tactics of corporate raiders. He vetoed so many prospective deals that he became known at KKR as "Doctor No." Kohlberg resigned in 1987 to form his own company but remained a limited partner in KKR. In 1990 Kohlberg sued his partners, alleging that they had illegally reduced his ownership stake in several buyout deals. The suit was settled under undisclosed terms.

Of the remaining founders, Kravis was the one who cast the higher profile. While Roberts, in California, avoided the limelight, "King Henry," as the media dubbed Kravis, took fashion designer Carolyne Roehm as his second wife. The couple was prominent on the social scene, contributing heavily to charities and maintaining a Manhattan duplex apartment plus homes in Colorado, Connecticut, and Long Island.

There seemed to be no limit to KKR's dominance at this time. Having raised $5.6 billion for its 1987 fund, the firm bought eight companies in the next two years for $43.9 billion, among them the more than $1 billion purchases of Owens-Illinois, Duracell, and Stop & Shop. If ranked as a single industrial company, the businesses KKR controlled would have placed it among the top ten U.S. corporations. When stock prices plunged in October 1987, KKR secretly bought chunks of several top-level U.S. corporations but was unable to sell their chiefs on the LBO idea.

KKR's biggest LBO—indeed the biggest of all time—was its acquisition of RJR Nabisco, Inc. for $30.6 billion. The bidding started with a $17.5 billion offer from Shearson Lehman Hutton. Other interested parties included Merrill Lynch and Forstmann Little, neither of which charged a fee when it sold companies, an annual fee to manage them, or directors' fees for having their executives sit on the boards of the companies they controlled.

KKR topped Shearson, only to have the ante raised in turn by Forstmann Little. In what unsympathetic outsiders described as high-stakes macho posturing and a fitting end to a decade of greed, Kravis won the battle but clearly overpaid for his prize.

KKR had to take 58 percent of the company itself. In 1990 it needed to pump in $1.7 billion more for a $6.9 billion recapitalization of RJR, which, after going public in 1991, lost more than $3 billion of its market value in the next two years. In 1995 KKR traded its remaining stake in RJR for ownership of Borden Inc.

KKR made other mistakes during 1987–88. Jim Walter Corporation (later Walter Industries), purchased for about $2.4 billion, later went bankrupt. Seaman Furniture Co., acquired for about $360 million, had to be restructured in 1989 to avoid bankruptcy and was in bankruptcy during 1992–93. Hillsborough Holdings Corporation, purchased for $3.3 billion, went bankrupt in 1989. American Forest Products, acquired from Bendix for $425 million, was sold at a loss.

Adapting and Thriving in the 1990s

After the completion of the RJR Nabisco deal in February 1989, KKR did not make another LBO acquisition for three years, not because of any loss of nerve but due to the collapse of the junk bond market, a growing reluctance of banks to lend for this purpose, and fewer corporate raiders to put companies into play. To some degree, KKR was a victim of its own success, since companies increasingly had put their houses in order before they became vulnerable to a takeover. "Paying off debt, getting rid of divisions that are not up to snuff—companies can do that for themselves now," a University of Chicago professor told a *New York Times* reporter in 1995.

Without lucrative LBOs to put into effect, KKR became less attractive to partners like the state pension funds, which then began complaining about its fees. In 1989 KKR had reported an annualized rate of return of 19.5 percent, well below its average. Investors wanted higher yields to compensate for high risk and the need to keep their money tied up until there was a payoff in the form of a company sale. Bad publicity concerning fired Safeway workers riled some limited partners, especially public pension funds whose constituents included unionized workers.

One alternative KKR tried was "leveraged buildups." The firm bought a piece of Macmillan Inc. in 1989 and turned it into K-III Holdings Inc., a publishing and information resources conglomerate that had made 52 acquisitions by 1997, when it was renamed Primedia Inc. This venture was unusual in that KKR took and continued to hold most of the equity itself. A

similar transaction was KKR's 1991 injection of $283 million into Fleet/Norstar Financial Group for the purchase of the assets of the failed Bank of New England. KKR also took "toehold" minority positions in companies such as ConAgra Inc., Texaco Inc., and First Interstate Bancorp, remaining a passive investor.

KKR consoled itself and stilled its critics by taking six prior LBO acquisitions public in 1991 for a combined estimated $6 billion, which meant a six-fold return to the investors in five years, not counting the firm's own fees. In 1992 KKR purchased American Re-Insurance Co. for $1.2 billion, an LBO acquisition at $10 a share. Keeping a one-fourth stake, KKR took the company public only four months later at $31 a share. Also in 1992, the firm raised $1.8 billion for a new fund.

Even so, as the 1990s continued, disillusionment over KKR's performance became more vocal. A *Fortune* article claimed in 1994 that since the early 1980s the firm had barely outpaced the Standard & Poor 500 stock index, at least for its two largest investors, the Oregon and Washington state pension funds. In its 1996 annual report, Oregon's state treasury said it was disappointed with the returns on more than half of its $2.1 billion investment in KKR funds, of which $1.2 billion was in the 1987 fund. Burdened by poor-performing investments in RJR Nabisco and K-III, this fund had an average annual yield of only 12.6 percent through 1996.

As the stock market roared ahead in the mid-1990s, KKR improved its record by cashing in some more of its acquisitions. The sale of Duracell, which had gone public in 1991 as Duracell International Inc., in 1996 to Gillette Co. for stock valued at $7.9 billion brought KKR $3.7 billion for an original investment of $350 million. Between the beginning of 1995 and September 1996 it sold, for $7 billion, stock originally acquired for $1.3 billion. This included American Re for $3.3 billion and Stop & Shop for $1.8 billion. In 1996 alone the firm sold five companies for $5.3 billion.

These gains were counterbalanced by some losers. Flagstar Corporation, in which the firm had invested $300 million in 1992, filed for bankruptcy in 1997. KKR put up $250 million for the $1.15 billion LBO in 1995 of the Bruno's Inc. grocery chain but wrote off the entire sum in early 1998, when the company's debt had reached about $1 billion. Spalding & Evenflo Cos., in which KKR had invested $420 million, was barely covering its interest payments in early 1998. Primedia (the former K-III) was still losing money after almost a decade because of the heavy cost of making payments on its acquisition debts.

KKR raised a record $6 billion for its 1996 fund. To raise this sum, the firm agreed for the first time to deduct losses from its profits and to reduce its transaction fees. Among the subscribers was the Oregon pension fund, which despite its misgivings committed to $800 million after a sales call by Roberts. For KKR the year was the firm's most lucrative ever, with Kravis and Roberts each believed to have collected $300 million. Kravis's personal fortune was estimated at more than $1 billion.

2000 and Beyond

KKR made dramatic forays into Canada in the early years of the 21st century, completing the two largest LBOs in the country's history in 2000 and 2002. Shoppers Drug Mart was acquired in 2000 for about $1.7 billion. Two years later, KKR took the directories unit of Bell Canada Enterprises private for C$3 billion ($1.9 billion). *Buyouts* magazine described the deal in 2003 as "[an] asset that offered stable, predictable cash flow and low capital requirements," all key selling points for KKR. It was, at the time, Canada's largest-ever LBO.

The firm also entered the European LBO market at the turn of the century, completing some of the largest deals the continent had seen. KKR initiated this effort in 1996, amassing a EUR 3 billion fund by 1999. Early acquisitions included Newsquest, a British newspaper publisher; insurance company Willis Corroon; and engineering firm TI Group. KKR made its biggest European LBOs to date in 2002. It took Legrand SA, a French manufacturer of electrical equipment, private for EUR 3.6 billion, and bought seven Siemens subsidiaries for EUR 1.7 billion. The Siemens companies were amalgamated under a holding company, Demag Holding s.a.r.l., and included Demag Cranes & Components, Gottwald Port Technology, Mannesmann Plastics & Machinery, Stabilus, Networks Systems, and Ceramics and Metering, with a combined annual sales volume of EUR 3.5 billion.

During this same period, KKR managed, for the most part, to avoid the telecom and dot-com debacle. In 2001, however, it had to write off its barely two-year-old, $210 million investment in Birch Telecom Inc. KKR made relatively small investments in Desktop.com, Starmedia, Mypoints.com, PlanetRX, and LivePerson as well. Its forays into the online world included a relatively modest partnership with Accel Partners to create Accel-KKR Internet Co., a venture capital firm charged with merging companies' on- and off-line capabilities.

KKR looked forward to completing a $610 million purchase of International Transmission Co., an electricity transmission company, in the first quarter of 2003. It was, at the time, the largest deal of its type, and KKR indicated that it would continue to look for deals in the electricity transmission industry.

Although the firm continued to enjoy success in the early years of the 21st century, the question of succession at KKR loomed large. Founding partners and cousins Henry Kravis and George Roberts were both due to turn 60 by January 2004, and even though both expected to continue with the company thereafter, they concomitantly worked to prepare the firm to outlast them. These preparations included shifting equity stakes in the firm to other partners, or, as KKR called them, "members." The principal owners also cultivated a cadre of legal, accounting, and investment banking professionals to carry on their legacy. An effort to encourage longtime institutional investors the Washington State Investment Board and the Oregon Investment Council to purchase ownership stakes in KKR failed, however. In fact, the firm's Millennium Fund drive actually accumulated less money than its previous pool. Jacqueline Gold of *Crain's New York Business* posited, "Without the charismatic and reassuring presence of its name partners, putting together a multibillion-dollar pot will be that much harder" in the future.

Principal Competitors

Hicks, Muse, Tate & Furst, Inc.; Clayton, Dubilier & Rice, Inc.; Forstmann Little & Co.

Further Reading

Anders, George, *Merchants of Debt: KKR and the Mortgaging of American Business,* Frederick, Md.: Beard Group, 2002.

Anreder, Steven S., "High-Wire Finance," *Barron's,* September 24, 1979, pp. 4–6, 8, 20.

Arenson, Karen W., "Kohlberg's Leveraged Success," *New York Times,* September 29, 1980, pp. D1, D5.

Baker, George, and George David Smith, *The New Financial Capitalists: Kohlberg Kravis Roberts and the Creation of Corporate Value,* Cambridge University Press, 1998.

Bartlett, Sarah, *The Money Machine: How KKR Manufactured Power and Profits,* New York: Warner Books, 1991.

Bianco, Anthony, "KKR Hears a New Word from Some Backers: 'No'," *Business Week,* April 15, 1991, pp. 80–82.

Bilefsky, Dan, "Benchmark Deal Sets KKR Up with European Base," *Financial Times,* March 16, 1999, p. 27.

Board, Laura, "KKR Drops U.K. Safeway Interest," *Daily Deal,* February 25, 2003.

Burrough, Bryan, and John Helyar, *Barbarians at the Gate,* New York: Harper & Row, 1990.

Carey, David, "Mediocrity at the Gates," *Daily Deal,* May 31, 2001.

Clow, Robert, "KKR's European Push Makes Up for Lost Time," *Financial Times,* January 24, 2003, p. 24.

Eichenwald, Kurt, "Kohlberg, Kravis Rouses Itself," *New York Times,* April 29, 1991, pp. D1, D7.

Farrell, Christopher, "King Henry," *Business Week,* November 14, 1988, pp. 125–27.

Gold, Jacqueline, "KKR on Fine Line of Succession," *Crain's New York Business,* December 23, 2002, p. 1.

Green, Leslie, "Kohlberg Kravis Roberts & Co.," *Buyouts,* March 12, 2001.

——, "Live Deals: KKR Makes Move into Utility Mart," *Buyouts,* February 21, 2001.

Holman, Kelly, "KKR-Backed Telecom Goes Bust," *Daily Deal,* July 29, 2002.

Hylton, Richard D., "How KKR Got Beaten at Its Own Game," *Fortune,* May 2, 1994, pp. 104–06.

Jereski, Laura, "How KKR Recovered from Some Trouble, Chalked Up a Big Year," *Wall Street Journal,* December 31, 1996, pp. 1–2.

Kleinfeld, N. R., "Kohlberg Collects Companies," *New York Times,* December 12, 1983, pp. D1, D5.

Kosman, Josh, and David Snow, "KKR Delves into Europe with $3B Fund," *Venture Capital Journal,* February 1, 1999.

——, "KKR Taps Merrill Lynch to Help Raise Euro Fund," *Buyouts,* May 31, 1999.

Lane, Amy, "DTE Energy Faces Challenge to Sale of Transmission Unit," *Crain's Detroit Business,* January 13, 2002, p. 4.

Leibowitz, Alissa, "News: Accel and KKR Merge Worlds," *Venture Capital Journal,* April 1, 2000.

Lipin, Steven, "KKR Is Back, and It Boasts Big War Chest," *Wall Street Journal,* September 16, 1996, pp. C1, C15.

Loomis, Carol J., "Ten Years After," *Fortune,* February 17, 1997, pp. 114–17.

MacFadyen, Ken, "Bell Canada Enterprises' Directories Unit," *Buyouts,* February 17, 2003.

Moriarty, George, "KKR Execs, Two VCs, Put $29M on Desktop Deal," *Buyouts,* Sept 13, 1999.

Morris, John E., "A Bridge Too Far?," *Daily Deal,* August 2, 2002.

Nathans, Leah J., "KKR Is Doing Just Fine—Without LBOs," *Business Week,* July 30, 1990, pp. 56–59.

Primack, Dan, "Bell Canada Sells Off Phone Directories," *Buyouts,* September 23, 2002.

Ross, Irwin, "How the Champs Do Leveraged Buyouts," *Fortune,* January 23, 1984, pp. 70, 72, 74, 78.

Rustin, Richard E., "Kohlberg Kravis Hones Its Takeover Technique," *Wall Street Journal,* September 25, 1980, pp. 35, 38.

Schifrin, Matthew, "LBO Madness," *Forbes,* March 9, 1998, pp. 130–31, 133–34.

Siklos, Richard, "Bumper Years Ahead for Buyouts," *Sunday Telegraph,* February 2, 2003, p. 7.

Sikora, Martin, "Transmission Carve-Outs Generate M&A Transactions," *Mergers & Acquisitions Journal,* January 1, 2003.

Sormani, Angela, "Senior Debt," *European Venture Capital Journal,* September 2002, p. S4.

Spiro, Leah Nathans, "KKR Plays a Slower Game," *Business Week,* June 29, 1990, pp. 96–97.

Truell, Peter, "At KKR the Glory Days Are Past," *New York Times,* August 10, 1995, pp. D1, D4.

—Robert Halasz
—update: April D. Gasbarre

Korea Electric Power Corporation (Kepco)

167 Samsong-dong, Kangnam-gu
Seoul 135-791
South Korea
Telephone: (+82) 2-3456-3633
Fax: (+82) 2-3456-3699
Web site: http://www.kepco.co.kr

Public Company
Incorporated: 1898 as Hansung Electric Company
Employees: 18,912
Sales: W 21.04 trillion ($17.53 billion) (2002)
Stock Exchanges: Korea New York
Ticker Symbol: KEP
NAIC: 221122 Electric Power Distribution

State-owned Korea Electric Power Corporation, also known as Kepco, is in the process of dismantling its more than 40-year monopoly of South Korea's electric power industry. Since 2001, Kepco has been restructuring its operations, splitting up its nonnuclear power generation operations into five separate, regional businesses—Korea South-East Power Co. (KOSEPCO), Korea Southern Power Co. (KOSPO), Korea Midland Power Co. (KOMIPO), Korea Western Power Co. (KOWEPO), and Korea East-West Power Co. (KEWESPO). The restructuring also includes plans to privatize these subsidiaries, with the first of the new companies, Kosepco, slated to be privatized by the end of 2003. As part of its restructuring, Kepco also has created a sixth business, Korea Hydro & Nuclear Power Co. (KHNP), which takes over all of the company's nuclear power and hydroelectric power generating facilities, accounting for nearly 40 percent of the group's total power generation capacity (with virtually no domestic resources, the group's coal- and gas-powered generators rely almost entirely on fossil fuel imports). Following deregulation of the domestic power generation market, Kepco will give up its monopoly on power distribution by 2009. In response, Kepco has begun to diversify its operations, primarily with a move into the international power generation arena. The company has been operating in the Philippines since the early 1990s, including the country's largest power plant, which began providing power in 2002. The company also expected to expand into China. Listed on both the Korean and New York Stock Exchanges, Kepco remains 54 percent controlled by the Korean government.

Royal Origins in the Late 19th Century

Soon after Thomas Edison connected the first electric light bulb, the Korean government, then in the waning decades of the final Han dynasty under King Kojong, sent a delegation to visit Edison and view his invention. Edison convinced the delegation of the need for electric lighting in King Kojong's Kyongbok palace. Orders for a generator were placed in 1884; political unrest, including an attempted coup, pushed back completion of the first generator, and the palace lights were not switched on until early 1887.

Initial reception of the new technology was limited, with many fearful of electricity as a supernatural force. The technology suffered a new setback when the original engineer assigned by Edison to install the generator died in an accidental shooting. Nonetheless, King Kojong remained supportive of the technology and ordered a new generator for Changdok Palace, which, at the time of its completion in 1897, was the largest power generator in the region. By 1891, the original Kyongbok power plant was replaced with a new and larger facility, which was completed in 1894.

By the end of the decade, the royal government had recognized the potential of electrical power and became determined to extend it to the public sector. In 1898, King Kojong granted authorization for the creation of a joint venture with two American businessmen, Henry Collbran and Harry Rice Bostwick, called the Hansung (or Seoul) Electric Company. The new company, 50 percent owned by the king himself, was charged with establishing a public electrical lighting network in Seoul, and contracted with Collbran and Bostwick Company to build an electric streetcar system as well.

Hansung Electric completed its first power plant in 1899 at Tongdaemun. By the end of that year, the company had succeeded in launching its streetcar service, and soon after had turned on its first electric lights in Seoul's Chongno Street. With a monopoly on Seoul's electricity and streetcar systems,

Company Perspectives:

KEPCO of the future will be a major world player that provides all customers with the best electric power products and services available.

Hansung Electric continued to build up its public lighting network into the turn of the century, and began offering electrical service to private homes as well.

The occupation of Korea by Japan following 1905 brought new competition to Hansung Electric. A group of Japanese businessmen set up a rival, gas-lighting system, which proved highly competitive for some time. Meanwhile, Hansung Electric's American owners were under increasing pressure to sell out to its Japanese rivals, in a deal that cut out the country's former ruler. Under Japanese occupation, Korea's electrical power system continued to develop, and a number of new companies were established, including Kyungsung Electric Company in 1915, the Chosun Electric Company in 1943, and the Namsun Electric Company in 1946. Nonetheless, the bulk of Japanese investments in power generation went to the northern half of the country—as Korea itself had virtually no natural fuel deposits, the country's power plants were established closer to Chinese coal supplies.

Japan's capitulation at the end of World War II led to the division of Korea into the Allied-dominated south and the Soviet-dominated north in 1945. In the initial postwar years, the northern half of the country continued to supply the southern half with electrical power. Yet the outbreak of the Korean War in 1950 caused the power grid between the two halves to be cut overnight—leaving South Korea, with its undeveloped power generation capacity, in economic chaos. Power shortages became commonplace, especially as the war destroyed much of South Korea's existing electrical power infrastructure. In the years following the war, the Korean government initiated a number of power-saving measures, such as not allowing elevators to stop at the first three floors of buildings, and barring escalators from early subway stations.

Government-Led Electrical Power Company: 1960s–80s

The military-backed coup of 1961 and the installation of a military government introduced a new period not only to Korea's economy but to its electrical power sector as well. In 1961, the government grouped together the three existing regional companies, Kyongsung, Namsun, and Chosun, to form a single, nationally operating electric power entity, Korea Electric Company, which became known as KECO.

While austerity measures continued through the 1970s, the government began ambitious investment and development programs that were ultimately successful in transforming South Korea into one of the region's financial and industrial heavyweights. Part of that development program included massive investments in boosting the country's power generation capacity.

Yet the government recognized early on that South Korea's lack of natural resources made it too dependent on foreign resources for its power supply. As early as 1962, the country initiated plans to develop its own nuclear power industry with the aim of reducing its reliance on fossil fuels. Backed by the United States, Korea launched its nuclear development program. In the meantime, the country was hit hard by the Arab Oil Embargo and the resulting worldwide recession in the early 1970s, stimulating its drive toward nuclear power capacity.

Korea brought its first nuclear-based power generation facility online in 1978. That plant, the Kori-1, was built by the United States' Westinghouse and boasted a capacity of nearly 600 megawatts. The country also began awarding contracts for new nuclear plants, with eight new plants to open by the end of the 1980s. In the meantime, the Korean government moved to take complete control of KECO, which was then renamed Korean Electric Power Corporation, or Kepco, a move that took place in 1982.

Throughout the 1980s, Kepco continued adding nuclear power facilities to its grid, bringing the country's total to nine by the end of the decade. The company also began planning its next phase of reactors—meant to bring the country's total to some 17 by the turn of the century. Yet now the company's awards went toward companies willing to include technology transfers in their bids, as Kepco sought to develop its own reactor designs in the late 1980s. In the meantime, the company's total nuclear output topped 4.75 million kilowatts by 1986, representing 26 percent of its total power generation capacity.

Preparing for Deregulation in the New Century

Kepco went public in 1989 as part of the Korean government's larger privatization program. In that year, the company, already one of Korea's largest nonfinancial corporations, listed some 21 percent of its stock on the Korean stock exchange. The government remained in control of the decision-making, however—particularly its policy of charging low rates to industrial and other customers, including farmers, in order to stimulate the economy. While this policy achieved its goal, it hampered Kepco's ability to invest in new power generation capacity. The company remained profitable, however, posting earnings of $557 million on 1993 revenues of $9.3 billion.

Kepco continued to target growth in its domestic market into the mid-1990s, announcing a five-year, $40 billion investment program to boost its generating capacity by more than 60 percent. The company, which listed its shares (as ADRs) on the New York Stock Exchange in 1994, also had adopted a new strategic direction: that of international expansion. This new strategy came in part because of increasing signs of the Korean government's interest in opening up the domestic power market to competition—a move that originally was expected to occur as early as 1997.

Kepco's first step onto the international front came in 1993, when it was awarded a contract to upgrade and operate a power generating facility in Minala, in the Philippines. In 1995, Kepco increased its presence in that country when it received a contract to relocate two of its existing Korean power plants to Cebu, also in the Philippines, which boosted the group's total generating capacity in the Philippines to more than 1,000 MW (as compared with its total Korean capacity of 28,000 MW).

Key Dates:

1887: The first electric lights are turned on in Korea's Kyongbok palace.
1898: Americans are contracted to build an electric network in Seoul, forming the Hansung (Seoul) Electric Company (50 percent owned by the King).
1910: Japan occupies Korea and takes over Seoul Electric.
1915: Kyungsung Electric Company is founded.
1943: Chosun Electric Company is founded.
1946: Namsun Electric Company is founded.
1950: Korean War cuts off South Korea from the North Korean electricity network.
1961: South Korean government leads the merger of Kyungsung, Chosun, and Namsun into the new Korea Electric Company.
1962: South Korea launches an investment program in nuclear power generation facilities.
1978: The first nuclear-powered generator in South Korea comes online.
1982: Korea Electric is taken over by the government and renamed Korea Electric Power Corporation, or Kepco.
1989: Kepco goes public with 21 percent of shares.
1999: Government announces deregulation of the domestic electricity market and the restructuring of Kepco.
2001: Kepco restructures by separating its power generation operations into six independently operating subsidiaries.

Calls for deregulation gathered steam in the late 1990s as the Korean economy reeled again from the crisis that had affected much of the region. Kepco began a new restructuring drive in preparation for the coming deregulation. Part of the company's preparation involved the hiring of a new chief executive—the first to be chosen through an open recruitment process. The new CEO, Chang Young-sik, launched the company on a restructuring drive, shedding a number of businesses—including its telecommunications investments, some of which were spun off into a new company, Powercomm, in 2000. Kepco also cut back its workforce by more than 3,700.

Nonetheless, Kepco remained hampered by a spiraling debt, which in the last half of the 1990s had more than doubled, topping W 33 trillion by 2000, including some $10 billion in foreign debt. By then the broad outline of the government's plans for the company were in place, involving the breaking up of Kepco into a number of independently operating power generating subsidiaries. But these plans met with growing resistance from the country's unions, forcing the company to make a number of concessions, including a pledge to retain majority control of the companies to be spun off. At the same time, analysts warned that Kepco would have to raise its rates—and especially its artificially low industrial rates—if the privatization effort was to succeed.

Massive strikes across the country forced the government to place Kepco's restructuring and the deregulation of the Korean market on hold until 2001. In that year, the company created six new subsidiaries, five of which—Korea South-East Power Co. (KOSEPCO), Korea Southern Power Co. (KOSPO), Korea Midland Power Co. (KOMIPO), Korea Western Power Co. (KOWEPO), and Korea East-West Power Co. (KEWESPO)—represented the company's regionally operating fossil fuel generating facilities and were slated to be sold off as privatized companies to foreign and domestic investors. The sixth company, Korea Hydro & Nuclear Power Co. (KHNP), which grouped the company nuclear and hydroelectric facilities, was to remain under Kepco's control.

The first of the companies slated for privatization was KOSEPCO, which was also the smallest. Initially slated for 2001, the sale, which faced continued resistance, appeared to be finally under way at the beginning of 2003, when the government promised to select its preferred bidder. At the same time, the government reiterated its determination to privatize all five of Kepco's power generating subsidiaries, with an eye toward full deregulation—including distribution to private homes—by 2009.

Before then Kepco expected to become one of the region's powerhouses, announcing plans to expand throughout the region. As part of that strategy, the company created a new subsidiary, Kepco International, in November 2002, which took over the operations of its former overseas division. At the same time, the company debuted its latest foreign venture, a 1.2 MW natural gas power plant in Ilijan, in the Philippines, the country's largest.

Kepco continued to seek new international projects in 2003, with bids on ten different projects in markets including Saudi Arabia, the United Arab Emirates, and Myanmar. In February 2003, the company announced plans to build a new 500 MW power plant in Indonesia, with construction slated to start in 2004. At the same time, Kepco was finalizing contracts to begin construction of two coal-fired power plants in China. Kepco expected to have the first of the two plants, which were to have a combined capacity of more than 600,000 MW, operational by the end of 2004. Kepco, which celebrated more than 100 years of history lighting Korea, expected to become a regional powerhouse for the new century.

Principal Subsidiaries

Korea Hydro & Nuclear Power Co. Ltd.; Korea South-East Power Co. Ltd.; Korea Midland Power Co. Ltd.; Korea Western Power Co. Ltd.; Korea Southern Power Co. Ltd.; Korea East-West Power Co. Ltd.; Korea Power Engineering Co. Ltd.; Korea Plant Service & Engineering Co. Ltd.; KEPCO Nuclear Fuel Co. Ltd.; Korea Electric Power Industrial Develop' Co. Ltd.; Kepco International Philippines, Inc.

Principal Competitors

State Power Corporation of China; Huaneng Power International Inc.; SembCorp Industries; Perusahaan Listrik Negara PT; Hongkong Electric Holdings Ltd.; Manila Electric Company.

Further Reading

Chon, Gina, "South Korea to Resume Sale of Power Plants," *Daily Deal*, April 2, 2002.

''KEPCO Eyeing Boosting Power Industry Efficiency Through Restructuring,'' *Korea Herald,* July 30, 2002.

''KEPCO's Aggressive Restructuring to Bring W2.3 Tril. in Profits,'' *Korea Times,* March 11, 1999.

Kim, Mi-hui, ''All Five Power Companies to Be Privatized,'' *Korea Herald,* Jan 28, 2003.

——, ''KEPCO to Expand Overseas Business,'' *Korea Herald,* November 15, 2002.

Kirk, Don, ''South Korea: Utility to Start Privatization,'' *New York Times,* October 10, 2002.

''Korea's Kepco to Decide on Prime Bidder for Kosep Next Month,'' *Asia Pulse News,* February 7, 2003.

Ward, Andrew, ''Korea Begins Kepco Sell-Off,'' *Financial Times,* July 16, 2002, p. 31.

—M.L. Cohen

Kotobukiya

Kotobukiya Co., Ltd.

3-3-3 Honjo
Kumamoto City 860
Japan
Telephone: (96) 366 3111
Fax: (96) 372 7470

Public Company
Incorporated: 1949
Employees: 2,235
Sales: ¥285.17 billion (US$2.29 billion) (2002)
Stock Exchanges: Osaka
NAIC: 445110 Supermarkets and Other Grocery (Except Convenience) Stores

Founded shortly after the end of World War II, Kotobukiya Co., Ltd. became the leading retailer in Japan's southern island of Kyushu. At its height, the company operated some 134-supermarket outlets under the name Kotobukiya and about 300 other specialty boutiques, selling everything from fashion to food and electric appliances. Like many Japanese retail chains, Kotobukiya provided the full range of shopping-related services, and was actively involved in the credit, travel, property leasing, and restaurant businesses. Hard hit by Japan's economic recession in the 1990s, the company was forced to file for bankruptcy protection in December 2001. The company sold off its retail outlets to a number of Japanese retailers, including Chiba Prefecture-based Aeon Co., and is now in the process of repaying ¥37.7 billion in liabilities before its final liquidation.

Origins of a Retail Chain: 1947

Kotobukiya originated in Kyushu, Japan's second most populated and industrialized island. The island is divided into seven provinces and contains the major industrial cities of Nagasaki and Fukuoka. It was in Nagasaki that Japan first had contact with the Western world in the 16th century and until 1868 it remained the only port open to foreign vessels.

Kotobukiya's founder, Sueko Suzaki, was born in 1904 in Saiki, a small town on the east coast of Kyushu, where she lived with her husband and family. After her husband was killed in World War II, she had to raise her family on her own. In postwar Japan there was limited opportunity for women to obtain employment, so in 1947, using her savings, she opened a small store of only 12 square meters selling handbags and cosmetics bags that she made herself. Suzaki named the shop Kotobukiya, which is another reading of the first Japanese character in the name Suzaki. Through her hard work, the shop flourished and Suzaki began selling decorative scrolls and other trinkets. Japan's defeat in World War II meant that in the early postwar years its economy was largely dominated by the United States and to some extent this also applied to consumer fashions. Realizing this, Suzaki began to stock items imported from the United States and gave her shop an American atmosphere.

Formulating a Strategy for Expansion: 1955–70

This expansion of the business caused Suzaki's eldest son Hajime to leave his job in a Tokyo tax office and return home in 1953 to help with the family business. The following year, in order to combat inflation and stabilize the economy, which was still fairly weak, the local authorities initiated controls that dictated prices for certain goods, making it easier for retailers and consumers to plan their finances. At the first company meeting in 1955, Sueko and Hajime Suzaki and the store's ten employees formulated their strategy for expansion. Novel promotional ideas were used to advertise the store; five female models were brought from Kyoto to promote the goods; and free samples were handed out. Then Kotobukiya began staff training, which was to become an important factor in the company's success. Employees were taught how to present the souvenirs sold in the store and how to serve the customer with respect.

In 1957, ten years after opening her first store, Suzaki opened another in the city of Miyazaki, south of Saiki. To raise money, half of the company's shares were sold to the employees. At the time the firm's capitalization was only ¥1.25 million—slightly less than $3,700. The two stores' combined shop floor area had increased to 1,800 square meters and a management system encouraging employee participation was introduced. The Miyazaki branch, located in a far more prosperous

---

Key Dates:

1947: Sueko Suzaki opens the original Kotobukiya, a 12-square-foot store where she sells her own handmade cosmetics and hand bags.

1955: Kotobukiya holds its first company meeting, during which Sueko, her brother Hajime Suzaki, and the store's ten employees formulate their strategy for expansion.

1957: Ten years after opening Kotobukiya, Suzaki opens a second store in the city of Miyazaki, south of Saiki.

1960: Kotobukiya Company is formed as a holding company.

1973: Kotobukiya becomes a listed company with its shares traded on the Fukuoka Exchange.

1976: The Company moves its listing to the Osaka Exchange.

1979: The 100th Kotobukiya store is opened in Kumamoto.

1980: Two new companies are formed: Kyushu Consultants, providing leasing and finance services, and Kotobukiya Land, dealing in real estate.

1983: The company implements "total quality control," a system subsequently used throughout Japanese business.

1995: Hajime Suzaki, the company's cofounder and top advisor, announces his resignation and plans to sell his family's 20 million shares in the company.

2001: Kotobukiya files for bankruptcy protection.

---

and populated area than Saiki, flourished. A Western products division was formed in 1960, and in the same year Kotobukiya Company was formed as a holding company. The year 1961 saw the opening of the company's first food supermarket in Saiki. The range of products sold in all the stores was enlarged to include processed foods and household items. In 1962 and 1963 several new stores—referred to as compact department stores—were opened, not as large as some of the bigger stores, but still selling a wide range of goods.

As president of the firm, Hajime Suzaki took the leading role in expanding the company and in 1963 visited the United States to observe retailing operations and methods. He studied inventory control and supermarket promotion and picked out aspects of U.S. retailing methods that he thought applicable to his own operation. One was the development of a strong brand image associated with the store, and he sought to apply uniform standards to all Kotobukiya stores so that customers could expect similar service in each branch. By 1966 capitalization had reached ¥40 million and, as a result of growing consumer demand, Kotobukiya continued to open new stores at the rate of about ten a year while closing down or moving smaller and less productive premises. That year, the original store in Saiki was closed and moved to a new location nearby. The company also began sending its store managers on overseas training courses and in the following year a formalized management training program was organized, with 13 new university graduates joining the company. With 400 employees, Kotobukiya was a medium-sized company and Hajime Suzaki decided to move it

to the city of Kumamoto on Kyushu's west coast. The four-story headquarters also contained a department store.

Diversification in the 1970s and 80s

With the large amount of real estate that the company owned or rented, Suzaki diversified successfully into property leasing. In 1970 a training program was set up for the sales staff—Japanese department stores provided, and the customers expected, excellent service and Suzaki strove to provide this by comprehensive staff training. In 1971 Kotobukiya opened Bouquet, its first specialty store in Kagoshima, which aimed to be the most modern in the region. The chain grew quickly, selling fashion goods aimed at the youth market. Frequent overseas trips to the United States and Europe by store managers meant that the company was well versed in the latest western fashion trends, many of which were copied in Japan.

In 1972 Kotobukiya formed a partnership with the Southern Japan Trust Bank to provide customers with credit services. The following year Kotobukiya became a listed company with its shares traded on the Fukuoka Exchange, moving to the Osaka Exchange in 1976. The range of goods sold at Kotobukiya's stores by then included electrical goods, leisure equipment, and imported liquor. The year 1977 marked the 30th anniversary of the company, and to celebrate the occasion Kotobukiya donated ¥100 million to local charities in Kyushu. In this year, sales reached the ¥100 billion mark—about $500 million—and new stores continued to be opened at the rate of about 12 per year. To cope with the necessary staffing requirements, a training center was opened, and in 1979 alone 1,400 people joined the company. The 100th Kotobukiya store was opened in Kumamoto and in 1980 two new companies were formed: Kyushu Consultants, providing leasing and finance services, and Kotobukiya Land, dealing in real estate. To remain competitive, the chain cut prices on groceries at its supermarkets. A new computer system allowed management to control stock more tightly and undercut smaller retailers. By 1981 the chain was ranked 19th among Japanese retailers and employed more than 10,000. Twenty-four-hour convenience stores were launched and an overseas trading company was set up to supply the stores with selected imported goods. For this purpose, a representative office was set up in Korea. Meanwhile, Kotobukiya entered two new areas of retailing, fresh fruits and marine products.

In 1983 the company implemented a system subsequently used throughout Japanese business—total quality control. Store managers were introduced to the system, the aim of which was to ensure that there was no price, stock, or quality variation across the chain and a computer system was used to verify this. At the frequent store managers' meetings, exchanges of ideas and information were encouraged. In 1984 Kotobukiya opened its first Sunpark leisure center and in the same year began issuing credit cards that could be used at Kotobukiya stores: there were 23,000 subscribers in the first year. In that year, the Japanese government promoted the industrial development of Kyushu and Shikoku, Japan's smallest island, under the Technopolis scheme and Kotobukiya donated ¥100 million to the project. The year 1985 marked the appointment of the first woman in charge of a Kotobukiya store—well overdue considering that in addition to having a woman as founder, over half of the company's staff were women.

Consolidation in the Late 1980s

Partly in response to overexpansion in the late 1970s and early 1980s and partly due to management plans to concentrate on larger stores, 19 branches were closed in 1985 resulting in job cuts—the workforce fell from 10,000 in 1982 to 6,000 by early 1986—and decreased revenues. Profits, however, remained steady. Hajime Suzaki was concerned that the bureaucracy of the company had become too large, and there was a management shakeup in 1986. The headquarters was reorganized into three divisions with 11 subdivisions. Early retirement was sought for some, and younger key staff were promoted. Responding to changing times, the company entered the video rental business and began importing directly from mainland China via a trading department set up within the company.

In response to the growing use of credit cards in Japan, Kotobukiya began accepting various cards and formed a partnership with Visa to issue a new card. The company began to consider permitting shopping by telephone, allowing customers at selected stores to arrange purchase and delivery from home or office. Kotobukiya, like most large Japanese companies at this time, took advantage of the booming Japanese stock market and engaged in *zaitech*—financial engineering—to generate profits. The company also looked to the European warrant market to raise capital, with a $100 million issue in the United Kingdom in 1988. Further consolidation occurred in 1988 and 1989 when 24 Kotobukiya stores were closed. This resulted in a less than 1 percent drop in sales during that period, indicating the soundness of management decisions. The management relied on its up-to-date computer system to identify the most inefficient stores.

In 1990 the company's founder Sueko Suzaki died at the age of 86, having long since retired from active management within the company she started. Following her death, her son Hajime took over as chairman of Kotobukiya, leaving the post of president open to a nonfamily member, Yutaka Yonekawa. Hajime's son Shigeru was a managing director in the company. Although the collapse of the Japanese stock market in 1990 and 1991 did not immediately weaken Japan's consumer spending boom, which had begun in the late 1980s, it affected corporate earnings considerably. Companies that had engaged in stock and real estate speculation were hit hard, although Kotobukiya was not as exposed as some companies. With the credit squeeze and raising of interest rates imposed by the Bank of Japan, funds for expansion and investment became increasingly scarce. In the wake of this, net operating profits decreased slightly in 1990 to ¥F5.6 billion or $39 million.

In 1990 the company pursued its policy of careful investment in training and facilities, concentrating on the expansion of point-of-sales information control systems and the refurbishing of stores to meet customer demand. Trade negotiations between Japan and the United States then emphasized the large-scale retail stores. The United States wanted to see certain retailing and distribution restrictions for foreign companies lifted to promote increased competition in this sector. Kotobukiya management conceded that retailing trends were hard to predict and it therefore responded to what it saw as current trends. Uncertain how long the consumer boom would continue, Hajime Suzaki and the management of Kotobukiya were content to adopt a cautious approach to expansion in the first half of the 1990s.

Suffering Under Economic Recession in the 1990s

By 1991, sales in Japan had begun to drop off considerably as the country entered recession. As Kotobukiya's sales dropped 1.5 percent to ¥135,735 million, the company was surpassed by its rival, Uneed, as the number one-selling supermarket operator in the Kyushu region. Still, Kotobukiya managed to offset the decline in sales with the increased efficiency of its point of sales system, thus maintaining solid profitability. As of yet, no major change of strategy seemed necessary. The company planned to continue its course of opening new stores, expanding existing stores, and freeing itself of unprofitable stores. In 1994, the company announced plans to open a women's wear shop in Taipei as a preliminary step to position itself to enter the mainland China market. Further, in February 1995, Kotobukiya became the first Japanese company to list bonds on the Hong Kong Stock Exchange, a move aimed at raising capital for the construction of new retail outlets.

In April 1995, however, in what was perhaps the first sign of trouble at Kotobukiya, Hajime Suzaki, the company's co-founder and top advisor, announced his resignation, as well as plans to sell his family's 20 million shares in the company, citing differences with Nishi-Nippon Bank, the company's main creditor bank and a significant force on its board of directors. Suzaki contended that Kotobukiya's survival would depend on the introduction of support from another major retailer, which he hoped to attain with the sale of his family's shares, about 20 percent of the total shares issued by the company. Nishi-Nippon opposed the sale. After various other attempts to raise capital proved insufficient, Kotobukiya announced in August 1999 that it would close its representative offices in Hong Kong, South Korea, and Shanghai within the business year, leaving one office in Taiwan as its only remaining overseas operation. The closures were deemed necessary to save the company an estimated ¥80 million annually.

Even with such drastic measures, circumstances for Kotobukiya did not improve measurably, and by September 2001, the company announced a negative net worth of ¥14.8 billion. Further, the company then held ¥170 billion in interest-bearing debt. After a failed attempt to secure a capital tie-up with Sun Live Co., another southwestern-Japan-based supermarket operator, Kotobukiya was forced to file for federal bankruptcy protection in December 2001, which further resulted in its delisting from the Osaka Securities Exchange.

Initially, Kotobukiya planned to cope with its financial difficulties by shutting down 44 of its 134 retail outlets, a 30 percent downsizing that entailed laying off all of its 2,200 full-time employees. Indeed, the company resolved to give up its status as the biggest supermarket in Kyushu, and to concentrate mainly on selling foodstuffs, rather than the broad range of household appliances and other goods it had formerly carried, in order to reduce costs. By January 2002, however Kotobukiya's restructuring plan was further thwarted by the refusal of many of its suppliers to deliver goods, fearing that the ailing company would be unable to make payments on them. Kotobukiya was subsequently forced to halt operations at all of its retail outlets. In February 2002, it laid off essentially all of its workforce.

After failing to find a single sponsor to take over the bulk of its operations, Kotobukiya resolved to parcel off its stores to a number of companies in hopes of securing re-employment agreements for its employees. The biggest buyer was Chiba Prefecture-based Aeon Co. (formerly Jusco Co.), a nationwide supermarket chain that agreed to take over 50 of Kotobukiya's outlets, for an estimated price of more than ¥10 billion. Aeon aspired to be one of the ten largest retailers in the world by 2010. Other prospective buyers of remaining Kotobukiya outlets included Hiroshima-based Izumi Co. and Kagoshima-based Taiyo Co.

By July 2002, Kotobukiya had submitted a ten-year rehabilitation proposal to the Kumamoto District Court. Under the plan, the company would repay ¥37.7 billion in debt by reshaping itself as a real estate management company and earning profits from the rental or sales of its various properties in Kyushu and Yamaguchi. Following the fulfillment of its repayment obligations, Kotobukiya planned to liquidate itself entirely. The company was among 14,687 cases of recession-induced bankruptcy in Japan in 2001, a postwar record.

Principal Subsidiaries

Gruppe Co. Ltd.; Kyushu Consultants Co. Ltd.; Kotobukiya Bakery Co. Ltd.; Kyushu Region Spar Honbu Co. Ltd.; Bouquet Co. Ltd. (90%); Tohya Department Store Co. Ltd. (50%); Tohya Shoji Co. Ltd. (50%); Sakura Department Store Co. Ltd. (55%).

Further Reading

"Distribution Industry Faces Major Power Shift," *Yomiuri Shimbun/Daily Yomiuri*, March 23, 2002.

"Failed Retailer Kotobukiya to Sell 50 Outlets to Aeon," *Japan Economic Newswire*, February 26, 2002.

"Failed Retailer Submits Rehabilitation Plan," *Japan Economic Newswire*, July 16, 2002.

"Failed Supermarket Lays Off All 13,000 Staff," *Japan Economic Newswire*, February 8, 2002.

"Founder of Kotobukiya to Resign from Board," *Japan Economic Newswire*, April 4, 1995.

"Japan's Corporate Failures Hit 2nd Post-War Record," *Japan Economic Newswire*, January 20, 2002.

"Kotobukiya Suffers Sales, Profit Drops," *Jiji Press Ticker Service*, April 17, 1991.

—Dylan Tanner
—update: Erin Brown

Liberty Travel, Inc.

69 Spring Street
Ramsey, New Jersey 07446
U.S.A.
Telephone: (201) 934-3500
Fax: (201) 934-3651
Web site: http://www.libertytravel.com

Private Company
Incorporated: 1951
Employees: 2,500
Sales: $1.4 billion (2001 est.)
NAIC: 561510 Travel Agencies

Liberty Travel, Inc. is the largest privately owned retail leisure travel agency in the United States. Liberty's travel agents sell primarily vacation packages, particularly those available through its sister company, wholesale travel provider GoGo Worldwide Vacations. Through extensive newspaper advertising, Liberty offers complete vacation packages inclusive of airfare, hotel, local transportation, and, in some cases, sightseeing and meals. Travel packages are available for destinations throughout the world and many cater to specific interests, such as skiing, golf, scuba diving, gaming, history and culture, adventure, spa and health resorts, romantic getaways, and family and singles vacations. Liberty agents provide corporate and group travel services as well. The company operates more than 200 travel offices in ten states, located primarily in New York, New Jersey, and Pennsylvania, with additional offices in Massachusetts, New Hampshire, Connecticut, Rhode Island, Delaware, Virginia, Maryland/Washington D.C., and Florida. At the company's web site, travelers can book cruises and vacation packages to the Caribbean islands, Bermuda, Mexico, Central America, Tahiti, Europe, and destinations throughout the United States. More than 60 travel agencies are affiliated with Liberty through a unique alliance program.

1950s Origins

Liberty Travel started in a small, one-desk office on 42nd Street in Times Square when founders Fred Kassner and Gilbert Haroche introduced to the travel market the idea of a complete vacation package, including transportation, hotel, and hotel transfers. The key component of this new concept involved pricing travel packages to resort destinations at rates affordable to the middle class. Kassner and Haroche accomplished this by negotiating special volume rates with hotels and, later, transportation companies. Their first organized package trips took customers to the Catskills Mountains in upstate New York and to Miami Beach, Florida. Liberty's success relied on newspaper advertisements to promote the low package rates. The company's first advertisement to appear in the *New York Times,* on December 23, 1951, promoted an eight-day trip to Miami Beach via train or plane for $99 per person plus tax, including hotel and taxi transportation to and from the hotel.

Liberty prospered in the 1950s, especially as commercial air travel became a regular part of American life. Kassner and Haroche brought mobility to the masses by making long distance vacation travel affordable to a growing, prospering middle class. By successfully selling low-cost packages at low season, the men enhanced their relationships with hotel operators who then provided Liberty with high-season reservations. Kassner and Haroche formed GoGo Tours to handle the wholesale aspect of the business, operating Liberty as a retail travel agency, specializing in popular honeymoon destinations and offering regular travel services in addition to selling packaged vacations.

By the end of the decade the company offered vacation packages to Europe, Mexico, Hawaii, Bermuda, and several Caribbean islands, such as Puerto Rico, the Bahamas, Jamaica, the Virgin Islands, and Barbados. Specialty trips to Europe included tickets to London theater productions and Moscow ballet. Newspaper advertisements continued to play an essential role in promoting low package rates and attracting customers. In the *New York Times* Liberty placed as many as four advertisements on different pages. A quarter-page advertisement that appeared in the *New York Times* on December 6, 1959, suggested several vacation options, while smaller ones focused on specific destinations. One of the four advertisements promoted a trip to Waikiki Beach in Honolulu, Hawaii, starting at $720 per person. The 16-day package included air transportation from New York City, hotel, and sightseeing; the trip included two nights in Los Angeles on the outbound trip and two nights in either San Francisco or Las Vegas on the return trip.

Although Liberty was criticized for using low rates to attract customers through advertising, its customers were clearly satisfied with available rates, given that the company grew and expanded. Liberty opened travel offices in Philadelphia and Miami Beach as well as in the Brooklyn and Queens areas of New York City.

In addition to attracting customers through low rates, Liberty applied other strategies, such as keeping its offices open every day of the week and offering the free use of Polaroid land cameras while on vacation. Another method Liberty used to attract a large volume of customers involved group and incentive travel. In the early 1960s the company advertised a free travel opportunity to an individual who planned a group trip for 15 friends or members of an organization; the person who initiated the trip traveled to that destination free of charge.

During the 1960s Americans became more experienced travelers and Liberty expanded its travel options, arranging package trips to more exotic or culturally interesting locations around the world, such as Tahiti, Tokyo, and Israel. While GoGo Tours, Inc. handled the wholesale operation of formulating vacation packages, Liberty's retail agents accounted for a large portion of sales at GoGo. Liberty expanded to accommodate new customers, opening several retail travel offices, for a total of 19 offices in New York City by 1970. Liberty opened offices in New Jersey, Connecticut, Pennsylvania, and Florida, as well as other areas of New York.

Competitive 1980s

Liberty endured and even prospered through many changes in the travel industry during the 1970s and 1980s. The energy crisis and a poor economy in the mid-1970s kept many people close to home. Deregulation in the 1980s resulted in a competitive atmosphere that resulted in lower airfares and, therefore, lower commissions to travel agents. The wider range of travel services, beyond airline ticketing, and the emphasis on low-priced vacation packages enabled Liberty to prosper and expand. In 1986 the company operated 130 travel offices in eight states and generated approximately $600 million in travel sales. Liberty accounted for approximately two-thirds of the sales volume at GoGo, receiving just less than $100 million in commissions from GoGo.

Liberty's advertising strategy continued to emphasize newspaper advertising as a means to reach a mass audience. The company reduced its level of advertising in the *New York Times* during the 1970s, but returned to an aggressive strategy as the economic situation improved during the 1980s. In 1987 the company spent $13.9 million placing advertisements in news-

papers nationwide, including 23 newspapers in the East. A full-page and five to ten quarter-page advertisements appeared in the *New York Times* every week.

Liberty participated in cooperative advertising with travel suppliers, either by being listed among other travel agents for a destination advertisement or by placing known brands and their logos in Liberty's print advertisements. A full-page advertisement in the *New York Times* could mention a national weekly rate for a car rental company, airlines involved in a package trip, or the rate for a specific destination hotel. All Liberty travel offices were listed at the bottom of the advertisements.

In the competitive atmosphere of the 1980s, Liberty began to experiment with a new form of advertising, interactive video kiosks. The videos showed views of popular resort destinations and offered a range of travel packages that could be purchased at the kiosk with a credit card. In 1987 Liberty placed ten kiosks in high traffic areas, such as airports, where the kiosks served customers making last-minute travel plans.

In 1988 Liberty initiated its first television advertising campaign, placing more than 25 commercials on New York City stations. The $3 million campaign focused on a one-week Hawaii package, including air transportation on American Airlines and a choice of 20 hotels. Liberty supplemented the television commercials with a quarter-page advertisement in the *New York Times*.

1990s: Innovation in Travel Promotion

During the early 1990s Liberty took an aggressively competitive stance in the travel industry by offering vacation packages at sale prices. In May 1993 the company offered 50 percent off of the lowest available airfares to more than 25 destinations, including popular resorts, when the customer purchased a vacation package. The ''Super Summer Sale,'' which ran the first two weeks of June, was the first time a retail travel agency offered air travel on sale.

The following year Liberty held similar sales. In conjunction with American Airlines, Liberty offered 35 percent off of air and hotel for Caribbean travel packages sold over four weeks beginning May 15 for travel between September 1 and November 19, 1994. From June 23 to June 26 the company held a cruise sale, with 18 cruise lines participating in the event.

To get an early foothold in the holiday travel market for the 1994–95 winter travel season, Liberty pre-purchased and reserved more than 10,000 airlines seats for travel during the Thanksgiving, Christmas, New Year's, and Presidents Day holidays. The seats covered travel packages to five Florida cities, Puerto Rico, Jamaica, St. Maarten, Hawaii, Las Vegas, Rome, and Athens.

As a strong economy in the 1990s increased demand for luxury vacations, the company decided to upgrade its offices and service. The company refurbished its offices, adding plush deck chairs for customer seating, and began to feature luxury accommodations and golf resorts in glossy travel brochures. The company developed its customer service training to emphasize open-ended questions in order to obtain information about customer travel interests.

Key Dates:

1951: Liberty Travel is founded, offering complete vacation packages to Miami Beach.
1959: Liberty promotes travel packages to Hawaii, the Caribbean, Mexico, and Europe.
1970: The company provides travel services through 19 offices in New York City, plus offices in New Jersey, Pennsylvania, Connecticut, and Florida.
1988: Liberty initiates its first television advertising campaign.
1993: Liberty is the first travel agency to offer air travel on sale.
1994: Sales reach $900 million through 171 travel offices.
1995: An Internet site is launched.
2001: Liberty introduces online booking for cruises.

Using the latest technology to promote its travel services, Liberty launched an Internet site in the fall of 1995. The web site provided information about travel destinations, hotels, and activities; customers could book travel by calling a toll-free telephone line or through one of more than 190 Liberty travel offices in nine states, including 33 offices in New York City; offices could be found by using an online locator feature. The site featured an interactive map and a free live chat room where travelers exchange ideas and share their experiences.

As new Internet technology developed, the web site provided real-time rates and availability and allowed customers to book vacation packages online. In 2001 Liberty launched a new web site in August, implementing Openpages' ContentWare. The software allowed Liberty to update and change web site content more readily, providing customers with more up-to-date information. Liberty licensed ProCruise, a cruise line booking tool that allowed customers to book a cruise through Liberty's web site. ProCruise allowed the company to provide real-time availability as well as deck plans and photos of cabin accommodations. Liberty added a custom weather forecast capability as well, providing weather reports to clients' travel destinations.

Challenges in the 21st Century

Liberty planned to continue expansion through the acquisition of small travel agencies and issued a press release in July 1996 that expressed the company's interest. Although 1,100 travel agencies responded, most were too costly to acquire, with only about 1 percent worth acquiring. Liberty developed an alternative to growth through acquisition by introducing an alliance program, offering owners of small travel agency owners an alternative to the difficulties of the times. Many travel agencies struggled with the advent of electronic ticketing and commission caps in the late 1990s. A slow economy and a soft travel market were exacerbated by the attack on the World Trade Center.

Introduced in 2002, the alliance program sought to create mutually beneficial relationships by offering agency owners an opportunity to take advantage of Liberty's profitability. The program allowed agencies the protection of a larger company by becoming independent contractors or full-time employees with health benefits and a 401k plan. Another option, the "royalty plan," provided a commission to retired agency owners. To participate in the program Liberty had three requirements: that the agency be located within 15 miles of an existing Liberty Travel office; that the travel agent have three years of leisure travel experience; and that the agency owner or independent agent be based in the United States. More than 60 agencies affiliated with Liberty within the first year.

Liberty took a new approach to travel advertising in 2002, adding a human face to convey the idea that Liberty provides not only travel information, but also offers assistance in making travel decisions. One advertisement featured an agent from the company's Philadelphia office and used a quote by that agent. Kay Howard is shown with the quote, "Vacations packages come in all shapes and sizes. Finding the right one for my clients, that's what I do best." (*Adweek Western Edition*, February 4, 2002, p. 31) The campaign involved ten different newspaper advertisements and featured the tagline, "Where travel begins."

In early 2003 Liberty joined a cooperative promotional effort initiated by the Mexican Tourism Board. Liberty's participation in the program involved print advertising in 44 newspapers nationwide and television commercials on 16 cable channels, such as the Travel Channel and the Discovery Channel. Mexico travel destinations promoted by Liberty included Cancun, Acapulco, Puerto Vallarta, Riviera Maya, and Los Cabos. The program tagline, "Closer Than Ever," implied the warmth of Mexican culture as well as the preference of Americans to stay close to home, given fears of terrorism, war in Iraq, and the outbreak of the SARS virus in Asia. Although Liberty could not measure the success of the Mexican Tourism Board promotion, popular travel destinations at this time included Mexico, as well as Hawaii, Las Vegas, and the Caribbean.

Principal Competitors

American Express Company; Carlson Wagonlit Travel, Inc.; WorldTravel BTI.

Further Reading

Butler, Simon, "Personal Touch," *Adweek Western Edition*, February 4, 2002, p. 31.
Cogswell, David, "GoGo for a New Age," *Travel Agent*, August 26, 1996, p. 82.
Dougherty, Philip H., "Liberty Travel to Start TV Effort on Sunday," *New York Times*, March 18, 1988, p. 4.
Fine, Phyllis, "Choosing Liberty," *Travel Weekly*, June 2, 1997, p. 18.
——, "The Liberty to Sell," *Travel Weekly*, July 23, 1998, p. 7.
Godwin, Nadine, "Video Sales Come of Age with Interactive Options; Three Major Systems Being Tested," *Travel Weekly*, March 23, 1987, p. 46.
"Liberty Adds to Cruise Stake," *Crain's New York Business*, September 25, 1989, p. 32.
"Liberty Alliance Program," *Travel Agent*, March 4, 2002, p. 45.
"Liberty Grows to Safeguard Travel Niche: Agency Expands to Luxury Segment, Adds 15 Offices," *Crain's New York Business*, October 21, 1996, p. 14.
Moss, Linda, "Liberty Travel Ignores Detractors, Packages Vacations at Cut-Rate Prices," *Crain's New York Business*, October 27, 1986, p. 3.

Parmar, Arundhati, "New Ads and Marketing Up Tourism to Mexico," *Marketing News,* April 14, 2003, p. 6.

Pasternack, Edward, "Liberty Travel Sets Up Site on Internet World Wide," *Direct Marketing,* October 1995, p. 9.

Rice, Kate, "Liberty Seeks Business of Agencies Closing Shop," *Leisure Travel News,* December 8, 1997, p. 28.

——, "New Web Site Lets Agents Sell On-Line," *Leisure Travel News,* December 6, 1999, p. 16.

Schaal, Dennis, "Liberty to Debut Cruise Booking Tool," *Travel Weekly,* May 21, 2001, p. 8.

"A Year for Vacations on a Shoestring," *Business Week,* July 7, 1975, p. 20.

—Mary Tradii

M.A. Bruder & Sons, Inc.

60 Reed Road
Broomall, Pennsylvania 19008
U.S.A.
Telephone: (610) 353-5100
Toll Free: (800) 622-1899
Fax: (610) 353-3963
Web site: http://www.mabpaints.com

Private Company
Incorporated: 1946
Employees: 772
Sales: $170 million (2002 est.)
NAIC: 325510 Paint and Coating Manufacturing

M.A. Bruder & Sons, Inc. is a family-run company that owns a regional chain of paint stores under the MAB Paints banner. With its headquarters located in Broomall, Pennsylvania, MAB boasts the top market share in the Philadelphia area, outpacing national brands like Glidden and Sherwin-Williams as well as the coating products merchandised by Sears. The MAB chain consists of 230 company-owned stores and a lesser number of independent dealers (about a third of the chain) covering 17 Eastern and Midwestern states. A typical MAB store is 3,500 to 5,000 square feet, a size the company has found to be large enough for periods of high demand while not leaving an excessive amount of unused space during the inevitable down cycle of the building industry, which drives the paint business. MAB avoids enclosed malls, preferring strip centers or stand-alone stores where professional painters are comfortable entering in paint-splattered overalls. MAB caters to both the do-it-yourself and professional customer, offering a wide range of architectural, industrial, maintenance, and commercial coatings. In addition, MAB stores sells painting-related products such as spray equipment, brushes, rollers, paint removers, and washers. The company produces its paints at manufacturing plants located in Philadelphia, Pennsylvania, Indiana, and Florida.

Company Established in 1899

The MAB name bears testament to the company's founder, Michael Albert Bruder, a pioneer of the commercial paint in-

dustry. He started out with a single store that opened in 1899 and was located in South Philadelphia at 16th Street and Passyunk Avenue. At the time, paint stores essentially sold the raw ingredients for paint—pigment, linseed oil, turpentine, and colorant—which were then mixed together at the job site. In addition to selling these bulk materials, Bruder began to mix paint himself and marketed the convenience of his ready-to-spread product, quickly finding a receptive base of customers among professional painters. With success came expansion, and Bruder opened new stores in the Philadelphia area, which later became dominated by two other family-run companies that would serve as MAB's main competition over the ensuing decades—even more so than the national chains that would one day enter the Philadelphia market. Those chains would learn that the local trio of paint companies had a stranglehold on the market. Buten Paint & Wallpaper, a retailer that sold paint made to its specifications, was formed in 1897. The other local company, Finnaren & Haley, Inc., actually had personal ties to MAB. Michael Bruder encouraged the original Mr. Haley and Mr. Finnaren to go into business together and served as a witness to the signing of their partnership agreement in 1913.

In 1932, Michael Bruder died and his son Thomas A. Bruder took over the company and carried on the task of growing the business, despite the economic difficulties brought on by the Great Depression. By the end of the 1930s, MAB operated 13 stores in the Philadelphia area. Business was enhanced during this period by the rising popularity of interior paints, as home owners began to paint their living room walls rather than rely on wallpaper. MAB helped to stimulate this emerging market of do-it-yourself customers by providing instructions on how to prepare and apply paint. During the 1950s, MAB expanded its reach in the Philadelphia market by adding stores owned by independent operators.

Third Generation of Bruder Family
Takes Over in 1967

Thomas A. Bruder, Jr. became the third generation of the Bruder family to take charge of the business, succeeding his father as president in 1967, aided by two other grandsons of Michael Bruder. Two years later, in 1969, MAB grew by external means, acquiring Smith Alsop Paint & Varnish of

Company Perspectives:

'On Time As Promised, Or We Pay'. You can find this service motto prominently displayed in all of our stores, on our business cards, and throughout all M.A.B. facilities. This simple statement, the guarantee that we will deliver on our promises to customers, puts into words one of the fundamentals of our company's century of success . . . a dedication to servicing the customer. From Specification writing and custom color matching to expedited job site delivery and technical support, M.A.B. personnel accept the responsibility for meeting the needs and expectations of our valued customers. Helping customers succeed is our key to success.

Terre Haute, Indiana, adding new locations in six Midwest states plus Alabama and Florida. Furthermore, MAB picked up two paint manufacturing plants in Terre Haute and Florida. Over the next twenty years, MAB devoted itself to internal growth, opening new stores in existing and new markets. To better serve the changing paint industry, MAB introduced many new products and created field sales service teams to better assist professional customers: builders, architects, and paint contractors. In 1981, the company upgraded its manufacturing operations by opening a new plant in Orlando, Florida. By the early 1980s, MAB was generating an estimated $85 million in annual sales, most of which came from the Philadelphia area, where the chain boasted nearly 100 stores and the lion's share of the local market. A distance second and third in Philadelphia, F&H had estimated annual sales just over $10 million and Buten just under $10 million. While the focus of all three area retailers was on the quality of the product, MAB was far more aggressive in its approach to television and radio advertising. The chain was reluctant to discount its paints, which management felt was unnecessary, instead opting to promote MAB's less expensive second line of paints.

A fourth generation of the Bruder family became involved in the running of the company. Thomas A. Bruder III first worked as a stockbroker during the 1980s at a time when the family considered taking MAB public. In the end, it was decided to keep the business private, and Thomas Bruder gave up trading to serve as MAB's marketing manager. The company was adversely affected by a downturn in the economy in he early 1990s. Deriving about three-quarters of its business from commercial or industrial customers, the company was hurt by a lack of new commercial construction. The do-it-yourself market, on the other hand, picked up some of the slack as many people decided to save money by doing their own painting. As a result, revenues were flat for 1991, but by carefully scheduling work and production the company was able to avoid laying off any of its 1,300 employees. MAB remained financially strong enough so that in 1992 it was able to acquire Paint America Co., a Dayton, Ohio-based maker and retailer of paints and coatings. The $4.8 million purchase brought with it 36 ''Warehouse Paint Centers'' stores mostly located in the Dayton and Cincinnati areas.

While MAB continued to produce a healthy profit, the Bruder family in the mid-1990s was becoming increasingly concerned about declining sales volumes. As part of a complete reorganization of the company, Thomas Bruder III took over as vice-president of sales, charged with turning around the company's sales efforts, which were handled by 74 account representatives along with managers and support staff. Bruder set a goal of increasing overall sales by 10 percent, but faced with an entrenched way of doing business, he turned to outside help, hiring a sales training and management development firm, Powers Training and Development of Conshohocken, Pennsylvania. A number of the sales reps were reluctant to embrace the changes that Bruder and Powers were promoting, with the result that within the next two years about half left the company. No one could recall the last time that an MAB store manager had been fired, yet now those who refused to adhere to the new system were quickly severed from the company, leaving some territories vulnerable to competition.

The changes instituted in MAB sales practices resulted in only modest gains in the late 1990s, but the company was not alone: the industry as a whole was experiencing flat growth. To attain growth, retailers were forced to increase market share, resulting in some consolidation. Rival Philadelphia paint company Buten, for example, was bought in 1994 by a national company, Beltsville, Maryland-based Duron Inc. Because MAB manufactured its paints locally it was still able to successfully compete with Duron, Sears, and Sherwin Williams, which could not provide as quick a turnaround on special orders. However, in order to continue to be successful MAB had to become increasingly more reliant on technology, which was not only instrumental in research and development efforts but also found a place in the store. By scanning a sample of a color a customer wanted to match, an in-store computer could read the values of the desired color, which could then be automatically mixed on site. MAB also began using computers to collect data on its customers, an activity that began in 1997 when it hired a marketing company. In addition to its traditional advertising program aimed at the general public, MAB was now able to use its data base to target commercial customers who were already using MAB coatings. MAB also invested money in research and development to fulfill the needs of its customers. For example, a number of schools, health-care facilities, and office buildings with environmental concerns asked for a non-odorous paint. In 1998, to address these concerns, MAB introduce Enviro-Pure, a coating that did not rely on volatile organic compounds and produced no odor.

Alliance With Kelly-Moore Established in 1999

In the mid-1990s, MAB attempted again to grow externally but was outbid in acquisition attempts in St. Louis and Fort Myers, Florida. The company was particularly interested in moving more aggressively into Sunbelt states where, because of warmer weather, outdoor painting took place year-round, making the business less seasonal than was the case in the Philadelphia market. In June 1999, MAB took an important step in expanding its business by forming a partnership with Kelly-Moore Paint Co., a San Carlos, California, paint manufacturer and retailer. Like Bruder, the Kelly-Moore 142-store chain had a strong regional presence in the West, as well as a few locations in Oklahoma and Arkansas. Because the territories of the two companies did not overlap they were able to form a marketing alliance that allowed both parties to bid on national contracts, a area in which regional suppliers were generally excluded. Terms of the agreement called for MAB to provide

Key Dates:

1899: Michael A. Bruder opens the first paint store in Philadelphia.
1932: Michael Bruder dies and is replaced by his son, Thomas A. Bruder.
1967: Thomas A. Bruder, Jr. assumes control of the business.
1969: Smith Alsop Paint & Varnish is acquired.
1992: Paint America Co. is acquired.
2000: Jim Renshaw is hired as general manager.

paint for projects on the East Coast and Kelly-Moore on the West Coast. The companies would have the added benefit of now being listed with just five other national paint manufacturers in the American Institute of Architects' MasterSpec Finishes directory, which provided architects from around the country with specifications, available colors, and special types of paint offered by the short list of paint manufacturers.

Although MAB could boast of a number of positive developments in the late 1990s, the company endured several years of flat results. As the larger players in the industry continued to buy up market share and were able to use their size to their advantage, companies in the middle range like MAB were hard pressed to keep their share of the business. MAB was still well entrenched in the fiercely loyal Philadelphia market and was still successful in landing contracts for the major jobs that provided close to 80 percent of its revenues. Among its more high-profile projects was the restoration of the Ben Franklin Bridge, the new Kimmel Center, and a new wing of the Philadelphia airport.

Nevertheless, it was clear that the company had to perform better within its market to just keep pace with the competition. While the company was still performing well, management detected that a complacency had set in which jeopardized MAB's future. To help the company revive growth, the Bruders looked to someone outside of their family and in the autumn of 2000 hired former Sherwin Williams division president Jim Renshaw to serve as its general manager. Over the next year and

a half, 30 percent of the sales force changed over and ten of 13 middle managers were replaced. In keeping with the Bruders' desire to bring fresh talent to the company, Renshaw hired six managers from outside the company, with only four of the positions filled by MAB insiders. In addition, MAB introduced new products and redesigned its stores, which then cut back on inventory by 19 percent. To support its all-important commercial business, MAB opened two commercial branches, one located in Philadelphia and the other in Chicago, to handle the kind of large-scale tinting jobs that the smaller stores were not equipped to handle.

MAB was also careful not to lose sight of its longtime practice of treating its major customers like partners. Contractors, who often had to wait 60 to 90 days for payment from their clients, appreciated the liberal credit terms MAB offered to accommodate their cash-flow situation. It was that local touch that Renshaw wanted to retain, and he also recognized the need to retain the bulk of MAB employees, who possessed the knowledge and rapport with customers that would continue to give MAB an edge over much larger national rivals.

In June 2002, after being in business for more than 100 years, MAB reached a significant milestone when its Philadelphia plant produced the company's billionth can of paint.

Principal Competitors

Benjamin Moore & Company; The Sherwin Williams Company; PPG Industries Inc.

Further Reading

Asher, James, "In the Phila. Market, 3 Colorful Firms Provide the Paint and the Competition," *Philadelphia Inquirer*, June 4, 1984, p. D6.

Briggs, Rosland, "It's Been a Colorful Century at M.A.B.," *Philadelphia Inquirer*, June 28, 1999, p. D1

Fredericks, Jen, "Profile: MAB Paints and Coatings," *Indiana Business Magazine*, October 1, 1996, p. 56.

Stone, Adam, "MAB Paints Brighter Future," *Philadelphia Business Journal*, April 19, 2002, p. 23.

Wood, Anthony R., "Family Firm Shows True Colors," *Philadelphia Inquirer*, February 3, 1992, p. D1.

—Ed Dinger

Maine & Maritimes Corporation

209 State Street
P.O. Box 789
Presque Isle, Maine 04769-0789
U.S.A.
Telephone: (207) 762-3626
Toll Free: (877) 272-1523
Web site: http://www.maineandmaritimes.com

Public Company
Incorporated: 1918 as Gould Electric Company
Employees: 146
Sales: $138.1 million (2002)
Stock Exchanges: American
Ticker Symbol: MAM
NAIC: 221122 Electric Power Distribution

Maine & Maritimes Corporation is the holding company for the subsidiaries Maine Public Service Company (MPS) and Energy Atlantic, LLC. MPS transmits and distributes electricity to both retail and wholesale customers in Aroostook County, the largest county east of the Mississippi River, and parts of Penobscot County, both in northern Maine. The company's service area of 3,600 square miles approximates the size of Rhode Island and Connecticut combined while servicing a customer base of 35,000. Energy Atlantic markets power and provides services to Maine's deregulated market. MPS maintains Maine and New Brunswick Electrical Power Company Ltd., an inactive Canadian subsidiary of MPS.

Rural Roots: 19th Century

In November 1886, Arthur R. Gould, a tobacco merchant in Bangor, Maine, sold his store and home to move to the northern Maine town of Presque Isle. His tobacco business thrived in this mill town in rural Aroostook County, and Gould soon took on private banking as well. As Gould was establishing himself in Presque Isle, Presque Isle Electric Light Company powered the lights for the city from its plant along the Presque Isle Stream.

Soon after Gould's arrival, he purchased a sawmill and a gristmill, gaining control of the dam and power rights of the stream. Following this purchase, Gould formed the Aroostook Lumber Company and became general manager of the light company. Gould was able to funnel the waste from his sawmill to the light plant for conversion to steam heat for the buildings along the city's Main Street. However, the light company was not profitable for its stockholders, and many were looking for a way out of their investment. Gould's business acumen provided just the win-win situation both he and the stockholders were looking for. Gould began to trade wooded lots of land he had purchased along the Presque Isle Stream in exchange for shares of stock. After a few years, Gould had acquired 90 percent of the stock in Presque Isle Electric Light Company.

As the population of Presque Isle grew, Gould's plant provided heat and light to homes and business, and the company inched toward profitability. In April 1904, however, fire destroyed the Aroostook Lumber Company and severely damaged the light company, which was adjacent to the lumber mill. At this time Gould was also looking towards alternate power sources besides the mill waste, and the Aroostook Falls located near the U.S.-Canada border appeared to be the most promising.

Maine and New Brunswick Electrical Power Company: 1903–26

In May 1903 a group of three Canadian men and two Americans had obtained a charter to form a corporate entity called the Maine and New Brunswick Electrical Power Company Ltd. Under the charter, the electric company was given all land and water rights privileges. An important provision to maintaining the charter was stipulated in that a plant had to be completed within six years to be located along the Aroostook River between the mouth of the St. John River and the U.S.-Canadian boundary. In 1904, John Stewart, a director of the charter, approached Gould to obtain the necessary financing for the plant. Gould accepted the deal provided he would receive the charter and corporation from Stewart and his associates. If the venture succeeded, Gould would pay the original group members the value of the company.

For the next several years as the managing director of the Presque Isle Electric Light Company, Gould worked to secure the capital for the venture and also negotiated the necessary

Company Perspectives:

Maine Public Service Company (MPS), now a direct subsidiary of Maine & Maritimes Corporation, is a transmission and distribution company dedicated to transmitting and distributing reliable, economical electric power to Northern Maine. MPS serves energy to approximately 35,000 retail customers in a 3,600 square mile area. Major business activities in the area center around agricultural and forest products. It is our aim to meet customer needs fully and efficiently, at the lowest possible cost, and highest reliability of service.

legal steps through the New Brunswick legislature and the Maine legislature that would ensure the fair operation of the plant to be built in New Brunswick, Canada. Construction of the Aroostook Falls Plant (later renamed the Tinker Plant) began in 1906 and was put into service October 17, 1907. The project included a 27-foot-high and 246-foot-long concrete dam, a 2,200-foot canal, a powerhouse with two 500 kilowatt generators, and 16 miles of transmission line that ran to Presque Isle and 50 miles of line that ran to Houlton, Maine. Although Gould fixed a price tag of $275,000 for the entire project, at the time of completion there were still numerous outstanding bills.

By 1909, the company provided power to seven communities in Maine and the towns of Perth-Andover in New Brunswick, while also reporting its first net earnings of $7,096.78. Although the company continued to grow and show profits, it became increasingly difficult to manage as an international company. The company's board of directors voted to split into two corporations: the Maine and New Brunswick Electrical Power Company Ltd., which would own and operate the Canadian properties, and Gould Electric Company which would own and operate the Maine properties. Gould Electric Company was incorporated January 1, 1918.

Change in Ownership: 1926–60s

During the early 1920s the holding company of Central Public Service Corporation of Chicago was shopping around for small utilities to purchase. In 1926 Central Public acquired all the capital stock of both Gould Electric Company and the Maine and New Brunswick Electrical Power concern. Arthur Gould and his son, Louis E. Gould, who was being groomed to take over the business, resigned from their posts as officers of the company. The Goulds' resignations signaled a shift from a locally owned and operated utility toward an absentee ownership and management. Colonel E.A. Pierce, director of the Chicago holding company, hired Iowa electrical engineer Lawrence Alline, whose father had roots in Maine, to take on the position of chief executive officer in 1926. Through the holding company structure Gould Electric acquired the capital of numerous small utility companies in Maine by exchanging Gould stock at $100 par value for the individual company's stock. On August 31, 1929, Gould Electric was granted charter rights to Aroostook County, and the company's name was changed to Maine Public Service Company (MPS).

With the stock market crash of 1929 and the Great Depression that followed, Central Public Service declared bankruptcy

in 1932. Operation of Central Public was taken over by Consolidated Gas and Electric Company, under which MPS remained a subsidiary until 1947. MPS withstood the lean years of the Depression with minimal construction and by the late 1930s was slowly gaining earnings and resuming construction. In 1939, the company built a new, modern 33,000-volt line that ran from the Tinker Plant to a substation in Presque Isle.

Prior to U.S. involvement in World War II, the northern Maine towns of Presque Isle and Houlton with proximity to the Canadian border were chosen as sites for Air Force bases, greatly changing the electrical needs of the largely agricultural communities. MPS applied for a permit to build a five-kilowatt steam plant to meet the higher demands for electricity, a particular concern should a drought occur and not enough power could be harnessed by the hydro plant. The company's request for a permit was turned down by the War Production Board because it was believed the increased usage would not continue after the war. MPS relied on purchasing power from Fraser Paper Company and Bangor Hydro in times of peak load or low water supply.

MPS achieved high growth during the war, with an increase in revenues between 1941 and 1945 of 50 percent, an increase in kilowatt hour sales of 82.5 percent, and an increase in customer base of 14.9 percent. MPS purchased the stock of Maine and New Brunswick Co. in 1941, operating as affiliated companies until 1942 when MPS became the parent company and Maine and New Brunswick became its subsidiary.

In April 1947 a public offering of MPS was made of 1.5 million shares at $22 per share. MPS shares were quickly snatched up, as 1,650 new stockholders from 39 different states invested. With a new board of directors, the company's primary focus became construction of a thermal plant to meet the increased consumer demands for electricity that had been established during the war. Then, in the fall of 1947, a drought swept throughout Maine; MPS was no longer able to purchase power from Bangor Hydro because that company no longer had surplus to sell. MPS was forced to issue rationing of power during the winter of 1947 and 1948 and was not able to return to full production until that March when spring runoff replenished storage facilities.

In December, during the energy crisis, the Maine Public Utilities Commission (PUC) authorized construction of a thermal plant and an added surcharge of one cent per kilowatt hour. News of a rate increase along with the demands of rationing during the harsh Maine winter quickly aroused public outrage, and MPS suffered enormous publicity damage. Stock in MPS dropped to as low as $10.50 a share during the emergency. In the end, the PUC allowed the surcharge effective for the month of December only, and allowed MPS to amortize the emergency expense over a five-year period. Although the emergency was over, its effect on company earnings lingered. In 1946, earnings per share were $2.17, in 1947 they were $1.53, and in 1948 they were $0.74.

Atomic Energy: 1970s–80s

Throughout the 1950s MPS slowly recovered its financial standing, and by 1961 MPS stock had reached $24 on the American Stock Exchange. The company had thus far provided

Key Dates:

1887: The Presque Isle Electric Light Company is formed.
1903: Maine and New Brunswick Electrical Power Company Ltd. is organized.
1905: Maine & New Brunswick Electrical Power Company acquires Presque Isle Light Company.
1918: Gould Electric Company is incorporated.
1926: Capital stock of Maine & New Brunswick and Gould Electric are acquired by Central Public Service Company, a Chicago holding company.
1929: Gould Electric's name is changed to Maine Public Service Company (MPS).
1942: MPS becomes parent company and Maine & New Brunswick Electrical Power Company is its subsidiary.
1966: Maine Yankee Atomic Power Company is organized.
1979: MPS purchases interest in Seabrook, New Hampshire, nuclear facility.
1986: MPS is able to sell its interest in troubled Seabrook investment.
1999: MPS sells its generation assets in anticipation of state deregulation. The company establishes Energy Atlantic, LLC.
2000: Deregulation in Maine takes effect March 1.
2002: MPS board of directors approves plan to reorganize as a holding company.
2003: Shareholders approve holding company structure and Maine & Maritimes Corporation is formed as holding company.

hydro, diesel, and steam energy, and by the 1960s MPS was ready to move toward a new, low-cost source. Plants in southern New England had experienced success with nuclear energy. In 1966 MPS joined ten other New England utilities, including Bangor-Hydro Company and Central Maine Power Company, to build a nuclear plant in Wiscasset, Maine. The 11 utilities formed the Maine Yankee Atomic Power Company and anticipated completing the plant by 1972. MPS's share in the venture was five percent or 35,000 kilowatts.

In 1978, after great success with the Maine Yankee Atomic plant, which was producing power below two cents per kilowatt hour, MPS, the state's third-largest electric utility, invested $34 million in the Seabrook, New Hampshire, nuclear plant. At the time of the investment, the estimated cost of the project was $2.36 billion. By 1981, huge cost overruns and delays had so hampered the construction that MPS was facing a bleak financial picture. At that time the estimated cost of the project had risen to $3.56 billion, leaving MPS with a share totaling $61.7 million.

The investment proved to be an albatross for MPS. By September 1981, MPS was granted a temporary rate hike totaling $1 million by the PUC, but there was growing concern that MPS would need to divest itself of its interest in Seabrook. In mid-1982 MPS attended hearings before the PUC again, this time requesting a $4.6 million rate hike and receiving only $1.6 million. MPS sought a buyer of its share, but there were no

takers. In July 1983 MPS was able to sell 200,000 shares of common stock, netting the company $5.5 million, but even this seemed a temporary relief for the troubled utility as the PUC had forecast the company's commitment at $130 million. In 1984, in an attempt to drastically reduce cash expenditures, MPS temporarily halted trade on the American Stock Exchange, reduced quarterly dividends 40 percent, and cut board of director's fees 25 percent.

Still struggling with debt in 1985, MPS requested a $5 million rate hike. At the time, public advocate Paul A. Fritzsche recommended that MPS merge with the state's largest electric utility, Central Maine Power (CMP). In May 1985 the PUC ruled that 47 percent of MPS's investment in Seabrook was imprudent and must be absorbed by the company and that 53 percent of the investment could be passed to customers through a $4.5 million yearly rate hike until the Seabrook project's completion.

Tensions rose later that year as more pressure was placed on MPS to merge with CMP following Fritzsche's conclusion that CMP residential customers paid an average five dollars less a month than MPS customers. MPS president G. Melvin Hovey protested any notion of a takeover. Ironically, amid MPS's bleak situation, the company was listed on *Forbes* "The 200 Best Small Companies in America." In May 1986 the PUC recommended that a merger of MPS and CMP was warranted economically, though the commission was unable to mandate the merger. That year MPS took its case to the Maine State Supreme Court and was able to fend off the merger.

Deregulation: 1990s

MPS slowly got back its financial footing in the 1990s and faced new challenges with deregulation measures. As a means to provide lower consumer utility costs, the PUC and the Maine State legislature hoped to deregulate the industry by the late 1990s so that consumers would be able to choose their energy supplier by 2000. Historically, Maine's energy suppliers included CMP, Bangor-Hydro, and MPS, and according to those in favor of deregulation, those companies represented a monopoly. Supporters also noted that New England charged higher rates than other regions in the United States and predicted rates would decrease with increased competition. Maine's three utilities were concerned about "stranded costs," the over $2 billion the companies had invested in operating costs to meet regulatory standards.

In early 1997 utilities were mandated by the Maine legislature to divest their generating assets by March 1, 2000. By September 1997, MPS placed all of its power plants up for sale, hoping to sell the seven plants by March 1, 1998. MPS president Paul Cariani stated, "We've put our generating assets out to bid early because the interest level of potential buyers seeking to own utility generation is high today. Our goal is to maximize the sale price to get the highest return to our customers and shareholders, thereby reducing the company's stranded investment to the greatest possible extent." In 1999 MPS sold its hydroelectric and fossil-fueled generating assets for $37.4 million to WPS Power Development, Inc., a subsidiary of the Wisconsin holding company WPS Resources Corporation. MPS continued to transmit and distribute service.

In January 2000, the PUC chose WPS Energy Services, Inc., another subsidiary of WPS Resources Corp., as the standard offer supplier of electricity in the MPS service territory. Beginning March 1, consumers who did not choose a power provider would be given service by WPS Energy by default. By 2003 the effects of deregulation fell mainly to large business consumers. For that market, standard offer rates were high, and this prompted companies to shop around for the best rates. However, most home customers used the standard offer service because the low standard rate did not attract a great deal of competition. MPS responded to the restructuring by offering "green power," renewable energy sources marketed as more environmentally friendly, through its subsidiary Energy Atlantic, LLC (EA). When introduced in 2000 EA was marketed as providing a cleaner source of energy from such renewable sources as waste wood, municipal trash, running water, and wind. While the price of renewable power was typically 25 percent higher than renewable sources, proponents of green energy claimed EA could compete by targeting those consumers who were willing to pay more for cleaner electricity. By 2003, the venture had achieved success in southern Maine, largely due to EA's contract as a residential standard offer service in CMP's service territory effective until February 2002. In northern Maine, where both home and business populations declined, EA was forced to exit the market, leaving WPS Energy Services the sole company marketing electricity in northern Maine.

Holding Company Structure in 21st Century

In October 2002, MPS announced that the company would seek to gain state and federal authority to reorganize as a holding company with MPS becoming a subsidiary of the proposed holding company. MPS president J. Nick Bayne stated in a company press release, "This strategic corporate alignment will give the Company the flexibility to implement a progressive growth and diversification strategy, while insulating the regulated utility's operations. Moving to a holding company is a more suitable corporate structure for responding rapidly to change and growth opportunities."

Securing overwhelming approval by stockholders at their annual meeting May 30, 2003, MPS announced the company would reorganize as the holding company Maine & Maritimes Corporation effective June 30, 2003. MPS shares trading under the ticker symbol MAP would be automatically converted to Maine & Maritimes shares traded under the symbol MAM. Following the reorganization MPS and EA would become subsidiaries of Maine & Maritimes. The inactive Canadian subsidiary Maine and New Brunswick Electrical Power Company would remain a subsidiary of MPS. As the company reached its centennial, its financial standing was solid with its best shareholder returns posted and management looked ahead to further growth.

Principal Subsidiaries

Maine Public Service Company; Energy Atlantic, LLC.

Principal Competitors

Central Maine Power Company; Bangor-Hydro Electric; Energy East; WPS Resources Corporation.

Further Reading

Allen, Scott, "Would Aroostook Be Better off If Their Utility Were Forced Out of Business?," *Maine Times,* May 10, 1985, pp. 14–15.

"Aroostook Power," *Maine Times,* May 7, 1982, p. 6.

Austin, Phyllis, "Seabrook and Maine," *Maine Times,* June 12, 1981, p. 18.

Brown, Wayne L. "Presque Isle, Maine, Electric Company Won't Accept New Customers," *Bangor Daily News,* February 25, 2003.

Burnett, Lee, "Electricity Competition in Aroostook," *Maine Times,* August 3, 2000, p. 12.

Clancy, Mike, "Aroostook Utility Faces Deficit," *Portland Press Herald,* December 1, 1984, pp. 1, 4.

"Electric Companies at Odds over Merger Study," *Portland Press Herald,* October 2, 1985, p. 14.

"Energy Company Awarded Contract for Northern Maine," *Portland Press Herald,* January 12, 2001, p. 3C.

Grant, Robert L., "Maine Public Service Conversion Seen Completed by July 1," *Dow Jones Business News,* June 2, 2003.

Hicks, Jonathan P., "Maine Utility Omits Quarterly Dividend," *New York Times,* February 27, 1985, p. D5.

Irwin, Clark T., Jr., "Ailing Utility among '200 Best,'" *Portland Press Herald,* October 28, 1985, pp. 1, 5.

——, "Seabrook Cost: Advocate Criticizes Lower Estimate," *Portland Press Herald,* October 18, 1984, pp. 1,10.

——, "Stockholders Must Bear Half of Seabrook 2 Costs," *Portland Press Herald,* May 11, 1985, pp. 1, 16.

"Maine Public Service Awarded Higher Rates," *Portland Evening Express,* May 11, 1985, p. 3.

"Maine Public Service, CMP Merger Proposed," *Portland Press Herald,* March 13, 1985, p. 12.

"Maine Public Service Cuts off Talks with CMP," *Portland Press Herald,* September 4, 1985, p. 11.

"Maine Utility Halts Trading on Its Stock," *Portland Press Herald,* October 18, 1984, p. 1.

"Maine's Main Supplier," *Electric Light & Power,* January 2000, p. 25.

"Northern Maine Power Firm Seeks Revenue Hike," *Portland Evening Express,* January 4, 1991, p. 4.

"Nuclear Costs Devastating to Aroostook," *Maine Times,* November 12, 1982, p. 6.

"Power Co. Charges Ahead with M&A Plan," *Corporate Financing Week,* June 5, 2000, p. 1.

"PUC Endorses Utilities' Merger," *Portland Press Herald,* May 16, 1986, p. 14.

"Second Utility Puts Power Plants on Block," *Portland Press Herald,* September 7, 1997, p. 4B.

Stetson, C. Hazen, *From Logs to Electricity: A History of the Maine Public Service Company,* Maine Public Service Company, 1984, 232 p.

"3 of Seabrook's Owners Face Selling Deadline," *New York Times,* January 9, 1985, pp. D1, D14.

Turkel, Tux, "Electricity Industry Reformers Pressured," *Portland Press Herald,* December 3, 1995, p. 1A.

——, "Restructuring Quietly Meeting Most Goals," *Portland Press Herald,* January 6, 2002, p. 1F.

——, "State Gets a New Power Choice," *Portland Press Herald,* March 14, 2000, p. 1C.

"Utilities: Takeover Debated," *Maine Times,* October 18, 1985, p. 9.

"Utility Announces Austerity Plans," *Portland Evening Express,* October 18, 1984, p. 40.

"Utility Nets $5.5 Million to Pay Seabrook Bills," *Maine Times,* July 1, 1983, p. 13.

—Elizabeth Henry

Manila Electric Company (Meralco)

Meralco Compound
Ortigas Avenue
Pasig City
Metro Manila 0300
Philippines
Telephone: (+63) 2-1622-0
Fax: (+63) 2-1622-8501
Web site: http://www.meralco.com.ph

Public Company
Incorporated: 1903 as Manila Electric Railroad and Light
    Company
Employees: 5,969
Sales: P 121 billion ($2.3 billion) (2002)
Stock Exchanges: Philippine
Ticker Symbol: MER
NAIC: 221122 Electric Power Distribution

The Manila Electric Company, or Meralco, is the Philippines' largest distributor of electrical power. The company holds the power distribution franchise for some 22 cities and 89 municipalities, including the capital city of Manila, as well as for the cities of San Juan, Las Piñas, Quezon, Malabon, Makati, Caloocan, Pasay, Mandaluyong, Paranaque, and Navotas. Meralco's 25-year franchise for these markets, awarded in 2003, gives the company control of the energy distribution services for an area of more than 9.3 thousand square kilometers and a population of more than 19.7 million—one-fourth of the Philippines' total population. The company boasts a coverage rate of more than 97 percent, the highest in the country. Each year, Meralco sells more than 23 million megawatt-hours (MWH), with residential and commercial sales each contributing roughly 35 percent, and industrial sales adding 30 percent. Formerly a power producer, Meralco purchases its power requirements primarily from government-owned National Power Corporation; since the beginning of the 2000s, however, the company has begun to purchase electricity from a number of newly established independent power producers, helping to lower its prices. Meralco also has started to diversify its operations in response to the deregulation of the Philippines power industry by extending into power gener-

ation, industrial construction and engineering, and other areas, including real estate development, e-commerce, and consultancy services. Meralco is led by Chairman and CEO Manuel M. Lopez, whose family, through direct and indirect holdings, retains control of some 25 percent of the company. The Lopez family, one of the country's most prominent, also controls conglomerate Benpres Holdings and other businesses.

Turn of the Century Beginnings

Electricity came to Manila in 1892 with the founding of La Electricista, which began providing electricity to residential customers. With the completion of a new power plant in 1895, La Electricista began providing street lighting service to the city as well. By the beginning of the 1900s, La Electricista boasted some 3,000 customers, as well as its streetlight business.

In 1903, the young government of the Philippines began accepting bids to operate Manila's electric tramway, as well as providing electricity to the city and its suburbs. The only bidder proved to be Charles M. Swift, a Detroit-based businessman, who founded a new company, The Manila Electric Railroad and Light Company, or Meralco, in 1903. Construction on the tramway began that same year. The following year, Meralco added its first electrical power operations by acquiring La Electricista. By 1906, the company boasted a yearly power output capacity of some eight million kWh.

Meralco built up a strong public transportation business in the decades leading up to World War II, building a 170-strong fleet of streetcars into the 1920s, before switching over to buses later in that decade. Yet the company's electric service grew even more strongly, overtaking its public transportation operations in terms of revenues by 1915. By 1920, the company's power capacity had grown to 45 million kWh. The company changed its official name to Manila Electric Company in 1919, although keeping the Meralco corporate name.

In 1925, Meralco, which had been registered in New Jersey, in the United States, was acquired by fast-growing power conglomerate Associated Gas & Electric Co. (AGECO), which had begun a massive expansion throughout the United States and Canada. Backed by AGECO, Meralco began acquiring a number of existing utilities in the Philippines, enabling the company to expand beyond its Manila city center base.

The company originally serviced its enlarged franchise area through small, diesel-powered generators added through its acquisitions. In the late 1920s, however, Meralco began construction on a new, large-scale power plant, the Botocan Hydro Station. Completed in 1930, the power plant was one of the region's largest construction projects of the time. The additional capacity allowed the company to begin hooking up customers throughout the metro Manila area. Meanwhile, Meralco opened its own retail store in order to sell home appliances—helping to drive demand for more power.

The Philippines government itself responded to the growing demand for electricity by establishing the National Power Corporation (Napocor), with Meralco signing a contract to purchase the entire output of Napocor's first facility. Meanwhile, Meralco's own power capacity continued to grow, reaching 184 million kWh by the outbreak of World War II.

Lopez Family Taking Over in the 1960s

The Japanese occupation of the Philippines placed Meralco under the control of the Taiwan Electric Company. By the end of the war, however, most of the former Meralco operations had been destroyed, along with the rest of Manila. Meanwhile, Meralco's parent company, AGECO, which had gone bankrupt and had been broken up, for the most part, in the 1930s, was reorganized under the name General Public Utilities.

Meralco was to remain under American control through the 1950s. In the meantime, as the newly independent Philippines began reconstructing after the war, Meralco quickly worked to restore electric service, and by 1947 had already topped its prewar capacity. By the beginning of the 1950s the company had fully restored service to its former metro Manila network, which included some 39 towns and cities. In the meantime, the company had abandoned its public transportation arm, selling its bus line to Fortunato Halili in 1948.

Demand for electricity grew strongly in the postwar era. By the early 1950s the company boasted more than 200,000 customers. It also continued to add capacity, adding new power plants in a five-year, P 45 million investment program started in 1950. The company also benefited from the rapid industrialization of Manila in the postwar era, and by 1958, the industrial market had become its largest source of revenues.

In 1962, a group of Filipinos, led by Eugenio Lopez, Sr., founded Meralco Securities Corporation (MSC) in order to acquire Meralco. The Lopez family was by then one of the Philippines' most prominent families, stemming from its con-

trol of the country's sugar sector since the middle of the 19th century. The family, through various holdings, also went on to become major forces in the Philippines' media sector, owning the ABS-CBN network and the *Chronicle* newspaper.

Meralco grew strongly under Eugenio Lopez's leadership, adding new power plants to increase capacity as its customer levels topped 500,000 by 1968. The company also abandoned the former management's reliance on U.S. suppliers for its infrastructure requirements, and instead began accepting bids from a variety of sources, helping to produce savings while achieving faster construction times. Meralco also began diversifying, launching Meralco Securities Industrial Corporation in order to build a petroleum pipeline between Batangas and Manila in 1967, and founding, in 1969, Philippine Electric Corporation in order to produce line transformers and other electrical equipment. Other expansion moves brought the company into banking and oil refinery operations.

Fall and Rise in the 1970s–80s

Lopez had supported Ferdinand Marcos in his presidential bids during the 1960s. Yet Lopez, through his media holdings, had grown increasingly critical of Marcos in the early 1970s. When Marcos declared martial law, the Lopez family was stripped of its assets, including its control of Meralco. Throughout the rest of the decade, Meralco struggled against a weakened economy and a series of natural disasters that destroyed a number of its facilities. Then, in 1979, the Marcos government named Napocor as the country's monopoly electrical power producer. Meralco's power generating assets were transferred to the state-owned body.

In the meantime, Meralco continued to expand its distribution business, linking up a growing number of towns and cities in the metro Manila region that had been unable to keep up with the surging demand for electrical power. By the mid-1980s, Meralco had signed on more than 60 new communities to its grid.

The revolution of 1986 that deposed the Marcos regime and brought Corazon Aquino to the presidency also restored the Lopez family's former holdings, including Meralco. One of Eugenio Lopez's sons, Manuel, took over as Meralco's president (and later became chairman and CEO) at this time.

Meralco then took steps to upgrade its network, which had been hit hard during the Marcos era and continued to experience difficulties in the economic upheavals of the latter half of the 1980s. In 1989, the company launched a large-scale investment program to upgrade its distribution system. At the same time, Meralco enhanced its customer service component by restructuring its organization into regional components.

Meralco went public in 1990. By then, however, the company faced a new difficulty. The surge in demand for electrical power—including a growing number of "pirates"—had overwhelmed the Napocor power generation monopoly. By the early 1990s, the Manila market became subjected to planned blackouts lasting up to eight hours per day and longer.

In response, the Philippines government called for the creation of a new generation of Independent Power Producers (IPPs), which were then given guaranteed contracts. Meralco joined this new market, backing the creation of First Private Power Corporation, building a 225 MW plant in Bauang. That

Key Dates:

1892: La Electricista is founded.
1903: Charles M. Swift is awarded a franchise to build the Manila electric tramway, founding the Manila Electric Railroad and Light Company (Meralco).
1904: Meralco acquires La Electricista.
1919: Meralco is renamed Manila Electric Company as electricity generation and distribution becomes the main business area.
1925: Associated Gas & Electric Co. (AGECO) of the United States acquires Meralco.
1930: Meralco inaugurates Botocan Hydro Station.
1948: The company sells off its bus operations, exiting the transportation market.
1950: The company begins a five-year, P 45 million investment program to restore and expand capacity.
1962: Eugenio Lopez, Sr., leads the Philippino buyout of Meralco.
1972: Meralco and other Lopez family businesses are taken away from Lopez after Ferdinand Marco declares martial law.
1979: Government-owned Napocor is granted a power generation monopoly, taking over Meralco's power generation operations.
1986: The revolution that topples Marco puts into motion the restoration of the Lopez family businesses, including Meralco.
1990: Meralco goes public on the Manila stock exchange.
2000: Meralco forms e-Meralco Ventures to create and invest in Internet and high-technology businesses.
2003: Meralco is granted a new 25-year franchise for the Manila electrical power distribution market.

plant came on line in 1994, with commercial operations starting the following year.

Facing Competition in the New Century

By then, plans had been laid for the deregulation of the Philippines' energy market. Although the actual legislation for deregulation was not enacted until 2001, Meralco began preparing for the coming competition in the early 1990s. In 1994, Meralco began working with Spain's Union Fenosa, which acquired a 9 percent stake in Meralco, to lead a new reorganization effort in the mid-1990s. The company also began diversifying its activities in order to reduce its reliance on electrical power distribution.

One of the company's first diversification efforts came with the creation, in 1994, of the Rockwell Center development project, on the site of the company's then-dormant Rockwell power station. That operation was created in partnership with the Lopez family's Benpres Holdings, formed a year earlier. The following year, Meralco joined with Union Fenosa to launch the IberPacific consulting firm.

The company continued to develop its diversified interests into the turn of the century. In 1997, the company formed a new unit, Corporate Information Systems, built around its IT ser-

vices component. In 1999, the company formed Meralco Energy, which specialized in providing energy-related services to industries and other large-scale energy users. The following year, the company moved into the e-commerce markets with the formation of e-Meralco Ventures, with the purpose of launching and investing in Internet and high-technology companies.

Meanwhile, Meralco's core power distribution business continued its growth. By 2001, it had extended its network to include 20 cities, then added two more cities, for a total of 114 municipalities by the end of 2002. By then, the company served nearly 4 million registered customers—with a total customer population of some 19 million.

Meralco received new contracts from the Philippines government in 2003, extending its franchise in the metro Manila market through another 25 years. The company's 100th anniversary celebrations that year were dampened somewhat, however, by a Philippines Supreme Court judgment ordering the company to pay back overcharges to customers from a four-year period. Estimates of the potential payback bill ranged up to P 28 billion ($500 million), a price Meralco claimed it was unable to pay. Indeed, by May 2001, the company, which had seen its request for a fee hike rejected amid a sales slump, reported a net loss of more than P 2 billion ($38 million) for 2002, prompting members of the government to call the Lopez family's management of the company into question. Despite this shadow over its anniversary celebration, Meralco was nonetheless able to look back on its history as a leading player in the development of the Philippines—and forward in its determination to remain one of the country's leading corporations.

Principal Subsidiaries

Corporate Information Solutions, Inc.; Meralco Industrial Engineering Services Corporation; Rockwell Land Corporation; Meralco Energy, Inc.; e-Meralco Ventures, Inc.

Principal Competitors

State Power Corporation of China; Huaneng Power International Inc.; SembCorp Industries; Perusahaan Listrik Negara, PT; Hongkong Electric Holdings Ltd.; Korea Electric Power Corporation.

Further Reading

Felipe, Cecille Suerte, "Lopez Family Trade Barbs on Meralco Ownership," *Philippine Star,* September 24, 2002.
Mariano, Dan, "What's Fair?," *Philippine Daily Inquirer,* December 5, 2002.
"Meralco Embraces Future with Confidence," *Asiamoney,* May 2000, p. 38.
"Meralco's Appeal Against 28b Peso Refund Rejected Company Says It Has No Money to Repay Customers," *Business Times,* April 11, 2003.
Robles, Raissa Espinosa, "Manila's Electric Bill," *Asiaweek,* June 15, 2001.
Rodrigo, Raul, *Phoenix: The Saga of the Lopez Family: 1800–2000,* Manila: Island Graphics Inc., 2002.
Sayson, Ian C., "Manila Electric Posts a Record Deficit," *Bloomberg News,* May 1, 2003.

—M.L. Cohen

Marshall & Ilsley Corporation

770 North Water Street
Milwaukee, Wisconsin 53202
U.S.A.
Telephone: (414) 765-7801
Fax: (414) 298-2921
Web site: http://www.micorp.com

Public Company
Incorporated: 1847 as Samuel Marshall & Co.
Employees: 12,625
Total Assets: $3.2 billion (2002)
Stock Exchanges: New York
Ticker Symbol: MI
NAIC: 522110 Commercial Banks

Marshall & Ilsley Corporation is the holding corporation for a major Midwest bank, M&I Bank. M&I is the largest bank in Wisconsin, with over 200 offices. It holds about 20 percent of all deposits in the state. The company has had a presence in Milwaukee and in Madison, Wisconsin, for over 150 years. The company began to grow markedly through acquisitions in the 1980s and 1990s, when it took over many smaller regional banks. M&I also has 25 bank locations in Arizona, and other offices in Florida and in Las Vegas. Its Southwest Bank affiliate operates seven banks in the St. Louis area and in Belleville, Illinois. M&I Bank also has a strong presence in the Minneapolis/St. Paul area. M&I operates a subsidiary company called Metavante that provides data processing services to banks throughout the United States and abroad. Metavante, headquartered in Brown Deer, Wisconsin, is one of the leading companies in the bank data services industry, with particular strengths in Internet banking and electronic billing and payment.

Frontier Days

Marshall & Ilsley Corporation was founded as Samuel Marshall & Co. in Milwaukee in 1847. Samuel Marshall was a Pennsylvania Quaker, born in 1820 in the small settlement of Concordville. When he was a teenager, Marshall was apprenticed to a relative who ran a hardware store. Marshall worked in the hardware store for five years, and then began to take exploratory trips out West to look for better business opportunities. After much cautious research, Marshall moved to Milwaukee at the age of 26. He set himself up as an exchange broker, renting space in a downtown cobbler shop. Banking was not legalized in Wisconsin until the following year. In addition, at this time there was no unified national currency, and each state issued its own paper money. Marshall acted as a clearing house for bills and notes of all kinds. His office also kept deposits and made loans. Marshall quickly met Milwaukee's movers and shakers, and his deposits grew quickly as wealthy businessmen patronized his office. Marshall was reputed to be an exceedingly cautious and sober man, and he was very skilled at weeding out counterfeit money and avoiding notes from shaky banks and institutions. He took on a series of partners before hooking up with Charles Ilsley in 1849. Ilsley grew up in Maine and, like Marshall, had come to Milwaukee looking for wider opportunities. The company became known as Marshall & Ilsley in 1850. Two years later, Wisconsin finally passed legislation allowing state-chartered banks. Marshall & Ilsley took out the first Wisconsin bank charter within weeks of passage of the law, and opened the State Bank of Madison with $50,000 in capital.

Civil War and After

The two owners' forethought saw their financial institutions through many hard times. Before the Civil War, Marshall & Ilsley had decided not to take notes from Southern banks, fearing that these banks' money would not be good in the chaos of the secession movement. Consequently, Marshall & Ilsley rode out the Civil War as one of the most stable banks in the state. (By this time, Marshall & Ilsley's Milwaukee institution was classified as a private bank.) After the war, Marshall & Ilsley took on two new partners. One was Ilsley's younger brother Frederick, the other was a German immigrant named Gustav Reuss. Reuss was able to bring in much business from Milwaukee's thriving German community. The bank also invested in many area industries, from real estate to mining.

Marshall & Ilsley was the largest private bank in Wisconsin by the mid-1880s. Though periodic banking panics had rocked other area banks, Marshall & Ilsley had never closed its doors,

Company Perspectives:

Marshall & Ilsley Corporation is committed to an environment in which . . . our Customers receive high quality financial services consistent with sound, honest and progressive business practices . . . our Employees are inspired to excel and grow, both personally and professionally, in an atmosphere of trust, integrity and respect . . . our Shareholders receive a favorable, long-term return on their investment . . . the Community becomes a better place to live as a result of our leadership and commitment.

as some did to avert runs on deposits, and it had enjoyed 40 years of relatively steady growth. In 1888 Marshall & Ilsley changed its status from private bank to state-chartered. This gave the bank a more formal management structure, allowing for succession when the founders retired. A few years later, Samuel Marshall and Charles Ilsley sold the State Bank of Madison. Now their business was all based in Milwaukee. Many Milwaukee banks failed or were rumored to be in bad shape during what became known as the Great Crash of 1893. The Marshall & Ilsley Bank, however, had long had a reputation for conservative management, and indeed, it had huge reserves of gold and stable U.S. bonds and treasury notes. As a result, Marshall & Ilsley actually benefited from the crash, drawing depositors from other banks.

New Leaders in the 20th Century

Samuel Marshall retired in 1901, though the octogenarian still came to the office every day. His partner Ilsley was 74 that year, and he became the bank's president. Other key figures at Marshall & Ilsley included Reuss, two of Marshall's sons, Ilsley's eldest son James, and John H. Puehlicher. Ilsley died suddenly of a heart attack in 1904, and Reuss became president. Reuss saw the bank through another nationwide banking panic in 1907. As in the 1893 crash, Marshall & Ilsley was untouched while other banks reeled. The bank had deposits of more than $3.2 million in 1907, and held almost $3.5 million in savings accounts. Founder Samuel Marshall died that year, having seen his bank rise to its strongest position yet after 60 years in business. Reuss retired the year after Marshall's death, and Ilsley's son James K. Ilsley became president. He led the bank until 1915. During his tenure, the bank constructed a new headquarters. Marshall & Ilsley stayed in this elegant columned building from 1913 until 1968.

Ilsley retired on the eve of World War I, plagued by health problems. John Cambell became the next Marshall & Ilsley president, but he too stepped aside after only a few years. John H. Puehlicher then took over the top job. Puehlicher became a nationally renowned banker. He and his family steered M&I Bank through the rest of the century. John Puehlicher had worked his way up from cashier, and at Cambell's retirement he was still only a minor shareholder. He had only gone to school through the sixth grade, but he had found many ways to continue his education. He initiated many educational outreach programs while he headed M&I Bank, arranging after-hours classes for bank employees and sponsoring programs to teach

schoolchildren and the general public about what banks did. He served as president of the Wisconsin Banking Association, and was a key figure in getting legislation passed that let state-chartered banks like M&I join the Federal Reserve system. Puehlicher also expanded the services M&I Bank offered. He created a trust department, and in 1924 debuted a special women's department. The bank opened a Ladies Lounge where women customers could do their banking as well as use writing desks and telephones.

Puehlicher was also a markedly conservative banker, like Marshall and Ilsley before him. As the stock market took off in the 1920s, Puehlicher spoke before national banking forums urging caution and restraint. The stock market crash of 1929 was followed by the Great Depression, but M&I yet again remained a singularly strong institution while other banks collapsed. Milwaukee was very hard hit, and in 1933 over 100 banks in Wisconsin failed. M&I had over $27 million in deposits in 1929, and total assets of more than $35 million. During the early 1930s the bank's assets shrank, dipping to just over $30 million by the end of 1932. But by 1935 the bank had recovered, and assets stood at more than $42 million. Puehlicher died in 1935. Like many of his predecessors, he suffered from heart trouble. His son Albert S. Puehlicher became M&I Bank's next president. Albert Puehlicher was only 38 when he succeeded his father, but he had been working at the bank since he was 15 years old.

Postwar Expansion

Albert Puehlicher saw the bank through the end of the Depression. During World War II, the bank invested heavily in the area's defense industry, making substantial loans to a Milwaukee shipbuilder and to companies in the metal and ordnance industries. After the war, returning veterans were eager to buy houses and start families. Housing was in great demand, and Milwaukee began to overflow into neighboring suburbs. M&I Bank grasped the trend, and soon became one of the area's leading home mortgage lenders. The bank also did much new business in consumer loans. This department had languished since its inception in the 1930s, but it soon became flourishing and profitable.

In 1958 Charles F. Ilsley, grandson of original partner Charles Ilsley and the chairman of M&I's board, retired at the age of 65. That year Albert Puehlicher reduced his day-to-day work at the bank, letting his son Jack become the effective president. Albert Puehlicher died in 1963, and Jack Puehlicher then became the official president. He oversaw the rapid expansion of the bank in the next decades. Even before he held the title of president, Jack Puehlicher put forward a plan that would let M&I move out into the suburbs. In 1958 the bank reorganized as a stock holding company called the Bank Stock Corporation of Milwaukee. This structure allowed the bank to buy up competitors, in an era where the opening of new branches was restricted by law. The holding company bought the Northern Bank, Milwaukee's fourth largest, in 1959. In 1961 it bought another Milwaukee bank, the Bank of Commerce. The three banks were held by one company, but maintained their own names and headquarters. An antitrust ruling ordered the combination broken up in 1969, and the holding company sold the Bank of Commerce. However, as a result of

Key Dates:

1847: Samuel Marshall establishes Milwaukee exchange brokerage.
1850: Name is changed to Marshall & Ilsley when Charles Ilsley becomes partner.
1888: Brokerage becomes state-chartered bank.
1920: John H. Puehlicher becomes bank president.
1958: Bank reorganizes as holding company.
1971: Holding company name is changed to Marshall & Ilsley Corporation.
2000: Spinoff is proposed for data processing unit Metavante.

the suit, the regulations governing where M&I could expand became clearer. The holding company got the go-ahead to buy other banks as long as they were in areas where there were no competing banks. The holding company changed its name to Marshall & Ilsley Corporation in 1971, and began buying up small banks throughout Wisconsin. M&I acquired nine small-town banks in the 1970s, and built several branch banks within a prescribed three-mile radius of Milwaukee. By 1985 M&I had made over 20 acquisitions. These for the most part kept their own names, adding the prefix M&I.

Acquisitions in the 1980s and 1990s

By the mid-1980s, M&I Corp. had assets of around $5.5 billion, and had grown to 33 locations, including several offices in Arizona. Other area banks had also been consolidating, and by 1987 Marshall & Ilsley was the second largest bank in Wisconsin, behind First Wisconsin, which had assets of $6.6 billion. In 1987 M&I announced that it was buying Marine Bank, the state's third largest. The combination would have made M&I again Wisconsin's largest bank, with assets of close to $10 billion. The move was seen as the crowning acquisition in Jack Puehlicher's career. He had worked assiduously to build the bank to its current size, and was about to pull off the biggest merger in Wisconsin banking history. However, before the deal could go through, another suitor appeared, and Marine was sold instead to Bank One Corp. of Ohio. The company moved ahead with a smaller acquisition, picking up the 29-bank Central Wisconsin Bankshares that year instead. M&I made several other small acquisitions over the next two years.

M&I's data services unit continued to grow in the late 1980s and early 1990s. This division sold software and handled computer processing for client banks around the country. It was a very profitable business, bringing in $20.2 million in net income in 1992 on sales of $151.6 million. M&I Bank was also very profitable compared to other banks its size, and it had one of the lowest proportions of bad loans in its portfolio. Jack Puehlicher retired in 1992, leaving James B. Wigdale in charge. Wigdale was the first man outside the Puehlicher family to head the bank since 1920. Wigdale brought off another large merger in 1993, buying Valley Bank. Valley had over 150 branches, and assets of $4.3 billion. The combination gave M&I a strong presence in the Fox River Valley area of Wisconsin. After the merger, M&I had assets of over $12 billion.

Changes of Direction in the 2000s

By the late 1990s, M&I Corp. held a 20 percent share of all bank deposits in the state of Wisconsin. Its next competitor, Firstar, held 12 percent. It also had more locations than any other bank in the state, with some 230. M&I continued to have very strong earnings, particularly from its data processing services unit. This division had been growing at around 25 percent annually since the mid-1990s, and it contributed as much as 20 percent of the firm's annual operating profit. The data processing unit was founded in 1964, when it began processing data for other area banks. The unit quickly moved ahead with new technology, pulling its president from IBM in 1976. It had 400 employees by the early 1980s, and its own headquarters in Brown Deer, Wisconsin. In 1995 the division began doing Internet banking for clients, and sales grew rapidly through the late 1990s. By 1999 the unit had over 1,000 client banks, but this grew precipitously over the next year, leaving it with 3,300 clients in 2000. These included 19 of the top 20 largest banks in the country. In mid-2000, M&I Corp. announced that it would spin off the data processing unit, releasing it as a publicly owned company called Metavante. At the same time, M&I announced it would cut back in some banking areas, such as issuing student loans and auto loans, and it would expand in its Sunbelt locations in Arizona, Florida, and Nevada. The data processing spinoff was expected to leave both the bank and the new company in better shape. Yet the public offering came at a bad time, when technology stocks in general started to decline. M&I twice cut the price it was offering for the new Metavante stock, and then decided to pull the stock offering altogether. Consequently, the renamed Metavante continued as part of M&I Corp. into the early 2000s. A year after the offering failed, retaining Metavante looked like a wise choice. The unit had continued to grow, despite overall straitened economic circumstances.

M&I also continued to make acquisitions, in 2001 picking up Harris Trust Bank in Phoenix and 11 Arizona branches of Fifth Third Bank as well. M&I also moved into Minneapolis, purchasing that city's National City Bancorporation for $250 million in stock in 2001. James Wigdale, who had led M&I since 1992, stepped down in 2001. He was succeeded by Dennis J. Kuester. Kuester had led the data services unit since 1985. Kuester continued M&I's expansion into far-flung locations. In 2002 M&I bought two more Minnesota banks, and then purchased Mississippi Valley Bancshares, a St. Louis-based bank that also had locations in Illinois and Arizona. M&I Corp. seemed in good shape in 2003, despite an increase in the amount of bad loans it had to write off. Though the national economy was still troubled, M&I announced a 12 percent gain in profits for the first quarter of 2003. But clearly, circumstances were different from the booming 1990s. In 2003 M&I's top managers all agreed to forego salary increases as the company looked for new ways to hold down costs.

Principal Subsidiaries

Metavante Corporation.

Principal Competitors

U.S. Bancorp.; Bank One Corporation; Wells Fargo & Company.

Further Reading

Gaskill, Warren, "M&I Corp. Makes Bid for Marine," *Capital Times* (Madison), June 29, 1987.

Gores, Paul, "Money in the Bank," *Milwaukee Journal Sentinel*, July 16, 2000, p. 12.

——, "Suddenly, M&I Feeds Acquisition Appetite," *Milwaukee Journal Sentinel*, May 6, 2001.

Kenney, Ray, "M&I Merger Is Seen As Crowning a Career," *Milwaukee Journal*, July 12, 1987.

Langill, Ellen D., *Powered By Our Past,* Milwaukee: M&I Corp., 1997.

Lassen, Tina, "Inside the M&I-Valley Merger," *Madison*, March 1994, pp. 41–44.

"M&I Managers to Forgo Year's Salary Increases," *Wisconsin State Journal*, March 28, 2003.

"M&I Officially Ends Its Bid for Marine," *Capital Times*, September 28, 1987.

Moyer, Liz, "M&I Commercial Run Takes It into St. Louis," *American Banker*, June 18, 2002, p. 1.

Newman, Judy, "M&I Expands into St. Louis," *Wisconsin State Journal*, June 18, 2002.

Norman, Jack, "Data Services Unit Launches M&I Stock to Record Highs," *Milwaukee Journal*, April 11, 1993.

——, "Quiet M&I Creates Buzz in Industry," *Milwaukee Journal*, August 9, 1992, pp. D1, D6.

Roth, Andrew, "Metavante Cuts Show Power Imbalance," *American Banker*, April 16, 2001, p. 1.

Schmelkin, Alissa, "M&I Shedding Seller Image," *American Banker*, May 13, 2003, p. 1.

Silver, Jonathan D., "Valley, M&I to Merge," *Capital Times*, September 20, 1993, p. 1A.

Spivak, Cary, and James E. Causey, "Attractive M&I Has Plenty of Options," *Milwaukee Journal*, July 12, 1998.

Wenzel, Judy, "In Banking, M&I Is a Quiet Giant," *Milwaukee Journal*, June 4, 1989.

—A. Woodward

Martz Group

239 Old River Road
P.O. Box 1007
Wilkes-Barre, Pennsylvania 18773
U.S.A.
Telephone: (570) 821-3838
Fax: (570) 821-3835
Web site: http://www.martzgroup.com

Private Company
Incorporated: 1912 as White Transit Company
Employees: 600 (est.)
Sales: $30 million (2002 est.)
NAIC: 485510 Charter Bus Industry

The Martz Group is a Wilkes-Barre, Pennsylvania-based family owned motor coach company that runs several bus lines on the eastern seaboard. All told, the company employs more than 500 people and operates some 300 motorcoaches. Affiliated companies of the Martz Group include Martz Trailways, operating out of Wilkes-Barre, Pennsylvania; Martz Lines, based in Philadelphia, Pennsylvania; Gold Line/Gray Line, offering sightseeing tours in Washington, D.C.; National Coach, operating out of Fredricksburg, Virginia; Franklin Motorcoach, based in Manassas, Virginia; Tourtime America, a Richmond, Virginia, operation; First Class Coach, located in St. Petersburg, Florida; and First Class Coach, in Orlando, Florida. In addition, the company operates a travel agency in Wilkes-Barre for air and cruise service. The Martz Group is headed by the fourth generation of the Martz Family.

Business Launched in 1908

The founder of the Martz Group was Frank Martz, Sr., who grew up the son of a grocer in the coal mining region of northeast Pennsylvania. According to family legend, the idea for starting the company occurred to him one day when he was forced to walk to a neighboring town. Thinking that others, especially weary miners, would be willing to pay for a ride, he created a makeshift transit company in 1908. The venture was based in Plymouth, Pennsylvania, at first using a touring car as a bus to provide service between the towns of Plymouth and Nanticoke.

The origins of the bus date back to France, where in 1828 the horse-drawn omnibus was introduced by private businessmen, accommodating as many as 50 passengers to traverse the muddy streets of Paris. Only two years later, in Great Britain, Sir Goldworthy Gurney invented a steam-powered stagecoach, while in New York City horsedrawn omnibus operators began to lay rails in order to provide a more efficient and comfortable ride. A convergence of these ideas would lead to the use of steam-powered trains providing mass transportation within and between cities. An eight-passenger omnibus using a gasoline-powered internal combustion engine developed in Germany in 1895 provided a more direct link to modern buses. In 1905, buses operated by sight-seeing companies were introduced to the streets of New York City. All early bus designs were actually based on a truck chassis, with a bus body simply mounted on top.

That Frank Martz was able to recognize at such an early date the potential for a bus operation in the backwaters of Pennsylvania was a reflection on a innovative spirit he exhibited throughout his life. His bus service charged a nickel a ride and was an instant success, prompting Martz to commission the White Motor Company, a Cleveland truck manufacturer with a nearby factory, to built a true bus for him. It was a Spartan affair featuring wooden cane seats, but it served its purpose. (It was so reliable in fact that for decades the bus still participated in parades and other events after it was retired from regular service and is still kept on a family estate.) Martz named his business White Transit Company and began to make regular runs between the mining towns of Pennsylvania's Wyoming Valley. In 1912, he incorporated the company and bought four more buses as part of an effort to expand the business and the number of routes he operated.

It was not until 1921 that the first vehicles featuring a chassis designed specifically for bus service were introduced in the United States by the Fageol Safety Coach Company of Oakland, California. The new "Safety Coach" buses, offering seven rows of four seats, were long and painted gray, prompting the nickname "Greyhounds." Martz created Frank Martz Coach

Company Perspectives:

The Martz organization employs over 600 people, operates over 400 motorcoaches, and is nationally known and respected within the industry.

Co. in 1922 in order to take advantage of the rising popularity of the bus and to provide inter-city bus service. This enterprise was incorporated in 1927, by which time it had established bus service between the Wilkes-Barre-Scranton area and New York City, Philadelphia, Albany, Utica, Syracuse, and Rochester. Elsewhere in America at the time, there were some 4,000 small independent bus operators. A pair of ambitious owners during this period joined forces and began to accumulate other small bus lines under the banner of Motor Transit Corporation, leading to the rise of a transcontinental bus service. In 1930, the company changed its name to Greyhound Corporation. By the end of the 1920s, in the meantime, Martz buses began running west to Buffalo, Cleveland, Detroit, and Chicago, resulting eventually in through-service from New York City and Chicago. Martz also provided service to Washington, D.C., and Atlantic City.

Martz Flirts With Air Travel in 1920

Martz displayed his creativity in a number of ways during the heyday of his business career. In 1926, he became involved in air travel, operating three airplanes that connected Wilkes-Barre, Buffalo, and Elmira, New York, with Newark Airport, which was the major facility serving the New York metropolitan area. A Martz slogan of the time was "By airway or highway." Frank Martz also introduced upscale bus service, anticipating modern motorcoaches that now have televisions as a standard feature. Martz, starting in 1930, offered what was called "Club Coach" service, outfitting two buses to resemble the living room of a house, with hostesses on board to cater to passengers on long trips. The service was so popular that the company ordered another 18 of these custom-made buses. Moreover, Martz was an early proponent of express schedules, eliminating local stops on major runs in order to offer their passengers shorter trips. By the early 1930s, Martz had some 150 buses operating out of ten garages spread between New York City and Chicago.

The Depression of the 1930s hurt Martz, as it did most businesses in America. In 1933, the airplane service was sold to what is now American Airlines. Martz, like other independent bus companies, faced stiff competition from larger and much better financed bus operations, in particular the growing dominance of Greyhound Corporation, whose lines covered most of the United States by 1936. The independents lacked a way to connect passengers between their lines, putting them at a major disadvantage operating against Greyhound. In February 1936, representatives from five bus companies met to form an umbrella organization that would become known as the National Trailways Bus System. Frank Martz was one of those executives, as was H.W. Stewart of Burlington Transportation Company, P.O. Dittmar of Santa Fe Trails Transportation Company, A.E. Greenleaf of Missouri-Pacific Stages, and A.T. Williams

of Safeway Lines. These men also comprised the managing committee of the new enterprise. Within two years, Trailways would include 40 bus companies.

Frank Martz was a Trailways' director for only a short period of time before he died. His son, Frank Martz, Jr., assumed control of the family transportation business as president. Although he inherited an innovative company, its operations were spread too far to allow it to be profitable under the difficult economic conditions of the 1930s. The company was heavily in debt, and a receiver was ultimately brought in by creditors in order to salvage the business. Most of the routes were lopped off, so that by the end of the decade Martz was essentially reduced to operating buses between Wilkes-Barre/Scranton, Philadelphia, Atlantic City, and New York City routes, which they still operate today. Trailways' membership no longer made sense, and Martz soon dropped its affiliation with the network.

The fortunes of Martz rebounded in the 1940s because of the boom in travel created by the war effort. The company continued to flourish during the postwar years. It was also during this period that Martz came into conflict with Greyhound over violations of protected territories, several times resulting in the two parties appealing to Pennsylvania's Public Utility Commission to moderate their dispute. In 1951, Martz renewed its affiliation with Trailways and moved its New York City operations into the newly opened Port Authority Bus Terminal, which consolidated interstate bus traffic into the city. Until then, Martz had used the Dixie Bus Terminal, one of eight facilities that had cropped up in a single square mile section of Manhattan, which resulted in both congested streets and cramped terminals.

Frank Martz, Jr. Dies in 1964 Accident

Control of the Martz Group changed hands in 1964 when Frank Martz, Jr. died in a helicopter accident while flying to Allentown to pick up auto parts. He was succeeded as president by his nephew Frank M. Henry, grandson of the company's founder. Henry continued to grow the business, adjusting to changing conditions in travel, which saw more people flying and a declining bus ridership. In 1972, Martz withdrew from its city transit business, which provided local bus service in the Wilkes-Barre area, and sold its routes to the Luzerne County Transportation Authority. In time, Henry was joined by his own son, Scott Henry, who went to work for the company full time in 1981. He learned all aspects of the business, working in the office, serving as a ticket agent/porter, and also working in maintenance. Father and son shifted the company's emphasis to tours and charters. In 1982, Martz built a five-story office/terminal complex on Public Square in downtown Wilkes-Barre, where the company housed its bus terminal and executive offices as well as its charter and tour office and travel agency.

Growth and Expansion: 1970s–1990s

Martz first expanded into the Washington, D.C., area with the purchase of Gold Line in Tuxedo, Maryland, in 1974. They later joined the Grey Line team in 1977 to offer individual per capita tours of Washington, D.C., and Williamsburg, Virginia. Service farther south was added in 1980 with the purchase of Gulf Coast Motor Lines in St. Petersburg, Florida; National

Key Dates:

1908: Frank Martz, Sr. launches a bus business.
1922: Frank Martz Coach is formed.
1936: Frank Martz, Sr., dies.
1964: Frank Martz, Jr., dies.
1972: The company withdraws from the city transportation business.
1986: The Florida market is entered.

Coach Works of Manassas, Virginia, in 1983; and First Class Coach of Orlando, Florida, in 1986. The Richmond, Virginia-based Tourtime America joined Martz two years later, providing tours of Colonial Williamsburg as well as excursions to Florida, New York, and New England. In 1994, Martz bought Franklin Motorcoach, a Virginia company that had been founded in 1953 as Franklin Charter Bus. It offered charter buses for educational, recreational, and sports-related activities in the Washington, D.C., and northern Virginia area.

In the 1990s, regional bus companies like Martz began to enjoy a renaissance due to a number of factors. They established many nonstop routes between major cities, such as between New York City and Washington, D.C., offering inexpensive fares to lure passengers away from both Amtrak and air shuttles. Commuter service between the Pocono Mountains of Pennsylvania and New York City became the backbone of the operation. Cuts in Amtrak service offered fresh opportunities for regionals, as did financial problems suffered by Greyhound, which cut services as a cost-saving measure. Far from the days of wooden seats, the contemporary buses operated by Martz featured plush seats as well as stereo music, televisions, and VCRs, making short rides and excursions an attractive option for both commuters and travelers. Moreover, the rising average age of the population worked in favor of the tour and charter businesses of Martz and other regional carriers. Following the terrorist attacks that occurred on September 11, 2001, bus operators like Martz saw business adversely affected. Later, the panic caused by a rash of sniper attacks in the Washington, D.C., and Virginia area resulted in customers avoiding travel for several months. Ridership slowly returned to normal, and Martz and other regional carriers looked forward to a new beginning in 2003.

Principal Divisions

Martz Trailways; Martz Lines; National Coach Works; Franklin Coach; National Coach; Tourtime America; First Class Coach, St. Petersburg, Florida; First Class Coach, Orlando, Florida.

Principal Competitors

Greyhound Lines, Inc.; Peter Pan Bus Lines.

Further Reading

Morgan-Besecker, Terrie, ''Martz Bus Started On Road to Success With Welcome Rides for Tired Miners,'' *Times Leader*, March 15, 1998, p. 1B.

Tomsho, Robert, ''Small Bus Lines Turn Aggressive and Win Riders,'' *Wall Street Journal*, December 28, 1994, p. B1.

Turfa, Pamela C., ''Family Operations in Pennsylvania Prove Successful, Long-lasting,'' *Tribune Business News*, July 16, 1998.

—Ed Dinger

metris

Metris Companies Inc.

10900 Wayzata Boulevard
Minnetonka, Minnesota 55305
U.S.A.
Telephone: (952) 525-5020
Fax: (952) 417-5613
Web site: http://www.metriscompanies.com

Public Company
Incorporated: 1996
Employees: 3,700
Sales: $1.4 billion (2002)
Stock Exchanges: New York
Ticker Symbol: MXT
NAIC: 522291 Consumer Lending; 522210 Credit Card
   Issuing

Metris Companies Inc., a financial products and services provider, has risen quickly in the industry by targeting the low- to moderate-income American consumer. The company issues credit cards through its subsidiary Direct Merchants Credit Card Bank, N.A. Besides consumer lending, Metris generates revenue through the sale of enhancement services, such as membership clubs and credit and purchase protection. Hard times in the early 2000s have hit both Metris and the consumers it serves, leaving the company with the challenge of regaining the profitability it had once enjoyed.

Data-Driven: 1940s to Early 1990s

Metris Companies Inc. was born out of Fingerhut Companies' obsession with data. Established in 1948, Fingerhut started out selling car seat covers on credit. From the get-go, the company kept detailed information on its customers. "Even as its product offering increased, Fingerhut did not use outside credit cards, did not seek payment histories from outside credit agencies, and did not report payment histories of its customers to any outside credit agency, which made its customer database proprietary in the truest sense of the word," explained Eric J. Wieffering in January 1994.

Fingerhut was also resilient. The direct marketer weathered the economic storms of the 1970s, capitalized on the consumer mail-order sale boom of the 1980s, and continued to grow and modernize its database. By 1994, Fingerhut was a $1.8 billion company with ten million households on its records. Of those, 6.7 million were deemed active buyers, according to Wieffering. To further exploit its database, the company had begun testing a range of financial products, such as life and property insurance and cobranded credit cards.

Fingerhut customers fell in the moderate- to low-income bracket, folks with little or no access to consumer credit. In 1994, Fingerhut tapped Ronald N. Zebeck to create a credit card program to serve that segment of the population. He formed the Direct Merchants Credit Card Bank and began offering MasterCard branded cards the next year. The Fingerhut Financial Services Corp. unit had 1.1 million cards and $1.06 billion in loans outstanding by mid-year, according to *American Banker*.

Needing capital for continued growth, Fingerhut renamed its financial services unit Metris Companies Inc. and sold 17 percent of the company for $16 per share in an October 1996 initial public offering. Its new name derived from a word denoting measurement, Metris held exclusive access to Fingerhut's database of households, where it drew more than half its card customers. Not limited to marketing credit cards, Metris used information gleaned from Fingerhut to market extended-service plans, membership clubs, card registration, and third-party insurance.

Prior to joining Metris, Zebeck had driven the highly successful introduction of the General Motors MasterCard in 1992. Partnered with Household Credit Services, the auto company issued a million cards in its first month. As CEO and president of a much smaller entity, Zebeck had to scale back his goals. Still, the fledgling company, whose typical customer earned between $15,000 and $35,000, made a sharp impression on the market.

"Metris has grown more rapidly than we assumed it would," said Joseph LaManna, an analyst with William Blair & Co., in a September 1997 *American Banker* article. "Its management team is very ambitious and we expect the company to be a lot bigger than it is today.''

The company's growth was helped by card registration deals with two big card issuers, Bank of America and Household. The move put Metris into competition with CUC International, the dominant provider of such fee-based card enhancements. Besides diversifying its revenue stream, Metris built its core credit card business through purchasing the credit card portfolios of other financial institutions. Year-end 1997 net income was $38 million, up 90 percent over the prior year, and Metris common stock traded at about $34 per share.

Spun Off and Climbing High: 1998–99

Metris stock continued to climb skyward, trading as high as $80 per share in the summer of 1998. Fingerhut spun off its creation in September; the 83 percent it still held given as a dividend distribution to stockholders. The spinoff took a significant chunk of Fingerhut earnings, and the business would have to find new ways to grow.

Meanwhile, Zebeck continued the tenacious pursuit of his goals. Metris held the 20th spot among credit card issuers in the country with nearly three million customers and $5 billion in receivables, according to *Corporate Report Minnesota* in November 1998. Profitability, not size, was Zebeck's main concern.

Zebeck continued down a path other financial institutions sought to avoid. ''He wants the person who's gone through a messy divorce and whose card was maxed out by an angry ex, or people who have not been offered a bank credit card in the past, such as the high school graduate who has recently entered the work force. He's also interested in attracting the Asian-American and Hispanic population, one of the fastest growing markets,'' wrote John Rosengren.

Metris's direct mail response was higher than the industry average. By and large, its potential customers were not receiving many other offers in the mail. On the down side, the company's write-off rate on bad debt exceeded the industry average. To compensate, Metris charged the majority of its customers annual fees, set higher interest rates on credit balances, and established relatively low credit limits. Its extensive Fingerhut data had allowed Metris to develop sophisticated statistical models to gauge risk.

Moreover, nearly 65 percent of Metris employees worked in the collections department. Their success rate was so good,

Metris had bought portfolios of bad debt on credit card accounts from other financial institutions.

Metris's choice of target market was itself the source of some skepticism. While Zebeck maintained that lower income Americans had just as much right to carry credit cards as did their more affluent counterparts, critics said people living paycheck to paycheck could ill afford to carry expensive debt.

Metris began having its own credit woes as 1998 wound down. The accounting practices of one of its competitors had come under federal scrutiny, putting downward pressure on Metris stock. A third quarter correction amplified the damage and hampered its plans to acquire another credit card portfolio. Then, in December 1998, private equity firm Thomas H. Lee Co. arrived on the scene.

Thomas H. Lee infused $300 million into Metris. A 29 percent stake in the company went for $37.25 per share. Capital-strapped Metris added a dividend of 9 percent for seven years to secure the deal. Ultimately, Thomas H. Lee would own 40 percent of Metris without additional payouts, according to *Buyout.*

Fingerhut could have ended its data-sharing agreement with Metris when Thomas H. Lee obtained a large stake in the company. Instead Fingerhut, which was purchased by Federated Department Stores Inc. in March 1999, switched to a nonexclusive agreement commencing in late 2001. Reliance on Fingerhut had been diminishing, but about 35 percent of Metris's credit card accounts still came from its former parent company's database.

After pulling in $57 million in profits in 1998, Metris barreled ahead in 1999. The company announced plans to move its Minnesota-based headquarters into a larger space and make operational expansions in Oklahoma and Florida. Entry into the Internet, a marketing effort which promised access to a new customer base, was also in the works.

Metris subsidiaries kept pace. Direct Merchants Credit Card Bank bought a $1.2 billion credit card portfolio from GE Capital, gaining 485,000 accounts. Metris Direct Inc. and Metris Recovery Services Inc. made agreements to perform customer service and collections activities, respectively, for GE Card Services, a unit of GE Capital.

Fall to Earth: 2000–03

More broadly speaking, Metris stock price rose with the overall strength of the credit card industry, but those days began to fade in early 2000. The industry faced an assortment of problems: rising interest rates, stalled loan growth, consumer privacy issues, charges of predatory lending activities, and calls for stricter capital requirements on subprime lending, according to *American Banker.* Zebeck, however, stayed the course and during the year acquired Banco Popular Inc.'s U.S. credit card portfolio. Metris also cobranded a credit card with the Puerto Rico-based banking company. The year ended with $195 million in net profits on $9.3 billion in receivables.

Nonetheless, Matthew Swibel, writing for *Forbes* in 2001, wondered if Zebeck's formula for profitability was losing its effectiveness. The rise in the number of delinquent accounts and the rate at which they were charged off looked troublesome. Some of its sales and marketing tactics drew the condemnation of federal bank regulators.

As subprime competitors Providian Financial Corp. and NextCard Inc. faltered, Metris worked to distinguish itself from them. David Wesselink, Metris vice-chairman, told *American Banker* the company concentrated on drawing the "near-prime" consumer. David Breitkopf wrote, "Mr. Wesselink cited the Hispanic market as one example of a market with a healthy near-prime segment." Moreover, Wesselink took pride in the company's credit risk management system and "industry-leading" loss reserves.

Yet, Metris was vulnerable. Despite its limited relationship with Fingerhut, when Federated Stores announced plans to shut the company down, Metris stock took a 14 percent drop. The January 2002 downturn followed a 10 percent drop which occurred only days earlier. Fourth quarter financial results had raised concerns about bad loans—both in terms of rising numbers and how they had been accounted for in the past.

More bad news followed in April, according to the *Business Journal*. Metris lowered figures on expected earnings and increased the figure for the previous year's bad loan write-offs. Additionally, its Direct Merchants Credit Card Bank subsidiary agreed to make operational changes at the behest of the Office of the Comptroller of the Currency (OCC), the chief regulator of the credit card business. Metris stock fell more than 30 percent with the news, trading about $13 per share.

Metris, which had been profitable each year since going public, faced its first losses. In December 2002, Ronald Zebeck was fired, and David Wesselink succeeded him as chairman and CEO. The company cut the workforce and made changes in senior management, in January 2003. Losses for 2002 totaled $33.9 million. Stock traded between $1 and $2 per share.

Wesselink, who had worked with Advanta Corp. and Household before joining Metris in 1998, had his work cut out for him. Metris faced the prospect of insolvency by mid-2003 if new funding sources could not be found. The company's own credit rating had been downgraded as the quality of its credit card portfolio eroded.

"The company finds itself in this precarious position partly because of the economy but also because of a decision that was made in 2001 to extend the credit limits of the company's most profitable customers," wrote Julie Forster in the *Star Tribune* in March 2003.

Coinciding with its change in credit limits, companies such as Target and Sears sought out customers for their new credit cards, tapping into Metris's market segment. When the economy slumped following the September 11th attack on the United States, people had trouble paying all their bills. High-pressure tactics by Metris to collect on the debt failed.

A financing agreement put a halt to Metris's downhill slide. A new operating agreement with the OCC was made. Collection improved and troubled accounts were sold. But, the company was not off the slippery slope quite yet, posting losses in the first quarter of 2003. Wesselink told *American Banker* Metris had moved closer toward profitability but would not speculate when that time might arrive.

Principal Subsidiaries

Direct Merchants Credit Card Bank, N.A.; Metris Direct, Inc.; Metris Receivables, Inc.

Principal Competitors

American Express Company; Bank One Corporation; Capital One Financial Corporation; Citigroup Inc.; MBNA Corporation.

Further Reading

Bloom, Jennifer Kingson, "Subprime Card Company on Scenic Route to the Net," *American Banker*, October 4, 1999, p. 17.

Breitkopf, David, "Metris Touts Merits of Its Own Strategy," *American Banker*, November 12, 2001, p. 1.

DePass, Dee, "Metris Reports $48 Million Loss," *Star Tribune*, January 30, 2003, p. 1D.

Feyder, Susan, "Metris Shares Fall on Fingerhut News," *Star Tribune*, January 18, 2002, p. 2D.

Fickenscher, Lisa, "Catering to Customers Others Shun," *American Banker*, September 16, 1997, p. 12A.

"Fingerhut Announces Filing of Registration Statement by Its Subsidiary," *Business Wire*, August 26, 1996.

Forster, Julie, "Metris Tries to Rebuild Its House of Cards," *Star Tribune*, March 17, 2003, p. 1D.

——, "Metris Wins $850 Million in Financing, Averts Crisis," *Star Tribune*, March 20, 2003, p. 1D.

Groeneveld, Benno, "Metris Plunges on Lower Numbers, Subsidiary Problems," *Business Journal* (Minneapolis/St. Paul), April 17, 2002.

"In Brief: Metris Closes Deal with Banco Popular," *American Banker*, August 31, 2000, p. 9.

Jean, Sheryl, "Credit Online: Metris Plans Internet Sales," *Business Journal* (Minneapolis/St. Paul), June 28, 1999.

——, "Metris Keeps Fingerhut Handy," *Business Journal* (Minneapolis/St. Paul), July 12, 1999.

Keenan, Charles, "Card Stocks in a Tailspin Despite Solid 4Q Profits," *American Banker*, February 14, 2000, p. 1.

Kosman, Josh, "Thomas H. Lee Credits Metris for Strong Returns," *Buyouts*, May 31, 1999.

Kuykendall, Lavonne, "1Q Earnings: Metris Posts Loss, But Says It's on Track," *American Banker*, April 17, 2003, p. 19.

——, "Little Detail on Metris Plan to Get Out of the Red," *American Banker*, January 30, 2003, p. 7.

——, "New Metris CEO Plans No Major Changes," *American Banker*, December 19, 2002, p. 5.

Meece, Mickey, "Fingerhut Planning to Spin Off Financial Unit in 4th Quarter," *American Banker*, September 17, 1996, p. 16.

Pender, Kathleen, "Tantalizing Notes Carry High Risks," *San Francisco Chronicle*, December 1, 2002, p. G1.

Rosengren, John, "Low Rider," *Corporate Report Minnesota*," November 1998, pp. 24+.

Swibel, Matthew, "Payback Time," *Forbes*, August 6, 2001.

Wieffering, Eric J., "I Can't Afford to Fail," *Corporate Report Minnesota*, January 1994, pp. 52–60.

—Kathleen Peippo

Midas Inc.

1300 Arlington Heights Road
Itasca, Illinois 60143
U.S.A.
Telephone: (630) 438-3000
Fax: (630) 438-3880
Web site: www.midasinc.com

Public Company
Incorporated: 1956
Employees: 1,900
Sales: $333 million (2002)
Stock Exchanges: New York
Ticker Symbol: MDS
NAIC: 336213 Gasoline Engine and Engine Parts
Manufacturing; 336322 Other Motor Vehicle
Electrical and Electronic Equipment Manufacturing;
33633 Motor Vehicle Steering and Suspension
Components (Except Spring) Manufacturing; 33634
Motor Vehicle Brake System Manufacturing; 33635
Motor Vehicle Transmission and Power Train Parts
Manufacturing; 336399 All Other Motor Vehicle Parts
Manufacturing; 441310 Automotive Parts and
Accessories Stores

Midas Inc. is the parent company for Midas International Corporation, a leading provider of automotive services related to exhaust, brakes, steering, suspension, climate control, and maintenance. The company also oversees Parts Warehouse Inc., a network of distribution sites designed to quickly deliver parts to Midas shops. The firm has over 2,000 franchised and company-owned stores in the U.S. and Canada and over 700 licensed and franchised locations in 17 countries across the globe. Once a private subsidiary of the Whitman Corporation, Midas was spun off in 1998 and now operates as an independent public company. Slowing sales and high costs have forced the company to restructure operations. Midas plans to exit the distribution business and sell off unprofitable stores.

Sherman Makes His Mark in the Automotive Service Industry: 1950s

In the early 1950s, the founder of Midas International Corporation, Nate H. Sherman, operated a family business in Chicago that manufactured car mufflers. As president of International Parts Corporation, Sherman was well aware of the developments in the automotive industry during the 1950s. The American economy was expanding rapidly, making the average person more prosperous than ever before. This prosperity translated into increased consumer demand for cars, and between 1950 and 1956 almost 40 million new automobiles were purchased. Technological innovations, such as 18-month mufflers and dual exhaust systems, were also changing the way cars were serviced. Sherman recognized that the independent service stations—the "mom and pop" corner gas stations—would no longer be able to meet the growing demand for automotive services. These developments convinced Sherman that he could develop a new type of service station where he could sell his mufflers directly to consumers and eliminate the need for distributors.

Sherman correctly predicted that consumers would prefer fast, efficient automotive service to the slower "mom and pop" service station. He felt that the best way to take advantage of the dramatic changes in the automotive market was to create a network of independent businesses that would be supported by a central company—in short, to begin franchising. In 1956, the entrepreneur formed the Muffler Installation Dealers' Association (M.I.D.A.S.) and convinced long-time friend Hugh Landrum to open the first Midas Muffler franchise shop. Located in Macon, Georgia, the shop installed and replaced mufflers as quickly and as efficiently as possible. In order to differentiate Midas from other service stations and to encourage return business, Sherman guaranteed to replace any muffler his shop had installed in a domestic car for as long as the motorist owned it. By the end of 1957, there were 100 Midas Muffler franchise shops independently operated in 40 states.

With his flair for marketing, Sherman began to revolutionize the automotive service industry. Consumer surveys taken throughout the 1950s indicated that most people did not understand how their own cars worked; because of their lack of mechanical knowledge, many of these people believed that they were overcharged or charged for unnecessary repairs at service stations. In addition, a large number of people were angry with the inadequate service or poor workmanship evident in fixing their cars. Sherman's marketing strategy was to directly involve the customer in making decisions about repairing the car. He instructed Midas Muffler shop owners to invite the motorists into the service bays to educate them about their cars and what needed repair. A written estimate that included an itemization of the repair work was given to each customer before the repairs were begun. Finally, Sherman suggested that all Midas shops install large windows to an area where customers could watch the repairs made on their cars.

Rapid Growth: 1960s–1970s

The accuracy of Sherman's predictions about the automotive industry and his marketing savvy helped Midas become one of the fastest growing franchises in the United States. By 1960, there were 319 Midas Muffler Shops in operation and a growing number of competitors both locally and regionally. In order to protect and increase its share of the automotive services market, Midas introduced shock absorber service in 1960. The company continued to grow, and in 1968 Midas purchased Huth Manufacturing Corporation, a firm that produced made-to-order bender machines. The benders provided automation to cut and weld tubing for a car's exhaust system. The Huth machines proved to be time savers, and, as muffler installers increased their demand for the benders, Midas's marketing network grew both in the United States and in foreign countries. The first Midas Muffler "Silencer" Shop opened in 1968 in Harlesden, England. By 1970, there were 577 Midas Muffler Shops operating throughout the United States, England, and Canada.

In 1972, Midas International was purchased by IC Industries, Inc., which subsequently renamed itself the Whitman Corporation. At that time, under the leadership of William Johnson, IC Industries divested most of its railroad holdings and began the transformation into a multinational conglomerate. Diversification into consumer goods and services was indicated by three major acquisitions: Pepsi-Cola General Bottlers, a soft-drink bottler located in the Midwest; Midas International; and Pet Inc., an evaporated milk company operating out of St. Louis.

As a wholly owned subsidiary operating within IC Industries' consumer products division, Midas benefited from the financial resources of its parent company. In 1974, Midas created the Midas Institute of Technology in Palatine, Illinois. This facility was designed to serve as a training center for new franchisees, managers, and automotive mechanics. In order to ensure the best service throughout its franchise network, em-

phasis was placed on developing good consumer relations and improving the technical skills of Midas employees. In 1978, Midas opened its 1,000th shop in the United States; during the same year, Midas also extended its muffler guarantee to customers with foreign cars. In 1979, Midas announced that it would provide brake service in all its shops. By 1980, there were 1,350 Midas Muffler and Brake Shops, with franchises in Australia, Belgium, Canada, England, France, Mexico, and Puerto Rico.

Continued Success in the 1980s

Midas continued to grow during the 1980s. The company manufactured its 50 millionth muffler in 1983 largely due to improvements in production. The company initiated a major expansion at its manufacturing facilities in Bedford Park, Illinois, and Hartford, Wisconsin, where it produced exhaust systems and other automotive parts for domestic and foreign cars, vans, light trucks, and even antique autos. With over 1,400 franchise outlets in the United States by 1985 and over 400 shops in foreign countries, Midas was three times larger than its closest competitor. Record revenues of $298 million were reported in 1984, an increase of 10 percent over the previous year. Also in the same year, Midas opened 74 shops in the United States alone. In the exhaust replacement market, Midas accounted for approximately 12 percent of the outlets but garnered about 25 percent of the business.

Near the end of 1984, *Entrepreneur* magazine ranked Midas as one of the top-ten franchisers in the country. Although the automotive products and services market was growing at an annual rate of over 10 percent, the market was far from saturated. Research had shown that as consumers kept their cars longer and as traditional service stations provided fewer automotive repairs, the demand for special repair stores continued to increase. Midas's own marketing research indicated that the company had the highest profile and best name recognition of all the competitors in the exhaust replacement industry. By taking advantage of these trends, Midas opened its 2,000th shop in 1986. In contrast, Car-X and Speedy Muffler King—both franchises that were controlled by Toronto-based Tenneco—Midas's closest competitors in the automotive services franchise business at the time, operated 434 shops combined. Meinecke Muffler Company, with 400 shops located primarily in the southern and midwestern parts of the United States, ranked third.

In 1986, Midas opened its New England Training Center in Taunton, Massachusetts. Because of the large number of applications for Midas franchises in the eastern part of the United States, the company duplicated the training services it had established in 1974 at the Midas Institute of Technology in Palatine. At the company's Hartford and Bedford Park manufacturing facilities, highly automated and computerized assembly lines were producing more than 1,000 mufflers per hour for both the domestic and foreign markets. In 1989, Midas manufactured its 100th million muffler. Midas also introduced computerized suspension and alignment services in all its shops during this time. With the increasing popularity of four-wheel-drive vehicles, the addition of smart suspension systems, and the use of four-corner struts by most car makers, Midas anticipated that the suspension market would ultimately grow larger

Key Dates:
1956: Nate H. Sherman forms the Muffler Installation Dealers' Association; Hugh Landrum opens the first Midas muffler franchise shop in Macon, Georgia.
1960: Midas begins offering shock absorber service.
1968: Huth Manufacturing Corp. is acquired.
1972: IC Industries Inc.—eventually known as Whitman Corp.—purchases Midas.
1979: The firm begins to offer brake service in all of its shops.
1986: The company opens its 2,000th shop.
1993: U.S. sales surpass $1 billion.
1998: Whitman spins off Midas.
2001: The company purchases 98 franchise locations.

and more financially rewarding than either the exhaust or brake markets.

In 1991, Midas celebrated its 35th year of operation by continuing to expand its franchise network. During the early 1990s, Whitman Corporation began acquiring muffler shops in Europe for Midas to operate and increased its name recognition in the United States through a major advertising campaign. By continuing to expand both in the United States and in such countries as England, Switzerland, and Austria, sales for the company grew rapidly. In 1992, sales and services provided by Midas shops accounted for 20 percent of Whitman Corporation's total sales. By the following year, U.S. retail sales had surpassed $1 billion.

Spurred by its franchising success, in 1993 Midas initiated an expansion campaign in Mexico. Under a franchise contract with Interamericana de Talleras SA de CV, Midas began opening retail and service outlets in major metropolitan areas. Management expected these outlets to grow at a rate of ten shops per year for the first few years and then increase rapidly. The goal was to open over 140 shops to service the nearly ten million registered automobiles and light trucks in the country.

The most recognized name in the muffler service and repair business, Midas was poised to take advantage of the growing used car market during the early 1990s. The unpredictable state of the world's economy resulted in people holding onto their cars longer than at any time in the past, and Midas planned to provide the repairs and services necessary to keep these cars on the road. With its continually expanding franchise operation and its ready access to the financial resources of its parent company, Midas appeared to be well positioned to remain the industry leader.

Overcoming Challenges: Mid-1990s and Beyond

The company began to face challenges in the mid- to late 1990s, however, due in part to heightened competition from the likes of Pep Boys and Penske Auto Centers Inc., companies that focused on the super auto center concept. As the competition was becoming well known for offering a vast array of services, Midas had to contend with the consumer perception that it only dealt with mufflers. To shore up its image, Midas launched a

$23 million advertising campaign in 1996 that focused on the company's other services, including alignment and suspension.

Meanwhile, franchisee relations with Midas's parent company were deteriorating and sales and store growth were languishing. In a move that was beneficial to both the muffler king and Whitman, Midas was spun off as an independent public company in January 1998. Under the leadership of new CEO Wendel Province, Midas immediately began to make changes in an attempt to revamp its brand, capture market share, and increase sales. To restore franchisee faith in the company, Province began selling company-owned stores in markets that directly competed with franchise locations. He then used the proceeds of those sales to give each franchisee $15,000 per store to pay for new signs and new paint in order to relate the company's "New Midas" campaign. To cut costs, the company moved its headquarters from downtown Chicago to Itasca, Illinois, and also shuttered a Midas factory.

Midas continued to face an upward battle as the exhaust market deteriorated further. In fact, during 1999 the market declined by 20 percent, making the company's transformation from just a muffler place to a multi-service auto shop crucial to its survival. During 2000, the company completed its "New Midas" North American campaign, which included store refurbishment and the addition of new services related to climate control and maintenance. The company also launched Parts Warehouse Inc., a network of distribution sites that delivered parts to Midas locations and other customers.

During 2001, the company switched gears and began an aggressive campaign to strengthen its company-owned holdings by purchasing 98 Midas locations in the United States. The strategy was designed to bolster profits, but during the following year the company reported a loss of $33.6 million. As earnings continued to decline, Province announced his retirement. McDonald's Corp. executive Alan Feldman was named his replacement and knew he had his work cut out for him. "It's clear to me we have our challenges," claimed the new CEO in a January 2003 *Crain's Chicago Business* article. Indeed, as the company planned to exit the wholesale distribution market and sell off many of its company-owned stores, Feldman's ability to bring the shine back to the Midas name remained to be seen.

Principal Subsidiaries

Midas International Corporation; Midas Illinois, Inc.; Midas Realty Corporation; Midas Properties; Muffler Corporation of America; Dealers Wholesale Inc.; Huth Inc.; International Parts Corporation; Parts Warehouse Inc.; Midas International Corporation; Insurance Services Management, Inc.; Progressive Automotive Systems, Inc.; Cosmic Holdings LLC; MDS Automotive Holdings B.V. (Netherlands); Midas Automotive International B.V. (Netherlands); Midas Canada Holdings, Ltd.; Midas Canada, Inc.; Midas Realty Corporation of Canada, Inc.; APWI Canada, Inc.

Principal Competitors

GKN plc; Monro Muffler Brake Inc.; The Pep Boys.

Further Reading

Arndorfer, James B., ''Profile: Former McD's Exec Brings Repair Kit to Midas' Shop,'' *Crain's Chicago Business*, January 27, 2003, p. 10.

Copple, Brandon, ''Life Is About Trust,'' *Forbes*, January 11, 1999, p. 55.

Haran, Leah, ''Midas Retools Image in New Ad Campaign,'' *Crain's Chicago Business*, March 25,1996, p. 32.

''Midas Makeover 'Is More Difficult Than I Ever Imagined,' '' *Business Week*, June 19, 2000.

Murphy, Lee H., ''Distribution Biz on Way Out as Midas Downsizes,'' *Crain's Chicago Business*, May 19, 2003, p. 16.

Strazewski, Len, ''Muffler Shops Search for Golden Touch,'' *Advertising Age*, May 16, 1985, p. 15.

Waters, Jennifer, ''Midas Looks to Cure its 'Muffler Vision,' '' *Crain's Chicago Business*, June 23, 1997, p. 4.

Willins, Michael, ''Midas CEO Bails as Expected Earnings Decline,'' *Motor Age*, November 2002, p. 108.

—Thomas Derdak
—update: Christina M. Stansell

Miele & Cie. KG

Carl-Miele-Straße 29
D-33332 Gütersloh
Germany
Telephone: (49) (52 41) 89-0
Fax: (49) (5241) 89-2090
Web site: http://www.miele.de

Private Company
Incorporated: 1899 as Miele & Cie.
Employees: 15,328
Sales: EUR 2.24 billion ($2.22 billion) (2002)
NAIC: 335221 Household Cooking Appliance
   Manufacturing; 335222 Household Refrigerator and
   Home Freezer Manufacturing; 335212 Household
   Vacuum Cleaner Manufacturing; 335224 Household
   Laundry Equipment Manufacturing; 335228 Other
   Major Household Appliance Manufacturing; 337124
   Metal Household Furniture Manufacturing; 337122
   Nonupholstered Wood Household Furniture
   Manufacturing

Miele & Cie. KG is Germany's third-largest manufacturer of household appliances and has a strong foothold in the European market as well. The company is best known for its durable washing machines, tumble dryers, rotary irons, dishwashers, built-in refrigerators, freezers, stoves and stove hoods, and vacuum cleaners. Miele & Cie. also makes commercial washing machines used in hotels, commercial dishwashers for restaurants, special washer-extractors for cleaning the protective suits of fire fighters, and washer-disinfectors for hospitals and medical laboratories. Professional appliances sold to businesses account for approximately 10 percent of total revenues. A line of built-in kitchen ensembles, which accounts for roughly 3 percent of sales, complements Miele's product range. Almost two-thirds of the company's sales are generated from exports. While Miele appliances are sold all around the world, the company manufactures almost all its components, including electronics, in Germany and Austria. This is done in order to insure Miele's high standards of quality. The company is owned and managed by the third-generation descendants of the two company founders.

Easing Housewives' Workload in the Early 20th Century

The initial purpose of the company, which was founded by mason Carl Miele and merchant Reinhard Zinkann in the Westphalian town of Herzebrock in 1899, was the production of cream separators used in farms to separate cream from milk. The eleven workers hired for the job—some tradespeople and the sons of local farmers—operated out of a small workshop on the premises of a former corn mill equipped with one drill and four lathes. Soon the company also started making butter churns with a stirring mechanism that freed the wives and daughters of local farmers from hand-churning. However, it was the decision to include washing machines in the product range that got the Miele enterprise off to a fast start. At the beginning of the 20th century, doing laundry was an exhausting task that involved arduous manual labor and often took several days to accomplish. The dirty laundry was soaked in soapy water over night and wrung out the next morning. After tough stains were rubbed out by hand, the laundry was thrown into a large wood-and-coal fired tub where it had to be manually agitated in the boiling water with a wooden paddle. The laundry was then rubbed by hand on a washboard before it was rinsed and wrung out several times. It was no surprise, then, that Miele's washing machines were soon in such great demand. Under the motto "forever better," the two company founders set out to ease the housewife's workload with a stream of innovative household appliances.

The first Miele washing machine looked very much like the butter churns the company was already making. It consisted of a wooden tub made from expensive oak and paddles in the form of a cross in the center of the tub. These paddles were moved manually by a crank or a lever. After the wooden lid was closed, the rotating cross—called the agitator—moved the laundry placed in the tub around in the hot, soapy water. The machine also included a wring function. Although the process still involved a great deal of manual labor, Miele's "Hera" washing machine, which was soon manufactured in greater numbers, was a welcome alternative to the old "laundry day." In 1904,

Miele introduced a new model that could be driven by a transmission belt. External motors with transmission belts had already been in wide use on family farms to operate cream separators and butter churns.

By 1907, the company had grown to a considerable size that included a workforce of 60 employees. In that year, Carl Miele and Reinhard Zinkann moved their business to Gütersloh, a city in northwestern Germany. The new property they purchased for the company was much larger and came with an iron foundry and an on-site railway connection. In 1907, Miele and Zinkann also established their first four regional sales offices. Four years later, a number of new production facilities were erected that enabled the company to build all the parts used in its products. These facilities included a foundry for non-ferrous metals; facilities for zinc-, nickel-, and tin-plating; an enameling plant; a pressing shop; and a sawmill. Carl Miele even invented a cleaner and cost-saving technology for zinc-plating that earned him a patent. By 1914, the year in which World War I started, Miele & Cie. employed more than 500 people. To ensure their loyalty, the company founders created an impressive benefits package. In 1909, they introduced a company health plan. One year later, over 200 flats were built for Miele employees. In the same year, Miele employees received their first Christmas bonus. A decade later, a company pension fund was created and more company-owned housing for employees was provided in Gütersloh. Another factory for manufacturing components for milk separators and electric motors was erected in Bielefeld, a city north of Gütersloh, in 1916.

Diversification in the Pre-World War II Era

Miele & Cie. kept refining its cream separators, butter churns, and washing machines. The first electricity-powered cream separator was introduced in 1910, followed four years later by the first electric washing machine. Since many households—especially in rural areas—did not have electricity yet, Miele built washing machines that could be powered by running water. For urban dwellers who already had power outlets in their apartments, the company manufactured a model with an electric motor mounted under the tub. The advent of the electric motor made it possible to design a greater variety of washing machines for different needs. By 1926, there were 24 different models of Miele washing machines on the market.

The 1920s and early 1930s saw a great number of Miele "firsts." In 1924, the company ventured into the growing market for commercial washing machines and tumble dryers. In 1926, Miele & Cie. started making milking machines. One year later, the company introduced the first Miele vacuum cleaner. In 1928, Miele's first electric rotary iron was launched, followed the next year by the first electric dishwasher for domestic use in Europe. In 1930, the company put an all-metal washing machine on the market. Two years later, the first Miele ice-box—a predecessor of the refrigerator—appeared.

Another area of new ventures for the company was in the production of motor vehicles. In 1912, Miele & Cie. was among the many manufacturers trying to get a share of the emerging market for automobiles. The company made passenger cars with two and four seats, limousines, and pick-up trucks, manufacturing over 120 vehicles before this business venture was finally abandoned. However, that was not the end of Miele & Cie.'s activities in the automotive arena. In 1924, the company began making bicycles, followed by a model with a supplemental electric motor in 1933. In the same year, Miele & Cie. introduced its first motorcycle.

Miele's constant stream of innovations helped the company survive the politically and economically unstable period between the two world wars. After World War I came to an end in 1919, the German economy was shaken by hyperinflation in the early 1920s, followed by the worldwide effects of the Great Depression, which was triggered by the New York Stock Exchange crash in 1929. Carl Miele and Reinhard Zinkann successfully led the company through these challenging years. Carl Miele died in 1938, Reinhard Zinkann in 1939. By that time, Miele & Cie. employed 2,700 people, and about 2,000 Miele products were produced daily and shipped to numerous countries around the world. The company had developed a network of warehouses, showrooms, and sales offices in Germany and abroad. Foreign sales offices had been established in Austria, Belgium, France, Poland, and Argentina in 1914, and the company's first subsidiary abroad was founded in Switzerland in 1931.

Second Generation Leadership during World War II and the Postwar Boom

In 1939, the year when a Hitler-led Germany declared war on Poland, the sons of the two company founders—Carl Miele, Jr. and Kurt Christian Zinkann—took over the leadership of Miele & Cie. For a limited period of time, they were guided by one of their fathers' most trusted employees, C.H. Walkenhorst, who had worked side-by-side with the two founders for many years. The war interrupted Miele & Cie.'s dynamic growth. The company was ordered to make whatever supplies the German military needed. At the same time, a small part of production capacity was still used to manufacture bicycles and wagons. Many of the company's factories and sales offices were badly damaged in Allied bombing raids on Germany.

After the war, Miele & Cie. adjusted to the very basic needs of the times and built coal-fired ovens from metal that survived the bombing raids. The company even resumed the manufacture of wooden tub washing machines and continued the production of wagons, which Miele had made since 1919. By 1949, Miele's product range was considerably smaller than before the war. However, the reconstruction years gave way to the "economic miracle" years of the 1950s and 1960s.

Key Dates:

1899: Carl Miele and Reinhard Zinkann establish a factory for cream separators.
1900: The company starts making washing machines.
1907: Business operations are moved to Gütersloh.
1916: The Bielefeld factory is built.
1924: The company starts making commercial washing machines and tumble dryers.
1929: Miele launches Europe's first domestic dishwasher with an electric motor.
1931: Miele's first subsidiary abroad is founded in Switzerland.
1969: The company starts making built-in kitchen ensembles.
1978: Miele introduces new computer-controlled appliances.
1980: The first subsidiary overseas is set up in Australia.
1986: Miele acquires laundry technology specialist Cordes in Oelde.
1990: The company takes over appliance manufacturer Imperial in Bünde.
1995: A Miele subsidiary is established in Singapore.
1999: The company celebrates its centenary.

To satisfy the exploding postwar demand for kitchen appliances, Miele & Cie. expanded its production capacities. New factories were built or acquired in Euskirchen, Lehrte, and Warendorf, Germany, and in Bürmoos, Austria. All but the latter were located in close proximity to company headquarters. At the same time, technological standards kept rising. Miele's first fully automatic appliances, a washing machine and a dishwasher, were launched in 1956 and 1960 respectively. The 1960s and 1970s brought more sophisticated control mechanisms based on microelectronics.

To free production and research capacities for household appliances, Miele & Cie. exited the bicycle and motorcycle market in 1960. In 1969, Miele & Cie. entered the rapidly emerging market for built-in kitchens, their strategy being that, instead of selling just one Miele dishwasher or refrigerator at a time, the company could sell a whole kitchen equipped with a number of Miele appliances to a single customer. Between 1973 and 1975, the company remodeled a newly acquired factory and transformed it into a production facility for built-in kitchens. Over the years, the range of Miele kitchen appliances grew more diverse. Miele's well-known dishwashers, refrigerators, and freezers were followed in the 1970s by electric and microwave ovens. Stove hoods, steam cookers, and built-in coffee makers and espresso machines later completed the company's product line.

Another natural extension of the company's activities was the manufacture of specialized washing machines for commercial use. In addition to larger and stronger washing machines for laundromats and hotels, Miele started manufacturing special washing machines for the protective suits of fire fighters. In 1984, the company launched a new line of commercial washing machines and tumble dryers called the "little giants," so named because they had a capacity of five to six kilograms. Miele also put out a number of medium-capacity appliances that were built to handle loads of up to 32 kilograms. In the 1980s, the company also refined its line of commercial dishwashers for restaurants and expanded into building special "dishwashers" for cleaning and disinfecting surgical instruments used in doctors' and dentists' offices, hospitals, and medical research laboratories.

Continuity and Growth in the 1990s and Beyond

In 1985, three of Miele's senior managers, including co-owner Kurt Christian Zinkann, passed away. One year later, CEO Carl Miele, Jr. died. They were succeeded by their sons—Rudolf Miele and Peter Zinkann. The grandsons of the company founders opened a new chapter in Miele & Cie.'s history. Reading the signs of the time, they strongly focused on international expansion. By the mid-1980s, the company had added foreign subsidiaries in Australia, South Africa, Ireland, and the United States in addition to their existing subsidiary in Switzerland. Over the next 17 years, the company's international operations extended to 31 countries. After the Soviet Union disintegrated in the early 1990s, Miele & Cie. expanded into many eastern European countries, including Russia. Another new target market of the 1990s was Asia, where the company founded subsidiaries in Japan, Hong Kong, and Singapore.

The reunification of the two German states in 1990 called for the reorganization of Miele & Cie.'s domestic sales and distribution network. After an almost 50-year absence from the eastern German market, Miele products were instantly popular again. The former sales office in Leipzig, which was lost after World War II, was reopened. Another large sales and distribution center was erected in Berlin later in the decade.

While the company invested heavily in conquering foreign markets, Miele & Cie. did not follow the trend to move production abroad in order to save cost. To the contrary, the company concentrated all manufacturing sites no further than a day's trip from company headquarters. Two acquisitions further expanded Miele's production capacity. In 1986, the company took over Cordes, a Westphalian specialist in laundry technology. Four years later, Miele & Cie. acquired Imperial, a manufacturer of built-in appliances and catering equipment.

Maintaining its emphasis on quality, Miele & Cie. disproved the widely held belief that in the 1990s, with rapid economic globalization under way, it was too expensive to maintain manufacturing facilities in a high-wage country such as Germany. As it turned out, customers were willing to pay premium prices for premium quality. To keep standards at the highest possible level, Miele & Cie. had started developing and manufacturing the microelectronic controls used in the company's appliances. A major strength of Miele's business strategy was the fact that the company's high standards of quality resulted in the longevity of its products. With an average life span of 20 years, Miele appliances were built to last. This policy earned the company top ratings from Germany's leading consumer advocate organization, Stiftung Warentest, and was expressed in the company's new slogan "Miele—a decision for life."

During the 1990s, Miele & Cie.'s sales kept growing. In 1990, the company's revenues passed the DM3 billion mark for the first time. In 1999, the year when the company celebrated its centenary, Miele grossed DM3.9 billion and employed a workforce of 14,364. In that year, 56 percent of the company's sales came from exports. Moreover, "Miele" was the most popular brand that was sold exclusively by special retailers in Germany and other European countries.

After over 100 years in business, Miele & Cie. was still jointly owned and managed by the two founders' grandsons. Over 60 shareholders—descendants from the Miele and Zinkann families—held shares in the company. At 72 and 73 years of age, in 2002 Rudolf Miele and Peter Zinkann, supported by three executive managers from outside the family, continued to co-manage the business over breakfast discussions from their glass-walled offices. In an era of national and international mega-mergers and acquisitions, they set out to dominate their niche in the global market, relying solely on the company's own resources and spending only the money they had already earned. In Rudolf Miele's opinion, the shareholder-value orientation of a public company would ultimately have a negative impact on product quality. With Marcus Miele and Reinhard Zinkann, the fourth generation was prepared to step in and carry on the family tradition.

Principal Competitors

BSH Bosch und Siemens Hausgeräte GmbH; AB Electrolux; Whirlpool Corporation; GE Consumer Products; Maytag Corporation; Alno AG; NOBILIA-Werke J. Stickling GmbH & Co.; Nolte Küchen GmbH und Co. KG.

Further Reading

"Die Küchen-Hersteller beschreiten einen langen Leidensweg," *Frankfurter Allgemeine Zeitung*, January 14, 2003, p. 16.

Fiswick, Andreas, "Miele an Firmenübernahmen und Börsengang nicht interessiert," *vwd*, October 20, 1999.

Helmer, Wolfgang, "Noch gelten die Grundsätze der Firmengründer," *Frankfurter Allgemeine Zeitung*, May 30, 1995, p. 20.

——, "Immer besser und noch immer aktiv," *Frankfurter Allgemeine Zeitung*, August 24, 2002, p. 16.

Liebs, Altrud, "Das Rührwerk im Butterfass," *Frankfurter Allgemeine Zeitung*, August 3, 1999, p. 2.

"Miele erzielt Rekordumsatz vor allem durch Wachstum im Ausland," *Frankfurter Allgemeine Zeitung*, August 27, 1999, p. 17.

"Miele glänzt wieder mit Rekordumsatz," *Frankfurter Allgemeine Zeitung*, August 24, 2002, p. 16.

—Evelyn Hauser

Mitsubishi Chemical Corporation

5-2, Marunouchi 2-chome
Chiyoda-ku, Tokyo 100-0005
Japan
Telephone: (03) 3283-6111
Fax: (03) 3283-5874
Web site: http://www.m-kagaku.co.jp

Public Company
Incorporated: 1950
Employees: 38,617
Sales: ¥1.78 trillion ($13.4 billion) (2002)
Stock Exchanges: Tokyo
Ticker Symbol: 4010
NAIC: 325110 Petrochemical Manufacturing; 325412
    Pharmaceutical Preparation Manufacturing; 325211
    Plastics Material and Resin Manufacturing; 325998
    All Other Miscellaneous Chemical Product and
    Preparation Manufacturing

Mitsubishi Chemical Corporation (MCC) was formed by the 1994 merger of Mitsubishi Kasei Corp. and Mitsubishi Petrochemical Co. As Japan's largest chemical concern, MCC and its network of subsidiaries manufacture petrochemicals, pharmaceuticals, functional materials and plastic-based products, specialty chemicals, carbon, and chemicals and products used in the electronics industry. The company began restructuring in the late 1990s due in part to weakness in the Japanese economy and is focused on streamlining operations and cutting costs in order to restore profitability.

Early History

The Mitsubishi industrial empire was founded by Yataro Iwasaki late in the 19th century and expanded rapidly into general trading and a variety of industrial occupations. So great was its influence that it became known as a *zaibatsu*, or "money clique." As Mitsubishi grew, it purchased factories from bankrupt or failing companies and established new divisions to operate them.

Nippon Tar was founded by Mitsubishi in 1934 to take over the operations of the Makiyama coking factory in northern Kyushu. Makiyama, which had been in existence since 1897, was modernized and reorganized. Renamed the Kurosaki plant, it later became Nippon Tar's primary facility for coke and coke products, fertilizer, and ammonia products. In 1936, the company's name was changed to Nippon Chemical Industries.

The following year, Japan became involved in military hostilities in China. By the end of 1941, Japan was at war with the United States and Great Britain. Chemical production was essential to the industries which manufactured ships, aircraft, and weapons. Nippon Chemical, by its association with Mitsubishi (famous for its deadly Zero fighter plant), was intimately involved in the Japanese war effort.

Japan surrendered to Allied powers in the late summer of 1945 and was placed under the administrative authority of an Allied military commander. The occupation authority enacted a series of industrial reorganization laws which included stringent anti-monopoly laws. The financial empires of the *zaibatsu*, principally Mitsui, Sumitomo, and Mitsubishi, were divided into thousands of independent companies.

When Nippon Chemical was separated from Mitsubishi in 1950, its glass making and rayon divisions were reestablished as separate companies called Asahi Glass and Shinko Rayon (later called Mitsubishi Rayon). The "new" Nippon Chemical Industries, a public limited company, was established in June of 1950.

In 1950, Japan was still recovering from the destruction and ruin caused during the war. Ironically, Japanese industries encountered a period of extreme growth later that year as the result of another war. The same month that Nippon Chemical resumed its operations, communist forces from North Korea invaded South Korea. Japan was used as a staging base for United Nations forces which were sent to Korea to repel the attack. As a result of their proximity to the battle, Japanese companies, including Nippon Chemical, were contracted to furnish a variety of provisions and supplies.

Nippon Chemical Changes Its Name in 1952

In 1952, the company's polyvinyl chloride (PVC) division was turned over to a company called Monsanto Chemical Industries (eventually known as Mitsubishi Monsanto), a joint

236

venture created by Nippon Chemical and Monsanto of the United States. Later that year, Nippon Chemical changed its name to Mitsubishi Chemical Industries Ltd. (or MCI), reflecting the company's growing ties with companies formerly associated with the Mitsubishi *zaibatsu*.

When an armistice was signed in Korea in 1952, many supply contracts with Japanese companies were canceled. Japan experienced a serious recession which forced hundreds of companies to merge in order to survive. In 1953, Mitsubishi Chemical absorbed the Toho Chemical company, later called the Yokkaichi plant, which produced ethyl hexanol and synthetic rubber and textile products. With additional resources and improving market conditions, Mitsubishi Chemical began to expand at a faster rate. The company established a carbide division and laid the groundwork for a petrochemical division.

By the end of the decade, Mitsubishi Chemical derived 38 percent of its revenues from coke, gas, and tar production. The rest of the company's operations consisted of agricultural chemical products (29 percent of revenues), organic chemical products (12 percent), sundries (12 percent), and inorganic chemical products (9 percent).

Mitsubishi Chemical constructed an aluminum rolling mill in 1963 under a joint venture with the Reynolds company of the United States. The mill was designated the company's Naoetsu plant and later became Japan's largest aluminum facility. During the 1960s, Mitsubishi Chemical constructed another coke plant at Sakaide, which was opened in 1969. Production of aluminum at the Sakaide plant commenced two years later.

In 1970, Mitsubishi Chemical resumed pharmaceutical manufacturing (suspended in the early 1950s), as part of its expansion into "bio-industry." The following year the company established the Mitsubishi-Kasei Institute of Life Sciences at Yokohama, which has since acquired an excellent reputation for research.

Overcoming Hardships: 1970s–1980s

The world oil crisis of 1973 compelled Mitsubishi Chemical Industries to reduce its work force in order to remain profitable. In addition, the company was forced to sell its aluminum division (later called Mitsubishi Light Metal Industries, Ltd.). As raw material costs continued to rise, particularly in petrochemicals, Mitsubishi Chemical placed greater emphasis on pharmaceutical and fine chemical production. It also initiated a program to reduce energy consumption. The company's financial position strengthened, and as oil prices began to fall, the petro-

chemical operations became less of a burden. The transfer of the light metals division to Mitsubishi Light Metal Industries was completed in 1976.

In 1983, the *Mainichi Shimbun* and *Nihon Keizai Shimbun*, two Japanese newspapers, reported that the United States Defense Department forced the American division of Mitsubishi Chemical to sell its Optical Information Systems unit to the McDonnell Douglas Corporation. Although the stories were denied, the reports said that Pentagon officials considered the company to be in possession of sensitive laser technologies that they felt could not remain secret unless controlled by an American company. The unit, which Mitsubishi Chemical purchased from Exxon in 1981, was reportedly sold for about $7 million.

In a continuing effort to expand its pharmaceutical division, Mitsubishi Chemical purchased the Mitsubishi Yuka Pharmaceutical company from the Mitsubishi Petrochemical Company in 1985. The transaction included the transfer of over 200 researchers to the company's research institute.

Mitsubishi Chemical lost ¥8.5 billion in 1983 and was forced to suspend dividends. This lowered demand for the company's stock and prevented it from recapitalizing, leaving Mitsubishi Chemical with a weak financial structure despite modest profits. In 1986, however, stronger profitability returned and a five yen dividend was reinstated.

Although it operated as independent company, Mitsubishi Chemical remained closely associated with other Mitsubishi companies. Managers of Mitsubishi Chemical regularly attended the *Kinyo-kai*, or "Second Friday Conference," a monthly meeting of Mitsubishi Corporation affiliated companies where joint business strategies were formulated.

During the mid-1980s, Mitsubishi Chemical declared that in the future it would emphasize its "functional products," namely pharmaceuticals and biotechnology products. Carbon products (coke) had been reduced to a 28 percent share of the company's revenues. The largest share of income was derived from petrochemicals (40 percent), followed by chemicals (17 percent) and agricultural chemicals (9 percent).

The company also branched out into the electronics sector. By 1985, the firm's information and electronics product division was gaining momentum through strategic partnerships and ventures, including tie-ups with U.S.-based Verbatim Corp. and SAE Magnetics to manufacturer floppy disks and rigid disks, respectively. In order to mark its diversification into these new fields, Mitsubishi Chemical changed its name to Mitsubishi Kasei Corp. in 1988.

The Creation of Mitsubishi Chemical Corp. in 1994

Operating under a new corporate moniker, Mitsubishi Kasei turned its attention to growth in the United States. In the early 1990s, it established Kasei Virginia Corp., a U.S. subsidiary created to oversee the production of high-tech products. As the company eyed international growth as key to future success, it set plans in motion to merge with Mitsubishi Petrochemical Co., Japan's largest petrochemical concern. According to a 1993 *Financial Times* article, the decision to merge came at "one of the most difficult times for Japan's petrochemical sector," which had been plagued with overcapacity and intense

---

Key Dates:

1934: Nippon Tar is established by the Mitsubishi industrial empire.
1936: The company changes its name to Nippon Chemical Industries.
1950: Nippon Chemical is separated from Mitsubishi and becomes a public limited company.
1952: The company changes its name to Mitsubishi Chemical Industries Ltd.
1988: The company adopts the name Mitsubishi Kasei Corp.
1994: Mitsubishi Kasei and Mitsubishi Petrochemical Co. merge to form Mitsubishi Chemical Corp.
1999: The company launches a major restructuring effort designed to cut costs during an economic slowdown.
2002: The firm sells its agricultural chemicals business.

---

competition. While Japan's Ministry of International Trade and Industry had been encouraging merger activity since the early 1980s, most of Japan's chemical firms remained independent, unwilling to relinquish control of their companies. The merger of the two Mitsubishi companies signaled a change in corporate thinking—that mergers may be necessary for survival.

The deal was completed in October 1994 and created the Mitsubishi Chemical Corp. (MCC), Japan's largest chemical manufacturer with sales surpassing ¥1 trillion. As the newly merged company focused on integration and global expansion, its domestic market was hit hard by both a downturn in the Japanese economy and a crisis that plagued Asia's financial institutions. As such, the firm began cutting costs while expanding into several areas. Its information and electronics division worked to strengthening its foothold in the data storage media market. The company also inked a deal with Asahi Glass Co. Ltd. to manufacture color filters for liquid crystal displays (LCDs). In its specialty chemicals business area, MCC partnered with U.S.-based Cargill Inc. to develop a low-calorie sweetener.

Japan's continued economic deterioration forced MCC to launch a major restructuring effort in 1999. The plan included plant closures, layoffs, cuts in spending, and spin offs of certain businesses. Overall, the company planned to save ¥40 billion per year as a result of the measures. Upon entering the new century, MCC made additional restructuring moves designed to shore up profits by focusing mainly on petrochemicals, specialty chemicals, and pharmaceuticals. The company made several key moves during this time period, including the divestiture of unprofitable businesses and the sale in 2002 of its agricultural chemicals business.

In 2001, the company announced the merger of its Mitsubishi-Tokyo Pharmaceuticals Inc. unit and Welfide Corp. The union created subsidiary Mitsubishi Pharma Corp., a company whose objective was to increase sales networks in both the United States and Europe by making key acquisitions and partnerships. In early 2003, MCC purchased Tonen Chemical Corp.'s shares in Japan Polychem Corp., a polyolefin joint venture created in 1996 by Mitsubishi and Tonen. After the purchase, Japan Polychem operated as a wholly owned subsidiary of MCC.

Under the leadership of president and CEO Ryuichi Tomizawa, MCC adopted a new management plan, the KAKUSHIN Plan, in 2002. Under this strategy, the company focused on restoring profits, intensifying research and development efforts, and consolidating the group into five major segments related to its core businesses. Meanwhile, the company's operating environment continued to pose challenges as Japan's economy remained stagnant. While MCC appeared to have a solid strategy in place, its future rested on both a domestic turnaround and the ability to successfully expand into international markets.

Principal Subsidiaries

ACT Research Center Inc.; Advanced Colortech Inc.; API Corp.; Chuo Rika Kogyo Corp.; Dia Fine Co. Ltd.; Dia Instruments Co. Ltd.; Dio Chemicals Inc.; Echizen Polymer Co. Ltd.; GenCom Co.; Japan Epoxy Resins Co. Ltd.; Japan Ethanol Co. Ltd.; Japan Polychem Corp.; Japan Unipet Co. Ltd.; Kawasaki Kasei Chemicals Ltd.; MCFA Inc.; Mitsubishi Chemical Engineering Corp.; Mitsubishi Chemical Functional Products Inc.; Mitsubishi Chemical Foam Plastics Corp.; Mitsubishi Chemical Logistics Corp.; Mitsubishi Engineering-Plastics Corp.; Mitsubishi Kagaku Foods Corp.; Mitsubishi Pharma Corp.; Nippon Rensui Corp.; Rhombic Corp.; ZOEGENE Corp.; Mitsubishi Chemical America Inc.; USR Optonix Inc. (U.S.A.); Verbatim Corp. (U.S.A.); Mitsubishi Chemical Europe GmbH (Germany).

Principal Competitors

BASF AG; Nippon Kayaku Co. Ltd.; Sumitomo Chemical Co. Ltd.

Further Reading

Carroll, Susan, ''Mitsubishi Chemical Unveils New Three-Year Restructuring Plan,'' *Chemical Market Reporter*, January 10, 2000, p. 20.
''Japan Polychem Corporation to Become 100%-Owned Subsidiary of Mitsubishi Chemical,'' *JCN Newswire*, January 22, 2003.
''M'Bishi Chemical to Become Mitsubishi Kasei,'' *Jiji Press Ticker Service*, May 30, 1988.
''Mitsubishi Chemical Details Restructuring Plan,'' *Chemical Week*, January 9, 2002, p. 6.
''Mitsubishi Chemical Launches Heavy Restructuring,'' *Chemicalweek Asia*, November 10, 1999, p. 3.
''Mitsubishi Chemical Plans U.S. Expansion,'' *Japan Economic Journal*, March 11, 1989, p. A2.
''Mitsubishi Companies to Merger Operations,'' *Financial Times* (London), December 29, 1993, p. 15.
''Mitsubishi Group Chemical Giants Plan Merger,'' *Nikkei Weekly*, December 27, 1993, p. 1.
''On the Threshold of the 21st Century, Reading the Future Is All Important,'' *Japan Economic Journal*, July 16, 1985, p. 7.
''Right Chemistry Eludes Mitsubishi Chemical,'' *Nikkei Weekly*, December 16, 2002.

—update: Christina M. Stansell

MITSUKOSHI

Mitsukoshi Ltd.

4-1, Nihombashi Muromachi 1-chome
Chuo-ku, Tokyo 103-8001
Japan
Telephone: (03) 3241-3311
Fax: (03) 3245-4559
Web site: http://www.mitsukoshi.jp

Public Company
Incorporated: 1904 as Mitsukoshi Dry-Goods Store
Company Ltd.
Employees: 7,632
Sales: ¥963.3 billion ($7.2 billion) (2002)
Stock Exchanges: Tokyo
Ticker Symbol: 8231
NAIC: 452110 Department Stores

As Japan's largest department store company, Mitsukoshi Ltd. maintains approximately 130 locations, both domestic and international, with stores across Japan and in the United States and Germany. The firm is also involved in real estate, logistics, and building services. Mitsukoshi fell on hard times during the 1990s due in part to the rise in Japan's consumption tax, falling consumer confidence, and an overall weakening of the economy. As a result, it has revamped its management practices and restructured business operations. Mitsukoshi operates as part of the Mitsui group, a large industrial group or *keiretsu.*

17th and 18th Century History

Mitsukoshi's origins date back past its establishment in 1904 as Japan's first modern department store to the nation's feudal days in the 17th century. The Lord of Echigo, head of the noble House of Mitsui, fled from the forces of a samurai who eventually unified Japan by subduing the protectors of the hereditary estates. Because Matsusaka, the place of refuge, was a busy market center near a popular port in a fertile province, the Lord of Echigo, no longer in a position to collect income from his estates, renounced his title in order to become a merchant. After an inauspicious effort operating a brewery of sake and soy sauce, a merchandising dynasty was launched through the work of the former lord's eldest son, Mitsui Sokubei Takatoshi, and his wife, Shuho, daughter of a successful merchant.

The drapery business they opened in 1673 was called Echigo-ya in recognition of the family's noble heritage, differentiating it from other businesses and attaching some prestige to its wares. A luxurious ambiance, in which transactions were discussed secondarily to elaborate social amenities, quickly attracted a loyal clientele, but the couple soon introduced some business practices that greatly broadened their customer base.

First, they maneuvered to become purveyors of textiles to the new government, which by that time had settled down under the thumb of the Tokugawa shogun to a lengthy period of peace and isolation from the outside world. Second, the couple opened a store where customers could view the merchandise and make cash transactions. This was a drastic departure from the practices of the late 17th century, when merchants made house calls on wealthy families—the only persons who could afford to buy—and would have to wait for payment until the lord of the manor collected the annual or semiannual rentals from tenants, who paid in rice rather than currency. That, in turn, would have to be converted into negotiable instruments by professional moneychangers or bartered for other goods.

Centralizing the purchase process in a store eliminated the transportation costs of making house calls, a saving that Echigo-ya could pass on to customers in the form of reduced prices. The couple also introduced fixed prices. This eliminated the uncertainty on both sides that had accompanied the traditional haggling and speeded the purchase process, making it possible to handle more transactions.

The success of the first store led to the opening of a second, in Edo, which became modern Tokyo. It also led to the establishment of a second business—a financial arm. Customers found it convenient to have a moneychanger on the premises, and the financial service eventually grew to gigantic proportions. It became known as the powerful Mitsui Bank, another independent member of the Mitsui group.

In pioneering consumer-oriented business practices, the change that had the greatest effect on attracting new customers was to make merchandise available in quantities small enough to be affordable for the common people. Previously, fabric had to be purchased by the bolt. Echigo-ya was the first store to allow the customer to limit the purchase to the amount needed. This resulted in an unprecedented volume of sales, and the couple was able to open additional stores in other urban centers during the following decades. It was not until the Bon Marche store was opened in Paris in 1852 that such practices became known throughout the occidental world.

Another legacy of the founders was the Mitsui House Code, derived from Takatoshi Mitsui's will in 1722. This was a guide for the Mitsui heirs for management of the family's companies, which were already proliferating through the country. It was also a code of ethics intended to ensure that the founders' principles and traditions of service would be followed by future generations. For example, Echigo-ya was so accommodating that an early patron wrote, "When ceremonial costumes are required in a hurry, the shop lets the servants wait and has the regalia made up immediately by several dozens of their own tailors. . . . This is an example of a really big merchant."

In the ensuing 150 years, trust in the Mitsui name grew to be so entrenched that when the Tokugawa shogunate was succeeded in 1868 by the restoration of the imperial government, Mitsui's financial arm became, for all practical purposes, its banker. The management system that the Mitsui House Code had established was no longer adequate, however, to handle the rambling empire of businesses and industrial enterprises that the Mitsui heirs were struggling to keep in order in the late 19th century. Japan's business climate had changed drastically with the opening of the nation to foreign trade and the new Meiji emperor actively encouraging openness to Western concepts. Moreover, the various Mitsui enterprises often did not work in harmony with one another, and each was bound by its own traditional ways of doing business.

Rizaemon Minomura, a talented manager, was recruited by the Mitsuis and given power of attorney to make any changes needed to solve the internal problems of the businesses, which by then represented almost all types of commercial, financial, and industrial enterprises. He was eminently successful. One of his methods was to release certain companies from direct control of Mitsui, but to retain a small share in businesses that were foundering as a result of mismanagement. One of these was the Tokyo Echigo-ya store.

The Tokyo Echigo-ya gained its independence in 1872, under the management of a related family named Mitsukoshi. The store prospered under its new management. Known first as the Mitsui Clothing Store, it became the Mitsui Dry-Goods Store in 1896 to reflect its expansion into additional lines of merchandise. Capitalizing on the Mitsui reputation for high quality and the growing popular fancy for Western-style fashions, the store brought in a designer from France to develop a

new apparel department. The designs caught on, along with other innovations, including a display of merchandise in the open, life-size poster displays at railway stations as well as a catalog sales department. Home delivery by auto was instituted in 1903. Stocking foreign-made goods also attracted customers.

Japan's First Modern Department Store: 1904–1930s

The following year, under new director Osuke Hibi, the store was reorganized as Mitsukoshi Dry-Goods Store Company and announced its metamorphosis into Japan's first modern department store, with newspaper advertisements emphasizing the convenience of one-stop shopping for an ever-increasing variety of merchandise, simulating "in part, the department stores of the United States." As well as adding items such as jewelry, luggage, food, and photography to its wares, Mitsukoshi also held events such as expositions and exhibitions to contribute to the cultural life of the area. This had the effect of elevating the status of the store and attracted so many new customers that additional Mitsukoshi stores were opened.

By 1914, the Mitsukoshi stores were firmly established as sources of high-quality merchandise that were accessible and affordable for most shoppers, and other stores had begun to copy their innovations. The new Renaissance-style building constructed to house the flagship store that year sported Japan's first escalator. Mitsukoshi was also firmly associated with cultural activities, having participated in the refurbishing of the Imperial Theater, among many community projects.

Japan's eventual entry into World War I did not slow Mitsukoshi's growth. If anything, wartime industries furnished employment that enabled many more persons to become customers. Reduced-price special sale days and the introduction of gift coupons also stimulated sales.

The Great Kanto Earthquake of September 1, 1923, marked a turning point for all Japanese department stores. Along with many other buildings in Tokyo, they were all burned to the ground. Small mobile units were quickly set up throughout the city to supply essentials to the people, many of whom had never before been customers. A large number of customers acquired in this way continued to shop at Mitsukoshi throughout the rebuilding process and remained loyal patrons. The new stores, built as high-rises with many architectural innovations, offered further convenience. They ended the practice of having customers remove their shoes at the entrance and pad through the stores in cotton slippers. Fashion shows were held and beauty salons added. Business burgeoned. In 1928, to reflect the great variety of goods and services offered, Mitsukoshi dropped the Dry-Goods part of its name and became Mitsukoshi Ltd.

In the 1930s, mobilization for war again created industrial activity that increased the number of workers who could become part of Mitsukoshi's customer base. The Mitsukoshi name had begun to be recognized overseas as a result of participation in world's fairs and other expositions in Europe and the United States, increasing the number of foreign customers. As part of the Mitsui group, Mitsukoshi profited from its association with Japan's top business-industrial conglomerate, or *zaibatsu*. However, government constraints on the business, instituted in 1938 and continuing throughout World War II, along with the wartime damage resulting from direct bombing, left Mitsukoshi in a greatly weakened state.

Postwar Growth

The trust in the company's integrity that had been built up over many generations enabled Mitsukoshi to begin the recovery period by successfully combating the black market with fixed prices. Working with the new government established during the Allied occupation of Japan, Mitsukoshi was able to make rapid progress in rebuilding its business. Reaching out to customers through its continuing involvement in cultural events, as well as adopting Western-style products and retail techniques, Mitsukoshi had recovered enough by 1954 to celebrate its 50th anniversary with exhibitions of fine art and the introduction of new fashions that quickly became popular.

The phenomenal recovery and growth of Japanese business and industry in general brought Mitsukoshi a host of new customers. As Mitsukoshi added new products made possible by Japanese technological advancement, a consumer boom resulted that carried through the 1960s and made it possible for Mitsukoshi to open overseas stores in such locations as Paris and Hong Kong, beginning in 1971. By 1974, Mitsukoshi's flagship store was importing Rolls Royces for purchase. During the 1970s, Mitsukoshi stores opened in London, New York, and Rome.

Mitsukoshi's profits dropped in the early 1980s. In September 1982, Mitsukoshi's directors dismissed Shigeru Okada from the presidency, and Akira Ichihara became president; in 1986 he became chairman of the board.

By 1985, the company's catalog sales, as well as its stores' travel, construction, and decorating departments, had become so large that they were reorganized as independent business divisions. Mitsukoshi continued opening new department stores, expanding existing ones, and establishing numerous specialty shops. In 1989, Mitsukoshi purchased 1.5 million shares of stock in Tiffany and Co. Mitsukoshi's president, Yoshiaki Sakakura, was appointed a director of Tiffany later that year.

During this time period, Mitsukoshi was still tied to the Mitsui group through the shares Mitsui held and through its own participation in the Mitsui group's leadership conferences. Like the rest of the Mitsui group, Mitsukoshi expanded through takeovers and joint ventures as well as through self-developed businesses. Mitsubishi recovered from World War II somewhat faster than the Mitsui group because all of its businesses were self-developed and therefore closer-knit and easier to control. That was why the Mitsui group had not regained its prewar *zaibatsu* number one position; however, its number two position, under the postwar *keiretsu* system, was not seriously threatened. Along with the Mitsui group, Mitsukoshi, too, appeared to be securely established as a front runner, both internally in Japan and worldwide. A sign of the ever-widening circle of Mitsukoshi activities was its joint venture with Marubeni Corporation in 1990 to set up cable television services in Europe.

Overcoming Problems: 1990s and Beyond

Problems arose in the 1990s, however, that threatened to usurp Mitsukoshi from its top spot. In 1992, the company was forced to forgo a costly expansion plan it had started in 1990 due in part to sluggish sales in its luxury goods segment. That year, the company also started to reorganize its executive and management structure, believing that mismanagement was the cause for much of the company's financial woes. By September 1992, the company was reporting major declines in pretax profits.

Mitsukoshi was dealt another blow in April 1997 when Japan raised its consumption tax from 3 to 5 percent. This tax increase, along with a crisis in Asia's financial sector, weakened consumer confidence. The company and its competitors began to feel the crunch as sales began to dwindle. Many of these companies had expanded significantly during the 1980s and early 1990s and were now left with too much floor space. According to a 1999 *Nikkei Weekly* report, sales per square meter of floor space declined by more than 30 percent from 1990 to 1999. Nevertheless, Mitsukoshi opened its new Fukuoka location in October 1997. Over 180,000 visited the store on its grand opening day.

Despite the challenging economic climate, Mitsukoshi was determined to enter the new century on solid ground. The firm launched a new management strategy in the late 1990s with five major goals—to secure strong sales and profitability, to bolster the performance of company businesses, to restructure financial operations in order to promote future growth, to adopt a new corporate culture, and to remain a good corporate citizen. As part of this plan, the firm sold off its interest in Tiffany and Co., set plans in motion to overhaul operations at three of its stores in the Kansai region, and stopped a golf course development project in the Chiba Prefecture. For the first time since it was listed in 1949, Mitsukoshi was forced to cancel its dividend payment in fiscal 1999.

Consumer spending continued its downward trend in the early years of the new century. Company sales declined for the third year in a row in fiscal 2000, prompting Mitsukoshi to look for new growth avenues. In 2000, the company launched its "Only You" e-commerce Web site and joined the Yahoo! Japan Shopping online shopping mall the following year, hoping that increased Internet sales would make up for lackluster traditional retail sales. During 2001, plans were set in motion to refurbish the Mitsukoshi Nihombashi store in preparation for its 100th anniversary celebration in 2004. Management hoped the revamped store would become a landmark in the Nihombashi area. A relocation strategy for the Osaka location was also in the works.

Taneo Nakamura took over the helm of Mitsukoshi in February 2002. Under his leadership, the company continued to divest unprofitable businesses and focused on entering high profit areas. In early 2003, the firm announced that it would merge four of its subsidiaries—Nagoya Mitsukoshi, Chiba Mitsukoshi, Kagoshima Mitsukoshi, and Fukuoka Mitsukoshi. Nakamura commented on the strategy in a 2003 *Japan Economic Newswire,* stating, "We will enhance our competitiveness and earning power by focusing management resources on our mainline department store operation."

Principal Subsidiaries

Nagoya Mitsukoshi Ltd.; Fukuoka Mitsukoshi Ltd.; Chiba Mitsukoshi Ltd.; Kagoshima Mitsukoshi Ltd.; Leo d'Or Trading Co. Ltd.; Niko Co. Ltd.; Mitsukoshi Sewing Co. Ltd.; Mitsukoshi Real Estate Co. Ltd.; Mitsukoshi Logistics Co. Ltd.; Mitsukoshi Environment Service Co. Ltd.; Mitsukoshi Enterprises Co. Ltd. (Hong Kong); Mitsukoshi U.S.A. Inc.; Mitsukoshi UK Ltd.; Mitsukoshi France S.A.

Principal Competitors

The Daimaru Inc.; Seibu Department Stores Ltd.; Takashimaya Company Ltd.

Further Reading

"Dull Sales Shelve Mitsukoshi Expansion," *Nikkei Weekly*, May 30, 1992, p. 24.

"Japan's Mitsukoshi to Trim Staff, Revamp Operations," *AsiaPulse News*, December 6, 1999.

Li, Sandy, "Retailers Fighting Pessimism," *South China Morning Post*, April 16, 2003, p. 3.

"Mitsukoshi Profits Plummet 95%," *The Nikkei Weekly*, September 12, 1992, p. 16.

"Mitsukoshi Sets Offering for its Tiffany Holdings," *WWD*, January 8, 1999, p. 11.

"Mitsukoshi to Merge 4 Subsidiaries in Reorganization," *Japan Economic Newswire*, January 30, 2003.

"More Pain for Major Department Stores," *Nikkei Weekly*, February 22, 1999, p. 7.

Roberts, John G., *Mitsui: Three Centuries of Japanese Business*, New York: Weatherhill, 1989.

"Stores Already Feeling That Wintry Chill," *Nikkei Weekly*, December 1, 1997, p. 6.

"Takashimaya Net Fall 41 Percent, Mitsukoshi Back in Black for Half," *WWD*, October 20, 2000, p. 22.

—Betty T. Moore
—update: Christina M. Stansell

Modine Manufacturing Company

1500 DeKoven Avenue
Racine, Wisconsin 53403-2552
U.S.A.
Telephone: (262) 636-1200
Fax: (262) 636-1361
Web site: http://www.modine.com

Public Company
Incorporated: 1916
Employees: 7,700
Sales: $1.09 billion (2003)
Stock Exchanges: NASDAQ
Ticker Symbol: MODI
NAIC: 33635 Motor Vehicle Transmission and Power
    Train Parts Manufacturing; 336322 Other Motor
    Vehicle Electrical and Electronic Equipment
    Manufacturing; 336399 All Other Motor Vehicle Parts
    Manufacturing; 336391 Motor Vehicle Air-
    Conditioning Manufacturing

Modine Manufacturing Company operates as a leading thermal management concern that serves the light truck, heavy equipment, HVAC (heating, ventilating, and air conditioning systems), and electronics markets. The company manufactures engine, charge-air, oil, transmission, HVAC systems, and gas recirculation (ERG) coolers and modulars used in both automotive and truck industries. During 2002, international customers were responsible for nearly half of Modine's revenues.

Origins and Early Growth

Modine Manufacturing Company was the brainchild of Arthur B. Modine, who graduated from the University of Michigan, Ann Arbor, in 1908 with a degree in engineering and became involved in a Chicago-based radiator repair business where he began experimenting with various radiator designs. In 1912, A.B. Modine moved to Racine, Wisconsin, and became a principle partner in Perfex Radiator (a predecessor to a company Modine Manufacturing would later acquire), where

Modine was actively involved in research, testing, and design of radiators. Following a business disagreement with a silent partner at Perfex over how that company should be managed and capitalized, Modine decided to establish his own company.

A.B. Modine founded Modine Manufacturing in 1916 to make radiators for farm tractors. He became president and treasurer of the company, which opened a one-room office adjacent to a small workshop in Racine. Soon after opening his office, Modine developed the company's first major product—the Spirex farm tractor radiator—a radiator core with a spiral fin put in the radiator cells which helped with the product's heat transferability.

In December 1916, Modine filed for a patent (issued seven years later) on his Spirex radiator and, in 1917, his radiator was literally called into service by the United States when it became standard equipment on World War I artillery tractors. By the end of 1918, the majority of leading tractor manufacturers were using the company's radiators.

In 1921, Modine Manufacturing entered the field of commercial building heaters after A.B. Modine developed a unit heater—a product enabling buildings to be heated without extensive ductwork—by putting a fan behind an automotive radiator and attaching the assembly to factory steam pipes in order to supply heat. During the early 1920s, Modine Manufacturing tried to market its Spirex radiator to Ford Motor Company, but because of the way the radiator's frame was designed, the Spirex was unsuitable for automobiles. By 1925, though, A.B. Modine had designed an automotive radiator, called the Turbotube, which helped Modine Manufacturing land its first major automotive contract that year when Ford adopted the radiator as standard equipment for the Model T. Ford quickly became Modine's principle customer and its major source of income, a role the auto maker would play in Modine's operations for the next 55 years.

Modine Manufacturing received a patent for its unit heater in 1928. That same year the company—boasting a wide mix of automotive, truck, and tractor customers—went public, issuing 100,000 shares of stock on the Chicago (later the Midwest) Stock Exchange. The October 1929 stock market crash did little to affect company sales that year, which climbed to a record

Company Perspectives:

Our vision is to pursue market leadership by being an innovative, customer-focused, global company delivering exceptional quality and value. We will grow our core business of heat transfer with superior technical solutions in systems, products, and services that we provide.

$5.5 million. But the following year, sales dipped below $4 million and by 1932, when revenues had plunged below $1 million, Modine Manufacturing suffered what would be its last annual loss ($165,000).

By the early 1930s, Modine Manufacturing had moved into the home-heating field and was offering a line of convection heaters for homes, including models targeting large, upscale houses. In 1932, the company landed a contract to produce radiators for Ford's new V-8 engine, which helped Modine Manufacturing pull out of the recession. Business continued to increase through 1937 and reached a peak for the decade that year when the company recorded $8.5 million in sales.

In 1940, Modine Manufacturing developed a vehicular wind tunnel and after the United States entered World War II, the company's technology was again enlisted by the government, with the wind tunnel used to test combat vehicles. During the war, while the wind tunnel was working on domestic soil, the company's convectors took to the sea, having been adapted to Naval vessels. The company also produced radiators for military tanks, tractors, trucks, and bulldozers during the war.

In 1946 A.B. Modine gave up his post as president and became chair of the board. Walter Winkel, who had been actively running the company since 1936 while A.B. Modine was involved in research and product development, succeeded the company founder as president. Two years later, Winkel died and C.T. Perkins became president.

Postwar Expansion

Modine Manufacturing benefited from the postwar boom in automobile sales, which helped to push annual revenues above $25 million in 1951. During the 1950s, the company began using aluminum to produce heat exchangers and, with the advent of air conditioning, it began producing all-aluminum brazed air-conditioning coils for passenger cars and trucks in 1956. That year, Modine Manufacturing received a patent for its concentric oil cooler, a device destined to become standard equipment on cars with automatic transmissions.

During the late 1950s and early 1960s, the company doubled its product line by securing new automotive contracts and introducing new applications for heat exchangers. In 1958, a smaller, more efficient prototype radiator helped Modine Manufacturing secure a contract to become the sole supplier of radiators for the new Ford Falcon. About the same time, Modine began supplying American Motors Corporation with a passenger-car radiator. During the early 1960s, the company extended its use of heat exchangers for buildings and introduced products for school heating and ventilation systems.

In 1961, Modine Manufacturing received a patent for its Alfuse chemical process, a means of fusing aluminum to aluminum that was used to produce condensers. That same year the company received a patent for its light-weight louvered serpentine radiator fin, which was bonded to radiator tubes in a serpentine fashion—as opposed to a plate-type fin bonded in parallel rows—and improved the efficiency of a radiator's heat transferring ability.

At the end of 1961, A.B. Modine retired from active service with the company he founded, although he remained on the corporate board as a director. C.T. Perkins was named to succeed Modine as chair beginning in 1962.

In 1963, Modine Manufacturing became the prime oil cooler and radiator supplier for Rambler. Ford, during the 1960s, steadily increased its production requirements, and Modine responded by producing an ever-growing list of truck radiators, aluminum heat exchangers, and aluminum oil coolers. The increased use of aluminum, which required separate production facilities, as well as the increased business from Ford and other auto makers, found the company facing the need to expand production capabilities. That expansion was led by E.G. Rutherford, who became president in 1963. During the next 11 years, Rutherford guided the steady growth of the company, which climbed from $34.5 million in sales to $110 million, while the number of its employees was doubled to 3,500 as production facilities grew from six to 13.

In order to facilitate such growth, in 1967 the company engaged in its first long-term borrowing. A.B. Modine, who was still a director, was adamantly against the company taking on debt, but the company's top management convinced the founder that the loan was necessary in order to accommodate the company's growth.

In 1969, Modine Manufacturing received a patent for its Flora-Guard unit heater for greenhouses. That same year the company made its first acquisition, Schemenauer Manufacturing, a privately-owned Ohio maker of unit ventilators and rooftop air-conditioning units.

In 1971, Modine introduced its BT Unit oil cooler, a more efficient type of cooler named after the British Thermal Unit. Two years later, the company received its first patent on a Donut oil cooler, originally designed for John Deere tractors but later finding successful applications on high-performance European automobiles.

Modine Manufacturing had been serving the aftermarket business informally for a number of years and, in 1972, established the subsidiary Modine Auto-Cool to produce and sell complete replacement radiators. In 1974, E.E. Richter was named president and Rutherford began a short stint as chair before dying unexpectedly the following year and leaving the position vacant.

Diversification in the Mid-1970s

Beginning in the mid-1970s, Modine began diversifying away from automotive radiators and entering new vehicular heat-transfer markets. During this period, the company introduced new products for heavy-duty trucks, as well as construction, industrial, agricultural, and drilling and mining equipment. During the latter half of the decade, Modine also expanded its production of oil coolers and condensers and evaporators for vehicle air conditioning.

In 1979, Modine established an international marketing group for export purposes and began leasing a New Berlin, Wisconsin, plant in order to manufacture automotive air conditioning condensers. By the end of the 1980, fiscal year annual sales were $200 million and Modine was the leading supplier of air-conditioning condensers for Japanese automobiles imported to the United States.

With nearly half of Modine's sales volume going to Ford, the automotive giant decided in 1979 to begin making its own light-truck radiators, which represented nearly 20 percent of Modine's product volume then. At that time, Modine's top ten customers accounted for up to 88 percent of Modine's sales, with much of that being geared to the original equipment automotive market. Ford alone was the source for 40 percent or more of all revenues.

During the 1980s, the company made a series of moves to lessen its dependence on the cyclical and recession-prone automotive original equipment market. In 1980, the company made its first aftermarket acquisition, Lake Auto Radiator Manufacturing Company, and entered the market for replacement radiator cores. Sales and earnings dipped slightly for the company's fiscal year ending in March 1980, and in October of that year Modine borrowed $10 million from the Wisconsin Investment Board. Sales continued to fall in the fiscal year 1981, and revenues dropped to $7.4 million, down from $14.4 million two years earlier.

In 1982, after years of research and development, Modine introduced its heavy-duty Beta-Weld radiator, the first radiator to feature welded tube-to-header joints. That same year, Modine began manufacturing operations outside the United States and established a joint venture in Canada to produce radiators for the aftermarket. In 1983, the Canadian venture, Ontario Limited, became the company's first wholly owned non-U.S. facility.

In fiscal 1983, Modine's sales followed the "double dip" recession and slid more than $30 million as profits dropped from $8.7 million to $3.8 million. In late 1983, having weathered the worst of the early 1980s recession, Modine restructured its management into a four-man executive office headed by Richter, as president and chief executive. Alex F. Simpson, Richard T. Savage, and B.K. Jacob were named group vice-presidents and members of the executive team. In early 1984, Modine switched its stock listing from the Midwest Stock Exchange to NASDAQ.

During the mid-1980s, Modine stepped up its market diversification and international expansion efforts and purchased joint or minority interests in several foreign producers of radiators and other heat exchangers. In 1984, Modine Manufacturing established the Holland joint venture NRF Holding B.V. and took 45 percent ownership in the overseas company designed to produce radiators for automotive aftermarkets and original equipment markets. Another joint venture was established that same year in Austria to produce aluminum condensers and evaporators for sale to European passenger car manufacturers.

In 1984, Modine also began a four-year program of acquiring North American aftermarket companies involved in the radiator core and distribution businesses. Acquisitions in 1984 included West's Radiator, Inc. of Indianapolis, a distributor and retail radiator repair shop, and Beacon Auto Manufacturing Company, Inc., a regional replacement radiator core maker and warehouse distributor.

The additional businesses, along with record auto and truck production and aftermarket sales, helped accelerate sales, which topped $300 million in 1985, while earnings soared to $21.5 million, 50 percent higher than ever. Acquisitions in the 1985 calendar year included Eskimo Radiator Manufacturing Company and Perfex Radiator Group of McQuay Inc., a heat-transfer business with sales to vehicular and industrial markets, with about $30 million in annual sales.

In 1985, the company also entered a joint venture in Germany with Windhoff G.m.b.H to produce heavy duty vehicular and industrial heat transfer products. That same year Modine established another joint venture in Mexico to produce radiators for the Mexican original equipment market.

The company received a patent on its Beta-Weld technology in 1985 and the following year introduced and received several patents for its PF (parallel flow) family of products. The PF condenser, a passenger car heat-exchanger, was designed to use less refrigerant and to reduce or eliminate the use of Freon, a chlorofluorocarbon that damages the ozone layer. In 1986, Modine sued the Allen Group's G & O Radiator for alleged infringement on its Beta welded-radiator technology.

An unusually cool summer, increased price competition in radiators for the automotive aftermarket, and the cost of assimilating Perfex into Modine operations contributed to a $1 million dip in earnings in 1986. A $1 million settlement with the Environmental Protection Agency over alleged violations of the Clean Water Act pushed earnings down almost another $1 million in 1987. A lower tax rate in 1987, along with a big boost in sales coming from acquisitions, helped put Modine's earnings back on the upswing the following year.

During the late 1980s, Modine acquired numerous manufacturers and distributors of radiator repair parts in its efforts to reduce dependency on original equipment markets. In 1987, the company purchased Stuart-Western Inc., a California manufacturer and distributor of automotive radiator cores, and Heatex Division of Howden Ltd., a Toronto-based manufacturer of radiators and radiator cores primarily for the Canadian automotive aftermarket. The two acquisitions brought Modine an additional $40 million in annual sales.

Additional acquisitions in 1987 further solidified Modine's growing radiator and radiator core manufacturing and warehousing operations. Added to Modine's operations that year were Durafin Radiator Corporation, Central Radiator, Inc., Carolina Cooling Supply Company, Inc., and Octagon Cooling Systems Distributors, Inc. By 1988, when Modine acquired NAYCO Distributors, Inc., the company's replacement radiator and radiator core businesses were the fastest growing markets for the company, representing a third of sales volume.

In 1987, Modine established a joint venture in Japan with Nippon Light Metal Ltd. The venture, Nikkei Heat Exchanger Company, was designed to manufacture and sell automotive heat exchangers to original-equipment manufacturers in the Japanese market. The following year, Modine acquired complete ownership of Windhoff, G.m.b.H. and in 1989 gained entire control of the joint venture it had established in Holland.

In February 1989, Richter was named chair and Savage became president and chief operating officer. That same year, Modine began a two-year acquisition program designed to expand its heating business and acquired Ted Reed Thermal, Inc., a Rhode Island-based heating equipment manufacturer with annual sales of $10 million. In the fall of 1989, Modine's commercial heating business unveiled a line of gas-fired, separated-combustion unit heaters. The following year, the company acquired Industrial Airsystems Inc., a St. Paul, Minnesota, manufacturer and marketer of heating and ventilating equipment for commercial facilities.

In 1990, Modine—in its largest acquisition ever—purchased the $60 million heat-transfer business of Sundstrand Corporation, a manufacturer of refrigeration and air-conditioning coils, secondary heat exchangers for high-efficiency residential furnaces, and copper and aluminum tubular components with operations in Michigan, Missouri, and Mexico. Sundstrand, which became the commercial products division in Modine's off-highway products group, brought with it customers that included original-equipment manufacturers of residential and commercial air conditioners, commercial refrigeration equipment producers, and residential heating systems producers—all representing new markets for Modine.

After five years of litigation, in 1990 Modine received an $18.6 million settlement from the Allen Group over the infringement lawsuit on Modine's Beta-Weld radiator technology. In 1991, Savage assumed the additional duties of chief executive officer when Richter retired from active employment after 44 years with Modine. By the time of the company's 75th anniversary in 1991, Modine's sales totaled nearly $500 million, stemming from more than 50 locations around the world.

In late 1991, Modine filed a lawsuit against two firms with parent companies in Japan—Mitsubishi Motor Sales of America, Inc. and Showa Aluminum Corporation—charging the companies with infringement of Modine's patents on its PF condensers. In April 1992, an International Trade Commission judge ruled in favor of Mitsubishi Motor Sales and Showa Aluminum, interpreting Modine's patent as covering only a narrow range of product types. Modine filed an appeal and, in November 1992, with that appeal still pending, the company announced it had licensed its PF condensers to a third Japanese firm, Nippondenso Company Ltd., a major competitor of Showa Aluminum. The deal added less than $10 million in annual sales. In July of 1993, the U.S. International Trade Commission reversed its earlier ruling, upholding Modine's patent but excluding the specific condensers used by Showa and Mitsubishi from Modine's patent coverage. The company planned to appeal the court's exclusion of the subject condensers at the Federal Circuit Court of Appeals for Patents.

During the late 1980s and early 1990s, Modine extended its Beta-Weld line of radiators to include new models for off-road construction and a variety of engine packages. It also introduced a long-life bus radiator core featuring Beta-Weld technology and a variety of charge-air coolers for trucks and vehicles with turbocharged or supercharged systems. Modine's expanded product mix, and its continued penetration into markets in heat-transfer businesses, helped the company break the half billion sales level for the first time in fiscal 1992.

Modine entered fiscal 1993 having, since the late 1970s, successfully cut much of its dependence on recession-prone major automobile manufacturers and broadened its share of the replacement radiator business. In its 1992 to 1993 fiscal year, Modine's top ten customers accounted for only one-third of its sales, down from three-quarters of all sales in 1977 when the company relied heavily on Ford and other major original equipment manufacturers for the bulk of its business. Since 1979, when Ford took its light truck radiator business in-house, Modine had not only diversified its automotive operations but also strengthened its nonautomotive operations as well, specifically in the field of commercial building activities.

However, as noted in a 1992 *Forbes* article, Modine remained "focused" on the business with which it began—heat exchangers. The company expected its cutting-edge leadership in heat-transfer technology—such as that which led to the development of PF condensers, light-weight aluminum radiators and parts, and Beta-Weld radiators—to pay ongoing dividends. To this end, in July of 1993 Modine acquired Langerer & Reich, a German limited partnership that produced charge-air coolers, oil coolers, radiators, and other heat-exchangers for the European market with sales in 1992 of $120 million.

1990s and Beyond

Modine's strategy for the remainder of the 1990s was to seek diversification and growth in heat-transfer and closely related fields, both in North America and abroad. Much of the company's expansion during this time period stemmed from its continued acquisition efforts. During 1995, the company acquired Signet Systems, a climate control systems supplier, and Radiadores Montana S.A., an automotive supplier based in

Spain. It also purchased full ownership in its Mexican joint venture Radinam S.A. Modine sold off its copper tubing business that year, signaling the company's strong commitment to its core operations.

In 1996, Modine secured a 45 percent stake in Constructions Mecaniques Mota S.A., a French company with a lucrative European vehicle manufacturer customer base. Core Holdings Inc. was added to the firm's arsenal two years later. During 1999, Modine's state-of-the-art $30 million Technical Center began operations in Racine, Wisconsin. The facility housed a new wind tunnel designed to simulate real-life conditions. ''This major investment strengthens Modine's reputation as a technological leader and helps position us for future growth opportunities,'' Donald R. Johnson stated in a 1999 *Aftermarket Business* article. Johnson was named president and chief operating officer of Modine in 1996 and became CEO in 1998.

Modine entered the new century intent on strengthening its position as a leading thermal management concern. The firm entered the exhaust gas recirculation (ERG) cooler market in 2000 and anticipated considerable growth from this new product area. Modine also gained a foothold in the electronics sector with its 2001 acquisition of Thermacore International Inc., a manufacturer of thermal management products used in the computer, telecommunications, networking, and semiconductor markets. The deal bolstered sales and gave the company access to growing markets.

During this time period, Modine focused on emerging technologies related to fuel cell development for automobiles. The firm also began to explore the possibility of utilizing carbon dioxide in air conditioning and heat pump systems. The company's focus on environmentally friendly products gained industry attention, and during 2002 Modine made *Business Ethics* magazine ''100 Best Corporate Citizens'' list for the third consecutive year. The firm took 62nd place based on a series of criteria related to its actions dealing with stockholders, employees, customers, the community, the environment, minorities, and women. Modine tied for first place in the environment category of the ranking.

David B. Rayburn was named president and CEO in 2003; Johnson planned to retire from the chairmanship in June of that year. While management had been shuffled over the past years, Modine's strategy had remained constant. The company continued to look for strategic, valuable acquisitions in order to expand its operations. With a focus on its core businesses and on new thermal management applications, Modine appeared to be hot on the trail of new growth opportunities.

Principal Subsidiaries

Industrial Airsystems Inc.; Manufacturera Mexicana de Partes de Automoviles S.A. (Mexico); Modine Inc.; Modine Acquisition Corp.; Modine Aftermarket Holdings Inc.; Modine Asia K.K. (Japan); Modine Austria Ges.m.b.H; Modine Holding Ltda. (Brazil; 99.9%); Modine of Canada Ltd.; Modine Climate Systems Inc.; Modine Export Sales Corp.; Modine Foundation Inc.; Modine Manufacturing Company Foundation Inc.; Modine of Puerto Rico Inc.; Radman Inc.; Modine Holding GmbH (Germany); Modine Transferencia de Calor S.A. de C.V. (Mexico; 99.6%); NRF B.V. (The Netherlands); Modine Climate Systems GmbH (Germany); Thermacore International Inc.

Principal Competitors

Delphi Corporation; Lennox International Inc.; Visteon Corporation.

Further Reading

''$30-Million Modine Tech Center Houses Wind Tunnel,'' *Aftermarket Business*, November 1999, p. 38.

Byrne, Harlan S., ''Modine: Record Share Net Is in Sight,'' *Barron's*, October 5, 1992.

Byrne, Harlan S., ''Modine Manufacturing Co.: Maker of Radiators Puts Its Trust in the Junk Out There,'' *Barron's*, May 28, 1990, pp. 53–54.

Carey, David, ''Using Its Strengths to Best Advantage,'' *Financial World*, November 14–27, 1984, pp. 83–84.

Cochran, Thomas N., ''Modine Manufacturing Co.: Radiator Maker Loosens Ties to Auto Industry's Cycle,'' *Barron's*, November 7, 1988, pp. 106–107.

Foran, Pat, ''Acquisitions Fire a Hot-Growth Period at Modine Manufacturing,'' *Milwaukee Business Journal*, August 27, 1990, p. 8.

Gordon, Mitchell, ''Modine's Move: Acquisitions, Lower Tax Rate Put Company Back into Record Territory,'' *Barron's*, June 1, 1987, pp. 61–62.

''Modine Intends to Acquire Core Holdings,'' *Aftermarket Business*, September 1998, p. 19.

''Modine Manufacturing Co.,'' *Business Journal-Milwaukee*, January 7, 2000, p. 35.

''Modine Manufacturing Co.,'' *Business Journal-Milwaukee*, December 29, 2000, p. 28.

Modine Manufacturing Company (75th Anniversary) Annual Report 1990–91, Racine, Wis.: Modine Manufacturing Company, 1991.

''Modine's President Picked to Replace Chief Executive Officer,'' *Milwaukee Journal Sentinel*, December 18, 1997.

''Modine Starts Year With New Logo,'' *Aftermarket Business*, February 1999, p. 16.

Rees, Matt, ''Staying Focused,'' *Forbes*, April 27, 1992, p. 136.

—Roger W. Rouland
—update: Christina M. Stansell

Motel 6

14651 Dallas Parkway, Suite 500
Dallas, Texas 75254
U.S.A.
Telephone: (972) 386-6161
Fax: (972) 702-5996
Web site: http://www.motel6.com

Wholly Owned Subsidiary of Accor S.A.
Incorporated: 1962
Employees: 20,410
Sales: $1.6 billion (Accor North America 2002)
NAIC: 721110 Hotels (Except Casino Hotels) and Motels

Famous for its ''We'll leave the light on for you'' tagline, Motel 6 operates as the largest economy motel chain in North America. The company is a subsidiary of French hotel giant Accor S.A. and has over 800 locations throughout the United States and Canada. Its extended-stay Studio 6 brand—launched in 1999—utilizes the company's traditional budget motel concept but offers travelers lodging options at weekly rates. Created by two former building contractors in 1962, Motel 6 stands as one of the most recognizable brands in the United States.

Origins

In the early 1970s, a new breed of motel operators began to emerge in the United States: a small group of companies no more than a decade old that promised to reshape an industry dominated by large and entrenched corporate giants. It was not the first time the lodging industry had undergone a radical transformation; years earlier the same large motel companies that stood atop the motel industry during the 1970s had captured an appreciable share of the overall lodging market from hotel operators by charging considerably lower room rates. Now, as these same motel companies reaped the rewards of their successful incursion of decades before, they found themselves vulnerable to attack by newer motel companies employing a similar strategy. In this latest revolution to sweep through the lodging industry, however, the motel industry turned against itself.

Leading this new attack against such larger motel chains as Holiday Inns and Sheraton were Scottish Inns of America, Inc., Chalet Suisse International, Inc., Days Inns of America, Inc., Econo-Travel Corporation, and a motel operator the *Wall Street Journal* referred to as the ''grandaddy of budget motel companies,'' Motel 6, Inc. Although the strategy employed by this relatively new band of budget motel companies was similar to the strategy once utilized by Holiday Inns and other large motel chains—charge lower rates than the competition—their approach was novel. Nearly all of the budget motel companies creating a stir in the lodging industry during the early 1970s were operated by management with professional backgrounds in construction rather than hotel management. Such was the case with Motel 6, one of the discount pack that would force motel industry stalwarts to rethink their marketing strategies.

Creating the Budget Concept: 1960s

Though it enjoyed an enviable market position in the early 1970s, Motel 6 was then only a decade old. Formed in 1962 by two Santa Barbara building contractors who specialized in low-cost housing projects, Motel 6 had clearly caught the motel industry by storm with its rapid growth. Midway through their careers as contractors, Paul A. Greene and William W. Becker decided to apply their talents to creating a motel that could charge rock-bottom prices yet still generate a profit, something they were aptly suited for given their construction experience. With $800,000 in cash, the two partners began formulating their plan to create a profitable bargain motel in 1960, starting initially with $4 per room per night as their target price. After exploratory research proved that figure too low, Greene and Becker raised their target price to $5 per night, then finally settled on $6 per night two years after beginning their design work. Once all the preliminary work was concluded and it was decided that a $6 nightly charge would cover land leases, mortgages, maid service, managers' salaries, and building costs, Greene and Becker set to work, opening their first Motel 6 in 1962. Their 54-unit complex in Santa Barbara was itself a notable achievement and an exception to the other motels scattered across the country.

While Greene and Becker were constructing their first budget motel, other larger operators, such as Holiday Inns, were creating increasingly luxurious properties, emulating hotels rather than countering them as they had first done. Amid this growing trend toward grander motels with their necessarily higher prices, Greene and Becker offered an alternative: a motel without the amenities of other motels but one that charged substantially less than its competition. There were numerous factors that enabled the two partners to charge $6 for a night's stay, chief among them the fact that they built the motel themselves. Other motel operators intent on securing a foothold in the budget motel market were, typically, businesspeople with hotel management experience—not construction experience—who set themselves to the task of creating and operating a budget motel after construction of their property was completed.

This was not the case with Greene and Becker. After spending two years developing a suitable model for their enterprise, Greene and Becker had designed nearly every aspect of their first Motel 6 to reduce costs wherever possible. The Santa Barbara property did not boast a dining facility, as did many large, higher priced motel chains. Beds were built flush to the floor to shorten the time required to clean each room, shower stalls were constructed with rounded edges to eliminate scrubbing in corners, glasses were replaced with Styrofoam cups, sheets were wash-and-wear, dressers were eliminated, television sets were outfitted with coin boxes that required a guest to deposit $.25 for six hours of viewing, and advertising for the motel relied exclusively on billboard announcements.

The first Motel 6 established a pattern for the many other Motel 6's to follow, a pattern that proved to be almost immediately successful. It was also a pattern predicated on ignorance of the motel industry, yet buttressed by expertise in the construction industry. As Becker later remarked to the *Wall Street Journal* regarding his company's genesis, "When we entered the business, we had the advantage of not knowing anything about it, so we weren't burdened by preconceived notions." Freed from the standard philosophy dictating other motel operators' actions, the company expanded. Four years after the first Motel 6 opened, there were 26 motels in operation, each built for 50 percent of the construction costs other motel properties required. The company generated more than $4 million in sales in 1966 and earned more than $750,000, double the figures recorded the previous year. From California, Greene and

Becker had moved into Utah, Nevada, and Arizona and were awaiting the completion of a 12-story motel in Waikiki and two more motels in Iowa, targeting any community that had a population base of at least 50,000.

Changes in Ownership: 1970s–1980s

By this time, Motel 6's advertising budget was less than it was at the company's inception four years earlier, declining as Motel 6 billboards were eliminated. But perhaps more remarkable—and more indicative of the chain's growing success—was its occupancy rate, the true measure of a lodging facility's success. In 1962, the company recorded a 53 percent occupancy rate, a figure below the national average, but by 1966 Motel 6 was registering an 84.9 percent occupancy rate, well above the national average of 67 percent. This gave Greene and Becker all the encouragement they needed to continue expanding their motel chain. As Motel 6's successes mounted during the late 1960s, outside investors began paying closer attention to the company's burgeoning growth, attention Greene and Becker welcomed. In a 1967 interview with *Newsweek*, Becker stated as much, auguring Motel 6's future course when he remarked, "We're sort of mavericks in this business, because we've done something that a lot of people said was impossible. Consequently, at times, we haven't had the full confidence of the financial community ... being acquired by a conglomerate would certainly make us accepted members." Shortly thereafter, the company was acquired by City Investing Company, giving it the financial wherewithal to expand at a robust pace.

By the early 1970s, Motel 6 and its group of budget-oriented competitors also had begun to draw the attention of their larger, more luxurious competitors by capturing some of their market share. In 1972, budget motels, the most active of which were companies with construction expertise rather than motel or hotel management expertise, accounted for between 2 and 3 percent of the lodging industry's aggregate revenues of $9 billion, up from essentially zero before the decade began. The sudden rise and encroachment of budget motels was sufficient to force larger motel chains to adapt to the changing market conditions. But as Motel 6 had demonstrated a decade earlier, driving overhead costs down was not something to be accomplished administratively; it was something to be realized, first and foremost, by paying assiduous attention to construction costs and design plans.

One of the pioneers of this revolutionary concept, Motel 6 moved forward with optimistic plans, bolstered by the growing presence and acceptance of budget motels across the country, particularly in the southwestern and western United States. The company now had roughly 110 motels stretched across 30 states, with plans to add 570 motels by the end of the decade. Those plans were dashed, however, as growth slowed during the balance of the 1970s, at least in terms of the company's hopeful prognostications. Proposing to operate 680 motels by 1979, Motel 6 only had 378 properties in operation by 1985, the year City Investing Company sold the motel chain to an investor group led by Kohlberg, Kravis, Roberts & Company (KKR) for $881 million. Although City Investing's divestiture of the budget motel chain was not directly related to Motel 6's laggard expansion—City Investing's shareholders had voted to liqui-

---

Key Dates:

1962: Paul A. Greene and William W. Becker open their first Motel 6 in Santa Barbara, California.
1966: The company generates more than $4 million in sales and earns more than $750,000.
1985: Motel 6 is sold to an investor group led by Kohlberg, Kravis, Roberts & Company.
1986: The firm launches a radio advertising campaign featuring Tom Bodett.
1990: Accor S.A. acquires Motel 6 for $1.3 billion.
1996: The company adopts a franchising strategy.
1999: Studio 6, an extended-stay budget lodging brand, is launched.
2002: Motel 6 celebrates its 40th anniversary.

---

date a majority of the company's assets to focus primarily on selling home insurance—there were clear indications that Motel 6 was suffering from potentially debilitating problems.

More alarming than the motel chain's slower-than-expected expansion was its consistently shrinking occupancy rate, which declined from over 90 percent during the early 1970s to 81 percent by 1981, and to 59 percent by the time of the sale by City Investing. Chiefly to blame for Motel 6's malaise were the same companies that had grown along with Motel 6 to be prodigious forces in the lodging industry during the 1960s and 1970s. By the 1980s competition among these companies had become intense, heightened after two decades of expansion that had blanketed the country with budget motels. In the drive to lure guests into its rooms, Motel 6 was losing ground and its expansion efforts were losing momentum. Meanwhile, its closest rivals began sprucing up their rooms, making them more hospitable, and consequently robbing Motel 6 of its historically high occupancy rates.

To enhance Motel 6's market position, the investor group led by KKR had several solutions in mind. Motel 6's new owners began adding amenities that Greene and Becker had previously eschewed, such as installing telephones and color television sets throughout the motel chain's properties, placing an emphasis on attracting business travelers to complement the company's primary clientele of weekend pleasure travelers and thus accelerating expansion. By far the most important change brought about by the company's new management was a major marketing push, the first advertising campaign put forth in Motel 6's history.

Spearheading the company's entry into the public spotlight was Joseph W. McCarthy, a former employee at Sheraton Corporation and Quality Inns who was hired by KKR in January 1986 to become Motel 6's president. Slated to air in the fall of that year, Motel 6's radio advertising campaign featured National Public Radio announcer Tom Bodett and his signature Motel 6 tag line, "We'll leave the light on for you." The advertisements were immediately successful and were quickly copied by fellow leading budget motel companies. Econo-Lodges hired comedian Tim Conway and Red Roof Inns hired Martin Mull, giving way to a new era in the budget motel

industry, an era with a humorous slant. By 1988, thanks largely to the company's advertisements, Motel 6's occupancy rate had stopped its steady decline and climbed to nearly 73 percent, 6 percent higher than the current national average.

Accor Takes Over in 1990

Once Motel 6's performance was invigorated by its radio advertising and the changes instituted by KKR, the motel chain stepped up its expansion efforts, hoping to improve upon or at least maintain its number two ranking in the United States. Trailing only Days Inns of America, Motel 6 increased its geographic presence in the late 1980s, expanding from 401 motels in 39 states in 1986 to 554 motels in 42 states by 1990. That year, the motel chain underwent its third change in ownership when Accor S.A.—a $4 billion French conglomerate with holdings in restaurants, hotels, motels, travel agencies, car rental companies, and restaurant voucher firms—purchased Motel 6 from KKR for $1.3 billion.

Accor, which owned a chain of motels in Europe similar to Motel 6 that were called Formule 1, had made its initial move into the United States in 1979 when it opened a hotel in Minneapolis, a move that proved to be only moderately successful. Six years later, the company launched its Formule 1 concept, a motel chain that met with immediate success. By the late 1980s, Accor was ready to make another attempt to enter the U.S. lodging market and the acquisition of Motel 6 provided the means. The addition of Motel 6's more than 550 establishments vaulted Accor to the number two position worldwide and gave Motel 6, which retained its existing management, a new infusion of cash to wage its advertising war and continue expanding. In 1991, Accor purchased 53 Regal Inns and Affordable Inns from RHC Holding Corporation, bolstering the motel chain's market position, while plans were formulated for Motel 6's advertising debut on television. With Tom Bodett continuing to serve as the motel chain's spokesman, Motel 6 began broadcasting its first television commercials in 1992, by which time it had ascended to the country's number one position, supported by the 672 motels that bore the Motel 6 name.

As Motel 6 entered the mid-1990s, it was competing for preeminence in the budget motel market in a decidedly different fashion than it had 30 years earlier, a change that was most discernible in the chain's advertising efforts. The rooms composing the Motel 6 empire had changed as well, becoming slightly more luxurious than the units Greene and Becker had first designed. However, one characteristic remained constant throughout the company's history: Motel 6 rooms were typically the lowest-priced lodging accommodations offered by any regional or national competitor in the country.

Challenges and New Developments in the 1990s and Beyond

Motel 6's rise to the top of the industry was not problem-free, however. During 1993, the company reported a loss of $40 million due in part to an industry downturn along with a bout of negative publicity related to a rape that occurred at a Fort Worth, Texas, location. Faced with the consumer perception that its motels may not be safe for travelers, Motel 6 sold off approximately 100 locations thought to be problematic and heightened security at each of its motels by installing new locks, security cameras, and even security guards at various locations. Profits continued to elude the company for the next several years. "The turnaround of Motel 6 has been more difficult than we expected," claimed CEO Georges Le Mener in a 1998 *New York Times* article, "but we are here for the long term."

Indeed, Accor's dedication to the Motel 6 chain was evident. The company returned to profitability in 1996 after a successful launch of its franchising campaign, which was designed to fuel expansion in the eastern United States. It also spent $600 million to upgrade each of its existing rooms. In addition, each new hotel was built with the firm's "Motel of the 21st Century" theme that included interior corridors, dataports in every room, a computerized front desk and office system, a swimming pool, and new security features.

Motel 6 also eyed the extended-stay market as a lucrative niche and began formulating a plan to launch its own extended-stay brand. In 1999, the company did just that when it added a second brand to its arsenal, marking the start of Motel 6's multi-branding strategy. Studio 6 was introduced as an extended-stay lodging facility that mirrored Motel 6's budget concept and offered travelers rooms with weekly rates. Growth continued to be at the forefront of Motel 6's strategy in the new century. The company's lofty expansion plans included adding 50 new franchise locations each year. By July 2000, Motel 6 had opened its 100th franchised hotel. In early 2003, its 150th franchise location was established in North Carolina.

The company celebrated its 40th anniversary in 2002 as one of the most recognized brands in the United States. With over 800 locations in the United States and Canada, Motel 6 continued to lead the economy motel industry. Over the past decade, Motel 6 and its parent had successfully battled changes in the industry and overcome damaging publicity. With a strong management team and solid strategy in place, the light at Motel 6 was sure to shine for years to come.

Principal Competitors

Days Inn Worldwide Inc.; Super 8 Motels Inc.; Travelodge Hotels Inc.

Further Reading

"Accor to Close 20 Motels; Cites Security Problems," *Wall Street Journal*, October 21, 1992, p. A11.

"Bedding Down the Budget-Minded," *Business Week*, August 27, 1966, pp. 57–59.

Charski, Mindy, "The Light Is Still On in Richards' New Motel 6 Ads," *Adweek*, June 2, 2003, p. 9.

"City Investing Completes Sale," *Wall Street Journal*, February 27, 1985, p. 14.

Dunkin, Amy, "Cheap Dreams: The Budget Inn Boom," *Business Week*, July 14, 1986, p. 76.

Fisher, Christy, and Ira Teinowitz, "Budget Motels Take to Humor Ads," *Advertising Age*, November 14, 1988, p. 65.

Hayes, Mary, "Motels Offer Rock-Bottom Rates to Those Wanting Bare Minimum," *Business Journal—San Jose*, February 24, 1992, p. 22.

Lehner, Urban C., "Economy Motels Lure Travelers with Prices as Low as $6 a Room," *Wall Street Journal*, December 26, 1972, p. 1.

"Lodging: The Inn Crowd," *Newsweek*, February 19, 1973, pp. 69–70.

McDowell, Edwin, "Not Just Leaving the Light On," *The New York Times*, October 28, 1998, p.C1.

"Motel 6 LP Acquires 46 Inns," *Wall Street Journal*, February 15, 1989, p. A4.

"Motels: Discount House," *Newsweek*, October 9, 1967, p. 85.

Reier, Sharon, "Bedroom Eyes," *FW*, June 9, 1992, pp. 56–59.

Riemer, Blanea, "This Buy-America Bandwagon Could Hit a Few Potholes," *Business Week*, July 30, 1990, p. 34.

Tanner, Lisa, "Motel 6 Seeks Growth Via Franchising," *Dallas Business Journal*, June 11, 1999, p. 8.

Teinowitz, Ira, "Hotels, Rental Cars Hope for Sonic Boom," *Advertising Age*, June 15, 1992, p. 3.

Totty, Michael, "Motel 6 Radio Ads Credited for Rise in Occupancy Rate," *Wall Street Journal*, May 12, 1988, p. 28.

Wade, Betsy, "Motels Turn Their Attention to Security," *New York Times*, May 24, 1992, p. 3.

Whitford, Marty, "Motel 6 Unveils Studio 6," *Hotel & Motel Management*, May 3, 1999, p. 1.

—Jeffrey L. Covell
—update: Christina M. Stansell

m·real

M-real Oyj

Revontulentie 6
FIN-02100 ESPOO
Finland
Telephone: (358) 1046 11
Fax: (358) 1046 94355
Web site: http://www.m-real.com

Public Company
Incorporated: 1986
Employees: 20,323
Sales: EUR 6.5 billion ($7.55 billion)(2002)
Stock Exchanges: Helsinki London Bavarian
Ticker Symbol: MRL
NAIC: 322110 Pulp Mills; 322121 Paper (Except
    Newsprint) Mills; 322130 Paperboard Mills; 322222
    Coated and Laminated Paper Manufacturing

M-real Oyj—known as Metsä-Serla Oy until 2001—operates as a leading supplier of paper and paperboard and is Europe's largest fine paper producer. The company offers a wide variety of products ranging from coated magazine papers used by magazine and catalog publishers to coated fine paper utilized in commercial printing. The firm also manufactures paperboard for consumer packaging used by the cosmetics, pharmaceutical, electronics, and food industries. The company's holdings also include the Map Merchant Group, which offers products made by M-real and other merchants to over 50,000 customers throughout Europe. M-real was created in 1986 by the merger between Metsäliiton Teollisuus Oy and G.A. Serlachius Oy. Osuuskunta Metsäliitto, the Finnish forest owners' cooperative, owns 38.5 percent of M-real.

History of G.A. Serlachius Oy

The history of what is now M-real begins in the 1860s, when a steep rise in the price of sawn wood in Europe made the exploitation of Finland's gigantic timber reserves economical for the first time. Even now Finland is one of the most densely wooded countries in the world, with a majority of its land area covered by forest. An engineer named Knut Fredrik Idestam started building a groundwood plant in Tampere in 1865. Three years later, when he moved to Nokia to build a second and bigger plant, he invited his friend Gustaf Adolf Serlachius, a pharmacist, to manage the Tampere mill. In 1868, Serlachius moved on from there to Mänttä, to start his own mill for grinding wood into pulp. It was successful enough to finance the building of a paper mill, with two paper machines, at the same site in 1881. Nine years later, this wooden building was destroyed in a fire: Serlachius's continuing prosperity enabled him to replace it with a brick and stone building containing three paper machines capable of turning out 5,000 tons each year. In 1913, the business, by then incorporated as a public company, came under the direction of the founder's nephew, Gösta Michael Serlachius. In spite of the disruptions caused by World War I and then by the civil war which followed Finland's declaration of independence from Russia, he pressed ahead with an expansion of the company, both by adding on a new plant at the Mänttä site—including a sulfite pulp mill in 1914 and a sulfite alcohol plant in 1918—and by acquiring other businesses, such as a saw mill at Kolho in 1916 and the Kangas fine paper mill at Jyväskylä in 1918. In 1917, Gösta Michael Serlachius acquired the Tampere Paper Board and Roofing Felt Mill, which Gustaf Adolf Serlachius had managed nearly half a century earlier. In the intervening years, it had passed through various hands, finally falling into bankruptcy when the delivery of a new corrugated board machine from Germany was delayed by the outbreak of World War I. The machine eventually arrived in 1920, and the mill, renamed Tako Oy in 1932, went on to produce a range of boards and building materials in its plants, some of which were used in the construction of the largest building in Tampere.

After 1918, and in line with the general trend in the Finnish forest industry, Serlachius abandoned the production of brown wrapping paper for the Soviet market, which was being torn apart by revolution, civil war, and foreign intervention, in favor of supplying newsprint to Finland's new market in western Europe. During this period, Finnish forest products were still mostly of a lower quality than those of rival companies in Norway and Sweden. Still, Serlachius and the other Finnish companies prospered, even in this new, more demanding mar-

Company Perspectives:

M-real's objective is to enhance its customers' business by providing them with excellent fibre-based products and value-added services for their needs in consumer packaging, communications, and advertising.

ket, because the low valuation of the Finnish markka kept their export earnings high, even during the Great Depression, when the Finnish forest industries maintained continuous output through the use of plant and equipment modernized during the boom years of the 1920s. By 1939, Finland was the world's leading exporter of paper.

Gösta Serlachius retained control of the company up to his death in 1942, when his son R. Erik Serlachius became managing director. The man who had overseen the expansion of the company into a large and diversified enterprise is commemorated in the Gösta Serlachius Museum of Fine Arts in Mänttä. This houses several hundred works of art collected by Gösta Serlachius or inherited from his uncle and passed into the hands of a fine arts foundation established in 1933. Gustaf Adolf Serlachius had been among the first patrons of Akseli Gallen-Kallela, generally considered Finland's greatest painter, and Gösta Serlachius, who shared his uncle's enthusiasm, assembled the largest private collection of this artist's work, now the main feature of the museum.

At the time of Gösta Serlachius' death, Finland was engaged in an alliance with Nazi Germany against the Soviet Union. In 1944, Finland surrendered to the Soviet Union, having failed to regain the lands—about 8 percent of its area—that it had ceded to Stalin after a brief war in 1939–1940. These two wars meant that the forest industry could not sell its products in Britain or the Americas, but it kept up production for its continental European markets. Some of the companies diversified: Serlachius began producing chemicals and switched from making newsprint to making printing paper during these years. Its plants in Tampere sustained some bomb damage and then had to contribute to the reparations demanded by the Soviet Union. These was also the further loss of land, which was a serious blow to the forest industry in general, since additional areas ceded to the Soviet Union in 1947 included 12 percent of Finland's forests, 20 percent of its wood- and pulp-producing capacity, and 10 percent of its paper and paperboard capacity.

It did not take Serlachius long to recover from the impact of these events. The company was now producing a range of papers, as well as paperboard, and in the late 1940s it expanded production of parchment paper at Jyväskylä, began producing impregnated wood at Kolho, and started work on the installation of its seventh paper machine at Mänttä. Paperboard production at Tampere prospered as the pre-packing of goods in cartons for delivery to retail outlets became the norm in Finland. The company also profited from selling pulp to the United States and returned to making newsprint. Another boost for the company's financial health was the fact that the prices of all kinds of paper products, as of other raw materials, rose sharply as the ending of rationing and the outbreak of the Korean War increased demand.

Finland's openness to international economic cycles cut both ways: when prices fell and recession set in at the end of 1951, the forest industry's expansion was slowed, and the levying of taxes on excess profits during the Korean War temporarily inhibited investment. Once the economy had recovered, Serlachius was able to begin production of copy paper and other special papers for technical uses at Jyväskylä and to modernize its plant at Tampere. In 1961, Serlachius began producing tissue paper using the eighth paper machine to be installed at Mänttä. This latest venture was so successful that another tissue paper machine was started up in 1965. The timber division of the company was also modernized, with the introduction of an automated saw mill at Kolho in 1963. In 1965, the company started to expand by acquisition as well as by internal growth, purchasing the Vammala plywood factory and the Lielahti mill, which produced dissolving pulp for use in the making of artificial silk. Serlachius's capacity for producing cartons was expanded in the 1980s with the acquisition of Järvenpään Kotelo Oy and Pak-Paino.

History of Metsäliiton Teollisuus Oy

The history of Metsäliiton Teollisuus was shorter than Serlachius's but organizationally more complex, since it was the creation not of a single founder and his successors but of a cooperative movement. It has its origins in 1934, when the Central Federation of Agricultural Producers set up Metsäliitto Oy, with Ilmari Kalkkinen as managing director, to supervise the export of products from its forestry department. Kalkkinen was also managing director of the Osuuskunta Metsäliitto, the cooperative organization of forest owners, which took over control of Metsäliitto in 1947. The company then diversified into sawn timber and impregnated wood, acquiring both a plywood factory at Hämeenlinna and pulp, paper, and paperboard mills and chemical plants at Äänekoski. These mills later became part of a subsidiary company, Metsäliiton Selluloosa Oy.

Kalkkinen retired in 1959 and was succeeded by Viljo A. Kytölä, under whom the board of directors and the management of the cooperative and of Metsäliitto were combined from 1960 onward. During the 1960s, Metsäliitto's plant and equipment were extensively modernized. In 1965, it became the main shareholder in Savon Sellu Mills and set up another pulp-producing subsidiary, Oy Metsäpohjanmaa-Skogsbotnia Ab. Meanwhile, Osuuskunta Metsäliitto established three more companies, Teollisuusosuuskunta Metsä-Saimaa, which operated sawmills; Oy Metsäliiton Paperi Ab, which had a paper mill at Kirkniemi; and Metsäliiton Myyntikonttorit, which brought together the cooperative's sales offices. In 1973, all these operations were reorganized. Osuuskunta Metsäliitto took responsibility for all wood procurement and marketing, with Metsäliiton Myyntikonttorit and Metsäliitto Oy as subsidiaries, while Metsäliiton Selluloosa Oy, renamed Metsäliiton Teollisuus Oy, became the parent company for the Metsäliitto groups' production activities, thus leaving Metsäliitto Oy as a timber procurement company and the largest supplier of timber in Finland. Following Kytölä's retirement, the managing directors of each of these bodies—respectively Mikko Wuoti and Pentti O. Rautalahti—became deputies to a single powerful president, Veikko Vainio. In 1980, all three were replaced, Vainio by Wuoti, Wuoti by Matti Puttonen, and Rautalahti by

Key Dates:

1868: Gustaf Adolf Serlachius moves to Mänttä to start his own mill for grinding wood into pulp.

1913: The business comes under the direction of Serlachius's nephew, Gösta Michael Serlachius.

1934: The Central Federation of Agricultural Producers sets up Metsäliitto Oy to supervise the export of products from its forestry department.

1947: Osuuskunta Metsäliitto, the cooperative organization of forest owners, takes over control of Metsäliitto.

1973: Metsäliitto is reorganized; Metsäliitto Teollisuus Oy becomes the parent company for the group's production activities.

1986: Metsä-Serla Oy is formed by the merger between Metsäliiton Teollisuus Oy and G.A. Serlachius Oy.

2001: The company changes its name to M-real Oyj.

Ebbe Sommar. By 1986, when Metsäliiton Teollisuus began negotiating the merger with G.A. Serlachius, its production units were making not only pulp, paper, plywood, and various kinds of board but also loghouses, saunas, doors, and windows.

A Merger Creates Metsä-Serla

The merger between Metsäliiton Teollisuus and G.A. Serlachius took effect on January 1, 1987, with Gustaf Serlachius as chairman of the board, Mikko Wuoti as his deputy, and Ebbe Sommar as managing director. The two groups were of similar size, for Metsäliiton Teollisuus had a turnover of Fmk2.5 billion and assets worth Fmk3 billion, while the equivalent figures for G.A. Serlachius were Fmk2.8 billion and Fmk3 billion.

Metsäliitto held nearly 57 percent of the shares in Metsäliiton Teollisuus at the time of the merger and came to hold the largest single portion of Metsä-Serla's shares, 27 percent, and votes, 48 percent, proportions which have risen slightly since the merger was completed. The other leading shareholders are the Gösta Serlachius Art Foundation, Gustaf Serlachius himself, and several Finnish insurance companies. The new company started out with 17 subsidiaries in Finland and 14 in other European countries.

Metsä-Serla's ten divisions faced serious problems, with excess capacity in eight divisions—magazine paper, fine paper, paperboard, domestic packaging, tissue paper products, chemicals, sawn timber, and building materials—alongside some success in international packaging and panel products. During its first year, the company brought a new fine-paper mill at Äänekoski into operation, disposed of seven subsidiaries not directly linked to forestry, and increased its majority shareholding in Oy Metsä-Botnia Ab, a bleached pulp producer. Profits rose by 17 percent, largely because demand for paper, cartons, tissue paper products, and building materials improved, but the company's work force was cut from about 13,200 to about 12,000. Production costs fell appreciably, compared with those in 1985, because a reform of Finland's energy tax and decreases in the prices of fuel oil and coal allowed the company, which derived 85 percent of its electricity from its own power

stations or from firms in which it has shares, to reduce its spending on energy.

Profits rose again in 1988 and in 1989 as demand grew in all the areas of Metsä-Serla's output. A new paper mill was started up at Äänekoski to help meet the rising demand. Early in 1989, Metsä-Serla bought the tissue paper and hygiene products company Holmen Hygiene from its Swedish parent company Mo Och Domsjo, renaming it Metsä-Serla AB. In 1988, this company had been the first in the world to produce unchlorinated tissue products. Metsä-Serla retained its plant in Sweden but sold off its factories in Belgium and Britain. The tissue paper products division became the second-largest producer of such products in western Europe, supplying half the market in the Nordic countries.

Following the acquisition of another pulp and liner board company, Kemi Oy, in which Osuuskunta Metsäliitto had had shares since 1950, the bleached pulp subsidiary Oy Metsä-Botnia Ab was reorganized in 1989 in order to reduce the company's need for pulp from other sources. One of its two mills, at Äänekoski, was absorbed into Metsä-Serla—to be run by a subsidiary called Metsä-Sellu—and the other, at Kaskinen, was assigned to a new Oy Metsä-Botnia Ab, which also took over Kemi Oy and Pohjan Sellu Oy in 1991. Metsä-Botnia was jointly owned by Metsä-Serla (around 30 percent); Osuuskunta Metsäliitto; United Paper Mills, Finland's largest forest products corporation; and the Tapiola Insurance Group. Metsä-Serla then acquired 30 percent of the shares of United Paper Mills itself. This action was seen as a hostile takeover bid but was justified by Metsä-Serla as an attempt to develop cooperation between the two groups, building on the Metsä-Botnia venture. In April 1990, it vetoed the long-awaited merger between United Paper Mills and Rauma-Repola but accepted the proposal two months later in return for seats on the board of the merged company Repola Oy and agreement on coordinating investments, marketing, and timber procurement. This agreement also led to the issuing of new shares in Metsä-Serla to Rauma-Repola Oy, which ended the year with a 7.6 percent holding, now owned by Repola Oy.

In April 1990, Timo Poranen succeeded Ebbe Sommar. Just two months later, Poranen announced that profits were likely to fall once again during 1990 and that the company still faced problems of excess capacity and rising production costs. Indeed, the whole Finnish forest industry was suffering from high production costs and an unfavorable exchange rate. The company's restructuring continued throughout 1990 with the purchase of 75 percent of the shares in a British paper merchant company, the Alliance Paper Group, and the transfer of the panel products division to Finnforest Oy, in which Metsäliitto had 90 percent of the shares and Metsä-Serla had 10 percent. Metsä-Serla also pressed on with the building up of its stake in United Paper Mills, so that by the end of the year it held 34.1 percent of voting rights. At 21.1 percent of the total shares, it was the biggest single shareholder in Repola Oy, the parent company of United Paper Mills, and the two groups generally cooperated on pulp mill investment. The company began disposing of these shares in 1996, however, when United Paper Mills merged with Kymmene.

Metsä-Serla's turnover in 1990 was nearly one and a half times the combined turnover of the companies which came together to create it in 1986. Its high level of diversification, and its close connections with Osuuskunta Metsäliitto, which represented nearly 130,000 owners of private forests, with Metsäliitto, the largest timber supplier in Finland, and with Repola Oy, the country's biggest private industrial corporation, provided the group with secure foundations for dealing with the turbulent nature of the European paper industry during the remainder of the decade.

Creating a New Look: 1990s and Beyond

The downturn in the global forest industry continued through the early 1990s. This eventually took its toll on Metsä-Serla's profits as well as the profits of its competitors. As such, the industry began to see a wave of restructuring, mergers, and the formation of alliances. Metsä-Serla returned to profitability during 1993, mainly due to its cost cutting efforts. The company divested both its sawmilling and chemicals business in 1995 and 1996, respectively, in moves that signaled the firm's focus was shifting back to its core operations.

During this time period, the firm's Finnish competitors were joining forces in large mergers that positioned them a step ahead of Metsä-Serla. The formation of United Paper Mill (UPM)-Kymmene Corp. and Enso Oy's purchase of Veitsiluoto left the company forced to make some key moves of its own. During 1996, the company acquired MD Papier, a German magazine and specialty paper manufacturer. It also formed a strategic alliance with the Finnish forestry group Myllykoski and purchased two production plants from UPM-Kymmene for $429 million in order to bolster its paperboard capacity. In 1997, the firm consolidated its pulp operations of Metsä Botnia and launched a public offering of its Metsä Tissue subsidiary. British fine paper wholesaler UK Paper was acquired in 1998 along with 94 percent of Medienos Plausas. That year, the company strengthened its tissue holdings with the purchase of Halstrick and Strepp in Germany.

Along with its acquisition and divestiture strategy, Metsä-Serla also focused on internal restructuring. This line of attack appeared to pay off, and by 1998 the company was posting near record results. Jorma Vaajoki, the company's CEO at the time, commented on the company's efforts in a 1999 *Pulp & Paper International* article, claiming that "catching up with our competitors is simply a confession that our results were lousy for a number of years. Our return on capital employed was not very good at all." Metsä-Serla's turnaround was successful, however, and by the end of the 1990s the firm was operating as Europe's largest coated and uncoated fine paper producer.

Buoyed by strong demand and rising prices, Metsä-Serla was optimistic as it entered the new century. The company focused on augmenting its coated paper and consumer packaging business, eyeing these divisions as key to maintaining a leading position in the European market. In late 2000, the company announced its plans to purchase a 72 percent interest in German-based Zanders Feinpapiere from International Paper Co. After the deal, Metsä-Serla controlled 23 percent of the European office papers market, which included printing papers and paper used for magazines.

The company made a bold move in 2001 when it changed its name to M-real Oyj. The new name stood for "making it real" and was designed to create a hip and more creative image for the company. "We want to highlight the timeless possibilities which paper affords for creativity, and intend to tie our product names in closely with our company names to create more direct contact with our company for the users of our products," remarked Jouko Jaakkola in a May 2001 *Paperboard Packaging* article. Jaakkola was named president and CEO of M-real in late 2001.

The company faced weakening demand for many of its products during 2002, resulting in lower sales and profits. While it continued to face challenges into 2003, company management remained convinced that the firm was on a successful track. With a new CEO and a new name, M-real was determined to remain a leading force in the European market and planned to seek out growth opportunities in Asia in the years to come.

Principal Subsidiaries

Alakoski Oy (52.78%); Oy Board International AB; Oy Hangö Stevedoring AB (75.33%); M-real International Oy; Forestia Oy (94.51%); Metsä Tissue Oy (65.58%); Tako Carton Plant Ltd.; Äänevoima Oy (45%); M-real Deutsche Hilding Gmbh (Germany); M-real Fine B.V. (The Netherlands); M-real Holding Belgium S.A.; M-real UK Holdings Ltd.; Map Merchant Holdings B.V. (The Netherlands).

Principal Operating Units

Consumer Packaging; Commercial Printing; Home & Office; Publishing; Map Merchant Group.

Principal Competitors

International Paper Co.; Store Enso Oyj; UPM-Kymmene Corp.

Further Reading

Brown-Humes, Christopher, "Metsa-Serla Returns to Profit," *Financial Times London*, February 19, 1994, p. 9.

Brown-Humes, Christopher, and Hilary Barnes, "Metsa-Serla Cuts Losses by Half to FM290m," *Financial Times* (London), February 22, 1993, p. 19.

Fales, Gregg, "Metsa-Serla Agrees to Zanders Takeover," *PIMA's North American Papermaker*, December 2000, p. 17.

Kenny, Jim, "Playing Catch-up with Metsa Serla," *Pulp & Paper International*, June 1999, p. 27.

Richards, E. G., ed., *Forestry and the Forest Industries: Past and Future*, Dordrecht: Martinus Nijhoff Publishers, 1987.

Tessieri, Enrique, "Metsa-Serla Falls Into the Red With Loss of FM41m," *Financial Times* (London), February 28, 1991, p. 18.

———, "Stuck from All Sides--Finland," *Financial Times* (London), May 24, 1991, p. 36.

—Patrick Heenan
—update: Christina M. Stansell

nutreco

Nutreco Holding N.V.

Prins Frederiklann 4
3818 KC Amersfoort
The Netherlands
Telephone: (+31) 33-422-6100
Fax: (+31) 33-422-6101
Web site: http://www.nutreco.com

Public Company
Incorporated: 1994
Employees: 13,237
Sales: EUR 3.81 billion ($3.8 billion) (2002)
Stock Exchanges: Euronext Amsterdam
Ticker Symbol: NUO
NAIC: 551112 Offices of Other Holding Companies;
    112511 Finfish Farming and Fish Hatcheries; 311119
    Other Animal Food Manufacturing; 311612 Meat
    Processed From Carcasses; 311615 Poultry Processing

Netherlands-based Nutreco Holding N.V. is a world-leading, vertically integrated feed and foods producer. The company is organized under two primary business divisions. Nutreco Aquaculture is the world's largest aquaculture company, manufacturing fish feeds, combining its various brand names, which included Trouw and Moore-Clark, under the single Skretting name in January 2003. Nutreco Aquaculture also operates salmon under the Marine Harvest name in Norway, Chile, Canada, Scotland, and Australia. The company also operates fish processing facilities in Chile, Norway, Scotland, and France. The second primary business division of the Nutreco group is Nutreco Agriculture, which encompasses breeding services and breeding stock production, as well as the production of specialist feed ingredients for pork and poultry farmers; Nutreco Agriculture also includes pork and poultry meat processing facilities, under brand names including Pingo Poultry, Sada, and Hendrix. In addition to these activities, Nutreco conducts a strong research and development component, working on animal genetics, as well as the development of other fish farming sectors, such as codfish. Nutreco, formed in 1994 from the animal feeds and aquaculture operations of BP

Nutrition, then in the process of being divested by British Petroleum, has been listed on the Euronext Amsterdam stock exchange since 1997. The EUR 3.8 billion company is overseen by Chairman R. Zwartendijk and CEO Wout Dekker.

Merging European Feed Producers in the 1970s

Although Nutreco itself was formed only in 1994, parts of the company stretch back to the early years of the 20th century. One of the oldest parts of what later became the Nutreco group was Skretting, founded in Norway in 1899. Skretting's original business was as an agricultural merchant, which later led the company into the production of animal feeds. The birth of the commercial fish farming sector in Norway, however, brought the company into manufacturing fish feeds in the 1960s. In 1963, Skretting became the first company to begin producing extruded salmon feed products. Soon after, Skretting focused its entire operation on production of fish feeds.

The Netherlands formed an important center for the later Nutreco. A primary component stemmed from the founding of Trouw Nutrition, by Adolph Trouw, in 1931. That company originally produced vitamin and mineral mixes for the feed industry, before expanding to become one of the world's leading feed producers.

Another important part of the later Nutreco was founded in The Netherlands in 1928 as Hendrix Voeders. Like Skretting, the Hendrix company started out as an agricultural products wholesaler, dealing in seeds, grains, manure, and potatoes, before turning to the production of animal feeds in the 1930s. Hendrix grew strongly through the 1940s, adopting new production methods. In the 1950s, Hendrix built new production facilities. By then, the company had begun diversifying its interests, adding a poultry breeding unit, which formed the basis of Nutreco's later Euribrid breeding group. Hendrix expanded further, adding a poultry brand, Pingo, to its operations.

In the 1970s, British Petroleum (BP), confronted with the loss of direct control of the OPEC-region oil production, went on a diversification drive. In 1975, BP targeted the feed market, creating, the new business unit BP Nutrition. That company went on a buying spree, acquiring a wide range of animal feed

256

Company Perspectives:

Mission: We are a global food company, inspired by consumer demands, creating value through sustainable modern aquaculture and agriculture.

Our activities span the globe and are characterised by a commitment to food safety through strict quality control and traceability. We begin with breeding fish and livestock to suit the range of current farming methods, and continue through feeds and farming, to the processing and marketing of fish and meat products—all in line with the requirements of modern consumers.

and aquaculture companies across Europe. Among the first of these was the purchase of a two-thirds share in Trouw in 1975, which placed the core of BP Nutrition in The Netherlands. That position was strengthened in 1979, when the Hendrix family sold out the Hendrix group to BP Nutrition as well, joining the growing number of companies, which by then included Spain's Sada and Nanta. The following year, BP Nutrition turned to Norway, which had become a center of the fish farming industry, where, through Trouw, it acquired Skretting.

BP Nutrition continued to expand both its feed and aquaculture operations, entering the South American feed market with the creation of Trouw Chile in 1981 and the launch of the Mares Aurstales fish farming operation. In 1986, BP Nutrition took a big step forward when it bought Purina Mills, the feed production arm of the United States' Ralston Purina. In that year, also, BP Nutrition added major Canadian fish feed producer Moore-Clark, which had focused on the Pacific Northwest salmon market, before expanding, under BP Nutrition, nationwide in 1990. BP Nutrition also began salmon farming operations in Canada, which followed on its extension into fish farming in South America, through Trouw Chile's acquisition of a fish farming operation in Chile in 1988.

By then, British Petroleum had acquired Standard Oil and Britoil. The downturn in the economy, coupled with the debt load from these acquisitions, forced BP to begin divesting its diversified operations, including BP Nutrition. By 1994, BP had, in large part, completed its divestment program. In that year, senior members of BP Nutrition's management team, including then-CEO Richard van Wijnbergen, set up a new company, Anchor Holding, which then joined with investment groups CinVen and Baring Capital Investors to lead a management buyout of BP Nutrition. The buyout, in a deal worth $550 million, created the world's largest aquaculture company, as well as one of the leading animal feed producers in Europe.

Following the management buyout, Anchor Holding changed its name to Nutreco and established its headquarters in Boxmeer, in The Netherlands. Despite Nutreco's market leadership—the company was the largest privately held feed supplier in Europe, including a 50 percent share of the worldwide market for salmon and trout feed, and was also one of Europe's main suppliers of poultry and pork breeding stock, and processed poultry and pork products—the company declined to go public immediately, preferring instead to build its own business track record.

Dual-Pronged Leader in the New Century

Nutreco's operations remained concentrated around two primary businesses, Hendrix and Trouw, which also included Skretting, through the 1990s. Growth was focused primarily on internal operations, such as Trouw's development of an organic salmon feed mix, launched in 1995. In 1997, the company opened a new experimental fish feed technology factory, in Stavanger, in the United Kingdom.

By then, Nutreco, seeking to accelerate its growth, decided the time was right for a public offering, and in May 1997 placed its shares on the Amsterdam stock exchange. The successful offering, which valued Nutreco at nearly $500 million, provided the basis for an extended acquisition drive that was to boost the company's sales by more than 50 percent in just four years. By the end of 1997, the company had made its first move into the Eastern European market, purchasing Polfarm, the leading premix feed maker in Poland.

Nutreco's acquisition spree gained speed in 1998, with the purchase of UT-Delfia, a $240 million per year animal feed maker. That month, also, the company took over Caicaen, a salmon farm in Chile. The company turned to Spain, acquiring Nanfor and Herca, then forming a joint venture between its Nanta subsidiary and Omsa de Alimentacion to develop pig farms in that country. The Eastern European market remained a Nutreco focus in 1998 as well, as the company began talks to acquire Pepees, a mixed feed producer. That acquisition, completed in October of that year, was followed by the purchase of a leading Dutch brooding chicken farmer, Gebroeders Van Erp, as well as pig breeders Bovar and Parvak, also in The Netherlands.

Fueling the company's acquisition campaign was its secondary offering, made in March 1998. Nutreco continued adding to its operations into 1999, with the purchase, through its French subsidiary Belanne Nueil, of Vendee Aliments, a manufacturer of animal feed with annual sales of just $9 million per year. Such small-scale purchases remained a key part of Nutreco's acquisition strategy, as the company added the egg production of W. Van Erp Holding, based in The Netherlands, the Hencu, Netherlands-based chicken processing arm of the United Kingdom's Hillsdown Holdings and, marking Nutreco's Nanta subsidiary's entry in Portugal, the livestock company Fabricas de moagem do Marco.

Yet Nutreco also was preparing two more significant acquisitions for 1999. On July 15 of that year, the company announced its agreement to acquire the Marine Harvest McConnell salmon farming and processing business from Booker Plc. Originally founded by Unilever in the late 1960s, Marine Harvest had pioneered the Scottish salmon farming market, which later grew to become one of the world's leaders. Marine Harvest was acquired by Booker in 1994, which merged it with its existing business, McConnell Salmon, forming a new subsidiary Booker Aquaculture, and taking on the trade name Marine Harvest McConnell. That business was one of the top four salmon producers in the U.K. market.

Two weeks after the Marine Harvest acquisition, Nutreco announced another significant purchase, this time of the BOCM Fish Feed Group, part of BOCM, which, although one of the United Kingdom's top animal feed producers—and a direct

Key Dates:

1899:   Skretting is founded in Norway as an agricultural merchant.

1928:   Hendrix Voeders is founded as an agricultural products wholesaler, which enters the animal feed business in the 1930s.

1931:   Adolph Trouw founds a company producing vitamin and mineral mixes for animal feeds, and later begins its own production of animal feeds.

1963:   Skretting begins producing extruded fish feeds, which becomes its sole focus.

1968:   Moore-Clark is founded in Canada.

1975:   British Petroleum establishes BP Nutrition and acquires Trouw.

1979:   BP Nutrition acquires Hendrix.

1980:   Trouw acquires Skretting.

1981:   Trouw Chile is founded.

1986:   BP Nutrition acquires Purina Mills and Moore-Clark.

1994:   Nutreco is formed from the management-led buyout of BP Nutrition.

1997:   Nutreco lists on the Amsterdam stock exchange.

2000:   Nutreco acquires most of Hydro Seafood from Norsk Hydro.

2003:   All fish feed operations are regrouped under the Skretting name.

competitor of Nutreco's Trouw subsidiary—had decided to exit the fish feed business. The addition of the BOCM Fish Feed operations gave Nutreco the number four leading fish feed group in the United Kingdom.

Following these acquisitions, Nutreco restructured its operations, creating two primary business groups, Agriculture and Aquaculture, and five secondary divisions: Aqua International; Aqua Feed Europe; Agri Northern Europe; Agri Iberica; and Agri International. By then, the company's annual revenues had been boosted past EUR 2.6 billion.

In March 2000, Nutreco made a move to cement its leading position in the worldwide aquaculture market, reaching an agreement with Norsk Hydro to acquire Hydro Seafood, the world's largest Atlantic salmon producer, with operations in the United Kingdom, Norway, Ireland, and France. The British mergers and monopolies commission, however, barred Nutreco from acquiring Hydro Seafood's U.K. operations, which represented some 20 percent of Hydro Seafood's business.

Nutreco had in the meantime continued to target new acquisitions. In Belgium, the company picked up Voeders Haeck, an animal feed producer, then entered Hungary with the purchase of the premix and feed operations of that country's Kornye. The company also reached an agreement to take over management of the poultry operations of the Spanish cooperative group Copaga. In September 2000, the company purchased a 56 percent stake in Cod Culture Norway, which had been developing technology that was expected to lead to introducing a new cod farming market. Also in 2000, Nutreco moved its headquarters in 2000 from Boxmeer to Amersfoort.

The turn of the century marked the entry into new territories. In 2001, Nutreco moved into the United States with the purchase of Ducoa's premix operations, giving it control of the third largest premix company in that market. That business formed the basis of a new Nutreco subsidiary, Trouw Nutrition USA. At the same time, Nutreco acquired shareholder stakes in two major Australian aquaculture businesses, Pivot Aquaculture, the South Pacific region's leading fish feed producer, and publicly listed Tassal, the region's top salmon producer. Meanwhile, in Spain, the company acquired Agrovic in its largest agricultural purchase to date, giving it a leading position in the Spanish feed market.

Nutreco slowed down its acquisitions in 2002, as it began a restructuring drive in order to enhance the operating synergies among its expanded operations. Nonetheless, the company acquired two new companies, those of Chisal, a salmon processor based in Chile, and Selko, a manufacturer of organic feed components. The company also joined a joint venture to build a premix plant for pig feed production in the Hunan province of China. At the beginning of 2003, Nutreco continued its restructuring. In January of that year, the company moved to regroup all of its fish feed operations under a single brand name, Skretting. By then, Nutreco, which had seen its sales top EUR 3.8 million, had firmly established its own name as a two-pronged, worldwide leader.

Principal Subsidiaries

Agrovic Alimentación S.A. (Spain); Atlantic Halibut AS. Hjelmeland (Norway; 62%); Cod Culture Norway AS (56.14%); Drucar S.r.l. (Italy); Euribrid España S.A. (94.87%); Fábricas de Moagem do Marco S.A. (Portugal); Gibson's Ltd. Launceston (Australia); Gruppo Sada p.a. S.A. (Spain); Hedimix B.V.; Hendrix Bacon UK Limited; Hendrix Feed (Xiangtan) Co. Ltd. (China; 50%); Hendrix Illesch GmbH (Germany; 90%); Hendrix Környe Kft (Hungary); Hendrix Meat Group B.V. (63%); Hendrix N.V. (Belgium); Hendrix Poultry Breeders B.V. (50%); Hendrix UTD B.V.; Hendrix UTD GmbH (Germany); Hifeed B.V.; Hifeed Romania S.r.L.; Hybrid International Inc. (United States); Hybro B.V.; Marine Harvest AS (Norway); Marine Harvest Canada Farming; Marine Harvest Fanad Ltd. (Ireland); Marine Harvest Norway; Marine Harvest Rogaland AS (Norway; 62%); Marine Harvest S.A. (Chile); Marine Harvest Scotland Limited (United States); rvest Valmer S.A. (France); Mowi AS (Norway); Nanta S.A. (Spain); Belgium N.V.; Pavo Deutschland GmbH; Piensos Nanfor S.A. (Spain; 50%); Piensos Nanpro S.A. (Spain; 50%); Pingo Poultry Farming B.V.; Plumex B.V. (50%); Reudink Biologische Voeders B.V.; Sada p.a. Canarias S.A. (Spain); Sada p.a. Catalunya S.A. (Spain); Sada p.a. Centro S.L. (Spain); Selko B.V.; Selko Latin America Ltda. (Brazil); Selko Mid-East Ltd. (Cyprus); Sistemas Pecuarios S.A. de C.V (Mexico); Skretting AS (Norway); Stimulan B.V.; Trouw (UK) Limited; Trouw Aquaculture Limited (Ireland); Trouw España S.A.; Trouw France S.A.; Trouw Nutrition Nederland B.V.; Trouw Nutrition Polska Sp. z.o.o.; Trouw Nutrition Portugal Lda; Trouw Nutrition USA LLC; Trouw Yem Ticaret Anonim Sirketi. Bodrum (Turkey; 99%); Yamaha Nutreco Aquatech KK (Japan).

Principal Competitors

Cargill Inc.; ConAgra Foods Inc.; Archer Daniels Midland Co.; Edison SpA; Eli Lilly and Co.; Land O'Lakes Inc.; Royal

Cebeco Group Cooperative UA; Cargill BV; Nisshin Seifun Group; ContiGroup Companies Inc.; Kerry Group PLC; Masterfoods; Glanbia PLC; Nestlé Purina PetCare Co.; Perdue Farms Inc.; Fenaco; Ebro Puleva S.A.; Hindustan Lever Ltd.; IMC Global Inc.; CJ Corporation; Compagnie Laitiere Europeenne SCA; Nippon Flour Mills Company Ltd.; Charoen Pokphand Northeastern PCL; Unicharm Corporation.

Further Reading

Howie, Michael, ''Nutreco Completes Acquisition of DuCoa Premix Business,'' *Feedstuffs,* June 4, 2001, p. 7.

''Nutreco Acquisition to Merge Pig Breeders,'' *Feedstuffs,* February 24, 2003, p. 6.

''Nutreco Completes Agreement to Acquire Agrovic in Spain,'' *Feedstuffs,* May 21, 2001, p. 7.

''Nutreco Opens First Premix Plant in China,'' *Feedstuffs,* November 4, 2002, p. 19.

''Nutreco Rescues Cod Culture Norway AS,'' *Nordic Business Report,* March 13, 2003.

Ross, David, ''Fish Farm Giant Proposed,'' *Herald,* March 14, 2000, p. 9.

—M.L. Cohen

Obie Media Corporation

4211 West 11th Avenue
Eugene, Oregon 97402
U.S.A.
Telephone: (541) 686-8400
Toll Free: (800) 233-6243
Fax: (541) 345-4339
Web site: http://www.obie.com

Public Company
Incorporated: 1996
Employees: 295
Sales: $44.8 million (2002)
Stock Exchanges: NASDAQ
Ticker Symbol: OBIE
NAIC: 541613 Marketing Consulting; 541850 Display
    Advertising; 541890 Other Services Related to
    Advertising

Obie Media Corporation specializes in the sale, design, production, and installation of "out-of-home" advertising, including transit posters, transit murals, billboards, urban wallscapes, and bus shelter and bench displays. With sales offices throughout North America, Obie Media has agreements with more than 40 local government transit districts in the United States and Canada to sell advertising space on district-owned vehicles, transit shelters, bus benches, stations, and kiosks. The company also owns and operates advertising faces on structures located in Washington, Oregon, California, Wyoming, Montana, and Idaho and leases outdoor building walls in Portland, Seattle, and Spokane.

1940s to Mid-1990s: From Sign Painting to Outdoor Advertising

In 1939, Gordon Obie started a sign-painting business in Bozeman, Montana, painting outdoor advertising displays. Known for his attention to detail and artistry, Obie's business thrived for two decades, and in 1959, having moved to Oregon, he began Obie Outdoor Advertising in Eugene. His son, Brian, joined him in the business in 1962. In 1968, Brian Obie became president of Obie Outdoor Advertising.

The father-son business took Gordon Obie's sign-painting venture one step further. The family business expanded steadily throughout the 1970s under Brian Obie's direction. Obie Outdoor Advertising moved from painting signs to marketing outdoor advertising space. In 1979, Brian Obie sold the assets of Obie Outdoor Advertising to 3M Media Corporation and signed a non-competition agreement with 3M.

Throughout the 1970s, too, Brian Obie became involved in Eugene politics; from 1973 to 1976, he served on the city planning commission; from 1977 to 1984, he was a Eugene city councilor. After serving as mayor of Eugene, Oregon, from 1984 to 1988, Brian Obie once again devoted his attention to business, this time Obie Media Corporation, a company he had cofounded in 1987 with a few billboards and a single transit advertising contract with Lane County Transit District.

Within several years, Obie Media had grown to cover 65 outdoor advertising markets along the West Coast, and the company undertook an aggressive sales program that targeted local small and medium-sized businesses, a client segment that traditionally had received little attention in the transit advertising business. Its revenue for 1995 was $8.3 million. By 1996, the company operated about 650 billboard display faces on 375 outdoor advertising structures in Washington, Oregon, Idaho, and California. It had 70 full-time employees and agreements with seven local government transit districts to sell advertising on nearly 1,200 vehicles. In 1996, Obie Industries Incorporated formed Obie Media Corporation as a subsidiary, which it subsequently spun off. Obie Media sold one million shares of common stock in an initial public offering in 1996, raising about $6 million, which it put toward paying down the company debt.

Mid-1990s to Late-1990s: Expanding Nationally As a Transit Advertiser

Throughout the mid-1990s, the company continued its strategy of focusing on transit advertising and of targeting small- to medium-sized businesses that could not finance other advertising methods, but had no problem paying Obie's $600 a month for a removable, vinyl billboard on the side of a bus. The company's chief financial officer in a 1998 *Business Journal* article attributed the company's rapid growth to the fact that it delivered "top-of-the-mind awareness in a very cost effective manner." "Traffic is increasing and more and more people are driving by billboards or waiting for . . . buses," he explained. Additionally, Obie's methods of advertising eliminated the need to strategize how to reach a particular segment of the population. "If you think about newspapers, there's a whole generation of people who don't read or subscribe to them. Because of the proliferation of broadcast signals, it's hardest to pinpoint an audience when, instead of three channels, you get 53," he said.

Transit advertising was a unique sort of business. Agreements with transit districts are typically awarded through a competitive proposal process. A transit agreement, typically three to five years in length, requires the transit advertising operator to guarantee the district the greater of a minimum percentage of the advertising revenues generated by the operator's use of the district's vehicles, benches, and shelters, with the operator often posting performance bonds or letters of credit.

In the late 1990s, Obie, feeling ready for a major push into the national advertising scene, began expanding outside the Northwest, establishing a hub and spoke system of regional sales offices. In 1997, the company landed contracts with several transit systems: Dallas Area Rapid Transit, Santa Cruz Metropolitan Transit System, Austin's Capital Metropolitan Transportation Authority, and Sacramento's Paratransit Incorporated. According to Obie's chief financial officer in a January 1998 issue of the *Register Guard*, the company, with accounts in 11 communities, and in three of the top 25 U.S. markets—Portland, Dallas, and Sacramento—had "a lot more to talk to the national advertising agencies about. . . . We're more attractive to national advertisers, and we're getting demand from national advertisers for our space. . . ." Revenue for 1997 was $13.3 million.

By 1998, the company's media business was booming as advertisers sought alternatives to the increasingly fragmented and costly television, radio, and print media markets. The company expanded again, this time eastward with the purchase of P&C Media in Pennsylvania. P&C, one of the oldest transit advertising firms, had started in 1941 as Philbin & Coine Inc.; it represented 16 markets in the eastern and midwestern United States at the time of acquisition. Obie also expanded into Canada through a seven-year contract with BC Transit in British Columbia to provide interior and exterior advertising displays for operations in Vancouver, Victoria, and 30 smaller municipal transit systems.

With the purchase of P&C, Obie became the second largest provider of transit ads in the United States. It had operations in 29 transit districts, including seven of the top 30 media markets. A major force in the outdoor media industry, Obie Media was firmly established in four distinct regions: Canada, the Northwest, the Southwest, and the eastern United States. Each region had its own sales, design, production, and administrative capabilities and drew in roughly $8 million in sales per year. The company's stock price had doubled since its initial public offering while its revenues edged close to $15 million a year. Obie Media Limited, a newly created subsidiary, oversaw the company's Canadian operations. In early 1999, Obie Media Limited opened an office in London, Ontario, to handle the company's contract with the London Transit Commission.

The late 1990s into 2000 saw a trend toward regional consolidation and heavy competition in the outdoor media industry, which up until then had been fragmented and consisted mostly of smaller players. Improved technology was also helping the industry as a whole to grow. Digital reproductions and computer painting created the possibility of more vibrant colors and more durable displays, according to the industry's Outdoor Advertising Association. Obie introduced its signature "Back Attack" product—an ad without a frame placed directly on the back of a bus. It also began to make use of "wraps," large vinyl appliqués that are wrapped around the sides and backs of buses. The design for the wrap was programmed into a computer and then digitally painted on a vinyl strip that matched the measurement of the vehicle to be wrapped.

The late 1990s were a period of stellar growth for Obie. Its sales for 2000 reached more than $51 million. In 2001, the firm, which employed 69 people, bought its second high-speed computerized printer so that it could increase in-house production of vinyl ads from 40 to more than 80 percent by the end of the year. The printers expanded Obie's digital production shop, which also employed about 20 artists in Eugene who hand painted ads.

In the past, Obie's billboard business had generated up to 90 percent of sales; however, with revenues from billboards dropping off to about 25 percent in the late 1990s, Obie turned its attention to signing up new transit districts as clients. From 1998 to 2001, Obie and its Canadian subsidiary generated a host of new contracts, and the company's revenues increased steadily. Throughout 1998 and 1999, Obie expanded in the midwestern and eastern United States and Canada. In the year 2000, Obie added to its East Coast clientele. In 2001, the Chicago Transit Authority signed on with Obie Media. Obie opened a major office in Chicago shortly after signing the contract with CTA, the second largest transit system in the United States.

In another aspect of its growth, the company also purchased the outdoor advertising assets of Sign Products and JOSCO Outdoor in Billings, Montana, and Empire Neon in Sheridan, Wyoming, in 1999. Despite record earnings of $2 million for the year on revenue of $22.7 million, Obie Media still required additional cash; thus, the company held its second public offering to pay down debt and increase its stability to borrow money to fund future acquisitions.

Overcoming Obstacles: 2000s

Early in 2000, Obie began to ramp up its local sales effort in many of its markets. By late 2000, it had 120 salespeople in the

Key Dates:

1939: Gordon Obie starts painting signs in Bozeman, Montana.
1959: Obie starts Obie Outdoor Advertising in Eugene, Oregon.
1962: Brian Obie joins his father's company.
1968: Brian Obie becomes president of Obie Outdoor Advertising.
1979: Brian Obie sells the assets of Obie Outdoor Advertising to 3M Media Corporation.
1980: Brian Obie restarts Obie Outdoor Advertising company, which lands its first transit advertising contract with Lane Transit District.
1987: Brian Obie founds Obie Media Corporation.
1996: Obie Media Corporation separates from its parent company, Obie Industries Incorporated, and launches its initial public offering.
1998: The company acquires P&C Media and creates its Canadian subsidiary, Obie Media Limited.

United States and Canada, 50 percent more than it had had the year before. Obie's three national sales offices achieved a 25 percent increase in sales during the first nine months of 2000 as compared to sales totals for the first nine months of 1999. During the summer of 2000, the company ranked second on the *Seattle Times'* "Northwest 100" list, commemorating its outstanding growth in sales, market value, and employees, plus best return on average equity during the previous two years.

By early 2001, though, the weakened national economy was hampering profits for Obie. Although sales doubled between 1998 and 2001, profits increased from $1.5 million for 1998 to only $1.6 million in 2001. Profits were suffering as a result of the company's contracts with transit districts, 80 percent of which guaranteed that Obie would pay a minimum amount or share a healthy percentage of sales revenues with the transit district. To solve this problem, Obie began to try to get its transit agencies to accept reduced guarantees.

Another problem arose in 2001 when the CTA fired Obie. Obie approached the CTA to say that it was unable to give bond security for 2002, "unable to meet . . . minimum guaranteed revenues for 2001," according to CTA authorities in a *Chicago Sun-Times* article. To cope with contract loss, the company laid off its 37 Chicago employees and 13 independent contractors who installed signs.

By 2002, however, Obie appeared to be bouncing back. The firm had trimmed costs, cutting about 4 percent of its employees. It was successful in renegotiating its share of revenue paid to transit agencies from 54 to 43 percent. In order to expand upon its national presence, Obie had developed a strategy based on developing regional operating centers; seeking new transit agreements; pursuing acquisitions; and expanding its national sales effort.

Principal Subsidiaries

Obie Media Limited (Canada); Obie Industries; OB Walls, Inc.

Principal Competitors

Clear Channel Communications Inc.; Gateway Outdoor Advertising; Infinity Broadcasting Corporation; Lamar Advertising Company; Mediacom; Omni: The Outdoor Company; Outdoor Systems Inc.; Pattison Outdoor; Urban Outdoor; Viacom Outdoor Group; Washington Transit Advertising.

Further Reading

Binole, Gina, "Obie's Clients Ride on the Side," *Business Journal (Portland)*, July 17, 1998.

DeSilver, Drew, "Obie Media Readies for National Advertising Push," *Register Guard*, January 7, 1998, p. 6D.

Herguth, Robert C., "CTA Faces $9 Million Loss Because of Botched Ad Pact," *Chicago Sun-Times*, December 6, 2001, p. 18.

Mair, Amy Tyler, "Obie Media Expands Business Advertising Market," *Business in Vancouver*, April 20, 1999.

Russo, Ed, "Chicago Transit Authority Fires Eugene, Oregon-Based Ad Agency, Costing 50 Jobs," *Register Guard*, December 7, 2001, p. 1E.

——, "Eugene, Oregon-Based Advertising Firm Anticipates Strong Sales," *Register Guard*, August 17, 2000.

——, "Eugene, Oregon-Based Outdoor Advertising Firm Faces String of Contract Disputes," *Register Guard*, July 30, 2000, p. 1D.

——, "Eugene, Oregon-Based Outdoor Advertising Firm on the Mend After Downturn," *Register Guard*, October 10, 2002, p. 1E.

Summerfield, Patti, "Competition Heats Up in Out-of-Home Category," *Strategy Magazine—The Canadian Marketing Report*, January 18, 1999, p. 7.

—Carrie Rothburd

PARSONS

The Parsons Corporation

<table>
<tr><td>

100 West Walnut Street
Pasadena, California 91124
U.S.A.
Telephone: (626) 440-2000
Fax: (626) 440-2630
Web site: http://www.parsons.com

Private Company
Incorporated: 1944 as Ralph M. Parsons Company
Employees: 9,500
Sales: $1.5 billion (2002)
NAIC: 541330 Engineering Services; 541310
    Architectural Services

</td></tr>
</table>

The Parsons Corporation is a leading international planning, engineering, and construction firm with operations in 46 states and 37 countries across the globe. Founded in 1944, the company serves both government and private clients and is involved in a wide range of markets, including federal services, water and infrastructure, aviation, roads and highways, bridges and tunnels, rail and transit, systems engineering, urban planning and design, and communications network. Parsons operates with four main global business units: advanced technologies, commercial technology, infrastructure and technology, and transportation.

Origins and Early Growth

The Parsons Corporation has gone through a number of configurations over the years. Ralph M. Parsons started his namesake company in 1944. Parsons was described in a *New York Times* profile as an "outstanding, self-made engineer" as well as a "first-class salesman" and an "accomplished manager of people." According to the profile, Parsons first demonstrated his ability to combine engineering and business at the age of 13, when he and his brother opened a garage and machine shop in Amagansett, New York. Parsons went on to study steam and machine design at the Pratt Institute, from which he graduated in 1916. After a brief stint in the Navy, he worked as an aeronautical engineer before turning his attention to oil refinery engineering. During World War II, Parsons formed an engineering partnership

that included Stephen D. Bechtel, who later became one of his chief rivals. Finally, in 1944 he founded The Ralph M. Parsons Company (RMPCo.) with capital of $100,000.

In 1945, American industry was able to turn to projects that had been delayed by World War II. Within three years, RMPCo., having reaped the benefits of such a business climate, grew to more than one hundred employees and expanded its services in architect-engineering, systems engineering, and design. During these first years, RMPCo. constructed plants and facilities for a number of companies, including Shell Chemical Corporation and Standard Oil Company of California. In addition, RMPCo. designed the Pt. Mugu Missile Test Center in California.

In an early major project, RMPCo. designed test facilities for the development of nuclear weapons at Los Alamos, New Mexico, in 1948. The following year, the company began its first overseas project with a water development program that included 125 wells in Taiwan. The company continued these efforts in 1950 with a survey on water resources conducted for the government of India.

During the early 1950s, RMPCo. expanded into the chemical and petroleum industries. The company engineered a sulfur recovery plant—which produced sulfur from hydrogen sulfide—in Baton Rouge, Louisiana, for Consolidated Chemical Industries, Inc. in 1951. During this decade the company also oversaw the construction of a number of refineries for natural gas and petroleum in Turkey and several European nations, including the world's largest in Lacq, France. Also, RMPCo. became involved in a number of advanced aviation projects during the 1950s, including high energy fuel development, programs to develop nuclear-powered aircraft for the U.S. Air Force and Navy, and the design of facilities at the National Reactor Test Station in Idaho for nuclear engine development. The company designed underground bulk fuel storage facilities for Strategic Air Command bases all around the world.

RMPCo. offered a diverse range of skills to clients, as demonstrated by the high-thrust rocket test station it designed at Edwards Air Force base during the mid-1950s. The station included control facilities, test stands, instrumentation, and laboratories, as well as systems for storing and handling fuel and

---

Company Perspectives:

The evolving requirements and expectations of our customers are dramatically changing the engineering and construction industry. In both the public and private sectors our clients are striving to improve quantitative and qualitative returns on capital investments, operate more productively, take advantage of the advances in technology, and reduce their risk profiles. At Parsons, we have responded to these fundamental shifts by enhancing our ability to deliver something more than our traditional engineering, construction, and program management services. We firmly believe that we must be in the business of providing professional, technical, and management solutions to our customers' most challenging problems.

disposing of hazardous waste. In 1958, the company began the first of many airport projects in the United States and around the world with the design and development of a large terminal in Saudi Arabia. Other international efforts during the late 1950s and early 1960s included additional petroleum refineries in Europe and several in Latin America. In all, RMPCo. provided architect-engineering services for construction facilities worth more than $2 billion between the late 1940s and the late 1950s.

RMPCo. gained some attention as a result of its expansion and numerous projects. One development that brought the company a higher profile, however, had little to do with engineering or construction. In 1958, Parsons purchased a 200-foot yacht, the Argo. During the next decade, the company entertained approximately two thousand people on board each year. Not surprisingly, the yacht provided a "great sales advantage," according to Parsons in the *New York Times*.

Success Continues in the 1960s

The purchase of Anaconda-Jurden Associates in 1961 brought significant involvement in mining and metallurgy. Renamed Parsons-Jurden Corporation, the new acquisition had experience in mining facilities around the world. Within the year, a copper concentrator was started in Butte, Montana. In addition to engineering such facilities, Parsons-Jurden was involved in other aspects of metallurgical projects, including geological and mineral surveys and feasibility and market studies.

Throughout the 1960s, RMPCo. continued with the types of projects they had successfully completed in earlier years. The company designed several major petroleum refineries in the United States and abroad, including a $100 million facility for Atlantic-Richfield in Cherry Point, Washington. New mining projects included an underground copper mine complex located in the Chilean Andes and designed for Cerro Corporation and a comprehensive mineral resources exploration and inventory program for India. RMPCo. also planned an expansion and modernization of Honolulu Airport, designed a terminal for Tunis/Carthage International Airport, and managed the construction of a $110 million airport complex in the Dallas-Fort Worth area. In addition, the company received a contract from the Federal Aviation Administration to expand and modernize air traffic control centers.

By the late 1960s, RMPCo. had designed 150 plants which produced sulfur from hydrogen sulfide. A $60 million natural gas processing plant engineered and constructed by the company in Alberta for Chevron Standard Limited in 1969 included the world's largest single sulfur recovery unit. During this time, RMPCo. also became involved in an even wider range of activities, some of which were experimental. The company engineered a saline water conversion plant in California and was involved in preliminary efforts to enable the countries of North America to collect unused runoff water in the sub-arctic. A test site designed and built by the company demonstrated that ballistic missiles could be fired from underground silos. RMPCo. also designed the first "lunar proving ground" to test flight hardware used in the Apollo moon flights.

Expansion as a Public Company: 1968 to the Late 1970s

RMPCo. had now become one of the nation's largest engineering and construction firms, with projects totaling $1.2 billion in 1968. In July of the following year, the company went public, selling a combination of stock worth about $7 million. A majority of the stock was sold on behalf of Parsons, who was serving as chairman of the company. Much of the remainder was sold to increase the working capital available for the company. In addition to the stock sale, RMPCo. began to explore more aggressively the possibility of acquiring companies. Parsons noted in the *New York Times* that these new practices represented quite a shift in his approach. He remarked that he would have to move beyond an adage from his childhood, "Never tell your friends where you shoot ducks"; now, he admitted, "We'll have to be more open."

During the early 1970s, RMPCo. did expand. The company acquired a controlling interest in an Australian engineering firm, adding approximately five hundred employees to its Australian operations. RMPCo. also formed a new company to aid in the integration of physical distribution services by providing warehousing, transportation management, and information services. This new company, called National Distribution Services, Inc., was the result of a joint effort between RMPCo., Eastern Airlines, and TRW Inc. In addition to this expansion, RMPCo. restructured its network of offices for improved efficiency. Activities in London were consolidated into one new facility, and a new office was opened in Australia. Finally, Parsons-Jurden moved from New York to Los Angeles, and RMPCo. consolidated its offices from four separate leased buildings in Los Angeles to a new headquarters facility in Pasadena.

Increasing concern with energy sources and pollution in the early 1970s provided opportunities for RMPCo. The company developed several new processes which helped decrease pollution. The Beavon Sulfur Removal Process reduced air pollution by increasing the amount of sulfur recovered from gases in gas processing plants and petroleum refineries, while the Double Contact/Double Catalysis process, applied in sulfuric acid plants, increased productivity as well as reducing emissions.

However, despite these apparently promising developments, demand for construction services was down in the early years of the decade, and RMPCo.'s revenue fell sharply, from $4.6 million in 1971 to $2.1 million the following year. The company attributed this development to a range of factors, including the unsettled condition of the economy, the lack of a coherent energy policy and uncertainty regarding energy requirements and supplies, the lack of government pollution standards, and pressures brought by environmental groups. The slump was short-lived, and by the mid-1970s revenues had begun a rapid and consistent rise. New projects, contracts, and acquisitions contributed to RMPCo.'s growth during these years.

On the international front, the Middle East was the main source of new foreign projects. RMPCo. was involved in the preliminary studies for and the design of Yanbu, a multi-billion dollar industrial city on the Red Sea in Saudi Arabia. In 1976, the joint venture company Saudi Arabian Parsons Limited was founded to help administer projects and pursue other opportunities in the Middle East. Along with another firm, Saudi Arabian Parsons Limited was selected by the government of Saudi Arabia to manage the construction of the new international airport in Jeddah.

That same year, RMPCo. began a major domestic undertaking: the company received a contract from the Federal Railroad Administration to manage the design and construction of a five-year, $1.75 billion program to modernize the Northeast Corridor, the passenger railroad route from Boston to Washington, D.C. RMPCo. was also involved in several projects with the Department of Energy, including an oil storage program, a synthesis gas plant, and the design of facilities and techniques for the handling of nuclear materials during the nuclear fuel cycle. In addition, Parsons became involved in an increasing number of "mega-projects," large, complex engineering ventures with multi-billion dollar budgets and decades-long schedules. One of Parsons' first such undertakings was a massive oil and gas production facility at Prudhoe Bay in Alaska. This project, the largest undertaken by private industry, required the transportation of hundreds of prefabricated modules to a site 350 miles north of the Arctic Circle.

In 1977, RMPCo. acquired two established engineering firms—De Leuw, Cather & Company of Chicago and S.I.P.,

Co., based in Houston. A leading engineering-design firm specializing in transportation systems, De Leuw, Cather & Company was involved in the Northeast Corridor railroad project as well as other ventures. Robert B. Richards, president and chairman of De Leuw, Cather—which retained its own corporate identity and management—was made a vice-president at RMPCo. S.I.P., Inc. provided RMPCo. with a strategic location: the Gulf Coast area, the site of much of the nation's petroleum, chemical, and gas processing industries.

Reorganization: 1978–79

Partly as a result of these acquisitions, and in an attempt to maximize the potential for future growth, RMPCo. management proposed a major reorganization of the company. Approved by shareholders on September 19, 1978, the reorganization divided RMPCo. into two separate corporations, although both were still owned by the same stockholders. In the United States, The Parsons Corporation was incorporated in Delaware as a holding company for RMPCo., De Leuw, Cather & Company, and S.I.P., Inc. Early in 1979, Parsons Constructors, Inc. (PCI), a new subsidiary intended to provide increased construction capability, was added to The Parsons Corporation. Shares of RMPCo. stock were converted to shares of The Parsons Corporation automatically at a one-to-one ratio. The company's management hoped that this restructuring would increase flexibility, aid growth, and make it easier to add subsidiaries.

On the international side, the plan was designed to improve the company's competitive position and provide tax savings. As a result of the reorganization, RMP International, Limited, was incorporated in the Cayman Islands. Shareholders of The Parsons Corporation received shares of RMP International, Limited, on a one-for-one basis. The shares of the two new corporations were required to be traded together.

In the years immediately following the reorganization, The Parsons Corporation continued to grow and to experience increasing revenue. In 1980, for example, Parsons was involved in almost 270 projects in 31 different countries. Revenue increased 25 percent in 1980 over the 1979 figure, and new records were established again in 1981 and 1982, when revenue reached $1.2 billion. William E. Leonhard—Chairman, President, and CEO of The Parsons Corporation—summed up the company's strategy this way: "The key to our continuing strength is a basic policy of providing engineering, construction, and related services, a business we fully understand, while diversifying both geographically and in terms of the industries we serve."

Returning to Private Company Status: 1984

In 1984, after fifteen years as a public company, Parsons began to explore the possibility of returning to private status. According to *Business Week*, provisions of the 1984 tax law made the purchase of companies by employee stock ownership plans particularly attractive. An additional reason for the move was offered in the *San Francisco Business Journal* by Marion Gordon, a Parsons spokesperson, who stated, "If you're not accountable [to shareholders and the public], it gives you more flexibility and the ability to map out big plans without the whole world looking on. This is a competitive industry and operating as a private company can provide a benefit in forming strategy.'' Chairman Leonhard similarly stated in the *Wall Street Journal* that he supported the plan ''so we could be in control of our own destiny.''

In October 1984, The Parsons Corporation returned to private ownership as a result of a $560 million buyout by the Employee Stock Option Plan. Almost immediately questions were raised about the deal, one of the largest such transactions in U.S. history. The U.S. Labor Department investigated charges brought by employee groups that executives who designed the plan benefited disproportionately, while employees were saddled with debt. The employees also argued that they had no meaningful input in the decision to go private and that they would be excluded from the process of shaping the country's future. In addition, some retirement experts expressed concern about the loss of a profit-sharing program of diversified stocks and bonds. Finally, the corporation was the target of several lawsuits. One suit, brought by employees in 1985, claimed that the purchase was a ''breach of fiduciary responsibility, misuse of corporate assets, and a termination of predecessor plans,'' according to the *Wall Street Journal*. Five years later, however, a federal court upheld the buyout.

Despite the difficulties resulting from the buyout, Parsons, now the largest 100-percent employee-owned company of its kind in the United States, continued to adapt and prosper. The company benefited from an increasing trend toward privatization, providing services to municipal governments in Chester County, Pennsylvania, for example. In addition, while opportunities in the Middle East decreased in the early 1990s, Parsons increasingly turned its attention to Asian markets.

Global Expansion and Diversification: Mid-1990s and Beyond

Success continued throughout the mid-1990s. During 1995, Parsons was named the top design firm in the United States based on domestic and international billings by trade publication *Engineering News Record*. The publication also ranked Parsons as the second-largest global design firm in the world. By this time, the company was involved in projects related to the Idaho National Engineering Laboratory, the Amoco Gas Terminal in the UK, the Kaohsiung Mass Rapid Transit System in Taiwan, and had various other international contracts in Argentina, Oman, Kuwait, Korea, Italy, Russia, and Thailand.

The firm strengthened its holding in 1995 by acquiring Gilbert/Commonwealth Inc., a company involved in power plant design and nuclear facility decommissioning. Parsons— now run by chairman and CEO Leonard J. Pieroni—then launched a restructuring effort in early 1996 that included a reorganization into four business units: Parsons Process Group Inc., Parsons Infrastructure & Technology Group Inc., Parsons Power Group Inc., and Parsons Transportation Group Inc. The strategy also included the creation of a new global business development unit designed to increase Parsons' international revenues, which by 1996 accounted for just 30 percent of overall revenues.

Parsons met with disaster, however, just four months after initiating its new strategy. While on a business trip with Com-

merce Secretary Ronald H. Brown and other business executives, Pieroni was killed when the plane carrying the group went down in Croatia. As the company mourned the loss of their leader, board members scrambled to elect a new CEO. James F. McNulty was given the task and promised to continue the company's current direction. ''My plans are to make Parsons into a big player in the global marketplace,'' McNulty commented in an April 1996 *Business Week* article. The authors of the piece pointed to the importance of McNulty's strategy, observing, ''It's a mission that Len Pieroni endorsed with his life.''

During the latter half of the 1990s, Parsons grew by diversifying into telecommunications, pharmaceuticals, and vehicle inspections. Annual revenues had more than doubled throughout the decade, growing from $1 billion in 1990 to $2.4 billion in 2000. Parsons continued to expand into the early years of the new century. The firm complemented its vehicle inspections business by adding Protect Air Inc. to its arsenal in 2000. The following year it acquired H.E. Hennigh Inc., a telecommunications general contracting firm, and bridge engineering concern Finley McNary Engineers Inc.

By now, the company had contracts with the Federal Aviation Administration to upgrade U.S. air-traffic control facilities and with Denver's Stapleton Airport to redesign its facilities. The firms other major domestic projects included the construction of the Olivenhain Dam in San Diego County, the expansion of the Seattle-Tacoma International Airport, and the Alameda Corridor rail project in Los Angeles, California. During 2003, the company was involved in the bidding process to repair postwar Iraq. While the majority of the work went to competitor Bechtel Group Inc., Parsons remained optimistic about future projects in the Middle East. With a solid strategy in place, company management felt confident the firm was headed in a positive direction.

Principal Operating Units

Advanced Technologies; Commercial Technology; Infrastructure and Technology; Transportation.

Principal Competitors

Bechtel Group Inc.; URS Corp.; Washington Group International Inc.

Further Reading

''And at Parsons This Week,'' *Business Week*, October 1, 1984, p. 50.

Armstrong, Larry, ''A Death in the Parsons Family,'' *Business Week*, April 22, 1996, p. 39.

Downey, Kirsten E., ''Vulnerable San Francisco Builder Takes Stock, Goes Public,'' *San Francisco Business Journal*, September 2, 1985, p. 1.

Foust, Dean, ''Turning to the Private Sector,'' *Philadelphia Business Journal*, December 29, 1986, p. 1.

Gottschalk, Earl C., Jr., ''Parsons's Acquisition by Employee Stock Plan Raises Some Questions about Who Benefited,'' *Wall Street Journal*, January 29, 1985, p. 4.

O'Malley, John, ''Certified Grocers of California Top Private Sector List,'' *Los Angeles Business Journal*, August 31, 1987, p. 17.

''Parsons Announces Organizational Restructuring,'' *Business Wire*, January 9, 1996.

"Parsons Employees Sue Firm and Others over Recent Buyout," *Wall Street Journal*, May 21, 1985, p. 24.

"Ralph M. Parsons Co. Went Public Last Week," *Chemical Week*, August 2, 1969, p. 10.

"Ralph M. Parsons Creates Two, New Corporate Entities," *Engineering News-Record*, September 28, 1978, p. 15.

Satzman, Darrell, "Staying Alive—Privately," *Los Angeles Business Journal*, October 29, 2001, p. 1.

Stone, Irving, "Architect-Engineers Build for Aviation," *Aviation Week*, October 8, 1956, pp. 62–64, 67, 69.

Streitfeld, David, and Nancy Cleeland, "War With Iraq: Finalists for Rebuilding Down to 2 Firms," *Los Angeles Times*, April 3, 2003, p. 1.

Williams, Fred, "Parson's Buy-Out Upheld," *Pensions and Investments*, July 23, 1990, p. 24.

Wright, Robert A., "Parsons, A Canny Hunter," *New York Times*, December 5, 1969, pp. 67, 73.

—Michelle L. McClellan
—update: Christina M. Stansell

Perkins Coie LLP

1201 3rd Avenue, Suite 4800
Seattle, Washington 98101
U.S.A.
Telephone: (206) 583-8888
Fax: (206) 583-8500
Web site: http://www.perkinscoie.com

Private Company
Incorporated: 1912
Employees: 1,400
Gross Billings: $157 million (2001 est.)
NAIC: 541110 Offices of Lawyers

Perkins Coie LLP is a law partnership whose clients are among the largest corporations in the world. Through 14 offices primarily located in the western United States, Perkins Coie's more than 500 lawyers serve clients such as The Boeing Co., AT&T Wireless, and Nintendo of America. The law firm is based in Seattle and operates internationally through offices in Taipei, Taiwan, London, England, and in Hong Kong.

Origins

The largest law firm in the Pacific Northwest at the beginning of the 21st century was founded not long after the beginning of the 20th century. It was a law partnership founded with a handshake. In 1912, Perkins Coie's two original partners first discussed forming their own firm while taking a walk along the streets of Seattle. The instigator of the discussion was George Donworth, Federal Judge of the Western District of Washington. To his side was Elmer Todd, U.S. Attorney for the Western District of Washington. Both men wanted to return to private practice, and Todd appeared to be the first of the two to follow through with his desire. Todd had received a partnership offer from William H. Bogle, who led a well-known Seattle law firm, but during his walk with Judge Donworth an alternative career choice arose. Donworth revealed his intention to resign as a judge and invited Todd to join him in forming a law partnership. The two men shook hands, and on May 1, 1912 opened their business. The new law firm of Donworth & Todd—known as

"the Donworth firm" during its formative years—began without any prospects. The law firm had no stenographer, no associates, and no clients.

Throughout Perkins Coie's history, the law firm was known for its business ties with some of the largest corporations in the world, a legacy established by the fledgling Donworth firm. The leap from having no clients to forging relationships with companies set to become corporate giants was aided greatly by Donworth & Todd's landlord. The firm rented three offices in the Hoge Building, owned by James D. Hoge, who introduced the law firm to several of its long-term, mainstay clients. Hoge's contributions as a networker began not long after the Donworth firm landed its first client. Several weeks after opening their doors, the two partners were hired by the Seattle and Lake Washington Water Way Co., a company originally formed to dig a canal through one of the major hills in Seattle. The firm's second client was provided by Hoge, who served as president of Union Savings and Trust Co.—a banking entity that evolved into Seattle First National Bank, or Seafirst—and hired Donworth & Todd as the chief counsel for his bank, providing a substantial and long-term source of revenue for the young firm.

Hoge's greatest gift to the fortunes of the Donworth firm arrived in 1914, when he introduced the partners to another Hoge Building tenant. Donworth & Todd's neighbor owned interests in real estate, timber, and a small airplane company located at the south end of Lake Union, several blocks away from downtown Seattle. The Hoge Building tenant was William E. Boeing. In 1916, Donworth, who controlled most partnership matters, drew up the articles of incorporation for Boeing's company, the Boeing Airplane and Transport Corporation. As the company matured into the multi-billion-dollar aerospace giant The Boeing Co., the Donworth firm, and later Perkins Coie, assisted in and benefited from the explosive growth recorded by its client, serving as its principal outside counsel.

Donworth & Todd's two-year anniversary also coincided with several other significant developments. The law firm hired its first associate in 1916, a lawyer name Nelson T. Hartson. That same year, Donworth & Todd gained another valuable client, providing ample work for Hartson and the firm's second associate, Donworth's son, Charles T. Donworth. The

Donworth firm was hired to manage the personal legal business of Colonel Alden Blethen and his family, the owners and publishers of *The Seattle Times*. The Blethens remained important clients until 1942, when Elmer Todd retired from the firm to become publisher of the newspaper.

During the law firm's formative years, a host of other companies—particularly lumber and pulp concerns—counted on the Donworth firm for their legal work. Among the list of early clients were Rainer Pulp and Paper, Grays Harbor Pulp and Paper, and Washington Pulp and Paper. Additional clients were gained in 1919 when Donworth & Todd merged with another law firm, Higgins and Hughes. Important clients obtained through the merger included the largest meat-packer in the western United States, Frye & Co., and pulp and paper manufacturer Zellerbach. The arrival of Higgins (Hughes was killed in World War I) necessitated the first of more than a dozen name changes for the Donworth firm, an ever-changing nomenclature determined by the departure and arrival of name partners. Following the 1919 merger, the firm became known as Donworth, Todd and Higgins.

The 1930s were years of symbolic change and gratifying stability for the law firm. Unlike the vast majority of companies of all types, the Seattle-based partnership escaped the ravages of the Great Depression, thriving while other commercial concerns floundered. Impressively, the law firm registered its success without its chief architect. In 1930, Donworth left the firm at age of 69, departing with his son to form another law firm, Donworth and Donworth. His departure created the need for a new name, Todd, Holman and Sprague, which paid homage to Hollister T. Sprague, who joined the firm in 1921, and a trial lawyer named Frank E. Holman, who was hired in 1928. In the severely harsh economic climate pervading the 1930s, Todd, Holman and Sprague expanded, more than doubling its personnel. The law firm added several important clients, including Puget Sound Power and Light Company, and managed to retain every one of its major clients.

As the law firm's client roster expanded during the ensuing years, a number of name changes eventually gave way to the modern version of its name. DeForrest Perkins joined as an associate in 1931. J. Paul Coie joined the firm in 1942. Perkins and Coie eventually became the principal name partners, giving the law firm the name of Perkins, Coie, Stone, Olsen and Williams by 1969. In 1985, the law firm followed the trend toward abbreviation that swept throughout the legal profession

and changed its name to Perkins Coie. By the time of the name change, both Perkins and Coie had retired.

After a half-century of serving clients in the corporate world, the partnership had earned the esteem of the legal profession in the Pacific Northwest, holding sway as one of the most prominent law firms in the region. The partnership's 50th anniversary party, celebrated under the name Perkins, Coie, Stone, Olsen & Williams, was attended by the 34 attorneys under its employ. Perkins Coie's prominence in the region's legal community stemmed not only from the size of the firm, but also from the company it kept. Since Judge Donworth's early association with Boeing, the predecessors to Seafirst, and the Blethen family, the firm had developed a reputation as the legal counsel to the region's biggest names in business.

By 1962, a half-century of growth had deepened the partnership's imprint on the regional legal and corporate community. The firm was known for serving just a few clients, but the size of it clients compensated for the relatively short list of its accounts. During this period, the partnership served as counsel for Boeing, Puget Power, Rayonier, and Pacific National Bank, among others, enjoying long-standing relationships that upheld the firm as a venerable member of the legal community. Further, Elmer Todd's decision to leave the firm to steward the fortunes of *The Seattle Times* had developed into a pattern. Numerous partners left the firm to head the businesses they had once provided legal counsel to, adding to the recognition of the firm. William Allen, a name partner during the early 1940s, left the firm to serve as chairman and president of Boeing. James Prince and Lowell Mickelwait later joined Boeing as vice-presidents. A string of executive appointments followed, including John Ellis to Puget Power, Richard Albrecht, Doug Beighle, and Ted Collins to Boeing, and Christopher Bayley to Burlington Northern.

A Legal Giant in the 1980s

The modern era of the firm's history began roughly at the same time Perkins Coie became the official name of the firm in 1985. The following year, Robert Giles was appointed managing partner of Perkins Coie, beginning a period of control over the firm that would continue into the 21st century. When Giles took the reins of command, the firm's revenues—measured by the dollar amount of its billings—stood at $41 million, a figure generated by the 189 attorneys working within the firm. Perkins Coie's 75th anniversary, celebrated two years after Giles appointment as managing partner, already revealed the hallmark of what would become Giles' legacy: growth. There were 267 attorneys on hand to mark the occasion, 109 of whom were partners. Based on the number of Perkins Coie attorneys, a support staff of 484 employees, and the billings they generated, Perkins Coie ranked as the largest law firm in the Pacific Northwest.

At roughly the same time that Perkins Coie celebrated its 75th anniversary, the partnership merged with another law firm based in Los Angeles. The deal made Perkins Coie the only law firm with substantial offices up and down the West Coast, from Alaska to California. The merger also set the tone for the 1990s, as the Giles-led firm fanned out and expanded geographically, giving it a sizeable profile in fast-growth regions both domestically and on the international front. In 1992, for instance, the partnership opened an office in Taipei, Taiwan, becoming the first Pacific Northwest law firm to open an office in an Asian country. Staffed with seven attorneys, who dealt with litigation, corporate matters, and licensing and acquisition activity, the Taipei office was the first of three foreign offices opened during the early 1990s. In 1993, when billings topped $100 million for the first time, Perkins Coie opened an office in Hong Kong. The following year, the partnership opened an office in London. The attorneys working these offices represented clients involved in the building of power plants and other infrastructure projects in countries such as Laos, Nepal, and China.

Perkins Coie: 1990s and Beyond

Billings from foreign operations provided essentially the only source of revenue growth during the first half of the 1990s, as Perkins Coie's domestic business stagnated. In an era of corporate streamlining, the partnership was forced to alter the way it conducted its business. The firm's clients wanted efficiency and cost-savings, causing Perkins Coie's billings and salaries to plateau. The hourly rates charged by associates and partners hardly increased during the first half of the decade. In 1990, associates billed out at between $85 an hour and $170 an hour. In 1996, associates billed out at between $90 an hour and $175 an hour. During the same time span, partners' hourly rates remained flat, ranging from $160 to $275 in 1990 and from $175 to $275 in 1996.

In response to the changing dynamics of the legal profession, Giles implemented several changes. Perkins Coie began offering incentive arrangements as an alternative to hourly billing, linking its fees to the result obtained for the client. The partnership also invested heavily in technology throughout the decade in an attempt to better communicate with clients and to deliver the firm's services more efficiently.

By the end of the 1990s, growth had returned to Perkins Coie. The partnership's billings and the number of attorneys it employed increased largely through the emergence and rapid growth of high-technology companies in the Pacific Northwest.

A new breed of high-technology entrepreneurs needed legal advice on issues ranging from corporate finance to intellectual property, and Perkins Coie fulfilled those needs. The partnership expanded its intellectual-property practice by forming a patent-litigation group. Perkins Coie also completed a significant merger late in the decade. In October 1998, the partnership absorbed the practice of a Silicon Valley firm, Hosie, Wes, Sacks & Brelsford LLP. The merger gave Perkins Coie 13 attorneys with a strong high-technology practice that included clients such as Yahoo!, Intuit Inc., and The Learning Company and strengthened its position in the Pacific Northwest. Perkins Coie's high-technology clients in Seattle increasingly were dealing with counterpart companies and venture capital firms in Silicon Valley. "We had to be seen as a player in the Bay Area to maintain our position in Seattle," Giles explained in a June 25, 1999 interview with the *Puget Sound Business Journal*.

As Perkins Coie entered the 21st century, its business continued to be grounded by its long-standing relationships with corporate heavyweights, particularly Boeing. There were a wealth of other important Pacific Northwest-based clients, such as AT&T Wireless and Nintendo of America, that added to the considerable sway of the venerable law firm, lending reassuring stability to the Giles-led enterprise. In the years ahead, Perkins Coie promised to be a fixture in the legal field, its legacy of legal work providing justifiable optimism for its future success.

Principal Competitors

Cooley Goodward LLP; Heller, Ehrman, White & McAuliffe LLP; Wilson Sonsini Goodrich & Rosati.

Further Reading

Bishop, Todd, "Perkins Weighs a Move," *Puget Sound Business Journal*, August 17, 2001, p. 13.

Erb, George, "High-Tech Boom Prompts Expansion at Law Firm," *Puget Sound Business Journal*, June 25, 1999, p. 29.

"First-Year Attorneys Vault the $100,000 Bar," *Puget Sound Business Journal*, February 18, 2000, p. 2.

Freeman, Paul, "Perkins Adjusts to New Legal Landscape," *Puget Sound Business Journal*, June 24, 1994, p. 46.

"Law of Supply, Demand; Big Legal Firms Regroup as Smaller Rivals Win Clients with Down-Home Ambiance, Lower Fees," *Seattle Times*, March 10, 1996, p. F1.

Neurath, Peter, "A Trend? Perkins' Newest Credo: Mediate, Rather Than Litigate," *Puget Sound Business Journal*, November 4, 1991, p. 27.

——, "Perkins Coie Opens Office in Taiwan, Eyes China Next," *Business Journal-Portland*, June 1, 1992, p. 5.

——, "Faster Growth Suits Perkins Coie Just Fine," *Puget Sound Business Journal*, June 27, 1997, p. 57.

—Jeffrey L. Covell

Pertamina

Jalan Medan Merdeka Timur Number 1 A
Jakarta 101110
Indonesia
Telephone: (21) 381-51114
Fax: (21) 384-3882
Web site: http://www.pertamina.com

State-Owned Company
Incorporated: 1945 as Perusahaan Tambang Minyak
    Negara Republik Indonesia
Sales: $19.4 billion (2001)
Employees: 24,000
NAIC: 211111 Crude Petroleum and Natural Gas
    Extraction; 324110 Petroleum Refineries

Pertamina operates as a state-owned company that controls the oil and natural gas industry in Indonesia. The company's activities include exploration, refining, production, transportation, and marketing. Indonesia's turbulent economy and its political and civil unrest over the past several years have forced many changes in Pertamina. The country's Oil and Gas Law 22, passed in 2001, includes provisions that will eventually turn the giant oil concern into a limited-liability company. Law 22 also intends to break up Pertamina's monopoly over the Indonesian energy industry by encouraging foreign competition and investment.

Early History

Since the 17th century, when much of the Indonesian archipelago came under the control of The Netherlands and its Dutch East Indies colonial administration, the region has been renowned for its vast natural resources, especially tin. Until the middle part of the 20th century, however, the country's oil deposits remained mostly untapped. History records that Indonesians in the Sumatra Strait successfully defeated attacking forces from the Portuguese armada by hurling oil-soaked fire balls at the foreigners and burning their vessels.

Dutch seafarers avoided a similar fate by arming their battleships with cannons to repel the fireballs from a safe distance.

With Indonesia a colony, the Dutch soon began tapping the country's oil reserves for their own gain.

In 1887, Adrian Stoop, a former engineer with Zijlker, a Dutch oil company, set up his own business in Surabaya. Having found oil deposits, he established a refinery at Wonokromo in 1890, and expanded with another one in Cepu, Central Java, in 1894. Two larger oil companies, Koninklijke Nederlandsche Petroleum Maatschappij and Shell Transport and Trading Company, were quick to assume the advantage over Stoop by setting up, in 1902, a joint venture in oil shipping and marketing operations in Indonesia. In 1907 the two Dutch concerns, impressed with each other's progress, merged into one group, which eventually became known as Royal Dutch/Shell, or Shell for short.

Other oil companies attempted at the turn of the century to establish a foothold in Indonesian oil mining. Most failed or were swallowed up, in part or whole, by Royal Dutch/Shell. For example, a number of foreign companies looking to explore in the Irian Jaya province in 1935 set up a joint company called Nederlandsche Nieuw Guinea Petroleum Maatschappij, with 40 percent of its shares held by Shell.

During the interwar years Indonesia had become the Far East's largest oil producer, and the prospect of the country's falling under Japanese control after the bombing of Pearl Harbor dismayed Indonesia's Dutch rulers. When the Dutch government realized Indonesia could no longer withstand a Japanese advance, many of the country's oil installations and facilities were destroyed. Before the Dutch army and the oil companies could complete the scuttling operation, the Japanese forces occupied a fair number of the remaining installations, putting them under the control of the invader's regional military commander.

Nationalizing the Oil Industry in the Mid-1940s

With the end of the war in 1945 and the proclaiming of Indonesia's independence in August of that year, to become fully effective in 1949, that country's anticolonial independence fighters, resuming the fight against Dutch rule, quickly seized on what remaining oil fields and installations they could secure

---

Company Perspectives:

Pertamina strives to be an excellent, progressive, and respected leading company. Our mission is to carry out business in energy and petrochemicals; to contribute added value for the shareholders, clients, workers, and the society and to support national economic growth; and to be a professionally managed, competitive company based on excellent values.

---

from the retreating Japanese. Recognizing this popular ferment, in September 1945 the Dutch administration included in the country's new constitution Article 33, which outlined the "people's desire" to develop their oil and gas sectors. In practical terms, Article 33 meant the establishment that month of a national oil company, Perusahaan Tambang Minyak Negara Republik Indonesia (PTMN-RI). In a wider sense, Indonesia started out on the road to reducing its dependence on foreign oil companies to tap its energy deposits and to managing the industry for its own gain.

At the same time, independence fighters in south Sumatra retained control of regional oil facilities and set up their own company, Perusahaan Minyak Republik Indonesia (PERMIRI). Elsewhere in Java, another oil company, Perusahaan Tambang Minyak Republik Indonesia (PTMN), held jurisdiction.

This postwar period was debilitating for Indonesia's oil industry, as rival independence movements used installations and facilities to gain advantage over the Dutch colonial rulers. For a time PERMIRI was able to run the Dutch blockade and sell oil to Singapore. By 1948, however, Dutch forces had ended exports of PERMIRI's supplies. In the same year, Dutch forces ended exploration at oil fields controlled by PTMN in Central Java.

After Indonesia's full independence in 1949, the country had to contend with foreign oil companies still tapping its most valuable oil and gas reserves. Royal Dutch/Shell and Standard-Vacuum Oil Company (Stanvac), two large foreign oil groups operating in the region, still had concessions to continue work in Indonesia until 1951. That year, Indonesia's house of representatives ordered the government to set up a state committee for mining affairs and to postpone granting concessions and exploration permits to foreign oil companies.

This was a modest first attempt by Indonesia to tap its oil and gas reserves for its sole gain. Plans were slow in developing. In 1954, the government forged a four-year agreement with Stanvac to give Indonesia greater input in how its oil industry was developed.

The Stanvac agreement expired in 1960, when the Indonesian government enacted Law 44, concerning oil and gas mining. Exploration and mining were now to be carried out only by the government, under the management of a state company. Hereafter, foreign companies such as Shell and Stanvac were no longer to be regarded as concession holders but as contractors, and had to renegotiate their agreements with the Indonesian government accordingly.

Again, plans were slow to bear fruit. Indonesia knew that it lacked the massive funds needed to explore and produce oil on its own. Negotiations, over which the United States took great interest and an eventual lead, were concluded in June 1963. The resulting agreement held that Shell, Stanvac, and Caltex, the major foreign oil companies operating in Indonesia, were to become contractors of PERMIGAN, PERMINA, and PERTAMIN, respectively. The foreigners would retain management of the oil installations, but 60 percent of profits from all activities would go to Indonesia.

Beyond profits, however, the Indonesian government was intent on maintaining general managerial responsibility for all oil exploring and drilling installations in the country. General Ibnu Sutowo, president-director of Pertamina, explained: "This does not mean that we insist on making every decision, but we do insist on making any decision we find necessary."

Although Indonesia remained, in large part, dependent on foreign oil companies, it had made an attempt to obtain crude oil on its own. In 1962, Indonesia joined the Organization of Petroleum Exporting Countries (OPEC), although at this time the oil-producing cartel was hardly the economic force it was to become during the 1970s.

The country's first state-owned oil company, Exploitasi Tambang Minyak Sumatra Utara (PT ETMSU), had been set up in 1957. After changing its name soon after to PT PERMINA, Indonesia made its first crude oil export on March 24, 1958, when the tanker *Shozmi Mam* carried 1,700 tons, worth about $30,000, to a foreign buyer.

Slowly, Indonesia established the infrastructure to produce its own crude oil on a lasting basis. PERMINA Oil Academy enrolled its first group of engineering students in 1962. In the same year, PERMINA purchased one aircraft for its operations and—a year later—secured approval from the government for the purchase of oceangoing tankers for crude oil exports.

By 1965, PERMINA had successfully drilled a total of nine oil fields, the resulting wells producing 21,000 barrels of oil per day. This progress instilled the Indonesian government with enough confidence to secure agreement from Shell to purchase all of Shell's assets for around $10 million over a period of five years after 1966.

The Emergence of Pertamina in the Late 1960s

It was not until 1971 that PN Pertambangan Minyak Dan Gas Bumi Negara (Pertamina) was established by the Indonesian government as the only national oil company that could extract oil and natural gas throughout the country. The state company had been formed earlier in 1968, again by government legislation, after the merger of PN PERTAMIN and PT PERMINA, the existing state oil companies. Under the 1971 legislation, Pertamina was to be run by a board of directors, headed by a president director, and five other directors. The state-owned company, headquartered in Jakarta, was to operate in close cooperation with the Indonesian government.

Pertamina needed the assistance of foreign oil companies. Under production agreements, the foreign contractors were to receive 40 percent of profits from exploration and drilling,

Key Dates:

1945: Article 33 of Indonesia's constitution establishes its first national oil company.

1960: The Indonesian government enacts Law 44 stating that exploration and mining are now to be carried out only by a state-owned company.

1968: Pertamina is formed by the merger of existing state oil companies.

1971: Pertamina becomes the only national oil company that can extract oil and natural gas throughout Indonesia.

1993: The company launches a restructuring program to cut costs.

1998: Indonesia's President Soeharto is forced to step down during a state of economic crisis and civil unrest.

2001: Law 22 is passed, which will end Pertamina's oil and gas monopoly.

while the Indonesian government carved out 60 percent of all gains. This all changed, however, in 1973 when the oil barrel price began to increase sharply. Pertamina renegotiated in 1974 complex agreements that stipulated that when the price of a barrel of crude oil climbed above a recognized base price, the incremental rise would be shared between the government and the contractor at a split of between 85-15 and 95-5 percent.

The West's growing thirst for energy supplies at this time gave tremendous impetus to the growth of Indonesia's LNG—liquefied natural gas—industry. The beginnings of LNG exploration dated back to October 24, 1971, when Bob Graves, exploration manager for Mobil Oil Indonesia, completed a drill-stem test on a wildcat well in the Arun oil field in North Sumatra. Graves had already drilled 14 holes in the field, an area of rice paddies, fish ponds, and coconut trees, but had found nothing. The 15th drill-stem test, Arun A-1, was successful. Alex Massad, Mobil Oil's exploration and production chief in New York, proposed further drilling in the area for natural gas, at a cost of 400,000. The directors at Pertamina recognized the potential for profits from Arun-1. The successful drilling of Arun-2 and Arun-3 in early 1972 confirmed the presence of large LNG reserves.

Mobil Oil was not alone in spotting Indonesia's rich LNG deposits. In 1971, Huffco, a Texas-based oil company drilling in palm swamps near the coast in east Kalimantan, drove a drill down the Badak-1 well site. Badak-1 produced a major gas discovery for Huffco.

On the strength of the Arun and Badak finds, Pertamina established a LNG unit, headed by Bambang Bramono, head of foreign gas marketing. The unit oversaw Mobil and Huffco development of their LNG finds. It soon became clear that Japan was to be Pertamina's main customer for natural gas.

The Indonesians' 50-year experience in the production of crude oil, and the political and economic machinations surrounding such endeavors, enabled them to gain the best advantage from LNG development. Pertamina extracted agreements from Mobil and Huffco that they would produce the natural gas, but that the Indonesian company would then sell it to foreign purchasers. All negotiations with prospective Japanese buyers, beginning in 1973, were headed by Indra Kartasamita, who worked in the company's sales and transportation division.

Contracts with foreign buyers followed, beginning in late 1972. Japanese electric utilities, including Kansai Electric Power Company, Chubu Electric Power Company, and Kyushu Electric Power Company, were among the first customers. Pertamina then signed a 20-year contract with Pacific Lighting Corporation, the parent of a California gas company. In 1979, Pertamina signed a five-year contract with Mitsubishi Oil Co., Ltd. of Japan, to double the latter's purchase of crude oil.

Pertamina's LNG operations were headed by General Ibnu Sutowo, who was directly responsible to Indonesian President Soeharto. Soedarno Martosewojo, a Pertamina director and chemical engineer, was appointed as LNG coordinator.

Once the taps that extracted LNG from deep below the Indonesian shorelines were switched on, production climbed steadily. It reached 312.6 billion standard cubic feet in 1976, compared with 150.8 billion in 1972. The LNG plant in Arun was fully completed in mid-1978, while the plant at Badak came onstream in July 1977, commencing production a month later. In 1990, the annual production from the two plants was 15.7 million tons and was exported almost entirely to Japanese users. There were also modest exports of LNG to South Korean users. Also in the pipeline was the export of 1.5 million tons of LNG to Taiwan each year, a market that was expected to open up in late 1990. This was agreed between the Chinese Petroleum Corporation and Pertamina in 1986. Then in 1995 the two companies signed a $6 billion deal, which would extend Pertamina's LNG export contract until 2018.

The rise in the price of oil following Iraq's invasion of Kuwait in August 1990 was expected to rejuvenate exploration and drilling in Indonesia. Over the five years since 1986, when the price of oil slipped to below $20 a barrel and remained static for a time, so too did the number of installations in Indonesia. During this period, 693 exploratory wells were drilled, comprising 385 wildcats and 308 delineation wells. These drillings saw a 35 percent success rate.

By mid-1989, the country had 78 onshore and offshore installations, covering 55 production contracts with foreign oil companies, and 18 joint operating arrangement areas. Of these installations, 29 were producing oil, while 49 were still in the exploration stage.

After its success in developing Indonesia's LNG deposits, Pertamina was eager to explore and tap geothermal energy sources around the country. In its early stages of development, steam production began at the first geothermal field in Kamojang, West Java. New fields set to begin production included those in Dieng plateau in Central Java, Mount Salak and Drajat in West Java, and Lahendong in North Sulawesi. Aside from expanding its crude oil production, LNG production enabled Indonesia to develop new markets in domestic gas uses, in fertilizer and petrochemical plants, refineries, and electric power generation.

Corruption and Change: The 1990s and Beyond

In 1993 and 1994, Pertamina launched a restructuring program designed to cut costs and increase efficiency. During the course of its efforts, however, the company became entangled in one of Indonesia's worst economic crises. By the mid-1990s, Indonesia was experiencing low employment, price increases, food shortages, and major devaluation of its currency, the rupiah. In fact, by December 1997, the rupiah had been devalued by nearly 40 percent over the course of one year. As the country's banks failed, the Indonesian government looked to the International Monetary Fund (IMF) for a bailout. The IMF agreed, offering approximately $23 billion in funds to restore the region's financial health.

Meanwhile, Soeharto's government was under attack for its corrupt policies. The president's 32-year reign came to an end in 1998 when he was forced to step down. His vice-president, B.J. Habibie, took over for a short while before Abdurrahman Wahid gained control in 1999. Wahid, nearly blind and suffering from two strokes, was eventually impeached in July 2001. Megawati Sukarnoputri was named his successor.

During this government shakeout, Pertamina experienced change of its own. While Soeharto had been in power, Pertamina had awarded 159 contracts to companies linked to Soeharto's family and friends. The *Oil and Gas Journal* claimed in July 1999 that "an independent report issued by Pricewaterhouse Coopers on July 9 revealed that graft and efficiency cost Pertamina about $6.1 billion in lost revenue during 1997 and 1998. The funds were lost due to embezzlement, illegal commissions, mark-ups on procurement contracts, and sheer inefficiency." Baihaki Hakim, a U.S. oil executive, was appointed CEO in 2000 and immediately began to overhaul Pertamina's corrupt business practices. By 2001, Hakim had issued the company's first financial report to the public, fired Soeharto cronies, cut jobs, and slashed more than $1 billion in costs. The new leader also changed the company's bidding process, making it more competitive, and began to file corruption charges against those who had defrauded Pertamina in the past.

Under President Megawati, the Indonesian government worked diligently to restore the country's financial health as well as its political stability. As part of its reform, Indonesia introduced its Oil and Gas Law 22, which would end Pertamina's monopoly over the country's energy resources and foster a competitive environment. Under the terms of Law 22, Pertamina's legal status was expected to change—turning it into a limited liability company—during 2003 in preparation for its eventual privatization in 2005. The company also would be forced to focus on its core operations and divest nonrelated assets and subsidiaries. The upcoming elections in 2004 threatened to overshadow the restructuring of the oil and gas sector, however, leaving Pertamina's future up in the air.

While Pertamina's role in the Indonesian oil and gas sector remained uncertain, the company continued with its internal strategy, which focused company efforts on becoming a global oil and gas company able to compete with the leading companies in the world. During 2001, Pertamina inked a deal with Petronas—Malaysia's state-owned oil company—that was worth approximately $3 billion. Under the terms of the deal, Pertamina would deliver LNG from the West Natuna gas field in the South China Sea to Malaysia. The company also kept its exploration business at the forefront of operations—it hoped to discover 118 million barrels of new oil reserves and 3.6 trillion cubic feet of natural gas reserves during 2003.

Principal Competitors

Petroliam Nasional Berhad; Singapore Petroleum Company Ltd.; Woodside Petroleum Ltd.

Further Reading

Abdullah, Ashraf, "First Pipeline Delivery of Natural Gas Launched," *Business Times Malaysia,* August 9, 2002, p. 5.

Bartlett, Anderson G., *Pertamina: Indonesian National Oil,* Jakarta: Amerasian Ltd., 1972.

"Big Changes Loom for Pertamina," *International Oil Daily,* November 19, 2002.

Hands Across the Sea: The Story of Indonesian LNG, Jakarta: Pertamina, 1985.

"Indonesia Considers Legislation That Would End Pertamina's 30-Year Petroleum Monopoly," *Oil and Gas Journal,* July 26, 1999, p. 27.

"Indonesia: Graft Won't Just Vanish," *Business Week,* June 1, 1998.

"Indonesia's Pertamina Misses Key Deadline for Corporate Revamp," *International Oil Daily,* April 3, 2003.

"Megawati's Short Honeymoon," *Business Week,* August 6, 2001.

"Pertamina Eyes 118 Million Barrels of New Oil Reserves in 2003," *Xinhua News Agency,* February 11. 2003.

Pertamina: History and Development, Jakarta: Pertamina, 1979.

Saragosa, Manuela, "Pertamina Signs Dollars 6bn LNG Deal with Taiwan," *Financial Times London,* October 27, 1995.

Shari, Michael, "Indonesia's Lone Ranger," *Business Week,* April 16, 2001.

——, "Megawati's Tightrope," *Business Week,* March 10, 2003.

—Etan Vlessing
—update: Christina M. Stansell

Petroliam Nasional Bhd (Petronas)

Tower 1, Petronas Twin Towers
Kuala Lumpur City Centre
50088 Kuala Lumpur
Malaysia
Telephone: (603) 20265000
Fax: (603) 20265050
Web site: http://www.petronas.com.my

State-Owned Company
Incorporated: 1974
Employees: 25,733
Sales: RM 67.1 billion ($17.6 billion) (2002)
NAIC: 211111 Crude Petroleum and Natural Gas
    Extraction; 324110 Petroleum Refineries

Petroliam Nasional Bhd, or Petronas, operates as a state-owned entity controlling Malaysia's oil and gas resources. The company and its subsidiaries are involved in nearly every aspect of the industry including upstream exploration, oil and gas production, downstream oil refining, marketing and distributing petroleum products, gas processing, gas transmission pipeline network operations, liquefied natural gas (LNG) marketing, and petrochemical manufacturing and marketing. Petronas has also diversified into shipping, automotive engineering, and property investment. During 2003, Malaysia's crude oil reserves were 3.2 billion barrels while its natural gas reserves reached 87.5 trillion standard cubic feet. Through its international activities, the country has access to additional reserves of 3.71 billion barrels of oil equivalent.

Petronas was not the first company to extract oil or gas in Malaysia. Oil was first found in what is now Malaysia at the end of the 19th century, and in 1910 Royal Dutch/ Shell, then as now one of the majors—the small group of leading private oil companies—first drilled for oil in Sarawak, then a British colony. It was still the only oil company in the area in 1963, when the Federation of Malaya, having achieved independence from Britain six years before, absorbed Sarawak and Sabah, both on the island of Borneo, and became Malaysia. The authorities in the two new states retained their links with Royal Dutch/ Shell, which brought Malaysia's first offshore oil field onstream in 1968.

Meanwhile the federal government turned to Esso, Continental Oil, and Mobil, licensing exploration off the state of Trengganu, in the Malay Peninsula, the most populous region and the focus of federal power. By 1974, however, only Esso was still in the area. It made its first discoveries of natural gas in that year and then rapidly made Trengganu a bigger producer of oil than either Sarawak or Sabah. By 1974, Malaysia's output of crude oil stood at about 81,000 barrels per day.

Setting Up a State Company: 1970s

Several factors converged in the early 1970s to prompt the Malaysian government into setting up a state oil and gas company, as first proposed in its Five Year Plan published in 1971. These were years in which power in the world oil industry began to shift away from the majors, which then controlled more than 90 percent of the oil trade, toward the Organization of Petroleum Exporting Countries (OPEC), as well as a proliferation of new private and state companies joining in the search for reserves. By 1985, the majors, reduced in number from seven to five, were producing less than 20 percent of the world total. It seemed that Malaysia would either have to join the trend or continue to leave its oil and gas entirely to Royal Dutch/Shell and Esso, multinational corporations necessarily attuned to the requirements of their directors and shareholders, rather than to the priorities the government of a developing country might seek to realize.

Further, an agreement between Malaysia and Indonesia, signed in 1969, had settled doubts and disputes about each country's claims over territorial waters and offshore resources at a time when both were heavily indebted to Organization for Economic Co-operation and Development (OECD) governments and banks as well as to the International Monetary Fund (IMF) and the World Bank. Setting up a state oil and gas company, through which the government could get international capital but avoid tangling with foreign oil companies or governments, had worked for Indonesia: why not for Malaysia as well? The oil crisis of 1973–74 made the government even

Company Perspectives:

Petronas's goal is to contribute to the well-being of the people and the nation where it operates. To fulfill this role, all of its business activities must be viable and profitable. Petronas's contributions—designed to assist in enhancing the quality of life of the people and help in the development of the nation—include the provision of quality petroleum and related products and services at a fair price; promoting and creating business and job opportunities in the petroleum industry; enlarging the country's industrial base; and ensuring a safe and clean environment.

more aware of Malaysia's dependence on foreign oil and foreign capital in general.

Another factor in the decision was that the technology had recently been developed for extensive exploration and drilling offshore. The local geography included a combination of broad basins of sedimentary rock with calm and shallow waters around the Sunda Shelf, making exploration for gas and oil relatively easier and more successful than in most areas of the world. Malaysian crude turned out to be mostly high quality with low sulfur content.

A final and crucial factor in the creation of Petronas, and its continuation in much the same form since, has been the political stability of Malaysia. Since the restoration of parliament in 1971, the country has been ruled by the National Front (Barisan Nasional), the heirs to the Alliance Party which had been dominant from 1957 to 1969 and the originators in 1971 of the New Economic Policy, which was designed to improve the economic position of Bumiputras—native Malays—relative to Chinese and Indian Malaysians and to foreign corporations. The difficulties this policy has caused for foreign companies and investors are outweighed by the benefits they believe they gain from Malaysia's political stability.

The Malaysian government chose to create a state company, rather than using taxes, production limits, leasing, or other familiar instruments of supervision. The government wanted, and needed, the cooperation of the majors but also sought to assert national rights over the use of the country's resources. A state company, having both supervisory powers over the majors and production activities of its own, was a workable compromise between allowing the majors full rein and excluding them, along with their capital and expertise, altogether.

Petronas was established in August 1974 and operates under the terms of the Petroleum Development Act passed in October 1974. It was modeled on PERTAMINA, the Indonesian state oil and gas company founded in 1971 in succession to PERMINA, which had been set up in 1958. According to the 1971 plan, Petronas's goals would be to safeguard national sovereignty over oil and gas reserves, to plan for both present and future national need for oil and gas, to take part in distributing and marketing petroleum and petrochemical products at reasonable prices, to encourage provision of plant, equipment, and services by Malaysian companies, to produce nitrogenous fertilizers, and to spread the benefits of the petroleum industry throughout the nation.

Having created Petronas, the government had to choose what forms its dealings with private oil companies would take. Starting with its legal monopoly on oil and gas activities and resources, it had several options: it could simply award concessions without taking part in production, management, or profits; it could try offering services at the supply end; or it could make contracts to cover profit-sharing, production-sharing, joint ventures—sharing both profits and costs—or all stages of the process, under "carried-interest" contracts. Petronas's first move was to negotiate the replacement of the leases granted to Royal Dutch/Shell on Borneo and to Esso in the Peninsula with production-sharing contracts, which have been the favored instrument, alongside joint ventures, ever since. These first contracts came into effect in 1976. Allowing for royalties to both federal and state governments, and for cost recovery arrangements, they laid down that the remainder would go 70 percent to Petronas and 30 percent to the foreign company. Esso began oil production in two offshore fields in 1978, exporting its share of the supply, unlike Petronas, whose share was consumed within the country.

Petronas went downstream for the first time in 1976, when it was chosen by the Association of South East Asian Nations (ASEAN) to begin construction on the second ASEAN joint industrial project, a urea plant. The subsidiary, Asean Bintulu Fertilizer (ABF), is based in Sarawak and now exports ammonia and urea all over the world.

Also in 1976, Malaysia became a net exporter of oil, but exports were at such a low level as to make the country ineligible to join OPEC. This situation benefited Malaysia, and Petronas, by allowing the company a degree of commercial and political flexibility and reinforcing Petronas's chief purpose, Malaysian self-reliance.

Petronas supervised its foreign partners' oil activities, taking no direct role in production until 1978, when the government saw to the creation of a subsidiary for oil exploration and production, Petronas Carigali. It began its work in an oil field off the Peninsula. Petronas retained its supervisory powers over all oil and gas ventures, particularly on issues of health and safety and environmental control.

Developing Natural Gas: Late 1970s to the Mid-1980s

The government was determined to develop Malaysia's natural gas as well as its oil. In 1974, it saw to the ordering of five tankers for liquefied natural gas (LNG) by the Malaysian International Shipping Company (MISC), of which it owned 61 percent. These were to take LNG exports out of Malaysia, save the cost of hiring foreign tankers, and expand the country's fleet under its own control—in contrast to cargo shipping, which was controlled by international conferences. Shell BV, the Royal Dutch/Shell subsidiary that was building the LNG plant off Sarawak with Japanese and Asian Development Bank aid, accepted production sharing with Petronas but baulked at sharing equity, transport management, or refining. Negotiations went on, pushing commencement further and further back, until 1977, when Petronas and the government, faced with the costs of maintaining the tankers between delivery and first use, surrendered management rights—leading to a repeal of part of the Petroleum Development Act—and settled for Petronas's taking 60 percent of equity in the

Key Dates:

1974: The Malaysian government creates Petronas.
1983: Petronas enters the refining and distribution market.
1985: The first stage of the Peninsular Gas Utilization Project is completed.
1990: Petronas begins oil exploration outside of Malaysia in Myanmar.
1994: Subsidiary Petronas Dagangan Bhd lists on the Kuala Lumpur Stock Exchange.
1997: Company headquarters are moved to the 88-story Petronas Twin Towers.
2003: The Malaysia LNG Tiga Plant opens.

new company Malaysia LNG. The Sarawak state government took 5 percent, and the other 35 percent was divided equally between Shell BV and the Mitsubishi Corporation. Production of LNG in Sarawak at last began in 1983.

After negotiations lasting from 1977 to 1982, Petronas had concluded contracts with Tokyo Electric Power and Tokyo Gas for the sale and delivery of LNG through to the year 2003. Malaysia LNG was to send almost the entire output of its Bintulu gas fields to Japan, under these contracts and another one, signed in 1990, to supply Saibu Gas of Fukuoka, in southwestern Japan, for 20 years from 1993.

When in 1982 Petronas Carigali formed an exploration and production company with Société National Elf Aquitaine of France, it allowed Elf better terms for recovering costs than it had offered in earlier ventures. This development came against the background of the government's imposition of a depletion policy on Petronas, Royal Dutch/Shell, and Esso in an attempt to postpone the exhaustion of oil reserves. These were then estimated to be about 2.84 billion barrels, and it was officially predicted that by the late 1980s Malaysia would be a net oil importer once again. By 1980, oil and gas already represented 24 percent of Malaysian exports, and the government decided to impose a tax on these exports at a 25 percent rate. The new policy and the new tax combined to cause Malaysia's output and exports of crude oil to fall in 1981 for the first time since Petronas was established. Output rose again, beyond its 1980 level, in the following year, but exports took until 1984 to surpass their 1980 level.

However, the depletion policy was being undermined by external circumstances. Through the early 1980s, a worldwide oil glut, which OPEC proved unable to control, forced the Malaysian government to increase production to offset deterioration in its balance of increased payments to a deficit of $1 billion. It became clear that this could only be sustained by relaxing the conditions for joint ventures between Petronas and the major oil companies. In 1982, the Petronas-government share, which had risen to 80 percent, was cut to 70 percent, and taxes on company income were also cut.

Petronas went into refining and distribution in 1983. It initiated the construction of refineries at Malacca and at Kertih in order to reduce its dependence on Royal Dutch/Shell's two refineries at Port Dickson and Esso's refinery in Sarawak. These two majors, and other foreign companies, already covered much of the domestic retail market, but the new subsidiary Petronas Dagangan was given the initial advantage of preference in the location of its stations. By 1990, 252 service stations carried the Petronas brand, all but 20 on a franchise basis, and another 50 were planned. Some were set up on grounds of social benefit rather than of strict commercial calculation.

As production from Royal Dutch/Shell and Esso's existing fields moved nearer depletion, the companies sought new fields and new contracts. In 1985, the government and Petronas revised the standard production-sharing contract, increasing the rate of recovery of capital costs from 30 percent to 50 percent of gross production in the case of oil and from 35 percent to 60 percent in the case of natural gas, abolishing signature, discovery, and production bonus payments and increasing the foreign partners' share of the profits. At first the drastic fall in oil prices during 1986, which cut Malaysia's income from exported oil by more than a third even though the volume of exports rose by 16 percent, discouraged interest in the new arrangements, but by 1989 Petronas had signed 22 new contracts with 31 companies from 11 countries. However, the contract period was still restricted to five years—compared, for example, with the 35-year contracts available in neighboring Singapore—and there was still a 25 percent levy on exported crude oil, a measure that was intended to promote the domestic refining industry. These conditions, cited as disincentives to foreign investment, were eventually relaxed over the next several years.

The government and Petronas aimed to encourage the replacement of fast-depleting oil within Malaysia itself and simultaneously to foster heavy industries which could help reduce the country's overwhelming dependence on exporting its natural resources. In 1980, petroleum products accounted for 88 percent of the country's commercial consumption of energy, the rest being provided from hydroelectric plants in Sarawak, too far away from the main population centers to become a major alternative. Five years later, gas accounted for 17 percent, hydroelectricity for 19 percent, coal for 2 percent, and petroleum products for 62 percent of such consumption, and about half of each year's gas output was being consumed in Malaysia.

The Petronas venture responsible for this shift in fuel use, and—along with Malaysia LNG—for Malaysia's becoming the third largest producer of LNG in the world, was the Peninsular Gas Utilization Project (Projek Penggunaan Gas Semenanjung), the aim of which was to supply gas to every part of the Peninsula. Its first stage was completed in 1985, following the success of smaller gasification projects in the states of Sarawak and Sabah, and involved the extraction of gas from three fields in the Natuna Sea, between the Peninsula and the island of Borneo; its processing in a plant at Kertih on the Peninsula's east coast; and its distribution to the state of Trengganu by pipeline and abroad via an export terminal.

Petronas's least happy venture was its ownership of the Bank Bumiputra, the second-largest, but least-profitable, of the commercial banks incorporated in Malaysia. Petronas spent more than M$3.5 billion over five years trying to rescue the bank from the impact of the bad loans it had made, starting with its support of the Carrian property group of Hong Kong, which collapsed in 1985, taking the bank's share capital down with it.

In 1991, Petronas sold the bank back to another state company, Minister of Finance Inc., and announced its intention to concentrate on oil, gas, and associated activities in future.

Just as Petronas was disposing of this liability, the crisis caused by the Iraqi regime's invasion of Kuwait culminated in military action against Iraq on behalf of the United Nations. Petronas had already raised Malaysia's oil production rate from 605,000 to 650,000 barrels per day in late 1990 as the crisis unfolded. This move only reinforced the company's awareness of the need to vary its policies, since, with known reserves of 2.94 billion barrels, and assuming no new major finds of oil, Malaysia risked seeing output decline to 350,000 barrels per day in 2000 and running down to depletion within another five years. This was exacerbated by the possibility that Southeast Asia in general would enjoy rapid economic growth in the 1990s, so that demand for oil there would rise twice as fast as demand in the relatively more sluggish, more mature economies of North America and Europe. The Malaysian government, and its state oil and gas company, was forced to decide what mixture of policies to adopt in response.

Battling Oil Depletion: Late 1980s

Fortunately for Malaysia, exploration was by no means at an end and could yet produce more reserves. The Seligi field, which came onstream at the end of 1988 and was developed by Esso Production Malaysia, was one of the richest oilfields so far found in Malaysian waters, and further concessions to the majors would encourage exploration of the deeper waters around Malaysia, where unknown reserves could be discovered. Meanwhile, computerized seismography made it both feasible and commercially justifiable to re-explore fields which had been abandoned, or were assumed to be unproductive, over the past century. In 1990, Petronas invited foreign companies to re-explore parts of the sea off Sabah and Sarawak on the basis of new surveys using up-to-date techniques.

Another way to postpone depletion was to develop sources of oil, and of its substitute, natural gas, outside Malaysia. Late in 1989, the governments of Vietnam and Myanmar (Burma) invited Petronas Carigali to take part in joint ventures to explore for oil in their coastal waters. In 1990, a new unit, Petronas Carigali Overseas Sdn Bhd, was created to take up a 15 percent interest in a field in Myanmarese waters being explored by Idemitsu Myanmar Oil Exploration Co. Ltd., a subsidiary of the Japanese firm Idemitsu Oil Development Co. Ltd., in a production sharing arrangement with Myanmar Oil and Gas Enterprise. Thus began Petronas's first oil exploration outside Malaysia. In May 1990, the governments of Malaysia and Thailand settled a long-running dispute over their respective rights to an area of 7,300 square kilometers in the Gulf of Thailand by setting up a joint administrative authority for the area and encouraging a joint oil exploration project by Petronas, the Petroleum Authority of Thailand, and the U.S. company Triton Oil. In a separate deal, in October 1990, the Petroleum Authority of Thailand arranged with Petronas to study the feasibility of transferring natural gas from this jointly administered area, through Malaysia to Thailand, by way of an extension of the pipelines laid for the third stage of the Peninsular Gas Utilization Project.

That project was on course to becoming a major element in the postponement of oil depletion. Contracts for line pipes for the second stage of the project were signed in 1989 with two consortia of Malaysian, Japanese, and Brazilian companies. This stage, completed in 1991, included the laying of 730 kilometers of pipeline through to the tip of the Peninsula, from where gas could be sold to Singapore and Thailand; the conversion of two power stations—Port Dickson and Pasir Gudang—from oil to gas; and the expansion of Petronas's output of methyl tertiary butyl ether (MTBE), propylene, and polypropylene, which were already being produced in joint ventures with Idemitsu Petrochemical Co. of Japan and Neste Oy of Finland. The third and final stage of the project was to lay pipelines along the northwest and northeast coastlines of the Peninsula and was completed in 1997.

Another new venture in 1990 was in ship-owning, since Petronas's existing arrangements with MISC and with Nigeria's state oil company would be inadequate to transport the additional exports of LNG due to start in 1994, under the contract with Saibu Gas. Petronas did not lose sight of the government's commitment to Malaysian self-reliance, and the company's second refinery at Malacca, completed in 1994, with a capacity of 100,000 barrels per day, promoted the same policy. The fact that it was built in a joint venture with Samsung of Korea, the Chinese Petroleum Corporation of Taiwan, and Caltex of the United States did not negate the policy, for the subsidiary company Petronas Penapisan (Melaka) had a decisive 45 percent of equity while sharing the enormous costs of and gaining advanced technology for the project. More to the point, a side effect of the refinery's completion was that Petronas was able to refine all of the crude oil it produced, instead of being partially dependent on refining facilities in Singapore.

Petronas, with its policies of promoting self-reliance, helping to develop associated industries, and varying the sources and uses of oil and gas, played an important role in the Malaysian economy as a whole. Under governments which—by current, if not historical, Western standards—were strongly interventionist, the contribution of oil taxes to the federal government's revenue hovered at around 12 percent to 16 percent until 1980, when it showed a marked increase to 23 percent, followed by another leap to 32 percent in 1981. From then until 1988 the proportion fluctuated between 29 percent and 36 percent. Petronas was not just another big oil company: it controlled a crucial sector of the economy and remained, for better or worse, an indispensable instrument of the state.

Expanding Globally: 1990s and Beyond

During the mid- to late 1990s, international exploration, development, and production remained key components in Petronas's strategy along with diversification. A key discovery was made in the Ruby field in Vietnam in 1994. That year, the firm also saw its first overseas production from the Dai Hung field in Vietnam and established its first retail station outside of Malaysia in Cambodia. In 1995, a subsidiary was created to import, store, and distribute liquefied petroleum gas (LPG). In addition, the company's polyethylene plant in Kertih began operations. Petronas marked a significant milestone during this time period—two of its subsidiaries, Petronas Dagangan Bhd and Petronas Gas Bhd, went public on the Kuala Lumpur Stock Exchange.

In 1996, Petronas entered the aromatics market by way of a joint venture that created Aromatics Malaysia Sdn Bhd. It also formed a contract with China National Offshore Oil Corporation and Chevron Overseas Petroleum Ltd. to begin exploration of block 02/31 of the Liaodong Bay area in China. While the Asian economy as a whole suffered from an economic crisis during 1997 and 1998, Malaysia was quick to bounce back due to successful government reforms. From its new headquarters in the world's tallest buildings, the Petronas Twin Towers, the state-owned concern continued its development in the oil and gas industry.

During 1997, Petronas heightened its diversification efforts. The firm set plans in motion to build three petrochemical plants in Kuantan as well as an acetic facility in Kertih. Its first LPG joint venture in China was launched that year and the company acquired a 29.3 percent interest in Malaysia International Shipping Corporation Berhad (MISC). In 1998, Petronas's tanker-related subsidiary merged with MISC, increasing Petronas's stake in MISC to 62 percent. That year, Petronas introduced the Petronas E01, the country's first commercial prototype engine. The company also signed a total of five new production sharing contracts (PSCs) in 1998 and 1999, and began oil production in the Sirri field in Iran.

Petronas entered the new century determined to expand its international efforts. The company forged deals for two new exploration plots in Pakistan and began construction on the Chad-Cameroon Integrated Oil Development and Pipeline Project. By 2002, Petronas had signed seven new PSCs and secured stakes in eight exploration blocks in eight countries, including Gabon, Cameroon, Niger, Egypt, Yemen, Indonesia, and Vietnam. The firm also made considerable progress in its petrochemicals strategy, opening new gas-based petrochemical facilities in Kerteh and Gebeng.

By 2003, Malaysia was set to usurp Algeria as the world's second-largest producer of LNG with the completion of the Malaysia LNG Tiga Plant. Prime Minister Mahathir Mohamad commented on the achievement in a May 2003 *Bernama News Agency* article, claiming that ''the Petronas LNG complex now serves as another shining example of a vision realized of a national aspiration, transformed into reality by the same belief among Malaysians that 'we can do it.' '' Indeed, Petronas had

transformed itself into a global oil company over the previous decade, becoming a national symbol for success. The company realized, however, that it would have to continue its aggressive growth strategy in order to insure its survival in the years to come.

Principal Subsidiaries

Petronas Carigali Sdn Bhd; Petronas Carigali Overseas Sdn Bhd; Petronas Assets Sdn Bhd; Petronas Maritime Services Sdn Bhd; Petronas Trading Corp. Sdn Bhd; Petronas Argentina S.A.; Petronas Australia Pty Ltd.; Petronas Thailand Co. Ltd.; Petronas Philippines Inc.; Petronas Cambodia Co. Ltd.; Petronas Technical Services Sdn Bhd; Petronas South Africa Pty Ltd.; Petronas India Holdings Company Pte Ltd.; Petronas China Company Ltd.; Petronas International Corp. Ltd.; Petronas Marketing Thailand Co. Ltd.; Myanmar Petronas Trading Co. Ltd.

Principal Competitors

ChevronTexaco Corp.; Exxon Mobil Corp.; Royal Dutch/Shell Group.

Further Reading

Akanni, Fred, ''Petronas Charges Into Africa,'' *Offshore*, February 1999, p. 18.

Creffield, David, *Malaysia*, London: Euromoney Publications, 1989.

Hamid, Hamisah, ''Asia Needs to Set Up Energy Stockpile,'' *Business Times Malaysia*, Ocotber 5, 2002, p. 1.

Klapp, Merrie Gilbert, *The Sovereign Entrepreneur*, Ithaca, NY: Cornell University Press, 1987.

Mehta, Harish, ''Foreign Firms Happy With KL-Viet Offshore Oil Accord,'' *Business Times Singapore*, June 30, 1992, p. 9.

''Oil MNCs Happy With Petronas' New Contracts,'' *Business Times Singapore*, August 7, 1992, p. 8.

''Petronas Makes Further Inroads Into Sudan's Oil Industry,'' *Business Times Malaysia*, April 29, 2003, p. 4.

''RM2.5 Bil Savings on the Cards for Oil Industry,'' *Star Malaysia*, October 11, 2000.

Tibin, Newmond, ''PM Says M'sia Must Improve Competitiveness in Oil and Gas Industry,'' *Bernama: The Malaysian National News Agency*, May 8, 2003.

Toh, Eddie, ''M'sia Resilient in Absorbing Shocks,'' *Business Times Singapore*, April 14, 2003.

—Patrick Heenan
—update: Christina M. Stansell

Pressman Toy Corporation

200 5th Avenue, Suite 1052
New York, New York 10010
U.S.A.
Telephone: (212) 675-7910
Fax: (212) 645-8512
Web site: http://www.pressmangames.com

Private Company
Incorporated: 1947
Employees: 300+
Sales: $75 million (2001 est.)
NAIC: 339932 Game, Toy, and Children's Vehicle
 Manufacturing

Family owned and operated, Pressman Toy Corporation is America's third largest games manufacturer. In addition to corporate offices located in Manhattan, Pressman operates a factory in New Brunswick, New Jersey, which produces some 85 percent of its products. Over the years, the company has shrewdly licensed popular film and television properties in order to develop and market best-selling games and other toys, including Disney's *Snow White* in the 1930s, *The Mickey Mouse Club* in the 1950s, hit television game shows *Wheel of Fortune* in the 1980s and *Who Wants to be A Millionaire?* at the end of the 1990s, and more recently *Spiderman,* the successful film based on the comic book hero. The company is run by the second generation of the Pressman family.

1920s Origins

After serving in the military during World War I, Pressman's founder, Jack Pressman, returned home to launch a Brooklyn toy company. As the nation's economy heated up and his business flourished, in 1925 he took on a partner, Max Eibetz, to look after the factory while he concentrated on merchandising. J. Pressman & Company's first major success was the 1928 acquisition of the rights to Chinese Checkers, a game that in fact had nothing to do with China. It was an odd (hence "chinese") variation of the game Halma, purportedly invented in England during the 1880s and played on a square board rather than the star shape employed

by Chinese Checkers. Whatever the truth of its origins, Chinese Checkers proved to be a boon to the fortunes of Pressman, and the company continues to sell the game today. Pressman added other indoor games, such as table tennis sets, as well as building sets and sewing kits for children's role playing and outdoor items like ring toss and golf.

In the 1930s, Pressman was one of the pioneers in the toy industry in licensing comic strip and film properties. In particular, the company launched a number of products based on Walt Disney's hugely popular movie *Snow White and the Seven Drawfs,* the first feature-length animated film. Also in the 1930s, Pressman sold licensed toys based on *Little Orphan Annie,* a newspaper comic strip created by Harold Gray in 1924. Another comic strip that Pressman licensed was *Dick Tracy,* launched by cartoonist Chester Gould in 1931.

Pressman reached a turning point in 1942 when Jack Pressman married Lynn Rambach, who became an active participant in the business. Within five years, Eibetz was out, the partnership dissolved, Lynn Pressman appointed vice-president, and the company renamed Pressman Toy Company. In addition, the business left Brooklyn for a larger, modern plant in Patterson, New Jersey, and executive offices in Manhattan. It was Lynn's influence that led to another major success for the company, the 1956 debut of the Doctor Bag, developed as a way to help children overcome their fear of doctors. Its success led to the introduction of the Nurse Bag, followed by licensed items that drew on the popularity of the Barbie Doll: the Barbie Nurse Bag and the Ken Doctor Bag. Also during the 1950s, Pressman took advantage of other licensing opportunities. It again teamed up with Disney, this time drawing on the new medium of television and another Disney success, *The Mickey Mouse Club.* A long line of Mickey Mouse club products were offered throughout the decade, as well as other Disney licensed items.

Jack Pressman's health began to fail in the 1950s, leading to his death in 1959. His widow took over as president, becoming one of the era's few women to serve in a top management position in the toy industry, the others being Ruth Handler, co-founder of Mattel and inventor of the Barbie Doll, and Beatrice Alexander, the founder of the Alexander Doll Company. Lynn Pressman served as president of the company for the next 20 years. Under her leadership, Pressman became one of the first toy makers to advertise a game on television and to hire fashion designers to design game boxes. She also continued the company's success with licensed products, including Superman and Lone Ranger games, a product based on the work of television puppeteer Sheri Lewis, and the Big League Action Baseball product, associated with such popular players of the period as Roger Maris, Carl Yastremski, and Tom Seaver.

New Generation of Leadership in the 1970s

In 1971, a second generation of the Pressman family became involved with the business when Jim Pressman graduated with an English Degree from Boston University after having worked summers at the company during his college days. One of his assignments after going to work for Pressman on a permanent basis was to relocate the factory to a larger property. He settled on the current New Brunswick production site and took charge of the relocation, a success that led to his mother appointing him president of the company in 1977, while she maintained the chairmanship.

Jim Pressman took over a business that was generating in the neighborhood of $4 million a year in revenues at a time when the toy industry was undergoing dramatic changes, with many small companies unable to survive a recession in the late 1970s. He took stock of the company and concluded that the strongest part of the business was its games. As a result, he rejected Pressman's scattershot approach of offering a wide range of products in favor of concentrating on games, in the process abandoning such staples as dolls and doctor's bags. Board games was a good business because they did not need heavy promotional budgets, relying instead on word-of-mouth. The company carved out a niche with classic board games, supplemented by an ability to spot popular trends and to capitalize on them. Pressman's timing proved fortuitous, as the board game business was soon revitalized by Selchow & Richter Co. after it introduced its highly popular Trivial Pursuit game, which also helped to break the prevailing $30 price barrier. Once again, it was Pressman's licensing efforts that proved a key element of success during the 1980s, in particular the home version of the hit syndicated television game show *Wheel of Fortune.* Pressman's Wheel of Fortune game grew to become America's top-selling game, which in just two years helped the toy company to double its annual sales to $30 million in 1985. Pressman then licensed other television game shows to produce board games, including the *New Newlywed Game* and *Jeopardy,* as well as launching a deluxe version of the Wheel of Fortune, resulting in revenues soaring to $54 million in 1986. Despite the importance of TV games to its bottom line, Pressman was experiencing growth in other areas as well. More than half of its sales came

from traditional games like checkers, Chinese checkers, and ring toss, and family games such as the Charade Game and Topple.

Pressman used some of its profits in the mid-1980s to move into a new gaming category that excited many in the industry, VCR games, spurred by the success of Parker Brothers video version of the Clue board game. Pressman's entries were Doorways to Adventure and Doorway to Horror, both of which they supported with generous ad budgets. In the end, however, VCR games failed to catch on with the public. Pressman had more success tapping into the rising importance of cable television for game licensing opportunities. In 1988, the company introduced a game based on Nickelodeon's *Double Dare,* resulting in another top selling product that grossed over $40 million for retailers. Television game shows, for both adults and children, were such a source of profitable games that the company even toyed with the idea of developing games that could be simultaneously pitched as television properties. One concept that Pressman tried to turn into a television show was a board game called Read My Lips, taken from President George H. Bush's 1988 presidential campaign, when he vowed not to raise taxes. In the Pressman game, players attempted to read the lips of their partners. The idea, as well as other attempts to launch television game shows, however, proved unsuccessful. In addition television tie-ins, Pressman manufactured a line of strategy games during this period, including Mastermind, Rummikub, and Tri-Ominos. An edgier game introduced by Pressman in the late 1980s was Therapy, in which the therapist asked the player-patient such questions as ''On a scale of 1 to 10, what is your sexual appetite?''

1990s and Beyond

In 1993, Jim Pressman succeeded his mother as chairman of the company while continuing to serve as president. She now took on the title of Chairman of the Board Emeritus. The retail environment for toys and games was becoming increasingly difficult for small companies, yet Pressman was able to succeed. An industry that was once dominated by a number of toy store chains became overly dependent on a handful of giant retailers, such as Wal-Mart, Kmart, and Target. As a result, fewer items were being stocked, forcing manufacturers to offer fewer products and making them less willing to take a risk: if the big three retailers opted not to carry an item, a manufacturer had a difficult time launching it. Moreover, retailers increasingly adapted a just-in-time approach to stocking its shelves, thereby placing enormous pressure on toy and game manufacturers, who had to truly believe in a product in order to approve the manufacture of a stock capable of supplying merchandisers in the fourth quarter Christmas season, when the lion share of retail business was done. Unlike some of the competition, which was becoming increasingly afraid to take a chance, Pressman had a number of factors working in its favor. The company was well established in the market and had low overhead, allowing it to offer low prices as well as the ability to put out a low-volume game simply because management liked it. Part of the company's secret to success was its decision to keep its operations low tech. Moreover, Pressman was receptive to ideas presented by independent toy inventors, an odd assortment of characters that the major companies preferred to ignore. Few of these pitch sessions resulted in commercial products, but remaining open to new ideas was a factor in maintaining Pressman's innovative spirit after being in business for several decades.

Pressman enjoyed a hit in the mid-1990s with Gooey Louie, a game for pre-schoolers in which players remove ''gooeys'' from the nose of a plastic head until the back of the skull popped open and the brain sprung out. In 1995, Gooey Looey was the best-selling game in its category. The company produced another highly popular game in 1997 with the introduction of Hydro Strike!, a pinball-type game in which players try to douse one another with water by hitting opposing targets with a marble. Hydro Strike! won awards from a number of magazines, including *Family Fun Magazine, Sesame Street Parents,* and *Zillions Magazine,* as well as television's CBS This Morning Toy Test. In 1998, Pressman was active on the licensing front, launching a line of games and puzzles based on the *Scooby Doo* cartoon program. Also in 1998, the company signed a licensing deal with IDG Books Worldwide, publishers of the For Dummies book series. Pressman contracted to produce three board games: Trivia for Dummies, Crosswords for Dummies, and Charades for Dummies.

Pressman signed a major licensing deal in 1999 when it successfully acquired the rights to produce a board game of *Who Wants To Be A Millionaire?,* which had become a phenomenal television hit. Pressman beat out industry giants, its track record with Wheel of Fortune Game as well as small company size providing an edge. According to the head of marketing at Celador Productions, the British licensor of *Who Wants To Be A Millionaire?,* ''We were looking for a company that would maintain the integrity of the show, and give it the

attention to detail that it deserves. Given their demonstrated success within the game industry and the passion they brought to this project, Pressman was our first choice.'' Although sales of the game when it was launched in 2000 were sluggish, at least in comparison to retailers high expectations, momentum picked up and carried through the holiday season. By the end of the year, the home version of *Who Wants To Be A Millionaire?* was the fourth-best selling toy introduced that year and the number one game in the world. In the process, it garnered a number of honors, including Best Licensed Toy of the Year by the Toy Manufacturers Association. The company was also named Licensee of the Year by Licensing Industry Merchandiser's Association, and Jim Pressman was named distribution entrepreneur of the year by Ernst and Young. Moreover, the company's balance sheet benefited greatly from sales of the game. Annual revenues grew to $75 million, approximately a 50 percent increase over the results of previous years.

Pressman followed up a successful 2000 by offering a second edition of Who Wants To Be A Millionaire in time for the 2001 holiday season. A year later, the company added a children's version of the game. Other popular offerings during this time included Fib Finder, a girl's lie detector game. Talking versions of Fib Finder as well as Gooey Louie were launched in 2003. Pressman enjoyed continued success in licensing popular cartoon and film characters, including the *Power Puff Girls* and products based on the 2002 movie *Spiderman.* In 2003, Pressman hoped to experience similar results from a line of products based on another comic book hero transferred to the big screen, the Incredible Hulk.

Principal Competitors

Hasbro; Mattel.

Further Reading

Applegate, Jane, ''The Little Toy Company That Could,'' *Record* (Bergen County, NJ), December 22, 1997, p. H08.
Pries, Allison, ''Plenty of Millions to Go Around,'' *Record* (Bergen County, NJ), July 18, 2001, p. B3.
Rigg, Cynthia, ''Toy Maker's Wheel Comes Up a Winner,'' *Crain's New York Business,* May 26, 1985, p. 3.

—Ed Dinger

PT Astra International Tbk

Jalan Gaya Motor Raya No. 8
Sunter II
Jakarta 14330
Indonesia
Telephone: (+62) 21-652-2555
Fax: (+62) 21-651-2058
Web site: http://www.astra.co.id

Public Company
Incorporated: 1957
Employees: 90,000
Sales: IDR 30.68 trillion ($3.73 billion) (2002)
Stock Exchanges: Jakarta Surubaya
Ticker Symbol: ASII
NAIC: 336111 Automobile Manufacturing; 321113
    Sawmills; 325131 Inorganic Dye and Pigment
    Manufacturing; 517110 Wired Telecommunications
    Carriers

PT Astra International Tbk is one of Indonesia's largest diversified conglomerates. The company's operations have long centered around its core automotive manufacturing and distribution business, which remains its largest division, at nearly 83 percent of total sales of IDR 31 trillion ($3.7 billion) in 2002. The opening of Indonesia's import market at the dawn of the 21st century, especially to fellow ASEAN economic community members, has forced Astra to adapt—in May 2003, the company sold off nearly all of its holdings in its longtime automotive manufacturing joint venture with Toyota. The move, the proceeds of which were earmarked toward paying down the company's $1 billion in debt, refocused Astra primarily on its automotive sales and distribution network, which remains the largest in Indonesia. The company holds the exclusive distribution rights to Toyota (the country's biggest selling brand), Peugeot, Daihatsu, BMW, Isuzu, and Nissan. The company also maintains manufacturing operations for certain Daihatsu and Isuzu vehicles, as well as the exclusive manufacturing and distribution rights for Honda motorcycles, the leading motorcycle brand in the country. Other Astra divisions include Financial Services, mostly to finance automo-

bile purchases, which accounted for 5.4 percent of sales in 2002; Agribusiness, which produced 6.6 percent of sales; heavy equipment manufacturing and wood-based production, which together added nearly 2.5 percent of sales. Nearly all of the company's operations are focused on the Indonesian market. The shakeup of the country's government, including the forced resignation of former President Suharto, has brought new leadership to Astra as well, in the form of Budi Setiadharma, who serves as President Director. Astra International is listed on the Jakarta and Surubaya stock exchanges.

From Juice to Cars in the 1960s

Astra International was founded in 1957, based on a small trading business operated by brothers Tjia Kian Tie and William Soerydadjaya, part of an ethnic Chinese family that had already lived in Indonesia for several generations, adopting the "Muslim" name of Soerydadjaya. The family had begun its trading activities by the 1940s, when it helped supply Indonesian forces, including troops led by Suharto, during the Indonesian war of independence in the 1940s. William Soerydadjaya also enjoyed personal ties with Sumitro Djojohadikusumo, long the country's top economist. The brothers' company initially operated as a distributor of fruit juices and other agricultural and grocery goods, before adding a small export business as well.

Astra's fortunes took off in the early 1960s, with the massive modernization program initiated by then-president Sukarno. Astra entered the import sector, focusing on asphalt and other construction materials needed for Sukarno's public works development effort. Although the Soerydadjaya family remained politically neutral—and built much of its later business empire on its reputation for integrity—it nonetheless carefully adhered to government economic policy.

The rise to power of Suharto in the mid-1960s represented new opportunities for the Soerydadjaya family. While avoiding the cronyism that marked much of the Suharto regime, the Soerydadjayas nonetheless benefited from their earlier support of the Indonesian independence movement. Therefore, in 1967, the company was granted a prized import license, backed by the U.S. government. Initially the company attempted to import

---

Company Perspectives:

PHILOSOPHY: 1. To be an asset to the nation. 2. To provide only the best service to our customers. 3. To respect individuals and promote teamwork. 4. To continually strive for excellence. VISION: 1. To be one of the best managed corporations in the Asia-Pacific region with an emphasis on building competence through human resources development, solid financial structures, customer satisfaction and efficiency. 2. To be a socially responsible corporation and to be environmentally friendly.

---

electrical generators made by General Motors Corporation (GM), a move that ended amid red tape. Instead, Astra replaced its generator order with GM with a fleet of 800 Chevrolet trucks, which Astra then sold to the Suharto government.

The government then turned to Astra for help in rescuing PN Gaya Motor. Originally established in 1927, Gaya Motor served as Chevrolet's entry into Southeast Asia, operating an assembly plant for Chevrolet vehicles. GM pulled out of Gaya Motor in 1954 with the coming to power of Sukarno's pro-Chinese government, and Gaya Motor then became government owned. By the end of the 1960s, a lack of investment had left Gaya Motor in poor condition, with outmoded production facilities and limited investment funds.

Astra agreed to purchase a 60 percent stake in Gaya Motor in 1969, paying more than the equivalent of $1 million. The move brought Astra into partnership with the Indonesian government. At first, Astra expected to continued to operate under an exclusive assembly and distribution relationship with Chevrolet. That contract, however, was denied the company. Instead, Astra began assembling cars for another, younger carmaker, Toyota Motor Corporation, which was just then seeking to enter the Indonesian market.

By 1971, Astra's connections with Sumitro—then Minister of Trade in charge of allocating the country's exclusive import agency contracts—received the rights to form the joint venture PT Toyota-Astra Motor, which became the exclusive agent for that automotive brand in Indonesia. Once again, Astra responded to the government's economic policy, which focused on so-called ''Import Substitution Industrialization,'' encouraging the growth of industry by requiring that finished goods destined for the Indonesian market be assembled in Indonesia itself, which was backed by restrictions on imports of finished cars imposed in 1969.

Astra quickly built up a list of exclusive agency contracts, adding Honda motorcycles in 1970, Peugeot/Renault in 1972, and Daihatsu in 1973. By the end of the decade, the company had succeeded in capturing some 40 percent of the total Indonesian automobile market.

The company also branched out into office equipment, assembling for Fuji-Xerox in 1970 (and becoming sole agent in 1976). The company became the exclusive assembler of heavy equipment in 1972, adding the Komatsu brand in 1973. The company's rise was aided by new legislation, which included an

outright ban on finished car imports by 1974 and an earlier ban on foreign investments in the country's growing automotive industry. (The Astra-Toyota joint venture was allowed to remain because it had been formed prior to the ban.)

Manufacturing in the 1980s

The Suharto government had by then begun to encourage the development of a full-fledged manufacturing industry, enacting legislation favoring the localization of car and motorcycle components. Astra responded by setting up the production of automotive batteries and motorcycle frames by 1973. By the end of the 1970s, the company had added production of electrical equipment, shock absorbers, Toyota car bodies, and car bodies for Daihatsu as well.

Into the 1980s, Astra's range of component production grew to include chassis frames in 1980, brake systems in 1981, rear axles and propeller shafts in 1982, transmissions in 1983, as well as engine assembly for both Toyota and Daihatsu vehicles. By then, the government's attention had broadened to establishing an export market for the country as well. Astra's response was to begin exports of a number of automotive components, including spark plugs and car batteries, as well as Toyota engines and Komatsu forklift frames.

Astra relied on the creation of joint ventures, chiefly with Japanese companies, in order to develop its export operations. The company quickly diversified beyond its core automotive operations, adding computers, televisions, and even, in the early 1990s, semiconductors. Meanwhile, the Soerydadjaya family, and especially William Soerydadjaya's son Edward, had expanded the family's fortune, through Summa International, into a number of new areas, notably property development, tourism, and, in 1989, banking, with the creation of Bank Summa.

By then, Astra had added a number of new brands to its exclusive automotive business, including Fiat, Isuzu, BMW, and Nissan Diesel. These new agencies allowed Astra to capture nearly 50 percent of Indonesia's fast-growing automotive market. Indeed, the country's steady economic growth had created a rising middle class as well as a high-flying wealthy class. At the same time, purchases of motorcycles became widespread among the country's large working class. Astra's control of Toyota and Honda gave it Indonesia's top-selling car and motorcycle brands.

Astra went public in 1990, listing on the Jakarta and Surubaya exchanges. The Soerydadjaya family retained control of the company, with more than 82 percent of its shares. Yet a shadow had begun to form across the family empire. Edward Soerydadjaya's expansion spree had saddled Summa International with debts of more than $350 million—debts that were backed up by the family's stake in Astra International. When Bank Summa collapsed, the Soerydadjaya family lost control of the company it had founded.

Astra then came under control of the Suharto family and its allies, although its management remained, for the most part, in place. William Soerydadjaya had long pursued a number of ''modern'' management techniques, including a policy of hiring top managers from outside of his own family. Faced with the impending end of the ban on imports of finished cars, which went through in 1993, Astra took steps to improve its own operating

Key Dates:

1927: Chevrolet founds KN Gaya Motors as its entry into the Asian market.

1954: The Indonesian government takes full control of Gaya Motors as GM exits the country.

1957: The Soerydadjaya family founds Astra International as a grocery trading company and then expands into imports of asphalt and construction materials.

1967: Astra is granted an import license by the new Suharto-controlled government; the company begins importing trucks for sale to the government.

1969: Astra pays $1 million to acquire 60 percent of KN Gaya Motors; the company begins assembling cars for Toyota.

1971: The company receives an exclusive license for Toyota in Indonesia, forming a Toyota-Astra joint venture.

1972: Astra begins production of car batteries.

1985: Astra begins to export company-manufactured automotive components, including spark plugs and Toyota car engines.

1990: Astra International goes public with listings on the Jakarta and Surubaya stock exchanges.

1992: The Soerydadjaya family loses control of Astra International.

1995: Astra begins to diversify its operations by acquiring palm oil, rubber, and other plantations.

1998: The collapse of the Suharto regime and Indonesian economy places 45 percent of Astra under the Indonesian Bank Restructuring Agency (IBRA).

2000: IBRA sells 40 percent of Astra to a consortium led by Cycle & Carriage Ltd.

2003: Astra sells 46 percent of its holding in Toyota-Astra's manufacturing operation, as it restructures around its automotive distribution and motorcycle businesses.

efficiency, boosting factory production levels to almost 100 percent capacity. Nonetheless, the Indonesian market remained protected, with import tariffs on automobiles based on the percentage of locally produced parts in the finished car.

Refocusing in the New Century

In the 1990s, Astra turned to a massive investment program to boost its component production, spending more than $800 million through the end of the decade, with another $300 million pledged at the beginning of the next. The investment was part of an effort to boost the technological scope of its automotive production, with the ultimate goal of creating a full-fledged Indonesian car, in response to the Suharto regime's desire to see the creation of a "national" automobile brand.

Astra's Japanese partners proved less than willing to transfer the necessary technology to the company. At the same time, terms of Astra's exclusive agency contracts for the most part barred it from exporting its production beyond Indonesia. Yet the Indonesian market remained relatively small and increasingly vulnerable to the volatile economic climate of the mid-1990s.

Astra took steps to reduce its reliance on the automotive market, which accounted for 80 percent of its sales in the late 1990s, by extending into a variety of diversified areas, including an entry into the agribusiness industry with the purchases of a number of palm oil, tea, rubber, and cocoa plantations in 1995. The company also expressed an interest in moving into the telecommunications sector.

Astra expansion had placed it deeply in debt, and especially burdened by a large load of foreign debt. The collapse of the Asian region's economies and the drastic devaluation of Indonesia's rupiah left Astra unable to pay off the $2 billion in foreign debt that had come due. At the same time, Indonesia slipped into recession, slashing automobile purchases, and sinking Astra into losses of some $200 million by 1998. In that year, the ouster of the Suharto regime placed that family's 45 percent stake in Astra under the control of the Indonesian Bank Restructuring Agency (IBRA), which had been charged with disposing of assets seized after the collapse of the country's banks.

Astra, which came under the leadership of Rini Suwandi (backed by the Suharto family) managed to restructure a large part of its debt payments, staggering them out over a seven-year period. By 1999, the company was once again posting profits. It also had been approached by a suitor seeking to acquire the company, the U.S.-based Newbridge & Gilbert, which happened to be advised by another Soerydadjaya son, Edwin (and who was slated to take Astra's CEO spot on completion of the opposition). Yet Suwandi blocked Newbridge & Gilbert's due-diligence efforts, and the takeover fell through.

In response, the IBRA sacked Suwandi and replaced him with Theodore Rachmat, who had served as Astra's president director and remained an ally of the Soerydadjaya family. By then, Astra faced a new threat, when the Indonesian government, which had joined the ASEAN Free-Trade Area, eliminated preferential tariffs for the country's automobile market. As it now became less expensive to import automobiles than to make them in Indonesia, Astra announced its intention to phase out its automobile and components manufacturing operations in favor of boosting its automotive distribution operations.

The IBRA at last found a new suitor for Astra in 2000, selling 40 percent of the company to a consortium led by Cycle & Carriage Ltd., based in Singapore and controlled by Hong Kong's Jardine Strategic Holdings. Cycle & Carriage, which also distributed Mercedes-Benz cars in the region, had long sought to acquire Astra, making several offers during the 1990s.

Under its new president-director, Budi Setiadharma, Astra restructured its operations, slashing its payroll and selling off a number of its holdings in an effort to reduce its debt still further. By the end of 2002, the company had succeeded in pushing its foreign debt down to $800 million, as well as rescheduling payments on some $200 million that were then due.

In February 2003, Astra launched a successful rights issue, raising more than $160 million—including $80 million from Cycle & Carriage, which boosted its own shareholding to more than 34 percent. That month, the company's longtime partner agreed to inject $180 million into the PT Toyota-Astra joint venture in order to expand its production capacity. Yet that agreement became merely a prelude to Astra's next deal—the sale of 46 percent of its stake in the joint venture to Toyota, leaving the company with just 5 percent. Astra then used the $226 million from the sale to pay down its debt. As part of the agreement, the two sides split Toyota-Astra into its manufacturing and distribution components, with Astra maintaining 51 percent control of the distribution arm.

Astra continued to look for buyers for its components manufacturing operations as it turned toward the new century. With its profits rising strongly, the streamlined company now intended to reinvent itself as Indonesia's leading automobile and automotive components distributor. At the same time, the company remained committed to its fast-growing motorcycle manufacturing and distribution operation.

Principal Subsidiaries

Astra Finance; Astra Industry; Astra Motor; Astra Resources; PN Gaya Motor; PT Toyota-Astra (51%).

Principal Competitors

Indomobil Suzuki International, PT; DaimlerChrysler Indonesia; Mekar Armada Jaya, PT; Krama Yudha Ratu Motor, PT; Prospect Motor, PT; Udatinda Group.

Further Reading

Butler, Charlotte, *Dare to Do: The Story of William Soeryadjaya and PT Astra International*, Singapore: McGraw-Hill, 2002.
Ford, Maggie, "Debt Deal Puts Astra on Track," *Asiamoney,* February 2003, p. 13.
"Indonesia's Largest Auto Firm Sells Subsidiary to Toyota," *Xinhua News Agency,* May 22, 2003.
Sato, Y., "The Astra Group: A Pioneer of Modernization in Indonesia," *Developing Economies,* December 1996, p. 247.
Sheri, Prasso, "Indonesia Sells Off Astra—to Asians," *Business Week,* March 24, 2000.

—M.L. Cohen

PTT Public Company Limited

PTT Public Company Ltd.

555 Vibhavadi Rangsit Road
Lard Yao, Chatuchak
Bangkok 10900
Thailand
Telephone: (+66) 537-2000
Fax: (+66) 537-3499
Web site: http://www.pttplc.com

Public Company
Incorporated: 1978
Employees: 4,342
Sales: THB 409.335 trillion ($9.87 billion)(2002)
Stock Exchanges: Thailand
Ticker Symbol: PTT
NAIC: 213111 Drilling Oil and Gas Wells; 213112
    Support Activities for Oil and Gas Field Exploration;
    324110 Petroleum Refineries; 324191 Petroleum
    Lubricating Oil and Grease Manufacturing

PTT Public Company Ltd., formerly the state-owned Petroleum Authority of Thailand before its privatization and public offering at the end of 2001, is that country's largest corporation, with revenues of more than THB409 trillion ($9.8 billion). The PTT is also one of the ASEAN (Association of Southeast Asian Nations) region's top 50 corporations. The PTT bills itself as a fully integrated oil and gas business combining upstream, transmission, and downstream operations in the domestic oil and natural gas market as well as the international oil trade markets. The PTT's Gas Business Group, which retains its former monopoly on Thailand's natural gas market, handles a gas supply capacity of 2,475 million standard cubic feet per day—more than 78 percent of which goes to fuel the country's state-controlled power sector. The company is also involved in exploration and production, as well as transmission through a pipeline network of 2,700 kilometers. PTT Oil is the group's oil marketing and oil trading arm, through which the company operates more than 1,400 service stations throughout Thailand. The company also operates a network of 1,015 LPG (liquified petroleum gas) retail outlets supported by 113 LPG bottling plants. The company's International Trading processes more than 12,000 million liters of crude oil, 2,400 million liters of condensates, and 4,300 million liters of finished oil products each year. The PTT is also involved in petroleum exploration activities in Thailand and abroad through its majority control of publicly listed PTT Exploration and Production Company (PTTEP). The PTT's final business group is its Petrochemicals and Refining wing, which consolidates the company's shareholdings in such companies as Thai Oil, Rayong, Star Oil, and Bangchak. Listed on the Thai Stock Exchange, the PTT remains controlled at 70 percent by the Thai government, which is unlikely to reduce its holding below 51 percent. The PTT is led by Chairman Manu Leopairote and President Visct Choopiban.

Developing a Domestic Oil Industry in the 1950s

As petroleum became increasingly important for building a modern state after World War II, the Thai government sought to lessen its country's reliance on imported oil, gasoline, and other finished petroleum products by creating the Defense Energy Department, which was attached to the Ministry of Defense and placed in charge of developing the country's own energy reserves. The country began drilling for oil in 1921 in the Fang basin in the north of Thailand, but by the early 1950s had found only small petroleum reserves. Because of the lack of good roads, the government, through the Ministry of Defense, commissioned a small, 1,000 barrel-per-day refinery to be built near the Fang basin wells in 1956.

For the most part, however, Thailand, like most of the developing world, remained dependent into the 1960s on a small group of dominant U.S. oil companies for their petroleum fuel supplies. The oil companies' dominance of the world market extended from exploration and drilling to the refining of the finished product. The discovery of vast oil reserves in the Middle East and the appearance of a number of new players in the market forced the major oil companies to begin shipping crude oil as more countries began building and operating their own refineries.

The Thai government had established the Oil Fuel Organization (OFO) in order to allocate the limited finished petroleum

---

Company Perspectives:

Vision and Mission: to be the preeminent Thai energy corporation, operating a fully integrated oil and gas business, which encompasses gas-based petrochemicals and total energy services, confident of being a regional leader and a high performance organization with accountability, integrity, and optimum stakeholder returns within a value-driven corporate culture.

---

imports in that country. At the time, Thailand's import market was dominated by Esso, Caltex, and Shell, which also controlled fuel storage in the region, a position that helped keep fuel prices high. The OFO sought alternative fuel sources and began accepting bids from foreign companies.

One of these companies was Summit Industrial Corporation, which had been set up in the United States after World War II by a group of native Chinese who had been students together at MIT. Summit originally operated as a trading company to the Far East that dealt in goods ranging from medicine to locomotive engines to consumer products. In the mid-1950s, Summit became interested in entering the oil trade as well. Backed by American Independent Oil Corporation, which had been granted the right to drill in the newly opened oil fields in Kuwait, Summit won the bid to supply the OFO. The company's initial shipment led to a three-year supply contract with the OFO. Summit then purchased land and established its own storage facilities.

In 1955, Thailand's Defense Energy Department had decided to build a larger multi-purpose refinery at Bangchak, near Bangkok. Although still quite small, at 5,000 barrels per day, the Bangchak facility was slated to produce not only diesel, kerosene, and gasoline but also aviation fuel. The initial contract was awarded to Japan's Niigata, which transferred the contract to a partnership between Fujicar Manufacturing Co., also of Japan, and Commentry Oissel, of France. The turnkey project finally got underway in 1960 but due to a series of delays was not completed until 1964—and failed its initial testing.

To complete the testing of the facility, the Defense Energy Department turned to Summit, which also began competing for the contract to operate the Bangchak site. In 1965, Summit signed an operating agreement with the government that granted the company permission to expand production to 20,000 barrels per day while operating on a tax-free basis. In exchange, Summit agreed to pay off the $20 million construction cost of the facility and turn it over to the government in 1980.

The facility's expansion was completed by 1968. By then, Summit had opened some 200 gasoline stations in Thailand; the company also became the supplier for the OFO's own network of service stations. In addition, Summit had built an asphalt production plant, supplying the government's road-building effort. By the mid-1960s, however, as new road construction slowed, Summit sought to unload the money-losing plant.

Thailand was by now experiencing a rapidly growing demand for fuel products in the country, and its two primary refineries—the Bangchak plant and a second, larger site built by Shell and operated through the Thai Oil Refinery Corporation—could not keep up with demand. The government agreed to the expansion of the refineries, with the Bangchak plant's capacity raised to 65,000 barrels per day. Summit's lease was then extended to 1990. At the same time, Summit sold its asphalt plant to Esso, which rebuilt the site and entered the Thai market with its own refinery.

Natural Gas to the Rescue in the 1970s

Thailand's hopes for finding large-scale domestic oil reserves were dashed by the mid-1970s. While a number of small reserves had been discovered, the country was still to remain heavily dependent on fuel imports. The Arab Oil Embargo and resulting worldwide crisis was especially crushing for Thailand.

Yet the country's exploration efforts had not been entirely in vain, as a number of important natural gas fields had been discovered. In response, the Thai government set up the Natural Gas Organization of Thailand (NGOT), which served as a counterpart to the OFO. With the deepening of the economic crisis, however, the Thai government moved to group all of its fuel operations under a single entity. The government passed legislation in December 1978, creating the Petroleum Authority of Thailand (PTT).

The PTT took over for the NGOT and the OFO and additionally became the nominal owner of the Bangchak refinery, which remained leased to Summit. The PTT began building its first natural gas pipeline, a 415-kilometer underwater pipeline stretching from the Erawan gas field in the Gulf of Thailand to an onshore site at Rayong. The Erawan field, which was exploited by Unocal, began producing gas in 1981.

Also in 1981, the PTT took possession of the Thai Oil Refinery's operations as part of the initial agreement. Another development in that year was the Thai government's direct negotiation of a crude oil supply contract with Saudi Arabia. This in turn led to the sudden termination of Summit's lease of the Bangchak refinery, which had been the site of frequent labor disputes, a rarity in Thailand. The PTT was now in direct control of more than two-thirds of the country's refinery capacity. Over time, the PTT stepped up its refinery capacity, and by 1991 the Bangchak facility alone had neared 250,000 barrels per day.

The PTT opened a second, 169-kilometer natural gas pipeline connecting the Erawan field directly to the state-owned electricity power plant in Bangkok in 1982. The company then constructed a network of six linked LPG terminals nationwide, a project which reached completion in 1985. By then, the PTT had opened its first gas separation plant in order to harvest by-products used in turn to launch a national petrochemicals industry. In 1985, the PTT formed the joint-venture National Petrochemicals Co. Ltd. That same year, the PTT entered the exploration business as well, forming PTT Exploration and Production Co. Ltd. (PTTEP).

In just a few short years, the PTT had grown from a starting capital of THB149 million into a fully integrated gas and petroleum company with revenues of more than THB26 billion. By 1988, the organization had expanded to include four major natural gas fields, including Erawan, and new sites at Baanpot,

Key Dates:

1921: Thai government begins its first oil exploration efforts in Fang basin.

1956: Defense Energy Department commissions a small refinery to process Fang basin oil reserves; Summit Industrial Corporation begins importing crude oil for Thai government.

1961: Construction begins on Bangchak oil refinery near Bangkok.

1965: Summit acquires a long-term lease and operating contract for Bangchak refinery; Thai Oil Refinery is created.

1978: Legislation creates a new Petroleum Authority of Thailand (PTT), which takes over from the Oil Fuel Organization and the Natural Gas Organization of Thailand.

1981: The PTT acquires Thai Oil Refinery and takes over Bangchak refinery.

1984: The company opens its first gas separation plant and enters the petrochemicals industry.

1985: The PTT establishes its own petroleum and gas exploration arm, PTT Exploration and Production Company (PTTEP).

1987: With increase in natural gas production, the PTT begins exporting excess fuel oil capacity.

1995: The PTT signs an agreement for natural gas production in Yadana field in Myanmar.

1996: PTTEP is spun off as a public company in preparation for the PTT's privatization.

2001: PTT Public Company is created and listed on the Thai Stock Exchange; Thai government sells 30 percent of the company.

2003: The company launches international exploration operations, through PTTEP, in Algeria and Oman.

Satun, and Platong. Unocal remained the primary operator of these fields, which had already produced more than one trillion cubic feet of natural gas by 1988. At that time, The Thai government had already decided to emphasize the use of natural gas for the country's fuel needs, leading the PTT to start exporting its excess fuel oil capacity in 1987.

A fifth Gulf of Thailand field was opened in 1989. The PTT had already contracted for its second gas separation plant, in Rayong Province, and this project was completed in 1991. The PTT, which had inherited the OFO's service station network, meanwhile continued expanding its operations in that area as well, becoming the dominant market player. By 1992, the PTT stations had debuted Thailand's first high-octane unleaded gasoline.

Privatized for the New Century

Thailand's booming economy stepped up demand for petroleum in the 1990s. In response, the PTT set up two new refinery companies in 1992: Rayong Refinery, in partnership with Shell Thailand, and Star Petroleum Refinery, in partnership with Caltex. The PTT's stake in each of the new ventures was around one-third of shares.

Demand for natural gas grew strongly in the 1990s as well, outstripping Thailand's own relatively small supply. Yet the PTT's expertise in the area made it an attractive partner for neighboring countries, such as Burma (Myanmar), where the PTT joined in the Yadana consortium to exploit the Gulf of Martaban in 1995. That deal involved the construction of the Yadana Natural Gas Pipeline on the Myanmar-Thai border, which began operations in 1998. The PTT opened a new domestic gas field, Tantawan, in the Gulf of Thailand in 1995. In 1997, the company negotiated a second gas supply contract in Myanmar, at the Yetagun field, which began delivery at the beginning of the next decade. In 1996, the PTT added a third gas separation unit, Khanom.

In the meantime, the PTT began preparing for its upcoming privatization, which was originally slated for 1999. Under the original privatization plan, the company was to spin off a number of its business units, a process that started with the public offering of PTTEP in 1996. The privatization stalled, however, amid growing concerns by labor unions over job security. At the same time, the PTT had been hit hard by the collapse of the Thai economy and the drastic devaluation of the baht, sinking the company into losses. At the beginning of 1999, the Thai government suggested its interest in spinning off PTT Gas as a separate company, a move that would have eliminated some 80 percent of the PTT's total revenues. By the end of the year, however, the PTT's privatization plan had been revised, calling for the proposed PTT Public Company Plc to retain all of its existing operations.

The PTT at last went public in November 2001, when the Thai government sold a 30 percent stake. The listing raised some $726 million for the government, which faced deadlines on its $17 billion debt to the International Monetary Fund. The government intended to reduce its stake, while pledging to maintain a minimum of 51 percent in the PTT. At the same time, the government reassured investors of its intention to maintain the PTT's monopoly on the Thai natural gas market.

Already the top corporation in Thailand, and one of the 50 largest in the ASEAN market region, the PTT targeted an increased presence in the international energy market. This effort was already underway during the 1990s, initiated by the purchase of a 35 percent stake in Petroasia, which in 1993 started opening service stations in China. The PTT had also long been in pursuit of expansion into neighboring Malaysia's large natural gas reserves, including the construction of a pipeline linking the two countries, and at the beginning of 2003 an inaugural project appeared imminent. In the meantime, the company's exploration wing had already begun its own international expansion, launching operations in Algeria and Oman.

At the same time, the PTT prepared for the liberalizaton of the country's natural gas market by splitting its natural gas business into two new, wholly owned companies—PTT Transmission Pipeline Co and PTT Distribution Pipeline Co. Backed by one of the region's strongest economies and most stable governments, the PTT had positioned itself to become a prime industry player in Southeast Asia.

Principal Subsidiaries

Clark Pipeline and Depot Company, Inc (Philippines; 50%); PTT Distribution Pipeline Co.; PTT Exploration and Production

Plc; PTT International Trading Pte., Ltd.; PTT Mart Co., Ltd. (49%); PTT Natural Gas Distribution Co., Ltd.; PTT Philippines Inc.; PTT Transmission Pipeline Co; Subic Bay Energy Co., Ltd (50%); Subic Bay Fuels Company, Inc. (50%); Thai Lube Blending Co., Ltd (49%); Thai Olefins Company Limited 59.71; Trans Thai-Malaysia (Thailand) Limited (50%); Vietnam LPG Co., Ltd. (Vietnam; 45%).

Principal Competitors

Chevron Texaco; Mitsui and Co. Thailand Ltd.; Siam Makro PCL; Unique Gas and Petrochemicals PCL.

Further Reading

"Algeria—Spurred by Soaring Profits; Thailand's PTT Exploration & Production Is Looking to Expand Overseas, with New Acreage in the Mideast and North Africa," *Petroleum Intelligence Weekly*, April 21, 2003, p. 6.

Greenfield, Sarah, "The Asian Energy Industry Begins to Branch out," *Petroleum Economist*, September 1995, p. 29.

Kazmin, Amy, "Thailand Hopes for Boost from Oil Sell-off," *Financial Times*, November 14, 2001, p. 16.

"Offload, Downsize and Survive," *Business in Thailand*, May 1999.

"Petroleum Authority of Thailand: A Finger in Every Pie," *Petroleum Economist*, March 1991, p. 17.

Praiwan, Ythana, "PTT Eyes Postwar Stake Sale," *Bangkok Post*, April 14, 2003.

"PTT's Natural Gas Unit to Be Split into Two," *Bangkok Post*, March 17, 2003.

"Thailand's Gas Growth Favors State PTT," *Petroleum Intelligence Weekly*, September 23, 2002, p.4.

—M.L. Cohen

QSC Audio Products, Inc.

1675 MacArthur Boulevard
Costa Mesa, California 92626
U.S.A.
Telephone: (714) 754-6175
Toll Free: (800) 854-4079
Fax: (714) 754-6174
Web site: http://www.qscaudio.com

Private Company
Incorporated: 1968 as Quilter Sound Company
Employees: 250
Sales: $80 million (2002 est.)
NAIC: 334310 Audio and Video Equipment
Manufacturing

QSC Audio Products, Inc. is a leading manufacturer of high-power sound amplifiers and speakers as well as computer control, signal transport, and digital signal processing products for audio applications. Many of the company's amplifiers utilize the firm's PowerWave switching power supply, which is significantly lighter in weight than standard designs for high-power amplifiers. Other QSC products include the QSControl remote audio monitoring system, the RAVE ethernet audio transport system, and the ISIS and QSC-ACE lines of speakers. The company's products are used in stadiums, concert halls, churches, and other public spaces where amplified sound is needed and have been chosen for such high-profile events as the Super Bowl, the Indianapolis 500, and the Academy Awards.

1960s Origins

The origins of QSC date to 1968, when Patrick Quilter borrowed money from his family and friends to form a small business in Costa Mesa, California. Quilter Sound Company, as the firm was named, initially produced guitar amplifiers for local musicians. Among its early offerings were the Quilter Sound Thing and the Duck Amp, as well as the PigNose amp, which was made for a larger company. At first Quilter rented a 400-square-foot garage space in an industrial park where a loose-knit staff helped build the equipment. An early recruit

was Barry Andrews, who had chanced upon Quilter when his motorcycle broke down near the firm's space. Needing help to build wooden enclosures for his gear, Quilter soon enlisted the new acquaintance, who was an experienced cabinet maker.

In the beginning, the small company was run in a relatively disorganized fashion, with Quilter focusing more on the construction of equipment than the bottom line. When Andrews asked if he could manage the books, Quilter readily agreed to let him. Andrews later brought in his brother John, who had worked summers for the company while attending the University of Southern California business school, and gave him control of the firm's finances. Quilter remained in charge of designing amplifiers, while Barry Andrews began to oversee sales and marketing. In 1975, the company was incorporated and its name changed to QSC Audio Products, Inc.

QSC had originally focused on production of guitar and box-type amplifiers, but after analyzing the market Quilter and the Andrews brothers decided to limit themselves to making professional power amplifiers. A larger manufacturing space was needed, and the firm moved into a 2,500-square-foot site on Placentia Avenue in Costa Mesa. New products were soon introduced, including a 150-watt monophonic amplifier and a 200-watt-per-channel stereo amp. A 300-watt stereo amp was added in 1977, which was then followed by six "A Series" models that put out as much as 325 watts per channel.

Expansion in the 1970s–80s

During the latter half of the 1970s, the company began to refine its manufacturing processes and the design of its products to improve reliability, sound quality, and cost. In addition to purchasing the best available parts, giving workers more training, and testing thoroughly for defects, designs were simplified so that production became less complicated.

In 1978, Quilter patented the AC Coupled Amplifier Circuit, which allowed the mounting of high-voltage transistors onto a grounded metal heatsink. The new design yielded greater cooling efficiency and power flow, was safer and more reliable to use, and further simplified the manufacturing process. Other QSC innovations of this period included a feature called Pow-

Company Perspectives:

QSC Values: quickly understand and exceed customer expectations; high quality is essential, low price is desirable; act with integrity and concern for others; people are our strongest asset; use the power of teamwork; work hard, have fun! QSC Business Focus: provide advanced power, signal, control, transport, and speaker products and services to audio professionals worldwide.

erLimit, which protected against short circuits. The company's products were by now gaining a sleeker look, which included LED displays and modular designs.

In 1982, QSC introduced its highest-power amplifiers to date, the Series Three line. The top-end model was capable of 1100 watts per channel and utilized convection cooling, a big plus over the sometimes noisy fan systems found in most power amps. This series soon became popular with customers in the touring sound industry who supplied audio systems for rock concerts and other live events. QSC's smaller Series One, which was introduced the same year, found a major customer in Dolby Laboratories, Inc. for use in their movie theater installations, then being adopted industry-wide as the standard for high-quality cinema sound.

In 1985, the MX 1500 amp debuted, and its combination of high power and a list price of less than $1,000 made it QSC's best seller to date. It was especially popular with musicians. Other MX series amps, which were based on the company's Series Three technology, were later added. QSC now had a total of 50 employees and had grown to occupy four buildings in the same industrial park in Costa Mesa.

In 1988, the company's EX Series bowed, the firm's first to incorporate a new ''open architecture'' design which could interface with digital, fiber optic, or computer control systems of other manufacturers. The initial model in the series, the EX 4000, put out 1600 watts per channel.

In 1993, QSC moved into a new 51,000-square-foot facility on MacArthur Boulevard in Costa Mesa. This location housed both manufacturing and corporate offices. The company's production capacity increased substantially, to 200 amplifiers per day, and its staff grew to more than 100.

QSC was now in the process of developing its most revolutionary product line to date. Based on its exclusive ''PowerWave'' switching power supply technology, the new PowerLight Series offered high power and great sound with a dramatic decrease in weight—as little as one-50th that of a standard amplifier. The new design used high-frequency switching, rather than the low-frequency type normally seen, and did not require the standard heavy transformers to convert power from AC to DC. The PowerLight line was introduced in 1994 and immediately began to win acceptance in the marketplace. The PowerWave technology would eventually be incorporated into six of the firm's eight amplifier lines.

The year 1994 also saw the principals in QSC invest in New Jersey-based Raxxess, Inc., a maker of audio equipment racks

and accessories, to help fund that firm's expansion to the West Coast. In 1995, the growing QSC was reorganized to improve customer service, and four sales managers were appointed to oversee the Retail/Musical Instruments, Engineered Sound, Cinema, and Touring/Live sound markets.

During this period, QSC was also beginning to branch out into other audio products, following several years of research by the firm's Advanced Systems Group design team. In 1997, the company introduced QSControl, which was a computer application that could be run on a personal computer to facilitate remote monitoring and control of audio amplification systems. Buyers included the Southeast Christian Church for use on its campus in Louisville, Kentucky, and Petronas Towers in Malaysia, where it was installed in a concert hall.

Another new QSC product, RAVE (Routing Audio Via Ethernet), allowed the transmission of up to 64 channels of digital sound via a standard ethernet network and featured open system architecture for use with off-the-shelf hardware. Users of RAVE included the Sydney Opera House in Australia and the Church of Jesus Christ and Latter Day Saints' campus in Salt Lake City, Utah.

The late 1990s saw QSC introduce more new lines of amplifiers, including the PowerLight-based PLX Series, which was geared toward the retail and musical instruments markets, the CX Series for professional sound contractors, the PTX Series for live and touring users, and the DCA Series for movie theaters. In 1998, the firm brought out its most powerful amplifier to date, the PowerLight 9.0 PFC. This model, which offered 4500 watts per channel in stereo or 9000 watts in monophonic mode, was chosen for use at a variety of high-profile events, including the Super Bowl, the Academy Awards, and the Grammy Awards. The new amp required as much as 40 percent less AC power than comparable models, which helped limit the strain placed on electrical supply systems.

QSC's continuing growth had by now forced it to lease additional manufacturing space off-site, and in September 1998 construction began on a new 81,000-square-foot plant next door to its headquarters, which would triple manufacturing capacity. The facility, which opened in July 1999, had taken two years to design and enabled production of the company's high-end models via a ''build-to-order'' system. Rather than keeping dealer shelves stocked with amplifiers, QSC streamlined its manufacturing process so that it could build an amp within several hours, shipping a freshly-built unit out the same day an order was received. Most of the company's amplifiers were redesigned to use a common ''motherboard,'' and a highly computerized materials handling system automatically routed the specific parts for each item to workers on the factory floor. The end result of the new system was a reduction in labor costs per unit of nearly half, as well as substantial savings on inventory expenses.

Late 1990s and Beyond

In November 1999, QSC arranged to partner with an Asian firm to produce a new low-cost series of amplifiers overseas. The following September, the company signed an agreement to license audio and video interface software and equipment from at the famed 500 mile auto race in May. The system relied entirely on QSC components, including speakers, amplifiers, signal transport, and sound processing equipment. QSC's products were now sold in over 80 countries around the world, and the company employed a staff of 250 to make as many as 1,500 amplifiers per day.

After 35 years in business, QSC Audio Products, Inc. had grown from a small producer of guitar amplifiers into a leading supplier of integrated sound systems for large-scale applications. The company's combination of innovative design, outstanding reliability, and high-tech manufacturing processes had earned it a reputation for quality that continued to attract a steady stream of customers.

Principal Competitors

Peavey Electronics Corp.; Harman International Industries, Inc.; Marshall Amplification PLC.

Digital Harmony Technologies, Inc., and in December 2001 QSC formed a strategic alliance with Audio Composite Engineering, Inc. (ACE) to produce loudspeakers using ACE's patented Composilite material. The new speakers would incorporate QSC amplifier, signal processing, and transport technologies.

In the summer of 2002, the company lost a dispute with Bose Corporation in the U.S. Court of Appeals over QSC's efforts to register PowerWave as a trademark, though the U.S. Trademark Trial and Appeal Board had initially ruled in favor of the firm. Bose had earlier trademarked the name ''Acoustic Wave'' for use on a line of audio equipment and argued that consumers would be confused by QSC's use of the name PowerWave on its products.

The fall of 2002 saw QSC unveil a new corporate logo as part of a complete visual makeover of the company's products. The move reflected the repositioning of the firm from amplifier maker to integrated audio systems supplier. During a transition period, the company would continue to supply its old logo design when requested and also made new logo graphics available for those wishing to upgrade the look of older components.

In 2003, QSC took on yet another high-profile job, installing a new sound system at the Indianapolis Motor Speedway for use

Further Reading

''Bose Wins Appeal on 'Acoustic Wave' Trademark,'' *Audio Week*, July 15, 2002.

Feare, Tom, ''Pump Up the Volume,'' *Modern Materials Handling*, March 31, 2000, p. 55.

Forger, Gary, ''Learning a New Song Without Missing a Beat,'' *Manufacturing Systems*, January 1, 2000, pp. 38–39.

''QSC Audio Goes Global,'' *The Music Trades*, December 1, 1999, p. 48.

''QSC Audio Products,'' *Pro Sound News Europe*, July 1, 1996, p. 45.

''QSC Audio,'' *Pro Sound News Europe*, April 1, 1997, p. 53.

''QSC Roars to Speedway,'' *Systems Contractor News*, April 1, 2003, p. 22.

''QSC Sets New Strategic Direction,'' *Pro Sound News Europe*, February 1, 1996, p. 28.

''QSC's New Factory of the Future,'' *The Music Trades*, February 1, 2001, p. 204.

''QSC to Double Production Capacity,'' *The Music Trades*, January 1, 1999, p. 32.

''Raxxess Expands; QSC Principals Invest to Fund Growth,'' *The Music Trades*, February 1, 1994, p. 76.

Young, Clive, ''QSC Debuts New Look,'' *Systems Contractor News*, October 1, 2002, p. 104.

—Frank Uhle

Red Robin Gourmet Burgers, Inc.

5575 DTC Parkway, Suite 110
Greenwood Village, Colorado 80111
U.S.A.
Telephone: (303) 846-6000
Fax: (303) 846-6094
Web site: http://www.redrobin.com

Public Company
Incorporated: 1969 as Red Robin Enterprises, Inc.
Employees: 9,211
Sales: $274.40 million (2002)
Stock Exchanges: NASDAQ
Ticker Symbol: RRGB
NAIC: 722110 Full-Service Restaurants; 533110 Owners
   and Lessors of Other Non-Financial Assets

Red Robin Gourmet Burgers, Inc. is a casual dining restaurant chain with a menu featuring a variety of burger sandwiches made with beef, chicken, fish, turkey, pot roast, and vegetarian substitutes. Red Robin owns and operates 100 restaurants scattered across 13 states. The company also franchises its concept, maintaining licensing agreements with 98 additional restaurants located in 17 states and in Canada. With a per person average check of $10, Red Robin relies heavily on the sales of its gourmet burgers, which account for 44 percent of the company's food sales. Aside from gourmet burgers, the Red Robin menu includes salads, soups, appetizers, and other entrees such as rice bowls and pasta. With a target market consisting largely of teens and pre-teens, Red Robin restaurants generate an average of $618,000 in annual profits.

Origins

Red Robin's presence in the casual dining industry was established in September 1969 when founder Gerald Kingen opened his first restaurant near the campus of the University of Washington in Seattle. The first restaurant, which offered gourmet hamburgers, found a receptive audience, leading Kingen to expand his concept by developing the format into a chain of restaurants.

Kingen, who named his company Red Robin Enterprises, Inc., opened his own units and, importantly, relied on franchising agreements to augment his own expansion. The decision to franchise the Red Robin concept proved to be a significant one in the development of the chain. Through franchising, and through one franchisee in particular, the chain drew its strength. Kingen's association with the company he founded later ended, but the franchising system endured, creating disciples of the gourmet burger format that extended the physical presence and geographic reach of the enterprise far beyond the efforts of its creator.

Of the numerous franchisees who would ally themselves to the Red Robin concept, none figured more prominently than Mike Snyder. A native of Yakima, Washington, a small city to the east of Seattle, Snyder became a Red Robin franchisee in 1979, when Kingen's ten-year-old company sold the 29-year-old Snyder the rights to open a Red Robin in his hometown. Snyder's first restaurant was a success, leading him to open other Red Robin units and to develop his own small chain of restaurants, which fell under the control of his company, The Snyder Group Company. While Snyder cobbled together his fiefdom of Red Robin units, Kingen pushed forward with his own expansion, fueled by the profits gleaned by Red Robin Enterprises. Several years after Snyder joined the ranks of Red Robin franchisees, Kingen reached a turning point in his career. Snyder, the young disciple, lost the mentor of the chain. New owners arrived, triggering changes that later required Snyder to correct.

By 1985, 16 years of expansion had engendered a chain of 22 Red Robin restaurants, which, two years earlier, had adopted Red Robin International, Inc. as its corporate title, a name change reflective of the company's expansion into Canada. It was at this point that Kingen decided he wanted out. He sold the company-owned restaurants to a Japanese-owned restaurant operator named Skylark Co. Ltd. The large, publicly traded company assumed control over the seven company-owned restaurants and presided over the 15 franchised restaurants. Skylark went to the whip and began expanding aggressively, using its considerable financial resources to inaugurate an era of unprecedented growth. The Red Robin chain grew quickly, but the growth was errant. Under the guidance of Japanese owners, the definitively American dining concept began to suffer from the cultural gap. The chain lost its focus, it lost its consistency as a concept, and became wayward strategically, hobbled by ambitious growth that greatly increased the physical stature of the company but left it rudderless as a niche-oriented casual dining chain. Sales at company-owned restaurants slumped and profits fell. Efforts were made to replace management, but the changes failed to correct the problems. Expansion continued as the situation worsened, characterizing a decade-long period of growth pocked by anemic financial performance. The search for a remedy eventually was found in Yakima. Snyder became Skylark's savior.

The Mike Snyder Era Begins in 1995

By 1995, a decade of control by Skylark had wrought discernible problems. The company-owned restaurants were generating sales nearly one-quarter below the total averaged by the chain's franchised units. The franchisees were recording better financial results than Skylark, and one franchisee in particular outperformed all: Mike Snyder. While the Skylark-owned restaurants floundered, The Snyder Group Company thrived, controlling 14 profitable restaurants. After years of trying to resolve the difficulties plaguing its company-owned units, Skylark turned to Snyder for help. In April 1996, the company appointed Snyder as president and chief operating officer of the beleaguered chain, hoping the successful franchisee could lend his salubrious touch to the company-owned restaurants.

Snyder made an immediate impression. Within a year of his appointment as president and chief operating officer, the company's board of directors selected him as chief executive officer. In May 1997, Snyder was elected as chairman of the board. His rapid rise through the executive ranks was attributable to the positive effect he had on Red Robin's financial health and the performance of the company's stores. Known as an aggressive operator before the perplexed Skylark board turned to him for help, Snyder wasted little time before he applied the management techniques he used at The Snyder Group Company to the whole of Red Robin. He paid close attention to costs and efficiency, succeeding in improving the profitability of the chain store by store. Snyder rallied the workforce, instilling a spirit of achievement and offering financial rewards for performance. Store managers, for example, were given bonuses for reaching sales objectives. A new upper-level management team was recruited and the restaurants' menu was expanded. As part of the program to streamline the operations of the restaurants, 10 of the units were deemed underperformers and shuttered.

Against the backdrop of Snyder's changes, the Red Robin chain improved its performance, taking on the luster exuded formerly only by certain franchised units. In 1995, the year before Snyder moved into corporate headquarters, company-owned restaurants generated average annual sales of $2.1 million. Individual stores averaged profit margins of 13 percent. After five years of Snyder-led management, the company-owned restaurants were generating average annual sales of $3 million. Profit margins swelled to 19.2 percent.

Encouraged by the achievements of the late 1990s, Red Robin made preparations for more aggressive growth during the first years of the new century. As part of the commitment toward growth, the company made several structural changes to better position itself for expansion. In 2000, the company completed a recapitalization and acquired the 14-unit Snyder Group Company, which gave Snyder a significant equity interest in Red Robin. Also, a private equity firm known as Quad-C invested $25 million in Red Robin, becoming the company's largest stockholder. Following these two transactions, the company implemented a system-wide reorganization, forming, in January 2001, Red Robin Gourmet Burgers, Inc. to facilitate the reorganization. In August 2001, the reorganization was completed, a process that entailed all the outstanding capital stock being ceded to Red Robin Gourmet Burgers, Inc. Red Robin Gourmet Burgers, Inc. became the company's new corporate title, although its business was operated primarily through Red Robin International, Inc.

Initial Public Offering in 2002

In its new guise, Red Robin prepared for a major leap in its evolution. In April 2002, the company filed a registration statement with the Securities and Exchange Commission for its initial public offering (IPO) of stock. Management hoped to raise $60 million in the offering, the proceeds from which were earmarked for expansion and debt reduction. The decision to convert to public ownership was indicative of the company's desire to expand, as management announced long-term plans to increase the size of the chain to 850 restaurants. With fewer than 200 restaurants in the months leading up to the IPO, the company would need all the capital it could secure considering that in 2001 it cost $1.7 million to build a new Red Robin unit.

Red Robin's announcement of its plans for an IPO and the revelation of its long-term growth plans caused industry pundits to assess the company's prospects. Some analysts were concerned that the company's' reliance on gourmet burgers as its mainstay product hamstrung its ability to increase profits. By 2002, the price of the company's signature burgers stood at $7, which was considered to be the plateau for burgers. In response, executives at the company's head offices in Greenwood Village, Colorado, pointed to the projected growth of Red Robin's core demographic. Teens and preteens constituted the bulk of the company's customers. Between 2002 and 2005, that sector of the population was expected to grow by two million people, reaching 33.6 million teens and preteens.

Red Robin made its public debut in July 2002. Although the offering was deemed a success by both those within and outside the company, the IPO failed to raise the $60 million hoped for three months earlier. Instead, the stock was sold for $12 per

---

Key Dates:

1969: Gerald Kingen opens the first Red Robin restaurant in Seattle, Washington.
1979: Mike Snyder, a Red Robin franchisee, opens his first restaurant.
1985: Kingen sells his stake in the company to Skylark Co. Ltd.
1996: Snyder is appointed company president.
2002: Red Robin completes its initial public offering of stock.

---

share, giving the company $42 million in net proceeds. To augment this infusion of capital, the company also entered into a three-year, $40 million revolving credit agreement in July 2002. Together, the proceeds from the IPO and the credit agreement gave the company the financial fuel to drive its expansion.

As Red Robin entered its first decade as a publicly traded concern, the company was concentrating on expanding in the Southwest, Midwest, and East Coast. During the year following its IPO, Red Robin achieved strides in extending its presence into these regions. In July 2002, the company opened two new restaurants, one in Fenton, Missouri, and another in Toledo, Ohio, increasing its presence in the Midwest to 27 restaurants. In September 2002, the company bolstered its presence in the Southwest by opening three company-owned restaurants in Arizona, giving it a total of eight corporate and franchise locations in the state. Next, in December 2002, the company returned to the Midwest, adding a new franchise partner, Kansas City, Missouri-base PB&J. Under the terms of the agreement, PB&J vowed to open seven Red Robin restaurants in Kansas by 2007. In October 2002, Red Robin signed another new franchisee, Wimberly, Texas-based Centex Red Bird LLC. Under the terms of the franchise pact with Centex, seven restaurants were slated to be opened in San Antonio and Austin by 2007.

Expansion continued in 2003, building on the 193 units in operation in January 2003. During the first two months of the year, the company opened two new restaurants in Omaha, the first units in Nebraska. In March 2003, when the first unit in San Antonio opened, the company opened a restaurant in Columbia, Maryland, its fifth unit in the state. The month also included the signing of another important franchise partner, Dallas, Texas-based Mandes Restaurant Group, LLC. Under the terms of the agreement with Mandes, eight new restaurants were slated for construction in the greater Dallas metropolitan market by 2008.

Principal Subsidiaries

Red Robin International, Inc.

Principal Competitors

Applebee's International, Inc.; California Pizza Kitchen, Inc.; The Cheesecake Factory Inc.

Further Reading

Berta, Dina, ''Bob Merullo: A Well-Done Menu and Beefed-Up Operations Send Sales Soaring at Red Robin,'' *Nation's Restaurant News,* January 27, 2003, p. 138.

Brand, Rachel, ''Red Robin: IPO, To Go Investors Expected to Give Englewood Chain $60 Million Smile to Expand, Pay Off Debt,'' *Rocky Mountain News,* June 8, 2002, p. 1C.

''Red Robin Gourmet Burgers Inc. Signed Wimberly, Texas-Based Centex Red Bird LLC to a Franchise Pact Calling for Seven Openings in San Antonio and Austin by 2007,'' *Nation's Restaurant News Daily,* October 23, 2002, p. 1.

''Red Robin Inks 7-Unit Pact for Conn., Western Mass.,'' *Nation's Restaurant News,* September 16, 2002, p. 112.

''Red Robin Raises $48M in IPO, Bucks Stock Slide,'' *Nation's Restaurant News,* July 29, 2002, p. 6.

''Taking the IPO Plunge,'' *Restaurants & Institutions,* June 1, 2002, p. 23.

—Jeffrey L. Covell

Samick Musical Instruments Co., Ltd.

424 Chongchon Dong
Pupyoung Gu, Inchon
Korea
Telephone: (+82) 32-453-33557
Fax: (+82) 32-453-33769
Web site: http://www.samick.co.kr

Public Company
Incorporated: 1958 as Samick Piano Co.
Employees: 1,555
Sales: W 171.5 billion ($143 million) (2002 est.)
Stock Exchanges: Seoul
Ticker Symbol: 02450
NAIC. 339992 Musical Instrument Manufacturing

Samick Musical Instruments Co., Ltd. is not only the world's largest manufacturer of grand pianos, it is one of the world's largest producers of musical instruments in general. The Inchon, Korea-based manufacturer produces a full range of pianos, electric and acoustic guitars, basses, banjos, autoharps, harmonicas, and other instruments. Samick produces more than 20,000 pianos per year in its Grand Piano Factory in Korea and in its 430,000-square-meter facility in Bogor, Indonesia. Samick's pianos are sold under the Samick name as well as under a variety of brand names, including Koher & Campbell and Knabe. The company also manufactures pianos for a number of other piano names, including Hyundai and DH Baldwin/ Wurlitzer. With a manufacturing capability of more than one million guitars per year in factories in Korea, Indonesia, China, and the United States, Samick also ranks as the world's leading stringed instrument producer. The company sells its guitars under its own brand names, including Samick, Abilene, Silvertone, and the Greg Bennett Signature Series. Samick also manufactures guitars for many other companies, including Fender and Gibson, at its stringed instrument factory in Korea and its Bogor, Indonesia, plant and operates a dedicated Upright Piano and Piano Action plant, as well as its own sawmill and woodworking facility in Korea, a smaller factory in California, and a plant in Harbin, China that produces wooden guitar and piano parts. Samick also operates its own research and develop-ment facility in Korea. Since the late 1990s, the company had been operating under bankruptcy protection and was acquired by a consortium led by Korean construction company Speco in November 2002. At the beginning of 2003, Samick announced that it had agreed to acquire 60 percent of Germany's Bechstein (which in turn acquired 15 percent of Samick) in a move designed to give Bechstein access to the fast-growing Asian market, while providing Samick access to Bechstein's technical expertise. Samick is led by former Speco president Kim Jong-sup.

Building a Korean Musical Instruments Firm: 1950s–1970s

With its economy and manufacturing capability devastated by the recent war, Korea began seeking to redevelop its manufacturing sector with a launch into new industries. Musical instruments became a target market, and the 1950s saw the emergence of a number of new companies, such as Seoul's Young Chang, founded in 1956. Two years later, there appeared another prominent Korean name in musical instruments, Samick. In that year, Hyo Ick Lee founded the Samick Piano Co. in Inchon. Like other Korean companies of the time, Lee's company initially acted as an importer for other brands—in Samick's case, the famous American piano brand Baldwin.

Samick quickly turned to manufacturing, however. In 1960, the company began building its own pianos, using imported parts, under its own name. The company's initial production remained limited to more easy-to-build upright piano models and in the early years were targeted at the domestic market. Samick and other Korean instrument manufacturers were aided by the country's educational system, which including musical education as part of the required curriculum.

By 1964, Samick's manufacturing confidence and capability had grown sufficiently for the company to make its first moves onto the more lucrative export market. At the same time, the company began to extend its production into other musical instrument categories, notably guitars. The boom in rock and folk music following the success of Elvis Presley, as well as the Beatles and other British Invasion groups, had created a worldwide demand for acoustic and electric guitars. Samick's own

Company Perspectives:

Samick Musical Instruments Co., Ltd. was established in 1958 with the purpose of "enriching human life" through music, the universal language. On the strength of our 43 years of extensive experience in the production of musical instruments, Samick has grown into the largest manufacturer of musical instruments in Korea and the world's largest piano company. We now pledge ourselves to the future, concentrating on the production of the world's finest quality instruments. We intend to make the musical needs of our valued consumers our top priority.

guitar production began in 1965, joining the flood of cheap (and often low-quality) Asian-made guitars that overwhelmed the market in that decade.

Nonetheless, Samick slowly moved toward a higher quality market. The company continued to improve its piano manufacturing techniques, and in 1970 its production abilities had developed sufficiently for it to launch its first grand pianos. At the same time, the company began to step up the quality of its guitar production. As part of that effort, Samick formed a joint venture with Texas-based International Music Company (also known as the Hondo Guitar Company). The new company introduced modern U.S. production methods to the Korean market, while taking advantage of the low-wage level in Korea to offer inexpensive, entry-level guitars.

Hondo initially produced a line of classical and folk guitars before adding its first electric guitars in 1972. By 1974, the company's electric guitars had achieved a certain level of quality, and Hondo became one of the largest-selling entry-level brands by the mid-1970s. Hondo added a variety of instruments to its line during the 1970s, including banjos, while continuing to make product improvements. By the end of that decade, Hondo was selling nearly 800,000 instruments per year before fading out in the 1980s.

Samick's thrust remained with its own brand, which was extended with the introduction of a line of harmonicas in 1971. In 1973, in recognition of the growing diversity of its musical instruments range, the company changed its name to Samick Musical Instruments Mfg. Co. Throughout the decade, Samick continued to modify its manufacturing methods in order to enhance product quality, and by the end of the 1970s the company had already become a major exporter of grand pianos at a time when the market for the larger pianos was growing steadily.

Samick continued to target the export market, especially the United States, where it opened a branch office in 1978. The lower production costs of Korean-made instruments made them attractive entry-level pianos, and a number of brands began contracting Samick to build their lower priced models. Such was the case with the Schumann piano brand, based in the United States, for which Samick produced pianos beginning in 1979.

By the late 1970s, the Korean musical instrument industry had largely caught up to its primary Japanese competitors in terms of quality, while at the same time retaining Korea's lower

production costs. Samick, too, had joined in the bid for higher quality by constructing new, automated production facilities that reduced the need for a large pool of expensively trained employees and at the same time enabled it to increase and maintain quality standards. The company opened its new guitar factory in 1979; the following year, it automated both its stringed instruments facility and its upright piano plant. That year, also, Samick opened a branch office in Germany, in order to introduce its brand to the European market. In 1982, the company established a full U.S. subsidiary, Samick Music Corporation.

Quality Growth in the 1980s

Throughout its more than twenty years in business, Samick had maintained close ties with Baldwin. In 1982, the two companies formed a joint-venture, Korean-American Musical Instruments Co. That company started up production in 1983, becoming the manufacturer behind Baldwin's entry-level Wurlitzer brand, as well as another brand, DH Baldwin.

That year also marked a new phase in Samick's own piano production. In March 1983, the company signed on Klaus Fenner, one of the world's most renowned piano designers, to provide design and technical assistance for Samick's grand piano production. By October of that year, Samick had completed a new dedicated grand piano factory, and in 1984 the company debuted its first Fenner-designed piano. That design won the prestigious Gold Prize award from the French piano specialist magazine *Diapason* in 1985.

Samick's quest for quality was to continue throughout the 1980s and was given a boost by the founding of the company's own research and development center, the Samick Musical Instruments Development Institute, in 1987. A major innovation introduced by the institute was a safety closing system for grand piano lids. The company also added a new piano line, that of digital pianos. In 1988, the company took a new step forward when it went public. That year it also acquired the prestigious Kohler & Campbell brand. Founded in New York in 1896, Kohler & Campbell was one of the largest piano companies in the United States during its heyday but had gone out of business in 1985. The addition of the Kohler & Campbell brand gave Samick an entry into the high-end grand piano market. The company then opened a U.S. production facility in California in 1989 for the Samick, Kohler & Campbell, and other piano brands.

Meanwhile, Samick's guitar and other stringed instruments had continued to make dramatic quality advancements, encouraging the shift of worldwide instrument production, and particularly of guitars, to Korea. The company became a major manufacturer for a number of well-known brands, including low-end models for the famed Fender and Gibson brands. Supporting Samick's growth was an expansion of its string instrument facility, as well as continued automation upgrades at its main piano and warehousing facilities.

By the end of the 1980s, Samick, which entered the export piano market under a variety of brand names, began to shift its emphasis to its own name as it established a reputation for affordable quality. By the beginning of the 1990s, Samick had already become one of the world's leading manufacturers of

Key Dates:

1958: Hyo Ick Lee founds Samick Piano Co. as an importer of Baldwin pianos for the Korean market.

1960: Samick begins production of upright pianos using imported parts.

1965: Samick begins production of acoustic guitars as part of its diversification into the broader musical instruments market.

1978: A branch office in Los Angeles is opened.

1979: Samick opens an automated guitar-production facility.

1982: The company establishes a U.S. subsidiary and launches Korean-American Musical Instruments Co joint-venture with Baldwin Piano & Organ Co.

1987: Samick Musical Instrument Development Institute is formed as a part of a research and development investment campaign; the company begins production of digital pianos.

1988: Samick goes public, listing on Seoul stock exchange, and acquires Kohler & Campbell piano brand.

1996: The company declares bankruptcy and begins to sell-off its diversified operations to refocus on musical instruments.

2000: Samick signs an original equipment manufacturer (OEM) agreement with Baldwin and launches a Fenner-designed line of pianos.

2002: Samick emerges from bankruptcy, being acquired by Korean construction group Speco.

2003: A high-end line of pianos is launched.

pianos, with exports topping $100 million, and the Samick brand itself had an established reputation.

Struggle and Recovery in the 1990s and Beyond

The rising standard of living in Korea led to increased wage and production costs, and the musical instrument industry began to look to new, lower-cost markets. Samick joined that trend, launching a wood processing subsidiary in Harbin, China, in 1990. In 1992, Samick took a step further, with the opening of a $30 million, 430,000-square-meter plant in Bogor, Indonesia. The new subsidiary, PT Samick Indonesia, began operation in 1993.

The Indonesian subsidiary gradually took over production of the company's entry-level instruments, beginning with acoustic guitars in 1993. By 1995, the facility had gained sufficient expertise to begin production of electric guitars as well, followed by upright pianos in 1996 and grand piano production in 1998. By the beginning of the new century, the Bogor site was producing some 15,000 pianos and 500,000 guitars each year, while Samick focused its Korean manufacturing capacity on higher end products. These, however, often featured wooden components produced by the Bogor plant.

By the end of 1995, Samick had claimed the number one spot for sales of grand pianos in the world, with more than 18,000 sold that year. Yet 1996 nearly spelled the end of the company when it was forced to declare bankruptcy amid the

economic turmoil in Korea and the rest of the Asian region. While the company's musical instruments business remained profitable, Samick had been hit hard by an attempt to diversify during the 1980s.

That effort had begun in 1986 with the formation of Samick Products Co. and had led the company into such areas as furniture, computer equipment, heavy industrial equipment, caster manufacturing and distribution, and even deep-sea fishing, complete with a fleet of tuna boats. Samick had hoped that the broader manufacturing base would give a stronger financial foundation for its musical instruments sales. Instead, the company found itself unable to turn a profit in most of its new ventures, winding up with a debt load as high as $400 million. In 1996, after defaulting on promissory notes of nearly W 13 billion ($10 million), Samick declared bankruptcy.

Samick's prominence as a musical instrument maker, and the division's relative health and strong growth, saved the company from going under. Its new administrators agreed to a restructuring in which Samick shed all of its money-losing businesses and regrouped around its musical products operations. By 1998, the company had succeeded in shedding nearly all of its failed businesses (a process completed in 2001) and most of its debt. The slimmed-down company was also able to report profits that year.

Samick remained under court protection into the next decade as it refocused on expanding its musical instruments sales. The company received a boost in 2000 with a $50 million original equipment manufacturer (OEM) contract to supply grand pianos to Baldwin, which itself had filed for bankruptcy the year before. The relationship between the two companies was to grow even stronger the following year when the former head of Samick's U.S. operation joined Baldwin as its new CEO. The year 2000 also marked the debut of the new and well-received "World" piano line designed by Klaus Fenner. Samick gained another boost when it acquired the rights to the highly regarded Knabe brand name as well. The company also launched a new "silent" piano system that year.

Samick at last found new owners in September 2002 when a consortium led by Korean construction company Speco purchased it for W 125 billion ($10 million) and retired nearly all of its remaining debt. Former Speco president Kim Jong-sup was named chairman of Samick. "You can consider this a brand new start for the company," Jong-sup told the *Korea Herald*. "Under brand new management, we will aim to become a top piano brand in the world not too far in the future."

Samick's new financial backing quickly produced results. In December 2002, the company announced that it had acquired 60 percent of Germany's Bechstein, a company which had been in business since 1853 and which had provided pianos for the likes of Franz Liszt and Claude Debussy. The deal was expected to give Samick access to Bechstein's technical expertise, while Bechstein, having acquired 15 percent of Samick as part of the deal, gained an entry into the fast-growing Asian market.

By April 2003, Samick appeared to have overcome its troubles. With revenue growth of nearly 30 percent, it pushed past the $200 million mark. With the launch of a new line of high-end Knabe-branded pianos, Samick was prepared to claim a place among the world's leading quality piano makers in the new century.

Principal Subsidiaries

HARBIN Samick Corp. (China); P.T. Samick Indonesia; Samick Europe GmbH. (Germany); Samick Japan; Samick Music Corp. (USA).

Principal Competitors

Kawai Musical Instruments Manufacturing Company Ltd.; Suzuki Metal Industry Company Ltd.; Peavey Electronics Corp.; Yamaha Corporation of America; Young Chang Akki Company Ltd.; Baldwin Piano and Organ Co.; Fender Musical Instruments Company; Gibson Guitar Corp.

Further Reading

Len, Samuel "The Beat Goes on at Samick," *The Korea Herald*, September 15, 1998.

Mi-hui, Kim, "Samick Plays New Tune in Global Piano Market with Investment," *The Korea Herald*, September 18, 2002.

"Number 1 in Grands," *Music Trades*, February 1996, p. 130.

"Samick Opens Indonesian Guitar Plant," *Music Trades*, February 1994, p. 143.

"Samick Realigns Top Management," *Music Trades*, October 2002, p. 26.

"The Top Growth Stories of 2002: Samick Music Corp. +29.20%," *Music Trades*, April 2003, p. 126.

Wassener, Bettina, "Bechstein Aims at Asian Market," *The Financial Times*, December 19, 2002, p. 26.

—M.L. Cohen

Sankyo Company, Ltd.

3-5-1, Nihonbashi Hon-cho
Chuo-ku, Tokyo 103-8426
Japan
Telephone: (03) 5255-7111
Fax: (03) 5255-7035
Web site: http://www.sankyo.co.jp

Public Company
Incorporated: 1913
Employees: 6,515
Sales: ¥548.9 billion ($4.1 billion) (2002)
Stock Exchanges: Tokyo
Ticker Symbol: 4501
NAIC: 325412 Pharmaceutical Preparation Manufacturing

As Japan's second largest pharmaceuticals company, Sankyo Company, Ltd. manufactures and markets a wide range of pharmaceuticals, medical devices and diagnostics, agrochemicals, food, cosmetics, veterinary drugs, and fine chemicals. The company spends heavily on research and development and has laboratories throughout the United States, Europe, and South America. Expanding globally and developing new drugs—especially those related to cardiovascular diseases—remain at the forefront of Sankyo's strategy.

Company Origins

While living in the United States Dr. Jokichi Takamine discovered a digestive enzyme and called the product Taka-Diastase. In order to import and sell the digestant in Japan, a company under the name of Sankyo Shoten was established in 1899. Contracting a sales agreement with Parke, Davis & Company, a U.S. drug firm, the product was manufactured in the United States, imported to Japan, and then distributed by Sankyo Shoten. Three years later, in 1905, the company began manufacturing Taka-Diastase in Japan. To augment production Sankyo's first plant was constructed in Shinagawa, Tokyo in 1908.

Other items were soon added to the product line. Dr. Umetaro Suzuki's vitamin B1 discovery in 1910 was marketed under the name Oryzanin. A cough depressant by the name of Brocin and a disinfectant called oxyfull were added to Sankyo's product line in the early 1900s. By 1913 the growing business was reorganized as a joint stock company and incorporated as the Sankyo Company, Limited. Dr. Takamine assumed the title of president. Later achievements included the production of salicylic acid, used as a mild antiseptic or pain reliever, and Dr. Hata's development of Arsaminol, an arsphenamine used as a treatment for syphilis and other infections.

In the 1920s production expanded into new areas. The Wakodo Company, established as a subsidiary, became an industry leader in infant care products. During this period Sankyo also initiated the research into and production of agricultural chemicals and enzymatics. Even the production of yeast for bakers was incorporated as a product item in 1932.

Postwar Growth

The Japanese pharmaceutical industry experienced unprecedented growth in the postwar years due to a new sense of health consciousness. In particular, worldwide breakthrough discoveries in medicine resulted in antibiotics amounting to more than 10 percent of Japan's total pharmaceutical production by 1963. Japanese pharmaceutical companies, however, did not actually participate in these discoveries; meaningful patent protection laws were significantly absent, making innovation subject to pirating. For this reason companies, allotting negligible amounts of money for research and development, depended on their foreign counterparts for innovative drugs. Industry developments eventually led to foreign companies seeking out Japan's expertise in antibiotics; in the interim, however, Sankyo played a major role in importing antibiotics.

Through a new licensing agreement with Parke, Davis & Company, Sankyo imported Chloromycetin, the tradename for antibiotic chloramphenicol. By 1950 Sankyo gained the necessary technical expertise from its foreign licensor to begin manufacturing Chloromycetin domestically. By 1966 this drug accounted for 80 percent of Sankyo's sales in antibiotics. As Japan's sole manufacturer of this popular pharmaceutical, Sankyo built a vast reserve of cash earned on large profits.

The establishment of the National Health Insurance system in the 1960s was not only important to Sankyo, but to the Japanese pharmaceutical industry at large. Under the new system patients were required to pay a fraction of prescription fees while the government assumed the majority of costs. Moreover, the system encouraged the generous prescription of medications since doctors profited from the difference between the official reimbursement price set by the Ministry of Health and the actual price for which the drugs were purchased. For this reason, the drug industry became one of Japan's most profitable industries. By 1961 the industry's annual growth rate reached 21 percent.

Sankyo benefited from these changes. Profits increased nearly 18 percent in 1963 due to the increase in sales of external medicines, food products, central nervous system drugs, and farm chemicals. Biotamin, a newly developed vitamin B1, recorded a monthly average sale of ¥150 million, making the sale of antibiotics and vitamins nearly half Sankyo's annual sales. At this time, the company's food product line included a non-caloric synthetic sweetener and a fruit juice clarification enzyme. Sankyo's agricultural chemical division produced more products than any other pharmaceutical company in Japan. Tachigaren, a soil fungicide and seed disinfectant developed by Sankyo, was awarded the Okochi Prize in 1969.

Sankyo's entry into foreign markets paralleled its growth in business. Joint ventures with overseas companies grew to include projects with AKZO, a pharmaceutical company in Holland; Miles Laboratories and Air Products, two companies in the United States; and pharmaceutical companies in Taiwan and India. Biotamin was well received on foreign markets and Cytochrome-C (sometimes spelled Titochrome C or Tytochrome C), an innovative new drug for the treatment of high blood pressure, was scheduled to be marketed abroad. This innovation marked one of Sankyo's first major discoveries that did not employ technical assistance from foreign companies.

The sale of Biotamin, Chloromycetin, and the newly developed Cytochrome now accounted for Sankyo's three major products. Biotamin became a popular item in overseas markets and Sankyo provided manufacturing knowledge to companies in France and Portugal. Although the basic patent right for Chloromycetin was scheduled to expire in 1966, Sankyo's market preeminence through affiliated patents mitigated the effects of losing exclusive marketing rights to this drug.

To facilitate growth two new plants were scheduled for construction. The Fukuroi site was chosen for the manufacture of soft drinks and seasonings and the Hiratsuka plant would house the manufacture of pharmaceuticals. Due to the fact that the main plant at Shinagawa was operating at capacity, the Hiratsuka site was designated the new main plant.

New Laws Encourage Development and Investment: 1970s–80s

Further changes in the pharmaceutical industry resulted in Japanese companies significantly increasing their research and development expenditures. The enactment of the 1976 patent protection laws marked an important date for the industry. Rather than depending on their foreign counterparts to develop drugs, Japanese pharmaceutical companies could invest in research without fear of pirating. Furthermore, an altered pricing system, placing newly developed drugs at a premium, suddenly made innovative drug research a highly lucrative business. The products of this research not only served to benefit the quality of domestic healthcare, but also began reversing the flow of technology from West to East.

Sankyo actively participated in this new development. During the 1970s Sankyo took a leading role in the development and production of drugs for the nervous system. The tranquilizer Serenal was developed with the intention of serving a growing number of people who experienced the stressful demands of modern lifestyles. The company submitted patent applications for the manufacture of the tranquilizer in more than 40 countries. Furthermore, upon the completion of the Hiratsuka plant, the company allotted funds to significantly increase research and development expenditures. Meanwhile, several other promising drugs existed in the development stage.

Prior to this new emphasis on research and development, a vast trade deficit existed between the large number of imported pharmaceuticals and the comparatively smaller number of drugs exported. Even as late as 1982 almost 80 percent of the drugs sold in Japan continued to be manufactured abroad or domestically with technology developed overseas. Recognizing the potential in developing a drug export trade, the government implemented further industry incentives with the 1980 Pharmaceutical Affairs Act of 1980. This act extended from three to six the number of years a company is ensured exclusive licensing rights with foreign companies. The new atmosphere encouraging industry export, coupled with the rising cost of research and development, compelled pharmaceutical companies to aggressively pursue foreign markets. Since millions of dollars were now spent on the development of a single drug, companies looked to foreign licensing as an attractive means of recovering investments in research and development.

Sankyo strengthened its long involvement with foreign markets during this period. In addition to the overseas introduction of Serenal, a joint venture in India was established. Uni-Sankyo supplied bulk medicine to the Indian market and also exported products to Asia and Africa. By 1986 Sankyo's licensing program and joint ventures grew to include agreements with Sandoz in Switzerland, Glaxo Holdings in the United Kingdom, and Du Pont, Squibb, and Upjohn in the United States. In a move to heighten the company's presence in the United States, Sankyo opened an office in New York.

Of the many drugs developed in Japan and actively pursued by foreign companies, a new family of highly effective third-generation antibiotics represented the drugs most in demand. Sankyo participated in the development and distribution of these medicines through the sale of Cefmetazon, a cephamycin-allied antibiotic, that was sold in the United States through a license agreement with Upjohn. Of similar technological importance was Sankyo's involvement in the development of drugs called enzyme inhibitors. By discovering the inhibitor for the enzyme instrumental in the synthesis of cholesterol, Sankyo developed a drug to inhibit heart disease, Mevalotin. This new drug was launched overseas in 1989 and by 1991 was responsible for ¥83 billion in sales.

Other lucrative products developed or marketed by Sankyo included an anticancer agent introduced in 1984. Sankyo acquired the rights to sell this agent, called Kurestin, which was developed by the Kureha Chemical Industry. In addition, Captoril, an anti-hypertensive drug, was also a source of income.

As the company expanded its business through innovation and overseas market penetration, the pharmaceutical industry underwent major changes. The per-capita drug bill by 1983 reached $95. To combat accusations of excessive profiting and to reduce the burden of national expenditures, official drug prices were reduced by more than 50 percent and patients were required for the first time to pay 10 percent of examination costs. As a result, nationwide drug production deceased for the first time since World War II and profits were negligible. Sankyo's net profits in relation to sales dropped from 3.9 percent in 1982 to 3.64 percent in 1983. Research and development expenditures, nevertheless, continued to increase. For this reason, by 1985 profits did not increase from the previous year despite the successful market introduction of Kurestin and a new anti-ulcer agent. Despite the changing configuration of the National Health Insurance system, Sankyo continued to be influential in both domestic and foreign markets and its earnings began to steadily increase. During 1991, profits increased by 30 percent over the previous year.

Overcoming Hardships: 1990s and Beyond

During the 1990s Sankyo placed increased importance on developing globally. The firm acquired an interest in Germany-based Luitpold-Werk GmbH & Co., which eventually became known as subsidiary Sankyo Pharma GmbH. In 1996, the company teamed up with Warner-Lambert Co. to create Sankyo Parke Davis, a U.S. company set up to market the diabetes drug Troglitazone—known as Rezulin in the United States—and cardiovascular agent Accupri. Sankyo eyed the venture as crucial to its global strategy and expected sales of Troglitazone, a treatment for diabetes, to be strong in both the United States and Europe. While the drug initially experienced stellar success, disaster loomed around the corner. Reports of possible toxic, and even deadly, side effects surfaced, resulting in a slew of lawsuits against the companies responsible for marketing the drug. By 2000, it had been pulled from the European, U.S., and Japanese markets. As a result, Sankyo's share price plummeted and the industry began to speculate that Sankyo could become a target for a hostile takeover.

To make matters worse, a series of patents related to Mevalotin were due to expire in 2002. The drug, responsible for nearly 40 percent of domestic pharmaceutical sales and much of the company's growth during the 1990s, was already seeing increased competition in the United States and, in 1999, shipments of the drug decreased for the first time. Domestic drug prices also were falling and the firm's product pipeline was considered lackluster by industry standards, leaving Sankyo's sales and profits in a vulnerable position. Then in 2000, the company's management took a blow when longtime chairman Yoshibumi Kawamura and his son Yoshinori resigned their posts due to a harassment scandal involving the latter.

With new blood at the helm—President Tetsuo Takato—Sankyo launched a turnaround effort. In order to bolster its presence in the United States, the firm acquired full ownership of Sankyo Parke Davis in 2001. That year it developed a new strategy focused on repositioning its businesses, creating new drugs, revamping its business processes, increasing its domestic market share, and strengthening its international sales force. As part of this new approach, the firm set plans in motion to spin off its agrochemicals and food additive business in 2003 in order to focus on pharmaceuticals. The company also announced a divestiture plan to sell off nonprofitable assets. Anti-hypertensive medication Olmesartan made its U.S. debut in 2002 under the name Benicar. This was the first drug over which Sankyo had independent control from start to finish and was considered a cornerstone in the company's globalization process.

Sankyo continued to face distinct challenges, however, as it worked to implement its strategy. New laws were encouraging foreign competition and threatened to weaken the company's domestic market share. The reforms were expected to continue through 2005, making it easier for overseas companies to sell drugs in Japan. "We are at the bottom now. If we can ride out our current problems, we should overtake market leader Takeda Chemicals Industries," President Takato optimistically claimed in a March 2003 *Nikkei Weekly* article. Indeed, only time would tell if Sankyo would emerge independently victorious or succumb to the impending industry shakeout.

Principal Subsidiaries

Nippon Nyukazai Co. Ltd.; Nippon Daiya Valve Co. Ltd.; Sankyo Chemical Industries Ltd.; Kyushu Sankyo Co. Ltd.;

Meguro Chemical Industry Co. Ltd.; Sankyo Grundstucks GmbH; Sankyo Trading Co. Ltd.; Sankyo Pharma GmbH; Luitpold Pharmaceuticals Inc.; Sino-Japan Chemical Co. Ltd. (52%); Sankyo Pharma Inc. (U.S.A.); F.P. Processing Co. Ltd.; Institute of Science and Technology Inc.; Sankyo Yell Yakuhin Co. Ltd.

Principal Competitors

Daiichi Pharmaceutical Co. Ltd.; Shionogi & Co. Ltd.; Takeda Chemical Industries Ltd.

Further Reading

Ando, Kiyoshi, "Sankyo Swallows Reform Medicine," *Nikkei Weekly,* March 24, 2003.

"A Dose of Reform for Japan's Drugmakers," *Business Week,* May 19, 2003.

Iida, Mihoko, "Diabetes Drug to Spearhead Sankyo Expansion Abroad," *Nikkei Weekly,* March 24, 1997, p. 12.

Marrow, David J., "Warner-Lambert Shares Plunge on Glaxo Move," *New York Times,* December 2, 1997, p. D1.

"Sankyo Ends Family Dominance," *Nikkei Weekly,* July 17, 2000.

"Sankyo Expects New Drugs to Fortify Bottom Line," *Nikkei Weekly,* May 23, 1992, p. 18.

"Sankyo Falls After Withdrawing Drug," *Financial Times London,* March 23, 2000, p. 41.

"Sankyo to Dispose of All Loss Making Units," *Pharma Marketletter,* March 24, 2003.

—update: Christina M. Stansell

SCANA Corporation

1426 Main Street
Columbia, South Carolina 29201-2845
U.S.A.
Telephone: (803) 217-9000
Toll Free: (800) 763-5891
Fax: (803) 217-8119
Web site: http://www.scana.com

Public Company
Incorporated: 1984
Employees: 5,369
Sales: $2.95 billion (2002)
Stock Exchanges: New York
Ticker Symbol: SCG
NAIC: 221121 Electric Bulk Power Transmission and
Control; 221122 Electric Power Distribution; 221210
Natural Gas Distribution; 234920 Power and
Communication Transmission Line Construction;
513310 Wired Telecommunications Carriers; 513332
Cellular and Other Wireless Telecommunications;
551114 Corporate, Subsidiary, and Regional
Managing Offices

SCANA Corporation is a diversified holding company head-quartered in Columbia, South Carolina. The company's core business is focused on the production, distribution, and sale of electricity and natural gas. Through its subsidiaries, SCANA provides services to more than one million natural gas customers in three southeastern states, in addition to providing electricity to over 550,000 customers in South Carolina. Following the deregulation of the Georgia natural gas industry in the late 1990s, SCANA quickly expanded into the promising new market, gaining nearly 500,000 new customers by the early 21st century. Along with its numerous energy holdings, SCANA operates an extensive telecommunications network through its subsidiary SCANA Communications.

The Emergence of Electric and Natural Gas Power in the 19th Century

Although SCANA was incorporated as recently as 1984, its history dates back to the establishment of the Charleston Gas Light Company in 1846, long before the appearance of the first light bulb or the commercial use of electricity. Lamps lighted by manufactured gas were the sleek and modern means of illumination, thanks to the inventor of manufactured glass, 17th-century Belgian chemist Jan Baptista van Helmont, and to William Murdock, a British engineer who invented gas lighting in 1802. Free enterprise and the spirit of invention were alive in South Carolina. In the 1840s gas lamps were aglow in the graceful streets of Charleston as the result of the establishment in 1846 of the Charleston Gas Light Company by a group of progressive businessmen. The year 1846 marked economic expansion everywhere; it was also the year that war began with Mexico, leading to the acquisition of California and most of the Southwest. The new company was also expanding: business blossomed, and street lighting in the beautiful southern port constantly improved.

The beginning of the Civil War in 1861, only 15 years after the establishment of the Charleston Gas Light Company, proved to be a severe blow to the company, mostly because of the Union blockade of Charleston's harbor, which meant a loss of raw materials. Despite these and other hardships, Charleston's thoroughfares continued to be lighted throughout the war years, that is, when raging city fires or federal bombardments did not interrupt service. The worst fire in Charleston's history took place in the first year of the war, destroying at least 500 private homes and numerous public buildings and churches in the very heart of the city and wiping out a high percentage of the company's customers. The quality of street lighting during this time deteriorated substantially. With no access to raw materials such as coal and oil, the company struggled to extract gas from local pine wood, which produced dim lighting for gas lamps. With the city occupied by the Union Army in 1864, Charlestonians were alarmed to see Union air balloons, filled with Charleston gas, looming in the sky for observation purposes. The end of the war brought little relief to the beleaguered

Company Perspectives:

SCANA is a group of southeastern focused companies with knowledge and experience in the energy industry. We are focused on providing quality energy solutions cost effectively to retail customers. This is achieved by the following: Building on demonstrated strengths in operational effectiveness and customer service; Being positioned as experts in residential and commercial markets; Leveraging core competencies to maximize efficiencies and profits; Pursuing growth through geographic, market and product expansions.

Charleston Gas Light Company, which for nearly two years was taken over by the federal government. Stockholders regained control of the company in 1866.

Columbia, the state's capital and home of the University of South Carolina, was even worse off than Charleston during the war. Gas illumination had arrived somewhat later in Columbia than in Charleston since the Columbia Gas Light Company had been established in 1852, six years after its counterpart, the Charleston Gas Light Company. Despite the relatively late start, the company boomed until the onset of the Civil War, whose effects were more severe in Columbia than in Charleston because of an invasion by General Sherman's troops and a terrible fire that erupted shortly after the Union army's occupation, reducing the new company to cinder and ashes.

Nonetheless, despite the deprivations of the postwar years and occupation by federal troops, population growth and the demand for lighting and gas surged, resurrecting the Columbia Gas Light Company and instilling new vigor in its Charleston counterpart. By 1871, the Columbia Gas Light Company had rebounded to the extent that high quality manufactured gas was efficiently carried through almost ten miles of mains. Eight years later, the still unknown inventor Thomas Edison created the first electric light bulb, inaugurating the revolutionary age of electricity.

Charleston was not far behind in acquiring the newfangled bulbs. By 1886 a strong competitor of the Charleston Gas Light Company emerged—the Charleston Electric Light Company. Soon the old gave way to the new, demand for electricity kept mounting, and after several mergers a newly reconstituted electric company arose in 1897 under the name Charleston Consolidated Railway, Gas and Electric Company. The company's name meant precisely what it implied: all gas and electric services in the greater Charleston area, including the city's public trolley system, would be provided by one company. The same consolidation had occurred in Columbia in 1892, when the Columbia Electric Street Railway, Light and Power Company emerged.

Mergers, Profits, and Regulation: 1900–45

With the advent of gadgets and home appliances powered by electric current still some years in the future, utility companies in the late 19th and early 20th centuries still had to devise inducements for people to use electricity. Profits for utility companies in those days were greatest from the electric trolley car systems; therefore, customers were encouraged to ride the trolleys as often as possible. Utility companies such as Charles-

ton Consolidated and Columbia Consolidated built dance halls, parks, even zoos, all within a stone's throw of the nearest trolley. In a state blessed with mile after mile of beautiful beaches, rail cars in South Carolina did a brisk business carrying summer crowds to the coast, with trolleys shuttling them to the nearest beach. In 1894 the first electrified textile mill in the world opened for business in Columbia, and 20 years later, a hydroelectric generating plant was built north of Columbia, at Parr Shoals. Gas manufacture was by no means dead, despite electricity being the preferred means of street and home lighting. The introduction and increasing popularity of gas stoves for cooking prompted a dramatic 160 percent increase in gas revenues for Charleston Consolidated between 1910 and 1925. Just before the United States entered World War I, Charleston boasted at least 5,000 gas ranges.

The United States' entry in World War I in April 1917 strained utility services to the limit, and drained them of ablebodied workers as well. With the timely addition of extra boilers to the Charlotte Street generating plant in Charleston, the amount of electricity produced in that city at least doubled. The strains of wartime production were exacerbated by the dire effects of a worldwide influenza epidemic that, by the time it had worn itself out in 1920, had taken the lives of more victims than the war. At least one-third of Charleston Consolidated's employees took ill, and recovery for the company was slow.

Postwar population growth and the popularity of electric home appliances such as irons, vacuum cleaners, and electric toasters put increasing demands on utility companies. Meanwhile the profitability of the trolley systems declined drastically in both Charleston and Columbia, undoubtedly because of the mass production of family cars and cheap oil prices. In fact, the last trolley car was replaced by bus systems in 1936.

The Roaring Twenties set some milestones for utility companies. In 1925 the ownership of Columbia Railroad, Gas and Electric Company fell to the Broad River Power Company, which was organized and owned by the New York firm of W.S. Barstow & Company. One year later, the South Carolina Power Company, in a merger of five Charleston utility companies that included the old Charleston Consolidated Railway, Gas and Electric Company, arose as a single powerful entity with a far reaching goal—rural electrification. By 1940 the South Carolina Power Company served 146 towns and villages, or 8,750 square miles. A similar expansion was undertaken in and around Columbia (the Midlands) by the Broad River Power Company, which changed its name in 1937 to South Carolina Electric & Gas Company.

These were heady years of growth and profit. By 1930 construction in South Carolina ended on the largest earthen dam in the world, sitting astride the 50,000-acre artificial Lake Murray that would provide generating power for the Saluda River Hydroelectric Plant; 5,000 residents in the area had to be relocated to make way for the gargantuan project.

By the time the plant went into operation, the effects of the 1929 stock market crash had reverberated throughout the economy, halting the booming expansion and profits of utility companies. A particular threat was the looming power of government, as embodied in the Public Utility Holding Company Act

| **Key Dates:** |

1846: Charleston Gas Light Company is founded.
1852: Columbia Gas Light Company is founded.
1892: Columbia Electric Street Railway, Light and Power Company is formed.
1897: Charleston Consolidated Railway, Gas and Electric Company is formed.
1925: Broad River Power Company acquires Columbia Railroad, Gas and Electric Company.
1937: Broad River Power Company becomes South Carolina Electric and Gas Company (SCE&G).
1950: SCE&G merges with South Carolina Power Company.
1984: South Carolina Electric and Gas Company merges with Carolina Energies, Inc. to form SCANA Corporation.
1997: SCANA sells subsidiary SCANA Petroleum Resources to Kelley Oil.
1998: SCANA begins marketing natural gas to customers in Atlanta, Georgia.

of 1935, which led to the creation of the South Carolina Public Service Authority. This public regulatory agency, established by the South Carolina legislature, soon began to acquire ailing or weak utility companies, which would have bloated the federal agency at the expense of private ownership. On the eve of World War II, the South Carolina Supreme Court put an end to the agency's power of acquisition.

During World War II the federal government encouraged voluntary energy conservation, but the South Carolina Power Company and the SCE&G did not decrease gas and electric services. Again the utility companies temporarily lost much of their workforce, hiring women as replacements for men serving in the armed forces. With the shortage of raw materials, private automobile use declined, and the bus transportation system in both Charleston and Columbia did a profitable business.

Unprecedented Expansion During the Postwar Boom: 1945–90

Compared to the boom in electric use following World War I, what followed World War II was a virtual explosion. So insatiable was the demand for electricity and electric appliances (the latter unobtainable during the war) that to meet these and other future needs, the South Carolina Power Company and SCE&G undertook a merger in 1950. The new corporation retained the name of South Carolina Electric & Gas Company.

Exciting new developments in the 1950s and 1960s held much growth and profit potential. These included the discovery of immense deposits of natural gas in Louisiana, Texas, and Mississippi, resulting in full conversion to natural gas in Columbia and Charleston by 1954, and the use of nuclear power to generate electricity, the demand for which was expected to rise continually. Gas revenues rose rapidly from $2.3 million to $13 million in the decade between 1953 and 1963.

Construction began in 1973 on SCE&G's most costly project to date: its first nuclear power facility (operated by SCE&G and two-thirds owned by the company) and hydroelectric plant facil-

ity on a 7,000-acre artificial lake, close to the original atomic power facility. Named after the then-president and chief executive officer of SCE&G, Vergil C. Summer, it was not to be completed until 1984, at a cost of $1.3 billion. Obstacles repeatedly delayed its completion, not the least of which was the skyrocketing price of energy resulting from the Arab oil embargo of the early 1970s, and the Three Mile Island nuclear power plant disaster in 1979. Leadership in this Herculean project fell to SCE&G President and Chief Executive Officer Arthur Williams, who retired before its completion. However, by 1990 the Summer Station was rated by the Nuclear Regulatory Commission as one of the five safest in the United States.

In 1984 SCE&G merged with Carolina Energies, Inc. (CEI), a holding company with six subsidiaries, to form SCANA Corporation. Within a few years SCANA comprised 11 subsidiaries, its latest acquisition being the Peoples Natural Gas Company of South Carolina. Three-quarters of its revenue was still derived from electricity production and service, while gas sales made up the remainder. SCE&G continued to be the largest component of SCANA.

In 1989 SCE&G faced the biggest challenge in its history: Hurricane Hugo, which left 300,000 customers without power. Well prepared for the disaster, SCE&G had enough spare parts and extra vehicles to enable its crews to work day and night to restore service. Over a two-week period employees of SCE&G, including workers borrowed by the company from 48 different utility companies in 15 different states, installed 731,000 new fuses and replaced more than ten million feet of wire. The following year the utility industry awarded SCE&G employees its most prestigious honor, the Edison Award, in recognition of their services.

During this period SCANA adopted an official environmental code, through which it began recycling three-quarters of the ash waste from its generators, as well as tons of office paper, and printing its annual reports on recyclable paper. Utility poles began to sport company-made nesting platforms for South Carolina's osprey population, and customers were encouraged by means of financial incentives to conserve electricity. Many of these environmental initiatives were in SCANA's best interests. For example, selling 75 percent of its ash waste to concrete and cement companies yielded a handsome savings of $2 million in dumping costs annually.

Having grown from a tiny gas light company to a huge corporation, SCANA, like all utility companies, faced formidable challenges in the closing decade of the 20th century. While economic recession in the early 1990s left the company unscathed, and dividends on its stock actually increased, deregulation in the utility industry forced it to re-examine its strategies. SCANA's plans for the future involved continuing to expand its growing interest in natural gas production, broadening its customer base by seeking gas markets out of state, and extending its investments in real estate, fiber optics, and communications.

Challenges and Opportunities in the Era of Deregulation: The 1990s

The early 1990s marked a period of extensive growth for SCANA Corporation. In an effort to gain a solid foothold in newly deregulated energy markets, the company began to look for ways to increase its customer base through the further diversification of its holdings. In November 1990, the company took a significant step toward becoming a major producer of natural gas, with the purchase of extensive gas reserves in Texas from Houston-based Tri-C Resources Inc. The agreement, worth $29 million, gave SCANA an initial daily production capacity of 12 million cubic feet of natural gas, and marked the company's inaugural foray into the production side of the natural gas business. The company further increased its natural gas properties the following February, with the $16 million purchase of offshore natural gas reserves from LLOG Exploration Co. in Louisiana. In June 1993 the company's oil and natural gas exploration subsidiary, SCANA Petroleum Resources, acquired NICOR Exploration and Production Company, significantly increasing SCANA's natural gas holdings in Texas and Louisiana, as well as expanding the company's production operations into Oklahoma. The purchase increased SCANA's overall natural gas reserves to 283 billion cubic feet.

During the mid-1990s, SCANA began to search for other diversification opportunities outside of its core utilities business. One area of potential growth was in the rapidly expanding telecommunications industry. SCANA already utilized an extensive system of fiber optic lines in the monitoring of its electricity supply networks; by 1994 the company's telecommunications arm, MPX Systems, owned 1,600 miles of cable throughout four states, and had plans to extend its network by more than a third over the coming years. With a substantial infrastructure already in place, SCANA hoped to play a major role in the future growth of emerging telecommunications technologies. In March 1996, the company acquired $75 million worth of shares in InterCel, a telecommunications firm dedicated to creating a Personal Communications Service (PCS) network throughout the Southeast. SCANA's investment infused InterCel with the venture capital it needed to enter the lucrative Atlanta, Georgia PCS market, giving it the potential to double its customer base in a relatively short span. SCANA made another $75 telecom investment in June 1998, when it acquired an additional 50,000 shares in InterCel's new incarnation, Powertel. The deal increased SCANA's overall stake in the PCS company to nearly 30 percent.

However, as the new century approached SCANA found its most enticing expansion opportunities in newly opened natural gas markets outside of South Carolina. As neighboring states North Carolina and Georgia forged ahead with deregulation, SCANA began to pursue an aggressive expansion strategy. In late 1998, Georgia prepared to open its natural gas industry to increased competition, SCANA began to market its services to customers in Atlanta, investing $3 million in advertising campaigns and in establishing six regional offices throughout the state. By May 1999 the company had added nearly 300,000 new customers in Georgia, a figure they eventually hoped to increase to 700,000. Within three years, SCANA had become such a significant presence in Georgia that, in June 2002, the Georgia Public Service Commission voted unanimously to allow the company to become the official provider of regulated natural gas service to the state's low-income customers. During this time the company also made significant inroads into the North Carolina energy market, effectively doubling its natural gas customer base with the $900 million acquisition of Public Service Co. in February 2000. Financing this growth activity forced the company to withdraw resources from some of its other recent ventures, which included dumping a significant portion of its wireless stock. The company even unloaded its nascent natural gas exploration operations, SCANA Petroleum Resources, selling the subsidiary to Kelley Oil for $110 million in October 1997. Although the company's earnings suffered initially, by the beginning of the new century its shift in strategy was already paying off, and the company's Georgia operations enjoyed profits of $4.4 million for the year 2000.

Yet while deregulation represented growth potential in Georgia, it posed a threat to SCANA's profitability in its home state. During the late 1990s SCANA was engaged in a pitched battle against deregulation in South Carolina; in late 1997, SCANA CEO Bill Timmerman had even begun to discuss the possibility of relocating the company outside of South Carolina, in the event deregulation made the state's utilities industry too competitive. Although the company's lobbying and marketing efforts eventually helped defeat the deregulation bill in the state legislature, it was clear that the issue of freeing up South Carolina's utilities markets was not going to go away. With the possibility of in-state competition still looming on the horizon, the challenge facing SCANA in the early years of the 21st century remained twofold: While the company needed to remain aggressive in its efforts to gain market share in unregulated markets in other states, at the same time it was compelled to remain highly attentive to its core South Carolina customer base.

Principal Subsidiaries

South Carolina Electric & Gas Company; PSNC Energy; South Carolina Pipeline Corporation; SCANA Energy Marketing, Inc.; Servicecare, Inc.; SCANA Communications, Inc.; Primesouth, Inc.

Principal Competitors

Dominion Resources, Inc.; Duke Energy Corporation; Progress Energy, Inc.

Further Reading

Leland, Isabella G., *Charleston: Crossroads of History,* Woodland Hills, Calif.: Windsor Publications, 1980.

Montgomery, John A., *Columbia, South Carolina: History of a City,* Woodland Hills, Calif.: Windsor Publications, 1979.

Pogue, Nell C., *South Carolina Electric & Gas Co., 1864–1964,* Columbia: State Printing Co., 1964.

Quinn, Matthew C., "SCANA Out of the Red in Georgia; Gas Marketer Makes $4.4 Million," *Atlanta Journal and Constitution*, February 13, 2001, p. 1C.

——, "SCANA Pushes to Forefront of Natural Gas Derby," *Atlanta Journal and Constitution*, October 18, 1998, p. 1R.

——, "SCANA to Be 'Last-Resort' Gas Supplier; Two-Year Contract Locks in Profit," *Atlanta Journal and Constitution*, June 19, 2002, p. 1D.

South Carolina Electric and Gas Company: Highlights of a Long History, Columbia, S.C.: SCANA Corporation, 1962.

Warren, John A., *SCANA Corporation, A History of Service,* New York: Newcomen Society, 1987.

Warren, Wendy, "South Carolina's SCANA Corp. Invests in New Wireless Communications," *The State*, March 7, 1996.

—Sina Dubovoj
—update: Erin Brown

Sears, Roebuck and Co.

3333 Beverly Road
Hoffman Estates, Illinois 60179
U.S.A.
Telephone: (847) 286-2500
Fax: (800) 427-3049
Web site: http://www.sears.com

Public Company
Incorporated: 1906
Employees: 241,000
Sales: $41.4 billion (2002)
Stock Exchanges: New York Chicago London
     Amsterdam Pacific Swiss EBS Dusseldorf
Ticker Symbol: S
NAIC: 452110 Department Stores; 454110 Electronic
     Shopping and Mail Order Houses; 441310 Automo-
     tive Parts and Accessories Stores; 442299 All Other
     Home Furnishings Stores; 444130 Hardware Stores

With a network of more than 870 full-line department stores and 1,300 freestanding specialty stores in the United States and Canada, Sears, Roebuck and Co. is the world's fourth largest retailer. For more than a century Sears has provided consumers with top brand names synonymous with durability and quality. Craftsman tools, Kenmore appliances, Diehard car batteries, and WeatherBeater paint are a just a few of its most recognized products; Sears also provides a variety of competitively priced apparel for men, women, and children featuring its own brands (Canyon River Blues, Covington, TKS Basics) and such staples as Levi's jeans and Nike athleticwear. A newer addition to its empire came with catalogue and online retailer Lands' End, acquired in 2001.

Humble Beginnings: Late 1880s to 1914

Sears bears the name of Richard W. Sears, who was working as a North Redwood, Minnesota, freight agent for the Minneapolis and St. Louis Railroad in 1886 when a local jeweler gave him an unwanted shipment of pocket watches rather than return them to the manufacturer. Sears sold them to agents down the line who then resold them at the retail level. He ordered and sold more watches and within six months made $5,000. He quit the railroad and founded the R.W. Sears Watch Company in Minneapolis.

Business expanded so quickly that Sears moved to Chicago in 1887 to be in a more convenient communications and shipping center. Soon customers began to bring in watches for repairs. Since he knew nothing about fixing them, Sears hired Alvah Roebuck, a watch repairman from Indiana, in 1887. A shrewd and aggressive salesman—a colleague once said of him, "He could probably sell a breath of air"—Sears undersold his competition by buying up discontinued lines from manufacturers and passing on the discounts to customers. At various times from 1888 to 1891, thinking himself bored with the business, Sears sold out to Roebuck but came back each time.

In 1888 the company published the first of its famous mail-order catalogues. It was 80 pages long and advertised watches and jewelry. Within two years the catalogue grew to 322 pages, filled with clothes, jewelry, and such durable goods as sewing machines, bicycles, and even keyboard instruments. In 1894 the catalogue cover proclaimed Sears was the "Cheapest Supply House on Earth."

The company changed its name to its current form in 1893, but Alvah Roebuck, uncomfortable with his partner's financial gambles, sold out his share two years later and remained with the firm as a repairman. Sears promptly found two new partners to replace Roebuck: local entrepreneur Aaron Nusbaum and Nusbaum's brother-in-law, haberdasher Julius Rosenwald. The company recapitalized at $150,000, with each man taking a one-third stake. The company continued to prosper; when the cantankerous Nusbaum was forced to sell out in 1901 after clashing with Sears, his interest was worth $1.25 million.

There was little harmony between the two remaining partners, Rosenwald and Sears. Sears believed in continuous expansion and risk-taking; Rosenwald advocated consolidation and caution. Rosenwald also objected to his partner's fondness for the hard sell in the catalogue and advertising copy. Had the Federal Trade Commission existed then, some of the company's advertising practices probably would not have passed muster—

but it should be mentioned that Richard Sears invented the unconditional money-back guarantee and stood by it.

In 1905 construction began on a new headquarters plant on Chicago's west side to consolidate all of the company's functions. To help raise the necessary capital, Sears went public in 1906. Yet Wall Street was leery of the incautious Richard Sears and he resigned as president in 1908 when it became clear he was obstructing the firm's progress. He was appointed chairman, but his heart was never in the job and he retired in 1913, never having presided over a board meeting. Sears died the following year at the age of 50. Near the end of his life, he summarized his career as a merchant: "Honesty is the best policy. I know, I've tried it both ways."

New Leadership and Growth: 1915 to the Late 1920s

Sears was now Julius Rosenwald's company to run and he did it with such skill and success he became one of the richest men in the world. Sales rose sixfold between 1908 and 1920, and in 1911 Sears began offering credit to its customers at a time when banks would not even consider lending to consumers. During this time the company grew to the point where its network of suppliers, combined with its own financing and distribution operations, constituted a full-fledged economic system in itself. Rosenwald's personal fortune allowed him to become a noted philanthropist—he gave away $63 million over the course of his life, much of it to Jewish causes and to improve the education of Southern blacks. As a result of the latter, he became a trustee of the Tuskegee Institute and a good friend of its founder, Booker T. Washington.

The depression of the early 1920s dealt Sears a sharp blow. In 1921 the company posted a loss of $16.4 million and omitted its quarterly dividend for the first time. Rosenwald responded by slashing executive salaries and even eliminated his own. He was also persuaded to donate 50,000 shares from his personal holdings to the company treasury to reduce outstanding capital stock and restore the firm's standing with its creditors. Sears thus weathered the crisis and benefited from the general prosperity that followed.

Rosenwald retired as president in 1924, retaining the chairmanship he had inherited from Richard Sears. He was succeeded by Charles Kittle, a former Illinois Central Railroad executive. In 1925 Sears began to take on its current shape when it opened its first retail outlet in Chicago. Seven more stores followed that year and by the end of the decade 324 outlets were in operation. Retailing became so successful for Sears that by 1931 the stores topped the catalogue in sales. The company's entry into retailing was the brainchild of vice-president Robert Wood, who was an executive at archrival Montgomery Ward

before Rosenwald hired him in 1924. Wood was always known as "the General" after serving as the U.S. Army's Quartermaster General during World War I. He had also been chief quartermaster for the construction of the Panama Canal. He much preferred business to the military, however, and his long career in merchandising earned him a reputation for genius.

For its first 40 years, Sears had targeted the U.S. farmer as its main customer, luring him with a combination of down-home earthiness and the tantalizing prospect of material luxury. Two postal service innovations—the rural free delivery system in 1891 and the parcel post rate in 1913—had helped target this consumer by making it affordable to reach remote locations by mail. Sears quickly became parcel post's largest single customer. Then Wood saw that automobiles would soon make urban centers more accessible to outlying areas, broadening the customer base for retail outlets. Thwarted by the conservative top management at Ward's, he wasted no time in implementing his vision at Sears. At first, the stores simply absorbed surpluses from the catalogue, but they soon began to offer a full range of goods. Sears also became the first chain to put free parking lots next to its stores. More than anyone else, it was Robert Wood who turned Sears into a leviathan.

Robert Wood Taking the Helm: 1929 to Mid-1940s

Charles Kittle died suddenly in 1928 and Wood succeeded him. In 1929 Sears arranged a merger between two of its suppliers, Upton Machine and Nineteen Hundred Washer Company, to form Nineteen Hundred Corporation, which changed its name to Whirlpool in 1950. Somewhat against its intentions, Sears became increasingly involved in the affairs of its suppliers, many of which were small companies whose outputs were almost entirely geared to its needs. Another leadership change occurred in 1932 when Julius Rosenwald died at the age of 69 and was succeeded as chairman by his son Lessing.

The onset of the Great Depression hurt sales from 1930 to 1934, but thanks to cost-cutting measures Sears posted a loss only in 1932. The company, in fact, had diversified in 1931 when it created its Allstate subsidiary (named after the company's own Allstate tires) to sell auto insurance. Wood saw it as another way to capitalize on the growing popularity of the automobile. He installed agent Carl Odell as general manager, an acquaintance who had suggested the idea as they commuted to work one day.

Lessing Rosenwald retired in 1939. Preoccupied with running his father's estate, he had never attended a board meeting. Wood succeeded him, and the power of chief executive passed from the presidency to the chairmanship. At about this time, however, Wood also became controversial because of his prominent support for America First, an isolationist organization from which Charles Lindbergh made his notorious anti-Semitic speeches. Wood dropped his backing once the U.S. entered World War II and publicly supported the war effort, but remained a strong critic in private ever after.

As war loomed, Sears benefited from increases in military spending and a consumer buying panic. In 1941 sales reached an all-time high of $975 million, a 30 percent increase over the previous year. Sales then leveled off, however, and raw material

Key Dates:

1886:   R.W. Sears Watch Company is founded in Minneapolis, Minnesota.
1887:   Richard Sears relocates to Chicago and Alvah Roebuck joins the fledgling company.
1888:   First mail-order catalogue is published.
1906:   Needing funds for expansion, Sears incorporates and goes public.
1911:   Sears begins offering its customers credit.
1925:   First Sears, Roebuck retail store is opened in Chicago.
1927:   Craftsman and Kenmore proprietary brands are introduced.
1945:   Annual sales top $1 billion for the first time.
1973:   The Sears Tower becomes the company's official headquarters in downtown Chicago.
1993:   Sears changes its image with a new advertising campaign.
1996:   Sears.com is launched.
2001:   Sears buys catalogue retailer Lands' End and introduces the Covington label.
2003:   Citigroup announces plans to purchase Sears' credit card business.

shortages made durable goods hard to come by. Even as late as 1946 Sears had to refund $250 million in orders that could not be filled. Military procurement, however, helped make up for the shortfall. During the war, Sears supplied the Armed Forces with just about everything that did not need gunpowder to make it work, and even a few things that did—as some factories belonging to Sears suppliers were converted into munitions plants by the War Department. Sears also began its first foreign ventures during and immediately after the war. In 1942 a store opened in Havana (later nationalized by the Castro government in 1960) and several opened in Mexico in 1947.

Wood's Postwar Expansion: Mid-1940s to 1960s

Once the war ended Sears flourished with sales up to $1 billion in 1945, which doubled the next year. Anticipating an economic boom, Wood launched an aggressive expansion program. Concentrating on the Sun Belt states, he located many of the new stores in the path of suburban expansion before the areas built up. One store in California was established on a dairy farm and had cows roaming around the parking lot when it opened. Thanks to the General's prescience, Sears left its rivals in its wake. In 1946 it held a small sales advantage over Montgomery Ward, but in 1954 posted sales of $3 billion while Ward, which had been slower to anticipate postwar trends, mustered only $1 billion. Sears also became a symbol of U.S. prosperity. In the late 1940s the Moscow bureau chief for the Associated Press reported that the most effective piece of foreign propaganda in the Soviet Union was the Sears catalogue.

At the same time, Sears became a widely hailed living experiment in corporate management. Wood had long wanted to decentralize the company and its postwar success gave him the luxury to remold it in his image of "corporate democracy." The mer-

chandising operations were carved up into five regional territories with each given a high degree of autonomy. Although buying operations remained centralized in theory, buyers were in fact allowed substantial independence. To its employees, many of them returned veterans (the company hired 50,000 people between 1946 and 1949 alone), Sears became, as author Donald Katz put it in *The Big Store,* "a place where country boys and infantrymen could speak their minds and still roam free."

During the early 1950s Sears began to stock more clothing as durable goods sales slackened. The new postwar suburbanites who bought their first homes had already filled them with all the Sears appliances they needed. At about this time the company strengthened its ties with its suppliers even further. Between 1951 and 1960 Sears acquired virtually complete control of Warwick Electronics, which made televisions, radios, phonographs, and tape players. In 1961 it effected a merger between 15 of its soft goods suppliers and created the Kellwood Company.

Robert Wood retired in 1954 at the age of 75, but retained power over appointment of his successors until shortly before his death (in 1969). A series of caretaker chairmen followed him, none of whom served more than six years. In 1963 the company posted sales of $5.1 billion, and an executive with the discount chain Korvette quipped that Sears was not only the number one retailer in the United States, but also numbers two, three, four, and five. Surveys showed that one in five U.S. consumers shopped at Sears regularly; its sales volume was greater than that of some entire industries. The company had become big enough to justify its own shopping center development subsidiary, Homart Development, which had been formed in 1960.

Retailing Giant Beginning to Falter: Late 1960s to 1980

In 1967 Sears posted $1 billion in monthly sales for the first time. In 1970 Allstate Enterprises, a subsidiary formed in 1960, acquired Metropolitan Savings and Loan Association, the first of several savings and loans it purchased over the next two decades. Also in 1970, construction began in Chicago on the 110-story Sears Tower. Completed in 1974, the Sears Tower was the tallest building in the world for many years and a symbol of corporate pride at a time when Sears dominated U.S. retailing unchallenged.

That era was fading, however, even as its monument rose above the Chicago skyline. Recession caused by skyrocketing oil prices led to a $170 million drop in profits in 1974 on only a modest sales increase, and financial performance remained flat through the middle of the decade. It became apparent to many that success had made Sears complacent and the company had long ignored some real problems. Competition was also getting serious. Specialty shops that filled the very malls anchored by Sears stores were cutting into market share, as were such discounters as the resurgent S.S. Kresge Co., which changed its name to Kmart Corporation in 1977. Hard times meant the company's shortcomings could no longer be obscured by success or justified in the name of tradition. Sears had to be shaken up, and it fell to Edward Telling, a company veteran who took the reins in 1978, to do it. Formerly head of the eastern territory, Telling had smashed local concentrations of power in the name of efficiency and proceeded to do the same for the parent company, centralizing all buying and merchandising operations. The once revolutionary territories were slowly eliminated.

Income declined from 1978 to 1980 and was subjected to intense scrutiny by Wall Street. Outsiders were not always impressed by Telling, a downstate Illinois native whose home-spun manner tended to conceal—often by choice—his erudi-tion and keen intellect. It was through his guidance that Sears undertook a major corporate reorganization in 1981.

Diversification and Its Consequences: 1981–91

Telling also saw the burgeoning financial services industry as one in which Sears should get involved. In 1981 Sears acquired the Los Angeles-based Coldwell Banker Company, the nation's largest real estate brokerage, and securities firm Dean Witter Reynolds Inc. Three years later, Sears launched Prodigy, an online service, with IBM and CBS. At the end of 1985 Telling retired and left a radically different company from the one he had inherited. He had reined in the once sprawling bureaucracy of Sears and taken the first steps toward diversifying into the burgeoning finan-cial services market. Telling was succeeded by Edward Brennan, who had headed up the merchandising division, and had always preached that Sears was just "one big store."

In 1985 the Discover Card was unveiled, a combined credit and financial services card that also offered savings accounts through Greenwood Trust Company, a bank acquired by All-state Enterprises earlier in the year. By this time it was esti-mated that one in every 30 living Americans had worked for the company in some way at some time. In 1987, perhaps con-ceding that the era of the big general merchant was over, the merchandise division launched a new strategy to turn Sears into a collection of specialty superstores. The next year Sears ac-quired Eye Care Centers of America, Pinstripes Petites, and Western Auto Supply as its workforce reached an all-time high of 520,000. Yet the surge of adrenaline anticipated by Coldwell Banker and Dean Witter failed to materialize.

As stock prices lagged, takeover rumors circulated and man-agement pondered ways to increase shareholder value and stave off possible attempts. In late 1988 Sears announced plans to sell Coldwell Banker's commercial real estate unit, the Sears Tower; it also planned to buy back some of its own stock. Further, Brennan, who had become company chairman in 1986, announced a new retail strategy of "everyday low prices" to reduce the number of sales and promotions. These new moves, however, provided unsatisfactory solutions. The Sears Tower went on the block during a commercial real estate glut in Chicago and no buyer was found. Lower prices squeezed profit margins because of the company's still-bloated cost structure. Merchandising profits fell from more than $700 million in 1986 to $257 million in 1990, as overall profits slid from over $1.3 billion to $892 million during the same period.

A Slimmer, Resurgent Sears: 1992–95

Whether or not Sears could sustain financial improvement through growing sales remained to be seen in the early 1990s. Brennan, representing the third generation of his family to work for Sears, was under considerable pressure from investors and the financial press to turn the company around and increase

outsider representation on the board of directors. In 1992 the company slashed 47,000 jobs and suffered a shocking year-end loss of almost $2.3 billion on sales of $53.1 billion.

To stave further losses and concentrate on the company's department store roots, Brennan began what became the largest restructuring ever: he sold the Eye Care Centers, the remainder of Coldwell Banker (residential real estate), and spun off Dean Witter and the Discover card services. The automotive group, under siege after a service fraud scandal and 20 percent sales dive, quit repairs to concentrate on selling tires and batteries, then filled vacant bays through a deal with Pennzoil's Jiffy Lube. In merchandising, Brennan's handpicked successor, Ar-thur C. Martinez, moved quickly and decisively to put a shine to the tarnished Sears image. Catering to female consumers (esti-mated at 70 percent of sales), Martinez launched a far-reaching advertising campaign on the "softer side of Sears," brought in more famous-name clothing items, and put the company's for-mer mainstay—the 101-year-old catalogue—out to pasture (smaller, specialized catalogues were later revived in 1994).

Year-end figures for 1993 supported the streamlining efforts and a $4 billion renovation program with lesser sales ($30.4 billion) but a return to profitability at $2.4 billion. By 1994 the Sears half-million-plus workforce had been whittled to less than 361,000, underperforming stores were closed, and others en-larged to include national brand names. The company was also finally relieved of the Sears Tower (put in trust for transfer in 2003) and freed of $850 million of debt. The next year was filled with more immense change—Brennan retired and was succeeded by Martinez, and Allstate, the country's largest pub-licly held property and casualty insurance carrier with over $20 billion in sales, was spun off. In addition, Martinez added further feminine touches to Sears with 152 "Circle of Beauty" in-store cosmetics boutiques providing skin care, fragrance, bath, makeup, and stress-relieving products.

To make way for the beauty lines, appliances, hardware and furniture were moved out of mall-based stores and into their own freestanding buildings (as Sears Hardware, Sears HomeLife and Sears franchise stores) to help serve the rural segment previously handled by the catalogue. Sears also fol-lowed rival J.C. Penney's lead and introduced its own line of denim sportswear under the Canyon River Blues label. Al-though Lee and Levi's jeans had always been big sellers at Sears, the private label ran about $10 less and debuted with a splashy media campaign in late 1995.

In just seven months Canyon River Blues apparel rang up $100 million in sales. Likewise, the newly upgraded jewelry and shoe departments gained double-digit growth while West-ern Auto, the company's stalwart auto titan, spawned a line of aftermarket merchandise stores called Parts America, opening 30 stores in 1995 and planning another 60 for the following year. While revenue climbed only a notch to $34.9 billion for 1995, net income was a sturdy $1.8 billion with retail profits hitting $1 billion for the first time.

Roller Coaster Ride: 1996 to 2003

Another success story in the late 1990s was the Sears credit card, which contributed mightily to the company's revenue by attracting 6.4 million new cardholders in 1996 alone, bringing the nationwide total to 55 million. Other highlights of the year included Martinez being named *Financial World*'s CEO of the Year and the purchase of Orchard Supply Hardware. Yet by the following year Sears had started to stall once again, so Martinez began trimming underperforming operations including selling off most of the firm's stock in Sears Roebuck de México S.A., bailing out of the Prodigy/IBM joint venture, and surprising investors in 1998 by getting rid of Western Auto and its Parts America chain. Also on the selling block were the underperforming HomeLife furniture stores, with a majority stake (over 80 percent) sold to a subsidiary of Citicorp. As the downward slide continued, executives jumped ship, thousands were laid off, and Martinez himself left Sears in 2000.

Martinez's successor came from within the ranks as Alan J. Lacy took the reins in October 2000 as president and CEO and added chairman by the end of the year. As a former CFO and head of card services, Lacy was an insider and reportedly well liked by both board members and Wall Street. Although Sears rallied briefly with strong appliance sales and growth in its credit card revenues, apparel sales were weak. The well known "softer side" campaign had garnered plenty of attention and early success, but the words had come to mean something entirely different in the minds of investors. Despite the soft sales, however, there were steady gains in footwear and a new housewares concept called "The Great Indoors."

In 2001 Sears aggressively touted its new gold MasterCard with a low introductory rate, hoping to convert many of its regular Sears credit cardholders to the more widely accepted format. Next came financing for the embattled HomeLife stores, but the move soon proved too little too late for the 133-store chain. Suffering a similar fate were the initially popular Circle of Beauty in-store boutiques (introduced in 1995); the beauty products line was discontinued in the summer of 2001 along with a fragrance joint venture with Avon (which continued a similar deal with rival J.C. Penney). A major makeover of the company's 867 stores was also underway, to better compete with J.C. Penney, Wal-Mart, Target, and rising star Kohl's Department Stores. While 2001 year-end revenues rose slightly from the previous year's figures ($41.1 billion *vs.* just under $41 billion), operating income fell from $1.3 billion in 2000 to $735 million for 2001 due to the various write-offs and cost-cutting measures. Cautiously optimistic, Lacy and his board members were soon ecstatic when share prices soared in early 2002, hitting $54 in April and $59 in May, seeming to herald the long-awaited turnaround.

The optimism, however, was short-lived. Sears had come to rely on its credit cards and financing operations too heavily. The Sears MasterCard, with 22 million cardholders, accounted for less than half the company's charge customers and the new card seemed to be cannibalizing its siblings. Lacy's solution was to convert all Sears account holders to the MasterCard. A good idea, yet with higher credit limits and newly launched cash advances, defaults were soon on the rise. Coupled with still-sluggish apparel sales, Sears faltered once again: stock prices plummeted and heads rolled. The year's only bright spot had been the June acquisition of catalogue and online retailer Lands' End, for $1.8 billion—though some worried what was seen as a good move for Sears was a bad move for Lands' End.

Would Lands' End prove the venerable retailer's savior? Or would the cost dimple an already taxed bottom line? In 2002 and 2003 these questions were answered—short-term at least—when Sears once again bounced back. Both Lands' End and a new basics label called Covington pumped up apparel sales, with revenues, income, and stock prices all gaining. Despite declines in credit card revenues, Sears continued to bolster its image with both consumers and Wall Street, for awhile. In 2003 such stalwarts as Wal-Mart and even fast-food giant McDonald's found themselves in a financial slump, and the same was once again true for Sears. Pink slips were given to hundreds of employees at the company's headquarters in Hoffman Estates, Illinois, and its credit card unit—formerly a cash cow—was up for sale. In July Citigroup announced that it would purchase the company's credit card business for $3 billion. In addition to the much needed cash resulting from the deal, which was expected to close by year-end, Sears would retain another $3 billion it had in the business as a portfolio reserve.

Once the world's largest retailer, Sears had suffered through almost four decades of turmoil. In 2003 the mass merchandiser was ranked fourth (behind Wal-Mart, Target, and Home Depot), with its future uncertain. Though updated full-line stores were making an impact with consumers, the instability of the economy and job losses made mall shopping more of a luxury than a necessity. Competition continued to be fierce—Wal-Mart and Target usually beat Sears in price, J.C. Penney spiffed up its teen lines, and upstart Kohl's attracted customers in droves with brand-new stores and numerous splashy advertising campaigns. While Sears continued to struggle with its identity, what had not changed were its famously dependable appliances (Kenmore), tools (Craftsman), and selection of sturdy, low-priced apparel. With new private labels including Covington and the acquisition of Lands' End, Sears endeavored to achieve the stability and sales it once took for granted.

Principal Subsidiaries

Lands' End; NTB (National Tire & Battery); Orchard Supply Hardware; Sears Canada Inc.; Sears Consumer Financial Corp.; Sears DC Corp.; Sears Hardware; Sears de México, S.A.; Sears Overseas Finance N.V. (Netherlands); Sears Roebuck Acceptance Corp.

Principal Divisions

Lands' End; Sears Auto Centers; Sears Hardware; Sears Home Improvement Services; Sears Optical; Sears Parts and Service; Sears Termite and Pest Control; The Great Indoors; National Tire Wholesale (NTW).

Principal Competitors

J.C. Penney Company, Inc.; Kohl's Department Stores, Inc.; Target Stores; Wal-Mart Stores, Inc.

Further Reading

Applebaum, Alec, "The Softer Side of Sears: A New CEO Tackles Fashion Troubles and More at the Retail Icon," *Money*, November 1, 2000, p. 44.

Baeb, Eddie, "Lenders Give Life Support to HomeLife...," *Crain's Chicago Business,* May 28, 2001, p. 4.

Berner, Robert, "The Fog Surrounding Lands' End," *Business Week,* March 10, 2003, p. 78.

"The Bottom Line," *Business Record (Des Moines, Iowa),* October 15, 2001, p. 22.

Bremner, Brian, and Michael O'Neal, "The Big Store's Big Trauma," *Business Week,* July 10, 1989.

Byrne, John A., "Strategic Planning," *Business Week,* August 26, 1996, pp. 46–52.

Chandler, Susan, "Where Sears Wants America to Shop Now," *Business Week,* June 12, 1995.

Emmet, Boris, and John E. Jeuck, *Catalogues & Counters: A History of Sears, Roebuck & Company,* Chicago: University of Chicago Press, 1965.

Jones, Sandra, "Big Store's Worry: Card Unit...," *Crain's Chicago Business,* October 14, 2002, p. 3.

Facenda, Vanessa L., "Popping Open the Sears Umbrella," *Retail Merchandiser,* May 2001, p. 16.

Katz, Donald R., *The Big Store: Inside the Crisis and Revolution at Sears,* New York: Viking, 1987.

McMurray, Scott, "Sears Fashions a New Future for Itself," *U.S. News & World Report,* May 13, 1996.

Omelia, Johanna, "Circle of Beauty Squares Off at Sears," *Drug & Cosmetic Industry,* November 1995.

Oneal, Michael, "Sears Faces a Tall Task," *Business Week,* November 14, 1988.

Pierce, J. J., "Designer Jeans at Sears, Kmart Textiles in Tiers," *Private Label,* November/December 1995, p. 7.

"Sears Restructuring Pays Off," *MMR,* February 10, 2003, pp. 7-9.

Sharoff, Robert, and Evan Clark, "Sears Profits Take a 27.9 Percent Dive in Period," *Daily News Record,* October 21, 2002, p. 8.

Siler, Julia Flynn, Laura Zinn, and John Finotti, "Are the Lights Dimming for Ed Brennan?" *Business Week,* February 11, 1991.

Sparks, Debra, "Arthur Martinez: *Financial World*'s CEO of the Year," *Financial World,* March 25, 1996.

Underwood, Elaine, "Jean-Etic License," *Brandweek,* May 29, 1995, pp. 1, 6.

Veverka, Mark, "That Softer Side of Sears Still Has Taste for Auto Grit," *Crain's Chicago Business,* May 29, 1995.

Weil, Gordon L., *Sears, Roebuck, U.S.A.,* New York: Stein and Day, 1977.

Worthy, James C., *Shaping an American Institution: Robert E. Wood and Sears, Roebuck and Company,* Urbana: University of Illinois, 1984.

—Douglas Sun
—update: Nelson Rhodes

Shaw's Supermarkets, Inc.

750 West Center Street
West Bridgewater, Massachusetts 02379
U.S.A.
Telephone: (508) 313-4000
Fax: (508) 313-3112
Web site: http://www.shaws.com

Wholly Owned Subsidiary of J Sainsbury PLC
Founded: 1860
Employees: 30,000
Sales: $4.4 million (2002)
NAIC: 45110 Supermarkets and Other Grocery (except
    Convenience) Stores

A wholly-owned subsidiary of U.K. supermarket giant J Sainsbury PLC, Shaw's Supermarkets, Inc. is the second-largest supermarket company in New England, behind Stop & Shop. Shaw's employs approximately 30,000 in over 185 stores in Connecticut, Massachusetts, Maine, New Hampshire, Rhode Island, and Vermont. With the purchase of Massachusetts-based Star Market stores and that company's natural food line Wild Harvest in 1999, Shaw's began operating Wild Harvest in-store departments in over 100 of its Shaw's locations.

19th-Century Humble Beginnings and Early Success

In 1860 Vermont native George C. Shaw moved to Portland, Maine, to embark on a business venture with starting capital of a little more than $900. He opened a small shop in downtown Portland and called it Shaw's China Tea Store. In a move to attract customers, Shaw employed an Asian man named Ah Foo who stood in a high profile window to serve as a tea expert. Soon, people came flocking to purchase teas at the China Tea Store. With success carrying tea and coffee, Shaw expanded the shop to include fresh foods and groceries. By 1872, Shaw opened a second store at 580 Congress Street in Portland. Increased sales prompted the company to open a larger facility at 585 and 587 Congress Street in 1881.

At the time George C. Shaw was expanding his stores in Portland, Maynard A. Davis of Poland, Maine, left the Pine Tree State in 1880 with $23 in his pocket. Davis journeyed to Pawtucket, Rhode Island, where he worked as a store clerk. By 1896, Davis and a friend had opened a public market in Providence, Rhode Island. However, Davis sold his interest in the company in 1899. At that time he moved to Massachusetts and started the Brockton Public Market (BPM). Soon after, he opened additional stores in New Bedford, Bridgewater, and Rockland, Massachusetts.

Shaw's and BPM's Growth and Expansion: 1919–79

In 1919 Davis bought controlling interest in George C. Shaw's, establishing it as a subsidiary of BPM. Davis remodeled the Shaw's stores to compete with national and other regional chains. Following the remodel, Shaw's stores were considered the most modern grocery store in New England and featured such items as fresh-baked bread, fresh roasted and ground coffee, and roasted turkeys. Clayton Baker and Elmer Batchelder operated the Shaw's chain in its early years as a subsidiary of BPM, building on the reputation established by George C. Shaw for specialty foods and services including telephone orders and delivery service.

In 1935 Maynard Davis's son, Halsey Davis, was named head of the George C. Shaw Co. in Portland, while his brother, Stanton Davis, became BPM president in Massachusetts. In 1947, in order to increase their private-label items and add a high quality house brand that could compete with national chain private-label brands, the Davis brothers entered their stores as charter members of the New England Food Buyers Association, a buying cooperative that later became known as Topco Associates of Chicago. By the mid-1970s, Topco would become the third-largest food distribution company in the United States.

As the population began to shift from the downtown urban centers to the suburbs, the Davis brothers saw the importance of expanding in shopping centers located outside the cities. In 1951, Shaw's opened its first supermarket outside of a downtown district in South Portland, Maine, at the Mill Creek Shopping Center. Soon after, other Shaw's supermarkets began to

---

Company Perspectives:

Shaw's is committed to being the supermarket of choice by satisfying the diverse and changing needs of our customers, associates, communities and business partners. We define ''supermarket of choice'' as follows: 1.) To our customers, we are a merchant who provides consistently high quality, innovative products and services, at competitive prices, in an environment that is safe, clean, convenient, and friendly; 2.) To our associates, we are an employer who provides opportunities for personal growth and long-term success based on performance and a work environment which respects differences and individual needs; 3.) To our communities, we are a neighbor who is socially responsible, charitable, and environmentally conscious; and 4.) To our business partners, we are a colleague who fosters relationships which are mutually beneficial and based on respect, honesty, and trust.

---

open in southern Maine. During that same period, BPM also continued to grow. In 1961, Stanton Davis initiated one central warehouse for both companies with the purchase of a three-story warehouse in Brockton, Massachusetts. By the late 1960s Shaw's supermarkets had expanded beyond the greater Portland market into other areas of the state, as well as northern Massachusetts and New Hampshire. With the combined growth of the Shaw's stores and the growth of BPM in southern Massachusetts, the brothers were prompted to build a new distribution center in East Bridgewater, Massachusetts, in 1972 that would serve both companies' stores.

Shaw's boasted $71 million in sales in 1973, and by 1974 Shaw's operated 19 stores and employed 1,500 full- and part-time employees. By 1979 Shaw's operated 22 stores in Maine, New Hampshire, and Massachusetts, and BPM operated 13 stores under the Shaw's name in Massachusetts for a total of 35 stores earning over $300 million in annual sales. That same year, the Bridgewater distribution facility was enlarged from 257,000 square feet to 434,000 square feet. Also in 1979, George C. Shaw Co. and BPM merged to form Shaw's Supermarkets, Inc.

J Sainsbury Acquisition: 1980s

By 1983, Shaw's had 41 stores in New England. In September of that year, Shaw's announced that it had entered into an agreement with J Sainsbury PLC, England's largest supermarket company with sales of $3.5 billion in 1982, to sell up to 25 percent of its stock, opening the door for Sainsbury to purchase up to 251,845 shares at $100 per share. Stanton Davis, chairman of Shaw's, maintained that controlling interest of the company would remain in the Davis family. At the time of the sale, Shaw's board grew from ten members to 12 to allow for two new spots to be occupied by Sainsbury representatives.

In 1986 when Shaw's owned 47 stores in New England and boasted 1985 sales figures of $14.8 million, the company announced it would go public with its stock. It was speculated that Sainsbury would retain 25 percent of the stock, Shaw's would retain 51 percent, and 24 percent would be available for the public, including a percentage of that offered to Shaw's employees.

This public offering never fully developed, and in early 1987 Sainsbury controlled 28.5 percent holdings of Shaw's. By mid-1987, Sainsbury gained majority control of the company with the purchase of 20 percent of the Davis family stock, bringing Sainsbury to hold 49.4 percent of Shaw's in the first stage of a two-stage sale. Shares were sold through Sainsbury's U.S. subsidiary Cheyne Investments of New York for $30 a share. Following the completion of this first sale through Cheyne Investments, a tender offer of $30 a share was made that would guarantee Sainsbury 74 percent of Shaw's. At the time Shaw's president and chief executive officer, David B. Jenkins, maintained that ''Shaw's management team looks forward with enthusiasm to drawing on Sainsbury's experience and resources as we pursue our growth strategy to become a more important factor in the supermarket industry.'' Sainsbury treasurer Ewan Davidson asserted in *Supermarket News* that while Sainsbury recognized the growth potential of Shaw's, they would continue to grow the company as a regional chain rather than on a national level. According to analysts at that time, while Sainsbury seemed to acquire Shaw's at a ''cheap'' price, Shaw's stood to benefit from Sainsbury's expertise in private-label sales.

Growth and Expansion: 1990s

Sainsbury invested $90.7 million in Shaw's in fiscal 1990, and the chain's profits rose significantly enough for the parent company to open five Shaw's stores in Massachusetts and one in New Hampshire. These store openings increased the total number of Shaw's stores to 74. With a recessionary climate in New England in 1992, Shaw's showed a profit loss of 16.5 percent in the first half of that year. Despite this loss, Shaw's opened three new stores by mid-1992 and planned an additional five new openings by year-end. By 1992 Shaw's was the third-largest supermarket chain in New England behind Stop & Shop and Hannaford Brothers.

As supermarkets faced stiffer competition from such discount store giants as Wal-Mart and warehouse clubs, Shaw's stood out with a comfortable growth record. At year-end 1994 Shaw's had $1.97 billion in sales and had plans to expand from 87 stores in Maine, New Hampshire, Massachusetts, and Rhode Island to over 110 by 2000. This forecasted growth was expected to come from the company's acquisition of small independent chains in the Boston area.

In 1995 Shaw's opened five new stores with a 45,000-square-foot format, purchased two stores from rival Stop & Shop, and bought eight former Almacs units in Rhode Island. In 1996 Shaw's operated 100 stores in New England, including stores in Connecticut, and boasted a 10.5 percent sales increase to $2.29 billion by March of that year. Also in 1996 Shaw's acquired 12 Edwards stores in Connecticut from rival Stop & Shop's parent, for $52 million. In 1997 Shaw's purchased four sites in New York state, planning to extend its reach beyond New England. The chain began site work on its first New York store, a 50,000-square-foot unit, in Nanuet, New York, in July 1997, and had begun pre-construction work for the opening of a 65,500-square-foot store in New Rochelle, New York, to be completed in 1998. By February 1998, however, Shaw's canceled its plans to enter New York and announced plans to sell its New York properties. Shaw's spokesman Bernie Rogan told *Supermarket News,* ''We decided not to go into New York, and

Key Dates:

1860: George C. Shaw opens small tea shop in Portland, Maine.

1872: Shaw opens second Portland store on Congress Street.

1899: Maynard A. Davis founds small grocery stores in Brockton and New Bedford, Massachusetts, calling stores Brockton Public Market (BPM).

1919: Davis buys the George C. Shaw Company, establishing it as a subsidiary of BPM.

1961: Stanton Davis purchases three-story warehouse in Brockton, Massachusetts, that both BPM and George C. Shaw's stores utilize.

1972: BPM becomes second supermarket in the United States to test scanning technology.

1978: Massachusetts BPM stores change name to Shaw's Supermarkets.

1979: Shaw's Supermarkets, Inc. is formed with merger of BPM and the George C. Shaw Co.

1983: England's largest supermarket company J Sainsbury PLC purchases 21 percent of Shaw's outstanding stock.

1987: Sainsbury acquires controlling interest in Shaw's.

1999: Sainsbury buys Massachusetts-based Star Market stores and distribution center to operate under Shaw's name, launching Shaw's to second-largest supermarket company in New England.

2002: Shaw's introduces self-checkout lanes, an industry first in New England.

instead to focus on Connecticut and the Boston area. We felt it was the smart thing to do, since this is our core market and we are gaining market share there.'' In April 1998, the six sites Shaw's held in New York were purchased for an undisclosed sum by the Stop & Shop Supermarket Co., officially ending Shaw's move into the New York market. Following Shaw's departure from New York and the company's aggressive growth in Connecticut, Sainsbury executives revealed that growth plans for Shaw's would slow in order for the company to focus on increasing profitability of its New England stores, including new stores in Vermont.

By late 1998, Shaw's slow growth received a quick boost when the company announced plans to acquire 53 Star Market stores in Massachusetts for $490,000 million. In operation since 1915 in urban locations in Massachusetts, Star Markets had been operating at a loss of $8 million to $9 million. When complete, the acquisition would place Shaw's just 20 stores short of New England's leading supermarket chain Stop & Shop. A significant gain for Shaw's in the acquisition also included Star Market's natural food line Wild Harvest. The Star Market sale was approved in July 1999. As part of the deal, Shaw's was required to sell three Shaw's stores and seven Star Market stores in Massachusetts, leaving Shaw's with a total of 44 Star Market stores that remained under the Star Market banner. In 2001 Shaw's had converted seven Star Market units to the Shaw's banner and had fully-integrated Shaw's private-label items and technology into Star Market stores, and were involved in converting the remaining 37.

Industry Innovators Past and Future

Dating back to George C. Shaw's hiring of Ah Foo to promote his specialty teas, Shaw's was at the forefront of industry innovations. In 1941, Shaw's was one of the first grocers in the United States to offer self-service in its stores. In 1947, the company began selling house label products and became a leader in private-label business. After Sainsbury—known as a leader in store brand business in the United Kingdom—acquired Shaw's in 1987, Shaw's grew its store brand program even more significantly. By 2002, Shaw's made up to 40 percent of net sales from private-label goods and produced over 5,000 private-label items. In January 2002, Shaw's introduced Signature brand, a line of higher quality private-label items. With its introduction, Shaw's carried 300 Signature brand food items and projected to carry 100 more items by year's end.

In 1967 BPM participated in a project known as COSMOS, an acronym for Computer Optimization and Simulation Modeling for Operating Supermarkets, an early computerized pricing strategy that was ultimately abandoned as computers of that generation did not have the file capacity to handle the multiple computations of COSMOS. Later, with the evolution of PC technology, the concept of COSMOS was reborn with the introduction of Direct Product Profit (DPP), a technology that Shaw's helped pioneer to improve store's space management.

Perhaps the most significant innovation for which Shaw's is recognized is its testing of cashier scanning in 1972. Data General Corporation approached BPM stores in 1972 looking for supermarkets to test their scanning system technology for checkout counters. Only two months behind Marsh Supermarkets of Yorktown, Indiana, BPM was the second supermarket company to test scanning technology. In 1974 BPM's Stoughton store became the third store in the United States to be outfitted with a pre-production supermarket scanning system. After two years of testing, Data General signed an agreement with Sweda to market their scanners. In 1977 the BPM store in Randolph, Massachusetts, went live with the Sweda Superscanner. By 1980 Shaw's had installed scanners in all of its stores and by 1982 had begun testing a computer-based replenishment system known as Supervised Re-Ordering (SRO).

Later developments in SRO allowed stores to gather and process sales and inventory data to create store orders for replenishment. Having experience in SRO and establishing paperless transactions of invoices and purchase orders through Electronic Data Interchange (EDI), Shaw's was in a solid position to benefit from cross-docking. By 1995, Shaw's moved 5 to 10 percent of weekly grocery shipments through its warehouses with minimal warehouse handling.

Attesting to Shaw's diligence in industry innovation, the company was awarded the *Supermarket Business* Award for Retailing Excellence in 1992. Shaw's was praised by the magazine, which stated, ''We honor the management and people of Shaw's for their historic role as a leader in supermarket technology and for their often frustrating and costly work on the leading edge . . . which . . . might better be termed 'the bleeding edge.' ''

In the late 1990s Shaw's again moved to stay ahead of its competitors with the testing of self-checkout systems, the first such system in New England. Shaw's began a pilot program of self-checkout lanes in 2000, and by early 2003 the company had self-checkout lanes in 52 store locations. Shaw's predicted that by year-end 2003, over 120 stores would be equipped with self-checkout systems.

Shaw's also sought to pioneer the grocery industry in terms of corporate environmental standards. In 1992, three years prior to governmental deadlines, Shaw's initiated the first existing store refrigeration system conversion to ozone-friendly refrigerants. In July 2001 Shaw's East Boston store received the first Energy Star label awarded by the Environmental Protection Agency for voluntary measures to increase energy efficiency and reduce air pollution. In 2003 Shaw's received the Climate Champions Award for corporations in the Northeast. Award presenter Michael Bradley maintained that Shaw's "has continually pursued energy-efficiency through measures in their stores and by seeking new technological solutions with their suppliers and vendors." While the environmental benefits of energy efficient practices proved significant, energy conservation also proved an added bonus to Shaw's bottom line. As reported in *PR Newswire* in 2003, "The Company estimates that Shaw's has helped to reduce air pollution by 50,000 tons of carbon dioxide per year and saved a total of more than $10 million in operating and energy costs since 1996."

In 2002 Shaw's announced its growth strategy for the next three years, which included plans to open 30 new stores at a cost of over $400 million as well as remodel and upgrade over 90 percent of its existing 186-store base. Analysts speculated whether the company must also secure a major acquisition to remain competitive with not only Stop & Shop but also warehouse clubs, Wal-Mart, and Target stores for grocery and nonfood item sales. Shaw's had earned a solid position with its parent company, having generated 17 percent of 2001 Sainsbury sales and 20 percent of its parent company's profits. President and Chief Operating Officer Paul T. Gannon maintained, "Some of the important factors [in targeting an acquisition] would be proximity to Shaw's, a willing seller and a company that's No. 1 or 2 in its markets in terms of market share." In April 2003 Shaw's opened a 56,000-square-foot-store in Boston's Back Bay in the Prudential Center. To keep abreast of the growing market for prepared foods, the store offered stir fry, sushi, olive, and pasta bars. With the opening of this showy Boston flagship store, Shaw's continued to carve its niche in the New England market and make new inroads into the urban market.

Principal Competitors

Stop & Shop; Hannaford Brothers; DeMoulas Super Markets.

Further Reading

Arditi, Lynn, "British Firm Buys Second New England Grocery Chain," *Knight Ridder/Tribune Business News*, November 27, 1998.

Balijko, Jennifer L., "Shaw's Set to Broaden Store Reach in New York," *Supermarket News*, September 30, 1996, p. 1.

"British to Buy Share of Shaw's," *Evening Express*, September 28, 1983, p. 1.

Cohen, Ted, "Shaw's Seeks to Go Public with Stock," *Portland Press Herald*, September 20, 1986, p. 1.

Fallon, James, and Max Wisenthal, "Sainsbury to Complete Acquisition of Shaw's," *Supermarket News*, June 29, 1987, p. 1.

Fallon, James, "J. Sainsbury to Accelerate Shaw's U.S. Expansion," *Supermarket News*, May 20, 1996, p. 22.

——, "Sainsbury Plans to Slow Shaw's Expansion," *Supermarket News*, May 18, 1998, p. 1.

——, "Sainsbury's Shift," *Supermarket News*, June 2, 1997, p. 1.

——, "Sainsbury to Open 6 Shaw's Units," *Supermarket News*, May 28, 1990, p. 36.

——, "Shaw's Operating Profit Falls 16.5% in First Half," *Supermarket News*, November 16, 1992, p. 9.

Fasig, Lisa Biank, "CEO of Shaw's Supermarkets Faces New Competition for Customers, Growth Plan," *Providence Journal*, July 14, 2002.

"Feds Approve Shaw's Purchase of Star Market," *Providence Business News*, July 12, 1999, p. 5.

Fensholt, Carol, "Presenting the 1992 Supermarket Business Award for Excellence to Shaw's Supermarkets, Inc.," *Supermarket Business*, December 1992, p. 23.

"First to Market: Shaw's Supermarkets Introduces Self-Checkout in New England," *Chain Store Age Executive with Shopping Center Age*, February 2002, p. 7C.

Gatlin, Greg, "New Store at Prudential Center Features Upscale, Gourmet Tastes," *Boston Herald*, April 24, 2003, p. O29.

Gattuso, Greg, "Shaw's Drops Plan for N.Y.; CEO Leaving for Petsmart," *Supermarket News*, February 16, 1998, p. 1.

"George C. Shaw and Co. to Celebrate 70th Milestone with Anniversary Sale," *Portland Sunday Telegram*, October 26, 1930, p. 8D.

Goad, Meredith, "Store Becomes Ozone Friendly," *Portland Press Herald*, June 9, 1992, pp. 1B-2B.

Hyde, Christopher, "When Giants Battle, Everyone's a Winner," *Biz*, January 1996, pp. 11, 14.

Irwin, Clark T., Jr., "Shaw's Markets Financial Charm," *Portland Press Herald*, October 17, 1986, p. 17.

O'Leary, Chris, "Shaw's Seeks to Move on 3 Cross-Docking Fronts," *Supermarket News*, December 18, 1995, p. 19.

"Maine-Born Grocery Head Dies in Brockton," *Portland Press Herald*, January 10, 1947, p. 14.

Philippidis, Alex, "Shaw's Supermarkets Begins Site Work on First Store in Westchester," *Westchester County Business Journal*, August 4, 1997, p. 8.

——, "Stop & Shop Acquires Shaw's Sites in New Rochelle, Yonkers," *Westchester County Business Journal*, May 4, 1998, p. 16.

Prenon, Mary T., "Shaw's Checks out of New York," *Westchester County Business Journal*, March 2, 1998, p. 5.

Schneider, Martin, "Shaw's Begins Star Conversion," *Supermarket News*, June 4, 2001, p. 4.

"Shaw's Cuts Energy Consumption," *Chain Store Age Executive with Shopping Center Age*, October 2001, p. 94.

"Shaw's Opens Sixth Store in N.H., 19th in Chain, 4 New Units in Year," *Portland Press Herald*, June 29, 1974, p. 117.

"Shaw's Supermarkets: 1983 a Year of Remodeling, Expansion," *Maine Sunday Telegram*, May 1, 1983, p. 30.

"Shaw's to Add 30 Stores, Remodel 170 Others," *Supermarket News*, July 29, 2002, p. 11.

"Shaw's to Open 13th Supermarket in North Conway, N.H., Next Fall," *Evening Express*, July 3, 1971, p. 113.

"Shaw's Ups Ante on Private Label with New Signature Brand," *Drug Store News*, March 4, 2002, p. 42.

Sleeper, Frank, "English Firm Buys Shaw's Supermarkets," *Portland Press Herald*, June 20, 1987, pp. 1, 18.

"Supermarket Chain Puts Environment First," *Chain Store Age Executive with Shopping Center Age*, November 1992, p. 118.

"Three Pioneers Saw the Future, Made it Work," *Supermarket News*, September 28, 1987, p. 10.

"35 Supermarkets Named Shaw's in Maine and Massachusetts," *Evening Express*, June 30, 1979, p. 71.

Unger, Harlow, "From Shore to Shaw's," *Super Marketing*, August 26, 1994, p. S46.

—Elizabeth Henry

Shred-It Canada Corporation

2794 South Sheridan Way
Oakville, Ontario L6J7T4
Canada
Telephone: (905) 829-2794
Toll Free: (800) 69-SHRED
Fax: (905) 829-1999
Web site: http://www.shredit.com

Private Company
Incorporated: 1988
Employees: 1,200
Sales: $130 million (2000 est.)
NAIC: 562119 Other Waste Collection

Shred-It Canada Corporation provides mobile document shredding services to over 120,000 companies and organizations around the world through 120 franchised operations and company-owned branches. Shred-It operates some 700 shredding trucks and employs more than 1,200 people. The company uses industrial-grade shredders that are far more powerful and faster than those found in the average office and are capable of destroying clothing, software, and on one occasion spare Academy Awards. Shred-It's main selling point is that it saves customers money. Clients contract Shred-It to provide shredding at a fraction of the salaries that would be paid to staff to do the work less efficiently. The demand for shredding has increased dramatically over the years, with the emphasis shifting away from the destruction of outdated documents to the shredding of more current materials as a way to protect business secrets, combating the recent phenomenon of "dumpster diving," in which industrial spies comb through the trash of rival companies in order to gain a competitive edge. To ensure security, Shred-It is circumspect in hiring and performs its work on-site, allowing customers to observe the shredders in operation. In between visits from the shredding trucks, customers store material slated for destruction in secure bins provided by Shred-It. In addition to Canada and the United States, Shred-It operates in Argentina, Belgium, Dubair, Hong Kong, Singapore, South Africa, South Korea, and the United Kingdom.

Origins in the Late 1980s

Shred-It's founder, Gregory Brophy, was the son of Irish immigrants who moved to Canada in 1957. His father was a butcher with business ambitions but a decided lack of focus, drifting from one idea to the next, from cocktail mixes to liquid fertilizers, nine failed startups all told. Gregory inherited his father's enthusiasm for business, especially salesmanship, but proved to be far more disciplined. When he was only 15 years old, he and his brother went into the driveway-sealing business after fixing up a used truck they bought for $250. They were able to do a dozen driveways a day at $50 each, the business drummed up at night when they made door-to-door cold calls. Brophy bought out his brother and stuck with the summertime job for six years before selling it. He also helped to fund his college education by running a small lawn care business. While attending school at McMaster University, he then used his savings to buy a three-bedroom house, which he converted into a seven-bedroom student residence, providing himself with a place to stay as well as earning spending money. Brophy was then able to use the equity in the property to buy ten more houses, so that by the time he finished his schooling with an MBA in 1988 at the age of 26 he had sold $1.25 million in real estate, earning a $300,000 profit.

Ready to launch a company of his own, Brophy considered a number of businesses, including a chemical manufacturing company, but his bid was turned down. He thought about buying a franchise in a new chain of chicken restaurants but dropped the idea after doing some personal research that convinced him the restaurants were not as popular as he had been led to believe. He also considered becoming a franchise for a furniture store chain. It was at this point that Brophy heard from a friend about someone in Ottawa who had mounted a 2,000-pound, refrigerator-sized industrial-grade shredder on a truck and was driving around the Canadian capitol destroying government and company documents on contract. Brophy was intrigued by the concept on a number of levels. His research indicated that some 70 percent of companies employed small, inefficient machines to shred their paperwork. Moreover, an increasing number of businesses were looking to outsource routine tasks in order to save money. Brophy recognized that the time saved by fully

---

Company Perspectives:

Shred-It is dedicated to being the World's Leading Mobile Shredding and Recycling company. We will achieve this goal on the strengths of our people. Shred-It will consistently deliver the greatest security, cost effectiveness, convenience and environmentally-friendly service available. We will earn a fair return on the investment in our systems, equipment and people. Above all, we will earn the confidence of our clients through a continued commitment to total customer satisfaction.

---

utilizing a high-powered shredder instead of relying on small office units would translate into cost savings for customers and a profit for an independent shredding operation. He also envisioned the possibility of a shredding business that could grow from market to market. In addition, the idea that the shredded material would be recycled appealed to him personally and would be a selling point to many customers as well.

Before Brophy was ready to invest in expensive equipment, he sought to sign up customers in advance. He visited major Toronto companies, hospitals, and government offices and made his pitch. The first to sign on was a General Electric plant located in a Toronto suburb, and within a month Brophy had lined up a dozen customers, enough business to keep a shredding truck busy at least on a half-time basis.

Bankers were not receptive to Brophy's business plan, but he was finally able to convince his bank manager to lend him $160,000. He cobbled together another $125,000 in seed money: $20,000 from savings, $70,000 on a second mortgage on a house he had acquired during his college real estate days, and a $35,000 Canadian government small-business loan. He acquired a truck and $70,000 shredder, able to destroy 1,200 pounds of paper per hour, then incorporated his company, naming it Shred-It. For the company's services Brophy established an hourly rate of $140, plus the cost of the operator. The first employee was a recent college graduate, whom Brophy paid $24,000 a year.

Shredding operations began on February 1, 1989, while Brophy continued to drum up new business, his office nothing more than a desk at an area electric company which he rented for $86 a month. To save money he even bartered shredding services for office supplies. His sales pitch was so persuasive, in fact, that within the month he had set up enough new business to justify the purchase of another truck. His banker, however, cautioned against moving too fast and turned down Brophy's loan request. Nevertheless, Brophy went ahead and bought the truck on his own, relying on credit cards and loans from family and friends, then convinced a leasing company to purchase the truck and lease it back to Shred-It.

In the company's first year in operation, some eight months long since its fiscal year ended September 30, Shred-It generated sales of $130,000, losing $30,000, although Brophy was able to pay himself $24,000 and the business was already starting to prove profitable. During the first full year in business, Shred-It posted sales of $470,000 and a $33,000 profit.

Despite initial success, the company was still not generating enough cash flow to fund the growth that Brophy felt was necessary in order to secure market share before better financed competitors entered the nascent industry, and bankers were still not willing to finance his ambitions. According to a *Forbes* profile, "His father's example steeled Brophy's resolve to focus on Shred-It's problem and solve it. 'My dad's experience,' he explains, 'taught me not to jump from business to business.'" It was one of Brophy's truck drivers who made a key contribution towards making Shred-It a more profitable business by reorganizing the truck routes to make the operation more efficient, allowing the mobile units to accommodate more customers each week. (The company also added weekend shredding to more fully utilize equipment.) As a result, trucks that had realized $3,500 in weekly business increased that amount to $5,200. In fiscal 1991, the company improved revenues to $753,000 and generated net earnings of $114,000. Brophy was also able to pay off the loan on his first truck. Now the bankers were approaching him to do business, and he was in a position to ask five major banks to put together a financial package and make a presentation at his office.

In 1992, Shred-It's revenues topped $1 million and Brophy prepared to take the business south into the United States. American banks, however, demanded U.S. credit references. One even refused to review the company's financial statements, which had been audited by a multinational accounting firm. According to Brophy, when he approached California banks in order to set up a Los Angeles branch of Shred-It, the best offer he received was a $50,000 credit line, contingent upon the deposit of $50,000 in a bank account. In the end, Brophy came up with $800,000 on his own to launch the Los Angeles office. It was clear, however, that lacking access to capital would prevent him from establishing the Shred-It name in the United States before others moved into the industry, achieved a major market share, and became difficult to dislodge. Moreover, Brophy lacked the personnel needed to launch widespread Shred-It operations. His solution to these problems was to augment Shred-It with franchise operations, selling rights to entire metropolitan areas for $45,000 and a 5 percent royalty on gross sales. Brophy placed ads in trade publications and attended trade shows, gradually selling franchises. By early 1997, Shred-It had 32 franchisees, mostly located in the United States. While Brophy provided franchisees with the Shred-It name, trucks, and canisters, as well as making available the company's expertise through a support center, he granted them the latitude to run their businesses as they saw fit.

Brophy's accomplishments were recognized in 1994 when he was named Emerging Entrepreneur of the Year for Ontario by the accounting firm of Ernst & Young, received the Young Entrepreneur of the Year award from the Federal Business Development Bank, and made the *Ontario Business Report* list of Ontario's Top 100 Entrepreneurs. Much of his success he credited to an advisory board of four retired executives he had assembled to help him chart the course of his business, including his father-in-law David Williams, a 36-year veteran of Sears Canada. Brophy met with the board every six weeks. Each adviser offered his expertise in a particular area: general management, operations, finances, and human resources. By the end of fiscal 1994, Shred-It was generating annual revenues in the $5 million range.

Key Dates:

1989:	Shred-It begins operations.
1993:	The company expands with franchises in the United States.
1996:	Shred-It opens a South American branch.
1998:	The company expands into Europe.

Moving Outside of North America: 1995 and Beyond

Shred-It also began to expand beyond the borders of North America. In 1995, an Asian franchise branch was established, followed the next year by a franchise operation in Buenos Aries, Argentina. Now with ten company-owned branches and 30 franchises, Shred-It posted company-wide sales of $21 million in fiscal 1996. That number would double in fiscal 1997, totaling some $42 million, then reach $81 million in fiscal 1998. Shred-It entered the European market in 1998, opening an office in Birmingham, England, as the company continued to post impressive gains.

Not only was the company expanding its operations, the demand for shredding was also growing at a fast pace. Despite years of hype about the paperless office, the consumption of paper tripled from 1980 to 1990, according to a study conducted by the University of Illinois. The use of paper was expected to grow at a 15 percent clip each year until 2010. Those numbers alone indicated that the demand for shredding services was certain to grow, providing a great deal of opportunity for Shred-It. Moreover, with the rise of "dumpster diving," security of documents was becoming an increasing concern for businesses (as well as individuals wary of identity fraud). To help solve a growing fraud problem, governments around the world began to enact legislation that mandated certain types of information be destroyed in a highly secure manner. Although the act of shredding took on negative connotations during the corporate scandals, such as the Enron affair, that shook the corporate world in the early years of the new century, the demand for shredding services only increased further. With a dominant position in the North American market and a toehold in four other continents, Shred-It was well positioned to fully take advantage of these favorable business conditions.

Shred-It opened a branch in South Africa in 2000. By the end of the year, the company had 82 branches located around the world, operating 260 shredding trucks. In 2002, Shred-It became the largest document destruction company in the United Kingdom following its acquisition of Shreddit PLC. As a result of this transaction and continued internal growth, Shred-It entered 2003 with 120 branches and 700 shredding trucks on the road. The company continued to enter new markets, the network growing ever larger, with North American branches set to open in South Carolina; Fresno, California; and Austin, Texas. Shred-It operations were also ready to start in France and Germany.

Principal Subsidiaries

Shred-It USA, Inc.; Shred-It International, Inc.

Principal Competitors

A C L Documents; Enviro Shred Inc.; Environmental Security Inc.

Further Reading

Goldfisher, Alastair, "Firm Proves Unholy Terror," *Business Journal*, October 13, 1997, p. 1.

Kroll, Luisa, "Fear of Failing," *Forbes*, March 24, 1997, pp. 109–11.

Picton, John, "Shred-It Making Piles From Little Pieces," *Toronto Star*, February 20, 1993, p. C3.

Roseman, Ellen, "A Future in Keeping Secrets," *Globe and Mail*, November 14, 1994, p. B6.

Steingberg, Carol, "Young and Restless: Three Young Franchisors Move into The Big Leagues," *Success*, April 1997, p. 73.

—Ed Dinger

THE SIAM CEMENT GROUP

The Siam Cement Public Company Limited

1 Siam Cement Road
Bangsue BKK 10800
Thailand
Telephone: (+66) 2586-3333
Fax: (+66) 2587-2199
Web site: http://www.siamcement.com

Public Company
Incorporated: 1913
Employees: 16,525
Sales: B 130.07 billion ($3.1 billion) (2002)
Stock Exchanges: Thailand
Ticker Symbol: SCC
NAIC: 327310 Cement Manufacturing; 322110 Pulp
    Mills; 322121 Paper (Except Newsprint) Mills;
    322130 Paperboard Mills; 322211 Corrugated and
    Solid Fiber Box Manufacturing; 322215 Non-Folding
    Sanitary Food Container Manufacturing; 325211
    Plastics Material and Resin Manufacturing; 325222
    Noncellulosic Organic Fiber Manufacturing; 327121
    Brick and Structural Clay Tile Manufacturing; 327122
    Ceramic Wall and Floor Tile Manufacturing; 327123
    Other Structural Clay Product Manufacturing; 327124
    Clay Refractory Manufacturing; 327320 Ready-Mix
    Concrete Manufacturing; 327331 Concrete Block and
    Brick Manufacturing; 327390 Other Concrete Product
    Manufacturing; 327420 Gypsum and Gypsum Product
    Manufacturing; 551112 Offices of Other Holding
    Companies

One of Thailand's largest companies, The Siam Cement Public Company Limited is a diversified conglomerate with operations focused around five strategic business units: Cement; Building Products; Distribution; Paper; and Petrochemicals. The company's paper operations are grouped under the holding Siam Pulp and Paper Plc, and focused on production of industrial paper, packaging products, and printing- and writing-grade paper. Under Siam Cement Industry, the holding company for the group's cement division, Siam Cement is one of the ASEAN region's leading producers of cement and concrete products under the Elephant, Tiger, CPAC, and other brand and trade names. The company's Cementhai Chemicals Co. holding encompasses its production of petrochemical products, which include polyethylene resins, olefins and polyolefins, polystrene and other chemicals. Siam Cement's building products division, grouped under Cementhai Building Products, is Thailand's leading maker of construction materials and building products, and includes the company's ceramic tile, sanitary fittings, roofing materials, concrete end-products, gypsum board, insulation products, and door production. Last, the group's Distribution division is responsible for the company's national and international trade and distribution operations, as well as logistics and warehouse services. In addition to these operations, the company has a list of diversified operations—ranging from CRT display production to tire manufacturing and steel production—slated for divestment since the late 1990s. Siam Cement is led by Chumpol Na Lamlieng, president and managing director. The Thai royal family owns more than 35 percent of the publicly listed company.

Royal Origins in the Early 20th Century

Despite a modernization effort backed by Siam's royal family in the mid-19th century, the kingdom remained heavily reliant on foreign imports at the beginning of the 20th century. The ascension of ruler King Rama VI in 1910 marked the start of a new period of industrialization in the country. Under the king's influence, a new company for the production of cement was set up in 1913, called Siam Cement. Leadership of the company was given to Norwegian native Oscar Schultz (the company was not to have a Thai-born head until 1974), but the royal family remained a primary shareholder.

Construction began on a plant in Bansue, with production starting in 1915. Early cement production was based on naturally formed marl (calcium carbonate) deposits. By the end of the decade, Siam Cement's annual production had topped 25,000 tons. By then, too, it also had begun supplying the export market, shipping cement to Singapore and Malaysia. The discovery of new marl deposits in Ban Mo enabled the company to step up production. In 1922, Siam Cement installed a second cement kiln, boosting its production capacity to 35,000 tons. A third kiln, added in 1928, pushed the company's total production capacity to nearly 110,000 by the end of the decade.

Siam Cement began its first diversification efforts in the late 1930s. At first, the company built this expansion effort around its core cement product, launching a roofing tile manufacturing operation, Siam Fiber-Cement Company. In 1942, however, Siam Cement entered a new field of operations, building a test facility for producing steel. That plant was damaged during Allied bombing raids in 1944, along with part of the company's Bangsue cement factory.

Postwar Expansion

Siam Cement rebuilt after the war, restoring the Bansue facility. In 1948, the company inaugurated a new cement site as well, in Tha Luang, adding some 130,000 tons of annual production volume. That year, also, the company completed its steel plant, becoming the first in Thailand to begin manufacturing steel and iron. Two years later, Siam Cement began production of steel bars as well. That activity enabled the company to establish a new division, the Iron and Steel Department, which began producing components needed for the company's machinery needs.

Siam Cement then extended its cement operations with the formation in 1952 of Concrete Products and Aggregate Co., or CPAC, which began producing its own range of concrete products. CPAC also opened a pre-stressed concrete facility that year. Meanwhile, Siam Cement neared completion of a new refractory brick facility, which began production in 1953.

Siam Cement continued to add to its production capacity, adding more than 600,000 tons of annual capacity by the beginning of the 1960s. The company stepped up its production effort over the next decade, particularly with the addition of a new plant in Thung Song, the company's first to use a lower-cost dry production method. That plant, which began production in 1966, added nearly 500,000 tons to the group's overall capacity.

As CPAC continued to add products, such as reinforced concrete pipes starting in 1961, Siam Cement created a new, dedicated distribution division to handle trading of its growing number of products. That subsidiary, called Construction Materials Marketing Company, began trading in 1962. Siam Fiber-Cement also expanded during the decade, adding asbestos cement pipe production in 1966, Glasolit translucent sheets in 1968, and asbestos cement sheet in 1969. During this time, Siam Cement launched production of white cement as well.

By the end of the 1960s, Siam Cement had added more than 1,000,000 tons of production capacity with the installation of several new kilns at its Bangsue and Tha Luang sites. An addition 570,000 tons of capacity came on line in 1971 at a new site in Kaeng Khoi.

Siam Cement's expansion led to a restructuring of its operations in 1972. Siam Cement Co. Ltd. now became a holding company, placing its manufacturing companies under a new Siam Cement Group structure. At this time the company adopted its symbol, a White Elephant. By then, the company had shed most of its steel operations, spun off in 1966 as Siam Iron and Steel.

Diversified Conglomerate in the 1980s

The appointment of Boonma Wongswan as general manager in 1974 marked the first time a Thai native took the leadership of Siam Cement. Wongswan was replaced in 1976 by Sommai Hoontrakool. The importance of Siam Cement in Thailand's economy was underscored by the fact that both Wongswan and Hoontrakool later became Finance Ministers in the Thai government.

The new management marked the beginning of a massive diversification program that saw Siam Cement grow into the country's leading conglomerate by the end of the 1980s. One of the company's first moves beyond its core cement and building materials market was the purchase of a stake in Siam Kraft Co. Ltd. in 1976. The company reinforced its position in that market in 1979 with the purchase of a stake in Siam Kraft Paper Company, as well as Thai Containers Ltd. These investments formed the beginnings of what was to become a core company division.

Siam Cement stepped up its diversification effort in the late 1970s. In 1978, the company began to target a series of overseas investments and joint ventures with foreign partners, forming a new subsidiary, SCG Corporation, for this purpose. SCG immediately went into business with the Prosperity Steamship Company of Hong Kong, creating Siam Prosperity Shipping. Meanwhile, Siam Cement itself formed a joint venture with Japan's Kubota that year in order to produce diesel engines for the Thai farm machinery market. At the same time, the company's international trade business had grown beyond its original construction materials market, prompting a change of name to Siam Cement Trading (SCT).

Siam Cement continued to invest in its cement business despite its increasingly diversified interests. In 1981, for example, the company debuted a new 1.6 million ton cement kiln at its Tha Luang plant. The company shut down its aging Bangsue plant that year; the new kiln in Tha Luang also allowed the

Key Dates:

1913: King Rama VI sponsors founding of Siam Cement in order to reduce the country's reliance on imported cement.

1915: Production begins with a capacity of 20,000 tons.

1938: The company begins producing roofing tiles in its first extension beyond cement.

1948: The company builds Thailand's first steel plant and begins producing iron and steel.

1952: The CPAC concrete products group is created.

1962: The company forms a distribution operation, the Construction Materials Marketing Company, later renamed Siam Cement Trading.

1976: The company invests in Siam Kraft Co., in its first diversification effort.

1983: A license to produce high-density polyethylene marks company's first entry into the petrochemicals market.

1990: The first of a series of reorganizations, into four core businesses, is implemented.

1998: The company announces plans to sell off noncore holdings.

2001: After sell-off fails, the company is restructured into six core businesses and two holding companies.

2003: Siam Cement creates a new Building Products division.

company to shut down its four oldest kilns at that plant as well. These moves marked the company's further shift into the dry production process.

Yet diversification remained the order of the day for the company. In 1982, it took over the Firestone's Thai tire production operation, which was renamed Siam Tyre Company. That year, Siam Fiber Cement launched production of gypsum board, as well as other materials for the construction industry. The following year marked the start of another important area, the petrochemicals market, as Siam Cement entered the market for polyethylene production.

By the late 1980s, Siam Cement had entered a bewildering variety of new businesses, ranging from CRT tube manufacturing, to polystyrene packaging, to car engine manufacturing, and ceramic floor tile production. The company's SCT subsidiary also had become a major distributor of computers to the Thai market.

Restructuring in the 1990s

Chumpol Na Lamlieng became president of the Siam Cement group and launched the company on a reorganization drive that grouped its widely diversified holdings under four primary business units: Cement; Construction Materials; Machinery and Electrical Products; and Paper and Packaging. Siam Cement's diversified investments continued, however, leading the company to restructure again into eight divisions, including new units for its ceramics, tire and auto accessories, and petrochemicals businesses. The company also embarked on an up-

grade program for its cement operations, boosting its total capacity to some 16 million tons in the early 1990s, placing it in a strong position not only in the fast-growing Thai construction market, but throughout the booming Asian Pacific region. By the middle of the decade, the company's production neared 20 million tons.

Siam Cement's position as Thailand's largest conglomerate made it vulnerable to the increasingly volatile economic conditions in the Far East. The sudden collapse of Thailand's economy in 1996—precipitating a regionwide economic crisis—hit Siam Cement hard, as its sales and share price dropped sharply and its heavy foreign debt, sparked by the devaluation of the Thai baht, soared.

Yet Siam Cement was to win praise for the transparency with which it faced its own economic crisis. The company called in a team of international consultants to help it perform a new and more drastic restructuring of its operations. The company now narrowed its strategic targets to only those business areas in which it could achieve regional leadership, namely, Cement, Petrochemicals, and Pulp and Paper. The company then began a sell-off program of its newly noncore operations, paying down its debt with the proceeds.

Siam Cement's restructuring hit a snag, however, when it found itself unable to find buyers, or at least suitable prices, for a number of the businesses it sought to sell. In 2001, therefore, the company restructured yet again, now grouping its operations into six primary divisions, Petrochemicals, Paper & Packaging, Cement, Construction Materials, Ceramic, and Distribution, and two holding companies for its other businesses and investments, Cementhai Holding and Cementhai Property. By 2003, the company had whittled its range of core business divisions down to five, creating a new Building Products division for its construction materials and ceramics products.

By then, Siam Cement's restructuring effort had successfully restored the company to the growth track, with revenues rising to B 130 billion ($3 billion) by the end of 2002. The company's petrochemicals unit had seen especially impressive gains, and by then accounted for 38 percent of the group's total sales. Paper & Packaging was also one of the primary growth areas for the company, accounting for 21 percent of sales. Yet the uncertain economic climate led the company to reduce its expansion efforts, at least for the short term. The company's business materials remained an exception, however, as the company announced in April 2003 its intention to spend up to B 850 million to meet the growing demand in that market. More flexible and focused, Siam Cement planned to lead Thailand's businesses into the 21st century.

Principal Subsidiaries

City Pack Co., Ltd.; Nippon Hi-Pack (Thailand) Co., Ltd.; Siam Cellulose Co., Ltd.; Siamkraft Industry Co., Ltd.; Thai Containers Chonburi (1995) Co., Ltd.; Thai Containers Industry Co., Ltd.; Thai Containers Ltd.; Thai Containers Ratchaburi (1989) Co., Ltd.; Thai Containers Songkhla (1994) Co., Ltd.; Thai Containers V&S Co., Ltd.; Thai Kraft Paper Industry Co., Ltd.; Thai Paper Co., Ltd.; Thai Union Paper Industry Co., Ltd.; Thai Union Paper Public Company Limited; The Siam Pulp and

Paper Public Company Limited; Cementhai Chemicals Co., Ltd.; Map Ta Phut Tank Terminal Co., Ltd.; Rayong Olefins Co., Ltd.; Rayong Pipeline Co., Ltd.; Thai Polyethylene (1993) Co., Ltd.; Thai Polyethylene Co., Ltd.; Thai Polypropylene (1994) Co., Ltd.; Thai Polypropylene Co., Ltd.; Siam Cement Industry Co., Ltd.; The Concrete Products and Aggregate Co., Ltd.; The Siam Cement (Kaeng Khoi) Co., Ltd.; The Siam Cement (Lampang) Co., Ltd.; The Siam Cement (Ta Luang) Co., Ltd.; The Siam Cement (Thung Song) Co., Ltd.; The Siam White Cement Co., Ltd.; Beijing Cementhai Ceramic Co., Ltd.; Cementhai Building Products Co., Ltd.; Cementhai Gypsum Co., Ltd.; PT. Surya Siam Keramik; Saraburirat Co., Ltd.; Siam Fiberglass Co., Ltd.; Thai Ceramic Co., Ltd.; Thai Ceramic Roof Tile Co., Ltd.; The CPAC Concrete Industry Co., Ltd.; The CPAC Concrete Products Co., Ltd.; The CPAC Roof Tile Co., Ltd.; The CPAC Roof Tile Industry Co., Ltd.; The Siam CPAC Block Co., Ltd.; The Siam CPAC Block Industry Co., Ltd.; The Siam Fibre-Cement Co., Ltd.; The Siam Moulding Plaster Co., Ltd.; The Siam Nawaphan Co., Ltd.; The Sosuco Group Industries Co., Ltd.; Tip Fibre-Cement Co., Ltd.; Cementhai Distribution Co., Ltd.; Cementhai Logistics Co., Ltd.; Cementhai Sales and Marketing Co., Ltd.; SCT Co., Ltd.; Aisin Takaoka Foundry Bangpakong Co., Ltd.; CRT Display Technology Co., Ltd.; Michelin Siam Co., Ltd.; Michelin Siam Marketing and Sales Co., Ltd.; Musashi Auto Parts Co., Ltd.; Siam Asahi Technoglass Co., Ltd.; Siam AT Industry Co., Ltd.; Siam Furukawa Co., Ltd.; Siam Lemmerz Co., Ltd.; Siam NGK Technocera Co., Ltd.; Siam Toyota Manufacturing Co., Ltd.; Siam Tyre Industry Co., Ltd.; Siam Tyre Industry Phra Pradaeng Co., Ltd.; Siam Yamato Steel Co., Ltd.; Thai CRT Co., Ltd.; Thai Electron Gun Co., Ltd.; Thai Engineering Products Co., Ltd.; Thai Tokai Carbon Product Co., Ltd.; Thai Tyre Mould Co., Ltd.; The Deves Insurance Public Company Limited; The Nawaloha Industry Co., Ltd.; The Siam Industrial Wire Co., Ltd.; The Siam Kubota Industry Co., Ltd.; The Siam Nawaloha Foundry Co., Ltd.; The Siam Steel Cord Co., Ltd.; The Siam United Steel (1995) Co., Ltd.; Toyota Motor Thailand Co., Ltd.

Principal Divisions

Paper; Petrochemical; Cement; Building Products; Distribution; Ceramics.

Principal Competitors

IFI; India Cements Ltd.; Lafarge S.A.; Holcim Ltd.; Ishikawajima-Harima Heavy Industries Company Ltd.; CRH Plc; Taiheiyo Cement Corporation.

Further Reading

Barnes, William, "Cost-Cutting Aids Siam Cement," *Financial Times,* February 15, 2000, p. 22.
——, "Restructured Siam Cement Posts 92% Rise," *Financial Times,* January 30, 2003, p. 29.
——, "Secretive Giant Finds That Stripping Is an Asset," *Financial Times,* April 27, 1999, p. 30.
Fein, Mark, "All Units Perform Solidly for Thai Cement Firm," *Knight Ridder/Tribune Business News,* May 12, 2003.
"Siam Cement Keeps Up the Fighting Spirit," *Business Day (Thailand),* December 21, 1998.
Treerapongpichit, Busrin, "Thai Cement Giant to Battle Foreign Rivals," *Knight Ridder/Tribune Business News,* November 19, 2001.

—M.L. Cohen

SEB

Skandinaviska Enskilda Banken AB

Kungsträdgårdsgatan 8
S-106 40 Stockholm
Sweden
Telephone: (46) 8 763-8000
Web site: http://www.seb.se

Public Company
Incorporated: 1972
Employees: 19,618
Total Assets: SKr 1.24 billion ($141.85 million)(2002)
Stock Exchanges: Stockholm
Ticker Symbol: SEBA
NAIC: 522110 Commercial Banking

Skandinaviska Enskilda Banken AB operates as the parent company of the SEB Group, a North European banking concern catering to corporations, institutions, and private individuals. SEB has over 670 branch offices throughout Sweden, Germany, and the Baltic states and serves over four million customers, with 1.3 million of these customers utilizing the group's e-banking services. SEB grew extensively during the latter half of the 1990s and into the new century through a series of strategic acquisitions. Its plans to merge with competitor Swedbank were thwarted in 2001 after the European Union Commission set forth strict conditions that threatened to devalue the union.

Sweden's banking regulations, framed and reframed over the years to relieve budget deficits incurred by its "cradle to grave" social welfare system, had grown into a complex web of restraint by 1971. The boards of two of Sweden's leading commercial banks met in September of that year to discuss a remedy: liquidating and transferring their assets and liabilities to a new bank that would be set up differently and have the ability to expand in different markets. Stockholms Enskilda Bank had been in operation since 1856 and Skandinaviska Banken since 1864. Both were respected institutions that had grown as much as their boards expected they could given the regulations according to which they operated.

Stockholms Enskilda Bank

The first privately owned bank in Stockholm, Stockholms Enskilda Bank was started by A.O. Wallenberg. The bank participated actively in the country's booming export economy from the start, using those profits to fund the building of the Swedish industrial infrastructure. When the boom broke, the bank found itself the owner of several businesses and the victim of large loan losses.

When Wallenberg retired, his two sons, K.A. and Marcus Wallenberg, succeeded him. K.A. developed the bank's international business, while Marcus took an active role in promoting the industrial development that took place in Sweden during the decades prior to World War I. Stockholms Enskilda Bank's development remained routine through the Depression and World War II. A third generation of Wallenbergs took over prior to World War II and continued serving Swedish commercial customers. During the 1960s, however, the industry underwent rapid expansion and larger companies began to demand increased financial resources. At the same time, government regulations made these demands difficult to meet. These circumstances combined with the international trend toward diversification caused Stockholms Enskilda Bank to begin to consider a major merger.

Skandinaviska Banken

Skandinaviska Banken had been a pioneer in commercial banking since its inception in April 1864 as Skandinaviska Kredit-Aktiebolaget i Göteborg. The idea of organizing a commercial bank to provide investment capital in Scandinavia dates back to the early 1860s, when C.F. Tietgen, a Danish banker, convinced several Swedish industrialists and bankers to help him create a new bank. The bank was to invest in shares in new industrial companies and later place the shares on the market. A third of the new bank's shares were to be sold in Sweden and the rest in major financial centers in Europe. Unfortunately, a sudden increase in the discount rates on the continent near the end of 1863 doomed this plan.

Nevertheless, in 1864 the bank was brought to life by Swedish industrialists and bankers, with Tietgen as the only

Company Perspectives:

SEB's business concept is to offer financial advice and to handle financial risks and transactions for companies and private individuals in order to: create real customer satisfaction, give shareholders a competitive return, and be seen as good corporate citizens of society. The group strives to be a leading North European bank based upon long-term customer relations, competence, and e-technology.

non-Swedish board member. Theodor Mannheimer, the first managing director of the new bank in Göteborg, and Henrik Davidson, who joined the bank's Stockholm staff when it opened an office there in 1865, had numerous contacts in Europe's financial centers. As their experience had been with private trading firms as well as banks, these two men were able to establish business agreements with major European banks quickly. One of their first transactions was to market an eight million mark government-railway loan for Hamburg Banco, which attracted much attention. Skandinaviska Banken had taken its first step toward becoming one of the largest foreign exchange dealers in the world.

The new bank opened branches in Sweden's major cities but was able to make contacts throughout the provinces without incurring the expense of opening an extensive branch network because it acted as agent for most of Sweden's provincial banks. A mounting tide of industrial activity around the turn of the century greatly increased the volume of business.

In 1910, following the restructuring of the Swedish banking system, Skandinaviska merged with Sweden's second-largest bank, Skånes Enskilda Bank, which had a number of provincial branches. A final merger 39 years later joined Skandinaviska with Göteborgs Handelsbank, adding another 40 provincial branches.

Skandinaviska was among the first banks in the country to introduce the check system, which attracted a large volume of new savings. Shortly after 1945, the bank introduced a commercial information service, providing expertise on economic conditions in foreign countries along with information on their markets, customs, laws, and currency. This service led to the publication of books and periodicals to communicate the information on a regular basis.

The Merger: 1971–72

On December 17, 1971, the Swedish government approved the Articles of Association of the Skandinaviska Enskilda Banken and granted it permission to take over the activities of the two original banks, commencing January 1, 1972. Shareholders in both banks exchanged their shares for shares in the Skandinaviska Enskilda Banken and many of the staff members of the original banks found positions in the new bank.

The investment management business was the new bank's first step outside the original framework of its operations. In 1974, S-E-Banken became the owner of Aktiv Placering A.B. in Stockholm. This wholly owned subsidiary was established to

manage the portfolios of individuals, offer legal services for families, and provide advice on taxes and life insurance. As legislation, securities markets, and other factors changed through the years, this subsidiary grew and acquired other subsidiaries both in Sweden and overseas. By the 1980s, it was managing about 40 mutual funds.

Although for many years Sweden protected its own banks by refusing to allow foreign banking within its borders, competition among Swedish banks for domestic business did not give any of them much potential for growth. Skandinaviska Enskilda Banken took a giant step into a lucrative new market when it went international in 1976.

Its first international acquisition was an interest in Deutsch-Skandinavische Bank in Frankfurt, Germany. The next step was the formation of Skandinaviska Enskilda Banken (Luxembourg) S.A. Then, in 1979, S-E-Banken reached halfway around the world to establish a subsidiary in Singapore to handle Southeast Asian business, creating Skandinaviska Enskilda Banken (South East Asia) Limited.

Deregulation Begins in the Late 1970s

During the late 1970s, as inflation and interest rates scaled new heights, there was a record amount of money in circulation. The Swedish government began to look for alternatives to the restrictive banking regulations in place and decided to pursue a course of gradual deregulation.

The first major step in deregulation was to relieve Swedish banks of the obligation to purchase new issues of the fixed-rate, long-term priority bonds that had been the traditional annual solution to the country's budget deficit. (Life insurance companies and pension funds, however, were still required to invest in them.)

The government next moved to allow Swedish banks to issue certificates of deposit, starting in 1980. These short-term, high-interest instruments became as popular in Sweden as they had become elsewhere and helped attract substantial numbers of new clients, many of whom went on to use additional bank services.

The Swedish savings rate had been sluggish for years, mainly because of Sweden's high income tax, which left households with little discretionary income. In addition, banks were allowed to offer only a relatively low interest rate on conventional savings accounts. The time was right for the introduction of new financial instruments offering better returns.

In the three years that followed the introduction of certificates of deposit, the government created several additional avenues for bank profits: Swedish treasury bills, a commercial paper market, and market-rate state bonds. S-E-Banken, already the front-runner in industrial corporation accounts, also led the nation in private business.

Svensk Fastighetskredit A.B. (SFK) began offering real estate financing and property management in 1961. As a wholly owned subsidiary, SFK financed single-family homes and commercial property and expanded steadily. In addition to conventional long-term, fixed-rate loans, SFK also made short-term and intermediate credit available for projects in the process of construction. A.B. Arsenalen and A.B. Garnisonen, subsidiaries established in 1965 and 1968 respectively, specialized in property management and related services such as appraisal, estate brokerage, construction management, and architectural services. These subsidiaries did not own property but became national leaders in property management.

In 1981, S-E-Banken created a new real estate-related subsidiary to fill its own needs for suitable premises for the bank's growing number of branches and subsidiaries: SEB-Fastigheter A.B. This subsidiary protected S-E-Banken's investments in existing properties by maintaining them and renovating them as needed to assure their continuing appreciation. It also invested in properties and constructed new buildings.

Growth and Deregulation Continues in the 1980s

The following year, 1982, was a banner year for acquisitions. Deutsch Skandinavische Bank, founded in 1976 in Frankfurt, opened a branch office in Hamburg, and subsidiaries were opened in two major trade centers. Skandinaviska Enskilda Banken Corporation was opened in New York, initially to handle transactions relating to business in Sweden but ultimately to gain a foothold in business involving American companies. With the growth of this business, branch offices were set up in New York and in the Cayman Islands to facilitate transactions involving such matters as the clearing of currency. In London, S-E-Banken established another wholly owned subsidiary, Enskilda Securities, Skandinaviska Enskilda Limited. Along with facilities such as FinansSkandic (UK), which had been in operation since 1964 and focused on corporate lending, the new subsidiary offered full-service banking to Swedish and international clients.

S-E-Banken had also entered into a partnership in 1969 with Scandinavian Bank, a consortium bank based in London, which was flourishing. The other two main partners were Bergen Bank of Norway and Union Bank of Finland. To outdistance competitors in their respective homelands, the three banks, with Privatbanken of Denmark, formed Scandinavian Banking Partners, an organization that made it possible to facilitate fast money transfers and cash management services for any client in any of the three countries. Sten Westerberg, then senior vice-president of S-E-Banken's international division, called the new organization "a cheap way of expanding in terms of costs, and more efficient than opening up subsidiaries."

Longstanding cooperative relationships with other banks throughout the world were an important factor in S-E-Banken's growth. During this time period, it maintained close relationships with more than 2,700 correspondent banks. At the same time, there was intense competition among Sweden's top four banks (Svenska Handelsbanken, PKbanken, and Götabanken were the other three at the time). All four were studying new approaches to retail banking in preparation for deregulation. Electronic banking was one instant success—pioneered by Götabanken, it was quickly emulated by the other leading banks, including S-E-Banken.

The heightened personal-banking activity that came with deregulation did not include a surge of new savings accounts; Sweden's savings rate continued to be low. Nevertheless, S-E-Banken found that adding new personal banking services and investment instruments resulted in a lucrative and less volatile rate of return than overdependence on the highly competitive money markets with their relatively narrow profit margins. (Within a few years of its inception, the Swedish money market had become the third largest in the world.)

As inflation and interest rates began to decline, the Swedish government took further steps toward deregulation. In 1985, it lifted its ban on foreign banking in its domestic market. Business was brisk, and S-E-Banken expressed no worry about the prospect of additional competition. Within a year, a dozen foreign banks had established facilities in Sweden but posed no immediate threat to any of the Big Four banks.

That same year government controls on interest rates and lending volume were removed, an occasion one banker described as "liberation day." With controls removed and the economy booming, the big banks' profits virtually doubled during 1986.

Also in 1985, S-E-Banken formed a new division, Enskilda Fondkommission, in Stockholm, to conduct investment banking in Sweden in cooperation with Enskilda Securities in London. In 1987, S-E-Banken opened additional facilities, notably Enskilda S.A., Paris, a subsidiary of London's Enskilda Securities. Additional branches were opened the following year in London, Hong Kong, New York, and Singapore.

At beginning of 1988, S-E-Banken established a new subsidiary in Stockholm called Kortbetalning Servo A.B. to develop new routines for redeeming credit and charge card bills, according to an agreement the bank had made with PKbanken and the Swedish savings banks. The bank's credit and charge card business conducted by the FinansSkandic A.B. subsidiary underwent a radical change beginning with S-E-Banken's 1987 purchase of the remaining shares in Kortgruppen Eurocard-Köpkort A.B. Eurocard operations remained an independent entity within the

FinansSkandic group; the credit card operations were merged with FinansSkandic's existing operation. FinansSkandic, as a group, led Sweden's credit and charge card market. It was also Sweden's largest leasing company. S-E-Banken, together with its Enskilda Securities subsidiary, also pioneered a new bond, denominated in Eurokronor. First issued in October 1988 by the World Bank, the bond sold out immediately.

While Skandinaviska Enskilda Banken's move into international banking had clearly been a success so far, the future posed a real challenge for the bank. In order to maintain its position, S-E-Banken knew it must continue to dominate in its domestic market while at the same time battling for a growing share of the European market—a market that stood to grow more competitive as the European Economic Community moved toward its ultimate goal of total economic integration.

Hardships and Further Expansion: Early 1990s and Beyond

While S-E-Banken worked to strengthen its position in the industry, it was forced to contend with a banking crisis that hit the region. In 1990, the company began to experience a slow down in profits due to overexposure to bad loans. The financial downturn continued over the next several years in the Swedish banking industry, forcing the company to report its first-ever operating loss in 1992. Contributing to that loss was an $83.6 million one-time charge related to the company's failed merger attempt with AB Skandia. Bjoern Svedberg was named CEO in 1992, becoming the third new leader in three years.

In early 1993, the company launched a restructuring program that included a major cost cutting program and a curtailing of international expansion. That year S-E-Banken returned to profitability. Progress continued and during the following year profits soared to five times the previous year's level. The purchase of Diners Club Nordic in 1994 signaled the bank's return to its expansion strategy.

The mid- to late 1990s proved to be an integral period in S-E-Banken's history. During 1997, the bank began to reorganize its operations under the leadership of CEO Jacob Wallenberg. Prompted by increased globalization, various demographic developments of its customers, new technology, and deregulation, S-E-Banken began to focus on broadening its product line as well as expansion in Northern Europe. During 1997, the company acquired insurance company Trygg Hansa AB. The following year, the bank launched the SEB brand, making Skandinaviska Enskilda Banken the parent company of the new SEB Group. It also began to close many of its branch offices due in part to the increased use of Internet banking, which proved to be much more cost efficient for the group.

SEB continued to make significant moves in the new century. Germany-based BfG was acquired in 2000 and eventually renamed SEB AG. The group also added three additional banks to its arsenal, including Eesti Uhispank, Estonia's second-largest bank, and the two largest banks in Latvia and Lithuania—Latvijas Unibanka and Vilniaus Bankas. As a result of these deals, SEB's financial position was greatly strengthened. In fact, from 1997 through 2002, the group's revenues and customer base doubled, its assets under management more than tripled, and it had positioned itself as a major North European player with over half of its staff and client base outside of Sweden.

SEB attempted to take its growth a step further in 2001 and announced merger plans with FöreningsSparbanken, or Swedbank, Sweden's second most-profitable bank. The union was called off in September of that year, however, after the European Union Commission laid forth harsh requirements that were necessary for completion of the deal. SEB felt the conditions devalued the merger and therefore called off the deal.

During 2003, the group continued to focus on increasing customer satisfaction, expanding its products and services and remaining cost-efficient. While many in the European financial sector experienced problems related to an economic slowdown, SBE stood on solid ground. "The 'big four' banks," claimed a June 2003 article in *The Banker*, "remain profitable and are seen as a beacon of stability in a difficult period."

Principal Divisions

Nordic Retail & Private Banking; Corporate & Institutions; SEB Asset Management; SEB Trygg Liv; SEB AG Group/ German Retail & Mortgage Banking; SEB Baltic and Poland.

Principal Competitors

Nordea AB; FöreningsSparbanken AB; Svenska Handlesbanken AB.

Further Reading

"Biggest Swedish Bank Acts in Bid to Survive Acute Financial Crisis," *The Wall Street Journal*, January 22, 1993, p. A6.

Jones, Colin, "Consolidation Continues," *Banker*, October 2000, p. 59.

——, "Time to Find Their Feet: The Failure of the Proposed Merger Between SEB and Swedbank May Give the Baltic Banks a Chance to Develop in Their Own Way," *Banker*, July 2002, p. 65.

Robinson, Karina, "Advantages in Abundance," *Banker*, December 2002, p. 38.

"SE Banken Had Fivefold Rise in 1994 Profit," *Wall Street Journal*, February 17, 1995, p. A5.

"Skandinaviska Enskilda Banken: Large Swedish Bank Posts First Operating Loss Ever," *Wall Street Journal*, June 9, 1992, p. A13.

"Skandinaviska Enskilda Banken: Swedish Group Posts Profit on Strong Rise in Revenue," *Wall Street Journal*, March 1, 1994.

"Sweden--Europe's Beacon of Stability," *Banker*, June 1, 2003.

—update: Christina M. Stansell

Smith-Midland Corporation

5119 Catlett Road
Midland, Virginia 22728
U.S.A.
Telephone: (540) 439-3266
Fax: (540) 439-1232
Web site: http://www.smithmid.com

Public Company
Incorporated: 1960 as Smith Cattleguard Company
Employees: 154
Sales: $26.9 million (2001)
Stock Exchanges: over the counter
Ticker Symbol: SMID
NAIC: 421320 Brick, Stone, and Related Construction
    Material Wholesalers

Smith-Midland Corporation is a Midland, Virginia-based company that specializes in the development, manufacture, licensing, marketing, and installation of precast concrete products for use in the construction, transportation, farming, and utilities industries primarily located in the Mid-Atlantic and Northeastern states. The company operates two manufacturing facilities, one in Midland and a second in Reidsville, North Carolina. Subsidiary Easi-Set Industries licenses Smith-Midland proprietary products to precast concrete manufacturers throughout the United States and Puerto Rico, as well as Belgium, Canada, New Zealand, and Spain.

Unlike other pre-cast concrete manufacturers, which are dependent on being the low bidder on construction projects, Smith-Midland has developed a long line of proprietary products that allows it to negotiate a price with customers. Research and development efforts have resulted in a number of innovations, such as the J-J Hooks positive connection highway safety barrier system. These self-aligning panels automatically hook into place, allowing for quick installation, smaller installation crews, and lower installation costs. The company's Parkway Stone Wall is an aesthetically pleasing wall for highway and roadside applications. Although actually a precast concrete panel, it looks like a stone wall and is designed for such uses as terrace walls,

property lines, and estate entrances. Another Smith-Midland development is Sound-Lok, a sound-absorbing concrete that the company uses in its Sierra Wall product, which has residential, industrial, commercial, and highway uses. The acoustical surface of Sound-Lok is comprised of a number of interlocking absorptive microcells that are similar to concrete in plasticity and hydration characteristics. Sound-Lok can be mixed and applied to an existing surface or mixed with regular concrete, as with the Sierra Wall system that relies on four-inch thick, steel reinforced concrete panels. They are joined together by a tongue and groove connection, which allows for easy and fast construction. With Sound-Lok, the Sierra Wall acts as a sound barrier, and because it comes in a variety of finishes it can be used to blend in with local architectural designs. In residential applications, the Sierra Wall can offer privacy between houses and apartments, screen a roadway, as well as serve as a windbreaker and security fence. In areas where residential and industrial uses conflict, or where shopping centers or other institutions are located close to residential areas, the Sierra Wall is used as an effective noise barrier that is able to blend in with the surrounding materials. Larger panels are used to construct sound barrier systems for highways. Smith-Midland's Easi-Set and Easi-Span precast, portable concrete buildings are able to serve a number of functions and have been erected as fiber optic regeneration huts, cellular phone facilities, switching stations, weather monitoring stations, rest rooms, sports dugouts, ticket booths, emergency generator shelters, and a multitude of storage facilities.

Smith-Midland is especially optimistic about the future of its Slenderwall architectural product, suitable for both new construction and recladding projects. This exterior wall system reduces thermal transfer while being isolated from the structural stresses of the building itself, including those that result from wind loading, steel frame movement, and siesmic shock. Because Slendwall is comprised of lightweight panels, customers save on shipping costs, and due to ease of construction they save on installation. Moreover, the finish of Slenderwall panels can be made to match the look of surrounding buildings, an important factor when working within a campus or similar environment. Finally, Smith-Midland continues to manufacture the product that established the business more than 40 years ago: the cattleguard.

Company Formed in 1960

Smith-Midland was founded in Midland, Virginia, in 1960 by David G. Smith, a farmer with an creative streak who was always looking to supplement his income with inventions, the most successful of which was his cattleguard. Like many cattle farmers, Smith was frustrated with having to stop and get out of his vehicle in order to open and close farm gates to prevent cattle from escaping a field. He was not the first to devise a cattleguard, but he was perhaps the first who tried to make a business out of selling his solution to others. In essence, the cattleguard was a shallow pit, about six inches in depth, covered by two inches of sand or crushed stone. For a 14-foot cattleguard, the pit would roughly measure 15 feet by 7 feet. The precast concrete fixture were slats that covered the pit, which vehicles could easily drive over but cattle were unable to step through. Side fencing prevented them from stepping around the pit. Makeshift versions relied on wood or pipe, which either wore out or became bent in the middle from use. The main selling point for the Smith Cattleguard was its longevity, which would save customers money in the long run, and the professional installation that relieved the farmer of a time-consuming task. Six months after starting his business, Smith was joined by his 22-year-old son, Rodney I. Smith, the current chairman, president, and chief executive officer of the company. With the passage of another six months, the two officially became partners, with Rodney Smith taking a lead in sales. He was responsible for creating the company's first advertisement, which attracted business from several states. For the first ten years or so, Smith Cattleguard used the family farm as the base for its operations, initially taking up a section of the farm machine shed. As business grew, the company increasingly usurped more space in the shed.

Smith Cattleguard traded on the success of its original idea and soon began to produce other pre-cast concrete farm products. The company introduced the fence line feed bunk for cattle feeding and the center line feed bunk, which allowed cattle to eat from both sides of a divided unit. In addition, Smith Cattleguard developed and sold an electrically heated automatic stock waterer and a concrete panel fence. After approximately five years in business, Smith Cattleguard expanded beyond farm products, supplying underground utility vaults and transformer pads for power companies. Later it introduced highway safety barriers, sound walls, and utility buildings into the product mix. Rodney Smith succeeded his father as president and chief executive officer of the company in 1965 and became chairman of the board in 1970. He also inherited his father's inventive talents, making significant improvements on the design of the original cattleguard as well as designing many of the company's later products. As the business expanded, Smith Cattleguard outgrew its facilities on the Smith farm. In the early 1970s, the company purchased a ten-acre site in Midland and built a factory, which ultimately became a 20-acre complex of office and production facilities. In the mid-1970s, due to the high cost of shipping pre-cast products, it purchased land and built a plant in Reidsville, North Carolina, in order to be competitive in the North Carolina market. In addition, a subsidiary, Smith Carolina, was formed to accommodate this business. Rodney Smith founded several other subsidiaries that would one day make up Smith-Midland. He created Concrete Safety System, the first company of its kind, dedicated to the leasing of precast concrete highway safety barriers to state highway departments and contractors. Smith also founded Easi-Set Industries, Inc., which was launched in 1978 to license the company's pre-cast products, the first full-service licensing operation in the industry. To promote both itself and the licensees, Smith Cattleguard became involved in cooperative advertising. To receive a discount, Midland Advertising & Design, Inc. was formed and proved to be instrumental in the success of the Smith-Midland companies.

Smith-Midland Corporation Name Adopted in 1985

After 25 years in business, and having diversified well beyond its original product, Smith Cattleguard changed its name to Smith-Midland Corporation in 1985. A third generation of the Smith family was now in line to become involved in the running of the business. Ashley Smith was named Vice-President of Sales and Marketing in 1990. During this period, the company began work on a light-weight wall cladding, its Slenderwall concept that was part of a devotion to research and development that had always been instrumental in the growth of Smith-Midland. The idea was to combine the properties of already accepted materials to create a functional highbred product. By early 1993, the company developed a prototype of the Slenderwall system, which joined precast concrete's durability with cold-form galvanized steel's light weight. The product was soon available for sale, enjoying strong growth, and because of its light weight was cheap enough to ship to job sites all along the East Coast, greatly enhancing Smith-Midland's marketing presence. Moreover, through Easi-Set Industries, Slenderwall started to be licensed to qualified manufacturers, further enhancing Smith-Midland's profile.

In October 1994, Smith-Midland completed a corporate restructuring in preparation for taking the company public. The business was now incorporated in Delaware, making the following entities wholly-owned subsidiaries: Smith-Midland Corp. (Virginia); Easi-Set Industries, Inc.; Smith-Carolina Corp.; Concrete Safety Systems, Inc.; and Midland Advertising & Design, Inc. The company's initial public offering was completed in December 1995, when 1 million common shares priced at $3.50 per share were sold, as were 1 million warrants priced at ten cents. The warrants permitted buyers the opportunity to purchase shares of common stock at $4 until December 13, 2000. The price of Smith-Midland quickly moved beyond that level. On its first day of trading on the NASDAQ Small Cap Market, Smith-Midland stock closed above $5. The company netted $2.8 million in the offering, using most of the proceeds to pay off debt and outstanding bills, with $600,000 earmarked for the expansion of its manufacturing capacity.

Although it was an innovative company with much promise Smith-Midland was hindered in its growth by the lack of enough cash flow to keep up with loans made by the Riggs Bank and Myers Trust. In 1998, the company arranged a $4 million term loan with First National Bank of New England, of which approximately $3 million was used to restructure current debt and the balance dedicated to further plant expansion and the purchase of new equipment. This funding arrangement was key to a five-year plan launched by the company to increase Smith-Midland's growth and profitability. Riggs and Myers were both repaid, while monthly payments for debt service was reduced by 40 percent, allowing for much better cash flow. In addition, First National Bank of New England provided a $500,000 revolving line of credit for additional operating funds.

Major Factory Renovation Completed in 1999

Smith-Midland completed a building renovation project in March 1999, gaining an additional 15,600 square feet of manufacturing space. Altogether, the company increased its indoor manufacturing capacity by 40 percent. Cost overruns, however, had an adverse impact on Smith-Midland's bottom line. Although a leader in its field, the company was still a relatively small company, and because it was unable to meet certain conditions it was delisted by the NASDAQ Small Cap and instead sold on the over-the-counter bulletin board. The investment in plant upgrades began to pay off in 2000 and 2001. Revenues topped $16 million in 2000 and approached $27 million in 2001, while net income improved from $593,373 to nearly $2 million during the same period.

In March 2003, Rodney Smith granted an interview to *The Wall Street Transcipt* in which he outlined his plans for Smith-Midland. He said he hoped that the licensing efforts of Easi-Set Industries would become ''the big money maker,'' spearheaded by the licensing of Slenderwall, the product which held the most promise. ''At this point there is no equivalent product to Slenderwall on the market anywhere in any country,'' Smith explained. ''Somebody always has to be first with anything major that's starting to be recognized in any given industry and we are in that position with this product. . . . When you look at all the individual components, every component is tried and proven for many years but we have assembled them in a new and a better way. Therefore, we don't have the resistance of people saying 'It looks great—come back in 20 years' because they know that all the components work.'' Slenderwall took a major step in gaining wider acceptance in the marketplace when in 2002 Smith-Midland secured an important $3.15 million contact to produce and install 68,000 square feet of Slenderwall panels to clad a 32-story New York City high rise hotel. The company's goal for Slenderwall according to Smith was to ''sign up 20 pre-casters in

North America with a goal of $14.5 million each in sales totaling $250 million a year from which our goal would be a 5 percent licensing fee. That by itself would be $12 million to $12.5 million a year of income.'' Because over the years Smith-Midland had arranged some 30 licenses, primarily for its J-J Hooks Concrete Safety Barrier and transportable buildings, it was well positioned to exploit the potential of Slenderwall. Nevertheless, Smith admitted that the company faced a challenge in convincing independent pre-casters that licensing a Smith-Midland product was a profitable idea, and it had to be vigilant about monitoring licensees to maintain quality control so that customers across the country would be assured of receiving a consistent and predictable product. In addition, Smith-Midland would assist licensees in selling the product, sending representatives with licensees to visit architects, as well as people to oversee installation. As a result, Rodney Smith asserted, customers ''will want to come back to us over and over again. It's essential that we monitor and train our licensees properly and then monitor their efforts and assist them.''

Although the economy was enduring a difficult stretch, Smith maintained that Smith-Midland was well suited to weather the storm. ''The bottom line on all this is we are one of the most diversified companies of pre-cast concrete companies in the country and when our competitors are out looking for work we are busy.'' Smith maintained that in the future the company would pursue its ongoing effort to reduce the cost of manufacturing, which would allow it to better compete in terms of pricing. In addition, Smith-Midland would continue to distinguish itself from other concrete pre-casters through its research and development program. According to Smith, ''We have about 12 projects in the R&D hopper. We like to bring out a major improvement on a new or existing product every 18 months or two years. This keeps us in a really different business model than other pre-cast manufacturers. Most pre-casters in America rely on being the low bidder for projects that somebody else creates. We have a whole line of products that other people do not have. Therefore, we get to negotiate for our work because we are good at R&D.'' While Smith-Midland appeared to be somewhat unappreciated by investors, there was good reason to believe that if the company was able to maintain its momentum in the coming years that situation would change.

Principal Subsidiaries

Smith-Midland Corporation (Virginia); Smith-Carolina Corporation; Concrete Safety Systems, Inc.; Midland Advertising & Design, Inc.; Easi-Set Industries, Inc.

Principal Competitors

Lafarge North America; Miller Building Systems; U.S. Concrete.

Further Reading

Hinden, Stan, ''Software Firm Looks For Security in Public Offering,'' *Washington Post*, February 19, 1996, p. F23.

''Smith-Midland Corporation (SMID),'' *The Wall Street Transcript*, March 3, 2003.

''Smith-Midland Ships Telecom Order,'' *Concrete Products*, September 1, 2002, PC8.

—Ed Dinger

Smoby International SA

B.P. 7
39170 Lavans-les-Saint-Claude
France
Telephone: (+33) 3-84-41-38-00
Fax: (+33) 3-84-42-83-24
Web site: http://www.smoby.com

Public Company
Incorporated: 1924 as Moquin Breuil
Employees: 1,408
Sales: EUR 208.54 million ($205 million)(2002)
Stock Exchanges: Euronext Paris
Ticker Symbol: SMO
NAIC: 339932 Game, Toy, and Children's Vehicle
 Manufacturing

Smoby International SA is France's leading toy manufacturer and number three in Europe. Posting sales of more than EUR 208 million, Smoby primarily targets the infant through age ten market with its stable of toy companies, which include Smoby, Ecoiffier, Monneret, Pico, Unice, and Smoby Baby (formerly Lardy). Smoby's catalog includes some 2,000 products grouped among several major categories, including infant to three years (15 percent of sales); role-playing (50 percent); outdoor (15 percent); and family (8 percent). While Smoby itself encompasses a wide range of toys, the brand is especially recognized for its plastic role-playing toys. Ecoiffier features a collection of educational and stackable and construction toys. Monneret's major product are tabletop soccer games. Spain's Unice is one of Europe's leading manufacturers of playing balls and balloons, and Pico, also based in Spain, is a leading maker of toy strollers and related toys. In addition, Smoby's Mob subsidiary produces plastic bottles and packaging, accounting for 12 percent of the company's sales. Located in France's Jura region, the heart of the country's toy-making industry, Smoby operates factories in France, Spain, and Romania and distribution subsidiaries in the United Kingdom, Switzerland, Italy, Germany, Argentina, and Hong Kong. International sales have become a strong component of Smoby's success, as some 57 percent of the group's sales come from outside France. In the early years of the new century, Smoby

has begun expanding beyond its core European market, which accounts for 93 percent of sales, with an entry into Brazil and Argentina and moves into the Asian region. Listed on the Euronext Paris Exchange, Smoby is led by Jean-Christophe Breuil, grandson of the company's founder.

From Pipes to Plastic: 1920s–1970s

For many French, the country's Jura region had long been synonymous for its two most important products: wood and toys. One of the most vibrant offshoots of the region's wood industry at the beginning of the 20th century was the production of tobacco pipes. The area surrounding Saint Claude was particularly active in this industry, with pipe-making workshops dating back to the 18th century. Early pipe production remained the province of artisans, but by the mid-1800s pipe-making had increasingly become industrialized. By the end of the century, more than a third of the total population was employed in the pipe-making industry, and by the outbreak of World War I the area contained some 50 factories.

Among these were companies operated by the Moquin and Breuil families. Both companies remained modest operations, however, until 1937, when Jean Breuil, born in 1908, whose family had founded its factory in 1924, married Georgette Moquin, whose brother led that family's pipe business. Breuil and Moquin went into business together, creating the new company SARL Moquin Breuil in 1939. In the meantime, cigarette smoking had already begun rising in popularity, steadily reducing demand for pipes. The company diversified its product lines, adding pens and mechanical pencils to its production, as well as wooden housekeeping products.

Moquin Breuil continued to grow during World War II and by the end of the war had three workshops in operation. The arrival of the Allied forces in France further stimulated the demand for cigarettes, and by the end of the 1940s the demand for pipes was shrinking dramatically. The company, by then led by Jean Breuil, decided to invest in a new material, plastic, and in 1947 the company acquired its first injection-molding machine.

The company now converted much of its production of household and housekeeping items to plastics. At the same time, it developed an important offshoot of this activity when it

Company Perspectives:

Play is more than having fun! It also means developing one's senses, physical ability, and language. And integrating the ideas of sociability, sharing, and exchanging. Finally, it's a training ground and preparation for tomorrow. At Smoby, we listen to children. By studying their behavior and identifying their desires, our experience grows each day. Smoby's strategy is based on values of complicity, creativity, and early-learning. Our mission is to create toys that will develop a child's independence and ability to adapt while stimulating the imagination. For this reason, we give importance to emotions and multiple sensory experience when conceiving our toys.

began producing a small line of plastic toys, another prominent industry in the Jura region. Through the 1960s, however, toys remained only a small part of the company's operations, accounting for just 25 percent of its sales. In 1967, however, the company joined with a number of other, dedicated toy makers, including Lardy, Clairbois, and Berchet, to form an export cooperative, Superjouet.

Focus on Toys in the 1980s

The major turning point for the Moquin Breuil company came at the end of the 1960s, when Breuil's son, Jean-Pierre, born in 1943, joined the company with his 20-year-old wife Dany. The pair took over the company's toy department in 1968 and became responsible for its development. The company's plastic production by then took place under the name Mob, a contraction of Moquin Breuil, and specialized in cheap plastic toys, which were picked up by the growing supermarket and hypermarket chains in the country. The company also produced toys as part of product bonuses, such as are found in cereal boxes or attached to laundry detergent containers. At the same time, Moquin Breuil, through Mob, launched into the production of plastic bottles, containers, and other packaging items.

Dany Breuil soon became the chief inspiration for the company's growth. With two young children at the beginning of the 1970s, and with the rise of child development theories favoring the necessity of play in a child's education, Breuil became interested in the educational aspects of toys. At the same time, Mob faced growing competition from the flood of cheap plastic toys from Japan, Taiwan, and elsewhere.

Under Dany and Jean-Pierre Breuil, the company began to invest in research and development in order to create a new line of higher-quality, educational toys. By 1978, the company had developed a new brand name, Smoby. The new line of toys—the company was to become synonymous with such role-playing toys as its grocery store and construction cranes—were a quick success, backed by strong investments in marketing. For its distribution, the company made use of supermarket and hypermarket channels, which had been quickly gaining on the traditionally small, city-center shops. The company also targeted the European market for sales.

By the early 1980s, the company's sales had topped FFr120 million. Over the next decade, toys became the company's primary focus, although it continued to build up its Mob pack-

aging operations, extending it into the pharmaceutical, food, and chemical industries. By the end of the 1980s, Mob contributed some 20 percent of the company's total sales.

Now known as Smoby, the company went public in 1983, listing on the Lyon Stock Exchange. The founding families nonetheless retained control of 58 percent of the company's stock, including 72 percent of its voting rights. Two years later, founder Jean Breuil retired, turning over leadership of the company to Jean-Pierre Breuil.

A new phase in Smoby's growth began in 1987 when the company acquired new plastics technology in the form of rotational molding. The new procedure, invented in the United States and adapted to meet European standards and market demand by Smoby itself, enabled the company to begin producing toys on a larger scale, and Smoby quickly established itself as one of the leading makers of outdoor slides, playhouses, and related products.

The launch of the company's first rotational molded toy, the ''Fée du Logis,'' became the company's first success in its newest market. Smoby continued adding to its rotational molding capacity over the next decade and expanded its range of large-scale designs to include some 25 models. Meanwhile, the company had successfully expanded internationally, opening distribution subsidiaries in Spain, Germany, England, and Switzerland. By 1991, Smoby's sales had risen to nearly FFr400 million.

The death of Jean-Pierre Breuil in 1992 placed Dany Breuil in the company's CEO spot. Joining Breuil was son Jean-Christophe, who, at age 20, abandoned his studies in international finance to help his mother keep the family business on track.

International Targets for the 1990s and Beyond

The 1990s were to mark a new period of expansion for Smoby. The company set itself an ambitious strategic target: that of becoming one of the top five toy makers in Europe by the end of the decade. As part of that strategy, Smoby decided to pursue growth through external expansion, starting with the acquisition of fellow Superjouet partner Lardy in 1993. That company, founded in 1952, had become a specialist in toys and other products (such as stuffed animals) for the early childhood years, and the addition of Lardy gave Smoby a strong boost in extending its own product range. It also encouraged Smoby to strike out on its own, and in 1994 the company, together with Lardy, left the Superjouet group, which later became Smoby's chief French rival, Berchet.

The year 1994 saw the next piece of the Smoby puzzle come into place when the company acquired Ecoiffier, a toy maker specializing in educational, creative, and construction toys while at the same time doing a strong business in the low-end toy segment. Like Lardy and Smoby, Ecoiffier had its roots in the Jura region and had risen to become one of France's toy leaders.

Smoby found new allies for its growth into the mid-1990s. Until the late 1980s, the retail toy market had been dominated by the supermarket and hypermarket circuit. Yet these stores tended to maintain limited toy departments outside of the crucial winter holiday period. In the early 1990s, however, a new

Key Dates:

1937: SARL Moquin Breuil founded to manufacture pipes and other wooden household items.
1947: Moquin Breuil begins producing plastic housekeeping items and toys under the Mob name.
1967: The company joins the Superjouet export cooperative.
1968: Jean-Pierre Breuil and wife Dany Breuil join the company and take over its toy operation.
1978: The company creates new toy brand, Smoby, while also developing its Mob plastic containers business.
1983: The company changes its name to Smoby and lists on the Lyon Stock Exchange.
1987: Smoby acquires its first rotation-molding machine, enabling it to begin making large-scale and outdoor toys.
1992: Dany Breuil takes over as CEO.
1999: The company signs a licensing agreement with Brazil's Gulliver to introduce the Smoby brand to the South American market.
2002: Jean-Christophe Breuil is named CEO.
2003: Founder Jean Breuil dies at the age of 95.

breed of toy specialists appeared in the French retail market in the form of such large scale "category killers" such as Toys "R" Us, Jouetland, Jouéclub, and other firms that introduced year-round toy shopping—as well as the floor space to display Smoby's large-scale products.

Smoby's own product range enabled it to cover the younger children's market. In 1996, the company acquired majority control (raised to full control in 2002) of another Jura-region toy maker, Monneret, which had already been in business at the beginning of the 20th century. Monneret had launched into plastic toy production in 1950 with the purchase of its own blow-molding press. By the time of its acquisition by Smoby, Monneret had become a market leader in its specialty of table-top soccer games yet had been struggling against losses in the mid-1990s. The addition of Monneret gave Smoby a link into the older children's segment while forcing the company to restructure its own operations as it worked to restore Monneret back to profitability.

Smoby returned to external expansion in 1998, turning to the international market for the first time in order to acquire Spain's Juguetes Pico. Based in Ibi, Pico specialized in manufacturing toy strollers, carriages, cribs, and related toys. The purchase not only helped reinforce Smoby's own toy range, it also gave it Pico's expertise in producing and working with tubes, which in turn enabled Smoby to enter the market for tricycles and scooters.

The purchase of Pico helped pushed Smoby's sales past the FFr1 billion mark ($150 million) in 1998, making Smoby the toy-making leader in France. The company was also on its way to achieving its long-term goal of becoming a leader in the European toy industry. By the end of the 1990s, more than 50 percent of the company's sales came from outside of France. By then, Smoby had made its first moves into the South American market, which was boosted in 1999 with a production and

distribution agreement with Brazilian toy producer Gulliver to bring Smoby's toys into that country. Meanwhile, Smoby had continued to invest in its Mob packaging subsidiary, adding a new production site in 1994, and acquiring Novembal Flaconnages, in the north of France, in 1998.

Smoby's next acquisition came at the beginning of 2001, when it once again turned to Spain, acquiring Unice. Founded in 1968 in Estella, in the north of Spain, Unice had become a leading manufacturer of play balls—backed by its patented method for applying illustrations to the ball surface—as well as balloons. The addition of Unice also added that company's recently established subsidiaries in Brazil and Mexico, both of which began production in 2001. Back at home, Smoby took its first step into the electronics market with the launch of a CD-ROM based on its popular Lilou doll.

By the end of 2002, Smoby had reorganized its holdings, absorbing Monneret and converting its Lardy brand into a new Smoby Baby brand. The company also entered into a joint-venture with leading Italian toy maker and distributor Giochi Preziosi. While rising raw materials prices and difficult economic conditions combined to depress the company's profits, Smoby continued to post strong revenue gains that year, topping EUR 208 million in sales. By then, Dany Breuil had turned over leadership of the company to son Jean-Christophe Breuil. Founder Jean Breuil died in April 2003 at the age of 95, having seen his company grow from a small pipe making workshop into one of the top three European toy companies.

Principal Subsidiaries

Ecoiffier; Euroball (50%); Giochi Preziosi France (49%); J 39 Distribution (80%); Juguetes Picó (Spain); MOB; Monneret Industrie; Monneret Jouets; Sjp (Spain); Smoby; Smoby Argentina; Smoby España; Smoby Hong Kong; Smoby International; Smoby Italia; Smoby Suisse; Smoby UK; Unice (Spain).

Principal Competitors

Mattel Inc.; Hasbro Inc.; Lego A/S; Little Tikes; Tomy Company Ltd.; Giochi Preziosi SpA; Simba Toys GmbH und Co.; Top-Toy A/S; Milton Bradley Co.; Berchet SA.

Further Reading

"A fini de jouer: Dany Breuil," *Nouvel Economiste*, November 9, 2001.
Chirot, Françoise, "Chez Smoby, le Père Noël est une femme," *Le Monde*, December 20, 1991.
Henriet, Monique, "Décès de Jean Breuil: Le monde du jouet en deuil," *La Voix de Jura*, April 30, 2003.
"Jean-Christophe Breuil: la force de la famille," *La Voix de Jura*, October 3, 2002.
"Le jurassien Smoby souhaite accelerer son internationalisation," *Les Echos*, September 29, 1999, p. 18.
"Smoby renoue avec une croissance a deux chiffres," *Les Echos*, September 27, 2001, p. 17.
"Smoby resiste malgre une conjoncture ardue," *Les Echos*, October 12, 2002, p. 12.
"Smoby to Acquire Spanish Balloon Manufacturer Unice," *European Report*, January 17, 2001, p. 600.

—M.L. Cohen

Sonic Innovations Inc.

2795 East Cottonwood Parkway, Suite 660
Salt Lake City, Utah 84117-7261
U.S.A.
Telephone: (801) 365-2800
Toll Free: (888) 880-0327
Fax: (801) 365-3000
Web site: http://www.sonici.com

Public Company
Incorporated: 1991 as Sonix Technologies, Inc.
Employees: 331
Sales: $68.02 million (2002)
Stock Exchanges: NASDAQ
Ticker Symbol: SNCI
NAIC: 334510 Electromedical and Electrotherapeutic
    Apparatus Manufacturing

Sonic Innovations Inc. makes and sells advanced digital hearing aids. The company was launched with digital signal processing (DSP) technology developed by a handful of professors in Utah and California. Sonic has five product lines; four of these—the Natura, Altair, Tribute, and Quartet—are available in a variety of models: behind-the-ear (BTE), in-the-ear (ITE), in-the-canal (ITC), mini-canal (MC), and completely-in-the-canal (CIC). The Adesso, the smallest digital hearing aid on the market, is an instant-fit CIC model. Sonic moved into international markets quickly. Europe ($14.2 million) and the rest of the world ($13.2 million) outside of North America accounted for a significant portion of the company's 2002 revenues of $68 million.

Origins

Sonic Innovations Inc. had its origins in the digital signal processing (DSP) research of Brigham Young University professors Doug Chabries and Richard Christiansen. Chabries developed a new algorithm for processing audio signals. On the way to developing a viable hearing aid, he was assisted by Thomas Stockham, a digital recording pioneer from the University of Utah, and Carver Mead, professor of electrical engineering at the California Institute of Technology. Mead designed the extremely small and powerful computer chip for the hearing aids.

The group formed Sonix Technologies, Inc. in Utah in May 1991 as they sought venture capital backing. Utah's Centers of Excellence program, created in 1987 to help the state's university researchers create commercial businesses, was an important early supporter.

By 1996, Sonix had raised $6 million in start-up money from several private groups. Sonix changed its name to Sonic Innovations Inc. that year, and Andrew Raguskus was made president and CEO in September 1996. Raguskus had formerly been an executive with two California companies: ReSound Corp., a hearing aid maker in Redwood City, and Sonic Solutions, a Navato-based designer of digital audio workstations. By the time of Sonic's first product launch in September 1998, the company had 82 employees. It was based in Murray, Utah, a suburb of Salt Lake City.

First Product in 1998

The company's first product, the Natura hearing aid, was rolled out in September 1998. The units sold for about $5,000 a pair, several times more than lower-end, conventional hearing aids but more than $2,000 less than the Widex Senso, a top-end digital model. Sonic was not the first to market; Oticon, Siemens and Widex were also selling digital units, which had been available since 1996. However, Sonic's product had some distinctive advantages.

Analog hearing aids had changed little since the 1970s, and they had many drawbacks. They amplified all noise equally, sometimes uncomfortably so. The high-pitched shriek of feedback was another unwelcome occurrence. Sonic Innovations revolutionized the industry in two ways. Its hearing aids sounded better than those of the competition, and they were small enough to be barely noticeable.

The Natura's computer chip, said to be the most powerful used in a hearing aid, was capable of processing sound much faster than traditional hearing aids. The Natura had nine channels, versus the three usually found in analog units. This al-

---

Company Perspectives:

Mission: to be the best hearing aid company in the world. Core Values: we are committed to delivering improved satisfaction to hearing impaired consumers; we are committed to delivering outstanding service & value to hearing aid dispensers; we are committed to continuous innovation; we are committed to practicing high standards of ethics, honesty, and professionalism; we are committed to providing value to our stakeholders.

---

lowed audiologists to dial in reinforcement for the specific frequencies of hearing loss in half-octave increments. This was important, since high frequency pitches were usually the first to be lost. The Natura claimed to help users distinguish conversation from background noise and could be tuned for two different listening environments.

Sonic's new hearing aid also simplified the buying process. Using proprietary EXPRESSfit software, the Natura was programmed via Palm Pilot, helping cut down on fitting time, and some versions were small enough to fit deep inside the ear canal, making them virtually invisible. The Natura's small size was possible due to miniature electronic components from AVX Corp. of Myrtle Beach, S.C.

Sonic faced a ripe market. The *Boston Globe* reported a survey that estimated half of users were unhappy with their hearing aids. Twenty-seven million people in the United States had problems hearing, yet one survey estimated only 10 to 20 percent of these used a hearing aid. Nevertheless, the worldwide retail market was valued at $5 billion a year, and hearing aid sales were increasing about 5 percent a year. This rate was expected to rise with the aging of the Baby Boomer generation.

During its first twelve months of sales, Sonic took in $30 million, and its loss rose 7 percent to $14.9 million. More than 40 percent of revenues came from one customer, Starkey Laboratories Inc., a hearing aid manufacturer itself.

International in 1999

With more than 300 million people around the world suffering some hearing loss, Sonic moved quickly to penetrate the global market. Distributor M-E Hearing Systems Pty. Ltd. launched the Natura in Australia in November 1999. The next year, Hoya Healthcare Corporation began distributing the company's products in Japan. International sales accounted for 28 percent ($8 million) of Sonic's net revenues in 1999. Sonic's total sales for the year ended December 31, 1999 were $28.7 million, producing a net loss of $14.9 million.

In 1998, Sonic set up a subsidiary to market in Europe. Sonic Innovations A/S was based in Denmark, home to three other leading high-tech hearing aid manufacturers. The company also had offices in Germany and Belgium. By the end of 1999, Sonic had moved its manufacturing operations from Salt Lake City to a new 12,000-square-foot facility in Eagan, Minnesota, a hearing aid industry center. In addition, Sonic moved its headquarters into 50,000 square feet of new office space in Salt Lake

City. The company had 125 employees there and 50 in Eagan, totaling 211 employees worldwide.

Public in 2000

Sonic Innovations Inc. listed shares on the NASDAQ stock exchange in May 2000. The fall-off in tech stocks at the time made it an unwelcoming market. However, Sonic's shares rose 50 percent from the original price of $14 in the first day of trading. One of the company's backers attributed this to the fact that the company had "real revenue and real products," uncommon commodities during the dot-com boom and bust. Sonic raised $54 million in the initial public offering.

By this time, the company had 225 employees and had just introduced a second hearing aid line, the Conforma. The Conforma was unique in that its soft foam shell allowed users to be fitted with the hearing aid in a single visit to an audiologist. Others required multiple visits for impressions to be made and the fit of acrylic shells checked over a period of one to two weeks. Sonic likened the convenience to that of the soft contact lens, which had tripled the contact lens market over three decades.

Another innovation introduced during 2000 was noise reduction, first available in the Natura 2SE model. By the end of the year, Sonic had introduced another hearing aid line, the mid-priced Altair.

Sonic also sold components to rival manufacturer Starkey Laboratories Inc. of Minneapolis. Starkey accounted for $7.3 million of Sonic's 1999 revenues. Sales of Sonic's own brands became more important when Starkey announced it was scaling back its orders in late 2000.

Net sales rose 80 percent to $51.7 million in 2000, while gross profit increased 119 percent to $25.5 million. The company posted a net loss of $2.2 million. It had lost $14.4 million the year before.

Sonic continued to acquire international hearing aid companies with distribution networks in 2001 and 2002. Sonic's Australian distributor M-E Hearing Systems had been created by the optometry company Laubman & Pank. After acquiring Laubman & Pank, new owner OPSM Protector sold M-E Hearing Systems and Hearing Aid Specialists Pty. Ltd. to Sonic for $5 million in July 2001. The acquisitions took the Sonic Innovations name. This added about $10 million a year to Sonic's revenues. M-E Hearing had 110 employees at the time of the purchase and produced 15,000 hearing aids a year. Sonic was planning to expand its operations as a supplier for markets in Australia, Southeast Asia, South America, and South Africa.

Sonic acquired seven international businesses in all in 2002; five of these were existing Sonic distributors. Sonic acquired its Danish hearing aid distributor, Omni-ReSound, in February 2002. It instantly gained a significant share of the Canadian market with the October acquisition of Ontario's Sentech Systems and Orsonique of Quebec. Sonic also acquired companies in Switzerland, Austria, the United Kingdom, and the Netherlands in 2002.

Key Dates:

1991: Sonix Technologies, Inc. is formed to market BYU hearing aid technology.
1996: Sonix becomes Sonic Innovations.
1998: The company's first product, the Natura hearing aid, is introduced.
1999: Sonic begins doing business internationally.
2000: Shares begin trading on the NASDAQ exchange; Conforma is introduced.
2002: The Adesso instant-fit hearing aid is introduced.

First Profits in 2002

The "adesso" instant-fit hearing aid was introduced in March 2002. The adesso was a completely-in-the-canal device that was virtually invisible when worn. It was aimed at first-time hearing aid wearers with mild to moderate hearing loss.

Net sales rose 19 percent in 2002, to $68 million. North American sales accounted for $39.7 million of the total, with the remainder divided between Europe and the rest of the world. The company logged its first profitable year with a net income of $32,000. However, demand in the global hearing aid market had begun to decline significantly.

Sonic countered sales declines by announcing product improvements at an industry convention in April 2003. The company continued to bolster its global distribution network through acquisitions. In May, it agreed to acquire German hearing aid distributor Sanomed Handelsgesellschaft mbH for an initial price of $13 million, plus another $4 million to $5 million based on financial performance. Sanomed's 2002 revenues were about $20 million. Germany was the world's second largest hearing aid market.

Principal Subsidiaries

Audifon U.K. Ltd.; Hearing Aid Specialists Pty Limited (Australia); Hoorcomfort Nederland B.V. (Netherlands); Hoortoestelcentrum Sneek B.V. (Netherlands); Omni ApS (Denmark); Omni Otoplast ApS (Denmark); Sonic Innovations AG (Switzerland); Sonic Innovations A/S (Denmark); Sonic Innovations Canada Ltd.; Sonic Innovations GmbH (Austria); Sonic Innovations Pty Ltd. (Australia); Star Medical Europe B.V. (Netherlands).

Principal Competitors

Phonak S.A.; Siemens GmbH; Starkey Laboratories Inc.; Widex A/S; William Demant Holding A/S.

Further Reading

Adams, Brooke, "Colleges Cash in on Brainpower," *Salt Lake Tribune*, December 26, 1999, p. C1.

Arnst, Catherine, "Now, High-Definition Hearing Aids," *Business Week*, October 26, 1998, p. 143.

"Australia's OPSM Protector to Sell Hearing Aid Unit to US Co.," *Asia Pulse*, July 25, 2001.

Carricaburu, Lisa, "S.L. Company Launches Hearing Aid That Better Mimics Inner-Ear Action," *Salt Lake Tribune*, October 7, 1998, p. D6.

Christopher, Alistair, "IPOs/Recent Issues: Sonic Innovations," *Venture Capital Journal*, July 1, 2000.

Collins, Lois M., "Sounds Good," *Deseret News* (Salt Lake City), October 11, 1998, p. M1.

"Computer-Programmed Hearing Aid Hits Market," *Greensboro News & Record* (North Carolina), October 7, 1998, p. B8.

Davis, Robert, "Finely Tuned Hearing Aid Controls the Quality of Sound," *USA Today*, October 6, 1998, p. 6D.

Eisenberg, Anne, "Hearing Aid's Flexible Cover Makes a Good Fit Easy to Get," *New York Times*, May 11, 2000, p. G3.

Goodman, Sherri C., "Lower Demand Hurts Maker of Hearing Aids," *Salt Lake Tribune*, January 1, 2003, p. D7.

Hailstone, Barry, "Hearing Aid Making All the Right Noises," *The Advertiser* (Australia), November 13, 1999, p. 7.

"Hearing Aid Campaign Generates Right Noise," *Healthcare PR & Marketing News*, February 4, 1999.

"Hearing Aid Sounds Like Improvement for Users," *Medical Industry Today*, May 9, 2000.

Jebsen, Per, "Rise in Sonic Innovations Shows IPO Market Revival," *National Post*, May 3, 2000, p. D4.

Milne, Chris, "Sound Expansion Ahead After Sell-Off," *The Advertiser* (Australia), Finance Sec., August 13, 2001, p. 26.

Mitchell, Lesley, "Program Turns Good Ideas into Companies," *Salt Lake Tribune*, December 2, 2000, p. B3.

"New Product Introductions Boost Sonic Stock Price," *Deseret News* (Salt Lake City), April 8, 2003, p. E1.

Oberbeck, Steven, "Sonic Innovations Files to Go Public," *Salt Lake Tribune*, February 24, 2000, p. D4.

Saltus, Richard, "Do You Hear What I Hear?" *Boston Globe*, January 31, 1999, p. 6.

"Sonic Innovations to Buy German Firm Sanomed," *Deseret News* (Salt Lake City), May 14, 2003, p. D10.

"Sonic Innovations Uses Digital Technology to Improve Hearing Aids," *Deseret News* (Salt Lake City), June 25, 2000, p. M7.

"Tiny Capacitors Aid Hearing," *High Tech Ceramics News*, July 1999.

Van Eyck, Zack, "Sonic Innovations Aims to Help World Hear," *Deseret News* (Salt Lake City), May 3, 2000, p. C3.

Wallace, Brice, "Sonic Faces 'Challenge' with Major Customer," *Deseret News* (Salt Lake City), October 26, 2000, p. B5.

—Frederick C. Ingram

SonoSite

SonoSite, Inc.

21919 30th Avenue Southeast
Bothell, Washington 98021
U.S.A.
Telephone: (425) 951-1200
Toll Free: (888) 482-9449
Fax: (425) 951-1201
Web site: http://www.sonosite.com

Public Company
Incorporated: 1998
Employees: 350
Sales: $73 million (2002)
Stock Exchanges: NASDAQ
Ticker Symbol: SONO
NAIC: 334510 Electromedical and Electrotherapeutic
   Apparatus Manufacturing

SonoSite, Inc. is the industry pioneer in point-of-care ultrasound devices, a new, technologically advanced breed of medical equipment that is far smaller than conventional ultrasound systems. Spun off from ATL Ultrasound in 1998, SonoSite produces and markets a line of ultrasound devices that weigh between 2.5 pounds and six pounds, which greatly increases the flexibility and cost-effectiveness of performing ultrasound examinations. The company sells its products on a worldwide basis, relying on a direct sales model that has improved its ability to articulate the advantages of its technological innovation.

Origins

SonoSite's niche within the medical equipment industry—a niche it created through its pioneering work—is predicated on technological advancements achieved roughly 40 years before the company's founding. During the late 1950s, ultrasound emerged as a safe and noninvasive method of medical diagnosis. By using low power, high frequency sound waves, ultrasound offered physicians real-time dynamic images of tissues and bodily fluids. A transducer placed on the skin or in a body cavity near the targeted area of a patient received sound waves reflected from the patient's tissues and bodily fluid. Based on the reflections

received by the transducer, the ultrasound system measured and organized the sound waves to produce an image for visual examination. At first, ultrasound was used to ascertain the general shape, size, and structure of internal soft tissues and organs. In later years, as the technology evolved, ultrasound was used in a variety of medical disciplines such as radiology, obstetrics, gynecology, and cardiology. Ultrasound grew to be an invaluable aid to medical practitioners, saving time, money, and lives.

During the 1990s, SonoSite sought to make a revolutionary change in ultrasound technology. The company aimed to make an ultrasound device drastically smaller than extant models, a goal, if achieved and if accepted by the medical community, that promised to radically alter the ultrasound market. The pursuit of this goal, however, began as a project undertaken by another company.

In 1994, a company named ATL Ultrasound began working on the design and specifications for a miniaturized ultrasound device for diagnostic imaging. The work by Bothell, Washington-based ATL eventually attracted the attention of the federal government, giving the project sufficient life to justify the formation of a division within ATL's corporate structure. In February 1996, the U.S. Office of Naval Research, under a grant through the U.S. Government Defense Advanced Research Projects Agency (DARPA), selected ATL among a consortium of entities to pursue further work with miniaturized ultrasound devices. DARPA, which awarded to ATL a two-year matching grant, was interested in a portable ultrasound device for use on the battlefield or for use in catastrophic events to diagnose victims of severe trauma. Aided by the grant and driven by its own financial investment, ATL stepped up its research and development of a portable, or "point-of-care," ultrasound device. In February 1997, exactly one year after the DARPA grant, ATL grouped its portable ultrasound activities into the Handheld Systems Business Group, the immediate predecessor to SonoSite.

The work performed under the DARPA contract was delivered to the U.S. Department of Defense on time and under budget in November 1998, yielding the first portable ultrasound prototype. By the time the Handheld Systems Business Group completed this project, however, it had moved on to other, potentially more lucrative work. It had, in fact, ceased to exist in name.

Company Perspectives:

Our corporate mission is to deliver revolutionary ultrasound-based visualization products and services that improve healthcare. Our goal is to lead in the design, development, and commercialization of high performance, all-digital ultrasound devices. We plan to reach this goal by maximizing the productivity of our U.S. and European direct sales forces, raising market awareness of the SonoSite brand name, maintaining product and technology leadership, providing education services to healthcare professionals, and expanding into new and existing ultrasound markets.

1998 Spin Off

Handheld Systems Business Group spent slightly more than a year within ATL's fold before its potential warranted the formation of a separate company. The final step in the evolution from project to division to company was made on April 6, 1998, when a new entity, SonoSite, was spun off as a separate company. Under the terms of the spin off, which included the company's initial public offering of stock at $11.75 per share, an arrangement was made between ATL and SonoSite. SonoSite entered into a cross-license agreement that gave it exclusive right to use certain ATL technology existing on April 6, 1998 or developed during the three-year period following April 6, 1998, but only in ultrasound systems weighing 15 pounds or less. For its part, ATL was given the exclusive right to use SonoSite technology existing on April 6, 1998 or developed by the company during the three-year period following April 6, 1998 in ultrasound systems weighing more than 15 pounds.

The management team that led SonoSite as it started out on its own was drawn from ATL's ranks. Heading the team was Kevin M. Goodwin, who began his career in the medical products industry as a national distribution manager for a company called American Hospital Supply Corporation. Goodwin left American Hospital to work for Picker International, where he was employed as area manager for the southwestern United States. Next, he landed a sales position at Baxter Healthcare. Goodwin distinguished himself during his tenure at Baxter Healthcare, becoming the top sales representative during his first year at the company's American General Healthcare division. Goodwin joined ATL in 1987 and continued to excel, earning a promotion to vice-president and general manager for ATL's operations in Asia Pacific, Latin America, Australia, and Canada (APLAC). During Goodwin's stint governing APLAC, the unit recorded growth at a rate eclipsing all other ATL units. In recognition of his performance, ATL's senior executives selected Goodwin to serve as vice-president and general manager of the Handheld Systems Business Group when the division was formed in February 1997. Goodwin was appointed president and chief executive officer of SonoSite upon its formation.

On the technological side of SonoSite, the company's principal executives were Blake Little and Dr. Juin-Jet Hwang. Little, who held a Bachelor of Science degree in electrical engineering from the University of Washington, joined ATL in 1988. While at ATL, Little served in various capacities, including presiding as senior manager of product development for the company's

Front-end Design group. In this position, Little was responsible for ultrasound system architecture, circuit board, and microchip design tasks. When the Handheld Systems Business Group was spun off, Little started as the director of ultrasound imaging development before being promoted to vice-president and director of engineering. Dr. Hwang earned his doctorate in electrical engineering from the University of Tennessee. In the years leading up to his involvement with SonoSite, Dr. Hwang authored more than 30 scientific publications and taught at several universities. In 1980, he joined a company called ADR Ultrasound, which was acquired by ATL three years later. At ATL, Dr. Hwang served as the principal project engineer and principal system architect for several ATL products. He first began working on the development of point-of-care ultrasound devices in October 1995. When the Handheld Systems Business Group was formed, Dr. Hwang was appointed its chief scientist. Concurrent with the formation of SonoSite, Dr. Hwang was named the company's chief technology officer.

SonoSite began its corporate life with control over potentially valuable technology but with no marketable product. Management believed, however, that the company could achieve financial viability once it opened a new market within the medical equipment industry. The company's survival, as was the case with most industry pioneers, depended on its ability not only to deliver a product to market but also on its success in convincing its potential customer base that the new technology was worth the investment. From its perspective, SonoSite's management was confident that healthcare providers would see the advantages of a portable, point-of-care ultrasound device. The size and complexity of traditional ultrasound systems generally forced physicians to refer patients to an imaging center, such as a hospital's radiology department, where a trained sonographer performed the examination. In contrast, SonoSite's technology promised ultrasound devices weighing roughly six pounds, far less than the 300-pound devices found in imaging centers. There were cost advantages as well, with handheld devices targeted for a sales price of roughly $25,000, as opposed to the $100,000 price tag of a traditional ultrasound system. In the years ahead, SonoSite's most difficult task would be convincing the healthcare industry that its portable devices were superior to the existing products on the market.

The process of preaching the advantages of a portable ultrasound device to the healthcare industry actively began not long after SonoSite's formation. In May 1998, the company received pre-market clearance from the U.S. Food and Drug Administration (FDA) for its ultrasound prototype, the SonoSite 180. The following month, SonoSite forged a U.S. distribution agreement with Physicians Sales and Service (PSS), a subsidiary of PSS World Medical. Through this agreement, the foundation was laid for the distribution of the SonoSite 180 system to private physicians' offices. In January 1999, the company opened up another distribution channel by signing an agreement with another PSS World Medical subsidiary, Diagnostic Imaging. Through the agreement with Diagnostic Imaging, a distribution channel was opened to market the SonoSite 180 system to hospitals, imaging centers, and radiologists. In March 1999, the company received another pre-market clearance for an improved version of the SonoSite 180 system. The FDA's approval covered ten clinical applications for the commercial

Key Dates:

1994: ATL Ultrasound begins work on a miniaturized ultrasound device for diagnostic imaging.
1997: ATL forms the Handheld Systems Business Group.
1998: The Handheld Systems Business Group is spun off as SonoSite, Inc.
1999: SonoSite ships its first products in September.
2002: SonoSite records its first profitable fiscal quarter.

version of SonoSite's handheld device, including obstetrical, gynecology, abdominal, and cardiovascular imaging.

In September 1999, SonoSite began shipping the SonoSite 180 system worldwide, marking the company's maturation into a genuine going enterprise. Improvements in the SonoSite 180 system followed, incorporating features that were offered in next-generation product lines, such as the SonoSite 180PLUS, which debuted in April 2001. Sales of SonoSite's devices were sluggish, however, falling short of the company's expectations. At the same time, SonoSite's losses mounted, forcing management to re-address the way in which it conducted its business. Belief in the technology had not waned, but the way in which the company promoted its products and broadcast the superiority of its technology had begun to become a topic of debate. SonoSite's financial problems, in the eyes of Goodwin, did not stem from technological issues but from the efficacy of the company's sales and marketing efforts.

Direct Sales Spurs Growth in the 21st Century

Goodwin's noted success in sales helped SonoSite begin to improve its financial position. In late 2000 and early 2001, the company started to assume far greater responsibility in its marketing efforts by shifting away from its reliance on third-party distributors and assembling a direct sales network in its place. By doing so, the company gained greater control over its approach to potential customers in the healthcare industry. The advantages of SonoSite's innovative technology could thereby be conveyed with greater persuasiveness than could be expected from third-party distributors, whose interests ran beyond focusing exclusively on marketing the SonoSite brand name.

The adoption of a direct sales model was credited with sparking SonoSite's financial growth. By the end of 2002, the company employed 50 direct sales representatives in the United States and 27 clinical application specialists. Overseas, the company continued to rely on third-party distributors in some areas, but direct sales operations had been established in the United Kingdom, France, Germany, and Spain. As the new sales and marketing approach was put into place, the company's financial status improved. In 2000, annual revenues more than tripled, rising to $32 million. In 2001, the final tally amounted to more than $45 million. In 2002, sales reached $73 million, 42 percent of which came from international sales. Profitability continued to be a nagging problem, however, but a glimmer of hope arrived at the end of 2002, providing justifiable cause for celebration at the company's Bothell headquarters.

In 2002, SonoSite posted a net loss of $7.7 million, far less than the $21.6 million recorded in 1999 and the $19 million registered in 2000, but a significant loss, nevertheless. Despite the sour news, the company's fourth fiscal quarter in 2002 marked a turning point in SonoSite's history. For the quarter, the company generated $25 million in sales and a profit of $869,000, the first profitable quarter in the company's history. Goodwin, in a February 14, 2003 interview with *Knight-Ridder/Tribune Business News,* explained the mood in Bothell. "People are very focused," he said, "and the intensity is high. There is an air of satisfaction that we passed through this gate, but don't think for a second that we'll rest on it."

As SonoSite prepared for the future, there were many challenging "gates" to pass through. Widespread acceptance of its technology remained only a hope by the time the company's fifth anniversary passed. By mid-2002, approximately 1,000 of the 5,000 hospitals in the United States had purchased a SonoSite product. A substantially smaller number of private-practice physicians had invested in the company's devices. In a June 3, 2002 article in *Business Week,* the magazine described the medical community's response to SonoSite's portable ultrasound devices as "moderately enthusiastic." On a more positive note, there was a rush of excitement about new products being produced by the company, a clamor that emanated from industry pundits. In 2002, SonoSite received regulatory approval for two new products, including an "imaging stethoscope" marketed under the name "iLook." Weighing 2.5 pounds, the iLook was a battery- or DC-powered ultrasound device with a touch-screen user interface that promised to give physicians immediate access to visual, diagnostic information in a variety of clinical settings. The introduction of the iLook 15 and the iLook 25 marked the next step in the technological revolution initiated by SonoSite, a company with much to prove, but also a company with considerable promise in the years ahead.

Principal Subsidiaries

SonoSite, Ltd. (United Kingdom); SonoSite France SARL; SonoSite GmbH (Germany); SonoSite Iberica, S.L. (Spain); SonoSite (Asia) Limited (China).

Principal Competitors

Acuson Corporation; Esaote S.p.A.; GE Medical Systems.

Further Reading

"Bothell, Wash.-Based Medical Device Firm SonoSite Posts first Quarterly Profit," *Knight-Ridder/Tribune Business News*, February 14, 2003.
"For SonoSight, a Strong Pulse," *Business Week*, June 3, 2002, p. 97.
McGrath, Courtney, "Good Things in Small Packages: Tiny SonoSite Seeks to Change How Doctors Examine Patients," *Kiplinger's Personal Finance Magazine*, March 2002, p. 66.
Ozretich, Joel, "Profitability May Be in Sight for Bothell's SonoSite," *Puget Sound Business Journal*, November 9, 2001, p. 27.
——, "SonoSite Shifts Tactics for Ultrasound Sales," *Puget Sound Business Journal*, February 9, 2001, p. 6.
Timmerman, Luke, "SonoSite Sees Big Rival Right Before Its Eyes," *The Seattle Times*, February 15, 2002, p. D1.

—Jeffrey L. Covell

Southern Financial Bancorp, Inc.

37 East Main Street
Warrenton, Virginia 20186
U.S.A.
Telephone: (540) 349-3900
Fax: (540) 349-3904
Web site: http://www.southernfinancialbank.com

Public Company
Incorporated: 1986 as Southern Financial Federal
   Savings Bank
Employees: 225
Total Assets: $1 billion (2002)
Stock Exchanges: NASDAQ
Ticker Symbol: SFFB
NAIC: 522110 Commercial Banking

Southern Financial Bancorp, Inc. is the holding company for Virginia-based Southern Financial Bank. Southern Financial has branches in northern central Virginia, and, since 2001, in Washington, D.C. To the delight of its shareholders, the community-oriented bank has been run by the notoriously thrifty husband-and-wife team of Georgia S. Derrico (chairman and chief executive officer) and R. Roderick Porter (president and chief operating officer). Derrico's son, Devon, was picked to lead the commercial-services department. With total assets of about $1 billion in 2002, Southern Financial is the 250th largest bank in the United States. The bank is also known as a leading originator of Small Business Administration (SBA) loans in the Richmond and Washington, D.C., areas. The company's niche, reported *FSB: Fortune Small Business* in 2003, is $2 million to $8 million loans for business owners, especially government contractors.

Born Into the S&L Crisis

The roots of the Southern Financial Federal Savings Bank don't reach back far. It was established in 1986 in a strip mall in Herndon, Virginia, a site, according to *FSB*, chosen for its proximity to a Kmart store. The thrift's first day of business was April 11, 1986, and it was profitable by that July. Start-up capital was a little more than $4 million.

Southern Financial was led by Georgia S. Derrico. Derrico had been head of corporate affairs at New York's Chemical Bank (later part of J.P. Morgan Chase & Co.) before organizing Southern Financial. She brought Chemical veterans with her to the new thrift, and most of Southern Financial's investors were from New York.

Derrico's career had a slow start before she was able to amass this kind of big-bank backing. She studied international affairs at St. Mary's, a women's college in Notre Dame, Indiana. Unable to break into the male-dominated corporate world of the 1960s with a bachelor's degree, she next pursued graduate studies at Johns Hopkins University and Columbia University, going to work for Chemical Bank in 1970 after earning her Master's.

Derrico and her husband, R. Roderick Porter, settled in Middleburg, Virginia, on a farm, where they enjoyed raising horses and bichon frisé dogs. Another reason for choosing that area were the opportunities afforded by its location in the heart of northern Virginia's high-tech corridor, near Dulles Airport and Washington, D.C.

At the time Southern Financial opened, the savings and loan industry was experiencing a massive crisis. In late 1989, the thrift applied for regulatory permission to convert its charter from that of a savings and loan to one of a national bank. It had assets of about $60 million and stockholder equity of about $7 million at the time, and was profitable. Banks were required to meet more stringent capital requirements than thrifts. However, they had more operational flexibility. Part of the reason for the change, Derrico told *American Banker,* was to distance Southern Financial from the sullied reputation of other savings and loans, which had given the industry a bad name by collapsing under the weight of numerous bad loans.

After two years, Derrico cancelled the tedious conversion process. By this time, Southern Financial had expanded to Middleburg and Winchester, Virginia, and had moved its headquarters from Herndon to Warrenton, Virginia, where cheaper rents could be found. Southern Financial had opened one new branch a year during each of its first 13 years, noted the *Richmond Times-Dispatch.*

Going Public in 1993

Southern Financial went public in 1993. Its initial public offering (IPO) sold out in ten days, raising $5 million. Most of the proceeds were earmarked for acquisitions from the Resolution Trust Corporation, the agency set up to sell off the remnants of failed savings and loans. Southern Financial had six offices and a staff of 35 at the time of the IPO, and its assets had grown 33 percent in one year to $103 million. Derrico and her husband owned 9.7 percent of shares after the offering.

American Banker noted that the thrift had been profitable through conservative and shrewd judgment calls. In the early 1990s, Southern Financial remained concentrated on residential mortgages, while its competitors lost bundles on failed commercial deals that ravaged the Washington market. Southern Financial removed its exposure to rising interest rates by maintaining variable-rate mortgages almost exclusively. However, by 2003, the mortgage business would be small compared to Southern Financial's main focus of $2 million to $8 million commercial loans for small businesses.

A Commercial Bank in 1995

Southern Financial was able to convert from a thrift to a commercial bank in late 1995, obtaining a state charter for that purpose and forming the holding company Southern Financial Bancorp, Inc.

Derrico's husband, R. Roderick Porter, who had been on the bank's board of directors since its founding, became president and chief operating officer in 1998, while his wife remained CEO. By this time, the bank had grown to record $250 million in total assets.

Porter had been in charge of the asset liability committee at Chemical, and had also been an executive at Morgan Stanley. With an investment banker as president, it was natural that

Southern Financial should start acquiring other banks. Vienna, Virginia-based Horizon Bank was acquired in October 1999, adding four branches and raising Southern Financial's total assets from $258 million to more than $400 million.

Horizon had been founded in 1990 by Riggs National veteran Richard Hall. The stock-swap deal valued Horizon at about $21.5 million. The timing of the deal surprised some observers, since most banks at that time were scrambling to ensure the Y2K integrity of their back office systems, rather than focusing on expansion.

Southern Financial also developed partnerships to extend its range of services. It entered a unique joint venture with Warrenton-based Piedmont Press in 1999. Piedmont/Southern Web Services was set up to help small businesses develop e-commerce web sites. Southern Financial initially had a 4.9 shareholding in the venture, but planned to increase that to a 51 percent majority holding. An online community directory of participating businesses was created and linked to Southern Financial's home page; merchants could take credit card orders through the site.

In June 1999, Southern Financial began offering stock brokerage services on its web site in partnership with Fleet Securities Inc.'s U.S. Clearing division. Southern Financial did not maintain its own retail brokerage office.

Another important acquisition in 1999 was that of Southern WebTech.com, a supplier of international banking software. This concern had been founded in 1978 in Connecticut as Darien Consulting Group by Aidan Harland, another Chemical Bank alumnus.

By 2000, Southern Financial's presence had spread to six Virginia counties. The company acquired First Savings Bank of Virginia in September of that year. First Savings had total assets of just $69 million, and it maintained two branches, bringing Southern Financial's total to 19 in a stock swap deal worth about $6 million. First Savings and the previously-acquired Horizon Bank were both based in Fairfax County, Virginia's most heavily populated and most affluent county.

Entering D.C. in 2001

Having evolved from a community bank to a regional one, Southern Financial opened its first branch within the District of Columbia in August 2001. Located in the Georgetown area, this was its 20th branch. One company official told the *Washington Times* that she expected the new location to lead to more Small Business Administration (SBA) loans. The SBA praised Southern Financial for its commitment to small business.

Another branch opened in Charlottesville in early 2002. That year net income rose 19 percent to $10 million, while total assets approached $1 billion. Southern Financial had a work force of 225 employees at the time.

In August 2002, Southern Financial bought Metro-County Bank of Virginia, Inc., based in Mechanicsville. The price was $17.1 million, which was paid in a combination of stock and cash. This acquisition brought with it five branches, including Southern Financial's first near the state capital of Richmond,

---

Key Dates:

1986: Southern Financial Federal Savings Bank founded.
1989: Southern Financial attempts to convert to a national bank structure.
1993: Initial public offering raises $5 million.
1995: Southern Financial becomes a commercial bank under a state charter.
1999: Horizon Bank is acquired.
2000: First Savings Bank of Virginia acquired.
2001: Washington, D.C., office opened.

---

and $92.3 million in assets. Metro-County had been in business just five years.

A few months after acquiring Metro-County, Southern Financial opened an international banking division in Richmond, which was a manufacturing hub boasting 3,000 exporters, 1,500 importers, and more than 160 foreign-owned companies. The bank already owned a producer of international banking software, Southern WebTech.com, noted *American Banker,* which helped save hundreds of thousands of dollars in start-up costs.

A company executive told *American Banker* that the city's four existing import/export banks had been acquired by competitors from out of state, leaving a niche for a local bank. Both CEO Georgia Derrico and COO R. Roderick Porter had experience with Chemical Bank's international divisions. Porter had managed offices in Tokyo and London.

In July 2003, Southern Financial acquired a lease for a brand new office in downtown Richmond, which would serve as the headquarters for the bank's International Trade Services Department. Begun as a community thrift 19 years earlier, Southern Financial had grown into a considerable regional player with assets of more than $1 billion.

Principal Subsidiaries

Southern Financial Bank; Southern Financial Capital Trust I; Southern Financial Statutory Trust I; Southern WebTech.com, Inc.

Principal Divisions

International Trade Services Department.

Principal Competitors

BB&T; Bank of America Corporation; First Virginia Banks, Inc.; Wachovia Corporation.

Further Reading

Atkinson, Bill, "Count-the-Pennies CEO in Va. Wins Top Marks," *American Banker,* January 11, 1994, p. 8.
——, "Southern Financial of Virginia, Fueled by IPO, Aims to Expand," *American Banker,* December 22, 1993, p. 6.
"De Novo Thrifts Show Highest Net Worths," *National Mortgage News,* December 15, 1986, p. 39.
Hazard, Carol, "Husband-and-Wife Team Run Sixth-Largest Bank Holding Firm in Virginia," *Richmond Times-Dispatch,* August 24, 2002.
——, "Metro-County Bank of Virginia Inc. to Become Southern Financial After Merger," *Richmond Times-Dispatch,* April 26, 2002.
——, "Warrenton, Va.-Based Bank Completes $17.1 Million Purchase," *Richmond Times-Dispatch,* August 16, 2002.
——, "Warrenton, Va.-Based Bank Opens International Department in Richmond," *Richmond Times-Dispatch,* March 25, 2003.
Heerwagen, Peter, "Community Banks Get Physical," *Quad-State Business Journal* (Winchester, Va.), September 2001, p. 12.
Hyman, Julie, "Southern Financial Buys First Savings," *Washington Times,* April 12, 2000, p. B8.
——, "Southern Financial Seeks OK to Open First Branch in District," *Washington Times,* March 26, 2001, p. D5.
——, "Warrenton, Va. Bank Gains Foothold in Northern Virginia with Acquisition," *Washington Times,* April 11, 2000.
Laval, Kevin, "Southern Financial Awaits Conversion," *Washington Business Journal,* March 5, 1990, p. 48.
Millner, Marlon, "Banking on the Internet: Local Financial Services Firms' Stocks Soar with Online Deals," *Washington Business Journal,* April 23, 1999, pp. 1f.
——, "Horizon Bank Finds a Buyer: Southern Financial," *Washington Business Journal,* March 26, 1999, p. 5.
Monahan, Julie, "High Tech Ways that Banks Stay High-Touch," *American Banker,* Community Banking Supplement, February 2000, p. 12A.
Reosti, John, "Duo Has Expansion Plans for Va.'s Southern," *American Banker,* September 10, 2001, p. 6.
——, "Richmond Newcomer Aims to Fill Vacuum," *American Banker,* March 24, 2003, p. 5.
Smith, Franklin, and Jeffrey Kutler, "Southern Financial, a Va. Thrift, Nears Conversion to National Bank," *American Banker,* June 4, 1991, p. 13.
"Va. Bank Offers Web-Based Broker Services," *American Banker,* June 18, 1999, p. 7.
Whitford, David, "For Love and Money," *FSB: Fortune Small Business,* July/August 2003, p. 72.

—Frederick C. Ingram

StanCorp Financial Group, Inc.

1100 Southwest 6th Avenue
Portland, Oregon 97204
U.S.A.
Telephone: (503) 321-7000
Toll Free: (800) 642-9888
Fax: (503) 321-6776
Web site: http://www.stancorpfinancial.com

Public Company
Incorporated: 1906 as Oregon Life Insurance Company
Employees: 2,465
Total Assets: $1.75 billion (2003)
Stock Exchanges: New York
Ticker Symbol: SFG
NAIC: 524113: Direct Life Insurance Carriers

StanCorp Financial Group, Inc. (''StanCorp''), located in Portland, Oregon, is the holding company for Standard Insurance Company, The Standard Life Insurance Company of New York, and two smaller subsidiaries, which collectively provide insurance, financial management services, retirement plans, and group and individual disability, life, and annuity products and dental insurance for groups. StanCorp was created as part of the process to convert Standard Insurance Company from mutual to stock ownership to enjoy the advantages of being a publicly traded company in a highly competitive and rapidly consolidating industry. StanCorp's subsidiary, Standard Insurance Company offers group and individual disability insurance and retirement products, as well as group life and dental insurance. The Standard Life Insurance Company of New York offers group life and disability insurance products for the New York market. StanCorp Mortgage Investors, LLC is devoted to originating, underwriting, and servicing small commercial mortgage loans. StanCorp Investment Advisers, Inc. provides performance analysis, fund selection support, and model portfolios to Standard Insurance Company Retirement Plans clients.

Lineage of StanCorp Begins in the 19th Century

The founder of the insurance company that would one day evolve into StanCorp was Leo Samuel, whose life was a true rags-to-riches story. At the age of 13, in 1860, he immigrated to America from Germany, accompanied by an uncle who promptly abandoned him once they arrived safely in New York City. Starting out with just a dollar in his pocket, Samuel managed to survive by selling newspapers during the day while learning English at night and began to nurture a dream of one day becoming a magazine publisher. A year later, he worked his way west, settling in Sacramento, California. The youngster began to work his way up in the publishing industry, soon advancing to an advertising sales job. His first publishing endeavor was a traveler's guide sold to steamboat passengers traveling between Sacramento and San Francisco. It was in 1871 that Samuel, still only 24 years of age, moved to Portland, where he published a variety of materials, from postcards to illustrated city directories, eventually launching an upscale magazine called *The West Shore,* which touted the Pacific Northwest. In the course of his publishing career, he made numerous contacts and friends in Oregon.

With the demise of his magazine in 1890, Samuel forged a mid-life career change, turning to the insurance industry, which was in its infancy and provided tremendous opportunity for growth during the period. He became an agent for Equitable Life Assurance Society of New York, one of the many large East Coast companies that dominated the insurance industry of the day, canvassing both Oregon and Idaho. He learned first-hand of the inequities facing the people who lived in the Pacific Northwest who did business with the eastern firms. Having the insurance companies located some 3,000 miles away meant that it usually took months to settle a claim. It also caused a lot of West Coast money in the form of premiums to flow to the East, only to be returned, at a price, to western banks to lend out for the development of the Pacific Northwest. The result was an economic drain on the area, which in effect enriched eastern investors, who made money coming and going on Oregon's wealth. Moreover, these firms and other financial institutions, especially the high-flying trust companies of the day, were corrupt and caused any number of scandals.

Company Perspectives:

*StanCorp Financial Group, Inc., through its principal sub-
sidiaries, has earned a reputation for high-quality, consistent performance. Responsive caring service, strong focused
growth, and disciplined financial practices all add up to a
company that dependably delivers on promises to customers.*

Equitable Life was one of the insurance companies that
came under government scrutiny in the early years of the new
century. Samuel traveled to New York in 1905 to try to learn
firsthand why Equitable Life was being investigated by New
York State and returned home somewhat sobered about his
employer and inspired with a new dream: to launch a local life
insurance company.

Samuel broached his idea with one of the people he be-
friended in the upper crust of Portland society, Abbot Mills,
president of First National Bank and a prominent businessman,
who then involved his business partner, Charles Adams. Samuel
won over Mills and Adams because the establishment of an area
insurance company would help to keep local capital within the
state. The idea also had practical merits because Portland, with
its healthy climate and excellent municipal water system,
boasted the lowest death rate in the United States.

By the end of 1905, Samuel already had a customer for a life
insurance policy, but when he approached the State of Oregon it
refused to license the insurance company until it established a
reserve fund of $100,000. Samuel, Mills, and Adams enlisted
the help of 81 wealthy Portland residents whom they approached to act as "guarantors." The guarantors pledged to
purchase at least one share of stock in the company, but no more
than two, with the further stipulation that they would receive no
profit from selling their shares. In addition, they could earn no
more than a 7 percent return on their investment each year. A
veritable Who's Who of Portland history signed up, and as a
result the Oregon Life Insurance Company was licensed by the
state on February 24, 1906. Although officially not a mutual
company, it acted as if it were, with the clear understanding that
when it was financially feasible the shareholders would be
bought out.

Leo Samuel Dies in 1916

The new company, with Samuel serving as general manager
and Mills as president, started out on a modest basis, at first
operating out of a one-room office. Mills's involvement with
the First National Bank, where he was president in 1903, led to
an intertwining of the fortunes of Oregon Life and First National Bank over the next quarter century. The conservative
investment philosophy of the Bank and other banking leaders
on the board guided Oregon Life's investments. Leo Samuel
died in 1916 before his dream of mutualizing Oregon Life could
be realized, but he did live long enough to see that the enterprise
was well established. Oregon Life expanded into Idaho in 1920
and Washington in 1921. All through the 1920s, while other
financial institutions made heavy commitments to the stock

market, the company continued to follow a balanced, conservative investment strategy, concentrating on local real estate investments and municipal, school, electrification, highway, water, and drainage bonds issued within its three state market.

With California growing rapidly in population and wealth, it
was natural for Oregon Life to look southward for new business
opportunities. Being a true mutual insurer was thought to be of
significant value in entering California, prompting the leaders of
Oregon Life to finally fulfill the dream of its founders. In 1929,
the company was formally mutualized, the original investments
of the 81 guarantors paid off, and the name of the business
change to Oregon Mutual Life Insurance Company. In that
same year the company began doing business in California. It
was also in 1929 that the stock market crashed, ushering in the
Great Depression. The fact that Oregon Mutual did not own and
had never owned common stock proved to be a major selling
point for its salesmen throughout the 1930s. The company's
policyholders were further served by Oregon Mutual's conservative approach to its investments because it allowed them to
borrow against the value of their policies, an important service
during those difficult economic times.

In 1944, Oregon Mutual entered Utah. During the postwar
economic boom, the company was eager to expand its business
even further but came to believe its efforts were hindered,
especially in the all-important California market, by having
Oregon as part of its name. Thus, in 1946, it changed its name to
Standard Insurance Company. Another key development in the
postwar years was the move into the group insurance market. In
1951, Standard Insurance Company, with absolutely no program in place, was able to win the group insurance contract for
the Oregon State Police and Penitentiary Guards Association.
Although it was entering a highly competitive field, the company had an edge over the better established New York insurers,
which were bound by a New York State law that prevented
them from bidding below the minimum rate that prevailed in
their home state. Group insurance proved to be such a boon for
Standard Insurance Company that by the end of the 1950s group
sales outstripped individual sales.

Standard Insurance Company entered Arizona in 1958,
Alaska and Nevada in 1959, and Montana in 1962. By 1963,
Standard Insurance Company had $1 billion of insurance in
force. Also in the 1960s, Standard Insurance Company entered
the mortgage business, but the product that would prove to be
the most instrumental in establishing Standard Insurance Company on a national level was long-term disability insurance
(LTD). The product was hardly unique and far from the least
expensive on the market, but the company worked hard to
establish a reputation for superior service by quickly settling
claims and making an extra effort to help customers' employees
receive rehabilitation so that they could return to their jobs as
soon as possible.

Connecticut Mutual Life Insurance Co. recognized what
Standard Insurance Company had accomplished, and in 1985
the two parties created a joint-venture in which Connecticut
Mutual marketed Standard Insurance Company's group insurance products. The arrangement was not entirely satisfactory for
Standard Insurance Company, which sold out to its partner after
two years, but the experience paid dividends. Standard Insur-

Key Dates:

1906: Oregon Life Insurance Company is formed.
1916: Founder Leo Samuel dies.
1929: The company is mutualized, becoming Oregon Mutual Life Insurance Company.
1946: The company's name is changed to Standard Insurance Company.
1998: StanCorp is formed as a holding company.
1999: Standard Insurance is demutualized; StanCorp goes public.

ance Company's next joint-venture, a reinsurance agreement with Wisconsin-based Northwestern Mutual Life Insurance Co., was successful and is still in place today.

With success came the confidence that Standard Insurance Company could succeed on the national level, and management made the commitment to apply for licenses and register its products in other states. By 1983, the company had offices established in 13 states and by 1987 was licensed to do business in 34 states. It boasted $1.4 billion in assets and $23 billion of life insurance in force. By 1989, the company was licensed in 49 states and the District of Columbia, electing to forego the state of New York (other than reinsurance) and its costly regulatory climate.

Mutuals Begin Converting to Stock Ownership in the 1990s

In the 1990s, long-time changes undertaken by mutual life insurance companies came to fruition when a number of them decided to convert to stock ownership in order to gain stock as a currency to use in acquisitions and thereby achieve greater growth. In 1992, the Equitable Life Assurance Society converted, followed by State Mutual Life Assurance in 1995, and Farm Family Mutual Insurance and American Mutual Life Assurance in 1996. When giant Prudential Insurance Company decided to convert to stock ownership in 1998, the industry reached a tipping point and the other major players made plans to follow suit. Standard Insurance Company considered converting to a stock company for more than year, then at a December 1997 meeting of its board of directors unanimously voted to pursue demutualization and take the business public. Over the course of the next year a plan was created and submitted to The Director of the Oregon Department of Consumer and Business Services for approval, and StanCorp Financial Group, Inc. was created as a holding company.

Conversion plans used by mutual insurance companies fall under three general types. A ''full'' demutualization plan compensates policyholders with stock in the newly formed holding company or with cash, all insurance policies remaining in effect. A ''subscription rights demutualization'' conversion offered no compensation to policyholders other than the right to purchase stock in the new company before the general public. Under the final option, the insurer formed a holding company, which was owned by policyholders and controlled a majority stake in the insurance company, now its subsidiary. On December 15, 1997, Standard Insurance Company's Board voted to pursue ''full'' demutualization, with policyholders receiving a number of StanCorp shares based on how long they held policies with Standard Insurance Company.

After receiving state and policyowner approval, Standard Insurance Company was officially demutualized in April 1999. Company executives, in conjunction with investment bankers Goldman Sachs, conducted extensive pre-IPO presentations to promote the offering, in just three weeks holding 70 meetings in 28 cities and five countries. The insurer pledged to expand its distribution and focus more effort into eastern markets, doubling the number of its sales representatives from 100 to 200. StanCorp's initial public offering (IPO) was conducted in April 1999, netting some $320 million. The stock then began trading on the New York Stock Exchange. The company quickly moved to keep its promises, opening five new group sales offices and hiring 19 new sales representatives. As a stock company, StanCorp continued to follow the conservative investment and bookkeeping practices that served it well as a mutual company. Although the company hoped to use its new status to achieve greater growth, management of Standard Insurance Company remained dedicated to its core insurance products and mindful of its commitment to provide excellent service and maintain the ability to pay benefits promised to policyholders. At the same time, StanCorp took steps to keep the company competitive in a changing marketplace and become a more full-service financial services company.

Continued Growth in the 21st Century

StanCorp took a number of positive steps in 2000. The company's presence in the East was bolstered by the opening of a customer service office in Portland, Maine. The company formed a subsidiary in White Plains, New York, named The Standard Life Insurance Company of New York and obtained a license from New York State to sell group life and disability products. A sales office was also established in New York. For years Standard Insurance Company had been accredited only for reinsurance in the heavily regulated New York market, but to further strengthen its market position in group life and disability StanCorp became licensed in New York, allowing it to bid on major group insurance accounts for companies headquartered in that state. Standard Insurance Company's commitment to the disability insurance business was reinforced by an agreement it signed in the fall of 2000 to acquire the individual disability insurance business of Minnesota Life Insurance Company. At the same time, it sold its individual life insurance business to Protective Life Insurance of Birmingham, Alabama. The transaction took effect on January 1, 2001.

In 2002, Standard Insurance Company strengthened its core business further by acquiring the group disability and group life insurance business of Teachers Insurance & Annuity Association, a transaction which placed Standard Insurance Company as the fourth largest provider of LTD and the ninth largest provider of Group Life. To finance the transaction, StanCorp raised $250 million through a ten-year debt-offering of 6.875 percent senior notes. In addition, the insurer continued to make progress in its national expansion efforts and in expanding its other lines, such as group dental coverage. By the end of 2002, over 70 percent of new sales were generated in the East and Midwest. It is now

America's fourth largest provider of long-term disability insurance and the fifth largest publicly traded company in Oregon. Given that the employee benefits market continues to grow despite a troubled economy, the conservatively managed StanCorp appears well positioned for ongoing growth.

Principal Subsidiaries

Standard Insurance Company; StanCorp Mortgage Investors, LLC; StanCorp Investment Advisors Inc.; StanWest Equities, Inc.; The Standard Life Insurance Company of New York.

Principal Competitors

Aon Corporation; Pacific Mutual Holding Company; UNUMProvident.

Further Reading

Brock, Kathy, "Standard Insurance Positions Itself for Growth," *Business Journal-Portland*, January 9, 1998, p. 8.

Frank, Gerry, "Duty To Make a Difference Not Confined to Any Age," *Portland Oregonia*, October 7, 1994, p. A28.

Giegerich, Andy, "Not Your Father's Insurer," *Business Journal-Portland*, December 31, 1999, p. 11.

Hollon, Jim, "Standard Turns History Upside Down," *Oregon Business*, March 1, 1998, p. 97.

Moody, Robin J., "Stancorp's Conservative Management Paying Off," *Business Journal*, May 9, 2003, p. 3.

Zolkos, Rodd, "More Mutuals Changing Structures," *Business Insurance*, March 9, 1998, p. 1.

—Ed Dinger

Stew Leonard's

100 Westport Avenue
Norwalk, Connecticut 06851
U.S.A.
Telephone: (203) 847-7214
Web site: http://www.stewleonards.com

Private Company
Founded: 1969
Employees: 2,000
Sales: $300 million (2002 est.)
NAIC: 445110 Supermarkets and Other Grocery (Except Convenience) Stores

Stew Leonard's, which bills itself as "the world's largest dairy store," has combined the atmosphere of a theme park with the business principles of a big box store to create a regional marketing phenomenon. Customers drive as much as 50 miles to shop at Stew Leonard's, where diversions include a petting zoo, robotic singing milk cartons, and employees dressed as farm animals dancing with customers in the aisles. Stew Leonard's sells an extremely limited list of products (less than one-tenth of the items in an average grocery store), but moves staggering quantities, including 13 million cookies, eight million ears of corn, and ten million quarts of milk per year. Managed by the Leonard family, the company maintains a distinctive corporate culture in which an emphasis on teamwork, slavish devotion to customer satisfaction, and nimbleness in the face of changing business needs coexist with a focus on showmanship that the company calls "The Wow!" In 1993 Stew Leonard's legions of fans were shocked to learn that the store's namesake, Stew Leonard, Sr., was convicted of tax evasion. The scandal, however, did not curtail the growth or popularity of the business.

Origins in the 1920s

The precursor to Stew Leonard's was the Clover Farms Dairy in Norwalk, Connecticut, which was founded by Charles Leo Leonard in 1921. Charles ran the business himself, out of his garage, and delivered fresh milk to local customers by horse and buggy. Leo Leonard, Jr., recalled: "He'd wake up at three

o'clock in the morning, drive to the farms to get milk, return and bottle it, then deliver it to his customers." In later years milk was delivered by trucks decorated with plastic cows that "mooed" for children. Charles's son Stew graduated from the University of Connecticut School of Agriculture and in 1951 joined his brother, John, in the business. By the end of the next decade, Stew had come to realize that the milk delivery business was in decline. At the same time, he was informed by the State of Connecticut that the dairy was in the path of a proposed highway, giving urgency to his desire to launch a new venture.

In 1969 Stew Leonard turned to retail, opening a 17,000-square-foot store—named simply "Stew Leonard's"—with seven employees selling eight items. During the first week, the store had 700 customers. By the end of the first year, there were 10,000 customers a week. Stew Leonard's quickly expanded beyond dairy products, adding meat, fish, produce, and bakery items. Stew's son, Stew Leonard, Jr., stocked shelves, worked cash registers, and made ice cream. After completing an undergraduate degree in accounting, Stew, Jr., received his MBA from the University of California at Los Angeles. He became president of the family business in 1982 and CEO in 1991, the same year that a second Stew Leonard's was opened, in Danbury, Connecticut, under the direction of his brother, Tom Leonard.

By that time the company had reached the $100 million mark in annual sales and had become a local landmark, providing a grocery experience unlike any other. Norwalk customers were greeted at the door by a life-sized plastic cow and a three-ton granite boulder featuring the store's motto: "Rule Number One: The customer is always right. Rule Number Two: If the customer is ever wrong, re-read Rule Number One." Rather than standard grocery aisles, a single path through the store led past a glass-enclosed milk processing plant, an in-store bakery, a fresh popcorn department, and a variety of diversions including banjo-playing dog robots atop the freezer case.

Secrets of Success

While the number of products offered at each Stew Leonard's store had grown from seven to approximately 800, this was still dramatically fewer than the 15,000 stocked by an

Company Perspectives:

Our philosophy is built upon the initials of our name—S.T.E.W. The S stands for satisfy the customer—it is everyone's most important job. The T stands for Teamwork, because teamwork makes it happen! The E stands for Excellence; excellence makes it better and assures great quality and freshness in everything we do. Finally, the W stands for WOW—the WOWs are all the fun reasons that Stew Leonard's is a great place to shop AND to work.

average supermarket, and any item selling fewer than 1,000 units per week was promptly removed from the shelves. According to Stew Leonard, Jr., the limited product list was a key element in the stores' success, allowing managers to stock only those items generating phenomenal sales and focus on moving them out the door quickly. "By focusing on turnover," he stated, "profit comes. I've repeatedly seen us bring items in at no profit in the beginning. Then, as customers started buying more, we were able to get better deals. Soon we were buying trailer loads. The next thing you knew, we were making money." Indeed, while customers frequently complained about the limited selection, sales per square foot were approximately five times that of the average grocery store, prompting an entry in the *Guinness Book of World Records* for the greatest sales per square foot of any food store in the United States. Stew Leonard, Jr., credited his computer system with allowing him to monitor sales with great precision and provide rapid feedback to department managers, who could then react promptly. Equally rigorous attention was paid to customer feedback. Stew Leonard, Sr., commonly wandered the aisles to chat with shoppers, and suggestion boxes were emptied each day, with suggestions typed up and delivered to managers by 11 a.m. the following morning. Regular focus groups also yielded innovations, such as making fish appear fresher by selling it on ice rather than wrapped in plastic—a change that doubled fish sales.

Stew Leonard's distinctive culture included a strong family orientation. Many Leonard family members held key roles, and more than half the non-Leonard employees also had at least one relative working at the company. (Said the perpetually aphoristic Stew, Sr., "I figure if we hire someone's daughter, she'll have two bosses: me and her mother.") Employees received rigorous training in customer service, the company strove to promote from within as much as possible, and outstanding performance was celebrated on a regular basis with plaques, gift certificates, dinners, and, for managers, profit sharing. Employee satisfaction was so high that turnover of full-time employees was half the industry average, and Stew Leonard's won a spot on *Fortune*'s list of "100 Best Companies to Work for in America." As Stew Leonard's growing fame brought a flood of visitors from companies hoping to emulate the retailer's success, the company set up Stew Leonard's University, in which store managers held seminars on their corporate culture and customer service techniques.

Stew Leonard, Sr., had become a folk hero. President Ronald Reagan presented him with an Award for Entrepreneurial Excellence. *Inc.* magazine reported that "probably no single-store proprietor has been more admired and celebrated than Stew Leonard." Business guru Tom Peters, who featured Stew Leonard's in his book *In Search of Excellence*, stated, "If you really try, you can make any product special. Leonard has proven it better than anybody I know." And the trade journal *Executive Excellence* profiled Stew Leonard, Sr., as a "management superhero," noting that his organization was built "on the concepts of care and trust."

Scandals in the 1990s

All the more shocking, then, when Stew Leonard, Sr., pleaded guilty to defrauding the Federal government of taxes on $17 million, in the largest criminal tax case in the history of Connecticut. With the help of three other company executives—Frank and Stephen Guthman (who were his wife's brothers) and Tiberio Belardinelli—Stew Leonard, Sr., had masterminded a decade-long conspiracy to skim profits from the store's cash registers. The conspirators used a sophisticated software program called Equity to alter sales records for the Internal Revenue Service, but kept a set of accurate figures to inform management decisions. The Equity software, which was designed to overwrite existing records and leave no trace that it had been run, was found hidden in a hollowed-out copy of the Business Directory of New England. Stacks of cash in $10,000 bundles were stashed in a safe hidden in a fireplace. The cash was then smuggled to the Leonards' vacation home in the Caribbean, packed in suitcases or "even disguised as baby gifts," according to government investigators. Prosecutors maintained that one of the brothers-in-law, Frank Guthman, embezzled additional money on his own behalf behind the backs of his colleagues.

"Well, I made a mistake," said Stew, Sr., when the news broke. "I'm very sorry. ... And I am prepared to take the consequences." He agreed to pay $15 million in taxes, interest, and penalties and was sentenced to 52 months in prison and three years of supervised probation. While authorities maintained that Stew, Jr., was aware of the conspiracy and altered records to cover it up, the conditions of his father's plea bargain guaranteed him immunity from prosecution.

The day after the guilty plea by Stew, Sr., the store faced more negative publicity as the Connecticut Department of Consumer Protection cited Stew Leonard's for underweight products and a raft of other labeling violations. With 1,232 violations on 2,658 items examined, the store's violation rate stood at 46 percent, in contrast to a statewide average of 7.2 percent. Stew Leonard's immediately launched a public relations campaign to control the damage, taking out ads, handing out flyers, and putting Stew, Jr., on a local radio talk show to rebut the charges. According to the Leonards, the violations were greatly exaggerated, and included many overweight products as well as some that were underweight. They maintained that the average discrepancy was a mere one-half ounce, adding, however, that "there's no excuse for any mistake, and we corrected every one of them before the inspector even left the store."

Stew Leonard's loyal customers were shocked, both by the tax-fraud scandal and the weight violations. The company's most influential cheerleader, Tom Peters, repudiated the business he had previously held up as a model, telling *Fortune*, "They were

Key Dates:

1921: Charles Leo Leonard founds Clover Farms Dairy in Norwalk, Connecticut.

1969: Charles Leonard's son Stew establishes the first Stew Leonard's retail grocery store, in Norwalk, with seven employees.

1986: President Ronald Reagan presents Stew Leonard with an Award for Entrepreneurial Excellence.

1991: Stew Leonard, Jr., becomes CEO; second store opens in Danbury, Connecticut, under brother Tom Leonard.

1992: Company makes the *Guinness Book of World Records* for highest sales per square foot of any food store in the United States.

1993: Stew Leonard convicted of tax fraud; company is fined for labeling products with incorrect weights.

1997: Tom Leonard indicted for tax fraud.

1999: Third store opens, in Yonkers, New York.

2002: Stew Leonard's named one of the "100 Best Companies to Work for in America" by *Fortune*.

selling charm as much as the big rock out front that says the customer is always first. The big rock is hollow." Industry observers expected sales to suffer; surprisingly, however, long-term effects were not discernible, as Stew Leonard's continued to prosper, even in the face of additional obstacles. In 1997 a proposed site in Orange, Connecticut, was turned down by zoning officials after bitter protests by citizens concerned about the traffic congestion that could be generated by the $25 million store. That same year, Tom Leonard was indicted by a grand jury on charges that, like his father, he had skimmed receipts and underreported income from 1992 to 1994. Also in 1997, the United Food and Commercial Workers union filed a complaint with the National Labor Relations Board (NLRB) alleging that Stew Leonard's had illegally opposed attempts to unionize employees. Without admitting wrongdoing, the company reached an agreement with the NLRB to post notices stating that the company would not interfere with attempts to unionize.

In 1999 a third Stew Leonard's was opened, in Yonkers, New York. The store was the largest in the chain, at 130,000 square feet, and employed 700 people. The Yonkers location expanded on the successes of the Connecticut stores with a sushi bar, kosher bakery, and wine shop. Despite protests by residents of nearby villages over traffic issues, Stew Leonard's was welcomed by Yonkers, which designated the store "Business of the Year." By 2003 the chain was serving 300,000 customers a week, sales had reached nearly $300 million, and Stew Leonard's was planning to open a fourth store, also in New York.

Industry observers debated the reasons behind the success of the Stew Leonard's chain. While Stew Leonard's held prices below those in neighboring stores, the price differences were not large enough to explain the volume of sales, and since prices were held down in part by selling larger packages, customers frequently complained that they left the store with more than they needed. Nor was the chain a one-stop shop, due to its limited number of products. The features that made Stew Leonard's entertaining for children or the occasional visitor could be perceived by other shoppers as a nuisance, along with the single aisle and frequently long drive to the store. Was the secret the store's vaunted focus on customer service? The "aw-shucks," folk-hero personas of the Leonards themselves? The mere distinctiveness of the Stew Leonard's shopping experience, which stood out in a sea of bland mega-chains? While no one could say for sure, observers commented with astonishment on the loyalty of Stew Leonard's customers—all of whom were always right.

Principal Competitors

Dairy Farmers of America, Inc.; The Kroger Co.; The Stop & Shop Supermarket Company.

Further Reading

Ain, Stewart, "Stew Leonard's Faces a Rough Landing," *New York Times*, March 9, 2003.

Auerbach, Jonathan, "They May Wait until the Cows Come Home to Get This Sign Up," *Wall Street Journal*, October 30, 1995.

Barrier, M., "A New Sense of Service," *Nation's Business*, June 1991.

Behar, Richard, "Skimming the Cream," *Time*, August 2, 1993.

Berman, Phyllis, "Like Father, Like Son," *Forbes*, May 20, 1996, p. 44.

Berton, Lee, "Executive Pay (A Special Report)—Off the Books: For Some Entrepreneurs, Skimming Cash Is Simply Part of Compensation," *Wall Street Journal*, April 12, 1995, p. R8.

Brown, Buck, "Succession Strategies for Family Firms—Tactics Include Splitting Helms among Siblings," *Wall Street Journal*, August 4, 1988.

Fox, Bruce, "The Customer Is Always Forgiving," *Chain Store Age Executive with Shopping Center Age*, November 1993.

Goldman, Ari L., "Weight Charges Filed against Stew Leonard's," *New York Times*, August 19, 1993, p. B8.

"Interview with Les Slater," *Review of Business*, Summer/Fall 1991, p. 10.

Kaufman, Joanne, "In the Moo: Shopping at Stew Leonard's," *Wall Street Journal*, September 17, 1987.

Lederman, Judith S., "All Together Now, Shout 'Wow!'" *New York Times*, July 21, 2002, p. 3(L).

Levy, Clifford J., "Store Founder Pleads Guilty in Fraud Case," *New York Times*, July 23, 1993, p. B1.

Millstein, Marc, "Stew Leonard's High-Turn Strategy," *Supermarket News*, December 26, 1988, p. 35.

Prenon, Marty T., "Attempt to Unionize Stew Leonard's Stirs Controversy," *Westchester County Business Journal*, January 1998, p. 3.

Rafalaf, Andrew, "One Dissatisfied Customer," *Fortune*, November 1, 2002.

Richman, Tom, "Runner-Up Stew Leonard," *Inc.*, January 1990, p. 50.

Rosen, Ellen L., "Traffic Fix Ordered for Stew Leonard Complex," *New York Times*, March 16, 2003.

Rosner, Hillary, "The Gospel According to Stew," *Brandweek*, March 25, 1996.

Steinberg, Jacques, "Connecticut Store Owner Sentenced in Tax Fraud," *New York Times*, October 21, 1993, p. B1.

——, "Papers Show Greed, Calculation and Betrayal in Stew Leonard Fraud Case," *New York Times*, October 22, 1993, p. B5.

Suters, Everett T., "Stew Leonard: Soul of a Leader," *Executive Excellence*, June 1991.

Vizard, Mary McAleer, "Stew Leonard's Taking Its Dancing Cows to Yonkers," *New York Times*, August 30, 1998.

Zwieback, Elliot, "What's Next for Stew Leonard's? Scandals Have Placed the Retailer's Image in Jeopardy," *Supermarket News*, August 2, 1993, p. 1.

—Paula Kepos and Michelle Hargrave

Strauss Discount Auto

91A Brick Plant Road
South River, New Jersey 08882-1097
U.S.A.
Telephone: (732) 390-9000
Toll Free: (800) 947-2637
Fax: (732) 390-9079
Web site: http://www.straussauto.com

Private Company
Incorporated: 1919 as R&S Home and Auto Stores
Employees: 1,500 (est.)
Sales: $150 million (2002 est.)
NAIC: 441310 Automotive Parts and Accessories Stores

Strauss Discount Auto is a privately owned regional aftermarket automobile parts chain, its headquarters located in South River, New Jersey. The company operates 96 stores in the Northeast: two outlets located in Wilmington, Delaware; 12 in the Philadelphia market; 35 throughout New Jersey; and the balance in the five boroughs of New York City and outlying suburbs. Strauss follows the superstore concept, offering service in addition to the sale of parts. All told, the Strauss chain has 360 bays and employs some 1,700 people. Although the model design of a new Strauss superstore is 13,000–14,000 square feet in size, featuring seven to ten service bays, the company adjusts the size of its stores to fit the available space, an imperative for the chain's expansion efforts in the highly congested New York City market.

R&S Home and Auto Established in 1919

The bulk of Strauss is the result of a merger between two well-established chains, R&S Home and Auto and Strauss Auto. The oldest of the two businesses was R&S Auto, founded in Newark, New Jersey, by Herman Schlenger and Harry Roth, the initials of their last names accounting for the name of the company. (According to a *New York Times* obituary, however, Herman's brother Henry was considered a co-founder of the company in 1922. Whether or not the business was started in 1919 or 1922, Henry would still have been only in his early 20s

when it began.) Over the next three decades, the R&S Auto chain added outlets throughout northern New Jersey. In 1954, R&S Auto opened its first superstore, a unique concept at the time, not only because it offered a service garage but also the simple amenity of customer parking. R&S Auto was led by Herman Schlenger's son, Donald, in the 1960s, a period of prosperity for the company-owned stores, and leased departments that operated within discount stores. When the national economy faltered in the early 1970s, a number of these discount operations failed, severely impacting the fiscal health of R&S Auto. In 1973, the company posted sales of $27 million, but business collapsed the following year, with sales totaling just $8.5 million. R&S Auto was forced to file for Chapter 11 bankruptcy protection, but it was not the only auto parts chain in such circumstances. Strauss Auto had also declared bankruptcy.

Not only did the Strauss family found an aftermarket auto parts chain that became a major component of what would one day become Strauss Discount Auto, it was also instrumental in the creation of a major competitor: Pep Boys—Manny, Moe & Jack. Strauss auto was founded by Issac (Izzy) M. Strauss, brother of Maurice (Moe) Strauss. Moe teamed up with Emanuel (Manny) Rosenfeld, Moe Radavitz, and W. Graham (Jack) Jackson, Philadelphia natives who became friends in the U.S. Navy during World War I and later formed Pep Boys. In 1921, they each chipped in $200 to launch an auto parts store, although at first Moe Strauss served as a silent partner because he worked at a rival store and could not afford to give up the job, having already failed twice at starting a business on his own. The partners rented a modest storefront in Philadelphia, so narrow that the shorter the name for the new enterprise the better. According to company legend, the young men were lounging in the store, drinking sodas and kicking around ideas for a suitable name, when one of them noticed a box of Pep Valve Grinding Compound, prompting the inspiration for "Pep Auto Supplies." They became the "Pep Boys" supposedly because a Philadelphia policeman made a habit of sending motorists in need of a replacement oil wick (used in the headlights of the day) to the "boys" at Pep. Moe Radavitz soon sold out his interest and Izzy Strauss replaced him as one of the partners. The Pep Boys became personalized in the early 1920s as Manny, Moe, and Jack, the caricatures of the founders becoming marketing and cultural icons. The original rendering of the trio included Graham Jackson, but when Izzy Strauss joined the business his face replaced Jack's. Because ''Manny, Moe and Izzy'' did not sound right to them, Jack's name was kept.

Izzy Strauss Launches Own Business in 1929

Izzy Strauss soon decided to strike out and launch his own auto parts store, but his caricature would forever link him to the Pep Boys, a future competitor of the chain he nurtured. When Izzy broke away, Pep Boys had a dozen stores in Philadelphia and were looking to expand to the growing California market, hardly competition for the business Izzy established in Brooklyn in May 1929. He started out with five stores and a warehouse. Like R&S Auto his business thrived in the postwar years, a period of unprecedented prosperity that came to a close in the early 1970s with the recession that drove both auto chains into bankruptcy. Investor Jerry Schottenstein salvaged both companies and installed Don Schlenger to run them.

Schlenger turned around both chains, became a partner in the business, and ultimately gained a controlling interest in it. In 1983, the companies were merged, creating R&S Strauss, the largest auto parts retailer in the Northeast, comprising some 70 stores that generated annual revenues in the range of $80 million. The company expanded beyond New York and New Jersey in 1987 when it acquired the bankrupt Penn-Jersey auto parts chain, in the process adding stores in Philadelphia and Delaware. A year later, Schlenger was ready to retire and sold R&S Strauss to a British holding company, Ward White, that owned auto parts stores in England. In an effort to enter the U.S. market, Ward White had already acquired the Whitlock and Rose Auto chains. Combined with R&S Strauss, the company owned 240 stores, generating approximately $250 million in annual sales.

Ward White's plans for America were scuttled when just six months after acquiring R&S Strauss the company became the victim of a hostile takeover by another British company, BOOTS, a health and beauty chain established in the mid-1800s that was branching into other retail areas. Uninterested in Ward White's vision for a U.S. auto parts empire, BOOTS soon put the three American auto parts chains on the block. Merrill Lynch Capital Partners acquired the assets, packaged them in a company named WSR (Whitlock-Strauss-Rose) Group, then put executives AL Woods and Mort Schwartz in charge.

By the early 1990s, the aftermarket for auto parts and services was a $125 billion-a-year industry. Although still very much a fragmented business, it was undergoing consolidation with a number of large chains attempting to gain a greater national presence, resulting in a highly competitive atmosphere. For Strauss, with its heavy concentration in the New York City market, this meant going up against a very aggressive Pep Boys chain, which until 1992 had not been involved in New York

City but was now looking to open as many superstore locations in the area as possible. Overall, Pep Boys boasted more than 350 stores, producing annual sales in excess of $1 billion. While WSR finished 1993 with 336 stores, it generated just $370 million in revenues for the year.

Merrill Lynch Capital Partners, dissatisfied with their investment in WSR, sacked management and installed an executive who was a veteran of corporate restructurings, Clark Ogle, charging him with dismantling the company. In 1994, four Whitlock outlets located in Pennsylvania and 26 stores operating under the National Auto Supply Stores banner in upstate New York were sold to Wheels Auto Discount Auto Parts, a division of Fay's Inc., whose primary business was a northeastern drugstore chain. Also in 1994, WSR sold the Rose Auto chain of 96 Florida stores to Auckland's Limited, a Canadian auto parts distributor, which paid nearly $15 million for the money-losing subsidiary. The sell-off was completed early in 1995 when Merrill Lunch Partners unloaded the rest of the Whitlock chain, a total of 80 stores, to Apex Automotive Warehouse, a midwestern auto parts wholesaler, for an undisclosed amount. Whitlock subsequently filed for Chapter 11 protection, and the business was liquidated in 1996. What was left of WSR were the Strauss assets. Unlike the Rose and Whitlock stores, many of the Strauss units offered auto service, which allowed it to be more competitive with rival chains such as Pep Boys.

Bankruptcy and Recovery: 1998 and Beyond

In 1995, WSR, doing business under the Strauss Discount Auto banner, was now a $135 million, 121-store chain, a third of its units located in the New York metropolitan area. At this point, Ogle stepped down in favor of Luke Beshar, formerly with the accounting firm of Arthur Anderson, who initiated a downsizing and restructuring effort. He was soon replaced as CEO by Terry Patterson, a rare woman executive in the auto parts industry. In 1997, she left for the top position at lingerie maker Frederick's of Hollywood. At this point, the Strauss chain had been reduced to 111 stores but was generating $175 million in sales.

In 1998, holding company WSR was sold to a group of private investors headed by Dan Gillings, a 30-year auto industry veteran. Almost immediately, in June 1998, the company filed a voluntary petition to reorganize under Chapter 11 of the U.S Bankruptcy Code. Maintaining that the goal was to position the Strauss chain as a regional market leader with fiscal stability, Gillings explained, ''After an intense review of the company's capital structure and financial commitments, we have determined that this reorganization is necessary so that Strauss can have a solid foundation on which to grow. . . . Daily operations will continue as usual, store hours will stay the same, and all aspects of the business will go on as before the filing.'' According to *Automotive Marketing,* however, ''There are those that say the bankruptcy was simply a ploy to escape years of debts and bad management decisions.'' Gillings brought back Al Woods to run Strauss during this transitional period.

In February 2000, Charon Investments LLC and Schottenstein Bernstein Capital Group, led by Charon's Glenn Langberg, made a successful bid to purchase the Strauss assets out of bankruptcy. After Woods resigned as president and CEO

Key Dates

1919: R&S Home and Auto is founded.
1929: Strauss Auto is founded.
1983: R&S and Strauss merge to form R&S Strauss.
1988: Ward White acquires Strauss to form WSR Group.
1995: WSR is dismantled, leaving Strauss as the company's main business.
1998: WSR declares bankruptcy.
2000: Strauss is bought by an investment group led by Glenn Langberg.

in July 2000, Langberg became chairman and CEO of the company. More experienced in real estate, he soon elevated a Strauss executive vice-president, Joe Catalano, to the job of president and chief operating officer to help him run the company. By now, the chain had shrunk to 90 stores, but having regained its footing Strauss was poised to once again open new stores. A newly created business plan envisioned the chain adding six to eight stores within the first year, all located in the company's current area of operation. Moreover, Strauss already had under construction two new superstores that would replace existing units in Blumfield, New Jersey, and Wilmington, Delaware, and also serve as a prototype for future expansion efforts. These stores, as large as 14,000 square feet in size with seven to ten service bays, extended the service department into the retail area. With new funding available, Strauss was also able to enhance its commercial business program for fleets. The company was soon able to sign up a major car rental agency as well as a number of livery services.

Because service was contributing as much as 40 percent of its sales, Strauss was interested in growing this segment of its business and management was committed only to opening stores that could at least offer light service business. In the New York City market, with its strict zoning laws and the scarcity of parcels of land large enough to accommodate a superstore, some flexibility was necessary. A store that opened in 2001 in the Canarsie section of Brooklyn, for instance, was limited to just two bays and light service, primarily mounting tires and installing batteries.

The new management team at Strauss undertook a number of initiatives to grow the business in 2001. It signed an agreement with an emergency auto roadside assistance service, 1-800-TOW-TRUCK, whereby the towing service would urge customers to have their vehicles taken to the nearest Strauss Service Center. In turn, all Strauss outlets would use the 1-800-TOW-TRUCK network for all their emergency roadside needs on an exclusive basis. Also in 2001, Strauss inked a deal with Wrenchead, Inc., an e-commerce provider, to maintain an electronic catalog service to be used in all of the stores. This initiative was part of a larger effort to use technology to make the chain more "customer-centric" and enhance the service business.

All of the Strauss stores were now linked by a high-speed Internet connection and shared a database that included as much in-depth information on a customer's car as possible, including the vehicle identification number, which could provide the vehicle's repair history. Not only would it enable Strauss mechanics to better service these vehicles, the system allowed the company to produce personalized marketing, such as reminders that a vehicle was due for maintenance. Strauss also relieved the customer of record keeping, retaining all information and providing receipts for customers as needed. In addition, Strauss turned to the Internet for marketing, buying banner ads on America On-Line, for instance, and offering online coupons that were gaining greater acceptance with customers. With a number of new store openings in the offing in the summer of 2003, Strauss was well positioned to enjoy another period of prosperity.

Principal Competitors

Advance AutoParts, Inc.; AutoZone, Inc.; The Pep Boys—Manny, Moe, & Jack.

Further Reading

Greenberg, Lisa, "Strauss Discount Gets 'Customer-Centric'," *Aftermarket Business*, May 2003, p.1.
"Strauss Auto Files Chapter 11," *Discount Store News,* June 22, 1998, p. 6.
Willins, Michael, "Strauss Discount Emerges From Bankruptcy with Equity Partner," *Aftermarket Business*, September 2000, p. 12.

—Ed Dinger

TB Wood's Corporation

440 North Fifth Avenue
Chambersburg, Pennsylvania 17201-1763
U.S.A.
Telephone: (717) 264-7161
Fax: (717) 264-6420
Web site: http://www.tbwoods.com

Public Company
Incorporated: 1897 as T.B. Wood's Sons Company
Employees: 950
Sales: $104.38 million (2002)
Stock Exchanges: NASDAQ
Ticker Symbol: TBWC
NAIC: 333999 All Other Miscellaneous General Purpose
  Machinery Manufacturing

TB Wood's Corporation is a leading innovator, designer, manufacturer, and marketer of electronic and mechanical industrial power-transmission products, which are used to transfer controlled power from an electric motor or internal combustion engine to a machine. Operating from 11 production facilities and with close to 950 employees in the United States, Mexico, Germany, India, and Italy, TB Wood's sells its products to North American and international distributors, original equipment manufacturers (OEMs), and end-users for manufacturing and commercial applications. In addition to such clients as Motion Industries and Kaman Industrial Technologies, among the largest distributors in the industrial power-transmission industry, TB Wood's markets its products through a network of some 1,000 independent distributors in North America. The company operates in two business segments: mechanical—which includes belted drives, couplings, and gearboxes—and the electronics industrial power-transmission segment—which consists of electronic drives and electronic-drive systems. TB Wood's standard AC drive products are programmable for specific applications in such industries as food processing, materials handling, packaging, heating and ventilating systems, and general machinery applications. The mechanical business seg-

ment (62.7 percent of net sales in 2002) offers a full line of stock and made-to-order products for the construction, oil field, specialized industrial machinery, food processing, mining, and agricultural equipment industries.

1800s Origins

In the United States, manufacturing processes remained simple and relatively slow until 1769, when James Watt made a breakthrough, adding a double-acting cylinder and gear to Newcomen's atmospheric pumping engine to provide the rotary motion needed for mechanical power to move other machinery. When Eli Whitney invented the cotton gin and introduced standard tooling, fixtures, jigs, and dies that allowed for interchangeable machine parts, mass production became possible—and the Industrial Revolution was on its way.

In 1857, T.B. Wood—a master mechanic and the shop superintendent of the Cumberland Valley Railroad—partnered with millwright Peter Housum, a designer and builder of machinery, to buy the Chambersburg, Pennsylvania-based Franklin Foundry & Machine Shop, which produced wood-burning stoves and specialized in "mill gearing." Judging from extant records of the Franklin Foundry, the two partners and their 24 employees also offered a variety of products, such as the pulleys, gears, couplings, rope sheaves, and flat belting that drove the mills and factories of that time. While the partners concentrated on building their business, the Southern States seceded and the nation was plunged into the Civil War. Colonel Peter Housum died in that war; T.B. Wood bought Housum's part of the business.

Franklin Foundry ironworks played a major role in the reconstruction of Chambersburg, a town nearly destroyed by the war. As two of T.B. Wood's sons joined the enterprise, it continued to focus on mill gearing and introduced new products, such as bridges, feed troughs, and a corn cob crusher labelled "The Miller's Friend." At their father's death in 1897, his sons took charge of the business and renamed it T.B. Wood's Sons. In 1899, Charles Wood—George's eldest son—joined the company as a partner; seven years later he became president of T.B. Wood's Sons Company.

Company Perspectives:

TB Wood's Corporation's primary goal is to grow net sales and profitability. The company's strategy for achieving this goal is to be a highly valued supplier to its customers by: (i) offering new and differentiated products and services, and (ii) distributing its products through a select group of distributors. The company's strategy also includes (i) continuous efforts to improve production efficiencies and otherwise reduce operating costs, and (ii) a program for external growth through strategic acquisitions and alliances both marketing and technical to further expand its product offerings and broaden its geographical market.

1900–50s: Ups and Downs

Under the leadership of the next generation of Woods, the company entered the power-transmission industry with the introduction of flat-belted and line-shaft mechanical drives, power transmission appliances, clutches, couplings, manila rope, and hangers. The company prospered and continued to expand until World War I.

Business declined in 1917, plummeted in 1921, recovered, and began to experience the effects of the Great Depression in the spring of 1930. According to company literature, TB Wood's did its utmost to keep employees on the payroll during this time, assigning available work as fairly as it could and even creating projects (painting, mowing grass, and other odd jobs) to keep employees at work. Under Roosevelt's New Deal, TB Wood's business slowly improved, growing steadily until World War II. Although the company was not directly involved with the production of armaments, it served the war effort through meeting heavy demand for its standard products, chiefly through subcontracts from the Chambersburg Engineering Company (CECO) for parts for the CECO forges. To meet demand, TB Wood's reopened its old Foundry No. 1 to make small parts for the CECO forges and Foundry No. 2 to make larger castings for the CECO forges and other standard products. Other subcontracts included the production of steel turret rings for tanks and heavy machine-gun mounts for P.T. boats.

By the end of World War II, TB Wood's had found a way to enhance its profits through a product of its own that became known as the Sure-Grip bushing. The company originally manufactured sheaves and pulleys and purchased its bushings from the Worthington Corporation. Adapting a new technology from Worthington, however, TB Woods soon secured its own license to produce and market interchangeable bores for sheaves and other shaft-mounted products. Demand for this Sure-Grip bushing increased.

In the mid- and late 1940s, major improvements to the company's machine shops were launched, as heavy molding machines and a large-capacity mechanized sand system were installed, eliminating much manual labor. Keeping up with technology continued to challenge the company during this time as well. While a rapid move to individual motors and drives for machines increased V-belt sales at TB Wood's, sales of lineshaft products, clutches, and hangers, as well as other older products decreased when replacement parts were no longer in demand.

To fill the void created by the discontinued products, TB Wood's began to market several new products in the 1950s, including mechanical variable speed-belted drives, synchronous-timing belt drive systems, and a newly patented Sure-Flex coupling product, which captured a significant segment of its market. The 1967 acquisition of Stratford, Ontario-based Bettger Industries Ltd.—a manufacturer of mechanical power transmission products—gave TB Wood's a wholly owned subsidiary with which it could reach the Canadian market. Next, an international molding machine placed in the foundry increased production of smaller castings.

1960s–90s: Continued Expansion

In 1968 Wood's entered the electronic drives market with Ultracon, the first of a new generation of drives which were versatile and offered powerful operating features and capabilities. A separate manufacturing subsidiary, Ultracon, Inc., was formed to manufacture the new product and its accessories.

In 1971, Wood's installed an eight-ton electric holding furnace in its foundry and only two years later replaced that with a 30-ton furnace. The foundry cleaning room was enlarged, as were the distribution centers located in Illinois and California. One of the company's most ambitious projects, installation of the Molding 2 high-pressure molding center, was completed in 1975; a new automatic molding machine reduced maintenance and improved the output of iron. In an alliance with U.S. Rubber Co. (Uniroyal), TB Wood's manufactured and marketed high torque drives and synchronous belted drive systems that replaced a large number of chain sprocket systems.

Since its inception in 1857, Wood's had used the coke-fired cupola method to make iron for castings. Because the removal of solid pollutants from the cupola exhaust required expensive maintenance and coke had become expensive—to name but two of many considerations—the foundry was converted to electric melting and replaced by a new facility in mid-1980. After 123 years of cupola melting, three 30/40-ton electric-induction furnaces were installed in a new melt building, which also housed a control room and a new metallurgical lab, as well as indoor storage of raw materials for the furnaces.

In the late 1980s, TB Wood's established a new machining facility in Trenton, Tennessee; this plant was the company's first manufacturing facility away from the Chambersburg area. It served as a satellite machine shop for the Atlanta, Chicago, and Dallas distribution centers and for the southern marketing region. Among the products introduced in 1981 was the Pro series of sheaves that provided maintenance-free service and eliminated the need for traditional oil lubricating systems. In 1984, TB Wood's further strengthened its position in the electronic controls business when it introduced its AC electronic drivers (inverters) to control electric motors.

Five generations of Wood family ownership and management had made TB Wood's a leading innovator of power transmission products. In December 1986 Thomas E. Foley bought the company. In 1991 he was joined by Michael L. Hurt who, as president, hired key managers to continue implementa-

Key Dates:

1857: T.B. Wood establishes a foundry and machine shop in Pennsylvania.
1897: Company is incorporated as TB Wood's Sons.
1900: TB Wood's enters the power transmission industry.
1930: The Depression slows down production; sales later improve under the New Deal.
1943: TB Wood's standard products help the war effort as well as its steel turret rings for tanks and machine-gun mounts.
1950s: The company markets its mechanical variable speed-belted drives and its new Sure-Flex coupling product.
1968: With its new Ultracon product, TB Wood's enters the electronic drives market.
1986: Thomas E. Foley buys the company.
1991: Michael L. Hurt succeeds five generations of Wood presidents.
1996: TB Wood's is traded on the New York Stock Exchange.
2001: Stock is moved to the NASDAQ.
2003: TB Wood's declares its 29th consecutive dividend since going public and buys back 100,000 shares of its stock.

tion of the company's growth strategy. They sought acquisitions and alliances to enhance product offerings, leverage fixed costs, and extend international market penetration. For example, the company bought several businesses that had a flexible coupling and mechanical variable-speed drive product line and two manufacturing facilities. In January 1994, TB Wood's acquired Plant Engineering Consultants, Inc., a manufacturer and marketer of integrated electronic drive systems for the fibers industry.

TB Wood's became a publicly held company in February 1996 when it completed an initial public offering (IPO) of its common stock on the New York Stock Exchange under the symbol TBW. Five years later, the company would move to NASDAQ and trade under the symbol TBWC.

In order to access technology and products that could not easily or effectively be made in its existing facilities, TB Wood's formed strategic technical and marketing alliances. For instance, in April 1992 Wood's set up a marketing and technical alliance for the development of high horse-power synchronous drives and introduced two new synchronous drives. In August 1992, the company entered into an alliance with Industry Uniserve Pty Ltd to sell AC electronic drives in Australia, New Zealand, and parts of Asia; in 1993 the company formed an alliance with Var-Spe S.p.a. to sell their hydrostatic variable speed drives in North America, and licensed Japan's Daido Precision for Form Flex couplings. In 1996 Wood's established electronic and marketing partnerships with Finland's Vaasa Controls and marketing agreements in Taiwan and Brazil. The company also owned 76 percent of a joint venture formed with Colorado-based Electron Corporation, a privately held foundry operation that specialized in gray and ductile iron casting solu-

tions and manufactured industrial mechanical power transmission products, especially belt-drive components. By 2002, TB Wood's would purchase Electron's share of that venture.

In 1996 TB Wood's acquired Grupo Blaju S.A. de C.V., and gained a leading market share position in belted drive systems components in Mexico as well as a cost-effective Mexican manufacturing operation. The purchase of Ambi-Tech Industries, Inc.—a leading manufacturer of electronic brakes—allowed for extension of an important TB Wood's product and support for growth in the electronics business. The November 1996 acquisition of Deck Manufacturing's line of gear couplings added to the fastest growing area of TB Wood's mechanical business. In December 1997, TB Wood's purchased Germany-based Berges electronic GmbH and its Italian subsidiary, Berges electronic S.r.l. The Berges companies, located in two of the most important European machinery markets were well-established developers, manufacturers, and marketers of variable frequency drives for AC induction motors.

TB Wood's continued to introduce new electronic and mechanical products, including an award-winning line of inverters in 1991. A 1993 strategic acquisition made the company a market leader in mechanical variable-speed drives and complemented its coupling line with a metallic disc product. During 1995–97, TB Wood's expanded the horsepower range of its AC drives with the installation of newly designed high-performance software.

In 1997 more than 30 percent of the company's sales came from internally developed products. In an interview for the July 7, 1997, issue of *Design News;* President Michael Hurt spoke of outsourcing as ''a passing fad'' popular in an era when Original Equipment Manufacturers (OEMs) and suppliers were farming out design. Hurt averred that given his company's talent to develop, manufacture, and sell its products, the company had to control its core manufacturing in-house. He was also of the opinion that ''rather than have . . . employees 'chase rainbows elsewhere' '' it was better to provide them with incentives to stay with TB Wood's.

2000 and Beyond

At the beginning of the 21st century, TB Wood's was a leading designer and marketer for the industrial power transmission industry. This industry consisted of three product categories: mechanical power transmission components, electronic drives, and gearboxes. For financial reporting purposes, Wood's classified its manufactured products into two business segments: the mechanical and the electronics industrial-power transmission business.

The mechanical business segment included a full line of stock and made-to-order products, such as belted drives, couplings, and gearboxes. The electronic business segment included electronic drives and electronic drive systems. TB Wood's standard AC electronic VFD products represented the major part of the company's sales of electronic drive products which were designed to meet electrical standards in both North America and Europe. The company's integrated electronic drive systems were uniquely configured for AC and/or DC electronic VFDs, had programmable logic controllers and in-house designed, custom-printed circuit boards and software.

When the economy began to spiral downwards in 2001, TB Wood's experienced some decreased demand for its products. In an April 2003 news release, President Hurt commented that while recovery from economic downturn was slow, he was pleased "with the growth of our targeted OEM programs, the initial demand for our new E-trAC(r)EF1 micro drive . . . and the increased output of our new Mexican plant." Sales of $104.38 million for the year 2002 were down 4.1 percent from the previous year. In response, the company continued to focus on matching costs with market demand; net inventory was reduced 16.2 percent and total debt dropped 16.9 percent. When the economy had not rebounded in 2003, TB Wood's saw the need to reduce employee work hours and eliminate several benefit programs. "Once the economy improves and inventory reduction activities end, we expect to return to our historical levels of performance," President Hurt affirmed. On April 3, 2003, the TB Wood's board of directors showed its belief in the future of the company by declaring the 29th consecutive dividend since the company's 1996 IPO. Moreover, on April 16, 2003, the board authorized the repurchase of an additional 100,000 shares of stock under the company's share repurchase program. Based on the company's resilience during its more than 146-year history, and the Board's confidence in Wood's viability, one could assume that Wood's would remain a leading and innovative provider of industrial-power transmission products—and again attain profitable growth.

Principal Subsidiaries

Berges electronic GmbH (Germany); Berges Electronic, S.r.l. (Italy); Industrial Blaju, S.A. de C.V. (Mexico); Plant Engineering Consultants, Inc.; T.B. Wood's Canada Ltd.; TB Wood's Inc.; TB Wood's (India) Pte Ltd.

Principal Competitors

Allen-Bradley; Asea Brown Boveri Ltd.; Emerson Electric Co.; Lovejoy, Inc.; Allen Bradley Martin Sprocket & Gear, Inc.; Rexnord Industries, Inc.; Rockwell Automation, Inc.; Siemens Corporation.

Further Reading

"CEO Interview: Michael L. Hurt, President, Discusses the Outlook for TB Wood's Corporation," *Wall Street Transcript Digest*, May 19, 1997.

Gross, Peter F., *T.B. Wood's Sons Company*, Chambersburg, Pa.: TB Wood's, 1982, 41 pp.

Kane, Les, and Stephany Romanow, "Sensorless Vector Drive Offers Flexibility, Enhanced Connectivity," *Hydrocarbon Processing*, June 2000, p. 117.

Maloney, Larry, "Outsourcing Is a Fad," *Design News*, July 7, 1997, p. 51.

Peiffer, Dave, "Integrated Motor Drive Cuts Installation Costs, Saves Space," *Design News*, August 25, 1997, p. 71.

TB Wood's Corporation Addendum, Chambersburg, Pa.: TB Wood's, 2001, 8 pp.

"TB Wood's to Enter Into a Joint Venture With Electron," *Foundry Management & Technology*, August 1999, p. 17.

—Gloria A. Lemieux

Trident Seafoods Corporation

5303 Shilshole Avenue Northwest
Seattle, Washington 98107
U.S.A.
Telephone: (206) 783-3818
Toll Free: (800) 426-5490
Fax: (206) 782-7195
Web site: http://www.tridentseafoods.com

Private Company
Incorporated: 1970
Employees: 4,000
Sales: $650 million (2002)
NAIC: 311711 Seafood Canning; 311712 Fresh and
Frozen Seafood Processing

Trident Seafoods Corporation is a vertically integrated harvester, processor, and marketer of seafood, operating onshore and offshore properties in Alaska, Washington, Oregon, and British Columbia, Canada. The company's fleet of processors and trawlers catch, can, and freeze pollock, salmon, crab, herring, and a variety of shellfish and groundfish. Trident pioneered vertical integration in the northwestern waters of the Pacific Ocean.

Origins

Revolutionary innovation in the offshore fishing industry was delivered by a native of Tennessee, an unlikely birthplace for an individual who would forever change the dynamics of doing business in the northwestern Pacific Ocean. Chuck Bundrant, Trident's founder, had escaped the landlocked confines of Tennessee long before he brought his vision to offshore fishing, however. In one of the most arduous occupations anyone could chose, Bundrant began his fishing career working on what tellingly was called the "slime line" at an Alaska crab processing plant. His time spent processing seafood for others sparked the genesis of Trident, a company whose birth was predicated on vertical integration—a business term signifying the ability of a single corporate entity to control the production of most, or all, aspects of its product, from raw material to distribution.

A vertically integrated sock manufacturer, for example, might own the cotton fields from which the socks were produced. That same company might own a packaging plant to package the socks it produced. Taken to a deeper lever, the sock manufacturer might own a distribution company to deliver its socks to market. Vertical integration, frequently sought after by commercial concerns of all types, gives the vertically integrated company greater control over its destiny. No longer subject to the whims of third-party enterprises, the self-reliant company is able to dictate its own way of conducting business and enjoy control over the supply and prices for virtually every component of its finished product. For Bundrant, vertical integration meant combining offshore fishing activities with onshore fishing activities, the union of fisherman and processor.

Bundrant's days on the slime line gave way to plans to become an entrepreneur in 1970. "It all started with one boat," Bundrant states on Trident's Web site. "We asked why we couldn't catch crab and process crab on the same vessel. They said it wasn't going to work." The question was innovative, the reaction typical of the response received by an industry pioneer. Bundrant's vision flew in the face of convention, but he pressed ahead regardless. The boat in question was the 135-foot *Billikin,* a vessel whose success blurred the line separating the often acrimonious relationship between fisherman and processor. At the time of Bundrant's idea to construct the *Billikin,* he was working as an Alaska king crab fisherman, as were his soon-to-be business partners, Kaare Ness and Mike Jacobson. The trio found themselves at the advent of a decade of robust growth in the business of harvesting crap. Vertical integration, the strategy underlying Bundrant's plans for the *Billikin,* promised to give the three fishermen a greater share of the profits available in the crabbing industry, particularly access to the lucrative business done on the docks.

Bent on processing crab where they caught it, Bundrant, Ness, and Jacobson designed the *Billikin* to include crab cookers and freezing equipment that enabled them to deliver a finished product. Once operational, the *Billikin* marked the beginning of a new era in the Alaska seafood industry, ushering in a time when fisherman would join the vastly more lucrative seafood processing industry.

Company Perspectives:

Trident believes that customer satisfaction is achieved through integrity, honesty, and on-time delivery of quality products, value pricing, and full service. We value long-term relationships with our customers. Our goal is to earn customer confidence and our pledge is to maintain a competitive profile. We will continue to listen to our customers and to exercise our creativity in developing new product lines to meet the ever-changing needs of the market place.

Trident was founded three years after Bundrant conceived the idea for the *Billikin*. At the time, in 1973, the fledgling enterprise was eased through its formative stage by the rising demand for fresh seafood, a demand that was global. The crucial first years of development were also aided by the expertise of several key individuals who joined Bundrant and his team in leading a revolution. A year after Trident's founding, Ed Perry, owner of San Juan Seafoods, a processing company based in Bellingham, Washington, joined the trio of fishermen, giving their company greater opportunities to fish and to process a spectrum of products, thereby diversifying Trident's business beyond harvesting crab. With a line, rather than a single item, of seafood to bring to market, the company enjoyed modest growth, gradually expanding its operations to meet growing market demand.

A decade after its formation, Trident had secured itself as a pioneering member of the seafood industry in the northwestern waters of the Pacific Ocean. At this point, the company could rely on seafood buyers in Europe and, most importantly, from the insatiable Japanese market. To serve these customers, as well as domestic purveyors, Trident's company-owned vessels and independent catcher vessels were delivering a full range of salmon, herring, shellfish, and groundfish products to the company's processing facilities in Alaska. The ability to serve these customers was measurably improved from 1984 forward by the arrival of Bob Eaton, a successful and inventive fisherman. Eaton joined the company's fold and pioneered new fishing technologies, assuming responsibility for managing the company's expanding fleet.

Industry Consolidation in the 1990s

By the 1990s, Trident ranked as a powerhouse in the regional seafood industry. After 20 years of expansion and innovation, the company enjoyed a solid presence along the western coast of the United States and Canada, operating facilities in Alaska, British Columbia, Washington, and Oregon. Toward the end of the decade, the processing industry experienced a period of consolidation, further erasing the distinction between onshore and offshore fishing companies. For many companies in the industry, survival, or at least the prospect of long-term growth, depended on the their actions during the period of consolidation. The smaller companies became the targets of larger companies, both the industry giants and medium-sized companies such as Trident. It was a situation that required companies in the seafood industry to either aggrandize through acquisition or become the target of those companies who did not

shy from acquiring. Bundrant sensed the gravity of the moment. Trident assumed the role of an acquirer, taking on an aggressive stance during this pivotal period of consolidation.

Trident's role as a consolidator began as the 1990s ended. In a classic example of vertical integration, the company, in early 1999, acquired a fish processing operation in Fife, Washington, 30 miles south of the company's Seattle headquarters. Before acquiring the Fife plant, Trident had served as one of the major suppliers to the facility, whose 120 employees produced surimi seafood and imitation crab. The Fife plant, acquired from Japan-based Nichirei Foods, gave Trident a modest boost to its operations yet considerably more control over the passage of its raw material—fish—through the processing stage and into the market.

At the time of the Nichirei transaction, a measure of Trident's stature could be taken. The company produced roughly 25 million pounds of pollock, cod, halibut, salmon, and tuna annually and operated more than 30 vessels, including four offshore processors and six onshore facilities in Alaska. Annual sales were approaching the half-billion-dollar mark. The dynamics of the company's business, which affected the conduct of its physical operations and influenced, to some measure, its acquisition of the surimi plant in Fife, were changing at this point due to new federal regulations on the fishing industry. In the years ahead, Trident responded to two forces, industry consolidation and federal legislation. A third force, emanating from an Alaska courtroom, would pock celebrations of the 30th anniversary of the inaugural sailing of the *Billikin*.

The 1998 American Fisheries Act dramatically changed the way in which Trident and other companies of its ilk conducted business. Before the legislation, fishing operators lived a decidedly frenetic life, their success dependent on catching as many fish as possible before the industrywide catch limit was reached. Once the fishing season started, operators took to the water, trying to catch more fish than they had the previous season and racing to catch more fish than their competitors. The 1998 American Fisheries Act legislated a different way of conducting business, establishing agreed upon quotas on the catch limit in the vast fishing grounds off Alaska. By creating fixed allocations based on each company's historical catch, the 1998 American Fisheries Act helped stabilize the fishing industry, freeing its operators from the mad dash to catch as much as possible as quickly as possible.

The 1998 American Fisheries Act changed not only the way in which Trident conducted its fishing activities but also the way in which the company defined its corporate strategy. With its quota of the total catch fixed by regulators, the company was forced to find other ways to fuel its growth. The years of catching an historically high number of fish were gone, so the company began delving into deeper levels of its business, going beyond the rewards engendered by vertical integration and striving to increase its revenues from value-added products. (An example of a value-added product in Trident's business would be to dip shrimp in a variety of batters and sell the battered shrimp for a higher price than plain shrimp). Bundrant explained the change in the company's strategic orientation. "We're trying to become more of a food company than just a seafood company," he said in a March 17, 2000 interview with the *Puget Sound Business Journal*. His objective, as stated in the same interview, was "how to add value and be able to sell everything we produce."

Bundrant's hopes for a bigger, more diverse Trident were realized in a signal 1999 acquisition, a transaction that met the challenges posed by the 1998 American Fisheries Act. Several months after acquiring the plant in Fife, Trident completed the purchase of Tyson Foods Inc.'s $180-million seafood assets, a deal that transformed the company into "the Microsoft of the waterfront," as hailed by the *Puget Sound Business Journal* in its March 17, 2000 issue. Tyson Foods was in the midst of exiting its non-core business interests and sharpening its focus on its chicken business, leaving the company's seafood assets, accumulated during the 1980s and early 1990s, up for grabs. Bundrant jumped at the opportunity, obtaining sea-worthy fishing vessels, associated fishing rights, and onshore processing plants that made Trident one of the largest competitors on the northwestern Pacific Ocean.

Following the Tyson Foods acquisition, Trident entered the 21st century exerting considerable sway in the industry. The company was supported by 12 processing plants in Alaska, Washington, and Oregon and a fleet of three at-sea processor boats. The addition of Tyson Foods' seafood assets enabled the company to begin processing onion rings, a symbolic step towards Bundrant's desire to transform the company from a seafood company into a food company. At the heart of the company, however, was its seafood business, which spanned the spectrum of fish and value-added fish products. Pollock, which accounted for about 45 percent of the company's revenues, served as Trident's mainstay, followed by salmon, a contributor of 25 percent of total revenues, with lesser percentages collected from catching and processing crab, shrimp, herring, shellfish, and groundfish. Trident's value-added and commodity products were primarily sold through restaurants and warehouses, but some of the seafood was sold at the retail level and marketed under such brands as Arctic Ice, Sea Alaska, Sea Legs, and Rubenstein.

Trident in the 21st Century

At the end of 2000, Trident acquired certain assets of a family owned processor and wholesaler named Depoe Bay Fish Co. Previously, Trident had been leasing Depoe's surimi facil-

ity, but the company acquired the plant in a deal that divvied Depoe's assets between Trident and Pacific Seafood Group. The acquisition represented yet another move toward consolidation orchestrated by Bundrant, but Trident's attention during the first years of the decade was focused not on consolidation but on the issues being debated in an Alaska courtroom. At issue, according to the company's attorney in the May 2003 issue of *National Fisherman,* was "the most important case, the most important thing, that Trident has ever been involved in."

In 1995, a lawsuit was filed by attorneys representing roughly 4,500 sockeye fishermen at Bristol Bay in Alaska. The lawsuit, aimed at a collection of processors that included Trident, sought $1.4 billion in damages as compensation for the alleged conspiracy to cheat gillnetters out of a fair price for their fish caught in the early 1990s. The case revolved around the marked price differences between 1988 and 1991, claiming collusion among the cabal of processors was responsible for the steep drop in prices paid at the docks in Bristol Bay. In 1988, processors paid more than $2 per pound for sockeye. In 1991, processors offered less than $.50 per pound. Executives for the processing companies maintained that market supply and demand dictated the precipitous decline in dock prices, with Bundrant voicing unequivocal disdain at the accusations of collusion. "I will never accede to this horseshit extortion," he exclaimed outside the Alaska courtroom, according to the May 2003 issue of *National Fisherman.* "I will never settle," he vowed. At the time of his pronouncement, Trident's position as an industry stalwart was secure, but the courtroom proceedings clouded the company's future. If Bundrant stood by his words, and the trial ended with victory by the gillnetters, the damage to Trident's operations promised to taint the company's fortunes as it moved beyond the 30th anniversary of the inaugural sailing of the *Billikin.*

Principal Subsidiaries

TT Acquisitions, Inc.

Principal Competitors

American Seafoods Corp.

Further Reading

Gibbs, Al, "Seattle-Based Seafood Processor Buys Fife, Wash., Plant," *Knight Ridder/Tribune Business News,* April 30, 1999.
Gorlick, Arthur C., "Trident Seafoods Acquires Tyson Seafoods," *Seattle Post Intelligencer,* May 29, 1999, p. B3.
Loy, Wesley, "In a Fix in the Bay: Processors and Fisherman Are Pitted against Each Other in a Billion-Dollar Lawsuit Over the Price of Fish," *National Fisherman,* May 2003, p. 24.
Robinson, Fiona, "Suppliers Vie for Sales Ranking," *Seafood Business,* February 2001, p. 1.
Smith, Rod, "Tyson Reaches Terms for Selling Seafood Business," *Feedstuffs,* June 7, 1999, p. 10.
"Trident Seafoods of Seattle Acquiring Nichirei Plant in Fife," *Seattle Post-Intelligencer,* May 1, 1999, p. B3.

—Jeffrey L. Covell

IIII

UNITED OVERSEAS BANK LIMITED

United Overseas Bank Ltd.

80 Raffles Place
UOB Plaza 1 048624
Singapore
Telephone: (+65) 6533-9898
Fax: (+65) 6534-2334
Web site: http://www.uob.com.sg

Public Company
Incorporated: 1935 as United Chinese Bank
Employees: 12,142
Sales: S$3.08 billion ($1.78 billion) (2002)
Stock Exchanges: Singapore
Ticker Symbol: UOBH
NAIC: 522110 Commercial Banking

United Overseas Bank Ltd. (UOB) is the second largest bank in Singapore and is staking a claim on the larger Asian-Pacific region. The bank offers the full range of commercial and corporate banking services, personal financial services, private banking and other asset management services, as well as corporate finance, venture capital, investment, and insurance services. The company also provides stockbroking services through its share of UOB-Kay Hian Holdings. Having established itself in the mature Singapore market—the company acquired rival Overseas Union Bank in 2002—UOB expects its future growth to come from its overseas operations. The company is already present, through subsidiaries and branch offices, in Malaysia, the Philippines, Indonesia, Thailand, China and Hong Kong, and Taiwan, as well as in South Korea, Japan, Australia, and Vietnam. Further abroad, the company operates branch offices in the United States, Canada, France, and the United Kingdom. In all, the company operates more than 250 offices worldwide. Although banking represents the company's primary business, UOB is also present in real estate, through a 40 percent stake in United Overseas Land; and in trading, through a 30 percent stake in Haw Par Corporation, which produces, among other products, Tiger Balm ointments. UOB continues to be led by Chairman Wee Cho Yaw, son of company founder Wee Kheng

Chiang. The Wee family remains the company's largest single shareholder, with a combined stake of some 20 percent.

Founding a Major Singapore Bank in the 1930s

Founded more than a century earlier, Singapore had become a thriving trade city and, like many countries in the region, home to a large native Chinese population. In the 1930s, a group of Chinese-born businessmen joined together to raise S$1 million in order to establish their own bank. Leading the group was Wee Kheng Chiang, of Chinese descent, whose father had built up a business empire in Malaysia and Singapore in the early part of the century. Wee was named CEO and chairman of the new bank, which was called United Chinese Bank to emphasize its links to the Chinese population in Singapore.

The Wee family eventually took control of the bank. When Singapore achieved its independent city state status in 1965, the bank's name was changed, becoming United Overseas Bank. In that year, the bank also took its first step onto the regional market when it opened its first foreign branch, in Hong Kong.

The bank remained a minor player, both in Singapore and especially in the Asia Pacific region when it went public in 1970, with a listing on what was at the time the Joint Stock Exchange of Singapore and Malaysia. By then, however, the Singapore government had begun a major push to modernize the state and, especially, rebuild it as one of the region's major financial centers. Wee, by then joined by son Wee Cho Yaw, had recognized that this political will was to have a far-reaching impact on the country's banking community, especially once the government inevitably opened the domestic financial market to foreign competitors. In order to survive, Singapore's banks, many of which were small, family-owned affairs, would be forced to grow.

During the 1970s, United Overseas Bank launched its own growth drive through a series of targeted acquisitions. In 1971, the bank bought up majority control of Chung Khiaw Bank, which not only strengthened its domestic network, but also gave it offices in Malaysia and Hong Kong. The Chung Khiaw acquisition also gave United Overseas Bank control of the Haw Par Corporation, which owned the famed Tiger Balm ointment brand.

United Overseas Bank's next acquisition came two years later, with the purchase of Lee Wah Bank, which also operated throughout Singapore and Malaysia. The following year, Wee Kheng Chiang, who had been given the honorary title of Datuk (''Sir''), turned over leadership of the family's holdings to Wee Cho Yaw. In that year, the company reinforced its new image as a major Singapore bank with the inauguration of its first office tower, the 30-story UOB Building.

United Overseas Bank continued to expand its operations through the late 1970s. While continuing to build on its presence in Singapore and Malaysia, the bank also stepped up its presence elsewhere in the region, notably in Hong Kong and in Tokyo, through Tye Hua Bank. The company also flirted with expansion into the United States, entering merger talks with American City Bank, based in Los Angeles. The two sides broke off discussions in 1981, however. Nonetheless, by the beginning of the 1980s, United Overseas Bank had opened branch offices in Los Angeles and New York.

At the start of the 1980s, United Overseas Bank Group claimed to be Singapore's largest, with more than 80 branches and total assets of nearly S$10 billion by 1983. The company also had begun building up a full range of financial services, including brokerage and other investment services. In the mid-1980s, UOB became one of the first to enter the slowly opening Chinese economy, opening a representative office in Beijing in 1986.

Acquisitions remained an important motor to United Overseas Bank's growth over the next decade. In 1984 the bank grew again with the addition of a controlling stake in Far Eastern Bank. That purchase was followed by the purchase of a majority share of Singapore's Industrial & Commercial Bank in 1987. The following year, United Overseas Bank took full control of Chung Khiaw Bank.

Consolidating for Regional Status in the 2000s

United Overseas Bank grew strongly through the 1990s, in part thanks to the roaring economic climate in its Southeast Asian region. During the decade, UOB began to position itself for the future, as the Singapore government began placing increasing pressure on the country's five largest banks—including state-owned DBS and Keppel Tatlee, the number one and four banks, respectively, and privately held Overseas Union Bank and Overseas-Chinese Banking Corporation (OCBC)—to consolidate.

By the mid-1990s, United Overseas Bank prepared to celebrate its 60th anniversary with the inauguration of a new headquarters complex, UOB Plaza, which was opened in 1995. By then, the bank had launched a streamlining effort. In 1994, UOB merged its Lee Wah Bank subsidiary's operations into its main

UOB business in both Singapore and Malaysia. Chung Khiaw's turn came in 1997, when that bank's Malaysian branches were placed under the United Overseas Bank signage. Two years later, the rest of Chung Khiaw's operations, including its branches in Singapore and Hong Kong, were converted to United Overseas Bank. This left the bank with just three primary brands, UOB, Far Eastern Bank, and Industry & Commerce Bank.

In 1998, amid the Asian economic crisis of the late 1990s, UOB faced even greater pressure to accede to government pressure for consolidation after the government merged its POSBank people's bank unit into DBS, creating Singapore's largest bank. Yet Wee continued to resist consolidation at home, turning instead to expansion abroad in order to become a stronger regional player.

In 1999, the company made two key foreign acquisitions. The first was of a 60 percent share of Westmont Bank, in the Philippines. That bank was then renamed United Overseas Bank Philippines, and gave UOB a branch network of 97 offices in that country. The second acquisition brought UOB into Thailand, with the purchase of 75 percent of Radanasin Bank—formed in 1998 from the ruins of more than 50 failed Thai banks—in a deal worth $388 million. That unit was then renamed UOB Radanasin Bank. Both the Thai and Filipino operations remained lossmakers into the next century, however.

In 2000, UOB began a new restructuring. The bank merged the operations of a financial services subsidiary, United Overseas Finance, into the overall UOB structure. Next, UOB agreed to merge its brokerage operations, which spanned Hong Kong, Indonesia, Malaysia, Philippines, and Thailand, as well as Singapore, with those of Kay Hian Holdings, a prominent Singapore brokerage, forming the joint venture UOB-Kay Hian Holdings Ltd.

Despite its resistance to local consolidation, UOB found its hand forced in 2001. The bank's main rival, government-backed DBS, launched a takeover attempt of Overseas Union that year, in a bid worth S$9.4 billion. Then OCBC offered nearly S$5 billion to take over the smallest of the top banks, Keppel Tatlee. UOB had no choice but to bid for one or the other of the two takeover targets. As Wee explained to the *South China Morning Post:* ''It gave me the opportunity. I had two options: either I counter-bid OCBC or DBS. So it gave me really one week of sleepless nights to think: 'In which direction I am going?' At the end of the day, I made a decision and recommended to the board that we should counter-bid DBS.''

UOB's offer for Overseas Union Bank came in at S$10 billion, beating out DBS. Perhaps more important, however, Wee made a personal visit to George Lien Ying Chow, the aging founder and chairman of family-owned Overseas Union—proposing a ''merger'' that would allow Lien to save face. The move, which contrasted sharply with DBS's hostile approach, won Lien's backing for the takeover bid. Wee later acknowledged, however, that he would have pursued the takeover even without Lien's approval.

The two sides reached agreement in September 2001, and by the beginning of 2002, integration of Overseas Union into the UOB network began. That process was completed at the beginning of 2003, when all of Overseas Union's branches were

Key Dates:

1935: Wee Khiang Cheng and others found United Chinese Bank Singapore.
1965: The bank changes its name to United Overseas Bank (UOB) after Singapore's independence; it opens its first foreign office in Hong Kong.
1970: UOB goes public on the Singapore and Malaysian stock exchanges.
1971: Bank acquires majority control of Chung Khiaw Bank.
1973: Lee Wah Bank is acquired.
1984: UOB acquires Far Eastern Bank.
1994: Lee Wah Bank operations are merged into UOB.
1997: Chung Khiaw Bank operations in Malaysia are merged into UOB.
1999: The Chung Khiaw restructuring is completed by merging Singapore and Hong Kong operations into UOB.
2000: United Overseas Finance is merged into UOB.

converted under the UOB signage. The addition of Overseas Union Bank's operations not only restored United Overseas Bank as Singapore's largest local bank, with more than $62 billion in assets, it also transformed it into a top regional competitor. The newly enlarged operation now controlled nearly 30 percent of the Singapore banking market, while boosting the share of domestic revenues to more than 90 percent of UOB's total.

This placed the bank on delicate ground. UOB could expect little additional room for growth in Singapore, which remained a relatively minor market in the region. Meanwhile, the Singapore government had begun granting banking licenses to an increasing number of foreign rivals—including such global and regional powerhouses as HSBC and Standard Chartered. UOB's only choice for future growth lay in continued regional expansion.

China became the obvious choice for expansion by the end of 2002. In August of that year, the bank opened a new full service branch office in Shanghai, which was followed by the upgrade of its Beijing office to a full service branch in November, bringing UOB's total Chinese presence to five branches. The company also was expanding its range of services in Hong Kong, particularly with a successful launch into the city's credit card market. UOB also eyed expansion into the Taiwan banking market as well.

Over the course of its nearly 70-year history, UOB had grown up with Singapore. At the beginning of the new century, United Overseas Bank now hitched its future as a regional player in the fast-growing Asian Pacific market.

Principal Subsidiaries

Far Eastern Bank; PT Bank UOB Indonesia; United Overseas Bank (Malaysia); United Overseas Bank Philippines; United Overseas Land Group; UOB Radanasin Bank (Thailand).

Principal Competitors

Bank of China; China Construction Bank; Agricultural Bank of China; Hongkong and Shanghai Banking Corporation Ltd.; Shinkin Central Bank; Kookmin Bank; Hang Seng Bank Ltd.; Woori Bank; Joyo Bank Ltd.

Further Reading

"It's Always the Next Deal," *South China Morning Post,* May 13, 2002.
Lim, Richard, "A Few Good Men," *Straits Times,* August 12, 2002.
Lloyd-Smith, Jake, "UOB Plans East Asian Expansion," *South China Morning Post,* March 9, 2002.
"A Merged Local Bank Will Still Be Small," *Straits Times,* June 8, 1998, p. SS3.
Montlake, Simon, "Singapore Bankers Take the Plunge," *Banker,* August 2002, p. 45.
"Outwards and Upwards," *Euromoney,* February 2001, p. 46.
Shih, Lee Han, "Can Wee Cho Yaw Pull Off Next Project?," *Business Times,* February 8, 2003.
"Singapore's United Overseas Bank Upgrades Beijing Office to Full Branch," *Xinhua News Agency,* November 6, 2002.
"UOB Sees Need to Expand Overseas," *Star,* June 21, 2002.

—M.L. Cohen

Vista Bakery, Inc.

3000 Mount Pleasant Street, Box 888
Burlington, Iowa 52601-0888
U.S.A.
Telephone: (319) 754-6551
Fax: (319) 752-0063
Web site: http://www.vistabakery.com

Wholly Owned Subsidiary of Lance Inc.
Incorporated: 1934
Employees: 500
Sales: $85 million (2002 est.)
NAIC: 311821 Cookie and Cracker Manufacturing

Vista Bakery, Inc. is a Burlington, Iowa-based manufacturer of cookies and crackers. A subsidiary of snack food manufacturer Lance, Inc., the company markets its own Vista brand of baked goods and also produces private label cookies and crackers for a number of retailers and wholesalers.

The Iowa Biscuit Years: 1907–33

Vista Bakery's roots stretch back to June 13, 1907, with the establishment of the Iowa Biscuit Co. J.M. Storrar served as the company's first president, and A.G. Oberle as vice-president.

In December 1907, six months after it was incorporated, the Iowa Biscuit Co. began producing baked goods at a rented facility on Third Street in Burlington. After approximately seven years of operation, volume and income tripled at the young enterprise. The company employed 50 to 100 workers, roughly 25 percent of whom were skilled laborers. Under the trademark of a wild rose and the slogan "Sweet and Clean," the company marketed its products to wholesalers and jobbers in select areas of the Midwest, including Iowa, western Illinois, and northeastern Missouri. Six traveling salesmen were charged with this important task.

By 1914, prosperity enabled Iowa Biscuit to relocate to a new, five-story facility adjacent to the one it had been renting. With 40,000 square feet of space, the new fireproof building was constructed specifically for the production of baked goods and contained a lunchroom for the company's employees and bathing facilities for bakers.

According to an early news account, a social welfare worker from Boston who inspected it dubbed the factory "absolutely perfect," which was a credit to company management. It was clean, well lighted and ventilated, and was designed with employee safety in mind. As the April 23, 1915 issue of the *Burlington Gazette* revealed: "In the matter of safety every device and appliance has been provided. The building is equipped with a complete sprinkler system; with fire-escapes at the southwest and northeast corners and stairways at the northwest and southeast corners. The machinery throughout is fully protected from contact. The equipment in the matter of machinery and appliances is of the most modern and up-to-date character and the management is in the hands of one of America's leading experts in the business."

The basement level of Iowa Biscuit's new plant was devoted to storing the raw materials used during production, including barrels of molasses and sacks of flour and sugar. An enormous Corliss engine, used to generate the plant's light and power, also was housed in the basement. Materials were taken to upper levels of the building via an elevator. On the fifth floor, a machine shook flour from emptied sacks so that they were clean upon their return to the mill. On the fourth floor, machinery stamped and cut cookies before they were manually placed onto racks in one of two large ovens. It also was on the fourth floor that marshmallow was applied to certain types of cookies. On the third floor, a process involving a mechanized wheel and vacuum system was used to clean tin boxes, and workers packaged cookies and crackers for sale. In addition to being used for box storage, the second floor also contained a department responsible for making ice cream sandwiches. Finally, the first floor of Iowa Biscuit's plant contained crackers, cookies, and cakes that were packaged and ready for sale.

Among Iowa Biscuit's earliest products were Perfect Biscuits; W.R. Graham Crackers; Iowa Flakes; W.R. Soda Crackers; Iowa Ginger Snaps; Neto Biscuits; Lemon Biscuit Squares; Vanilla Wafers; Iowa Oyster Crackers; Animal Cookies; Oyster Crisps; Dutch Tea Rusks; Peanut Wafers; Select Soda Crackers;

Company Perspectives:

Our quality extends beyond the cookies and crackers themselves to Vista Bakery's commitment to 'Leadership, Quality, and Service You Can Clearly See.'

Baby Soda Crackers; Kenwood Sugar Wafers; Lemon Snaps; and W.R. Oatmeal Crackers.

The Midwest Biscuit Years: 1934–79

An important development took place in late 1934, when Frank J. Delaney purchased Iowa Biscuit Co. and renamed the enterprise Midwest Biscuit Co. Delaney's involvement would have an enormous impact on the organization and assure its future success.

Born in 1887 in Chicago, the son of Thomas and Wilmer Delaney, Frank Delaney was a seasoned biscuit and cracker industry veteran, with 35 years of experience. His interest in the industry began in 1900, not long after the National Biscuit Co. (later Nabisco) was formed. Delaney's cousin, Orrin S. Goan, managed National Biscuit's Tenth Avenue bakery in New York and had previously worked in Chicago at National Biscuit's Kennedy Biscuit Works. Inspired, Delaney found employment at Kennedy Biscuit for $5 per week, working for a man named C.W. Sample.

Delaney eventually was transferred to National Biscuit's general sales department on La Salle Street when a strike closed the Kennedy plant. This proved to be an excellent opportunity, and Delaney saw his scope of responsibility increase. Before long, he was handling sales at the city and national level for National Biscuit. Upon the recommendation of A.H. Vories, then head of sales, Delaney relocated to Freeport, Illinois, and worked as a national salesman for three years. Subsequent promotions brought him to other Illinois cities, including Peoria and Galesburg.

Prior to his acquisition of Iowa Biscuit, Delaney served as an executive at a number of different companies including the Loose-Wiles Biscuit Co. of Omaha, Nebraska (where his cousin Orrin Goan was general manager); the Shelby Biscuit Co. of Memphis, Tennessee; Penick & Ford, Ltd., Inc., of New Orleans; and the cracker department of Continental Baking Corp.'s Taggart Bakery in Indianapolis. His performance at the Shelby Biscuit Co. was especially remarkable. According to a 1932 issue of *Cracker Baker*, thanks to Delaney and his colleague F.S. Vories, "a very unprofitable small business with nine salesmen was developed into an exceedingly profitable one employing 56 salesmen and operating four agencies." According to the publication, Delaney's success at Shelby was noticed by executives at Penick & Ford, "who engaged him to organize and develop a department to service the baking trade, and especially the biscuit and cracker industry, with molasses. This work not only gave him the opportunity of renewing old acquaintances made through his 25 years spent in the industry, but also a broad knowledge of the industry."

With Delaney serving as president, Henry S. Walker as vice-president, and Delaney's wife Eileen as secretary, Midwest Biscuit made preparations for the future. While the company would retain its hometown image, plans were made to modernize the plant in a number of ways including the addition of new equipment. In addition, Delaney announced that a completely new line of quality biscuits, crackers, and cakes would be introduced. Until his death from a heart attack in March 1947, Delaney was successful at growing Midwest Biscuit and increasing awareness about the company and its reputation for quality throughout the Midwest.

One important aspect of Delaney's legacy was the construction of a new $150,000 plant on Mount Pleasant Street in West Burlington. Plans for the new facility, located on 17 acres, were announced in the fall of 1946 and it was completed in 1947 after Delaney passed away. The new plant—and Midwest Biscuit—played an important role in the city of Burlington's strategy for growth and development following the end of World War II. During the war, the city had prospered because of an ordnance plant that employed 13,000 workers. However, when the plant switched to standby status, employing only 300 to 400 people, the city implemented a strategy to attract new companies to the area and to help existing ones expand.

Following the war, Midwest Biscuit continued to prosper. The company enjoyed several decades of steady growth. During this time, the plant that was built in 1947 was expanded in several stages. Although the Midwest remained Midwest Bakery's primary market, the firm gradually extended its reach, serving distributors and supermarket chains in 34 states and Canada. By the late 1970s the company employed 170 workers and recorded annual sales of about $10 million. It sold products under the Vista Pak trade name, and also produced private label products for others.

Lance Takes Control: 1979–95

Midwest Biscuit's steady growth and success made it an attractive candidate for acquisition. Thus, some were not surprised when Charlotte, North Carolina-based snack food manufacturer Lance, Inc. announced that it intended to acquire Burlington's oldest commercial baking concern in July 1979 for cash. At the time, Frank Delaney's sons, Frank J. Delaney, Jr., and R.H. (Dick) Delaney, led the company as chairman and president, respectively. Frank had joined the company in 1938 and Dick in 1940. The two men agreed to remain with the company long enough to ensure a smooth transition in ownership.

Lance's acquisition of Midwest Bakery was ultimately completed on November 5. The new parent company initially left things unchanged, although it noted that expansion would be needed at some point in the future because of Midwest Biscuit's continued progress. During the mid-1980s, Paul Stroup, who eventually became chairman of Lance, became Midwest Biscuit's president. He served in that capacity until 1989, when he was transferred to Lance's headquarters.

By the early 1990s, things continued to go well for Midwest Biscuit and Lance. The firms weathered the economic recession of the early 1990s, and Midwest Biscuit saw sales and net income increase in 1991. The company developed a strategy to increase market penetration for its Vista and private label products in the southeast. Subsequently, a plant was established in

Key Dates:

1907: The Iowa Biscuit Co., Vista Bakery's predecessor, is founded.

1914: Production takes place in a new, fireproof facility spanning five stories and 40,000 square feet.

1934: Frank J. Delaney purchases Iowa Biscuit Co. and renames the enterprise Midwest Biscuit Co.

1947: A new, $150,000 plant is erected on a 17-acre site in West Burlington.

1950: Several decades of steady growth and development begin.

1979: Charlotte, North Carolina-based snack food manufacturer Lance, Inc. acquires Midwest Biscuit Co. in a cash deal.

1992: Midwest Biscuit establishes a plant in Columbia, South Carolina.

1995: Midwest Biscuit changes its name to Vista Bakery.

1996: In order to control costs, Lance closes the Vista Bakery plant in South Carolina and moves the majority of operations to Burlington.

2000: Product volume reaches 165 million pounds, almost doubling from 84 million pounds in 1995.

2003: Vista Bakery's reach includes the United States, Canada, Mexico, and a number of select international markets.

Columbia, South Carolina, and production started there in fall 1992. At this time, Midwest Biscuit's private label clients included a number of well-known grocery chains including Aldi, Cracker Shop, Eagle, Hy Vee, and Lady Lee.

Focused on the Future: 1995 and Beyond

During the mid-1990s, several important changes took place at Midwest Biscuit. Most of these represented a natural evolution, as the company strived to stay progressive after nearly 100 years of continuous operation.

Perhaps the most significant change occurred in July 1995 when, after 60 years, Midwest Biscuit changed its name to Vista Bakery. As Lance's vice-president, Gerry Smith, explained in the July 30, 1995 issue of the *Hawk Eye*, "By changing our name we are matching our corporate name with our brand name. A customer in California who's seen the name Vista on our packaging will connect with the name better." Smith said that Midwest Biscuit's workers approved the name change.

In September 1995, Vista's president, Gary Martin, retired after a 33-year career with the company. Lance appointed Dean Fields, a 32-year veteran of the snack food industry, as Vista Bakery's new general manager. Fields eventually was named president. By this time, approximately 500 workers were employed at the Burlington plant, which operated six ovens. Vista produced private label products for hundreds of companies throughout the United States and Canada.

In order to control costs, Lance closed the Vista Bakery plant in South Carolina in 1996 and moved two of its three ovens to Burlington, along with makeup and packaging systems, and in-

gredient handling. In Burlington, operations were expanded to include six cookie lines and two cracker lines. One of the cookie lines was set up so that it could make crackers if necessary. The move caused total product volume to almost double, increasing from 84 million pounds in 1995 to 165 million pounds by 2000. Vista added several new crackers to its product line in early 1996. Among these were fat-free saltines, low-fat regular and cinnamon graham crackers, and four types of snack crackers: smoked bacon, cheddar cheese, garden vegetable, and sesame wheat.

During the mid-1990s, Vista began efforts to modernize its 313,000-square-foot plant to accommodate growth and meet the increasingly demanding needs of private label customers, who expected national brand name quality. The company devoted additional resources to quality assurance, as well as research and development. These efforts were supported by improvements in technology. In the October 2001 issue of *Baking & Snack*, Laurie Gorton summarized a few of the things Vista had done to stay at the forefront of the industry, explaining: "Electronics make lines flexible. On-line monitoring verifies quality standards. Robots speed distribution staging. Computers forecast needs, and plant-wide data networking is in the offing."

Unlike the early days of Iowa Biscuit Co., when operations took place in a five-story building, by the early 2000s Vista's plant was set up so that cookie and cracker production more or less took place on one floor. Although mixing and formulation occurred in a three-story tower, the company's eight oven lines were set up in straight, parallel lines. This made it possible for ingredients to be processed, baked, packaged, placed on pallets, and moved to the warehouse in a streamlined manner. Due to space limitations, Vista relied on "just-in-time" delivery with many of the companies that supplied ingredients for its products, often receiving several shipments of packaging materials and raw ingredients each day.

By the early 2000s, Vista had extended its reach even further. In addition to the United States and Canada the company marketed its products to Mexico and a number of select international markets. Approximately 80 percent of its production was attributable to private label customers. Vista's plant operated around the clock, five to six days per week, depending on demand. With its efforts devoted largely to the private label sector, the company had learned to be very responsive to its customer base, putting it in a strong position for future success. As Tyler Cook, vice-president of sales, said in the October 2001 issue of *Baking & Snack*: "We make chocolate crème sandwich cookies for 20 or 30 customers, but we are able to do different things for each client that individualize their products. To be successful in private label, you have to be flexible. Every client is different. What's important at Vista is that we have a large facility with plenty of capacity and that our people are nimble and flexible in making decisions."

Principal Competitors

Bake-Line Group LLC; Ralcorp Holdings Inc.; Parmalot Bakery Division.

Further Reading

Allen, Don, "Burlington Solves Postwar Problems," *Des Moines Sunday Register*, September 1947.

"Company History," Burlington, Iowa: Vista Bakery, Inc., 2003.

Delaney, Steve, "Vista Bakery Launches New Era in Burlington," *Burlington Hawk Eye,* January 7, 1996.

"F.J. Delaney Manager Taggart Biscuit Co.," *Cracker Baker,* 1932.

Gorton, Laurie. "Exceeding Expectations," *Baking & Snack,* October 2001.

"Lance Plans Purchase of Assets of Midwest Biscuit for Cash," *Milling & Baking News,* July 24, 1979.

Martin, Mitch, "New Name for Bakery," *Burlington Hawk Eye,* July 30, 1995.

"Midwest Biscuit Co. to Be Sold," *Burlington Hawk Eye,* July 17, 1979.

"Midwest Biscuit Sale Complete," *Burlington Hawk Eye,* November 6, 1979.

"Vista Supreme Lowfat Crackers," *Snack Food,* February 1996.

—Paul R. Greenland

W.B Doner & Co.

25900 Northwestern Highway
Southfield, Michigan 48075
U.S.A.
Telephone: (248) 354-9700
Fax: (248) 827-0880

Private Company
Incorporated: 1937
Employees: 930
Sales: $121.5 million (2003 est.)
NAIC: 541810 Advertising Agencies

W.B. Doner & Co. is the largest independently-owned advertising agency in North America. The firm offers a full range of services that include creation of advertising campaigns, media buying, public relations, account planning, sales promotion, and direct marketing. Doner works with many well-known clients including Mazda, Blockbuster Entertainment, Minute Maid, Owens Corning, Arby's, DuPont, HGTV, May Department Stores, and La-Z-Boy. The Michigan-based company has offices in several U.S. cities as well as in Canada and the United Kingdom.

1930s Origins

The roots of W.B. Doner & Co. date to 1937, when Wilfred Brodcrick "Brod" Doner founded an advertising agency in Detroit. Doner, who was just 23, gradually built up the firm's client base during the late 1930s and 1940s. By the early 1950s, when the company had begun doing television commercials, its accounts included Speedway 79 Gasoline and E-Z Pop popcorn.

In 1954 Doner won the account of National Brewing Company, based in Baltimore, and when that firm offered a building for Doner to use, the agency added an office there. It opened in January 1955 and was headed by a new recruit, 26 year-old Herbert Fried. Fried had studied business and marketing, and had worked for several agencies in Chicago before joining Doner. Though National Brewing was the only account in Baltimore for the first two years, the office later began to win work for other clients such as First National Bank.

During the 1960s Doner continued to grow, creating memorable ad campaigns for the likes of Colt 45 Malt Liquor and Hygrade Ball Park Franks. For the latter, the firm came up with the classic "They plump when you cook 'em," slogan, which debuted in 1966. Another notable Doner campaign, for Tootsie Roll, asked the question, "How many licks does it take to get to the center of a Tootsie Pop?" The tagline was introduced in 1968 and used for many years afterwards.

New Leadership in the 1970s

In 1973 Herb Fried was named chairman and CEO of the company, having already served as president since 1968. Fried remained in the Baltimore area, and the firm designated its Detroit and Baltimore offices as co-headquarters. To keep up with the activities of both branches, Fried took frequent trips to Detroit. During the 1970s Doner's work included the "Scrubbing Bubbles" campaign for Dow and the creation of the Vlasic Stork character for Vlasic Pickles. The decade also saw the firm add a number of important new accounts, including United Brands' Chiquita Banana division, May Department Stores Co., Lionel Trains, and Dutch Boy, Inc. Doner had acquired a reputation for creating advertisements that produced sales on the retail level, and many clients sought it out for this specialization.

Though the firm's clients typically paid the agency the industry standard 15 percent of billings (meaning the total advertising budget), this began to change in the late 1970s. Doner began to work with its clients to find less rigid ways of charging them for their advertising services, and in some cases accepted fees based on the sales results of its advertising.

In 1981 several key members of Doner's Baltimore staff left to form a rival agency, Smith, Burke and Azzam. They took an estimated 30 percent of the office's clients with them, including restaurant chain Roy Rogers and hotel franchiser Quality International. Doner subsequently filed suit against the parties involved—Roger Gray, Barry L. Smith and Eugene Azzam—settling the claim for a reported $300,000.

During the 1980s the company continued to come up with creative and successful campaigns for a variety of clients. The "Zoo Stars" ad for the Detroit Zoo, which featured talking

Key Dates:

1937: Wilfred Broderick Doner founds an ad agency in Detroit, Michigan.

1955: Firm opens a second office in Baltimore, Maryland, run by Herb Fried.

1960s: Memorable slogans include "They plump whey you cook 'em" for Hygrade.

1973: Herb Fried named chairman and CEO.

1986: Chicago office opened with purchase of Lou Beres and Associates.

1988: Doner wins $30 million British Petroleum retail account; London office opens.

1995: Purchase of GGK London.

1997: $240 million Mazda account is won.

1998: Firm wins $160 million Blockbuster account.

2003: Baltimore office closed and its operations moved to Southfield.

animals, won a number of awards, and was later adopted as the official commercial of the National Zoo Association. Ads for Canadian Tire and Klondike bars were well-received during the early 1980s as well, with the "What would you do for a Klondike bar" line being used for years afterwards. The company was also hired to work for the Michigan State Lottery. In 1984 an office was opened in Toronto, which joined an existing location in Montreal to give Doner offices in Canada.

The year 1985 saw the company begin working for Little Caesar's, the Detroit-based pizza restaurant chain which then had 700 locations. Over the next three years Doner's ads helped the chain double this amount of outlets and triple the number of markets it served.

In 1986 Doner bought the Chicago-based ad agency Lou Beres and Associates, which handled billings of some $17 million and accounts that included Turtle Wax and Florsheim. Owner Beres was retained to serve as managing director of the office, which would employ approximately 25 and take on the name of its new parent. The move was made in part to serve the new G. Heileman Brewing Company account, which was worth $4 million in billings. In 1987, Doner also added an Hispanic unit to handle specialized advertising.

New Clients in the Late 1980s

In early 1988 Doner scored a major coup when it was assigned the British Petroleum (BP) worldwide retail gasoline account. The work had grown out of a small job done for Standard Oil in 1984 to promote six auto repair shops in Toledo, Ohio. This later led to contracts with sister companies Gulf, Sohio, and Boron, and after BP took control of Standard the new parent company selected Doner to boost its profile around the world, an assignment which was expected to involve some $30 million in annual billings. Doner would create the ads, with media-buying handled by BP's agencies in its various international markets. To service the account Doner opened an office in London, and this soon helped bring in other foreign assignments. Over the next four years Doner's overseas work jumped from 5 percent to 30 percent of its total billings.

The late 1980s saw other major clients such as Arby's, La-Z-Boy, Iams, and B.F. Goodrich added to the firm's roster. Memorable work of the era included a series of television spots for Red Roof Inns which featured comedian Martin Mull. By 1989 Doner was planning campaigns worth more than $300 million in billings, and taking in $52.1 million in revenues. The firm employed a staff of 550, 325 of whom worked in the Detroit suburb of Southfield, where the company had moved into new offices in October 1988. Some 140 other staffers were in Baltimore, with the rest in satellite offices in Boston, Chicago, Cleveland, St. Petersburg, Florida, London, Toronto, and Montreal. Doner had no presence in the advertising Mecca of New York, but despite its "outsider" status, in March 1989 the firm was named runner up as Agency of the Year by the influential trade publication *Advertising Age,* which ranked Doner the 26th largest agency in the United States.

In January 1990 founder and patriarch Brod Doner passed away at the age of 75. More than 40 years after starting the company he had remained a vital presence there, at the end serving as president of its executive committee. His guiding philosophy had been, as Herb Fried told *Crain's Detroit Business,* "creativity comes first, and everything else is secondary." Doner was praised for his ethics and family-oriented values, and his professional way of conducting business. Because of his personal convictions, the company had never taken assignments from cigarette makers or the National Rifle Association.

After Doner's death, the firm expanded its executive committee from two to six members and gave Herb Fried the position of chairman. Other changes that took place at this time included the sale of the Chicago office and the opening of a new one in Dallas to serve an account with Ford dealership associations in that area. A joint venture was also formed with Grey Advertising, Inc. of New York to do work for the BP account, with Grey handling media buying and other services through its network of European offices. In 1991 Doner bought into Luscombe & Partners, the fourth-largest independent advertising agency in Australia.

Challenges in the 1990s

In early 1992 Doner laid off 24 employees due to declining revenues caused by the stagnant U.S. economy. A number of the firm's clients, including the Ford dealerships and the Michigan-based appliance store chain Highland Superstores, were seeing drastic sales declines, which left them with fewer dollars to spend on advertising. The company was also hurt by the decision of the Michigan State Lottery to find a new agency, and the bankruptcy of long-time client Eckerd Drug Stores. Some new accounts were landed during the year, however, including Rose's Stores, a 217-outlet chain of discount department stores located in the southeastern United States.

In June 1992 Doner president Jim Dale was promoted to the jobs of CEO and chairman, while Herb Fried kept his role as chairman of the executive committee. A 25-year company veteran, Alan Kalter, who was based in Detroit, was given the job of president. At the same time Steve LaGattuta, vice-chairman of international business development, resigned. LaGattuta had been credited with boosting the company's international profile, but was reportedly upset at having been passed over for the president's job. Since Brod Doner's death about a dozen key executives had left the company, which was still trying to redefine itself in his absence.

In 1993 Doner lost the Vlasic pickle account, which it had held for 27 years. Vlasic had recently been purchased by Campbell Soup Company, which was consolidating its advertising with several other agencies. Doner had also recently lost Hygrade Food Products Corporation, which had been acquired by Sara Lee.

The company's fortunes began improving at the start of 1994 with the signing of six major new accounts worth $40 million in billings. These included Frank's Nursery & Crafts, Musicland Stores Corporation, National Car Rental System, Inc., and National Tire Warehouse, which was owned by Sears.

In the spring of 1994 Doner formed a public relations division at its Baltimore co-headquarters. Additional accounts added during the year and into early 1995 included supermarket chain Kroger (for its Michigan stores), Prudential SeniorCare, and G. Heileman Brewing, which the firm had lost four years earlier. Coca-Cola also tapped the agency for a Christmas season promotion and other tasks. The year was strong for Doner, with billings increasing nearly 20 percent, to $450 million.

In April 1995 chairman and CEO Jim Dale announced he was leaving the company to pursue a writing career. The CEO role was taken by Allen Kalter, while Herb Fried became chairman. After his elevation to the top post, Kalter announced that Doner would establish a series of "centers of excellence" at the firm's 11 offices worldwide. These would consist of specializations in different areas, such as direct marketing (already in place in Baltimore), automobile and retail advertising (established in Southfield), and media, promotions and research, which would be added later. Though Doner's Southfield office was twice as large, Baltimore had typically been the home of the firm's top officer, and at times the two co-headquarters competed against each other for business. In some instances, such as the recently-won Coke assignment, both agencies claimed they would be performing the work, though it was later determined that it would actually be done in Southfield.

In October 1995 Doner bought GGK London, an offshoot of GGK International, whose clients included Equifax and Marie Curie Cancer Care. GGK London was merged into Doner's existing London office, which then took the name Doner Cardwell Hawkins, after two former GGK executives who helped run the operation. Doner had recently won a number of important new accounts, including Lowe's Home Improvement Warehouse, lawn equipment maker Cub Cadet, and ABC Warehouse, a Michigan-based appliance chain.

The year 1996 started off on a solid note when G. Heileman Brewing expanded Doner's assignment to cover its entire advertising program. Other new work included U.S. Cellular's $25 million account; Color Tile, worth $20 million; Hill Stores Co. of Massachusetts, with billings of $10 million; and Nordic Track, which billed for $5 million.

In April Doner restructured its media planning operations, consolidating the work in Southfield. The firm then spun off its rapidly-growing Doner Direct unit, which handled direct marketing. Doner Direct employed 30 and had accounts worth $48 million in billings. It remained headquartered in the firm's Baltimore office.

On August 4, 1996, Doner suffered a catastrophe when the company's Southfield headquarters building was ravaged by fire. The blaze, which started after hours in an empty office, extensively damaged the second floor of the structure, where much of the firm's creative work was done. Fortunately, most of the crucial computer data files were salvaged. Temporary quarters were hastily secured, and some employees worked from home in the fire's immediate aftermath.

The disaster did not scare away clients, however, and new accounts brought in during the latter half of the year included Loyola University Medical Center and the $15–$20 million ad work of the Bennigan's and Steak & Ale restaurant chains, owned by S&A Restaurant Corporation. Early 1997 saw the addition of Bush Brothers & Co., the leading maker of baked beans in the United States, an account that was worth $5 million in billings.

In the spring of 1997 the company formed Doner Public Affairs in its Florida office to provide consulting services for political candidates. Its first client was New York Mayor Rudolph Giuliani, then seeking reelection. Doner hired noted political advertising expert Adam Goodman to run the agency. He had worked with a number of Republican candidates including Senator Trent Lott and Wisconsin Governor Tommy Thompson. During the year Doner also added the work of Stroh Brewery Co., which had acquired G. Heileman in August 1996, and Florists' Transworld Delivery (FTD).

In October 1997 Doner won its biggest assignment to date, triumphing over a number of larger agencies to secure the North American advertising for Mazda Motor of Japan, whose sales had been in decline. The $240 million account was a feather in Doner's cap, as the firm had never been the agency of record for an automaker, though it had worked for a number of regional Ford dealership groups over the previous 17 years. To avoid a possible conflict of interest, Doner gave up this work, which was worth $100 million, and also opened an office near Mazda's U.S. headquarters in Irvine, California. In December the firm's Canadian unit, Doner Shur Peppler, was renamed Doner Canada, and plans were laid for expansion there, due largely to the new Mazda assignment. Doner's annual revenues now stood at $62.6 million.

In January 1998 Herb Fried sold his majority ownership stake in the firm, ceding the chairmanship to Alan Kalter, though he stayed involved as a consultant. At that time Doner named Southfield as its sole headquarters, letting 24 of the 195 Baltimore employees go a few weeks later. Major accounts for Arby's and Bush Brothers were shifted to Southfield as well. Work that stayed in Baltimore included Ikon Office Solutions and the newly-won Teligent, which billed for an estimated $5–$10 million.

In June 1998 Doner moved back into its Southfield headquarters, 22 months after the building had been gutted by fire. In the reconstruction process a third floor was added, increasing the usable space to 106,000 square feet. In the months after the fire the firm had added 90 employees at the location, for a total of 405.

Doner was experiencing a growth spurt, and when the $160 million Blockbuster video store account was won in the fall, it put the firm above $1 billion in annual billings for the first time.

The company was now working on upgrading its own image, and asked media outlets to refer to it as ''Doner,'' rather than ''W.B. Doner and Co.'' The company's official name was not changed, though it filed an ''also doing business as'' notice with the state of Michigan. During 1999 the firm won the $60 million Progressive Corporation insurance account and other work from AutoTrader.com and ADT Security Services, Inc., though it lost $15 million in billings from long-term client Iams. For 1999 Doner's revenues topped out at nearly $100 million, with the company now employing 832. *Adweek* magazine named the firm one of its agencies of the year, ranking it fourth in the country in terms of management, growth, and creative effort.

2000 and Beyond

The year 2000 was another strong one for Doner, which saw billings top $1.5 billion, helped in part by the acquisition of such major new accounts as Owens Corning and Serta. New ads for Mazda, with their ''Zoom-Zoom'' tagline, helped further boost the carmaker's sales, which had been on an upswing since Doner had begun working for the company.

In 2001 Doner won assignments to work for cable giant Cox Communications, as well as Sherwin-Williams, Mail Boxes, Etc., and PNC Bank, among others. The firm's revenues for the year hit $114.2 million, though billings dropped to $1.2 billion as the U.S. economy faltered.

In 2002 Doner was chosen to create ads for Helzberg Diamonds, Heinz Pet Products, and DuPont's Corian and Zodiaq product lines. In March, legal proceedings began in a lawsuit filed in 2000 against Doner and Mazda by rock musician Rob Zombie, who claimed unauthorized use of one of his songs in a Doner-created spot. The company settled with Zombie for an undisclosed amount. By fall the busy firm was looking for additional office space in Southfield, having already outgrown the addition to its headquarters there. Doner was now handling work worth $1.6 billion in billings.

In June 2003 Doner announced it would close its Baltimore office, moving all operations there to Southfield. The move came amid rapid consolidation in the advertising industry, which left Doner as the largest independently-owned agency in the United States. The decision to combine the firm's two main offices was a response to the new climate, according to Herb Fried, as well as due to the relative difficulty of recruiting top talent to Baltimore and the dwindling opportunities there for local advertising work. Detroit had by now evolved into one of the major U.S. advertising centers, though still ranked behind New York, Chicago, and Los Angeles.

After more than 65 years in business W.B. Doner & Co. had established itself as the largest independent advertising agency in the United States. Since its founder's passing in 1990 the firm had doubled in size, with its ad billings increasing nearly five-fold. The company's strong emphasis on producing retail results helped bring it new business despite the struggling U.S. economy, as did its proven track record and history of many memorable campaigns.

Principal Divisions

Doner Canada; Doner International (United Kingdom); Doner Cardwell Hawkins (United Kingdom); Doner Direct; Doner Public Affairs; Doner Automotive.

Principal Competitors

Omnicom Group, Inc.; The Interpublic Group of Companies, Inc.; WPP Group plc.

Further Reading

Beatty, Sally Goll, ''Mazda Hands Image Campaign Over to Underdog W.B. Doner,'' *Wall Street Journal*, October 29, 1997, p. B6.

Bernstein, Marty, ''Rocker Zombie Sues Mazda Over Music,'' *Automotive News*, May 20, 2002, p. 17.

Bloomquist, Randall, ''Doner Growth Fueled by 'Prodigal Sons','' *Business Review*, December 30, 1985, p. 2.

——, ''Doner Push Into Chicago Caps a Sizzling Summer,'' *Business Review*, September 15, 1986, p. 33.

Byland, Kathleen, ''Creative Still Drives Doner,'' *Crain's Detroit Business*, July 30, 1990, p. E10.

Elliott, Stuart, ''Mazda Hopes New Agency's Ads Will Reverse Sales, Image Problem,'' *Houston Chronicle*, March 8, 1998, p. 2.

Fitzgerald, Nora, ''Doner's Direct Course in Baltimore Leads to Layoffs, Account Shifts,'' *Adweek Southwest*, February 23, 1998, p. 3.

''Golden Days,'' *Baltimore Sun*, June 22, 2003, p. 1D.

Kiley, David, ''Doner Aims to Focus its Double Vision,'' *Adweek—Eastern Edition*, June 8, 1992, p. 9.

McConnell, Bill, ''Old Animosity Leads Doner to Spurn Ad Competition,'' *Daily Record*, February 20, 1992, p. 1.

——, ''Recession Forces Doner Layoffs,'' *Daily Record*, February 5, 1992, p. 3.

Moore, M.H. and Halliday, Jean, ''Doner Bolsters its U.K. Presence with Acquisition,'' *Adweek Southwest*, October 30, 1995, p. 46.

Raphael, Steve, ''Doner CEO Sees Growth Ahead After Static 1990,'' *Crain's Detroit Business*, February 20, 1991, p. 1.

——, ''W.B. Doner Struggles to Find Stability, Spirit, Niche,'' *Crain's Detroit Business*, December 20, 1993, p. 1.

Serafin, Raymond, ''W.B. Doner Poised to Become Global Agency,'' *Crain's Detroit Business*, June 13, 1988, p. 19.

Serwach, Joseph, ''Bigger, Better and Back Home,'' *Crain's Detroit Business*, June 22, 1998, p. 1.

——, ''W.B. Doner Regroups in Wake of Fire,'' *Crain's Detroit Business*, August 12, 1996, p. 26.

Smith, Jennette, ''Adding Business: Winning Streak Has Independent Ad Agency Doner Looking for More Space, Beefing Up Staff,'' *Crain's Detroit Business*, November 11, 2002, p. 3.

''W.B. Doner at 60: Doner Downplays Detroit and Baltimore Rivalry,'' *Advertising Age*, March 3, 1997, p. C4.

—Frank Uhle

Watson Pharmaceuticals Inc.

311 Bonnie Circle
Corona, California 91720
U.S.A.
Telephone: (909) 493-5300
Fax: (909) 493-5836
Web site: http://www.watsonpharm.com

Public Company
Incorporated: 1985 as Watson Laboratories, Inc.
Employees: 3,729
Sales: $1.2 billion (2002)
Stock Exchanges: New York
Ticker Symbol: WPI
NAIC: 325412 Pharmaceutical Preparation Manufacturing

Watson Pharmaceuticals Inc. develops, manufactures, and sells proprietary (brand) and off-patent, or generic, pharmaceutical products. The company offers more than 140 generic products as well as 30 branded products marketed through three divisions: general products, nephrology, and women's health. Watson was formed in 1985 and grew significantly during the 1990s by making key acquisitions. During 2002, more than 178 million prescriptions were filled with a Watson product—the company reported that 11 times every second of every 12-hour business day, a company product was dispensed by a U.S. pharmacist.

Watson Pharmaceuticals was launched in the mid-1980s, when the market for generic drugs was blooming. Generic drugs are off-brand drugs that are chemically the same as their brand-name cousins. When a pharmaceutical company develops and patents a new drug, the patent protection typically allows the inventor to sell the drug (at a premium) for several years free from direct competition. Once the patent protection terminates, however, other companies are free to copy and produce the same drug. The generic drug industry began to emerge as a force in the early 1980s, when many pharmaceutical goods that had been developed in the 1970s lost their patent protection. When the manufacturers of those proprietary products continued to charge high prices, generic drug makers jumped into the game, offering drugs that were identical in effect but much lower in price.

Coming to America in the Late 1960s

Enter Taiwan native Allen Chao. Chao had left Taiwan in 1968 to study pharmacy sciences in the United States. After only five years, Chao earned his doctorate in industrial and physical pharmacy at Purdue University. He then took a job with pharmaceutical developer and manufacturer G.D. Searle & Co. There, in a span of five years, he rose from a position as researcher to the director of new product and new pharmaceutical technology development. After a few years in that post, however, Chao was restless. He wanted to strike out on his own and build a pharmaceutical company from scratch.

Chao's motivation to start his own enterprise came partly from his parents: "You know, you'll never win the Nobel Prize," Chao's mother told him after he went to work with G.D. Searle, according to *Forbes*. In fact, Chao's parents had originally hoped that their son would return to Taiwan to run the family pharmaceuticals manufacturing business. When Chao's father realized that his son was going to begin a career in the United States, he sold the business and he and his wife moved to California to retire. Throughout his career at Searle, Chao's mother prodded him to start his own company. She got her wish in 1983, when Chao left G.D. Searle and launched the venture that would become Watson Pharmaceuticals.

Developing a Formula for Success in the 1980s

Chao's long-term goal was to build a fully integrated pharmaceutical company that, like Searle, developed and marketed its own drugs. Such a venture, however, typically required massive sums of money to fund the research and development of new drugs. Of import were the huge costs and risks related to getting a new drug approved for market by the Food and Drug Administration (FDA); if a proposed drug failed to receive FDA approval, which was often the case after months or years of FDA studies, a larger company could suffer greatly and a start-up company would likely be destroyed. Lacking the resources needed to launch a fully integrated drug company, Chao decided to start with generics.

The chief appeal of the generic segment of the pharmaceutical industry for Chao was that drug approval was much less

Company Perspectives:

Watson pursues a strategy of generating revenue through established brand and generic businesses, capitalizing on the Company's proven ability to support the development and commercialization of a broad range of brand and generic pharmaceutical products.

complicated; the FDA had already accepted the original drug and had only to complete cursory research to ensure that the generic counterpart was safe. Although generic drugs did not offer the huge profit margins intrinsic to patented products, many generic producers were able to profit handsomely. Success in the industry depended in large part on the generic drug producer's ability to move quickly to fill a void in the marketplace, but also on its ability to minimize overhead costs related to production, packaging, marketing, and distribution.

Joining Chao in the start-up was David S. Hsia, who started out as vice-president of product development and would later become senior vice-president of scientific affairs. Although the generics strategy reduced their capital requirements, Chao felt that they still needed about $4 million to develop their first generic drug, and possibly as much as $2 million more to achieve FDA approval. Few investors were interested. Venture capital companies snubbed the entrepreneurs, and the banks in Chicago (where Chao originally wanted to locate the company) would not even loan him money against the family's personal property in California.

Unable to find start-up capital from conventional sources, Chao returned to California and tapped his connections in the Taiwanese community. Family members and friends eventually contributed nearly $4 million, which helped the founders to land another $1.5 million from U.S. venture capital firms. All the while, Chao and Hsia scurried to develop the company's first drug, Furosemide, a treatment for high blood pressure. Chao and Hsia incorporated their venture in January 1985 as Watson Laboratories, Inc. The name was an amalgamation of "Hwa," Chao's mother's maiden name, and "son," Americanized into "Watson." By the end of 1985 Watson Pharmaceuticals had received FDA approval for Furosemide, which it began selling almost immediately.

Watson was able to turn a profit in its first full year of sales. The company used cash flow from that first drug to fund the development of other generics, or off-patent drugs. Watson survived a period of more than two years in the late 1980s during which it received no new drug approvals from the FDA. Despite that hindrance, however, Watson continued to profit and to research a string of new generics. Sales rose to about $13.25 million in 1988 as net income inched up to $259,000. Despite heavy investments in ongoing research and development, Watson managed to boost profits to $1.26 million in 1989, from sales of nearly $21 million.

Watson's successful development efforts following the introduction of Furosemide provided the formula for its work on Loxapine, a tranquilizer used to treat schizophrenia. Chao began developing a generic substitute for the original patented product in 1986, and it eventually won the FDA's blessing. At that time, the market for the drug was only $10 million. Soon the sales volume of the drug more than doubled and Watson was able to capture a full 50 percent of the market. By 1996, Watson was still the only pharmaceutical company selling a generic version of the original drug.

Loxapine was a good illustration of Watson's unique operating stratagem. It was true that Chao was competing in the typically low-margin generics industry. But his company had managed to avert many of the downsides of generics manufacturing by pursuing a singular market approach. Rather than target the markets for big drugs that were coming off patent, such as Tagamet and Valium, Chao decided to chase smaller market segments that were of less interest to the big generics manufacturers. Watson was willing to chase drugs with markets of less than $30 million annually, while its bigger competitors often ignored drugs with less than $150 million in annual sales.

Watson was able to profit, though, because it was often the only company competing in its selected niches. The big drugs, in contrast, were often copied by as many as ten or more generics manufacturers that competed fiercely on price. In addition to pursuing smaller market niches, Watson focused on developing drugs that were difficult to duplicate. That tactic allowed the company to utilize its advanced research and development arm to generate relatively high profit margins, even in the generics industry. To find those high-margin, small-market drugs, Watson's researchers regularly plied public records, searching for little-known drug prospects with big potential.

Imitation Leading to Innovation in the 1990s

Success at developing generics for niche drug markets allowed Watson to post steady gains in the early 1990s. Sales increased from $23.4 million in 1990 to $34.7 million in 1992, while net income more than quadrupled during the same period to about $2.4 million. In 1993, moreover, sales nearly doubled to $67.6 million, a hefty $12.2 million of which was netted as income. The big jump in 1993 was the result of several new drug introductions. By late 1993, in fact, Watson had the exclusive right to produce 17 generic products, and was also making about 40 drugs for other companies. It also had about a dozen new products in its research and development pipeline that were awaiting FDA approval.

Bolstering its niche market strategy in this period were Watson's efforts to develop proprietary value-added delivery systems that enhanced its generics and gave it an edge in the marketplace. For example, Watson would develop a generic substitute for a drug that was typically administered to the patient through a syringe by a trained professional. Watson might then create a new dose delivery system—such as a patch worn on the skin or a device that administered the drug through the nose or mouth—that allowed the patient to administer the drug. Not only would Watson benefit from revenue from the new delivery technique, but it would profit from an often significantly expanded market for the drug.

To take advantage of rising sales, Chao and fellow executives pursued an aggressive plan to expand Watson's manufacturing operations. To that end, they had taken Watson public in February of 1993 with a stock sale that raised $25 million. A

Key Dates:

1985: Allen Chao and David S. Hsia incorporate their generics venture as Watson Pharmaceuticals Inc.
1993: Watson goes public; sales reach $67.6 million.
1995: Circa Pharmaceuticals is acquired.
2000: The firm purchases Schein Pharmaceutical Inc.
2003: Oxytrol, the first transdermal product to treat overactive bladder, gains FDA approval.

subsequent offering brought a total of more than $100 million to Watson's war chest. The cash was used to add manufacturing capabilities. For instance, Watson purchased the patent on an injection-molding technology that would let Watson make suppository products that were less waxy and messy. The money also was used to fund research and development of new generics and delivery systems. Of importance, Watson's cash surplus allowed Chao to move closer to his initial goal of making the company a fully integrated pharmaceutical firm.

Toward Full Integration: Mid-1990s and Beyond

Watson's revenues rose to $87 million in 1994 as it introduced new drugs to market. The company followed those gains early in 1995 with the acquisition of Circa Pharmaceuticals, another maker and marketer of generics. Circa had formerly operated as Bolar Pharmaceutical Co. before being disgraced in a fraud and bribery scandal. In 1989, in fact, the FDA announced that several of its employees had accepted bribes from various generic drug makers. Watson was not involved in the scandal. Bolar, on the other hand, ultimately lost nearly all of its government drug approvals and was fined $10 million (the largest penalty ever levied against a generic drug maker). In addition, several Bolar executives went to jail.

By 1995 Circa, after changing its name from Bolar, was staging a recovery. Chao saw an opportunity to buy the company at a reasonable price and add a number of drugs and related proprietary products to its own portfolio. Watson paid the equivalent of about $600 million for the company. Management at the two companies planned to work together to create a global, one-stop shop pharmaceutical company that sold both generic and proprietary products. After the merger was complete, Watson's product line had grown to include more than 80 different drugs (variations of 30 major pharmaceutical products). Sales for 1995 increased to $153 million, reflecting the merger as well as revenue growth related to new and established products.

Despite the challenges presented by such rapid growth, Chao remained focused on his goal of making Watson a fully integrated, global pharmaceutical company. To that end, Watson entered two joint ventures with Chinese companies that would allow the company to begin manufacturing and marketing its products to Chao's native region. The company also was working to develop its own patented drugs through joint ventures and partnerships with other drug makers. The firm's strategy, which centered on internal product development and making both strategic alliances and acquisitions, remained at the forefront of company operations.

As such, Watson's acquisition pace heightened during the late 1990s. In 1997, the company completed two important purchases that brought it closer to its goal and also gave it a foothold in the branded pharmaceuticals market. In February, the firm inked a deal with Oclassen Pharmaceuticals Inc., a California-based manufacturer of branded dermatology products. It then created a new sales division designed to market Oclassen's branded Microzide, a drug created to treat hypertension. The company also agreed to purchase generic pharmaceutical manufacturer Royce Laboratories Inc. that year. The transaction added a slew of new products to the firm's developmental pipeline.

In October 1997, Watson secured the U.S. rights to four G.D. Searle & Co. branded off-patent oral contraceptive products, marking the firm's commitment to expand its women's health business. In 1998, it acquired the rights to three additional products. This division became increasingly important for the company—between 1996 and 2001 Watson's oral contraceptive product line experienced a compounded annual growth rate of 32 percent. Watson entered the diagnostic device sector of the industry in 2002 when it launched PapSure, an in-office cervical screening exam designed to aid in the detection of cervical cancer. That year it also teamed up with OMJ Pharmaceutical Inc. to develop and launch brand-equivalent oral contraceptives.

Watson entered the new millennium on solid ground. By now, it had acquired TheraTech Inc., a Utah-based drug delivery company, and had received FDA approval for its generic anti-smoking gum product, the first generic of its kind. During 2000, the firm doubled in size with its purchase of competitor Schein Pharmaceutical Inc., a manufacturer of nearly 100 generic products. The deal, valued at approximately $694 million was completed in August. This was followed by the purchase of Makoff R&D Laboratories, which strengthened Watson's presence in the kidney disease, or nephrology, sector.

While the company had pursued an aggressive acquisition strategy during the late 1990s and into 2000, it also had been active in the product development arena. In 2002, the company set plans in motion to launch Oxytrol, the first Watson product developed internally from start to finish. The branded drug was the first transdermal, or skin, patch designed to treat overactive bladder. The company faced a major setback, however, when the FDA declined its approval in March 2002. Determined to see the drug reach fruition, Watson went back to the drawing board and resubmitted the product after additional testing. In February 2003, Oxytrol was approved.

By now, it was evident that founder Chao's strategy had indeed paid off. In 2003, Watson was operating as the fifth largest pharmaceutical company in the United States, based on prescriptions dispensed, and the third largest generic drug company in the nation. Sales reached $1.2 billion in 2002 and were expected to continue their upward climb. With a strong focus on both its generic and branded businesses, Watson Pharmaceuticals appeared to be well positioned for continued growth in the years to come.

Principal Subsidiaries

Watson Laboratories Inc.; Watson Pharma Inc.; The Rugby Group Inc.; Rugby Laboratories Inc.; Royce Laboratories Inc.;

Watson Laboratories Inc.; Watson Laboratories Caribe Inc.; Makoff R&D Laboratories Inc.; Nicobrand Limited (Northern Ireland); Watson Pharmaceuticals (Asia) Ltd.

Principal Competitors

Amgen Inc.; Johnson & Johnson; Merck & Co. Inc.

Further Reading

Darlin, Damon, "Still Running Scared," *Forbes,* September 26, 1994, p. 127.

McAuliffe, Don, "Corona Drug Company Plans 1994 Expansion," *Press Enterprise,* October 14, 1993.

——, "Corona Drug Firm Capitalizes on New Technology," *Press Enterprise,* August 2, 1993.

——, "Stock Selloff Puzzles Watson as Plant Expansion Continues," *Press Enterprise,* February 24, 1994.

——, "Watson Pharmaceuticals' Profit Slips Because of Acquisition Cost," *Press Enterprise,* November 3, 1995, p. 9E.

Pascual, Psyche, "California's Watson Pharmaceuticals Buys Miami-Based Generic Drug Maker," *Business Press,* January 6, 1997.

Sanchez, Jesus, "Deal Would Create a Generic Drug Giant," *Los Angeles Times,* March 31, 1995, p. 2D.

Unger, Michael, "Circa Pharmaceutical to Merge," *Newsday,* March 31, 1995, p. 69A.

"Watson Expects Strong Year," *Chain Drug Review,* February 17, 2003.

"Watson Pharmaceuticals to Acquire TheraTech," *Chemical Market Reporter,* November 2, 1998, p. 16.

"Watson to Acquire Schein," *Drug Store News,* June 26, 2000, p. 108.

"Watson to Buy Competitor Schein," *Drug Topics,* June 5, 2000, p. 10.

White, Ronald D., "Watson Profit Rises on Strong Drug Sales," *Los Angeles Times,* May 7, 2003, p. 2.

—Dave Mote
—update: Christina M. Stansell

Wilbert, Inc.

2913 Gardner Road
Broadview, Illinois 60155
U.S.A.
Telephone: (708) 865-1600
Fax: (708) 865-1646
Web sites: http://www.wilbertinc.com;
http://www.wilbertonline.com

Private Company
Incorporated: 1933 as Wilbert W. Haase Company
Employees: 1,200
Sales: $200 million (2002 est.)
NAIC: 327390 Other Concrete Product Manufacturing;
326130 Laminated Plastics Plate, Sheet, and Shape
Manufacturing; 326140 Polystyrene Foam Product
Manufacturing; 326150 Urethane and Other Foam
Product (Except Polystyrene) Manufacturing; 812210
Funeral Homes and Funeral Services

The Wilbert name has been a fixture in the funeral services industry since the early 1900s, though the company went through several incarnations before becoming Wilbert, Inc. first in 1967 and again in 1997. Reorganized as a holding company in 1997, Wilbert, Inc. oversees two distinct yet complementary divisions: the Funeral Services unit (consisting of the well known Wilbert Funeral Services, Inc.) and the Industrial Plastics unit (home to Thermoform Plastics, Inc. and a number of smaller specialized plastics firms). While both of Wilbert's divisions are at the forefront of their business sectors and comprised of several subsidiaries, not all of the Industrial Plastics companies work within the burial or funeral field.

In the Beginning: 1850s–80s

The Wilbert story begins with the emigration of Ferdinand Haase from Germany and his arrival in New York in 1849. He traveled through Buffalo, Detroit, and Chicago, but the harsh winter weather drove him south to New Orleans. Ferdinand worked at several jobs before being summoned home to help his parents settle their affairs and travel to the United States. By 1851 the Haase family acquired 55 acres along the Des Plaines River outside Chicago. Ferdinand, meanwhile, had found time to meet and wed a woman named Minnie Zimmerman.

Over the next two decades Minnie and Ferdinand had seven children and lived in both Germany and Illinois. Haase had amassed a substantial amount of land around the Des Plaines River and farmed, raised cattle, and even opened some of his property up as a resort. In addition, he sold a parcel to Concordia University (now Dominican University) for a graveyard and had discovered Native American burial mounds on other parts of his land. In addition to the Pottowattomie burials, the Haase family had begun to bury its own dead in the early 1850s. By the 1860s Ferdinand considered turning some of his acreage into a cemetery for nonfamily members as well. In 1874 Ferdinand and his two oldest sons, Emil and Leo, opened Forest Home Cemetery in Forest Park, Illinois, which included a museum housing the Native American artifacts.

The Haase land in and around Forest Home was rich in rock and clay and much of the cemetery's early operation was made possible by mining gravel and selling it to local merchants for a number of uses, including concrete. Ferdinand's inquisitive and hardworking son Leo began to show a flair for geology; the 17-year-old soon realized the value of the sand, topsoil, and stone beneath the family's land. In 1880 Leo founded the L.G. Haase Manufacturing Company to sell concrete products such as cemetery lot markers, burial vaults and covers, benches, tiles, and irrigation basins. Leo believed imagination was akin to a force of nature, calling it "the most important force outside of gravity," according to *Service & Innovation: The Wilbert Way*. Leo more than proved this adage by not only inventing many uses for concrete, but patenting the machinery he designed to make these products.

While Forest Home Cemetery and L.G. Haase Manufacturing Company began to thrive in the 1880s, Leo was elected highway commissioner and later village clerk of Forest Park. His connections were vital in bringing telephone lines into the area; he also learned surveying and architecture during his political tenure. With help from his brother William, Leo even designed and built a suspension bridge from Forest Home

---

Cemetery across the Des Plaines River to other Haase family land. Yet one of Leo's most important contributions was in company promotion: he created business card paperweights, listing the costs of various services and cemetery plots on a small paper placed inside attractive pieces of glass.

Serving Death: 1890s–1930s

In 1892 William Haase and his wife welcomed twins, Wilbert and Wesley, into the Haase clan. Though Wesley perished before his second birthday, Wilbert was a bright and spirited child. He was raised among the growing acreage of Forest Home Cemetery and took over L.G. Haase Manufacturing Company at the age of 20 in 1902. The now legendary Leo, Wilbert's uncle, had retired and moved to the West Coast leaving the Haase family assets in Wilbert's capable hands. By the onset of World War I, Wilbert was married and the father of one child and expecting another with his wife Gertrude. While most young men his age were abroad fighting, Wilbert built up the family's concrete business and made sure Forest Home was one of the Chicago area's finest cemeteries.

For Wilbert, like Leo before him, death was a business like any other—comprised of supply and demand. Since Haase burial products were made for Forest Home Cemetery as well as funeral directors in the region, supply and demand usually balanced. Yet occasionally the unthinkable happened and demand was out of proportion to supply. One of these instances came during the influenza outbreak that swept through the Midwest in 1918 and 1919. The death toll reached into the thousands and the L.G. Haase Manufacturing Company was one of the few companies able to meet the dramatically increased demand. After most of the influenza burials were completed, Wilbert bought L.G. Haase from the family for $19,000 and rechristened it American Vault Works (known as American Wilbert). Wilbert ran the new company himself and incorporated it in May 1924.

Wilbert Haase had proven himself not only an astute businessman, but an adventurer as well. He had taken up flying (advertising American Vault Works on the side of his biplane) and had traveled the world. He was fascinated by the preservation techniques of the Egyptians and was determined to make an airtight, waterproof burial vault. It took two years of trial and error, but Wilbert introduced the first waterproof burial vault made of concrete and lined with asphalt in 1930. Rivals cried foul and took the firm to court, accusing Wilbert of false advertising. They were wrong; the vault was indeed waterproof

and Haase not only applied for a patent but established a second company to sell licensing rights for the revolutionary new burial vaults. The Wilbert W. Haase Company was formed in 1930 and by the time it was incorporated in 1933, sister firm American Vault Works was serving the burial needs for most parts of Chicago and its suburbs, with plants on the South side, the North shore, and in Forest Park.

Another Haase invention changed the burial industry forever: the WilbertWay Vault Handling Device took the arduous task of lowering caskets into burial vaults and made it a one-man operation. Haase patented the WilbertWay in 1938 and was pleased it not only cut back on manpower, but on the presence of nonfamily members at the grave site. He believed funerals should be as private and dignified as possible, undisturbed by outsiders or workers who had no relationship to the deceased.

Changes: 1940s–70s

By the 1940s the W.W. Haase Company had licensing agreements with vault companies in several states, issued 50-year guarantees for its waterproof vaults, and had added decorative symbols (for groups like the Knights of Columbus, American Legion, Masons, etc., as well as the Star of David for Jewish decedents). The firm and its licensees had also created the Wilbert Manufacturers Association (WMA) in 1944 and begun an advertising campaign touting its sturdily built vaults, "Asphalt for Waterproofing, Concrete for Strength." Wilbert himself had cut back his duties to devote more time to other pursuits, such as his love of flying. He not only flew search missions for the Army Air Corps during World War II, but later took over the daily operations of a Wisconsin airport near his vacation home.

By 1948 the WMA bought the W.W. Haase Company and introduced a new vault lining to escape the dangerous and super-heated use of asphalt. "Plasco," a hybrid of the words plastic and coating, became the liner of choice for the company's vaults. During this time Wilbert Haase retired, leaving his business legacy in the hands of nonfamily members. Two years later, in 1950, the famed Forest Home Cemetery was sold and land next to American Wilbert's manufacturing plant was purchased in Broadview, Illinois. This stretch of land became Wilbert W. Haase Company's new headquarters, complete with offices and warehouse space to house its growing line of burial vaults, including a new copper-lined vault called the Triune. The move also marked a new era, one in which the firm initiated regular national advertising campaigns in such influential publications as *Life* magazine, *Ladies' Home Journal,* and the *Saturday Evening Post.*

Entrepreneur and adventurer Wilbert W. Haase, a guiding force behind the Wilbert empire for decades, died in Wisconsin in 1959, at the age of 66. He was buried in the famed Forest Home Cemetery, founded by his ancestors. The company nurtured by Haase continued to grow and prosper during the next decade; the two-millionth vault was produced in 1963, the same year President John F. Kennedy was entombed in a specially designed Wilbert vault.

The end of the 1960s brought several changes of note for Wilbert. In 1966 the company bought Thermoform Plastics, Inc.

Key Dates:

1851: The Haase family buys acreage on the Des Plaines River outside Chicago.
1874: Ferdinand, Emil, and Leo Haase open Forest Home Cemetery in Forest Park, Illinois.
1880: Leo Haase founds L.G. Haase Manufacturing Company and begins making concrete burial vaults.
1919: American Vault Works is founded.
1930: The Wilbert W. Haase Company is formed to license its waterproof burial vault technology.
1937: The first cremation urns are introduced.
1938: American Vault Works is the world's largest manufacturer of asphalt-lined concrete burial vaults; the WilbertWay Vault Handling Device is patented.
1955: The company marks its 25th anniversary and produces its one millionth Wilbert burial vault.
1967: The firm is renamed Wilbert, Inc., and Thermoform Plastics, Inc. becomes part of the business.
1973: Wilbert sells its four millionth burial vault.
1988: The WilbertWay Casket Lowering Device is introduced.
1990: American Industrial Technologies, Inc. becomes part of Wilbert.
1997: Wilbert is reorganized into two divisions.
2001: Matthews International acquires the firm.
2002: Wilbert acquires several plastics firms for its Thermoform unit.

as a joint venture with the H.B. Fuller Company. The St. Paul, Minnesota-based firm produced a new polystyrene vault liner called "Strentex" (strength + texture), which was not only strong but when bonded with an epoxy called Unidex formed an airtight seal. Strentex was soon the liner of choice and replaced the traditional asphalt-lined vaults that made American Wilbert an industry leader. The following year, 1967, the Wilbert W. Haase Company was renamed simply Wilbert, Inc., and a few months later the newly rechristened company bought out Thermoform partner H.B. Fuller.

While Strentex was touted for its immense strength and durability, American Wilbert paired it with a host of other materials, including stainless steel, bronze, and copper, for a variety of vault models. During the next decade, American Wilbert continued to produce its world renowned burial vaults but also segued into caskets. To establish itself in the casket market, Wilbert, Inc. acquired two casket manufacturers, one in Michigan and the other in Indiana, to service funeral directors in the tristate area of Indiana, Illinois, and Michigan. While the casket venture floundered several years later, Wilbert's plastics unit, Thermoform, flourished.

Death Never Takes a Holiday: 1980s–90s

In the 1980s Wilbert had an expanding line of vaults and urns, including models for men, women, and children. By the end of 1981 Wilbert had sold more than six million vaults and was bringing in over $15 million in sales annually. Innovations for the 1980s included the WilbertWay Casket Lowering De-

vice, which worked with the already in-use WilbertWay Vault Handling Device; a new Research & Development department in the company's Broadview headquarters; and the conception and production of more than two dozen new cremation urn designs. Another sophisticated top of the line vault, the Wilbert Bronze, called "the Cadillac of the industry" by Wilbert insiders, was built in 1986 and formally introduced to the funeral industry in 1987. It was considered a "high-tech" vault with a bronze top and lining, as well as concrete placed between two molded layers of plastic. To keep up with ever increasing demand, land next to Wilbert's manufacturing plant in Broadview was purchased for expansion and parcels in St. Paul were acquired for Thermoform's burgeoning plastics business.

In the early 1990s Thermoform moved into its new headquarters in Minnesota and purchased American Industrial Technologies, Inc. (AIT), a producer of specialized adhesives and coatings. Since AIT's adhesives worked well with Thermoform's molded plastic products, the acquisition was a good fit. In 1992 Wilbert created the Funeral Service division to broaden its marketing efforts to funeral directors; two years later, in 1994, the company was one of the first in the death care industry to introduce "pre-need" contracts for healthy customers who wanted to make arrangements for their future funeral needs.

By the mid-1990s Thermoform was booming, providing liners for Wilbert's vaults as well as handling lucrative contracts for a wide range of products in the plastics industry. After acquiring Plastivax and TransPak-USA, Thermoform had entered the plastic pallet market, selling molded pallets for retailers and factories to ship materials. No longer considered simply a business unit of the legendary Wilbert, Thermoform was among the top five industrial thermoform producers in North America for 1999, as ranked by *Plastics News* and sales for the year reportedly topped $55 million. Parent company Wilbert also remained at the top of its field, having restructured itself as a holding company in 1997 over its two very successful business units—Thermoform Plastics Inc. and Wilbert Funeral Services, Inc.

A New Century: 2000s

At the turn of the millennium Wilbert, Inc. was embroiled in a takeover attempt of York Group Inc., a Houston-based casket and vault producer. The two companies had begun merger talks early in 2000 which unraveled by May. Rebuffed by York's leadership, Wilbert began buying up the casket maker's common stock over the summer and into the fall. By early 2001 Wilbert had become York's largest shareholder with over 14 percent of the firm's stock; York, however, fought Wilbert every step of the way, which included selling its vault division to Doric Products Inc.

While waiting for the York imbroglio to settle, Wilbert bought out the thermoforming units of Altrista Corp. and the assets of Morton Customs Plastics LLC in the fall of 2001, both of which became part of its Thermoform Plastics unit. The York saga ended in December, when the casket maker agreed to a takeover by the Pittsburgh-based Matthews International Corporation, an adversary of Wilbert. Despite its missteps with York, Wilbert remained the world's largest vault producer, the established favorite for heads of state and titans of industry (Dwight D. Eisenhower, John F. Kennedy, Herbert Hoover,

Lyndon B. Johnson, Robert F. Kennedy, Adlai E. Stevenson, Conrad Hilton, Richard J. Daley, and Harold Washington) as well as legends of the stage and screen (Louis Armstrong, Elvis Presley, Rosalind Russell, Frank Sinatra, and John Wayne). For those who might wish to tout the Wilbert name while still living, the company created an online shopping service featuring everything from golf bags and denim jackets to pen sets, travel mugs, and stadium blankets.

Principal Subsidiaries

American Industrial Technologies, Inc. (AIT), Synergy World; Thermoform Plastics, Inc. (TPI); Trienda; Wilbert Funeral Services, Inc.

Principal Competitors

Hillenbrand Industries Inc.; Matthews International Corporation.

Further Reading

Bregar, Bill, ''Thermoform Plastics Buys Trans-Pak USA,'' *Plastics News,* May 31, 1999, p. 29.

Cecil, Mark, ''Will York Bury the Hatchet with Wilbert?'' *Mergers & Acquisitions Report,* May 21, 2001.

——, ''York Is Determined Not to Go Gently into Wilbert's Grasp,'' *Mergers & Acquisitions Report,* April 2, 2001.

Greer, Jim, ''Funeral Firm Buys York Stock After Casket Maker Buries Merger,'' *Houston Business Journal,* September 29, 2000, p. 16.

——, ''York Group Buries Deal for Sell Off; Mulls Next Move,'' *Houston Business Journal,* May 11, 2001, p. 2.

Madlern, Susan L., ed., *Service & Innovation: The Wilbert Way,* Broadview, Ill.: Wilbert, Inc., 1998.

Mohr, Michele, ''Standing on Solid Ground: Wilbert Vaults Help Put the Perpetual in Perpetual Care,'' *Chicago Tribune,* May 5, 1996, p. 1.

Pryweller, Jim, ''Burial Products Maker Revamping Operations; Wilbert Consolidating Biz of Newly Acquired Facilities,'' *Crain's Chicago Business,* February 25, 2002, p. 37.

Schodolski, Vincent, ''Cemeteries Head Off a Grave Matter,'' *Chicago Tribune,* December 1, 1996, p. 6.

Van Matre, Lynn, ''Treating Funerals in a New Way,'' *Chicago Tribune,* June 23, 1998, p. 1.

—Nelson Rhodes

Willbros Group, Inc.

Plaza 2000 Building
50th Street, 8th Floor Apartado 6307
Panama City 5
Panama
Telephone: (507) 2-13-0947
Fax: (507) 2-63-9294
Web site: http://www.willbros.com

Public Company
Incorporated: 1908 Williams Brothers Corporation
Employees: 4,620
Sales: $583.7 million (2002)
Stock Exchanges: New York
Ticker Symbol: WG
NAIC: 213112 Support Activities for Oil and Gas Field
   Exploration

With experience going back nearly 90 years, Willbros Group, Inc. is one of the world's leading pipeline construction specialists, with a specialty in logistically difficult projects, including pipelines crossing the Andes mountain chain, the Wyoming desert, the Amazon river, and work on the Trans-Alaskan pipeline. Originally part of The Williams Companies, Willbros is registered in Panama, although the company has long operated its administrative headquarters from the United States. In 2000, the company moved its administrative headquarters from Tulsa to Houston. Willbros provides turnkey oil field production and pipeline construction services, as well as engineering, construction, and other specialty services in more than 55 countries worldwide. The company's primary focus is on the United States, West Africa, and the Middle East, although it has also participated in projects in South American and the Australian and Asia Pacific regions. Willbros has been on an expansion drive at the turn of the century, with a series of acquisitions including Rogers & Philips in 2000, MSI Energy Services of Canada in 2001, and Mt. West Fabrication Plants & Services in 2002. Willbros posted sales of nearly $584 million in 2002. The company is led by chairman Larry Bump and vice-chairman, president, and CEO Michael Curran and is listed on the New York Stock Exchange.

Developing a Pipeline Construction Business in the 1920s

Willbros had its start at the turn of the century of the 20th century when two construction workers who were also brothers, Miller and David Williams, founded Williams Brother Corporation in order to finish a sidewalk paving contract in Arkansas that had been abandoned by their employer, the original contractor. The first great oil boom of the time, Oklahoma, led the brothers to begin laying pipelines in 1915. That activity quickly became one of the company's primary businesses, and in 1919 Williams Brothers moved their headquarters to Tulsa.

Over the next two decades, the company became an important figure in the pipeline and gas field construction industry, highlighted by its award, in 1942, as the principal contractor for two War Emergency Pipelines. The "Big Inch" and "Little Big Inch" connected the East Texas oil fields to ports in New Jersey. In this way, the U.S. government was able to thwart the presence of German submarines and deliver crucial fuel oil to the northeast. The first leg of the Big Inch pipeline was completed by 1943, and by 1944 oil arrived at its final destination in Linden, New Jersey.

Williams by then had started it first international contract—building a pipeline in Venezuela. Joining the company for that project was David Williams, Jr. and his cousin, John Williams, who interrupted his education at Yale University for the project. Another member of the Williams family, Charles Williams, son of the older brother of David and Miller Williams, joined the pipeline business during this time.

The company continued to win international projects, particularly in South America, in addition to its operations in the United States, including a contract to build a 370-mile pipeline in Bolivia in 1947. Two years later, Miller and David Williams retired, selling the business to David, Jr. and John and Charles Williams, as well as a number of the company's executives.

The discovery of vast oil reserves in the Middle East presented a natural market extension for the company in the 1950s. In 1951, Williams joined in on the construction of the Trans-Arabian Pipeline, building the 400-mile leg connecting Jordan,

Syria, and Lebanon. In the mid-1950s, Williams added the Persian Gulf to its sphere of operations, completing the southern portion of the Trans-Iranian pipeline in 1957. The following year, the company added another large-scale project in Iran, participating in the Kharg Island oil export terminal.

Meanwhile, Williams had continued to develop its pipeline business in the United States, notably with the contract to build a 625-mile pipeline system in Alaska, the first pipeline constructed in that state. In addition to the pipeline itself, Williams oversaw construction of the pipeline's support operations, including tank farms, pump stations, and docks.

Williams went public in 1957. In 1960, the company expanded into gas pipelines, building a 2,175-mile pipeline, the Mid-America Pipeline, as well as its support operations, including delivery terminals, storage facilities, and pump stations. At the same time, Williams continued to look abroad for work, and in 1962 entered Western Africa with a contract to build the 170-mile TransNiger Pipeline.

Splitting Off in the 1970s

A major moment in Williams' history came in the mid-1960s when the company constructed a 390-mile pipeline connecting Santa Cruz to Sica Sica in Bolivia—a project that reached an elevation of nearly 14,800 feet above sea-level, making it the world's high pipeline and helping establish the company's reputation for its ability to complete "logistically difficult" projects under the most extreme conditions. The Bolivian project was completed in 1965, in time for the company to begin a new project, the 175-mile Fahud-Muscat crude oil line, which brought the company into Oman for the first time.

A significant moment in Williams history came in 1966, when the company acquired the Great Lakes Pipe Company. Subsequently renamed the Williams Brothers Pipe Line Company, the purchase extended the company from the construction of pipelines to their ownership. It also marked a step in the company's transition to a stronger focus on the natural gas market.

In 1967, Williams began another high-profile, logistically difficult project, the construction of a crude-oil pipeline cross the Andes mountains in Colombia. This undertaking represented the first of five Andes mountain projects for the company. In 1970, Williams began work on a new Andes mountain project, this time with the construction of the Trans-Ecuadorian Pipeline. Completed in 1972, that project led the way to two more challenging projects, the launch of the Trans-Alaskan Pipeline in 1974 and, in a joint-venture, of a pipeline and pump station project in the western Amazon river basin in Peru.

In the late 1960s, the company had begun making a series of acquisitions designed to diversify its range of businesses. By the mid-1970s, the company, which changed its name to The Williams Companies in 1972, encompassed operations including propane sales, fertilizers, chemicals, and metals, as well as pipeline ownership. The company had also stepped up its interest in natural gas, and in 1974 set up its own gas exploration and production wing.

Williams' expansion led it to lose interest in its historic core pipeline construction business, and in 1975 it sold off that operation in a management buyout, which formed a new company, registered in Panama, called Willbros Group. In 1979, however, Willbros, in a move to retire its debt, sold 60 percent of its shares to Heerema Holding Construction Inc. Originally formed in Venezuela in 1948, Heerema had become a specialist in offshore petroleum platform construction in the mid-1950s. Heerema acquired completed control of Willbros in 1986.

Throughout the 1980s, Willbros racked up a string of projects, including a 505-mile carbon dioxide pipeline in the American Southwest, the All American Pipeline System. Completed in 1983, the pipeline stretched over 1,200 miles and included 23 pump stations.

Expanding Focus for the New Century

In the mid-1980s, Willbros once again performed work for the U.S. government when it developed and built a new "rapid deployment fuel pipeline distribution and storage system." Started in 1984, that system was delivered to the U.S. Army and deployed during the first Persian Gulf War in 1990. It was used again during the 1995 conflict in Somalia.

That project highlighted Willbros' expansion beyond its focus on construction with a heightened emphasis on its engineering expertise during the 1980s. This development enabled the company to win a contract providing project management, engineering, and procurement and support services for the modification and expansion of the Great Lakes Gas Transmission System, starting in 1988. The following year, Willbros began supplying engineering and other support services for the Kern River Gas Transmission System, which crossed from Wyoming to California.

Heerema decided to exit the pipeline construction and engineering market in 1992, and sold Willbros in a new management buyout led by Larry Bump and other members of the company's management, backed by investors including Dillon, Reed & Co. That year, the company began a new contract for the reconstruction of the oil field gathering systems in Kuwait. The company also began working in Russia, setting up a subsidiary there, as it started work as part of a consortium building a pipeline connecting the Kazakstan oil fields to the Black Sea.

Willbros went public in 1996, listing its shares on the New York Stock Exchange. The following year the company made a secondary offering. By then, Willbros had begun to target a number of new markets, particularly the booming Asian countries, including Pakistan in 1995 and Indonesia in 1996. The collapse of the Asian economies in the late 1990s, however, limited Willbros' growth in the region.

Key Dates:

1908: David and Miller Williams found Williams Brothers Corporation in Arkansas.

1915: The company begins pipeline construction operations in Oklahoma.

1919: Williams moves its headquarters to Tulsa as it begins to specialize in pipeline construction.

1939: The company takes on its first international venture, a pipeline project in Venezuela.

1942: Willbros is named principal contractor of Big Inch and Little Big Inch War Emergency Pipeline projects.

1949: David, Jr., Charles, and John Williams buy the company from David and Miller Williams.

1957: Williams goes public.

1966: The Great Lakes Pipe Line company is acquired in a move to transition to the natural gas market.

1972: The company changes its name to The Williams Companies.

1975: Williams exits the pipeline construction market and spins off those operations in Willbros management buyout.

1986: Hereema Holding acquires full control of Willbros.

1992: Willbros is spun off from Hereema in a new management buyout led by CEO Larry Bump.

1996: Willbros goes public on the New York Stock Exchange.

2000: The company refocuses on the North American market.

2003: The company plans to enter the Chinese market.

The company found stronger markets in the United States, where it constructed a 45-mile gas pipeline system connecting Texas and Mexico in 1998. The following year, the company turned to Australia, forming a joint-venture to build a pipeline with a total length of 492 miles. Nonetheless, the United States, with its booming economy, became the company's strategic target through the end of the decade. Whereas Asia and West Africa had been the source for much of the company's sales in the first half of the decade, by the beginning of the next, the North American market accounted for more than half of total sales, which climbed from $252 million in 1997 to more than $390 million in 2001. The company's refocus in that year enabled it to pull away from three years of losses, with a profit of more than $19 million.

Acquisitions formed a significant part of Willbros' growth at the turn of the century. In 2000, the company paid $7 million to acquire Houston-based pipeline construction company Rogers & Philips, which itself had been formed in 1992. (Also in 2000, the company moved its administrative headquarters from Tulsa to Houston.) Willbros' acquisition drive continued into 2001 with the purchase of MSI Energy Services Inc., based in Alberta, Canada. Formed in 1988, MSI gave Willbros its first base of operations in that country.

Larry Bump, who had served as company CEO since 1979, retired to the chairman's position in 2001, naming Michael Curran as the company's new CEO, president, and vice-chairman. Curran maintained the company's growth through acquisition, leading the September 2002 purchase of the Mt. West Group of companies, which, with offices in Oregon, Colorado, and Wyoming, not only added some $60 million to Willbros' annual sales but also enabled it to gain coast-to-coast coverage of the U.S. market. In addition, the acquisition of Mt. West gave Willbros the potential of diversifying into the larger energy sector.

By the end of 2002, Willbros sales had soared to nearly $584 million. In 2003, the company prepared a return to the Far East, specifically an entry into the highly promising Chinese market. In May of that year, the company formed a partnership agreement with local groups Sinopec Jianghan Petroleume Group and Joanghan Oilfield Construction and Engineering Company. After nearly 90 years in business, Willbros had successfully repositioned itself as a full-service engineering and construction group focused on the worldwide energy sector.

Principal Subsidiaries

Constructora CAMSA, C.A.; MSI Energy Services Inc.; Mt. West Group; Nigeria and West Africa Marine; Rogers & Phillips, Inc.; The Oman Construction Company Ltd; Willbros (Nigeria) Limited; Willbros (Overseas) Limited; Willbros Engineers, Inc.; Willbros International, Inc.; Willbros Offshore (Nigeria) Limited; Willbros USA, Inc.

Principal Competitors

Halliburton Inc.; Schlumberger Ltd.; Bechtel Inc.; BHP Billiton Ltd.; Technip Italy SpA; Chevron Exploration and Production Services Co.

Further Reading

Perin, Monica, ''Pipeline Firm Willbros Moves HQ to Town After Houston Acquisition,'' *Houston Business Journal*, March 24, 2000, p. 7.

''Willbros Completes Acquisition of MSI Energy Services,'' *Canadian Corporate News*, October 12, 2001.

''Willbros Completes Mt. West Transaction,'' *Electric Light & Power*, November 2002, p. 17.

''Willbros Unit to Build Pipeline in Bolivia,'' *Houston Business Journal*, December 21, 2001, p. 3.

—M.L. Cohen

Winegard Company

3000 Kirkwood Street
Burlington, Iowa 52601
U.S.A.
Telephone: (319) 754-0600
Fax: (319) 754-0787
Web site: http://www.winegard.com

Private Company
Incorporated: 1954
Employees: 325
Sales: $95.6 million (2001)
NAIC: 334220 Radio and Television Broadcasting and
    Wireless Communications Equipment Manufacturing;
    334290 Other Communication Equipment
    Manufacturing; 334310 Audio and Video Equipment
    Manufacturing; 334419 Other Electronic Component
    Manufacturing; 335312 Motor and Generator
    Manufacturing

Based in Burlington, Iowa, Winegard Company manufactures a wide variety of reception equipment for home, commercial, and mobile markets. The company's more than 1,000 different products fall into one of four main lines: outdoor/rooftop TV and FM Antennas, electronics, and accessories; satellite antennas and mounts; mobile off-air and satellite TV antennas and mounts; and medical telemetry antenna and accessories. In addition to serving customers throughout the United States, Winegard markets its products internationally.

Origins in Radio

The inspiration for the Winegard Company came from John Winegard, a Burlington, Iowa, native who became interested in radios at a young age. As a student in the seventh grade Winegard constructed a one-tube radio. As his accomplishment flowered into a hobby, Winegard furthered his knowledge by reading large numbers of technical articles and building radios for others.

John Winegard graduated from high school in 1939 and found employment as a radio repair apprentice. Moving to Cedar Rapids, Iowa, he was hired by the Collins Radio Co., an equipment manufacturer. After receiving additional communications training from the U.S. Army Air Corps during World War II, Winegard established a radio shop in Omaha, Nebraska, but eventually returned to Burlington.

When John Winegard arrived back in Burlington, television was an emerging medium that interested him greatly. Because of his training, it also was a medium he understood technically. In 1948, Winegard began making TV antennas, one of which was used to receive Burlington's very first TV picture. In fact, he constructed an antenna that enabled large numbers of Burlington residents to watch the 1949 inauguration of President Harry Truman.

Winegard eventually began making antennas with Dr. Eugene Gulick, another Burlington resident who was interested in television. Although aluminum was in short supply because of the Korean War, the two men made antennas in Gulick's basement, and sold them as they could, using much of the proceeds to treat their wives to Saturday night dinners. They soon made their first ''commercial'' sale, manufacturing three antennas for Block & Kuhl Co., a local appliance shop. The antennas made it possible for Block & Kuhl to receive broadcasts from Chicago station WBKB.

As demand for antennas increased, the enterprise moved to the two-car garage of John Winegard's parents in Burlington. Dr. Gulick eventually exited the picture, and Winegard found a new business partner named John Wells. Together, they formed the Wells Winegard Co. Antenna orders quickly started to pour in, and the company was forced to find a larger facility at Eighth and Maple Streets. In the winter of 1951, expansion necessitated a move to an even larger facility on Mt. Pleasant Street.

In 1952, John Winegard developed the first antenna capable of receiving more than one channel; the earliest models were designed to only receive channels 4 and 5. Ultimately branded as the Clipper, the new product hit the market in 1953. Demand for TV antennas continued to skyrocket, and before long Winegard's production was lagging more than a month behind schedule. These conditions prompted another move, this time to a 7,000-square-foot facility on Scotten Boulevard.

Starting Out Strong: 1954–59

In 1954, an important milestone took place when John Winegard bought out his partner and renamed the enterprise Winegard Co. At this point in time, the firm was worth an estimated $500,000 and had a payroll of about $231,000. It employed 22 salespeople and as many as 70 production workers who manufactured approximately 1,200 antennas per day. Among Winegard Co.'s earliest products was a $17.95 antenna called the Interceptor. According to the company, Winegard was the first in its industry to market antennas nationally, which was accomplished through magazine advertisements. In addition, it offered anodized antennas that were more resistant to the effects of weather than untreated aluminum antennas. By mid-1955 Winegard was one of four companies leading the industry. In addition to 48 states, the company had established a foothold in several international markets including Belgium, Canada, and Sweden.

During the mid-1950s, Iowa Governor Leo Hoegh presented John Winegard with a merit citation for his rapid success. However, things were not all positive. A setback occurred in October 1956 when fire from a welder's torch caused an estimated $100,000 in damage to the firm's manufacturing facility. Unfortunately, the fire happened during Winegard's busiest time of the year. Still, no employees were seriously injured and some inventory was spared and relocated to the company's new 25,000-square-foot facility that was nearing completion. After the fire, Winegard continued to prosper. By the end of the 1950s its product base had grown to include 156 different models of antennas, up from 30 three years earlier.

Reaching New Markets: 1960–89

Progress continued at Winegard Co. throughout the 1960s, with several noteworthy developments occurring late in the decade. In 1968 the company introduced a new closed circuit TV outlet intended for use in commercial buildings. It also nearly doubled the size of its delivery fleet, increasing the total number of semi trucks to five. Early the following year, Winegard introduced its new Color Wedge line of outdoor antennas.

During the late 1960s, nearly 450 employees worked at the company's two locations in Burlington: a part fabrication plant at 2840 Mount Pleasant Street and two plants at 3000 Kirkwood Street. At the latter site, Plant No. 1 was used as a base for administration, engineering, antenna production, and shipping. Plant No. 2 was devoted to the production of electronic equipment used for TV and FM radio reception. In July 1969, Winegard expanded its production facilities for the fifth time

when construction commenced on a 30,000-square-foot addition to Plant No. 1. Complete with a new parking lot for 80 vehicles, the new structure would serve mainly as a warehouse so that existing storage space could be used for additional production.

John Winegard's engineering skills continued to attract national attention during the 1960s. As the company explained on its web site: "In addition to innovative and progressive TV antenna designs, [Winegard] was recognized in the 1960s for designing tracking antennas for Dr. James Van Allen to track early satellites." Winegard Co. also received an award for contributing to the Apollo 11 space mission in 1969, which took astronauts Neil A. Armstrong, Michael Collins, and Edwin E. Aldrin to the moon. The company provided the Houston Space Center with amplifier systems that were used in its television-viewing amphitheater.

During the 1970s, the scope of Winegard Co.'s offerings expanded to include satellite TV reception equipment. Among its products were master TV systems for consumers and organizations like hospitals, motels, and schools. The company also developed an electronic antenna called the Sensar, a version of which was still being sold in the early 2000s. (In a total departure from the antenna business, John Winegard also founded the Pzazz! Restaurant Complex in Burlington during this time.)

After seven years of development work, Winegard's first satellite receiver hit the market in 1983. At the time, leading pay television services like HBO did not scramble their signals, allowing those with receivers to view a wide variety of satellite programming for free. This led to an explosion in satellite equipment sales in 1984–85. By 1985, half of Winegard's revenues were attributable to satellite receivers. However, broadcasters quickly began to scramble their signals, which had a negative effect on the equipment market. At Winegard, receiver sales fell by 50 percent in 1986.

Although scrambled signals represented a small setback for equipment manufacturers, Winegard could foresee the satellite sector's emergence as a strong competitor to cable television. It continued to devote research and development resources to this market, focusing on the development of a two-foot diameter dish. Winegard also developed a remote controlled receiver, similar to the units that eventually became standard when services like DirecTV and DISH Network exploded in popularity during the early 2000s. As described in the July 12, 1987 issue of the *Hawk Eye*: "About the size of a videocassette recorder, the receiver permits viewers to select, from a hand-held control, any of hundreds of channels without adjusting the satellite dish. It will not require the viewer to determine on which satellite a particular channel is located, or the direction the satellite must face to receive the signal."

During the 1980s John Winegard moved to Colorado, then home to his company's design facility, and eventually retired. His son, Randy Winegard, succeeded him as president. On the company's web site, a retired executive commented on John Winegard and his importance to the company's success, explaining: "People say John Winegard was a brilliant engineer, and that's true. One of his greatest strengths was engineering. Today, people talk about 'manufacturability' and that is exactly how John Winegard designed his products back in the 50's.

Key Dates:

1948: John Winegard begins making homemade TV antennas, one of which is used to receive Burlington, Iowa's first TV picture.

1950: With business partner John Wells, Winegard forms the Wells Winegard Co.

1952: Winegard develops the first antenna capable of receiving more than one channel.

1954: Winegard Co. is formed when John Winegard buys out Wells and renames the enterprise.

1969: Winegard receives an award for contributing to the Apollo 11 space mission that put American astronauts on the moon.

1983: Winegard markets its first satellite receiver.

1980s: John Winegard retires and is succeeded by his son, Randy Winegard.

1990s: Winegard begins manufacturing TV reception equipment for the RV market.

2003: Winegard's products number more than 1,000.

I would ask him why he designed a part a certain way and he would answer by showing me why it would be easier to put together that way. He had a keen understanding of the process. What people don't realize is that he was an effective marketer too. He had an overall grasp of business.''

John Winegard's knack for developing effective manufacturing processes had been of considerable benefit to his company throughout the years. Under his son's leadership, the company focused on ways to make operations even better. In 1985 Winegard installed a resource planning software application developed by Cincom Systems, Inc. According to *Computerworld*, the addition of the MRPS (Manufacturing Resource Planning System) successfully coordinated production and inventory data for Winegard's distribution warehouse, as well as its fabrication and assembly facilities. In addition to cutting material costs, the company was able to lower freight charges by nearly 15 percent, reduce inventory by almost 30 percent, and improve its inventory turn rate by 25 percent. As the publication explained, the MRPS software ''enabled the company to eliminate obsolete and excessive inventory and to order the right amounts of parts at the right times.''

By 1989 Winegard's pursuit of quality and efficiency continued as the company focused on simplifying the way its products were made. Randy Winegard and his management team instituted a plan to review manufacturing processes, seeking valuable input from the company's 500 workers. The ultimate goal of the initiative—which uncovered a number of unnecessary production steps—was to enable Winegard to make the best equipment as cost effectively as possible. In the February 26, 1989 issue of the *Hawk Eye*, Randy Winegard said: ''It's a myth in American manufacturing that you have to pay more for quality. . . . Management has to lead by example. You can't just say you're committed. You've got to get involved.''

As part of its simplification efforts, the company said it would consolidate operations in several different ways. For example,

Winegard announced that operations at its 100,000-square-foot facility in Chariton, Iowa, and the Evergreen, Colorado, research and development office would relocate to Burlington. In addition to a goal of reducing its then 300,000 square feet of manufacturing space by roughly 50 percent, traditional forms of incentives were eliminated in order to shift production workers' focus from quantity to quality.

Positioned for Success: 1990 and Beyond

During the 1990s, Winegard expanded the scope of its product offerings again by manufacturing satellite TV reception equipment for the recreational vehicle (RV) market. Its first offering was an expensive six-foot dish used primarily by owners of large motorcoaches. According to *RV Business*, the company's expansion effort became more aggressive midway through the 1990s, at which time DirecTV made it possible for customers to use a more affordable 18-inch dish to receive programming.

Growth also began to heat up in the home satellite market, and by June of 1995 Winegard had a long-term agreement with Sony Corp. to manufacture accessories and home installation kits. The company also announced that it would supply as many as one million 18-inch satellite dishes to AlphaStar Digital, a subsidiary of Canada-based Tee-Comm that planned to provide satellite TV service in the United States. The deal with AlphaStar meant a potential production increase of 500 dishes per day.

In addition to supplying its DirectSat satellite dish antenna, Winegard's arrangement with AlphaStar involved various accessories and installation kits. Best of all, it meant that 40 to 50 new jobs could be added to the company's workforce, which by this time consisted of approximately 200 employees. Related expansion plans—involving a new assembly line and more parking spaces—were announced, and Winegard sought approval to rezone residential land adjacent to one of its light industrial facilities in order to accommodate a 50- by 200-foot addition.

By 1996, Winegard had much to celebrate. By this time it had been recognized many times with different awards, including seven consecutive Dealer's Choice Awards. The company employed some 300 people in a plant that occupied 110,000 square feet. To produce the latest generation of satellite antennas, Winegard added an 800-ton press to its manufacturing operations, as well as new computer-operated equipment. With 34 patents to its name, the company marketed four different lines of products: rooftop TV and FM antennas and accessories; medical telemetry antennas; marine and recreational vehicle TV antennas; and satellite antennas and mounts.

The RV market had become a very important component of Winegard's business by 1998, accounting for some 40 percent of sales. Although the RV aftermarket initially constituted the lion's share of the company's RV sales, by the late 1990s nearly 70 percent of its RV business came from original equipment manufacturers (OEMs). Winegard continued to serve the RV and mobile markets with innovative products into the twenty-first century. For example, in 2003 the company added three new devices to its line of Entertainment Select Video Distribution Switches. These units allowed RV owners to switch between a variety of sources including DVD players, VCRs, satellite TV, cable TV, and standard TV antennas.

By the early 2000s, Winegard Co. had truly evolved from its origin during broadcast television's earliest days. Over the span of nearly 50 years the company's product offerings had grown to more than 1,000. This remarkable growth had occurred in tandem with the emergence of new markets like direct-to-home satellite broadcasting, the use of medical telemetry devices, and the demand for home-style entertainment in recreational vehicles. The fact that communications technology—especially in the realm of entertainment—continues to become more pervasive should bode well for Winegard into the 21st century.

Principal Competitors

Hughes Electronics Corporation; Motorola, Inc.; Thomson S.A.

Further Reading

Delaney, Steve, ''Good News Keeps Flowing,'' *Burlington Hawk Eye*, July 23, 1995.

——, ''TV Satellites Signal Winegard,'' *Burlington Hawk Eye*, July 12, 1987.

——, ''Winegard Touts Its Simple Manufacturing Process,'' *Burlington Hawk Eye*, February 26, 1989.

''Firm Cuts Inventory with Resource Planning Package,'' *Computerworld,* March 11, 1985.

Marshall, Grant, ''Burlington Linked To Apollo Voyage,'' *Burlington Hawk Eye*, July 16, 1969.

Martin, Mitch, ''Winegard Eyes Plant Expansion,'' *Burlington Hawk Eye*, June 13, 1995.

Olson, Lee, ''Winegard Company Expands Operations,'' *Burlington Hawk Eye*, June 5, 1955.

Sogard, Bob, ''Winegard Co. Swept By Fire,'' *Burlington Hawk Eye*, October 16, 1956.

''Winegard Co. Adds Plant Facilities,'' *Burlington Hawk Eye*, July 6, 1969.

''Winegard Thrives in RV Satellite Niche,'' *RV Business,* June 1998.

''Winegard Video Switches,'' *RV Business,* April 2003.

—Paul R. Greenland

INDEX TO COMPANIES

Index to Companies

Listings in this index are arranged in alphabetical order under the company name. Company names beginning with a letter or proper name such as Eli Lilly & Co. will be found under the first letter of the company name. Definite articles (The, Le, La) are ignored for alphabetical purposes as are forms of incorporation that precede the company name (AB, NV). Company names printed in bold type have full, historical essays on the page numbers appearing in bold. Updates to entries that appeared in earlier volumes are signified by the notation (upd.). Company names in light type are references within an essay to that company, not full historical essays. This index is cumulative with volume numbers printed in bold type.

Bulkships, **27** 473
Bull. *See* Compagnie des Machines Bull S.A.
Bull-GE, **III** 123
Bull HN Information Systems, **III** 122–23
Bull Motors, **11** 5
Bull Run Corp., **24** 404
Bull S.A., **III** 122–23; **43** 89–91 **(upd.)**
Bull Tractor Company, **7** 534; **16** 178; **26** 492
Bull-Zenith, **25** 531
Bulldog Computer Products, **10** 519
Bulley & Andrews, LLC, 55 74–76
Bullock's, **III** 63; **31** 191
Bulolo Gold Dredging, **IV** 95
Bulova Corporation, I 488; **II** 101; **III** 454–55; **12** 316–17, 453; **13** 120–22; **14** 501; **21** 121–22; **36** 325; **41** 70–73 **(upd.)**
Bumble Bee Seafoods, Inc., **II** 491, 508, 557; **24** 114
Bumkor-Ramo Corp., **I** 539
Bunawerke Hüls GmbH., **I** 350
Bundall Computers Pty Limited, **56** 155
Bundy Corporation, 17 62–65, 480
Bunker Ramo Info Systems, **III** 118
Bunte Candy, **12** 427
Bunzl plc, IV 260–62; **12** 264; **31** 77–80 **(upd.)**
Buquet, **19** 49
Burbank Aircraft Supply, Inc., **14** 42–43; **37** 29, 31
Burberry Ltd., 41 74–76 **(upd.);** **47** 167, 169
Burberrys Ltd., **V** 68; **10** 122; **17** 66–68; **19** 181
Burda Holding GmbH. & Co., 20 53; **23** 85–89
Burdines, **9** 209; **31** 192
Bureau de Recherches de Pétrole, **IV** 544–46, 559–60; **7** 481–83; **21** 203–04
The Bureau of National Affairs, Inc., 23 90–93
Bureau Veritas SA, 55 77–79
Burelle S.A., 23 94–96
Burger and Aschenbrenner, **16** 486
Burger Boy Food-A-Rama, **8** 564
Burger Chef, **II** 532
Burger King Corporation, I 21, 278; **II** 556–57, **613–15**, 647; **7** 316; **8** 564; **9** 178; **10** 122; **12** 43, 553; **13** 408–09; **14** 25, 32, 212, 214, 452; **16** 95–97, 396; **17** 69–72 **(upd.)**, 501; **18** 437; **21** 25, 362; **23** 505; **24** 140–41; **25** 228; **26** 284; **33** 240–41; **36** 517, 519; **56** 44–48 **(upd.)**
Burgess, Anderson & Tate Inc., **25** 500
Bürhle, **17** 36; **50** 78
Burhmann-Tetterode, **22** 154
Buriot International, Inc., **53** 236
Burke Scaffolding Co., **9** 512
BURLE Industries Inc., **11** 444
Burlesdon Brick Co., **III** 734
Burlington Coat Factory Warehouse Corporation, 10 188–89
Burlington Homes of New England, **14** 138
Burlington Industries, Inc., V 118, **354–55**; **8** 234; **9** 231; **12** 501; **17** 73–76 **(upd.)**, 304–05; **19** 275
Burlington Mills Corporation, **12** 117–18
Burlington Motor Holdings, **30** 114
Burlington Northern, Inc., IV 182; **V** 425–28; **10** 190–91; **11** 315; **12** 145, 278

Burlington Northern Santa Fe Corporation, 27 82–89 **(upd.);** **28** 495
Burlington Resources Inc., 10 190–92; **11** 135; **12** 144; **47** 238
Burmah Castrol PLC, IV 378, **381–84**, 440–41, 483–84, 531; **7** 56; **15** 246; **21** 80; **30** 86–91 **(upd.);** **45** 55
Burmeister & Wain, **III** 417–18
Burn & Co., **IV** 205
Burn Standard Co. Ltd., **IV** 484
Burnards, **II** 677
Burndy, **19** 166
Burnham and Co., **II** 407–08; **6** 599; **8** 388
Burns & Ricker, Inc., **40** 51, 53
Burns & Wilcox Ltd., **6** 290
Burns-Alton Corp., **21** 154–55
Burns Companies, **III** 569; **20** 360
Burns Fry Ltd., **II** 349
Burns International Security Services, **III** 440; **13** 123–25; **42** 338. *See also* Securitas AB.
Burns International Services Corporation, 41 77–80 **(upd.)**
Burns Philp & Company Limited, **21** 496–98
Burnup & Sims, Inc., **19** 254; **26** 324
Burpee & Co. *See* W. Atlee Burpee & Co.
Burr & Co., **II** 424; **13** 340
Burr-Brown Corporation, 19 66–68
Burrill & Housman, **II** 424; **13** 340
Burris Industries, **14** 303; **50** 311
Burroughs Corp., **I** 142, 478; **III** 132, 148–49, 152, 165–66; **6** 233, 266, 281–83; **18** 386, 542. *See also* Unisys Corporation.
Burroughs Mfg. Co., **16** 321
Burroughs Wellcome & Co., **I** 713; **8** 216
Burrows, Marsh & McLennan, **III** 282
Burrups Ltd., **18** 331, 333; **47** 243
Burry, **II** 560; **12** 410
Bursley & Co., **II** 668
Burt Claster Enterprises, **III** 505
Burthy China Clays, **III** 690
Burton-Furber Co., **IV** 180
Burton Group plc, V 20–22. *See also* Arcadia Group plc.
Burton J. Vincent, Chesley & Co., **III** 271
Burton, Parsons and Co. Inc., **II** 547
Burton Retail, **V** 21
Burton Rubber Processing, **8** 347
Burton Snowboards Inc., 22 118–20, 460
Burtons Gold Medal Biscuits Limited, **II** 466; **13** 53
Burwell Brick, **14** 248
Bury Group, **II** 581
Busch Entertainment Corporation, **34** 36
Bush Boake Allen Inc., IV 346; **30** 92–94; **38** 247
Bush Brothers & Company, 45 71–73
Bush Hog, **21** 20–22
Bush Industries, Inc., 20 98–100
Bush Terminal Company, **15** 138
Business Communications Group, Inc. *See* Caribiner International, Inc.
The Business Depot, Ltd., **10** 498; **55** 353
Business Expansion Capital Corp., **12** 42
Business Express Airlines, Inc., **28** 22
Business Information Technology, Inc., **18** 112
Business Men's Assurance Company of America, III 209; **13** 476; **14** 83–85; **15** 30
Business Objects S.A., 25 95–97
Business Post Group plc, 46 71–73

Business Resources Corp., **23** 489, 491
Business Science Computing, **14** 36
Business Software Association, **10** 35
Business Software Technology, **10** 394
Business Wire, **25** 240
Businessland Inc., **III** 153; **6** 267; **10** 235; **13** 175–76, 277, 482
Busse Broadcasting Corporation, **7** 200; **24** 199
Büssing Automobilwerke AG, **IV** 201
Buster Brown, **V** 351–52
BUT S.A., **24** 266, 270
Butano, **IV** 528
Butler Bros., **21** 96
Butler Cox PLC, **6** 229
Butler Group, Inc., **30** 310–11
Butler Manufacturing Co., 12 51–53; **43** 130
Butler Shoes, **16** 560
Butterfield & Butterfield, **32** 162
Butterfield & Swire. *See* Swire Pacific Ltd.
Butterfield, Wasson & Co., **II** 380, 395; **10** 59; **12** 533
Butterick Co., Inc., 23 97–99
Butterley Company, **III** 501; **7** 207
Butterworth & Co. (Publishers) Ltd., **IV** 641; **7** 311; **17** 398
Buttrey Food & Drug Stores Co., 18 89–91
Butz Thermo-Electric Regulator Co., **II** 40; **12** 246; **50** 231
Butzbacher Weichenbau GmbH & Co. KG, **53** 352
Buxton, **III** 28; **23** 21
buy.com, Inc., 46 74–77
Buzzard Electrical & Plumbing Supply, **9** 399; **16** 186
BVA Investment Corp., **11** 446–47
BVD, **25** 166
BWAY Corporation, 24 91–93
BWP Distributors, **29** 86, 88
Byerly's, Inc. *See* Lund Food Holdings, Inc.
Byrnes Long Island Motor Cargo, Inc., **6** 370
Byron Jackson, **III** 428, 439. *See also* BJ Services Company.
Byron Weston Company, **26** 105
Bytrex, Inc., **III** 643

C&A, 40 74–77 **(upd.)**
C&A Brenninkmeyer KG, V 23–24
C.&E. Cooper Co., **II** 14
C&E Software, **10** 507
C.&G. Cooper Company, **II** 14; **20** 162
C & G Systems, **19** 442
C & H Distributors, Inc., **27** 177
C&J Clark International Ltd., 52 56–59
C & O. *See* Chesapeake and Ohio Railway.
C&R Clothiers, **17** 313
C&S Bank, **10** 425–26
C&S Co., Ltd., **49** 425, 427
C&S/Sovran Corporation, **10** 425–27; **18** 518; **26** 453; **46** 52
C & S Wholesale Grocers, Inc., 55 80–83
C&W. *See* Cable and Wireless plc.
C-COR.net Corp., 38 118–21
C-Cube Microsystems, Inc., 37 50–54; **43** 221–22
C.A. Delaney Capital Management Ltd., **32** 437
C.A. La Electricidad de Caracas, **53** 18
C.A. Pillsbury and Co., **II** 555

The Dow Chemical Company, I 323–25,
334, 341–42, 360, 370–71, 708; **II** 440,
457; **III** 617, 760; **IV** 83, 417; **8 147–50**
(upd.), 153, 261–62, 548; **9** 328–29,
500–1; **10** 289; **11** 271; **12** 99–100, 254,
364; **14** 114, 217; **16** 99; **17** 418; **18**
279; **21** 387; **28** 411; **38** 187; **50 160–64**
(upd.)
Dow Corning, **II** 54; **III** 683, 685; **44** 129
Dow Jones & Company, Inc., IV
601–03, 654, 656, 670, 678; **7** 99; **10**
276–78, 407; **13** 55; **15** 335–36; **19**
128–31 (upd.), 204; **21** 68–70; **23** 157;
47 100–04 (upd.)
Dow Jones Telerate, Inc., **10 276–78**
DOW Stereo/Video Inc., **30** 466
Dowdings Ltd., **IV** 349
DowElanco, **21** 385, 387
Dowell Australia Ltd., **III** 674
Dowell Schlumberger. *See* Schlumberger
Limited.
Dowidat GmbH, **IV** 197
Dowlais Iron Co., **III** 493
Down River International, Inc., **15** 188
Downe Communications, Inc., **14** 460
Downingtown Paper Company, **8** 476
Downyflake Foods, **7** 429
Dowty Aerospace, **17** 480
Doyle Dane Bernbach, **I** 9, 20, 28, 30–31,
33, 37, 206; **11** 549; **14** 159; **22** 396
DP&L. *See* Dayton Power & Light
Company.
DPCE, **II** 139; **24** 194
DPF, Inc., **12** 275; **38** 250–51
DPL Inc., 6 480–82
DQE, 6 483–85; 38 40
Dr. August Oetker KG, 51 102–06
Dr. E. Fresenius KG. *See* Fresenius
Aktiengesellschaft.
Dr. Gerhard Mann Pharma, **25** 56
DR Holdings, Inc., **10** 242
Dr. Ing he F. Porsche GmbH, **13** 413–14
Dr. Karl Thomae GmbH, **39** 72–73
Dr. Martens, **23** 399, 401
Dr. Miles' Medical Co., **I** 653
Dr Pepper/Seven Up, Inc., I 245; **II** 477;
9 177–78; 32 154–57 (upd.); 49 78
Dr. Richter & Co., **IV** 70
Dr. Solomon's Software Ltd., **25** 349
Dr. Tigges-Fahrten, **II** 163–64; **44** 432
Drackett Professional Products, III 17;
12 126–28
DraftDirect Worldwide, **22** 297
Draftline Engineering Co., **22** 175
Dragados y Construcciones. *See* Grupo
Dragados SA.
Dragon International, **18** 87
Dragonair, **16** 481; **18** 114. *See also* Hong
Kong Dragon Airlines.
The Drake, **12** 316
Drake Bakeries, **II** 562
Drake Beam Morin, Inc., IV 623; **44**
155–57
Drake Steel Supply Co., **19** 343
Drallos Potato Company, **25** 332
Draper & Kramer, **IV** 724
Draper Corporation, **14** 219; **15** 384
Drathen Co., **I** 220
Dravo Corp., **6** 143
Draw-Tite, Inc., **11** 535
Drayton Corp., **II** 319; **17** 324
DreamWorks SKG, 17 72; **21** 23, 26; **26**
150, 188; **43 142–46**
The Drees Company, Inc., 41 131–33

Dreher Breweries, **24** 450
Dresdner Bank A.G., I 411; **II** 191,
238–39, 241–42, 256–57, 279–80,
281–83, 385; **III** 201, 289, 401; **IV** 141;
14 169–70; **15** 13; **47 81–84**
Dresdner Feuer-Versicherungs-Gesellschaft,
III 376
Dresdner RCM Global Investors, **33** 128
The Dress Barn, Inc., 24 145–46
Dresser Industries, Inc., I 486; **III** 429,
470–73; 499, 527, 545–46; **12** 539; **14**
325; **15** 225–26, 468; **16** 310; **18** 219;
24 208; **25** 188, 191; **52** 214–216; **55**
129–31 (upd.)
Dresser Industries, Inc., **55** 194, 221
Dresser Power, **6** 555
Dressmaster GmbH, **53** 195
Drew Graphics, Inc., **13** 227–28
Drew Industries Inc., 28 106–08
Drewry Photocolor, **I** 447
Drexel Burnham Lambert Incorporated,
II 167, 329–30, **407–09,** 482; **III** 10,
253, 254–55, 531, 721; **IV** 334; **6**
210–11; **7** 305; **8** 327, 349, 388–90,
568; **9** 346; **12** 229; **13** 169, 299, 449;
14 43; **15** 71, 281, 464; **16** 535, 561; **20**
415; **22** 55, 189; **24** 273; **25** 313; **33**
253. *See also* New Street Capital Inc.
Drexel Heritage Furnishings Inc., III
571; **11** 534; **12 129–31; 20** 362; **39** 266
Dreyer's Grand Ice Cream, Inc., 10
147–48; **17 139–41; 30** 81; **35** 59–61
Dreyfus Interstate Development Corp., **11**
257
DRI. *See* Dominion Resources, Inc.
Dribeck Importers Inc., **9** 87
Drip In Irrigation, **26** 494
Drogueros S.A., **39** 188
Drott Manufacturing Company, **10** 379
Drouot Group, **III** 211
DRS Investment Group, **27** 370
Drug City, **II** 649
Drug Emporium, Inc., 12 132–34, 477
Drug House, **III** 9
Drug, Inc., **III** 17; **37** 42
Drummond Lighterage. *See* Puget Sound
Tug and Barge Company.
Drummonds' Bank, **12** 422
Druout, **I** 563; **24** 78
Dry Milks Inc., **I** 248
DryClean U.S.A., **14** 25
Dryden and Co., **III** 340
Drypers Corporation, 18 147–49
Drysdale Government Securities, **10** 117
DSC Communications Corporation, 9
170; **12 135–37**
DSL Group Ltd., **27** 49
DSM Melamine America, **27** 316–18
DSM N.V., I 326–27; **III** 614; **15** 229; **56**
94–96 (upd.)
DST Systems Inc., **6** 400–02; **26** 233
DTAG. *See* Dollar Thrifty Automotive
Group, Inc.
DTE Energy Company, 20 197–201
(upd.)
Du Bouzet, **II** 233
Du Mont Company, **8** 517
Du Pareil au Même, 43 147–49
Du Pont. *See* E.I. du Pont de Nemours &
Co.
Du Pont Fabricators, **III** 559
Du Pont Glore Forgan, Inc., **III** 137
Du Pont Photomask, **IV** 600
Duane Reade Holding Corp., 21 186–88

Dublin and London Steam Packet
Company, **V** 490
Dublin Corporation, **50** 74
DuBois Chemicals Division, **13** 149–50;
22 188; **26** 306
Ducatel-Duval, **II** 369
Ducati Motor Holding S.p.A., 17 24; **30**
171–73; 36 472
Duck Head Apparel Company, Inc., 8
141–43; **30** 159; **42 118–21**
Duckback Products, Inc., **51** 190
Ducks Unlimited, **28** 306
Duckwall-ALCO Stores, Inc., 24 147–49
Duco Ltd., **25** 104–05
Ducommun Incorporated, 30 174–76
Ducon Group, **II** 81
Ducros, **36** 185, 187–88
Dudley Jenkins Group Plc, **53** 362
Dudley Stationery Ltd., **25** 501
Duff & Phelps Credit Rating, **37** 143, 145
Duff Bros., **III** 9–10
Duffy Meats, **27** 259
Duffy-Mott, **II** 477
Duke Energy Corporation, 27 128–31
(upd.); 40 354, 358
Duke Energy Field Services, Inc., **24** 379;
40 354, 358
Duke Power Company, V 600–02
Dumes SA, **13** 206
Dumez, **V** 655–57
Dumont Broadcasting Corporation, **7** 335
The Dun & Bradstreet Corporation, I
540; **IV** 604–05, 643, 661; **8** 526; **9**
505; **10** 4, 358; **13** 3–4; **19 132–34**
(upd.); 38 6
Dun & Bradstreet Software Services
Inc., 11 77–79; 43 183
Dunavant Enterprises, Inc., 54 88–90
Dunbar-Stark Drillings, Inc., **19** 247
Duncan Foods Corp., **I** 234; **10** 227
Duncan Toys Company, 55 132–35
Duncanson & Holt, Inc., **13** 539
Dundee Acquisition Corp., **19** 421
Dundee Bancorp, **36** 314
Dundee Cement Co., **III** 702; **8** 258–59
Dunfey Brothers Capital Group, **12** 368
Dunfey Hotels Corporation, **12** 367
Dunhams Stores Corporation, **V** 111
Dunhill Holdings, **IV** 93; **V** 411
Dunhill Staffing Systems, Inc., **52** 397–98
Dunkin' Donuts, **II** 619; **21** 323; **29** 18–19
Dunlop Coflexip Umbilicals Ltd. *See* Duco
Ltd.
Dunlop Holdings, **I** 429; **III** 697; **V** 250,
252–53
Dunlop Ltd., **25** 104
Dunn Bennett, **38** 401
Dunn Bros., **28** 63
Dunn-Edwards Corporation, 56 97–99
Dunn Manufacturing Company, **25** 74
Dunn Paper Co., **IV** 290
Dunning Industries, **12** 109
Dunoyer. *See* Compagnie de Saint-Gobain
S.A.
Dunwoodie Manufacturing Co., **17** 136
Duo-Bed Corp., **14** 435
Dupey Enterprises, Inc., **17** 320
Dupil-Color, Inc., **III** 745
Duplainville Transport, **19** 333–34
Duplex Products, Inc., 17 142–44, 445
Dupol, **III** 614
Dupont. *See* E.I. du Pont de Nemours &
Company.
Dupont Chamber Works, **6** 449

406, **426–30**, 431–33, 437–38, 454, 466, 506, 508, 512, 515, 522, 537–39, 554; **V** 605; **7 169–73 (upd.)**, 230, 538, 559; **9** 440–41; **11** 353; **14** 24–25, 291, 494; **12** 348; **16** 489, 548; **20** 262; **23** 317; **25** 229–30; **26** 102, 369; **27** 217; **32 175–82 (upd.)**; **45** 54

Exxon Mobil Corporation, **40** 358; **50** 29; **54** 380, 385

Eye Masters Ltd., **23** 329

Eyeful Home Co., **III** 758

Eyelab, **II** 560; **12** 411

Eyes Multimedia Productions Inc., **51** 286–87

EZ Paintr Corporation, **9** 374

EZCORP Inc., 43 159–61

EZPor Corporation, **12** 377

F. & F. Koenigkramer Company, **10** 272

F&G International Insurance, **III** 397

F. & J. Heinz, **II** 507

F & J Meat Packers, Inc., **22** 548–49

F & M Distributors, **12** 132

F. & M. Schaefer Brewing Corporation, **I** 253, 291, **III** 137; **18** 500

F & M Scientific Corp., **III** 142; **6** 237

F&N Foods Ltd., **54** 116–17

F & R Builders, Inc., **11** 257

F.A. Computer Technologies, Inc., **12** 60

F.A. Ensign Company, **6** 38

F.A.I. Insurances, **III** 729

F.A.O. Schwarz. *See* FAO Schwarz

F. Atkins & Co., **I** 604

F.B. McFarren, Ltd., **21** 499–500

F.C. Internazionale Milano SpA, **44** 387

F.E. Compton Company, **7** 167

F. Egger Co., **22** 49

F.F. Dalley Co., **II** 497

F.F. Publishing and Broadsystem Ltd., **IV** 652; **7** 392

F.H. Tomkins Buckle Company Ltd., **11** 525

F. Hoffmann-La Roche & Co. A.G., I 637, 640, **642–44**, 657, 685, 693, 710; **7** 427; **9** 264; **10** 80, 549; **11** 424–25; **14** 406; **32** 211–12; **50 190–93 (upd.)**

F.J. Walker Ltd., **I** 438

F.K.I. Babcock, **III** 466

F. Kanematsu & Co., Ltd. *See* Kanematsu Corporation.

F.L. Industries Inc., **I** 481, 483

F.L. Moseley Co., **III** 142; **6** 237; **50** 223

F.N. Burt Co., **IV** 644

F. Perkins, **III** 651–52

F.S. Smithers, **II** 445; **22** 405

F.W. Dodge Corp., **IV** 636–37

F.W. Means & Company, **11** 337

F.W. Sickles Company, **10** 319

F.W. Williams Holdings, **III** 728

F.W. Woolworth & Co. Ltd. *See* Kingfisher plc.

F.W. Woolworth Co. *See* Woolworth Corporation.

F.X. Matt Brewing Co., **18** 72; **50** 114

Fab-Asia, Inc., **22** 354–55

Fab Industries, Inc., 27 142–44

Fab 9, **26** 431

Fabbrica D' Armi Pietro Beretta S.p.A., 39 149–51

Fabco Automotive Corp., **23** 306; **27** 203

Faber-Castell. *See* A.W. Faber-Castell Unternehmensverwaltung GmbH & Co.

Fabergé, Inc., **II** 590; **III** 48; **8** 168, 344; **11** 90; **32** 475; **47** 114

Fabri-Centers of America Inc., 15 329; **16 197–99**; **18** 223; **43** 291

Fabrica de Cemento El Melan, **III** 671

Fabtek Inc., **48** 59

Facchin Foods Co., **I** 457

Facit, **III** 480; **22** 26

Facom S.A., 32 183–85; **37** 143, 145

Facts on File, Inc., **14** 96–97; **22** 443

FAE Fluid Air Energy SA, **49** 162–63

Fafnir Bearing Company, **13** 523

FAG Kugelfischer Georg Schafer AG, **11** 84; **47** 280

Fagerdala World Foams, **54** 360–61

Fagersta, **II** 366; **IV** 203

Fahr AG, **III** 543

Fahrzeugwerke Eisenach, **I** 138

FAI, **III** 545–46

Failsafe, **14** 35

Fair Grounds Corporation, 44 177–80

Fair, Isaac and Company, 18 168–71, 516, 518

Fairbanks Morse Co., **I** 158, 434–35; **10** 292; **12** 71

Fairchild Aircraft, Inc., 9 205–08, 460; **11** 278

Fairchild Camera and Instrument Corp., **II** 50, 63; **III** 110, 141, 455, 618; **6** 261–62; **7** 531; **10** 108; **11** 503; **13** 323–24; **14** 14; **17** 418; **21** 122, 330; **26** 327

Fairchild Communications Service, **8** 328

The Fairchild Corporation, **37** 30

Fairchild Dornier GmbH, 48 167–71 (upd.)

Fairchild Industries, **I** 71, 198; **11** 438; **14** 43; **15** 195; **34** 117

Fairchild Semiconductor Corporation, **II** 44–45, 63–65; **III** 115; **6** 215, 247; **10** 365–66; **16** 332; **24** 235; **41** 201

Fairclough Construction Group plc, I 567–68

Fairey Industries Ltd., **IV** 659

Fairfax, **IV** 650

Fairfield Communities, Inc., 36 192–95

The Fairfield Group, **33** 259–60

Fairfield Manufacturing Co., **14** 43

Fairfield Publishing, **13** 165

Fairmont Foods Co., **7** 430; **15** 139

Fairmont Hotels and Resorts Inc., **45** 80

Fairmont Insurance Co., **26** 487

Fairmount Glass Company, **8** 267

Fairport Machine Shop, Inc., **17** 357

Fairway Marketing Group, Inc., **24** 394

Fairway Outdoor Advertising, Inc., **36** 340, 342

Faiveley S.A., 39 152–54

Falcon Drilling Co. *See* Transocean Sedco Forex Inc.

Falcon Oil Co., **IV** 396

Falcon Products, Inc., 33 149–51

Falcon Seaboard Inc., **II** 86; **IV** 410; **7** 309

Falconbridge Limited, IV 111, 165–66; **49 136–39**

Falconet Corp., **I** 45

Falley's, Inc., **17** 558, 560–61

Fallon McElligott Inc., 22 199–201

Falls Financial Inc., **13** 223; **31** 206

Falls National Bank of Niagara Falls, **11** 108

Falls Rubber Company, **8** 126

FAME Plastics, Inc., **18** 162

Family Bookstores, **24** 548. *See also* Family Christian Stores, Inc.

Family Channel. *See* International Family Entertainment Inc.

Family Christian Stores, Inc., 51 131–34

Family Dollar Stores, Inc., 13 215–17

Family Golf Centers, Inc., 29 183–85

Family Health Program, **6** 184

Family Life Insurance Co., **II** 425; **13** 341

Family Mart Group, **V** 188; **36** 418, 420

Family Restaurants, Inc., **14** 194

Family Steak Houses of Florida, Inc., **15** 420

Famosa Bakery, **II** 543

Famous Amos Chocolate Chip Cookie Corporation, **27** 332

Famous Atlantic Fish Company, **20** 5

Famous-Barr, **46** 288

Famous Dave's of America, Inc., 40 182–84 4

Famous Players-Lasky Corp., **I** 451; **II** 154; **6** 161–62; **23** 123

Famous Restaurants Inc., **33** 139–40

FAN, **13** 370

Fancom Holding B.V., **43** 130

Fannie Mae, 45 156–59 (upd.); **54** 122–24

Fannie May Candy Shops Inc., **36** 309

Fansteel Inc., 19 150–52

Fantastic Sam's, **26** 476

Fanthing Electrical Corp., **44** 132

Fantle's Drug Stores, **16** 160

Fantus Co., **IV** 605

Fanuc Ltd., III 482–83; **17 172–74 (upd.)**

Fanzz, **29** 282

FAO Schwarz, I 548; **46 187–90**; **50** 524

Faprena, **25** 85

Far East Airlines, **6** 70

Far East Machinery Co., **III** 581

Far Eastern Air Transport, Inc., **23** 380

Far Eastern Bank, **56** 363

Far West Restaurants, **I** 547

Faraday National Corporation, **10** 269

Farah Incorporated, 24 156–58

Farben. *See* I.G. Farbenindustrie AG.

Farbenfabriken Bayer A.G., **I** 309

Farberware, Inc., **27** 287–88

Farbro Corp., **45** 15

Farbwerke Hoechst A.G., **I** 346–47; **IV** 486; **13** 262

Farine Lactée Henri Nestlé, **II** 545

Farinon Corp., **II** 38

Farley Candy Co., **15** 190

Farley Industries, **25** 166

Farley Northwest Industries Inc., I 440–41

Farm Credit Bank of St. Louis/St. Paul, **8** 489–90

Farm Electric Services Ltd., **6** 586

Farm Family Holdings, Inc., 39 155–58

Farm Fresh Catfish Company, **54** 167

Farm Fresh Foods, **25** 332

Farm Journal Corporation, 42 131–34

Farm Power Laboratory, **6** 565; **50** 366

Farmcare Ltd., **51** 89

Farmer Bros. Co., 52 117–19

Farmer Jack, **16** 247; **44** 145

Farmers and Mechanics Bank of Georgetown, **13** 439

Farmers and Merchants Bank, **II** 349

Farmers Bank of Delaware, **II** 315–16

Farmers Insurance Group of Companies, 23 286; **25 154–56**; **29** 397

Farmers' Loan and Trust Co., **II** 254; **9** 124

Hodgkin, Barnett, Pease, Spence & Co., **II** 307

Hoechst AG, **I** 305–06, 309, 317, **346–48**, 605, 632, 669–70; **IV** 451; **8** 262, 451–53; **13** 75, 262–64; **18** 47, 49, 51, **234–37 (upd.)**, 401; **21** 544; **22** 32; **25** 376; **34** 284; **35** 455–57; **38** 380; **50** 420

Hoechst Celanese Corporation, **8** 562; **11** 436; **12** 118; **13** 118, **262–65**; **22** 278; **24** 151; **26** 108; **54** 51–52

Hoeganaes Corporation, **8** 274–75

Hoenig Group Inc., **41** 207–09

Hoerner Waldorf Corp., **IV** 264; **20** 129

Hoesch AG, **IV** 103–06, 128, 133, 195, 228, 232, 323

Hofbräubierzentrale GmbH Saarbrücken, **41** 222

Hoffman Enclosures Inc., **26** 361, 363

Hoffmann-La Roche & Co. *See* F. Hoffmann- La Roche & Co.

Hoffritz, **27** 288

Hofmann Herbold & Partner, **34** 249

Hogan & Hartson L.L.P., **44** 220–23; **47** 445–46

Högbo Stål & Jernwerks, **IV** 202

Högforsin Tehdas Osakeyhtiö, **IV** 300

Hogue Cellars, **50** 520

Hohner. *See* Matth. Hohner AG.

Hojalata y Laminas S.A., **19** 10

Hojgaard & Schultz, **38** 436

Hokkaido Butter Co., **II** 575

Hokkaido Colonial Bank, **II** 310

Hokkaido Dairy Cooperative, **II** 574

Hokkaido Dairy Farm Assoc., **II** 538

Hokkaido Electric Power Company Inc., **V** 635–37

Hokkaido Forwarding, **6** 428

Hokkaido Rakuno Kosha Co., **II** 574

Hokkaido Takushoku Bank, **II** 300

Hokoku Cement, **III** 713

Hokoku Fire, **III** 384

Hokuetsu Paper Manufacturing, **IV** 327

Hokuriku Electric Power Company, **V** 638–40

Hokusin Kai, **IV** 475

Hokuyo Sangyo Co., Ltd., **IV** 285

Holberg Industries, Inc., **36** 266–69

Holbrook Grocery Co., **II** 682

Holcemca B.V., **51** 29

Holcim, Ltd., **51** 27, 29

Holco BV, **41** 12

Holcroft & Company, **7** 521

Hold Everything, **17** 548–50

Holden Group, **II** 457

Holderbank Financière Glaris Ltd., **III** 701–02; **8** 258–59, 456; **39** 217. *See also* Holnam Inc

Holding di Partecipazioni Industriali S.p.A., **52** 120, 122

N.V. Holdingmaatschappij De Telegraaf, **23** 271–73

Holec Control Systems, **26** 496

Holes-Webway Company, **40** 44

Holga, Inc., **13** 269

Holgate Toys, **25** 379–80

Holiday Corp., **16** 263; **22** 418; **38** 76; **43** 226

Holiday Inns, Inc., **I** 224; **III 94–95**, 99–100; **6** 383; **9** 425–26; **10** 12; **11** 178, 242; **13** 362; **14** 106; **15** 44, 46; **16** 262; **18** 216; **21** 361–62; **23** 71; **24** 253; **25** 386; **27** 21. *See also* The Promus Cos., Inc.

Holiday Magic, Inc., **17** 227

Holiday Mart, **17** 124; **41** 114–15

Holiday Rambler Corporation, **7** 213; **25** 198

Holiday RV Superstores, Incorporated, **26 192–95**

Holland & Barrett, **13** 103; **31** 346, 348

Holland & Holland, **49** 84

Holland America Line, **6** 367–68; **26** 279; **27** 90–91

Holland Burgerville USA, **44 224–26**

Holland Casino, **23** 229

Holland Electro B.V., **17** 234

Holland Hannen and Cubitts, **III** 753

Holland House, **I** 377–78

Holland Motor Express, **14** 505

Holland Studio Craft, **38** 402

Holland van 1859, **III** 200

Hollandsche Bank-Unie, **II** 184–85

Hollandse Signaalapparaten, **13** 402; **50** 300

Holley Carburetor, **I** 434

Holley Performance Products Inc., **52** 157–60

Hollinger International Inc., **24 222–25**; **32** 358

Hollingsead International, Inc., **36** 158–60

Hollingsworth & Whitney Co., **IV** 329

Hollostone, **III** 673

Holly Corporation, **12 240–42**

Holly Farms Corp., **II** 585; **7** 422–24; **14** 515; **23** 376–77; **50** 492

Holly Sugar Company. *See* Imperial Holly Corporation.

Hollywood Casino Corporation, **21** 275–77

Hollywood Entertainment Corporation, **25 208–10**; **29** 504; **31** 339

Hollywood Park, Inc., **20 297–300**

Hollywood Park Race Track, **29** 118

Hollywood Pictures, **II** 174; **30** 487

Hollywood Records, **6** 176

Holme Roberts & Owen LLP, **28 196–99**

Holmen AB, **52 161–65 (upd.)**

Holmen Hygiene, **IV** 315

Holmen S.A., **IV** 325

Holmens Bruk, **IV** 317–18

Holmes Electric Protective Co., **III** 644

Holmes International. *See* Miller Industries, Inc.

Holmsund & Kramfors, **IV** 338

Holnam Inc., **III** 702; **8 258–60**; **39** **217–20 (upd.)**

Holophane Corporation, **19 209–12**; **54** 255

Holson Burnes Group, Inc., **14 244–45**

Holsten Brauerei AG, **35** 256, 258

Holt Manufacturing, **III** 450–51

Holt, Rinehart and Winston, Inc., **IV** 623–24; **12** 224

Holt's Cigar Holdings, Inc., **42 176–78**

Holthouse Furniture Corp., **14** 236

Holtzbrinck. *See* Verlagsgruppe Georg von Holtzbrinck.

Holvick Corp., **11** 65

Holvis AG, **15** 229

Holyman Sally Ltd., **29** 431

Holyoke Food Mart Inc., **19** 480

Holzer and Co., **III** 569; **20** 361

Holzverkohlungs-Industrie AG, **IV** 70

Homart Development, **V** 182

Home & Automobile Insurance Co., **III** 214

Home and Community Care, Inc., **43** 46

Home Box Office Inc., **II** 134, 136, 166–67, 176–77; **IV** 675; **7 222–24**, 528–29; **10** 196; **12** 75; **18** 65; **23** **274–77 (upd.)**, 500; **25** 498; **28** 71

Home Builders Supply, Inc. *See* Scotty's, Inc.

Home Centers of America, Inc., **18** 286

Home Charm Group PLC, **II** 141

Home Choice Holdings, Inc., **33** 366–67

The Home Depot, Inc., **V 75–76**; **9** 400; **10** 235; **11** 384–86; **12** 7, 235, 345, 385; **13** 250, 548; **16** 187–88, 457; **17** 366; **18 238–40 (upd.)**; **19** 248, 250; **21** 356, 358; **22** 477; **23** 232; **26** 306; **27** 416, 481; **31** 20; **35** 11–13; **39** 134; **43** 385; **44** 332–33

Home Entertainment of Texas, Inc., **30** 466

Home Furnace Co., **I** 481

Home Insurance Company, **I** 440; **III** **262–64**

Home Interiors & Gifts, Inc., **15** 475, 477; **55 202–04**

Home Nutritional Services, **17** 308

Home Office Reference Laboratory, Inc., **22** 266

Home Oil Company Ltd., **I** 264; **6** 477–78

Home Products International, Inc., **18** 492; **55 205–07**

Home Properties Co., Inc., **21** 95

Home Properties of New York, Inc., **42** **179–81**

Home Quarters Warehouse, Inc., **12** 233, 235

Home Savings of America, **II** 181–82; **10** 342–43; **16** 346; **28** 167; **47** 160

The Home School, Inc., **41** 111

Home Shopping Network, Inc., **V 77–78**; **9** 428; **18** 76; **24** 517; **25 211–15** **(upd.)**; **26** 441; **33** 322

Home Telephone and Telegraph Company, **10** 201

Home Telephone Company. *See* Rochester Telephone Corporation.

Home Vision Entertainment Inc., **31** 339–40

HomeBase, Inc., **II** 658; **13** 547–48; **33** **198–201 (upd.)**

HomeBuyers Preferred, Inc., **51** 210

HomeClub Inc., **13** 547–48; **16** 187; **17** 366. *See also* HomeBase, Inc.

Homécourt, **IV** 226

HomeFed Bank, **10** 340

Homegrocer.com Inc., **38** 223

Homelite, **21** 175

Homemade Ice Cream Company, **10** 371

Homemakers Furniture. *See* John M. Smyth Co.

HomeMax, Inc., **41** 20

Homer McKee Advertising, **I** 22

Homes by Oakwood, Inc., **15** 328

Homeserve.net Ltd., **46** 72

Homestake Mining Company, **IV** 18, 76; **12 243–45**; **20** 72; **27** 456; **38 229–32** **(upd.)**

Hometown Auto Retailers, Inc., **44** **227–29**

HomeTown Buffet, Inc., **19** 435; **22** 465. *See also* Buffets, Inc

Homette Corporation, **30** 423

Homewood Stores Co., **IV** 573; **7** 550

Homewood Suites, **9** 425–26

Hominal Developments Inc., **9** 512

Hon Industries Inc., **13 266–69**; **23** 243–45

Rijnhaave Information Systems, **25** 21
Rike's, **10** 282
Riken Corp., **IV** 160; **10** 493
Riken Kagaku Co. Ltd., **48** 250
Riken Kankoshi Co. Ltd., **III** 159
Riken Optical Co., **III** 159
Riklis Family Corp., 9 447–50; **12** 87; **13** 453; **38** 169; **43** 355
Riku-un Moto Kaisha, **V** 477
Rinascente Group, **12** 153; **54** 220
Ring King Visibles, Inc., **13** 269
Ring Ltd., **43** 99
Ringier America, **19** 333
Ringköpkedjan, **II** 640
Ringling Bros., Barnum & Bailey Circus, **25** 312–13
Ringnes Bryggeri, **18** 396
Rini-Rego Supermarkets Inc., **13** 238
Rini Supermarkets, **9** 451; **13** 237
Rinker Materials Corp., **III** 688
Rio Grande Industries, Inc., **12** 18–19
Rio Grande Oil Co., **IV** 375, 456
Rio Grande Servaas, S.A. de C.V., **23** 145
Rio Grande Valley Gas Co., **IV** 394
Rio Sportswear Inc., **42** 269
Rio Sul Airlines, **6** 133
Rio Tinto plc, 19 349–53 (upd.); **27** 253; **42** 395; **50** 380–85 (upd.)
Rio Tinto-Zinc Corp., **II** 628; **IV** 56, 58–61, 189–91, 380; **21** 352
Rioblanco, **II** 477
Riordan Freeman & Spogli, **13** 406
Riordan Holdings Ltd., **I** 457; **10** 554
Riser Foods, Inc., 9 451–54; **13** 237–38
Rising Sun Petroleum Co., **IV** 431, 460, 542
Risk Management Partners Ltd., **35** 36
Risk Planners, **II** 669
Rit Dye Co., **II** 497
Ritchie Bros. Auctioneers Inc., 41 331–34
Rite Aid Corporation, V 174–76; **9** 187, 346; **12** 221, 333; **16** 389; **18** 199, 286; **19 354–57** (upd.); **23** 407; **29** 213; **31** 232; **32** 166, 169–70
Rite-Way Department Store, **II** 649
Riteway Distributor, **26** 183
Rittenhouse and Embree, **III** 269
Rittenhouse Financial Services, **22** 495
Ritter Co. *See* Sybron Corp.
Ritz Camera Centers, 18 186; **34 375–77**
Ritz-Carlton Hotel Company L.L.C., 9 455–57; **21** 366; **29 403–06** (upd.)
Ritz Firma, **13** 512
Riunione Adriatica di Sicurtà SpA, III 185, 206, **345–48**
Riva Group Plc, **53** 46
The Rival Company, 17 215; **19 358–60**
Rivarossi, **16** 337
Rivaud Group, **29** 370
River Boat Casino, **9** 425–26
River City Broadcasting, **25** 418
River North Studios. *See* Platinum Entertainment, Inc.
River Oaks Furniture, Inc., 43 314–16
River-Raisin Paper Co., **IV** 345
River Ranch Fresh Foods—Salinas, Inc., **41** 11
River Steam Navigation Co., **III** 522
River Thames Insurance Co., Ltd., **26** 487
Riverdeep Group plc, **41** 137
Riverside Chemical Company, **13** 502
Riverside Furniture, **19** 455

Riverside Insurance Co. of America, **26** 487
Riverside Iron Works, Ltd., **8** 544
Riverside National Bank of Buffalo, **11** 108
Riverside Press, **10** 355–56
Riverside Publishing Company, **36** 272
Riverwood International Corporation, 7 294; **11 420–23; 48 340–44** (upd.)
Riviana Foods, **III** 24, 25; **27 388–91**
Riyadh Armed Forces Hospital, **16** 94
Rizzoli Publishing, **IV** 586, 588; **19** 19; **23** 88; **54** 19, 21
RJMJ, Inc., **16** 37
RJR Nabisco Holdings Corp., I 249, 259, 261; **II** 370, 426, 477–78, 542–44; **V** **408–10, 415; 7** 130, 132, 277, 596; **9** 469; **12** 82, 559; **13** 342; **14** 214, 274; **17** 471; **22** 73, 95, 441; **23** 163; **24** 273; **30** 384; **32** 234; **33** 228; **36** 151, 153; **46** 259; **49** 77–78; **56** 190–92. *See also* R.J Reynolds Tobacco Holdings Inc., Nabisco Brands, Inc.; R.J. Reynolds Industries, Inc.
RKO. *See* Radio-Keith-Orpheum.
RKO-General, Inc., **8** 207
RKO Radio Sales, **6** 33
RLA Polymers, **9** 92
RM Marketing, **6** 14
RMC Group p.l.c., III 734, **737–40; 34 378–83** (upd.)
RMF Inc., **I** 412
RMH Teleservices, Inc., 42 322–24
RMP International, Limited, **8** 417
Roadhouse Grill, Inc., 22 464–66
Roadline, **6** 413–14
Roadmaster Industries, Inc., 16 430–33; 22 116
Roadmaster Transport Company, **18** 27; **41** 18
RoadOne. *See* Miller Industries, Inc.
Roadway Express, Inc., 25 395–98 (upd.)
Roadway Services, Inc., V 502–03; 12 278, 309; **14** 567; **15** 111
Roaman's, **V** 115
Roan Selection Trust Ltd., **IV** 18, 239–40
Roanoke Capital Ltd., **27** 113–14
Roanoke Electric Steel Corporation, 45 368–70
Roanoke Fashions Group, **13** 532
Robb Engineering Works, **8** 544
Robbins & Myers Inc., 13 273; **15 388–90**
Robbins Co., **III** 546
Robeco Group, **IV** 193; **26** 419–20
Roberds Inc., 19 361–63
Roberk Co., **III** 603
Robert Allen Companies, **III** 571; **20** 362
Robert Benson, Lonsdale & Co. Ltd., **II** 232, 421–22; **IV** 191
Robert Bosch GmbH, I 392–93, 411; **III** 554, 555, 591, 593; **13** 398; **16 434–37** (upd.); **22** 31; **43 317–21** (upd.)
Robert E. McKee Corporation, **6** 150
Robert Fleming Holdings Ltd., **I** 471; **IV** 79; **11** 495
Robert Gair Co., **15** 128
Robert Garrett & Sons, Inc., **9** 363
Robert Grace Contracting Co., **I** 584
Robert Half International Inc., 18 461–63
Robert Hall Clothes, Inc., **13** 535
Robert Hansen Trucking Inc., **49** 402
Robert Johnson, **8** 281–82

Robert McLane Company. *See* McLane Company, Inc.
Robert McNish & Company Limited, **14** 141
Robert Mondavi Corporation, 15 391–94; 39 45; **50 386–90** (upd.); **54** 343
Robert R. Mullen & Co., **I** 20
Robert Skeels & Company, **33** 467
Robert Stigwood Organization Ltd., **23** 390
Robert W. Baird & Co., **III** 324; **7** 495
Robert Warschauer and Co., **II** 270
Robert Watson & Co. Ltd., **I** 568
Robert Wood Johnson Foundation, 35 375–78
Robertet SA, 39 347–49
Roberts Express, **V** 503
Roberts, Johnson & Rand Shoe Co., **III** 528–29
Roberts Pharmaceutical Corporation, 16 438–40
Robertson Building Products, **8** 546
Robertson-Ceco Corporation, 8 546; **19 364–66**
Robertson, Stephens & Co., **22** 465
Robin Hood Flour Mills, Ltd., **7** 241–43; **25** 241
Robin International Inc., **24** 14
Robinair, **10** 492, 494
Robinson & Clark Hardware. *See* Clarcor Inc.
Robinson Clubs, **II** 163–64
Robinson-Danforth Commission Co., **II** 561
Robinson Helicopter Company, 51 315–17
Robinson-Humphrey, **II** 398; **10** 62
Robinson Industries, **24** 425
Robinson Radio Rentals, **I** 531
Robinson Smith & Robert Haas, Inc., **13** 428
Robinson's Japan Co. Ltd., **V** 89; **42** 191
Robinsons Soft Drinks Limited, **38** 77
Robot Manufacturing Co., **16** 8
Robotic Simulations Limited, **56** 134
Robotic Vision Systems, Inc., **16** 68
ROC. *See* Royal Olympic Cruise Lines Inc.
ROC Communities, Inc., **I** 272; **22** 341
Roccade, **39** 177
Roch, S.A., **23** 83
Roche Biomedical Laboratories, Inc., 8 209–10; **11 424–26**. *See also* Laboratory Corporation of America Holdings.
Roche Bioscience, 14 403–06 (upd.)
Roche Holding AG, **30** 164; **32** 211, 213–14; **37** 113; **50** 421
Roche Products Ltd., **I** 643
Rocher Soleil, **48** 315
Rochester American Insurance Co., **III** 191
Rochester Gas And Electric Corporation, 6 571–73
Rochester German Insurance Co., **III** 191
Rochester Instrument Systems, Inc., **16** 357
Rochester Telephone Corporation, 6 332–34; 12 136; **16** 221
Röchling Industrie Verwaltung GmbH, **9** 443
Rock Bottom Restaurants, Inc., 25 399–401
Rock Island Oil & Refining Co., **IV** 448–49
Rock Island Plow Company, **10** 378
Rock of Ages Corporation, 37 329–32
Rock Systems Inc., **18** 337

Uni-Cardan AG, **III** 494

Uni-Cast. *See* Sturm, Ruger & Company, Inc.

Uni-Charm, **III** 749

Uni Europe, **III** 211

Uni-Marts, Inc., 17 499–502

Uni-President Group, **49** 460

Uni-Sankyo, **I** 675

Unibail SA, 40 444–46

Unibank, **40** 336; **50** 149–50

Unic, **V** 63

Unicapital, Inc., **15** 281

Unicare Health Facilities, **6** 182; **25** 525

Unicco Security Services, **27** 22

Unice, **56** 335

Unicel. *See* Rural Cellular Corporation.

Unicer, **9** 100

Unichem, **25** 73

Unichema International, **13** 228

Unicoa, **I** 524

Unicom Corporation, 29 486–90 (upd.). *See also* Exelon Corporation.

Unicomi, **II** 265

Unicon Producing Co., **10** 191

UniCorp, **8** 228

Unicorp Financial, **III** 248

Unicredit, **II** 265

UniCredito Italiano, **50** 410

Uniden, **14** 117

Unidrive, **47** 280

UniDynamics Corporation, **8** 135

Unie van Kunstmestfabrieken, **I** 326

Uniface Holding B.V., **10** 245; **30** 142

Unifi, Inc., 12 501–03

Unified Energy System of Russia. *See* RAO Unified Energy System of Russia.

Unified Management Corp., **III** 306

Unified Western Grocers, **31** 25

UniFirst Corporation, 16 228; 21 115, 505–07

Uniflex Corporation, **53** 236

Uniforce Services Inc., **40** 119

Unigate PLC, II 586–87; 28 488–91 (upd.); 29 150. *See also* Uniq Plc.

Unigep Group, **III** 495

Unigesco Inc., **II** 653

Uniglory, **13** 211

Unigroup, **15** 50

UniHealth America, **11** 378–79

Unijoh Sdn, Bhd, **47** 255

Unik S.A., **23** 170–171

Unilab Corp., **26** 391

Unilac Inc., **II** 547

Unilever PLC/Unilever N.V., I 369, 590, 605; **II** 547, **588–91; III** 31–32, 46, 52, 495; **IV** 532; **7** 382, **542–45 (upd.),** 577; **8** 105–07, 166, 168, 341, 344; **9** 449; **11** 205, 421; **13** 243–44; **14** 204–05; **18** 395, 397; **19** 193; **21** 219; **22** 123; **23** 242; **26** 306; **28** 183, 185; **30** 396–97; **32 472–78 (upd.); 36** 237; **49** 269

Unilife Assurance Group, **III** 273

UniLife Insurance Co., **22** 149

Unilog SA, 42 401–03

Uniloy Milacron Inc., **53** 230

UniMac Companies, **11** 413

Unimat, **II** 265

Unimation, **II** 122

Unimetal, **IV** 227; **30** 252

Uninsa, **I** 460

Union, **III** 391–93

Union & NHK Auto Parts, **III** 580

Union Acceptances Ltd., **IV** 23

Unión Aérea Española, **6** 95

Union Aéromaritime de Transport. *See* UTA.

Union Assurance, **III** 234

Union Bag–Camp Paper Corp., **IV** 344–45

Union Bancorp of California, **II** 358

Union Bank. *See* State Street Boston Corporation.

Union Bank of Australia, **II** 187–89

Union Bank of California, 16 496–98. *See also* UnionBanCal Corporation.

Union Bank of Canada, **II** 344

Union Bank of England, **II** 188

Union Bank of Finland, **II** 302, 352

Union Bank of Halifax, **II** 344

Union Bank of London, **II** 235

Union Bank of New London, **II** 213

Union Bank of New York, **9** 229

Union Bank of Scotland, **10** 337

Union Bank of Switzerland, II 257, 267, 334, 369, 370, **378–79; 21** 146. *See also* UBS AG.

Union Battery Co., **III** 536

Union Bay Sportswear, **17** 460

Union Camp Corporation, IV 344–46; 8 102; **39** 291; **47** 189

Union-Capitalisation, **III** 392

Union Carbide Corporation, I 334, 339, 347, 374, 390, **399–401,** 582, 666; **II** 103, 313, 562; **III** 742, 760; **IV** 92, 374, 379, 521; **7** 376; **8** 180, 182, 376; **9** 16, **516–20 (upd.); 10** 289, 472; **11** 402–03; **12** 46, 347; **13** 118; **14** 281–82; **16** 461; **17** 159; **18** 235; **22** 228, 235; **43** 265–66; **48** 321; **50** 47; **55** 380

Union Cervecera, **9** 100

Union Colliery Company, **V** 741

Union Commerce Corporation, **11** 181

Union Commerciale, **19** 98

Union Corporation. *See* Gencor Ltd.

Union d'Etudes et d'Investissements, **II** 265

Union des Assurances de Paris, II 234; **III** 201, **391–94**

Union des Coopératives Bressor, **25** 85

Union des Cooperatives Laitières. *See* Unicoolait.

Union des Mines, **52** 362

Union des Transports Aériens. *See* UTA.

Union Electric Company, V 741–43; **6** 505–06; **26** 451

Union Electrica de Canarias S.A., **V** 607

Unión Electrica Fenosa. *See* Unión Fenosa S.A.

Union Equity Co-Operative Exchange, **7** 175

Union et Prévoyance, **III** 403

Unión Fenosa, S.A., 51 387–90; 56 216

Union Fertilizer, **I** 412

Union Fidelity Corporation, **III** 204; **45** 26

Union Financiera, **19** 189

Union Financière de France Banque SA, 52 360–62

Union Fork & Hoe Company. *See* Acorn Products, Inc.

Union Gas & Electric Co., **6** 529

Union Générale de Savonnerie, **III** 33

l'Union Générale des Pétroles, **IV** 545–46, 560; **7** 482–83

Union Glass Co., **III** 683

Union Hardware, **III** 443; **22** 115

Union Hop Growers, **I** 287

Union Laitière Normande, **19** 50. *See also* Compagnie Laitière Européenne.

Union Levantina de Seguros, **III** 179

Union Light, Heat & Power Company, **6** 466

Union Marine, **III** 372

Union Minière. *See* NV Umicore SA.

Union Mutual Life Insurance Company. *See* UNUM Corp.

Union National Bank, **II** 284; **10** 298

Union National Bank of Wilmington, **25** 540

Union of European Football Association, **27** 150

Union of Food Co-ops, **II** 622

Union of London, **II** 333

Union Oil Associates, **IV** 569

Union Oil Co., **9** 266

Union Oil Co. of California, **I** 13; **IV** 385, 400, 403, 434, 522, 531, 540, 569, 575; **11** 271. *See also* Unocal Corporation.

Union Pacific Corporation, I 473; **II** 381; **III** 229; **V 529–32; 12** 18–20, 278; **14** 371–72; **28 492–500 (upd.); 36** 43–44

Union Pacific Resources Group, **52** 30

Union Pacific Tea Co., **7** 202

Union Paper Bag Machine Co., **IV** 344

Union Petroleum Corp., **IV** 394

Union Planters Corporation, 54 387–90

L'Union pour le Developement Régional, **II** 265

Union Power Company, **12** 541

Union Rückversicherungs-Gesellschaft, **III** 377

Union Savings, **II** 316

Union Savings and Loan Association of Phoenix, **19** 412

Union Savings Bank, **9** 173

Union Savings Bank and Trust Company, **13** 221

Union Steam Ship Co., **IV** 279; **19** 154

Union Steamship Co. of New Zealand Ltd., **27** 473

Union Steel Co., **IV** 22, 572; **7** 550

Union Sugar, **II** 573

Union Suisse des Coopératives de Consommation. *See* Coop Schweiz.

Union Sulphur Co., **IV** 81; **7** 185

Union Supply Co., **IV** 573; **7** 550

Union Tank Car Co., **IV** 137

Union Telecard Alliance, LLC, **34** 223

Union Telephone Company, **14** 258

Union Texas Petroleum Holdings, Inc., I 415; **7** 379; **9 521–23; 22** 31

Union-Transport, **6** 404; **26** 243

Union Trust Co., **II** 284, 313, 315–16, 382; **9** 228; **13** 222

The Union Underwear Company, **I** 440–41; **8** 200–01; **25** 164–66

Union Wine, **I** 289

Unionamerica, Inc., **III** 243; **16** 497; **50** 497

UnionBanCal Corporation, 50 496–99 (upd.)

UnionBay Sportswear Co., **27** 112

Unione Manifatture, S.p.A., **19** 338

Uniphase Corporation. *See* JDS Uniphase Corporation.

Uniplex Business Software, **41** 281

Uniq Plc, **52** 418, 420

Weyerhaeuser Company, **I** 26; **IV** 266, 289, 298, 304, 308, **355–56**, 358; **8** 428, 434; **9 550–52 (upd.)**; **19** 445–46, 499; **22** 489; **26** 384; **28 514–17 (upd.)**; **31** 468; **32** 91; **42** 397; **49** 196–97

Weyman-Burton Co., **9** 533

WFSC. *See* World Fuel Services Corporation.

WGM Safety Corp., **40** 96–97

WH Smith PLC, 42 442–47 (upd.)

Whalstrom & Co., **I** 14

Wharf Holdings Limited, **12** 367–68; **18** 114

Whatman plc, 46 462–65

Wheat, First Securities, **19** 304–05

Wheaton Industries, 8 570–73

Wheatsheaf Investment, **27** 94

Wheel Horse, **7** 535

Wheel Restaurants Inc., **14** 131

Wheelabrator Technologies, Inc., I 298; **II** 403; **III** 511–12; **V** 754; **6 599–600**; **10** 32; **11** 435

Wheeled Coach Industries, Inc., **33** 105–06

Wheeler Condenser & Engineering Company, **6** 145

Wheeler, Fisher & Co., **IV** 344

Wheeling-Pittsburgh Corp., 7 586–88

Wheelock Marden, **I** 470; **20** 312

Whemco, **22** 415

Whemo Denko, **I** 359

Wherehouse Entertainment Incorporated, 9 361; **11 556–58**; **29** 350; **35** 431–32

WHI Inc., **14** 545

Whippet Motor Lines Corporation, **6** 370

Whippoorwill Associates Inc., **28** 55

Whirl-A-Way Motors, **11** 4

Whirlpool Corporation, I 30; **II** 80; **III** 572, 573, **653–55**; **8** 298–99; **11** 318; **12** 252, 309, **548–50 (upd.)**; **13** 402–03, 563; **15** 403; **18** 225–26; **22** 218, 349; **23** 53; **25** 261; **50** 300, 392

Whirlwind, Inc., **6** 233; **7** 535

Whiskey Trust, **I** 376

Whistler Corporation, **13** 195

Whitaker-Glessner Company, **7** 586

Whitaker Health Services, **III** 389

Whitall Tatum, **III** 423

Whitbread PLC, I 288, **293–94**; **18** 73; **20 519–22 (upd.)**; **29** 19; **35** 395; **42** 247; **50** 114; **52 412–17 (upd.)**

Whitby Pharmaceuticals, Inc., **10** 289

White & Case LLP, 35 466–69

White Automotive, **10** 9, 11

White Brand, **V** 97

White Brothers, **39** 83, 84

White Bus Line, **I** 448

White Castle System, Inc., 12 551–53; **33** 239; **36 517–20 (upd.)**

White Consolidated Industries Inc., II 122; **III** 480, 654, 573; **8** 298; **12** 252, 546; **13 562–64**; **22** 26–28, 216–17, 349; **53** 127

White Discount Department Stores, **16** 36

White Eagle Oil & Refining Co., **IV** 464; **7** 352

White Fuel Corp., **IV** 552

White Industrial Power, **II** 25

White Miller Construction Company, **14** 162

White Motor Co., **II** 16

White Mountain Freezers, **19** 360

White Mountains Insurance Group, Ltd., 48 428–31

White-New Idea, **13** 18

White Oil Corporation, **7** 101

White Rock Corp., **I** 377; **27** 198; **43** 218

White-Rodgers, **II** 19

White Rose, Inc., 12 106; **24 527–29**

White Star Line, **23** 161

White Stores, **II** 419–20

White Swan Foodservice, **II** 625

White Tractor, **13** 17

White Wave, 43 462–64

White Weld, **II** 268; **21** 145

White-Westinghouse. *See* White Consolidated Industries Inc.

Whiteaway Laidlaw, **V** 68

Whitehall Canadian Oils Ltd., **IV** 658

Whitehall Company Jewellers, **24** 319

Whitehall Electric Investments Ltd., **IV** 658

Whitehall Labs, **8** 63

Whitehall Petroleum Corp. Ltd., **IV** 657–58

Whitehall Securities Corp., **IV** 658

Whitehall Trust Ltd., **IV** 658

Whitewater Group, **10** 508

Whitewear Manufacturing Company. *See* Angelica Corporation.

Whitman Corporation, 7 430; **10** 414–15, **553–55 (upd.)**; **11** 188; **22** 353–54; **27** 196; **43** 217

Whitman Education Group, Inc., 41 419–21

Whitman Publishing Co., **13** 559–60

Whitman's Chocolates, **I** 457; **7** 431; **12** 429

Whitmire Distribution. *See* Cardinal Health, Inc.

Whitney Communications Corp., **IV** 608

Whitney Group, **40** 236–38

Whitney Holding Corporation, 21 522–24

Whitney National Bank, **12** 16

Whitney Partners, L.L.C., **40** 237

Whittaker Corporation, I 544–46, **III** 389, 444; **34** 275; **48 432–35 (upd.)**

Whittar Steel Strip Co., **IV** 74; **24** 143

Whitteways, **I** 215

Whittle Communications L.P., **IV** 675; **7** 528; **13** 403; **22** 442

Whittman-Hart Inc. *See* marchFIRST, Inc.

Whitworth Brothers Company, **27** 360

Whole Foods Market, 19 501–02; **20 523–27**; **41** 422–23; **47** 200; **50 530–34 (upd.)**

Wholesale Cellular USA. *See* Brightpoint, Inc.

The Wholesale Club, Inc., **8** 556

Wholesale Depot, **13** 547

Wholesale Food Supply, Inc., **13** 333

Wholesome Foods, L.L.C., **32** 274, 277

Wholly Harvest, **19** 502

WHSC Direct, Inc., **53** 359

Whyte & Mackay Distillers Ltd., **V** 399; **19** 171; **49** 152

Wicanders Group, **48** 119

Wicat Systems, **7** 255–56; **25** 254

Wichita Industries, **11** 27

Wickes Companies, Inc., I 453, 483; **II** 262; **III** 580, 721; **V 221–23**; **10** 423; **13** 169–70; **15** 281; **17** 365–66; **19** 503–04; **20** 415; **41** 93

Wickes Inc., 25 533–36 (upd.)

Wickman-Wimet, **IV** 203

Wicor, Inc., **54** 419

Widows and Orphans Friendly Society, **III** 337

Wielkopolski Bank Kredytowy, **16** 14

Wien Air Alaska, **II** 420

Wienerwald Holding, **17** 249

Wiesner, Inc., **22** 442

Wifstavarfs, **IV** 325

Wiggins Teape Ltd., **I** 426; **IV** 290

Wilbert, Inc., 56 377–80

Wild by Nature. *See* King Cullen Grocery Co., Inc.

Wild Harvest, **56** 317

Wild Leitz G.m.b.H., **23** 83

Wild Oats Markets, Inc., 19 500–02; **29** 213; **41 422–25 (upd.)**

WildBlue Communications Inc., **54** 406

Wildlife Conservation Society, 31 462–64

Wildlife Land Trust, **54** 172

Wildwater Kingdom, **22** 130

Wiles Group Ltd., **III** 501; **7** 207

Wiley Manufacturing Co., **8** 545

Oy Wilh. Schauman AB, **IV** 300–02; **19** 463

Wilhelm Fette GmbH, **IV** 198–99

Wilhelm Weber GmbH, **22** 95

Wilhelm Wilhelmsen Ltd., **7** 40; **41** 42

Wilkins Department Store, **19** 510

Wilkinson, Gaddis & Co., **24** 527

Wilkinson Sword Co., **III** 23, 28–29; **12** 464; **38** 365

Willamette Falls Electric Company. *See* Portland General Corporation.

Willamette Industries, Inc., IV 357–59; **13** 99, 101; **16** 340; **28** 517; **31 465–468 (upd.)**

Willbros Group, Inc., 56 381–83

Willcox & Gibbs Sewing Machine Co., **15** 384

Willetts Manufacturing Company, **12** 312

William A. Rogers Ltd., **IV** 644

William B. Tanner Co., **7** 327

William Barnet and Son, Inc., **III** 246

William Barry Co., **II** 566

William Benton Foundation, **7** 165, 167

William Bonnel Co., **I** 334; **10** 289

The William Brooks Shoe Company. *See* Rocky Shoes & Boots, Inc.

William Burdon, **III** 626

William Byrd Press Inc., **23** 100

William Carter Company, **17** 224

William Colgate and Co., **III** 23

William Collins & Sons, **II** 138; **IV** 651–52; **7** 390–91; **24** 193

William Cory & Son Ltd., **6** 417

William Crawford and Sons, **II** 593

William Douglas McAdams Inc., **I** 662; **9** 403

William Duff & Sons, **I** 509

William E. Pollack Government Securities, **II** 390

William E. Wright Company, **9** 375

William Esty Company, **16** 72

William Gaymer and Son Ltd., **I** 216

William George Company, **32** 519

William Grant Company, **22** 343

William H. Rorer Inc., **I** 666

William Hancock & Co., **I** 223

William Hewlett, **41** 117

William Hill Organization Limited, 49 449–52

William Hodges & Company, **33** 150

William Hollins & Company Ltd., **44** 105

William J. Hough Co., **8** 99–100

William Lyon Homes, **III** 664

INDEX TO INDUSTRIES

Index to Industries

AUTOMOTIVE

CONGLOMERATES

FINANCIAL SERVICES: BANKS

FOOD PRODUCTS

HOTELS

INFORMATION TECHNOLOGY

MINING & METALS

The Timberland Company, 13; 54 (upd.)
Tommy Hilfiger Corporation, 20; 53 (upd.)
Toray Industries, Inc., V
Tultex Corporation, 13
Unifi, Inc., 12
United Merchants & Manufacturers, Inc., 13
United Retail Group Inc., 33
Unitika Ltd., V
Vans, Inc., 16; 47 (upd.)
Varsity Spirit Corp., 15
VF Corporation, V; 17 (upd.); 54 (upd.)
Walton Monroe Mills, Inc., 8
The Warnaco Group Inc., 12; 46 (upd.)
Wellman, Inc., 8; 52 (upd.)
West Point-Pepperell, Inc., 8
WestPoint Stevens Inc., 16
Weyco Group, Incorporated, 32
Williamson-Dickie Manufacturing Company, 14
Wolverine World Wide Inc., 16

TOBACCO

American Brands, Inc., V
B.A.T. Industries PLC, 22 (upd.)
British American Tobacco PLC, 50 (upd.)
Brooke Group Ltd., 15
Brown & Williamson Tobacco Corporation, 14; 33 (upd.)
Culbro Corporation, 15
Dibrell Brothers, Incorporated, 12
DIMON Inc., 27
800-JR Cigar, Inc., 27
Gallaher Group Plc, 49 (upd.)
Gallaher Limited, V; 19 (upd.)
Holt's Cigar Holdings, Inc., 42
Imasco Limited, V
Imperial Tobacco Group PLC, 50
Japan Tobacco Incorporated, V
Philip Morris Companies Inc., V; 18 (upd.)
R.J. Reynolds Tobacco Holdings, Inc., 30 (upd.)
RJR Nabisco Holdings Corp., V
Rothmans UK Holdings Limited, V; 19 (upd.)
Seita, 23
Standard Commercial Corporation, 13
Swisher International Group Inc., 23
Tabacalera, S.A., V; 17 (upd.)
Universal Corporation, V; 48 (upd.)
UST Inc., 9; 50 (upd.)
Vector Group Ltd., 35 (upd.)

TRANSPORT SERVICES

Aéroports de Paris, 33
Air Express International Corporation, 13
Airborne Freight Corporation, 6; 34 (upd.)
Alamo Rent A Car, Inc., 6; 24 (upd.)
Alexander & Baldwin, Inc., 10
Allied Worldwide, Inc., 49
Amerco, 6
American Classic Voyages Company, 27
American President Companies Ltd., 6
Anschutz Corp., 12
Aqua Alliance Inc., 32 (upd.)
Atlas Van Lines, Inc., 14
Avis Rent A Car, Inc., 6; 22 (upd.)
BAA plc, 10
Bekins Company, 15
Boyd Bros. Transportation Inc., 39
Brambles Industries Limited, 42
British Railways Board, V
Broken Hill Proprietary Company Ltd., 22 (upd.)
Budget Group, Inc., 25
Budget Rent a Car Corporation, 9

Burlington Northern Santa Fe Corporation, V; 27 (upd.)
C.H. Robinson Worldwide, Inc., 40 (upd.)
Canadian National Railway System, 6
Canadian Pacific Railway Limited, V; 45 (upd.)
Cannon Express, Inc., 53
Carey International, Inc., 26
Carlson Companies, Inc., 6
Carolina Freight Corporation, 6
Celadon Group Inc., 30
Central Japan Railway Company, 43
Chargeurs, 6
Chicago and North Western Holdings Corporation, 6
Christian Salvesen Plc, 45
Coach USA, Inc., 24; 55 (upd.)
Coles Express Inc., 15
Compagnie Générale Maritime et Financière, 6
Consolidated Delivery & Logistics, Inc., 24
Consolidated Freightways Corporation, V; 21 (upd.); 48 (upd.)
Consolidated Rail Corporation, V
Crowley Maritime Corporation, 6; 28 (upd.)
CSX Corporation, V; 22 (upd.)
Danzas Group, V; 40 (upd.)
Deutsche Bahn AG, 46 (upd.)
Deutsche Bundesbahn, V
DHL Worldwide Express, 6; 24 (upd.)
Dollar Thrifty Automotive Group, Inc., 25
East Japan Railway Company, V
Emery Air Freight Corporation, 6
Emery Worldwide Airlines, Inc., 25 (upd.)
Enterprise Rent-A-Car Company, 6
Eurotunnel Group, 37 (upd.)
EVA Airways Corporation, 51
Evergreen International Aviation, Inc., 53
Evergreen Marine Corporation (Taiwan) Ltd., 13; 50 (upd.)
Executive Jet, Inc., 36
Exel plc, 51 (upd.)
Expeditors International of Washington Inc., 17
Federal Express Corporation, V
FedEx Corporation, 18 (upd.); 42 (upd.)
Fritz Companies, Inc., 12
Frontline Ltd., 45
Frozen Food Express Industries, Inc., 20
GATX Corporation, 6; 25 (upd.)
GE Capital Aviation Services, 36
Gefco SA, 54
Genesee & Wyoming Inc., 27
The Go-Ahead Group Plc, 28
The Greenbrier Companies, 19
Greyhound Lines, Inc., 32 (upd.)
Grupo TMM, S.A. de C.V., 50
Grupo Transportación Ferroviaria Mexicana, S.A. de C.V., 47
GulfMark Offshore, Inc., 49
Hanjin Shipping Co., Ltd., 50
Hankyu Corporation, V; 23 (upd.)
Hapag-Lloyd AG, 6
Harland and Wolff Holdings plc, 19
Harper Group Inc., 17
Heartland Express, Inc., 18
The Hertz Corporation, 9
Holberg Industries, Inc., 36
Hospitality Worldwide Services, Inc., 26
Hub Group, Inc., 38
Hvide Marine Incorporated, 22
Illinois Central Corporation, 11
International Shipholding Corporation, Inc., 27
J.B. Hunt Transport Services Inc., 12
John Menzies plc, 39

Kansas City Southern Industries, Inc., 6; 26 (upd.)
Kawasaki Kisen Kaisha, Ltd., V; 56 (upd.)
Keio Teito Electric Railway Company, V
Keolis SA, 51
Kinki Nippon Railway Company Ltd., V
Kirby Corporation, 18
Koninklijke Nedlloyd Groep N.V., 6
Kuehne & Nagel International AG, V; 53 (upd.)
La Poste, V; 47 (upd.)
Leaseway Transportation Corp., 12
London Regional Transport, 6
Maine Central Railroad Company, 16
Mammoet Transport B.V., 26
Martz Group, 56
Mayflower Group Inc., 6
Mercury Air Group, Inc., 20
The Mersey Docks and Harbour Company, 30
Metropolitan Transportation Authority, 35
Miller Industries, Inc., 26
Mitsui O.S.K. Lines, Ltd., V
Moran Towing Corporation, Inc., 15
The Morgan Group, Inc., 46
Morris Travel Services L.L.C., 26
Motor Cargo Industries, Inc., 35
National Car Rental System, Inc., 10
National Express Group PLC, 50
National Railroad Passenger Corporation, 22
Neptune Orient Lines Limited, 47
NFC plc, 6
Nippon Express Co., Ltd., V
Nippon Yusen Kabushiki Kaisha, V
Norfolk Southern Corporation, V; 29 (upd.)
Oak Harbor Freight Lines, Inc., 53
Ocean Group plc, 6
Odakyu Electric Railway Company Limited, V
Oglebay Norton Company, 17
Österreichische Bundesbahnen GmbH, 6
OTR Express, Inc., 25
Overnite Transportation Co., 14
Overseas Shipholding Group, Inc., 11
Pacer International, Inc., 54
The Peninsular and Oriental Steam Navigation Company, V; 38 (upd.)
Penske Corporation, V
PHH Arval, V; 53 (upd.)
The Port Authority of New York and New Jersey, 48
Post Office Group, V
Preston Corporation, 6
RailTex, Inc., 20
Railtrack Group PLC, 50
Roadway Express, Inc., 25 (upd.)
Roadway Services, Inc., V
Royal Olympic Cruise Lines Inc., 52
Royal Vopak NV, 41
Ryder System, Inc., V; 24 (upd.)
Santa Fe Pacific Corporation, V
Schenker-Rhenus AG, 6
Schneider National, Inc., 36
Securicor Plc, 45
Seibu Railway Co. Ltd., V
Seino Transportation Company, Ltd., 6
Simon Transportation Services Inc., 27
Smithway Motor Xpress Corporation, 39
Société Nationale des Chemins de Fer Français, V
Southern Pacific Transportation Company, V
Stagecoach Holdings plc, 30
Stelmar Shipping Ltd., 52
Stevedoring Services of America Inc., 28
Stinnes AG, 8

WASTE SERVICES

GEOGRAPHIC INDEX

Geographic Index

NOTES ON CONTRIBUTORS ──────────────────────────

Notes on Contributors

BIANCO, David. Writer, editor, and publishing consultant.

BRENNAN, Gerald E. California-based writer.

BROWN, Erin. Business writer and researcher.

COHEN, M. L. Novelist and business writer living in Paris.

COVELL, Jeffrey L. Seattle-based writer.

DINGER, Ed. Bronx-based writer and editor.

FIERO, John W. Writer, researcher, and consultant.

GASBARRE, April Dougal. Michigan-based business writer and researcher.

GREENLAND, Paul R. Illinois-based writer and researcher; author of two books and former senior editor of a national business magazine; contributor to *The Encyclopedia of Chicago History* (University of Chicago Press) and *Company Profiles for Students.*

HAUSER, Evelyn. Researcher, writer and marketing specialist based in Arcata, California; expertise includes historical and trend research in such topics as globalization, emerging industries and lifestyles, future scenarios, biographies, and the history of organizations.

HENRY, Elizabeth. Maine-based researcher, writer, and editor.

INGRAM, Frederick C. Utah-based business writer who has contributed to *GSA Business, Appalachian Trailway News,* the *Encyclopedia of Business,* the *Encyclopedia of Global Industries,* the *Encyclopedia of Consumer Brands,* and other regional and trade publications.

LEMIEUX, Gloria A. Researcher and writer living in Nashua, New Hampshire.

PEIPPO, Kathleen. Minneapolis-based business writer.

RHODES, Nelson. Business editor, writer, and consultant in the Chicago area.

ROTHBURD, Carrie. Writer and editor specializing in corporate profiles, academic texts, and academic journal articles.

STANSELL, Christina M. Writer and editor based in Farmington Hills, Michigan.

TRADII, Mary. Writer based in Denver, Colorado.

UHLE, Frank. Ann Arbor-based writer; movie projectionist, disc jockey, and staff member of *Psychotronic Video* magazine.

WOODWARD, A. Wisconsin-based business writer.